The Principles of Knitting

Methods and Techniques of Hand Knitting

JUNE HEMMONS HIATT

Illustrations by Jesse Hiatt

A TOUCHSTONE BOOK

PUBLISHED BY SIMON & SCHUSTER

NEW YORK   TORONTO   LONDON   SYDNEY   NEW DELHI

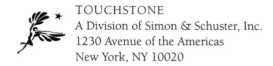

TOUCHSTONE
A Division of Simon & Schuster, Inc.
1230 Avenue of the Americas
New York, NY 10020

First Touchstone hardcover edition February 2012

TOUCHSTONE and colophon are registered trademarks
of Simon & Schuster, Inc.

For information about special discounts for bulk purchases,
please contact Simon & Schuster Special Sales at
1-866-506-1949 or business@simonandschuster.com.

The Simon & Schuster Speakers Bureau can bring authors to your
live event. For more information or to book an event contact the
Simon & Schuster Speakers Bureau at 1-866-248-3049 or visit our
website at www.simonspeakers.com.

Manufactured in the United States of America

10 9 8 7 6 5 4 3 2 1

Library of Congress Cataloging-in-Publication Data is available.

ISBN 978-1-4165-3517-1

Artwork of the first edition by Kelly J. Hall, Joanna Lynch,
and Beverly J. Beckman has been digitally reproduced and
appears again in this edition.

Frontispiece: Photograph by Corey Lesh

To Rob and Jesse
For more than can be said
. . . again

CONTENTS

Part Five: Stitch and Color Patterns

Part Six: Pattern Design

Part Seven: Materials

Part Eight: Working a Project

INTRODUCTION TO THE SECOND EDITION

In rereading the original introduction to this book, written more than twenty years ago, I was pleased to find that it has withstood the test of time. The sentiments and thoughts expressed there have stayed with me and seem to still be relevant.

However, two things have profoundly changed. The emergence of knitting events held nationally throughout the year and the pervasive influence of the Internet have bound knitters together in a community without boundaries; these developments sustain them in this craft to an extent that was unimaginable before.

After *The Principles of Knitting* went out of print in the mid-1990s, it was this community that soon began asking, emphatically, for it to be put back into their hands. It was deeply gratifying to learn how much the first edition had come to mean to so many knitters, and a deep sense of responsibility to them persuaded me to find a way to republish it.

And so ten years ago I took the first, tentative steps toward deciding what to do about this book. The physical materials necessary to reprint it had been lost, and scanning it for a facsimile was simply not an option I would consider. Therefore, the first task was to type the text back into the computer. While this might seem daunting, I type fast, and the process of doing this had the benefit of requiring careful reading of a text I had not revisited in a long time. As I worked my way through it, I gained ideas about how it might be improved for a second edition.

Initially, I thought I would rewrite about seven chapters, and then do no more than a good edit of the remaining material to polish things up a bit. That plan did not survive long. As any of you who have remodeled an old house will understand, a new kitchen can make the living and dining rooms look shabby, and then the bedrooms and bathrooms are no longer satisfying, and over time the whole house is made over and extensions added on.

So it was with the second edition of *The Principles of Knitting*. Techniques and concepts have been clarified and presented in ways that should make them more accessible, explanations have been rethought and instructions refined, sentences polished up and repetition rooted out, and new material added.

The book has grown to roughly 450,000 words from the previous 350,000, there are an additional 100 pages and more than 900 illustrations (still too few in this highly visual age, but as many as could be managed). The heft of this book proves that while knitting may seem to be a simple craft, there is indeed quite a lot to say about it.

Still, I must apologize for how long this has taken me. Perhaps the scale and detail justify the delay to some extent, and I can only hope that you will find it has been worth the wait. I think it is a better book: better written and better organized, and with a wonderful new design that should help you navigate through it more easily.

Those of you who are new to *The Principles of Knitting* will find that it is not quite like other books on techniques, and so there are suggestions here for how to best make use of it. I also want to reassure beginning knitters that the book was written with you in mind, and there is information below that should help you get started in this wonderful craft.

How to Use This Book

Most knitting books are the equivalent of cookbooks: a variety of techniques are presented with a brief description, followed by instructions and a drawing or two. In a book of that kind, you can dip in anywhere and extract something of interest without regard to what goes before or after it; each recipe, each knitting technique, stands on its own. *The Principles of Knitting*, both the original and this new edition, is an entirely different type of book in several respects.

It does not simply provide instructions for *how* to do a technique, with the expectation that you would learn in a rote fashion, but instead it provides the knowledge you need to truly master the craft. Therefore, each technique is *explained*; how it works, what its characteristics are, how it can be expected to behave in the fabric, and how it compares to other, similar techniques.

Developing this material required me to test every technique, and for all similar ones, to test them in the same way so they could be compared. If it was a cast-on, for instance, I used the same yarn, the same needles, the same number of stitches. I tried each edge with a ribbing, with Stockinette, with a pattern that drew in and one that opened out, like lace. In each case, I noted its appearance and measured how far it would stretch and how well it recovered. This general approach was used throughout the book.

My goal was to let the knitting itself teach me what it was capable of doing. In some cases, this process overturned my assumptions, or that of received opinion about a technique; at times it revealed new insights into how a technique could best be used, suggested a variation on the theme, or even an entirely new technique.

In writing up the information, related techniques were grouped together and their pros and cons discussed. Therefore, you will miss some of what is most useful in the book if you simply lift one technique out of context, as if selecting a recipe from a cookbook. Instead, I suggest that you read the introduction to each chapter, as well as those under the main headings, and then glance at the first few paragraphs describing each related technique to get a sense of what they are all about.

This will not only help you select whichever technique is particularly suitable for the purpose you have in mind at the moment, but it will also give you a sense of what might be in the book that you would like to learn about at another time and for a different purpose. I think you will find that while some techniques are generalists, suitable for many purposes and used often, many others are specialists, just right for only certain applications—but it is good to know they are there for when you need them.

Looking through the material in this way before starting any new project will deepen your understanding of techniques that may already be familiar to you. In some cases, you may decide to substitute a technique discussed in this book for one recommended in a published pattern. If you are planning to design something of your own, it could suggest approaches you would otherwise not have considered, but that will improve the results.

You may never have reason to explore some of the chapters in this book, and that is fine. Should you decide to learn how to do Twined Knit or Inlay, or work a Double-Fabric, that material will be there waiting for you. However, there are several chapters that I strongly recommend everyone read, regardless of their skill level, because they are relevant to whatever you might want to make.

If I had to select just one chapter that I thought was the most important in the book, it would be Stitch Gauge. I know this subject is a frustrating one for many knitters. But the method recommended here is new, and I think you will find that it not only provides you with an easier way to find gauge, but also gives you results that are far more accurate and reliable.

You will also find suggestions for what to do if you cannot match the gauge recommended in a pattern, which is common. And if you tend to dismiss the whole idea of doing a gauge, I hope to persuade you to reconsider. In addition to finding the gauge itself, which is important enough, there are other significant benefits that come from making a swatch that more than outweigh the relatively small amount of time it takes.

I also encourage you to read the chapters on Fibers and Yarns, which will help deepen your understanding of the basic materials of the craft. While the information contained there is relatively brief in light of the vast amount written on the subject, it is intended specifically for knitters and will help give you a better sense of what to expect from yarn as you work with it, and from the garment that you will wear.

Also important is the chapter on Cleaning and Dressing a Knit, which has information about how to dress a swatch before you find the gauge, as well as how to dress a garment the very first time and care for it thereafter.

Finally, I suggest you read the first chapter in the book, which discusses Knitting Methods. If you are an experienced knitter you may find tips for how to improve some aspect of the method you already use, as well as suggestions for how to teach someone else to knit. But I also strongly recommend that every knitter learn more than one method; it really does not matter which one.

All methods have pros and cons—tasks they excel at and those they are less well suited for—and being able to switch to a different method that better suits a particular project is a great advantage for any knitter. Furthermore, there is always the possibility that an injury will prevent you from knitting in your customary way, and it is nice to have an alternative that will allow you to keep working.

In trying a different method, you may even discover that the one you learned first and grew accustomed to is not ideal for your hands, or perhaps for the kind of knitting you like to do best, and that your enjoyment of the craft could be enhanced by using a different method for most of what you make.

Terminology

As you go through this book, you may encounter terms that are unfamiliar to you, or which differ from those you have seen in use elsewhere. This can be confusing; therefore, I want to repeat here some information from the Introduction to the First Edition that explains something about how I settled on a few of the more important terms that are used throughout the text:

In doing the research, I found that identical techniques were often referred to by different names or symbols in different books. In trying to decide which name was most appropriate, I found there was often no way to choose among the alternatives. In some cases I have simply abandoned all of them and settled on a term that conveys a sense of the operation performed or the resulting appearance. I hope I have not added to the confusion.

There is also a difficulty with certain relative terms commonly used in knitting, particularly "right side" and "wrong side," or "front" and "back." Both "right side" and "front" are generally used to refer to that side of the fabric which will show when the garment is worn. But "front," for example, could also mean the part of the garment worn on the front of the body, or it could be used to refer to the side of the work that happens to be facing the knitter.

For the sake of consistency and clarity, I will use "inside" and "outside" to refer only to the faces of the fabric as it is intended to be worn or used. "Front" and "back" will be used only to refer to particular pieces of the garment, as in the front part of a sweater. "Right" will be used only with "left," as in the right or left side of a stitch or the right or left side of the fabric as you are looking at it.

When we are discussing the position of the work in relation to the knitter, the position of the knitter's hands, or the placement of yarn or needles, I will use the terms "nearside" and "farside," meaning that side closest to the knitter or farthest away at that particular moment.

If You Are a Beginner

This is a big book and looks daunting, but I want to assure you that beginners were very much in my mind as I wrote; in fact, every instruction is written for someone learning the technique for the first time.

A good foundation in technique is the best way to start a new craft, because it will allow you to take pride in your first efforts; this builds your confidence and encourages you to continue. You can get started with a limited number of very basic techniques, and I think you will be surprised to find how many wonderful things you can make with so few of them. Then for each new project you take on, learn one or two more; this will give you a sense of how easy it is to develop new skills, and as your knowledge grows, you will soon be capable of taking on even the most challenging projects.

But first things first: you must start by learning how to put some stitches on a needle, which is called casting on. The simplest way to do this is to begin by attaching the yarn to the needle with a Twist Start or a Slip Knot, either of which will serve as the first stitch; then use Knit Half-Hitch Cast-on to add 20 or 30 more. This cast-on technique is fun to do and there is a good set of drawings accompanying the instructions that will help make it easy to learn.

Next, turn to the chapter on Knitting Methods, read the introductory material, and then start with the Right-Hand Method, which is described first. It is the easiest one to learn: the material is written with beginners in mind, and so includes instructions for how to hold the yarn and needles, and how to work the two most basic stitch techniques, Knit and Purl (which are actually just two sides of the same stitch). Practice just those two stitches until your hands have learned to do them well enough that you no longer have to think about every step.

Then turn to the more detailed information about Knit and Purl in the chapter The Stitches; this material will enrich your understanding of the structure and characteristics of the basic stitch. While you are there, also read about Turned Stitches, Slip Stitches, and Twist Stitches. These are simple variations of the basic stitch, and they appear alone or in combination with other types of stitches in many patterns; familiarity with them will give you a good foundation of knowledge to build on later.

Following this, you will want to learn a few techniques that allow you to shape a fabric. This is done with what are called increases and decreases; the former add stitches to the number on the needle so the fabric will get wider; the latter remove stitches so the fabric will get narrower. Unless you want to knit scarves forever, you will want to learn how to do this. For general information, first read through the relatively short chapter on Shaping, and then learn a small assortment of specific techniques that you can use for most everything.

Decreases are quite simple and all you need to know to begin with are how to do a Knit Right Decrease and a Knit Left Decrease (the latter has two variations, but they both do the same thing).

There are far more increases to choose from, but you will manage just fine if you learn about the Yarnover and the Turned Yarnover, the Running Thread Increase, and perhaps the Rib Increase, all of which are very easy to do. Eventually you will want to learn the Raised Increase because it is so good at what it does, but save that for later because it is slightly more challenging.

Then, when you are done with whatever you have made, you will need to know how to cast off, which is the technique used to remove the stitches from the needle in a way that gives the fabric a finished edge and prevents the stitches from running down and spoiling everything. The basic Chained Cast-Off is easy to do and serves nicely for almost every purpose.

Before you embark on your first pattern, also read the chapters on Written Stitch Patterns and Written Garment Patterns. These will explain how to read pattern instructions, which use a specialized set of terms and abbreviations that make it possible to write the material in a very concise way. Patterns can look quite mysterious and complicated at first glance, but they are actually fairly simple to read once you get the idea of how they are done, and they will quickly seem familiar to you.

Finally, whenever you do not understand a term used in the discussion or instructions, please turn to the Glossary in the back of the book for definitions.

So take up needles and yarn and join us in this creative and satisfying craft.

INTRODUCTION TO THE FIRST EDITION

Even the simplest hand-knit garment in this day and age is a luxury. In an era when ordinary men and women measure their lives and activities by tenths of seconds on digital watches, taking the time to knit a sweater, hat, or scarf must be justified by more than utility. If we simply wanted to keep warm, machine-knit garments would do the job. Why, then, do hand knits remain popular?

From the beginning of the machine age, people have expressed concern for the loss of individuality that mass-produced objects imply. The inherent uniqueness of anything handmade is a reassuring reflection of the individuality of each human being; it is a gesture of defiance against anonymity and monotony. Against a background of mass-produced objects, things handcrafted have taken on the luster of art. What had once been simply a fisherman's sweater or a peasant's warm mittens have come to be seen as desirable luxuries far from the small world in which they originated. As a result, the craft of knitting has been taken up by people who have no need to make their own clothing.

I don't think we can deny that the same motives are at work in knitting that operate when we acquire any other luxury object. In addition to aesthetic appreciation, there is both the awareness of the work and skill that went into its creation and the aura of status we assume in owning or wearing it. However, these are probably insufficient in themselves to impel most people to spend the long, long hours necessary to knit a garment. Fortunately, there is something about knitting that makes it an intrinsically pleasant activity.

Central to the appeal of knitting is that it works like meditation. Everything becomes quiet, still, and peaceful, and all the turmoil of life seems to succumb to the silent rhythm of the needles and the orderly progression of the stitches. There is a simple, sensual pleasure in the colors and textures of the yarns, and for me, inveterate adherent of the work ethic that I am, it provides an excuse to sit still, for after all I am accomplishing something worthwhile. I also find I do my best thinking when I knit, and I often keep a pad of paper nearby to jot things down as they come to mind.

In addition, knitting offers a creative outlet that accommodates itself nicely to busy lives. The tools and materials represent a modest investment, and the basic techniques are easily learned. The work is eminently portable, accompanying the knitter on vacations or to committee meetings, or helping to fill the empty hours on an airplane. Best of all, the result of the knitter's efforts is something attractive, practical, and unique. A hand-knit garment is also a special way of giving to the ones you love. When I see my husband or child wearing a sweater I have knit, I often think how every inch of the yarn has passed through my hands—it is almost as if I have my arms around them. The sweater is like a cozy talisman I have given them to wear out into the world.

However much we enjoy knitting, and hand-knit garments, there is no knitter who is not aware of the amount of time it takes to knit something. For some time now, in response to knitters wanting "quick knits," bulky yarns and large needles have become a major part of a yarn store's stock in trade, with patterns showing simplified styling and gauges of three or four stitches to an inch. Creativity has been expressed with color and texture rather than with detail or styling, and yarn manufacturers have responded with blended, fluffy yarns.

There is no doubt that this cheerful experimentation enlarged the domain of knitting to its benefit, but it did so to some extent at the expense of quality. Garments knit up with the idea of doing something quick and fun seem to have a short lifespan; they look dated, like last year's fad, all too soon. Certainly there is a place in our lives for things that are fun and ephemeral, but they should not be the sum of our efforts. There is a reawakened interest in classic style and the durable object, and I think the time is right for knitting to rediscover its more serious side as well. Instead of two quick knits you could as easily create one really choice sweater that will be treasured for a lifetime.

If you are going to knit something with more complex styling, a more difficult stitch, and finer yarn and needles, you will also want a mastery of technique that does justice to the effort. This book is intended to help you achieve just that. Of course, it will also help you make that next quick knit a better garment and one that is more satisfying to wear. Technique is the dry side of any art or craft, but it allows you to realize your ideas. How many of us have invested long hours in a knitting project only to have the result a disappointment because our skills were not adequate to the task?

Do not think, however, that you must master every esoteric element of knitting before you can turn out a quality garment. Far from it! Truly special knits that you would be proud to wear or give as a gift are possible using only a handful of the most elementary skills. And for all its emphasis on technique, this book was not meant to encourage technicians.

Those who knit up someone else's designs, however perfectly they do it, are good technicians and not masters of the craft. This is not to say that patterns and kits don't have a place in knitting—they most certainly do. You may not always have time to design your own garment—it can be twice as time consuming as simply knitting one—and there will always be occasions when even the most expert knitter will find that a kit or a commercial pattern is exactly what is needed. I think, however, that if you limit yourself to these you are missing half the fun and all the rewards of knowing that the finished product is uniquely yours.

Besides, what knitter has not been in the situation of discovering, in the back of the closet during spring cleaning, some yarn purchased three years ago? Perhaps you still like the yarn but wouldn't dream of making it up in the pattern you originally bought it for. Then, there is always that time when what you want to do more than anything else is to knit, but you've run into problems and the yarn store is closed—or you're on vacation and a store is miles away. Or perhaps you saw a gorgeous sweater in a store and you can't find a knitting pattern like it, or the pattern is close but the neckline or the sleeve is wrong.

My hope is that the information in this book will give you the confidence in your skills that will liberate you from dependence on instructors and patterns so you can create a garment that is exactly what you wish it to be. Knowing how a knitting pattern is put together, and how the stitches and techniques work, will help you to recognize errors when they occur in a commercial pattern (and they do), or to make any changes required to make a garment fit properly. You will be able to add elements to a pattern that the designer did not suggest, and as your confidence grows, you will want to begin to design your own patterns.

I do not believe in rote learning, nor in faithful adherence to recipes, so you will find few formulas here. I did not want to simply tell you how to do something; rather my goal was to explain the techniques so that instead of just going through the motions you would truly understand what you were doing. With this in mind, I have tried to be sensitive to the problems of description. Too often knitting books contain instructions that are incomplete, convoluted, or impossible to follow. Instead, the instructions here are given in a detailed, often lengthy, step-by-step manner. Please do not confuse length with difficulty. I think you will find these full descriptions easier to follow than the often brief and cryptic ones found in other books. I have also been most detailed in those descriptions likely to be of importance to a beginning knitter. As the techniques become more esoteric I become more brief, assuming that the knitter who would be interested in these needs less in the way of description.

In doing the research, I found that identical techniques were often referred to by different names or symbols in different books. In trying to decide which name was most appropriate, I found there was often no way to choose among the alternatives. In some cases I have simply abandoned all of them and settled on a term that conveys a sense of the operation performed or the resulting appearance. I hope I have not added to the confusion.

There is also a difficulty with certain relative terms commonly used in knitting, particularly "right side" and "wrong side," or "front" and "back." Both "right side" and "front" are generally used to refer to that side of the fabric which will show when the garment is worn. But "front," for example, could also mean the part of the garment worn on the front of the body, or it could be used to refer to the side of the work that happens to be facing the knitter.

For the sake of consistency and clarity, I will use "inside" and "outside" to refer only to the faces of the fabric as it is intended to be worn or used. "Front" and "back" will be used only to refer to particular pieces of the garment, as in the front part of a sweater. "Right" will be used only with "left," as in the right or left side of a stitch or the right or left side of the fabric as you are looking at it.

When we are discussing the position of the work in relation to the knitter, the position of the knitter's hands, or the placement of yarn or needles, I will use the terms "nearside" and "farside," meaning that side closest to the knitter or farthest away at that particular moment.

If you have read this far, you will have become aware that this is an affectionate but critical look at this fine old craft. Few knitters stop to really think about the techniques they use, but work the way they do because that's the way they were taught, and the well-worn path is the most comfortable one. Therefore, even the most advanced knitter will have a legacy of methods that may not really be the best in a given situation. I have gone back to the beginning and have questioned, examined, and tested even the most fundamental aspects of knitting, trying to look at each with new eyes. I wanted to know why a technique behaved the way it did, under what circumstances it worked best, and whether or not it could be improved or if there was an alternate method that worked better. In some cases, I found that what many believe to be separate techniques are simply different ways of doing exactly the same thing. I have tried to be exhaustively thorough, even including techniques that you should know about just so you can avoid them. In addition, there are countless regional variations and little oddments of knowledge that are not generally known. I have sought out and tested any obscure technique that I could find, rejecting some and delighting in others that I hope will find wider use.

This is meant to be a reference book, dipped into from time to time as the need arises, and is intended for every knitter, beginning, intermediate, or advanced. The beginning knitter should concentrate on the most basic techniques until they are mastered, and only then go on to something more complicated. If you are an intermediate knitter, it would be a good idea to review familiar techniques before delving into new material to make sure you are using the best methods of working, and then use the book as a reference when you want to try something new. As you keep knitting and solving problems associated with realizing your ideas, you will soon join the ranks of the expert knitters.

When I began this book, I already considered myself something of an expert knitter. Well, pride goes before the fall, and needless to say I completely underestimated the amount of time such an inquiry would take and how much there was to learn. Speaking from experience, I can unhesitatingly recommend to the most self-confident knitter that even the first chapters on fundamentals be read carefully. Just as I did, I think you may find some of your most cherished and dependable techniques called into question. On the whole, I hope the book will deepen your understanding, hone your skills, and provide you with new ideas and challenges.

ACKNOWLEDGMENTS

Writing is a solitary occupation, but making a book out of what is written requires the help and participation of others. During the ten years it took to create this new edition of *The Principles of Knitting*, I was blessed with the support, encouragement, and contributions of a great many wonderful, capable, and talented people.

As I suggested in the dedication, it is impossible to adequately express how grateful I am to my dear husband, whose belief in me and this book was constant, and whose generosity and patience throughout were extraordinary. He steadied and sustained me through all the ups and downs of this big, complicated project. My multi-talented son, Jesse, revised and improved many of the original graphics and managed to create new ones that blended in with the old ones. He was a joy to work with; always patient with my requests and revisions, and ready for any challenge. It was especially convenient that we keep the same night-owl schedule; he was literally there for me at almost any time. The book would never have been possible without both of them; their love and support means everything to me.

I also want to thank Muriel C.M. Sarik, who patiently scanned all the original artwork for me. In addition, she and her husband, Christopher B. Becker, have been family friends who have helped me in countless thoughtful and considerate ways over the years. I think they know how much they mean to me and how grateful I am, but it is nice to have the opportunity to express it publicly.

On a day-to-day basis, quiet, patient companionship was offered by Rufus, our orange tabby, and by Harley, our amazing African Grey Parrot. His "Whatcha doin'?" signaled I had been at it too long, and that it was time for a break and a cup of tea. He never failed to amuse, delight, and divert me; his uncanny ability to speak clearly was almost like having someone else in the office, which helped assuage my sense of isolation.

Midway through the revision, there were practical matters to deal with. I had the great good fortune of being introduced to Jennifer Joel of International Creative Management (ICM), who agreed to become my agent. She and ICM attorney John DeLaney worked with patience and persistence over many months on the details of a contract with Simon & Schuster, which assured that the second edition of this book would have a good future. Jenn was also there for me at every turn with help, information, and welcome advice; it made a huge difference to have her in my corner.

It was a great pleasure to have Michelle Howry as my editor and Project Manager at Touchstone Publishing, a division of Simon & Schuster. No writer could ask for more sensitive feedback on precious sentences and paragraphs than she provided to me, nor could they have a better advocate for their book than she was for mine. She offered subtle insight and diplomatic, thoughtful advice every step of the way; it was both a privilege and a wonderful experience to work with her and she has my heartfelt gratitude.

Stacy Creamer, publisher; David Falk, associate publisher; and Sally Kim, editorial director, remained steadfast in spite of all the challenges. Their patience with the difficulties and delays we experienced in bringing this big book back to life, and their extraordinary generosity throughout has not only earned my gratitude, but I am humbled by their belief in me and *The Principles of Knitting*; all of you who care about the book owe them a big "thank you."

The important matters of paper, binding, and printing were in the capable hands of Twisne Fan and George Turianski in the Production Department. Marcia Burch and Justina Batchelor in the Publicity Department are working to help bring the book out into the world again, and Allegra Ben-Amotz, assistant to Ms. Kim, helped with many details in the Editorial Department. I also want to thank Michelle for arranging to have Rosy Ngo help acquire some of the photos we used, and to assist with background research on fibers. Megan Looney provided assistance with the bibliography.

The book was designed and copyedited at Wilsted & Taylor Publishing Services in Oakland, California. It is truly difficult to overstate how important their contribution has been. Christine Taylor and LeRoy Wilsted are well-known for their dedication to the venerable craft of book making, and I can testify to their consummate professionalism and skill. They and their entire staff exhibited an extraordinary attention to detail in regard to text and image, as well as a sensitivity and patience with this author and her book that was beyond all expectation. It was an immense privilege to work with them.

I am delighted with Jody Hanson's wonderful new design for the entire book and its cover. It is not just lovely to look at, but the tasteful choice of fonts and layout will enhance the reader's experience. Jody patiently adjusted all the headings, each image and its caption, and all the lines of text so everything was clear and readable on the page. Nancy Evans, copy editor, and Jennifer Brown, proofreader, did far more than polish my prose and correct my lapses in grammar and punctuation. As knitters, they provided invaluable feedback on the clarity and accuracy of the instructions and discussions, and also made welcome suggestions regarding organization and content that improved the text in ways both large and small. They were also tireless in making sure that all of the cross-references pointed to exactly the right place.

Eagle-eyed Melody Lacina made sure that every word, every detail, every line was in place, exactly where it should be. Jennifer Uhlich did the extensive index, which is so important to a book of this kind, with great accuracy and insight as to what would be needed. And Mary Lamprech, Andy Joron, and Yvonne Tsang helped all of them and me in innumerable ways. Their combined efforts have made this new edition of *The Principles of Knitting* incomparably better than it would have been otherwise; any remaining errors and omissions are mine alone. I was also touched and honored by the sweet welcome I received from Willa, Christine and LeRoy's shy greyhound, whenever I visited the Wilsted & Taylor offices.

Finally, I want to thank several people who played background roles, but ones for which I am very grateful.

Most of the swatches I knit up for new photographs were done with Gems Merino from Louet, a superb, worsted-spun yarn that was designed by Trudy Van Stralen. She and her husband, Jan, became good friends during the time I worked on the book, and I always looked forward to their visits, phone calls, and encouragement.

I also want to thank Linda Ligon of Interweave Press. Knitters everywhere owe her a debt of gratitude for all the wonderful books she has published over the years, many of which I turned to during this project. She has also become a friend (and owing to a lucky escape, has remained one), who checked in from time to time to encourage me; it helped a lot to hear from her.

My dear friend Candi Jensen, author and producer of the Emmy-nominated TV program *Knit and Crochet Today*, would periodically drag me away from my desk. We went to lunch and museum shows, indulged in knitting-world gossip, and simply enjoyed each other's company thoroughly. During the last year, when the book took over my life, her visits for tea and cookies provided a welcome break; it always meant so much to have her come by and cheer me along.

And my epistolary friend, Ted Myatt, has been sending his good wishes from afar throughout the entire time I worked on the book. He would check on me from time to time, and his letters always brightened my day; as modest as he is, he probably does not realize how much this meant to me over the years.

And last, but by no means least, I want to honor knitters everywhere who have contributed so much to this craft, and say a special "thank you" to those who believed in this book and waited so patiently for it to return.

Part One

LEARNING AND METHODS

CHAPTER 1

Knitting Methods

All knitting methods produce the same stitches and the same fabric, but they differ in how the yarn and needles are held. With one method, the yarn is in the left hand; with several others it is held in the right hand, and with another it is passed around the back of the neck or pinned to the front of the clothing. The method used to hold the yarn determines how it is wrapped around the needle and what movements are used to form the stitches.

While the various methods are often associated with certain regional knitting traditions, the craft now belongs to the world; therefore, in this book they are primarily identified by the way they are done rather than by geographic association. Indeed most people today knit the way they do not because they belong to a particular knitting culture, but more or less by chance; they use whatever method was first taught to them by a relative, a friend, a neighbor, someone at the local yarn store, or an instruction book.

Furthermore, we are no longer bound by either custom or chance and are free to choose the way we knit based on an analysis of the merits of each method. Each offers certain advantages and disadvantages in terms of speed, fatigue, ease in working different techniques, or control of tension with particular yarns. Every knitter's hands are unique, and we all differ in our dexterity and ability to tolerate the repeated motions required to make the stitches; anyone can be faced with injury or fatigue, which can make it difficult or impossible to continue with a project. In short, it is nice to have options.

For all of these reasons and more, I strongly recommend that every knitter consider learning at least two methods; three is even better. No doubt you will settle on one as your favorite, but when you realize the advantages that knowing the others can provide, you may wonder why you did not acquire these skills earlier. For instance,

you might choose one method when working in the round and another when working flat; prefer one for textured yarns but a different one for smooth yarns; or find one works best with stitch patterns and another for color patterns.

It must be said that while learning to knit initially is relatively painless, learning another method when you already know how is more of a struggle—it is all too easy to give up and return to the comfort of the familiar. Aside from counseling patience, the best suggestion I can offer is one often recommended to beginners: practice on a swatch and then throw it away. Next, make a scarf in a fuzzy colorful yarn that will hide any irregularities, and promise yourself that you will be uncritical about the results. Once you have learned a second method, I think you will find learning a third or even a fourth is considerably easier.

The first method discussed here is the easiest one for a novice to learn, and therefore that material includes the basics of making Knit and Purl stitches so someone new to knitting can follow the instructions. The instructions for the other methods are less detailed, not because they are less important, but because I assume they will be of interest to those who already know how to knit but would like to learn another method and need no instruction in how to Knit and Purl.

Overall, the material is organized on the basis of how the methods relate to one another; simply because the method for beginners happens to be one where the yarn is held on the right, those that are similar to it are discussed next. The methods that hold the yarn on the left follow, and then the one where the yarn is wrapped with the thumb.

With the exception of the method for beginners, the variations in each of these categories are discussed in the order of which ones are more common. Those that have been widely taken up around the world because they are so very good at what they do get most of the attention, while others that are less common but interesting or useful for one reason or another get briefer mention.

In addition to the descriptions of each method, you will find tips for how to improve efficiency and speed, reduce stress and fatigue, and make a smooth, even fabric; even if you regularly work with a particular method, you might find something of interest there. Also included is information on the pros and cons of each method: none of them is perfect nor is any ideal for all circumstances, and this will give you a sense of why you might want to work with one or another method, depending upon circumstances.

Origins of Names for Knitting Methods

Here in the United States, the names we use for the different knitting methods reflect our historical ties to England, where they carried the yarn in the right hand. To distinguish this method from others, we began to refer to it as "English knitting." However, the same method had long been used in many parts of Europe (fourteenth-century paintings of the Madonna from northern Italy and Germany show her knitting in the round and carrying the yarn on her right finger). It is fair to say that knitters from France or Spain who also knit that way do not think of themselves as knitting "English-style."

The English originally called the Left-Hand Method "German knitting," but after two world wars this name had negative associations for many knitters, and, as the method came into more common use elsewhere in Europe, the name gradually changed to "Continental knitting." However, left-hand methods were known quite a bit earlier in Central Europe and Russia, where knitters are unlikely to think of themselves as working in "Continental style."

Unfortunately, these regional names give the impression that knitting originated in Europe, when in fact the oldest examples of the craft have been found in the Middle East; it seems to have spread from there throughout the world by means of trade and exploration.

Yet another method that is common in the Middle East and around the Mediterranean area spread to South America several hundred years ago with the Spanish explorers, but it is only now becoming better known in Europe and North America. With it, the yarn is carried around the neck or pinned to the bodice.

The history of knitting is incomplete, much has yet to be learned, and this is not a history book. But it does seem safe to say that the regional names long in use in the United States are somewhat inappropriate and, therefore, I have decided instead to use terms that reflect something of how each method is done.

General Information

Before going on to a discussion of the particular knitting methods, I want to provide you with some information that is useful for all of them.

If you are new to knitting, you might want to just skim through this now for what you need to know to get started, and then reread it after you have learned the fundamentals. Also, you might find it helpful to look at the material in the Introduction to the Second Edition about Terminology, which includes some definitions of terms you will encounter here.

If you are already a knitter, you might want to read through this just to see if something is new to you or provides insight into some aspect of a method that you were not familiar with before.

Basically, this information tries to make explicit many of the things we take for granted once we already know how to knit; it should be of use to any knitter, beginning or experienced, and may be particularly helpful to the latter when teaching someone else.

❖ *Position of Hands*

For every method but one, the hands are on top of the needles, palms down, with the forefingers and thumbs close to the tips. The forefinger and perhaps the thumb of one hand is used to manipulate the yarn and maintain tension. The other thumb and forefinger are also busy; they are used to stabilize the needles where they meet, to encourage a needle to enter or exit a stitch, to put downward tension on the fabric to make it easier to work a stitch, or to hold a stitch out of the way in order to make it easier to insert the needle tip into the stitch next to it.

As you work, the growing weight of the fabric can contribute to fatigue. It helps to tuck your elbows firmly into your waist (and keep them there), and lower your hands so the growing weight of the fabric can rest in your lap. This position also prevents you from tensing your upper arms and shoulders, which can cause aches and pains later.

When learning any new method I recommend you use a smooth knitting yarn of medium thickness in a light, neutral color and a pair of 8- to 10-inch-long needles in size 4 or 5. I do not recommend long straight needles for any purpose. The problem is that a very small motion of just an inch or so at the tip of the needle will cause a very large motion of several inches at the other end. Even if you support the fabric in your lap, the needle must still move, and you will be doing a minor version of weight lifting with every stitch; this not only adds to fatigue but can contribute to repetitive motion injuries. If you cannot accommodate all the stitches you need for a particular project on needles no more than 10 to 12 inches long, change to circular ones (see Circular Needles).

❖ *Tensioning the Yarn*

A certain amount of tension is applied to the yarn at all times. This does several things: it maintains the yarn in position in your hand or on your finger ready to form the next stitch, and also keeps it wrapped on the needle as the next stitch is formed. In addition, the combination of the size of the needle and the tension you apply to the yarn determines the size of each stitch.

However, the tension on the yarn must vary slightly as you work. The yarn needs to slip through your hand as it is wrapped around the needle, and then it must be stayed as the new stitch is made. This alternation in tension is quite subtle and with practice becomes automatic; it is the primary skill required to produce a fabric with even stitches (and should you need them, there are additional tips below in Problems with Tension or Yarn Twist).

It is fair to say that there is no ideal way to tension the yarn; it is partly a matter of anatomy (everyone's hands are different), partly what kind of yarn you are using, and perhaps what kind of stitch or color technique you are working with. It is quite common to change how the yarn is held, depending upon circumstances.

With one of the knitting methods discussed below, the function of manipulating the yarn and tensioning it is combined; it is held by the same thumb and forefinger that are used to wrap the yarn. With others, the yarn is often wrapped several times around the forefinger that does so. However, with most methods, these two functions are separated; the yarn is carried on one finger near the needle tip and the tension is provided either by wrapping the yarn around one or more other fingers of the hand, or simply by holding it in the palm.

Here are the most common ways to tension the yarn separately, regardless of the method used (although there are endless variations on this theme):

- The yarn is passed from the ball to the palm of the hand, up between the fourth and fifth fingers, and then completely around the fifth finger at its base; from there it passes under the two middle fingers, then over the top of the forefinger to the needle.
- The yarn is passed under the fifth finger, over the fourth finger, under the middle finger, and then over the back of the forefinger.

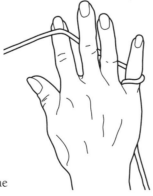

Yarn Tension: Common method of tensioning yarn.

- The yarn passes across the palm, up between the forefinger and middle finger, across the back of the last three fingers and across the palm again to the forefinger.
- The yarn simply lies in the crease between the palm of the hand and the fingers, and is held in place there when the fingers grip the needle.

❖ *Knitting Direction*

All but two of the methods are described for working the stitches in the most common way, by starting with the needle bearing the stitches held in the left hand, and with the empty needle in the right hand. As the stitches on the left needle are worked and discarded into the fabric, new stitches accumulate on the right needle.

Some people prefer the Reversed Method, working in the opposite way with the needle bearing the stitches in the right hand, the empty needle in the left, and the new stitches passing from the right needle to the left; people who are left-handed often favor this method. It is also possible to combine these two approaches in a method called Bi-Directional. These are discussed in Optional Methods, below, where you will also find a brief discussion about being left-handed and whether this affects the choice of knitting method.

❖ *Stitch Position*

The instructions describe how to wrap the yarn and form stitches that sit on the needle in what is considered standard position for most methods, with the right side of the stitch on the nearside of the needle.

However, with two of the Left-Hand Methods, all or some of the stitches are placed on the needle in the "turned" position, with the left side of the stitch on the nearside of the needle instead. The yarn and needles are held in the same way, but different motions are required to form the stitches.

Methods with Yarn to Right

There are two primary ways to knit with the yarn carried in the right hand. With one, the yarn is held between thumb and forefinger, with the other it is held on the right forefinger. There are also two variations of the latter method; with each of them the needle is held in a unique way, but in other respects they are much the same.

For all of these, the yarn supply is placed on the right side, so more can be drawn off without getting caught in the work at hand.

The first method is the one I recommend if you are learning how to knit. Once you are comfortable with working this way, then you can explore the other methods; as mentioned above, it is a good idea to know how to do at least two of them.

❖ *Right-Hand Method*

I think of this method as the Cinderella of knitting because it is all too often dismissed as slow and awkward. I am impressed by what it offers to many people as a primary method to use for everything they make, and to others as an option for certain projects.

The great value of the method is that the yarn is both held and tensioned by the right thumb and forefinger. There is no need to acquire the skill of using these definitively human tools since we have all practiced doing so since infancy; they allow the most refined and precise control for any task.

For this reason I recommend the Right-Hand Method to beginning knitters as the best one to learn first. Because everyone already knows how to use their thumb and forefinger, the focus can be on learning stitch formation instead of how to hold and tension the yarn. This means there is considerably less initial frustration and even the first thing made is likely to be of good quality, which is an encouragement to continue.

The Right-Hand Method is also a very good option if you lack dexterity, whether because of youth or age, injury, or disability; if you have found that the method you previously used has become difficult to manage, this one is worth trying.

However, lest you be tempted to think it is a method only for beginners or for those whose hands are not cooperative, I want to recommend that those of you who primarily use some other method consider learning the Right-Hand Method as an option. There is no aspect of knitting that cannot be accomplished with it, and it provides exceptional control when working even the most difficult stitch techniques.

Furthermore, the exact control of tension it provides is a great asset when a smooth, even fabric is needed or when a highly textured or slippery yarn proves hard to manage; it is ideal for working with ribbon yarns, for instance. In short, it could well become the method you turn to when faced with some of the most challenging tasks in knitting.†

While this is not the fastest method, it is more than acceptable in that regard (most knitters work at a nice steady pace, no matter what method they use), and there are tips included below that help make the motions smooth and efficient. It is not the best method to use for a Stranded Color pattern; the Right-Finger Method and the Left-Hand Method are much better choices, especially when combined.

---

† I also gave the Right-Hand Method considerable attention in the first edition of *Principles of Knitting*, and for the same reasons mentioned here. This gave many people the erroneous impression that it was my favorite, when it is simply one of the four methods I rely upon. My mother taught me to knit this way when I was very young; I remain fond of it and use it often, but by the 1980s when I originally wrote this book, it was no longer my primary method.

Learning to Knit

If you have never knit before, the first step is to put about 20 to 30 stitches on the needle. This is called *casting on*, and I recommend you use a technique called Knit Half-Hitch Cast-On. It is fun to learn and easy to do, and you do not need to know how to knit in order to use it and get started.

Once you gain some facility with holding the yarn and needles and making basic Knit and Purl stitches (these terms actually refer to the two sides of the same stitch), you will want to read more about them in the chapter The Stitches. Also included there are definitions of the component parts of a stitch and an explanation of the structure of a knitted fabric and how it is made.

When learning how to knit, you will be making a small square of flat fabric; later you can learn how to do circular knitting, which allows you to make something in the round like a tube (or, of greater interest, a sweater with no seams, or a hat, or a sock). To find out more about the characteristics of both approaches, see Circular and Flat Knitting.

Holding the Yarn and Needles

Place the ball of yarn to your right; take up the needle holding the cast-on stitches in your left hand, and the empty needle in your right hand. Sit in a comfortable position, with your elbows at your sides, and your hands holding the needles no higher than your waist. The most important thing is to relax; tension causes fatigue and stitches that are too tight.

1. Hold needle with stitches on it in left hand, palm down, with thumb and forefinger about one inch back from tip and other three fingers curled under needle to brace it against hand; yarn will be hanging from first stitch on needle.
2. Hold empty needle in right hand in same way. Reach last three fingers of right hand under yarn and scoop it up; let it settle in gap between middle finger and forefinger and trail loosely over back of hand.
3. Bring two needle tips close together, with about a one-inch gap between them. Yarn should pass on farside of right needle tip, from first stitch on left needle to right hand.
4. Grasp yarn lightly with right thumb and forefinger and rest these fingers on top of needle until it is time to wrap yarn; return to this default position after forming each stitch.
5. Hold needles with tips up at a slight angle—imagine a clock face and point one tip toward number ten, and other toward number two.

Forming the Knit Stitch

As mentioned above, Knit and Purl refer to the appearance of the two sides of the basic stitch in the fabric. When you make a Knit stitch, that side of the stitch will appear on the nearside of the fabric as you work; Purl will be on the other side. When you make a Purl stitch, that side of the stitch appears on the nearside, and Knit will be on the other side.

1. Move tip of right needle to nearside of left needle and insert it into center of first stitch *from left to right*, sliding it under other needle and out on farside. Both needles are now in stitch, with left needle pointing up to right on nearside, and right needle pointing up to left on farside.

Right-Hand Method for Knit: Step 1. Hold yarn and needles as shown and insert right needle into first stitch on left needle.

2. Pinch left thumb and forefinger together to support two needles just *below* where they cross. Hold on to yarn with right thumb and forefinger and then release right needle (if supported correctly, it will not slide out of stitch), and lift right hand an inch or two.

3. Drop left hand down slightly to right, moving crossed needle tips below right hand, and then wrap yarn: under right needle tip, up between two needle tips and then over top of right needle to farside again. Allow enough yarn to slide through fingers to wrap yarn firmly but not too tightly around needle.

Forming the Knit Stitch: Step 3. Wrap yarn under right needle.

Forming the Knit Stitch: Step 3. Drop left hand under right hand to wrap yarn for stitch.

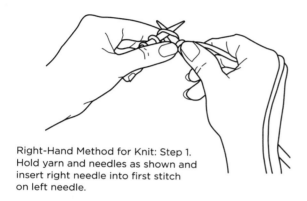

4. Move left hand back up into position, and move right hand down to pick up right needle again; maintain some tension on yarn at all times.

5. With right hand back in starting position, use right needle tip to pull yarn wrapped around it under left needle and through stitch to nearside; at same time use left needle to lift original stitch over yarn.

6. Discard (drop) original stitch from left needle by simultaneously sliding left needle out of stitch and using right needle tip to push it off.

7. Repeat Steps 1–6 with each stitch on left needle. When all original stitches have been Knit and dropped off left needle, and same number of new stitches are on right needle, this completes one row of knitting.

8. Transfer needle with new stitches from right hand to left, and empty needle from left hand to right, turning tips so they face one another again at center, and work next row in same way.

Forming the Knit Stitch: Step 5. Pull yarn through stitch to nearside.

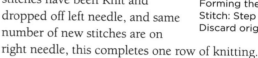

Forming the Knit Stitch: Step 6. Discard original stitch.

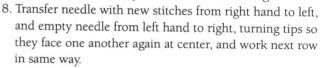

After discarding the first stitch in Step 6, notice that it encircles the base of the new stitch on the right needle. The yarn is now attached to the new stitch, and as you Knit it should always be in position on the farside of the right needle.

Also notice that after working the first stitch, the two needles are then tied together by a strand of yarn that passes from the discarded stitch below the right needle to the next stitch on the left needle; this strand is called the *running thread*. Keep the needle tips close together because, if the running thread is stretched too tight, it will be difficult to insert the needle into the next stitch.

Knit another row and watch the process carefully as you make each stitch. When you discard a stitch from the left needle, the head of the stitch will be dropped on the farside of the right needle, out of sight. On the nearside, the lower portion of the stitch will be visible below the right needle, and it will look like a little V; this is the Knit side of the stitch.

After you have done one row and turn to begin a new one, you will see a double row of little horizontal nubs below the left needle. The nubs in the top of the row are the heads of the discarded stitches; those in the bottom are the running threads that pass between the new stitches on the needle above.

Each time you Knit a row, you will put Vs above nubs, and on the farside nubs will appear above Vs. After completing several rows of knitting, examine the fabric. It will have a corrugated appearance made up of horizontal rows of little nubs separated by rows of little Vs. This is called the Garter Stitch pattern; it lies very flat, looks the same on both sides, and is vertically resilient (in fact, you may have to stretch it out to see the Knit stitches because the Purl stitches close around them).

The Subtleties

After you have practiced doing a few rows and start to gain confidence, here are a few things to pay attention to that will help you work more quickly and smoothly.

- Your left thumb and forefinger should always be positioned on either side of the fabric between the crossed needle tips; pinch the fabric right below the first few stitches so the needles just rest on top of your fingers.

- The slight movement of the left hand to bring the needle tip below the right hand is important; it makes the motion of wrapping the yarn more efficient and increases speed. This is done not by moving your hand from the wrist, but by dropping your left forearm from the elbow; your hand and wrist should remain in a straight line.

- *Always keep your elbows at your sides.* There is never any reason to move your entire right arm when wrapping the yarn around the needle. Simply lift your right hand from the needle and drop the crossed needle tips under it; your hand should move only an inch or two in order to wrap the yarn.

- Keep your hands down low over your lap. This supports the weight of the fabric as it grows from the needles, frees your hands to manipulate the stitches, and reduces strain on elbows and shoulders. Relax. Maintain the tension on the yarn with your hand; tensing your body will not help.

- While it is easiest to describe inserting the right needle into the center of the stitch, in fact, the left needle is equally engaged in putting the stitch on the right needle.

    Once you have moved the tip of the right needle to the left of the next stitch at its base, slide the stitch down onto it with the left needle; the right needle will automatically pass through the stitch and come out on the farside.

- The circumference of the needle acts as a gauge that determines the amount of yarn allotted to each stitch. Wrap the yarn around the *shaft* of the needle; if the yarn is wrapped around the tip of the needle instead, your stitches will tend to be too tight.

- Maintain tension on the yarn as you draw the new stitch through the original one; if this is not done, the stitches will be too loose, or a stitch may even slip off the needle before you can pull it through.

- Fussing with the yarn slows you down. Having the ball of yarn on your right side helps to maintain it in position between your fingers so it will not get caught between

hand and needle. Also, you can simply raise your right arm to draw more yarn out of the ball, which allows for a quick return to the knitting.

- As you work, pause from time to time to push a group of stitches up closer to the left needle tip, and smooth some of the new stitches down along the right needle.

Forming the Purl Stitch

The second step in becoming a knitter is to learn how to Purl. When working as described above, the Knit side of the stitch was on the nearside of the right needle; to make a Purl stitch, the head of the stitch is discarded on the nearside instead. To do this, the needle is inserted into the stitch and the yarn is wrapped in slightly different ways, as follows:

1. Hold yarn and needles as before, with one bearing stitches in left hand, and empty needle in right hand, but always keep yarn on *nearside* of right needle.
2. Move tip of right needle to nearside of left needle tip and insert it directly into first stitch from *right to left*; tips of needles will cross, with right needle pointing to left on nearside, and left needle pointing to right on farside.

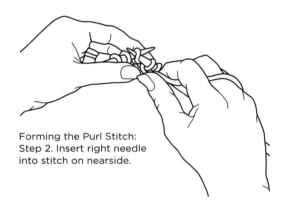

Forming the Purl Stitch: Step 2. Insert right needle into stitch on nearside.

3. Support cross of needles with left thumb and forefinger and release right needle. Drop left hand under right hand, as before, and wrap yarn down between crossed needle tips and under right needle tip to nearside. Move hands back into position, and pick up right needle again.

Forming the Purl Stitch: Step 3. Wrap yarn over needle.

4. Maintain tension on yarn and use tip of right needle to draw yarn under left needle and through original stitch toward farside.
5. With new stitch on right needle, simultaneously pull left needle

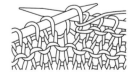

Forming the Purl Stitch: Step 4. Draw new stitch through to farside.

back slightly, and then slide right needle against original stitch so it drops off toward nearside.

6. Repeat these steps across row; with all stitches now on right needle, turn needles and exchange them from right to left hand and work next row in same way.

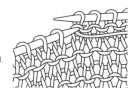

Forming the Purl Stitch: Step 5. Discard stitch.

As you Purl, notice that the little nubs now appear below the right needle where you can see them. If you look on the other side of the fabric, you will see the little V shapes of the lower half of the stitches.

Practice Purl, just as you did Knit, until it feels almost automatic. Do not be surprised if you discover that you are still making Garter Stitch. Of course you are! If you Purl every stitch and every row, you will be stacking nubs on top of Vs with results no different than if you Knit every row, stacking Vs on top of nubs.

However, where you changed from working one way to the other, you will see two rows of Knit, on one side of the fabric, and two rows of Purl on the other. If you always work a row of Knit when there are Knit stitches below the left needle, and then work a row of Purl above Purl stitches, you will make Stockinette, which is the most common pattern in all of knitting; try that next. And then, to learn to make patterns that combine Knit and Purl on the same row, see the chapter on The Stitches.

Common Knitting Errors

When first learning to knit, it is difficult to absorb so many little details all at once, and you need to be patient and give your hands time to learn; trust that they will find their way. It is a bit like learning to ride a bicycle—very awkward at first, and then so easy you will no longer have to think about it.

When you make a mistake, just go on as best you can, and promise you will not be hard on yourself; even expert knitters make mistakes. With practice you will make fewer of them, and learn how to fix the ones you do make. What is important as you work on this first practice swatch is simply to pay attention to your errors and analyze how they happened; this feedback will help you learn not to repeat them. The ones that are most common to beginners are fairly easy to watch for.

Location of Yarn

Make sure the yarn is always on the farside of the needles when you Knit, and on the nearside when you Purl. If the yarn is not in the correct position when you Knit or Purl a stitch, it will pass over the needle; you may not be aware of this when it happens, but on the next row you will encounter a strand on the needle that does not look like a normal stitch.

This is called a Yarnover, and it is a very important stitch technique when used appropriately, but it should not be used by accident; it adds an extra stitch to the fabric with a hole under it (this is called an Eyelet, and is the basis of all lace knitting).

Since this is merely a practice swatch, if you find a strand like that on the needle, just drop it off; in time, you will make this mistake less frequently and later you can learn how to fix it so you have no holes in your fabric where you do not want them.

To prevent this from happening in the future, always check the position of the yarn before you begin to work; if necessary, move it *between* the two needle tips to the nearside for Knit or farside for Purl before making the next stitch.

Dropped Stitches

If a stitch drops off the needle, just pick it up as best you can and go on; make sure the right side of the stitch is on the nearside of the needle. If a stitch drops off and you do not catch it right away, it will unravel a few rows down, leaving an open "ladder" in the fabric, and you will have one fewer stitch on the needle.

To prevent this from happening, keep your stitches away from the tips of the needles; the first stitch should sit on the shaft of the needle just back from where it starts to taper down to the tip.

Once you are comfortable making the stitches, you will want to read the information on how to pick up dropped stitches and put them back on the needle in the correct position (see Repairing a Dropped Stitch).

Split Stitches

Another common error made when you are first learning is to insert the needle through the yarn instead of into the center of the stitch. This causes what is known as a *split stitch*, which will look like a thin loop of yarn on the surface of the fabric.

Here again, the important thing is simply to notice the stray yarn and understand how this happened; later, you can learn how to undo the stitches back to the one that is split and correct it (see Unraveling Stitches). For now, concentrate on preventing this from happening. The trick is to slide the tip of the right needle against the shaft of the left needle as you insert it into the stitch; maintain contact between the two needles because a stitch can be split only when the tip is exposed.

❖ Right-Finger Methods

The Right-Finger Method has become one of the most common ways to knit, and for good reason: it is not only very fast, but it can also be used successfully for any kind of knitting project. In addition, it is an excellent choice to pair with the Left-Hand Method for working color patterns (see Two-Hand Stranding).

For all its speed and versatility, however, it is more difficult to learn how to manage the yarn with this method, and it will take some practice before you feel comfortable and can achieve a smooth, even fabric.

Right-Finger Knit and Purl

I am going to assume that you already know how to Knit and Purl and all that is needed here is a description of how to hold the needles and yarn and form the stitches.

1. Use an option discussed above for wrapping yarn around fingers of right hand for tension. Hold needles with palms down and fingers close to tips.
2. Hold right forefinger up at an angle on farside, an inch or so above needle tip and nearly parallel to it. Rest finger against yarn, to maintain tension on it at all times.
3. Simultaneously insert right needle into stitch and use left needle to put stitch on right needle.
4. Wrap yarn around needle tip with a slight flick of the finger, returning it immediately to default position. Back of hand will rotate slightly toward nearside, however, wrist and forearm should remain in a straight line.

The finger movement used for both Knit and Purl, and the motion used to bring the yarn between the needles to the nearside or farside when shifting from one to the other, are basically the same. However, for Purl, the back of the hand is rotated slightly farther toward the nearside to position the forefinger at a better angle in relation to the right needle tip.

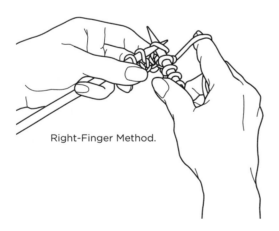

Right-Finger Method.

This similarity between Knit and Purl is one of the great advantages of the method, because it means you can do both of these primary stitches with equal facility, speed, and tension. Forming the stitches requires little movement of the hands and no movement of the wrists, which means you can knit for long stretches without fatigue or risk of injury.

Furthermore, because the yarn is drawn firmly to the right, the area between the needle tips remains fully visible, which can be a great advantage when executing complex stitch techniques. The direction in which the yarn is pulled also helps to maintain the wrapped yarn on the needle, and draws the new stitch to the right.

The Right-Finger Method is a direct descendent of a much older one that is now little used; see the Knitting Belt or Sheath Method, below; while the latter has some limitations, it is worth learning because it is perhaps the fastest and least tiring of all, and allows precise control of tension.

Common Problems

- If the yarn is too long between the last stitch made and the forefinger, the distance your finger needs to move in order to wrap the yarn will increase, which reduces speed. Adjust the length of the yarn so your finger just clears the needle tip when wrapping it.
- If you have trouble clearing the needle tip with your right forefinger, move your hand closer to the tip. As you move your finger to wrap the yarn, relax your grip on the right needle so the opposite end drops down in your hand slightly; the tip will move up to meet the yarn.
- Alternatively, use your right thumb somewhat like a fulcrum; as you reach your forefinger toward the needle tip, bend your thumb and slide your palm along the needle without dropping it.
- Some knitters find it works to slide their hand forward along the needle shaft to wrap the yarn; if this helps, you might also want to try the technique described for the Right-Hand Method: drop the left hand down slightly to the right to bring the crossed needle tips to meet the yarn.

Supported-Needle Methods

The Right-Finger Method evolved out of a much older one that was common in many places in Europe until the late nineteenth and early twentieth centuries (and no doubt elsewhere).

The Knitting Belt or Sheath Method is still used, most famously in the Shetland Islands, and its great advantage is that the right needle is supported, which frees the right hand to manage stitch formation and tension control. A closely related technique is the Underarm Method.

Knitting Belt or Sheath Method

In nineteenth-century Great Britain, this method was used by knitters who helped feed and clothe their families by making socks, sweaters, and shawls for personal use and for sale. They were paid not for their time, but for what they produced, so there was an incentive to make high-quality goods as quickly as possible, and the knitting method they used is fast and extremely efficient.

One of the devices used to hold the needle is an oval leather pouch stuffed with horsehair; it is attached to a belt that is fastened around the waist or hips. The leather has holes punched in it, and one end of a double-point needle is inserted into whichever hole will position it at the most convenient angle. With the needle supported in this way, the right hand is free to work more swiftly as a shuttle and keep the stitches flowing.

Another device that serves the same purpose is a wood or bone sheath about 8 to 10 inches long with a hole drilled in one end to receive the needle; it is tucked into the waistband or belt. Some are contoured to fit the body comfortably and many were beautifully carved; knitting sheaths are frequently seen in museum collections of craft tools.

Absent a belt or a sheath, knitters might tie some goose feathers together, stick the bundled quills into their waistband or apron tie, and insert the knitting needle into the vanes. If there were no geese in the yard and nothing else was at hand, the needle could be tucked under the right arm, which eventually became a knitting method as well (see Underarm Method, below).

The fixed needle also frees the knitter from a seated position; drawings often show nineteenth-century British women knitting as they walked to market or went about their chores. The yarn was carried in a bag or on a hook that hung from the waist or was pinned to the bodice. Traditionally, one end of the knitted fabric was also pinned to the skirt so the work could be dropped to attend to a task or pick up a child (or catch a goose).

The yarn is held in the same way as for the Right-Finger Method, and wrapped on the needle with a swift flick of the forefinger. Hand, wrist, and forearm are kept level and the elbows are down at the sides.

Knit and Purl are done with nearly identical motions and facility, and there is no difficulty in working any stitch technique. The motion required is so small that it is possible to work very quickly and for long periods of time with little fatigue; an expert knitter using a belt or sheath can achieve phenomenal speed.

Furthermore, the method is ideal for working color patterns, and this is the technique used in the Shetlands to make those glorious Fair Isle sweaters. Both yarns can be held on the right, or the second yarn can be held as for the Left-Hand Method, discussed below.

Working with the needle supported in this way is also particularly suited to making small items in the round on double-point needles because the right hand is held above, out of the small circle formed by the fabric and away from all those needle tips; you might want to learn this method just to use it for socks.

Perhaps the reason this style of knitting is not more widespread is that it is somewhat difficult to find the knitting belts and sheaths. Also, the technique is traditionally done with long steel double-point needles in sizes smaller than 3 mm (typically no larger than American size 0 to 2). Although double-point needles of any length can be used, if you wanted to use anything larger than a size 3 or 4 you would need a sheath with a bigger hole, or you could use an awl to enlarge a hole in the stuffed pouch.

Working with a Belt or Sheath

To use a knitting belt, fasten it around your waist or hips with the pouch positioned just forward of the right side of the body. It is traditional to have it at the waist, but you can wear it lower on the hips if that helps to position the needles at a comfortable angle. An advantage of the belt is that it will work with needles in a range of sizes.

A knitting sheath is tucked into the waistband, or into a belt worn at the waist. There is a hole in the end of the sheath that is correct for just one needle size, so you would need a sheath for each size. If you are working with long needles, the sheath is positioned farther around to the side; for shorter needles, it is worn forward, on the right front of the waist.

To try this, work with a relatively thin yarn and use a pair of solid steel or aluminum double-point needles in a size no larger than about 2.5 mm (American size 3). The needles are under some stress with this method and need to be relatively strong; wood and bamboo are likely to break, a hollow needle may crumple, and plastics are not stiff enough. It is traditional to use needles as long as 14 to 18 inches, but the technique can be done with needles of any length.

1. Fasten sheath at waist or hip and insert right needle into whichever hole in pouch will position it so tips of needles can be centered, roughly at or just below waist level when working.

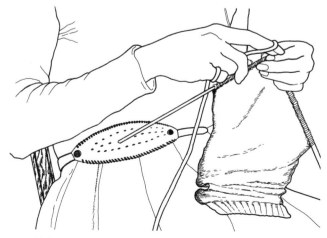

Knitting Belt in use.

2. Perch hand above right needle, with just tips of thumb and middle finger on top of needle; or, rest pad of thumb on top of needle. Relax hand; there is no need to grip needle. Left needle is held in usual way, palm down.

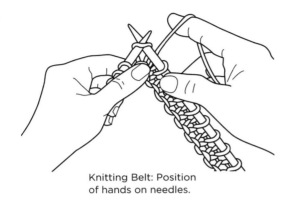

Knitting Belt: Position
of hands on needles.

3. Tension and hold yarn as for Right-Finger Method, with forefinger extended up, about an inch to farside and slightly to right of needle tip; lean finger against yarn held at tension, ready to form a stitch.
4. Use left needle to put stitch on fixed right needle, as to Knit or Purl.
5. Pass yarn around needle tip with a quick flick of forefinger. The hand, wrist, and forearm should remain straight and level at all times.
6. Use left needle to lift original stitch over yarn for discard.

Tips for Using a Belt or Sheath
• You will notice that because the right needle is fixed, the left needle does most of the work. Instead of inserting the right needle tip into the stitch, use the left needle to put the stitch on the right needle tip. Instead of using the right needle to pull the yarn through the original stitch, use the left needle to lift that stitch over the new stitch and off the right needle tip.
• In addition to the movements used to make the stitches, there are several others that help to keep the stitches flowing up to and away from the needle tips. While the pause taken to do this each time is relatively brief, it adds up, and it is worth learning how to minimize the time this takes because it will improve the speed at which you can work.

   As necessary, stop and push a fairly large group of stitches up toward the left needle tip. Bunch them tightly together; use your thumb and forefinger to hold the first few safely on the needle and your little finger to keep the group of stitches collected in the palm of your hand. Then, as the new stitches are made, use your right thumb and middle finger to "walk" them down the right needle away from that tip.

• Somewhat different hand positions can be used, depending upon the position of the needle and its length (and to some extent, on the material of which it is made).

   If the needle is positioned relatively low, you can perch your hand above the needle and use the thumb and middle finger as a fulcrum. As you wrap the yarn, tilt the back of the hand very slightly toward the nearside. This hand position is also advantageous when working with short needles.

   A sheath offers few options for positioning the needle, and it is more likely to be up relatively high. As a result, you may prefer to rest the pad of the thumb on the needle (and with a longer needle, even the forearm), and allow the weight of your hand to push the needle down slightly.
• As mentioned above, the technique puts stress on the needles and some materials are not strong enough. The length of the needle is unimportant, although it is traditional to work with 14- to 18-inch-long spring steel needles, which are inherently flexible, a characteristic that can be used to increase efficiency and speed. The needle is flexed down slightly when inserted into a Knit stitch, and then allowed to flex back up to assist pulling the new stitch through; it is allowed to flex up when inserted into a Purl stitch, and flexed down to draw the new stitch through.

   When using needles made of other materials, somewhat the same thing can be done by simply bending an ordinary, stiff needle down using the pouch or sheath as a fulcrum; the resistance set up will cause the needle to rise again when released.

   Also keep in mind that there is considerable motion required of the left needle, and the longer it is, the more movement there will be at the end opposite the active tip, which causes fatigue; a needle about 12 inches long is a satisfactory compromise. If you prefer to work with longer needles, try to minimize "wagging" the end of the left needle; work low in your lap to support the weight of the fabric. Also, use an up and down motion to put the stitches on the right needle instead of a twisting one to reduce the stress on your wrists.
• To make a circular garment of any size, simply use as many double-point needles as you need for the number of stitches. When working flat with a large number of stitches, use three needles, one active and two for the stitches; keep one folded out of the way on your lap until needed.
• And an important warning: when switching from one needle to the next, grasp the tip of the needle to remove it from the sheath or belt. If you grab the needle down close to the belt or sheath and it resists coming free, you may find yourself with a handful of stitches and an empty needle. Trust me on this—I speak from experience.

Underarm Method

This is no doubt a descendent of the Knitting Belt or Sheath Method. The right needle is tucked up under the arm, which would be a quite natural solution for anyone who normally worked with a belt or sheath but found themselves without one at hand. In time, this evolved as a method of its own; perhaps the belts or sheaths came to be seen as inconvenient, or had been left behind a generation or two ago and were eventually forgotten.

The method requires working with long needles and holding the right arm firmly at the side to keep the needle in position, and as a result the work is held quite high. While this might be an advantage for those whose vision is not good, it can force the arm, hand, and sometimes even the shoulder into a somewhat awkward position.

The position of the hand is like that described for using long needles when working with a Knitting Sheath, above, with the pad of the thumb and perhaps the entire forearm resting on the top of the needle.

If the needle is up high enough, it begins to make sense to put the back of the hand under the right needle, allowing it to rest in the crook between thumb and forefinger, which is probably the origin of the following method, Parlor Knitting.

Regardless of the position of the hand, the method is otherwise the same as the Knitting Belt or Sheath Method, above.

Parlor Method

This method is a descendent of the Supported-Needle family; I called it "pencil knitting" in the first edition of this book because the right needle is held somewhat as you would a pencil. I later came across the name "parlor knitting" in Richard Rutt's fine book *A History of Hand Knitting*, and find it delightfully apt.†

When middle-class Victorian women took up knitting as an activity to occupy quiet hours in the parlor after dinner (along with many other needle arts), this was the method they adopted. Perhaps they knew about the knitting belts and sheaths but did not want things of that sort to compromise the beauty of their dinner clothes; they apparently thought that propping a needle under the arm lacked a certain refinement and wanted to distance themselves from the working-class origins of the craft.

However, they apparently did like the idea of holding the needle from underneath because the hand took on such an elegant position, quite like daintily raising a cup when sipping tea.

† Richard Rutt, *A History of Hand Knitting* (London: B. T. Batsford, 1987; Loveland, Colo.: Interweave Press, 2003), pp. 17–20; citations are to the Interweave Press edition.

1. Tension and hold yarn as for Right-Finger Method, above. Hold left needle in usual way, palm down.
2. Place right hand under other needle so it rests in hollow between thumb and forefinger and grasp it between thumb and forefinger, as for holding a pencil. Place hand far enough forward on needle that forefinger can clear needle tip to wrap yarn.
3. To move finger forward in order to wrap yarn, spread thumb and forefinger apart (with thumb acting somewhat like a lever), and/or slide hand along shaft of needle slightly.

For Purl, rotate back of hand toward nearside to bring forefinger in better alignment with right needle tip.

I have also seen knitters carry the yarn on the middle finger and, after it is wrapped around the needle, use their forefinger to hook the yarn and draw it firmly to the right. While this works reasonably well, it does mean that the shuttle finger is even farther from the needle tip, especially for Purl.

The elegance of the hand position comes at some cost, because without the support of belt, sheath, or underarm, the weight of the needles and growing fabric rest primarily on the thumb. Furthermore, some of the fabric is bunched up between thumb and needle and the hand is trapped under the needle, which both restricts its motion and inhibits the flow of stitches down along the needles.

The stability of the needle depends upon pinching it slightly between the thumb and joint of the forefinger, and it can be difficult to apply the force needed for some of the more complex stitch techniques.

It is unfortunate to list so many negatives about a method that many knitters use quite happily (although these are not new criticisms; it was also made fun of in print during Victorian times). I know that those who work this way find it comfortable, achieve impressive speed, and make beautiful fabrics; nevertheless, it must be said that other methods present fewer problems than this one does, and offer many advantages that it does not in terms of efficiency and comfort.

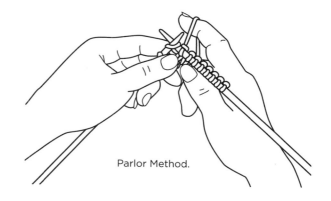

Parlor Method.

Methods with Yarn to Left

While much is unknown about the history of knitting, there is good reason to believe that the Left-Hand Methods arose out of a very old technique that was done with hooked needles (which are still used in some parts of the world), and these, in turn, developed out of an even earlier knowledge of crochet.

Several variations of the Left-Hand Method exist, and all of them carry the yarn on the left forefinger, just as for crochet. They differ only in how the yarn is wrapped for the stitches, and in the position of the stitch on the needle.

With the Left-Hand Method that is used primarily in Europe and North America, the stitches are on the needle in what we think of as the standard position, with the right side of the stitch on the nearside of the needle. For the Turned Method, which is more common in Central Europe, Russia, and the Middle East, the stitches are turned on the needle, with the left side of the stitch on the nearside of the needle. The Combined Method (sometimes called Eastern Combined), borrows from both of these, and has proved increasingly popular of late.†

❖ *Standard Left-Hand Method*

This is an extremely fast and efficient method and can be successfully used for any purpose, but it is particularly effective for working circular fabrics, primarily in Knit. It is also ideal for doing Stranded Color patterns, especially when carrying one yarn in each hand. The motions used for working this way are quite different than those used for the methods where the yarn is carried on the right.

Left-Hand Knit

1. Place yarn at left side and hold needles, palms down, in usual way; tension yarn with one of methods described above, either on little finger, in palm, or wrapped more than once on forefinger; yarn should come off nearside of finger and pass to stitch.
2. Hold left finger on farside of needle tip, parallel to it, no more than about ¼ to ½ inch away; strand of yarn should pass on farside of needle from last stitch formed to forefinger and will be directly behind next stitch to be worked.

Left-Hand Knit: Wrapping yarn for Knit stitch.

3. On nearside, insert tip of right needle into stitch as to Knit and then move it over and down on farside of strand of yarn passing to forefinger.

---

† Mary Thomas discusses the "Eastern Combined" method in *Mary Thomas's Knitting Book* (London: Hodder and Stoughton, 1938; New York: Dover Publications, 1972).

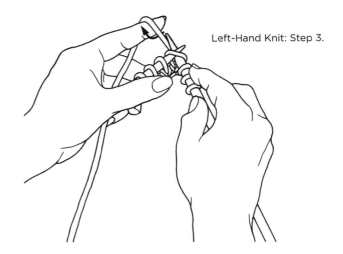

Left-Hand Knit: Step 3.

4. Use right needle to draw yarn through original stitch to nearside and simultaneously use left needle tip to lift stitch over yarn. Withdraw left needle from stitch to discard it, and also use right needle tip to push stitch off.

Left-Hand Purl

1. With yarn on nearside of needle, insert right needle into stitch from right to left as for Purl; move needle up nearside of strand of yarn, over top, and down on farside.
2. Make a quick downward motion of needle tip, which will cause yarn to slide to right, past point where two needles cross.
3. Maintain this contact between two needles to keep yarn in place and then slide right needle tip against shaft of left needle to draw yarn under it and out farside.

Left-Hand Purl: Wrapping yarn for Purl stitch.

The Details

Most Left-Hand knitters hold the forefinger very close to the needle tip and parallel to it with the yarn between stitch and finger kept short. Others hold their finger up away from the needle tip as for crochet; when in this position, it is helpful to position the middle finger of the left hand behind the yarn and the stitch being worked to guide the needle tip.

The forefinger is normally held still and the needle is used to catch, or hook the yarn to draw it through the stitch; for this reason the method is often referred to as *picking*, in contrast to the Right-Hand Methods, which are called *throwing* because the yarn is wrapped by moving the forefinger or hand.

Holding the finger still is not universal, however; many

Left-Hand knitters move the forefinger to pass the yarn around the needle tip, more or less as for the Right-Finger Method; some do this for Purl, others for both Knit and Purl. Some hold the yarn still with the forefinger and use the middle finger to push it over or under the needle; others actually work as for the Right-Hand Method and hold the yarn between thumb and forefinger.

The Left-Hand Method is extremely fast and efficient when working in Knit, but even knitters who love using the method complain of problems with Purl, to the extent that they begin to avoid it whenever possible. They have difficulty in forming the stitch, and with maintaining the same tension for both Knit and Purl.

These problems arise because the motions used for Knit and Purl are very different, and also because the path of the yarn around the needle for Knit is much shorter than the one used for Purl. The combination of these two things can enlarge the Purl stitches. While this difference is not particularly noticeable in a pattern of mixed Knit and Purl, it can be quite obvious in Stockinette when it is worked flat, with alternating Knit and Purl rows.

The direction in which the yarn is held is the primary factor in the problem because it determines the motions needed to wrap the yarn and form the stitches. The new stitches need to be drawn through to the right but the yarn is pulled to the left, as it is for crochet; in the absence of a hooked tip, this can make it difficult to keep the wrapped yarn on the needle.

When doing crochet, the yarn is attached to the last stitch in the fabric and lies directly below the hook, closer to the vertical and perfectly aligned to make the next stitch. However, when the yarn is held in the same way for knitting, it is connected to a stitch on the right needle and is therefore drawn closer to the horizontal.

When working Knit, the yarn is perfectly positioned for the next stitch, and it can be drawn through without difficulty; actually, it is far easier to make a Knit stitch with this method than it is with any other (although it may present problems with techniques that involve more than one stitch).

But in order to make a Purl stitch with the yarn held as for crochet, a considerable amount of motion is required on the part of both needles and wrists to capture the yarn and bring it through the stitch, which can lead to fatigue and repetitive motion injuries.

As an alternative, some people wrap the yarn by moving the forefinger sharply down on the nearside, below the left needle tip (some knitters use the middle finger), and then hold it there in order to keep the yarn on the needle while pushing it through the stitch.

In addition, because the yarn passes across the gap between the needles, it is difficult to see the first stitch on the left needle. For a plain Purl stitch, you hardly need to look where

to go and this is not really an issue. However, when working complicated techniques, many knitters find it necessary to hold the yarn out of the way so they can see to insert the needle, and it can be difficult to draw the yarn through if more than one stitch is involved.

As a result of these difficulties with Purl, many knitters use the Combined Left-Hand Method, below, which makes use of a different method for doing Purl. However, before turning to that method, first let us look at the Turned Left-Hand Method; it is like a mirror-image of the Standard version, and, as you will see, instead of difficulties with Purl, it presents some minor problems with Knit.

❖ Turned Left-Hand Method

This method is probably older than the version described above and is apparently more common in Central Europe and Russia; it has some interesting similarities with the Thumb Method, which is common in the Middle East and around the Mediterranean, where knitting seems to have originated.

With this approach, the left side of the stitch is on the nearside of the needle; for more information, see Turned Stitches.

If you want to try this, use Knit Half-Hitch Cast-On to put the first stitches on the needle, but take the yarn off the forefinger by passing the needle under the yarn, instead of over it so the stitches will be turned.

There are two versions, and they differ in how Purl is made.

Turned Left-Hand, Version One

- To make a Purl stitch, hold yarn on nearside; move right needle to farside and insert into turned stitch from left to right and then under left needle tip to nearside (tip of right needle will point left). Move needle tip over yarn and down on nearside so yarn wraps *under* needle; pull stitch through to farside. New stitches will be in turned position on right needle.

Turned Left-Hand Purl, Version One. Yarn is wrapped under needle.

- To make a Knit stitch, move right needle to farside of left needle and insert into turned stitch directly from right to left; move needle tip *under* yarn to farside; lift tip up to catch yarn and draw through to nearside. New stitches will be in turned position on right needle.

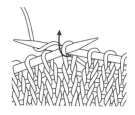

Turned Left-Hand Knit, Version One. Yarn is wrapped over needle.

In this version, it is Knit that presents something of a problem. Because the yarn is close to the horizontal, it tends to pop off the needle before it can be drawn through the stitch;

pressing the right forefinger against the needle tip helps keep it in position.

Actually, that is a movement you might want to try when working a Purl stitch with the Standard Left-Hand Method, but use your right thumb instead; it works quite well.

Turned Left-Hand, Version Two

• Work Knit as described above for Version One.
• To work Purl, retain yarn on *farside* of fabric. Move right needle tip around on farside of yarn, insert into stitch from *left to right*, and then tip it up on farside of left needle tip (*do not allow right needle to pass under left needle*) and rotate into position so it points left.

Turned Left-Hand Purl, Version Two. Retain yarn on farside.

Move needle *over* yarn and retrace path of needle to draw yarn back through stitch from nearside to farside.

In spite of how complicated the motion used for Purl may seem at first, it is actually quite easy to do. It is the same motion used for Knit when working with the Thumb Method, described below.

❖ *Combined Method*

This method is, as its name suggests, a combination of the two methods; Knit is worked as for the Standard Left-Hand Method, above, and Purl is formed as for Version One of the Turned Left-Hand Method.

This is a much faster and easier way to make a Purl stitch, and Knit and Purl can then be worked with equal speed and facility. Furthermore, the simpler motions used make it easier to maintain consistent tension on the yarn, and the distance the yarn travels between one stitch and the next is the same for Knit and Purl. When these factors are combined, the result is a much more even fabric. However, it presents challenges of a different kind.

The instructions are for working Stockinette flat, with alternating Knit and Purl rows. Start with a Purl row, and work as follows:

• For all Purl rows, work as described for Turned Purl, above: Move needle over yarn and down on nearside so yarn wraps *under* needle; new stitches on right needle will be in turned position.
• For all Knit rows, work as for Standard Left-Hand Method, above: Move right needle to farside of left

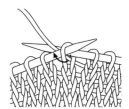

Combined Method: Knit a turned stitch farside; wrap yarn under needle.

needle and insert into turned stitch from right to left; move needle over yarn and down on farside so yarn wraps *under* needle; new stitches will be in standard position on right needle, with right side of stitch on nearside of needle.

Having the stitches in standard position after Knit rows, and in turned position after Purl rows, works very well for Stockinette. It even works well for ribbing because it becomes quite natural to work into the nearside of a standard stitch for Purl, and into the farside of a turned stitch for Knit.

However, the method is problematic when used for patterns of mixed Knit and Purl, because some of the stitches will be in one position, some in the other, and which ones are turned can change row by row. As a result, it is necessary to check each stitch to see how to work it and, when necessary, a Purl farside is more awkward to do.

Having stitches in different positions on the needle can also present difficulties when working some of the more complex stitch techniques, because instructions are written on the assumption that the stitches will all be on the needles in the standard position.

Nevertheless, if you find that this method suits you, it is certainly possible to translate the instructions for any stitch technique and then adjust the position of the stitches as necessary to produce the correct result in the fabric; those techniques you use most often will become familiar and then present no problems.

Optional Methods

Regardless of whether you prefer to hold the yarn to the left or right, there are two other methods that are worth consideration.

With one of them the work begins with the needle bearing the stitches in the right hand and the new stitches accumulate on the left needle.

The other method combines this with the standard way of working; on one row the stitches flow from the left needle to the right; on the next, from the right needle to the left.

❖ *Reversed Method*

This method is relatively rare, but seems to be favored by knitters who are left-handed (for a discussion of handedness and knitting, see below). You will also want to learn how to do this if you are interested in the Bi-Directional Method, below.

The yarn may be held on the right forefinger, in which case it is the equivalent of working as for a Left-Hand Method (the yarn is held in a direction opposite to the flow of the stitches). And as with that method, the most common way to work is to use the needle to catch the yarn, although some knitters wrap the yarn by moving their finger instead.

If the yarn is held on the left forefinger, the method is the equivalent of working as for the Right-Finger Method (the yarn is held in the same direction as the flow of the stitches). And, of course, regardless of whether the yarn is to left or right, you could also hold it with thumb and forefinger as for the Right-Hand Method.

The motions used to work the stitches and wrap the yarn are discussed at some length in Reversed Knit and Purl, and they can take some getting used to, but no more so than when learning any new method.

It is a good idea to practice by doing a swatch of Garter Stitch, first working several rows in Knit, and then, when you are reasonably comfortable with that, switch to working every row in Purl. Once you have developed some facility with both, next try something like a Double Rib, to gain practice switching from Knit to Purl and back again.

❖ *Bi-Directional Method*

This method is used only when making a flat fabric. It is done by working one row in the standard way, with the new stitches flowing from the left needle to the right needle; and the next row with the Reversed Method, described above.

The great advantage of the method is that there is no need to turn the needles and exchange them from one hand to the other. This makes it an especially nice approach to use for small things like heel flaps for socks, when doing Short Rows, or for even smaller things like Bobbles.

If you enjoy working this way, it is important to take tension into account because, in effect, you will be working the Right-Hand Method on one row and the Left-Hand Method on the next unless you switch the yarn from one hand to the other at the end of every row. See the discussion in Problems with Tension or Yarn Twist, below, for suggestions about what to look for, and how to even out your tension if you find you are having a problem.

❖ *Knitting for the Left-Handed*

The material world we live in is designed for the right-handed, but knitting requires us to be ambidextrous. There is no necessity for a left-handed person to learn a special way to knit because both hands have critical roles to play.

Nevertheless, left-handed knitters often take up the Left-Hand Method of working, apparently with the idea that holding the yarn that way ought to be more comfortable for them. However, with that method, the left hand is usually relatively motionless, while the right hand does most of the work.

Some take up the Reversed Method, perhaps with the intuitive sense that if their handedness is opposite that of most people in society, then working in the other direction should

suit them better, although with that method, the yarn could be held in either the left or right hand.

I live with someone who is left-handed and have talked to many left-handed people about how they cope in a world designed for right-handed people—door knobs, tools, writing methods—so many things we righties take for granted pose a daily challenge for lefties. My impression is that even lefties who were blessed with parents and teachers who never tried to turn them into righties become quite ambidextrous out of necessity. Therefore, it seems to me that left-handed knitters should have fewer problems using any method. In short, all of the methods are yours to learn, if you choose. Just as there are many right-handed people who knit holding the yarn on the left, someone who is left-handed should have no difficulty holding the yarn on the right.

Should you follow my recommendation to add at least one other method to your set of knitting skills, please do not attribute the natural awkwardness that overcomes everyone when learning a new way of working to the fact that you are left-handed; I can assure you that we all feel the same way.

Methods with Yarn in Center

The two knitting methods described here are undoubtedly among the oldest known, and they remain in use in countries around the Mediterranean, as well as in South America. Mary Thomas, writing in 1938, mentions French shepherds working this way while on stilts, all the better to keep watch over their flocks.†

The yarn is not carried on either the right or left side, but is instead wrapped around the neck or pinned to the front of the clothing; the left thumb is used to wrap the yarn on the needle tip.

❖ *Thumb Method*

Because the yarn travels directly toward the knitter, and is therefore on the nearside of the needles, this is a method that favors the Purl stitch; the Knit stitch requires somewhat more motion but is not difficult to do. It is also very easy to maintain even tension when working this way, because that function is entirely separate from stitch formation and requires no special skill.

The method is fun to do and offers many advantages; I recommend you try it.

Cast on in the usual way, hold the needle bearing the set of stitches in your left hand and the empty needle in your right hand, palms down. Set the yarn down on the right and pass the strand behind your neck.

---

† Mary Thomas, *Mary Thomas's Knitting Book* (London: Hodder and Stoughton, 1938; New York: Dover Publications, 1972), p. 16.

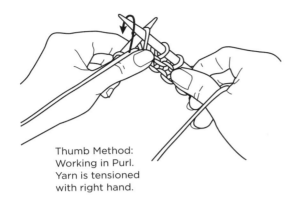

Thumb Method:
Working in Purl.
Yarn is tensioned
with right hand.

Hold the yarn to the ball in your right hand; a common method is to pass it under the fourth and fifth fingers, over the middle finger, and under the forefinger. Position hands at about waist level, with the yarn held at tension between the left needle, your neck, and your right hand.

Thumb Method: Purl

1. Insert needle into stitch on nearside from right to left. Move left thumb under yarn to catch it; with a quick motion, flip it over needle and drop it down between crossed needle tips.

2. Use right needle to draw new stitch through to farside; simultaneously use left needle to lift original stitch over yarn and discard it on nearside.

Thumb Method: Purl.
Pass yarn over needle.

Thumb Method: Knit

1. Move yarn to farside of right needle tip; it will pass over needle toward neck.

2. Insert needle into stitch from left to right, and then slide tip up on *nearside* of left needle and point it to left (it will be in same position as for Purl).

3. Wrap yarn over needle tip with thumb as described in Step 1 for Purl. Rotate right needle tip back to right, around needle tip to farside, and then down through stitch to nearside; use left needle to lift original stitch over yarn and discard it on farside.

Thumb Method: Knit.
Bring yarn over right
needle to nearside.

The movement of the needle tip within the Knit stitch is complicated to describe but quick enough to do and easily learned (and is a mirror image of the method used for Purl in the Turned Left-Hand Method, above).

After inserting the needle into the stitch, instead of allowing it to slide under the left needle tip, rotate it up and around to the left on the nearside so it looks just as it does when you Purl; after wrapping the yarn, just repeat the motion in reverse to draw the yarn through the original stitch.

As you will see when you try this method, the thumb operates quite independently and the motion used is minimal, which means this is not a tiring way to work. Also, it is easy to maintain a constant tension on the yarn because that function is completely separate from the movements used to manipulate the needles and wrap the yarn for a stitch.

Because Purl is the simpler motion, that stitch is preferred in most situations where Knit would be used by knitters who work with the Standard Left-Hand Method or with any Right-Hand Method. Garter Stitch, for instance, is done entirely in Purl. And Purl is also used for working a circular fabric; the Knit side of the fabric faces into the circle, instead of being on the outside.

For color patterns, both yarns are passed around the neck; one is passed around to the left and tensioned in the left hand, the other is passed around to the right and tensioned in the right hand. Simply reach your left thumb either over or under the other yarn to pick up the one needed next.

Actually, patterns using more than two colors in a row are common in the knitting traditions where this method is used because managing multiple colors is so easy. Two yarns are passed around the neck from the left and held in the right hand; one or two other yarns are passed around the neck from the right and held in the left hand; the arrangement keeps them well-separated at the needle.

Aside from the fact that you might feel a bit trussed up in yarn, the only difficulty with this method is that the developing pattern is not visible because the outside of the fabric is on the farside of the needle.

However, you can still check your progress by looking at the arrangement of the stitches on the needles, and that of the stranded yarns on the inside of the fabric, which are visible. The inside of the fabric will show a reverse of the pattern, with dark strands covering a light motif, and vice versa. Those who have always worked this way find this perfectly normal and have no problem with it, and with practice, so might you.

This is actually a marvelous way to work a color pattern because the motions are so simple and it is so easy to maintain an even tension on the yarns and, therefore, make a beautiful fabric. The only difficulty with the method is that having the yarn around your neck can be irritating, or can leave lint on your clothing. While it is customary to pin the yarn to your bodice, some garments are too loose or not strong enough to sustain the pull of the yarn tension. I have tried attaching a hook to my waistband instead, and it works quite well; as long as the yarn is directed straight toward you from the needles, and is angled high enough to allow the thumb easy access under it, the system will work fine.

❖ *Hook Method*

A very old version of the Thumb Method makes use of a set of four or five needles that are hooked at one end and pointed at the other. When used for working in the round, the hook in the right hand will be facing the tip of the needle held in the left hand.

These needles are also ideal for use with any of the Left-Hand Methods, where the yarn is held as it would be for crochet; because the hook catches the yarn so effectively, it is just as easy to do Purl as it is to do Knit. This makes it possible to maintain an even tension and work very quickly.

While it is possible to work flat, the two hooks will be facing each other, which is considerably more awkward. The left hook has to be kept positioned so it does not interfere with discarding the stitch, or, at the very least, the stitch must be lifted well off the needle so it does not get caught.

Problems with Tension or Yarn Twist

Regardless of how you choose to knit, it is important to develop a consistent tension so that all the stitches are a similar size and your fabric looks nice and even. To some extent this is simply the result of practice, and your hands will find their way. However, if you remain unsatisfied with the results you are getting, there are some tips below that you can try.

Also, it is common for yarn to gain twist as you knit, causing it to kink up on itself and tangle; not only can this be annoying, but also it can cause bias in the fabric that is impossible to remove. You will find suggestions below for how to prevent and correct for this problem.

❖ *Analyzing Tension*

To see if your tension is uneven, make a swatch in Stockinette, 4 to 6 inches square, and dress it to relax the fabric (see Dressing a Swatch).

Then examine the swatch to analyze what kind of a problem you might be having. There are four possibilities: uneven tension across rows, a gradual change in tension over the length of the fabric, an abrupt change of tension somewhere within the fabric, and uneven tension on Knit and Purl rows.

Uneven Tension Across a Row

Examine the Knit face of the fabric, looking for any irregularities in the appearance of the stitches. If you notice that some stitches in each row are larger than the others, this usually indicates you are having a problem with how you are tensioning the yarn. Another clue that this is the case is if you frequently have to stop and rewrap the yarn.

Experiment with different ways to wrap the yarn on your fingers; see Tensioning the Yarn. Cast on about 20 stitches and

try each method, working as many rows as needed until you begin to feel comfortable with it. Then dress the swatch to see which method made the most difference. Select the one you felt the most comfortable with, and before going on to make something you care about, make another, larger swatch to give your hands time to learn the new method.

Change in Tension over Length

If what you see in the fabric is a gradual change in tension over the length of the swatch, this could be because you were tense when you started to knit, and then began to relax because of its calming effect. If you have troubles on your mind, or are just wound up after a day at work, it can take 10 or 15 minutes before you fall into a comfortable rhythm with your knitting. If you are aware that this happens to you often, you can take steps to work around it.

Put on your favorite music, have a cup of tea nearby, make sure your chair is comfortable, prop up your feet—you get the idea; do what it takes to get yourself in a frame of mind where you can relax and enjoy your knitting. Before you pick up the needles, roll your shoulders forward and back, and shake out both hands to loosen them up. Let your arms hang down limp for a minute or two; take a deep breath and just stare out the window for a while doing *nothing*.

Consider keeping an ongoing warm-up project of some kind in your workbasket. Make scarves for your friends and family in colorful, textured yarns that will hide any inconsistencies in your tension. Or use that time to try out a new yarn or some stitch or color patterns you are curious about; once you have loosened up a bit, then pick up your more important project.

It is also common to have a change in tension over the length of a gauge swatch, or after working the first few inches of a new project. In many cases, this is simply the result of being unfamiliar with a stitch or color pattern when you first begin; once you have learned a pattern, your gauge will become more even. The solution is to practice the pattern on a Test Swatch before you make the larger Gauge Swatch.

Abrupt Change in Tension

If you see a line across the fabric, this usually indicates that the stitches below it are a different size than those above it. Something like this might not be apparent in a small swatch; it is more often seen when changing from working circular to working flat, such as after dividing a circular fabric at the armholes. However, it can also be the result of any change in the way you are knitting. If you change the type of needle, or the manner of tensioning the yarn, your gauge can change; for more information about this, see The Five Variables in the chapter Stitch Gauge.

Change in Tension on Knit and Purl Rows

Next, turn the fabric over and look at the Purl side. If what you see are pairs of Purl rows with a deeper "gutter" in between, this indicates that the tension when you Knit is different than it is when you Purl (see the illustration in The Knit and Purl Stitches in the chapter The Stitches). The gutter is evidence of a row of stitches that is larger than those on either side.

This can happen with any knitting method, but it is particularly common when working Purl with the Left-Hand Method because such very different motions are used to make the Knit and Purl stitches. The problem can often be solved by working with the Combined Method described above, which makes it much easier to maintain a consistent tension as you work; unfortunately, it is only really practical for working Stockinette or ribbing.

If you prefer to use the Standard Left-Hand Method, there are a few things you can do to even out your tension.

- First, try different methods of wrapping the yarn on your fingers until you find a way to put more tension on the yarn for the Purl rows.
- Second, get in the habit of tightening the yarn *after* forming a Purl stitch; move your finger up sharply before making the next stitch. This will draw some of the extra yarn out of the new stitch, and with a little practice the motion should become automatic and feel quite natural.
- Third, try the suggestion above of "trapping" the yarn on the needle with your right thumb; this helps keep it from loosening as you draw the new stitch through.

When using one of the Right-Hand Methods, the movements used for Knit and Purl are so similar that it is a little more difficult to discover what is causing uneven tension. However, usually it is simply a matter of developing a new habit. Knit a long Test Swatch in Stockinette while paying close attention to your tension on the Purl rows; if necessary, find another way to wrap the yarn on your fingers.

Enlarged Stitches in Left Knit Columns

Another common problem with tension shows up primarily in Double Ribbing, or with any decorative stitch pattern that has several columns of Knit next to columns of Purl. This has to do with the distance the yarn must travel for a Purl stitch, and you will find an explanation for it in The Knit and Purl Stitches.

❖ *Knitting Methods and Yarn Twist*

A well-made knitting yarn is "balanced," which means that when it is spun and plied, the amount of twist added to a single ply will be offset by the amount of twist used to ply several single plies together (see Yarns). A yarn that is balanced will be relaxed when it hangs free. As a yarn is given additional twist, it will become thinner and tighter, and will begin to kink up on itself; if a yarn is untwisted, it will get softer and looser and the plies will begin to separate.

If you want to see twist in action, take the end of the yarn in your right hand, and hold it tight with your left hand about 3 to 4 inches away; twist the end with your fingers several times to the right; if you then move your hands together, it will kink up on itself. Let the end drop and it will spontaneously unspin and hang relaxed again. Take the end in your hand again and twist it to the left and you will see the plies begin to separate.

Most knitting yarns are what is called "S ply," which means the singles were spun by twisting them to the left and several singles were then plied together by twisting them to the right.

The conventional way to wrap the yarn around the needle for both Knit and Purl (under the needle to the nearside and over it to the farside), adds twist to an S-ply yarn with every stitch. You will also see twist accumulate in the tail of yarn when using one of the Compound Half-Hitch Cast-On techniques. In addition, a certain amount of twist will also be added to the yarn when it is drawn out of the ball, as well as when you turn the fabric as you work.

If the twist is allowed to accumulate in the yarn, the fabric will start to go on the bias; this is permanent and cannot be corrected by blocking or steaming (see Dressing a Fabric). Therefore, it is important to take steps as you work to maintain the yarn in as close to a balanced state as possible; there are several easy things you can do.

- Twist will be added to a yarn when it is drawn off the top of a center-pull ball or a cone. If possible, place the cone or ball on a reel arrangement of some kind so you can draw the yarn off the side instead. If nothing else, put the ball on your finger and let it spin as you unreel some yarn from the outside. Alternatively, just leave the ball on the ball-winder, and draw it back out through the eye of the metal guide arm. For an even simpler solution, put a skein on an umbrella swift and draw the yarn off of it (and save the bother of winding a ball).
- When working flat, turn the tip of the needle toward you at the end of an outside row, and away from you at the end of an inside row (or vice versa, but be systematic). When working circular, "undo" the round at the join—spin the needles and fabric back in the other direction before starting the next round.
- The Combined Method of knitting provides a means of balancing the twist on the yarn stitch-by-stitch; with that method, the yarn is wrapped in one direction for a Knit stitch and in the other direction for a Purl stitch, and one offsets the other. As discussed above, this works very well for a flat fabric made entirely in Stockinette, and works

reasonably well for ribbings, but presents challenges when used for other kinds of stitch patterns and, of course, does not help for circular knitting if no Purl is being used.

However, if you are knitting in the round on double-point needles, here is a little trick you can try: Work all stitches on first needle Knit Under (wrap in the usual way); the new stitches will be in standard position. Work all stitches on next needle Knit Over so the new stitches will be in turned position (see Turned Stitches). Continue to alternate in this way needle-by-needle; on subsequent rounds, Knit all stitches in standard position nearside, and those in turned position farside. You could do the same thing on a circular needle by setting Ring Markers to divide the stitches into four equal groups.

- If twist has accumulated in the yarn, it is easy enough to rebalance by letting either the needles and fabric, or the ball, hang free and unspin. Stop working when you have about a yard of yarn between the needles and the ball and use one of the following approaches:

  To let the needles untwist, hold the yarn against the ball so no more will pull free, raise it up, and drop the needles and fabric (the stitches will tighten on the needle from the hanging weight of the fabric and will not slip off); let everything spin until it slows to a stop. If there was a lot of twist in the yarn, it might spin too far and have to unspin again in the other direction before it re-balances.

  Or, attach the yarn to the ball by making a big half-hitch in the yarn and tightening it around the ball, or stick a short double-point needle, a cable needle, or a tapestry needle into the side of the ball and wrap the yarn around it a few times, or use a convenient Bead Stopper (see Tools). Take hold of the yarn near the needles and raise it up to let the ball hang free and unspin the extra twist.

  To see if the yarn has rebalanced, let it hang down in a U-shape and bring the two sides close together; if the yarn has too much twist, the two strands will actively ply together; if the yarn is balanced, they will hang relaxed, or only twist a few times around each other.

- When casting on, periodically drop the tail of yarn from your thumb and let it hang free to untwist.

CHAPTER 2

Circular and Flat Knitting

Conventionally, a garment is worked from the bottom edge to the top, but it is also possible to work from the top down, from side to side, or at an angle. Sections of the garment can be constructed separately as flat pieces and then sewn together; this is called "flat knitting" or "working flat." Or the entire garment can be worked "in the round," also called "circular knitting," to form an interconnected set of tubes that requires no assembly of any kind.

The two approaches are often interchangeable, but in some situations one or the other is clearly required or makes the most sense for the type of item that will be made. The only shape that cannot be made flat is a Medallion, although oddly enough, it is a flat fabric (see Uncommon Shapes). There are, however, several types of garments, such as socks and mittens, that *could* be made flat, but this is almost never done because they are so much the better for being seamless. Working in the round is only slightly more limiting; only a few types of Intarsia color patterns can be done in the round, the shaping of some garment styles can be more challenging, and of course things like scarves and shawls are flat fabrics.

For all of these things, the decision about whether to work flat or in the round is more or less made for you, but when there is a choice, you might want to weigh the pros and cons of using one approach or the other; some of the factors to take into consideration are discussed below.

Working flat is quite straightforward and is described along with the instructions for learning how to knit in the chapter Knitting Methods; most of the other things you need to know to work that way are found elsewhere in this book, except for how to use circular needles to make something flat, which is discussed here.

In order to work circular, however, you will need the additional information below, which begins with a discussion of the different kinds of needles that can be used, how to cast on, and how to draw the edge into a round

to begin. Also included is information on which kinds of needles are suitable for different projects, and why you might choose to work with one type rather than another.

These instructions are followed by a discussion of various methods used to make openings in the fabric to accommodate armholes and sleeves, and about working a garment from the top down.

Circular Knitting

Circular knitting is done with two different types of needles. The traditional double-point needles have tips at both ends, and come in lengths from 4 to 18 inches; these can be used to make a circular fabric of any circumference.

Circular needles were introduced relatively recently and consist of two short tips, 4 to 6 inches in length, attached to each end of a flexible cable. These are very convenient to work with and have largely supplanted double-point needles, except for making small items.

Regardless of what kind of a needle you work with, the process is the same: instead of working back and forth in rows as for a flat fabric, you work around and around.

However, because the yarn passes from the last stitch at the end of one round to the first stitch at the beginning of the next, instead of the horizontal rows of a flat fabric, a circular fabric is a spiral, which can have an effect on its appearance; for more information, see Rows or Spirals.

❖ Double-Point Needle Sets

Double-point needles come in all sizes and in various lengths, usually in sets of four or five; the minimum that can be used is three. One needle is reserved for use in the right hand, and the stitches are distributed to the others. Whether to work with a set of four or five needles is basically a matter of preference or what the stitch multiple is, but a stitch or color pattern may determine a particular distribution, or the demands of a garment pattern may dictate a certain arrangement.

For instance, when decreasing the crown of a hat in four

sections, it would be easier to work with the stitches of each section on a separate needle; in other situations, there may be more stitches on some of the needles than others.

You can cast on directly to the double-point needles and divide the stitches among them as you do so, or cast on to a single needle first, and then transfer and distribute the stitches to multiple needles.

Three-Needle Cast-On for Double-Points

These instructions are written for working with the stitches distributed on three needles, one-third on each.

1. Take up first double-point needle and cast on one-third total number of stitches. Push stitches about an inch back from tip of needle.
2. Take up second double-point needle and line up on nearside of cast-on edge below first needle, extend tip about ½ inch to left of other needle, and have both yarns on farside.
3. Cast on next stitch; slide it down second needle until it is adjacent to last stitch cast on to other needle; tighten yarn firmly between two needles. Continue to cast on second third of stitches; push both sets of stitches down along needles together, as necessary to make room for new ones.
4. Rotate first needle on running thread between two sets of stitches, down on right, up on left, and reposition parallel to second needle; align needle tips. Two sets of stitches will then be side by side, with first stitch cast on at left side.

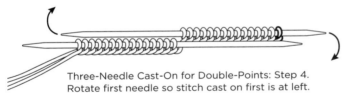

Three-Needle Cast-On for Double-Points: Step 4.
Rotate first needle so stitch cast on first is at left.

5. Take up third double-point needle and hold with other two as described in Step 2; cast on remaining third of stitches.
6. Turn three needles around together so yarn is at right on farside.

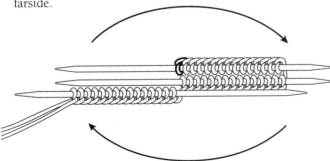

Three-Needle Cast-On for Double-Points: Step 6.
Turn all needles around so yarn is at right.

7. Take right tip of needle on nearside (with first stitch cast on), and swing across to left, so opposite tip passes *over* center needle. Take right tip of needle on farside (with yarn to last stitch cast on), and swing to left *over* center needle. Bring two tips together in center.

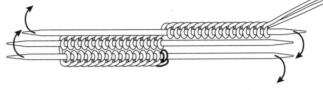

Three-Needle Cast-On for Double-Points: Step 7.
Swing right tips of first and third needles toward you.

8. To join round and begin to work, see Circular Knitting on Double-Points, and also Tips for Joining the Round, below.

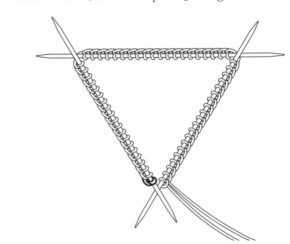

Three-Needle Cast-On for Double-Points:
Needles in position to join the round.

Four-Needle Cast-On for Double-Points

Either by preference, or when necessary to cast on more stitches, you can work in a similar way with four needles; it is slightly more complicated because extra steps are required.

1. Work Steps 1–5 of Three-Needle Cast-On for Double-Points, above.
2. Rotate first and second needles together on running thread that passes to third needle; with needles parallel again, align tips.

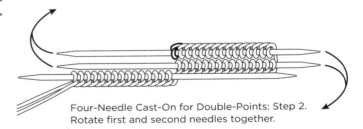

Four-Needle Cast-On for Double-Points: Step 2.
Rotate first and second needles together.

3. Pick up fourth needle, position on nearside of other three, and cast on next set of stitches.

4. Rotate needle on farside (bearing first cast-on stitch) up on right, down on left, and position parallel with other needles again. First and fourth sets of stitches are at left; second and third sets of stitches are at right.

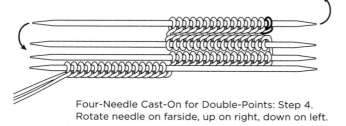

Four-Needle Cast-On for Double-Points: Step 4. Rotate needle on farside, up on right, down on left.

5. Turn all four needles so first and last stitch cast on are pointing toward you.

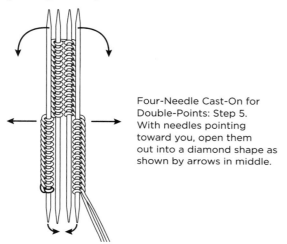

Four-Needle Cast-On for Double-Points: Step 5. With needles pointing toward you, open them out into a diamond shape as shown by arrows in middle.

6. Open needles, moving tip with yarn from right into center, and tip with first stitch from left into center, until four needles form a square.

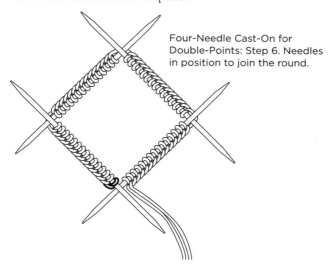

Four-Needle Cast-On for Double-Points: Step 6. Needles in position to join the round.

7. To join round and begin to work, see Circular Knitting on Double-Points, and also Tips for Joining the Round, below.

Preliminary Cast-On with Single Needle

Here is an alternative method that is a good choice when you will be casting on a large number of stitches. Put them all on a straight needle first, and then transfer them to a set of double-point needles.

1. Use one double-point needle (longer than others, if necessary), and cast on full number of stitches.

2. Starting at end where yarn is attached, slip one-third of stitches to second double-point needle.

3. Pick up third double-point needle in right hand and hold on nearside of cast-on edge; slip next third of stitches. Third set of stitches is now alone on first needle used for casting on.

4. Check that cast-on edge is lined up below all needles; draw right tip of second needle, and left tip of first needle toward center on nearside to form triangle with third needle in between.

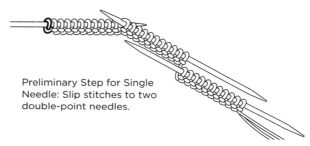

Preliminary Step for Single Needle: Slip stitches to two double-point needles.

Alternatively, cast on to a single needle, and transfer half of stitches to second double-point needle; begin working as described for the Shetland Three-Needle Method, below. If you prefer, instead of continuing with that method, you can distribute the stitches to four double-point needles as you do the first row.

Circular Knitting on Double-Points

There are three challenges when learning how to work with a set of double-point needles—how to join the round to begin, where to put your hands to avoid getting stabbed by all those points, and how to manage the intersection between needles.

Here are the most basic instructions for how to begin, along with some tips for how to hold the needles. You will find several suggestions for how to neatly join the first and last stitches cast on so the edge stays smooth in Tips for Joining the Round, below; add whichever of those options you prefer in the future.

1. Pick up needle bearing first stitch cast on in left hand.

2. Pick up empty needle in right hand, pick up yarn (which is attached to last stitch), and move it to nearside or

farside of empty needle as necessary to Knit or Purl first stitch, and then tension yarn to draw needle to right with last stitch cast on as close to tip of left needle as possible.

3. Place tip of empty needle *over* needle to right and insert into first stitch on left needle, wrap yarn, drawing it up very firmly, and Knit.

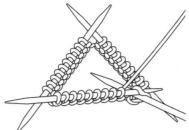

Circular Knitting on Double-Points: Step 3. Yarn wrapped on empty right needle for first Knit stitch.

4. After stitch is formed, tighten it again on right needle; work next stitch with firm tension as well. Resume normal tension and work remaining stitches.

5. Immediately after discarding last stitch, tuck tip of right needle under tip of needle bearing next set of stitches to left; slide stitches back from right needle tip about 1 inch, drop it, and let it hang from fabric.

6. Transfer empty needle from left to right hand. Pick up next needle in left hand; arrange opposite tip of that needle so it is on top of one to its left; slide stitches to right tip to begin.

7. Repeat Steps 3–6.

Always arrange the two needles you are holding in your hands so the opposite tips are on top of the needles to either side; this leaves your grip unimpaired.

When you get to the last few stitches on the

Circular Knitting on Double-Points: Working with a set of four needles.

left needle in Step 4, you might find it easier to hold if you place your left thumb under the adjacent needle and your forefinger over it; the tip will stick up within the circle formed by your fingers.

It is important to control the tension on the stitches at the intersection of two needles so the running thread passing between them will not stretch out, which causes a distinctive, unsightly vertical line in the fabric, often referred to as a "ladder."

As described in Step 1, when working the first stitch on a needle, always position the empty needle tip *over* the needle tip to the right; this brings the three needle tips as close together as possible and places the least stress on the running thread. If the empty needle is inserted into the stitch from below the needle to the right, it will lie within the intersection and make it impossible to draw the two stitches close together.

Tightening the yarn firmly as you work the first two stitches as described in Steps 2 and 3 is also very important.

You may see it recommended to shift the intersection between needles on every round to avoid creating a ladder. In other words, after working a group of stitches on one needle, you would knit one or two stitches off the next needle before picking up the empty needle. The number of stitches on each needle remains constant; the individual stitches are simply redistributed, from one needle to the next. The idea is that if the problem is staggered it will not be as obvious, but instead of solving the problem, this approach can simply leave a spiral of irregular stitches in the fabric.

Redistributing Stitches

From time to time when working a pattern, you may find it necessary to redistribute the number of stitches on the respective needles (perhaps with more on one than the others), or change from working with three to four needles, or vice versa.

Use one of the following methods:

- To move the stitches to the needle at the left of the one you are working on, work all the stitches on that needle until only those to be moved remain. Transfer the needle to your right hand, slide the remaining stitches to the left tip, and then slip them to the next needle. With the needle in your right hand now empty, begin to work the next set of stitches. Transfer the stitches at the end of each set to the following needle in the same way, until all stitches are redistributed.

- To move stitches to the needle in your right hand, after completing one set, put the empty needle down, pick up the next needle to the left, and work the number of stitches to be transferred, adding them to the right needle. Then set the right needle down and pick up the empty needle again and work the remaining stitches on the left needle. This can be awkward to do with three needles, but works well with four.

- Or, pick up an empty needle in your right hand, a needle with stitches in your left hand; slip as many stitches as needed for a new set to the right needle. If you were working with three needles, there will now be four needles in the stitches. Transfer the partial set from your left to right hand, pick up the next needle, and slip as many as needed to complete that set. Repeat to complete the redistribution and then begin to work again.

Shetland Three-Needle Method

Shetland knitters often work with just three double-point needles instead of the usual four or five as described above; they arrange the stitches on two needles and work with the third. The technique is primarily used when working with long double-point needles and a Knitting Belt or Sheath, but will work with needles of any size and with any knitting method.

It can be challenging to manage all the needle tips and make a smooth transition between one needle and the next when working with double-point needles, but with this approach, there is one less intersection between the needles and two fewer tips to deal with.

1. Cast on to a single double-point needle.
2. Slip half of stitches to second double-point needle.
3. Fold needle bearing first stitch around to farside of second and hold both needles as one in left hand. Running thread connecting two sets of stitches will be at left; last stitch cast on (with yarn attached) is on farside at right. Slide both sets of stitches to right needle tips.
4. With third, empty needle in right hand, begin to work stitches on near needle. For Knit, bring yarn between two needle tips; for Purl, bring it to nearside of both. Work first stitch with firm tension, as usual. For a Knit stitch, right needle tip will emerge between two needles.

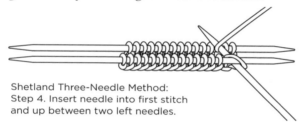

Shetland Three-Needle Method:
Step 4. Insert needle into first stitch
and up between two left needles.

5. After working several stitches, two needles in left hand will begin to separate; insert left forefinger down between them.
6. After a few more stitches, three needles will form a triangle; release needle on farside and continue with one on nearside.
7. At about midpoint of row, place needle on farside between forefinger and middle finger of right hand. For last few stitches, needles in right hand will be nearly parallel.
8. With all stitches worked on one needle, turn needles as for flat knitting, slide stitches to tip of second needle, and begin next row in same way.

It is a bit awkward to work the first and last few stitches on the needle, but your hands will find their way, and I think you will discover that it all goes rather smoothly.

However, working this way is really only worth it when making something wide, because the difficulty at each end is offset by a greater number of stitches that can be done in the usual way in the middle. For a similar approach that is in many respects easier, see either the Two Circular Needles Method or the Three Circular Needles Method, below.

Also see Tips for Joining the Round, below, for information that applies to all methods used for circular knitting.

❖ Circular Needles

A circular needle has two pointed needle shafts connected by a length of fine-diameter, flexible nylon cord. At most, the needle tips are roughly the length of your hand and some have a slight bend built into the shaft to make them more comfortable to hold and to work with; the smallest can only be grasped with a few fingers.

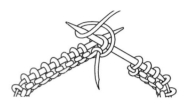

Flat Knitting on a Circular Needle:
Working first stitch in Purl.

The needles come in all the standard sizes and the nylon cord comes in various lengths. The needle measurement is tip-to-tip and the shorter the length, the smaller the needle shafts; the shortest length that is comfortable to hold when drawn into a circle is generally twelve inches.

A circular needle of any length can be used for flat knitting, but when working an item in the round, the length of the needle must be less than the circumference of the fabric or you will not be able to join the stitches into a circle. For smaller items, the alternative is to use the Two Circular Needles Method, the Looped Needle Method, described below, or the Singular Double-Fabric technique.

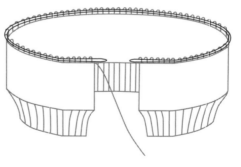

Flat Knitting on a Circular Needle: A sweater with center front opening.

Flat Knitting on a Circular Needle

Using a circular needle to make a flat fabric is little different from working with straight needles. Simply treat the two needle tips as if they were separate; to begin, work as follows:

- Last stitch cast on will have yarn to ball attached. Slide this stitch up close to one needle tip, and hold in left hand. Take up empty needle tip in right hand; hold yarn in left or right hand according to preferred method. Knit one row; at end of row, needle tip in left hand will be empty. Turn work, transferring empty needle tip to right hand and needle tip bearing stitches to left hand. Work next row, and repeat, row by row.

Circular Knitting on a Circular Needle

1. Cast on number of stitches required for full circumference of fabric. Push stitches close to both needle tips and draw them into a circle with yarn coming off first stitch on right needle tip.

Circular Knitting on a Circular Needle: Working first stitch; notice Ring Marker on right needle.

2. Examine cast-on edge carefully to make sure it lies flat below needle and at no point passes over it. If edge circles needle, spin it around and back into place.
3. Knit first stitch on left needle; running thread will then span gap between two stitches and join cast-on edge into a circle.

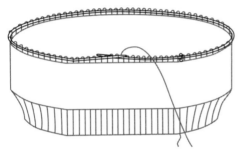

Circular Knitting on a Circular Needle: A Circular garment.

Casting on to a circular needle can often feel like working with a live snake; it does wiggle about without the weight of a fabric to stabilize it. This makes it more likely that the edge will spiral around the cable; it may be impossible to fix this if you have used Stranded Cast-On or Alternating Cast-On because they have less initial structure than most other edges.

To help keep the edge aligned properly, see Cast-On Edge Markers. This technique is used to insert a contrast-color yarn into the edge as you cast on; it is used as a way to keep count of stitches while casting on, but is equally useful in making sure they are not twisted over the needle.

Another way to keep the edge under control is to cast on as for the Shetland Three-Needle Method, above, and then begin working with the circular needle on the first row. If you are dealing with a lot of stitches, you may not have double-point needles long enough to do this, but if you can crowd them together enough to fit, it works quite well.

Also see Tips for Joining the Round, below, for information that applies to all methods used for circular knitting.

Two Circular Needles Method

If you like making small things like mittens and socks but are not comfortable with double-point needles, use two circular needles instead—one for each half of the stitches.†

The length of the needle does not matter, but it is usually easiest to work with the shortest one that has a tip comfortable in your hands.

1. Cast on required number of stitches for circumference of garment and distribute stitches, half to each needle.
2. Slide set of stitches cast on last onto cable of needle with yarn to right; running thread that joins two sets of stitches is at left.
3. Pick up needle bearing other set of stitches in left hand and bring to nearside; slide right tip of needle into stitches. Reach across to left on nearside to pick up other tip of *same* needle and bring tips together as when working flat.
4. Draw yarn firmly across gap between two circular needles and work across that set of stitches. With all stitches now on needle tip held in right hand, draw tip out to left so stitches are on cable.
5. Turn, as for working flat; drop needle from right hand, pick up other needle, and bring to nearside to work other set of stitches.
6. Repeat Steps 3 and 4, always turning as when working flat, and always working each set of stitches with tips of same needle.

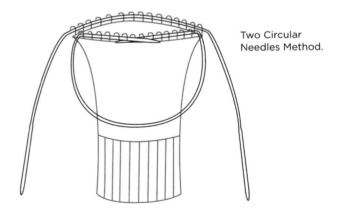

Two Circular Needles Method.

As you will see, the tips of the needle not in use will hang down from the work on the farside, out of your way. You will find it easy to start each set of stitches with the other set relaxed on the thin cable. Also, the running threads that pass

---

† I first read about this technique in an online forum; my understanding is that it was introduced by Joyce Williams, who is also the author of *Latvian Dreams: Knitting from Weaving Charts* (Pittsville, Wisc.: Schoolhouse Press, 2000).

between the two are less likely to stretch out, which keeps the intersection neat, and there is less need to draw the yarn up tightly when starting the first stitch.

Another way to reduce strain at the intersection is to hold the cable of the needle not in use in your left hand along with the needle you are working on. This also helps keep the dangling needle tip from bouncing around, which is one of the complaints knitters have about working this way. It also helps to work as low in your lap as possible, or even tuck one or both tips of the needle not in use into the fabric once there is enough of it to provide an anchor.

Three Circular Needles Method

You can also work with three circular needles in a variation of the Shetland Three-Needle Method, above, and it is easier to manage doing so with circulars than it is with straight needles, except for how lively they can be. Work as follows:

- Hold third, empty needle in right hand, and first set of stitches on its needle in left hand. Work across those stitches; when that needle is empty, use it to work next set of stitches.

Looped Needle Method

One of the limits of working on a circular needle is that the length of the needle must be smaller than the circumference of the fabric. If you do not have the right length needle on hand, here is a clever way to work small items in the round using just one circular needle of any length; in fact, it is better if the cable is relatively long.†

Cast on and then work as follows:

1. Pull needle tips out of stitches so all of them are on cable.
2. Fold cables together so yarn attached to last stitch cast on is at right on farside. Find midpoint of stitches and use one needle tip or fingers to draw bend in cable out between two stitches to form loop at left; needle tips are hanging to right.
3. Push set of stitches on nearside onto needle tip and hold in left hand. Pick up other needle tip in right hand; if necessary, draw some cable out of other set of stitches to right until it is long enough to loop around and bring needle tips together. There are now two cable loops, one on each side.
4. Draw yarn across intersection between two sets of stitches and begin to work. When last stitch of set is worked, loop in cable at left will release.

---

† For more details about working this way, see Bev Galeskas, *The Magic Loop: Working Around on One Needle; Sarah Hauschka's Magical Unvention* (East Wenatchee, Wash.: Fiber Trends, 2002).

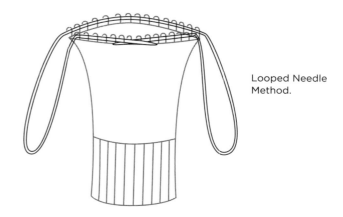

Looped Needle Method.

5. Turn as for working flat; remaining loop in cable will then be at left side; set of stitches just completed is now on farside; next set on nearside. Repeat Steps 3 and 4.
6. Repeat Steps 3–5.

This works well enough if you do not have the kind of needles you would ordinarily use for the number of stitches. However, there will be two big loops jutting out to each side and bouncing around, and there is considerable tension on the running threads between the two sets of stitches, which can leave visible evidence in the fabric.

If you have the option, it seems the Two Circular Needles Method is less trouble and is easier on the fabric. Or try the method discussed below.

❖ Circular Knitting on Straight Needles

And finally, for working very small things in the round such as thumbs for a mitten or fingers for a glove, for which any number of double-point needles is a nuisance, there is a way to knit in the round on two single-point needles using the Singular Double-Fabric technique.

As you will see, the method is not restricted to small things—you could make an entire sweater using it, or two sleeves, or two socks at the same time—and it is very easy to do.

❖ Tips for Joining the Round

As mentioned above, there are two aspects of joining the round that are important to deal with; lining all the stitches up under the needles, and smoothing out the jog in the edge. The following suggestions apply to working in the round with any of the needles described above.

Line Up the Edge

Before joining the round, make sure the cast-on edge lies entirely below the needle and has not twisted around it.

One very easy way to manage this is to insert a contrast-color yarn into the edge as you cast on; see Cast-On Edge

Markers. This not only makes it obvious if the edge has twisted over the needle, and makes it clear when you have fixed it, but it also allows you to do a very quick count of the number of stitches cast on before you begin.

If you began to work without realizing the edge was twisted, it will become obvious as you work the first round; fortunately, you will have one last chance to correct it.

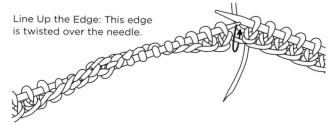

Line Up the Edge: This edge is twisted over the needle.

- Work to end of first round. Pass left needle tip under running thread; rotate entire edge over left needle until twist in edge disappears. The twist will be absorbed by the running thread that joins the round and will not be noticeable.

Irregularity at Lower Edge

Here are several suggestions for how to smooth out or hide the jog at the lower edge. The first one gives the best result but is more complicated to do and requires planning ahead; the others are adequate and simpler to manage.

Pullover Join

This may seem a bit complicated the first time you try it, but it is easy enough once you get the idea, and it is quite effective at smoothing out the edge.

1. Begin with a Twist Start and cast on all stitches with preferred method; place one more stitch than needed on first needle; use Simple Left Half-Hitch Cast-On for last stitch on third or fourth needle (this positions tail of yarn on farside).
2. To join round, hold needle bearing first stitch cast on in left hand and needle bearing last, Simple Cast-On stitch in right hand.
3. With yarn farside, slip first stitch from left to right needle, pull Simple Cast-On stitch over and off. Begin to work remaining stitches on needle.

There are several things to notice here. The first stitch is a Twist Start, and therefore has no knot or half-hitch at its base; the last Simple Cast-On stitch is a half-hitch. After the half-hitch is pulled over the Twist Start, the two will look just like all the other stitches in the edge. It is important to use the Left Half-Hitch version when casting on, so it will lie in the same direction as the others in the edge; an additional advantage is that then the tail is on the inside of the fabric, which is convenient when hiding it later.

The pullover functions as a decrease, which eliminates the extra stitch cast on in Step 1. And because the first stitch is slipped and not worked as you begin the round, it pulls the left corner of the edge up into alignment with the one on the right side of the join. However, because you Slip the first stitch, you will need to Knit the next stitch, regardless of what the stitch pattern might otherwise require, so the strand will be on the inside of the fabric.

Decrease Join

- Begin as described in Step 1 above, but cast on last stitch in same way as other stitches (do not use Simple Cast-On). To join round, Slip first stitch cast on to left needle and join it to last stitch cast on with Right Decrease. Retain new stitch on right needle to equalize stitch count.

Threaded Stitch Join

For this version, do not cast on an extra stitch (as is done for the versions above).

1. Hold needle bearing last stitch cast on in right hand and needle bearing first stitch cast on in left hand. Slip last stitch to left needle.
2. Insert right needle tip into first stitch as to Purl and into second stitch as to Knit and draw second stitch through first (see Threaded Stitch); retain this stitch on right needle and other stitch on left needle. This joins the round.
3. Pick up empty needle and yarn in right hand, work stitch now first on left needle, and then work remaining stitches on left needle.

The two stitches at the intersection are exchanged by drawing one through the other to join the round. The one drawn through to the right needle is the first stitch cast on; because it is slipped, and not worked, it helps draw the edge into alignment.

Double-Yarn Join

If you have used a Knitted Cast-On, and have a tail of yarn at one needle tip and the yarn to the ball at the other needle tip, try this:

- Knit first stitch of first round with main yarn and tail of yarn held as one; drop tail of yarn and continue.

Sewn Method

Fortunately, if you forget to deal with the jog at the edge on the first round, you can usually tidy things up later, and, in fact, this works well enough that you may prefer to use it in any case.

- Thread the tail of yarn into a tapestry needle and sew a stitch that closes the gap and duplicates the appearance of the edge; see Edges and Seam Corners. As you hide the end, pull the left side of the jog up firmly to draw it into alignment as best you can.

❖ Constructing Circular Garments

The great challenge of making any circular garment is how to make the necessary openings for the armholes and neckline. The simplest and most direct way to do so is to divide the stitches at the underarm and change from working in the round to working flat. However, there are several reasons to avoid having to do this.

First, in many cases this would require the use of Purl on inside rows, and many knitters find that stitch slower to do, and/or they have trouble maintaining even tension on Knit and Purl rows; this can cause a change in the gauge and leave visible evidence in the fabric; see The Five Variables in the chapter on Stitch Gauge. Also, many people find that it is more difficult to work a color pattern in Purl.

Two approaches solve these problems by making it possible to work the entire garment in the round. One is traditional, and involves cutting the fabric open; the other is a newer concept, and involves working the garment from the top down, making the upper bodice and upper sleeves simultaneously.

Openings in a Circular Fabric

Two traditional methods can be used to construct the body of a sweater as a tube, working from waist to shoulders, and later open it to allow for armholes, or to divide the front for a cardigan.

The Steek

A Steek is basically an internal selvedge that makes it possible to cut the fabric open for armholes, neckline, and center front opening in a way that keeps it from unraveling; for more information, see Steeks: Selvedges for Cut Openings.

The technique is a very old one. There are examples of fashionable garments in European museum collections from the sixteenth and seventeenth centuries that were made of fine silk, and the fabric was cut and assembled as for a garment made of woven fabric. Traditional Scandinavian garments often had little or no shaping; the fabric was cut as needed and the raw edges were often bound with decorative woven fabric (see Sewing Wovens to Knits), and Fair Isle sweaters are typically cut open to make armholes. There are even situations where it is advantageous to cut out the armholes and neckline in a flat fabric, just as you would for a woven.

In most designs of this kind, stitches are picked up along the cut edges to add knitted borders at center front openings, and around the armholes to add sleeves worked from the top down; see Picking Up Stitches. Unfortunately, the only sleeve style that can be worked in the round in this way is a straight, unshaped tube (see Bodice and Sleeve Design); a shaped sleeve cap requires the use of Short Rows, which are done as for flat knitting. For an alternative, see Working from the Top Down, below.

If this is the approach you want to use, keep in mind that many stitch and color patterns do not look the same upside down, which means the sleeve and the bodice may have a slightly different appearance. Before deciding how to work, you might want to make two Test Swatches, dress them so you can really see the pattern, and then turn one with the cast-on edge up and set them side by side.

Cutting a circular fabric open does avoid the necessity of seaming the sides of the bodice and the lower sleeves, and sewing sleeves into armholes. However, it must be said that seams of this kind are quick and easy to do (see Finishing Techniques), while Steeks are rather complicated, requiring several steps and special skills that take considerably more time and effort.

Furthermore, instead of a tidy pair of selvedges on the inside of the seam, there will be a rather bulky and somewhat ragged machine- or hand-sewn edge. However, a cut edge can be bound or faced for a nicer finish (see Sewing Wovens to Knits), and the little fringe left by the following method (or the Knotted Steek method) is not only softer, but quite charming.

Knitting Flat on Outside Only

As an alternative to a Steek, you can divide the fabric at the underarm but continue to work only on the outside of the fabric, as follows:

1. Divide the work at the armholes, placing half of stitches on a holder. Continue to work on a circular or long double-point needle, but on just one section.
2. At the end of every row, break yarn, slide stitches to tip of needle on right side, and reattach yarn. Work every row as an outside row.
3. Every other row, tie two ends together with Square Knot and cut ends short.
4. At top of armhole, shape shoulder with Short Rows.
5. Work other set of stitches in same way; bring two sets of shoulder stitches together and use Joinery Cast-Off; repeat on other shoulder.

The result will be a charming little fringe all around the armholes (and see the Knotted Steek, which is another way to do the same thing). This avoids the more complicated steps required to secure the fabric prior to cutting the opening, and the fringe forms a much less bulky join when the sleeve is added.

Working from the Top Down

Another popular way to avoid Purl and sewing up seams is to work an entire garment from the top down, making the upper sleeve and upper bodice as one.†

---

† For a comprehensive introduction to this approach with several options for designs, see Barbara G. Walker, *Knitting from the Top* (New York: Schoolhouse Press, 1996).

Many knitters also like this approach because they want to try a garment on while it is being made to check for fit and length (this is done with socks and mittens, as well). However, the dimensions of a fabric change when it is dressed the first time, so trying on a garment as it emerges from the needles does not usually provide a very accurate sense of how it will really fit later. Please see the discussion in Stitch Gauge about the kinds of changes a fabric undergoes when it is washed and blocked; you will also find information there about how to check the gauge and dimensions of a work in progress.

Another aspect of working this way is more problematic. In designs of this kind, it is common for the armhole and sleeve cap shaping to be done with paired increases set along four lines, two front and two back. This seems at first glance to make sense because the slope of the sleeve cap and that of the armhole must be the same length so they will fit together.

However, as explained in Armhole and Sleeve Cap Design, correct shaping of the cap and armhole of a set-in sleeve requires two entirely different patterns because the widths and lengths of the two areas are not the same. A raglan sleeve actually requires four patterns, since the front and back armholes are different as well. In other words, working entirely in the round from the top down imposes a compromise in terms of how well the garment will fit, although the results can be reasonably successful in a loose garment because a knitted fabric is forgiving.

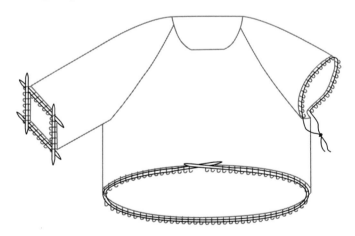

Working from the Top Down: Sleeve at left on double-point needles; sleeve at right on holder; bottom of garment on circular needle.

Also, many designs of this type require the extensive use of Short Rows, such as for the shoulder and neckline area and some sleeve cap designs. But of course, this is also done flat and so requires working inside and outside rows; if you have difficulty with different tensions on Knit and Purl rows, this could be problematic.

Working from the top down does make it easier to alter the length of the bodice or sleeves later, should you need to do so. All that is necessary is to pull out the cast-off edge and make whatever adjustment is needed. Do keep in mind that the characteristics of the yarn may have changed with wear and cleaning, and using the same yarn to make something longer may not be entirely successful. Consider adding a stripe between the old and new yarn, or do the entire change in a different color.

Finally, while there are a wealth of cast-on techniques to choose from, there are very few options for casting off. Most conventional garments start with a ribbing, and Alternating Cast-On is ideal for this purpose because it is very resilient; to accomplish the same thing when working in the other direction requires Grafted Cast-Off, which is a sewn technique, and a lot more trouble to do.

Flat Pieces, or a Whole Garment?

When there is a choice about whether to work flat or in the round, you might want to give some thought to several other pros and cons.

❖ *Wear and Tear*

When working flat, only one small section of the entire garment occupies your lap or your knitting bag at any time; the project remains relatively small and portable from beginning to end.

It is far less effort to turn a single section of a garment at the end of each row than it is to spin a full garment in your lap, and it takes less time overall. Indeed, there is often no need to move the fabric in your lap; you can simply twist it on itself at the end of one row, and then untwist it for the next.

This means the fabric is subjected to less handling as it is made, which is especially important for fragile yarns or those with a tendency to pill. And since each section is put away until it is time to assemble the garment, everything stays cleaner, a particularly important consideration for light colors.

❖ *Mistakes*

Should you make a mistake that requires ripping out rows in a flat fabric, you will lose, at most, half as much work as you would with a fabric made in the round. Indeed, if you find an error when working from the top down on both bodice and sleeves simultaneously, the loss is even greater. Of course, this will matter less if the item is small or the stitches are large and there are fewer of them.

It is also possible to drop one stitch, or even a narrow section of stitches, and unravel down to the error to fix it (see Correcting Mistakes in the chapter Working a Project). When I first tried this, I thought it very clever indeed. However, it soon became clear that it was a tedious and time-consuming task, and difficult to do well enough to leave no evidence in the fabric of what happened. In the end, it took far more time than if I had ripped out and reknit everything, and I would have enjoyed it more.

❖ *Rows or Spirals*

A flat fabric consists of rows stacked one on top of the other and, when the garment is sewn together, they will be perfectly aligned on either side of the seam.

A circular fabric consists of a spiral; the running thread passes from the last stitch at the end of one round to the first stitch at the beginning of the next. This creates a step, or jog at the intersection, which makes its first appearance at the cast-on edge and continues the entire length of the fabric.

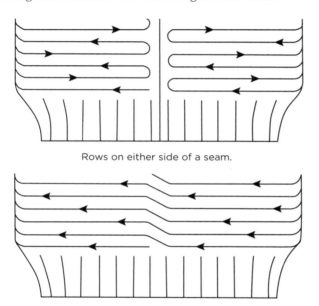

Rows on either side of a seam.

The spiral structure of a circular garment.

If the fabric is made in plain Stockinette or in a decorative pattern that has a vertical orientation, the jog may be scarcely noticeable. However, with patterns that create horizontal stripes (of which there are many), the jog at the end of each round is

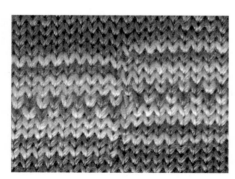

Jog in a color pattern at the join between rounds.

quite visible at every color change; it is less so if the stitches are small or the pattern is complex enough to distract the eye.

Short of working flat and seaming, there is no way to avoid this entirely, but here are several suggestions for how to mitigate the problem.

Stripe Insertion

One very easy way to deal with the jog is to place several columns of plain stitches at either side of the garment (where seams would be). This creates a vertical stripe in the fabric that interrupts the horizontal pattern and makes the jog at the join between rounds considerably less noticeable. Planned well, the stripe simply looks like an integral, intentional part of the design.

Decorative Pattern Placement

Many patterns have solid stripes set above and below sections that contain discontinuous decorative motifs. You may be able to locate the pattern so that the plain stitches between motifs fall at the intersection between rounds, instead of the motif itself, which will eliminate some of the problem caused by the jog; for more information, see the suggestions in Coordinating Stitch and Garment Patterns.

Slip Stitch Method

The jog is most visible on a row where a color change takes place. This could be the first row of a stripe, or when changing from a stripe to a section of plain background. Here is a way to make the jog at this transition point somewhat less noticeable.

1. Begin working with new color at start of round.
2. At beginning of second round, Slip first stitch purlwise; complete round.

This pulls the first stitch of the new color up into the second round and eases the appearance of the jog.

Of course, if done in the same place every time there is a color change, there will be fewer stitches in that column. Therefore, the technique works best with stripes that are fairly deep so fewer Slip stitches are needed; with narrower stripes, it may eventually cause some distortion in the fabric.

As an alternative, you can shift the start of the round one stitch to the left at every color change. In other words, when working the next stripe, start the new color on the second stitch instead of the first, and Slip it on the next round. For the stripe above that, start the new color on the third stitch, etc.

Either variation will ease the jog in a plain stripe (especially if you are working with a thin yarn and the stitches are small), but it does not entirely disappear. Also, this only works well with plain stripes; for more complex color patterns that do not have several rows of solid color, it is not of much help.

Raised Increase Method

Another solution that helps to pull the jog on the first row of a color change into alignment is to use a variation of the Raised Increase.

1. Introduce new color and work one round.
2. On second round, lift stitch below first stitch onto left needle; Knit the two stitches together.

This raises the first stitch with the new color up into the second round and eases the jog, and it is reasonably effective if the stitches are small.

However, it does thicken the fabric, and as with the Slip Stitch solution described above, it is most successful if used infrequently. This depends on the pattern having multi-row stripes or plain background areas near other pattern elements; it is less successful when motifs straddle the join.

❖ Seams

Certain kinds of designs and some fabrics benefit from having a seam, while others are best without any. For these things, the decision about whether to work flat or in the round is easy to make.

For close-fitted items like socks, mittens, hats, or camisoles, a seam is normally thought of as an unwelcome and unnecessary intrusion. While seams are not necessarily uncomfortable in wear (argyle socks have always had them), they are likely to stretch open, which makes them unsightly.

When a fabric is airy and open or the garment style loose and fluid, a seam could impair the intended effect. A seam can also be difficult to manage in a fulled fabric and tends to be very bulky; for more information see Designing a Fulled Project, as well as Sewing Fulled Knits.

On the other hand, seams can add support to a heavy garment or one made with fibers that lack resilience, and they contribute important definition to certain garment styles. Also, it is considerably easier to manage relatively complex shaping patterns by working flat pieces and seaming them together; in some cases it is only possible to accomplish what is needed by doing so.

Even relatively simple styles often benefit from the definition or support of a seam. For instance, many knitters feel that a circular bodice set over a ribbed edge tends to take on the shape of a barrel because it lacks the structure a seam provides. Perhaps this criticism has some validity, but my sense of the matter is that too much is made of it because the garment style is inherently shaped that way, but if you want to make it look slimmer and straighter, a seam will help.

For those who prefer to work in the round, one solution proposed for the barrel effect is something called a Seam Stitch. This is no more than a Slip Stitch worked every other row where a seam would be if the garment were worked flat.

The idea is to tighten the stitch column so it will provide the structure and definition of a seam.

However, a Slip Stitch column will have only half as many stitches as there are in the surrounding fabric, and this can constrict the fabric somewhat. A little steam and stretching will often help, but much depends on the nature of the stitch pattern used for the main fabric; if the garment is heavy or the fabric is loosely knit it might simply stretch out on either side of the Seam Stitch.

Before deciding whether to use this method, therefore, test the effect on your Gauge Swatch first (and make it a little longer than usual to get a real sense of what will happen). Also, a Slip Stitch column is the equivalent of a Vertical Foldline, and it tends to fold out, not in, which somewhat defeats the purpose. Whenever it would suit the surrounding pattern, you might find it more effective to use a column of Purl instead, because it tends to recess into the fabric.

Seams offer another great advantage that has nothing to do with whether or not they are important to the garment. A selvedge functions as a tiny closet where you can tie on new balls of yarn and hide the ends. Of course, there are ways to do these things in the middle of a fabric when necessary (see Tying On Yarn, and Hiding Ends of Yarn), but all of them tend to be more challenging and time-consuming to do, and provide less satisfactory results. And as discussed above, a seam solves the problem of aligning the rows of a horizontal stitch or color pattern.

In many cases, however, it does not matter if seams offer some convenience or would benefit the style or appearance of the garment, because the decision is not made on its merits—many knitters choose to work in the round simply because they want to avoid seams. If the problem is that you do not know how to sew a seam that would be acceptable, that can be overcome with a little patience and practice and the information in Seams in the chapter Finishing Techniques. If you know how to sew, but do not like it, then it is a matter of deciding whether the trade-offs are worth it to you.

❖ Working in Purl

Many knitters who use the Standard Left-Hand Method complain of difficulty with Purl and as a result choose to work in the round almost exclusively as a way to avoid it. This is a viable option and solves the problem if you primarily work in Stockinette, whether plain or with color patterns, and there are many designs that can be accomplished in this way.

However, if you are tempted by a project that requires fairly extensive use of Purl, or one that has to be made flat, rather than decide not to make it at all, please see the discussion of the alternative Left-Hand Methods that present fewer problems with Purl to see if one of them will help.

Or, take up the challenge to learn one of the Right-Hand

Methods to use for just those occasions; there is no problem working Purl with any of them. Indeed, for some things you might want to consider the Thumb Method, which makes Purl easier to do than Knit.

❖ Stitch Patterns

The instructions for most published stitch patterns are written for working flat, with inside and outside rows (see Written Stitch Patterns). No doubt this is done so you can try the pattern on a small flat swatch before deciding whether to use it.

These patterns need to be rewritten before they can be used for a circular fabric. In many cases, this is quite easy—no more than changing all the inside Purl rows to outside rows done in Knit—but it can be more challenging on patterns where inside rows also contain special techniques or a mixture of Knit and Purl stitches.

Charted stitch patterns are easier to follow when working in the round than when working flat because they show only the outside rows (see Charted Stitch and Color Patterns). To work flat, any symbol for a technique used on an inside row needs to be translated into its Purl version, and many people find this challenging to do.

Unfortunately, few written patterns make it clear whether a pattern is suitable for working circular or flat. Some may contain edge stitches that are used to balance a pattern on both sides of a flat fabric, but these are not needed for a circular fabric, in which case it is important to recognize and eliminate them; for more information, see Edge and Selvedge Stitches.

The Garter Stitch pattern is often favored by knitters who like to avoid Purl when working a flat fabric because it is done by using Knit on both inside and outside rows. However, if you like the stitch pattern and want to use it when working something in the round, it will be necessary to Purl every other row. While there is a way to do Garter Stitch in the round entirely in Knit (see Circular Intarsia Worked in Rows), the results are not very satisfactory because the join between rounds tends to be distorted.

❖ Color Patterns

It is advantageous to work color patterns in the round because the outside of the fabric is on view at all times and it is easy to see the pattern develop and keep your place. One of the preferred ways to do Stranded Color patterns is to work with two yarns at the same time, most commonly with one yarn in each hand, and this is easier to do when working in the round. There are alternative ways to hold the yarn when working flat and using these kinds of color patterns; see Stranded Pattern Methods.

One option discussed there is to hold both yarns in the right hand, because this presents little problem with Purl. Not mentioned there is the option of using the Thumb Method, which is traditionally used for doing elaborate color patterns, often with more than two colors, while working in Purl on the inside of a circular fabric. In this case, it is Knit that is slightly more difficult to do, but the method does lend itself to doing color patterns in a flat fabric, and it is easier to manage the yarns and maintain even tension than with almost any other method.

Unfortunately, Intarsia patterns—with one lovely exception—are difficult, if not impossible, to work in the round; see Intarsia in the Round.

❖ Summary

As the discussion above makes clear, the pros and cons regarding whether to work flat or in the round are numerous. Each approach brings benefits as well as challenges or problems. But there are also personal factors that weigh into the decision.

Many knitters put more value on how they feel while knitting and prefer to use familiar techniques. Working in the most comfortable and satisfying way is far more important to them than whether the garment might have been somewhat improved by using another approach. Basically, the benefits or compromises of working in one way or another are inconsequential to them. This is entirely understandable because the pleasure of knitting is an essential part of what we all love about the craft.

There are also knitters who enjoy making traditional garments like ganseys or Fair Isle sweaters in a completely authentic way, in which case the question of how to work is decided beforehand. Their focus is primarily on the challenges of working a stitch or color pattern.

Other knitters enjoy improvisation and do not want to be bothered with a lot of planning ahead of time; they like to develop their ideas as they go and enjoy the challenge and creativity of working in the round and seeing the garment and fabric emerge simultaneously from their needles.

Some knitters are more interested in contemporary garment styles. They may like to design for themselves and enjoy the challenge of making something fashionable with complex or subtle shaping. More often than not the emphasis is on using whatever techniques are suitable to the project and the method of knitting is less important.

My hope is that the material in this book will provide you with the knowledge and skills to work in whatever way you find satisfying.

Part Two

CONSTRUCTING A FABRIC

CHAPTER 3

Casting On

Casting on (or binding on, as it is sometimes called) refers to the process of placing the first stitches on the needle in order to begin knitting. In most cases, these stitches will form the lower edge of the fabric. A surprising number of techniques can be used for this purpose, and each one produces an edge with unique characteristics. This makes it possible to select one that will be compatible with the style of the garment and the stitch pattern used for the main fabric.

For instance, you might want to choose an edge that is quiet and unobtrusive for a tailored garment, but something more decorative for a dressy style. Furthermore, an edge with good stretch and resilience is necessary for ribbed cuffs and waistbands, but would not be needed for a fabric that is firm and inelastic.

A glance through this chapter might cause you to think there are simply too many choices. But take heart, because the material is organized into groups of related techniques, each no more than a variation on a theme; having learned the definitive one, the others in the group will seem familiar. You will probably find that no more than four or five methods become favorites because they work well for almost everything you knit. Nevertheless, it is worth knowing at least something of the others so you can select an alternative for those projects that require a more specialized edge.

To sort out this issue and find the techniques you prefer, first read the introduction and general discussion at the start of each group. This will give you a general idea of what each type of technique has to offer; then learn only those you think will prove the most useful for the kind of knitting you do. As a rule, the basic technique, discussed first within each group, may be the only one you will need. Should a new project require something different, come back to this material and add one of the variations to your repertoire at that time.

General Information for Casting On

Here are some helpful hints that apply to any of the cast-on techniques. These include how to select the correct needle size for an edge, how to attach the yarn to the needle, and, when necessary, how to calculate the amount of yarn to allow.

❖ Needles

It is usually easier to cast on with a straight needle rather than a circular one, since it provides greater stability for the hand. Also, the cast-on edge tends to stay lined up under a straight needle, which makes it easy to space the stitches out to make an accurate count. In contrast, the edge often spirals around the thin cable of a circular needle and it can be difficult to set it right again to work the first row of stitches. This is more of a problem with some techniques than others; one solution is to cast on to a straight needle and then begin the first row with a circular needle if you prefer; for circular work, either join the round on the second row, or slip all the stitches to a circular needle or a set of double-point needles before beginning to work; see Circular Knitting.

❖ Attaching the Yarn

The first step in casting on is to attach the yarn to the needle; there are three ways to do so. The Simple Cast-On Start and the Twist Start are very easy to do and both accomplish the same thing; either will serve as the first stitch, but will not be secure on the needle until you cast on the next stitch. A Slip Knot is somewhat more challenging to do, but it works well for any purpose, and will stay put until you are ready to begin; with some techniques you have the option of using it for the first stitch, or dropping it off the needle later.

Simple Cast-On Start

The most elementary way to begin a Simple Cast-On is to do barely anything at all (the result is the same as the Right Twist Start, below):

• Hold end of yarn under needle in right hand and yarn to ball in left hand and begin to cast on; after second loop is on needle it is safe to drop yarn end.

Twist Start

This technique is not suitable for the Knitted Cast-On techniques, but works nicely with several of the Finger Cast-Ons. It is not only very quick and easy to do, but leaves a neat, unobtrusive corner on the fabric.

It is no more than a loop of yarn around the needle that is twisted on itself, either to the right or to the left. In most cases it does not matter which version you use, but when it does, this will be specified in the instructions.

After putting the Twist Start on the needle, your hands will be in position to begin casting on. Maintain tension on the strands until you have added the first stitch, or the loop will come undone.

Left Twist Start

1. Pick up yarn to ball in left hand, end of yarn in right hand.
2. Extend left thumb and forefinger and, with right hand, wrap yarn up nearside of left thumb, over back of thumb and forefinger, then down farside of forefinger.
3. Add second strand to first in palm of left hand and grasp both firmly; spread finger and thumb apart to put tension on strand.
4. Insert needle tip down into circle formed by thumb, forefinger, and strand, and then move needle tip under strand between thumb and forefinger toward nearside and back into starting position to wrap yarn (tip of needle will move clockwise).

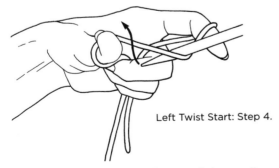

Left Twist Start: Step 4.

The yarn will make a full circle around the needle and, where the two strands cross beneath it, the one to the thumb will pass to the left of the one to the forefinger; if you turn the tip of the needle toward you, you will see that the loop crosses on itself to the left.

Right Twist Start

To twist the yarn in the other direction, work as follows:

• Work as above, but move needle tip up under strand toward farside and back into starting position to wrap yarn (tip of needle will move counterclockwise).

Where the two strands cross beneath the needle, the one to the thumb will pass to the right of the one to the forefinger; if you turn the tip of the needle toward you, you will see that the loop crosses on itself to the right.

Slip Knot

The most common way to begin casting on is to make a Slip Knot and place it on the needle; it works with every technique, and is secure on the needle.

You can count the knot as the first stitch, in which case it will be visible at the corner of the fabric. Alternatively, do not include it when you count the cast-on stitches; drop it from the needle when working the first row, or, when finishing the corner, undo the knot by pulling the yarn end free.

There are two ways to make a Slip Knot.

Slip Knot: Method One

1. Hold yarn to ball in left hand and pick up yarn in right hand a minimum of 10 to 12 inches from end.
2. With right hand, form yarn into loop about 2 inches in diameter; pass end of yarn over loop, drop on farside, and hold loop in position with left hand.
3. Take up knitting needle in right hand, insert tip through loop, then around strand of yarn on farside from right to left; catch strand on needle and pull loop through to nearside.

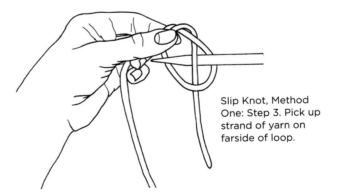

Slip Knot, Method One: Step 3. Pick up strand of yarn on farside of loop.

4. With left hand, pull down on both strands of yarn to tighten Slip Knot on needle.

If you prefer, you can reach your fingers through the loop to catch the strand and draw it through, instead of using the tip of the needle.

Slip Knot: Method Two

Here is another way of doing the same thing. I really like this method—once you get the hang of it, it is very quick to do. This Slip Knot is particularly good for any of the Finger Cast-On techniques that start with a "tail" of yarn, because when the knot is complete, your fingers will already be in the correct position to begin casting on.

1. Hold yarn to ball in palm of left hand and pick up yarn in right hand a minimum of 10 to 12 inches from end.
2. Extend first two fingers of left hand, pointing to right. Starting on nearside, wrap yarn twice around these two fingers, as follows: Over top, straight down farside close to tips of fingers, under and up nearside toward left, crossing second wrap over first, over fingers again and then straight down farside; add end of yarn to other strand in palm of left hand. The wrapped strands should form an X on nearside of fingers, and will be parallel on farside.
3. With needle held in right hand, pass tip to nearside of first parallel strand and to farside of second parallel strand; catch that strand on needle and draw it back through the circle to the right to form loop.

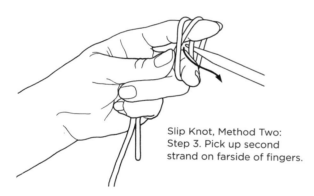

Slip Knot, Method Two:
Step 3. Pick up second strand on farside of fingers.

4. Drop strands of yarn off fingers; immediately insert fingers between two strands below knot and spread them apart to tighten it and begin to cast on.

❖ Yarn Requirements for Edge

Cast-on techniques differ in how long a tail of yarn to allow before attaching the Twist Start or Slip Knot to the needle.

Yarn Allowance for Knit Cast-Ons

The Knit Cast-On techniques begin close to the end of the yarn, and there is no need to be very precise about how much of an end to leave.

- Allow a length of yarn that will be easy to thread into a sewing needle and hide on the inside during finishing; 10 to 12 inches is usually sufficient.

- If you are working a flat fabric and plan to seam the edge, you might want to allow an end long enough to use for sewing up as well. See Yarn Butterfly for Seaming, below.

Yarn Allowance for Finger Cast-Ons

For a Simple Cast-On, allow the same amount of yarn as for the Knit Cast-Ons, above. All the other Finger Cast-On techniques require two strands of yarn, one for the stitches and the other for the baseline that attaches the stitches securely to the needle. In most cases, these are part of a single supply of yarn divided into two portions.

The baseline strand, commonly called the "tail," is an allowance of yarn measured from the end to where it is attached to the needle. While it is possible to make a close estimate of how much yarn to allow for the tail, it is frustrating to come up short and have to rip everything out and start over again.

Here is a precise way to calculate the length of yarn required for a baseline:

1. Estimate a length of about 1 to 2 feet from end of yarn, make Slip Knot, and cast on 10 stitches.
2. With left thumb and forefinger, pinch tail of yarn where it emerges from last stitch cast on. Slide all stitches except Slip Knot off needle and unravel.
3. Measure length of tail yarn between fingers and needle; this is amount of yarn required for baseline of ten cast-on stitches. Multiply that measurement by one-tenth the number of stitches you plan to cast on.

Walking Off the Measurement

If you do not like math, "walk off" the measurement instead.

1. Complete Steps 1–3 above.
2. Double length of unraveled tail yarn; this is now enough yarn for a baseline of 20 cast-on stitches.
3. Hold doubled length of yarn between left and right hand and count by 20s to measure off as many more equal lengths of yarn as needed.
4. Make Slip Knot at that point and begin casting on.

Casting On with Two Yarns

To guarantee that you will not run out of yarn for the baseline, you can use two balls of yarn of the same color (or one end from the inside, the other from the outside of a center-pull ball). For a decorative effect, see Contrast-Color Half-Hitch Edges, below.

Working with two yarns in this way is a particularly useful trick when casting on a large number of stitches, in which case the consequence of miscalculating the amount of yarn for the tail would be a great deal of wasted effort.

- Leave ends of each yarn long enough to make it easy to hide them during finishing. Tie two yarns together with Slip Knot and place it on needle; do not count knot as first stitch.
- After casting on, drop knot from needle when working first row of stitches and untie when convenient.

Yarn Butterfly for Seaming

If you plan to work a flat fabric and seam the side edge, measure off extra yarn to the baseline strand to use for sewing up. An added benefit of doing this is that there will be no tail of yarn left at the corner to hide when finishing.

A strand about twice the length of the seam is usually more than sufficient for sewing up. After casting on, gather the remaining strand into a Yarn Butterfly, as follows:

1. Spread fingers of hand apart and wrap yarn in "figure 8" pattern around forefinger and thumb, or thumb and small finger.
2. Turn yarn on itself to form small half-hitch loop, pull wrapped yarns from one finger through this loop and then tighten to secure; make second loop and repeat.
3. Allow Butterfly to hang at end of work until needed for seaming.

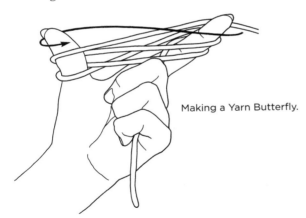

Making a Yarn Butterfly.

❖ Cast-Ons and Stitch Formation

Most of the cast-on techniques require a basic understanding of stitch formation even when no stitches are yet present. For instance, you will frequently encounter an instruction to insert the needle tip into a loop or under a strand of yarn "as to Knit" (in other words, from left to right when the needle is horizontal), or "as to Purl" (from right to left).

Also, some of the techniques require an understanding of the position of a stitch on the needle; in standard position, the right side of the stitch is on the nearside of the needle, while in "turned" position, the left side of the stitch is on the nearside instead. The position of the stitch on the needle is also related

to whether a cast-on stitch will be twisted by working into it on the nearside or farside.

And from time to time a strand will be positioned on the needle "as for a Yarnover." For more information about all of these fundamental concepts, please see The Knit and Purl Stitches, Turned Stitches, Twist Stitches, and Yarnovers.

Finger Cast-On Techniques

The methods discussed here rely on the use of the fingers to manipulate the yarn in order to place the first stitches on a needle. Two major families of techniques are done in this way, and both of them contain quite a few variations.

The Half-Hitch family is by far the largest group, and it also contains the single most useful and versatile method of all; if you had to choose just one to learn, the Knit Half-Hitch Cast-On would be it. The many variations on this technique range from the simple to the complex, with each seemingly small change in method producing an edge with rather different characteristics. Despite how many there are, as you will see, once you have mastered the primary one, the others will be easy to learn.

This large category of cast-ons all share a common foundation: a rudimentary knot, or crossed loop, called a half-hitch. Knitters often refer to this as an "e-loop," from its resemblance to the cursive form of the letter.

In knot making, a half-hitch is normally wrapped around something like a post or another section of a rope. In knitting, a half-hitch is wrapped around the base of each stitch and, when done in a series, these form the baseline (or lower edge of the knitted fabric), which also secures the stitches on the needle.

Simple Half-Hitch, discussed first, consists of just the half-hitch baseline; the stitches are added later, in a second step. The Compound Half-Hitch Cast-Ons combine the two steps, with the baseline and the stitches made at the same time.

The Wrapped Cast-On family contains techniques that create very attractive and useful edges, but they have more limited applications. One is used only for ribbing or Double-Fabrics, another is purely utilitarian and never used for a finished edge, and several are used primarily to start at the center of a fabric instead of at an edge, such as for the toe of a sock. These may be used less often, but they are ideal in certain situations.

Also included are instructions for provisional cast-on techniques (for edges that will later be removed), as well as those for casting on at the side or within the fabric.

❖ Simple Half-Hitch Cast-Ons

The Simple Cast-Ons are no doubt the oldest and by far the easiest ways to put stitches on a needle. Other more efficient or versatile techniques have largely supplanted these, and they now play a rather minor role in knitting. Nevertheless, it is helpful to understand the structure of these edges, since they form the basis for the closely related Compound Half-Hitch Cast-Ons, which are far more common. One of the remaining useful applications for this cast-on is that it offers a precise way to control the amount of yarn in the baseline of the cast-on edge; for more information on why this can be important, see Tips for Simple Half-Hitch Cast-Ons; in some circumstances, it is also a practical way to add stitches to a side edge, or within the fabric (see Side or Mid-Fabric Cast-Ons).

Use a straight needle, allow 10 to 12 inches of yarn, and begin with one of the methods described above for attaching the yarn to the needle.

Right and Left Simple Cast-On

A Simple Cast-On consists of no more than a series of half-hitches looped on to the needle. There are several ways to hold the yarn, and you can cross the loops to the right or left. The choice of how to work is a matter of what you are comfortable with, or how you want to work the first row of stitches, since the outcome is much the same.

Simple Right Half-Hitch

This is by far the most common way to work. The yarn is held on your left thumb, and the loops on the needle will cross to the right.

1. Hold needle in right hand and use Simple Cast-On Start or Slip Knot and hold in place with right forefinger about an inch back from tip of needle; hold yarn to ball in palm of left hand.
2. Move left thumb down farside of strand between needle and hand, then under strand and up on nearside. Yarn now passes from palm, up nearside and across back of thumb, and between thumb and forefinger to needle.
3. Maintain slight tension on yarn, insert tip of right needle under yarn on outside of thumb from left to right, as to Knit. Transfer loop to needle and release yarn from thumb.

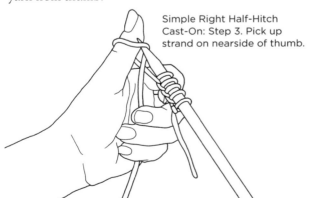

Simple Right Half-Hitch Cast-On: Step 3. Pick up strand on nearside of thumb.

4. Tighten yarn gently around needle with downward movement of left hand; wrap yarn on thumb again as before.
5. Repeat Steps 2–4 until number of loops required is on needle.
6. Work first row of stitches as follows:
   - Circular fabric: Knit or Purl all loops farside.
   - Flat fabric: to Knit, work first loop nearside and all others farside; to Purl, work all loops farside.

Simple Left Half-Hitch

Work as described above, but with the following modifications:

1. To wrap yarn, move left thumb down nearside of strand to needle, then under and up on farside; yarn passes from palm up farside and across back of thumb and then to needle.
2. Reach needle tip around on farside of thumb and pick up strand from left to right, as for Purl farside.

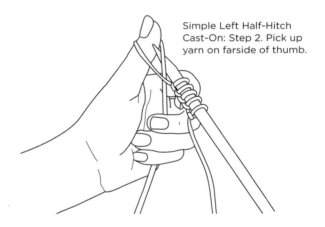

Simple Left Half-Hitch Cast-On: Step 2. Pick up yarn on farside of thumb.

3. Tighten yarn gently around needle with downward movement of left hand; wrap yarn on thumb again as before.
4. Repeat Steps 1 and 2 to cast on as many stitches as required.
5. Work first row of stitches as follows:
   - Circular fabric: Knit or Purl all loops nearside.
   - Flat fabric: to Knit, work all stitches nearside; to Purl, work first stitch farside and all others nearside.

Simple Half-Hitch Variations

While it is most common to wrap the yarn on the thumb, here are two alternatives that are also easy to do and result in exactly the same edge. With the first, the yarn is held on the forefinger. With the second, hold the yarn in your right hand and the needle in your left; the movements used to wrap the yarn are a mirror image of those described above.

Simple Half-Hitch from Forefinger

- Wrap yarn as for Right or Left version, above, but on left forefinger instead of on thumb; otherwise work in same way.

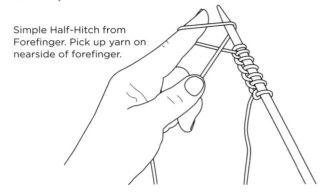

Simple Half-Hitch from Forefinger. Pick up yarn on nearside of forefinger.

Simple Half-Hitch from Right Thumb

- To cross loops to left, use Simple Right Half-Hitch, above; to work first row, use instructions for Simple Left Half-Hitch.
- To cross loops to right, use Simple Left Half-Hitch, above; to work first row, use instructions for Simple Right Half-Hitch.

Tips for Simple Half-Hitch Cast-Ons

- *The main advantage of a Simple Cast-On is that the needle acts as a gauge to measure off a precise amount of yarn to each loop. This is important because, collectively, the amount of yarn in each of them will determine how compatible the edge will be with the fabric.*

  The ideal needle size for the cast-on edge may not be the same as the one used for the stitch pattern. Use Test Swatches to find the needle size that will make an edge that is neither too constricted, nor too loose.

- *It can be difficult to insert the needle into the loops of a Simple Cast-On when working the first row of stitches. Keep the needle tips close together so the strand between two loops remains somewhat slack.*

- *For information on how to cross the loops more than once, see Twisted Half-Hitch Cast-On.*

- *As you cast on, the yarn may either unply, or ply more tightly. To correct this, let the tail hang loose from time to time; to rebalance the yarn, push the stitches back several inches from the tip of the needle, hold the yarn, drop the needle, and let it spin; see Knitting Methods and Yarn Twist. The stitches will not come off the needle because the hanging weight tightens the first loop, but if you are concerned, put a stitch guard on the tip.*

❖ *Compound Half-Hitch Cast-Ons*

This is a large group of closely related cast-on techniques. I think of them as "compound" techniques because they simultaneously create the same edge as a Simple Half-Hitch Cast-On plus the first row of stitches. It is equivalent to casting on and working the first row at the same time, and you can do so as to either Knit or Purl, or in a combination of the two.

There are quite a few variations on this theme and all of them are well worth knowing about, since each allows you to vary the edge—either to make it more compatible with the fabric above, or to change its appearance.

Most techniques of this type are done with a single needle held in the right hand and two strands of yarn held in the left hand; one strand is used for the edge and the other for the stitches. There are several variations on this that are discussed below.

Holding Yarn and Needle

To begin, measure off an initial length of yarn, called the "tail,"† to use for the baseline. As a rule, allow ½ to 1 inch per stitch for the tail of yarn; the thicker the yarn, the more you will need. You will not waste very much yarn using this rough guideline, but for a more precise approach, see Yarn Requirements for Edge.

1. Calculate tail of yarn, make Slip Knot, and place on needle with tail on nearside. With needle in right hand, hold knot about an inch back from tip with right forefinger and grasp two strands of yarn firmly in palm of left hand.
2. Insert left thumb and forefinger between strands, spread them apart slightly, and then move left hand and needle apart to place moderate tension on strands between needle and fingers.
3. Hold left hand with thumb and forefinger pointing up and palm facing tip of needle; fingertips and needle tip should be about 2 to 3 inches apart.

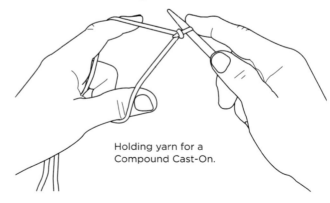

Holding yarn for a Compound Cast-On.

---

† This technique is frequently called "Long-Tail Cast-On," although it is only one of a great many cast-on techniques that make use of a tail of yarn in this way. Some are variations on this theme, while others are entirely different.

A Slip Knot is usually more compatible with this edge than a Twist Start, but the latter could also be used.

In Step 3, the tail of yarn should travel from the needle across the top of your left thumb and down the nearside into your palm; the yarn to the ball should travel from the needle across the top of your left forefinger and down the farside and then join the other strand in your palm.

Basic Half-Hitch Cast-Ons

The most basic form of this relatively large group is undoubtedly the most common cast-on used in knitting, and for good reason: it is fast, easy to do, and produces a handsome, moderately resilient edge that is suitable for nearly everything you might have occasion to knit. It is justifiably popular among knitters, and for many it is the only cast-on used.

The edge has Knit and Purl sides, although many knitters are only familiar with how to do the Knit version. Once you understand how to do the Purl version, you can control which side of the edge appears on the outside of the fabric, and of course this also gives you the option of making an edge that is perfectly compatible with any ribbing.

While you can use a Twist Start for this cast on, the Slip Knot is more compatible because it is similar to a half-hitch around the base of a stitch; the Twist Start lacks the stitch, and thus pulls the corner up, out of line with the rest of the edge.

Knit Half-Hitch Cast-On

1. Slide tip of needle up under strand on nearside of thumb from left to right as to Knit and draw it to right, creating open half-hitch loop between thumb and needle; do not drop yarn from thumb.
2. Move needle tip over strand between forefinger and needle, down farside and under. Right side of strand will be on nearside of needle and will look like a Yarnover.

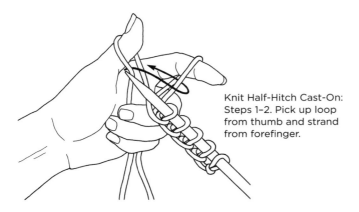

Knit Half-Hitch Cast-On: Steps 1–2. Pick up loop from thumb and strand from forefinger.

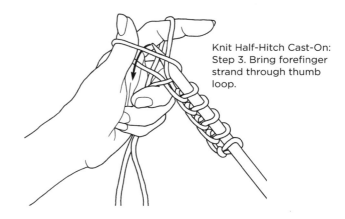

Knit Half-Hitch Cast-On: Step 3. Bring forefinger strand through thumb loop.

3. Bring strand on needle from farside to nearside through loop held by thumb.
4. Allow loop to slide off thumb below needle, and then pick up tail of yarn on thumb as before. Place tension on yarns and gently tighten both stitch and loop.
5. Repeat Steps 1–4, to cast on as many stitches as required.

As you work, notice that the strand from your forefinger forms a half-hitch that encircles the base of the stitch on the needle; when these stitches are worked, they will form the first row of the fabric.

If you are familiar with the Left-Hand Method of knitting, you will undoubtedly notice similarities with this cast-on technique. The loop on the thumb is the equivalent of a stitch on the left needle, and the yarn on the forefinger is wrapped on the needle and drawn through the loop as it would be to make a Knit stitch with that method. As you gain familiarity with the cast-on, you will find that the motions are a combination of moving the needle, and moving your fingers and/or hand.

To add additional stretch to the edge, you may encounter advice to cast on with a larger needle than used for the fabric itself, or even two needles held as one. However, the size of the needle determines only the size of the stitches in the first row and has no effect on the baseline, which is what determines the elasticity of this edge; Contrast-Color Half-Hitch Cast-On reveals the structure quite clearly.

To add a moderate amount of stretch to the baseline, leave a space between one stitch and the next equal to the width of the yarn; this will slightly elongate each half-hitch. Tighten the thumb strand gently, just enough to make each half-hitch neat and consistent with its fellows. For more precise control over the amount of yarn in the edge, use Simple Half-Hitch Cast-On, above, or, for a fully elastic edge, see Double-Needle Cast-On.

The Knit side of the edge has smooth sloping strands and

will be on the nearside as you cast on; the Purl side has tiny nubs. Both are attractive but look quite different.

- If you are working in the round, the Knit side of the edge will be on the outside of the garment when you begin.
- If you are working flat, when you turn to begin the first row, the Purl side of the edge will then be on the nearside. You can decide which side of the edge you want to have on the outside of the fabric by starting the stitch pattern either with an inside or outside row; if necessary, start with the last row of the pattern repeat, instead of the first. Or, use Purl Half-Hitch Cast-On, below.

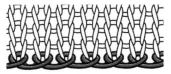 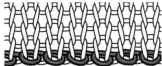

Knit Half-Hitch Cast-On Edge. Appearance on nearside while casting on.

Purl Half-Hitch Cast-On Edge. Appearance on farside while casting on.

Purl Half-Hitch Cast-On

Here are two ways to work if you prefer to have the Purl side of the edge on the nearside as you cast on; when working flat, this means the Knit side of the edge will be on the nearside after turning to begin the first row. The structure and appearance of the edge will otherwise be the same.

Method One

In this version, the stitches are made with the yarn held on the forefinger. This will seem awkward the first few times you do it but is quite easy once you get the hang of it.

1. Hold needle and yarns as for a Compound Half-Hitch Cast-On, but move strand on forefinger to nearside of needle.
2. Slide tip of needle under strand on nearside of thumb from right to left as to Purl; draw it to right, creating open half-hitch loop between thumb and needle; do not drop yarn from thumb.
3. For stitch, pass needle over, then under strand to forefinger to catch it on needle as for a Yarnover, with right side of strand on nearside of needle.

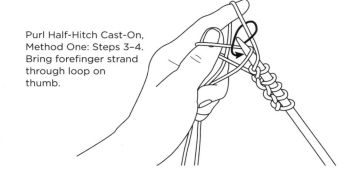

Purl Half-Hitch Cast-On, Method One: Steps 3–4. Bring forefinger strand through loop on thumb.

4. Move needle toward nearside and then back through loop from nearside to farside; move needle back into starting position.
5. Drop loop off thumb below needle and pick up yarn under newly formed stitch in same way as before; tighten stitch and baseline on needle.

Notice the similarity between these movements and the manner of working a Purl stitch when using the Left-Hand Method of knitting.

Method Two

With this version, the tail of yarn is held on the forefinger and forms the baseline; the yarn to the ball is held on the thumb and forms the stitches.

1. Hold needle and yarn as for a Compound Half-Hitch Cast-On.
2. Move needle to nearside of strand from forefinger to needle and to farside of strand passing from forefinger to palm; insert tip up under this strand to form loop.

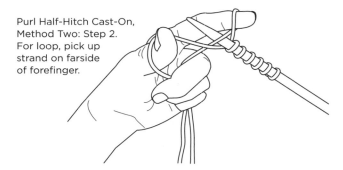

Purl Half-Hitch Cast-On, Method Two: Step 2. For loop, pick up strand on farside of forefinger.

3. For stitch, pass needle tip under strand between needle and thumb, then up nearside to catch on needle as for a Yarnover. Alternatively, move your thumb to do this instead of moving the needle, or a little of both.

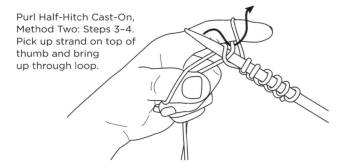

Purl Half-Hitch Cast-On, Method Two: Steps 3–4. Pick up strand on top of thumb and bring up through loop.

4. Move needle tip back under and up through loop formed between forefinger and needle.
5. Drop loop off forefinger and pick yarn up again below newly formed stitch as before; tighten stitch and baseline in usual way.

Ribbed Half-Hitch Cast-On

Once you have learned the Purl versions of this cast-on, then of course you can alternate the Knit and Purl to make an edge suitable for a ribbing, or for any pattern of mixed Knit and Purl stitches. However, because with one version the stitches are made from the yarn, and with the other they are made from the yarn on the forefinger, when either Purl method is combined with Knit Half-Hitch Cast-On, the result will be edges with a similar appearance but with a different structure and behavior.

Alternating Yarns Version

A cast-on done by alternating Knit Half-Hitch Cast-On with Purl Half-Hitch Cast-On Method Two, which has stitches made from the thumb yarn, will create a very resilient edge.

Each strand of yarn is used first for a stitch, next for a half-hitch; therefore, they can borrow from each other for additional stretch.

Ribbed Half-Hitch Cast-On: Alternating Yarns Version. Yarns alternate between stitches and baseline.

Separate Yarns Version

When both the Knit and Purl Half-Hitch stitches are made with the yarn from the forefinger, the baseline will be made entirely from the yarn on the thumb. As a result, the edge will have no more resilience than one done either with all Knit or all Purl Half-Hitch.

Ribbed Half-Hitch Cast-On: Separate Yarns Version. Baseline from thumb yarn, first row of stitches from forefinger yarn.

Half-Hitch Cast-On for Two Hands

This method creates exactly the same edge, except you hold the baseline yarn on your left thumb and the yarn for the stitches on your right forefinger, as in the Right-Finger Method of knitting.

This is a particularly quick and easy method to use when mixing Knit and Purl along the edge, especially when done in conjunction with a Knitting Belt or Sheath, or some other method of support for the needle. It is also used for Twisted Half-Hitch Cast-On, Method Three.

Knit Half-Hitch for Two Hands

1. Allow tail of yarn and place Slip Knot on needle.
2. Wrap tail of yarn around left thumb as for Simple Right Half-Hitch Cast-On; hold needle and yarn to ball in right hand as for Right-Finger Knitting.
3. To form loop, insert needle tip under strand on nearside of thumb from left to right as to Knit; do not drop from thumb.
4. Wrap yarn for stitch around needle with right finger as for Knit, and then bring needle through loop on thumb (or move thumb to pass loop over needle tip).

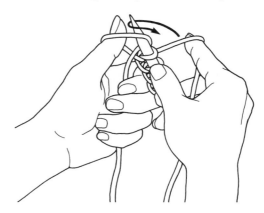

Knit Half-Hitch for Two Hands: Steps 3–4. Pick up loop as to Knit; wrap yarn with right forefinger.

5. Drop loop below needle, and then pick up yarn below new stitch and wrap on thumb as before; tighten baseline and stitch on needle.

Purl Half-Hitch for Two Hands

1. Work as described above, but move yarn on right forefinger to nearside of needle.
2. To form loop, insert needle tip under strand on nearside of thumb from right to left as to Purl, wrap yarn and draw strand through loop; drop loop from thumb.

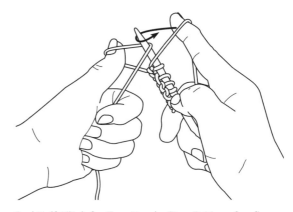

Purl Half-Hitch for Two Hands: Step 2. Move forefinger strand to nearside of needle; pick up loop as to Purl.

Mirror-Image Cast-On

If you use the Reversed Method, or if for any reason you find it awkward or difficult to maneuver yarn and needle when they are held as described above, try holding the yarns in your right hand and the needle in your left, as follows:

Knit Mirror-Image Cast-On

1. Allow tail of yarn and place Slip Knot on needle.
2. With needle in left hand, hold the two yarns in right hand as for basic Knit Half-Hitch Cast-On, with tail yarn on right thumb and yarn to ball on left forefinger.
3. To form loop, insert needle tip under strand of yarn on nearside of thumb from right to left; do not drop yarn from thumb.
4. Move needle under strand on forefinger and then up on farside; yarn should pass over needle and resemble a Yarnover, with right side of strand on nearside of needle.
5. Draw strand through loop and then drop loop from thumb below needle; pick up yarn on thumb as before and tighten stitch and half-hitch.

Purl Mirror-Image Cast-On

There are two ways to do the Purl version of this cast-on technique.

Method One

1. Hold needle and strands of yarn as described above.
2. Move yarn on right forefinger to nearside of needle tip.
3. To form loop, move needle under strand on nearside of thumb from left to right.
4. Move strand on forefinger under needle on nearside, swing needle down, and catch strand to pull it through loop to farside.

Method Two

1. Hold needle and yarns as described above, but with tail yarn on forefinger, yarn to ball on thumb.
2. To form loop, move needle over strand from forefinger to needle, and pick up strand from forefinger to palm from right to left.
3. Move needle over thumb yarn to nearside, then back under to farside to pick up strand as for a Yarnover.
4. Draw strand through loop, then drop loop from forefinger below needle, pick up yarn on forefinger as before, and tighten stitch and half-hitch.

Right-Left Half-Hitch Cast-On

When a Knit or a Purl Half-Hitch Cast-On is done in the usual way, the half-hitches in the baseline slope up to the right. However, as with Simple Cast-On, it is possible to turn the half-hitches so they slope up to the left.

While that in itself is an insignificant change, when you combine the right and left versions, the result is an entirely different edge, in which each strand passes from the right side of one stitch to the left side of the next. This makes the edge somewhat prone to snagging and less elastic; however, it is quite attractive.

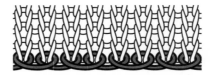

Right-Left Half-Hitch Edge. Notice baseline strand passes across two stitches.

1. Hold needle and wrap yarn on forefinger in usual way, but wrap yarn on thumb in opposite direction, from palm up farside and across back of thumb to needle (see Simple Left Half-Hitch Cast-On).
2. To form loop, move needle tip down on farside of strand from thumb to needle and then under strand from thumb to palm from right to left.
3. Pick up forefinger strand in usual way for Knit Half-Hitch Cast-On, and draw up through loop on thumb to form stitch. Pick up yarn again; tighten stitch and half-hitch on needle.
4. For next stitch, wrap yarn on thumb in usual way, from palm up nearside and across back of thumb to needle; work a Knit Half-Hitch Cast-On.
5. Continue to alternate right and left versions to cast on required number of stitches.

Tighten the half-hitches in the baseline gently as you work, so as not to restrict the edge, but do not work too loosely or they will be prone to snagging.

Twisted Half-Hitch Cast-On

Twisting the half-hitch an extra turn or two changes both the appearance and behavior of the edge. The Knit side of the edge is particularly attractive, with an interesting woven appearance. Many knitters claim that a Twisted Half-Hitch edge is more elastic than a plain one; however, the comparisons I have made do not show this to be the case. The extra twists at the base of the stitch absorb some of the yarn in each stitch, which makes it impossible for the edge to stretch out as much as an open stitch can.

To work this cast-on edge, the only modification required in the basic technique is to wrap the yarn and/or pick up the strand for the half-hitch in a slightly different way. Nevertheless, there are a surprising number of variations on this slight change.

Some of these work best when done as for a Simple Half-Hitch Cast-On, while others also work when done as a Compound Half-Hitch Cast-On. Try them all and pick the one that is comfortable for you; the result will be the same.

Twisted Half-Hitch: Method One

The variations of this method use Simple Half-Hitch Cast-On; the half-hitches are placed on the needle in the usual way, but they are twisted when worked on the first row.

• Use Simple Right Half-Hitch Cast-On, and on first row Knit or Purl all loops nearside.
• Or use Simple Left Half-Hitch Cast-On, and on first row Knit or Purl all loops farside.

Twisted Half-Hitch: Method Two

With this method, the half-hitch is crossed by picking up the loop from the thumb in a different way, and this works well for Simple Half-Hitch Cast-On. It is also possible to work this way with Knit or Purl Half-Hitch Cast-On, but both are more challenging to do, especially the Purl version.

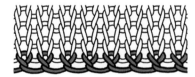

Twisted Half-Hitch Edge.

Twisted Simple Half-Hitch Version

• Wrap yarn on thumb as for Simple Right Half-Hitch Cast-On, move needle tip to left and under strand on nearside of thumb and then under strand on farside of thumb. Pick up this strand on needle and draw back under one on nearside; drop loop from thumb and pick up yarn as before and repeat.

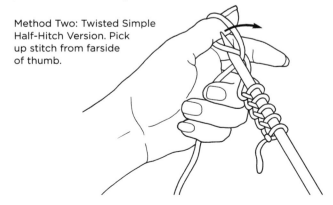

Method Two: Twisted Simple Half-Hitch Version. Pick up stitch from farside of thumb.

Twisted Knit Half-Hitch Version

• Pick up loop from thumb as above, and then hook thumb down to open loop. Pick up yarn from forefinger in usual way and draw down through loop to nearside; drop loop below tip of needle; tighten stitch on needle and half-hitch at base, and repeat.

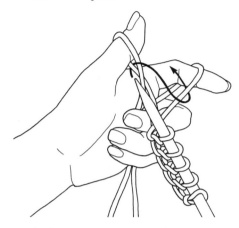

Method Two: Twisted Knit Half-Hitch Version. Pick up loop; take strand from forefinger.

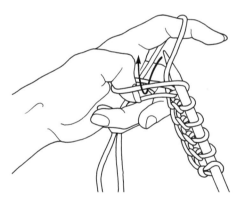

Method Two: Twisted Knit Half-Hitch Version. Hook thumb down to open loop, and then draw new stitch through.

Twisted Purl Half-Hitch Version

1. Move stitch yarn to nearside of needle and hold in place with tip of right forefinger.
2. To pick up loop, move needle to nearside of strand from thumb to palm, then over and under strand from thumb to needle; draw strand forward to form loop and drop thumb down to open it.
3. Pass needle over yarn to forefinger, down farside, and under again to catch strand and then bring needle tip down on nearside and up through loop; allow strand held on top of needle to roll down to nearside as stitch is formed.
4. Drop loop from thumb, tighten yarns as before, and repeat.

Twisted Half-Hitch: Method Three

With this version, the yarn is transferred from thumb to forefinger. It works well for Simple Half-Hitch Cast-On and is particularly useful for Half-Hitch Cast-On for Two Hands, especially if you work with a Knitting Belt.

Twisted Simple Half-Hitch Version

- For Simple Cast-On, wrap yarn on thumb in usual way, move forefinger over strand between thumb and needle, and then under strand on nearside of thumb from left to right as to Knit; transfer loop from thumb to forefinger. Pick up strand on nearside of forefinger as to Knit and transfer half-hitch to needle.

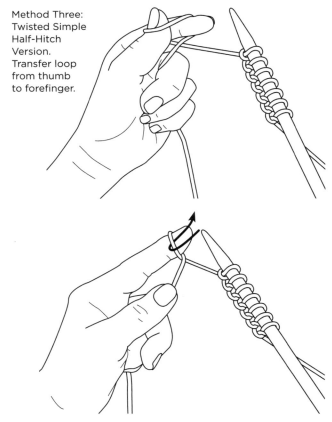

Method Three: Twisted Simple Half-Hitch Version. Transfer loop from thumb to forefinger.

Method Three: Twisted Simple Half-Hitch Version. Pick up loop from forefinger.

Twisted Half-Hitch Version for Two Hands

- For Knit, transfer loop from thumb to forefinger as described above, insert needle into loop from left to right as to Knit, and then use right finger to wrap yarn to form stitch.
- For Purl, move stitch yarn to nearside of needle, form loop as described above, and then insert needle into loop from right to left as to Purl; use right finger to wrap yarn to form stitch.

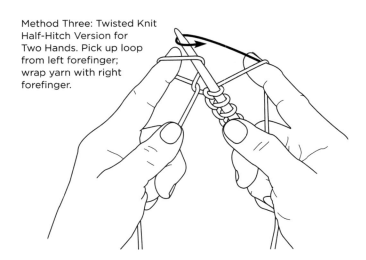

Method Three: Twisted Knit Half-Hitch Version for Two Hands. Pick up loop from left forefinger; wrap yarn with right forefinger.

Twisted Half-Hitch: Method Four

This version also works for either Simple Cast-On or Half-Hitch Cast-On for Two Hands. It seems a little complicated at first, but goes quite smoothly with practice.

Twisted Simple Half-Hitch Version

1. Wrap yarn from palm up nearside of thumb, across back of forefinger, and then to needle.
2. Swivel back of hand toward you, thumb down, forefinger up; strand between thumb and forefinger will cross over strand between forefinger and needle.
3. To pick up loop, move tip of needle nearside and to left of strand between forefinger and thumb, and then under strand between forefinger and needle.
4. Drop yarn off forefinger, then immediately pick it up as before, tighten loop on needle, and repeat.

Twisted Half-Hitch Version for Two Hands

- For Knit version, pick up loop as described above, wrap yarn as to Knit and draw through loop. Drop yarn from forefinger, and then pick up as before and tighten half-hitch below stitch on needle.

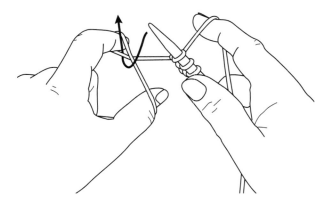

Method Four: Twisted Knit Half-Hitch Version for Two Hands. Swivel thumb down and pick up strand under forefinger.

- For Purl version, start with stitch yarn on nearside of needle, pick up loop by moving needle over and then under strand between forefinger and needle, and then wrap yarn as to Purl and draw through loop.

Double-Needle Cast-On

This cast-on was introduced in the first edition of this book. I developed it because the Compound Half-Hitch Cast-Ons, while attractive and easy to do, are not sufficiently elastic in many cases. Double-Needle Cast-On creates a handsome, unobtrusive, fully expandable edge suitable for use with any stitch pattern, and it holds its shape with wear.

Furthermore, it handles a scalloped or serrated edge with aplomb. Let us consider for a moment why this last feature is so useful. Stitch patterns with a scalloped or angular edge often curl up to the outside, forming little "cups" that cannot be steamed out to make them lie flat. Why does this happen?

If you were to measure along every little curve or angle of an edge of this kind, and compare that measurement to one taken across the straight width of the fabric, you would find an enormous difference—the edge can sometimes be twice as long as the fabric is wide. Unfortunately, the baselines created by most cast-on techniques have only enough yarn to form a straight edge, and they cannot stretch out enough to follow the contour created by a stitch pattern of this kind.

A Double-Needle Cast-On provides additional yarn to the edge because the stitch is placed on one needle and the half-hitch is placed on another, smaller needle; the latter acts as a gauge to measure out a precise amount of yarn to the baseline. This assures adequate yarn for expandability and allows the edge to accommodate itself to any contour created by the stitch pattern.

However, even when done on a small needle, these half-hitches are larger than normal and would normally be prone to snagging. To correct for this, the stitch yarn is passed under the needle between each stitch, which binds the baseline to the fabric and keeps the half-hitches neat.

The instructions will seem complicated at first, but keep in mind that this is just another variation of Knit Half-Hitch Cast-On; with practice, the technique goes smoothly, although it is never quick to do. As with any Compound Cast-On edge, there is a Knit and Purl side, so either begin your stitch pattern accordingly, or, if you are working flat and want to have the Knit side of the edge when you turn to begin, use one of the Purl versions.

Knit Double-Needle Cast-On

1. Allow for tail of yarn and place Slip Knot on needle; hold yarn and needle as for Knit Half-Hitch Cast-On.

2. Take up second, smaller needle; line it up under first one, holding two needles as one. Slip Knot will be on top, larger needle, and two yarns will hang down on either side of smaller needle below.

3. With tips of both needles, pick up yarn on nearside of thumb to form loop.

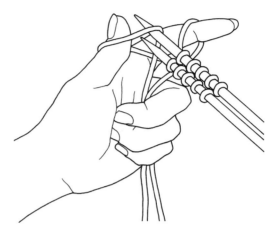

Knit Double-Needle Cast-On: Step 3.
Pick up loop from thumb.

4. Move needles toward farside, allowing forefinger strand to pass between needle tips to nearside. Then bring top needle back under to nearside so strand wraps over top of needle as for a Yarnover.

5. Move both needles from farside to nearside through loop formed between thumb and needles.

6. Move lower needle back under top strand of loop so it passes between needles; drop loop from thumb onto lower needle to form half-hitch.

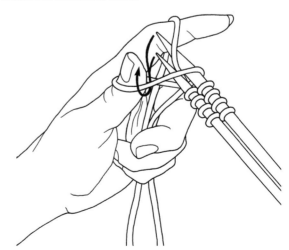

Knit Double-Needle Cast-On: Steps 5–6.
Pass forefinger strand over top needle, and then bring through loop.

7. Pick up strand on thumb below needles as before; tighten stitch gently on top needle and half-hitch firmly on bottom needle.

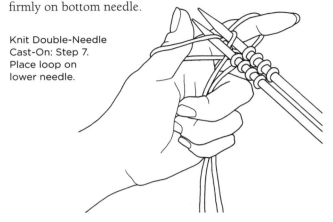

Knit Double-Needle Cast-On: Step 7. Place loop on lower needle.

8. Place tension on strands between needle and left hand, rotate needle tips over strands to farside, and then under yarns to nearside, so tips draw complete circle around the two yarns.

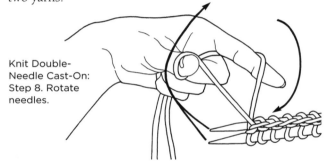

Knit Double-Needle Cast-On: Step 8. Rotate needles.

9. Continue in this manner, first making a stitch and then rotating the needles, to cast on required number of stitches. Pull bottom, smaller needle out of stitches and begin to work.

In Step 8, as you rotate the needles around the yarns, the two needles themselves should rotate around each other in your right hand, with the top one

Double-Needle Cast-On Edge.

going down the farside, under, and up into position again; these movements pass the stitch yarn under the baseline.

After you have worked a row or two, stretch the material out to its maximum. This smooths out the funny little loops left when you pulled out the bottom needle, and at the same time you will see how beautifully expandable this edge is.

All Compound Cast-On techniques have an effect on the twist of the yarn, and the rotation step used in this one exacerbates the problem. Drop the tail of yarn from time to time

to allow it to rebalance, and then let the needle hang from the yarn to spin the other strand back into balance as well.

If you prefer to make an edge that is identical to Knit Half-Hitch Cast-On, work Double-Needle Cast-On with a second needle of a very small size, eliminate the rotation in Step 8, and tighten the half-hitch in the baseline firmly. While the baseline will not be tied to the fabric, using the second needle for the half-hitches will help make the edge consistent.

Purl Double-Needle Cast-On

Yes, it is possible to do this cast-on technique in Purl and, therefore, also to mix Knit and Purl stitches along the edge. As discussed above, there are two ways to work a Purl Half-Hitch Cast-On—one method forms the stitches from the yarn on the thumb, the other from the forefinger.

Method One

This is the easiest way to do a Double-Needle Cast-On in Purl. The stitches are taken from the thumb yarn, and the baseline from the yarn held on the forefinger.

If you want to use this method for an edge with alternating Knit and Purl, there is no need to do the rotation to bind the baseline stitches to the fabric because the yarns switch position between baseline and stitch, which accomplishes the same thing.

1. Hold yarn and needles as described above.
2. To form loop, insert top needle from right to left, as for Purl, under strand of yarn passing from forefinger to palm.
3. Wrap strand passing between needle and thumb around top needle as for a Yarnover.
4. Bring both needles under and up through loop between forefinger and needle.
5. Drop loop from forefinger below both needles, pick yarn up on forefinger again, and tighten stitch and half-hitch in usual way.
6. Rotate needles as described in Knit version, Step 8, above.
7. Repeat Steps 2–6 for as many stitches as required.

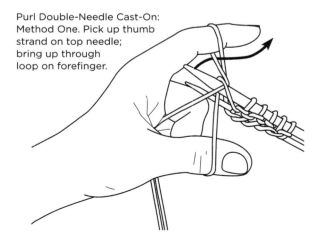

Purl Double-Needle Cast-On: Method One. Pick up thumb strand on top needle; bring up through loop on forefinger.

Method Two

This version is a little more awkward to learn, but then goes smoothly. In this case, if you plan to alternate Knit and Purl, the rotation step is advisable because the forefinger yarn is used for all stitches.

1. Hold yarn and needles as described above.
2. To position yarn for Purl, pass forefinger yarn between two needles to nearside, and then over top of needle to farside; when in position, strand will look like Yarnover.
3. Pass both needles as for Purl under strand on nearside of thumb to form loop; strand from Step 2 and loop are now on top needle.
4. Pass forefinger yarn between needles to nearside, and then over top needle as for a Yarnover; three strands are now on top needle.
5. Move both needles to nearside, and then back through loop to farside; yarns will roll around top needle to nearside and Purl stitch will form below top needle.
6. Move interlaced strands at top of loop between needles to farside and then drop loop from thumb onto lower needle. Pick up yarn on thumb again and tighten stitch and half-hitch in the usual way.
7. Rotate needles as described in Knit version, Step 8.
8. Repeat Steps 2–7 for as many stitches as required.

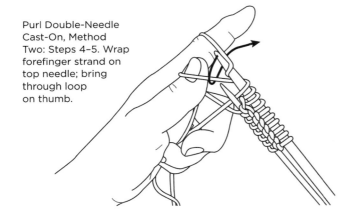

Purl Double-Needle Cast-On, Method Two: Steps 4–5. Wrap forefinger strand on top needle; bring through loop on thumb.

Rotated Half-Hitch Cast-On

The Double-Needle Cast-On rotation step can also be used when doing a Half-Hitch Cast-On with a single needle. The result is a very neat, trim edge and both sides are attractive, but quite different in appearance; the Purl side has a strong resemblance to Picot Cast-On. It is nice with any kind of pattern, but is particularly effective with Single Rib.

- Work Knit Half-Hitch Cast-On, and rotate needle between each stitch as for Knit Double-Needle Cast-On (Step 8).

Rotated Half-Hitch Cast-On with Single Rib.
Above: Knit face of edge. Below: Purl face of edge.

- If you prefer, you can use Purl Half-Hitch Cast-On instead. For Knit Half-Hitch Cast-On, rotate needles toward farside; for Purl Half-Hitch Cast-On, rotate needles toward nearside.

    You can also alternate Knit and Purl Half-Hitch, changing the direction of the rotation after each one.

Contrast-Color Edges

You can make any of the Half-Hitch Cast-Ons more decorative by using yarns of different colors or textures, or both, for the baseline and/or the stitches. This is also the best way I know of to display the actual structure of the edge.

Because you will use more than one supply of yarn for these techniques, there is no need to measure off a tail of yarn for the baseline, but do allow an end of each yarn long enough to weave the ends in during finishing. Tie the yarns together with a Slip Knot and place it on the needle. Do not count this as a first stitch; at the end of the first row of knitting, let it drop from the needle and later untie it.

Contrast-Color Half-Hitch Edges

- This first version results in an edge made up of half-hitches in a contrast color. Hold contrast-color baseline yarn on thumb and yarn for stitches on forefinger. Work Half-Hitch Cast-On for required number of stitches.
- In this next version there will be a one-row stripe of contrast-color stitches between the baseline of half-hitches and the main body of the fabric. Hold main color on

thumb for baseline, and hold contrast-color yarn on fore-finger to form stitches. After casting on, begin to work with main color. For smooth color transition, work one row of Knit on outside; for more information, see Color Patterns with Purl.

Contrast-Color Half-Hitch Edge.

- For a very bold edge, select several relatively thin yarns of different colors and/or textures to carry on thumb for baseline; carry a single strand of main color on forefinger.
- There is a technique mentioned in Sheila McGregor's *The Complete Book of Traditional Scandinavian Knitting* called the "Dala Floda" cast-on from Dalarna, Sweden.† The needle is held in the left hand, and two contrast-color yarns are held in the right hand. First, one yarn is wrapped over the left finger and needle, and then the other yarn is wrapped around the needle as for Knit; then the first strand is lifted over the second and off the needle with the left finger. It is very awkward to do and the result is a Contrast-Color Half-Hitch Cast-On edge.

Contrast-Color Edges for Ribbing

It is also possible to use a contrast color for a Ribbed Half-Hitch Cast-On edge. I find this works best if the ribbing itself is done in a single color; it can also be used for a ribbing done in contrast-color vertical stripes, although I think an Alternating Cast-On edge is better for that purpose. Here are some variations:

- Carry main yarn on forefinger and contrast-color yarn on thumb; make both Knit and Purl stitches from forefinger yarn; color will be flecked below Purl stitches. Continue ribbing with main color yarn.
- Carry yarn as above, but make Knit stitches with one yarn, Purl stitches with the other. Where to carry the contrast yarn, on thumb or forefinger, depends on whether you will continue flat or in the round, and you will need to plan ahead.

---

† Sheila McGregor, *The Complete Book of Traditional Scandinavian Knitting* (New York: St. Martin's Press, 1984), p. 33.

To work ribbing, change to main color, and work Knit columns above Knit cast-on stitches done in contrast color; work Purl columns above Purl cast-on stitches done in main color.

- For vertical stripe ribbing, decide which color to use on Knit columns, as only one face of this ribbing can be used on outside of garment. Work as above, and continue same colors for stitch columns as were used for cast-on stitches.

Braided Cast-Ons

Here are several versions of a decorative Cast-On technique done with two or three yarns in either solid or contrast colors or textures, or doubled for a bolder effect. There are many variations of these techniques in the Scandinavian and Baltic knitting traditions.

They are slow to work, however, so they are most often used for small things like the edge of a sleeve, mitten, or sock. However, if you have the patience, these edges are suitable for any number of stitch patterns and garment styles, and they deserve to be more widely used than they are. In addition, Herringbone Braid is a closely related stitch technique that is done within the fabric rather than at the edge, and it is very compatible when placed in close proximity or directly adjacent to one of these cast-ons (also see Double Slip Chained Cast-Off).

You can do Braided Cast-Ons with the yarns held in the left hand, as for Half-Hitch Cast-On, or with one held on the left and the other on the right, as for Half-Hitch Cast-On for Two Hands.

Two-Yarn Braided Cast-On

This version is done with two yarns, either in the same or in different colors, which alternate between the stitches and the baseline. The edge will be made up of what looks like a horizontal chain of Knit stitches.

To work with one strand of yarn, measure off a tail of yarn, make a Slip Knot, and place it on the needle; this will serve as the first stitch. To work with two strands of yarn, allow ends long enough to weave in during finishing, tie them together with a Slip Knot, and place it on needle; drop the knot from the needle after the first row and untie later for finishing.

1. Use Knit Half-Hitch Cast-On to add one stitch.
2. Move yarn from forefinger under tip of needle to nearside and pick up on thumb; move yarn from thumb to right under shaft of needle to farside and pick up on forefinger.
3. Repeat Steps 1 and 2 to cast on all stitches; after making each one, use previous baseline yarn for next stitch, and previous stitch yarn for baseline, always changing yarns in same direction.

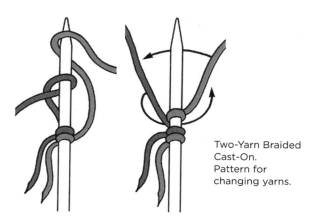

Two-Yarn Braided
Cast-On.
Pattern for
changing yarns.

Tricolor Braid Cast-On.
Shown with Garter Stitch above edge.

If you prefer, you can change the yarns in the opposite direction, moving the yarn on the thumb to the right under the tip of the needle, and the yarn on the forefinger to the left under the shaft of the needle. The important thing is to be consistent.

Two-Yarn Braided Cast-On.

Tricolor Braid Cast-On

Here is a braid edge done in much the same way as the ones above but, as the name implies, with three different colors instead of two. The first set of instructions is for different ways to handle the three yarns; the second is a color variation.

Method One

This is done like the Two-Yarn Braided version, holding the yarns as for Knit Half-Hitch Cast-On; of the three yarns, the two active ones are held on the left in the usual way; the third is held against the shaft of the needle by the right hand, out of the way until needed.

1. Tie ends of three yarns together in single Slip Knot and place on needle; do not count as first stitch; drop from needle when working first row.
2. Carry two yarns in left hand, one on thumb, one on forefinger; hold third yarn under needle with right hand.
3. Work one Knit Half-Hitch Cast-On stitch in usual way.
4. Release yarn held under needle; transfer baseline yarn from left thumb to right hand and hold this strand under needle. Pick up yarn used for previous stitch on thumb; pick up yarn previously held under needle on forefinger. Cast on next stitch.

Always transfer yarns in same direction, around to right, or around to left. If you prefer, use Knit Half-Hitch for Two Hands, holding one yarn on left thumb, one on right forefinger, and change yarns in same direction.

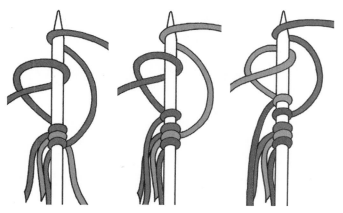

Tricolor Braid Cast-On. Pattern for changing yarns.

Method Two

• For a nice variation, maintain one yarn on your left thumb at all times, and use forefinger to alternate the other two yarns to the stitches, always changing from one to the other in the same direction.

The result is a complex edge with a narrow chain composed of two parallel lines of sloping strands. The upper line is in one color, while the lower line and the stitches have alternating colors.

By the way . . .

Here are some suggestions for how to manage the yarn and make the best use of this edge.

• *With any Braided Cast-On, the yarns will wind together as you work. You can push the entwined yarns down closer to the balls of yarn for a time, but eventually it will become difficult to continue. See the suggestions in Twined Knit for how to cope.*

• *When used with a Stockinette fabric, this edge has a tendency to roll up to the outside, making the bottom of the edge, with its little chain of stitches, more prominent. It is attractive, but if you prefer to have it lie flat, work a few rows of Seed Stitch or Garter Stitch above the edge.*

• *As with any Half-Hitch Cast-On edge, there is a Knit and Purl side, with the former on the nearside as you cast on; the Purl side is also attractive, adding a row of little nubs above the braid.*

To use the Purl side of a Braid edge when knitting flat, turn and start with an outside row of your pattern. If you plan to use a stitch pattern of mixed Knit and Purl stitches, work the first row in plain Knit to avoid broken color flecks and then begin your main pattern; for more information on why this intermediary row is important, see Color Patterns with Purl.

Alternatively, if you are working a circular pattern, or simply prefer to do so, work the cast-on with Purl on the nearside; see Purl Half-Hitch: Method Two, with stitches taken from yarn on forefinger, or Purl Half-Hitch for Two Hands. As above, if you will be using a pattern of mixed Knit and Purl stitches, work first round in plain Knit.

Knotted Cast-On

This cast-on and the Channel Island Cast-On are edge techniques often used for "ganseys" (also called guernseys, or jerseys), the traditional sweaters worn by the fishermen of the coastal communities of Great Britain. Both are variations of a Compound Half-Hitch Cast-On.

The Knotted Cast-On technique produces a handsome, highly textured, and very expandable edge. When done with a contrast-color yarn, or one that is textured or thicker, as the baseline strand, the effect is quite striking. It is best to maintain a firm tension on the thumb strand and use a relatively small needle size for this so the edge does not splay out (unlike other Compound Half-Hitch Cast-On techniques, in this case, the size of the needle does make a difference); try several Test Swatches to find the best needle size to use.

The version given here is easier to do than the traditional method, which is discussed below the instructions.

Knotted Cast-On Edge.

1. Use Knit Half-Hitch Cast-On to place twice as many stitches as required on needle. Turn.
2. [Pull second stitch on left needle over first and discard. Knit or Purl remaining stitch.] Repeat between brackets across row.
3. To begin first row, slide stitches to edge where yarn is.

The Purl side of the edge is considerably nubbier, and this can be further enhanced if you also work the first row above it in Purl.

Traditional instructions for this edge say to cast on two stitches, pull one over, cast on two more, pull one over, etc. The problem with this is that you must pick up a second needle to work the pullover step, and then set that needle down and pick up the yarn again to cast on the next two stitches. It is far easier to work as described above, and the result is the same. Or, if you prefer, use a double-point needle and do just the pullovers in Step 2 as for a Slip Chained Cast-Off; slide the remaining stitches to the edge where the yarn is, and then work the first row.

Channel Island Cast-On

This is a very traditional cast-on from Great Britain with a bold, handsome appearance that resembles Knotted Cast-On. It is also identical in structure to Picot Cast-On, which is an easier and somewhat more versatile way to make the same edge. However, this method appears in many books as if it were an entirely different edge; try both methods and decide how you want to work.

The technique is normally worked as for Half-Hitch Cast-On for Two Hands, although it can certainly be done with both yarns carried on the left. The half-hitch cast-on stitches are made with a doubled strand of yarn wrapped twice on the thumb in the opposite direction from the way it is usually done, and then a Yarnover is placed between each cast-on stitch.

1. Tie three strands of yarn together in a Slip Knot and place on needle; discard Slip Knot after working first row.
2. Hold yarns as for a Half-Hitch Cast-On, with single yarn for stitches on left or right forefinger, and doubled yarn for baseline on thumb. To wrap baseline, move thumb down nearside of strand, then under and up on farside, and repeat for second wrap; yarn will travel from top of thumb to needle.
3. Insert right needle tip up under both strands on nearside of thumb to form loop, wrap yarn on needle as for Knit, and draw stitch through loop. Drop loop and tighten at base of stitch; rewrap yarn on thumb as before.
4. Use yarn on right finger to make Yarnover.
5. Repeat Steps 3–4 to cast on as many stitches as required; end with Step 3.

The doubled yarn on the thumb creates a relatively large knot in the baseline below every other stitch. However, if you examine the knot closely you will find it is actually identical in structure to a Purl Half-Hitch Cast-On, but when done in this unusual way, it is much more difficult to tighten into place.

❖ *The Wrapped Cast-Ons*

These cast-on techniques are all done by wrapping the yarn in a simple way around the needle. However simple they are in structure, they provide surprisingly versatile and interesting edges.

Stranded Cast-On is entirely utilitarian and not used for a visible edge, while Alternating Cast-On is excellent for ribbings, since it is not only resilient but also, in effect, invisible. These two join Knit Half-Hitch Cast-On in the small list of essential techniques that every knitter should know how to do because they are so useful and produce such excellent results.

Both of these techniques can also serve as provisional cast-ons, which make it relatively easy to free the first row of stitches in order to work them at another time in another way. There are many reasons to do this, such as to match the top and bottom edges of a scarf, or to add a border to a lower edge; see Working in the Opposite Direction. A provisional cast-on edge is also ideal if you plan to graft two sections of fabric together; see Grafting.

Also included here are several traditional methods used to start fabrics worked from the center to the edges, such as for sock toes and mittens worked from tip to cuff, or for a Medallion fabric; for more information, see Uncommon Shapes. In addition to the standard techniques, you will also find a modification of Alternating Cast-On that is considerably more effective than those normally used.

Stranded Cast-On

This cast-on technique produces an edge that is altogether too homely to remain visible; however, it is a good backstage player. Stranded Cast-On does not really form an edge at all; the result is merely a strand of yarn or cord strung through the running threads of the new stitches on the needle. Despite its rudimentary nature, however, this cast-on can be useful in several ways.

First, and most important, it is the technique of choice for making a Gauge Swatch. Both Stranded Cast-On and its mate, Stranded Cast-Off, create unrestrained edges that allow the fabric to lie flat for accurate measurement; for why this is important, see Stitch Gauge.

Second, the technique has long been used to make a provisional edge.† While I no longer think it is the best technique for this purpose—the modification of Alternating Cast-On works so much better—Stranded Cast-On is easier to do and in some circumstances more effective; see Provisional Cast-Ons, below.

Finally, Stranded Cast-On is ideal when you need a simple drawstring, since it makes it possible to insert any sort of cord, regardless of size, into an edge while casting on.

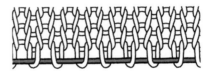

Stranded Cast-On Edge.

Basic Stranded Cast-On

To work this edge, use a straight needle rather than a circular one, because it is important to keep the edge perfectly lined up under the needle; if you prefer to work the fabric with a circular needle, begin to use it on the first row after casting on. While the instructions seem lengthy, the technique itself is very simple to do once you understand how it works.

To Cast On

1. Allow tail of yarn slightly longer than fabric will be wide; place a Right Twist Start on needle and count this as first stitch; hold two strands as for a Half-Hitch Cast-On.

---

† Mary Thomas mentions this cast-on as being in common use in her book on techniques, *Mary Thomas's Knitting Book* (New York: Dover Publications, 1972).

2. Reach needle tip over, down nearside and under strand to thumb, then over and down farside of strand to forefinger. Bring forefinger strand under one to thumb and return to starting position.

Stranded Cast-On: Step 2.

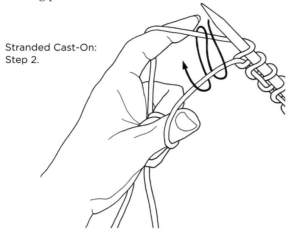

3. Pass needle over and down farside of strand to forefinger, then up again on nearside so strand passes over top of needle; return to starting point.

This will look like a Yarnover.

Stranded Cast-On: Step 3.

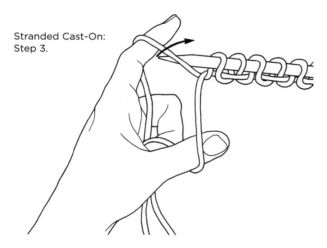

4. Alternate Steps 2 and 3 to cast on; end with Step 2.

The stitch placed on the needle in Step 2 will be drawn under the baseline strand to the nearside and will resemble a Knit stitch; the stitch placed on the needle in Step 3 will look like a Yarnover.

For an odd number of stitches, place a Left Twist Start on needle as first stitch, and then alternate Step 3 followed by Step 2; end with Step 2. It is easiest to end the cast-on sequence with Step 2 because the "Knit" stitch is slightly more secure on the needle. However, you can also end with the Yarnover in Step 3; just draw the baseline strand around the main yarn to hold it in place on the needle as you begin to work.

Work cast-on firmly and keep baseline strand aligned below needle; if it spirals around the needle it can be difficult to set right again.

A Stranded Cast-On edge will unravel unless you maintain a constant tension on both yarns as you work. Once you finish casting on and work the first stitch, the edge will be secure. To stop and count stitches, pinch the two strands beneath the needle tip to keep the stitches in place; do not let go. To set the work down temporarily, work a temporary Simple Half-Hitch Cast-On stitch; remove it from the needle before you continue.

As insurance against having too few stitches, cast on several more than needed; after working the first row, make a final count and drop any extra stitches; they will unravel and become part of the baseline strand and the extra yarn can be pulled in under the stitches (if you used a Slip Knot, undo it).

To Work First Row

After casting on, make sure baseline strand is wrapped once around stitch strand and hold it securely to prevent the last stitch from unraveling as you begin to work.

- For flat fabrics, draw baseline strand to nearside along cast-on edge, hold against needle, and transfer it to left hand. Begin to work first row of stitches with main yarn; drop strand when convenient.
- For circular fabrics, add one temporary Simple Half-Hitch Cast-On to secure edge until time to join round, and then drop temporary stitch from needle and unravel it. Hold baseline strand under right needle, and draw main strand of yarn across gap between needles to join round and work first stitch.

By the way, if you use Stranded Cast-On followed by just one or two rows of Single Rib and then remove the baseline strand, the result will be an "invisible" edge. No, it will not unravel, but it will be loose and unsightly; it is much easier to accomplish the same thing with Alternating Cast-On (below), and the result is far more successful.

Alternating Cast-On

Here is a wonderful cast-on method to use for Single or Double Rib, or for a Double-Fabric, and it is fast and simple to do. It creates a slightly rounded, fully expandable edge that consists of nothing more than the first row of stitches; there is no cast-on edge in the usual sense of that term. You may have seen this edge on machine knits; here is how to do it on a hand knit.

In addition to the versions of Alternating Cast-On discussed here, there are two others that are not used to create a finished edge, which are discussed below. One of these is used to make a Provisional Cast-On; the other is used to start a fabric at the center, such as when working a sock from the toe up, or a mitten from tip to cuff; see Cast-Ons for a Center Start.

These instructions assume you will be working flat and plan to do a Knit/Purl ribbing sequence on an even number of stitches; the first and last stitches are selvedges. Once you are familiar with the technique, you can alter the sequence to suit your project, and eliminate the selvedges for circular fabrics.

Alternating Cast-On Edge.

Alternating Cast-On for Single Rib

Use a needle at least one or two sizes smaller than the one to be used for the ribbing itself. Hold yarn as for a Compound Half-Hitch Cast-On, work firmly, and maintain tension on yarn at all times.

These instructions are for working flat; the slight adjustments needed for working circular are given below.

1. Allow for tail of yarn and place a Right Twist Start on needle; consider this as first selvedge stitch.
2. To form a "Knit" stitch, reach tip of needle over, down nearside, and under strand of yarn that passes between needle and thumb; then bring needle over and down farside of strand that passes from needle to forefinger. Bring this strand back under first strand and return to starting position.

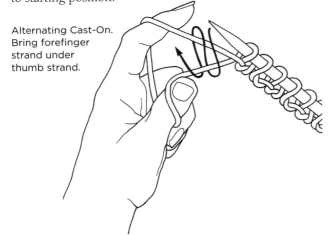

Alternating Cast-On. Bring forefinger strand under thumb strand.

3. To form a "Purl" stitch, reach tip of needle over and down farside of strand that passes from needle to forefinger, then under and up nearside of strand from needle to thumb. Bring this strand back under and up farside of first strand and return to starting position.
4. Alternate Steps 2 and 3 to add as many stitches as required; add one Knit Half-Hitch Cast-On to serve as last selvedge stitch.

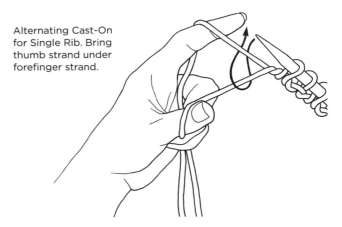

Alternating Cast-On for Single Rib. Bring thumb strand under forefinger strand.

5. Turn. Change to needle size required for ribbing. Work selvedge stitch according to preference, then begin Knit/Purl Single Rib sequence; at end of row, work last selvedge stitch.

In Step 2, both sides of the stitch will pass under the baseline strand and up the nearside to the needle; it will look like a Knit stitch. In Step 3, both sides of this stitch pass under the baseline and up the farside to the needle and it will look like a Purl stitch.

Work with a consistently firm tension and make sure that the yarns cross in a straight line underneath the needle.

As with Stranded Cast-On, nothing secures these stitches against unraveling, so do not let go of the two strands. If you need to stop and count stitches, pinch the two strands with your left fingers to hold the last stitch in position. If you must set the work down, work one Simple Half-Hitch Cast-On stitch and remove it from the needle before you continue.

Once you understand how to form the Knit and Purl stitches of this cast-on, you can alter the sequence as you please, working either as for Knit/Purl or Purl/Knit, and casting on an even or uneven number of stitches; use a Right Twist if the following stitch will be a Knit, or a Left Twist if the following stitch will be a Purl. A Slip Knot is not as compatible with this edge as the Twist Start.

If you plan to work in the round, use the Twist Start to begin and a Simple Half-Hitch Cast-On at the end; treat the first as a Knit stitch, and the last as a Purl.

Alternating Cast-On for Double Rib

Until now, there has been no "invisible" cast-on edge for Double Rib that was comparable to Alternating Cast-On for Single Rib. Since many people prefer Double Rib, I was determined to find a

Alternating Cast-On for Double Rib Edge.

solution, and here it is. I do not find it quite as elastic as the other, but it looks very nice and I think you will be pleased.

To Cast On

Use two balls of yarn and a pair of needles one or two sizes smaller than you plan to use for the ribbing.

1. Measure off tails for both yarns and hold as one, with tails on thumb and strands to balls of yarn on forefinger; begin with a Twist Start.
2. Use Alternating Cast-On as described above; place half required number of stitches on needle.
3. Allow tail on one yarn long enough to hide on inside during finishing and break off; continue with other yarn.

Note that each cast-on stitch will be composed of two strands on the needle.

To Work First Row

Take up second needle of same size used for casting on; turn if you are working a flat fabric, or join round if working circular.

1. Work two Knits, one into each strand of first "Knit" cast-on stitch, and then two Purls, one into each strand of next "Purl" cast-on stitch. Alternate in this way to establish pattern on first row.
2. On next row, change to size needle required for ribbing, and continue in Double Rib.

To work the first stitch of each pair, pull the second one away slightly to isolate it. If the two stitches are crossed where they emerge from the baseline half-hitch, straighten them out before working them for the best result.

The edge is, of course, the same on both sides. Also, you can adapt the method for any sequence; either start with Purl or use an uneven number of pairs, just as for Alternating Cast-On for Single Rib.

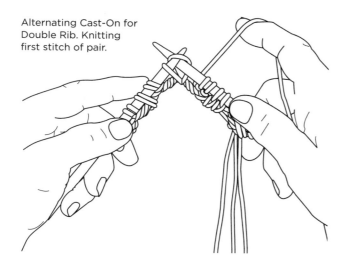

Alternating Cast-On for Double Rib. Knitting first stitch of pair.

Alternating Cast-On for Multicolor Ribbings

There are several ways to handle more than one color yarn when you plan to work ribbings with vertical stripes, one color for the Knit stitches, the other for the Purl stitches. Try one or the other of the following to see what works best for your project.

As always, establish the Knit and Purl columns of the ribbing above the equivalent of the "Knit" and "Purl" stitches in the edge.

- Work Alternating Cast-On with a single color yarn; work Single Rib using a contrast-color yarn for the Knit stitches and the color used to cast on for the Purl stitches.
- Work Alternating Cast-On with two colors, one on the thumb, the other on the forefinger; for the Single Rib, match the colors of the stitch columns to those used for the cast-on stitches.
- Work Alternating Cast-On for Double Rib with two colors. Hold two strands of one color on the thumb, two strands of the other color on the forefinger. Then begin Double Rib, matching the colors of the stitch columns to those in the cast-on edge.

Picot Cast-On

This technique, which Barbara Walker calls Picot Ribbing in her *Second Treasury of Knitting Patterns*,† is quite charming. It combines Half-Hitch Cast-On and Alternating Cast-On, and on the Purl side, the half-hitch forms a little "picot" or tiny knot below every other stitch.

This edge is resilient and quite attractive, and it is particularly effective with Single Rib if the Knit columns of stitches rise above the little knot. It also makes a nice edge for a Double-Fabric.

Interestingly enough, Picot Cast-On is identical in structure to the very traditional Channel Island Cast-On from Great Britain. It is not easy to see that this is the case because the two are done in such a very different manner. The method used for Channel Island Cast-On is unnecessarily complicated and somewhat awkward to do, so feel free to substitute this approach instead.

It was the Purl side of Channel Island Cast-On that was preferred, and the method may have been developed in order to have that face of the edge on the outside when working in the round. However, it is just as easy to do Picot Cast-On in Knit as in Purl, so you can choose which side of the edge to have visible no matter how you plan to work.

Also, Picot Cast-On was originally described as being done with one strand for the baseline, but it is certainly possible to borrow the notion from Channel Island Cast-On of dou-

---

† Barbara G. Walker, *A Second Treasury of Knitting Patterns* (New York: Charles Scribner's Sons, 1970), p. 329.

bling the baseline strand to create a bolder effect. Furthermore, when done with a contrast color for the baseline you will see how very interesting both sides of this edge are and, in fact, you may be hard-pressed to choose between them. To take this one pretty step further, set a bead on the half-hitch; see Beads and Sequins.

Hold yarn as for a Compound Half-Hitch Cast-On and work as follows:

Knit Picot Cast-On

1. Place a Twist Start on needle; consider this as first stitch.
2. Work one Knit Half-Hitch Cast-On stitch, and then one Knit Alternating Cast-On stitch; repeat these two steps, ending with a Knit Half-Hitch Cast-On for an even number of stitches.

Picot Cast-On with Contrast-Color Edge. Above: Purl side. Below: Knit side.

For an odd number of stitches, start with a Slip Knot followed by a Knit Alternating Cast-On, and then a Knit Half-Hitch Cast-On.

Purl Picot Cast-On

1. Start as described above, but carry baseline strand on forefinger and stitch strand on thumb.
2. Work one Purl Half-Hitch Cast-On, Method Two, taking loop from forefinger strand and stitch from thumb strand.
3. Work one Purl Alternating Cast-On, drawing thumb strand under forefinger strand to form equivalent of Yarnover on needle.
4. Alternate Steps 2 and 3 for required number of stitches. For an even number of stitches, end with Step 2.

Provisional Cast-Ons

There are several situations where it is valuable to have a cast-on edge that can be removed easily to free the stitches. This might be the case if you want to match the cast-on and cast-off edges, or add a decorative border to the freed stitches of a bottom edge; both of these applications are discussed in Working in the Opposite Direction. A Provisional Cast-On is also useful when you need to Graft bottom and top edges together.

Stranded Cast-On is traditional for this purpose; it is very

easy to do and it is relatively easy to free the stitches and pick them up again on a needle. Alternating Cast-On is new to this role; it is more challenging to do, but there is no need to free the stitches or pick them up because they will already be on a needle, waiting for you at the bottom of the fabric.

Stranded Provisional Cast-On

To use Stranded Cast-On as a provisional edge, it is done exactly as described above, but with a smooth cord or tightly spun yarn in a contrast color for the baseline strand. Something of that kind is much easier to remove when it is time to pick up the stitches along the edge, and a contrast color makes it easier to see where to insert the needle. For more information, see Working in the Opposite Direction in the chapter Picking Up Stitches.

To pick up stitches, use a cable needle several sizes smaller than used for main fabric. Turn fabric upside down, and start where baseline strand emerges from last stitch cast on.

1. Pull up on baseline strand to enlarge stitch slightly, insert needle tip into stitch, and then withdraw baseline strand; repeat across row.
2. Begin working picked-up stitches with whatever size needle is required for new section of fabric; make sure each stitch is on needle in standard position, with right side of stitch on nearside of needle.

If you use a small-size needle, you can wait to pull out the baseline strand until you have several stitches picked up.

Alternating Provisional Cast-On

Here is a modification of Alternating Cast-On that is a remarkably good way to make a provisional edge. Instead of inserting a strand of yarn or cord as a stitch holder at the lower edge as Stranded Cast-On does, this method borrows the approach used in Double-Needle Cast-On and inserts a second needle instead.

The first row of stitches for the main fabric is cast on to one needle, and another row of stitches is simultaneously cast on to the other. This second needle functions as a stitch holder and is left to hang at the bottom of the fabric until it is time to finish the lower edge in some way. Then all you need to do is pick it up, slide the stitches to the tip of the needle, and begin.

The Knit face of the cast-on edge will be on the nearside as you work; it is possible to work so as to have the Purl face on the nearside, but it is a little more awkward to do.

Use two cable needles (the type that have straight tips, not the ones with a bend in them), and work as follows:

Knit Version

1. Measure tail of yarn as for a Compound Half-Hitch Cast-On. Place Slip Knot or Right Twist Start on lower

cable needle and hold both needles parallel in right hand, tips aligned. Hold yarns with left hand in usual way.

2. Make equivalent of Knit Alternating Cast-On stitch— move both needles under thumb strand as usual, but catch forefinger strand with just top needle. Move needles back under thumb strand and return to starting position. Hold new stitch in position on needle with right forefinger when making next stitch.

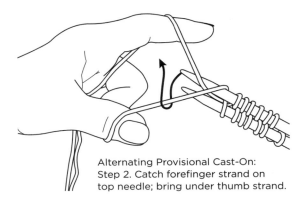

Alternating Provisional Cast-On:
Step 2. Catch forefinger strand on
top needle; bring under thumb strand.

3. Pass thumb strand over lower needle from nearside to farside, as for a Yarnover. Hold new stitch in position on needle with right thumb while making next stitch.

4. Repeat Steps 2 and 3 until number of stitches needed for width of fabric is on top needle, and equal number is on bottom needle; end with Step 2.

5. Draw tip of bottom needle out so all stitches are on cable and let hang at bottom; begin to work stitches on top needle.

Purl Version

1. Measure tail of yarn, place Slip Knot or Left Twist Start on lower cable needle and hold yarn and needles as described above.

2. Make equivalent of a Purl Alternating Cast-On stitch; move both needles over forefinger strand to farside, and then back under to nearside; catch thumb strand on top needle as for a Yarnover. Move both needles back under forefinger strand and return to starting position. Hold new stitch in position on needle with right forefinger while making next stitch.

3. Pass forefinger strand under needle tips to nearside and then between two needles to farside.

4. Repeat Steps 2 and 3 to cast on equal number of stitches on both needles; for an even number of stitches, end with Step 2.

5. Draw tip of bottom needle out so all stitches are on cable and let hang at bottom; begin to work stitches on top needle.

When thumb strand is wrapped on top needle in Step 2, it will first pass over top needle from nearside to farside and then between the two needles to the nearside again. It helps to point the needle tips up slightly in order to catch the yarn.

After moving the yarn between the needle tips in Step 3, when you then repeat Step 2, the yarn will be drawn under the needle to form a new stitch. You will see Purl nubs forming between the two needles.

The two cable needles can be of the same or different sizes. If, for instance, you know that the pattern you plan to work down from the stitches at the lower edge requires a different size needle, then use it as the lower needle when casting on.

In the Knit version, the forefinger strand is used for the stitches on the top needle; in the Purl version, it is the thumb strand. This may be relevant if you want to work the cast-on in two colors.

Cast-Ons for a Center Start

Several kinds of garments worked in the round are started on a very few stitches at the center of a fabric instead of at an outside edge. The most common examples are socks or mittens worked from the tip up, and Medallion fabrics, which are flat fabrics worked in the round (the latter can be started at the outer edge and worked in, but are more often started at the center).

Three rather rudimentary techniques have traditionally been used to cast on for this purpose, all of them done in a very similar manner. They are also alike in that, when there are only five or six stitches involved, the needles get skittish and one or the other will inevitably escape below the sofa, or wherever—usually more than once.

Fortunately, the first technique described here tames the needles and makes all this much easier to do. The other, more traditional methods that can be used to start at the center of a fabric are also described, as well as an assortment of other solutions to the challenge of starting a project in this way.

Alternating Cast-On for Center Start

The modification of Alternating Cast-On, described above for use as a Provisional Cast-On, also works very well as a way to start a fabric in the center. For this application, however, both needles remain in use so you will need to be familiar with how to work in the round with two circular needles (see Two Circular Needles Method).

1. Work as for Alternating Provisional Cast-On, placing half of the stitches needed on one needle, half on the other. Pull tip of lower needle to one side so all stitches are on cable.

2. Draw tips of top needle together and work across those stitches; then pull tip of needle to left so all stitches are on cable.

3. Pick up second needle, push stitches to tip closest to yarn and draw tips together; pull yarn up firmly to bridge gap between the two needles, and work across second set of stitches. Pull tip of needle to left so all stitches are on cable.

4. Pick up first needle again, push stitches to tip, pull yarn up firmly to bridge gap, and work across those stitches again to close the round.

5. Continue in this manner, working first the stitches on one needle and then those on the other, always leaving the other set on a cable as a holder; begin to increase according to pattern.

Starting a Medallion fabric in the center.

Double-Fabric Center Start

It is also possible to start a fabric at the center with a pair of straight needles using Alternating Cast-On for a Center Start and the Basic Double-Fabric technique.

1. Work as described in Step 1, above.
2. Use Basic Double-Fabric technique to work several rounds; after first round, begin to work increases as necessary, according to pattern.
3. When there are enough stitches to make it easy enough to work, change to a set of double-point needles or a pair of circular needles and continue in the round.

Circular Needle Wrap

This technique requires a pair of short circular needles; for more information on how to continue with the same needles after casting on, see Two Circular Needles Method.

To begin, place a Slip Knot on one needle and then slide it onto the cable; continue as follows:

1. Hold tail of yarn and pair of circular needles in left hand, center cable of needle bearing Slip Knot below tip of other needle.
2. With right hand, wrap yarn firmly around both needle and cable, up farside and then down nearside, one full circle for every two stitches needed; wraps should be as close together as possible. To finish, bring yarn up farside, then between cable and needle tip to nearside.

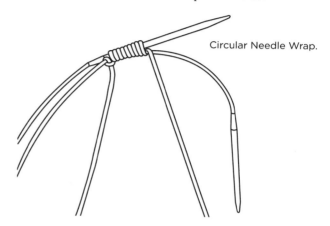

Circular Needle Wrap.

3. Bring tips of top needle together and Knit first set of wraps. Draw one tip of this needle to left so new stitches are on its cable.

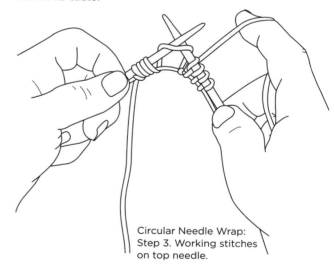

Circular Needle Wrap: Step 3. Working stitches on top needle.

4. Turn as for flat knitting, bring other needle to top, and push second set of wraps from its cable to right tip; drop Slip Knot from needle and hold tail of yarn to left, to maintain tension on first wrap. Draw needle into a circle and Knit second set of wraps.

5. Continue to work in round according to pattern.

It is important to wrap the yarn in the direction described above; if it is wrapped the other way, the stitches will twist when you work them.

The unequal size of the paired needle tip and cable prevent the first stitches at the center of a fabric from being too large. Check the effect on a Test Swatch or two before you begin.

If the stitches are too small, use the cable and a larger needle tip, and then change to the needle size needed for the fabric in Step 3. Alternatively, wrap the yarn around two smaller needle tips instead of a cable and a needle tip; see Double-Point Needle Wrap, below.

This technique can also be used as a Provisional Cast-On, but the version done with Alternating Cast-On is so much better for that purpose that there is no reason to do so.

Double-Point Needle Wrap

If you do not have a pair of circular needles of the right size on hand, you can use a set of straight double-point needles in the traditional manner instead. To keep stitches from enlarging, use needles one or two sizes smaller than planned for the fabric. This technique requires a tail of yarn long enough for the wrap and to work one round of stitches, as well.

Double-Point Needle Wrap.

1. Hold pair of needles in left hand and wrap as described in Circular Needle Wrap, but with tail of yarn.
2. Push stitches to right needle tips, and then draw lower needle to right so wraps are centered and will not fall off.
3. Bring tail of yarn to nearside between needles; pick up third needle and use tail of yarn to Purl wraps on top needle. Draw this needle to left so new stitches are at center.
4. Turn, pick up lower needle, and push wraps to right tip. Purl second set of wraps; drop tail of yarn.
5. Turn to Knit side; push both sets of stitches to tips of needles so main yarn is at right side. Begin to work next round in pattern and distribute stitches among three or four needles.

It is actually traditional to start working in Knit, but using Purl as in these instructions is easier to do; however, this is what makes it necessary to use the tail of yarn for the first round.

Also, it does not work to combine a double-point needle and a cable needle for this—it is impossible to push the stitches off the cable and past the bend in the needle tip when the time comes to do so.

Figure-8 Wrap

This method produces the same result as the methods above, but the wraps tend to be somewhat more secure as you work the first stitches. However, there is more yarn in the wraps, so it is even more important to use smaller needles so the first stitches will not be enlarged. Do a sample or two before you decide how to work.

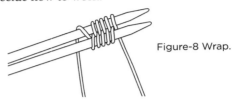

Figure-8 Wrap.

1. Hold needles as described in one of methods above, and wrap yarn around tips in a figure-8 pattern, alternating Steps A and B to make as many wraps as required.

   Step A: Up farside and over top needle, down nearside and between two needles to farside again.

   Step B: Down farside and under bottom needle, up nearside and between two needles to farside again.
2. Push wraps to center of lower needle; push wraps on top needle to tip and Knit.
3. Push new stitches to center of top needle, pick up lower needle, and push wraps to right tip. With lower needle now on top, Knit wraps farside, so they will not twist.

You can also use the approach described for the Double-Point Needle Wrap, above. Wrap the needles with the tail yarn and Purl them, and then turn to the Knit side and continue with the main yarn. However, it is more difficult to Purl the wraps farside in Step 3.

Tab Start

Here is a variation of a Wrapped Cast-On that is started by knitting a small square or rectangle around which stitches are later picked up to continue in the round.

1. Use one of Cast-Ons for a Center Start, above, and work both sets of wraps.
2. Push one set of new stitches to center of straight needle, or onto cable of circular needle, and let hang below other needle.
3. On other set of stitches, work several rows, number depending upon row gauge and size of tab needed.
4. With Knit face of fabric on nearside, use third needle to pick up into each selvedge stitch on one side of the tab.
5. Knit across second set of stitches (those on needle that was left hanging).
6. Take fourth needle and pick up into selvedge stitches on other side of the tab.
7. With stitches now on four needles, begin to work circular.

Alternatively, you can work just one set of wraps and continue on those stitches to make the tab. Then, as you begin to work in the round, pick up stitches along the first side of the tab, and only then work the second set of wraps.

Slip Knot Start

This method starts with a Slip Knot that you can tighten at the center of the fabric, and it can be done in Purl using either a knitting needle or a crochet hook. It is awkward to get started, but if you want a minimum of stitches at the center, this will do the trick.

Purl Slip Knot Start

1. Make Slip Knot on two or three fingers of left hand. Hold needle in right hand.
2. Wrap yarn around needle as for a Purl-to-Purl Yarnover.
3. Insert needle tip from right to left into Slip Knot, wrap yarn, and Purl.
4. Repeat Steps 2 and 3 once or twice more; end with a Step 3.
5. Work as for Double-Fabric Center Start, or transfer to three double-point needles immediately.

Work several rounds before you tighten Slip Knot so it does not constrict the work; there is no hurry.

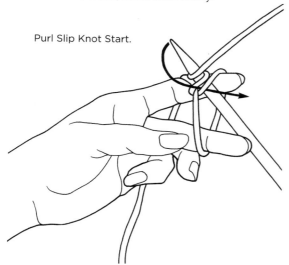

Purl Slip Knot Start.

Crochet Slip Knot Start

This version is done with a crochet hook.

1. Work as described above, but hold crochet hook in right hand; allow stitches to accumulate on hook.
2. Transfer stitches to double-point needles; tighten Slip Knot when convenient.

Three-Stitch Start

All of the above techniques start the fabric at the center with several stitches. In some cases, even these few are too many.

Here is a technique that reduces the number of stitches to the bare minimum.

1. Use double-point needle and cast on three stitches with Picot Cast-On; work with firm tension. Slide stitches back to right tip of needle.
2. With second needle, Knit first stitch, work Bar Increase on second stitch, and Knit third stitch; four stitches are now on needle.
3. Turn. Slip two stitches to second needle, and then fold it to left so two needles lie parallel with Purl faces to inside.
4. Slide stitches to right needle tips; yarn is attached to stitch on needle held on farside.
5. Take up third double-point needle and begin working in round using Shetland Three-Needle Method, starting with first stitch on needle held nearside. Work increases according to pattern, and when there are enough stitches, redistribute them to three needles and work with a fourth.

❖ Miscellaneous Cast-Ons

The following techniques do not fit neatly into any of the above categories, but often contain elements of one or more of them.

Corded Cast-On

Two techniques are commonly recommended for making a "tubular" or "invisible" edge for use with Single Rib. The result resembles the corded edges that can be done on picked-up stitches at a side edge, or as a cast-off (see Attached Cords); these can be quite handsome, and are especially decorative when done with a contrast-color yarn.

However, I do not understand how this type of edge came to be thought of as invisible, because its appearance is actually quite bold; perhaps this is because it lacks the distinctive baseline common to edges done with most other cast-on techniques. The edge is also frequently recommended as "elastic," and, therefore, suitable for use with Single Rib, but I am even more puzzled by this because it does not seem to be true; the edge is basically a tiny hem of Stockinette. (Both Double-Needle Cast-On and Alternating Cast-On are better choices for a resilient edge.)

To compound these problems, the two most common ways to make an edge of this kind are unnecessarily complicated. Fortunately, the two alternatives discussed here rescue the situation; both are easy to do and produce a nice corded edge.

It is important to try the technique you want to use on a fairly large swatch to see how compatible the edge is with the fabric above; if necessary, you may need to adjust the needle size or the number of stitches so the edge neither pulls in nor splays out.

Tubular Edge with Chained Cast-On

This version of a corded edge is found in many instruction books. It is started on a Chained Provisional Edge, and while the result is satisfactory, there are quite a few steps involved; for a much simpler way to accomplish the same thing, see the Double-Fabric Corded Edge, below.

1. Work Chained Provisional Edge with contrast-color yarn; use main yarn to pick up stitches in chain.
2. Work three to five rows, depending upon gauge and how thick cord should be.
3. Pick up running threads from first row and use Joinery Decreases to form cord.
4. Remove Chained Edge.

Step 3 is done as for working a Horizontal Welt; the contrast-color edge makes it clear which strands to pick up.

Tubular Edge with Simple Cast-On

This method is often recommended for making a corded edge for Single Rib, but it is more complicated to do than the Double-Fabric version below and offers no benefit. After casting on, there will be an uneven number of stitches on the needle.

1. Use Simple Cast-On to place half required number of stitches, plus one, on needle.
2. Knit these stitches, working a Yarnover between each one.
3. Work three to five rounds of a Basic Pattern for Double-Fabric.
4. Unravel half-hitches in baseline and begin Single Rib pattern.

After completing Step 2, the odd-numbered stitches will have a half-hitch at the base; those in between will be Yarnovers. To establish the pattern in Step 3, use the Yarnovers as the base for the stitches on the inside face of the cord and the other stitches for the outside face of the cord. This makes a Stockinette cord that is half as wide as the fabric would be if the same number of stitches were worked side-by-side.

Double-Fabric Corded Edge

Here is an easier way to make a Stockinette corded edge; there is no need to pick up stitches or unravel a cast-on edge.

1. Use Alternating Cast-On to place twice the number of stitches needed for width of fabric on needle.
2. Work three to five rounds of a Basic Pattern for a Double-Fabric, depending on gauge and size of cord wanted.
3. Work Joinery Decreases across row.
4. Continue with main fabric.

An edge of this kind tends to curl to the outside if followed by plain Stockinette; if this is a problem, work one row of Purl on the outside or a few rows of Garter Stitch above the Welt before starting the main pattern.

For an interesting, decorative variation, you can also use a Knit Half-Hitch Cast-On instead of Alternating Cast-On. This will create a chain of stitches at the bottom of the cord, which can be further enhanced if done in a contrast color; hold the contrast-color yarn on your thumb, and the main yarn on your forefinger. And, by the way, if you add a few more rows to the cord, it will turn into a hem; see Double-Fabric Hems.

Double-Fabric Cord for Single Rib

With a slight modification, the same cord can be done as an edge for Single Rib; while it is attractive, it will reduce the resilience of the ribbing. Nevertheless, the edge has interesting decorative possibilities when done in a contrast color or different yarn texture, and can be very effective when used with a ribbing done in a vertical stripe; see Color in Ribbing Patterns.

- Use a needle one or two sizes smaller than planned for ribbing. Work as described above, but do not do Joinery Decreases in Step 3. Instead, change immediately to Single Rib, working Knit stitches on columns of stitches forming outside of the cord, and Purl stitches on those forming inside of cord.

Side or Mid-Fabric Cast-Ons

There are times in knitting when it is necessary to widen the fabric abruptly at a side edge, or to add stitches within the fabric, such as for a buttonhole or pocket opening. In these cases, increases will not suffice and the additional stitches have to be cast on instead. This has traditionally been done with either Simple Half-Hitch Cast-On or Knit Half-Hitch Cast-On, and both will do the job.

However, here are three alternatives that are not only easy, but produce very satisfactory edges. The only compromise involved is that they all require an extra strand of yarn for the baseline, leaving two ends to hide during finishing.

The instructions here are for working at a side edge, but you can do the technique in the same way within the fabric. Measure off a separate strand of yarn long enough for a baseline of new cast-on stitches.

Compound Cast-On at Side Edge

1. Work across to end of row and with needle bearing stitches in right hand, take up strand of yarn for baseline and press end against nearside of fabric with thumb.
2. Pick up baseline strand on left thumb and main yarn on left forefinger as for working a Compound Half-Hitch Cast-On.

3. Cast on required number of stitches, then abandon baseline strand.
4. Turn, work across new stitches and remaining stitches of row, according to pattern.

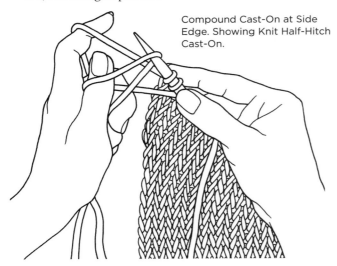

Compound Cast-On at Side Edge. Showing Knit Half-Hitch Cast-On.

Half-Hitch Cast-On for Sloped Edge

You can use the same technique to cast on for a sloped edge, either adding the stitches in small groups called "steps" (see Stepped Cast-Off), or casting on all of those needed and then sloping the edge with Short Rows.

1. Begin as above and cast on first group of stitches; use Knit Half-Hitch Cast-On to add stitches on outside; Purl Half-Hitch Cast-On to add stitches on inside.
2. Drop baseline strand, turn; slip first cast-on stitch, and with main yarn work in pattern across row.
3. Turn, work back across row, including group of newly cast-on stitches at left side. Pick up baseline strand on thumb and cast on next group of stitches.
4. Repeat Steps 2 and 3 to cast on required number of stitches.

The Slip Stitch in Step 2 smooths the turning point between steps.

As an alternative, you could also cast on the full number of stitches required and use Increasing Short Rows to slope the edge.

Provisional Cast-On at Side Edge

One of the Provisional Cast-Ons can also be very useful for certain types of side edges; here are two examples.

- For a garment worked from side to side, after completing first sleeve, use Stranded or Alternating Provisional Cast-On to add stitches at side edge; complete bodice, and then use Stranded Cast-Off or place stitches of opposite

side edges on holder; complete second sleeve. To finish, pick up stitches of both side edges and use Joinery Cast-Off to seam sides.
- For garment worked from bottom up, add all stitches for a dolman sleeve with a Provisional Cast-On and use Short Rows to contour; pick up stitches later and seam with Joinery Cast-Off.

Knitted and Chained Cast-Ons

Two groups of techniques are described here. The first is composed of methods that are done in a way that closely resembles knitting itself, which makes them very easy to learn and, therefore, particularly suitable for beginners. These are attractive, all-purpose edges that are recommended in every book and, for many knitters, are the only cast-ons used.

However, Knitted Cast-Ons are not as quick as the Finger Cast-Ons, there are fewer of them to choose from, and they are less versatile. As a result, they are now used less than before; nevertheless, they are suitable in certain circumstances, and all are worth knowing about. Also included with this group is a brief discussion of knitted borders that can be used to substitute for a true cast-on edge.

The techniques in the second group all produce an edge identical to a Single Crochet Chain, as well as to the basic knitted edge, above. These are quite versatile and are particularly well suited to stitch patterns that produce a contoured edge. Of course, if you are comfortable with a crochet hook, you needn't stop with Single Crochet, since a wealth of patterns can be used in the same way.

There is no need to worry about measuring off a tail of yarn for any of these techniques; none of them requires any more than one long enough to hide on the inside during finishing or to sew a seam.

❖ *Knitted Cast-Ons*

This fundamental technique produces an attractive and moderately resilient edge, although if done too loosely, it is prone to snag or pull out of shape with wear.

The edge and the first row of stitches are both made from a single strand of yarn. Because they are interconnected in this way, the edge can borrow yarn from the first row of stitches for stretch, making it fairly resilient.

There are several variations, all of them involving no more than a small change in the method of working, but each produces surprisingly different edges.

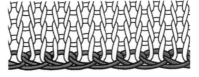

Knit Cast-On Edge.

Knit Cast-On

1. Place a Slip Knot on left needle and count as first stitch.
2. Knit one; do not discard stitch on left needle.

Knit Cast-On: Step 2.
Knit first stitch on needle.

3. Transfer new stitch directly from right needle to left needle; do not turn stitch as it is transferred.

Knit Cast-On: Step 3.
Transfer new stitch from right to left needle.

4. Reinsert right needle into new stitch as to Knit and tighten stitch firmly around both needle tips.
5. Repeat Steps 2–4 for required number of stitches.

Tightening the stitch around both needle tips in Step 4 helps make each stitch a consistent size, and also provides more yarn to the edge for resilience.

Examine the edge and you will see that there are a series of strands, each one spanning two stitches, from the left side of one to the right side of the other. The longer these strands are, the more likely it is that they will snag. To minimize this problem, make the stitches of the edge no larger than necessary. Use a few Test Swatches to see how the edge behaves with the stitch pattern you plan to use and adjust your needle size accordingly.

Purl Cast-On

If you can Knit it on, you can certainly Purl it on, and knowing how to do so means you can control which side of the edge will be on the nearside as you begin to work.

1. Place Slip Knot on left needle and count as first stitch.
2. Purl one, but do not discard.
3. To make next stitch, insert left needle tip into farside of new stitch on right needle, wrap yarn on right needle, and Purl. Repeat this step as many times as necessary.

Purl Cast-On: Step 3.
Purl first stitch on needle.

The maneuver in Step 3 is equivalent to transferring the stitch back to the left needle, then reinserting the right needle as to Purl, but is much quicker.

This is a much faster way to work than the Knit version, above, and is ideal if you are planning to work circular; when you turn the work to begin, the Knit side of the edge will then be on the nearside.

Knit-Purl Cast-On

If you can Knit it on and Purl it on, it follows that you can use both in whatever sequence needed to make the edge compatible with the pattern for the fabric.

While this method will produce a quite satisfactory edge for a fabric done in a pattern of mixed Knit and Purl stitches, there are techniques with greater elasticity that are more suitable for ribbing; see Alternating Cast-On and Double-Needle Cast-On.

Some tips for Knitted Cast-Ons

- *This edge is identical to that produced by working a chain of Single Crochet and then knitting into one side of each stitch; see Crochet Cast-Ons.*
- *If you find the edge is constricted or does not have sufficient elasticity, use a larger needle, or hold two smaller needles as one instead; if it seems too loose, use a smaller needle. However, keep in mind that the size of the needle also determines the size of the stitches in the first row of the fabric, and too large a difference between it and subsequent rows will be noticeable. If necessary, stretch the edge out to encourage it to borrow some yarn from the stitches, and then steam it gently so the edge and the fabric settle in together.*
- *As with the Compound Cast-Ons, the two sides of the edge have a different appearance. Because the stitches accumulate on the left needle, there is no need to turn it in order to begin working a flat fabric; instead, you will need to turn in order to being working in the round. The method used to cast on will determine the appearance of the edge below the first row. Start with either an inside or outside row of a stitch or color pattern, depending upon which side of the edge you prefer.*
- *Because the edge is separate from the stitches of the fabric, you have the option of casting on with a contrast-color yarn or one that is textured.*
- *Knit Cast-On is commonly used to add stitches at a side edge in order to widen the fabric abruptly, such as for a dolman sleeve, or to cast on within a fabric, such as for buttonholes or pockets. However, I think a better result can be achieved by using one of the techniques discussed in Side or Mid-Fabric Cast-Ons.*

Open Knit Cast-On

This variation looks very nice under a lace stitch, because it produces tiny eyelets along the edge. These openings are also very convenient should you want to add a fringe.

An edge of this kind looks best with Knit stitches above it, at least for a row or two; however, it seems to lose distinction when used for a ribbing.

Open Knit Cast-On. Turn new stitch as it is transferred.

- Work as described in Knit Cast-On above, but insert left needle tip on nearside from right to left to turn new stitch as it is transferred.

  Do not withdraw the right needle after transferring the stitch; instead, tuck it under the left needle tip into position to work the next stitch.

This is not a particularly elastic edge, but if done with a larger needle than the one that will be used for the pattern, it has adequate stretch.

The strands that pass from one stitch to the next are rather long; however, each is twisted in a way that makes it less prone to snagging than is the case with the basic Knit Cast-On.

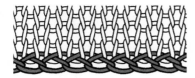

Open Knit Cast-On Edge.

Woven Knit Cast-On

The edge produced with one of these variations has a complex, woven appearance that has little tendency to curl, making it a good choice for a tailored garment without ribbing.

However, take care to balance it with a compatible stitch pattern, for it is quite dense and inelastic and will not do with a pattern that widens. Use a Test Swatch to determine the best needle size.

- Use either Knit Cast-On or Open Knit Cast-On. Knit first row of stitches through farside so they cross.

Oddly enough, the Open Knit Cast-On version produces an edge that is more tightly woven than the Knit Cast-On version.

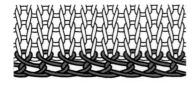

Woven Knit Cast-On Edge.

Cable Cast-Ons

This technique produces an edge that is neat and uniform, and it is often recommended as "strong." If strength is defined as dense and inelastic, it certainly qualifies. However, as with a reed that bends in the wind, the resilience of a knitted garment is its true strength, and an edge that does not stretch has more of a tendency to break.

On the other hand, this edge is quite handsome, and it is an excellent choice for stitch patterns that share its firm characteristics. The two sides have a different appearance, and both are attractive.

Knit Cable Cast-On

1. Place Slip Knot on needle and use Knit Cast-On to make one additional stitch.
2. For all subsequent stitches, insert right needle tip from nearside to farside between first two stitches on left needle. Wrap yarn as to Knit, draw new stitch through, and transfer it directly to left needle. Repeat for required number of stitches.

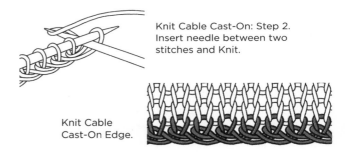

Knit Cable Cast-On: Step 2. Insert needle between two stitches and Knit.

Knit Cable Cast-On Edge.

Purl Cable Cast-On

- Work as described above, except insert right needle between first two stitches on left needle from farside to nearside and Purl.

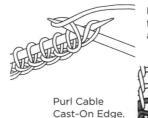

Purl Cable Cast-On. Insert needle from farside between two stitches and Purl.

Purl Cable Cast-On Edge.

❖ Knitted Border Cast-Ons

As with the crocheted edges discussed below, there are a great many beautiful borders knit narrow and long that can be used as a substitute for a true cast-on edge. These can be worked first, and then the stitches for the main fabric are picked up along the selvedge of the border; see Picking Up Stitches.

Alternatively, the stitches along the lower edge of the garment can be started with a Provisional Cast-On, and then the border is worked and attached at the lower edge at the same time; see Picking Up to Join. In either case, the columns of stitches in the border will run perpendicular to those in the main fabric.

Also, any stitch pattern can be worked down from stitches that have been freed from the lower edge. You might do this to lengthen a garment, for instance, or simply to add some color or texture that was absent in the original design. For more information, see Working in the Opposite Direction.

Here is just one example of the first type of border, a very narrow knitted edge that is worked separately before picking up the stitches for the fabric along one side.

Eyelet Cast-On Border

This border is quaint, highly decorative, and very easy to do. It has a good deal of lateral spread, so it works well with stitch patterns that widen, but it can also be frilled or ruffled by using it with a pattern that compresses, such as a rib.

The edge tends to look best when done with a relatively small needle; test a few sizes before you begin the actual border to see what works best with the stitch pattern you will use for the garment.

1. Place Slip Knot on small needle, and make one additional stitch with Half-Hitch Cast-On. Transfer needle with two stitches to left hand, and hold second needle in right hand.
2. With yarn farside, wrap yarn over top of right needle to nearside, and then back under to farside to make a Turned Yarnover with left side of strand on nearside of needle.
3. Insert right needle into farside of two stitches on left needle as for a Left Decrease, wrap yarn over needle, and Knit; new stitch will be in turned position on needle.

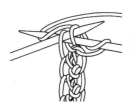

Eyelet Cast-On Border: Step 3.
Knit 2 farside, wrap yarn over needle.

4. Transfer new stitch and Yarnover directly to left needle.
5. Repeat Steps 1–4 until chain is as long as required for cast-on edge.
6. Knit last two stitches together farside without forming a new Yarnover, leaving one stitch on needle.
7. For open Eyelets, transfer needle to right hand and pick up chain in left hand; with right needle, pick up and Knit stitches into Yarnover loops on one side of chain. To twist the Yarnover closed, pick up with a needle held in the left

hand and insert into Yarnover from nearside to farside; use needle in right hand to Knit the turned strand farside.

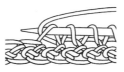

Eyelet Cast-On Border: Step 7.
Pick up stitches along edge.

As you work, there should always be two stitches on the left needle, always in the Turned position; no stitches accumulate on the right needle.

Because the technique makes use of a Left Decrease, it is easier to turn the stitches and the Yarnovers as they are made instead of having to turn each one with the needle tip prior to the decrease; for more information, see Turned Stitches.

For open Eyelets along the edge, Knit into the nearside of each Yarnover; to close the Eyelets, work into the farside of the Yarnovers, as for a Twist Stitch.

Eyelet Cast-On Border for Old Shale pattern.

❖ Chained Cast-Ons

These cast-on techniques all produce an edge that is structurally identical to a Single Crochet Chain; the variations are merely in how they are done. When used as an edge for a knitted fabric, this is traditionally done with a crochet hook, and then a knitting needle is used to pick up stitches into the chain. However, there is an easier way to accomplish the same thing in one step by using a hook paired with a knitting needle, or, if you are not comfortable with a crochet hook, with two knitting needles instead.

A Chained Cast-On edge is quite decorative and nicely elastic, and, perhaps more important, it exactly matches a Chained Cast-Off. This makes it very nice to use when both the top and bottom edges of a fabric will be visible, such as on a blanket or a scarf.

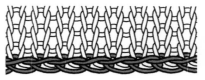

Chained
Cast-On Edge.

In addition, this technique is often used as a provisional cast-on, to make an edge that can later be removed to free the stitches. It works quite well for this purpose; however, see Provisional Cast-Ons for alternatives.

Also included here is Double-Chained Cast-On, a closely related technique done with two colors that produces a beautiful braided effect along the edge.

Single Crochet Cast-On

All that is needed for this cast-on is to crochet a simple chain, and then pick up stitches into it with a knitting needle. Two different edges can be made from the same chain, depending upon how the stitches are picked up.

Single Crochet Chain

1. Place Slip Knot on crochet hook; hold yarn as for Left-Hand Method of knitting.
2. Pass hook over yarn, down farside, and under to nearside again to wrap yarn on hook as for a Yarnover. Bring tip up on nearside and hook yarn; draw through Slip Knot.
3. With one stitch on hook, repeat Step 2 to chain number of stitches needed for cast-on edge. Transfer last stitch from hook to knitting needle.

The chain consists of a series of loops on one side and a series of nubs, like a little spine, on the reverse. The yarn that runs between one loop and the next is equivalent to the running thread in knitting, and forms the nubs.

Picking Up in Chain: Method One

There are two ways to pick up into a Single Crochet Chain.

This first method is traditionally recommended for an edge that will later be removed; see Chained Provisional Edge.

- Insert needle from nearside to farside under nub on back of chain and Knit.

Single Crochet Cast-On: Method One. Picking up stitches into nub.

Picking Up in Chain: Method Two

This method results in an edge that is the same as Knit Half-Hitch Cast-On.

- Insert needle from nearside to farside into center of loop in chain and Knit.

Single Crochet Cast-On: Method Two. Picking up stitches into loop.

Hook and Needle Chained Cast-On

Here is a more efficient way to accomplish the same edge as when using Method One for picking up stitches along a Single Crochet Chain, above; it creates the chain and places the stitches on the knitting needle at the same time and is related to Horizontal Chain Stitch.

This is done with a knitting needle in your left hand and a crochet hook in your right, and it may seem awkward at first—but once you get the hang of it, it is quite easy to do.

1. Place Slip Knot on crochet hook held in right hand; hold knitting needle in left hand.
2. Hold yarn on left forefinger as for crochet or Left-Hand Method of knitting; yarn should pass from hook, under knitting needle, to finger.
3. Hold hook against nearside of needle and chain one stitch firmly; yarn will now pass over knitting needle.

Hook and Needle Chained Cast-On: Step 3. Draw wrapped yarn through stitch on hook.

4. With either right forefinger or hook, return yarn under knitting needle to farside so it is in same position as in Step 2.

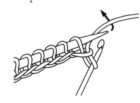

Hook and Needle Chained Cast-On: Step 4. Return yarn under needle.

5. Repeat Steps 3 and 4 until there is one less stitch than required on left needle. Transfer last stitch on crochet hook to needle.

The new stitch is formed when the hook draws the yarn over the needle; the crocheted chain of stitches forms the edge below the needle.

Aside from how efficient it is, another advantage this version offers is that the needle and hook can be different sizes, offering precise control over the respective sizes of the stitches and the loops in the chain.

Two-Needle Chained Cast-On

If you are not comfortable with a crochet hook or do not have one on hand, here is an alternate approach that can be done with two knitting needles. It creates the same edge as the Hook and Needle Chained version, above; however, it is slower and somewhat more awkward to do.

The first instructions here are for the Purl version of the technique, since I find it goes along very smoothly; the Knit version is below, if you prefer to use it.

Purl Two-Needle Chained Cast-On

1. Place Slip Knot on needle and hold in left hand; hold second needle in right hand.
2. With yarn nearside, wrap yarn around right needle as for Purl-to-Purl Yarnover.

Purl Two-Needle Chained Cast-On: Step 2. Purl-to-Purl Yarnover.

3. Maintain firm tension on yarn and Purl stitch on left needle. Transfer new stitch from right needle to left needle.

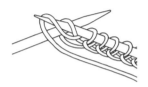

Purl Two-Needle Chained Cast-On: Step 3. Purl stitch on left needle.

4. Repeat Steps 2 and 3 to cast on as many stitches as needed.

The Yarnovers are the new stitches and will accumulate on the right needle; the discarded stitches form the chain baseline. There will never be more than one stitch on the left needle; it is used only to work the Purl stitch.

Take care to work evenly; with both needles inserted into the stitch, tighten yarn firmly before purling. Keep a watchful eye on the chain of stitches in the baseline, since they have a tendency to enlarge. To make each stitch the same size, after transferring the stitch to the left needle, place tension on the yarn and then pull up on the stitch with the left needle to draw yarn out of the chain at the base of the previous Yarnover.

Knit Two-Needle Chained Cast-On

It is easy enough to adapt these instructions if you prefer to work in Knit; substitute the following for Steps 2 and 3:

- With yarn nearside, Knit stitch on left needle. Transfer this stitch to left needle and repeat.

  When the yarn is held nearside, it will go over the needle as you Knit the stitch, automatically forming the Yarnover.

Chained Provisional Edge

As mentioned above, a Chained Cast-On is often recommended as a provisional edge because it is easy to remove; to free the stitches, simply unravel the chain. While it is not as easy to do as Stranded Provisional Cast-On, it is easier to free the stitches; for another alternative, see Alternating Provisional Cast-On, which eliminates the need to free the stitches and pick them up.

All of the Chained Cast-On methods described above can be used to make a provisional edge, but either the Hook and Needle or Two-Needle variations are more efficient. The version of the technique described here makes use of what is known as "waste" yarn—any available yarn, ideally in a contrast color; it will be discarded when freed stitches are picked up.

1. Use a contrast-color waste yarn and make a chain equal to or greater than number of stitches required.
2. Extend last loop several inches and tighten yarn at base to serve as temporary knot; break yarn.
3. Begin to work fabric with main yarn.
4. To unravel cast-on edge, untie temporary knot or draw end from extra chain, pull on yarn to free stitches, and then pick them up on needle.

The extra stitches cast on in Step 1 are insurance against having too few; at end of first row, make a final count and drop those you do not need. Or, if using a hook, crochet a few extra stitches in just the chain (do not add extra stitches to the needle), and then break the yarn and pull the end through the last stitch.

If you are concerned that stitches might unravel as you pick up the edge, use one of the following approaches:

- Free only a few stitches at a time, pick them up, and then unravel a few more.
- Alternatively, cast on with waste yarn and then add several rows of Stockinette; change to main yarn and start stitch or color pattern.
- To free stitches, remove Chain and unravel all but two of these extra rows. Draw waste yarn out of stitches one by one, pick them up on needle, and then rip back one more row, stitch by stitch, to make sure they are all on needle in correct position, with nearside of stitch on nearside of needle.

Chained Loop Cast-On

For a more decorative edge, work Chained Cast-On and skip some chains as you pick up stitches.

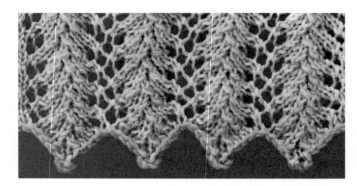

Chained Loop Cast-On. Extra loops at tips of indented edge.

- One chain between each stitch will produce an Eyelet effect.
- Skipping several chains will create a loop between one stitch and the next; these are not only decorative, but can serve as convenient hangers for fringe.

This approach works well for stitch patterns that create a deeply indented edge since the chain can accommodate itself to the extra length required. For an explanation of why extra length is important for an edge of this kind, see the discussion in Double-Needle Cast-On.

Double-Chained Cast-On

Here is a lovely version of a two-color Chained Cast-On that Nancy Bush wrote about in *Folk Knitting in Estonia*.† The edge consists of a pair of chains in alternating colors that share a center strand; one leans toward the outside, one is along the very bottom of the edge. It is a pretty effect, but very slow to execute, so it is traditionally reserved for smaller items like mitten or sock tops, or the wrist edge of a sleeve.

The method of working is very closely related to Hook and Needle Chained Cast-On, as well as to the Braided Cast-Ons, both described above, and like them it is compatible with the Twined Knit technique for making a Herringbone Braid within a fabric.

Handling the yarns requires patience, and it is important to maintain firm, even tension in order to create a consistent edge. Also, the yarns wind around one another, stitch by stitch, so it will be necessary to stop now and then to untangle them; the easiest way to do so is to hold the needle up, tip down, and spin it in your fingers until the yarns have separated again.

This is a slight modification of the traditional method, which I find somewhat easier to do.

† Nancy Bush, *Folk Knitting in Estonia: A Garland of Symbolism, Tradition and Technique* (Loveland, Colo.: Interweave Press, 1999), p. 43.

1. Tie two yarns together in Slip Knot and place on needle.
2. Add two Simple Cast-On stitches, one with each yarn. Transfer needle with Slip Knot and two stitches to left hand.
3. Purl first stitch on left needle with contrast-color yarn.
4. Move yarn last used between needles to farside and to right; draw second yarn under it and then between needle tips to nearside for next stitch. Tighten newest chain stitch under needle to match size of others.
5. Make a Purl-to-Purl Yarnover on right needle, and then Purl stitch on left needle. If working Step 5 for first time, drop Slip Knot.
6. Transfer new stitch from right to left needle.
7. Repeat Steps 4–5 to cast on as many stitches as required.

After dropping the Slip Knot the first time you work Step 5, there should never be more than one stitch on the left needle. The Yarnovers form the new stitches and will accumulate on the right needle.

❖ *Crocheted Edges*

There are a great many beautiful crochet patterns for edgings of various kinds. Pattern books most often show them applied as decorative finishes on woven fabrics for things like hand towels, pillow cases, and table runners.

These patterns can just as easily be used for the edge of a knitted item of any kind, whether for the ends of a scarf or shawl, to decorate the wrist of a sweater, or as a finish for a neckline or center front opening.

Depending on the circumstances, you can make the edge and then pick up stitches into it, as described above for a Single Crochet Chain, or you can pick up stitches along the edge of a knitted fabric and then crochet the border. For more information, see Picking Up Stitches.

CHAPTER 4

Selvedges and Steeks

selvedge consists of one or two columns of stitches at the side edge of a flat fabric. These stitches are worked according to small specialized patterns that create edges with various desirable characteristics. Some selvedges are particularly attractive when used for the visible edge of a fabric, while others make it easy to seam the edge or pick up stitches along it, and several leave a decorative detail along the join between two fabrics. However small they are, selvedges are important because few decorative patterns used across the full width of a fabric will create edges that serve these purposes quite as well.

Also included here is a discussion about Steeks. This technique makes it possible to knit a garment entirely in the round all the way to the shoulders, and later cut the fabric open for the armholes and/or for a center front opening. There are two primary advantages to working this way. First, there is no need to divide the fabric at the armholes and continue flat, which can cause a change in gauge, and second, it is easier to work a color pattern accurately if the outside of the fabric remains visible at all times. Also, while a Steek is thought of as a technique exclusive to circular knitting, almost in a category of its own, in fact it is a form of Selvedge and has some interesting applications for knitting flat, as well.

Selvedges

There are two categories of selvedges here. First are the basic selvedges that consist of a single stitch at the edge of a fabric. These may serve either practical or decorative purposes, depending upon how they are used. The second group of selvedges all have two stitches, and these are exclusively decorative, although they may be used for a seamed edge as well as a visible one.

❖ Basic Selvedges

Stockinette Selvedge and Chain Selvedge are used by most knitters for most projects, and for good reason. They serve equally well for a visible edge or for seams, and, when seamed, can be turned to the outside for a decorative detail. However, they do have quite different characteristics, and there are good reasons to select one or the other depending upon the project at hand.

The other two basic selvedges are nice for a visible edge because they provide more texture; one is related to Garter Stitch and the other resembles it, but is more open.

The Selvedge patterns below are designed to work the same way on both side edges of a fabric. However, for those situations where one selvedge is seamed and the other remains visible, you will find it easy enough to adapt these patterns to the circumstances.

Here are some tips that you will find useful when working any of them.

Tips for Basic Selvedges

- Always work the selvedge pattern according to the instructions regardless of how you work the stitches of the main fabric. In other words, work the selvedge stitch at the beginning of the row, and then move the yarn nearside or farside if necessary to Knit or Purl the first stitch of the main pattern. Similarly, at the end of the row, work the last stitch of the main pattern, and then move the yarn into position to Knit or Purl the selvedge stitch.

- If the selvedge is picked up or seamed, it will be absorbed in the join and no longer contribute to the width of the fabric. Therefore, it is necessary to calculate the total number of stitches required for the width of the garment according to stitch pattern and gauge, and then add the selvedge stitches. For more information, see Seams, and Picking Up Selvedges.

- If a selvedge will serve as the visible edge of the fabric, it does contribute to the overall width and is included in the calculation of how many stitches to use overall. While this represents a negligible amount with a thin yarn and a gauge with a relatively high number of stitches per inch, it can make a difference when the yarn is thicker.

- Complex stitch techniques or shaping are normally set within the fabric and away from the edge; see Shaping a Fabric. This is done to keep a visible edge neat and consistent. However, this is also important when an edge will be seamed or picked up into; these techniques make use of the space between the selvedge and the main fabric, and any shaping done there will make it more difficult to create a smooth, even join between two fabrics.

- Because the selvedge itself will be turned to the inside of the garment when seamed, it can serve nicely as a convenient little "closet" where you can hide yarn changes or carry alternating yarns up from one color pattern area to another; see Stranding Yarns Up Edges.

Stockinette Selvedge

This all-purpose selvedge is very easy to do, and when left visible, it forms a neat, quiet edge. It is a nice edge to seam or pick up into since there is one stitch per row, which makes it easy to join two fabrics together evenly with the rows to each side of the join perfectly lined up, and can also be used for joining two edges without sewing (see Linked Seam). Furthermore, the edge is quite attractive when turned to the outside; for more information, see Turning Selvedges to Outside.

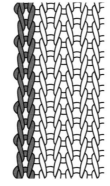

Stockinette Selvedge.

- Outside Row: Knit first and last stitches.
- Inside Row: Purl first and last stitches.

A Stockinette Selvedge looks much like a normal column of Knit stitches; however, along the very edge there is a little nub every other row, formed as the yarn doubles back through the stitch below to the one above. Because the selvedge curls to the inside of the fabric (more or less depending upon your primary stitch pattern), these nubs are not particularly visible and you will find them quite convenient for counting rows—two rows for every nub.

Chain Selvedge

A Chain Selvedge looks like a crocheted chain, with each stitch spanning two rows, and is attractive as a visible edge. It is less bulky than a Stockinette Selvedge when it has stitches picked up into it or is seamed, and the seam can be turned to the outside. It is also a good selvedge to use when working with more than one color (see Managing Stranded Yarns).

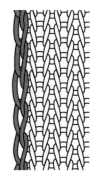

Chain Selvedge.

1. First Row Only: Work selvedge stitch at beginning and end of first row.
2. Outside Row: At beginning of row, Slip 1 knitwise; at end of row, Knit 1.
3. Inside Row: At beginning of row, Slip 1 purlwise; at end of row, Purl 1.

Step 1 produces a neater corner at the cast-on edge. Be consistent about working the last stitch of every row in pattern: Knit on an outside row, Purl on an inside row.

Frankly, I have a troubled relationship with this Selvedge. In my hands, at least, the stitches in the left Selvedge tend to enlarge and the adjacent column of stitches is irregular. This is not only unsightly, but one side of the fabric becomes longer than the other.

A Stockinette fabric is ruthless in revealing any irregularity in the stitches adjacent to the selvedge. Fortunately this is less evident with most textured stitch patterns, especially when using a soft yarn, and it tends to even out if the edge is seamed or has stitches picked up along it.

I get a better result with the yarn held on the left instead of the right, or, when holding the yarn on the right, if I work the Purl row from left to right. This suggests the problem has something to do with the direction in which the yarn is held in relation to the direction in which the stitches are moving. If you share this problem, here are a few other tricks you can try:

- Slip first and last stitches of row; work these stitches on return row.
- Or, work first stitch of every row; Slip last stitch of every row.

These are similar, in that after the turn, you will find the yarn attached to the second stitch on the needle, and you must draw it to the right to work the first stitch.

Garter Stitch Selvedge

This very old, very common selvedge technique is quite attractive,
with bold little knots along the
edge; it looks particularly handsome alongside smooth stitch patterns that provide textural contrast.
It is, to borrow a phrase from
Rudyard Kipling, "nice, but
nubbly,"† which makes it ideal
for a visible edge but not, perhaps,
the best choice for a seam.

Garter Stitch Selvedge.

Of course, there is no need to
work selvedge stitches in a special
way for a fabric made in Garter Stitch; simply work all the
stitches of the row in pattern, from first to last.

Add one stitch on each side for the selvedges and work every row as follows:

• Knit first and last stitch of every row.

If you look carefully, you will notice that the right and left
sides look slightly different when used on a fabric other than
Garter Stitch. Should you really, truly want them to match exactly, work as follows:

1. Outside Row: Purl first stitch, Knit last.
2. Inside Row: Knit first stitch, Purl last.

Slip Knot Selvedge

This technique produces an edge that is similar in appearance to a Garter Stitch Selvedge but is not as elastic. It has a
pair of vertical strands with a tiny knot at the base, and there
is an eyelet between the selvedge and the adjacent column of
stitches.

1. Outside Row: At beginning of row, with yarn nearside,
   Slip first stitch purlwise; at end of row, Knit 1.
2. Inside Row: At beginning of row, with yarn farside,
   Slip first stitch purlwise; at end of row, Purl 1.

It is important to maintain firm tension on the slipped stitch
as you work the second and third stitches on the needle so the
edge stays neat, especially at the left edge; see the discussion
in Chain Selvedge, above.

❖ Double Selvedges

Here are some selvedge patterns made with two stitches instead
of one. All are decorative enough to serve as a visible edge and

---

† Rudyard Kipling, "How the Whale Got His Throat," in *Just So
Stories* (London: Macmillan, 1902).

will help an edge to lie flat and neat. Because of their inherent
elasticity, they adapt particularly well to a contoured edge.

The first two are simple and easy to do and good for almost
any purpose. The third one creates a more open edge, which
makes it particularly compatible with lace. The last three can
all serve as a visible edge, but they are ideally used when two
fabrics are to be joined, whether by seaming or picking up
stitches, because one of the two selvedge stitches will remain
on the outside of the fabric to form a decorative vertical line.

Double Garter Stitch Selvedge

This technique multiplies all of the
good characteristics of Garter Stitch
Selvedge, since it lies very flat and
has greater vertical elasticity. Add
two stitches at each side for the
selvedges.

Double Garter Stitch
Selvedge.

• Knit first two stitches and last two
  stitches of every row.

Of course you can use three or four,
or however many stitches you care
to, but at some point it becomes a
border, not a proper selvedge.

Seed Stitch Selvedge

This is another attractive two-stitch
selvedge that will steam nice and
flat, is easy to do, and also has good
resilience. I think it is prettier than
the Double Garter Stitch Selvedge.

Seed Stitch Selvedge.

• On Every Row: Work first
  two stitches, Knit 1, Purl 1;
  work last two stitches Purl 1,
  Knit 1.

Yarnover Selvedge

This puts a Yarnover at the beginning of each row, making the selvedge quite open and decorative.
Because a Yarnover adds a stitch,
the next two stitches are worked
as a decrease to maintain the stitch
count. Add two stitches at each side
for this selvedge and work with a
firm tension.

Yarnover Selvedge.

1. Outside Row: At beginning of
   row, with yarn nearside, Knit Left
   Decrease; at end of row, Knit 2.

Yarn will pass over right needle automatically to form Yarnover at edge.

2. Inside Row: At beginning of row, wrap yarn over empty right needle as for Purl-to-Purl Yarnover, and then Purl Right Decrease; at end of row, Purl 2.

Stockinette and Garter Selvedge

This method creates a Stockinette Selvedge adjacent to a column of Garter Stitch that is very attractive for an unseamed edge. However, if seamed, there will be a double column of Garter Stitch on the outside, with one column from each fabric on either side of the seam, or a single column of Garter Stitch adjacent to a border done on picked-up stitches.

1. Outside Row: Knit two stitches of selvedge at beginning and end of row.
2. Inside Row: At beginning of row, Purl 1, Knit 1; at end of row, Knit 1, Purl 1.

To decorate the join even more, crochet a contrast-color chain up the columns of Garter Stitch, working into the little Purl nubs that alternate row by row. Alternatively, weave in a contrast-color yarn or ribbon under the nubs. Either approach adds a very nice touch along a button band, for instance.

Chain and Garter Selvedge

This is nearly the same as the selvedge above, but with a Chain Selvedge; use this version if you want to reduce bulk in a join. When done neatly, this Selvedge can also be turned to the outside for a very decorative effect. The result will be a double chain on either side of a seam, or a single chain adjacent to a border done on picked-up stitches.

Chain and Garter Selvedge.

• At beginning of row, Slip 1, Knit 1; at end of row, Knit last two stitches.

Chain and Purl Selvedge

This version has a Chain Selvedge next to a column of Purl and it is a lovely Selvedge when left visible; the Purl column is, of course, a column of Knit on the inside, so the edge looks very nice on both sides of the fabric. Also, the Chain tends to turn toward the Purl column, hiding it; this effect is enhanced if the edge is seamed, which forces the Chain to the outside where it will lie nested in the Purl column, flush with the surface of the fabric.

1. Outside Row: At beginning of row, Slip 1 knitwise, and with yarn nearside Purl 1; at end of row, Purl 1, Knit 1.

Chain and Purl Selvedge. Outside edge on left; inside edge on right.

2. Inside Row: At beginning of row, Slip 1 purlwise, and with yarn farside, Knit 1; at end of row, Knit 1, Purl 1.

Steeks: Selvedges for Cut Openings

In some areas of Great Britain and northern Europe, and no doubt elsewhere, there is a traditional method of making a circular garment in which the fabric is worked entirely in the round to the shoulders. The result is a tube that must be cut open to make the armholes; a cardigan or jacket would also be cut open at the center front.

Steek, an old Scots word, is the term commonly used today to refer to the multistep process needed to prepare the fabric so it will not ravel when cut open. The word has a suitably incisive sound and colloquially it refers variously to a stitch in sewing or knitting, to locking or latching, or to binding something.

The method was originally employed for very simple garment styles with little or no shaping. It is still used in the same way by knitters who enjoy making garments in an authentic, traditional manner, as well as by many others for a wider variety of garment styles. The approach is also favored by those who like to use complex multicolor patterns, which are easier to follow with the outside of the fabric in view at all times. Also, because there is no need to change from working circular to flat at the armholes, there is no risk of a difference in gauge, which can happen when two areas are worked in a different way (see The Five Variables, in the chapter Stitch Gauge).

As you will see below, however, it is not actually necessary to work a Steek in the traditional way in order to cut open a knitted fabric, nor is it necessary to restrict the general concept of making a Steek to working in the round. It is also possible to knit a flat rectangle of fabric and cut out and assemble the various garment pieces much as one would a woven fabric, using some of the same techniques that would be employed to make a Steek in a circular one. This suggests the need for a slight change in the concept of what a Steek is and what steps are essential to it; to be more precise, it is really a method used to make an interior selvedge, one set within a fabric that will be cut, which is why you find the discussion in this chapter.

A variety of techniques can be used for the different steps that are necessary to shape and finish a fabric in this way, but the material here includes instructions only for those used to make an internal selvedge of some kind. For more information on how to secure the stitches and cut a fabric, whether it has a proper Steek or not, see Sewing and Cutting Steeks, Seams for Wide Selvedges, and Bound Edges. Also see Picking Up a Cut or Knotted Edge.

❖ *Making a Steek*

For a traditional Steek, the garment is worked in the round to the base of the armhole. Next, a certain number of stitches are set aside at the underarm; how many depends upon the gauge and the size of the garment (see Bodice and Sleeve Design). These may be cast off or placed on a holder and, once they have been secured in some way, a Steek is introduced to replace them.

There are two main types: a Knitted Steek is a set of stitches that are worked along with all the others, while a Knotted Steek employs strands to span the armhole opening.

Knitted Steek

Most Steeks are worked on a set of stitches cast on immediately above those cast off or placed on hold at the base of the planned opening. The number of stitches to add for the Steek is a matter of preference and gauge, but usually it is more or less equal to those set aside at the base. Knit Cast-On or Simple Cast-On is commonly used for this purpose, but also see Side or Mid-Fabric Cast-Ons.

These stitches are then worked along with all the other stitches on the needle and the knitting just continues round and round with no break in the rhythm.

To finish, the stitches at each side of the Steek are sewn so they will not unravel, and the fabric is cut down the center of the area to open the armhole. Once the fabric is opened, the extra columns of stitches in the Steek serve as selvedges, half at each side of the opening, and are turned to the inside when the sleeve is attached.

There really is nothing more to it than that, but here are some suggestions for things that will help when you make a Steek:

- It is useful to distinguish the stitches of the Steek in some way, both as an aid in maintaining the pattern in the main fabric as you work, as well as serving as a guide when it is time to sew and cut the opening.

  If you are working with a single yarn, place Yarn Markers on either side of the Steek, or use a different stitch

pattern of some kind to distinguish the area from the main fabric.

If you are using two color yarns, alternate the yarns to the stitches of the Steek as you knit each round; this serves to carry both of the strands across the Steek as well as to identify it clearly.

- Consider working a Vertical Foldline at each side of the Steek to help it turn neatly into place on the inside of the garment when seaming or picking up stitches on the edge. This also serves to mark off the stitches of the Steek from those of the garment itself.

  A foldline of this kind is similar to a Chain Selvedge, and you might consider seaming or picking up stitches along it so as to leave it on the outside.

- Instead of casting off and casting on again at the base of the Steek, use the Placeholder Opening technique and knit the stitches that would normally be cast off with a short length of contrast-color yarn. Slip these stitches back to the left needle and work across them with the main yarn to begin the Steek. Tie the two ends of the Placeholder yarn together so it will not come out. The stitch columns that continue above the marked area constitute the Steek. When the Steek is cut open, remove the marker yarn and pick up these stitches.

- Alternatively, continue to work a few rows above the base of the armhole, and then stop and thread a bit of contrast-color yarn into the group of stitches below, or insert a stitch holder, picking up the right side of each stitch; see Tools.

- If it is necessary to attach a new supply of yarn, do so at the center of the Steek. The strands left behind will be

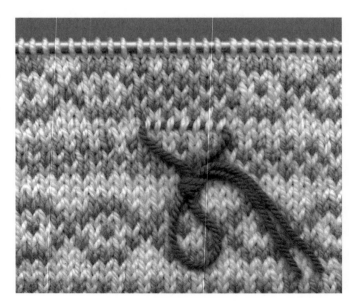

Stitches on Yarn Holder at base of Steek.

Knotted Steek fringe on inside.

eliminated when you cut the opening, and there will be no need to hide the ends on the inside of the garment.

Knotted Steek

This interesting method is seen in Shetland Fair Isle sweaters, and it produces a very different kind of selvedge. Instead of adding stitches to span what will be the opening, measured lengths of yarn are used instead. These yarns are later cut open and knotted off to each side.

This is an especially nice way to work because there are no extra Steek stitches to knit and no sewing is needed to secure the area before cutting it open. Even better, instead of a bulky selvedge with an unsightly cut edge, all that remains is a lovely little fringe that will be turned to the inside when the edge is seamed or when stitches are picked up along it. I find the fringe charming and only you will see it, but it can be covered with a Facing if you prefer to hide it; see Faced or Bound Edges.

Some people do not like using a Knotted Steek because stitches on either side of the area become rather loose and unruly as you work, although everything gets tidied up nicely at the end and it is quick and easy to do.

At position of Steek, cast off stitches at base of armhole or place on holder and proceed as follows:

1. Wrap yarn around needle four or five times, and then continue to work next stitches on left needle.
2. On next round, drop previously wrapped yarn from needle, then wrap yarn again in same way. Continue in this way, dropping previous wrap and making a new one on each round.

3. To open Steek, cut down center of loose strands. To find center of strands, fold fabric so two sides of armhole are lined up, one on top of the other, insert one blade of a scissors under a group of strands, pull them taut at center, and cut.
4. Take a pair of adjacent strands, tighten up any loose stitches at side of armhole, making them the same size as all others, and then tie strands in Square Knot. Repeat with two strands on opposite side of opening and continue in this way until all strands have been knotted.
5. Repeat Steps 3 and 4 until all strands are tied, and then trim yarn ends evenly along each edge to about 1 inch.

The number of wraps to use in Step 2 depends upon your gauge. The point is to leave long enough ends after the strands are cut open so you can tie the knots; 6 to 8 inches is usually sufficient.

Knitted and Knotted Steek

Here is an approach that combines the best aspects of both the Steeks described above.

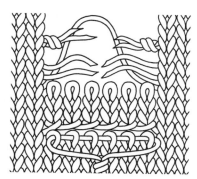

Knitted and Knotted Steek. Stitches on hold at base of armhole; Steek stitches cast on and later cut and knotted.

1. Cast on and work as described in Making a Steek, above.
2. At top of garment, place stitches of Steek on holder until time to finish armhole; do not cast off.
3. To finish, remove holder and unravel stitches to release strands that span opening. Cut strands and finish as described in Knotted Steek, above.

Offset Knots

If you prefer to offset the knots and fringe away from the edge of the opening, work as follows:

1. Work as described above, but add four to six extra stitches to those cast on for Steek.
2. At top, cast off extra stitches at each side of Steek; place remaining stitches at center of Steek on holder.
3. To finish, remove stitches from holder and unravel, cut strands at center, and knot to each side. Turn knots as well as extra columns of stitches to inside to serve as Selvedges.

For an edge that will remain visible, a wider selvedge of this kind can serve as a self-facing (see Facings), in which case, consider the use of a Vertical Foldline.

Twice Knit Steek

Twice Knit is a stitch technique that creates an extremely dense fabric. It is an interesting option for a Steek because it will not unravel when cut, particularly if done in wool. It makes a very stable selvedge, but can be bulky.

Twice Knit Steek. Partially cut with Yarn Holder still in place.

• Work as for Knitted Steek, above, using Twice Knit for stitches of Steek. Cut Steek open down center.

These stitches can tighten up; work with a gentle tension. After you cut the edge, there will be a few stray yarn bits, but just brush them away gently; the edge will stay intact.

A Twice Knit fabric appears to have a slight bias, which makes knowing where to cut the opening somewhat difficult unless it is marked beforehand. Here are some suggestions:

• Use a Yarn Marker, carrying it up at the center of the Steek row by row as you knit.
• Or, after garment is finished, place a ruler at the center of the Steek and mark the cutting line with a chalk marker, as you would when sewing a woven fabric.

❖ Shaping for a Cut Opening

It is possible to knit a straight tube and later cut a nicely curved armhole or even a neckline without any need to use one of the techniques described above for making a Steek. While this means you would be making quite a large area of fabric that will later be cut away, the benefit is that it is unnecessary to follow a pattern to shape the opening, which can save time and effort.

On the other hand, if you prefer to contour the opening as you work, there are two ways to do so. With the first method, the shaping is placed within the main fabric much as you would do when working flat—in this case, on either side of several columns of stitches that serve as an internal selvedge, or Steek.

With the other method, the shaping is set within the Steek instead of within the main fabric and eliminated when the area is cut open. This is an excellent approach to use when the position or appearance of the shaping techniques would otherwise conflict with a complex stitch or color pattern.

Shaping Next to a Steek

1. Thread a strand of yarn into stitches at base of armhole or use stitch holder, as described above in suggestions for a Knitted Steek; continue working in round. Stitch columns above marker or holder form Steek.
2. Place decreases needed to shape armhole within main fabric, one or two stitches away from Steek on each side.
3. To finish, secure Steek and cut fabric open.

The number of stitches in the Steek remains constant; you might find it helpful to carry Ring Markers on your needle to clearly set off the area, or simply work those stitches with a different stitch pattern of some kind.

Shaping Within a Steek

1. Secure stitches at base of armhole as described in Step 1, above.
2. To shape armhole, work Double Decreases or paired Single Decreases set at center of stitch columns that constitute Steek.
3. To secure selvedge prior to cutting, sew between decreases and main fabric on one side, across base of armhole, and then up between decreases and main fabric on other side. Cut through decreases to open fabric.

The number of stitches in the Steek must remain constant; therefore, for every decrease, one stitch from the main fabric should become part of the Steek. Because of this shift, it may be easier to use a length of contrast-color yarn as a Stitch Column Marker to define the area instead of carrying Ring Markers on the needle; or, as above, simply work the Steek in a different stitch pattern of some kind.

The sewn line will cut across columns of stitches because of the way the shaping is done.

Shaped Steek for a Flat Fabric

The concept of offsetting the shaping to the area of a Steek in order to leave a stitch or color pattern undisturbed can be applied to a flat fabric as well.

1. Work several rows above where armhole should begin, using Stockinette on stitches that will be cast off at base of armhole.
2. Cast those stitches off and then continue shaping armhole according to pattern, working decreases on first and second stitch columns at edge of fabric.

Shaped Steek for flat fabric. All decreases placed at edge; sew and cut off excess selvedge.

3. To finish, sew within Steek between shaping and main fabric—across base of armhole, curve around corner, and then up to shoulder.
4. Cut away extra stitch columns at edge to leave a narrow sewn selvedge.

Work the Steek with a distinctive stitch pattern, or insert Stitch Column Yarn Markers on either side as a guide. The decreases used for shaping will be cut away with the extra stitch columns.

CHAPTER 5

Casting Off

Casting off is the process by which the stitches are taken off the needle in a secure manner so they will not unravel. In most cases, this also creates the finished, visible edge of the fabric.

The first set of closely related techniques discussed below are those most often used. You should find these familiar and easy to learn, since they are all based on basic stitch techniques. In one way or another, they create an edge with the same structure and appearance as a simple crocheted chain and, in fact, it is possible to use a crochet hook for this purpose. In addition, there are variations of the basic techniques that can be used to join two sets of stitches in the equivalent of a seam, or to attach a border to the edge stitches.

Those in the second group are all sewing techniques, done by drawing yarn through the stitches with a needle. These are less often used and more challenging to do; however, when appropriate, nothing else serves quite as well.

Also, several of these techniques make it possible to match the appearance of the cast-off and cast-on edges, which is ideal for items like a scarf or a blanket.

Chained Cast-Offs

There is but one Chained Cast-Off, but there are several ways to make the same edge. The only criteria for choosing among the different methods is to find which one is comfortable for you to do and produces the best result in your hands. In addition, there are some variations of the basic technique that can be used to adjust the width of the edge to make it more compatible with the fabric, and a few of them are quietly decorative.

In most cases, a cast-off is done as you work the last row of stitches, either on the inside or outside of the fabric, in plain Knit or Purl, or in a more complex stitch pattern. However, the characteristics of the last row will have an effect on the appearance of the edge, and you may want to adjust your method of working to achieve the result you want; for more information, see General Tips for Chained Cast-Offs, below.

Also note that it is not necessary, nor often advisable, to use the same size needle for the cast-off as was used for the fabric itself. The size of the needle held in the right hand determines the size of the stitches in the finished edge and, therefore, its width and its relative stability or resilience. To guarantee that you will make an edge that is compatible with the fabric, first try several needle sizes by casting off the stitches of a Test Swatch; if the first size you try does not seem suitable, rip the edge out and try a different one.

Pullover Chained Cast-Off, described first, is the fundamental technique, and the "pullover" step that gives it its name is merely a way of pulling one stitch through another so it cannot unravel; the variations of the basic technique that follow may have different ways of accomplishing the same thing, but the results will be much the same.

For all of these techniques, when you have cast off all but one stitch, break the yarn, pull the end through the stitch, and tighten to secure it and keep the edge from unraveling. Should it be necessary to undo a Chained Cast-Off edge, simply free that last stitch, pull on the yarn, and it will "unzip." If you plan to pick up the freed stitches, pull the yarn gently and free only a few stitches at a time so they do not run down before you can get them on the needle.

❖ Basic Chained Cast-Off

The first version of this basic cast-off is by far the most common method used; it employs a Pullover technique to secure the edge (one stitch is pulled over the next and then discarded). The next version makes use of a decrease technique, and the third is done with a crochet hook. These are all different ways of producing the same edge; simply select whichever method you find easiest to use.

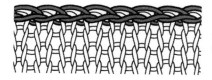

Basic Chained
Cast-Off.

Pullover Chained Cast-Off

The instructions are for working in Knit, but you can use Purl, or a mixture of Knit and Purl, if you prefer, but this will have a subtle affect on the appearance of the edge; see Working in Pattern, below.

1. To begin, Knit first stitch.
2. With one stitch on right needle, Knit 1.
3. With two stitches on right needle, on nearside reach left needle past first stitch, and insert from left to right into second stitch; pull it over first stitch and off needle.

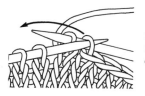

Pullover Chained Cast-Off.
Pull second stitch over first and
discard beneath needle.

4. Repeat Steps 2 and 3 across row; there should never be more than two stitches on right needle. With one stitch remaining, break yarn and secure last stitch.

The stitch pulled over and discarded will encircle the base of the stitch remaining on the right needle. As this is repeated with each stitch in turn, a horizontal chain of stitches will form on the top edge of the fabric.

Decrease Chained Cast-Off

Here is another way to work the same edge; it is also easy to do, and it produces nice, even stitches. Instead of the Pullover technique, however, this version uses the equivalent of the Slip Slip Knit version of a Left Decrease.

Knit Decrease Chained Cast-Off

1. To begin, Slip 1 knitwise.
2. With one stitch on right needle, Slip 1 knitwise.
3. Insert left needle tip from left to right into nearside of two stitches on right needle; wrap yarn as to Knit, lift both stitches over yarn and off needle.
4. Repeat Steps 2 and 3 across row; secure last stitch.

Purl Decrease Chained Cast-Off

The same cast off is much easier to do in Purl; use it when convenient to cast-off on an inside row in Purl, or on the outside, if suitable.

1. To begin, Purl 2 together.
2. Return new stitch to left needle; Purl returned stitch and next stitch together.
3. Repeat Step 2 across row; with one stitch remaining on right needle, break yarn and pull through stitch to secure.

Crochet Chained Cast-Off

You can create exactly the same edge holding a crochet hook in your right hand.

1. To begin, Slip first stitch from left needle to hook.
2. Slip 1 stitch. There are now two stitches on hook.
3. Hook yarn and draw through both stitches. One new stitch remains on hook.
4. Repeat Steps 2 and 3 across row; secure last stitch, as above.

For a slightly quicker way to do the same thing, begin as above, and then with one stitch on hook:

- Insert hook into first stitch on needle as to Knit or Purl, wrap yarn on hook, and draw through stitch on needle and stitch on hook with a single, smooth motion.

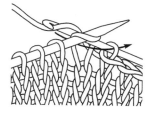

Crochet Chained Cast-Off.
Draw yarn through stitch on
needle and stitch on hook.

❖ Pullover Chained Cast-Off Variations

The following variations of the basic Pullover Chained Cast-Off technique, above, provide the means to control how even the edge is, to adjust its width in relation to the fabric, or to add a decorative touch.

Suspended Chained Cast-Off

This method of working a chained edge is a little more awkward to do, but you might want to try it if you have trouble making a consistent edge. The trick is to retain the pulled-over stitch on the left needle while working the next stitch. This not only helps to make the stitches more even, but enlarges them slightly so the edge will not be too tight. The technique is relatively easy to work in either Knit or Purl.

Knit Suspended Chained Cast-Off

1. To begin, Knit first stitch.
2. With one stitch on right needle, Knit 1.
3. With two stitches on right needle, pull second stitch over first, but do not discard; retain this stitch on left needle tip.
4. Tighten remaining stitch on right needle, and then move needle tip to nearside, past suspended stitch, and Knit next stitch on left needle; discard that stitch and suspended stitch together.

Knit Suspended Chained Cast-Off: Step 4. Hold pulled-over stitch on left needle.

5. Repeat Steps 2–4 across row. When two stitches remain on right needle, pull second over first; secure last stitch.

Purl Suspended Chained Cast-Off

1. To begin, Purl first stitch.
2. With one stitch on right needle, Purl 1.
3. With two stitches on right needle, pull second stitch over first, but do not discard; retain this stitch on left needle tip.
4. Tighten remaining stitch on right needle, and then move needle tip to nearside, past suspended stitch; Purl second stitch on left needle; discard that stitch and suspended stitch from left needle together.
5. Repeat Steps 2–4 across row. When two stitches remain on right needle, pull second over first; secure last stitch.

Purl Suspended Chained Cast-Off: Step 3. Hold pulled-over stitch on left needle.

Picot Chained Cast-Off

This technique is worked like a Pullover Chained Cast-Off, but has an additional stitch inserted between each one pulled over. This creates a tiny eyelet effect along the edge that you might use to add a decorative note, to add more stretch to an edge that requires it (such as a sock top), or to add extra length to an edge to accommodate the contour of a scalloped or indented pattern. Aside from being decorative, the openings are also very accommodating if you want to attach fringe.

Knit Picot Chained Cast-Off

1. To begin, Knit first stitch.
2. Knit 1; with two stitches on right needle, pull second over first as for Pullover Chained Cast-Off, above.
3. On nearside, insert left needle into remaining stitch on right needle, wrap yarn and re-Knit stitch.
4. Repeat Steps 2–3 across row; secure last stitch.

If you need more ease and larger Eyelets, work twice into the stitch in Step 3.

If it is only additional stretch that is required, and the Eyelet is not desirable or simply too large, the effect can be minimized by working with a smaller needle in the right hand.

Crochet Picot Chained Cast-Off

It is really easiest to do this variation using a crochet hook.

- Work as for for Crochet Chained Cast-Off, but chain one extra stitch between each cast-off step.

Of course, once you have the hook in hand, all sorts of decorative crochet edges become possible and there is no reason to stop with a simple chain such as this.

Yarnover Chained Cast-Off

This method is used only to add extra length to an edge, and does not change its appearance. While it is effective, it seems to me you can achieve the same result with less trouble by using a larger needle when casting off. However, if you do not have one at hand, this will do the trick.

Knit Yarnover Chained Cast-Off

Work as for Pullover Chained Cast-Off.

- To begin, Knit first stitch. With one stitch on right needle, Yarnover, Knit 1, pull right stitch and Yarnover over left stitch together and discard.

As you will see, the Yarnovers initially protrude from the edge in an unsightly way; however, if you stretch the edge out to encourage adjacent stitches to absorb all the extra yarn from each Yarnover, the stitches in the cast-off edge will enlarge. Alternatively, leave the Yarnover strands the way they are and use the strands as a base for adding fringe.

Crochet Yarnover Chained Cast-Off

1. To begin, Slip 1 stitch from left needle to hook, wrap yarn, and draw through stitch.
2. With one stitch on hook, wrap yarn on hook to make equivalent of a Yarnover.
3. Slip 1 stitch from left needle to hook, wrap yarn, and draw through slipped stitch. There are now three stitches on hook—two stitches flanking a Yarnover.

4. Wrap yarn on hook and draw through all three stitches.

5. Repeat Steps 2–4 to complete cast-off; secure last stitch.

Slip Chained Cast-Off

With this version of a Pullover Chained Cast-Off, the stitches are not worked prior to the Pullover step. The result is a very consistent, precise edge. As it is normally done, the edge is also very stable and inelastic, which is why the technique is most often used for buttonholes or a shoulder line, where these characteristics are desirable.

However, it is possible to make the edge more resilient and compatible with almost any fabric, and then it is the consistency of the stitches that becomes its most desirable quality.

The cast-off is worked in two stages. First, the larger needle is used to work one row; it acts as a gauge to measure off a precise amount of yarn for each of the new stitches. On the next row, the stitches are cast off, but they are not worked when this is done; therefore, they will remain the size they were when made on the previous row (because the stitches are not worked, needle size does not matter for the second step). A needle one or two sizes larger than that used for the pattern of the fabric is usually sufficient, but it is a good idea to try the cast-off on a Test Swatch before working the edge on your fabric; if the first attempt is not satisfactory, try a needle one size smaller or larger. The structure of the edge is exactly the same as any other Chained Cast-Off, however, because of the way it is made, it will not unravel as easily; it is necessary to pick each stitch free of the next one.

Basic Slip Chained Cast-Off

1. With circular or double-point needle of larger size held in right hand, work last row of fabric in pattern.
   - If working flat, do not turn; drop yarn and slide stitches to opposite needle tip.
   - If working circular, drop yarn and simply continue with first stitch of next row.
2. To begin cast-off, Slip first stitch of row knitwise.
3. With one stitch on right needle, Slip 1 knitwise; with two stitches on right needle, pull right stitch over left and discard. Repeat across row; secure last stitch.

Crochet Slip Chained Cast-Off

This edge is also easy to do with a crochet hook. First work the preparatory row on the larger size knitting needle as described in Step 1, above, and then hold a crochet hook in your right hand and work the Pullover step as follows:

1. Preliminary step to begin cast-off: Slip 1 stitch to hook knitwise.

2. With one stitch on hook, Slip next stitch knitwise, and draw it through stitch on hook in one motion. Repeat across row; there will never be more than one stitch on hook. Secure last stitch.

Double Slip Chained Cast-Off

Here is a decorative variation that produces a double chain along the edge.

- Work one row of Horizontal Chain Stitch, followed by Slip Chained Cast-Off.

❖ General Tips for Chained Cast-Offs

Here are several suggestions for working a Chained Cast-Off that will help refine the edge. There is a discussion of the interaction between the cast-off edge and the last row of your stitch pattern, some additional tips for how to adjust the width of the edge, and how to neaten up the corners and finish off the last stitch.

Working in Pattern

The characteristics of the stitches discarded into the fabric as you cast off will affect the appearance of the edge in subtle, but significant ways; it is important to take this into consideration if the edge will remain visible.

- If the last row or two is in Stockinette, a Chained Cast-Off edge will tilt toward the Knit side, obscuring the last row of stitches. If you want it to remain visible and the edge to be less obvious, work the cast-off in Knit on the inside of the fabric, or in Purl on the outside.
- If the last rows are a mixture of Knit and Purl, the chain of cast-off stitches will ride along the top of the edge, and the stitches in the row below will be more visible on the outside.
- If the pattern in the last row of the fabric contains complex stitch techniques that might cause irregularities in the edge or make the cast-off difficult to do, work the cast-off on a plain row instead. Or, work the last row in pattern, and then use Slip Chained Cast-Off.

Adjusting Width of Edge

It is important to make the edge compatible with the fabric, so it is neither constricted nor splayed out; the most common problem is that it is too tight.

- To ensure that the stitches are large enough and are all of an even size, tighten the yarn firmly while you still have both needles inserted into the stitch during the Pullover step. At this point the stitch will be slightly enlarged and the needles will prevent you from tightening the stitches too much.
- As an alternative to changing the size of the needle held

in your right hand, you can increase or decrease the stitch count slightly prior to casting off. Use whichever shaping techniques blend in best with your stitch or color pattern (see Increases and Decreases), and distribute them evenly across the width of the fabric, either as you cast off or on the row below; see Horizontal Shaping in the chapter Calculations for Pattern Design.

Corner Selvedge Stitches

On a flat fabric, the selvedge stitches at the corner of a cast-off edge can be problematic since they tend to enlarge, and become unsightly. If the fabric is seamed, these corner stitches will be hidden on the inside, but if the edge will be visible, it is best to neaten them up as much as possible. Here are a few tips that will help.

The First Stitch

- If you are using a Chain Selvedge, work the first stitch of the cast-off row instead of slipping it. Then, before you work the next stitch, use the left needle to pull up on the new stitch, drawing yarn out of the selvedge stitch below it; retighten the stitch on the right needle and begin casting off.

The Last Stitch

The last stitch is the worst offender. The movement of the needle as you work across the last row tends to enlarge this stitch at the expense of those next to it. Here are several suggestions for how to tighten it up, listed in order of my preferences as to which ones work best.

- If you have used a Chain Selvedge, work the first stitch of the row *prior* to the cast-off row instead of slipping it; maintain a firm tension on the yarn as you work this stitch and the next one.
- Slip Chained Cast-Off makes it easy to control the size of the last stitch because it will be the one with the yarn attached, and it can then be snugged down very neatly.
- Alternatively, with one stitch remaining on the left needle, pick up the running thread and work a Running Thread Increase, or Twisted Running Thread Increase. Work the last stitch, and then pull the two stitches to the right over the last one worked.

  Working into the running thread draws yarn out of the following selvedge stitch, which helps to tighten it up. While this can leave a tiny gap below the increase, it is usually hidden by the chain edge.
- You may encounter the suggestion to work a Right Decrease on the last two stitches, but this pulls the corner in at an angle and does not really tighten up the last stitch.

I do not think it is as successful as any one of the suggestions above.

- If all else fails, and you still have an unsightly left corner, take a needle tip and work yarn out of the selvedge stitch and into the adjacent stitches in the rows below the cast-off edge. Start by tugging up on the running threads that go into and out of the selvedge stitch, and then gently ease the extra yarn into the fabric nearby, making the stitches as even as possible.

Securing the Last Stitch

After the cast-off is complete, the last stitch is normally secured by drawing the yarn through it; however, this can be unsightly on a visible edge. To finish it more neatly, thread the end of the yarn into a sewing needle and work in one of the following ways before hiding the tail on the inside (see Hiding Ends of Yarn).

Finishing Flat Fabric Edge

The idea here is to use the end of yarn to duplicate the appearance of the top selvedge stitch at the corner.

1. Complete cast-off and break off yarn, leaving 10 to 12 inches; draw end of yarn up through last stitch and thread into sewing needle.
2. Pass sewing needle from nearside to farside behind both strands of second selvedge stitch below corner, and draw yarn through.
3. Pass sewing needle back down through last cast-off stitch.
4. Hide yarn end within selvedge or on inside of fabric in the usual way.

If you do not have a sewing needle at hand, you can do this with a crochet hook as well.

Finishing Circular Fabric Edge

This technique is used to duplicate the appearance of a cast-off stitch that joins the end of the edge to the beginning.

1. Break yarn and pull through last stitch, as above; thread yarn through sewing needle or use crochet hook.
2. Insert sewing needle under both sides of first cast-off stitch, and then down into center of last cast-off stitch, coming out on inside of fabric.
3. Hide yarn end on inside of fabric in usual way.

Finishing a Circular Fabric Edge. Duplicate the shape of a stitch to close the gap.

Specialized Cast-Offs

The following variations of the basic Chained Cast-Off technique are used when something more than a plain edge is needed. Two of them can be used to create a sloped edge, and several others can be used to simultaneously cast off and seam two edges together.

❖ *Sloped Cast-Off Edges*

Several areas of a garment require sloped edges, such as shoulders, necklines, or the top of sleeve caps. The traditional way to make a slope of this kind is to use Stepped Cast-Off. For this technique, the total number of stitches to be cast off is divided into small groups called "steps," each of which requires two rows to complete. Details on how to develop a pattern of this kind can be found in Steps and Points, and also in Charting an Acute Slope.

Unfortunately, there is a good reason why this is called Stepped Cast-Off, because the way the technique is normally done leaves a definite jog between each step. While an edge of this kind is usually absorbed either by a seam or picked-up stitches and will not be visible, the method discussed here smooths out the turning points between the steps and makes a slope that is no more difficult to do, easier to seam, and nice enough to be on display. For an even smoother edge, however, see the Short Row Sloped Edge, below.

Stepped Cast-Off

For an edge that slopes up to the left (as seen on the outside of the fabric), start on the outside of the fabric; for one that slopes up to the right, start on the inside. Maintain the stitch pattern as best you can as you work.

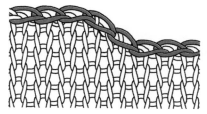

Stepped Cast-Off.

1. Slip first stitch of step knitwise, Knit 1, pull Slip stitch over and discard; continue with Chained Cast-Off until last stitch of step remains on right needle; do not cast it off. Continue in pattern to end of row, turn.
2. Work back across next row until two stitches remain on left needle.
   If on outside, work a Knit Right Decrease.
   If on inside, work a Purl Left Decrease. Turn.
3. Repeat Steps 1 and 2 for next step; continue in this way until all steps have been cast off.

Two things about these instructions help ensure a smooth slope.

- Using a Slip stitch at the beginning of each step smooths the transition between two steps.
- Working the correct decrease at the turning point makes it slant in the same direction as the slope of the edge.

Short Row Sloped Edge

A technique called Short Rows can also be used to create a slope, but it is done within the fabric, and the slope is completed before you reach the last row and are ready to cast off; the result is a very smooth and even edge, with no awkward steps in sight. However, Short Rows can be more challenging to do than a Stepped Cast-off and can also interfere with stitch or color patterns; both techniques have merit, so decide which one to use based on the circumstances.

❖ *Joinery Cast-Off*

This technique is a combination of Joinery Decreases and Pullover Chained Cast-Off and it makes it possible to join the stitches of two separate garment sections and cast off simultaneously. The method is very easy to do and the result is a seam with the stitch columns of the two fabrics lined up perfectly, head to head, with a single, slim chain of cast-off stitches on the inside. It has moderate resilience, and, when worked firmly, provides good support for areas such as shoulders. If the garment design requires a sloped edge, this is done first with Short Rows.

Joinery Cast-Off Seam.

Basic Joinery Cast-Off

The two fabrics to be joined are both worked to the row below the cast-off edge and then positioned face-to-face. Pairs of stitches, one from each fabric, are first linked with a simple decrease, done as to Knit or as to Purl, and the resulting new stitches are then cast off. As for any Chained Cast-Off, you can control the size of the stitches in the edge, and therefore its relative stability or elasticity, by holding a larger or smaller needle in the right hand as you work.

To work this cast-off, hold the needles bearing the stitches of the two fabrics parallel in your left hand, with the outside faces of the fabrics together and the inside faces visible nearside and farside. Line up the tips of the needles and have at least one of the yarns available at the right side, preferably on the near needle. Continue as follows:

Knit Joinery Cast-Off

1. Insert right needle as to Knit into first stitch on near needle, and then into first stitch on far needle; Knit Two Together as for a Right Decrease (stitch on near needle must be left stitch of decrease pair).
2. With one stitch on right needle, Knit next pair of stitches together as in Step 1.
3. With two stitches on right needle, pull second stitch over first as for Pullover Chained Cast-Off, leaving one stitch on needle.
4. Repeat Steps 2–3 to complete cast off.

Purl Joinery Cast-Off

I find this version slightly easier to do; the result will be the same.

• Work as above, but in Step 1 insert right needle as to Purl into first stitch on far needle, and then into first stitch on near needle; Purl Two Together as for the Purl version of a Right Decrease.

Purl Joinery Cast-Off.

Crochet Joinery Cast-Off

It is also easy to do a Joinery Cast-Off with a crochet hook.

1. Insert hook from left to right into first stitch on near needle, and then into first stitch on far needle; catch yarn and draw through both stitches, and discard them from left needles.
2. With one stitch on hook, work next pair of stitches together on left needles as in Step 1.
3. With two stitches on hook, draw left one through right one (do not wrap yarn on hook).
4. Repeat Steps 2–3 to cast off.

Single Needle Joinery Cast-Off

If you have trouble working with the stitches on two needles, first intersperse them on a single circular or double-point needle that is at least one size smaller, and then cast off.

To transfer the stitches, hold the two needles bearing the stitches in your left hand, positioned as described above, and a double-point needle or circular needle in your right hand.

1. Slip one stitch from far needle, and then one from near needle; stitch from near needle is left stitch of each pair slipped. Continue alternating one stitch from each needle until all are interspersed on right needle.
2. Transfer needle now bearing stitches to left hand and slide stitches so supply of yarn is at needle tip.
3. Begin Joinery Cast-Off, working each pair of stitches with a Right Decrease; with two stitches on right needle, work Pullover step, as described above.

Reverse Joinery Cast-Off

For a very handsome, decorative effect, work Joinery Cast-Off so the horizontal chain of stitches is visible on the outside of the garment.

Reverse Joinery Cast-Off. Seam turned to outside.

• Place *inside* faces of fabric together and cast off as described above.
• Also, consider casting off with a yarn in a contrast color, or alternatively, work the last row on each fabric in a contrast color, and then cast off with either that yarn or the main yarn, or use the Slip Joinery technique, below.

Slip Joinery Cast-Off

This variation is done using Slip Chained Cast-Off, and offers the same advantages. Because of the perfection of the edge, it is particularly attractive when turned to the outside of the garment, as described in Reverse Joinery Cast-Off, above.

This approach can make a very firm join, with little or no stretch. To provide more ease, work the last row of one fabric with a larger needle; only the stitches of one fabric will form the chained edge so there is no need to do this with both. Try this on a pair of Test Swatches to find the appropriate needle size.

Hold the needles bearing the stitches in your left hand; if you have enlarged one set of stitches, hold the needle bearing those stitches on the farside, and the one with the normal-size stitches on the nearside. Slide both sets of stitches to the tip of the needle *opposite* where the yarn is attached, and work as follows:

Basic Slip Joinery Cast-Off

1. Insert right needle knitwise into first stitch on near needle, and then into first stitch on far needle; Slip these two stitches together to right needle (do not work them). Pull right stitch (belonging to fabric on near needle) over left.
2. With one stitch on right needle, Slip next pair of stitches to right needle as in Step 1.
3. With three stitches on right needle, pull middle stitch over stitch to left.
4. With two stitches on right needle, pull right one over left one.
5. Repeat Steps 2–4 across row until one stitch remains; draw yarn through to secure.

Slip Joinery Cast-Off with Crochet Hook

Hold two needles parallel in your left hand and a crochet hook in your right hand; hold yarn on your left forefinger.

- Work as above, but in Step 1, pull left stitch through right stitch as it is slipped from left needle; work Step 2, and then combine Steps 3 and 4, pulling left stitch through other two stitches.

Two-Row Slip Joinery Cast-Off

- Work all decreases to join two sets of stitches on one row; on next row use Slip Chained Cast-Off.

Joinery Cast-Off for Ribbing

To join two sections of ribbing, it is necessary to plan ahead so the columns of Knit and Purl stitches line up properly.

For instance, if you establish a Single Rib with a Knit/Purl sequence on an even number of stitches, the first stitch of every row will be a Knit and the last stitch of every row will be a Purl.

When this is done on both fabrics, and they are positioned with the outside faces of the fabrics together for joining, the last Purl stitch of one section will be facing the first Knit stitch of the other section. The same would be true for a Double Rib, with a Knit 2/Purl 2 sequence.

To line up the columns of stitches in both fabrics, Knit-to-Knit and Purl-to-Purl, there are two options:

Joinery Cast-Off for Single Rib

- Work on an even number of stitches, and start one fabric Knit/Purl, and the other Purl/Knit. Same type of stitch will be on right side of one fabric, left side of other, and they will face each other when joined.
- Or, work on uneven number of stitches so first and last stitch of both fabrics are the same; Knit 1/Purl 1 across row, ending with Knit 1.

Joinery Cast-Off for Double Rib

- Begin one fabric Knit 2/Purl 2, and begin the other Purl 2/Knit 2.
- Alternatively, use a pattern multiple of four plus two, so the sequence on both fabrics is Knit 2/Purl 2 across the row, ending with Knit 2.

Although it is important to line up the columns of Knit and Purl stitches, it is not necessary to maintain the ribbing pattern while casting off; use either all Knit Two Together or all Purl Two Together; it will make no difference in the outcome.

Joinery Cast-Off for Side Seams

Joinery Cast-Off is also an excellent method to use to join the seams of a garment worked from side to side.

1. Use Stranded Provisional Cast-On or Alternating Provisional Cast-On to start first side edge; work garment section and at other side edge place stitches on holder, leave on cable of circular needle, or use Stranded Cast-Off.
2. To assemble garment, place two sets of side stitches on separate needles with outside faces of fabric together and use Joinery Cast-Off; repeat with second set of stitches on other side of garment.

If you want to work the sleeve as one with the body, see Side or Mid-Fabric Cast-Ons for how to add the stitches needed using one of the techniques mentioned in Step 1.

Also consider using Reverse Joinery Cast-Off to turn the seam to the outside as a decorative element.

This technique can also be used for dolman sleeves, which are cast on at each side of a bodice worked up from lower edge. Use a Provisional Cast-On as in Step 1, above, to add all the stitches at once, and then use Short Rows to slope the edge; repeat the Short Row pattern at the other edge before joining the two sets of stitches to seam the sleeve.

Sewn Cast-Offs

The cast-off techniques discussed here are done with sewing techniques rather than knitting, and three of them are important to know about. The first, Stranded Cast-Off, like its mate Stranded Cast-On, is utilitarian and not used for a visible edge; Double Stranded Cast-Off is a variation that is useful for gathering an edge. For something like a shawl or scarf, where both ends will be visible, Half-Hitch Cast-Off provides a means of duplicating the appearance and structure of a Half-Hitch Cast-On edge; Backstitch Cast-Off is less often used, but it makes a nice edge and is worth knowing about. And, finally, Grafted Cast-Off is an ideal technique for ribbings, where it is important to preserve elasticity; it creates an "invisible" edge equivalent to Alternating Cast-On.

Most of these are relatively slow to work and require some practice in order to produce a good result. However, in situations where an edge of this kind is appropriate, the outcome is well worth the extra effort required.

First, here are some suggestions for how to work.

❖ *General Tips for Sewn Cast-Offs*

- Use a blunt needle with a large eye, suitable for working with yarn; these are often called tapestry needles; see Tools. To thread the needle, wrap the yarn around the eye of the needle and pinch it in place as tightly as possible. Draw the pinched end off the needle and push the doubled yarn through the eye; extend the loop to pull the end through. Allow an end long enough to hide during finishing.

- Be careful not to split the yarn of a stitch with the needle; the result will be untidy and difficult to correct; make it a habit to wiggle the needle slightly while it is inside the stitch to make sure it has cleared. Maintain a gentle, even tension as you pull the yarn through the stitches, and stretch the edge out from time to time to make sure you are not making the edge too tight or too loose. Check frequently, since it can be tedious to correct a problem once you have gone too far.

- Sewn techniques present a problem because the entire length of yarn must be pulled through each stitch and may begin to fray. Yarns that are highly textured or softly spun can be particularly difficult to manage, and some may be impossible to use at all for this purpose. In some cases it may be best to use an entirely different and more suitable yarn; you can also turn challenge into opportunity and consider a contrast color to add a decorative touch.

- If you plan to use a separate strand of yarn for casting off, allow a 10- to 12-inch tail to weave in later and thread sewing needle. Hold tail on inside of fabric, insert sewing needle up into Purl nub below first stitch on needle, pass yarn over knitting needle, and then pass sewing needle down through same Purl nub below; yarn should duplicate path of first stitch so it contains two strands instead of one. Begin casting off.

- If you are working with a yarn that begins to thin and weaken, it is best to abandon that strand and start a new

one. However, with every new strand introduced there will be two ends of yarn to hide during finishing; see Hiding Ends of Yarn. Done neatly on the inside, right below the cast-off edge, they should not be apparent nor will these changes restrain the edge in any way.

❖ *Basic Sewn Cast-Offs*

Here are three very elementary techniques that you can use for a sewn cast-off edge. None are attractive, but they are useful, particularly the first.

Stranded Cast-Off matches Stranded Cast-On, and, like that technique, it produces a completely unrestrained edge, which makes it ideal for gauge swatches. It is also frequently used as a temporary stitch holder or as a gathering strand—for instance, at the top of a stocking cap—although Double Stranded Cast-Off (the second technique here) may be a better choice.

The third technique, Backstitch Cast-Off, does not resemble any cast-on technique, but it is easy to do and is rather attractive.

There is little abrasion of the yarn with any of these techniques, and there should be no problem using the yarn you are knitting with unless it is highly textured.

Stranded Cast-Off

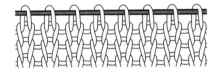

Stranded Cast-Off Edge.

1. Measure length of yarn equal to width of fabric, plus a 10- to 20-inch allowance; thread yarn in sewing needle.
2. Slip stitches directly from knitting needle to sewing needle one or two at a time; with a small group of stitches on sewing needle, draw yarn through and repeat.

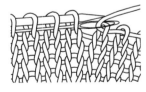

Stranded Cast-Off: Step 2. Thread yarn through stitches on left needle.

If you plan to use this technique as a temporary stitch holder, a firm, smooth yarn or cord in a contrast color will be easy both to see and to remove when the time comes to free the stitches and pick them up again.

Double Stranded Cast-Off

While this technique isn't attractive enough to serve as a visible edge, it often works a bit better than Stranded Cast-Off for gathering, since it pulls the stitches together more evenly and tends to hold the edge better.

Allow a length of yarn one and a half times the width of the fabric, thread sewing needle, and work as follows:

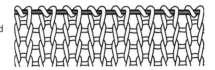

Double Stranded Cast-Off Edge.

1. On nearside, insert sewing needle into first two stitches on nearside from right to left, as to Purl.
2. Draw yarn through and drop first stitch from knitting needle.

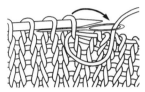

Double Stranded Cast-Off: Steps 1 and 2. Thread yarn through two stitches, discard one.

3. Repeat across row, always inserting needle into two stitches and dropping one.
4. Pass yarn a second time through last stitch to secure.

Backstitch Cast-Off

Backstitch Cast-Off Edge.

1. On nearside, insert sewing needle from right to left through nearside of first two stitches as to Purl; draw yarn through.
2. Insert sewing needle into first stitch as to Knit and draw yarn through; drop stitch from needle.

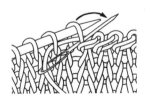

Backstitch Cast-Off: Step 2. Work first stitch again, and then discard.

3. Repeat Steps 1 and 2 across row.

❖ Half-Hitch Cast-Off

This cast-off technique provides a perfect match for Half-Hitch Cast-On in both appearance and structure, and is just as versatile. The edge can be done as for Knit or Purl, on the inside or outside of the fabric.

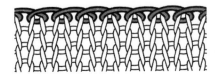

Knit Half-Hitch Cast-Off Edge.

To decide how much yarn you will need for the edge, see the method described in Yarn Allowance for Finger Cast-Ons, which serves equally well for casting off. (If you are really organized and have inordinate amounts of foresight, you will write that figure down when you are casting on, knowing that you will need it later for casting off.) Measure from the last stitch worked, leave an allowance, break the yarn at that point, and thread the end through a sewing needle.

Knit Half-Hitch Cast-Off

1. On nearside, insert sewing needle into second stitch on left needle as to Knit and pass sewing needle under knitting needle and out of stitch on farside. Draw yarn through stitch and tighten gently, pulling first two stitches together side by side.

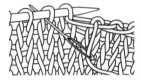

Knit Half-Hitch Cast-Off: Step 1. Work second Knit stitch.

2. On nearside, insert sewing needle into first stitch as to Purl. Draw yarn through stitch and tighten gently; drop first stitch from knitting needle.

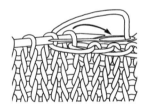

Knit Half-Hitch Cast-Off: Step 2. Work first Knit stitch again, and then discard.

3. Repeat Steps 1 and 2 across row.
4. With one stitch remaining on knitting needle, insert sewing needle into stitch as in Step 1, above, and then back under strand that runs between this stitch and preceding one. Tighten to form a Slip Knot.

Purl Half-Hitch Cast-Off

1. Bring yarn under needle tip to farside. Insert sewing needle into second stitch on left needle from farside as to Purl; pass sewing needle under knitting needle and out of stitch on nearside. Draw yarn through stitch and tighten gently to pull first two stitches together side by side.
2. Insert sewing needle into first stitch as to Knit. Draw yarn through stitch and tighten gently; drop first stitch from knitting needle.
3. Repeat Steps 1 and 2 across row.
4. With one stitch remaining on knitting needle, insert sewing needle as in Step 1, above, and then under strand that runs between this stitch and preceding one. Draw yarn through and tighten gently.

❖ *Grafted Cast-Off for Ribbing*

To preserve the elasticity of a ribbed edge, such as at a neckline, the wrist of a sleeve worked from top down, or for the tops of socks or mittens worked from tip to cuff, you can use a variation of the Grafting technique as a sewn cast off.

Grafting is commonly used to join two fabrics, but for this application the result is a rounded edge that looks like Knit stitches—it is identical to Alternating Cast-On. As with that technique, this approach is ideal for a Single Rib or for a Double-Fabric, and it also works well for a Double Rib.

Because the technique replicates the form and size of the stitches, it is necessary to calculate the length of yarn needed. If you had the foresight to calculate the figure for stitches per yard when developing the Stitch Gauge, you will have no trouble deciding how much is required to graft the edge. If not, you can safely use a variation of the method for determining how much yarn to allow for a tail when casting on (see Yarn Allowance for Finger Cast-Ons), but measure the amount of yarn used for the stitches, not the amount used for the half-hitches in the edge. And it is always better to have too much than too little, so add a bit extra.

The grafting can be done with the stitches on the needle, which is safest, or off the needle, which makes it somewhat easier to see what you are doing, but you take the risk that stitches will unravel.

Grafted Edge for Single Rib

There are two ways to graft an edge with the stitches on the needle, and the basic version is described first. If you have trouble making a nice, even edge when working this way, there are two alternatives that involve transferring the stitches to a pair of needles in order to separate the Knits and Purls. I find one of them a decided improvement over the normal way of doing this, but the result will be the same regardless of how you work, so choose the method you find easiest to manage.

Always sew into each stitch twice before dropping it from the needle. Pass yarn under needle tip, not over it, to change from working farside or nearside.

Grafted
Single Rib Edge.

One-Needle Grafted Edge

These instructions are for grafting an edge for a Single Rib fabric that begins with a Knit Stitch. Sew through every stitch twice before dropping it from the needle, and as you work, always pass the yarn under the needle tips to move the yarn from nearside to farside or vice versa, never over the needle. Thread sewing needle with yarn and work as follows:

1. On nearside, insert sewing needle into first Knit stitch from right to left as to Purl and draw yarn through; do not discard stitch.

2. From farside, insert sewing needle between first Knit and Purl, and then into Purl stitch as to Knit; draw needle and yarn through toward farside.

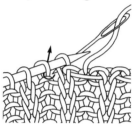

Grafted Cast-Off: Step 2.
Working Purl stitch as
to Knit.

3. On nearside, insert sewing needle into first Knit stitch from left to right as to Knit; draw yarn through and drop stitch from needle. Adjust size of last stitch made to match others in grafted edge. A Purl stitch is now first on left needle.

Grafted Cast-Off: Step 3.
Working Knit stitch.

4. On nearside, insert sewing needle into next Knit stitch from right to left, as to Purl; draw yarn through.

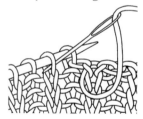

Grafted Cast-Off: Step 4.
Working Knit stitch as
to Purl.

5. On nearside, insert sewing needle into first Purl stitch from right to left, as to Purl; draw yarn through and drop stitch from needle. Adjust size of last stitch made to match others in grafted edge. A Knit stitch is now first on left needle.

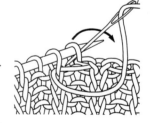

Grafted Cast-Off: Step 5.
Working Purl stitch.

6. Repeat Steps 2–5 to cast off.

The maneuver in Step 2 is a little tricky—pass the sewing needle under the knitting needle from the farside, move the tip around the side of the Purl stitch, and then back through the center of the stitch to the farside.

Basically this is a four stitch "repeat" pattern—sew two stitches as to Knit and discard one; sew the next two stitches as to Purl and discard one. If you want a little refrain to help you remember how to work, try:

- Knit-Knit-Discard, Purl-Purl-Discard.

Because you will be sewing into each stitch twice, here is another way to remember the pattern:

- Sew into a Knit stitch the first time as to Purl, the second time as to Knit.
- Sew into a Purl stitch the first time as to Knit, the second time as to Purl.

Two-Needle Grafted Edge

With this method, first transfer the stitches to two double-point needles, one for the Knits, the other for the Purls. Re-arranged in this way, the work will resemble a Double-Fabric, with the Knit side of all the stitches facing out, half on the nearside, half on the farside. To put it another way, it is as if you were holding two fabrics together, ready to be joined by Grafting them together and, in fact, it works exactly the same.

To Transfer Stitches

Use needles at least one size smaller to hold transferred stitches; they will tighten up when divided between the two and this makes them easier to handle.

1. Hold needle bearing stitches in left hand, and hold two double-point needles parallel in right hand.
2. Alternate slipping a Knit stitch to near needle, and a Purl stitch to far needle; repeat to transfer all stitches.
3. Slide stitches to tips of needles so yarn is at right side.

To Graft Stitches

Calculate yarn length needed and thread sewing needle.

1. On nearside, insert sewing needle into first Knit stitch from right to left, as to Purl; do not discard stitch.
2. On farside, insert sewing needle into first Purl stitch from left to right, as to Knit. Draw yarn through.
3. On nearside, insert sewing needle into first Knit from left to right, as to Knit. Draw yarn through and drop stitch from needle.
4. On nearside, insert sewing needle into next Knit stitch from right to left, as to Purl; draw yarn through.
5. On farside, insert sewing needle into first Purl stitch from right to left, as to Purl. Draw yarn through and drop stitch from needle.
6. Repeat Steps 2–5.

When you drop the stitch from the left needle in Steps 3 and 5, draw the yarn up to neaten the last grafted stitch and make it the same size as the previous ones.

Circular Needle Grafted Edge

Here is another way to work, and it has become my favorite because it is easier to make a neat, even edge. Instead of a pair of double-point needles, use two circular needles.

1. Transfer stitches as described above, Knits on one needle, Purls on other. Draw needle tips out so all stitches rest on cables.
2. Follow instructions for Two-Needle Version, above; however, in this case, always draw yarn from one stitch to next over cables; leave all stitches on cables until grafting is complete.

Use circular needles in a very small size so they can be drawn out of the edge easily after it is complete. Even if you are grafting a small edge, use long circular needles; it helps if the tips are dangling well out of the way so they do not catch the sewing yarn as you work.

For a circular fabric, transfer one-half of the stitches to the pair of circular needles, do the Grafted Cast-Off on those; then transfer the other half of the stitches to the circular needles, and repeat.

When working this way, it can be more difficult to insert the needle the second time into a stitch; if necessary, pull down on the fabric to enlarge the stitch.

Off-Needle Grafted Edge

It is also possible to graft the edge with the stitches off the needle; however, the risk of splitting a stitch or having one run down is high. Nevertheless, you may prefer to work this way when dealing with a well-behaved yarn, or if you do not have double-point needles available. This also makes it easier to see what path the yarn should take and to make all the stitches the same size. To be on the safe side, however, remove the stitches in small groups from the needle, instead of all at once.

Once off the needles, the Knits and Purls will separate, the Knits tilting toward the nearside, the Purls tilting toward the farside, leaving a little channel in between. You will be looking down into the channel as you work, where all you will see are the Purl nubs of both sets of stitches.

First sew a pair of stitches on the nearside of the channel, then sew a pair of stitches on the farside of the channel. Always pass the sewing needle through the first stitch of a pair from the outside to the inside of the channel, and through the second stitch of the pair from the inside to the outside (this forms the running thread between the two stitches); then draw the yarn across the channel to sew the next pair (this forms one side of the new grafted stitch).

1. Remove four to six stitches from needle.
2. Work Pair on Nearside: Insert sewing needle into first stitch from outside to inside of channel and then into next stitch from inside to outside; draw yarn through.

Off-Needle Grafted Cast-Off: Step 2. Working a pair of Knit stitches.

3. Work Pair on Farside: Insert sewing needle into first stitch from outside to inside of channel and then into next stitch from inside to outside; draw yarn through.

Off-Needle Grafted Cast-Off: Step 3. Working a pair of Purl stitches.

4. Adjust length of yarns that cross the channel between pairs to make sewn stitches even; repeat Steps 2 and 3, dropping next group of stitches off needle after completing previous group.

When you take the stitches off the needle, you may find it helpful to pinch the fabric below them with your left thumb and forefinger so they will not unravel as you sew. Also, pull the tip of the knitting needle to the right a bit to prevent any other stitches from falling off.

Here is a little phrase to help you remember the pattern:

• Pair on nearside, into channel and back out; pair on farside, into channel and back out.

Grafted Edge for Double Rib

A Double Rib edge is grafted in much the same way as a Single Rib one; however, because it has a four-stitch repeat of two Knits and two Purls, it is difficult to handle on a single needle. Therefore, it is best to either take the stitches off the needle entirely or place the Knits and Purls on two separate needles. The circular needle method described above is especially useful for this purpose; however, these instructions work equally well for either approach.

Whether the stitches are off the needle, or on two needles, pairs of stitches will separate, one pair tilting toward the nearside, the other away toward the farside, leaving a channel in between where all you will see are the Purl sides of all the stitches.

Grafted Edge for Double Rib.

You will be working into pairs of stitches, two on the nearside, then two on the farside. Because this is Double Rib, and because you will work into each stitch twice, the first time you work into a pair the two stitches will be set close together, but when you work into the next pair on that same side they will be separated by a pair of stitches on the other side.

Each time you work into a pair, the needle should pass into the first stitch from outside to inside and into the second stitch from inside to outside; this makes the equivalent of a running thread between the two. Each stitch will be sewn into twice, and the first stitch of each pair should always have a strand of yarn in it. When you start to work a pair on the other side, the yarn will be drawn across the gap in the middle and this will form one side of a stitch. As you work, adjust the length of yarns that pass across the channel to make the sewn stitches in the edge even.

1. Preliminary step: Remove 6 to 8 stitches from needle. Insert sewing needle into first stitch on nearside from inside to outside; draw yarn through. Then reach past next stitch on nearside and insert sewing needle into first stitch on farside from inside to outside. Continue as follows.
2. Sew nearside pair that is side-by-side.
3. Sew farside pair that is side-by-side.
4. Sew nearside pair that is separated by two stitches on farside.
5. Sew farside pair that is separated by two stitches on nearside.

Grafting a Wide Ribbed Edge

As mentioned above, the yarn is subject to abrasion as it is drawn through each stitch for a sewn cast-off edge, and this is especially the case with softer and more delicate yarns. This is a particular problem with ribbings, which usually have a relatively large number of stitches per inch.

If you see the yarn begin to thin and weaken, it is best to abandon that strand and begin working with a new one. Here is a method you can use to weave the ends into the ribbing; they will be quite hidden on the inside and will not restrain the edge in any way.

Grafting a Wide Ribbed Edge. Weaving in yarns on wide edge.

1. Change yarns after Knit stitch in Single Rib, or between two Purl stitches in Double Rib.
2. Abandon original strand, leaving end of yarn about 8 to 10 inches long hanging on inside of fabric.

3. Pick up new strand, leaving an end of same length on inside, and continue to cast off.

4. To finish each pair of strands left at a yarn change, thread left end into a sewing needle, and then wrap two strands around each other to interlock them. Weave first end down along one side of the column of Knit stitches to left, duplicating path of yarn in stitches.

5. Thread second end into sewing needle, adjust interlock of two yarns at edge as necessary, draw yarn parallel to Purl stitch below cast-off edge, and then weave it down side of Knit column to right as before.

For a Double Rib, the interlock will be between two Purls; weave each strand through an adjacent Purl stitch before hiding end in column of Knit stitches as described above.

CHAPTER 6

Shaping a Fabric

One of the wonderful things about knitted fabrics is how very accommodating they are. A sweater may consist of no more than one large tube for the body and two smaller tubes for the sleeves and serve its purpose quite well; indeed, most traditional garments, many of them very beautiful, are made that way. However, as we all know to our respective despair or delight, a human body does not consist of simple shapes, and the most comfortable garment is undoubtedly one that is designed with our particularities in mind. Furthermore, there is no reason to restrict our sense of style to such severely basic designs, since it is possible to knit far more subtle and complex ones.

The three types of techniques discussed here can be used in various ways to change strictly horizontal or vertical edges into slopes or curves, transform a flat fabric into one with volume, and turn straight tubes into contoured ones. When applied according to the information found in the section on Pattern Design, these tools make it possible to knit custom fitted garments in any style imaginable.

Increases and Decreases are small, simple techniques that are used to change the number of stitches on the needle; as the stitch count changes, the width of the fabric will change as well. The Short Row technique makes it possible to work partial rows, adding more length in some areas of the fabric than in others. This causes the stitch columns and side edges to slope and changes the interior contour of a fabric. Finally, Regauging is a very simple way to change the size of stitches, and thereby the Gauge, and, as a result, it affects both length and width.

Increases and Decreases

The most common and versatile means of shaping a garment consists of the adroit placement of Increases or Decreases, either within the fabric or along the edges. Increases add stitches to those already on the needle, making the fabric wider; Decreases remove them, making it narrower. You will find the detailed instructions for these techniques in the chapters on Increase and Decrease Techniques and Increase and Decrease Stitch Patterns, where their role in various decorative and utilitarian stitch patterns is discussed; the material here focuses entirely on how they are used to change the contour of a fabric.

For this purpose, "shaping units," individual increases or decreases of whatever kind, are positioned according to a pattern developed with the use of the Stitch Gauge and the information found in Calculations for Pattern Design and in Charted Garment Patterns. Shaping units can be arranged vertically, either at a side edge or within the fabric, or distributed horizontally, across one or several rows.

Here are some examples of how shaping of this kind can be used.

❖ *Vertical Shaping*

Nearly every garment is shaped with techniques that are arrayed in a vertical line along the side edge of the fabric (or where seams would otherwise be in a circular fabric), primarily because this is where the change is needed, but also because their presence will be less noticeable there. The edge will take on the shape of a slope or a curve, but the stitch columns within the fabric and the lines of any stitch or color pattern will stay their courses as if nothing has happened. This is the method used to widen a bodice between waist and chest, or a sleeve from wrist to underarm, as well as to slope or curve the opening edge of an armhole or a neckline.

The same kinds of patterns that are used along vertical edges can also be applied within a fabric. This kind of shaping is used to make darts in a fitted bodice, as well as for sock toes or the crown of a hat, and to make the beautiful segmented areas of a contoured lace shawl (see Medallions). When this is done, the result is far more noticeable, because the columns of stitches will converge toward or flow out of the vertical line along which the techniques have been placed.

Vertical Edge Shaping

Shaping techniques placed at the sides of a fabric and distributed over several rows will cause a straight vertical edge to slope or curve. The number of stitches added or removed, and the distribution of the shaping units along the edge, determine the angle of the slope or the shape of the curve.

Regardless of whether the selvedge will remain visible or will be seamed, the shaping units are normally placed adjacent to it, within the fabric. This is done to leave a visible selvedge undisturbed and attractive, but it is also done when the edge will be seamed or have stitches picked up into it because these techniques make use of the space between the selvedge and the remainder of the fabric and the result will be less than satisfactory if shaping has been placed there.

As mentioned above, shaping is positioned in exactly the same places in a circular garment as it is in a flat garment—where the seams would be, if they were present.

Vertical Slopes

If a relatively large number of stitches must be added within a short distance, the change will be abrupt; if a few stitches are added over a longer distance, the change will be slow. For instance, if the increases or decreases are worked on every row, the fabric will become wider or more narrow quickly, and the edge will angle sharply away from the vertical. If the shaping is worked every other row, the change will be more gradual, and it will be more gradual still if there are more rows in between each technique.

Where the shaping units are placed will affect the appearance of the change. When a series of increases is set immediately adjacent to the selvedge, the new columns of stitches

will rise vertically, above the sloped edge. When a series of decreases is set next to the selvedge, the edge will cut across the top of the columns of stitches that have been eliminated.

However, when the shaping is set within the fabric, slightly away from the edge, the columns of stitches in between will slope parallel to the edge, forming a narrow border. The practice of setting the shaping within the fabric to create this decorative effect along the edge apparently became popular with the introduction of inexpensive, factory-made knitwear that was cut and sewn from knitted cloth in much the same way a garment would be made from woven cloth. In reaction, knitters began

Sloped Edges. Left: Increases placed within fabric.
Right: Decreases placed within fabric.

to place the shaping slightly within the fabric to make it more visible and serve as evidence that the item was handmade. Of course, once this design feature was accepted as a mark of quality and fashion, it was incorporated into the better machine-knit garments as well. Its origins being long forgotten, it remains a design feature in many garments and serves the purpose of drawing the eye to the seams, much as piping or top stitching does in a garment made of a woven fabric.

Curves

The kind of curve used for a shaped armhole or neckline is no more than a series of short slopes, each one set at a slightly different angle. For instance, if the first inch of an edge has

Sloped Edges. Left: Increases placed at selvedge.
Right: Decreases placed at selvedge.

Curved Edge.

shaping done on every row, and over the next 2 inches it is done every other row, and then over the following 3 inches only every fourth or fifth row, the result will be three different slopes, first acute, then moderate, then slight. Because a knitted fabric is so resilient, these straight segments will smooth out into a gentle curved line.

Here again it is the Gauge of your particular fabric that determines how to work. While it might seem a bit of a bother to develop and work several different patterns to make a curve when a simple slope might serve, it is easier to do than you might think and for a garment that requires a more refined fit, it is definitely worth it; for more information, see Charting a Curve.

Vertical Interior Shaping

When shaping is used to contour the interior of a garment, such as for bustline darts, or a hat, for instance, it creates a visible line in the fabric that will be more or less obvious depending upon the technique used.

The pattern may consist of a series of increases or decreases set one above the other; Left and Right versions can be alternated row by row to stagger the effect, or they can be set facing one another in pairs; there are also double versions of these techniques that can be used for an even more decorative effect (see Double Decreases).

Here are some examples of this kind of shaping.

Vertical Darts

Vertical darts can be set below the bust line in a bodice, at the top of a skirt, or perhaps at the back neckline (horizontal darts are done with Short Rows, which are described below). In these situations, the shaping is used not only to change the width of the fabric, but also to create volume and contour to accommodate the natural shape of the body and refine the fit.

The area of fabric that has more stitches will protrude relative to the area with fewer stitches. If the Dart is made with increases, the new columns of stitches will flow up from each side of it at an angle; if it is done with decreases, the stitch columns on either side of those that were eliminated will flow toward the dart.

The type of pattern used is the same as for a slope at a side edge; see Charts for Internal Shaping.

Segments

In certain kinds of strongly contoured garments, shaping units are often set in several lines spaced across the fabric. The lines that contain the shaping may be vertical, sloped, or even curved, and they are intended to cut across the remaining columns of stitches, forming wedge-shaped areas. These defined spaces have always tempted the imagination of knit-

ters and they are commonly filled with a stitch or color pattern to enhance the effect.

A hat, for instance, might have three or four lines of decreases evenly spaced around the crown; this both contours the fabric and creates rounded triangular spaces within it as the lines converge.

Medallion fabrics are also shaped with multiple slopes or curves, however, for this purpose they are done in such a way that instead of adding volume and contour at the interior, the fabric remains flat and the outer edges are drawn into angles, changing a square or rectangle into some form of a polygon.

Gussets are small triangular sections of fabric introduced within a fabric to provide wearing ease, such as at the underarm of traditional sweaters, which otherwise have minimal shaping for the armhole. The first half of a gusset is done with increases, and the second half with decreases.

In mittens, small gussets are commonly set below the thumb to accommodate its shape, and in the nicest and most comfortable gloves, you will find tiny gussets set between the fingers for comfort and wearing ease.

❖ Horizontal Shaping

Shaping that takes place across the width of a fabric is less often needed, but is equally useful when appropriate. This is most commonly done at the transition between two different stitch patterns, either to create gathering or to prevent it.

Wherever a shaping unit is placed, the adjacent stitch columns will (at least temporarily) move at a slight angle to accommodate a newcomer introduced by an increase or to fill a space once occupied by a neighbor removed by a decrease. For this reason, the approach is particularly useful when vertical shaping would interfere with a decorative pattern of some kind; instead it can be distributed across the fabric and hidden quite successfully. If there are only a few shaping units and they are widely distributed, their presence may be difficult to discern, particularly when obscured by a stitch or color pattern or a textured yarn.

The edges of a flat fabric are also affected by horizontal shaping. If the fabric is unrestrained at the sides, the edges will fan out as the fabric responds to the change, but within a few inches they will become vertical again. If the sides of the fabric are forced to remain vertical, such as by a seam, or because the garment is done in the round, the abrupt change in width will create overall volume. A common example is a bodice or sleeve that puffs out over a narrower ribbing at waist or wrist.

Abrupt Horizontal Change

Multiple increases spaced evenly across a single row within a fabric will cause the new portion of fabric to puff out, forming soft gathers. If decreases are used instead, the original fabric will be gathered by the new, narrower section. Shaping of this kind can also be concentrated in certain areas to position gathering where it is wanted, for instance, at the center back of a garment above the ribbing, or at the center of the sleeve above the back of the hand.

Conversely, the same type of pattern might be used to prevent any alteration in the width of the fabric when changing from a stitch pattern with one gauge to a pattern with a different gauge, or to control the fit and the amount of gathering that occurs when changing from a ribbing to the main pattern above it; see Average Gauge for Ribbing.

This kind of shaping is also used after picking up stitches, and for the same reason—to change from the number of stitches picked up evenly along an edge, to the number needed for the new fabric; see Picking Up Stitches.

Gathering can also be achieved by Regauging, discussed below, which is a method of radically altering the gauge so the width of the fabric changes. Also, there is a stitch pattern called Ruching that has somewhat the same effect.

Gradual Horizontal Change

When shaping units are distributed across a row, and the pattern is repeated several times with plain rows worked in between, the fabric will change size less abruptly, taking on its new dimensions and contour more gradually.

Shaping of this kind is sometimes used to narrow the yoke area of a garment without creating the obvious lines that would appear if the shaping units were arranged vertically at the armhole. The approach is helpful when a color pattern forms a circle around the area below a neckline; the shaping can be tucked into the background across the width of the fabric, leaving the motif undisturbed.

A similar shaping pattern can also be used to narrow a garment that has a pattern of vertical stripes, so they gradually converge toward the top.

Short Rows

Here is a fascinating technique that can be used to form sloped or curved edges or to add contour within the fabric. Whereas Increase and Decrease techniques change the number of stitches on the needle (and thereby affect the width of the fabric), Short Rows change the number of rows in only some of the stitch columns, which differentially affects the length of the fabric. The most common application is to slope a shoulder line or contour the heel of a sock, but there are many other interesting ways to make use of Short Rows.

To work the Short Rows, some of the stitches on the needle

are inactivated, either all at once or gradually. All of the inactive stitches remain on the needle, and the respective number of active and inactive stitches changes row-by-row in a stepwise fashion. Each "step" requires two rows. At the end of one shortened row, it is necessary to turn the work within the fabric, instead of at a side edge, in order to work back again on the next row; this is called a "turning point."

To prevent a gap from forming in the fabric between each step, the yarn is wrapped around the first stitch on the left needle to tie two steps together where they meet. This "wrap," and the stitch it encircles, are later worked together with the equivalent of a decrease, which is done in a way that hides the wrap on the inside where it will not be seen.

The columns of stitches that remain active, and those that are reactivated, will each have several more rows than those that are inactive; as a result, they will begin to travel at an angle above the Short Rows. This change in direction is quite visible, and the partial rows will also interrupt any stitch or color pattern.

The basic instructions are written for working Short Rows in a plain Stockinette fabric; however, you will find suggestions below for how to use the technique with other stitch or color patterns, as well as a discussion of various applications of the technique.

❖ *Decreasing Short Rows*

In this version of Short Rows, the number of active stitches on the needle is gradually reduced, so each row worked is shorter than the last. When the Short Row pattern is completed, all of the stitches that were temporarily set aside are reactivated and work continues as before.

To try this, make a swatch of 30 stitches and work in Stockinette for about an inch before beginning the pattern. There will be four steps in the pattern, each of which contains five stitches. References to the right or left side of the fabric are as seen on the outside. When moving the yarn to make the wrap at the turning point, always pass it between the needle tips to nearside or farside as specified.

Slope from Left to Right

The slope created in this way will go from the left side edge of the fabric up to the right.

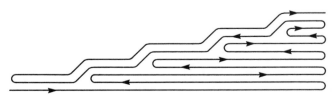

Decreasing Short Rows. Slope is from left up to right.

Working the Short Rows

1. On outside, Knit across row until first step of five stitches remains on left needle.
2. To make wrap, with yarn farside, Slip 1 purlwise, yarn nearside, return slipped stitch to left needle, yarn farside. Turn. (This wraps yarn around first inactive stitch on left side of turning point.)

Decreasing Short Rows: Step 2. Wrap stitch on left needle.

Path of wrapped yarn around stitch.

3. On inside, Slip 1, place firm tension on yarn to Purl next stitch, and then work as usual across remaining stitches. Turn.

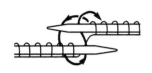

Decreasing Short Rows: Step 3. Strand past Slip Stitch and Purl.

4. On outside, Knit to next turning point (each time working five fewer stitches in the row) and repeat Steps 2 and 3.
5. Continue in this way, inactivating one step of five stitches on each outside row, until there are twenty inactive stitches and ten active stitches.

The Slip stitch in Step 3 eases the transition between steps. If you prefer, you can Slip this stitch from the right to the left needle before turning to the inside of the fabric. Drawing the yarn firmly past the Slip stitch to work the first stitch after the turn ensures that the wrap will not be too loose.

Working Wrap on Outside

1. On outside, Knit ten stitches to first turning point.
2. Yarn is wrapped around base of first stitch on left needle. To join wrap and stitch together, use an equivalent of a Right Decrease in one of the following ways:
   - Slip wrapped stitch to right needle, insert left needle under wrap and into stitch; transfer stitch and wrap back to left needle as one; Knit wrap and stitch together.

Working Short Row Wrap on Outside: Step 2.

- Or, with wrapped stitch on left needle, reach right needle under wrap, and then insert into stitch; Knit wrap and stitch together.
3. Knit four remaining stitches of step.
4. At next turning point, repeat Steps 2 and 3.
5. Continue in this way, joining a stitch and wrap at each turning point to reactivate remaining stitches of row.

With all the stitches active again, work another inch or so of fabric, and then examine the slope created in the swatch and the direction of the columns of stitches above it. Also, turn the fabric over and notice the appearance of the wraps on the inside of the fabric.

Slope from Right to Left

In this case, the Short Rows start at the right edge of the fabric and slope up to the left; therefore, the turning points and the wraps are handled on the inside of the fabric in Purl.

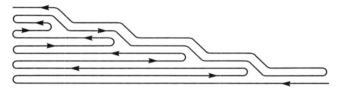

Decreasing Short Rows. Slope is from right up to left.

Working the Short Rows

1. On inside, Purl across row until first step of five stitches remains on left needle.
2. With yarn nearside, Slip 1, yarn farside, return slipped stitch to left needle, yarn nearside. Turn.
3. On outside, Slip 1, draw yarn up firmly to Knit next stitch, and then continue across row with normal tension. Turn.
4. On inside, Purl to next turning point (each time working five fewer stitches in the row) and repeat Steps 2 and 3.
5. Continue in this way, inactivating one step of five stitches on each inside row, until there are twenty inactive stitches and ten active stitches.

Working Wrap on Inside

1. On inside, Purl to first turning point.
2. Yarn is wrapped around base of first stitch on left needle. To join wrap and stitch together, use an equivalent of a Left Decrease in one of the following ways:
   - Slip wrapped stitch knitwise. Reach left needle under wrap and then into turned stitch; transfer both turned stitch and wrap back to left needle and Purl Two Together farside.

- Or, reach right needle around to farside and lift wrap onto left needle with right side on nearside of needle. Purl wrap and stitch together.
3. Purl four remaining stitches of step.
4. At next turning point, repeat Steps 2 and 3.
5. Continue in this way, joining stitch and wrap at each turning point to reactivate remaining stitches of row.

❖ Increasing Short Rows

With this method of working Short Rows, an entire set of stitches is inactivated immediately and the number of active stitches increases step by step, and, instead of working all the turning points and then all the wraps, they are done together. As a result, starting with the second step, it will be necessary to cross the previous turning point, joining that wrap and stitch together, and then work to the next turning point and make a new wrap. While Decreasing Short Rows are far more common, there are times when working this way is necessary—and, in some cases, the two are combined.

As before, try this on a swatch of thirty stitches, with a pattern of five stitches in each of four steps.

Slope from Right to Left

1. On inside, Purl ten stitches to first turning point; next twenty stitches on left needle are now inactivated.
2. With yarn nearside, Slip 1, yarn farside, return slipped stitch to left needle, yarn nearside. Turn.
3. On outside, Slip 1, draw yarn up firmly to Knit next stitch, and then work at normal tension across remaining stitches of row. Turn.
4. On inside, Purl to first turning point. Join next stitch and wrap together with equivalent of Purl Left Decrease as described in Slope from Right to Left: Working Wrap on Inside, above. Decrease includes first stitch of next step.
5. Purl four remaining stitches of step; at second turning point, repeat Steps 2–4.
6. Continue in this way, each time joining stitch and wrap from previous row, and then working across to the next turning point and making another wrap, until twenty stitches set aside in Step 1 have been reactivated.

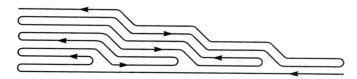

Increasing Short Rows. Slope is from right up toward left.

Slope from Left to Right

1. On outside, Knit ten stitches to first turning point. Next twenty stitches on left needle are now inactivated.
2. With yarn farside, Slip 1, yarn nearside, return slipped stitch to left needle, yarn farside. Turn.
3. On inside, Slip 1, draw yarn up firmly to Purl next stitch, and then work at normal tension across remaining stitches of row. Turn.
4. On outside, Knit to first turning point. Join next stitch and wrap together with equivalent of Knit Right Decrease as described in Slope from Left to Right: Working Wrap on Outside, above. Decrease includes first stitch of next step.
5. Knit four remaining stitches of step; at second turning point, repeat Steps 2–4.
6. For each step, work wrapped stitch from the previous row, and then work across to next turning point and make another wrap; continue in this way until twenty stitches set aside in Step 1 have been reactivated.

❖ Additional Information for Short Rows

The material presented below includes some aspects of dealing with turning points that will help you "see" the work so you understand better what to do, and also explains some of the reasoning as to why the different steps involved are done as described.

This is followed by a discussion of the effect that Short Rows have in a fabric, along with some suggestions for ways to fit them into a stitch or color pattern with the least amount of distortion. Also included is a collection of alternative methods for wrapping the yarn at a turning point; you may prefer one of these to the method described above, or you may find that one or the other works better in certain circumstances.

Basics of Wrapped Turning Points

Here are some additional tips for working Short Rows that you may find helpful.

- At each turning point the last active stitch is on the right needle, and the first inactive stitch is on the left needle. Wrap the inactive stitch starting with the yarn on the inside of the fabric. The yarn will travel from right to left on the inside, left to right on the outside, and then back to the inside.
- You may find it helpful to place a Ring Marker on the needle at each turning point as it is made (see Markers); this makes it easy to identify the wrapped stitches when it is time to close the gaps.
- After wrapping the stitch and turning to the other side, Slip the first stitch; this helps smooth the transition between the two rows of each step.

- After the Slip stitch, place relatively firm tension on the yarn to work the next stitch. If the wrap is too loose, it will not close the turning point; if it is too tight, it will distort the fabric. Try this on a Test Swatch first, because the tension that works best for a firm fabric may not be as successful for a softer, more open one.
- Work the wrap and the stitch together with a Knit Right Decrease on the outside, or a Purl Left Decrease on the inside, so the decrease slopes in the same direction as the Short Row slope.

Effect of Short Rows in the Fabric

- Decreasing Short Rows: The number of active stitches on the right needle will decrease step-by-step; the number of inactive stitches on the left needle will increase. The turning points will be at the top of the Short Row section, parallel to the first full row of reactivated stitches.
- Increasing Short Rows: The number of active stitches on the right needle will increase step-by-step; the number of inactive stitches on the left needle will decrease. The turning points will be at the bottom of the Short Row section, parallel to the last full-width row.
- For either method, if there are the same number of stitches in each step, and the same number of steps, the resulting slope will be set at the same angle in the fabric.
- Each step requires two rows; therefore, the angle is determined by how many stitches are in each one. In a fabric of the same gauge, if there are more stitches in a step, the angle will be shallower than if there are fewer stitches in a step.
- The columns of stitches above the Short Rows, as well as the side edge of the fabric, will be perpendicular to the slope created, and set at an angle in relation to the stitch columns in the rest of the fabric.

Alternative Wrap Methods

Other methods can be used to wrap the stitch at the turning point. Keep in mind that the wrap is no more than an elongated running thread; here are three alternatives that can make it tighter or looser, or that simply offer an option for how to work. To try any of these, you might want to use the same number of stitches and the pattern described for the basic Short Row instructions, above; however, only one turning point is described here.

Reverse Wrap Option

When the inactive stitch is wrapped as described in the basic instructions above, it will be tied neatly to the inside of the fabric once it is joined together with the stitch. However, if it is too tight and distorts the fabric, wrapping it in the other direction will make the strand slightly longer.

Work as follows:

- To wrap stitch when working on outside, bring yarn nearside, Slip 1, yarn farside; return slipped stitch to left needle.
- To wrap stitch when working on inside, bring yarn farside, Slip 1, yarn nearside; return slipped stitch to left needle.

No Wrap

Some older patterns do not include a wrap, leaving a hole in the fabric at each turning point, much like an Eyelet. Depending on how you choose to look at it, this is either an error or a decorative element. These openings might be pretty for something like a bust dart or the shoulder slope of a fancy sweater, or might fit in well with a lace pattern.

Running Thread Wrap

Instead of wrapping the running thread around the stitch at the turning point, it is possible to pick it up later, when it is time to close the gap. This method makes a wrap that is tighter than any of the others and it is somewhat more complicated and challenging to do. However, if you have forgotten to wrap a stitch at the end of a Short Row, you can use this method to fix the problem.

Try using the tip of your needle, but if you find it difficult to manage, use a cable needle instead (see Tools).

1. At turning point, do not wrap stitch; turn.
2. Slip 1; continue across row; turn.
3. Work back to turning point and work wrap in one of following ways.
   - On outside, work across to turning point; reach around on farside (or turn to inside of fabric) and insert tip of left needle *down* into running thread that passes across first stitch to second in row below right needle; lift strand onto left needle and then join it and next stitch with Knit Right Decrease.
   - On inside, Slip next stitch knitwise and then replace on left needle in turned position; insert tip of left needle up under running thread that passes across first stitch to second in row below right needle (it will be in turned position), join strand and next stitch with Purl Left Decrease.

I have seen instructions that suggest attaching a safety pin to the yarn after slipping the first stitch in Step 2, so the pin rides on the running thread while you continue to work. When it comes time to close the turning point, the pin is used to lift the running thread onto the needle as described above, and is then removed.

This works reasonably well, but fussing with all the little pins, one for each turning point, will make things go very slowly; with a little practice, you will learn to find the running thread with the tip of your needle, if this is the method you prefer to use, and it is much quicker to work that way.

Yarnover Wrap

Instead of wrapping the yarn around the inactive stitch, you can place a Yarnover on the needle and then work it together with the stitch when you reactivate it. Because the Yarnover is wrapped around the needle, it will be slightly longer than a strand that is passed around the base of a stitch, as described above.

Working on Outside

1. Knit to turning point; turn.
2. On inside, place Purl-to-Purl Yarnover on right needle, Slip 1, and continue across row. Turn.
3. To close gap, work to turning point and join stitch and Yarnover with Knit Right Decrease.

Working on Inside

1. Purl to turning point; turn.
2. On outside, yarn nearside, Slip 1, Knit 1 (yarn will pass over needle to form Yarnover); continue across row. Turn.
3. To close gap, work to turning point and join stitch and Yarnover with Purl Left Decrease (slip both Yarnover and stitch knitwise, and then Purl Two Together farside).

Short Rows and Decorative Patterns

When Short Rows are used to shape a shoulder line, the only evidence of their presence is the slope of the seam. However, when Short Rows are used within the fabric, the angled stitch columns above the area will be quite obvious, and the slope created will interrupt any stitch or color pattern.

Also, it can be a challenge to do Short Rows while working a pattern that employs complex stitch or color techniques. Depending on the kind of pattern you are using, the result will be more satisfactory if you position the Short Rows where they will least affect the pattern. It is helpful to work out the approach you want to take beforehand with the help of a small garment chart of the area around the Short Rows that shows the slope pattern; see Coordinating Stitch and Garment Patterns. Pencil in the stitch or color symbols (or draw lines representing the repeats) so you can see exactly how the pattern and the slope will relate.

When working Short Rows in a fabric made with a pattern that contains complex stitch techniques, use one of the following methods to minimize the interference of one with the other and maintain the appearance of the stitch pattern as much as possible.

Short Rows and Stitch Patterns

- Change the number of stitches in adjacent steps in order to place the wrap on a stitch that will be worked in plain Knit on the outside. For instance, if each step would normally have six stitches, work seven in one and five in the next.
- Alternatively, move the Short Rows up or down a row or two so you can close the turning points and reactivate the stitches on a plainer row.
- Substitute plain Knit stitches for any complex stitch technique that would fall at a turning point, moving the technique to a nearby stitch.
- If a wrap occurs on a Purl stitch that is on the outside of the fabric, there will be two "nubs"—one is the head of the stitch, and the other is the wrap. Make sure to pick up the wrap when working the decrease that closes the gap.
- In some cases, the turning point will blend in better if you do not work the wrap and stitch together. The wrap will then remain at the base of the stitch and look like a Purl nub, and it will be just as effective in preventing a gap. You might also consider leaving the wrap in place if it is on a Knit stitch, but the pattern would look more consistent if there were a Purl stitch there, instead.
- Lace patterns have paired Decreases and Yarnovers; if a pair falls at a turning point, do not work either of them in order to maintain the stitch count, or shift both to another position; alternatively, work the Yarnover on one row and the decrease on the next, or vice versa.

Short Rows and Color Patterns

Color patterns present the same set of challenges and solutions that stitch patterns do when working Short Rows, but the disruption of the pattern can be even more obvious. You might find it worthwhile to shift things around a bit.

- When working a Stranded Color pattern, if possible, separate the steps of the Short Row pattern, working them only on plain rows. In other words, work to the first step, wrap, turn, and work back. On next row, work wrap and stitch together and continue to end of row; continue with decorative pattern. On the next plain row, work the second Short Row step of the pattern; repeat until all of the steps have been worked. If the plain rows are too far apart to make this practical, try to position the turning points in background areas of the pattern, instead of within a motif.
- Depending upon the nature of the pattern, you may find it helpful to wrap the stitch at the turning point with both yarns held as one; this anchors the yarn that is being stranded at the turning point, so it is not left hanging several stitches back.

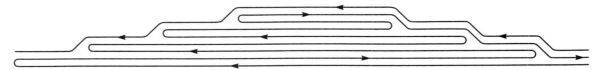

Short Row Dart Pattern. More rows at center than at sides.

• When the Short Row pattern is complete, reactivate the stitches using just the background yarn, leaving the contrast-color yarn within the fabric; work to the end of the row, turn, work back to innermost point of the slope, pick up the second yarn, and complete the remainder of the row in pattern. Work the next rows of the pattern on all the stitches.

Mosaic Patterns are less problematic because only one yarn is used at a time; simply substitute plain Knit for any Slip stitch that falls at a turning point.

For Intarsia Patterns, you may want to shift the turning points away from any area where there is a color change, but in some cases it might work to wrap the yarn around a stitch at the turning point instead of interlocking it with the other yarn.

Short Rows and Garter Stitch
Garter Stitch is a special case. You can achieve a very satisfactory result doing Short Rows in this pattern, but only if you abandon all the rules; best of all, the result looks just as nice on both sides.

1. Knit to turning point, yarn nearside, Slip 1, yarn farside, return Slipped stitch to left needle.
2. Turn to other side, Knit across row (do not Slip first stitch after turn).
3. To reactivate stitches, simply work across turning point, leaving wrap at base of stitch, where it will resemble a Purl stitch.

❖ Applications
Now that you understand the principles, let us take a look at how Short Rows can be used to alter the contour of a knitted fabric. Some of these applications are traditional and commonly used, some have only limited utility, but they are all worth knowing about, and once you are familiar with how the technique works you may find innovative ways of your own to put it to use; also see the information on using Short Rows for color block patterns in the chapter on Color Techniques.

Short Row Shoulder Lines
One of the simplest and most effective ways to use Short Rows is to slope a shoulder line. Once you have completed the slope, join the stitches of the back and front garment sections either by Grafting, or with Joinery Cast-Off.

This produces a much smoother and more refined shoulder line than a Stepped Cast-Off and a sewn seam. However, the latter is often an easier method to use when dealing with a complex stitch or color pattern; while not included here, it is in effect a Short Row technique.

Short Row Shoulder.

Short Row Darts
There are several areas in a garment where horizontal darts can be used to enhance the fit and comfort of a garment, and you can use either Decreasing or Increasing Short Rows; for more information on designing Darts, see Measurements and Schematics. The most common place to use darts, of course, is at the side edge of a bodice to add shaping for the bust line.

Also, tailored jackets often include darts at the elbow to curve the sleeve in an anatomically correct way, which not only adds to comfort but provides ease to reduce stress on the garment in wear; this is particularly helpful with a fitted sleeve.

Contoured Lower Edge
In some cases, Short Rows can be used to advantage along a cast-on edge in much the same way they are used to slope a cast-off edge.

• For instance, to shape the lower edge of a bodice back or sleeve, cast on the full width and then work Increasing Short Rows to curve the edge from the center up toward the sides; this can be done immediately after casting on, or above a ribbing.
• To shape a dolman sleeve, cast on all of the stitches at the

side edge, and then use Increasing Short Rows, gradually activating the cast on stitches from the bodice toward the wrist; for more information, see Side or Mid-Fabric Cast-Ons.

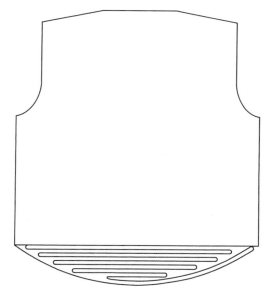

Contoured Lower Edge.
Lower edge of back shaped with Short Rows.

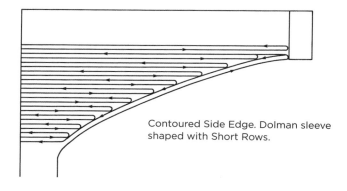

Contoured Side Edge. Dolman sleeve shaped with Short Rows.

Sock Heels

The most common use for Short Rows is to turn sock heels. There is no room here for a full discussion of the many different styles of socks beyond mentioning in a very general way how this technique is used for this purpose.

The most traditional heel consists of a square flap below the ankle followed by a small set of Short Rows, paired with decreases to cup the heel. Another popular heel style eliminates the flap. Instead, the first half of the heel cup is shaped with Decreasing Short Rows, and the second half with Increasing Short Rows.

When using Short Rows to shape the heels of socks, no wrap is required because a true decrease joins the two stitches

on either side of the turning point, simultaneously reducing the number of stitches on the needle and closing the gap.

In fact, working a sock is an excellent way to get a sense of how Short Rows can be used to form a cup shape. The same general concept, done on a larger scale, can be used to shape a baby bonnet or a hood for a jacket.

Short Row Miter

A variety of border patterns, many of them lace, are knit narrow and long and then sewn onto an edge or joined to stitches picked-up along it; see Picking Up to Join. If the border must pass around a corner (such as on a square shawl or blanket, for instance) it will need a Miter, a corner done with Short Rows that causes the fabric to turn at a right angle.

First use Decreasing Short Rows to inactivate all but one of the border stitches, creating the slope at the corner, and then reactivate them with Increasing Short Rows. To make sure the corner turns out nice and square, work out the pattern for the slope as you would for any other; see Miters, or Steps and Points.

Short Row Curves

Short Rows can also be used to form curved side edges, such as for the corner on a blanket or shawl, or to create an entire collar worked narrow and long. Unlike the curved edge of something like an armhole, however, Short Rows curve the entire fabric, from one side to the other.

This is done with a series of small, wedge-shaped pattern repeats, one set on top of the other. Because one side of the wedge has more rows than the other, the whole fabric takes on a smooth, consistent curve. To change the nature of the curve, several different Short Row patterns can be used. Plain rows can be inserted between repeats of the pattern, or the pattern

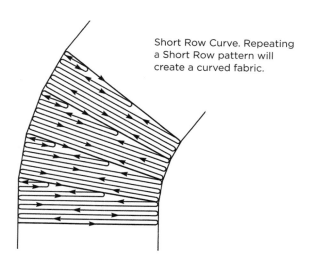

Short Row Curve. Repeating a Short Row pattern will create a curved fabric.

can be flipped over so it curves from right to left in one area, and left to right in another.

For instance, a Short Row pattern that changes direction in that way could be used to make a border that will be attached to a neckline and center front opening, where the inward curve of the neckline is different from the outward curve at the transition between neck opening and center front opening.

While this may seem complicated, in fact it is not that difficult to do, and you will find a very easy method of working out a pattern of this kind in Charting a Curve.

Short Rows and Yokes

Yokes in sewn garments can be used not just for decorative effect, but also as a means of subtly shaping a garment. Unlike a sewn garment, where the yoke is a separate piece of fabric, a knitted yoke is normally delineated with no more than a change of color or stitch pattern, or perhaps a stripe or welt, but this serves equally well as a place to hide the shaping. Simply insert Decreasing Short Row darts at the side edge between bodice and yoke; because the eye is drawn to the yoke, the darts will not be noticeable. For more information on Darts, see Measurements and Schematics.

Figure Irregularities

Few figures are truly symmetrical, and a garment that appears to fit well does so because it conforms gracefully to the particular body, regardless of its irregularities. Short Rows can be used in very unobtrusive ways to help customize the fit of any garment.

For instance, to provide additional length at the center of a garment for a prominent upper chest bone or for a rounded upper back, work Increasing Short Rows in the upper bodice area.

You can also add a yoke below the waistline of a skirt and position darts at each side of the front and/or back to add extra length at the center to accommodate a prominent abdomen.

Similarly, if one shoulder is higher than the other, you can use a different Short Row pattern for each shoulder; see Customized Fit.

Regauging

Regauging is a technique used to change the contour and density of the fabric by changing the size of the needle. This changes the size of the stitches, which alters the gauge.

The great advantage of the technique is that the number of stitches on the needle can remain the same because the shaping is done without the use of increases or decreases. This makes Regauging a good choice to use in situations where it is desirable to continue a stitch or color pattern without interruption; it is ideal for ribbings.

Regauging. Sample shows effect of Regauging in Single Rib.

There is a limit to how much shaping can be done in this way, however, because Regauging alters the overall appearance and feel of the fabric. Nevertheless, many stitch patterns, particularly ribbing or lace patterns, camouflage the change to a great extent—and in some applications, the alteration in the characteristics of the fabric is used as a decorative detail.

❖ Applications

There really are no instructions necessary for this technique because it is so very simple. Instead, here are some examples of how Regauging can be used to improve the fit or appearance of a garment. Once you understand the concept, you will find it easy to apply the technique whenever it seems appropriate.

Turned-Back Ribbing

A ribbing that is turned back on itself—such as a sleeve cuff, hat brim, or turtleneck collar—will fit better and be more comfortable in wear if it is regauged so the circumference of the outer portion is slightly larger than the inner portion. It is best to do this without changing the number of stitches on the needle so the ribbing is uninterrupted.

Turned-Up Sleeve or Hat Ribbing

For a hat brim, or a sleeve worked up from the wrist, cast on and work the outer portion of the cuff on a larger needle, and then step down twice in size, first for the fold and then for the inner portion, as follows:

1. Make a swatch and determine number of stitches for cuff using wrist measurement and Average Gauge for Ribbing.

2. Cast on required number of stitches using needle two sizes larger than that used to determine gauge.
3. Work length of outer portion of cuff.
4. Change to needle one size smaller and work three to five rows for fold.
5. Change to needle one size smaller and work length of inner portion of cuff.
6. Change to correct size needle for main fabric and continue above ribbing.

Turtleneck

In this case, start on stitches picked up around the neck opening and increase the needle sizes instead of decreasing them.

1. Make swatch and determine number of stitches for collar using actual neck opening measurement and Average Gauge for Ribbing.
2. Pick up stitches and work inner portion of collar with needle used to determine gauge.
3. Change to needle one size larger and work three to five rows for fold.
4. Change to needle one size larger and work outer portion of collar.

Collars and Ruffles

Regauging can also be used to create a flat collar, or to make a ruffle for a neckline, or for a peplum at the lower edge of a bodice or sleeve. These decorative elements can be started at the cast-on edge and worked toward the garment, or started on stitches picked up along an edge and worked out from it.

The instructions here rely entirely on Regauging, but there are also ways to combine that technique with increases or decreases if a change in needle size is insufficient to achieve the effect you want. To work out the pattern for something like this, see Charted Garment Patterns.

It is also possible to work an item of this kind narrow and long, as described in Short Row Curves, above, and attach it to the main fabric along a side edge, either with a seam, or to picked-up stitches (see Picking Up to Join).

Flat Collars

It is quite easy to do a regauged flat collar in ribbing because the fabric is so resilient that the planning need not be all that precise. These instructions are for starting at the neckline edge, which is the easiest way to work. The needle sizes will gradually increase and the collar will flare out across the shoulders.

Flat Ribbed Collar

Use a small size needle for this, since a firmly knit ribbing will provide more support for the collar at the neck.

1. Make swatch and determine number of stitches for collar using neck opening measurement and Average Gauge for Ribbing.
2. Multiply row gauge by length of collar to find total number of rows needed.
3. Divide rows into three sections for regauging, one for each needle size. To allow for change in row gauge, subtract one or two rows from section done with largest needle and add these to section done with smallest needle.
4. Pick up stitches around neck edge and begin working with needle used to find gauge.
5. At beginning of each new section, change to a needle one size larger than that used for previous section.

Flat Collars in Other Stitch Patterns

You can make a collar of this kind using any stitch pattern, but they are particularly nice done in lace. Here again, it helps to work a few rows of relatively dense ribbing at the neck edge to provide flexibility and support before beginning the collar pattern.

Two gauges are required, one for the ribbing, and one for the collar stitch pattern; they will be quite different, and it will be necessary to space decreases across the fabric in order to change from one to the other; see Horizontal Shaping, above.

1. Calculate number of stitches required for collar at neckline using Average Gauge for Ribbing. Pick up stitches around neckline with smallest needle and work a half inch or so of ribbing.
2. Use neck opening measurement and gauge for collar stitch pattern to calculate number of stitches to use for main collar pattern.
3. Space as many decreases as required across a plain row between ribbing and collar pattern. Begin to work collar pattern, changing needle sizes as described above.

Ruffles

A ruffle is started in the same way as the flat collar described above, but it requires evenly distributed increases to create the initial fullness. Regauging can then be used to increase the gathering without interfering with any stitch pattern.

Here again, this pattern starts at the fabric and is worked out to the cast-off edge, but I think it will be clear how to reverse the process and start by casting on instead (a particularly nice approach to use for a lace pattern that creates a scalloped edge, but the collar would need to be sewn on).

1. Work as described above for a flat collar and, after ribbing is complete, adjust to number of stitches needed for stitch pattern of ruffle.

2. Use gauge of ruffle stitch pattern to calculate number of rows to work; divide rows into three sections and shift several rows between third and first sections to compensate for gauge change, as described for Flat Ribbed Collar.
3. Continue with same needle used for ribbing and work first section of ruffle.
4. Use needle one size larger for rows in next section, and then increase needle size again for last section.

Should the Regauging technique alone not be adequate to add as much fullness as required, more increases can be made use of within the ruffle, as well. You could, for instance, distribute a set of increases across the last row of each segment of the ruffle, just before changing needle size to Regauge, or introduce several columns of plain stitches between each repeat in the pattern and work increases or decreases in that area only, distributing them evenly over all the rows.

Fitted Garments
Here are several ideas for how to use Regauging to change the contour within a fabric in order to add subtle shaping without the use of Increases or Decreases.

Bodice Waistline
If you want a garment to draw in somewhat around the waistline, use Regauging either in addition to, or instead of, shaping at the side seam or using vertical darts. Start the Regauging about 2 inches below the waist and finish 2 inches above. Use a needle one size smaller for the first inch, and then a size smaller than that for the next inch or two; then reverse the process and step up the needle sizes over the next 2 inches.

Socks
Regauging is a very useful way to refine the fit of socks, especially when you want to avoid conventional shaping in order to preserve the integrity of a stitch or color pattern.

To make knee-high socks for someone with a large difference between the calf and ankle measurements, regauge this area, using the largest size needles for the calf area and progressively smaller needles between calf and ankle and between calf and knee. Use gauge and detailed measurements of the area to determine how many rows to assign to each needle size; see Average Gauge for Negative Ease, as well as Negative Ease in Measurements and Schematics.

Also, a denser fabric will wear better; use needles one size smaller to work the stitches of the heel and sock tip. Similarly, if you are using double-point needles, you can work just the sole of the sock, or the palm of a mitten, with smaller needles than used for the rest of the fabric.

Skirts
For a skirt gathered at the waist, regauge the area just below the waistline by changing the needle sizes to reduce the volume caused by the gathering. Be careful to check the measurements so there is still sufficient width to pull the garment over the hips.

For a skirt with a zipper, use Regauging instead of darts at front and back; this helps firm up the fabric in this area to provide additional support for the weight of the garment.

Hems
Regauging can also be used to reduce the inherent bulk of Hems and Facings.

CHAPTER 7

Picking Up Stitches

This is a wonderfully versatile technique that can be used to join one section of fabric to another without sewing. All you need to do is use a knitting needle to draw loops of yarn through the stitches of an existing fabric in order to create a new set of stitches. This technique is often used to add a collar to a neckline, or a border to a center front opening.

Most often, a new portion of fabric is worked out from the stitches picked up along an edge of the original one. However, it is also possible to join the side of a new fabric as it is worked, row-by-row, to the set of picked-up stitches. This is a nice way to add one of those lovely border patterns that are knit narrow and long as trim along an edge, and the technique can also be used to insert one fabric between two others, joining it at both sides.

In addition, several less-well-known applications are discussed here, such as how to pick up stitches within the interior of a fabric. This is a good way to join an element such as a pocket, or to add some decorative trim such as a small ruffle that runs from shoulder or neckline to the lower edge of the fabric.

Also included here is material on how to free the stitches of the lower edge in order to work in the opposite direction, as well as how to separate a fabric in order to make an alteration of some kind.

Perhaps because these applications are so common, many patterns say little more than how many stitches to pick up and provide no information as to how to go about it or how to space them across the fabric. This chapter should help fill in the details so you can deal with these situations.

General Information

Before we turn to the instructions, here is some general information that I think you will find helpful regardless of which of these techniques you want to use or how you want to apply them.

❖ Gauge

When working any project that involves picking up stitches, it is important to take into consideration the Stitch Gauge of both the original and the new fabric, since they are rarely the same.

For instance, if you pick up stitches along a side edge for a new section that will lie perpendicular to the original, you will be attaching columns of stitches to rows. In this case, it is the row gauge of the original fabric that determines how many stitches there are to pick up into, and the stitch gauge of the new fabric that determines how many new stitches are required. Gauge is also a factor when two side edges are joined and each fabric has a different stitch pattern, or when stitches are picked up along an edge that is a mixture of rows and stitch columns, such as around a neckline.

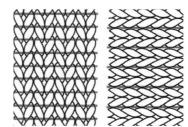

Relationship of rows and stitch columns.

The smoothest and most attractive join between two fabrics is achieved by picking up into every stitch, whether along an edge or within the fabric, and then working increases or decreases on the first row to change the number of stitches to that needed for the new fabric. While it is also possible to pick up the exact number of stitches required by skipping some stitches or drawing more than one new stitch through others, this approach results in an irregular join that is more likely to have gaps or to bunch up in places.

You will find more information about developing a pattern for either adjusting the number of stitches or spacing the new, picked-up stitches evenly along the join in Adjusting Number of Stitches.

❖ *Tools for Picking Up*

Many people pick up stitches with one needle, wielding it much like a crochet hook. This approach works well when picking up along Chain Selvedge, or when dealing with a somewhat loosely knit fabric. However, I often find it easier to work with two needles when dealing with most other selvedges, especially when picking up along something other than a plain, straight edge.

The pickup is easier to do and the results are often better if the size of the needle used is smaller than that used for the fabric itself. A thin needle held in the left hand is easier to insert into the strands along the edge, and distorts nearby stitches less as you work. The needle held in your right hand will determine the size of the new stitches; if it is a size or two smaller than what you plan to use for the border, any increases or decreases necessary to adjust the stitch count will be somewhat less noticeable; after these increases are made, switch to the border needle.

You can also pick up stitches by holding a crochet hook in the right hand and the yarn and a knitting needle in the left, although it can be awkward to transfer the new stitches from hook to needle. Actually, the ideal tool to use is an unusual type of circular needle, sometimes called a "cro-needle" (see Tools), that has a crochet hook at one end, a knitting needle tip at the other, and a cable in between. The first, most basic instruction below includes information for how to work with all of these tools; all the other directions assume the work is done with one or two knitting needles.

❖ *And an Alert*

If you find it necessary to unravel picked-up stitches, what you may find is a selvedge turned somewhat ragged and homely. When the new stitches are introduced, the selvedge and the adjacent column of stitches are pushed apart, which can elongate the running thread and stretch the selvedge stitch out of shape. You can pick up along the edge again and all will be set right; however, if you decide that picking up is not the right approach, you will need to find a way to hide the damage.

Therefore, if you are at all unsure about picking up the stitches, or uncertain about which of the approaches you want to use, try things first on a Test Swatch; if you do not like the result, you will not have spoiled your fabric and can try something else.

Should you be faced with a damaged edge, keep in mind that sewing one piece of fabric to another is an acceptable substitute for picking up stitches in any situation; see Seams. Alternatively, you can cover a free edge with a fabric binding or a knitted one as described in Facings.

Picking Up Selvedges

There are three basic ways to pick up stitches along a selvedge. You can draw the new stitches under the entire selvedge (in effect, between the selvedge and the adjacent column of stitches), under the inner half of the selvedge stitch (closest to the fabric), or under just the outer half (at the very edge). It is also possible to draw the yarn under the running threads so the yarn does not pass around the adjacent selvedge stitches, which, while rarely done, can be useful on occasion.

You can pick up as to Knit or as to Purl, depending upon what is convenient and whether you want to work from the bottom of an edge up to the top or from top to bottom, and you can also turn the selvedge to the outside. Each of these approaches will produce somewhat different results, and the various selvedges have distinctive characteristics that will affect the outcome.

Also, the standard approach is to start the pickup on the outside of the fabric at the right corner and work across the edge to the left in a manner similar to working across a row in Knit. However, there are times when it is necessary, or more convenient, to start at the other end of the edge, which requires working on the inside of the fabric in a manner similar to doing a Purl row. These are both described in the basic instructions; however, in those that follow it is assumed you will understand how to proceed if you want to work in Purl.

The first section of instructions here, Picking Up Stockinette Selvedge, can be considered definitive, since the basic principles involved apply with relatively minor (albeit important) variations to all the other methods. Once you understand the concepts, it is easy to make use of them in different circumstances and with whatever tools you prefer.

❖ *Picking Up Stockinette Selvedge*

It is very easy to pick up one new stitch for every row along a Stockinette Selvedge. The result is a neat and tidy join with the new fabric firmly attached to the original.

Tie on the yarn at the right corner (see Tying On Yarn), and hold the fabric with the outside facing you and the selvedge up, so the stitch columns are horizontal.

Picking Up Full Selvedge

With this approach, the loop of yarn is drawn under the full selvedge stitch. You will want to insert the needle into the space bounded on the top by the two strands of the selvedge stitch, on the bottom by the first stitch within the fabric, and on either side by the running threads that pass between these stitches. The running threads of the new picked-up stitch will wrap around the running threads between the selvedge and the first column of stitches in the fabric.

Border on Picked-Up Stitches. Full selvedge turned to inside.

Picking Up with One Needle

Hold the needle in your right hand and the edge of the fabric in your left hand. It helps to put some tension on the edge to open it up somewhat so you can see where to insert the needle each time; then, pull the edge taut with your left hand, or pull the selvedge up slightly with the needle to make it easier to draw the new stitch through the edge.

Picking Up as to Knit

• Insert right needle tip under both sides of selvedge stitch from nearside to farside, wrap yarn as to Knit, and draw new stitch through fabric. Continue in this way, bringing one new stitch under each selvedge stitch.

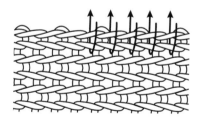

Picking Up Full Selvedge as to Knit. Pick up both sides of stitch.

Picking Up as to Purl

• Insert right needle tip under both sides of selvedge stitch from farside to nearside, wrap yarn as to Purl, and draw new stitch through fabric. Continue in this way, bringing one new stitch under each selvedge stitch.

Picking Up with Two Needles

Hold a small size needle in the left hand, and one of whatever size you prefer in the right.

Picking Up as to Knit

• Insert tip of left needle from nearside to farside under both sides of selvedge stitch. Treat two strands of sel-

vedge now on left needle as a stitch, insert right needle as to Knit, wrap yarn, and draw new stitch through.

Picking Up as to Purl

• Insert tip of left needle under selvedge stitch from nearside to farside, insert right needle into these strands as to Purl, wrap yarn, and draw new stitch through.

Picking Up with Crochet Hook

Hold crochet hook in right hand and knitting needle in left hand; hold yarn on left as for crochet or Left-Hand Method of knitting. Unlike the methods above, in this case it is necessary to work across the edge from *left to right*.

The Knit version is very easy to do; the Purl version is somewhat awkward.

Picking Up as to Knit

• With yarn farside, insert hook under full selvedge stitch, catch yarn, and draw new stitch through edge; transfer stitch to left needle in standard position, with right side of stitch on nearside of needle. Repeat in selvedge stitch to right and continue in same manner across edge.

Picking Up as to Purl

• With yarn nearside, insert hook from farside to nearside under full selvedge stitch, catch yarn, draw stitch through edge to farside, and transfer to needle. Repeat in stitch to right.

This necessitates holding the tools slightly on the farside of the edge.

Picking Up with Cro-Needle

If you have one of these wonderful tools, with a hook on one end of a cable and a knitting needle tip on the other, you will find it makes picking up stitches very easy to do under any circumstances.

For this method, it is necessary to pick up the stitches using a "tail" of yarn, similar to that used for Finger Cast-On techniques. To determine how much yarn to allow for picking up the number of stitches needed, work as described in Yarn Allowance for Finger Cast-Ons; however, measure the amount of yarn used for the *stitches* instead of the amount used for the baseline.† To pick up, start using the yarn at that point, holding hook end of cro-needle in right hand, and tail of yarn to left as for crochet or the Left-Hand Method of knitting; work from

† For a rough estimate, wrap the yarn around the needle ten times, unwrap yarn, measure the length, and then multiply to find how much is needed; add a bit extra to compensate for error. Or, use the figure for Stitches per Yard if you did that calculation when developing the Gauge.

right to left on outside of fabric as to Knit, or inside of fabric as to Purl.

1. Insert hook under selvedge stitch, catch yarn, and draw new stitch through fabric; repeat across row.
2. Return to first stitch at other end of cro-needle where main supply of yarn is attached, and with a conventional straight or circular needle in right hand, begin to work new fabric on picked-up stitches; set cro-needle aside after first row.

Picking up with a tail of yarn in this way also works in any situation in which it would be advantageous to start working the new section of fabric with the first stitch picked up instead of with the last, even when you use a regular double-point or circular needle.

Picking Up Partial Selvedge

Picking up into one or the other side of the selvedge stitch will create a looser join, but the selvedge will be less bulky on the inside of the fabric. The running threads of the new stitches will pass through the center of the selvedge stitches.

The instructions are written for working on the outside of the fabric in Knit, but you can certainly follow the same principles described above and work on the inside in Purl, if necessary.

Picking Up into Inner Strand

With this version, the outermost strands of the selvedge stitches will lie along the join on the inside, between the two fabrics.

Picking Up with One Needle

- Insert needle from nearside to farside under strand that lies closest to fabric, and Knit.

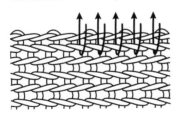

Picking Up into Inner Strand of Selvedge. Pick up strand closest to fabric and Knit.

Picking Up with Two Needles

- Insert left needle from nearside to farside to pick up strand closest to fabric, insert right needle into strand, and Knit.
- Due to angle of strand, it may be easier to insert left needle under strand from farside to nearside. Strand will be turned on needle; therefore, Knit farside so it does not cross.

Picking Up into Outer Strand

This version produces a very nice result that blends in well, because the strands of the selvedge stitches that lie closest to

the fabric are left on the outside and cover the join somewhat. Work with either one or two needles, as follows:

- Insert needle from nearside to farside under outer strand of selvedge stitch and Knit.
- Or, for a join that is too loose, pick up outer strand and Knit it farside so it will twist; for more information, see Twist Stitches.

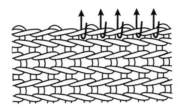

Picking Up into Outer Strand. Pick up strand at very edge of fabric and Knit.

❖ *Picking Up Chain Selvedge*

A Chain Selvedge consists of one stitch for every two rows in the fabric. It is very easy to pick up into because each selvedge stitch is relatively large and there is an obvious space below it. Because of this, it is easy to work with just one needle held in the right hand, however, working with two needles can minimize distortion of the fabric and the edge. Use whichever method you prefer; the instructions serve for both.

The resulting join is considerably looser and less bulky than when the pickup is done on a Stockinette Selvedge, as described above. If the original and the new fabric are also relatively soft and open, the result can be very satisfactory; however, a soft open join is not always appropriate and it is all too easy for a Chain Selvedge to stretch out of shape. Fortunately, there are several ways to tighten up the join, giving this edge more versatility than it might otherwise have.

Once again, these instructions are for picking up on the outside as to Knit; should you need to pick up on the inside in Purl, use the approach described above for a Stockinette Selvedge.

Picking Up Full Selvedge

This is the easiest way to work, and even though the full selvedge is turned to the inside, there will be less bulk on the inside than is the case with a Stockinette Selvedge because there are half as many stitches.

- On outside of fabric, insert needle from nearside to farside under both sides of selvedge stitch and Knit.

Picking Up Partial Selvedge

For a softer, looser join, you can pick up into either the inner or outer side of a Chain Selvedge. This is often a good method to use when joining something to the edge of a lace fabric, since there will be no bulk whatsoever and the loose attachment blends well with an open fabric.

Picking Up into Inner Strand

This method turns the outer strand of the selvedge to the inside.

- On outside of fabric, insert needle from nearside to far-side under half of selvedge stitch lying closest to fabric and Knit.

Picking Up into Outer Strand

This leaves the inner half of the selvedge stitch visible on the outside of the fabric; it is quite attractive and works to hide the join.

- On outside of fabric, insert needle under half of selvedge stitch at edge and Knit, or on inside of fabric as to Purl.

If you find the result is too open, but want to use a Chain Selvedge to reduce bulk in the join, work so as to twist the strands, as described below.

Twisted Chain Selvedge

If it is necessary to tighten up the join between two fabrics, you can pick up so as to twist a Chain Selvedge to either the right or the left; the result has a woven look that is quite attractive.

In order to twist the selvedge stitch, once you insert the needle into it, treat it just as you would a normal stitch; for more information, see Twist Stitches.

Inner Strand Twisted Left
- Insert left needle from nearside to farside under half of selvedge stitch closest to fabric, insert right needle into strand on farside, and Knit.
- Alternatively, insert right needle under strand from far-side to nearside and insert left needle into picked-up strand on nearside; with both needles in strand, Knit.

Inner Strand Twisted Right
- Insert left needle from farside to nearside under half of selvedge stitch closest to fabric, insert right needle into picked-up strand on nearside, and Knit.

Twisted Outer Strand

In this case, not only is the outer strand twisted, but the inner strand will remain visible on the outside of the fabric; the result has a more complex appearance than the version above.

- Use either variation described above, but pick up into outer half of selvedge stitch instead.

Picking Up Every Row

When there is a large discrepancy between the number of stitches needed for the new fabric and the number of stitches

available in a Chain Selvedge, it may be better to pick up one stitch for every row instead of one in every selvedge stitch. This will minimize the adjustment necessary; for more information, see Adjusting Number of Stitches. Also, if the Chain Selvedge is too loose or inconsistent in some way, this will also help even out the edge.

Picking Up Between Running Threads

With this version, the pickup is done between each running thread leading into the Selvedge, and the result is the same as if you picked up along a Stockinette Selvedge.

If you examine a Chain Selvedge (see drawing in Selvedges and Steeks), you will see a fairly large space below the selvedge stitch, with a pair of running threads on each side. It is easy enough to insert the needle into the space below the selvedge stitch, but more difficult to do so between the pairs of running threads, since they lie very close together. Once you are familiar with the structure of the edge, it goes along reasonably well. It helps to do the pickup with a relatively thin needle held in the left hand.

- Insert needle into gap below selvedge stitch, between two pairs of running threads, and pick up one stitch; for next stitch, insert needle between two running threads of one pair.

Picking Up Twice into Selvedge

In this case, the pickup is done by working separately into each of the two strands of the selvedge stitch.

- Insert left needle under both halves of selvedge stitch from nearside to farside. With both strands on needle, treat them as two stitches and Knit first strand, which is the outer half of selvedge stitch, and then Knit second, inner strand.

If you plan a Single Rib border, there is no need to alternate picking up as to Knit and then as to Purl, since a portion of the inner strand of the selvedge stitch will remain visible below the first new stitch of the pair and will resemble a Purl nub; establish your pattern on the first row to take advantage of this. Unfortunately, if the number of stitches picked up is more than what you need, it is difficult to change because any decreases would interfere with the pattern; however, you can change the gauge by working with a thinner needle to make the new fabric narrower; most ribbings are much improved by doing so, in any case.

Picking Up with Added Yarnover

This version leaves tiny holes, or Eyelets, along the join. They are quite attractive and the selvedge is no longer in evidence on either side of the fabric.

- Pick up under full selvedge stitch and then make a Yarnover; alternate in this way across edge. On first row, work Yarnover farside to twist it.

There are several other ways to handle these Yarnovers on the first row.

- When spacing decreases across first inside row of picked-up stitches, use Purl Left Decreases, with Yarnover as left stitch of each pair. If working on outside, use Knit Right Decreases, with Yarnover as right stitch of each pair.
- As with working twice into selvedge, this is also compatible with Single Rib; establish pattern on first inside row by working each Yarnover as Knit, so it will be in Purl on outside, or if working on outside, use Yarnovers as basis for Knit columns.

Also see Picking Up to Enclose an Edge for another application of this technique.

❖ Picking Up Garter Stitch Selvedge

You have several options for picking up stitches along a Garter Stitch Selvedge. As described for the Chain Selvedge above, you can pick up one stitch per row, or one every other row. If you are dealing with fabric made entirely in Garter Stitch, which is generally quite compressed, it is probably best to pick up every other row. If it is merely a Garter Stitch Selvedge along a fabric made with some other stitch pattern, picking up one stitch for every row might be preferable.

However, consider the gauges of the original and new sections of fabric. In order to minimize the number of increases or decreases required, select the method that results in the number of picked-up stitches closest to what you need for the new section. After you decide upon the number of stitches to pick up, then decide how you want to work into what is actually a rather complicated edge.

The most obvious aspect of a Garter Stitch Selvedge is the series of little knot-like Purl nubs along the edge, one for every other row. The knot is made when the selvedge stitch at the end of one row is reknit at the beginning of the next row and doubles back on itself; to add to the complexity of the knot, the running threads passing into and out of the stitch are pulled in close as well.

It can be a challenge to decide which of the strands in the little knots would be best to pick up; however they can be ignored if you prefer, because in between them are simple Knit stitches, no more than two neat strands, and these are very easy to deal with.

Picking Up Every Two Rows

Here are two options for picking up one stitch every other row.

- Pick up into Knit stitch lying between the knots; insert left needle under just top strand, or under both of them, and then Knit.

You can also pick up into one of the two strands in the knot, and the result is good, although it is somewhat more challenging to work this way; it helps to use relatively thin needles. Try this on a Test Swatch beforehand, because which strand you use, and whether it is knit nearside or farside, will change the appearance of the join. Be very consistent about how you work, always picking up the same strand in each knot, and always knitting the strand in the same way, because any change will be obvious.

- Insert left needle into strand on nearside of knot, or into one on farside and Knit. To cross either strand, Knit farside.

Picking Up Every Row

Here are two ways to pick up one stitch for every row along a Garter Stitch Selvedge.

- Insert needle under both strands of Knit selvedge stitch; Knit first, outer strand on needle and discard, and then Knit second, inner strand.
    This is similar to working under both sides of a Chain Selvedge stitch.
- Combine methods above, picking up once into top strand of Knit stitches in selvedge, and then into one of the strands in knot.

❖ Other Methods of Picking Up

The instructions above assume you will be picking up along a nice, straight, consistent selvedge and turning it to the inside of the fabric, but that is not always the case. Here you will find some suggestions for how to pick up adjacent to the selvedge, how to turn the selvedge to the outside for a decorative seam, or, conversely, how to hide it completely. Also included are tips for picking up along a sloped or curved edge, which can present challenges, as well as how to pick up stitches into a woven fabric in order to add trim of some kind.

Picking Up Running Threads

This is a somewhat unorthodox approach, but in certain circumstances it may be worth considering. Instead of drawing a new stitch under a selvedge stitch, draw it under the running threads that lie between the selvedge and the first column of stitches.

- On outside, insert left needle from left to right under running thread that lies between selvedge and first column of stitches, bringing tip of needle through to outside of fabric; insert right needle into strand as to Knit, wrap yarn, and draw new stitch through.

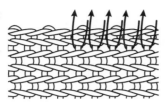

Picking Up Running Threads. Pick up running thread between selvedge and next stitch.

The entire selvedge will be turned to the inside and will have a row of Purl nubs above it. The result is a very firm and even join, but one that is also quite bulky. However, if you have a border that persists in turning to the outside of the garment, this forces the selvedge firmly down against the inside of the fabric and will usually correct the problem.

Turning Selvedges to Outside

A neatly done selvedge turned to the outside as you pick up stitches is not only quite decorative, but serves nicely to camouflage the join between two fabrics.

All that is necessary, beyond first making a neat selvedge, is to pick up using one of the methods described above, but work on the inside in Knit, or the outside in Purl.

- A Stockinette Selvedge, done neatly and consistently, will look very attractive when turned to the outside, where it forms a tidy chain.
- A Garter Stitch Selvedge is also nice when turned to the outside, since it forms a nubby cord. If you pick up one stitch per row, the edge will tighten and the result will be a bold cord on the outside. If you pick up one stitch every two rows, the result is softer and more subtle.
- A Chain Selvedge turned to the outside is, perhaps, the most successful of these choices, since not only is the chain of stitches pleasing to the eye, but also the join is considerably less bulky; see the illustration in Picking Up to Join.

Seed Stitch border joined at side edge, with Chain Selvedge turned to outside.

- The technique described in Picking Up Running Threads, above, can also be quite decorative when done so the edge turns to the outside, since it places a row of Purl nubs between the picked-up stitches and the fabric.

Also, if you alternate Knit and Purl as you pick up the running threads in this way, it makes a very nice base for a Single Rib border.

- There are also three Double Selvedges that are decorative when just the selvedge stitch of the pair is turned to the outside. The first two consist of either a Stockinette or Chain Selvedge at the edge, with an adjacent column of Garter Stitch. These look very nice and are easy to do, but I like the third one, Chain and Purl Selvedge even better—the selvedge stitch nests inside the column of Purl stitches, lying almost flat on the surface of the fabric.

Picking Up a Shaped Edge

It is always best to work any increases or decreases needed to slope or curve the side of the fabric one or two stitches away from a selvedge. This leaves the selvedge stitches, and the space between the selvedge and the first column of stitches in the fabric, unaffected, and it will be easier to pick up along the edge.

However, if you have included some selvedge stitches in an increase or decrease, it is better to turn all the strands involved to the inside when picking up by inserting the needle into the space between where the shaping technique is and the next unaffected stitch within the fabric. This will make the selvedge bulkier, but it will help minimize any visible distortion at the join.

A curved edge often has a small group of stitches that have been cast off or placed on a holder, such as at the center front of a neckline or the bottom of an armhole. There is frequently a gap at the intersection of a horizontal section of this kind and the adjacent curved or sloped section that can be challenging to close neatly when picking up.

Here are a few suggestions for making a pickup of this kind as even and consistent as possible.

- Pick up running thread within gap at each side and Knit or Purl farside so it will cross. If necessary, use this technique in addition to one of those that follow.
- If stitches are on a holder, transfer to right needle. Work a Left Raised Increase into last of these stitches, then pick up stitches around neckline; work a Right Raised Increase into first of the stitches that were on hold, and then work across those stitches.
- If stitches were cast off, work into right side of first stitch immediately below edge, pick up into outer strand of all cast-off stitches, and then work into left side of stitch below last one cast off in same way.

Picking Up into Woven Fabrics: knitted border on a doily. Photograph by Joe Coca; from Nancie Wiseman, *Lace from the Attic: A Victorian Notebook of Knitted Lace Patterns* (Loveland, Colo.: Interweave Press, 1998).

- If more is needed to close gap, also work a Left Raised Increase on stitch below selvedge to right of those on hold or cast off, and a Right Raised Increase into stitch below selvedge to left of them.

Picking Up a Cut or Knotted Edge

If you are dealing with a cut edge, you will not have knitted selvedge stitches available for picking up. The edge may have been secured by hand or machine sewing, or with knots to keep it from unraveling; for more information, see Steeks: Selvedges for Cut Openings.

However the edge was finished, pick up one stitch per row, as follows:

- Use one of methods described above for a Stockinette Selvedge. On outside, insert needle into spaces between first uninterrupted column of stitches and sewn or knotted edge, so that rough Selvedge is turned to inside of garment.

Picking Up to Enclose an Edge

This is a rather clever technique that makes it possible to pick up in a way that encloses the selvedge on both sides. It is most often used for a Single Rib border, but can be adapted for use with other types of patterns.

1. To pick up around edge, use Picking Up with Added Yarnover.
2. Work two to four rows using the Basic Double-Fabric technique.
3. Revert to single thickness fabric (see Double to Single Fabric). Begin Single Rib or other border pattern.

The result is similar to the join used for necklines on machine knits and it can be quite attractive. You might also want to consider it when adding a border to a fabric that will be visible on both sides, such as a shawl, and it can also be a nice way to handle an unattractive or cut edge, although the join tends to be bulky.

For a smooth, neat edge, it is important to try this on a Test Swatch before deciding how to work, since needle size is critical. You will find other tips for how to produce a successful result in the instructions for the technique Double-Fabric Enclosed Edge.

Picking Up into Woven Fabrics

Some very interesting designs can be made by combining knitted and woven fabrics. The charming Scandinavian jackets often seen in textile museums that have woven fabric bodices and knitted sleeves are wonderful examples. On a smaller scale, you could add a knitted lace collar to a blouse or ribbed cuffs and waistband to a jacket. Traditionally, the technique has also been used to add knitted trim to the edges of household items such as linen table mats, pillowcases, and hand towels.

You can, of course, simply sew the woven fabric to the knitted one (see Sewing Wovens to Knits), but you can also pick up stitches along the edge of a woven fabric and either knit a border out from the edge, or join the side edge of a narrow border to the picked-up stitches as you knit it (see Picking Up to Join).

Here are some suggestions for how to pick up a new set of stitches along a woven edge.

- The finished edge may or may not remain visible, depending upon how you work and the spacing of the stitches you pick up, but it is a good idea to finish it first with a tiny hem or edge stitching so it will not ravel.
- Mark off fractional inch or centimeter increments around edge with tailor's chalk as a guide for evenly distributing the stitches while picking them up.

  Or, if you are dealing with a curved edge and don't have a soft measuring tape, fold the fabric in half and mark, fold in quarters and mark, and so on, dividing each space into smaller and smaller areas.

  Alternatively, to create a guide for picking up, sew a line of contrast-color stitches adjacent to the hemmed edge, setting the stitch length to produce however many you need per inch; remove stitching later.

- Instead of picking up the stitches with a knitting needle, first add an edge of Single Crochet to the fabric, easing head of hook through threads. Then, pick up new set of stitches for knitted portion by working under crochet chain as if it were a Stockinette or Chain Selvedge.

If necessary, use an awl to make preliminary openings along the edge at each mark you made. Gently ease the threads apart, and then insert the crochet hook into the hole formed.

- Or, use hook to draw yarn through fabric and transfer each new stitch to knitting needle, or use a cro-needle; see Tools.

❖ *Adjusting Number of Stitches*

As mentioned in the introduction to this chapter, it is almost always necessary to adjust the number of stitches on the needle after picking up because the gauge of the new fabric is unlikely to match that of the original. For more information, see Stitch Gauge, as well as the information in Charting Horizontal Shaping in Charted Garment Patterns; or, for a different way to do the same thing, see Step and Points for Horizontal Shaping in Calculations for Pattern Design.

Here are some tips for how to make these kinds of adjustments according to the pattern you develop.

Increases and Decreases

When it is necessary to adjust the number of stitches on the needle, it is easy to choose among the decreases because there are so few of them; however, there are more options with increases, and it depends upon the particular circumstances of your pattern which one will work best. Here are some suggestions:

- When picking up under the full selvedge, on next row use the equivalent of a Raised Increase as necessary; reach the needle down on the inside and work the increase on the inner strands of the selvedge stitches.

  If you picked up into one side of the selvedge, work the increase on the remaining strand.

- If you are planning to work a Single Rib pattern on the picked-up stitches, Rib Increases done on the first row will blend in well.

- While picking up on a Chain Selvedge, insert a Yarnover between some of the new stitches, according to your pattern; see Picking Up with Added Yarnover. To help the increases blend in, twist the Yarnovers when working them on the next row; see Turned Yarnovers.

  Alternatively, on the next row, work the Yarnovers so they remain open, leaving evenly spaced Eyelets in the join.

Adjusting Stitches for Slopes and Curves

When picking up along a slope or curve, keep in mind that the edge will have a longer measurement for the same number of rows than one that is straight; see Picking Up a Shaped Edge.

To calculate the number of stitches needed for the new section of fabric, use a flexible tape to measure the edge, and multiply that length by the gauge of the new section of fabric. For more information, see Stitch Gauge, as well as the information in Charting a Curve.

Necklines present an additional challenge, because they will have stitches at center front and back, either cast-off or on a holder, and selvedge stitches at each side.

• To determine number of stitches needed along each side of neckline opening, compare stitch gauge of new fabric with row gauge of main fabric.
• To determine number needed at center of neckline opening, compare stitch gauge of new fabric with stitch gauge of main fabric.

Spacing a Pickup

As mentioned above, it is possible to space the stitches along the edge as you pick up instead of adjusting the number later. I do not find this a particularly effective approach, since it tends to create an uneven join between the two fabrics. However, for a simple pickup, particularly on a fabric done in a textured yarn that will hide the join, it can be satisfactory, and it is certainly quick and easy to do. This is especially true if you want to reduce the number of stitches—all that is necessary is to skip a Selvedge stitch from time to time, according to the pattern you work out.

A Garter Stitch Selvedge works quite well for this purpose since it is nice and nubbly, and the natural compression of the fabric and its texture will hide any irregularities. It also offers a variety of strands to pick up into and one or the other will make a neat job of spacing things out, depending on the circumstances.

I do not recommend spacing stitches along a Chain Selvedge as you pick up because the structure of the edge is too soft and loose. Wherever you slip a selvedge stitch, or work twice into one, there will be a visible inconsistency in the join.

Nevertheless, if you want to increase into only some of the selvedge stitches along an edge, there are some techniques mentioned in Picking Up Every Row along a Chain Selvedge that can be used in this way as well. The important thing is to space the increases out evenly.

Try some of these approaches on the selvedge of a Test Swatch to decide which one works best for your project.

Picking Up to Join

As mentioned in the introduction of this chapter, in most cases the picked-up stitches are treated as if they had been cast on

and the new section of fabric is worked out from that edge. However, it is also possible to join a new section of fabric to stitches picked up along a selvedge, row-by-row as it is worked. You can also work in the same way to add a new section of fabric to stitches freed and then picked up along a bottom or top edge of a fabric.

This technique is commonly used to attach elements of a design that are worked narrow and long, such as a button band for a center front opening or a border around the edges of a shawl. There are any number of beautiful patterns (many of them lace) that can used in this way for collars, for instance, or to trim the lower edge of a sleeve or bodice.

In addition to these traditional applications, the technique also makes it possible to insert a new section of fabric within another, either vertically or horizontally, by joining it at both sides. You might choose to work this way because the insert has a very different gauge, or because you want to set a decorative stitch pattern perpendicular to the one used for the main fabric.

The instructions for how to add a vertical border to a side edge are given first; this is the most basic type of join. As you will see, the methods used for a horizontal join, as well as for insertions, are done in much the same way. Also included are instructions for how to join something like a collar to a curved edge or a border to more than one side of something like a shawl, which involves navigating around the corners. Finally, there is a discussion of various aspects of incorporating an element like this into a garment design.

❖ *Vertical Joins*

For a vertical join, the side edge of the new fabric is attached row-by-row to stitches picked up into the selvedge of the original fabric. Once joined, the stitch columns of the two fabrics will lie parallel to each other.

Basic Vertical Join

Allow tail of yarn sufficient for casting on number of stitches needed for width of border, plus additional to hide on inside during finishing. Leave tail hanging at corner of fabric and begin picking up stitches along edge with main yarn.

1. Pick up stitches into selvedge, using one of the methods described above. Turn.
2. On first row, work evenly spaced increases or decreases to adjust number of stitches as necessary; tail of yarn and main yarn will now be together at needle tip.
3. Use a Finger Cast-On with tail of yarn as baseline and main yarn for stitches and add number of stitches required for width of border to needle bearing picked-up stitches (see Side or Mid-Fabric Cast-Ons); in addition to

Joining a Vertical Border to picked-up stitches.

border stitches, add one stitch for border selvedge, and one stitch for join between border and main fabric.

4. Work border stitches in pattern toward join; with one border stitch remaining on left needle, work decrease to join border stitch to next picked-up stitch.
5. Turn, work stitches of border out to edge.
6. Repeat Steps 4 and 5 to attach border.

To help you maintain the pattern, you might want to place a marker between the two border stitches closest to the join. You will find several choices for decreases to use below.

General Information for Vertical Joins

As you can see, there are a great many variables when joining one fabric to another in this way. Here are some suggestions regarding what kind of needles to use, recommendations about which decrease to use in different circumstances, as well as some options for how to pick up the stitches that were not discussed above.

Needles

- To keep stitches from dropping off as you work, use a circular needle to pick up; pull opposite tip out while working on project, and pull both needle tips out so cable will act as a stitch holder when work is set aside.
- If there are a great many picked-up stitches on left needle, or if garment is heavy, use cable needle bearing picked-up stitches as a holder. Transfer several stitches at a time from circular needle to a short double-point needle held in left hand and use it and needle in right hand to work border stitches and join.

- Consider working border from right to left on one row, and left to right on next so there is no need to turn work; see Bi-Directional Method for more information.

Choice of Decrease

The type of decrease to use depends in part on whether you are joining the left or right side of a new fabric. If you are joining the left side of the new fabric, you will be working toward the join on the outside of the main fabric; if you are joining the right side of the new fabric, you will be working toward the join on the inside.

You can use either a Right or Left Decrease for either side; however, each one produces a different appearance and the choice between the two depends upon whether you want to have a border stitch or a main fabric stitch visible at the join. For more information, see Decreases.

- If a Knit Left Decrease is used to join left side of border, facing stitch of join will be from border.
- If a Knit Right Decrease is used instead, facing stitch of join will be from main fabric.
- If a Purl Right Decrease is used to join right side of border, facing stitch will be from border.
- If a Purl Left Decrease is used instead, facing stitch of join will be from main fabric.

Number of Picked-Up Stitches

A join of this kind can be done on the same number of picked-up stitches as there will be rows in the attachment, or on half the number of stitches. Which way you choose to work will change the appearance of the join, as will the type of decrease used.

Joining to Half as Many Stitches

If there are half as many picked-up stitches as rows in the border, the border will be joined every other row. There are two options:

- Work joining decrease, turn, work border stitches to outer edge.
  The stitch column at the join will have a slight zigzag appearance.
- Or, work joining decrease, turn, Slip 1, work border stitches to outer edge.
  The slipped stitch is the one formed on the joining decrease, and it will form an attractive chain of stitches on the outside of the fabric.

Joining to Equal Number of Stitches

In this case, every row is joined to a picked-up stitch; the result is a neat and tailored column of stitches at the join.

1. Work joining decrease on last border stitch and first picked-up stitch; immediately work second decrease that includes new stitch from previous decrease and next picked-up stitch.
2. Turn, Slip 1, and work border stitches to outer edge.

In Step 1, the last stitch of one row is part of the first decrease, the first stitch of the next row is part of the second decrease.

Picking Up While Joining

It is also possible to pick up the stitches along the selvedge one at a time as you work the new section of fabric and just before each one is needed for the joining decrease. There are two approaches described here: the first has several options for how to work, but the results are problematic; the other is decorative, but somewhat limited.

Join and Turn Selvedge Inside

This is a quick and easy approach (and therefore tempting), *but* there are several problems with it.

First, in order to adjust the number of stitches, either some selvedge stitches must be worked into twice or some must be skipped, which does not produce as smooth a join as when the stitches are all picked up ahead of time (see Spacing a Pickup).

Second, the join will be considerably thicker because the running thread between one picked-up stitch and the next wraps around the entire selvedge instead of nesting beneath it.

Nevertheless, for a short and simple pattern, you might prefer this approach. To begin, cast on number of stitches required for border and work first row toward join as described for Basic Vertical Join, above.

- To work join on outside row, Slip last stitch of border knitwise, pick up and Knit one stitch into selvedge, and pass slipped stitch over new stitch and off needle, as for a Left Decrease.
- To work join on inside row, Slip last stitch of border, pick up one stitch into selvedge as to Purl, insert left needle into farside of both this new stitch and slipped border stitch, and Purl Two Together.
- Alternatively, Slip last border stitch knitwise, Purl selvedge stitch, and pull border stitch over.

Join and Turn Selvedge Outside

This technique is nice if you want to simultaneously pick up and join a Garter Stitch border, or a border with an intermediary pattern of Garter Stitch, to a Chain Selvedge (also see Cord with Visible Selvedge for another application).

1. Allow tail of yarn; instead of Slip Knot, pull loop through first stitch at lower corner to serve as joining stitch. Pick up tail and main yarn and add stitches for border to needle with a Half-Hitch Cast-On.
2. Work border toward join; with yarn farside, Slip joining stitch knitwise, pick up stitch under full selvedge as to Knit, and pass Slip stitch over picked-up stitch.
3. Turn, Slip joining stitch purlwise, yarn farside, tighten Slip stitch on needle, and then Knit border stitches.
4. Repeat Steps 2–3 for length of border.

The joining stitches and the selvedge stitches will form a double chain on the outside, lyng between the main fabric and the border. If the border is in a contrast color, the two stitch columns of the chain will be in different colors.

The border has a tendency to flip to the inside of the fabric unless it is steamed thoroughly to encourage it to lie flat. Of course, the success of this approach depends on being able to stretch the Garter Stitch to fit the length of the main fabric, because there is no way to adjust the number of stitches available in the edge.

Joining a Garter Stitch Border with
Chain Selvedge turned to outside.

❖ Horizontal Joins

The same basic concepts discussed above for a vertical join can also be used to join a border of any kind to a top or bottom edge. In a sense, this is a cast-off technique because it also serves to finish and secure the edge and there is no need to pick up stitches (also see Corded Cast-Off). For joining to a cast-on edge, however, either use a Provisional Cast-On or unravel the cast-on edge as described in Removing Cast-On Edges, and then pick the stitches up. The Vertical and Horizontal Join techniques are combined when adding a border around all four sides of something like a shawl or blanket.

Depending on the nature of your project, you may want to determine the Row Gauge of the border and then adjust the number of stitches in the last row of the fabric before joining it, or work as described for Picking Up While Joining and perhaps just adjust your needle size and use some steam to help the border fit itself to the fabric.

Here are the instructions for adding a Garter Stitch border in this way, but there are a great many narrow border patterns available that could be used in the same way.

Horizontal Garter Stitch Border

A Garter Stitch border will have two rows in the border for every stitch used for the join; calculate the gauge of the border and adjust the number of stitches in the main fabric accordingly.

Joining a Garter Stitch Border to a top edge.

1. Cast on number of stitches required for width of border.
2. Knit toward join; with two stitches remaining on left needle, work Knit Left Decrease. Turn.
3. Knit to edge of border; turn.
4. Repeat Steps 2 and 3 for length of edge.
5. On last row, cast off toward join; with 1 stitch on right needle and two on left needle, work Knit Left Decrease; with last two stitches on right needle, pull second stitch over first to complete edge.

Edge Border

Here are the instructions for how to attach a border to the top or bottom of an existing fabric. There is no need to pick up stitches in the sense used in this chapter; instead, work as follows:

1. For stitches at a top edge, do not cast off; work one row to adjust number of stitches to that needed for number of rows in border pattern.

   For stitches at a bottom edge, start main fabric with Stranded Provisional Cast-On, or Alternating Provisional Cast-On, or pick out existing cast-on edge to work border; see Working in the Opposite Direction.
2. Attach border to these stitches in same way as described above for Vertical Join.

❖ *Insertions*

The joinery techniques discussed above can also be used to insert one section of fabric between two others; instead of joining at one side as the material is worked, it is joined on both sides. This requires two sets of picked-up stitches—on the left side of one fabric, and on the right side of the other. The technique makes possible some very interesting design applications that would be difficult to do in any other way.

Vertical Insertion

It can be a challenge to combine two different stitch patterns in one fabric, particularly if they have radically different gauges.

For instance, should you want a garment with a center front lace panel and the sides done in a plain or textured pattern, the ideal needle size to use for the respective patterns is likely to be different.

It is possible to work the panel separately and sew it into place or even to work with two different size needles. The former approach is a perfectly good option, but the latter may be a problem if the number of rows required for the length of the panel is different from that required for the fabric at each side; for more information about coordinating two patterns in this way, see Swatches for Vertical Patterns in the chapter on Stitch Gauge.

Instead, you can work the panel as an insertion, using whatever size needles it requires, and simultaneously join it to stitches picked up along each side section of a main garment piece made separately. Because you can adjust the number of stitches picked up along the two selvedges to exactly that needed for the number of rows in the new fabric, the resulting join will be very smooth. Also, see Integrated Edges, below, for suggestions about how to handle the top and bottom edges of an insertion of this kind.

1. Make two sections of garment that will be to either side of decorative panel. Using separate needles, pick up stitches along right side of one and left side of other garment section for joining center panel.
2. Determine number of rows to work in panel, according to its gauge and length of fabric to each side.
3. Work one row to adjust number of picked-up stitches on each needle to either equal total number in panel, or half number in panel, depending upon joining technique to be used (see Number of Picked-Up Stitches, above).
4. Using separate needle, cast on stitches for width of insertion panel, plus two additional stitches for join at each side.
5. Begin to work panel, joining new fabric at end of an outside row to set of picked-up stitches on one side, and at end of an inside row to set of stitches on other side.

Horizontal Insertion

It is also possible to insert a panel into a fabric horizontally, so the stitch columns are perpendicular to those of the main fabric. This is a good way to handle an Epaulette Shoulder, which is a perpendicular strip of decorative fabric introduced between the front and back shoulders.

This approach might also be used to introduce a bit of decorative trim within the fabric, perhaps at the base of a yoke, or several inches above the lower edge of a bodice or sleeve. Any number of narrow patterns designed for edgings are suitable for this, and the trim could be done with a contrast-color yarn or one of a different type. For a nice transition between three fabric sections joined in this way, consider using one of the Intermediary Patterns for Joins, below.

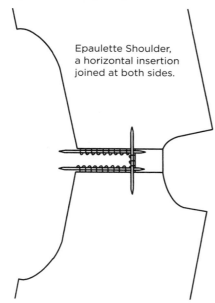

Epaulette Shoulder, a horizontal insertion joined at both sides.

Basic Horizontal Insertion

Here is an example of how to insert some horizontal trim across the width of the fabric.

1. In main fabric, work to row below position of insertion; adjust number of stitches to equal number of rows in insertion pattern; place stitches on cable needle to act as holder.
2. Use Alternating Provisional Cast-On and two separate needles to cast on number of stitches equal to number of rows in insertion pattern.
3. On set of stitches cast on for main fabric, work one row to adjust number of stitches to that needed for width of garment, and work to top of garment section.
4. With separate pair of double point needles, cast on stitches for width of insertion; begin to work, joining on one side to stitches on holder from Step 1, and on other side to stitches on holder that were cast on in Step 2.

The cast-on used in Step 2 creates two sets of stitches: one is the set you will next work up from in Step 3 to make the fabric above the insertion; the other is the set that will be used to attach the insertion in Step 4; these remain temporarily on hold on the second needle.

Horizontal Trim with Free Edge

These instructions are for a piece of trim such as a narrow ruffle that is inserted horizontally and hangs down on the face of the fabric. As it is worked, the rows of the trim are joined on one side to the stitches of the fabric. There are three ways to work.

Version One

1. Work to row before position of insertion in main fabric; work one row to adjust number of stitches to that needed for rows in trim pattern.
2. On separate needle, cast on number of stitches required for width of trim. Work trim pattern and join at one side to main fabric. Inside row of trim is on same side of needle as outside row of main fabric.
3. At opposite side edge of garment, cast off trim stitches when working toward main fabric.
4. Turn to inside of main fabric and fold trim down on outside. Pick up heads of stitches in row *below* where number of stitches was adjusted in Step 1 (that row has same number of stitches needed for main fabric above trim) and continue on these stitches to complete remaining portion of garment section.

Version Two

1. Work as described in Step 1, above.
2. Cast on and work trim separately.
3. Pick up stitches along one edge of trim; work one row and adjust number of stitches to match number in main fabric.
4. Hold needle bearing stitches of main fabric, and needle bearing picked-up stitches of trim parallel; work Joinery Decreases to link the two fabrics.

Version Three

• The same general ideas can be applied to stitches picked up through the fabric; see Picking Up Within a Fabric.

About gathers . . .
Calculate the number of rows needed to gather the ruffle carefully to get the effect you want. It is tempting to simply use twice as many rows in the ruffle as there are stitches in the width of the fabric, but this may create too much gathering. Try several possibilities on a swatch before deciding how to work; it may be best to adjust the number of stitches in the width to that needed for a smooth join, and then return to the original number after joining the trim.

❖ *Joining to Shaped Edges*

For the most part, joining the side of a new fabric to a curved or sloped edge is much the same as joining to one that is straight. The only real difference is in how to calculate the adjustment from the number of stitches picked up to that needed for the border, since this may require dealing with a row gauge in some areas, and a stitch gauge in others, as discussed in Picking Up a Shaped Edge. The information below on setting a sleeve cap into an armhole is a good example of how to use the Insertion technique to join something to a shaped edge.

Another challenge is joining a border that travels around all the edges of a garment—such as the four sides of a shawl, or the lower edge, center front opening, and neckline of a cardigan sweater or jacket—since there will be corners to deal with that require Short Row patterns.

Collars and Ruffles

- To attach side of flat collar done in pattern worked narrow and long, pick up stitches around neckline opening, work one row to adjust number of stitches according to gauge, and then join one side of collar as described above for a straight border. To curve a flat collar for this purpose, see Short Row Curves in Shaping a Fabric.
- A ruffle is likely to have considerably more rows than there will be picked-up stitches. First find number of rows required for ruffle, and then pick up on edge of main fabric in one of the ways described above; on next row, radically increase number of stitches to adjust number of stitches for join.
- If doubling number of stitches picked up is not sufficient, or if it looks too crowded, also use Short Rows within the ruffle.

Corners

A border joined at the side to picked-up stitches may be worked continuously around two or more sides of a fabric. This will involve both vertical and horizontal edges, and the border will need a Short Row Miter pattern at any place where it changes direction.

For instance, to work a continuous border around all sides of something like a shawl, here are some basic guidelines:

Continuous Border for Shawl

1. Pick up stitches on all four sides of fabric and adjust number of stitches to that needed for attachment rows.
2. At first corner, use Stranded Provisional Cast-On or Alternating Provisional Cast-On to add stitches for border.
3. Work half of miter pattern on these stitches using Increasing Short Rows, and then begin to work border, joining one side of border to each side of fabric, and working full miter pattern at each of next three corners.

4. After joining border to last side of fabric and returning to first corner, work other half of miter pattern using Decreasing Short Rows.
5. Graft last row of half miter made in Step 4 to Provisional Cast-On edge of half miter made in Step 3.

Joining a Jacket Border

To work a continuous border around the edges of a garment with a center front opening, work as follows:

1. Pick up stitches on all edges of garment, starting at center back neck.
2. Use a Provisional Cast-On to add stitches for border.
3. Begin to work and join border, using Short Row patterns at side of neck, where neckline meets vertical center front opening, and at bottom of opening.
4. When border is complete, graft last row to Provisional Cast-On edge at center back neck.

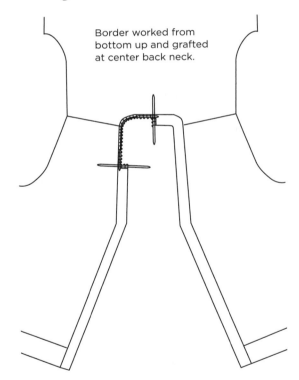

Border worked from bottom up and grafted at center back neck.

Joining Sleeve to Armhole

When working flat, it is possible to join a shaped sleeve cap to stitches picked up around an armhole. The advantage of this approach is that the sleeve will be set precisely in the armhole, with no guesswork, as there often is when sewing a sleeve into place.

This is basically done like a Vertical Insertion; however, the technique requires the use of two sets of shaping techniques; one set is used to join the sleeve to the stitches picked up around the armhole; the other is used to shape the sleeve cap.

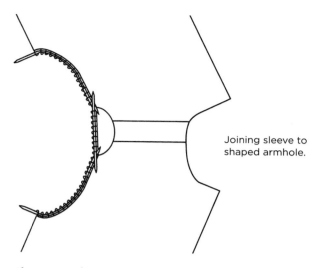

Joining sleeve to shaped armhole.

The pattern for the sleeve cap remains the same—increases if worked from shoulder down, decreases if worked from armhole up. Set the techniques used for shaping the sleeve cap one or two stitches away from the Joinery Decreases used to join the cap to the picked-up stitches around the armhole.

Here are some tips for how to work:

- Both sleeve cap and armhole will need selvedges at each side for join.
- Use circular needles to pick up stitches around armhole and adjust number to that needed for rows in sleeve cap.
- Work sleeve on separate needles, either from bottom up or from top down.
- When working from top down, seam shoulder first, work cap to bottom of armhole, pick up stitches at underarm of bodice front and back, and work sleeve to wrist; seam sleeve arm and bodice.
- When working from bottom up, sew bodice side seams, work sleeve to underarm, and use Joinery Decreases or Grafting to join stitches at underarm of bodice front and back with those at each side of sleeve. Work sleeve cap, joining at both sides; seam shoulder to finish.

It is very easy to work a simple, unshaped sleeve (one without a sleeve cap) in the round from the armhole to the wrist, but it is not possible to make a shaped sleeve cap when working from the top down, except as described above or by means of Short Rows, which are also worked flat.

It is possible to work the upper sleeves and bodice of a garment together in the round from the top down, but this also requires some use of Short Rows, and necessitates a compromise in the shaping of the sleeve cap, which would normally have considerably fewer rows than the armhole; for more information, see Bodice and Sleeve Design, as well as the discussion in Circular and Flat Knitting, Working from the Top Down.

❖ *Design Details for Joined Fabrics*

When planning for a design element of this kind, there are some subtle but important things to take into consideration. For instance, in addition to the width of a border or insertion, the picked-up stitches and the join itself can add some length or width to the fabric, and this may be worth taking into consideration when planning a design.

Also, you will want to give some thought to the appearance of any visible edges, especially in regard to integrating one or more of them with other elements of the garment, such as where a center front border meets the neckline.

And finally, there are a few decorative intermediary patterns that can be inserted between the main fabric and the join.

Width or Length of Join

When calculating the overall width of the fabric, it is not quite sufficient to simply add in the width of the joined section. Both the picked-up stitches and the join itself will have some effect on the width as well, and your gauge determines whether this is a minor issue or not.

Calculating Effect of Join

To determine what, if any, effect the join will have on the length and width of the fabric, here are some details to keep in mind:

- Calculate the basic number of stitches required for the section to be added, and then add two selvedge stitches. For a Vertical Insertion, both selvedge stitches will be used for the join, one at each side. For a border, one selvedge stitch is for the join, and one will serve as the visible edge.
- In most cases, the selvedge of the main fabric will be absorbed by the pickup and will not add to the width. However, if only the outer side of the selvedge stitch is picked up, the result may be rather open and loose, and it will contribute something to the width.
- If one row is worked to adjust the number of stitches after picking up, it will also contribute to the length or width.
- The picked-up stitches will be absorbed in the decrease used for the join, and will not contribute to the width.

In sum, three stitches, and perhaps the original selvedge, as well, have an effect on the width. Depending upon the gauge, this could add anywhere from one-quarter to 1 inch in length or width to the fabric—and of course that will double if there is a border on two sides.

Integrated Edges

With most Joinery applications, it is also important to give some thought as to how to handle the other edges. A border on a vertical edge, for instance, will at the least require a nice selvedge for the side opposite the join, because it will remain visible. In addition, the top and bottom edges require consideration, depending on how they relate to the main fabric.

This is also true of a Horizontal Join, but in this case, the top and bottom edges of the new section will be adjacent to the sides of the main fabric, and may be visible if those edges are not seamed.

Bottom Edges

The bottom edge of a Vertical Join can start at either the cast-on edge or just above the lower border of the main fabric. Here are some suggestions for how to integrate this edge in an attractive way.

Border Cast-On Edge

With this approach, the fabric and the border or insertion share a single cast-on edge.

1. Cast on number of stitches for width of fabric, plus those for border, and three selvedge stitches, one each for border and fabric to be used for join, and one for visible edge of border; place cast-on border stitches and two selvedge stitches on holder. Work main fabric.
2. Transfer border stitches from holder to needle; pick up stitches along selvedge of main fabric, and work border, joining at side.

Insertion at Cast-On Edge

1. Cast on number of stitches for width of fabric, plus those for insertion, and four selvedge stitches, one for each side of main fabric and two for sides of insertion.
2. Place insertion and two selvedge stitches on holder. Complete two sides of main fabric.
3. Transfer insertion stitches from holder to needle; pick up stitches along each side of main fabric sections, and work insertion, joining at both sides.

Insertion Above Bottom Border

- For a vertical border or insertion that starts above a ribbing or any other type of border at lower edge, work as described above, but complete lower border to depth required before placing stitches for vertical border or insertion on holder.

Top Edges

The stitches at the top of a center front border or insertion may be cast off, or placed on hold and later picked up with the stitches of the main fabric for a neckline or collar. The stitches at the top of an insertion that is set to one side of

the garment section will end at the shoulder line and will require a slope.

Top Border Edge

1. Work main fabric to length equal to planned border; place stitches on hold or leave on cable of circular needle.
2. Work border to same length, joining at side.
3. Cast off stitches of border toward main fabric, and then reactivate stitches of main fabric and complete garment section, shaping neckline and shoulder according to pattern.

If border stitches will be picked up later for collar or other neckline finish, place them on hold instead of casting them off.

Top Insertion Edges

- If insertion is for flat piece, like a shawl or scarf, work each side section length required and then place stitches on holders; when insertion is complete, reactivate stitches of side pieces and cast off across all three sections.
- If insertion ends at a shoulder, the slope at top edge of insertion and those in two areas of fabric to each side are done separately (insertion will be attached to fewer rows on one side than the other). With slope complete, work across all three sets of stitches together to cast off.

Side Edges for Horizontal Joins

When a new fabric is joined horizontally and runs perpendicular to the main fabric, care must be taken to integrate the bottom and top edges of the insertion with the side edges of the main fabric. Of course, it is no problem if the edges will be seamed, but if they will remain visible, it poses a challenge.

One easy way to camouflage the transition is to crochet either a plain or decorative edge that runs continuously along the sides of both sections of fabric.

Here is another approach that blends the selvedges at the side edges of the main fabric, and the first and last rows of the insertion:

1. Use a Provisional Cast-On to start the border or insertion; after attaching do not cast off last row.
2. Pick up all stitches along selvedge on one side of main fabric, and those cast on for insertion; turn and immediately cast off all stitches.
3. Repeat on other side to incorporate stitches in last row of insertion.

Intermediary Patterns for Joins

When attaching two fabrics at their side edges, there are several ways to make the join more decorative by introducing a narrow intermediary pattern between the main fabric and the border. This can also be an effective way to distract the eye from the pickup row and any increases or decreases required if that area is not attractive. For this purpose, consider a highly textured stitch pattern or color pattern, or choose a stitch pattern that is relatively firm and tailored if you think the border needs support.

Both of these approaches are very simple; one is worked along with the border, the other on the picked-up stitches.

Parallel Intermediary Pattern

1. Pick up stitches along side edge of main fabric and cast on sufficient stitches for width of border, plus two or three extra stitches for intermediary patterns, and one for the join.
2. Work border stitches according to pattern, work intermediary stitches in Garter or Seed Stitch, or some other simple decorative pattern, and then work join on last stitch of border and first stitch of main fabric.

Work in the same way for joining an Insertion, just add the extra stitches for the intermediary pattern at both sides.

Perpendicular Intermediary Pattern

With this approach, the rows of both border and fabric will run in the same direction, while the rows of the intermediary pattern between the two will be perpendicular to them.

• Pick up stitches along selvedge, and work intermediary pattern before adding stitches for border.

  Adjust number of stitches needed for join either before or after working this pattern, whichever works best in the circumstances.

Picking Up Within a Fabric

The techniques discussed here are used to pick up stitches within a fabric instead of at an edge, like those above. This is a good way to apply things like pockets, flat collars, or ruffles to the interior of a finished fabric without sewing.

For instance, stitches can be picked up within a fabric for the base of a pocket, leaving just the sides to sew down later. Or you can pick up stitches between a neckline ribbing and the main fabric to introduce a flat collar, or above the ribbing of a sleeve to add a lace ruffle.

Design details of this kind lend themselves particularly well to improvisation. Various applications of the techniques can be used to add details you may not have thought of in the planning process, or to liven up an existing garment that has come to seem too plain.

While picking up stitches within the fabric is quite similar to doing so along an edge, it can be more of a challenge to keep track of exactly where to work next—particularly on a slope,

if the yarn texture obscures the stitches, or if the stitch pattern is complex. Also, once you are under way and the fabric is no longer lying nice and flat, things can get into even more of a muddle. It is often best to lay the fabric flat and mark the pickup line with a length of contrast-color yarn or embroidery thread beforehand, or, even better, plan ahead and insert a Yarn Marker as you work.

As always, it is best to pick up evenly into every stitch and then adjust the number of stitches as necessary on the next row according to the gauge of the fabric that is added; see Adjusting Number of Stitches.

The instructions assume you will be picking up into a plain Stockinette fabric, a pattern of mixed Knit and Purl, or any decorative pattern that has some plain stitches to pick up into. In fact it is somewhat easier to work into Purl stitches, because the nubs make easy targets for your needle. If this is something you are planning ahead of time, consider working a row or column of Purl stitches on the outside of the fabric where the pickup will occur to define the area clearly; this makes the pick-up process very easy to do.

Two methods can be used—holding the yarn on the outside of the fabric, or holding it on the inside and drawing each stitch through the fabric to the outside. As with picking up along an edge, I find it easier to do this with two needles and that is the way the instructions have been written. However, it can also be done with one needle, as shown in the illustrations; they were drawn this way to make it easier to see what to do.

❖ Picking Up on the Outside

With this method, the new stitches can be drawn either under the heads of the stitches in the original fabric, under the running threads between the stitches, or through the sides of the stitches. The pickup can be done horizontally along a row, or vertically along a stitch column.

Both the new, picked-up stitches as well as the running threads that pass between each one will be on the outside of the fabric; therefore, plan the pickup so the attached fabric will hide the running threads of the new stitches (for instance, under a ruffle or inside a pocket). If you work as to Knit, the running threads of the new, picked-up stitches will be above the needle; if you work as to Purl, they will be below the needle.

There are two ways to control for this, by how you hold the fabric, with the top up, down, or sideways, and whether you work as to Knit or as to Purl. In either case, the pickup can be done horizontally, across a row, or vertically, along a column of stitches.

Picking Up Stitch Heads

With this approach, the new stitches will be drawn through the center of the existing ones, which works very well when the pickup is done along a row of the fabric. However, when the pickup is done vertically, along a stitch column, it generally means that half of the original stitches will remain visible, while the other half will be hidden by the new portion of fabric. If that is not acceptable, the solution is to pick up into the running threads, which is described below. It is generally easiest to do this with the fabric turned on its side, with stitch columns running horizontally.

Picking Up Stitch Heads in a Row

The instructions are written for a pickup that starts on the right and works across a row to the left.

- Insert left needle into center of first stitch in pickup row, and then out center of stitch in row above; insert right needle into picked-up stitch and either Knit or Purl. Repeat, working into center of next stitch to left in same row.

Picking Up along
a row as to Knit.

Picking Up Heads in a Stitch Column

The instructions are written for a pickup that starts at a lower row and works up a stitch column.

1. Insert left needle into center of first stitch in pickup column, and then out center of second stitch in row above, and Knit or Purl.
2. Insert left needle into center of second stitch, and then out center of third stitch in row above, and Knit or Purl.
3. Repeat in this way, working up the column of stitches and inserting needle into each stitch twice.

Picking Up Running Threads

On some occasions it makes more sense to pick up into the running threads instead of the stitch heads, and it is done in exactly the same way as working into the stitch.

This approach works best when you plan to pick up along a stitch column, since the new stitches will emerge between two stitch columns instead of from within the stitches, leaving a full column visible on the outside.

On the other hand, having the new stitches emerge between two stitch columns is not ideal when the pickup is done horizontally, along a row. The only reason you might choose to work this way is if a complex stitch pattern makes it difficult or impossible to work into the center of the stitches.

Picking Up Side of Stitch

In this case, the new stitch is drawn under one side of the stitch. If you pick up into the right side of the stitch, the new stitch will emerge between two stitch columns (which works best when picking up vertically, along a stitch column). However, if you pick up into the left side of the stitch instead, the new stitch will emerge from the center of the original one (which works best when picking up horizontally, along a row).

While it is a matter of preference how to hold the fabric for this purpose, I find it easiest to work with the stitch columns vertical.

Picking Up Stitch Sides in a Row

- Insert left needle between two stitch columns, pick up left side of stitch, insert right needle into picked-up stitch, and Knit or Purl. Repeat with stitch in same row of next stitch column.

Picking Up Stitch Sides in a Column

- Insert left needle into center of stitch, pick up right side of stitch, insert right needle into picked-up stitch and Knit or Purl. Repeat with next stitch in same column, one row up.

Picking Up Stitches in a Column.
Pick up right side of stitch as to Purl.

❖ Picking Up Through the Fabric

With this approach, the pickup is done in much the same way as described above (on the outside of the fabric), but the yarn supply is held on the inside, which makes this somewhat awkward to do. However, the advantage is that the running threads of the new stitches remain on the inside where they will not be seen.

While the yarn for the pickup is held on the inside, it is necessary to have the main supply of yarn available on the outside of the fabric in order to work the new fabric. One solution is to pick up with a separate strand of yarn held on the inside and then to continue, attaching the main yarn to the picked-up stitches on the outside; the other is to pick up with a tail of the yarn drawn through to the inside, leaving the main supply on the outside.

You can pick up the stitches with a knitting needle, but the best tool to use for this purpose is a cro-needle, which has a crochet hook on one end of a cable and a conventional needle tip on the other end (see Tools). Alternatively, you can also use a conventional crochet hook to draw the stitches through the fabric, and then transfer each one to a knitting needle as you go.

Picking Up with Separate Strand

This is easy enough to do, but leaves three tails of yarn on the inside to hide during finishing. However, if you will be picking up a relatively large number of stitches and are concerned that a fragile or softly spun yarn might fray, or if you are working with a highly textured yarn that would be difficult to pull through the fabric, then this is the approach to use.

Attach the yarn on the inside of the fabric so it will not pull through as you work; a clever way to do this is to thread it through the holes of a big button and tie a knot. Alternatively, weave the tail in on the inside as you would during finishing, but do so before you start. See Button-Stop, and Hiding Ends of Yarn.

1. With separate supply of yarn, allow 8–10 inches tail to hide in finishing, and attach to inside in one of ways described above.
2. With outside of fabric on nearside, hold yarn on farside and reach tip of needle through fabric, either into center of stitch or between two stitches. Wrap yarn and draw new stitch through to outside.
3. Pick up as many stitches as required; break off yarn leaving another 8–10 inches tail and attach to inside, as in Step 1.
4. Take up main yarn, pull an 8–10 inch tail through from outside to inside and tie to inside, as well. Begin working on picked-up stitches.
5. Return to hide tails of yarn on inside during finishing.

If you are using a crochet hook or a cro-needle, work as follows:

- Wrap yarn on left finger held under fabric, and reach cro-needle hook through fabric to catch loop of yarn.
- Work in same way with crochet hook, but work from left to right and have knitting needle on outside of fabric to your left; transfer each stitch from hook to needle as it is drawn through the fabric.

Picking Up with Tail of Yarn

This leaves only one end of yarn on the inside, which is far more convenient when finishing. The trick is to draw a tail of yarn through to the inside and use it for picking up the new stitches through the fabric.

1. Calculate length of yarn required for number of stitches needed by using method described for Picking Up with Cro-Needle.
2. With main yarn supply on outside of fabric, pull entire tail through to inside; fasten main supply of yarn to outside with coilless safety pin near where pickup will begin, as described above.
3. On outside, start where tail of yarn was drawn through

fabric and pick up stitches with one of the methods described above; when done, attach end of yarn on inside with coilless safety pin.
4. Return to right tip of needle, unpin main yarn supply where it is secured to outside, and begin to work new section of fabric.

Working in the Opposite Direction

There are occasions in knitting when it may be necessary to work down from a lower edge—perhaps to add a border, to make the top and bottom edges match, or to make alterations or repairs. You might also have occasion to separate a fabric if you want to lengthen a sweater for a growing child, replace a worn-out ribbing, or simply revitalize a style that no longer suits your wardrobe. In these cases, you can divide the fabric wherever it seems best and work either up or down from the freed stitches.

When this is planned for, it is ideal to start with Stranded Provisional Cast-On or Alternating Provisional Cast-On, which makes it easy to reactivate the stitches when the time comes. If this was not anticipated, either separate the fabric along a row above the cast-on edge, or unravel the baseline of the edge to free the stitches. Alternatively, it is possible to pick up stitches along a cast-on edge, leaving it in place; the edge can be turned to the outside as a decorative element.

Before we turn to the instructions on how to remove the edges, however, it is important to understand something about the structure of a knitted fabric when it is upside down.

❖ Upside-Down Fabric Structure

Whether you free the stitches along a cast-on edge or separate a fabric, it would seem simple enough to just begin to work. However, when working down from a set of stitches, things do not line up in quite the same way as when the fabric is right side up, and it is important to understand why and take this into consideration.

If you turn a Stockinette fabric upside down, it seems to look exactly the same as it does right side up; however, there has been a subtle metamorphosis. A good way to see what is happening is to make a swatch with two colors alternating stitch by stitch to create vertical stripes. With the top edge up, there will be nice neat columns of Knit stitches, but when turned bottom side up, the two sides of each Knit stitch are transformed into what appears to be halves of adjacent stitches instead (it is also important to take this into consideration when choosing stitch and color patterns for a garment worked entirely from the top down; see Working from the Top Down).

In addition, a count of the freed stitches along the bottom edge of a fabric will show that there is one less stitch than there is at the top. To get a good visual sense of the explanation for this, hold up your hand with the fingers spread. Think of the tips of your fingers as the top of the stitches and the connection between one finger and the next as the running threads. You have five fingertips, equivalent to five stitches, and four connections, equivalent to running threads, right?

Stockinette Upside Down. Vertical color stripes show how the appearance changes when the fabric is upside down.

Freed Lower Edge of Single Ribbing. One stitch is highlighted to show how the appearance changes with fabric upside down.

Now turn your fingers down instead of up. The four connections are now the heads of stitches and the five fingertips are the equivalent of running threads. Looked at this way, there is one less "stitch" and one more "running thread" than before. Actually, it is not really one stitch less, but one-half stitch less at each side of the fabric.

In spite of all this, if both the original and the new section of fabric are worked in Stockinette and made with the same yarn and needles, there will be no obvious difference between the two, particularly if the yarn is fine and the stitches small. With a thicker yarn, the discrepancy in the number of stitches will make more of a difference to the width of the fabric (especially if there are visible edges, such as on a scarf), and it may be necessary to tuck an increase in somewhere to restore the stitch count.

However, if either the original or new portion of fabric is worked in a stitch or color pattern of some kind, any attempt to continue in the same way will be quite obvious, since there will be a little jog in the stitch columns on the row where the fabric was divided. There are several tricks for getting around this problem, but just adding in the missing stitch is generally not the solution. Instead, it is best to turn the situation to decorative advantage by introducing some new element between the new and original sections of fabric. For instance, even a row or two of a different pattern or color will provide a visual break between one portion and the other so that the offset will not be noticeable.

❖ *Removing Cast-On Edges*

Freeing the edge stitches is much easier to accomplish with some casting-on techniques than with others. If you have planned for this and used Alternating Provisional Cast-On, the

stitches at the lower edge will already be on a needle waiting. Stranded Provisional Cast-On is also designed for this purpose, and makes it easy to free the edge stitches when the time comes. However, if you have used any other cast-on edge, it will be necessary to pull out the baseline, stitch by stitch. The important thing is to carefully pick up every one of the freed stitches on a needle as you go; while a Single Rib or Seed Stitch will not unravel, all or parts of most other edges will, and the more complicated the stitch pattern, the more challenging it is to put things right again.

It helps to work with the fabric on a table, or at least in your lap, so the needle is supported as you pick up the newly freed stitches. It is also a good idea to use a thin needle, because it is easier to insert into the stitches and will pull less on adjacent ones. Once all the stitches have been picked up, change to the needle size needed for the new portion of fabric.

Removing Stranded Cast-On

Stranded Cast-On is commonly used for this purpose since it is both easy to do and easy to remove when the time comes to pick up the stitches along the lower edge of the fabric. Work as follows:

• Hold fabric with lower edge up and needle in right hand. Pull up on end of strand to lift first stitch; insert needle into stitch as to Purl, with right side of stitch on nearside of needle; pull strand out of stitch. Repeat across row.

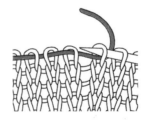

Removing Stranded Cast-On. Pick up stitch with fabric upside down.

If you find it difficult to pick up the stitches so they are in the correct position on the needle, just pick them up as best you can and put things right as you work the first row. Or, after picking up, transfer the stitches to a needle of the correct size, checking each one as you do so. The important thing is to get each stitch safely on the needle before you move the strand so there is no risk that any will unravel, since this can sometimes be difficult to correct.

You will probably save time in the long run by capturing each stitch on a needle as it is freed from the baseline. If you are working with a well-behaved yarn, it is also possible to free all of the stitches before picking any of them up on the needle, or, more sensibly, to free them in groups. However, there is quite a bit of drag as the strand is withdrawn, and as you try to free one stitch it is all too easy for some of the other stitches to unravel.

Removing Half-Hitch Cast-On

A Half-Hitch Cast-On edge is somewhat tedious to remove, but easy enough to do. Rather than practice on your garment, do so on a small swatch with the edge done in a contrast color; see Contrast-Color Baseline. This reveals the structure of the edge very well, making it easier to see what you are doing.

Keep in mind that each half-hitch is wrapped around the base of a stitch, and that the strand passes through each stitch twice, in opposite directions. When upside down, the strand will look as though it is passing through the center of adjacent stitches; for more information on why this is so, see Upside-Down Fabric Structure, above. Also note that the strand passes through each stitch twice, in opposite directions.

You can work on either the inside or the outside of the fabric, but it is somewhat easier to identify the path of the strands on the Purl side.

Hold fabric as described above, and work as follows:

1. Pull up on end of yarn to identify path it takes, insert needle under strand that leads to tail, tease a loop of yarn out of first stitch, and then use your fingers to pull it free.
2. With one strand remaining in stitch, pull up on yarn to enlarge stitch and insert needle as to Purl, picking it up with right side of stitch on nearside of needle.
3. Pull first strand out of next stitch still in edge, and remove remaining strand from picked-up stitch on needle.
4. Repeat Steps 2 and 3 across row; if necessary, cut yarn short from time to time so there is less to pull through each stitch.

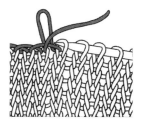

Removing Half-Hitch
Cast-On: Step 2.

Removing Knit Cast-On

In this case, the baseline strand travels from right to left and spans three stitches—out of the one on the left, past the one in the center, into the one on the right—before it then emerges out of the one in the center. The loops formed are interlocked within each stitch as well.

Removing Knit Cast-On
as in Step 3, above.

Despite this rather complex structure, removing the edge can be done much as described above for Removing Half-Hitch Cast-On, with one slight difference:

- In Step 3, above, pull yarn out of second stitch to left, and then from picked-up stitch on needle.

Removing Alternating Cast-On

In an edge made with Alternating Cast-On, adjacent stitches are made from different strands of yarn and it cannot be unraveled; therefore, it is necessary to separate the fabric above the edge. If you are interested in why this is the case, turn to the instructions for this technique in the chapter Casting On, and look at the illustration with the book turned upside down.

❖ Retaining a Horizontal Edge

If the cast-on edge is attractive, consider retaining it to form a visible horizontal line between the main fabric and a section worked on picked-up stitches. The same thing can be done with a cast-off edge at the top of a fabric. You can work directly up or down from these stitches as with any others, or join a border to them as described above.

The edge can also be used as a foldline for a facing added at the bottom or top of a fabric (see Facings).

Picking Up Half-Hitch Cast-On Edge

If you decide to leave a Half-Hitch Cast-On edge in place, the result will have a different appearance depending upon whether the Knit or Purl face of the edge was used on the outside of the fabric.

Knit Half-Hitch on Outside

The result will be a horizontal line of sloping strands on the surface of the fabric.

- Turn edge up with inside of fabric facing; pick up as to Purl, inserting needle down into Purl nubs adjacent to strands of cast-on edge.

Purl Half-Hitch on Outside

In this case, there are two ways to work. With the first, there will simply be a row of Purl nubs left visible on the outside of the fabric; the half-hitches are turned to the inside. With the other, both the row of Purl and the half-hitches will be on the outside; this has a more pronounced surface texture.

- To leave just row of Purl on outside, turn edge up with outside of fabric facing, and pick up as to Knit, inserting needle up into half-hitch strands.
- Or, turn edge up with inside of fabric facing; pick up as to Purl, inserting needle down into Purl nubs below half-hitches in second row of fabric.

> **For any other edge . . .**
> *If you are removing an edge made with any other technique, make a Test Swatch with that cast-on and try one of the methods above to see what it will look like if all or some of the strands are left on the outside of the fabric after picking up.*

Picking Up Chained Cast-Off Edge

As with a Half-Hitch Cast-On edge, a Chained Cast-Off edge is also very attractive when left on the outside of the fabric when picking up stitches. Work as follows:

- On inside of fabric, pick up as to Purl, inserting needle down into Purl nubs directly below cast-off edge.

Picking Up to turn Cast-Off Edge to Outside. Decorative pattern done with Slip stitches and stranding on outside.

Replacing Cast-On with Cast-Off

For an interesting border between the main fabric and one done on picked-up stitches, you can replace a cast-on edge with a Chained Cast-Off one. This will form an attractive, horizontal chain of stitches. Use a Provisional Cast-On in order to do this, or remove the bottom edge as described above and work as follows:

1. Work on outside of fabric and use a Chained Cast-Off across row of picked-up stitches.
2. Turn to inside and pick up as to Purl, inserting needle up into Purl nubs directly below newly cast-off edge; work new section of fabric below cast-off.

If all you want to do is make the top and bottom edges match, simply work Step 1.

❖ *Separating a Fabric*

The most common reason to separate a fabric is to remove a worn, stretched-out ribbing or to rescue a still-useful garment that has a stain or a hole in the bodice or sleeve. You can divide the fabric to eliminate the problem, and then rework it in one of the ways suggested in Tips and Applications, below.

When you have spent a lot of time knitting something, the thought of cutting it apart can produce a certain amount of dithering and procrastination. But if you will not be able to wear it in its current condition, you really have nothing to lose, so gather your courage and forge ahead. The task is actually easy once you get under way.

The instructions assume that the lower portion of the fabric is to be removed and a new portion worked down from the freed stitches.

Freeing the Stitches

1. For a garment worked flat and sewn together, first pull out seams. Pull fabric taut on either side of seam just above lower edge of garment, cut one strand of sewing yarn, and unravel seam to about 2 inches above where fabric will be divided; repeat on other side.
2. If possible, select a plain row to pick up, and remove stitches in row below. Start close to edge, or near beginning of a round, and use needle tip to pull one stitch out firmly to enlarge it; cut loop.
3. Insert needle tip into stitch to pick up, and then unravel yarn; see Picking Up Freed Stitches. Work toward selvedge or beginning of round first, and then in other direction to free and pick up all stitches of row. Cut end of yarn short periodically, to make the work go faster.

Once you have all the stitches picked up and safely on the needle, slip them from one needle tip to the other to check that each one is in the correct position, and that no stitch has unraveled or is split; if you do not anticipate many problems, do this as you work the first row. For stitches that have unraveled a row or two, see Dropped Stitches for information on how to work them back into position.

If you plan to salvage both sections and introduce a new section of fabric between them, you will need to pick up both sets of freed stitches on separate needles; the best way to do this is to use a pair of double-point or circular needles, one for each set of stitches. Pick up the stitches at the edge of the upper fabric section first, because these are more difficult to manage if they unravel, and with them safely on the needle, pick up those from the lower section.

Separating a fabric.

Tips and Applications

There are several situations where it might be useful to separate a fabric in this way; here are some ideas and suggestions for how to work.

- If a ribbing is worn or stretched out, it is relatively easy to remove and rework it from the top down; separate the fabric on a plain row, above ribbing.

  If it is necessary to replicate the edge, see Sewn Cast-Offs for edges that match various cast-on techniques.

- Alternatively, cast on and work the ribbing up, and then graft it to the main fabric.

  Keep in mind that grafting works best over short widths because the yarn will begin to fray. Therefore, a repair of this kind might work well for a sleeve, but could be more of a problem for a bodice; see Grafting for more information on how to deal with wider fabrics.

  Graft the two sections back together where the join will be unobtrusive, such as just above the ribbing where any slight gathering will obscure it, or at a row adjacent to a change in stitch or color pattern.

- To lengthen an existing garment, keep in mind that both the fabric and the yarn will have changed with time and repeated cleaning; even if you have some of the original, unused yarn on hand, the two will not match. Reusing the unraveled yarn is often the best match because it has undergone the same wear; see Recycling Yarn.

  If necessary, separate new and old yarn with a stripe of some kind done in a yarn of a different color or texture, or just use a new yarn in a contrast color and/or texture for the entire alteration.

  Alternatively, use the technique described in Horizontal Insertion to introduce a decorative stripe that runs perpendicular to the rest of the fabric. This is also a clever way to avoid Grafting two sections of a wide fabric together.

- In some circumstances, Joinery Cast-Off can be used to reattach separated and reworked sections of a fabric.

  There is no way to hide the resulting seam, but you can turn the cast-off edge to the outside instead, where it will form a decorative chain of horizontal stitches. Use a contrast color to make it more decorative; to make it blend in more, place it between two areas of stitch or color pattern. Work the cast-off with a needle size large enough to make it resilient and compatible with the surrounding fabric.

- If a cast-on edge is too tight or has a broken thread, remove it, pick up the stitches, and immediately cast off again. See Replacing Cast-On with Cast-Off, above.

CHAPTER 8

Openings

Many functional elements, such as buttonholes and pockets, require openings in a knitted fabric. These features are usually located on the front of a garment and call a great deal of attention to themselves; therefore, it is important that they be done well.

Buttonholes are the most common openings and, fortunately, there are quite a few techniques that can be used to make them. This allows you to create an opening that best suits the garment style, the type of yarn used, and the size of the button.

Pockets also have a rather commanding presence on the front of a garment. Simple patch pockets are easy to do and offer great scope for creativity. The type of pockets that require an opening in the fabric and a lining are more complicated; however, none of the techniques used is difficult.

Buttonholes

Buttonholes in a knitted fabric make me rather unhappy. I think they generally look better when hidden by a button. Nevertheless, we must have them, and fortunately there are some techniques you can use to make quite nice ones (or at least improve those that are less than ideal).

Any knitted buttonhole is best kept as small as possible, since a knitted fabric will stretch to allow the button to pass through. For those occasions when a larger, sturdier buttonhole is needed or large decorative buttons play a prominent role in the design, there are ways to stabilize the opening so it will not stretch out of shape. More time and care are required to manage this successfully, but the result is superior.

There is no formula for the number of stitches or rows to use for a buttonhole; your gauge will determine the size of the opening. In other words, the same number of stitches or rows will produce a small buttonhole in fine yarn and a large one in a thicker yarn. As always, try out what you want to do on a Test Swatch first.

❖ Yarnover Buttonholes

This first group is composed of buttonholes that all rely on a Yarnover to help create the opening, and they are very easy to do. They range in size from tiny round buttonholes to fairly large vertical ones.

Small Eyelet Buttonholes

One or another variation of this buttonhole has been traditionally used for baby garments; however, it is perfectly appropriate any time a small button will be used, even for something like an elegant evening sweater. These also work nicely for drawstrings.

Since an Eyelet makes a round opening rather than a slit (as is the case with the typical buttonhole), the button must be somewhat larger than the opening in order to stay in place. For this reason, the technique is generally used only with finer yarns.

Basic Eyelet Buttonhole

Many of you will find this technique familiar, since it makes use of the fundamental unit of all lace patterns: a paired Yarnover and decrease (see Eyelets, Mesh, and Lace). There are several variations; use whichever one you find easiest to work or that is the most compatible with your pattern.

Basic Eyelet Buttonholes. Left Decrease Version on left; Right Decrease Version on right.

Left Decrease Version

- Work a Left Decrease followed by a Yarnover.

Right Decrease Version

- Work a Yarnover followed by a Right Decrease.

Even Smaller Eyelet Buttonhole

If you are making a relatively loose, open fabric, this might be a better alternative.

- Work an Open Running Thread Increase, either after a Left Decrease, or before a Right Decrease.

Single Rib Eyelet Buttonhole

To make a nearly invisible buttonhole in a Single Rib fabric, work as follows:

- With a Knit stitch first on left needle, work a Left Decrease followed by a Yarnover.
- Or, with a Purl stitch first on left needle, work a Yarnover, followed by a Right Decrease.

In other words, the Yarnover replaces the Purl stitch, which should be the backing stitch of the decrease so it is hidden on the inside of the fabric. This recesses the opening between two columns of Knit stitches.

Narrow Eyelet Buttonhole

Here is a new version of an Eyelet Buttonhole with a shape that is narrow instead of round. It is more trouble to work than the smaller buttonholes, above, but the result is so superior I am sure you will not mind. This is a very neat, quiet, and orderly little buttonhole. The technique can also be used in a horizontal series to create openings through which to thread ribbon.

1. On inside, work to position of buttonhole and make a Yarnover; continue to end of row.
2. On outside, work to stitch before buttonhole, Slip 1 knitwise, Knit Yarnover, but do not discard strand; pull Slip stitch over new stitch.
3. Insert needle into stitch to left of Yarnover, then under Yarnover strand, and Knit Two Together.

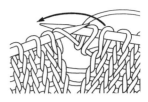

Narrow Eyelet Buttonhole: Step 2. Decrease to right of buttonhole.

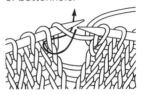

Narrow Eyelet Buttonhole: Step 3. Decrease to left of buttonhole.

In Step 2, the equivalent of a Left Decrease is used to join the Yarnover and the preceding Knit stitch; the Yarnover is retained on the needle. In Step 3, a Right Decrease is then used to join the same Yarnover strand and the following stitch. The strand will be hidden behind the two decreases.

It is possible to start the buttonhole on an outside row, but the decreases are somewhat more difficult to do on an inside row in Purl.

Notice that this buttonhole is made between two columns of stitches, rather than in one, which helps to keep it narrow. And because of the type of decreases used, the columns of stitches on either side are uninterrupted. These two qualities combine to make it very unobtrusive.

Rib Increase Eyelet Buttonhole

This is a charming little buttonhole of a useful size, and it has a tiny "picot," or little knot at the top, which is formed by the type of increase used.

1. On outside, work to position of buttonhole and make a Double Yarnover.
2. On next row, work a Rib Increase on Yarnover, dropping extra wrap.
3. On final row, work a Left Decrease on preceding stitch and first increase stitch; and then a Right Decrease on next increase stitch and following stitch.

Rib Increase Buttonhole.

In other words, the two stitches worked on the Yarnover strand are removed on the next row by the decreases; the stitch columns on either side of the buttonhole continue relatively undisturbed.

Large Yarnover Buttonholes

The next three techniques are similar to those above, but these are worked over more rows and therefore require more than one Yarnover.

Two-Row Yarnover Buttonhole

1. On outside, work to position of buttonhole and make a Double Yarnover.
2. On next row, with yarn near-side, Slip Double Yarnover, dropping extra wrap; make a second Yarnover.
3. On final row, work to stitch preceding buttonhole; Slip 1 knitwise, Knit two Yarnover strands together (do not discard), and pull slipped stitch over new stitch as for a Left Decrease.

Two-Row Yarnover Buttonhole.

Next, insert right needle into stitch to left of buttonhole, and under both Yarnover strands; Knit stitch and strands together as for a Right Decrease.

Using a Double Yarnover in Step 1 elongates the strand so it can stretch over two rows. Both of the Yarnovers will be hidden behind the facing stitches of the two decreases.

Four-Row Yarnover Buttonhole

1. On inside of fabric, work to location of buttonhole. Turn to outside, and work back across row on same side of buttonhole. Turn to inside and work to buttonhole again. There are now three rows on one side of buttonhole.
2. Make Yarnover to cross opening, and continue to end of row on other side of buttonhole. Turn to outside.
3. On outside, work to stitch before buttonhole; Slip 1 knitwise, Knit Yarnover strand but do not discard it, pull Slip stitch over new stitch and off needle.
4. Turn to inside, and work back across row on same side. There are now three rows on other side of buttonhole.
5. Turn to outside and work to buttonhole; Knit Right Decrease on Yarnover strand and following stitch; continue across row.

Four-Row Yarnover Buttonhole.

The two decreases are done on different rows; the equivalent of a Left Decrease in Step 3 on one side of the buttonhole, and a Right Decrease in Step 5 on the other side.

You could begin the buttonhole on the outside of the fabric, but the Left Decrease is more difficult to manage in Purl.

If you find that the first Yarnover does not have enough yarn to span the rows, use a Double Yarnover in Step 2, dropping extra wrap when working it with the decrease in Step 3.

Six-Row Yarnover Buttonhole

The technique above can also be applied to a six-row buttonhole, but it makes a fairly large opening that may need to be stabilized; see Sewn Finishes for Buttonholes, or Buttonhole Facings.

1. Start on inside and work as in Step 1 and 2, above, but add two more rows for a total of five on first side; use a Double Yarnover to span opening and continue across row.
2. Turn and work to stitch before buttonhole; Slip 1 knitwise, Knit Yarnover strand but do not discard it, pull Slip stitch over new stitch and off needle; retain Yarnover strand on needle. Turn and work third row.
3. Turn and work fourth row to buttonhole; repeat decrease as in Step 2, again retaining Yarnover on needle. Turn and work fifth row.
4. Turn and work sixth row to buttonhole; Knit Right Decrease on Yarnover strand and following stitch. Complete row.

❖ Divided Vertical Buttonholes

This method of working a vertical buttonhole is found in every knitting technique book. Because the fabric is divided at the bottom of the buttonhole, it can be made over any number of rows; the basic concept is the same as that used to work vertical or sloped pocket openings.

Vertical buttonholes tend to look nicer than the horizontal ones discussed below, but their behavior can be problematic. In wear, the button will push against the long side of the buttonhole, causing it to widen and enlarge. At its worst, the edge of the button band will take on a scalloped appearance and the button may pop out of the opening, especially on a snug garment.

Because of this, vertical buttonholes of this kind benefit from the application of a woven fabric facing on the inside of the garment to stabilize them (see Buttonhole Facings).

The first two versions discussed both involve breaking off the yarn and reattaching it again; one is for an even number of rows, the other for an uneven number. This leaves two ends of yarn at the buttonhole; they can be used to reinforce the edges of the opening, but otherwise will need to be hidden on the inside during finishing. The third method does not leave yarn ends at the opening, but may present problems with some stitch or color patterns.

Vertical Buttonhole—Even Rows

1. Work to lower point of buttonhole; leave all stitches on left needle in waiting. Turn and work a minimum of two more rows on fabric at right side of buttonhole; end with tips of needles at opening and drop yarn.
2. Attach a second supply of yarn to first stitch on left needle and work an even number of rows on fabric at left side of buttonhole, one less than worked on right side; end with tips of needles at buttonhole and break off second yarn.
3. Turn, pick up original yarn dropped at end of Step 1 and work across top of buttonhole to rejoin two sides.

If a Test Swatch shows that a buttonhole has a tendency to gape, make a Left Raised Increase at the beginning of Step 1, before turning to work rows at side of buttonhole. Then, before dropping yarn at the top, work a Left Decrease on the last two stitches on the needle to restore the stitch count.

This helps fill in the opening somewhat; the technique can also be used for any of the similar buttonholes described below.

Vertical Buttonhole—Odd Rows

1. Work Step 1 of Vertical Buttonhole, above, but break off original yarn at opening.
2. Leave stitches of first side in waiting, reattach same yarn to first stitch on left needle, and work second side of buttonhole same number of rows as first, ending at selvedge.
3. Turn and work final row directly across top of buttonhole to rejoin two sides.

As above, leave adequate tails of yarn to reinforce opening or hide on inside.

Vertical Buttonhole—Slide Method

Here is a new version with no ends at the buttonhole to worry about; instead, there will be one at each selvedge, where they are easier to hide. This makes use of the Slide technique, so it is necessary to work on double-point needles or a circular needle.

1. On outside, work across row to position of buttonhole and leave stitches on other side of buttonhole in waiting; turn.
2. On inside, work second row back to selvedge; break yarn. Do not turn.
3. Still on inside, pick up needle bearing stitches on other side of buttonhole, Slide stitches so selvedge is at needle tip, reattach yarn and work across to buttonhole; turn to outside, and work back to selvedge.
4. There are now two rows on either side of buttonhole. Turn to inside and work across entire row, closing top of buttonhole and rejoining two sides of fabric.

This is a two-row buttonhole, but it is easy enough to work it over four rows; an uneven number of rows is impossible. You can, of course, start the buttonhole on an inside row.

The Slide technique used in Step 3 will change the sequence of rows in a stitch pattern, so inside and outside rows are switched. While some stitch techniques may be more difficult to do on the inside, most are manageable; it is easiest to adjust the working method if you are using a charted pattern.

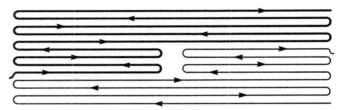

Vertical Buttonhole: Slide Met chapter hod.

There is no avoiding this for the two rows on either side of the buttonhole, but you can correct the one above the opening if you prefer. Break the yarn at the end of Step 3, Slide the stitches to the other needle tip, and reattach the yarn on the right side; in Step 4, work across the row on the outside.

Vertical Buttonhole for Single Rib

To help a vertical buttonhole blend in with a Single Rib pattern, try the following:

1. Work to location of buttonhole. With Purl as first stitch on left needle, divide fabric and work rows on right side of buttonhole as described above.
2. To begin left side, work a Right Decrease on first two stitches.
3. After completing rows on left side, work a Rib Increase at top of buttonhole to restore stitch count, and then continue across full row to close opening.

The decrease at the bottom of the opening removes the Purl stitch, leaving two columns of Knit on either side; depending on how you work the buttonhole, use a Knit/Purl or Purl/Knit Rib Increase at the top, as necessary to restore the correct sequence of stitches in the Single Rib pattern.

Sloped Buttonhole

For a decorative element, you can make a buttonhole that slopes by decreasing on one side and increasing on the other. The two edges will not match perfectly, but a satisfactory result can be had if you work as follows:

1. Use a Right or Left Decrease on two stitches at one side of buttonhole; decrease should slope in same direction as opening.
2. On other side of buttonhole, work a Yarnover at beginning of each row. On return row, work Yarnover so it is twisted to right or left, toward fabric and away from opening (see Turned Yarnovers, and Twist Stitches).

❖ *Horizontal Buttonholes*

Functionally, a horizontal buttonhole is a better style than a vertical one because the button rides in the corner of the opening, where it tends to cause less distortion at the edge of the fabric.

Two quite different approaches can be used to make a buttonhole with this orientation and shape. The first is done by casting off to make the opening and casting on again to close it; the buttonhole requires no further finishing. There are two variations; the first is the traditional method; the second is an improvement of that technique, but it is somewhat more challenging to do.

The other type of buttonhole is done by using a separate, contrast-color yarn to knit the stitches of the opening; these stitches act as a "Placeholder" and are later removed in order to finish the opening in one of a variety of ways. There are more options in regard to the appearance and behavior of this buttonhole, but some of them take care and patience to achieve.

Traditional Horizontal Buttonhole

This is the traditional method of working a Horizontal Buttonhole, and it is found in every knitting book. However, I do not find the result very attractive and I rather doubt anyone else does either. Nevertheless, it must be mentioned, not only because it is such a standard, but also because it introduces the basic concept at work here. An improved method is discussed below.

1. Knit to position of buttonhole.
2. Use Pullover Chained Cast-Off to remove as many stitches as required for size of opening, according to gauge.
3. Continue across row and turn; work back to buttonhole.
4. Use Simple Half-Hitch Cast-On or Knit Cast-On to replace number of stitches cast off; continue with work.

When you examine the finished buttonhole you will see several rather obvious problems. There is a gap at the lower right corner and the bottom edge is offset slightly in relation to the top. Furthermore, the two edges have a very different appearance and, worse, the whole thing splays wide open.

In short, there is really little to recommend this but its simplicity, although it can be

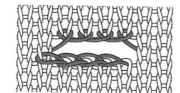

Traditional Horizontal Buttonhole.

improved somewhat by using one of the sewn finishing techniques discussed below. If you want a horizontal buttonhole that looks quite nice the minute it is done, try the following technique instead.

Improved Horizontal Buttonhole

Perhaps this should be called the "Improved, Improved Horizontal Buttonhole," because it is not the one introduced with this name in the first edition of *Principles of Knitting*. That version was the best I could come up with at the time, but when I looked at it again, I was still not happy with the result.

Here is a new modification that solves almost all the problems seen in the traditional version, above. The two edges match, the corners are neat, and the buttonhole remains tidy. It is really quite an acceptable buttonhole and can be taken out in public without apology.

As with the other version, this one is made by casting off, and then immediately casting on again. However, in this case the techniques used are Slip Chained Cast-Off and Two-Needle Chained Cast-On. The cast-off is very easy, but the cast-on can be a challenge to do evenly and it is a good idea to practice on a Test Swatch a few times before using it for a buttonhole in a garment.

You might find it helpful to read through these instructions once before you begin.

1. On outside, work to location of buttonhole, Yarnover, Knit 1, pull Yarnover strand over stitch; do not count this as a stitch cast-off for opening.
2. Drop yarn and remove number of stitches required for opening with equivalent of Slip Chained Cast-Off, as follows: [Slip 1, pull second stitch on right needle over first]; repeat sequence between brackets. After final Pullover, return last slipped stitch to left needle.
3. To begin casting on stitches at top of buttonhole, pick up yarn at right side of buttonhole and, with left needle, reach across cast-off edge and lift Purl nub through which yarn supply passes and Knit it; Slip new stitch to left needle.
4. [Make Yarnover on right needle, Knit 1; transfer new stitch to left needle]; repeat sequence between brackets. Number of Yarnovers should equal number of stitches cast off; retain last new stitch on right needle.
5. To complete buttonhole, Slip 1 stitch from left needle, pull last cast-on stitch over it, and tighten at base. Return slipped stitch to left needle and then Knit it; continue across row.

Improved Horizontal Buttonhole.

In Step 1, the Yarnover strand will wrap around the stitch at its base; it is decorative and helps make a tidy corner. The first stitch pulled over in Step 2 will have this Yarnover at its base.

The top edge of the buttonhole is done with Two-Needle Chained Cast-On. The Yarnovers accumulate on the right needle and serve as new stitches to replace those cast off. Each new stitch made is returned to the left needle and re-knit. When discarded, these stitches form the chain along the upper edge that matches the Chained Cast-Off along the lower edge; the number of stitches in the two edges should be the same. Before making the next Yarnover, tighten up the discard stitch so it matches the others before returning the new stitch to the left needle.

And finally, the last pullover done in Step 5 makes a neat corner and the appearance of the two corners will be the same.

Placeholder Opening

This technique can be used for several different kinds of openings, including thumb holes in mittens, or heels in socks, as well as for a pocket style discussed below; it is also a clever way to make a buttonhole.

1. Take strand of contrast-color yarn about 10 to 12 inches long and work stitches of buttonhole.
2. Slip stitches back to left needle.
3. Take up main yarn again, work across contrast-color stitches, and continue.
4. Return later to remove contrast-color yarn, pick up stitches, and finish buttonhole opening.

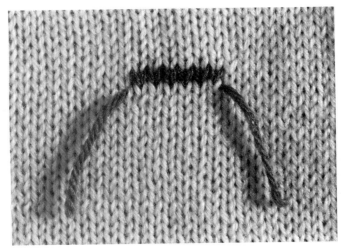

Placeholder Opening.

If you have any concern that the Placeholder yarn will pull free, tie the two ends together in a Slip Knot.

While it is easy enough to insert the Placeholder yarn into the fabric, finishing a buttonhole of this kind requires a certain amount of time and care. As mentioned above, there are several ways to do so and the result can be very satisfying. You can use the Sewn Half-Hitch Cast-Off for buttonholes, or one of the options in Knitted Finishes for Buttonholes, both described below.

❖ *Edge, Border, and Loop Buttonholes*

There are many ways to make buttonholes at the edge of a center front opening or in the join between the main fabric and a border.

Buttonholes in Sewn-On Borders

- For a border made separately and sewn to a side edge, skip buttonhole-size spaces along edge as you attach it. Run tapestry needle through selvedge stitches of either garment or border, or weave it through running threads, alongside the space left for the buttonhole, and then begin sewing two fabrics together again.
- To make button loops with a Knitted Cord, estimate additional overall length needed for number of loops required. Make cord and leave its stitches on a holder at top; begin to sew cord to fabric at bottom, spacing loops along edge; if necessary, adjust length of cord at top, and then cast off.

Also see below for suggestions about making button slits or loops when attaching a cord of this kind to picked-up stitches.

Buttonholes on Picked-Up Edges

There are several nice ways to make buttonholes between the main fabric and a border done on picked-up stitches.

Slit Buttonholes for Picked-Up Border

1. Pick up stitches along edge to bottom of first buttonhole. See Picking Up Selvedges.
2. Use Simple Half-Hitch Cast-On or Knit Cast-On to add number of stitches required to span length of opening. Skip same number of stitches in selvedge for opening and then begin to pick up stitches again.
3. Repeat Steps 1 and 2 for each buttonhole.
4. Turn and work border out from picked-up stitches.

Loop Buttonhole on Picked-Up Edge

This approach uses the technique described in Attached Cords to make buttonhole loops on a set of stitches picked up along a side edge (see Picking Up to Join).

1. Pick up stitches along edge. Turn and add stitches for cord to needle and begin working as for Cord on Picked-Up Stitches.
2. For each loop wanted along edge, work cord for several rows without attaching it to fabric, and then begin attaching it again to next picked-up stitch, forming a loop.

Slit Buttonhole on Corded Edge

This approach also uses the Cord technique, but leaves vertical slit buttonholes along the edge.

1. Pick up stitches along edge.
2. Turn and work one row, casting off number of stitches needed for each buttonhole, leaving gaps in row.
3. Turn, add number of stitches needed for cord, and begin to work the Cord, attaching it to stitches along edge. At each cast-off area along edge, work Cord for number of rows needed to span buttonhole opening without attaching it, and then begin attaching it again to next set of stitches.

Crochet Edges with Buttonholes

Edges or borders done with crochet are very successful on knitted fabrics. Not only is there a wide variety of decorative patterns to choose from, but crochet also produces a firmer fabric that holds its shape well.

- As with knitted methods described above, work crochet chain past number of selvedge stitches to create a slit buttonhole of required length, or crochet loops of whatever size needed; then begin to work into selvedge again.

Interior Button Loops

It is also possible to knit loops set an inch or so within the fabric for a toggle closure; however, unless the loops are stabilized on the inside of the fabric, they tend to pull yarn out of adjacent stitches. To secure them, use one of the techniques described in Sewing on Buttons. To make loops, use one of the following methods:

Button Loop, Version One

This version makes a loop by reknitting a stitch as many times as necessary to make a chain.

1. Knit 1. Insert left needle into nearside of new stitch, wrap yarn as to Knit, and pull stitch over to discard; stitch will twist to right on discard (see Twist Stitches).
2. Rework new stitch on left needle as many times as necessary to make chain of length needed.
3. To draw chain into loop, simply work next stitch and continue across row.

After working Step 3, there will be a gap at the right side of the loop that will be closed when you work across it on the next row.

Button Loop, Version Two

This version is done in much the same way, but the chain is located between two stitches; this is convenient if you want to fit it in between stitch pattern elements.

1. Make Running Thread Increase; work chain on this new stitch as described above in Version One.
2. To form loop, slip first stitch on left needle knitwise, pull last new stitch of chain over slipped stitch and off needle (this is a Left Decrease).

   Or, reach left needle down on farside and pick up running thread on which first stitch of chain was made, place on right needle, and then pull chain stitch over picked-up stitch and off needle.

Button Loop, Version Three

This version uses the Knitted Cord technique described in Uncommon Shapes.

1. Knit three stitches of fabric and Slip them back to left needle. Draw yarn past stitches on inside of fabric and Knit three stitches again. Repeat to make cord length needed for loop.
2. Slip three cord stitches to left needle, [with right needle pick up Purl nub below first stitch at base of cord, place picked-up stitch on left needle, and Knit Two Together]; repeat between brackets to join each of remaining two stitches of cord to Purl nubs picked up in same way.

❖ Buttonhole Finishing

While some of the openings described above can be considered complete when you have finished knitting them, many benefit from additional finishing—and some require it. If a buttonhole is going to be subjected to hard wear, if the yarn used for the garment is softly spun, or if the fabric was worked with a loose tension, it helps to reinforce the edges with one of the techniques described here. This also tends to stabilize the opening so it does not stretch out with wear.

A finished edge will blend in best if it is done with the same yarn used for the garment; however, if the yarn is not suitable for this purpose, substitute any smooth yarn that is compatible. If the yarn you have available is too heavy for the purpose, consider removing one or more of the plied strands to reduce the thickness (for more information, see Unplying Yarn).

To add a decorative element, use a contrast color around the opening; for this purpose consider wool needlepoint yarns, crewel embroidery yarns, or cotton or silk embroidery threads instead—all of which have a range of colors to choose from and are intended for sewing. Silk buttonhole thread may also serve well for a tailored, sporty garment, although the color selection is more limited.

Whether or not you use one of the methods discussed here to finish the edges of the buttonholes in your garment, to my way of thinking the nicest way to complete a set of buttonholes is to back the entire edge with a grosgrain ribbon or other woven fabric backing. This prevents both the buttonholes and the edge from stretching out of shape and it looks very nice on the inside when the garment is worn unbuttoned. See Woven Facings, as well as Buttonhole Facings.

Sewn Finishes for Buttonholes

Several sewn methods can be used to finish the larger Yarn-over or vertical buttonholes. You might want to do this to camouflage an imperfect buttonhole, to correct one that is too large or has stretched, or to decorate a plain one with a contrast-color yarn. Use one of the techniques discussed here to fix the size of the opening before you begin; this will help you sew evenly.

Tips for Sewn Finishes

To ensure that a buttonhole is the correct size (and if you have several, that they are equal in size), use one of the techniques discussed here to stabilize the opening before you begin to sew; this will also help you sew evenly. Also included here is a tip for attaching the sewing yarn.

To Stabilize Buttonholes

- Use woven tape, such as that used to stabilize seams in a sewn garment; cut two lengths longer than the buttonhole opening. Mark finished length of buttonhole on tape with pen or pencil. Use sewing thread to baste one tape on either side of opening, slightly away from edge; remove tape after sewing buttonhole.
- Use lightweight adhesive tape; put one strip perpendicular to each corner of opening and two strips parallel to it (one above, one below) just outside stitching area.

   Adhesive tape may not adhere to a knit very well, and it will pull some fiber out of the yarn when removed, but for a flat fabric done in a smooth yarn this easy fix may work just fine.

- Or, simply baste around opening, slightly away from edge, with a strand of contrast-color embroidery thread or smooth yarn, draw opening up to exact size needed, and then tie two ends of basting strand together to hold in place; remove after finishing.

To Tie on Yarn

- To secure the yarn end so it does not pull free as you begin to sew, hold it on the inside of the fabric; hide both ends when you are done.
- Alternatively, weave in first end before beginning to sew, in effect hiding it ahead of time; then weave the other end in afterward (see Hiding Ends of Yarn).

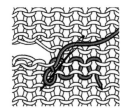

Weaving yarn in on inside for sewn finish.

To Sew Openings

To sew around a buttonhole opening, use what is called a tapestry sewing needle for this purpose (see Tools); it has a wide eye that is easy to thread, and a blunt tip that will not pierce the yarn.

Overcast Stitch

This is a very quick and simple finish for a horizontal or vertical buttonhole that needs to be stabilized a bit. The result is not attractive enough for use on a garment done in a smooth yarn where it will be fully visible, but it is fine for something done with a soft or textured yarn that obscures it somewhat.

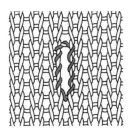

Overcast Stitch on vertical opening.

1. Insert sewing needle from nearside to farside and draw yarn through; work once or twice into center of each stitch around opening.
2. Bring yarn to inside, tie one end to other with a Simple Knot tucked up against corner of opening, and then hide ends of yarn.

To help keep the buttonhole from gaping open, you can also work an optional "bar tack" at each corner. Just wrap the yarn once or twice through the fabric at each corner; the bar should be slightly wider than the buttonhole and perpendicular to the opening.

Concealed Finish

If you want to stabilize a vertical opening against stretching out of shape but prefer not to see the results, sew on the inside as follows:

1. Insert sewing needle down under head of first stitch at bottom of opening, draw yarn through; insert sewing needle under head of stitch above in same way. For a Backstitch Seam, continue in this way up one side to top of buttonhole.
2. Insert needle from bottom up under head of stitch at top left of buttonhole, draw yarn through, and then into head of stitch below in same way. Continue in this way down other side to bottom of buttonhole.
3. Tie two ends in Simple Knot and hide ends on inside.

The stitches double back on themselves, which locks them in place; do not draw them up too tightly or opening will be constricted. You can do the same thing around a horizontal buttonhole, sewing in much the same way into the Purl nubs just above and below the edge of the opening.

Buttonhole Stitch

This classic finishing technique is often recommended for horizontal buttonholes but can also be used for vertical ones. It has a rather commanding appearance when done with yarn, resulting in a bold, decorative finish. If you prefer to have the buttonholes blend in as much as possible, work with a finer yarn or silk buttonhole thread, or split a ply from your knitting yarn.

You may come across other ways to work buttonhole stitch in various needlework books, but all produce the same result. This version is simple and effective.

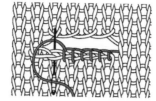

Buttonhole Stitch.

For a horizontal buttonhole, work as follows:

1. Pass sewing needle from inside to outside between two stitches at lower right corner of buttonhole.
2. With left finger, hold yarn above opening on nearside. Insert needle from nearside to farside into center of next stitch to left (yarn will form loop between finger and fabric); bring needle out buttonhole opening to nearside and through center of loop.
3. Drop loop from left finger and draw yarn up gently to form sewn stitch.
4. Repeat across lower opening edge, working once into each stitch, and once between each stitch, always bringing needle out opening and through loop.
5. At corner, either work two or three Buttonhole Stitches, fanning them around corner, or use a bar tack of two or three vertical strands.
6. Turn fabric upside down and repeat across other edge of opening; work second bar tack or buttonhole-stitch fan at other corner.
7. To finish, draw two ends of sewing yarn to inside, tie with Simple Knot, and hide ends.

The important thing is to work the stitches evenly around the opening, each one the same size. One of the sewn strands will be at the very edge of the opening, and another will be perpendicular to it, below the edge.

If the yarn twists up as you work, periodically roll the needle between thumb and forefinger in the direction opposite the twist to undo it, or let the needle dangle from the work long enough for it to unwind itself.

To use this technique to finish an Eyelet or vertical buttonhole, work along the selvedge stitches of the opening. Because a stitch is taller than it is wide, adjust the method as follows:

• Enclose each full selvedge stitch with two buttonhole stitches, working twice between each pair of running threads. Work bar tacks at top and bottom corners to help hold opening together.

Draw strand up very gently to make stitches about same width as stitch columns in knitted fabric so opening does not enlarge.

Duplicate Stitch Finish

This is a bold finish for a vertical buttonhole that stands out from the fabric; use a sewing needle and the same yarn as for the garment, or one in a contrast color.

• To begin, pass sewing needle through to outside at center of stitch at lower right corner of buttonhole. Use Duplicate Stitch on every stitch around edge of opening, stranding yarn up on inside between one stitch and the next; then bring yarn to inside and hide ends.

For illustrations that may help you understand the path the yarn must take, see Stockinette Selvedge.

Sewn Half-Hitch Cast-Off

A Sewn Half-Hitch Cast-Off is an excellent finish for a Horizontal Buttonhole done with a Placeholder Opening, leaving a narrow line of strands around the opening. It is very easy to do because the Placeholder stitches will be in a contrast color, which helps you see exactly where to sew. Also, because that yarn remains in the fabric while you work, it both defines the width of the opening and prevents it from stretching out of shape; if the sewn stitches do not look right, you can gently pull them out and try again without the risk of things falling apart.

Work from left to right, across the row of stitches immediately below the Placeholder stitches. Then turn the fabric upside down and work back across the row on the other side of the Placeholder stitches. As you sew, always bring the needle out *above* the yarn, and carefully tighten up each stitch as you go to make all of them the same size.

Buttonhole with Sewn Half-Hitch Cast-Off. Placeholder stitches not yet removed.

1. To begin, pass needle from farside to nearside through stitch in row below, and to left of first Placeholder stitch. Insert needle into stitch to right, and then out same stitch to left.
2. To continue, insert needle two stitches to right, and then out stitch to left. Repeat to right corner.

3. Insert needle into stitch to right of last Placeholder stitch, and then out stitch in row above. Turn fabric upside down.

4. Insert needle into stitch to right, and then back out same stitch to left.

5. Continue across other edge as in Step 2, above.

6. At opposite corner, insert needle from nearside to farside into stitch below one in Step 1 so last two strands lie parallel.

7. On inside, tie two ends of yarn together in Simple Knot, and hide ends.

It is also possible to do something similar around the edges of a vertical buttonhole. Just work into the center of the selvedge stitches around the opening in the same manner as described above, two over, one back, from left to right. Use the equivalent of a little bar tack, a stitch perpendicular to the opening, to turn the corner.

Knitted Finishes for Buttonholes

Another way to finish a buttonhole done with a Placeholder Opening is by working a Chained Cast-Off around the opening. This can be done with either knitting needles or a crochet hook, and the result is a bold chain of stitches around the opening. Done neatly, it makes a very nice, stable buttonhole.

The freed stitches of the buttonhole can also be hemmed to the inside using a combination of a knitted and a sewn finish; this is a challenging technique, but the result can be very nice.

Chained Cast-Off Finish

This finish requires first picking up the stitches around the buttonhole on a pair of double-point needles, and then removing the Placeholder stitches and casting off the picked-up stitches. You can do this on either the outside or inside of the fabric.

While this seems challenging, it is not difficult to do, and one of the advantages is that the stitches can be worked in Knit, Purl, or even in Single Rib as you cast off. Also, you can work with thinner needles and yarn to reduce the size of the stitches in the edge. There is also a crochet version below.

Buttonhole with Chained Cast-Off.

Picking Up Around Opening

Pick up the stitches above and below the buttonhole before removing the Placeholder stitches. To make this easy to do,

use a pair of short double-point needles or two small circular ones that are one or more sizes smaller than those used for the fabric itself—one for the stitches below the opening and one for those above.

1. With first needle, start at right corner of buttonhole and pick up right side of every stitch in row below Placeholder stitches.

2. Turn work upside down and, with second needle, start at right corner and again pick up right side of every stitch with Placeholder yarn in it.

3. With all stitches safely on needles, remove Placeholder yarn.

You will notice that the first and last stitches of the opening have only one strand of Placeholder yarn in them, while all the others have two.

Also, after picking up there will be one more stitch on the top needle than on the bottom one; for more information on this, see Working in the Opposite Direction.

If you prefer to pick up on the inside, it is quite easy, since the contrast-color Placeholder yarn outlines the area very clearly. Work as follows:

• Working from right to left, insert first needle down under each Purl nub in row below Placeholder Opening; insert second needle down under running threads in row above opening, and then remove stitches.

To Cast Off Opening Edge

1. With separate strand of yarn, start at right corner and work Chained Cast-Off on stitches of lower edge of opening; pick up new stitch under right side of stitch at corner. Turn fabric around.

2. Start with stitch picked up at corner and cast off across top edge in same way; pick up once into side of stitch at other corner. Turn fabric around.

3. Elongate last stitch, cut yarn leaving a 10–12 inch end, and thread through blunt sewing needle.

4. Pass strand from right to left under both sides of first cast-off stitch, and then down through center of last cast-off stitch (see Finishing Circular Fabric Edge). Turn to inside, knot two ends of yarn together gently, and hide them on inside.

You can also cast off in Purl on the outside, or use a mixture of Knit and Purl if that would blend in with your fabric better. Either of these will cause the cast-off edge to turn up into the opening a bit instead of lying flat on the face of the fabric.

Crochet Chained Cast-Off Finish

You can do the same edge described above with a crochet hook instead of a knitting needle. There are two versions: one is done much like the method above; the other is done *before* removing the Placeholder stitches.

Crochet Chain with Stitches Removed

- Work as described above, but insert hook into each stitch around Placeholder Opening as to Knit; with two stitches on hook, pull first through second.

Crochet Chain with Stitches in Place

Here is an even quicker, more efficient way to work the same edge. Use a crochet hook to work the chain around the Placeholder Opening, and pull the Placeholder stitches out after you are done.

To work so Knit stitches are on the outside of the fabric below the cast-off edge, work on the *inside*, as follows:

1. Start at upper right corner, in row above Placeholder stitches, and insert hook up into first Purl nub with strand of contrast-color Placeholder yarn passing through it. Wrap yarn on hook and draw loop through stitch.
2. Repeat with nub to left; draw second loop through first; one loop is left on needle. Repeat across top of buttonhole and then work once into side of stitch at corner.
3. Turn fabric around so lower edge of buttonhole is now on top and work back across in same way, working last chain into side of stitch at corner.
4. Elongate last stitch so it will not unravel, and then use tip of needle to remove Placeholder stitches; turn to outside and finish as described in Step 4 of Chained Cast-Off Finish, above.

To place Purl stitches on the outside around the cast-off edge, work on the *outside* as follows:

- Work as described above, but start at lower right corner and insert hook into right side of first stitch with contrast-color yarn passing through it.

Hemmed Finish

Here is another, interesting finish for a buttonhole done with a Placeholder Opening that creates a tiny hem around it. This requires patience and practiced skill to do well, but for a tailored garment such as a jacket or coat that would benefit from a subtle buttonhole, this technique has much to recommend it.

1. On inside of fabric, pick up stitches around opening on pair of needles as described above and remove Placeholder stitches.
2. With separate yarn, Knit each stitch on lower needle, and then once into side of stitch at corner. Turn and Knit

across top needle, and once into side of stitch at other corner. There will be two extra stitches temporarily on needle.
3. Thread yarn into tapestry needle and sew each stitch down on inside; insert needle up under second Purl nub below first stitch on lower needle, and then into stitch as to Purl; drop stitch from needle. Repeat until all stitches have been sewn down on inside.

Hemmed Buttonhole.

Sew as evenly as possible and do not draw up yarn too tightly.

Working in Knit on the inside of the fabric places a round of Purl at the edge of the opening on the outside; it will serve as the equivalent of a foldline.

As you will see, the buttonhole will look thickened because there are now two layers of stitches plus sewing yarn in the area around the opening. You can reduce the bulk somewhat by removing one ply from the yarn before knitting the stitches and/or sewing them down with something like buttonhole thread instead of yarn. Finally, a little steam should settle things in nicely, especially if you finger press the buttonhole; however, if the fabric is smooth, the buttonhole might benefit from actually pressing the fabric (see Steaming and Pressing).

Hemmed and Faced Finish

It is also possible to sew the freed stitches to an edge faced with ribbon using one of the following suggestions:

- Work as for Steps 1 and 2 above, but pick up the stitches on the outside of the fabric and Purl instead. Make buttonholes in a ribbon facing, line up openings, and sew ribbon to inside around buttonhole edge with thread. Draw each knitted stitch in turn off needles, through opening to inside, and sew to ribbon with a small stitch or two.
- Alternatively, cut two strips of a fine iron-on interfacing for knits and fuse to inside on either side of opening. First sew knitted stitches to interfacing and then sew opening in ribbon to opening in knit fabric, to completely hide the stitches from sight.

Machine-Sewn Buttonholes

Machine-made buttonholes are a subject of some controversy. Many people object to the intrusion of machine work on a handmade garment and will not have them under any circumstances. Others are sufficiently dismayed with their knitted buttonholes that they are willing to compromise their principles on this matter. Still others think machine buttonholes are so superior they wouldn't bother with those lumpy handmade ones. I am not fond of rigid rules of any sort, and I think you should do whatever you please!

If you prefer machine-made buttonholes, keep in mind that if done badly they will be just as homely as poorly constructed handmade ones. If you do not have an excellent sewing machine and a familiarity with making buttonholes, I do not recommend you try this; it would be far wiser to plan from the outset to take your completed garment to a professional. Inquire at your local yarn or fabric store for the name of a tailor or dressmaker. Ask to see samples done on a knitted fabric before you give them your precious garment, or even pay them to work a sample buttonhole on a swatch you provide.

Should you decide to make your own sewn buttonholes, I must emphasize again the importance of practicing on a Test Swatch done just like your garment—a strip 3 to 4 inches wide and 10 to 12 inches long will give you a good length to practice on. Keep in mind that a machine-sewn buttonhole will have no stretch, so the size should be calculated exactly as one would a buttonhole on a woven fabric.

Here are some suggestions that may improve the outcome; one or another of these should prove useful, depending upon your circumstances:

- Thread in four short Yarn Markers to serve as guides for sewing—two perpendicular to each end of buttonhole and two parallel to opening at each side—separated by width of presser foot.
- Stabilize buttonhole with one of methods described in Tips for Sewn Finishes, above, or use stabilizer available in sewing stores that can be torn off after stitching.
- The buttonhole foot on most machines is designed to hold a stabilizing thread or cord underneath. The stitching encases the cord to create a more pronounced "bead," or raised line of stitching.
- If necessary, use a "walking" foot attachment on machine. These are designed to draw stretchy and bulky fabrics evenly under the needle.
- Consider using buttonhole or machine embroidery thread; adjust the needle size and tension as necessary.
- If the buttonhole maker of your machine sews too narrow a bead, try using the regular zigzag stitch instead; or, as a second step, sew over the buttonhole stitch with a wider zigzag. Alternatively, work a narrow machine-made buttonhole, and then overcast the stitched edge by hand with yarn.

Sewing on Buttons

Buttons sewn to a knitted fabric also benefit from support on the inside of the garment. For suggestions, see Sewing on Buttons in the chapter on Finishing Techniques; also included there are several ideas for how to remove delicate or valuable buttons from the garment before cleaning so they will not be damaged.

Pockets

All of the fundamental techniques used to make pockets are described elsewhere in this book, including how to cast off, pick up stitches, work fold lines for hems and borders, and sew linings and hems into place. What you will find here, therefore, has to do with how to apply these techniques to make pockets of different styles.

There are basically just two kinds of pockets, with many variations on the theme. A patch pocket is a separate piece of fabric that is sewn to the outside, while an integral pocket consists of an opening in the fabric with a lining on the inside of the garment.

Patch pockets are, of course, the simplest of all, and since they are added to a completed garment, they require little or no advance planning. They also offer great scope for decorative enhancement, because they can be made with patterns and materials different from those used for the main fabric, and can easily be replaced when worn or to change the look of a garment.

An integral pocket has a more subtle, tailored appearance, since only the opening itself is visible on the outside of the garment, and it requires the use of somewhat more advanced techniques than a patch pocket does. There are a variety of ways to finish the opening and make a lining, and these can be done while working the garment or added later.

❖ Patch Pockets

A patch pocket consists of no more than a piece of fabric sewn to the outside of the garment with one edge left open. At its simplest, the patch is knitted in the same yarn used for the garment, and, for a very discreet look that blends in, also worked in the same stitch or color pattern as the garment and sewn into place so everything lines up.

For a more decorative pocket, you can use a contrast color or textured yarn, a different stitch or color pattern, or even add some beads or sequins. Instead of knitting the pocket, consider crochet, a firmly woven fabric, or even a natural or artificial leather, since these materials hold their shape very well and can add a very interesting design detail.

There are several options for how to position the pocket opening, which is really no more than deciding which edge to leave open. You could, for instance, knit a square but sew it onto the fabric with the opening at the side instead of the top, or set it at an angle. Even a slight modification in the shape of the patch makes a difference, such as working one corner of a rectangle with a sloped or curved edge for the opening.

Patch Pocket Edges

When designing the shape and surface pattern of a patch pocket, the only criteria are personal taste, the characteristics of the yarn, and compatibility with the garment. However, the open edge requires special consideration, because you will want it to remain stable in wear.

This can be achieved through the use of certain stitch patterns, by working a hem at the edge, or by applying a small facing of some kind. All of these options are the same as discussed in Horizontal Pocket Edges, below. You might also want to consider selecting an edge pattern that can be used on all four sides of the pocket to define it.

Sewing a Patch Pocket

Attaching the pocket to the outside of the garment is quite straightforward; see Sewing Within a Fabric, or Grafting a Patch Pocket. To make sure the pocket is positioned accurately for sewing, see Yarn Markers.

Also take into consideration how to handle the Selvedges; the most basic kinds are necessary for any seam and will be hidden on the inside of the pocket, but there are also some that can be turned to the outside for a decorative note.

If you plan to use a woven fabric as a pocket, see Sewing Wovens to Knits. That information would also be useful if you want to stabilize the inside edge of the pocket with a woven facing or face all four edges with a decorative woven binding.

And finally, consider lining the entire pocket with a woven fabric to help it hold its shape. This is a particularly good approach if the yarn is softly spun, fragile in any way, or the stitch pattern you would prefer to use is not firm enough to serve well as a pocket.

❖ *Horizontal Pockets*

A pocket with a horizontal opening is the easiest style to work as an integral part of the knitted fabric. All that shows on the outside of the fabric is the opening itself; the lining is on the inside of the garment.

You can work to the row where you want the opening and stop to make the entire pocket before continuing on the garment section. Alternatively, you can use the Placeholder

Pocket Opening, below, which is no more than an enlarged version of a technique used to make a buttonhole, or the very similar Stitch Holder Opening; either of which will allow you to finish the edge and make the pocket lining after the garment section is complete.

And finally, on occasion you may want to add a pocket to a completed garment. Perhaps you are unsure of its proper placement and want to try on the garment before deciding where the pocket should go, or want to add a pocket to a garment completed long ago in order to give it a new look. For these situations, you can use a technique that Elizabeth Zimmermann named, most appropriately, the "Afterthought Pocket."†

There are a wide variety of ways to finish the edge of the opening, from plain to fancy, but there are only two types of pocket linings. One consists of a single layer of fabric sewn to the inside of the garment, while the other has two layers forming a pouch that hangs free on the inside.

Pocket Openings

Here are four techniques that can be used to make a horizontal opening in a knitted fabric to accommodate a pocket lining. As mentioned above, you can mark the position and return to finish the pocket later, stop and complete it before going on, or make an opening later.

Placeholder Pocket Opening

This method is used if you prefer to finish the entire pocket after the garment section is complete. The technique is the same as that used to make a buttonhole with the Placeholder Opening, just done on a larger scale.

1. Work to position of pocket and use separate contrast-color yarn to insert Placeholder stitches in width of opening; continue with garment section.
2. To finish pocket, pick up stitches around opening.
3. Finish visible edge of opening and make lining using one of methods described below.

Stitch Holder Opening

If you are working with a fairly complex stitch pattern, you might want to place the stitches of the pocket opening on holders instead of using Placeholder stitches. With this approach, the stitches do not need to be picked up later; they are ready for finishing whenever you are.

1. Work to position of pocket; transfer pocket stitches from left needle to holder.
2. With main yarn and separate strand for baseline, use

---

† Elizabeth Zimmermann, *Knitting Workshop* (Pittsville, Wisc.: Schoolhouse Press, 1981), p. 108.

Provisional Cast-On at Side Edge to add an equal number of pocket stitches to those on right needle.

3. Work across remainder of row, and complete garment section above position of opening.

4. To finish pocket, return to stitches on hold for lower opening edge and Stranded Cast-On stitches for upper edge, and make lining with one of methods described below.

Afterthought Pocket

Should you want to add a horizontal pocket to an already finished garment, it is possible to remove a row of stitches to make the opening, and pick up the freed stitches in the rows above and below to work as for the Placeholder Pocket Opening, above.

Here is the basic information for how to do this; for more details, also see Separating a Fabric.

1. Determine row and width of pocket opening; if necessary, insert Yarn Markers, pins, or small stitch holders at each side to define number of stitches to remove.

2. Use thin double-point needle and pick up right side of each stitch in row below stitches marked for opening. Turn fabric upside down and repeat with second needle in row above opening.

3. Insert tapestry needle or knitting needle into center stitch of those marked for removal and pull to form loop; slip point of scissors into loop and snip yarn. Working from center toward one side and then toward other side, pull yarn free from stitches on needles above and below opening.

4. Secure ends of unraveled yarn on inside (see Hiding Ends of Yarn) and proceed as described in the Placeholder Pocket Opening, above.

The whole process is really quite simple once you overcome your fear of snipping that first stitch.

The traditional method is to snip the yarn and begin to unravel, picking up the freed stitches on two needles as you go, but it provides a certain peace of mind to have the stitches already picked up and on needles ahead of time. This is particularly true if you are doing this on any fabric made in a complex stitch or a color pattern, in which case it is also best to position the opening so you can pick up into the plain rows above and below and remove a pattern row.

In-Process Opening

Here are the steps to follow should you want to complete the entire pocket at the point of insertion before going on to finish the garment section.

The instructions are slightly different depending upon what kind of a lining you make; see Pocket Linings, below.

1. Work to position of pocket opening.

2. Secure garment stitches on right needle, or place on holder; these remain inactive until pocket is complete.

3. Take up separate needle and work across pocket stitches using pattern chosen to finish visible edge. Secure garment stitches on left needle as described in Step 2; leave inactive on other side of pocket opening.

4. Take up second needle for pocket stitches and complete edge pattern; make lining with one of methods described in Pocket Linings, below.

Horizontal Pocket Edges

The nicest edge for a pocket is one that will remain stable in use and not stretch out of shape. Beyond that, however, there are a wide variety of options, from a plain cast-off edge or a simple foldline with a small hem to borders done in different stitch patterns or colors.

Cast-Off Edge

The quickest and easiest way to finish the edge of a pocket opening is to simply cast off the stitches. Unfortunately, a plain cast-off edge presents the same problems at the corners as a Traditional Cast-Off Buttonhole does, which can result in a less than ideal finish.

Instead, use the method described for casting off the lower edge of the Improved Horizontal Buttonhole, Steps 1 and 2, since this will help neaten corners.

Pocket Borders

To add a decorative element to the opening and stabilize the edge at the same time, make a border using a non-curling stitch pattern such as Single Rib, or select one that is firm and not resilient. Because an edge of this kind involves a different stitch pattern than is used for the main fabric, it may require a change in needle size and/or a slight adjustment in the number of stitches.

You can start the border just below the opening edge and work it as part of the main fabric, or add it above the opening after separating the main fabric.

Border Below Opening

- Place Ring Markers on needle to define stitches of pocket opening and work border pattern on these stitches; continue primary pattern on stitches to each side. Once border is complete, divide fabric for opening, finish edge, and make lining as described in Pocket Linings, below.

Extended Border

A border added to serve as the pocket edge that rises above the opening in the fabric is somewhat more complicated.

After dividing the fabric, work the stitches of the border with a separate supply of yarn as follows:

1. Allow adequate tail of yarn to sew one side of border to main fabric.
2. On first row, increase one or two stitches at each side to make border slightly wider than pocket opening and allow for selvedges. Begin border pattern.
3. On last row, begin cast-off on side where border yarn was tied on; after casting off, draw yarn through last stitch and break off, allowing sufficient length to sew other side to fabric.
4. Make Pocket Half Lining and incorporate into main fabric as described there; complete garment section.
5. To finish pocket edge, use first yarn end to sew one side edge of border to outside of fabric above opening and second yarn end to sew other side (see Sewing Within a Fabric).

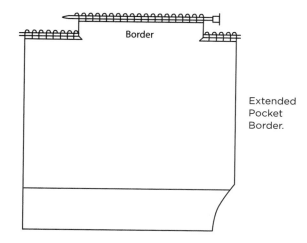

Border

Extended Pocket Border.

You can allow a longer length of yarn in Step 1, and place stitches on holder instead of casting off in Step 3. To finish, use the same yarn to sew first side, continue with Sewn Cast-Off across top, and then sew the other side.

Crochet Border

Many beautiful crochet patterns are intended for use as edgings, and they tend to be more firm than knitted edges. You could crochet just a narrow edging along a cast-off edge, or use a more complicated pattern as an extended border. For a fancier edge, consider working a bit of crocheted lace that would hang down from the pocket edge instead (or in addition to an extended border; crochet makes this sort of thing very easy to do).

Hemmed Pocket Edge

A hemmed border provides a very discreet finish for the opening, but can add a certain amount of bulk. Work as follows:

1. On stitches of opening, work a Purl Foldline, or a Picot Foldline.
2. On next row, increase one or two stitches at each side of border and work sufficient rows for small hem; at a minimum work two or three rows, or for a full hem as much as 1 or 2 inches.
3. To finish, graft both sides and free stitches of hem edge to inside, or cast off stitches and sew three sides of hem to inside.

There are several ways to reduce the bulk of this hem. If the yarn is cooperative, you can remove one or two plies, breaking it off 6 to 8 inches beyond increase row. Alternatively, make the fabric softer and more open by using Regauging; eliminate the increases in Step 2 and change to a needle one or two sizes larger to work the hem.

Instead of a hem, you could line the inside of the cast-off edge of a pocket opening or an extended border with grosgrain or satin ribbon to stabilize it just as for a button band on a center front opening (see Sewing Wovens to Knits).

Pocket Linings

There are three approaches to making a lining for a pocket.

A half lining consists of one piece of knitted fabric sewn to the inside of the garment. It is less bulky than a full lining but, because it is attached to the fabric, it will be more evident on the outside, and also has a tendency to distort the garment somewhat when full of hands, or keys, or treats.

The full pocket lining is basically a pouch that hangs free on the inside. Because it consists of two pieces of fabric, it is bulkier than the half lining, but since it is not sewn to the garment, it will not cause as much distortion when the pocket is in use.

Finally, a woven fabric makes an excellent lining of either sort and, while somewhat unorthodox, is definitely worth consideration.

Half Lining

A lining of this kind is worked separately, from the bottom up, and the stitches of the lining are then inserted between the stitches of the two sides of the main fabric, which have been on hold. The sides and bottom of the lining are later sewn to the inside of the garment.

1. Take up separate set of needles and yarn, and cast on same number of stitches as for pocket opening, plus a minimum of four extra stitches (two at each side), to make lining slightly wider than opening and provide selvedge for sewing.
2. Work length of lining, the number of rows determined by pocket design and row gauge.
3. Break off yarn, allow sufficient length for sewing around three sides, and wind end into Yarn Butterfly.

4. Take up needle bearing garment stitches on one side of pocket opening and, if necessary, work across row so yarn is at corner of opening.

5. Pick up needle bearing lining stitches in left hand, with outside of lining and outside of garment section facing in same direction; continue across lining stitches.

6. Pick up needle bearing garment stitches on other side of opening and complete row to incorporate lining; finish garment section above pocket opening.

7. To finish pocket, position lining carefully on inside below pocket opening, and pin or baste into place; sew two sides and bottom to main garment fabric. For more information, see Sewing Within a Fabric.

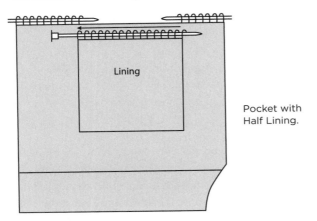

Pocket with Half Lining.

Full Lining Worked Flat

With this method, the lining is worked down from the stitches of the front opening edge. When it is twice the length needed, it is folded up into position and the lining stitches are inserted between the two sets of stitches for the garment section, as described above for the Half Lining. This pocket lining hangs free on the inside of the garment.

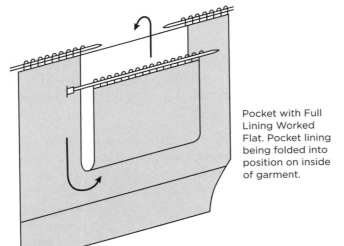

Pocket with Full Lining Worked Flat. Pocket lining being folded into position on inside of garment.

1. Work a foldline on the stitches of the opening. On next row increase a minimum of four stitches, two at each side, to make lining slightly wider than opening edge and allow selvedge for sewing.

2. Work as many rows as needed for length of front half of lining; Knit face of lining should be on *inside* of pocket.

3. Work second foldline for bottom edge of pocket, and then repeat same number of rows for second half of pocket lining. On last row, decrease extra stitches at each side to return to original stitch count.

4. Incorporate stitches of lining between two sets of stitches of garment as described above for Half Lining, Steps 5 and 6.

5. To finish, sew sides of pocket together to form pouch.

Full Lining in the Round

If you have used a Placeholder Opening, a Stitch Holder Opening, or plan to do an Afterthought Pocket, you can work the lining in the round. If you prefer to use a set of double-point needles, pick up stitches above and below opening on four needles and work with fifth. Alternatively, work with a pair of small circular needles, or pick the stitches up on two straight double-point needles and use the Shetland Three-Needle Method.

Pick up stitches on inside of fabric, and work outside of lining in Purl, as follows:

1. Knit one row of stitches on lower opening edge to create Purl Foldline on outside.

2. Begin working pocket lining in Purl. Draw yarn between two needles to join one side and work across stitches of upper opening edge to start back half of lining. At end of row, draw yarn between two needles to join round.

3. On second round, increase a minimum of two stitches at each side to make lining slightly wider than opening.

4. Work as many rounds as needed for length.

5. Use Joinery Cast-Off to close lower edge of lining.

To help the pocket lie flat, consider working a Vertical Fold-line at each side.

Reducing Bulk of Linings

To reduce the bulk inherent in a lining of this kind, it helps to use a thinner yarn and smaller size needles, with the change occurring about an inch below the opening so it will not be visible in wear.

Because this change will not be seen, use any yarn you have on hand or consider removing one or two ply from the garment yarn (see Unplying Yarn). This might be too much fuss for a large pocket, but for a small one it is worth consideration; for information on how to estimate the amount of yarn needed, see Calculating Yarn Requirements in the chapter Stitch Gauge.

To maintain pocket lining width when working with different size yarns and needles, use a Test Swatch to calculate a quick Gauge to use for this portion and adjust the number of stitches when changing from one yarn to the other.

For Half Lining

• With finer yarn and smaller size needles, cast on and work lining until it is about an inch short of length needed. Change to main yarn and needle size, adjust number of stitches as necessary, and complete last few rows of lining; then integrate between sides of main fabric, as described above.

For Full Lining

1. Work foldline for opening edge and about 1 inch of lining.
2. Switch to thinner yarn and smaller needle size, adjust number of stitches as necessary, and work first side of pocket lining.
3. Work foldline at bottom of pocket; make second side of pocket lining with same number of rows as in Step 2.
4. Return to main yarn and needle size and work remainder of lining with same number of rows as in Step 1.
5. Incorporate lining between sides of main fabric as described above.

Woven Fabric Linings

There is no rule that says you have to knit a pocket lining, and there are good reasons to use one made of a firmly woven fabric instead.

A woven fabric pocket, whether done as a half lining or a full one, will contribute a minimum of bulk to the garment, will not stretch out of shape with wear, and can readily be replaced if it becomes worn. You can make your own pocket lining pattern or use one from a sewing pattern of a similar type and size as the garment you are knitting.

The information here is for making a lining of this kind for a horizontal opening, but the concept applies equally well for a pocket made with a Vertical or Sloped opening, both of which are described below.

Woven Half Lining

1. Finish lower opening edge of pocket.
2. On separate needles, knit small facing, 1 or 2 inches long, in same manner as making a Half Lining, and then incorporate these stitches with those on either side of opening; complete garment above pocket.
3. Cut out pocket from woven fabric and finish all edges.

4. Sew top edge of woven pocket to bottom edge of knitted facing. Pin or baste two sides and bottom of lining, and side edges of knitted facing to inside of garment, and sew into place; see Sewing Wovens to Knits.

Woven Full Lining

You will need two facings, one for the opening edge of the pocket, and one extending down from the fabric above the opening.

1. Finish lower opening edge with foldline and work facing 1 to 2 inches as for Hemmed Pocket Edge, above; cast off.
2. To make facing for other side of lining, work as described for Woven Half Lining, Step 2.
3. Cut out pocket lining from woven fabric, fold into position, and sew sides; finish top edges so they will not fray.
4. Sew top edges of pocket lining to bottom edges of knitted facings.

Pocket Flaps

To make a flap that will hang down and cover the opening, here are several options for how to work:

• Knit flap separately and sew it into place.
• Alternatively, cast on and work flap from bottom up; insert flap stitches between those of main garment sections as for the Half Lining, above. Then cast on and make lining; cast off at top and sew edge behind flap on inside.

   Or, join top of lining and top of flap stitches with Joinery Decreases, and then insert lining and flap together between stitches of main garment.
• If you prefer, work flap on stitches picked up on outside of fabric (see Picking Up Within a Fabric).
• Or, make either a half or full lining and, at top of back lining, work foldline and then length of flap. Pick up stitches at base of flap foldline and insert these stitches between those of main garment sections.

❖ *Vertical or Sloped Pockets*

For a vertical or sloped opening, the fabric is divided and the two sides are worked separately for the length of the opening and then rejoined, just as for a Vertical Buttonhole. The pocket lining is normally worked on stitches added to one side of the main fabric, but it can be made separately and attached to small facings done at the opening.

A vertical opening requires little calculation, since it is no more than the length of the opening times your row gauge. However, for a sloped edge, you will need to work out a pattern for the placement of the decreases. See Charting a Gradual Slope, or, if you prefer a mathematical approach, see Steps and Points for Gradual Slopes.

Also, use your gauge to determine how many stitches and rows are required for the pocket lining; it needs to be wide enough for the hand, and should extend several inches below the lower corner and a row or two above the upper corner of the opening.

A circular garment divided for a vertical or sloped opening of this kind will, by necessity, be worked flat for the length of the opening. This can sometimes cause a visible change in gauge; see the Five Variables in the chapter Stitch Gauge.

In the following instructions, the "lining side" refers to that half of the divided garment section that has the lining attached to it. The "facing side" refers to the half of the divided garment section that has the finished, visible edge for the pocket opening; later the bottom and side of the lining will be sewn to it on the inside.

Making a Sloped Pocket Opening

At the lower point of the pocket opening, divide the fabric, place the stitches of the lining side of the garment section on a holder, and proceed as follows:

The Facing Side

1. Continue to work facing side of garment. Work decreases along opening edge to form slope.
2. When pocket opening is length wanted, work last row of facing side of garment section toward pocket opening; place stitches on hold.

To make a decorative border along the opening edge, work ½ to 1 inch in a decorative stitch pattern of some kind.

The Lining Side

The pocket lining needs to be wider than the opening of the pocket. To determine the number of stitches for the lining, add enough stitches for 1 or 2 inches to the number of stitches decreased for the sloped pocket opening.

1. On separate needle, cast on number of stitches required for width of pocket opening.
2. Work several inches of lining for portion of pocket below bottom point of opening. Work last row of pocket lining toward lining side of garment section with outsides of both facing in the same direction.
3. Hold needle with lining stitches in right hand and needle bearing stitches of lining side of garment in left hand; work across those stitches with pocket lining yarn to join two sets of stitches.
4. Work garment side and pocket lining together as one until length matches that of opening edge on facing side; end last row at lining selvedge.

5. On next row, count across stitches and place Ring Marker on needle to define the 1 or 2 inches of extra stitches added to pocket for additional width.

To check to see if you have positioned the Ring Marker correctly, add the number of stitches before the marker on the lining needle, to the number on the facing needle; the result should equal the number of stitches on the needles before the fabric was divided for the pocket. The extra stitches belong to the top of the pocket lining.

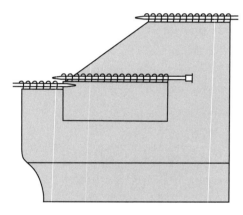

Sloped Pocket Lining on inside of garment; work across pocket lining stitches and then across stitches of lining side of garment.

To Complete Pocket

1. Work across stitches of lining side of garment to Ring Marker and remove it.
2. Pick up needle bearing stitches of facing side of garment and position it parallel to needle with stitches at top of lining. Hold needle bearing remaining stitches of lining side of garment in right hand.
3. Use Joinery Decreases to attach lining stitches to facing stitches, and then continue across row to rejoin two sides of garment and close top of pocket opening.
4. At your convenience, sew sides and bottom of pocket lining to inside of garment.

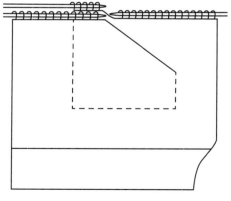

Completing Sloped Pocket. On outside, join stitches at top of lining to stitches of facing side of garment.

Instead of using Joinery Decreases, you can either cast off lining stitches at top and sew to inside, or you can Graft free stitches to inside.

Vertical Pocket Edges

There are several ways to finish the edge of a vertical or sloped pocket opening. The simplest, of course, is to use a decorative selvedge of some kind.

Here are some other suggestions:

- Work a decorative stitch or color pattern on about 1 inch of stitches adjacent to opening on facing side. Work decreases to slope edge adjacent to selvedge, or stitches of the main fabric next to the border pattern.
- For extended border along edge, pick up stitches along facing side of opening and work border perpendicular to opening (see Picking Up Stitches). Cast off and then sew side edges of border to outside of lining side of garment at top and bottom corners.
- Alternatively, an extended border can be done by casting on extra stitches at lower point of opening on facing side of garment, and then casting them off at the top; sew side edges of border to outside of lining side.
- To stabilize opening edge, line inside with woven facing or decorative ribbon, as described above for a Horizontal Pocket Edge, or even encase edge with facing (see Facings).

Woven Fabric Lining for Vertical Edge

If you prefer, you can attach a pocket lining of woven fabric, as described above for a Horizontal Pocket Lining. A lining of this kind is best sewn slightly away from the pocket opening so it will not be visible. To do this, work a border of some kind on the facing side of the garment, and a small extension on the lining side of the garment and sew the pocket to these (see Sewing Wovens to Knits).

After dividing the fabric for the opening, work as follows:

1. Work facing side of garment with border or hem at opening.
2. On lining side make small extension to serve as facing; with separate needles, cast on enough stitches for about 1 inch width and work 1 inch in length.

   This extends facing below lower point of opening.
3. Hold needle with stitches of facing in right hand, and stitches of lining side in left hand, and work across to join facing. Work lining side of garment same length as facing side of garment.
4. Cut out and sew pocket with opening at side; finish edges. Sew open side edge of front portion of pocket lining to inside along border or hem on facing side of garment. Sew other side edge of pocket to edge of small facing on lining side of garment. Sew top and bottom edges of knitted facing to inside of garment near opening.

CHAPTER 9

Hems, Facings, Pleats, and Tucks

In the first half of the twentieth century, many knitting patterns were available for elegant blouses, skirts, and dresses that were done in fine yarns. These designs sometimes included features such as pleats, tucks, hems, or facings, which double or triple the thickness of the fabric. Things of this kind can be bulky when done in garments made with the heavier yarns that have been popular more recently; therefore, they are now rarely seen except in machine knits.

This is unfortunate—these techniques are worth consideration for garments made with any yarn, and several methods discussed here can be used to reduce the inherent thickness of a folded fabric. The challenge is not so much in the techniques themselves, which are easy enough to do, but in knowing when and how to make use of them successfully.

Hems and Facings

A hem is a portion of a fabric folded back on itself along the edge of a garment and fastened to the inside; it is used to finish and stabilize an edge so it will hold its shape. A facing is used for the same purposes as a hem, but it is a separate piece of fabric sewn to the inside of the garment during finishing. Because facings are not an integral part of the main fabric, there are a great many more options for how to make them than hems, and it is easier to refine the fit. They can be done with a different yarn or stitch pattern than that used for the main fabric, or can even be made from a woven fabric, which is in many ways preferable.

While hems and facings are almost always used to finish the edges of sewn garments, there are a variety of border patterns that better serve many of the same purposes for hand knits, so they do require some justification.

The primary reason to use a hem or facing is when an edge needs to be tamed but it would be best to hide the means of doing so. For instance, when the ideal stitch pattern for a border would otherwise not lie flat and smooth, or when the appearance of a garment design with an overall pattern would be compromised by a border of any kind, a hem or facing can provide the solution. Last, but by no means least, facings can be applied later to help restore the shape of a well-loved, but worn garment.

A casing is a doubled area of the fabric that is intended to hold a drawstring or elastic. When used at the edge of a garment, such as the waistline of a skirt or the lower edge of a sleeve or jacket, it is simply a hem by another name and is made in exactly the same way. However, a casing set within the fabric, such as for the waistline of a dress, is made like a facing, by sewing a separate piece of fabric into place; for one knitted into the fabric, see Double-Fabric Insertion.

Regardless of what stitch or color pattern you plan to use for the garment itself, the instructions here assume that a knitted hem or facing will be made in Stockinette, since it is plain, smooth, and easy to do. Also, if the main fabric is made with a textured stitch or color pattern, a hem made in the same way would be too bulky. In the general tips that follow the instructions, you will find some suggestions for suitable cast-on and cast-off techniques, how to attach a hem or facing to the main fabric so it is as unobtrusive as possible, and various ways to use gauge to refine the fit.

❖ Hems

It is easy to include either a horizontal or a vertical hem in a basic garment design. The pattern is generally quite straightforward because it simply needs to replicate the shape of the main fabric when folded into place, and the size should be in proportion to the garment. A horizontal hem is normally 1 to 3 inches deep, a vertical hem usually no more than 1 or 2 inches wide, but these may be wider for larger garments like a coat or jacket.

However, even though a hem is worked as an integral part of the garment, it may require a separate gauge to determine the number of stitches and rows required, particularly if it is made with a different stitch pattern or yarn than that of the main fabric. Also, if the side edges of the garment are shaped, the hem will require the same shaping at the sides, but done in reverse. In other words, for something like an A-line skirt, the hem will be slightly narrower where it is sewn to the inside, and wider at the edge of the garment, and this may require a separate pattern. Information on Gauge and tips for how to attach the hem to the inside of the fabric can be found in Tips for Hems and Facings.

Of equal importance to the success of a hem is the foldline, which will form the finished edge of the fabric. A foldline for a horizontal hem is made with a one- or two-row pattern; for a vertical hem, it consists of one or two stitch columns. Here are several patterns; some are very plain, some more decorative.

Horizontal Foldlines

There are five horizontal foldlines below; the first two are soft and rounded, the third is crisp and well-defined, and the last two are decorative.

The instructions assume that you will start with a cast-on edge, work the rows needed for the hem in Stockinette, and then add a foldline. After the foldline, change to the pattern for the main fabric; if necessary, adjust the number of stitches according to gauge. To finish the garment, fold the hem into place and fasten it to the inside.

For a hem on a garment worked from the top down, or for something like a casing at the top of a skirt, just reverse the sequence, working the foldline first and then the hem.

Rounded Horizontal Fold

This is basically no foldline at all, but even so it has its place and requires some minimal planning. Because a soft knitted fabric does not fold crisply, a hem without a foldline will have a rounded edge, although it can be encouraged to flatten a bit with a little steam. A rounded edge can be quite attractive for certain garment styles and the Filled Hem, below, even exaggerates the effect.

Depending upon how thick the fabric is, the folded edge may absorb a few extra rows just going around the bend, and this can result in a hem that is shorter than anticipated. To compensate, add one to three extra rows for the fold.

If you want to be more precise about planning this, work as follows:

- Make swatch in hem pattern; measure full length of swatch and divide in half. Then fold swatch in half as for hem and remeasure.

  Compare two measurements; if folded one is shorter than the other, use gauge to determine how many rows are needed to compensate for rounded fold.

Twist Stitch Foldline

For a soft, unobtrusive edge that will lie flatter than the Rounded Horizontal Fold above, work as follows:

1. On inside row, use needle three to four sizes larger than that used for main fabric and Purl one row for foldline.
2. On next row, return to original size needle and Knit all stitches farside to twist them; see Twist Stitches.

Of course you could Knit the foldline on an outside row with the larger needle and Purl all stitches farside on the next row, but that is slightly more awkward to do.

Purl Foldline

This is the most common method used for a foldline and it is very easy to do; it produces a crisp, tailored edge suitable for most purposes.

- Work single row of Purl on outside of fabric.

Purl Foldline.

Picot Foldline

Here is a charming foldline done with a row of Eyelet Insertion; it is often seen on baby garments, but I think it is a nice touch on something for a grown-up as well.

Picot Foldline.

Flat Picot Foldline

This version is for working flat and the first and last stitches of the pattern are selvedge stitches; to work circular, see below.

1. On outside row: Knit 1 [Knit Right Decrease, Yarnover]; repeat between brackets; end Knit 1.
2. On next row, Purl.

The decreases will form little pointed "teeth" separated by gaps created by the Yarnovers.

Circular Picot Foldline

- To work circular, eliminate selvedge stitches and use basic pattern repeat in Step 1 for one round. On next round, Knit.

Spaced Picot Foldline

Here is a slight variation that spaces the Yarnovers farther apart:

- Insert one or two extra stitches between every paired decrease and Yarnover; work next row or round as above.
- Alternatively, consider working all stitches except the Yarnovers so they will be in Purl on outside of fabric; this will make an "interrupted" Purl foldline.

Horizontal Chain Foldline

Horizontal Chain Stitch is a decorative stitch technique that makes a very handsome foldline for a hem or casing. Several variations on the theme are discussed in Increase and Decrease Stitch Patterns, but the Cast-Off Chain Stitch version is the easiest to do.

Vertical Foldlines

A vertical hem, such as for a center front opening, is worked on extra stitches added at one side of the main fabric. For a garment that is worked side-to-side, the same approach can be used to create a hem at the bottom or a casing at the top.

The foldline for a vertical hem is worked the length of one or two stitch columns. There are several nice patterns here; some are inconspicuous and do no more than help form a flat edge, while others are quite decorative.

The instructions are for the foldline only; it is assumed you will work the hem stitches in Stockinette and the remaining stitches of the row in whatever pattern is needed for the main fabric.

Rounded Vertical Fold

A vertical hem worked without a foldline will have a nice rounded contour. A little steam will flatten it somewhat, but not entirely. Conversely, if you want to plump it up a bit, see the Filled Hem.

Slip Stitch Foldline

A column of Slip stitches is by far the most common way to create a foldline for a Vertical Hem. This pattern creates an attractive, elongated column of stitches at the edge and the structure helps turn the hem to the inside quite smoothly.

Slip Stitch Foldline.

1. On outside row, with yarn farside, Slip foldline stitch purlwise.
2. On inside row, Purl foldline stitch.

To encourage the hem to lie flat and to keep adjacent stitch columns neat and even, strand the yarn very firmly past the Slip stitch to work the next stitch.

Beaded Slip Stitch Foldline

Here is a modification of the same foldline that I think produces a handsome edge. The foldline stitch is wrapped with the yarn before stranding past it; the result is a tidy beaded look along the edge.

1. On outside row, with yarn farside Slip foldline stitch purlwise, yarn nearside, return foldline stitch to left needle, yarn farside, Slip foldline stitch; tighten wrapped yarn firmly around base of Slip stitch and Knit next stitch.
2. On inside row, Purl foldline stitch.

Twist Stitch Foldline

This produces a subtle, slightly corded edge; it requires two stitches for the foldline.

Twist Stitch Foldline.

Twist Stitch Foldline at Right Edge

1. On outside, work Knit Right Twist Stitch on two foldline stitches.
2. On inside, Purl first stitch of foldline pair and Slip second stitch; strand firmly past Slip stitch to Purl next stitch.

Twist Stitch Foldline at Left Edge

1. On outside, work Knit Left Twist Stitch on two foldline stitches.
2. On inside, Slip first stitch of foldline pair and strand firmly past Slip stitch to Purl next stitch.

❖ Facings

Facings offer a great many more options for how to handle an edge than hems do. Not only is it easier to make them exactly the right shape, but it is also easier to make a facing with the characteristics that are best suited to the garment. Facings can be knitted in the same or a different yarn and made so the fabric is considerably thinner; they can be made straight, curved, or on the bias, and they can be used to line an edge or wrap around it. Woven facings are in many ways superior to those that are knitted, due to the wide variety of fabrics and trims that can be used for this purpose; they can be cut straight or on the bias, and in any width suitable for the nature of the project.

Which type of facing to use depends upon the characteristics of each type, the work it needs to do, and the shape of the edge. All of them will prevent an edge from curling, but some will also preserve the resilience of the edge, while others will add stability so it does not stretch out of shape. Detailed instructions for all of these are included here, and there is more general information regarding gauge, how to handle edges, and how to sew a facing into place in Tips for Hems and Facings, below.

Knitted Straight or Contoured Facings

Straight, rectangular facings serve much the same purpose as a simple hem, but can provide more control over how much resilience the edge retains. Contoured facings can be precisely shaped to fit curved edges such as necklines and armholes, and they generally do not change the resilience of the main fabric. Both can be made wide and short, or narrow and long.

Straight Facings

A plain, rectangular facing is no more than an inch or two wide and the length of the relevant edge of the garment. It is usually made separately and sewn into place, but can also be done on picked-up stitches (see Facings on Picked-Up Stitches, below).

Making a facing of this kind is so straightforward it really does not require detailed instructions. However, it is important to decide how to position the facing on the garment because a knitted fabric exhibits more stretch widthwise, along the rows, than it does lengthwise, along the stitch columns. Therefore, a facing set with its stitch columns running parallel to those in the main fabric will share its characteristics and have no effect on resilience. In contrast, if the stitch columns of the facing are set perpendicular to those of the main fabric, it will counteract the natural resilience.

To develop a pattern for a straight facing, work as follows:

- To make a facing narrow and long, multiply stitch gauge times width of facing and row gauge times length of edge.
- To make a facing wide and short, multiply stitch gauge times length of edge and row gauge times width of facing.

Contoured Facings

A contoured facing is used to finish a shaped edge, such as an armhole opening or a neckline. In order for the facing to lie flat and smooth on the inside of the fabric, it must replicate the contour of the garment in the area it covers. Keep in mind that the shape of the curve might change over its length, or the curved portion might occupy only part of an opening.

For instance, an armhole has a relatively deep curve at the bottom, and little or no curve between there and the shoulder. A neckline might be straight at the back and sides, but have relatively deep curves at the corners and a shallow curve at the center front. Both of these are examples of concave curves (ones that bend in), and they have a smaller measurement along the outer, visible edge of the opening and a larger one where the facing is sewn to the inside of the garment.

The kind of curve sometimes seen at the transition between a center front opening and a neckline is convex (one that bends out). It will have a larger measurement along the outer edge and a smaller one on the inside where the facing is sewn into place.

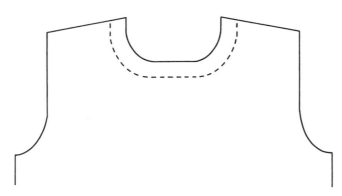

This neckline has a concave curve. The outer measurement is smaller than the inner measurement.

A curved facing can be worked wide and shallow, in which case it is shaped either with increases or decreases distributed across some of the rows, or with Regauging. Alternatively, it can be worked long and narrow and shaped with Short Rows.

Wide Curved Facing

For a concave facing worked wide, the number of stitches to use is determined by gauge and a measurement of the length of the edge; see Formulas for Width and Length.

- If facing is started at outer edge, it is shaped with increases.
- If facing is started at inner edge, it is shaped with decreases.
- The shaping techniques are distributed across several rows. To control degree of curve, use more shaping in some areas, less in others; see Horizontal Shaping in the chapter Calculations for Pattern Design.

Regauged Facing

Regauging is another technique that can be used to shape a facing that is worked wide and shallow, and it is much simpler to develop the pattern for this than for the method above. It is also easier to work, as all that is necessary is to change the size of the needle twice.

This approach creates a consistent curve rather than one that changes contour. However, as the needle size increases, the fabric becomes softer and it is then amenable to being stretched out more in some areas than in others. This means you can shape it with steam before attaching it to the garment and then ease it along the curve as it is sewn to the main fabric; once it is in place, add a little more steam to help it settle in.

Regauging a curved facing in this way also reduces its bulk, since the portions done with the larger needle sizes will be progressively more open. In fact, a simpler form of the technique is one of the methods that can be used to refine any hem or facing; see Regauging in Tips for Hems and Facings.

1. Make several Test Swatches to determine optimum needle sizes. Use smallest size needle to make a swatch and determine Gauge; find number of stitches and rows needed for facing.
2. Divide rows into three groups; subtract one row from third group and add it to first group.
3. Work largest group of rows with smallest size needle, change to needle one size larger for second group, and then to largest size needle for third group.

The little bit of math in Step 2 has the effect of dividing the total number of rows into three sections with one less row in each of them; this compensates for the change in row gauge.

The tightly knit side of the facing will provide more support for an edge than the loosely knit side; therefore, this type of facing is more successful when used for a concave curve.

Short Row Facing

For a facing made long and narrow, shaping must be done with Short Rows in the same manner as for making a curved collar.

For this purpose, a small Short Row pattern unit is developed that creates a wedge shape, with one side edge longer than the other. This pattern is repeated over the length of the facing as many times as necessary to create the curve needed; see Short Row Curve.

For a curve with a contour that changes, you can intersperse plain rows between the Short Row pattern repeat, or the repeat can be used only in some areas and not in others. Alternatively, it may be necessary to develop two different Short Row patterns, one for the area with a greater curve, the other for the area with a lesser curve.

Facings on Picked-Up Stitches

Straight or Contoured Facings can also be worked on stitches picked up along an edge. This is a good approach to use for a contoured facing on a neckline or armhole, since it leaves only one edge to sew into place. A facing can also be applied later to correct a garment edge that has stretched out of shape.

Hem picked up on Half-Hitch Cast-On edge.

Here you will find some general information about how to work in this way; for more detailed instructions, see Picking Up Stitches.

- To add a facing of this kind to a top or bottom edge, remove the cast-on or cast-off edge and pick up the freed stitches, work a Horizontal Foldline, and then the facing.
- If the cast-on technique is one that is difficult to remove, separate the fabric an inch or so away from the edge (see Separating a Fabric).
- Or, if the cast-on or cast-off edge is attractive, it can be left in place. The stitches are then picked up in such a way that the edge remains on the outside of the fabric to serve as a decorative foldline.
- A facing can also be added to a center front opening on stitches picked up along the selvedge. Here again, you can pick up the stitches and then work a conventional foldline, or pick up so the selvedge is turned to the outside of the fabric to serve as one.

While a wide facing is normally worked out from the picked-up stitches, a narrow one can also be joined to stitches picked up along one side (see Picking Up to Join).

- When adding a facing to a neckline or armhole, pick up the stitches around the opening in the usual way and work either a Wide Curved Facing or one that is Regauged, as described above.

Knitted Bias Facings

A knitted bias facing is made by working a series of increases along one side edge and a series of decreases along the other. This shaping causes the columns of stitches to travel at an angle relative to the side edges of the fabric; the stitch columns emerge out of the increases, travel up across the fabric and are then absorbed into the decreases.

If the positions of the increases and decreases are switched from one side to the other, the stitches will travel up in the other direction. Bias facings are always knit narrow and long because the effect is lost if done wide and shallow (although the bias effect is retained in fabrics with sufficient length).

A facing of this kind can be applied flat along the inside edge of a fabric, or be used to wrap an edge that has been cut (see Steeks: Selvedges for Cut Openings). It is also possible to make Double Bias Facings, with columns of stitches converging on a foldline at the center. If a bias casing is used to wrap an edge, it adds a certain amount of width to the fabric; a narrow one will be rounded like a cord, while a wider one done with a foldline will lie flat like a self-faced border.

As with a normal fabric, a bias facing will have greater stretch along the rows than along the stitch columns. However, because everything is set at an angle, regardless of where a facing of this kind is placed it will provide both support and some resilience because the facing and the main fabric will not stretch in the same direction.

Bias facings have a tendency to curve toward the side that has the increases because they constrict the edge somewhat, shortening it relative to the one with the decreases. If the curve is slight, it can usually be straightened with a bit of steam, but a strong curve is permanent. Some increases cause more of a curve than others, so the selection of which one to use is important. Also, the degree of curve can be changed over the length of the facing by changing the type of increase used, which allows you to contour it to fit the shape of an opening such as an armhole or neckline.

Here are a few basic patterns, with some suggestions for variations. I recommend you do several Test Swatches before deciding how to work. Make these several inches long and give them a good dose of steam when you are done to see how the fabric will behave before you decide how to work.

Single Bias Facing

This pattern is easy to work and results in nice smooth edges on both sides.

Left Single Bias Facing. Yarnover Increase on right edge, Knit Right Decrease on left edge.

Left Single Bias Facing

1. Outside Row: With yarn nearside to form Yarnover, Knit first stitch; Knit across row; with two stitches remaining on left needle, work Knit Right Decrease.
2. Inside Row: Slip 1, tension yarn firmly to Purl next stitch; Purl across row to last stitch; Purl Yarnover farside to twist it toward fabric.

Right Single Bias Facing

1. Inside Row: With yarn farside, Purl first stitch, forming Turned Yarnover on right needle; Purl across row; with two stitches remaining on left needle, work Purl Left Decrease.
2. Outside Row: Slip 1 knitwise, Knit across row to last stitch; Knit Yarnover nearside to twist it toward fabric.

A few suggestions . . .

The edge decreases in these patterns are, in effect, part of a Chain Selvedge. You will have to judge how firmly to work the first two stitches in the row above the decrease. If you draw the yarn too tightly, the edge will constrict; too loosely, and it will lengthen.

For alternative increases, try either a Knit Bar Increase or a Knit/Purl Rib Increase done on the last stitch of a row; this will place the Purl nub at the very edge, instead of within the fabric.

Single Bias Curved Facings

In order to make a Single Bias Facing take on a curve, all that is necessary is to use the same pattern, above, and either a different increase technique or a slightly different position or method for the decrease.

Single Bias Curved Facing. Raised Increase on right; Right Decrease adjacent to Stockinette Selvedge on left.

Increase Options for Curved Facings

Work either of these adjacent to a Stockinette Selvedge:

- A Yarnover that is twisted when worked will constrict the edge somewhat and draw the facing into a curve; try it twisted toward or away from the edge to see which version you prefer; see Turned Yarnovers.
- Alternatively, work a Knit Raised Increase on the second stitch on the outside for a left bias facing, or use a Purl Raised Increase on the second stitch on the inside for a right bias facing.

Decrease Options for a Curved Facing

As mentioned above, the edge with the decrease tends to lengthen relative to the one with the increases, and even a slight change will alter the degree of curve the facing has. Here are some options:

- Place decrease adjacent to either a Stockinette Selvedge or a Chain Selvedge.

Alternatively, use this slightly unorthodox method of making a decrease:

- With two stitches on left needle, pull second stitch over first and discard; Knit or Purl remaining stitch.

    The stitch pulled over encircles the other at its base and tends to relax the edge somewhat more than a conventional decrease, encouraging it to curve.

To change the degree of curve, but maintain the same combination of increases and decreases, substitute a plain row for a patterned one from time to time.

- If one pattern row is eliminated, there will be three plain rows between the pattern rows.
- Or, work a pattern row on the inside followed by two plain rows; the pattern rows will alternate, one on an inside row, the next on an outside row.

Knitted Double Bias Facings

A Double Bias Facing is, in effect, two Single Bias Facings with columns of stitches that converge on a center foldline. Here again, there are straight and curved versions. A facing of this kind can be used to enclose an edge, or it can serve as a self-faced border that extends out from the edge. In the latter case, the facing will add width to the fabric; take this into consideration when planning the overall design.

The bias effect is created either by placing a series of double increases at the center of the facing, with decreases at each side edge, or with double decreases at the center and increases at the sides. For more information, see Bias Stitch Patterns.

- If the increases are at center and decreases are at side edges, columns of stitches will slope up from center toward edges.
- If decreases are at center and increases are at side edges, columns of stitches will slope up from edges toward center.

The behavior of the fabric will be the same regardless of the direction of the bias, so it is only a matter of deciding how you want to work and which technique produces a foldline that appeals to you.

Here are two patterns that work quite well, one for a straight facing, the other for a curved one.

Facing with Center Double Decreases

This version has the same increases used in the Left and Right versions of the Single Bias Facing, above, with a Double Decrease in the center.

Double Bias Facing. Center Double Decrease in middle, Yarnover Increases twisted toward fabric at sides.

1. Cast on twice number of stitches required for folded width of facing, plus one for foldline.
2. Outside Row: With yarn nearside to form Yarnover Knit first stitch, Knit to three center stitches and work a Knit Center Double Decrease; Knit to end of row.
3. Inside Row: With yarn farside to form Turned Yarnover Purl first stitch; Purl across row, Purl last stitch farside.

On all outside rows after the first, the last stitch will be a Turned Yarnover; Knit it nearside to twist it toward the fabric.

Facing with Center Double Increases

This version has a pair of Yarnovers on either side of a center Knit stitch and decreases at each side edge.

1. Cast on twice number of stitches required for folded width of facing, plus one; Purl one row.
2. On outside, work Knit Right Decrease; Knit to center stitch, work Turned Yarnover, Knit 1, Yarnover; Knit to last two stitches, Knit Left Decrease.
3. On inside, Purl to center three stitches. Purl first Yarnover farside, Purl center stitch, Purl Turned Yarnover nearside; Purl to end of row.

The two Yarnovers are twisted, one to the right, one to the left.

Curved Double Bias Facing

Here is a bias foldline that employs an increase at the center that will pull the entire strip into a pronounced curve when it is folded.

1. Cast on twice number of stitches required for width, plus one extra for foldline.
2. On outside, Knit Right Decrease; Knit to center stitch, work a Running Thread Increase, Slip 1, work second Running Thread Increase; Knit to end of row, work Knit Left Decrease.
3. On inside, Purl across row.

Barbara Walker provides an alternate version of a curved double facing in her book *A Second Treasury of Knitting Patterns*† that has two center stitches worked plain, flanked by Raised Increases. The foldline is a little bulkier than the version I have given here, but try them both and see which one you prefer.

Curved Double Bias Facing. Foldline at right.

Faux Double Bias Facing

A straight Single Bias facing folds lengthwise quite readily and, with the application of a little steam, will lie flat. However, if you prefer the look of a foldline, one of the two techniques here can be used to give it the semblance of one. This is not quite as satisfactory as a true Double Bias Facing, but it is easier to work.

Slip Stitch Double Bias Foldline

Cast on uneven number of stitches and use one of the patterns for Single Bias, above, with the following change.

• On inside rows, Slip center stitch, stranding yarn firmly on nearside to Purl next stitch.

Because the columns of stitches flow past the center of the fabric, the Slip stitches will not be stacked one on top of the other as they would be in a vertical fabric. This means there is less of a visual cue for where to work the Slip stitch on each row, and it is necessary to count across to the center stitch. Also, the stitch count changes temporarily on the pattern rows, which can throw your count off, so it is much easier to do this on the inside, plain rows instead.

† Barbara G. Walker, *A Second Treasury of Knitting Patterns* (New York: Charles Scribner's Sons, 1970).

Twist Stitch Double Bias Foldline

- If facing is intended for a curved edge, cast on even number of stitches, work as for a Single Bias Facing, and use Twist Stitch Foldline on two stitches to right or left of center.

  Work so foldline stitch slants in same direction as bias; if up toward left, use a Left Twist Stitch; if up toward right, use a Right Twist Stitch.

Woven Facings

Grosgrain ribbon is commonly used to face the center front edges of a garment and provide support for buttons and buttonholes. However, other kinds of woven fabrics can also be used as facings, and they can be extremely useful in some applications. For instance, these kinds of facings are ideal for supporting the armhole of a sleeveless garment, a shaped neckline, or the open edge of a pocket.

A vast number of woven fabrics on the market are quite suitable for use as a facing on a hand-knit fabric. Any of these lightweight materials will add little or no bulk and need only be cut to length and sewn into place (see Sewing Wovens to Knits).

Furthermore, it is much easier to adjust the fit of a woven facing simply by trimming the facing or by stretching or shrinking it to fit with steam and easing it into place when sewing. I have come to prefer them for these good and practical reasons, but also because they can add a beautiful grace note to the interior of the garment.

- Woven tapes are readily available in several widths and a wide range of colors, and are suitable if you want something plain.
- For an alternative that can be both functional and beautiful, there are hundreds of ribbons to choose from, both solids and patterns, as well as a wide variety of lace trims. Any of these can be mitered to fit a corner, such as for a center front opening (see Mitered Hems and Facings, below).

  Grosgrain ribbon has long been used as a facing for the button and buttonhole bands of a center front opening. Petersham is a special type of grosgrain traditionally used for hats; it has a woven edge that allows it to be shaped into a curve with steam and is softer than conventional grosgrain. This makes it a good choice for facing something like a neckline or sleeveless armhole, and it can be sewn inside a garment edge to support the shape and maintain the fit, or outside to make a trim.
- Many fabric stores now offer a selection of soft bias silk ribbon in a wide variety of color blends and solids. These

can provide adequate support for soft fabrics, and because they are bias can be shaped with steam to fit a contoured edge. If you cannot find a ribbon in just the right color, it is also possible to cut bias strips from any suitable fabric for use as a facing.

- A great many elastic trims are available today that are specifically intended for stretch woven and knitted fabrics. Some are decorative and intended to be seen, others are plain and functional, but all serve equally well to stabilize an edge while preserving its resilience.
- It is also possible to make a facing that exactly replicates the shape of the area around the opening, as is done for sewn garments. Any number of woven fabrics would be suitable for this purpose; however, also consider a stretch woven or even a lightweight commercial knit fabric.

  To make the facing the right size and shape, it may be possible to find a sewing pattern with similar proportions that you can alter, or you can draw your own pattern; for more information, see Drawing Schematics, and also see Linings.

❖ *Mitered Hems and Facings*

For a garment with hems or facings on two or more sides, such as the lower edge and center front opening of a jacket, increases and decreases are used to remove excess fabric to form a miter. If this is not done, the corner would be four layers thick with the two sections folded into place.

There are two ways to make a mitered hem or facing. The horizontal and vertical hems can be worked separately and the miter at the corner is then sewn together. Alternatively, the two sections of the hem can be worked at the same time and the corner mitered with either increases or decreases.

The instructions here are for knitted hems and for facings done on picked-up stitches. There is also a note below regarding woven facings, which are much easier to do.

Making Miters

Here is the basic information you will need to develop a pattern for a miter:

- Measurement of inner edge of horizontal portion of hem or facing (where it is sewn to fabric), is equal to width of fabric, minus width of vertical portion.
- Measurement of inner edge of vertical portion of hem or facing is equal to length of fabric, minus depth of horizontal portion.
- To develop pattern for miter, find gauge, and then see Charting a Curve.

Hem with Sewn Miter

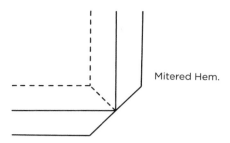

Mitered Hem.

With the following two methods, the horizontal and vertical hems are worked separately and the miter is then sewn together; one is started on a cast-on edge, the other on picked-up stitches. Both have advantages and disadvantages, and which one to use depends on the project and personal preference.

Mitered Hem from Cast-On Edge

With this method, the horizontal hem is first worked up from a cast-on edge; stitches for the vertical hem are then added at the side and these are worked together with the main fabric. One hem will have a horizontal foldline, the other a vertical foldline, and the miter is sewn together.

1. Cast on number of stitches required for width at inner edge of horizontal hem.
2. Work rows of hem, increasing according to pattern to slope edge at corner for miter.
3. When number of stitches equals that needed for full width of garment section, and hem is length required, work horizontal foldline.
4. On first row of main garment section, add one stitch for vertical foldline at side edge; continue to increase row by row according to slope pattern for miter to add stitches required for width of vertical hem.
5. Complete full length of garment section, working on stitches of main fabric, plus vertical hem and foldline.
6. To finish, seam angled edges of hem to form miter, fold hem into place, and either sew or graft edges to inside of garment.

Mitered Hem on Picked-Up Stitches

For this approach, the horizontal hem is worked down from the lower edge of the fabric, and the vertical one out from the side edge. Done this way, both will have matching horizontal foldlines, and the mitered corner is sewn together.

1. Work lower edge with Stranded Provisional Cast-On or Alternating Provisional Cast-On, or, if necessary, remove

cast-on edge; pick up these stitches for horizontal hem (see Working in the Opposite Direction).
2. Work horizontal foldline on first row, and then number of rows for hem, working decreases for miter at one side.
3. Pick up stitches for vertical hem along Selvedge; see Picking Up Selvedges.
4. Work horizontal foldline on first row, and then number of rows for hem, working decreases for miter at one side.
5. Sew side edges of facings together at corner to form miter; sew or graft hems to inside of fabric.

Continuous Hem with Miter

Instead of working the horizontal and vertical hems separately and sewing the miter together, you can also work them as one. The stitches for both hems can be cast on and worked toward the garment, shaping the miter with increases. Alternatively, stitches for both hems can be picked up along the two sides and worked out from the garment, shaping the miter with decreases. The latter is the easiest way to work; when done this way, the miter is formed at the corner with increases or decreases.

Continuous Hem from Cast-On Edge

1. Cast on sufficient stitches for width of horizontal portion of hem, plus number of stitches needed for full length of vertical portion of hem.
2. Work number of rows required for depth of hem, using increases for mitered corner, according to pattern.
3. Work horizontal foldline on all stitches of hem.
4. Continue with main garment section on stitches of horizontal hem, and join vertical hem row-by-row at side with decreases composed of one stitch of vertical hem, and one from main fabric (see Picking Up to Join).
5. Sew both edges of hem to inside of garment during finishing.

Continuous Hem on Picked-Up Stitches

1. On circular needle, pick up stitches for horizontal hem along a Provisional Cast-On edge, or remove a cast-on edge; then pick up for vertical hem into selvedge stitches at side.
2. Work horizontal foldline across all stitches on first row.
3. Knit hem, using decreases for mitered corner according to pattern.
4. To finish, either graft free stitches to inside, or cast off and sew edge in place.

Miters for Woven Facings

When dealing with a woven facing, a miter is quite straightforward. If the facing fabric is relatively fine, the miter can simply be folded into place and sewn. For a facing done in a heavier fabric, where bulk would be a concern, the miter is seamed and trimmed.

1. Draw lines for miter on fabric with chalk marker.
2. Line up two pieces of fabric and sew miter with relatively small stitches; trim the selvedge to about ⅛ to ¼ inch, tapering to almost nothing at the outer corner.
3. Press selvedges open on inside.

❖ *Tips for Hems and Facings*

The best hems and facings do their work in the background without calling attention to themselves. This can be achieved by taking into consideration several details in regard to how the hem or facing is made. As mentioned above, the hem or facing may have a different stitch pattern from that used for the main fabric, and it will then require its own gauge. Also, it is important that the edges are soft and resilient, and are attached to the fabric in an unobtrusive way so they do not compromise the characteristics and behavior of the garment.

Here are some suggestions for how to refine a hem or facing in order to solve these problems.

Stitch Patterns for Hems and Facings

In all of the instructions above, it was assumed that any hem or facing is done in Stockinette, and indeed that is the most common way to work; however, they need not be plain.

There is an old tradition of using a hem or facing as a convenient place to knit the name or initials of the maker or wearer, or perhaps a date or a tender message in either a stitch or color pattern. And even if that is not what you have in mind, do consider an alternative to Stockinette. Here are a few other suggestions.

For something that is both utilitarian and decorative, a simple lace pattern or Eyelet Mesh would certainly reduce the bulk of a hem or facing. I am a great believer in making garments attractive on the inside, and something like this could be lovely if it came into view occasionally.

If you do want to use a different stitch pattern of some kind, the gauge will not be the same as that of the main fabric; see Gauge for Hems and Facings, below. For a facing, simply cast on the number of stitches required; for a hem, it will be necessary to adjust the number of stitches at the foldline to make the transition to the main fabric.

For something much bolder, try the following.

Filled Hem

While in most cases the challenge is to reduce the bulk of a hem or facing, my next task is to tell you how to make it plump.

For a distinctive border, turn the hem over a bit of batting or soft filling of some kind.

- A filled hem done without a foldline will take on the appearance of a soft cord at the edge of the garment.
- For a filled hem with a Purl Foldline, allow a few more rows in the hemmed portion of the main fabric than in the hem itself so the outer fabric will protrude a bit. Secure the hem a row or two *above* where it would normally be. Try on a Test Swatch to make sure foldline remains at bottom of garment.
- Also consider working the outer area of the hem in something like a Seed Stitch, not just to give it some texture, but to help it stretch a bit around the filling.

Gauge for Hems and Facings

Typically, the hem or facing is done in Stockinette regardless of how the fabric is made—one made in a textured stitch or color pattern would be too bulky. Therefore, unless the main fabric is also done in Stockinette, you will need to calculate a separate Stitch Gauge in order to find out how many stitches and rows are needed to make the hem or facing fit properly. You will also need a gauge if the hem is made in a lighter, more open pattern than the main fabric to reduce its bulk.

Coordinating Gauges

When the gauges of a horizontal hem and the main fabric are different, it is necessary to distribute a certain number of either increases or decreases across the last row of the hem, prior to working the foldline (or at the top of a garment in the first row of a casing after the foldline), in order to change to the number of stitches needed for the main fabric. To work out a pattern for something like this, see Horizontal Shaping.

The gauge for a vertical hem worked out from the edge on picked-up stitches can be handled just as you would a horizontal hem. Develop a gauge and calculate how many stitches are needed for the width, and then adjust the number of stitches on the first row after picking up the stitches.

A vertical hem done in a different stitch pattern and worked with the main fabric at the side edge can be problematic because the two row gauges are unlikely to match. In most cases, it is best to use a facing instead.

A facing is quite straightforward, because you work it according to its own gauge, make it exactly the size needed, and sew it into place.

Regauging

You may be able to avoid any change in the number of stitches needed for a hem, and improve its characteristics at the same time, by using Regauging. The hem can be made more open by using a larger size needle, or by using the same size needle and a thinner yarn on the same number of stitches.

You might also use Regauging to make a hem less dense and bulky even when both the main fabric and the hem are in Stockinette, however, in that case, it would be necessary to adjust the number of stitches on the needle between one and the other.

Negative Ease

The circumference of the inside of a garment is slightly smaller than the outside, and this differential is greater in a heavier fabric than in a lighter one. Unless the thickness and/ or the width of the hem or facing is adjusted slightly, it will have a tendency to push against the outer fabric, causing it to bulge out in an unsightly way. This can be prevented by making the hem or facing thinner, either with a more open stitch pattern or by Regauging, as discussed above, or by using the concept of Negative Ease, which reduces the width by a small percentage.

- For a hem, use normal gauge to calculate number of stitches required for width; reduce this number by 5 percent.
- For a hem or facing done narrow and long, use row gauge; reduce this number by 5 percent.

Stretch and steam the hem or facing to fit when securing it to the inside of the garment.

This is an especially good approach to use if you have worked the hem or facing in a light, open pattern or have Regauged it, since it might not otherwise support the edge adequately; if necessary, reduce the width by 10 percent. Try this on the swatch you used to calculate the gauge of the main fabric, or make a Test Swatch large enough to judge the effect.

Hem and Facing Edges

The long edges of a hem or facing need to be sufficiently resilient so they will not restrict the normal behavior of the main fabric. Most selvedges will work fine, but Chain Selvedge is the softest. Here are some suggestions for cast-on and cast-off techniques that work well for this purpose.

- The most resilient edge is one that has free stitches that you can graft into place, instead of sewing. For a hem, start with Stranded Provisional Cast-On or Alternating Provisional Cast-On; for a casing or something worked on picked-up stitches, use Stranded Cast-Off.
- If you prefer to sew the edge into place, use Alternating Cast-On, followed by one row of Single Rib for a resilient edge with no bulk, or use Simple Cast-On with a slightly larger needle than you might otherwise use in order to soften it with slightly enlarged stitches.

- For a top edge, use a Sewn Cast-Off, or work a Chained Cast-Off in such a way that it retains adequate stretch.
- For a narrow facing that will encircle an opening, such as a neckline or armhole, graft the top and bottom edges together where they meet.

Attaching a Hem or Facing

It is important to fasten the hem or facing to the inside of the garment as invisibly as possible so the attachment will neither show through on the outside, nor impair the resilience of the fabric.

The instructions for the techniques used for this purpose can be found in the chapter Finishing; therefore, the discussion here covers only how they apply to hems and facings in particular.

Sewn Hems and Facings

- For information on sewing the inner edge of a knitted hem or facing into place, see Sewing Within a Fabric.
- For tips on how to attach woven facings, see Sewing Wovens to Knits.
- It is often helpful to insert a Yarn Marker into the main fabric along the row or stitch column where you will attach the hem or facing to act as a guide for sewing evenly, particularly if the fabric is done in a complex stitch pattern.

Grafted Hems

- The Grafted Hem technique is a method of sewing that replicates the shape of a knitted stitch and maintains the resilience of the fabric.
- Because grafting is done on free stitches, it is necessary to eliminate any cast-on or cast-off edges (see Hem and Facing Edges, above).

Joinery Decrease Hem

A hem can be attached to the fabric with Joinery Decreases, as for the Double-Fabric Hem.

1. Start with Stranded Provisional Cast-On or Alternating Provisional Cast-On; work hem and foldline, and then work same number of rows above foldline as below.
2. If necessary, pick up stitches along cast-on edge.
3. Fold hem into position with needle bearing stitches of cast-on edge held on farside of needle bearing active stitches; work across row with Joinery Decreases.

This is easy to do, but may leave a noticeable indentation on the outside of the fabric unless the hem has been refined in some way; there are suggestions for how to do this in Gauge for Hems and Facings, above.

For an interesting alternative, you can use the Double-Fabric technique to make the hem and complete it with Joinery Decreases in this way; with that approach, the cast-on edge serves as the foldline. The same technique can be used to make a casing; for more information, see both Double-Fabric Hems and Double-Fabric Casings.

Pleats

Pleats are vertical folds within the fabric that are fastened only at the top. In practical terms, they are used to add ease and movement to a garment without creating the kind of fullness that gathers do. In addition, the vertical lines they establish are not only attractive but also visually elongate a garment.

How much width the pleats contribute is varied by their size and number, while the decorative effect is determined by their position in the garment, the direction of the folds, and the relationship of one pleat to another. This latter characteristic is most often used to define different types of pleats. For example, Knife Pleats are relatively narrow and are all folded in the same direction. A Box Pleat consists of a pair of wide pleats that are folded toward one another and meet at the center, while an Inverted Pleat is reversed, with a pair of pleats set side-by-side, but folded away from one another.

Pleats done in any of these ways are normally secured in position only at the top; these are most commonly seen in skirts, but might also be used on the peplum of a jacket, or tiny pleats could be set at the wrist of a sleeve.

Because pleats require a free edge, some thought should be given to how to work the first few rows so it will lie flat and smooth. Either use a simple stitch pattern as a tiny border, such as a Seed Stitch, or perhaps a Double Rib steamed open and flat in finishing, or consider a very thin woven facing made of a fabric that will fold crisply—a hem would be far too bulky.

Pleats fastened at both the top and bottom edges are used to provide movement ease in the middle of a garment. For instance, Box or Inverted Pleats are commonly placed at the center or side back of a jacket, or sometimes on the front or even down the length of a sleeve.

And last, but by no means least, decorative stitch patterns can be used to create some of the effect and appearance of pleats in a knitted fabric. These are very attractive when used for skirts, peplums, or ruffles, are considerably less trouble to do than true pleats, and because they do not need to be folded into place there is no additional bulk.

❖ *Basic Pleat*

A pleat consists of three layers: the overlay, which is the outer, most visible portion; the foldback in the middle; and the un-

derlay. Each pleat requires two vertical foldlines, one that is visible on the outside of the garment between the overlay and the foldback, and another on the inside between the foldback and the underlay.

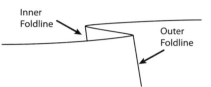

Pleat structure: Overlay is to left of Outer Foldline, Turnback is between two foldlines; Underlay is to right of Inner Foldline.

There are several steps involved in working pleats. First, of course, it is necessary to calculate the additional number of stitches required, then to establish the position of the foldlines on the first row of the fabric. The last step involves folding the pleat into place at the top and securing it.

Pleat Proportions

To calculate the number of stitches to add for each pleat, keep in mind that the stitches of the underlay are a portion of those that make up the basic width of the garment; you only require extra stitches for the widths of the foldback and overlay.

1. Use gauge to find number of stitches needed for width of garment.
2. Find number of stitches needed for folded width of pleat and double this number. Use half for pleat foldback, half for pleat overlay; stitches for foldlines are included.
3. Multiply number of stitches needed for one pleat by number of pleats; add to number of stitches for width of garment in Step 1.

Pleat Foldlines

A Slip Stitch Foldline is generally used for pleats, with the yarn stranded very firmly past the slipped stitch to encourage the pleat to fold as flat as possible. One foldline faces out, the other in, and the yarn must be stranded accordingly.

Outer Foldline

- Slip foldline stitch, stranding yarn on *inside* of fabric. On next row, work foldline stitch as Knit on outside of fabric.

In other words, if you are working flat, Purl the foldline stitch on an inside row; if you are working in the round, Knit the foldline stitch.

Inner Foldline

- Slip foldline stitch, stranding yarn on *outside* of fabric. On next row, work foldline as Knit on inside of fabric.

Therefore, if you are working flat, you will want to Knit the foldline stitch on an inside row; if you are working in the round, Purl the foldline stitch.

Establishing a Pleat Pattern

It is important to establish the foldlines in the correct position immediately after casting on and continue them in pattern the full length of the fabric; the position of the inner and outer foldlines in relation to the different parts of the pleat will determine how it folds.

1. Cast on full number of stitches needed for width of fabric, including those for pleat foldback, underlay, and foldlines.
2. Work one row (on inside of fabric if working flat); count stitches and place markers at location of each foldline.
3. On outside row, establish pleat pattern in one of following ways:

Pleat Folded to Right

- At first marker, work inner foldline stitch; at second marker work outer foldline stitch.

Pleat Folded to Left

- At first marker, work outer foldline stitch; at second marker work inner foldline stitch.

Securing Pleats at Top

The pleat is folded into position and secured at the top of the garment section, and since many styles continue above this point, it is important to consider how to handle the transition.

For a pleated skirt, make the waistband firm enough to support the shape, and line it, if necessary. A dress with a pleated skirt could also have a waistband, perhaps in a firmly knit ribbing, but in some cases it may make sense to cast off as the pleats are made in order to provide a firmer edge and more support for the garment; pick up stitches for the bodice along the cast-off edge, or make the bodice separately and sew it to the skirt edge. When there are pleats within a bodice or jacket, the transition is smoother if they end at a yoke, because this avoids the need to include the bulk of folded fabric in a shoulder seam.

However this transition is handled, the method suggested here for securing the pleat "grades" the transition from three layers of fabric to two and then to one, which reduces bulk at the top of the pleat and leaves the outer fabric as undisturbed as possible.

To make it easier to do this, set markers on the needle to the right and left side of all the stitches of the pleat on the row below where it will be secured. Then, the stitches of the underlay and the foldback are slipped to separate double-point needles, one or two sizes smaller than the size used for the fabric. The

pleat is folded into place according to the pattern established on the first row and a Pullover technique is used to join these two parts of the pleat, and then Joinery Decreases are used to attach the overlay.

To avoid confusion in the instructions when referring to the different needles used, those bearing all the stitches are called the main needles; the double-point needles bearing the stitches of the pleat sections are designated A, B, and C.

While forming the pleat, there are times when the main needles are not in use; use tip protectors or push the stitches back from the needle tips so they will not fall off (circular needles work well for this purpose), and support the weight of the work in your lap or on a table.

Graded Right Pleat

These instructions are for a pleat folded to the right as you look at it on the outside of the fabric; it will face to the left in wear.

1. On outside, work across row to pleat; set Right Main Needle down. Slip stitches of underlay from Left Main Needle to double-point Needle A.
2. Slip stitches of inner foldline and foldback from Left Main Needle to second double-point Needle B; equal number of stitches should be on Needles A and B.
3. Swing left tip of Needle B and Left Main Needle to right on nearside, folding first part of pleat into position. Push stitches back from tip of Left Main Needle and let it hang from front of fabric.
4. Hold Needles A and B parallel in left hand, with Needle A and underlay stitches on farside, and Needle B and foldback stitches on nearside with inner foldline stitch now at left.

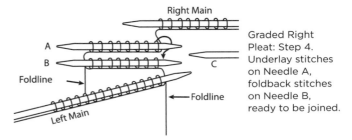

Graded Right Pleat: Step 4. Underlay stitches on Needle A, foldback stitches on Needle B, ready to be joined.

5. With Needle C in right hand, transfer first stitch from Needle A on farside to Needle B on nearside, pull stitch now in second place on Needle B over transferred stitch, and discard; Slip remaining stitch of pair to Needle C; stitches in these steps are not worked.
6. Repeat Step 5 until stitches of underlay and foldback have been joined (pulled-over stitches will encircle underlay stitches at base of stitches on Needle C).

7. Pick up Left Main Needle and hold parallel to Needle C; outer foldline stitch is at right tip of Main Needle followed by overlay stitches.

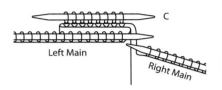

Left Main

Right Main

C

Graded Right Pleat: Step 7. Overlay stitches on Left Main Needle folded into position, ready to be joined to remaining pleat stitches on Needle C.

8. Pick up Right Main Needle and work Knit Joinery Decreases on two sets of pleat stitches, inserting needle tip first into stitch on Left Main Needle, and then into stitch on Needle C.
9. With all stitches of pleat joined, continue row.

Graded Left Pleat

These instructions are for a pleat folded to the left as seen when looking at the outside of the fabric; it will face to the right in wear.

1. On outside, work across row to pleat; set Right Main Needle down at side. Slip stitches of overlay and outer foldline stitch from Left Main Needle to double-point Needle A.
2. Slip stitches of foldback and inner foldline stitch from Left Main Needle to double-point Needle B. Equal number of stitches should be on Needles A and B.
3. Draw right tip of Needle B to left on nearside and move Left Main Needle to right in order to fold first part of pleat into position. Bring Right Main Needle and Needle A to nearside as well; position them out of the way for next step.
4. Hold two needles parallel in left hand, with Left Main Needle and underlay stitches on farside, Needle B and foldback stitches on nearside, and inner foldline stitch at right. Work pullovers as in Step 5 of Graded Right Pleat, above.
5. Move Needle A and Right Main Needle back to right; place Needle C with joined stitches on farside of Needle A with overlay stitches; outer foldline is last stitch on near needle.
6. Use Right Main Needle to work Knit Joinery Decreases on two sets of pleat stitches, inserting needle tip first into stitch on Needle A and then into stitch on Needle C.
7. With all stitches of pleat joined, continue row.

Cast-Off Pleat

• To cast off fabric once pleats are secured, work as described above, and use Joinery Cast-Off instead of Joinery Decreases for stitches of pleat in Step 6.

Securing Pleats at Bottom

There are some applications that require a pleat to be secured at the top and the bottom, such as at both the yoke and waist of a jacket, or at the top and bottom of a sleeve.

Here are some suggestions for how to work.

Working Down from Secured Pleat

A relatively easy approach is to use a Stranded Provisional Cast-On or Alternating Provisional Cast-On and work any lower border down from these stitches after the pleat is folded into position and secured.

1. Work main body of fabric and secure pleat at top. Return to pick up stitches at lower edge, fold pleat into position, and use graded method, above, to secure pleat.
2. Work ribbing or other border down from lower edge.

Grafting Pleat to Lower Border

Another approach involves casting on stitches for the pleat above a border. This works reasonably well for a fairly narrow pleat but could be difficult to manage with a wide one because the stitches of the foldback and underlay need to be introduced within a small space. Use a small circular needle or a pair of double-point needles; once you are a few inches above the edge they will no longer be necessary.

1. Work border or ribbing; at position of pleat, place number of stitches equal to underlay on holder.
2. Use technique for Side or Mid-Fabric Cast-Ons to add number of stitches required for two sections of pleat, plus foldlines, to stitches already on right needle. Complete main fabric.
3. To finish, pick up stitches of underlay and foldback and fold into place. Join with graded method, above; graft remaining overlay stitches to those on hold in ribbing or border.

❖ Stitch Pattern Pleats

Many stitch pattern books include instructions for patterns that give the illusion, and even some of the effect, of pleats. These make use of the tendency of columns of Knit stitches to protrude and columns of Purl stitches to recede (see Basic Knit and Purl Patterns). However, even if you do no more than work inner and outer foldlines as if there were pleats, the fabric will take on a slightly fluted appearance.

Welts and Tucks

Both Welts and Tucks are somewhat like pleats in that they are folds made within the fabric, but they differ in that they are fixed into place. This means they can be placed horizontally as well as vertically, and when used across the length or width of a fabric they do not add fullness as a pleat does. However, it is also possible to make partial ones that create the effect of gathering.

Welts and Tucks are made in a similar way, but a Welt consists of only a few rows and protrudes like a cord from the surface of the fabric,† while a Tuck is composed of more rows and requires a foldline so it will lie flat against the underlying fabric. Both of them can be fixed in place using stitch techniques, or they can be sewn into position later. The latter approach is worth consideration because it is not only easy to do, but often produces a superior result as well; it also offers an interesting way to alter a garment that is too wide or too long by adding a Welt or Tuck even where you did not plan to have one.

We will start with the Welts, since they are simpler and introduce the technique nicely.

❖ *Welts*

There are horizontal and vertical versions of Welts, and you can also make partial ones that do not run the full width or length of the garment. They provide great visual interest to the surface of a fabric and are often used to define areas of a design.

For instance, a vertical Welt could be used to highlight a center front border, while a horizontal one might set off the shoulder yoke of a bodice. If a series of partial Vertical Welts were placed somewhere at the top of a garment—shoulder, center of neckline, or sleeve—the result would be equivalent to gathering the fabric, leaving fullness below. Small partial Welts, either horizontal or vertical, can also be treated like a stitch pattern and scattered across a fabric to create a pronounced surface texture. In addition, the stitch technique Rouleau Welt creates the illusion of a Horizontal Welt.

Horizontal Welts

Here are the basic instructions for working Welts, which generally consist of no more than three or four rows, the number being determined by your gauge and the effect you are trying to achieve.

Welts tend to widen and it may be necessary to temporarily reduce the stitch count on these rows or use a smaller size needle to Regauge them; use a Test Swatch to decide how to work.

To fasten a Welt into place, the stitches in the last row are worked together with stitches picked up below the first row using Joinery Decreases; these same techniques are used when making a Tuck (see below).

---

† In British knitting terminology, a border done in Double Ribbing is often called a Welt, because of the protruding, rounded Knit columns.

Horizontal Welts.

To make it easier to see which row of stitches to pick up, it helps to insert a Yarn Marker into the row below the Welt as you work, or weave it in later with a tapestry needle. Work the rows of the Welt and then secure it as follows:

Joining Welt on Outside

1. Working on outside of fabric, reach around to farside and insert right needle tip up under first Purl nub in row below Welt and lift stitch onto left needle in standard position, with right side of stitch on nearside of needle.
2. Knit raised stitch and next stitch together.
3. Repeat Steps 1–2 across row.

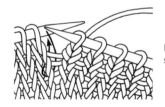

Horizontal Welt. Picking up stitches on outside.

Joining Welt on Inside

• To work on the inside, Slip 1, insert left needle tip up under Purl nub in row below Welt and lift it up; return slipped stitch to left needle and work two stitches together with a Purl Decrease.

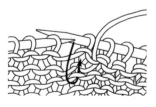

Horizontal Welt. Picking up stitches on inside.

Alternative Method for Joining Welt

It is also possible to pick up all the stitches in the row below the Welt on a separate needle, and then use Joinery Decreases across the entire row. For this purpose, use a circular or double-point needle in a smaller size than that used for the fabric, and work as follows:

1. On inside, start at right side edge and insert needle down into each Purl nub in row below first row of Welt.
2. With all stitches picked up, hold this needle parallel to needle bearing stitches at top of Welt. Depending upon location of yarn, either return to right needle tip and use Purl Joinery Decreases to secure Welt, or turn to outside and use Knit Joinery Decreases.

Seamed Welt

Instead of using Joinery Decreases, you can sew the Welt into place.

1. Work extra rows for Welt and then continue with fabric.
2. To finish, fold fabric to outside at center row of Welt and, on inside, sew top and bottom rows together (see Sewing Within a Fabric).

If you use a different stitch pattern for the Welt than for the main fabric, it will be easy to see where to sew. If not, consider inserting Yarn Markers in the row above and below the Welt to guide you.

Rouleau Welt

You can also create the illusion of a Welt by simply taking advantage of the tendency of Stockinette to curl at the edges;

Rouleau Welt. Stitches picked up below Welt on inside to continue fabric above it.

see Fabric Edge Curl. For instance, if a neckline or wrist edge is not finished with a border of any kind, a Stockinette fabric will curl to the outside forming what looks quite like a proper Welt. The effect is enhanced if the stitches are worked on a smaller needle size than would be normal for the yarn in order to make a firm fabric.

You can also create a Rouleau Welt within the fabric by working several rows in Stockinette and then casting off; pick up the stitches at the base of the "welt" and continue the fabric above it. The rouleau will curl down, exposing the Purl side of the fabric.

Vertical Welts

The two stitch techniques described here can be used to make a Vertical Welt, or it can be sewn into place like a horizontal one.

Vertical Sewn Welt.

For either of them, add three or four extra stitches for the Welt to those cast on for the width of the garment; the number of stitches to add depends upon your gauge.

To start a Welt within the fabric, such as above a lower border or ribbing, use one of the Double Increases, instead.

Unless the Welt is drawn very tightly together, it can add a slight amount of width to the fabric; this is less likely if it is sewn into place instead of done with a stitch technique. Test the method you want to use on a swatch that is wide enough for you to judge the effect.

Slip Stitch Welt

Here is a vertical Welt made on the same principles used to create a separate Knitted Cord.

1. On first row, work stitches of Welt.
2. On second row, Slip Welt stitches to left needle; strand yarn very firmly past them on inside to work next stitch.
3. Repeat Steps 1 and 2 for length of fabric.

Because the stitches of the Welt are worked on one row and slipped on the next, they will have half the number of rows as the surrounding fabric, and as with a Vertical Foldline, this may constrict the fabric lengthwise. Try the Welt pattern on a relatively large Test Swatch and apply enough steam to help it relax to get a good sense of whether this will be a problem; if it is, work the stitches of the Welt at a slightly looser tension, or try one of the following approaches:

- Use a double wrap on the center stitch of the Welt in Step 1; on the return row, drop the extra wrap when slipping that stitch, and then take up extra yarn into all three stitches as evenly as possible as you slip the others. If you are working circular, double wrap the first stitch of the Welt instead.
- Alternatively, place a Yarnover before or after the Welt, depending on whether you are working flat or circular; drop it, and then draw the extra yarn it provides into the stitches of the Welt as you Slip them.

Wrapped Welts

Two other stitch techniques, either a Couching Stitch or a Wrap Stitch, can also be used to work Welts. In both cases, the yarn that pulls the columns of stitches together will show on the outside, making them quite decorative. Unlike the Slip Stitch method, above, these will have the same number of rows as the surrounding fabric and, therefore, will not distort the fabric.

- Work a series of these stitch techniques, always on same column of stitches, and spaced every other row for pronounced effect, or somewhat farther apart for softer one.

❖ Tucks

As mentioned above, Tucks are made in much the same way as Welts, but they are larger and have a foldline, which allows them to lie flat on the fabric. Unlike the Welts, there are no stitch techniques that can be used to make these, but it is certainly possible to use stitch or color patterns to make them even more decorative.

Horizontal Tucks

The Tuck described here is made just like a Welt, but it requires more rows with a Horizontal Foldline in the middle. For a different, and very efficient approach, see Insertion Welts and Tucks, which are done with a Double-Fabric technique.

The rows of the Tuck will not add to the length of the garment; however, the join might add a very small amount. If you plan to make a series of them, check the effect on a swatch. If

necessary, adjust the number of stitches before and after making the Tuck.

First, develop a pattern for the Tuck. As with Welts, Tucks tend to widen slightly when folded into place; you might want to reduce the width using either Negative Ease or Regauging.

If the Tuck will be in a different stitch pattern from the main fabric, make a swatch and calculate a separate gauge. Then adjust the number of stitches on the needle before making the Tuck, and again when it is finished in order to return to the original number of stitches.

Horizontal Tuck.

1. Calculate number of rows required for depth and multiply times two, half for overlay, half for foldback; add one row for foldline.
2. Work to position of Tuck; if main fabric is not Stockinette, work one row of Purl on inside of fabric to serve as inner foldline, and then continue as follows:
3. Work half number of rows needed for Tuck; work outer, visible foldline (see Horizontal Foldlines); and then work second half of rows required for Tuck.
4. To fix Tuck in position, pick up Purl nubs of inner foldline as described for Welts, above, and use Joinery Decreases to join two rows of stitches together.

If a garment with a Horizontal Tuck will be seamed at the side edges, there are two methods that can be used to mitigate the bulk caused by the folded fabric.

- For a Tuck that will be sewn together, seam sides of garment first, and then fold Tuck into position and sew; folded Tuck will cross seam on outside.
- A Tuck made with Joinery Decreases will already be sewn into position; include only outer edge of Tuck in side seam. After seaming, turn to inside and loosely stitch Tuck foldback and underlay together; as an option, tack sewn edge of Tuck to seam.

Vertical Tuck

A Vertical Tuck is worked the entire length of the fabric on extra stitches cast on at the bottom, along with all the others; it is then sewn into place.

1. To develop a pattern for a Tuck, calculate number of stitches needed as for a Pleat, including inner and outer foldlines, and work in the same way.

2. At top, fold into place and work as described for Securing Pleats at Top.

3. To finish Tuck, on inside, fold into place along length and sew stitches of inner foldline to running threads of outer fabric using equivalent of a Running Thread Seam.

4. To finish bottom edges, see suggestions in Securing Pleats at Bottom.

Part Three

DECORATIVE TECHNIQUES

CHAPTER 10

The Stitches

The structure of a knitted fabric is deceptively simple—no more than little interconnected loops of yarn called stitches. But these loops can be configured in a great many ways, and as their form is changed, so is their character, with each one contributing something different to the fabric of which it is a part.

A "stitch technique" is used to give each stitch a particular shape in the fabric; it consists of a specific way to insert the needle into an existing stitch and wrap the yarn around it in order to make a new one. This chapter introduces the techniques used to make all the stitches, from the most fundamental to the most specialized. As the alphabet stands to language, these stitch techniques are to knitting, and they can be varied or combined in one way or another to create a multitude of decorative and practical patterns.

Included are instructions for how to do the techniques, a description of the structure, characteristics, and behavior of the resulting stitches, and typical ways in which they can be used in patterns. The material is organized into groups of related stitches and their variations and, by necessity, the discussion of each one is approached as if the reader has never encountered it before. This begins with the Knit and Purl techniques, which are the foundation for all the others.

Because the information is presented in such an elementary way, more experienced knitters may be tempted to skip past the initial material on Knit and Purl and some of the other basic techniques that are already familiar. However, I want to encourage everyone, regardless of skill level, to read through even those instructions because the discussions make explicit certain aspects of the basic stitches that are often taken for granted, and these fundamentals have implications for all the other techniques. In doing so, you might glean only one or two new insights, but these could prove valuable.

Once you are familiar with these techniques and

understand how they can be applied, you will be able to learn any new stitch pattern more quickly and will find it easier to prevent and correct common errors as you work. In addition, if you are interested in designing, a knowledge of the characteristics that each stitch technique imparts to a fabric will help you select a pattern that is suitable for a particular yarn and garment style.

For novice knitters, the necessary organization of the material presents some challenges. In order to learn how to do these stitches, you must already understand how to hold the yarn and needles and cast on the first stitches. If you have not already done so, therefore, read the section If You Are a Beginner (see the Introduction to the Second Edition), which includes recommendations for the Knitting Methods and Casting-On techniques that are easiest for a beginner to use. There is also information there on various terms used here that may be new to you.

To work your way through this material, cast on 20 or 30 stitches to make a small practice swatch. Relatively short single-point needles are easiest to use for something small like this, and it is best to work with a medium-thickness, light-colored yarn so you can see the stitches clearly; it also helps if the color of the needles provides some contrast with that of the yarn. The instructions are written for working flat, but information is included for adapting the techniques as necessary when working circular (for more information, see Circular and Flat Knitting). The illustrations show the yarn held to the right, but stitch formation is the same if the yarn is held to the left (see Knitting Methods).

The Knit and Purl Stitches

Before we go on to the details of the basic stitches, it will be helpful to give some consideration to the word "Knit," which has its origins in the word "knot," and which is used in so many different ways it can lead to some confusion. Knit is the name of the craft, it is what we do when we make a fabric in this way, and it is the generic name of the most basic stitch form, the simplest shape the loop can take in the fabric.

Furthermore, every stitch in the fabric has two "faces," each with a distinctively different appearance. The way the basic stitch looks on one side of the fabric is called Knit; the way it looks on the other side is called Purl.

In other words, while it is common to speak of a "Knit stitch" or a "Purl stitch," these are not different stitches, but merely two aspects of the same one. If you use the technique that makes a Knit stitch, the Knit face of the stitch will appear on the side of the fabric facing you, while the Purl face of the stitch will be on the other side of the fabric; if you use the technique that makes a Purl stitch, the Knit face of the stitch will appear on the other side of the fabric. While there are many specialized techniques described here, they can all be thought of as variations of this basic stitch form, and all of them will also have both Knit and Purl versions.

The material on Knitting Methods has a full discussion of the different ways the yarn and needles can be held. What is described here is the direction in which the work progresses, the position of the stitches on the needles, and the details of how the yarn and needles are moved in order to manipulate them.

The Standard method of working, described first, is the most common one; it is the method that most pattern instructions, including those in this book, assume you will be using. The needle holding the existing stitches is held in the left hand and the work progresses across the set of stitches, one-by-one, from right to left.

The Reversed Method is used less often, but works just as well: the existing set of stitches is held in the right hand, and the work progresses from left to right instead. The motions required to make the stitches are different, but their position on the needle and resulting form in the fabric are exactly the same.

The third method, Turned Stitches, is combined with the Standard Method in one way or another rather than being used by itself, and an understanding of how it works is very important. Some aspects of it are used in specialized ways to facilitate working various stitch techniques, and the Purl version is used for all purposes by many knitters as their standard way of working.

Also included here are instructions and information about the most basic stitch patterns that are made up of just Knit and Purl—Stockinette, Reverse Stockinette, Garter Stitch, and Ribbing. These are such essential patterns that they appear in almost every knitted garment, and an understanding of their structure and characteristics is not only important for this reason, but because it will help clarify the nature of patterns made with other techniques as well.

❖ *Standard Knit and Purl*

For this method, the needle bearing the set of stitches is held in the left hand, with the tip pointing to the right; the second needle is held in the right hand with the tip pointing to the left. To make a new stitch, moderate tension is placed on the yarn, the right needle is inserted into the first stitch on the left needle and the yarn is wrapped around the tip, which is then used to draw the strand of yarn through the stitch.

The new stitch is held on the right needle and the original one is "discarded," meaning it is dropped from the left needle into the fabric. As each stitch is worked and discarded in turn, there will be one less stitch on the left needle and one more on the right needle; the supply of yarn will always emerge from the last new stitch made.

When all the stitches have been worked and discarded in turn, you will have completed one "row" (for definition, see below); transfer the now-empty needle to your right hand, and the needle bearing the new stitches to your left hand, and begin the next row.

Here are the details of how to make these two forms of the basic stitch.

Standard Knit Stitch

To make a Knit stitch, always hold the yarn on the farside of the needle and work as follows:

1. On nearside, insert right needle tip from left to right into center of first stitch on left needle and allow it to pass under needle to farside. Needles cross each other within stitch, with right needle tip on farside of left needle.

2. Wrap yarn up between needle tips and then over right needle to farside.

3. Use right needle tip to draw wrapped yarn up and back through center of stitch toward nearside; simultaneously use left needle tip to lift original stitch over yarn and drop it on farside. Maintain new stitch on right needle.

Standard Knit Stitch: Step 2. Wrap yarn around right needle tip.

Standard Knit Stitch: Step 3. Draw yarn through stitch.

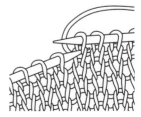

Standard Knit Stitch: Step 3. Discard original stitch below right needle.

4. Repeat these steps until all stitches have been worked and discarded.

Maintain even tension on the yarn as you work, and be careful not to drop a stitch from the left needle before drawing a new stitch through because it will come undone (unravel), and revert to a strand of yarn, as could one or more stitches below it.

Notice that the discarded Knit stitch lies below the right needle and encircles the base of the new stitch; the top of the stitch is on the farside and only the two sides of the stitch are visible. The yarn passes into it from farside to nearside on the right, travels over the needle to form the new stitch, and then reenters the Knit stitch from nearside to farside; from there it passes to the ball of yarn. The strand of yarn that lies between two stitches is called the "running thread."

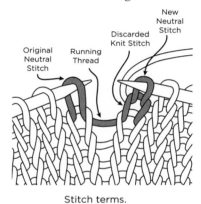

Stitch terms.

When you look at the Knit stitch in the fabric, all that can be seen are the two sides of the loop forming a little V-shape. The stitch is narrow at the bottom where it emerges from the stitch below and wider at the top where the next stitch is drawn through it in turn.

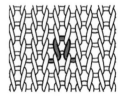

Standard Knit Stitch.

Standard Purl Stitch

To make a Purl stitch, always hold the yarn on the nearside of the needle, and work as follows:

1. On nearside, insert right needle tip from right to left directly into center of first stitch. Needles cross each other within stitch, with right needle tip on nearside of left needle.
2. With both needles now in stitch, wrap yarn down between needle tips, and then under right needle toward nearside.
3. Move right needle tip down and back to draw wrapped yarn through stitch toward farside;

Standard Purl Stitch: Step 2. Wrap yarn around needle.

simultaneously use left needle tip to lift original stitch over yarn and drop it on nearside.

Standard Purl Stitch: Step 3. Draw new stitch through.

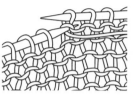

Standard Purl Stitch: Step 3. Discard original stitch.

4. Repeat these steps until all stitches have been worked and discarded.

Notice that the yarn passes into the discarded stitch from nearside to farside, over the needle to form the new stitch, back through the stitch from farside to nearside and then to the ball of yarn.

The only part of a Purl stitch that is visible in the fabric is the top of the discarded stitch; it looks like a small horizontal strand and is called the "Purl nub." Just below and to each side of the Purl nub is another pair of strands that look just like it; these are the running threads that belong to the new stitch above.

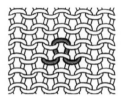

Standard Purl Stitch.

Making a Knitted Fabric

Once you are familiar with how to make the basic Knit and Purl stitches, the next thing to understand is how they are used to make a fabric. Here are some basic definitions:

Stitch Form

The stitches on the needle are "neutral"—they do not yet have a distinctive shape, or "form." It is only when a technique is used to manipulate a stitch in some way and it is discarded into the fabric that it becomes a Knit or Purl, or one of the other kinds of stitches described below.

Stitch Position

In European-derived knitting traditions, the standard position, or "mount" of a neutral stitch on the needle is with the right side of the stitch "leading" on the nearside of the needle and the left side of the stitch "trailing" on the farside.† In some

---

† These terms were coined by Priscilla Gibson-Roberts, who uses them to discuss the differences between European, Middle Eastern, and some contemporary methods of knitting in Priscilla A. Gibson-Roberts and Deborah Robson, *Knitting in the Old Way: Designs and Techniques from Ethnic Sweaters* (Fort Collins, Colo.: Nomad Press, 2004).

other knitting traditions and for some special techniques, the stitch is positioned with the left side "leading" on the nearside and the right side "trailing" on the farside; see Turned Stitches, below, for more information, and also the discussion in Knitting Methods about the Turned Left-Hand Method and the Combined Method.

Rows, or Rounds

The process of drawing new stitches through the entire set of stitches on a needle, one after the other, is called knitting a "row." As the work progresses, the neutral stitches remaining on the

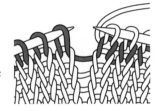

A row.

first needle, and those that have been given a form and discarded into the fabric, are all part of the same row. The new set of stitches that accumulate on the second needle are part of the next row.

Within the fabric, a single row normally consists of a set of stitches that are formed with a continuous strand of yarn and sit side-by-side in a horizontal line. There are exceptions—in some cases individual stitches may occupy more than one row, and in many color patterns the stitches in a row are made with more than one yarn.

A knitted fabric is constructed from the bottom up; with the stitches of each row drawn through the stitches of the row below. A series of rows, one on top of the other, constitutes the length of the fabric.

Path of Yarn

In a flat fabric, the yarn travels through the rows in a zigzag path, from right to left on one row, left to right on the next. In a circular fabric, the yarn travels in a spiral path, always in the same direction, and a row is often referred to as a "round."

Because the yarn travels from stitch to stitch horizontally, a basic knitted fabric has more stretch widthwise than it does lengthwise. When it is stretched from side to side, the running threads borrow yarn from the stitches and elongate; the stitches become shorter and wider, and the spaces between them enlarge.

Stitch Columns

The individual stitches are also aligned vertically, each one emerging from the one below it. A single set of stitches related in this way is referred to as a "stitch column," and a series of stitch

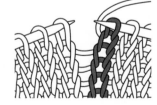

A stitch column.

columns sitting side-by-side constitute the width of the fabric.

The fabric is less expansive in the vertical dimension because the stitches in each column are not connected by a continuous strand of yarn; they are related only by virtue of their position. Nevertheless, when stretched lengthwise, the stitches will become somewhat taller and narrower and the stitch columns will draw closer together.

❖ Reversed Knit and Purl

This is an alternative knitting method that is no more than a mirror image of the one above, with the needle bearing the existing stitches held in the right hand; the new stitches will accumulate on the left needle. The structure of the stitches in the fabric is the same as with the standard method.

Some knitters prefer this method and use it all the time. Others use it for flat knitting in combination with the Standard method, working from right to left on one row and left to right on the next. Even if you do not use this method often, it can be very useful to know how to do so when working on something very narrow because there is no need to turn at the end of a row; for more information, see Bi-Directional Method.

The only difficulty in using this method is that any instruction for how to work a particular technique, in this book or any other, will be written for the Standard Method, described above, and will need to be "translated" for use with the Reversed Method. However, even complex patterns generally include only one or two specialized techniques that will pose a challenge in this regard, and knitters who use the method regularly become fairly adept at making the changes needed.

Reversed Knit Stitch

Hold the needle bearing the existing stitches in your right hand and the second needle in your left hand; with yarn held on farside work left to right, as follows:

1. On farside, insert tip of left needle from left to right into center of first stitch.
2. With both needles now in stitch, wrap yarn over left needle from farside to nearside and then down between needle tips and back toward farside.
3. Pull new stitch through toward nearside and hold on left needle; discard original stitch from right needle.

Reversed Purl Stitch

Hold needles as described above, but with yarn on nearside, and work as follows:

1. On farside, insert left needle tip from right to left into center of first stitch and then under right needle to nearside.
2. With both needles now in stitch, wrap yarn up between the two, over top of left needle, and down on nearside.
3. Pull new stitch through and hold on left needle; discard original stitch from right needle.

❖ *Turned Stitches*

The Basic Knit or Purl techniques described above are done with all the stitches on the needle in standard position, and the right needle tip held on the nearside of the left needle when inserted into a stitch. However, if the right needle tip is positioned on the farside of the left needle when it is inserted into a stitch that is in standard position, the discarded stitch will twist on itself instead of lying flat and open in the fabric. This is done for decorative reasons in some stitch patterns (see Twist Stitches); but when not wanted, it is an error.

Some techniques require the neutral stitches on the needle to be "turned," with the left half of the stitch on the nearside of the needle. When a Turned Stitch is worked, the result is the opposite of what happens with a stitch in standard position; if the right needle is positioned on the nearside of the left needle when inserted, the stitch will twist on itself; if it is positioned on the farside, it will not.

There are two ways to turn a new stitch on the needle.

An individual stitch can be turned as needed using the Slip Stitch technique. This may be done to twist the stitch in a decorative pattern, but more commonly it is used as one step in more complex stitch techniques where it is used instead to prevent this.

The method discussed here, however, is used to turn all the new stitches of a row by changing the way the yarn is wrapped around the needle. In European-derived knitting traditions, this is normally done only when making an entire fabric in a Twist Stitch pattern. However, it is the standard way of working in some other knitting traditions where it does not have that effect, and the two are sometimes combined by knitters who hold the yarn on the left beause it makes it easier to work Purl and doing so produces a more consistent fabric; see Turned Left-Hand Method, and Combined Method.

Regardless of which method you use, you will find it very useful to understand the relationship between the position of a stitch on the needle and how a stitch is formed because it is a significant factor in many stitch techniques; the material on Slip Stitches and Twist Stitches will also help make this clear.

The following instructions specify whether to work into the stitch from the nearside or farside of the left needle; most published pattern instructions use the terms "Knit back," or "Purl back" for the latter; for more information on the terms used in this book, see Terminology.

Knit Over

With this method of wrapping the yarn on the needle for a Knit stitch, the new stitches will be in turned position on the right needle, while those discarded into the fabric will be normal Knit stitches.

There are two options: the first is used when you start with the existing stitches in standard position on the needle; the second, when they are in turned position.

Stitches in Standard Position

- On nearside, insert needle from left to right into stitch, slide tip under left needle to farside, wrap yarn *over* right needle, down between needle tips and back to farside; pull new stitch through and discard stitch on left needle.

Knit Over with stitch in Standard Position.

In other words, Knit stitch nearside, wrap yarn over.

Stitches in Turned Position

- On farside, insert needle from right to left into turned stitch, wrap yarn *over* right needle, down between needle tips and back to farside; pull new stitch through and discard stitch on left needle.

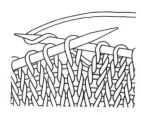

Knit Over with stitch in Turned Position.

In other words, Knit farside, wrap over.

Purl Under

This produces the same result, but in Purl; the new stitches will be in turned position on the right needle, while those discarded into the fabric will be standard Purl stitches in the fabric.

Here again, there are two options for how to wrap the yarn on the needle depending on whether the existing stitches are in standard or turned position on the needle.

Stitches in Standard Position

- On nearside, insert needle into first stitch from right to left as to Purl, wrap yarn *under* right needle tip, and then up between needle tips to nearside; pull new stitch through and discard stitch on left needle.

Purl Under with stitch in Standard Position.

In other words, Purl nearside, wrap under.

Stitches in Turned Position

- On farside, insert needle into center of first stitch from left to right; slide tip below left needle to nearside. Wrap yarn *under*, then up between needle tips to nearside. Pull new stitch through and discard original stitch.

Purl Under with stitch in Turned Position.

In other words, Purl farside, wrap under.

Sixteenth-century silk waistcoat, Brocade pattern with
embroidery. Norsk Folkemuseum, Oslo, Norway.

❖ *Basic Knit and Purl Patterns*

Many complex decorative stitch patterns are made up of no
more than Knit and Purl stitches that are combined in a variety of ways. Lest you think that a fabric made with just two
stitches must be rather plain, consider that there are examples of exquisite knitting in the textile collections of museums done in just that way. It is fair to say that you need only
Knit and Purl stitches to equip you for a lifetime of knitting,
but I certainly would not want to discourage you from learning about all the others discussed below and in the following
chapter.

In the meantime, here is a small group of the most fundamental Knit and Purl patterns: Stockinette, Garter Stitch,
Ribbing, and Seed Stitch are used more often than any others. They are commonly used for entire garments, for borders,
or serve as the background for other stitch or color patterns.

Stockinette and Reverse Stockinette

The Stockinette pattern has only Knit stitches on the side of
the fabric that will be visible in wear or in use; Reverse Stockinette has only Purl stitches on the side that will be visible.
Since these are two sides of the same stitch, the pattern names
merely distinguish the respective sides of the fabric, or specify
which side is to remain visible when worn.

The patterns are done in a slightly different way depending
on whether you are working a flat fabric, or a circular one.

Stockinette Worked Flat

1. Knit all stitches on left needle to make one row.
2. Transfer right needle, now bearing new stitches, to left
   hand, giving it a half turn so needle tip is to right. Transfer
   empty needle to right hand, tip pointing left. Purl sides of
   discarded stitches are now below needle in left hand.

3. Purl all stitches on needle to make next row.

4. Alternate rows in this manner, always working Knit when there are Knit stitches below left needle, and Purl when there are Purl stitches below left needle.

Reverse Stockinette is simply the other side of the same fabric and, therefore, done in the same way.

Stockinette Worked Circular

• Knit every round.

The Knit face of the fabric will always be on the nearside as you work, the Purl face of the fabric on the farside.

You could, of course, work an entire Reverse Stockinette fabric by Purling every round; however, most people prefer Knit to Purl. Therefore, if you want Purl on the outside, simply work in Knit and turn the fabric inside out before finishing the garment.

Of course, if you are making stripes of Reverse Stockinette within a fabric that contains other stitch patterns, it will be necessary to Purl every round.

Stockinette Characteristics

Stockinette seems to have earned its name because it traditionally served as the smooth, utilitarian pattern used for stockings, but it is by no means restricted to that. It is, by far, the most common stitch pattern in knitting, and for good reason.

General Appearance

In appearance, a Stockinette fabric has a vertical effect overall, which is produced by the V-shapes of the Knit stitches lined up in columns. While attractive enough on its own, Stockinette also serves as the neutral background for a wide variety of more highly textured and decorative stitch techniques. It is also used for most color patterns, because it is quiet and does not compete for attention with the design.

With Reverse Stockinette, the Purl nubs and their companion running threads dominate visually, and together they create a rough surface texture and a strongly horizontal effect that draws the eye to the rows.

While Purl is less often used as the primary pattern on the outside of the fabric, it certainly can be, and it is particularly effective at enhancing the qualities of highly textured yarns. More often, however, Reverse Stockinette is used in combination with Knit, as well as with many other stitch techniques that produce a smooth decorative effect, for the contrasting surface texture it provides.

There are two characteristics of a Stockinette fabric that are important to take into consideration. One is the tendency of the fabric to curl at the edges, and the other is the challenge of working it with a sufficiently even tension.

Fabric Edge Curl

Left to its own devices, the edge of a fabric done entirely in Stockinette will curl, and it becomes apparent why if you consider what a stitch looks like from the side.

A stitch is narrow at the bottom where it is pulled through the stitch below; at the top it is arched back and widened out where the stitch above is pulled through it in turn. Think of the stitch like a little soldier at attention, heels together, shoulders thrust back, and chest puffed out.

With all the stitches in this posture the fabric is placed

Stockinette with curl at side edges.

under a certain amount of tension and the side edges of the fabric will curl toward the Purl face. This curl is strong enough that a very narrow fabric will form a tight scroll shape; a wider fabric will flatten in the middle and the curl will be evident only at the sides. A similar but opposite effect can be seen at the top and bottom edges; they curl toward the Knit face of the fabric, as if the little soldiers had slumped over, and were standing at ease.

This tendency to curl is occasionally something of a nuisance, but it is easily tamed by using some combination of Knit and Purl stitches for borders at the edges. In mixed patterns of that kind, the Knit stitches on the outside of the fabric lean back, and the Purl stitches lean forward; each cancels out the effect of the other and the fabric will lie flat.

On the other hand, the curl can also be taken advantage of to add a charming design element to a garment. Several rows of plain Stockinette worked at the top or bottom edge of a fabric create a decorative effect called a Rouleau, the French word for "roll."

Stockinette showing curl at bottom edge.

Tension

Stockinette is so commonplace and seemingly so easy to do that knitters typically underestimate its challenge. In fact, it is one of the most difficult stitch patterns to handle successfully because the smooth surface betrays any uneven tension or error in technique.

It takes practice to develop the skill of maintaining sufficiently even tension on the yarn to do justice to Stockinette; even slight differences in stitch size will be more obvious in this fabric than would be the case in one with more surface texture. While you are learning to knit, therefore, it helps to work with more softly spun or textured yarns, or ones with variegated colors, because these tend to hide any irregularities.

Reverse Stockinette with uneven row tension.

Uneven tension is particularly troublesome for many knitters when working flat, since it can be difficult to maintain even stitch size on alternating Knit and Purl rows. The problem is most evident on the Purl side of the fabric, where you will see what looks like pairs of closely set rows separated by wide "gutters," which are really rows of enlarged stitches that were worked at a looser tension.

Knitters who work with the yarn on the right find it relatively easy to adjust their tension on Knit and Purl rows to even out stitch size. Knitters who work with the yarn on the left, however, use very different motions for Purl than those that are used for Knit, which makes this adjustment somewhat more difficult, although with practice it can be done; another solution is to use Purl Under instead; see Problems with Tension or Yarn Twist in the chapter Knitting Methods for more information.

Garter Stitch

The Garter Stitch pattern consists of one-row stripes of alternating Knit and Purl, and the fabric looks exactly the same on both sides.

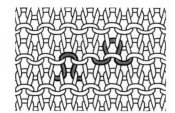

Garter Stitch fabric. Alternating rows of Knit and Purl on both sides.

Garter Stitch Worked Flat

• Knit every row.

Garter Stitch Worked Circular

• Knit one row and Purl the next.

It is also possible to work Garter Stitch in the round entirely in Knit; however, it requires two balls of yarn and working inside and outside rows as for a flat fabric; for more information, see Stitch Patterns in the chapter Circular and Flat Knitting.

Garter Stitch Characteristics

A fabric done in Garter Stitch lies very flat, because the curved posture of each stitch in the Knit rows is balanced by the opposite curl of each stitch in the Purl rows. This alternating curl compresses the fabric, giving it great vertical elasticity and resilience. As a result, a Garter Stitch fabric has far more rows per inch than a Stockinette one, it will be considerably thicker, and it requires considerably more yarn and, it must be said, time, for an equivalent size fabric.

It is common to assume that the gauge of Garter Stitch is balanced, with twice as many rows as stitches. While this may be true when the fabric first emerges from the needles, and depends upon working at a consistent tension, it is not a stable characteristic, since the gauge may change radically with wear. There are several reasons for this, such as the size and weight of the garment, whether the fabric was knit firmly or not, and the type of yarn used (with resilient wool holding its shape better, for example, than cotton). These factors can be taken into consideration in the design process; see Drop: The Effect of Gravity, and also Weighted Gauge Measurement.

Garter Stitch is often used for entire garments, particularly because its inherent resilience provides some flexibility with size and fit. This is also an asset when it is used for the border of a fabric done in another stitch pattern, since it is relatively easy to adjust it to fit the adjacent fabric with the application of a little steam, making it less important to take gauge differences into account. These characteristics, as well as the fact that Garter Stitch is so easy to work, ensure its utility and popularity.

Horizontal Ribbing

You can also make horizontal stripes of alternating Knit and Purl that are wider versions of Garter Stitch. Because of the fabric's tendency to curl, the smooth Knit rows will be slightly recessed, and the textured rows of Purl will protrude, which compresses the fabric and gives it a strong surface texture.

However, these stripes are at their boldest when they

Horizontal Ribbing. Stripes contain different number of rows. Garter Stitch at bottom.

have only a few rows; the more there are, the more the fabric will flatten out. Also, the tendency to curl is easily subdued in the process of cleaning or steaming the garment unless care is taken to preserve it; even the hanging weight of the garment may diminish it with time.

Vertical Ribbing

Ribbing (often called Welting in Great Britain), consists of alternating vertical columns of Knit and Purl stitches. The two most common patterns are Single Rib, which consists of one Knit, one Purl, alternating across the width of the fabric, and Double Rib, which has two Knits, two Purls.

In contrast to the horizontal nature of Garter Stitch and horizontal stripes described above, in vertical ribbings it is the columns of Knit stitches that protrude and those in Purl that recede; seen in cross-section, the patterns look like a corrugated tin roof. These patterns lie flat overall and have great horizontal elasticity, and they are commonly used for borders at the lower edges of bodices and sleeves, and to finish necklines and center front openings.

Because the yarn is held on the farside of the needle to make a Knit stitch, and on the nearside for a Purl stitch, it must always be brought between the needle tips when changing from working one to the other. In this book, the instruction to move the yarn in this way is "yarn nearside" or "yarn farside." Most other knitting books use the terms "front," or "forward," and "back," but for reasons I discussed in the Introduction, I find those terms ambiguous; see Terminology.

When changing between Knits and Purls, it is all too easy to make the mistake of passing the yarn over the needle instead of between the needle tips. However, this will form what is called a Yarnover, which adds a stitch to the needle with an opening below it. In an appropriate setting this is desirable—the Yarnover technique is a basic increase and is also essential in lace patterns where it is used to make Eyelets; in the wrong setting, it leaves an unsightly hole in the fabric and an unwanted stitch on the needle.

Single Rib

This is a trim, tailored, and elastic fabric. A fabric of Single Rib will be about 30 percent narrower than one made of Stockinette using the same yarn, needle size, and number of stitches.

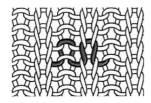

Single Rib. One column of Knit, one column of Purl.

1. With yarn held on farside of needle, Knit 1, move yarn between needle tips to nearside, Purl 1; alternate these two stitches across the row.
2. On subsequent rows, always work a Knit stitch above a Knit in the row below, a Purl above a Purl.

Double Rib

This is a more pronounced rib; a fabric done with the same yarn, needles, and number of stitches will be about 40 percent narrower than one done in Stockinette and 20 percent narrower than one in Single Rib. However, this is only true when the fabric is first made, because Double Rib is considerably softer and is more prone to lose its elasticity and flatten out with time and wear.

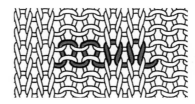

Double Rib. Two columns of Knit, two columns of Purl.

1. With yarn held on farside, Knit 2 stitches; move yarn between needle tips to nearside, Purl 2 stitches; alternate stitch pattern two-by-two in this way across row.
2. On subsequent rows, always work Knit stitches above Knit stitches, and Purl stitches above Purls.

Gauge for Ribbing

While most patterns and instruction books recommend that a ribbing be done on a needle one or two sizes smaller than what will be used for the remainder of the garment, I think that should be considered a minimum; in fact, you can hardly use a needle too small. The more stitches there are packed into every inch of the fabric, the more elasticity it will have and the less likely it is that the ribbing will stretch out and lose its resilience with wear. This will take more time and yarn, but the results are superior.

Also, it is just as important to do a gauge for a ribbing as for any other stitch pattern; see Average Gauge for Ribbing. Use that gauge to determine the number of stitches required for the width of the border, and then adjust the number when making the transition to the pattern for the main body of the garment; see Horizontal Shaping in the chapter Calculations for Pattern Design, and also Charting Horizontal Shaping.

> **The Knit stitch on the left . . .**
> When there are two or more columns of Knit stitches in a pattern element, as there are in Double Rib, the leftmost stitch of the group tends to enlarge. This is primarily because of the position of the stitches when on the needle and the relative distance the yarn has to travel when Knit and Purl stitches are made.
>
> The shortest distance a running thread must span is between two Purl nubs on the same side of the needle. The distance it travels is longer if the two nubs are on different sides of the needle, as they are when a Knit and a Purl are side-by-side.
>
> Also, when stitches are in standard position on the needle, with the left side of a stitch on the farside of the needle, the "default" position of the yarn is on the farside where it travels straight down the needle and out through the Purl nub. When the yarn is brought to the nearside to make a new Purl stitch, the nub exerts a slight resistance that lengthens the running thread further. In contrast, the running thread will be shorter when a Knit stitch follows a Purl stitch because there is less resistance when the yarn is returned to the farside; it is, in a sense, going "home."
>
> There are three ways to correct this uneven tension in the Knit column.
>
> • Place very firm tension on the yarn when you move it nearside to Purl—and I do mean firm. Pull the Purl nub from the farside all the way under the right needle where you can see it, and do not relax the tension on the yarn until after Purling the next stitch.
> • Or, after making a Purl stitch and returning the yarn to the farside, tighten the new stitch on the right needle before making the next stitch.
> • An alternative is to work the Purl stitches by wrapping the yarn under the needle (see Purl Under, above), which shortens the distance the yarn travels when it is wrapped around the needle.
>
>   There are some limitations to this approach: it is problematic when working more complex patterns of mixed Knit and Purl, as well as those with other types of stitch techniques; see the Combined Method in the chapter Knitting Methods.

Seed and Double Seed Stitch

These closely related stitch patterns provide all the texture Purl makes possible, but because they have an equal number of Knit stitches mixed in, they are more attractive than plain Reverse Stockinette, and the fabric lies perfectly flat. These patterns are handsome when used for an entire garment, are very effective as a background for various decorative motifs, and serve nicely for borders.

Seed Stitch

Seed Stitch is perhaps the most common texture pattern of this kind, imparting a nice nubby quality to a fabric. It is basically a broken Single Rib, with the pattern staggered on each subsequent row.

Seeded Chevron. Seed Stitch alternating with Stockinette and Reverse Stockinette.

On an even number of stitches, work as follows, always moving the yarn between the needles, farside for a Knit stitch and nearside for a Purl stitch:

• Alternate Knit 1, Purl 1 across one row, and Purl 1, Knit 1 on next row.

In other words, always work a Knit stitch on top of a Purl, and a Purl stitch on top of a Knit.

The pattern is the same for working flat or circular.

Double Seed Stitch

These two variations of Seed Stitch are the equivalent of a broken Double Rib; the instructions are written for working flat, but are the same for working circular, except there is no need to turn at the end of a row.

Here again, work on an even number of stitches, moving the yarn between the needle tips as necessary for Knit and Purl.

Version One
1. [Knit 2, Purl 2]; repeat between brackets across row. Turn.
2. [Purl 2, Knit 2]; repeat between brackets across row. Turn.
3. Repeat Steps 1 and 2 for pattern.

Version Two
1. [Knit 2, Purl 2]; repeat between brackets across row. Turn.
2. Repeat Row 1, working Knit stitches on top of Knit stitches, Purl on top of Purl. Turn.

3. [Purl 2, Knit 2]; repeat between brackets across row.
   Turn.
4. Repeat Row 3.
5. Repeat Steps 1–4 for pattern.

This forms little four-stitch blocks of alternating Knit and Purl.

It is easy enough to alter the pattern to work on an uneven number of stitches; just keep the principle in mind and stagger the stitches on each row.

Seed Stitch Characteristics

These patterns are good examples of how radically different a fabric can be as the result of no more than a small change in the relationship of the stitches. While made in a way that resembles ribbing, instead of drawing in, these fabrics spread out. Seed Stitch, for instance, can be as much as 30 percent shorter and 18 percent wider than Stockinette when done with the same yarn, needles, and number of stitches.

When used for a border, therefore, it is important to do a separate Stitch Gauge and adjust the number of stitches when changing from one pattern to the other (see Horizontal Shaping in the chapter Calculations for Pattern Design); if the difference is not large, a little steam may be enough to fit the border to the rest of the fabric. You might also consider working a border of this kind using a smaller-size needle.

Brocade Patterns

The term brocade is used for woven fabrics with elaborate motifs that are slightly raised on the surface of a plain background. The word has its origins in the Latin *brocchus*, which means "projecting," and *broccare*, which means "to stud with nails." This also seems apt for patterns created by setting Purl stitches on the smooth face of a Knit background, since the Purl nubs do resemble little nail heads.

Clustered together, the Purls can be used to create squares,

Biscuit Brocade. Pattern with mixed Knit and Purl stitches.

Dutch wool petticoat in figurative Brocade pattern; probably late seventeenth century.
Victoria & Albert Museum, London, England.

diamonds, diagonal lines, zigzags, butterflies, flowers, or windmills—any shape that can be reduced to the simple geometry of stitches. And, of course, if you create a motif made of Purl stitches set on a Knit background and then turn to the other side of the fabric, you will find the same motif in Knit stitches on a Purl background. Because these patterns are reversible, they are favored for things like blankets and shawls; when used for a conventional garment with an inside and an outside, you may be hard-pressed to decide which side to use.

Slip Stitch

There is probably no simpler technique in all of knitting. When instructions call for a Slip stitch, all that is necessary is to move a stitch from the left needle to the right needle without working it. This simplicity is quite deceptive, however, because a Slip stitch plays many and various roles, some obvious, and others quite subtle.

❖ Basic Slip Stitch

A true Slip stitch is transferred from the left needle to the right needle as if to Knit or to Purl, and left unworked until a later row; drawn up in this way, it will be elongated. The yarn is stranded past the slipped stitch in order to work the next stitch, and positioned either on the inside of the fabric, where it will be hidden, or on the outside, where it will remain visible and add a decorative element.

It is important to strand the yarn past a Slip stitch at a gentle tension so it has sufficient length; if it is too tight, it will draw the two flanking stitches together, and if it is too loose, those stitches will take up the extra yarn and enlarge.

Some stitch techniques also make use of Slip stitches as a temporary step, usually to facilitate manipulating the stitches in some way; in these cases the stitch is not drawn up into a row above and does not remain as a true Slip stitch within the fabric.

Slip Stitch Purlwise

A stitch slipped purlwise remains in standard position, with the right side of the stitch on the nearside of the needle.

Strand on Inside

1. If working on outside row, hold yarn on farside, insert right needle into first stitch on left needle as to Purl, and withdraw left needle to transfer stitch. If working an inside row, hold yarn on nearside instead.
2. Either maintain yarn on farside, or move yarn between needle tips to nearside, as necessary, to strand yarn past Slip stitch and Knit or Purl next stitch.
3. On next row, work Slip stitch either as to Knit or Purl according to pattern.

Slip Stitch Purlwise: Step 1. With yarn on inside, transfer stitch directly from left to right needle.

The discarded Slip stitch occupies two rows instead of one.

Strand on Outside

• Work as described above, but in Step 1, hold yarn on nearside of fabric when working an outside row, and on farside if working an inside row.

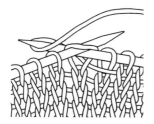

Slip Stitch. Knitting stitch after Slip stitch with yarn stranded on outside.

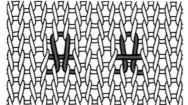

Slip Stitches. Left: Yarn stranded on inside of fabric. Right: Yarn stranded on outside of fabric.

Slip Stitch Knitwise

With this approach, the stitch will be in turned position after it is slipped, with the left side of the stitch on the nearside of the right needle (for more information about the position of the stitch on the needle, see Turned Stitches).

1. Move yarn to inside or outside of fabric, as necessary (see instructions above); move right needle to nearside and insert into first stitch on left needle as to Knit and then withdraw left needle to transfer stitch.

Slip Stitch Knitwise. Insert needle into stitch as if to Knit.

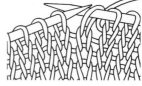

Slip Stitch Knitwise. Transfer stitch to right needle in turned position.

2. With stitch on right needle now turned, work next step of a pattern, as required.
3. On next row, work slipped stitch either as to Knit or Purl according to pattern.

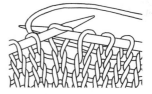

Slip Stitch Knitwise. Yarn stranded past Slip Stitch on inside.

> **Longer Slip stitches . . .**
> *In some patterns, Slip stitches are carried up another row or two, although beyond three rows it is best if the stitch is first Elongated to give it enough yarn to span the distance; see below.*

Basic Slip Stitch Patterns

The Slip Stitch technique appears in many patterns and to surprisingly different effect. Slip stitches may be used repeatedly throughout a fabric without being particularly noticeable, while in patterns where they are used less frequently, they may be the dominant visual element, creating striking surface texture or distinctive motifs. The technique also plays a major role in some interesting color patterns.

Twill Patterns

Simple diagonal patterns, zigzags, or diamond motifs can be created by slipping one or more stitches over one or more rows, with the yarn stranded on the inside of the fabric, and then shifting the pattern unit one stitch to right or left on subsequent rows.

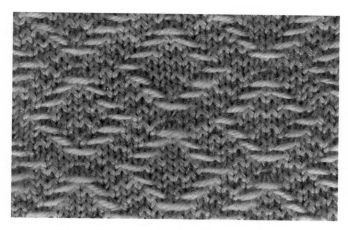

Woven Diamond. A Multiple Slip Stitch pattern.

Fabrics of this kind have a handsome, tailored appearance, and, when worked with a needle size that would be normal for the thickness of the yarn, they tend to be firm and dense. Because the Slip stitches were given only enough yarn to occupy one row, when drawn up across two, the entire fabric is compressed vertically.

This density makes these patterns suitable for garments that need to hold their shape well, like suits or skirts. Also, a jacket or coat done in a Slip Stitch pattern would be somewhat more windproof because the horizontal strands cover the spaces between the stitches (for a related technique that makes a truly windproof fabric, see Twined Knit). And in the Heel Stitch pattern, every other stitch is slipped every other row, making socks last longer.

Of course, the fabric can be softened simply by the use of a larger needle, in which case the surface texture would be of primary interest.

Stripes and Flecks

When Slip stitches are worked repeatedly in a single column, the result is a vertical line that seems to float on the surface of the fabric. When several columns of Slip stitches are spaced across the width of the fabric, it produces a subtle, elegant effect that looks like textured pinstripes. A single column of Slip stitches is also used to make foldlines for hems and pleats (see Slip Stitch Foldline).

In some patterns, Slip stitches are pulled at an angle using Crossed Stitch or Cable techniques, to create sinuous lines that travel across the surface. When this is done to individual Slip stitches that are scattered across the fabric, it creates a flecked effect on the surface.

Puff Patterns

"Blister" or "puff" patterns are done by drawing Slip stitches up several rows on either side of a group of stitches, which forces the area in between to bunch up and protrude from the fabric. In some cases, the number of stitches bracketed in this way is temporarily increased to exaggerate the effect.

Slip Stitch Color Patterns

Several types of color stitch patterns make use of Slip stitches with contrast colors stranded on the outside to create tweed or flecked effects. Also, Mosaic patterns are done with Slip stitches pulled over a two-row stripe in a contrast color with the yarn stranded on the inside; for more information, see Color Stitch Patterns.

❖ Multiple Slip Stitches

It is also possible to slip two or more adjacent stitches; when the yarn is stranded past them it will be that much longer. The length of the strand is, of course, determined by the number of stitches slipped and the gauge of the fabric; the only practical limit on this is the problem of snagging when the garment is worn. A strand of about half an inch is probably safe, although it can be longer if caught up on a later row with the Lattice Technique (see below).

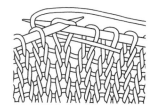

Multiple Slip Stitch. Stranding past two Slip Stitches on outside of fabric.

To ensure that a strand is long enough to span the Slip stitches without compressing the fabric, work as follows:

- Move yarn to nearside or farside, as necessary. Slip stitches, and then stretch them out on right needle as far as possible; move yarn into position to work next stitch.

Lattice Techniques

A strand passed on the outside of Multiple Slip Stitches can be caught up at its center by a stitch in a later row so it forms a little tent-like float on the surface; a stitch motif of this kind usually consists of three or five stitches (always an odd number). If the same stitches are slipped again on subsequent rows, this leaves several parallel strands on the outside of the fabric, multiplying the effect.

There are two methods that can be used to pick up one or more strands of this kind. A third technique is also discussed here, but it is more complicated to do and the result is less successful; it appears in some patterns and is included so you will recognize it and can substitute one of the others, if you prefer.

Multiple Lattice. Three strands drawn up into row above.

Version One

On outside of fabric, work as follows:

1. With tip of right needle, reach under strand on nearside and pick it up in turned position, with left side on nearside of needle.
2. Knit first stitch on left needle, drawing new stitch first through original stitch and then under strand on right needle from farside to nearside; discard stitch and strand together.

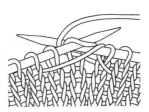

Lattice Technique, Version One: Step 2. Knit stitch and strand together.

Notice that the strand is caught at the base of the new stitch.

Version Two

This produces the same result as the version above; use whichever one you prefer.

1. Lift strand onto left needle in standard position, with right side of strand on nearside.
2. Insert right needle under strand and into first stitch on left needle as to Knit, wrap yarn in normal way, and draw new stitch under strand and through stitch; drop them from left needle together.

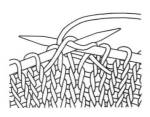

Lattice Technique, Version Two: Step 2.

To pick up the strand in Step 1, either pass the right needle between the fabric and the strand to pick the latter up and put it on the left needle, or move the left needle tip down on the nearside and up under the strand to catch it on the needle directly.

Version Three

In this version, the strand is pulled up one less row than with the methods above; the path of the yarn through the stitch distorts the pattern somewhat, and the technique involves extra steps; for all these reasons, I think you will find one of the others more useful.

1. With tip of right needle, reach down on nearside and under strand to pick it up in turned position, with left side on nearside of needle.
2. Wrap yarn around needle as to Knit and draw loop under strand.
3. Knit first stitch on left needle, and then pull loop holding strand over new stitch and off needle.

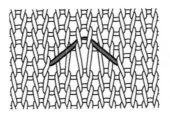 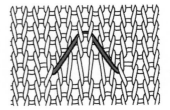

Two-Row Lattice.   Three-Row Lattice.

Elongation

This group of very simple techniques allows you to make some of the stitches longer than those in the rest of the fabric. There are several ways to elongate stitches; the method to use depends on what effect is needed.

Needle Elongation is used to enlarge all the stitches of a row to create the equivalent of a stripe, and Stitch Elongation is used when only a few of the stitches need to be larger.

Elongated stitches are found in a variety of patterns; they are usually manipulated in some way by other techniques and can take on a variety of forms. Most often, they are Slipped and carried up several rows, and then Twisted, Crossed, or Wrapped at their base or in the middle; they also frequently appear in Threaded Stitch patterns.

In addition, the technique provides an easy way to add openwork to a fabric, as well as texture and contour to nearby rows, which have to find their way around these longer stitches. It is also used in a utilitarian way to enlarge stitches that would otherwise be too tight and cause unwanted compression of a fabric.

❖ *Needle Elongation*

This technique elongates an entire row of stitches; the effect it produces is related to Regauging, a method of changing the gauge of the fabric by changing just the needle size.

Elongation Stripes

Stripes of this kind can be done with a different yarn, perhaps in a contrast color, and/or the elongated stitches can be worked on the next row with a different stitch technique than that used for the main fabric. Also, if the length of the stitches is planned carefully, a ribbon can be threaded through them.

Needle Elongation Stripes.

- In right hand, hold needle two or more sizes larger than that being used for fabric, and work across row. For next row (or round) set larger needle aside and return to original needle size.

Any change in the needle size will be visible, but, as a rough estimate, a needle four sizes larger will make the stitches approximately 50 percent larger. A stripe with multiple rows of elongated stitches will, of course, have a different gauge than that of the rest of the fabric. However, Elongation affects the row gauge more than the stitch gauge; a little judiciously applied steam and the weight of the garment in wear will elongate the stitches and draw in the extra width. Take this extra length into consideration when planning the pattern, particularly if there are multiple stripes planned for the design.

A somewhat similar effect can be achieved not by changing the needle size, but by using a much thinner yarn for the rows of the stripe.

Combo, or Condo Knitting

You can also hold two needles of very different sizes to work an entire fabric, instead of just for a row or two. That this would be called "combo knitting" makes sense to me, since it suggests "combining" two different needles, but why it might be called "condo knitting," as it sometimes is, seems a mystery. Perhaps combo was heard wrong, but I did come across a funny story that claimed condo was the correct name because knitting this way was very popular in the 1970s with people who lived in condominiums in Florida.

There are circular needles available with tips in two different sizes that are intended for this sort of thing, but these give no choice as to their respective sizes. Far better to use a set of interchangeable needles if you have them (see Tools) or just use whatever needles you have on hand in sizes that will give you the effect you want.

❖ *Stitch Elongation*

Here are two ways to elongate only some of the stitches on the needle, rather than all of them. One method is done using the Yarnover technique, the other by wrapping the yarn on the needle more than once when making a stitch.

Yarnover Elongation

This technique is a good method to use when the elongation is one step in a more complex stitch technique.

The pattern is written for working a flat fabric.

1. Work a Yarnover after each stitch that will be elongated.
2. On next row, drop Yarnover from needle, insert right needle into next stitch and pull up to draw in extra yarn; Knit or Purl elongated stitch in normal way.

Seafoam—a Yarnover Elongation pattern.

For a circular fabric, make the Yarnover before the stitch to be elongated so it precedes the stitch on the next round.

To elongate the stitch more, either work a Double Yarnover, or work one Yarnover on either side of the stitch in question.

Wrap Elongation

This method is used to elongate individual stitches or small groups of stitches, but it can also be used to enlarge an entire row if you do not have a needle size large enough to produce the effect wanted with Needle Elongation. Also, see Veil Stitch, below, where a wrap technique of this kind is used to create an entire fabric.

1. Work stitches to be elongated in normal way, either Knit or Purl, but wrap yarn two, three, or four times around needle for each one.

Wrap Elongation: Step 1.

2. On return row, Knit or Purl elongated stitch, dropping extra wraps as stitch is discarded.

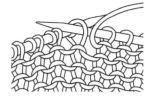

Wrap Elongation: Step 2.

Each wrap added in Step 1 will add roughly half again as much to the length of yarn provided to the stitch.

After working elongated stitch in Step 2, pull up on needle and tug down on fabric to encourage stitches to take up the extra yarn.

This technique and Yarnover Elongation appear in some Slip Stitch and Drop Stitch patterns, which call for an elongated stitch to be pulled up over several rows. The same approach is also seen in Threaded Stitch patterns, where one group of stitches is pulled through another.

Veil Stitch

Here is a lovely old stitch pattern that makes an open, net-like fabric of Elongated stitches that are twisted twice. It requires a rather elaborate wrap around the needle to work each stitch, but once you get the hang of it, it goes very quickly.

Knit every row, as follows:

1. Insert right needle into first stitch on left needle as to Knit.
2. Wrap yarn on right needle as to Knit, and then under and up nearside of left needle tip, over top to farside, and then wrap around right needle again as to Knit.
3. Original stitch and wrapped stitch cross on left needle, forming an X. Draw right needle through to nearside at bottom of X, below left needle; discard stitch and wrap together.

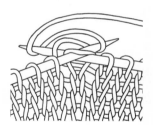

Veil Stitch: Step 2. Wrap yarn around both needle tips.

Veil Stitch: Step 3. Draw new stitch through X-strands.

Veil Stitch.

Wrap Stitches

This simple technique offers some nice textural possibilities. All that is necessary is to wrap the yarn around several stitches, either with a moderate tension so as to leave horizontal strands on the outside of the fabric, or with the yarn pulled tight to cluster the stitches together. Patterns may include two or more stitches and call for one wrap or several, and the appearance of the wrap can be changed somewhat by a slight change in the method of working.

The Wrap technique appears in some patterns where it is used to draw stitch columns together in a way that resembles smocking. It can also be used to create an overall fabric texture, although a similar effect is more easily achieved with the Pullover technique. One of the more charming applications I have seen was in a little floral bouquet motif where several stems made of Slip stitches were wrapped together to create a bouquet.

Smocking pattern made with Wrap Stitch.

❖ Single Wrap

There are two variations on this technique: one wraps a pair of stitches before they are worked, and the other wraps them afterward. Try both and see which works best given the circumstances at hand. All stitches are slipped purlwise.

Version One

With this method, the wrap will lie at the base of the discarded stitches.

- To work on outside: With yarn farside, Slip two stitches to right needle, yarn nearside, return two stitches to left needle, yarn farside, Knit two.
- To work on inside: With yarn nearside, Slip two stitches to right needle, yarn farside, return two stitches to left needle, yarn nearside, Purl two.

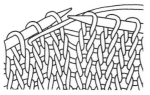

Single Wrap Stitch: Version One. Making the wrap.

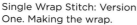

Single Wrap Stitch: Version One. Wrap shown in fabric.

Version Two

With this method, the stitches are worked first, and then wrapped. The strand will lie at the base of the new stitches instead of at the base of the discarded stitches; in other words, one row up.

- To work on outside: Knit two stitches, yarn nearside; Slip two new stitches to left needle, yarn farside, return two stitches to right needle.
- To work on inside: Purl two stitches, yarn farside; Slip two new stitches to left needle, yarn nearside, return two stitches to right needle.

To add slightly more texture, work wrapped stitches in Purl on outside of fabric.

❖ Multiple Wrap

To wrap the stitches more than once, it helps to use a cable holder, a tool used for making Cable stitch patterns (see Tools).

Basic Multiple Wrap

1. Knit stitches to be included in wrap.
2. Transfer new stitches from right needle to cable holder.
3. Wrap yarn around stitches on cable holder first to right on inside, and then to left on outside; repeat as many times as needed to create effect wanted.
4. Transfer stitches from cable holder to right needle and continue row.

Variations on Multiple Wraps

- If wrapped loosely, there will be multiple horizontal strands lying on the surface of the fabric. When done tightly, the wrapped stitches will be clustered together, forming a pronounced texture.

Little Bells—Multiple Wraps and Bobbles.

- Or, you can slip the stitches onto the cable holder from the left needle, wrap them, and then Knit them off the holder, but once they are wrapped this becomes more difficult to do.

Knit Below

The Basic Knit Below technique involves knitting into a stitch one or more rows below the first stitch on the left needle (machine knitters call this "tuck stitch").

In some stitch patterns it is used to create subtle effects, most often for what are known as Brioche fabrics, which have a wonderfully soft texture. In other types of patterns, the results can be quite bold, particularly if done with the Multi-Stitch Knit Below version, which involves working more than one row down.

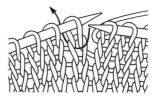

Basic Knit Below. Knit into stitch below left needle.

❖ Basic Knit Below

This is a very simple technique; instead of working into the next stitch on the left needle, work into the one immediately below it.

- Insert tip of right needle from nearside to farside into center of stitch directly below first stitch on left needle, wrap yarn as to Knit, pull new stitch through, and discard stitch above.
- Work in same way for Purl, but insert tip of needle into stitch from farside to nearside.

Once the stitch below is worked and the one on the needle discarded, the latter will lose the form of a stitch, and the result is a metamorphosis.

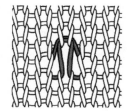

Knit Below Stitch.

When the upper stitch unravels, it is transformed into a Yarnover —it will have exactly the same structure—and the lower stitch is drawn up a row, changing into a Slip stitch. What you will see in the fabric is a Slip stitch tucked under what looks like a little tent formed by the Yarnover. In fact, the same stitch form can be achieved by combining a Yarnover and a Slip stitch on one row, and then working them together on the next; see the Alternative Brioche Method, below.

Because the Knit Below technique requires a plain stitch on either side to anchor the strand, it can be worked no more frequently than every other stitch. And because it combines the stitches of two rows, it can only be worked every other row in the same stitch column. However, these limitations are minor and you will find a wide variety of patterns that use the technique to create wonderful fabrics with beautiful texture.

Knit Below Brioche Patterns

The fabrics made with these techniques have a cellular structure and excellent thermal properties. In fact, it would be difficult to find an alternative that could make a cozier jacket, shawl, or blanket, and their best qualities are exhibited when they are done with soft yarns.

Here are three sample patterns for you to try. The second is no more than a slight variation on the first, while the third one demonstrates how a small change in the pattern can produce a very different look in the fabric.

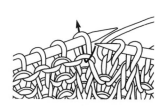

Brioche, or Fisherman's Rib.

Brioche Rib

This is the most basic pattern of the kind; it is often called Fisherman's Rib and it is reversible. Cast on an uneven number of stitches (this balances the pattern at both sides), include two selvedge stitches, and work as follows:

Brioche Rib Worked Flat

1. Preparatory Inside Row: Knit. Turn to outside.
2. Knit 1, [Knit Below, Knit 1]; repeat between brackets across row; turn.
3. Purl 1, [Knit 1, Knit Below]; repeat between brackets across row; end Knit 1, Purl 1.
4. Alternate Steps 2 and 3 for length of fabric.

Brioche Rib Worked Circular

1. Preparatory Row: Knit.
2. [Knit Below, Knit 1]; repeat between brackets for one round.
3. [Purl 1, Purl Below]; repeat between brackets for one round.
4. Alternate Steps 2 and 3 for length of fabric.

Staggered Brioche Rib

To stagger the pattern, work six or eight rows in Knit as described above, and then continue with an equal number of rows in Purl, as follows:

Staggered Brioche Rib Worked Flat

1. Knit 1, [Purl Below, Purl 1]; repeat between brackets across row; end Purl Below, Knit 1; turn.
2. Purl 1, [Purl 1, Purl Below]; repeat between brackets across row; end Purl 2.

Staggered Brioche Rib Worked Circular

1. [Purl Below, Purl 1]; repeat between brackets for one round.
2. [Knit 1, Knit Below]; repeat between brackets for one round.

Honeycomb Stitch

To give you an idea of how interesting these patterns can be, here is one that makes a beautiful fabric that really does look like a honeycomb; it is not reversible. Even though it is worked as for Garter Stitch, the Purl stitches disappear.

Honeycomb Stitch.

For a Flat Fabric

Cast on an even number of stitches, and work as follows:

1. Inside Row: Knit across row; turn.
2. Outside Row: [Knit 1, Knit 1 Below], repeat between brackets across row, end Knit 2; turn.
3. Inside Row: Knit across row; turn.
4. Outside Row: Knit 2 [Knit 1 Below, Knit 1], repeat between brackets across row; turn.
5. Repeat these four rows for pattern.

Always work plain Knit on the stitches that have a Knit Below under them—they will have what looks like a Double Purl nub under the needle (two strands instead of one)—and work the Knit Belows only on stitches that have a normal, single Purl nub below them.

For a Circular Fabric

1. Purl one round.
2. [Knit 1, Knit 1 Below], repeat between brackets to end of round.
3. Purl one round.
4. [Knit 1 below, Knit 1], repeat between brackets to end of round.

Alternative Brioche Method

As mentioned above, the Brioche family of patterns can be done using two distinctly different techniques, the Knit Below method discussed here, and the Yarnover-Slip Brioche method discussed in the chapter Increase and Decrease Stitch Patterns. The sample patterns above, Brioche Rib and Honeycomb Stitch, produce exactly the same fabrics as the ones made with the patterns you will find in the latter chapter so you can compare the two methods.

There is a wide variety of these kinds of patterns, including some in color. Once you understand how both techniques are done, you should find it relatively easy to rewrite a pattern written for one method if you prefer to use the other.

Tips for Brioche Patterns

Brioche fabrics tend to be compressed and wide, with gauges that have more rows and fewer stitches per inch than normal; make several Test Swatches to select the needle size that produces a fabric that feels right to you. When calculating Gauge, count rows carefully and remember that what looks like a single Knit stitch is really a Slip stitch that spans two rows.

These proportions also mean it is important to work the top and bottom edges in a way that will accommodate a wide fabric. This is not a problem if you begin above a ribbing, but if you plan to start the pattern directly above the edge, consider using Double-Needle Cast-On or Alternating Cast-On, since they will expand as needed. If you decide to use the latter, work the first row in Single Rib and plan the cast-on so that when you start the first row of the pattern, the Knit Below stitches will be worked into Purl stitches. At the top, use a larger needle and a Chained Cast-Off, or try one of the sewn cast-off techniques, done loosely.

The patterns above have a Stockinette Selvedge; it is smoother, but more trouble to do than a Garter Stitch Selvedge, which would also work well. Alternatively, consider one of the Double Selvedges, which are particularly compatible with these patterns.

Shaping a Brioche fabric can pose a challenge because the technique requires paired Knit and Knit Below stitches. In order to maintain the pattern, work any increases or decreases directly adjacent to the selvedge and then adjust how you start the next pattern row accordingly. If shaping is required within the fabric, it will be necessary to add or remove an entire pattern unit of two stitches; either work a single increase or decrease in the same position on each of two rows, or use a double version of the technique.

Because the structure of a Brioche fabric is complex, if you need to correct an error, it is best to unravel stitch by stitch; to undo several rows, take the stitches off the needle and unravel down to the row above the error, pick up the stitches again, and then unravel one more row stitch by stitch. When a Brioche stitch is off the needle, you will see a stitch with a Yarnover crossing it; pick both up together and on the next row use a Knit Two Together to join them into a Brioche stitch again.

❖ Multi-Stitch Knit Below

It is just as easy to Knit two, three, or four rows below as it is to Knit one row down. When several Multi-Stitch Knit Below techniques are placed in fairly close proximity, the stitches in between will protrude, which creates highly textured effects. Done in a slightly different way, the technique can be used to draw a single stitch up from more than one row below, turning it into the equivalent of a long Slip stitch.

Basic Multi-Stitch Knit Below

- Insert right needle into stitch two, three, or even four rows below first stitch on left needle.

As with Basic Knit Below, any stitches above the one worked into will unravel once the discard stitch is released from the left needle; there will be one strand for every row, all caught up by the new stitch.

A Multi-Stitch Knit Below pattern.

Unraveled Knit Below

Some pattern instructions may instruct you to unravel several stitches before working the stitch in the row below. In general, this is more trouble to do and the effect will be the same, but it is helpful if you are working with yarns that do not unravel easily on their own, or are so highly textured that it is difficult to locate the correct stitch.

1. Drop first stitch off needle. Insert tip of needle under running thread alongside dropped stitch and pull up gently until stitch unravels; repeat as necessary to reach stitch needed in row below.
2. Insert left needle tip from nearside to farside into unraveled stitch and under all strands above it; stitch and strands should be in standard position, with right sides on nearside of needle.

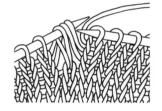

Unraveled Knit Below: Step 2.

3. Knit picked-up stitch and all strands; drop original stitch and strands from left needle.

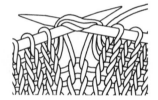

Unraveled Knit Below: Step 3.

If the yarns are difficult to unravel but you can see which stitch to work into, insert the right needle into the stitch first, and then drop the stitch above from the left needle and use it to undo the stitches.

Knit Below Ladder

A Multi-Stitch Knit Below can also be worked without including the strands.

- Unravel to stitch in row below, reach down on nearside to pick up just stitch, leaving strands behind, and Knit.

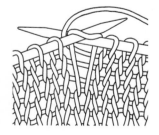

Knit Below Ladder. Working stitch without strands.

The stitch becomes a long Slip stitch with a backdrop of strands that will spread apart, creating a small, round, barred opening in the fabric that is quite charming.

Threaded Stitch

With the Basic version of this technique, one stitch is pulled through another and then both are worked separately. The first stitch will encircle the second and only half of it will be visible on the outside of the fabric, slanting either to right or left. In ap-

pearance, the result somewhat resembles a Pullover technique (see Pullovers in Increase and Decrease Stitch Patterns).

It is also possible to do the technique using pattern units of four, six, or even eight stitches, with half the stitches pulled through the other half; an Elongation technique is normally used to enlarge the stitches first.

You will find few stitch patterns that use this technique, but it is very attractive and deserves wider use. Threaded Stitches can be worked across a row to form stripes, stacked into columns, spaced across a fabric to make a spot pattern on a background of some other stitch, or used for an all-over pattern.

❖ *Basic Threaded Stitch*

The Right and Left versions of the Threaded Stitch are defined by the slope of the visible, encircling stitch, and there are multiple options for how to work each one. While it does not make any difference how you do the Right Threaded version, because the outcome will be the same, the two methods used for the Left Threaded version produce slightly different results.

In most of these patterns, the first stitch is temporarily slipped knitwise; this is done only to make it easier to work in the last step.

Right Threaded Stitch

Three methods can be used to do this technique. The left stitch of the pair will encircle the other and slope up to the right.

Method One

This can be done in one quick motion if the stitches are not too tight on the needle.

1. Slip 1 knitwise; replace turned stitch on left needle.
2. Insert right needle tip into second stitch as to Knit, and then move tip to nearside of first stitch before passing it under left needle; wrap yarn and pull through new stitch. Lift second stitch over first stitch and discard.

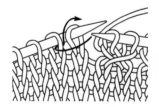

Right Threaded Stitch, Method One: Step 2. Knitting second stitch.

3. Knit turned stitch farside and discard.

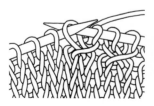

Right Threaded Stitch, Method One: Step 3. Knitting turned stitch farside.

Method Two

1. Slip 1 knitwise; replace turned stitch on left needle.
2. On nearside, insert right needle tip into second stitch as to Purl and lift it over first stitch, placing it in first position on tip of left needle; withdraw right needle.
3. Hold stitch now second on needle away from first with left finger, reinsert right needle into first stitch as to Knit, wrap yarn, draw through new stitch, and discard.
4. Knit turned stitch farside and discard.

Method Three

This alternative is easier to do because there is no need to turn the first stitch, but it is worked on the Purl side, as follows:

1. Pull second stitch over first to tip of needle and Purl; discard.
2. Purl remaining stitch of pair; discard.

Left Threaded Stitch

Two methods can be used for the left version of a Threaded Stitch; however, only the first one makes a matched pair with the Right Threaded Stitch, while the second does not. If you are going to use only a Left Threaded Stitch, either will do.

An all-over pattern in Left Threaded Stitch.

Method One

1. Slip 1 knitwise; replace turned stitch on left needle.
2. Reach right needle tip through first stitch and insert into second stitch as to Knit; pull second stitch through first and then Knit it; discard that stitch from left needle.

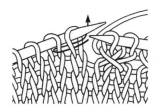

Left Threaded Stitch, Method One: Step 2.

3. Knit turned stitch farside and discard.

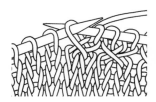

Left Threaded Stitch, Method One: Step 3.

The first stitch is Turned and then worked farside so it will not cross on discard; this is done merely to make it easier to work the technique.

Here is a slightly faster way to work:

• Slip stitch knitwise to right needle, and then insert left needle into farside of turned stitch; needles will then be in position to draw second stitch through first.

Basic Threaded Stitch, showing Left and Right versions.

Method Two

In this case, the first stitch is not turned and will cross on discard; therefore, it does not look exactly like the Right Threaded version. Nevertheless, if you like it and do not plan to pair right and left versions, you may prefer to work this way because it is easier to do.

1. Insert right needle into first stitch as to Purl, and then into second stitch as to Knit. Pull second stitch through first, wrap yarn and Knit; discard.
2. Knit second stitch farside and discard.

In Step 1, you may find it helpful to hold the first stitch back on the left needle with your finger as you draw the second stitch through it.

❖ Threaded Stitch Variations

Basic Threaded Stitch can be varied in several ways. You can enlarge a whole row of stitches with Needle Elongation, or increase the number of stitches that are included in each unit of the pattern.

Bold Threaded Stitch

A fabric done entirely in Threaded Stitch can be rather dense. Use a Test Swatch to select a needle size that produces the kind of fabric you want. For stripes, use the Needle Elongation technique; the enlarged stitches also make it easier to do this technique.

A stripe done with Bold Threaded Stitch.

1. To work row below Threaded Stitch pattern row, hold needle two or three sizes larger than that used for main fabric in right hand.
2. Return to main needle and work Basic Threaded Stitch on every pair of stitches across row.

Multiple Threaded Stitch

Here is an example of a Left Threaded Stitch pattern done with six stitches, three to be threaded through the other three. For a Right Threaded Stitch version, work in exactly the same way, but do the pattern row on the inside of the fabric in Purl instead of on the outside.

1. On one row, work an Elongation technique on all six stitches of pattern unit: either wrap yarn twice for each one, or work Yarnover after each one.
2. On next row, Slip six stitches to right needle, dropping Yarnovers or extra wraps.
3. With left needle tip, pick up second set of three stitches on right needle and pull them over first set.
4. Hold set of stitches on left needle in position with forefinger, and then transfer remaining three stitches on right needle back to left needle as well.
5. Knit the six stitches, one at a time.

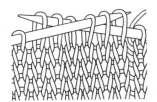
Multiple Threaded Stitch: Step 3. Pull second set of three over first set.

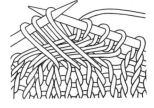
Multiple Threaded Stitch: Step 5. Knitting last three stitches.

The number of stitches involved is optional; it is possible to pull just two-through-two, or enlarge it and do four-through-four, but I have never seen more than that used. And, of course, you might prefer asymmetry and pull three through two, etc.

Openwork Cross—a Threaded Stitch pattern.

Faceted Diamond. A pattern with Knit, Purl, and Twist Stitches.

Twist Stitches

A Twist Stitch is turned at its base to right or left so the two sides of the stitch change places. Instead of looking like a V in the fabric, therefore, it will somewhat resemble an X. One side of the stitch will be visually dominant, sloping up to the left or to the right, while the other side will be partially hidden; the Purl face of the stitch is unchanged.

In patterns where only some of the stitches in a row are done this way, a simple knitting technique is used to twist the stitch in one direction; to twist it in the other direction, the stitch is first turned with Slip Stitch Knitwise.

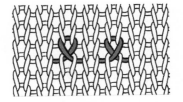
Left and Right Twist Stitches.

There are also patterns for making an entire fabric of Twist Stitches, and for these, it is necessary to turn an entire row of stitches as a preparatory step prior to twisting them; see Turned Stitches.

A change of mind . . .

When I was writing the first edition of The Principles of Knitting, *the term Crossed Stitch seemed firmly established as the name for this technique; however, that was not always the case. In many older books, a stitch that was turned on itself was referred to as a Twist, or Twisted Stitch, while a pair of stitches that were crossed over each other was called Crossed or Cross-Over Stitch.*

To my way of thinking, the latter use of the terms makes considerably more sense—a single thing can be twisted on itself, but it takes two things to make a cross—and I always regretted not using them. I decided to do so in this edition, with some trepidation and the hope that this does not add to the confusion everyone probably shares about which is which.

❖ Individual Twist Stitches

Twist Stitches are tighter and firmer than a standard, open Knit stitch and have a raised, embossed look—especially when a single column is set against a contrasting background. Because of this they are frequently used as vertical elements that bracket other aspects of a pattern, or to create lines of stitches that travel across a fabric.

There is a knitting tradition in Germany and Austria that makes extensive use of Twist and Crossed Stitch techniques (see below). These elaborate, yet refined patterns have a crisp definition that is quite unique and beautiful; there is a welcome new translation of Maria Erlbacher's *Twisted-Stitch Knitting*, a collection of old patterns from Austria that defines the style.†

Left Twist Stitch

The right half of the stitch will be most visible on the outside of the fabric, sloping up to the left and partially hiding the other half.

Knit Version

This is very easy to do; it is the version most often used in patterns.

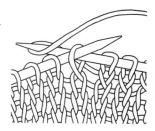

- With stitch in standard position, move right needle to farside of left needle; insert into stitch from right to left and Knit.

Knit Left Twist Stitch.
Knit stitch farside.

---

† Maria Erlbacher, *Twisted-Stitch Knitting: Traditional Patterns and Garments from the Styrian Enns Valley*, English translation by Char Dickte (Austria, 1982; English edition, Pittsville, Wisc.: Schoolhouse Press, 2009).

Purl Version

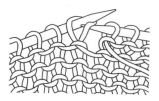

- With stitch in standard position, move right needle to farside and insert into stitch from left to right and Purl.

Purl Left Twist Stitch.
Purl stitch farside.

Right Twist Stitch

The left half of the stitch will be most visible on the outside of the fabric, sloping up to the right and partially hiding the other half.

Knit Version

This is not as easy to do as the left version, above, and so is used only when necessary.

- Slip 1 knitwise and replace turned stitch on left needle; move right needle to nearside, insert into turned stitch from left to right, and Knit.

Beaded Chain. A pattern with Twist Stitches on a Purl ground.

Purl Version

If you need a Right Twist Stitch, it is easier to do in Purl on the inside of the fabric than in Knit on the outside.

- Slip 1 knitwise, replace turned stitch on left needle; move right needle to nearside, insert into turned stitch from right to left, and Purl.

Or, for an even faster way to work:

- Slip 1 knitwise, insert left needle into stitch on farside; with both needles in stitch, Purl.

> **To sum up . . .**
>
> *If a stitch is in standard position and you Knit or Purl it farside, it will twist to the left; if a stitch is in turned position, and you Knit or Purl it nearside, it will twist to the right.*
>
> *Left Twist is easier to do and more common in patterns; the abbreviated term in pattern instructions here is "Knit farside" or "Purl farside." In most other published books of instructions and patterns, the terms are usually something like "Knit back" or "Purl in back of stitch"; for more information, see the discussion of terms in the Introduction to the Second Edition, under Terminology.*
>
> *Because Right Twist is less often used, and because it is normal to work into the nearside of a stitch, "Knit nearside" or "Purl nearside" are less often used.*

❖ Twist Stitch Fabrics

A fabric made entirely, or primarily of Twist Stitches has some very interesting characteristics because the stitch creates bias. When all the stitches of a fabric are twisted in the same way, the entire fabric will slant in that direction as well and take on the shape of a trapezoid.

If all the stitches in several rows are twisted to the right, followed by several rows with stitches twisted to the left, it will create a Chevron pattern in the fabric consisting of areas of alternating bias and side edges in a zigzag shape. A pattern of this kind would make an interesting scarf or shawl.

Some patterns make use of blocks of Twist Stitches and the bias they create is strong enough to pull the remaining areas of the fabric on the bias as well.

The bias can be overcome entirely by combining equal numbers of Right and Left Twist Stitches in close proximity, either alternating them across a row, or row by row, so the effect of one cancels out the other. Doing so creates a fabric with a flat, tailored appearance; the stitch columns look plaited and there is more space between them because the individual stitches are narrower.

The techniques used to make Twist Stitch fabrics rely on the concepts discussed in Turned Stitches in order to position the stitches on the needle so they can be twisted in the direction needed; the instructions use the terms "wrap under" or "wrap over," or "Knit Under," "Purl Over," which are explained there. The patterns are written for working a flat fabric, with alternating rows of Knit and Purl; only a small change is required to work in the round.

Bias Twist Stitch Fabric

To twist every stitch of the fabric in the same direction, work in one of the following ways.

Right and Left Bias Twist Stitch Fabric.

Left Bias Twist Fabric

Start with all stitches on needle in standard position.

1. All Outside Rows: Knit farside.
2. All Inside Rows: Purl farside.

To work circular, use only outside row pattern.

Right Bias Twist Fabric

This pattern requires stitches in turned position; you can start with them in standard position and work the preparatory row to turn them, or, if you know how to do so, adjust the method of casting on to turn the stitches of the first row, and then begin with Step 2.

1. Inside Preparatory Row: Slip 1 knitwise, insert left needle into farside of turned stitch on right needle, and, with both needles in stitch, Purl Under; repeat across all stitches of row.
2. All Outside Rows: Knit nearside, wrap over.
3. All Inside Rows: Purl nearside, wrap under.

For working circular, do one row Knit Over to turn all stitches on needle, or adjust cast-on technique to turn them; for all subsequent rows, use only the outside row pattern.

It is somewhat awkward to work into the nearside of a turned stitch. It helps to have the stitch as close to the tip of the needle as possible, and then pull down on the fabric below it to open up a little room so you can insert the right needle.

Balanced Twist Stitch Fabric

To create a subtle, all-over texture pattern and cancel the tendency to bias, work one row of Left Twist Stitch, followed by one row of Right Twist.

Balanced Twist Stitch Fabric.

To Work Flat

1. All Outside Rows: With stitches in standard position, Knit farside, wrap over.
2. All Inside Rows: With stitches in turned position, Purl nearside.

The alternative, working Knit on turned stitches and Purl on stitches in standard position, is more difficult to do and the result is the same.

To Work Circular

1. First round: Work as in Step 1, above.
2. Second round: With stitches in turned position, Knit nearside.
3. Alternate Steps 1 and 2 for length of fabric.

About ribbon knits . . .

In the mid-twentieth century, Balanced Twist Stitch was frequently used with silk or rayon ribbon to make exquisite blouses, dresses, and suits. The ribbon was drawn off a spool and wrapped carefully around a relatively large-size needle so it would lie flat and not be crushed within the stitches. In finishing, the fabric was pressed to flatten the Twist stitches, giving the surface a scale-like appearance, and the garments were often lined to preserve their shape.

Twist Stitch Ribbing

Here are three variations of a Single Rib made with Twist Stitches; they look the same on both sides and will not bias.

The same concepts can be applied to make a Double Rib as well. These patterns make handsome borders that lie nice and flat.

Cast on an even number of stitches; the patterns are the same whether done flat or circular.

Left Twist Single Rib

Work every row as follows:

- [Knit 1 farside, Purl 1 farside]; repeat between brackets across row.

Right Twist Single Rib

This requires all stitches to be turned on the needle when cast on or with a preparatory row, as described for Right Bias Twist Stitch, above.

- [Knit 1 nearside, wrap over; Purl 1 nearside, wrap under]; repeat between brackets across row.

Balanced Twist Stitch Rib

To make a balanced version of the ribbing, combine the two patterns above; the stitches will zigzag in the columns, twisting to the left on one row, to the right on the next.

Start with stitches in standard position.

1. [Knit 1 farside, wrap over; Purl 1 farside, wrap under]; repeat between brackets. Discarded stitches are twisted to left; new stitches are turned.
2. [Knit 1 nearside, Purl 1 nearside]; repeat between brackets. Discarded stitches are twisted to right; new stitches are in standard position.

Two Ribbing patterns in Twist Stitch. Above: Left Twist Stitches. Below: Knits with Left Twist; Purls not twisted.

Twist Ribbing Characteristics

Some books claim that a Ribbing done with Twist Stitches is tighter and more elastic than a conventional ribbing, but I have not found this to be the case. If the two patterns are compared using separate gauge swatches, each made with the same yarn, needle, and number of stitches, there is a rather large difference in the results.

With the swatches I did, Single Rib had a gauge of 7.0 stitches per inch, whereas Twist Single Rib had 5.7 stitches per inch; the Twist Rib fabric was not only wider, but was less resilient. Patterns of this kind are attractive, however, and serve nicely for a border where elasticity is not important.

Crossed and Cable Stitches

Crossed Stitches and Cable Stitches are first cousins. Both types of patterns are done by switching the positions of adjacent stitches on the needle, to either the right or the left, so when discarded they will cross over one another in the fabric.

Cable techniques are used for pattern units that contain a minimum of four stitches, which, because of the number involved, require a special tool to manipulate them into position. Crossed Stitch techniques are used when just two stitches are involved and, because there are so few stitches, the tool is not needed. As a result there are more options for how to work the latter, and in some cases the resulting structure is different from that of a true Cable; also, the types of patterns that can be done with these two techniques are quite different.

❖ *Crossed Stitches*

The first method discussed below works exceedingly well and is very easy to do; there is really no need to look further. However, the other methods accomplish much the same thing, and, while sometimes limited or problematic in one way or another, they have their place and in some patterns may be preferable.

Crossed Stitches can be done in either Knit or Purl, but the pattern is, with one welcome exception, decorative only on the Knit side. Once the two stitches have been worked and discarded into the fabric, one will be the visible "facing" stitch that slopes up to right or left, and the other will be the "backing" stitch, which is largely hidden.

There are decorative patterns that use Crossed Stitches for entire fabrics and the effects can be subtle, lending no more than a slight ridge or small sideways curl to the stitches. In other patterns, the results are more obvious, such as a basket-weave pattern made of alternating rows of Right Crossed Stitch and Left Crossed Stitch. When done with a needle size normal for the yarn, the result would be suitable for a potholder or an extremely durable and windproof jacket; however, using a larger-size needle makes a more supple fabric, suitable for many other kinds of garments.

Crossed Stitches are more often spread across a Purl background, forming the dominant decorative element in a pattern. Stacked one on top of another and worked on every other row, columns of Crossed Stitches are tight and quite embossed; these can be used to bracket a column of lacy openwork or might be tucked in alongside larger Cable stitch patterns. There are also strikingly beautiful effects that can be created by shifting the Crossed Stitches to right or left on subsequent rows to create zigzag and serpentine lines.

> **A name change . . .**
>
> As discussed above in "A change of mind . . . ," in the first edition of The Principles of Knitting, I called a stitch that was turned on itself a Crossed Stitch, and a pair that crossed each other a Twist Stitch, because those seemed to be the most common names for the techniques in stitch pattern books at that time. However, in many older knitting books, and in some books today, the names are just the opposite—a single stitch turned on itself is called a Twist Stitch, and two stitches that trade places are Crossed or Cross-Over Stitches.
>
> I prefer the latter use of the terms because they better match the structure of the respective stitches and I have decided to use them here.

Knit-Together Crossed Stitches

This is an excellent way to make Crossed Stitches. It is easy and results in a very neat, trim, and consistent appearance. Most important, the Right and Left Crossed Stitches are perfect mirror images of each other, which is not true of the other methods discussed below.

Wickerwork. Right and Left Knit-Together Crossed Stitches.

This technique makes use of either a Knit Right or Purl Right Decrease, with two stitches worked together, but one of the pair is then worked a second time. There is one important variation, which has a distinctive look of its own.

Right Crossed Stitch

The instructions are for working on the outside of the fabric in Knit, or on the inside in Purl, but it is only the appearance of the stitch on the outside that matters, where the facing stitch of the pair will slope up to the right.

Knit Version

1. Knit first two stitches on left needle together. Retain stitches on left needle; there is one new stitch on right needle.
2. Insert needle between same two stitches to Knit first stitch again and then discard them.

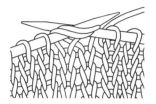 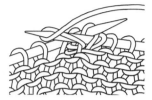

Knit-Together Right Crossed Stitch: Step 1. Knit two stitches together.

Knit-Together Right Crossed Stitch: Step 2. Knit first stitch alone.

Purl Version

1. Purl second stitch on left needle. Retain stitches on left needle; there is one new stitch on right needle.
2. Purl first two stitches on left needle together; discard both.

Purl Version of Knit-Together Right Crossed Stitch: Step 1. Purl second stitch.

Purl Version of Knit-Together Right Crossed Stitch: Step 2. Purl two stitches together.

Left Crossed Stitch

In this case, the facing stitch of the pair of stitches will slope up to the left on the outside of the fabric.

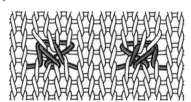

Knit-Together Left and Right Crossed Stitches.

Knit Version

1. Slip 2 stitches knitwise, one at a time; return to left needle in turned position.
2. Knit second stitch farside, and then Knit first and second stitch together farside; discard both.

 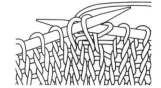

Knit-Together Left Crossed Stitch: Step 2. Knit second turned stitch farside.

Knit-Together Left Crossed Stitch: Step 2. Knit two stitches together farside.

Purl Version

1. Slip two stitches knitwise, one at a time; return to left needle in turned position.
2. Purl two turned stitches together farside, and then insert needle between two stitches to Purl first stitch farside. Discard both stitches from left needle.

 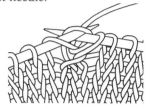

Purl Version of Knit-Together Left Crossed Stitch: Step 2. Purl two together farside.

Purl Version of Knit-Together Left Crossed Stitch: Step 2. Purl first stitch farside.

Why turning the stitch is important . . .
Many stitch patterns that use a Left Crossed Stitch do not say to turn the stitches first, and as a result both will become Twist Stitches in the fabric. This is quicker to do, but it does not look like the Right Crossed version and the difference is quite obvious when the two are in close proximity.

Ribbed Leaf Pattern. Right and Left Knit-Together Crossed Stitches.

Reversible Crossed Stitch Ribbing

There are numerous patterns that employ Crossed Stitches in one guise or the other, but I do not recall coming upon this one anywhere; unlike most of them, it is reversible and makes a lovely ribbing.

For a Flat Fabric

Use a relatively small size needle to encourage resilience and cast on a multiple of four stitches, plus four extra. Two of these are edge stitches, which are used to balance the pattern so it looks the same on both sides, and two are selvedge stitches, one at each side (see Edge and Selvedge Stitches).

Reversible Crossed Stitch Ribbing patterns.
Bottom: Crossed every row.
Middle: Crossed on two rows, then two rows plain.
Top: Right and Left Crossed combination.

1. Knit 1, [Knit Right Crossed Stitch, Purl 2], repeat between brackets, end Knit Right Crossed Stitch (the edge stitches), Knit 1.
2. Purl 1, [Purl 2, Knit Right Crossed Stitch], repeat between brackets, end Purl 3.
3. Alternate these two rows for length of ribbing.

For a four-row pattern, work Steps 1 and 2 followed by two rows of plain Double Rib; continue selvedge stitches at beginning and end of rows.

For a zigzag effect, use a four-row pattern: Work first two rows of repeat as described in Steps 1 and 2, above. For second two rows of repeat, work Step 1 again, but in Step 2 substitute a Knit Left Crossed Stitch. Continue in this way, alternating Right and Left Crossed Stitch versions every other row.

For a Circular Fabric

While the advantage of this pattern is that it is reversible, it is so attractive, you might want to use it for a circular fabric even if the other side will not be seen.

- Cast on a multiple of four stitches (there is no need to add the edge and selvedge stitches), and work Step 1 on every round, or alternate the pattern as suggested by introducing plain rows and/or alternating Right and Left Crossed Stitches.

Cable-Type Crossed Stitch

The structure of this Crossed Stitch is the same as a tiny two-stitch Cable. The facing stitch tends to be a little larger and looser than when done with the Knit-Together Crossed Stitch method above, but you may prefer this in some applications.

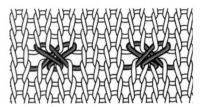

Cable-Type Crossed Stitches.

Right Cabled Crossed Stitch

It is customary to work Crossed and Cable stitches in Knit on the outside of the fabric, where you can see the results of what you have done. However, the Purl version of this is actually easier to do, and you might want to use it if you can adjust the rest of the pattern so you can work on the inside.

Knit Version

1. Insert right needle tip into second stitch as to Knit, and then move it around nearside of first stitch and under left needle tip; wrap yarn and pull new stitch through.

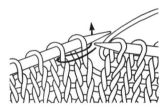

Right Cabled Crossed Stitch, Knit Version: Step 1. Knit second stitch, moving needle around first stitch.

2. Knit first stitch in normal way and discard both stitches from left needle together.

In Step 1, push the first stitch toward the needle tip slightly so it is out of the way so you can insert the needle into the second one.

Purl Version

- Insert right needle into nearside of second stitch on left needle and Purl, and then Purl first stitch; discard both stitches from left needle together.

Right Cabled Crossed Stitch, Purl Version. Purl second stitch, then first.

Left Cabled Crossed Stitch

In this case, it is the left version that is easiest to do in Knit, but it can be done in Purl when necessary.

Knit Version

1. Slip first stitch purlwise, second stitch knitwise; return both stitches to left needle, maintaining turned position of second stitch.
2. Knit second stitch farside, and then Knit first stitch nearside and discard both.

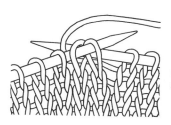

Left Cabled Crossed Stitch, Knit Version: Step 2. Knitting second stitch farside.

Purl Version

1. Slip first stitch purlwise, second stitch knitwise; return both stitches to left needle, maintaining turned position of second stitch.
2. Purl second stitch farside, and then Purl first stitch normally and discard both together.

Left Cabled Crossed Stitch, Purl Version: Step 2. Purling second stitch farside.

It might seem easier to turn both stitches, but it is then more difficult to separate the first one from the second in order to work it alone.

Crossed Stitch Drop Technique

The Drop Stitch method is another way to make a Cable-Type Crossed Stitch, not a separate technique. It is just what it says it is—the first stitch of the pair is dropped off the needle and then picked up again after you have worked the second one. Since there is no need to use a cable holder, this is quick and convenient for tiny one-over-one Cables, especially when using a wool or any highly textured yarn that will not unravel easily.

Work on outside of fabric, as follows:

* For a Left Crossed Stitch, drop first stitch from left needle to nearside and pinch against fabric with finger; work next stitch, and then insert left needle into dropped stitch to pick it up again and work it.
* For Right Crossed Stitch, work as above, but drop stitch from left needle on farside.

Left Crossed Stitch Drop Technique. Pick up stitch on nearside and Knit.

Always pick up the stitch so it is in standard position on the needle or, if you pick it up turned, work it farside so it will not cross.

Wrapped Crossed Stitch

This readily suggests itself as a way to do a Crossed Stitch, but it has a rather different appearance in the fabric. With this way of working, the first stitch is "wrapped" on the farside by the yarn stranded past it to work the second stitch, and on the nearside when the second stitch is pulled past it. The final appearance of the stitch will only be fully apparent when the new stitches are worked on the next row and discarded into the fabric.

The facing stitch tends to be enlarged even when done with a firm tension; the backing stitch, if it is seen at all, looks like a little Purl nub, which may help this version of a Crossed Stitch blend in nicely with a Purl or Seed Stitch background.

Right: Cable-Type Crossed Stitch. Left: Wrapped Crossed Stitch.

Right Wrapped Crossed Stitch

1. On nearside, insert needle into second stitch on left needle as to Knit, allowing tip to emerge on farside; wrap yarn and draw through new stitch.

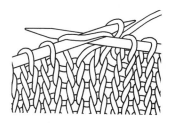

Right Wrapped Crossed Stitch: Step 1. Knit second stitch.

2. Knit first stitch; discard both stitches from left needle together.

Left Wrapped Crossed Stitch

While it is possible to do this in Knit, it is more difficult; if a left version is needed and your pattern permits, work on the inside of the fabric in Purl instead.

1. On farside, insert right needle into second stitch on left needle as to Purl (tip should pass under needle and emerge on nearside); wrap yarn and pull through new stitch.

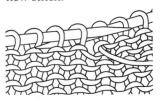

Left Wrapped Crossed Stitch: Step 1. Purl second stitch from farside.

2. Purl first stitch; discard both stitches from left needle together.

Rotated Crossed Stitches

Here is another way to make a Crossed Stitch, and it is related to the Rotated Cable; the two stitches are temporarily slipped together so they change places, and then they are worked. The right and left versions match reasonably well, but are slightly different structurally.

Right Rotated Crossed Stitch

The two stitches are crossed using a Slip Stitch technique that turns them at the same time; the Knit and Purl versions differ in how to work the turned stitches so they will not become Twist Stitches in the fabric.

Knit Version

1. Slip two stitches together by inserting right needle as for Knit Two Together. Stitches will cross; first stitch on left needle will then be first on right needle and both will be in turned position.
2. Return both stitches to left needle one at a time, maintaining their crossed and turned position.
3. Knit first and then second stitch farside; discard them together from left needle.

If you prefer, the stitches can be returned to standard position as they are transferred back to the left needle, in which case they can be worked nearside, but it is easier to do as described.

Purl Version

1. Slip two stitches by inserting right needle as for Knit Two Together.
2. Return both stitches to left needle, one at a time, inserting left needle tip into stitch on nearside from right to left to restore them to standard position.
3. Purl first stitch, and then second one.

Left Rotated Crossed Stitch

This is the same basic idea, but the stitches are slipped from the farside to cross them to the left.

Knit Version

1. Slip two stitches together by inserting right needle on farside from left to right.
2. Return both stitches to left needle, one at a time, inserting left needle tip into stitch on farside from right to left to restore them to standard position.
3. Knit first stitch, and then second one.

In this case, it is easiest to work the stitches if you "unturn" them as they are transferred back to the left needle.

Purl Version

1. Work Steps 1 and 2 as in Knit Version, above.
2. Purl first stitch, and then second one.

Multi-Stitch Cross-Over

The final variations possible with Crossed Stitch make use of more than two stitches. You could, for instance, Knit the fourth stitch, and then the first, second and third; or Knit the fourth, and then the third, second, and first. The stitches will bunch up to produce a knot-like effect, so this does not resemble either a true Crossed Stitch or a Cable, but it is attractive in its own way. To open it up a bit, enlarge the stitches first with an Elongation technique.

❖ *Cable Stitches*

As discussed above, the Cable technique is used to switch the positions of several stitches on the needle, and it creates far more dramatic patterns than the little Crossed Stitches do. The stitch columns of cable patterns look like they have been braided and they protrude boldly from the surface of the fabric.

A garment covered with the sinuous lines of cable stitches looks daunting to the knitter who has never tried to make one; however, these fabrics are more works of care and patience than of advanced skills. It is the complexity of the design and the need to follow the pattern accurately that sets the challenge, since the technique itself is quite simple (albeit slow and somewhat tedious to do).

A rich trove of cable patterns is available since the technique seems to invite creativity and elaboration—especially since the patterns are all remarkably compatible with one another and can readily be combined in novel arrangements. Furthermore, a garment made with these kinds of patterns is also quite practical because the fabric has a dense, resilient structure that is warm, supple, and durable.

Basic Cables

A cable pattern unit is comprised of two, three, or even four sets of adjacent stitch columns with a minimum of two stitches in each set. These stitches are worked plain for several rows and then on the pattern row, one set is drawn past another so they change places. To do this, the first set of stitches is temporarily removed from the left needle onto a holder of some sort while the second set is worked, and then the first set is worked in turn. There are endless variations on this theme, but nothing more complicated than that.

The small tool used for this technique is called a cable holder, or cable needle. There are two types; one has straight ends with a dip in the center for the stitches to nest in, the other is curved somewhat like a fish hook, and both have two tips; see Tools. The choice between them is a matter of preference; either will do the job, as will a plain, short knitting needle—toothpicks or even common nails could be used, and no doubt have been when the proper tool was not available, but they are less than ideal.

Cables are often done in Knit set on a Purl background and with few exceptions are not reversible. Patterns typically call for the cable step to be done on an outside row, where it is easy to see what to do. However, it is certainly possible to work on the inside of the fabric in Purl, so those instructions are included as well (however rarely they may be used). Nevertheless, any reference to the direction in which the cable crosses, to right or left, is as seen when looking at the outside of the fabric.

Once the cabled stitches are discarded into the fabric, those that remain visible are referred to as the "facing" stitches; those obscured behind them are called the "backing" stitches.

Right Cable

This cable unit is made up of four stitches; the two facing stitches will slope up to the right.

Knit Version

Work on the outside of the fabric, as follows:

1. Slip two stitches purlwise from left needle to cable holder and move it to farside.
2. Knit next two stitches on left needle.

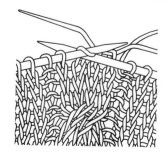

Basic Right Cable: Step 2. First set of stitches held on farside; knit second set.

3. Return two stitches from cable holder to left needle, and then Knit them; or, slide two stitches to other tip of cable holder and Knit them off directly.

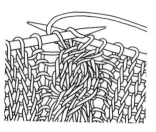

Basic Right Cable: Step 3. Knit set of stitches returned to left needle.

In Step 1, you can either drop the cable holder and allow it to hang from the fabric until needed, or pinch it against the fabric with your fingers if you are concerned it might slip out of the stitches.

Purl Version

This version is done on the inside in Purl; the cable will cross to the right on the outside of the fabric.

- Slip two stitches to cable holder and move it to farside. Purl next two stitches on left needle, then Purl stitches off cable holder, or return them to left needle and Purl.

Left Cable

In this case the two facing stitches will slope up to the left on the outside.

Knit Version

Work on the outside of the fabric, as follows:

1. Slip first two stitches purlwise from left needle to cable holder; retain it on nearside.
2. Knit next two stitches on left needle.

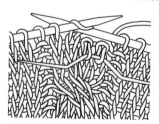

Basic Left Cable: Step 2. First set of stitches held on nearside; knit second set.

3. Return two stitches to left needle, and then Knit them; or slide them to other tip of the cable holder and Knit them off of it directly.

Basic Left Cable: Step 3. Knit stitches from cable holder.

Purl Version

This version is done on the inside in Purl; the cable will cross to the left when viewed from the outside.

- Slip two stitches to cable holder and retain it on nearside. Purl next two stitches on left needle, and then Purl two stitches on cable holder, or return them to left needle and Purl.

Tips for Working Cables

Working the stitches directly off the cable holder eliminates a step, and anything that makes the technique faster to do is worthwhile. The stitches are somewhat more secure on the hook-shaped holder; if you are using one of these, take the stitches onto the holder with the short end, and Knit them off the long end.

To make it easier to knit the stitches directly off the holder, slip them to the holder knitwise to turn them, and then, when the time comes, work them farside from the holder so they will not twist in the fabric.

Also note that as the two sets of stitches are pulled past each other, a gap may form to each side. To mitigate this, draw the yarn up firmly as you work the first stitch of the cable and the first stitch after the cable.

By the way, you can set the cable holder down when not needed, but fumbling for it under the seat cushions of the sofa will only slow you down that much more; stick it into your knitting where you can find it.

Basic Cable Stitch Patterns

In most Cables, both the facing and the backing stitches are worked in Knit with the Cable itself set off on a background of Purl or Seed Stitches. However, a Cable can also be done in Seed Stitch, or with a mixture of Seed and Stockinette set against a Purl background.

Alternatively, only the facing stitches of the cable might be done in Knit, with the backing stitches done in Purl so the latter blends in with the background. Instead of the customary plaited look of a traditional Cable, this creates a single raised, sinuous line that travels across the face of the fabric.

Using the same basic Cable techniques described above, it is also possible to cross two stitches over one, three over three, two over three, four over two, and many other combinations. An eight-stitch cable unit of four over four is generally the outside practical limit beyond which the stitches will not stretch (although you could use an Elongation technique first to make this possible). Instead, larger patterns are made with six or eight stitches cabled in pairs to make complex, intertwined plaits.

Written patterns use a variety of abbreviations to indicate which cable technique to use. I prefer a very simple notation

Four Rib Braid.
A pattern with right and left cables.

that serves for any type of cable; for instance, "RC 2/2" means the cable unit has four stitches, and two will be crossed to the right past the other two, while "LC 3/3" means three crossed to the left past the other three. Fortunately, charted Cable patterns are easy to read, and it is not difficult to learn how to modify an existing pattern or even design a new one; for more information, see Charted Stitch Patterns.

If you are designing a garment with cables, keep in mind that these highly textured patterns draw the fabric together widthwise, and will require more stitches per inch than fabrics that lie flatter; see Gauge for Multiple Patterns for more information; and, for information about how to position the stitch patterns on the garment, also see Coordinating Multiple Stitch Patterns.

Introduced Cables

Most cables run from the bottom to the top of the fabric, and the number of stitches needed for the width is the same for the full length of the fabric. However, Elsebeth Lavold, in her book *Viking Patterns for Knitting,*[†] presents patterns with cables that are introduced within the fabric; she starts them with pairs of Raised Increases, and ends them with pairs of decreases. The new stitches add volume so the cable can protrude; if this were not done, it would pull existing stitches together, making the overall fabric narrower.

---

† Elsebeth Lavold, *Viking Patterns for Knitting: Inspiration and Projects for Today's Knitter*, translated by Robin Orm Hansen (North Pomfret, Vt.: Trafalgar Square, 2000).

Seed Stitch Cable.

In order to have the new stitches in Knit on the outside of the fabric, and leave the Purl stitches of the background undisturbed, the Raised Increases may be done by working both the original and the new stitch as either Knit or Purl, or the two stitches may be mixed and worked as Knit/Purl, or as Purl/Knit. Which way to do the increases depends on their position and whether you are working on the inside or outside of the fabric.

Basic Introduced Cable

Here is how to introduce a four-stitch cable unit in this way. The instructions are for working flat, but once the concept is understood, working in the round should be no problem.

To Begin the Cable

1. Outside Row: At position of new cable work a Purl/Knit Left Raised Increase, and then a Knit/Purl Right Raised Increase on two background stitches.
2. Inside Row: Work two new stitches of cable unit in Purl (so they will be in Knit on the outside).
3. Outside Row: Work a Knit/Knit Left Raised Increase on first new cable stitch; work a Knit/Knit Right Raised Increase on second one.
4. To continue, work cable according to pattern.

Step 1 introduces two new Knit stitches between the original Purl background stitches. Step 3 introduces two more; the number of stitches in the Purl background remains the same.

To End the Cable

1. Outside Row: Work Knit Left Decrease on first pair of cable stitches, Knit Right Decrease on second pair; two stitches of cable remain.
2. Inside Row: Work a Purl Left Decrease joining a background stitch and a cable stitch, and then a Purl Right Decrease joining a cable stitch and a background stitch.

The beginning of the cable is done over three rows, the end is done over only two; if it seems appropriate, add a row between the latter two steps: Purl the two remaining cable stitches in Step 2, above, and work the final pair of decreases in Knit on the next row.

Alternative Introduced Cable

Here is a slight modification that I think gives a nice start to a cable of this kind.

1. On outside, work two background stitches in Knit to start new cable unit.
2. On inside, work a Purl/Purl Left Raised Increase and a Purl/Purl Right Raised Increase on these two stitches.

After working Step 2 there will be four Knit stitches for the cable; the outer ones were background stitches, the two in the center are increases.

If you think two new stitches for the cable are sufficient, begin the pattern. If you prefer to add two more, use one of the following options:

- On outside, Knit first stitch of cable unit, on second stitch work Knit/Purl Left Raised Increase, on third stitch a Purl/Knit Right Raised Increase, and Knit last stitch.

  This places a pair of Purl stitches in the center of the four-stitch cable unit, which pushes the right and left sides apart.
- To add background stitches at each side, instead of in between the new cable stitches, work a Purl/Knit Right Raised Increase on the first of the four stitches, and a Knit/Purl Left Raised Increase on the last.

Other Cable Techniques

Here are some variations on the basic Cable technique. One is reversible, the second has three sets of stitches, the next intersperses the stitches with one another, and in the last one they simply spin around front to back.

Reversible Ribbed Cable

Most cables only look good on the Knit side, but it is possible to make a reversible one by doing it in Single Rib. Because columns of Knit stitches naturally close over columns of Purl stitches in a ribbing, and because what is Knit on one

Ribbed Cable on Seed Stitch Ground.

side is Purl on the other, the cable on both sides of the fabric will appear to be made up only of Knit stitches. This illusion is encouraged by the tight waist of the cable so even the rows in between will look the same. In every other respect, this is a conventional cable.

However, there are two limitations.

First, there is not much choice as to size because the minimum number of stitches that is effective is eight—a four-over-four cable. Any more than that would be difficult to manage, and any less is not effective.

When the eight stitches are done in Single Rib, four will be Knit, four will be Purl. The four Knit stitches belong to the cable on one side; the four worked as Purl will appear as Knit on the reverse and belong to the cable on that side. Once the cable has been made and the two sets of four stitches are pulled tightly past one another, the result looks quite like a normal four-stitch cable, crossed two-over-two on both sides.

The second limitation has to do with the background. Most cables are set against Purl because it highlights them so well. However, that will not work here because what is Purl on one side is Knit on the other, and the cable with the Knit background would simply blend in with it and lose distinction. The solution is to use Seed Stitch for the background since it is the same on both sides and contrasts well with the Knit stitches of the cable. It can be tricky to do this, however, because both the cable and the background patterns alternate Knit and Purl; it helps to place Ring Markers on either side of the cable stitches.

Or make the entire fabric in Single Rib; this produces a very soft effect and is easier to do. To provide more contrast between the cables and the background, stretch the fabric slightly widthwise when dressing it to open up the ribbing (see Dressing a Fabric).

Axis Cables

These Cables are made with three sets of stitches; the center stitch or stitches remain in position while only the ones at each side cross; this is done with two cable holders.

Center Stitches on Nearside

This is a six-stitch cable with the pairs of flanking stitches crossing behind the two stitches in the center.

1. Slip two stitches to first cable holder and move to farside; slip two stitches to second cable holder and retain on nearside.
2. Knit two stitches from left needle.
3. Knit two stitches from cable holder on nearside; Knit two remaining stitches from cable holder on farside.

Center Stitches on Farside

Here the two pairs of flanking stitches cross on the outside, in front of the two stitches in the center.

1. Slip two stitches to first cable holder and retain on nearside; slip two stitches to second cable holder and move to farside.

Chain Link—an Axis-type Cable.

2. Knit two stitches from left needle.

3. Knit two stitches from cable holder on farside; Knit two remaining stitches from cable holder on nearside.

Interspersed Cables

Here is another interesting cable variation, in which a number of stitches are transferred to the cable holder and then interspersed with stitches on the left needle one by one.

These instructions are written for working all stitches in Knit, but the effect can be heightened if the facing stitches are worked in Knit and the backing stitches are worked in Purl.

Left Interspersed Cable

1. Transfer up to four stitches to cable holder and retain on nearside.

2. [Knit one stitch from left needle, Knit one stitch from right side of cable holder]; repeat between brackets until all stitches on holder are interspersed with equal number on left needle.

Right Interspersed Cable

- Follow the steps as for Left Interspersed Cable, but move cable holder to farside.

Rotated Cables

Here is an interesting, simple way to make a cable. It has a narrower waist than the others because the outside stitches trade places; there will be gaps at either side, which should be considered part of the effect. If it seems too tight, use an Elongation technique on the stitches of the cable unit when working the previous row.

Rotated Cable patterns.

1. Transfer four stitches to cable holder.

2. Turn cable holder to left or to right, so stitches do an "about face."

3. Knit all stitches off cable holder.

The stitches will be tight, so do not try to return them to the left needle.

You might also try this with either three or five stitches done in Single Rib to make it reversible.

CHAPTER 11

Increase and Decrease Techniques

Increases and Decreases are specialized stitch techniques with a wide variety of practical and decorative applications. In their most basic form, they are used to shape a garment—increases add new stitches to the number already on the needle, which makes the fabric wider; decreases remove stitches, making it narrower. You will find a detailed discussion of how they are used for these purposes in the chapter Shaping a Fabric.

However, the same techniques are also used in a great many decorative stitch patterns, and, when used in these ways, Increases and Decreases are always paired to prevent any change in the number of stitches on the needle. A pattern may consist only of these pairs, or they may be combined with any number of other stitch techniques. You will find an extensive discussion of the various ways in which these techniques can be applied following the instructions.

As you will see, there are quite a few Increases. Some are highly decorative, others are more subtle, but they all have their uses. There are considerably fewer Decreases, and most of them have quieter personalities; nevertheless, there are good reasons to choose one over another in particular circumstances, and in the right setting they may be a prominent visual element in a pattern. You should feel free to change the technique used in a pattern if it would make it easier to work or produce a more satisfying outcome.

There are Knit and Purl versions of all of these techniques, and many of them also make use of the concepts discussed in Turned Stitches. In addition, there are "single" and "double" as well as "multiple" versions of the techniques that make it possible to add or remove more than one stitch in a single place; before going on to the instructions, I want to clarify these terms because they can be a bit confusing.

Counting Stitches

- To make a "single" increase, two new stitches are worked on one existing stitch; one of the new stitches replaces the discard stitch, and the other one increases the total number of stitches on the needle.

  In other words, the term "single" refers to the results—how many stitches are added to or subtracted from the total number on the needle—not how many stitches are made in one position.

- It is also possible to make a single increase on a running thread, the strand that lies between two stitches. In this case, only one new stitch is made because there was none in that position before; in other words, there is no discard stitch to replace.

- A Yarnover is a special form of a running thread increase; it is made between two stitches and adds one new stitch to the total number on the needle.

  In the next row, the Yarnover is treated as if it were a normal stitch; if a single increase is made on it, two new stitches are needed: one replaces the discarded Yarnover strand, and the other is the increase.

- To make a "double" increase, three stitches are worked on an existing stitch or a Yarnover; one to replace the discard stitch and two that add to the number on the needle.

  If a "double" increase is used on a running thread, only two new stitches are made, because both add to the number on the needle. Here again, the word "double" refers not to how many stitches are worked, but to how many are added to or subtracted from the total number on the needle.

- Decreases work in the same way but in reverse. A "single" decrease involves reducing two stitches to one; a "double" decrease involves reducing three stitches to one.

- Finally, a "multiple" increase or decrease simply means that the technique is used to add or subtract more stitches than a "double," but the number varies and needs to be specified in the pattern instructions.

Increases

It may seem as if there are a great many increases, but most of the variations are no more than ways to work a technique in Knit or Purl, or to the right or left of a stitch. These may seem to be minor differences, but they can be very important.

For instance, the appearance of a stitch pattern can be radically altered by nothing more than changing from one version of a technique to another. Or it may be difficult to use one type of increase in close proximity to a certain stitch technique, while another might work fine. And when used for shaping, a particular increase technique might be quite obvious when used in one setting, yet blend in nicely in a different one.

The first four techniques discussed here (Bar, Rib, Raised, and Understitch) are all done by working more than once into an existing stitch. The others are worked between two stitches, which is in many respects much simpler.

❖ Bar Increases

The "bar" in the name of this technique refers to what looks like a Purl nub that lies below one of the two new stitches formed by the increase. As you will see, this is not done with the Purl technique, but occurs because the head of the discard stitch twists on itself. There is also a tiny hole under the bar and these two features make the increase quite noticeable in a smooth fabric, but it is less so in a highly textured one.

These qualities can be used to decorative advantage when multiple increases are set row by row in close proximity. In contrast, this increase can be quite unobtrusive when used with a stitch pattern that includes a combination of Knit and Purl stitches where the "bar" will blend in.

Single Bar Increases

The first version, below, is very easy to do, while all the others require several extra steps and are, therefore, only used when necessary.

Knit Left Bar Increase

There will be two new stitches on the right needle: the right one will have a Knit below it, while the left one will have the "bar" that looks like a Purl.

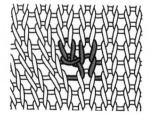

Knit Left Bar Increase.

1. Knit into first stitch on left needle; do not discard.
2. Knit into same stitch on farside; discard.

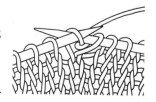

Knit Left Bar Increase: Step 2. Knit into same stitch on farside.

Purl Left Bar Increase

This version is done on the inside; on the outside, it will look like the Knit Left version.

1. Purl 1 farside; discard stitch will twist to left.
2. Move left needle tip to farside and insert from left to right into discard stitch below right needle and pick up right side of stitch; with strand on needle in standard position, Purl.

Knit Right Bar Increase

In this case, the right stitch will have what looks like a Purl below it, while the left one has a Knit.

1. Slip 1 knitwise; replace turned stitch on left needle.
2. Knit turned stitch nearside and discard; discard stitch will twist to the right.
3. On nearside, insert left needle tip from right to left into discard stitch below right needle and lift stitch up; right side of lifted stitch will be on nearside of needle; Knit as if it were a normal stitch.

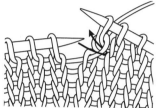

Knit Right Bar Increase: Step 3. Knit into discard stitch.

Purl Right Bar Increase

Here again, this is done on the inside of the fabric; the result will look like the Knit Right version on the outside.

1. Slip 1 stitch knitwise; replace turned stitch on left needle.
2. Purl turned stitch farside; do not discard.
3. Purl into nearside of same stitch and discard.

> **By the way . . .**
> *There were only two Bar Increases in the first edition of this book: the Knit Left and Purl Right versions, above; their partners here are new. Also, there was a Turned Bar Increase in the previous edition, included because it seemed to make the little hole below the bar smaller, but I no longer think this is the case and have dropped it.*

Double Bar Increase

The Double Bar Increase is similar to the single version, but the results are distinct. In this case, the discard stitch is crossed on itself several times, which clusters the new stitches tightly together at their base. In some stitch patterns this is just what is wanted, but if the result seems too tight, you can substitute a Double Rib Increase or a Knit Double Yarnover Increase and either will leave things a bit more relaxed.

Work this increase in the same way on a stitch or a Yarnover.

- In a single stitch, Knit or Purl into the nearside, the farside, and then the nearside again.

Paired Bar Increases

This is only a double increase by virtue of proximity; it is no more than two Single Bar Increases placed side-by-side. The technique is especially nice when the arrangement is repeated in a vertical column because it creates the illusion of a center stitch flanked by the two little bars. While the bars are really to the left of each stitch of the pair, one will fall to the left of the second stitch and the other to the right of it, making it the center of attention while the first stitch goes unnoticed.

- Work a Knit Left Bar Increase into each of next two stitches.

You can, of course, take this concept and use it in other ways:

- Work a Knit Left Bar Increase followed by a Knit Right Bar Increase; bars of two increases will sit side-by-side.
- Work a Knit Right Bar Increase followed by a Knit Left Bar Increase; bars of two increases will be separated by two Knit stitches.

❖ Rib Increases

A Rib Increase is made in nearly the same way as the Bar Increase, but the result is quite different and more decorative because it stretches the discard stitch open, leaving a larger Eyelet-like hole in the fabric.

Single Rib Increase

Whether this increase is worked on a stitch or Yarnover, it will add one new stitch to those on the needle. It can also be worked on a running thread, in which case it functions as a double increase, adding two new stitches; see Double Running Thread Increases.

1. Knit 1; do not discard.
2. Yarn nearside, Purl into same stitch, and then discard.

Single Rib Increase: Step 2. Move yarn nearside and Purl same stitch.

Needless to say, this technique can certainly be done with a Purl stitch first and a Knit stitch second, so work in whichever way seems most compatible with the stitch pattern you are using. The variations produce stitches with an identical structure, one the mirror-image of the other—if you work the increase on the outside using a Knit stitch first, a Knit stitch will be the first of the pair on the inside, as well.

Either way, there will be a small nub between the two new stitches, formed where the yarn switches from one side to the other for the second stitch. This nub will be more obvious when the increase is worked at a loose tension; when done on a Yarnover, it can sometimes cause an Eyelet to look somewhat heart-shaped.

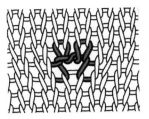 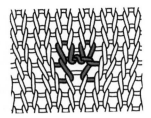

Knit/Purl Single Rib Increase.

Purl/Knit Single Rib Increase.

Double Rib Increase

The double version of a Rib Increase leaves a larger opening in the fabric, which is why it is commonly used in Eyelet and Lace patterns. The base of the new stitches will have a ridge where the yarn has passed back and forth between each stitch. For an alternative that softens the effect, see the Multiple Yarnover Increase, below, which can be used as a substitute in any pattern that calls for this technique.

Whether worked on a stitch or a Yarnover, this increase will add two new stitches to the number on the needle.

- Work three times into a single stitch: yarn farside, Knit; yarn nearside, Purl; yarn farside, Knit.

If necessary to blend in with surrounding pattern, work Purl, Knit, Purl instead.

For another variation, see Rib Increase on a Running Thread, below.

Multiple Rib Increase

This version is done in the same way as the Double version, above. Whether worked on a stitch or Yarnover, this increase will make five new stitches on one, increasing the number on the needle by four; the technique is not used on a running thread because it is too tight.

Always bring yarn farside for a Knit stitch, nearside for a Purl stitch.

- Work five times into a single stitch: Knit, Purl, Knit, Purl, Knit.

To blend in with a surrounding pattern, of course, you can start and end the sequence with Purl instead.

❖ Raised Increases

Instead of working twice into one stitch, as with the Bar or the Rib Increases, in this case, you will work into both the stitch on the left needle and the one below it. The appearance of the increase will change depending upon whether you work into the one below from the right or left side of the original stitch.

A Raised Increase is very unobtrusive; therefore, it is an excellent technique to use in almost any situation where you do not want to call attention to the change in the fabric. It is also a good choice for a color pattern, because you can use different yarns for each stitch of the increase. There are several variations of both the Single and Double versions.

Single Raised Increases

The technique is easiest to do on the right side of the original stitch; it is slightly more complicated to work on the left side, so those versions are only used when necessary. Because the technique requires working into a stitch in the row below, it cannot be used in every row of the same stitch column; when necessary to work on the next row, shift the increase to an adjacent stitch column.

The instructions are written for working one or both of the stitches involved in the increase in either Knit or Purl, so you can blend it in with the surrounding pattern or work on the inside or outside of the fabric. And as you will see, the technique is done in a slightly different way depending upon whether there is a Knit or Purl stitch below the first stitch on the left needle.

In all cases, work as close to the tips of the needles as possible to avoid stretching out the stitch on which the increase is made, and shift the yarn to the nearside or farside of the needle in the usual way before a Knit or Purl stitch.

Right Raised Increases

These versions are used when increasing on the right side of a stitch.

Knit Version

Use this version if there is a Knit stitch below the first stitch on the left needle.

1. Move right needle to farside and insert it up under Purl nub below first stitch on left needle; raise this stitch onto left needle with right side of strand on nearside of needle. Original stitch is now second on left needle.

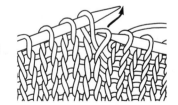

Knit Right Raised Increase: Step 1. Lift stitch below onto left needle.

2. Knit or Purl raised stitch, discard; Knit or Purl original stitch and discard.

If necessary, pull original stitch slightly to left in order to work the first stitch.

If you find the original stitch stretches out too much, try this method:

- Insert right needle tip down into Purl nub below first stitch on left needle (do not lift stitch onto left needle); wrap yarn as to Knit and draw new stitch through; or, insert right needle tip up under Purl nub and Purl.

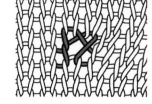

Knit Right Raised Increase.

The challenge is to insert the needle cleanly into the stitch below without splitting the yarn or catching any of the stitch above. It helps to use your left thumb to push the fabric below the needle up on the farside so you can see the target better.

Purl Version

Use this version if there is a Purl stitch below the first stitch on the left needle.

1. On nearside, insert right needle tip up under Purl nub below first stitch on left needle, raise stitch up and place on left needle in turned position.
2. Knit or Purl raised stitch farside, and then Knit or Purl stitch above it nearside.

Or, try the following alternative:

- Insert right needle down into Purl nub, wrap yarn and Purl; or, insert right needle up under Purl nub, and Knit farside; then Knit or Purl stitch above.

Left Raised Increases

In order to place the increase on the left side of the original stitch, the latter must be worked first; the stitch to raise will then be found two rows below the right needle, under the discard stitch.

Knit Version

Use this version if there is a Knit stitch below the first stitch on the left needle.

1. Knit or Purl first stitch on left needle and discard.
2. Move left needle tip to farside and insert up under Purl nub of stitch two rows below right needle (below discard stitch); raise stitch up in turned position, with left side of stitch on nearside.

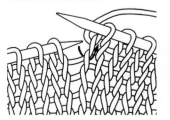

Knit Left Raised Increase: Step 2.

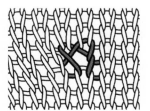

Knit Left Raised Increase.

3. Knit or Purl raised stitch farside.

The turned stitch is worked farside to prevent it from twisting (see Twist Stitches).

Purl Version

Use this version if there is a Purl stitch below the first stitch on the left needle.

1. Knit or Purl stitch in position of increase and discard.
2. On nearside, insert left needle tip up under Purl nub of stitch two rows below new stitch on right needle and raise it in standard position, with right side of stitch on nearside.
3. Knit or Purl raised stitch.

Slip Raised Increase

In some situations, this variation may produce a slightly more subtle result; try it and see if it works for you.

- For right version, Knit or Purl raised stitch, and then Slip original stitch with yarn stranded on inside of fabric.

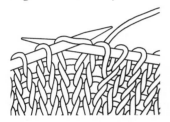

Slip Raised Increase. Knit stitch after increase; strand yarn on inside.

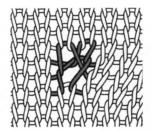

Slip Raised Increase.

- For left version, Slip original stitch with yarn stranded on inside, and then raise stitch one row below and Knit or Purl.

Unlike the Left Raised Increase, above, in this version the original stitch is not worked; therefore, the stitch into which you increase is only one row down, not two.

Double Raised Increases

Several variations of the Raised Increase can be used to place three stitches where one had been. Each has a unique appearance that can be enhanced further when a series is placed in a vertical column; this can only be done every other row.

Double Raised Increases. Right: Version One. Left: Version Two. Decreases in center.

Version One

This version leaves a tiny hole in the fabric.

- Work a Right Raised Increase into first stitch on left needle; with two new stitches now on right needle, work a Left Raised Increase into other side of same stitch below, now two rows down.

Version Two

A very slight change in method makes a rather large difference in the outcome; in this case the center stitch is twisted and it pulls everything together very neatly.

- Work Right Raised Increase below first stitch on left needle; Knit stitch above farside and discard; with two new stitches now on right needle, work Left Raised Increase into other side of same stitch below, now two rows down.

Version Three

This is not technically a double increase because it requires more than one base stitch, but it serves the same purpose. The result is a center column of distinctive vertical strands; it is attractive, tailored, and has no holes.

Double Raised Increases. Right: Version Three. Left: Version Four. Decreases in center.

- On three stitches, work a Left Raised Increase on first stitch, Knit center stitch, and then work a Right Raised Increase on third stitch.

Version Four

This version requires two base stitches, and it produces what looks almost like a column of Slip stitches.

- On two stitches, work a Left Raised Increase on first stitch, and a Right Raised Increase on next one.

❖ Understitch Increase

This simple technique is worked in a manner very similar to the Raised Increase, although it is considerably easier to do. Instead of being unobtrusive, however, it creates an opening and tends to thicken the fabric below the new stitch. This may be desirable with some highly textured stitch patterns; however, if you want the opening but not the bulk, a Rib Increase or the Open Running Thread Increase might be a better choice.

Right Understitch Increase

- Insert right needle tip from nearside to farside into center of stitch below first stitch on left needle, wrap yarn and Knit; Knit or Purl stitch on needle.

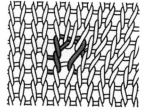

Right Understitch Increase.

Left Understitch Increase

This is more awkward to do, and would be used only when necessary.

- Knit or Purl stitch to be increased, insert left needle from nearside to farside into center of stitch below discarded stitch (two rows below needle), and then insert right needle into this stitch as well; wrap yarn and Knit. For Purl, insert needle from farside to nearside instead.

❖ Running Thread Increases

This is a very common increase. The new stitch is worked on the running thread, the strand that passes horizontally between two stitches. The result in the fabric is structurally the same as a Yarnover; however, it is made in a different way and the opening it can leave in the fabric will be smaller.

Single Running Thread Increases

The Open version leaves a small hole in the fabric that can be used for decorative effect, especially when several increases are placed in close proximity. The Twist version closes the hole, but still has a distinctive, if more subtle appearance; it will be visible in a smooth fabric, but less so in a textured one.

Open Running Thread Increase

This increase can be done using both needles or just one. The latter may be quicker to do in certain circumstances, but it can sometimes prove difficult to draw the new stitch under the running thread without the help of the second needle.

Two-Needle Version

- Insert left needle tip from nearside to farside under running thread that lies between needle tips and pick up strand with right side on nearside of needle; Knit or Purl into strand as for a normal stitch.

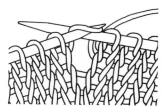

Single Running Thread Increase with two needles. Knit into lifted strand.

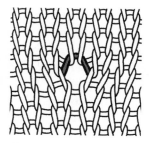

Running Thread Increase.

One-Needle Version

There are two ways to work; choose whichever one works best for you.

- Yarn farside, insert right needle under running thread from nearside to farside, wrap yarn and Knit.
- Or, yarn nearside, insert right needle under running thread from farside to nearside, wrap yarn and Purl.

Twisted Running Thread Increase

Twisting the running thread on itself produces a quiet, attractive little increase. When several are placed in close proximity, they can be used for a subtle decorative effect.

Because there is so little yarn in a running thread, the resulting stitch is rather tight and may be more obvious in the fabric than when a similar increase is made on a Yarnover strand.

The Left Twist version is easiest to do; therefore, the Right Twist version is only used when its appearance is more compatible with a nearby stitch technique or an adjacent edge.

Left Twist Version

- Insert left needle tip under running thread from nearside to farside to pick it up in standard position, with right side on nearside of needle. Knit or Purl strand farside.

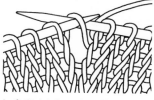

Left Twist Running Thread Increase. Knit into farside of lifted strand.

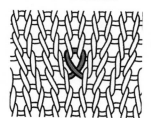

Left Twist Running Thread Increase.

To make this easier to do, hold the needle tips close together to reduce the tension on the running thread.

Right Twist Version

- Insert left needle under running thread from farside to nearside to pick up strand in turned position, with left side on nearside of needle. Knit or Purl strand nearside.

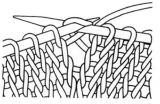

Right Twist Running Thread Increase. Knit into nearside of turned strand.

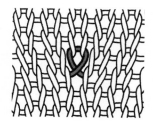

Right Twist Running Thread Increase.

Double Running Thread Increases

A pair of Running Thread Increases on either side of a stitch make a very effective double increase and, depending upon how this is done, the result varies from subtle to decorative. When it is necessary to make two new stitches on a single running thread, the Rib Increase works best.

Paired Running Thread Increases

One or another of the versions below are commonly seen in Chevron patterns, where they are set in vertical columns. When used individually, their appearance will be less dramatic, but still distinctive; simply choose whichever one blends in best with the surrounding stitch pattern.

Version One

This produces two columns of tiny Eyelets flanking a center stitch.

Paired Running Thread Increases. Right: Version One. Center: Version Two. Left: Version Three. Columns in between contain decreases.

- Work an Open Running Thread Increase on either side of a center Knit stitch.

Version Two

This is only slightly different, but the center stitch column looks tighter and neater.

- Work as above, but Knit center stitch farside so it will twist to the left.

Version Three

Here is a very attractive version, with a slightly embossed and elongated center column of stitches; the Eyelets have virtually disappeared. This is handsome in Chevron patterns and makes a beautiful foldline for a Bias Facing.

- Work as above; Slip center stitch.

Version Four

In this case the center column of stitches has a somewhat beaded look, since one stitch is prominent and rounded, while the one above it is very tiny.

Right: Paired Running Thread Increases. Version Four. Left: Rib Increase on a Running Thread. Column in between contains decreases.

- Work a Right Twist Running Thread Increase; Knit one; work a Left Twist Running Thread Increase.

Rib Increase on a Running Thread

This decorative increase leaves an opening in the fabric; the technique is a single increase, but when done on a running thread, it adds two new stitches where none were before.

- Insert left needle under running thread from nearside to farside; work a Knit/Purl or Purl/Knit Single Rib Increase on strand, as necessary to blend it in with the surrounding pattern.

❖ Yarnovers

A Yarnover is made by passing the yarn over the needle between one stitch and the next, which in effect elongates the running thread. This adds the equivalent of a new, neutral stitch to the right needle, which will be given a particular form in the fabric only when it is worked on the next row.

If it is then worked so it remains open, the Yarnover strand will be drawn up, leaving a hole beneath the new stitch, which is known more politely (and more deservedly) as an Eyelet. If the strand is worked farside so it twists, it tends to relax into the fabric somewhat because of the extra yarn it contains, and looks more like a normal Twist Stitch than if the same thing is done with a Twisted Running Thread Increase. The strand can be twisted to the right or the left, depending upon what looks best within a stitch pattern or in relation to a nearby edge; to twist it to the right, the Yarnover strand needs to be turned on the needle; see Twist Stitches.

A Yarnover has two somewhat contradictory roles to play. It serves as a very simple increase technique; however, it is less often used for shaping than for decorative purposes where either of its two attributes, the hole it can make and/or the strand itself contribute something to the effect created. In these situations it is always paired with a decrease to prevent any change in the number of stitches on the needle.

With a decrease as its constant companion, the Yarnover then becomes the primary technique used to create all of the astonishing variety and beauty of knitted lace (see Eyelets,

Mesh, and Lace). It also appears in many other types of stitch patterns where its presence may be far more subtle.

Many pattern instructions that specify a Yarnover do not indicate exactly how to make it. While it is very easy to do, the motions used to pass the yarn over the needle are somewhat different depending upon what sort of stitch precedes and follows it. Furthermore, there are subtle differences in how to make a Yarnover depending on whether you hold the yarn to the right or left; this has been taken into consideration in the instructions.

Basic Yarnovers

While these formulas may look like a lot to keep in mind, common sense should serve you well. The important thing to remember is that a Yarnover should sit on the needle in the same position as a normal stitch, with the right side of the strand on the nearside; a quick look will reveal whether it is on the needle correctly. (In certain circumstances, the Yarnover will need to be in turned position on the needle, but this is an exception and will always be specified in a pattern.)

Knit-to-Knit Yarnover

Knit the stitch preceding the Yarnover, and then work in one of the following ways, depending on how the yarn is held.

- If yarn is held to right, move it between needle tips to nearside and Knit next stitch. Yarn will automatically pass over needle to farside, forming Yarnover.
- If yarn is held to left, move right needle over and down farside of yarn, and then under it to nearside; yarn will now be on top of needle, forming Yarnover. Knit 1. If necessary, hold Yarnover back from tip of right needle to Knit stitch.

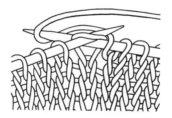

Knit-to-Knit Yarnover. Bring yarn to nearside, Knit next stitch.

Knit-to-Purl Yarnover

Knit the stitch preceding the Yarnover and then work in one of the following ways, depending on how the yarn is held.

- If yarn is held to right, move it to nearside between needle tips, over needle to farside, and then back between needles to nearside again. Purl 1.

Knit-to-Purl Yarnover. Bring yarn to nearside and wrap around needle to nearside again; Purl next stitch.

- If yarn is held to left, move right needle over yarn to farside, under to nearside, and then over to farside again. Purl 1. If necessary, hold Yarnover back from needle tip to Purl stitch.

The wrap in Step 2 is a long way around—give it a good tug or the Yarnover may be larger than desirable.

Purl-to-Purl Yarnover

Purl the stitch preceding the Yarnover and then work in one of the following ways, depending on how the yarn is held.

- If yarn is held to right, pass it over right needle to farside, and then between needle tips to nearside again. Purl 1.
- If yarn is held to left, move right needle under yarn to nearside, and then up and over it to farside again. With yarn on nearside, Purl 1.

Purl-to-Purl Yarnover. With yarn on nearside, wrap yarn around needle to nearside again; Purl next stitch.

Purl-to-Knit Yarnover

Purl the stitch preceding the Yarnover and then work in one of the following ways, depending on how the yarn is held.

- If yarn is held to right, retain it on nearside and Knit next stitch. Yarn will pass over needle to farside, forming Yarnover.

Purl-to-Knit Yarnover. With yarn on nearside, Knit next stitch.

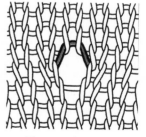

Yarnover Increase.

- If yarn is held to left, move right needle under yarn to nearside; yarn will pass over needle to farside; Knit next stitch.

Turned Yarnovers

When a Yarnover is used as a basic increase, it is normally twisted to the right or left to close up the hole it would otherwise leave in the fabric. This is done in the same way as described for a normal stitch; see Twist Stitches.

Working a Left Twist is quite straightforward; simply Knit or

Purl a stitch or a Yarnover that is in standard position by inserting the right needle into it on the farside. However, a Right Twist requires turning a stitch or Yarnover on the needle first and then working it as to Knit or Purl by inserting the right needle into it on the nearside (for a general explanation, see Turned Stitches). You might do this if you want mirror-image increases in a fabric, and it also is called for in some specialty applications.

The Yarnover can be turned immediately before it is worked by slipping it to the right needle knitwise and then slipping it back to the left needle in the turned position. Or it can be put on the needle in the turned position as it is made by wrapping the yarn in the opposite direction from that described above; this is sometimes more convenient. Work as follows:

- Knit-to-Knit Turned Yarnover: Wrap yarn over needle to nearside and then under needle to farside; Knit next stitch.
- Knit-to-Purl Turned Yarnover: Maintain yarn on farside and Purl next stitch; it will automatically pass over needle to form Yarnover.
- Purl-to-Purl Turned Yarnover: Bring yarn between needles to farside and then Purl next stitch; yarn will automatically pass over needle to form Yarnover.
- Purl-to-Knit Turned Yarnover: Bring yarn between needles to farside, over needle to nearside, and then between needles to farside again; Knit next stitch.

Double Yarnovers

Some stitch patterns require an elongated Yarnover strand, either to make a larger opening in the fabric or because the strand will be used in a way that makes this necessary. To do this, simply wrap the yarn twice around the needle; on the next row, drop the extra wrap before working the Yarnover in one way or another.

It is a very simple procedure to wrap the yarn more than once, but as with the basic method, everything depends on the nature of the stitch before and after the Yarnover. If a stitch technique requires more than two wraps, it will be specified in the pattern and requires no more than repeating the wrapping step described below.

Knit-to-Knit Double Yarnover

Knit the stitch preceding the Yarnover, and then work in one of the following ways.

- If yarn is held to right, move it between needle tips to nearside, over needle to farside, and then back between tips of needle to nearside. Knit next stitch; yarn will pass over needle to form second Yarnover.
- If yarn is held to left, move right needle over and down

farside of yarn, and then under it to nearside; repeat a second time forming double wrap. Knit 1.

Knit-to-Purl Double Yarnover

Knit the stitch preceding the Yarnover, and then work in one of the following ways.

- If yarn is held to right, move it between needles to nearside, over needle to farside, and then back between needle tips to nearside; repeat a second time to form two full wraps. Purl next stitch.
- If yarn is held to left, move right needle over it to farside, under to nearside, and repeat for second wrap; hold wraps away from needle tip with right fingertip. With yarn now on nearside of both needles, move right needle to farside of yarn again and then insert into stitch on left needle and Purl.

Purl-to-Purl Double Yarnover

Purl the stitch preceding the Yarnover, and then work in one of the following ways.

- With yarn held to right, wrap it over needle to farside and then back between needle tips to nearside. Repeat a second time to form two full wraps. Purl next stitch.
- With yarn held to left and on nearside, move right needle under it to nearside, and then over and under it again; with yarn now on nearside of both needles, hold Yarnovers back with fingertip, move right needle to farside of yarn again, and then insert it into stitch on left needle and Purl.

Purl-to-Knit Double Yarnover

Purl the stitch preceding the Yarnover, and then work in one of the following ways.

- With yarn held to right, wrap it over needle to farside and then back between needle tips to nearside; Knit next stitch; yarn will pass over needle to form second Yarnover.
- If yarn is held to left, pass needle under it to nearside, over to farside, and under to nearside again; with yarn now on farside of both needles, hold Yarnovers out of way with fingertip, insert right needle into stitch and Knit.

Specialized Yarnover Increases

Here are a few specialized forms of the Yarnover that can be used in one way or another as increases in decorative stitch patterns.

Half-Hitch Increase

This is another variation on the Running Thread/Yarnover theme. Instead of using a plain Yarnover to elongate the strand, you can use Simple Cast-On instead. This adds a tiny bit more yarn to the strand because it is twisted on itself as it is being put on the needle.

Right Twist Version

1. Wrap yarn on thumb as for Simple Right Half-Hitch Cast-On; add new stitch to right needle.
2. On next row, work in one of following ways:
   - To cross strand, Knit or Purl nearside.
   - To leave strand open, Knit or Purl farside.

Left Twist Version

1. Wrap yarn on thumb as for Simple Left Half-Hitch Cast-On; add new stitch to right needle.
2. On next row, work in one of following ways:
   - To cross strand, Knit or Purl farside.
   - To leave strand open, Knit or Purl nearside.

Crossed Stitch Yarnover Increase

This is a new increase that I am quite pleased with. It is ideal for use in situations where there will be Right or Left Decreases nearby, since the two techniques are rather compatible in appearance and structure. It is also an excellent choice for use with a Knit-Together Crossed Stitch technique, because this is no more than a variation of it; if you tuck this increase into a pattern of that kind just right, it will be nearly invisible.

Only the Knit versions of the technique are included here, but it is also possible to work in Purl, if necessary. The instructions for the Knit-Together Crossed Stitch are accompanied by illustrations that should help you understand how they can be turned into increases, and will also make clear how to work the Purl versions.

Note that the technique can only be done in the same position every other row, and it requires two stitches as a base, not one, as is the case with other increases.

Right Crossed Version

1. Knit Two Together; do not discard.
2. Tighten first new stitch on right needle and move yarn nearside for Yarnover; Knit first stitch of pair again; discard. There are three new stitches on right needle; one in middle is Yarnover.
3. On return row, Purl Yarnover farside to cross it, or nearside to leave it open.

Left Crossed Version

1. Slip two stitches knitwise, and return them to left needle in turned position. Knit second stitch farside; do not discard.
2. Tighten new stitch on right needle and move yarn

nearside for Yarnover; Knit both stitches together farside; discard. There are three new stitches on right needle; one in middle is Yarnover.
3. On return row, Purl Yarnover farside to cross it, or nearside to leave it open.

Double Yarnover Increase

This technique can be worked on a stitch, on another Yarnover that was made in the previous row, or on a running thread. It is often used as one step in a more complex technique, and it is common in lace patterns.

There will be three new stitches; if worked on a stitch or a Yarnover, one replaces the discarded stitch and two are additions; if worked on a running thread, three are added to the number on the needle. There is a Knit version and a Purl version.

Knit Version

This version will have two Knit stitches flanking what looks like a little Purl nub in the center.

- Knit; retain stitch or strand on left needle. Move yarn to nearside for Yarnover, Knit same stitch again; discard stitch or strand from left needle; there are three new stitches on right needle; one in middle is a Yarnover.

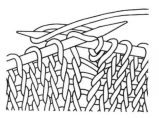

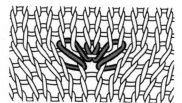

Knit Double Yarnover. First stitch and Yarnover on right needle; Knit same stitch again.

Double Yarnover Increase.

Purl Version

This version will have two Purl stitches flanking a Knit stitch in the center. Use it on the inside of the fabric, or on the outside if that would make it blend in better with the surrounding stitch pattern.

- Yarn nearside, Purl stitch or strand on left needle; do not discard. Make Purl-to-Purl Yarnover, and then Purl same stitch or strand; discard.

Work with a firm tension, because a Yarnover made this way is slightly larger than others.

Multiple Yarnover Increase on Stitch

With this version, there will be five new stitches on the right needle: three stitches with Yarnovers between them. One of the new stitches replaces the discard stitch, so there will be four additional stitches on the needle.

- Knit; retain stitch on left needle; yarn nearside for Yarnover, Knit same stitch again; yarn nearside for Yarnover, Knit; discard stitch from left needle.

Multiple Yarnover Increase on Yarnover

This version is somewhat more complicated to do, but makes it possible to add three new stitches to the number on the needle. It is done on a Yarnover that was made in the previous row, and starts with a Double Yarnover Increase, above, but adds an extra step.

There are two versions: one if the increase is followed by a Knit stitch, the other if it is followed by a Purl. The instructions are written for holding the yarn to the right, but it is easy to do the technique with the yarn held to the left; simply move the needle instead of the yarn, as described for the Basic Yarnovers, above.

Knit Version

1. Knit 1 on Yarnover; do not discard strand. Yarn nearside to make Yarnover, Knit strand again; do not discard. There are three new stitches on right needle, two Knits on either side of a Yarnover; original Yarnover strand remains on left needle.
2. Move yarn nearside and then pass it over right needle and hold on farside to form another Yarnover and position yarn for next stitch. Insert right needle into first stitch on left needle as to Knit, and then pass tip from nearside to farside under original Yarnover strand; wrap yarn on needle and draw it under that strand and through stitch; discard strand and stitch from left needle together.

There will be five new stitches on the right needle; two Yarnovers in between three Knit stitches. The first stitch replaces the original Yarnover, the last one replaces the stitch following the Yarnover, so only the three in the middle are additions to the number of stitches on the needle.

Purl Version

1. On Yarnover strand, Purl 1, Yarnover, Purl 1, Yarnover; do not discard. These are Purl-to-Purl Yarnovers; there are four new stitches on right needle.
2. With yarn nearside, insert right needle tip from farside to nearside under original Yarnover strand, and then into next stitch as to Purl; wrap yarn and draw it through stitch and under strand. Discard strand and stitch from left needle together.

Decreases

To make a decrease, two stitches are worked together as if they were one. There is but one decrease technique, with variations. Which variation you use, and where you place it in the fabric, will determine whether the result is decorative or barely discernible. And, as with the Increases, there are Single, Double, and Multiple versions.

A decrease makes its presence known in two ways. One stitch of the pair will be the "facing stitch," which slants to either the right or the left on the outside of the fabric; the other stitch will be the "backing stitch," and will be hidden from view. The column of stitches that contains the facing stitch will continue above the decrease, while the column that contains the backing stitch will stop on that row.

In many situations it does not matter which decrease you use; however, in certain circumstances it may. For instance, when working a stitch or color pattern, you might want to use the decrease to remove a background stitch, instead of one that belongs to a motif. Or, you might consider whether to work the decrease so the facing stitch slants to either the right or the left in relation to a nearby edge or to other pattern elements.

❖ Single Decreases

A single decrease technique is used to combine two stitches, leaving one stitch on the needle. The instructions provide several options for how to work Right or Left slanting decreases in either Knit or Purl; which one to use is a matter of preference, because the outcome is basically the same.

There are also Twist versions of the decreases, which can be useful when working with a Twist Stitch pattern of some kind.

Right Decreases

The standard Knit and Purl versions of the Right Decrease are by far the most common techniques used, and with good reason, since they are neat, unobtrusive, and very easy to do. On the Knit side, the left stitch of the decrease pair is the facing stitch and slants up to the right; the right stitch of the pair is the backing stitch.

Knit Right Decrease

The first version of the Right Decrease is the common Knit Two Together that you will encounter in pattern instructions. The second version is just another way to do exactly the same thing, and is an option for those who hold the yarn to the left.

Knit Two Together Right Decrease

- Insert right needle knitwise into first two stitches on left needle, wrap yarn in normal way, and draw through both stitches. Discard two stitches from left needle together; one new stitch remains on right needle.

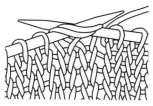

Knit Two Together Right Decrease.

Knit Right Decrease.

Pullover Knit Right Decrease

If you hold the yarn to the left, begin with it on the farside of the needles and work as follows:

1. Move left needle to farside of yarn so it passes over tip of that needle.
2. Move right needle to nearside of yarn and insert it as to Purl into first two stitches on left needle; pull these stitches over strand of yarn, and discard (or pull them over one at a time).
3. Slip new stitch from left needle to right needle.

Purl Right Decrease

These two variations produce the same structure as the Knit version, but are done in Purl for use on the inside of the fabric. Here again there are two ways to work; the first is customary; the second is an option for those who hold the yarn on the left.

Purl Two Together Right Decrease

1. Insert tip of right needle from right to left into first two stitches on left needle and Purl.
2. Drop two stitches from left needle together; one new stitch is on right needle.

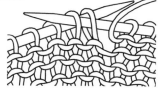

Purl Two Together Right Decrease: Step 1.

Slip Purl Pullover Right Decrease

If yarn is held to left, you might prefer this method.

1. Slip 1 purlwise; Purl 1.
2. Pull second stitch on right needle over first and discard.

Insert left needle into stitch on nearside or farside, whichever is easiest for you given position of yarn.

Left Decreases

There are two common ways of working a Knit Left Decrease, and both produce the same result. However, neither method

is as quick to do as a Knit or Purl Right Decrease, which is why a Left Decrease is used only when it is essential to the appearance of a pattern or when it is necessary to have mirror-image pairs.

The basic structure of a Left Decrease is the same as a Right Decrease, but the right stitch is the facing stitch and slants up to the left, and the left stitch is the backing stitch.

Unfortunately, the facing stitch of the left version tends to enlarge slightly. In many cases this is not a problem, but it can be quite noticeable when right and left decreases are placed in close proximity; see Paired Right and Left Decreases, below, for information on how to mitigate the problem.

Knit Left Decrease

Here again, there are two ways to work, and regardless of which one you use, the result is the same. You may find, however, that one or the other makes it easier to work the Pullover step after a particular stitch technique.

Slip Slip Knit Left Decrease

1. Slip two stitches knitwise, one at a time, from left to right needle.
2. On nearside, insert left needle from left to right into two turned stitches on right needle, wrap yarn as to Knit, and pull both stitches over yarn and discard.

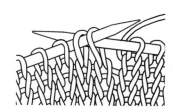

Slip Slip Knit Left Decrease: Step 2. Knit two turned stitches farside.

Slip Knit Pullover Left Decrease

While this method will seem quite different when you do it, the result is identical to the Slip Slip Knit Decrease, above.

1. Slip one stitch knitwise, and then Knit next stitch.
2. On nearside, insert tip of left needle from left to right into turned slipped stitch (now second stitch on right needle), and pull over new stitch and discard.

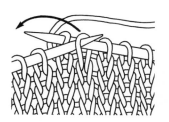

Slip Knit Pullover Left Decrease: Step 2. Pull turned stitch over new stitch.

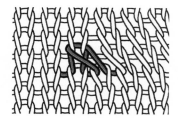

Knit Left Decrease.

> **An explanation . . .**
> *Whether you Slip one or both stitches, it is important that you turn them first so they will not twist; for more information, see Turned Stitches. A decrease with a twisted facing stitch will be quite obvious and can be used to decorative advantage (see Twist Stitch Decreases, below), but in most circumstances it is not desirable.*

Purl Left Decrease

Working a Left Decrease in Purl improves its appearance on the Knit side somewhat, because the facing stitch is less likely to enlarge than with the Knit version.

Slip Slip Purl Left Decrease

1. Slip 2 stitches knitwise, one at a time, from left to right needle.
2. Insert left needle into near-side of both slipped stitches and transfer them back to left needle in turned position.
3. On farside, insert right needle tip into two stitches from left to right and under left needle to nearside.
4. Wrap yarn as to Purl and draw through new stitch; discard both original stitches.

Slip Slip Purl Left Decrease: Step 3. Purl two turned stitches together farside.

Purl Slip Pullover Left Decrease

The Slip Slip Purl method, above, can be awkward to do with yarns that are not resilient, particularly if you hold the yarn to the left; here is an alternative, although it is slower to do. Work this decrease firmly so the new stitch will not enlarge.

1. Purl 1, Slip 1 knitwise.
2. Return both turned stitch and new stitch to left needle, maintaining each in their respective positions.
3. On farside, use right needle to pull second stitch on left needle over first; return first stitch to right needle; tighten new stitch before continuing.

Twist Stitch Decreases

The decreases discussed above are suitable for every purpose; however, it is also possible to work any decrease so the discard stitches are twisted. The result is quite noticeable in the fabric, especially when done repetitively, and it is ideal for shaping a fabric made with a Twist Stitch pattern.

Right Twist Stitch Decrease

1. Slip 2 stitches knitwise, one at a time.
2. Transfer stitches back to left needle in turned position.
3. Knit or Purl Two Together.

Left Twist Stitch Decrease

- Knit or Purl 2 stitches together through farside.

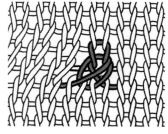

Right Twist Stitch Decrease.

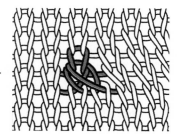

Left Twist Stitch Decrease.

> **Paired Right and Left Decreases**
> *While it is common to use mirror-image pairs of decreases to shape the two sides of a garment, this can be problematic because the facing stitch of a Left Decrease tends to be larger than that of a Right Decrease. This is odd, since the structure of the two is the same; there may be something about the different path the yarn takes through the two stitches that causes this.*
>
> *When the yarn passes through the stitch in a direction opposite that of the slanted facing stitch, as it does in the Knit Right and Purl Left Decreases, it remains tidy. However, when the yarn moves through the stitches in the same direction as the slanted facing stitch, as it does in the Knit Left and Purl Right Decreases, it tends to enlarge. Why it does this remains a mystery.*
>
> *The difference in the appearance of the two decreases is only a problem in a smooth fabric or when a pair is set close together; done in a textured yarn, or set within a complex stitch or color pattern, it will not draw the eye.*
>
> *If you want the pairs to match as closely as possible, here are some tips; try one or the other to see what works best for you given the circumstances at hand.*
>
> - *Pair a Knit Right Decrease with a Purl Left Decrease, keeping in mind that the latter will be one row above the former; this will not be noticeable in a wide fabric where they are far apart.*
> - *When working the Slip Slip Knit version of the Left Decrease, draw the new stitch through, drop the right discard stitch first, and then pull up on the left discard stitch before discarding it. This will draw some yarn out of the facing stitch.*

- *Alternatively, Slip the first stitch knitwise, as usual, and then pull up on the second stitch before slipping it, tightening up the first.*
- *Work as for a Slip Knit Pullover, slipping the first stitch knitwise as usual, but Knit the second stitch farside so it will twist. The latter will be the backing stitch and hidden from view; twisting it tightens up the facing stitch a bit.*
- *In the row below the planned decrease, use Purl Under for these two stitches (wrapping yarn under needle instead of over); this gives them a little less yarn. On the return row, work the left decrease farside so the stitches will not twist.*

❖ Double Decreases

As with the increases, above, the basic decrease techniques can be modified to remove more than one stitch at a time from the needle. For the most part, the differences in how they are made are less significant than how they are used.

The first ones discussed are all Double Decreases, meaning that one new stitch is formed on three discard stitches, reducing the total number of stitches on the needle by two. Right and left pairs of single decreases can also be used as the equivalent of Double Decreases, usually in situations where repetition enhances the subtle appearance they have in the fabric. And there are also several ways to do Multiple Decreases, which remove more than two stitches in one position.

In the following variations, one of the three discard stitches will be the dominant, facing stitch on the outside of the fabric; the others will slant behind it and are hidden from view.

Center Double Decreases

With this version, the center stitch is the facing stitch on the nearside, the left stitch is on the farside, and the right stitch is between the other two.

Knit Center Double Decrease

1. Insert right needle into first two stitches on left needle as to Knit and slip together to right needle.
2. Knit next stitch.

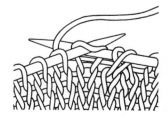

Knit Center Double Decrease: Step 2. Knit third stitch.

3. Pull two slipped stitches, one at a time or together, over new stitch and off needle.

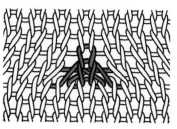

Center Double Decrease.

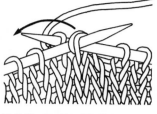

Knit Center Double Decrease: Step 3. Pull two slipped stitches over new stitch.

In Step 1, the two stitches will cross each other; the one that was first on the left needle will be first on the right needle, and each will be turned, with the left side of the stitch on the nearside.

Purl Center Double Decrease

1. Slip 2 stitches knitwise, one at a time.
2. On nearside, insert left needle into slipped stitches from right to left and return them to left needle.
3. Yarn nearside, insert right needle into three stitches on left needle and Purl; discard all three stitches together.

In Step 1, the two stitches are turned. In Step 2, they will cross each other as they are slipped back to the left needle; they will no longer be in the turned position, so they can be worked nearside.

Right Double Decreases

With this version, the decrease will slope to the right; the left stitch is the facing stitch, the right stitch is on the farside, and the center stitch is between the two.

The facing stitch can become enlarged with this version; to minimize this, work close to the tips of the needles.

Knit Right Double Decrease

- On nearside, insert right needle from left to right into first three stitches on left needle and Knit.

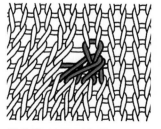

Knit Right Double Decrease.

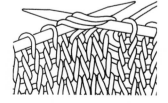

Knit Right Double Decrease. Knit three stitches together.

- Or, with yarn held to left, use equivalent of Pullover Knit Right Decrease, above; lay yarn over left needle and pull stitches over it.

Purl Right Double Decrease

- On nearside, insert right needle from right to left into first three stitches on left needle and Purl; discard all three stitches together.
- Or, with yarn held to left, use Slip Pullover Purl Right Decrease; Slip 2 stitches, Purl 1, and then pull two stitches over new stitch.

Left Double Decreases

There are several ways to do both the Knit and Purl versions of this decrease; all of them slope to the left and look the same, although two have slight differences in structure. Try them all and choose the one you find easiest.

Knit Left Double Decrease

There are three versions here. The first two produce the same result in the fabric; while the third is structurally different, it will look the same.

Version One

The right stitch is the facing stitch; the left stitch is on the farside.

- Slip 2 stitches knitwise, one at a time, and Knit next stitch. Pass two turned slipped stitches over new stitch and off needle, either together or one at a time.

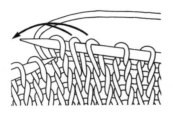

Knit Left Double Decrease, Version One. Pull two slipped stitches over new stitch.

Version Two

- Slip 3 stitches, knitwise, one at a time. Wrap yarn around right needle as to Knit and pull slipped stitches over wrapped yarn.

Pull all three stitches over together, one at a time, or one and then two, however it is easiest for you to work.

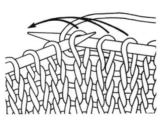

Knit Left Double Decrease, Version Two. Wrap yarn and pull three slipped stitches over new stitch.

Version Three

Here the center stitch is on the farside and the left one is in the middle, a difference that is barely discernible.

- Slip first stitch knitwise. Knit next two stitches together. Pass turned Slip stitch over new stitch and off needle.

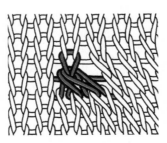

Knit Left Double Decrease.

Purl Left Double Decrease

There are two ways to work: the first matches the appearance of the first Knit version, above, but is not as easy to do; the second is easier and matches the third version.

Version One

- Slip 3 stitches, knitwise, one at a time. Return stitches to left needle in turned position. Reach around on farside, insert needle into all three stitches from left to right, and Purl.

Version Two

The version above can be difficult to do, particularly if you are working at a firm tension or with a yarn that is not resilient; this is a reasonable alternative, although it requires more steps.

- Purl two stitches together, and Slip next stitch knitwise. Return both Slip stitch and new stitch to left needle. On nearside, insert needle into turned stitch on left needle and pull it over new stitch and discard; Slip new stitch to right needle.

You can simplify this slightly by not turning the third stitch, but it will then twist when worked. This changes the appearance slightly, but that may not matter, and it is both easier to do and the result is attractive.

❖ Multiple Decreases

Some stitch patterns require more than two stitches to be removed at once. One solution is to work several single decreases in close proximity. However, in some cases the goal is to bunch the stitches closely together to produce a more textured effect in the fabric. Here are several options.

Slip Pullover Multiple Decreases

These two combine a Left and Right Decrease.

Five to One Variations

One new stitch is made on five existing stitches; this reduces the total number of stitches on the needle by four.

- Slip 2 stitches knitwise, one at a time, Knit three together, pull two slipped stitches over new stitch and discard.
- Or, Slip 3 knitwise, one at a time, Knit Two Together, pull the three slipped stitches over the new stitch and discard.

Four to One Variation

In this case, one new stitch is made on four existing stitches; this reduces the total number of stitches on the needle by three.

- Slip 2 stitches knitwise, one at a time, Knit Two Together, pull two slipped stitches over new stitch and discard.

Wrap Pullover Multiple Decreases

These are all very easy ways to do a multiple decrease. With two of the versions all the stitches involved in the decrease slant to the right or left. The other two are similar to those above, where the stitches converge in the center.

Because they make use of the Pullover technique, these decreases are particularly useful when working with a yarn that is not very resilient and you find it difficult to insert the needle into several stitches at the same time.

These techniques can be used to remove three or more stitches; the number used in the instructions can be changed to fit your circumstances.

Version One

With this decrease, one new stitch is made on four existing stitches, reducing the total number of stitches on the needle by three. All the discarded stitches will slant to the right.

1. Bring yarn nearside, and then wrap it over *left* needle to farside.
2. Move right needle to nearside and pull four stitches to left of yarn over it and discard them from left needle.
3. Slip new stitch to right needle.

Pull the stitches over one at a time, in pairs, or all together, as you prefer.

Version Two

This is just like the version above, but the decrease slants to the left in the fabric.

1. Slip 4 stitches knitwise, one at a time.
2. Wrap yarn around right needle as to Knit.
3. Move left needle to nearside and pull turned slipped stitches over yarn and discard them.

Pull the stitches over singly, in pairs, or all at once, as you prefer.

Version Three

This decrease is worked on five stitches, reducing the stitch count on the needle by four; the stitches converge in the center, but the facing stitch slants to the right.

1. Slip 3 stitches knitwise.
2. Wrap yarn over *left* needle from nearside to farside.
3. Move right needle to nearside and pull two stitches to left of yarn over it and discard them.
4. Slip new stitch to right needle.
5. Move left needle to nearside and pull three turned slipped stitches to right of new stitch over it and discard them.

I have seen a variation of this decrease in several pattern books that calls for pulling the last stitch over first. This results in a very tight cluster, and is rather difficult to do.

Version Four

Here, four stitches are used in the decrease, reducing the number on the needle by three; the stitches converge in the center, but the facing stitch slants to the left.

1. Slip 2 stitches knitwise, one at a time to right needle.
2. Wrap yarn over *left* needle.
3. Move right needle to nearside and pull two stitches to left of yarn over it and discard them; Slip new stitch to right needle.
4. Move left needle tip to nearside and pull two turned slipped stitches to right of new stitch over it and discard them.

CHAPTER 12

Increase and Decrease Stitch Patterns

In this section, you will find information on the kinds of stitch patterns that achieve their effects primarily with the Increase and Decrease techniques discussed in the previous chapter. The decorative surface textures and fabric structures that can be made with just these two types of techniques are remarkable in their variety.

The Surface Relief patterns are used to produce depth and strong texture throughout an entire fabric, or in large areas of one, as well as for isolated motifs that protrude from the surface, such as the ever-popular Bobbles. Additive patterns create charming decorative elements such as loops and bows that look as if they were added to the surface rather than being worked into the fabric. The more subtle Surface Floats make use of strands of yarn that skim across the surface; these can also be used to decorate entire fabrics or can be arranged in stripes or motifs of various shapes and sizes.

There are also techniques that are only used for entire fabrics, like the Brioche patterns (which can also be made with the Knit Below technique described in The Stitches), and the related but very different Tunisian patterns. Twice Knit patterns make very dense fabrics with somewhat limited utility, but there are ways to adapt the technique to enlarge the possibilities considerably.

Then there are the Bias patterns, which cause the stitch columns to slope in one direction or another. These are commonly used to make handsome tailored fabrics, but they also appear in the Eyelet and Lace patterns that make openwork fabrics, ranging from those with discreet Eyelets scattered across a smooth fabric, to gossamer webs of exquisite delicacy and beauty.

Surface Relief Patterns

In this section you will find a discussion of how various Increase and Decrease techniques can be applied to create a fabric with a pronounced surface texture. In patterns of this type, an increase technique is used to add several stitches in one location, and these are then decreased again to restore the stitch count. Some patterns of this kind are intended to provide texture for an entire fabric, but more often the techniques are placed in limited areas to create stripes or motifs of various kinds, or they are combined with other techniques in more complex stitch patterns.

The first type of pattern is called Ruching, and it is used to make stripes of horizontal gathering within the fabric; it produces a very nice effect with little effort. Next are the Cluster Stitches, which are tightly worked pairs of Multiple Increases and Decreases that produce little bumps on the surface of the fabric. Following these are the Embossed Motifs, which are often put to use in patterns that form charming representative shapes in relief on the fabric, such as bells, flowers, or leaves.

And last, but by no means least, are the popular Nubs, Knots, and Bobbles, which are round shapes that protrude from the fabric. While the subtle little Nubs are sometimes used for an entire fabric or for large areas within it, their bigger, bolder cousins the Knots and Bobbles are normally part of another stitch pattern, and are often found keeping company with Cables.

❖ *Ruching*

Ruching is a French word that means "gathering." The term is commonly used in fashion design to refer to a narrow piece of gathered, ruffled, or pleated trim that is either inserted between two pieces of fabric, or applied to the surface of one. Because trim of this kind is flexible, it is often placed in sinuous lines or drawn into tight circles to form flowers.

While you could knit a piece of trim of this kind and apply

it in exactly the same way as a woven one (see Applied Materials), a knitted ruching pattern is no more than a gathered stripe within a fabric. These can be repeated for the length of the fabric, each one separated by a few rows done plain or in another decorative pattern, or two or three ruched stripes might be set above the cuff of a sleeve or at the lower edge of a bodice.

To enhance the effect, the ruching can be worked in a different color or with a yarn of a different texture. And if the garment section is worked side-to-side, the ruching will be vertical in wear; for a similar effect, it could be worked on stitches picked up along a center front opening before working a border.

Horizontal stripes of Ruching are traditional in knitting, but there is no technical reason to limit the technique in this way; a diagonal or sinuous line of ruching could travel across a garment section. This requires drawing the design first on the schematic and then on a garment chart in order to develop a stitch pattern for the location of the increases and decreases; for more information, see Measurements and Schematics, and Coordinating Stitch and Garment Patterns.

Ruching is most successful if confined to a relatively narrow width of no more than about an inch or two, or the effect begins to dissipate. Also keep in mind that the narrow rows of the fabric, not the ruched areas, define its overall width.

There are two ways to work: Increase Ruching and Regauged Ruching.

Ruching.

Increase Ruching

1. Increase into every stitch across row, doubling number of stitches on needle.
2. Work number of rows required for depth of ruching, according to gauge.
3. Decrease every stitch across row, restoring original number of stitches to needle.

The Raised Stitch Increase works well for this and the decrease is a simple Knit or Purl Two Together. Other increase techniques could be used, depending upon which one would blend in best with the pattern in the row below where the ruching begins.

Regauged Ruching

Instead of changing the number of stitches to create ruching, you can Regauge the fabric instead; this is much easier to do because it does not use increases and decreases, and the result is quite different because the ruched area of fabric will be lighter and more open than the main fabric. Use a Test Swatch to determine the needle size to use for the best result.

There are three alternatives, depending upon what you want the ruched fabric to look like.

- Continue main stitch pattern, but use needles two or three sizes larger to work number of rows required for depth of ruching, and then change back to original needle size for main fabric.
- Instead of changing needle size, use a stitch pattern that is more open than the main fabric, or perhaps use Needle Elongation.
- Alternatively, instead of creating ruching by enlarging the stitches and widening the fabric so it will gather, use a stitch technique above and below an area to gather it; Single Rib works nicely for this, or you might want to try something firmer, like Twice Knit.

❖ Cluster Stitches

This effect is created by setting several increase and decrease pairs in close proximity. Cluster Stitches are found in a great many patterns, and are used both on their own or combined with other techniques to create entire fabrics that have charming, bumpy surface textures. When done on relatively small needles, the fabric will be thick and warm; when done on larger needles, the texture can be quite open, because the decreases pull the stitches together and leave little gaps between one cluster and the next.

In addition to being used for all-over patterns, a series of cluster stitches can be placed in horizontal, vertical, or diagonal lines; groups can be set between motifs done with other stitch patterns; or the clusters can be used like Purl stitches on a Knit ground to create textured geometric motifs.

What you will find here are brief descriptions of how the concept can be applied; as you will see, even a small change in the type of technique used, or just its placement, can have a rather large effect on the structure and appearance of the fabric. Once you are familiar with how these patterns work, you will not only recognize ones new to you in pattern books, but also understand how easy it is to vary them and create your own.

Paired Clusters

Here are some examples of how paired increases and decreases can be used to create clusters; specific patterns vary in terms of the particular technique used.

- To make an individual Cluster Stitch, work one of the Double Increases immediately followed by a Double Decrease.
- Alternatively, work the increase on one row, and the decrease on the same stitches in the row above.
- For a stripe, Knit Two Together on every pair of stitches across the row. On the return row, either work a Bar Increase on every stitch, or a Running Thread Increase between every stitch in order to restore the stitch count.
- A somewhat bolder version calls for a Knit Three Together across the row, and on the return a Multiple Yarnover Increase on every stitch.

Coral Knot. A Cluster Stitch pattern.

Simultaneous Clusters

Some patterns use multiple increases and decreases in the same location. A few examples of this would be:

- Purl three together but do not discard; Yarnover, Purl same three stitches together again.
- Or, Purl three together, Knit three together, Purl three together, all on same three stitches, without discarding in between. This is more difficult to do than the version above.
- Alternatively, Knit three together, Knit first stitch again, and then Knit remaining two stitches together.
- This one is subtle: Work a Raised Increase, and do not discard; transfer new stitch to left needle, and Knit Two Together.
- For a bolder version of the one above, use a Double Raised Increase and then work a Double Decrease on the three new stitches. Or, work a Double Decrease on the next three to restore the stitch count.

❖ *Embossed Motifs*

These patterns are done by adding several extra stitches in one small area and then either gradually decreasing them over several rows, or doing so all at once on the last row of the motif. Because the extra stitches are confined in a small area, they will puff out from the surface of the fabric.

When using a pattern with Embossed Motifs it is important to check the gauge on a swatch large enough to show the effect they will have on the width of the fabric; most of the extra stitches protrude from the face of the fabric, but they do add a bit of width overall. Also, the side edges may be scalloped or wavy instead of straight, which is attractive on an exposed edge, but may need special handling if the item is seamed; see the discussion on how to handle irregular fabric edges in Tips for Bias Stitch Patterns, below.

Note that the overall stitch count on the needle changes from row to row; if you need to check the number of stitches, do so on a pattern row where it has returned to normal.

Cast-On Motifs

This technique produces some of the more charming and decorative of the embossed patterns. The additional stitches, for the motif are formed with casting on rather than with increases, creating an opening at the base of the motif.

1. On outside of fabric, work to location of motif; turn to inside. Use Cable Cast-On, Woven Knit Cast-On, or Hook and Needle Chained Cast-On to add number of stitches required for base of motif, plus one. Turn to outside.
2. Transfer extra cast-on stitch to left needle, and work it and next stitch together with Right Decrease; continue with row.
3. Work additional stitches along with rest of fabric for as many rows as required, decreasing according to pattern to restore original stitch count, using one of options described below.

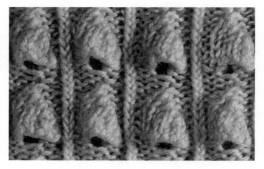

Carillon. A Cast-On Embossed Motif.

The extra stitch added and then removed with the decrease in Step 2 helps eliminate a gap that often appears between the lower left corner of the motif and the main body of the fabric.

Increase Motifs

In this case, the motif can begin with a Double or Multiple Increase, or the increases can be spaced over several rows. As a result, there will be no gap at the base as there is with the semi-detached method above. Once the extra stitches have been added, any of the approaches described below for how to handle the decreases can be used.

The motifs are usually divided by a few stitch columns of Purl, which helps them puff out and sets them off visually. In some patterns of this type, however, the repeats are nested side-by-side and staggered vertically; as one motif is decreased, the adjacent motif is increased and the number of stitches on the needle remains constant at all times; as a result, the motifs will lie more flat.

Decreases for Embossed Motifs

In some patterns, the motif stitches are worked with the main fabric for several rows and then decreased all at once using a Double or Multiple Decrease. In others, the decreases are worked within the motif, row by row, until the stitch count is restored. Regardless of what the stitch pattern calls for, keep in mind that you can create different effects by changing the type of decrease used or its position.

- If left decreases are placed on the right side and right decreases on the left side of the motif, the facing stitches of each decrease will slant toward the center of the motif and will be quite decorative.
- With right decreases on the right side and left decreases on the left side, the facing stitches of the decreases will slant toward the edge of the motif, leaving the stitches at the interior of the motif smooth and undisturbed.
- If all of the decreases are placed along one side of the motif, the stitches within the motif will slant on the bias; see Bias Stitch Patterns.
- In some patterns, Center Double Decreases are placed in the middle of the motif, creating a strong vertical line with the stitches converging behind it.

Picked-Up Motifs

Another type of motif that protrudes from the surface can be done by picking up stitches instead of casting on or using an increase technique. Two very different types of effects can be achieved with this technique.

Intarsia-Type Motif

An Intarsia-type motif is introduced on one row, worked separately from the main fabric with its own yarn supply, and then rejoined on a later row; it is attached only at the bottom and top, not at the sides. The stitches used for the motif are replaced in the background by picked-up stitches. These kinds of things are fun and easy to do, and you can add them to a fabric done with many other kinds of stitch or color patterns.

To determine the length of yarn required for each motif, work one motif as a sample, unravel it and measure the yarn used, and then add an allowance for ends to hide on the inside during finishing.

Left: Candle Flame: An Embossed Motif. Increases and decreases at center of motif.

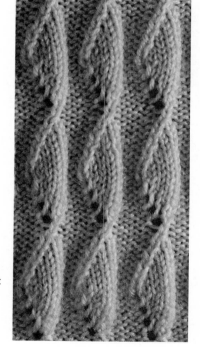

Right: Fuchsia: An Embossed Motif. Yarnover Increases at lower left; decreases at upper left.

1. Work across row to position of first motif and push stitches back from tip of right needle.
2. With strand of motif yarn and separate circular needle held in right hand, work number of stitches from left needle required for width of motif; push these stitches back from tip of needle onto cable, and let hang on outside of fabric.
3. Return to main yarn and right needle and pick up stitches below first row of motif: Reach down on farside and insert right needle tip up under Purl nub below first stitch on left needle; lift this stitch onto left needle in standard position and Knit it, as you would for a Raised Increase. Repeat for each stitch of motif.
4. Continue across row to position for next motif, drop main needle again, pick up circular needle, attach another strand of yarn, and repeat Steps 2 and 3; work across row in this way, adding as many more motifs as needed to circular needle, and always picking up equal number of stitches from under each motif on main needle.
5. At end of row, push main stitches back from needle tips, pick up circular needle bearing motifs, and work each one separately with its own yarn as many rows as required by pattern.
6. Let needle with motifs hang on outside of fabric again and return to stitches of main fabric; work same number of rows as were done in motifs.
7. On outside, work across row to position of first motif, bring needle bearing stitches of motif up parallel to left needle and use Joinery Decreases to attach motif to main fabric; continue across row, joining each motif in same way.

An Intarsia-type Motif worked on separate stitches and twisted before being reattached.

In Step 3, you can insert the needle down under the Purl nub and Knit it without lifting the stitch onto the needle, but it may be harder to draw the yarn through for the new stitch.

Intarsia Motif Applications

Here are some ideas for different ways to make these charming add-ons.

- If you know how to do so, use the Bi-Directional Method for working these little motifs; they will go much faster.
- A Stockinette motif will curl at the side edges, and if narrow enough it will roll into a cord; if you prefer flat motifs, use something like Seed Stitch instead.
- The motifs can be shaped with increases and/or decreases, or you can pull the center together into a "waist" with a Wrap technique or a Cable technique.
- Alternatively, in Step 7, transfer stitches of each motif to a small double-point or cable needle; turn the needle to twist the motif to right or left before working the Joinery Decreases.
- If you want the motifs to loop out from the surface somewhat, work the main fabric one or two fewer rows than used in the motif, or work the motif a few more than in the main fabric.
- It is not necessary to reattach the motifs directly above where they began. To pull the motif on a diagonal, attach it several stitches to the right or left; adjust number of rows in motif to provide adequate length, if necessary.
- Or, work the motif on the bias, with increases set on one side, decreases on the other, or use a Twist Stitch pattern to create bias and then, when attaching at the top, position the motif to one side or the other.

Welting Patterns

There are other, highly textured patterns that can be done by picking up stitches within the fabric and joining them to stitches on the needle in the same manner as for Welts. While the kind of Welt described in Hems, Facings, Pleats, and Tucks is worked across the full width of the fabric, stitch patterns can make use of the same techniques for partial Welts, perhaps no more than an inch or so wide, set in various arrangements in the fabric. You can work the Welts in Purl or Garter Stitch set against a background of Knit, and/or work them as for Intarsia with separate strands of contrast-color yarn.

❖ Nubs, Knots, and Bobbles

These techniques all create round shapes that protrude from the surface of the fabric. In size, they range from the discreet little Nubs, through the medium-size Knots, and on up to the flamboyant Bobbles.

A certain number of extra stitches are introduced in one place, these are immediately worked in some way, and are then removed with decreases. The Nubs are quite elementary and present no challenges. However, the Knots and Bobbles increase not only in size, but in complexity; a glorious sweater covered with Cables and Bobbles is a testament to patience and perseverance.

Nubs

These are the smallest members of the family; sometimes they are called "peppercorns," which describes them perfectly. Because they are so tiny, they are most often found distributed all over a fabric in fairly close arrangement, used as a quieter companion pattern for a bolder one, or clustered to create a geometric motif of some kind.

With any of these variations, work the stitches firmly to make the nub neat and prevent gaps forming between it and the stitches on either side.

Peppercorn Stitch. A Chain Nub pattern.

Chain Nub

This is tiny, even by Nub standards, but has the advantage of being very easy to do. All that is necessary is to work one stitch several times—not horizontally, as one would with a multiple increase, but vertically as for a Single Crochet Chain.

1. On outside, work to position of Nub; Knit 1 stitch and discard, wrap yarn around right needle tip as to Knit, use left needle tip to pull new stitch over yarn and off needle. Pull up on new stitch to tighten discard stitch before continuing.
2. Repeat wrap and pullover once or twice more to create Nub of size required.
3. Place firm tension on yarn to Knit next stitch, and then continue row.

Chain Nub. Wrap yarn and pull new stitch over.

Three stitches seem to be the happy medium; two are a little small, although they will be visible, while four start to hang down and turn into the Chain Loop. Also, the outcome is a little nubbier and more effective if done in Purl.

Running Thread Nub

This version is worked between two stitches, which eliminates the gaps that can appear on either side of a Nub. This feature also makes it easy to introduce Nubs into a pattern that does not have them, since nothing else needs to change.

1. Work a Running Thread Increase, and then rework new stitch to make Chain Nub as described above.
2. Knit next stitch, and then with left needle tip pull Nub stitch over new stitch and discard; continue row.

Step 2 is done somewhat like a Left Decrease.

If the Nubs are placed close together, consider working them with a contrast-color yarn and the Stranded Color technique.

Double Running Thread Nub

Here is a slightly bolder version, and, because the Nubs are larger, they tend to stay in place better on the outside of the fabric; this is especially important if the fabric is somewhat loosely knit.

1. Work Rib Increase on running thread to add two stitches.
2. Slip two stitches to left needle, draw yarn to right and Knit them; repeat three or four times in Stockinette, Reverse Stockinette, or Garter Stitch.
3. To finish, work two Nub stitches with Left Decrease, Knit 1, and then pull remaining Nub stitch over new stitch and discard.

Instead of turning in Step 2, use the Bi-Directional Method or Slip the two stitches to the left needle and draw the yarn to the right to re-knit.

For an alternative to the decrease used in Step 3, Knit the two Nub stitches, Knit the next stitch, and then pull both of the Nub stitches over the new stitch and discard them.

Five-Stitch Nub

This is a nice compact little nubbin, and it is quick and easy to do (it is actually a form of Cluster Stitch).

1. Work a five-stitch Multiple Rib Increase or Multiple Yarnover Increase.
2. With five new stitches on right needle, work a Wrap Pullover Multiple Decrease.
3. Push Nub toward outside of fabric with left forefinger; work next stitch with firm tension on yarn, and continue across row.

Knots

Now we move up to the Knots, which have one plain row worked in between the increases and decreases. These instructions rely on a Multiple Yarnover Increase that makes five new stitches; it produces a Knot that is well centered, although other increase techniques could also be used.

Center panel in Bouquet, a Knot pattern.

Slip Stitch Knot

This Knot is compact and fairly symmetrical. It is intermediate in size between the Five-Stitch Nub above and the Double Decrease Knot, below.

1. On outside: Work a Multiple Yarnover Increase. Turn.
2. On inside: Draw yarn up firmly and Knit or Purl these five stitches. Turn.
3. On outside: Slip stitches to right needle and then work a Wrap Pullover Multiple Decrease, or see decrease suggested in Step 3 of Double Decrease Knot, below.

Double Decrease Knot

This is somewhat larger and more nicely centered—altogether, an excellent Knot.

1. On outside: Work a Multiple Yarnover Increase. Turn.
2. On inside: Draw yarn up firmly and Knit or Purl these five stitches. Turn.

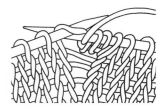

Double Decrease Knot: Step 1. Five-stitch Knit Yarnover Increase.

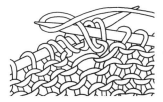

Double Decrease Knot: Step 2. Purl five stitches on inside.

3. On outside: Work a Knit three together Right Decrease, followed by a Slip Slip Knit Left Decrease; pull second stitch on right needle over first and off needle.
4. Work next stitch with firm tension to close gap and continue row.

The center stitches of the Knot will be the facing stitches of the decrease, which helps them to protrude.

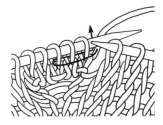

Double Decrease Knot: Step 3. Knit three together followed by Left Decrease.

No need to turn . . .
With either of these Knots, you can use the Bi-Directional Method on the plain row in the middle, and eliminate the need to turn the fabric.

Bobbles

Now let's turn to the Bobbles, which are just bigger Knots. The bigger they get, of course, the more work they are, and no Bobble is quick to do. Perhaps, like puppies and children, it is only because they are so charming that we put up with all they ask of us.

There are almost as many ways to create a Bobble as there are patterns containing them, and some of them are less than ideal. Those included here are quite satisfactory, and there is also a new one that I think is really an improvement— I hope you like it as well as I do.

The Better Bobble

Begin on the outside of the fabric and work as follows:

1. Work a Knit Double Yarnover Increase. With three new stitches on needle, turn.
2. Purl 1, Purl Double Yarnover Increase, Purl 1. With five stitches on needle, turn.
3. Knit 5, turn.
4. Purl Left Decrease, Purl 1, Purl Right Decrease; turn.

Hollow Oak pattern. Bobbles, Cables, and Seed Stitch on Purl background.

5. Slip 2 together knitwise, Knit 1, pass two Slip stitches over.
6. Tighten remaining Bobble stitch on needle, maintain firm tension on yarn, and work next stitch; continue across row.

There are several new things to notice here. First, the increases and decreases require two rows. This adds to the symmetry of the Bobble. Second, the final decreases are planned so the outside stitches converge behind the center stitches, allowing the Bobble to protrude as much as possible.

To make the first decrease in Row 4 easier to do, use Knit Under on the last two stitches of Step 3; this turns these stitches in preparation for the left decrease in Step 4; see Turned Stitches.

To pull the fabric more firmly around the Bobble, after Step 5 reach down on the inside and pick up the Purl nub of the stitch the Bobble was made on and then Purl it together with the final Bobble stitch on the needle.

Many patterns call for slipping the first stitch of each row of the Bobble, but this enlarges these stitches and tightens those within the Bobble, making them less prominent; I find the result rather unattractive.

You may also encounter advice to "lock" the last stitch of the Bobble by working it one more time and tightening the discard stitch firmly; while this neatens up the last stitch, it also adds length and causes the Bobble to droop. I think it is better to just put good tension on that stitch as you work the next one.

Consider working all rows in Knit for a Garter Stitch Bobble, or, for an even nubbier version, work so the Bobble is entirely in Purl on the outside.

One-Way Bobbles

Without question, Bobbles are slow to do because of the need to turn the work after each tiny row; this becomes particularly tiresome when the fabric has grown heavy. Here are several ways to eliminate the turns and still produce a very smooth, handsome Bobble.

Version One

1. Work a five-stitch Multiple Yarnover Increase.
2. Slip five stitches to left needle, draw yarn firmly across farside, and Knit five.
3. Repeat Step 2 once or twice, depending on size of Bobble required, drawing yarn less firmly across farside on center rows than on first and last rows to allow Bobble to take on rounded shape.
4. To complete Bobble, Slip five stitches to left needle; Knit Right Decrease, Knit 1, Knit Left Decrease; Slip 3 left,

Slip 2 together knitwise, Knit 1, and pass two Slip stitches over to make a Center Double Decrease.

Version Two

- Work as described in Version One, but use a pair of short, double-point needles to work Bobble; Slide stitches from left point to right point at end of every row instead of Slipping stitches from one needle to the other.

  Support the fabric in your lap, and push the other stitches back from the main needle points somewhat so they don't slip off during Bobble-making.

This approach also allows you to use a smaller-size needle for the Bobble than for the main fabric, which helps to give it a very neat, compact appearance.

Version Three

- Use Bi-Directional Method, working right to left on one row, left to right on next.

Of course, you will need to learn how to work the increases and decreases required on the return rows, but if the pattern calls for a lot of Bobbles, it would be worth doing so because then you will never need to turn at all. If you find it a challenge to manage increases and decreases when working that way, just use it for the plain rows in the middle.

Running Thread Bobbles

As with a Knot, a Bobble can be worked as easily on a running thread as on a stitch. This makes it easy to introduce Bobbles into a pattern that does not already include them, either between two motifs or pattern repeats, or even within one that has an even number of stitches, since the Bobble will then act as the center stitch.

- Work Better Bobble, above, on running thread; work last Bobble stitch together with an adjacent stitch using either a Left or Right Decrease, with bobble stitch as backing stitch of decrease.

Attached Bobble

There is one remaining problem with the methods described above, and that is the stubborn tendency for gaps to appear on either side of a Bobble regardless of how diligent you are in working the first and last stitches with a firm tension.

The way to eliminate these gaps is to use a technique borrowed from another area of knitting entirely; Bobbles are, after all, a form of Short Rows, and that technique provides the solution.

In this version, the Bobble is the same—the only difference is that during its construction the two stitches to either side of the Bobble are wrapped with the yarn as for Short Rows; these wraps are then worked together with adjacent stitches in two final steps.

While Bobbles are already somewhat tedious to do, and this adds a few more steps, I think the outcome is worth it. Here is a Bobble that is plump, symmetrical, and firmly attached to the fabric with no gaps.

1. On outside: Work a Knit Double Yarnover Increase, turn.
2. Purl 1, work a Purl Double Yarnover Increase, Purl 1. To make first wrap: Slip 1 stitch from left to right needle, yarn farside, return stitch to left needle, yarn nearside. Turn.
3. Knit 5. To make second wrap: Slip 1 stitch from left to right needle, yarn near-side, return stitch to left needle, yarn farside; turn.
4. Purl Left Decrease, Purl 1, Purl Right Decrease; turn.
5. Slip 2 together knitwise, Knit 1, pass two Slip stitches over.

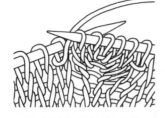

Attached Bobble: Step 3. Wrapping stitch to left of Bobble.

The first wrapped stitch to the left of the Bobble is dealt with immediately as you continue the row; the wrap to the right will be taken care of on the next row.

To Work First Wrap

1. Slip wrapped stitch at left side of Bobble to right needle.
2. Insert left needle tip up into wrap and then into stitch and slip back to left needle; join wrap and stitch with Knit or Purl Two Together, depending upon stitch pattern.

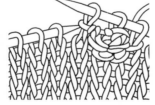

Attached Bobble, First Wrap: Step 2. Lift wrap onto right needle, and Slip wrap and stitch together to left needle.

The wrap will become the backing stitch of the decrease, hidden on the inside of the fabric.

To Work Second Wrap

- If working flat, on next row, work stitch holding Bobble and then Slip next stitch knitwise, insert left needle tip up under wrap and into turned stitch and slip back to left needle; join wrap and stitch with Purl Two Together farside.
- If working circular, work to right side of Bobble and complete second wrap.

The Bigger Better Bobble

Here is a grand Bobble, constructed on the same principles as the Attached version, above. It can be done without the Short Row Wraps, of course, but because it contains an extra row, the gaps will be even larger without them, and I think the outcome is much nicer if they are used.

1. On outside: Work a Knit Double Yarnover Increase; turn.
2. On inside: work three new stitches: Purl 1, Purl Double Yarnover Increase, Purl 1; turn.
3. On outside: Knit 5. To make first wrap: Slip 1, yarn nearside, Slip 1 left, yarn farside; turn.
4. On inside: Purl 5. To make second wrap, Slip 1, yarn farside, Slip 1 left, yarn nearside; turn.
5. On outside: Work Left Decrease, Knit 1, Right Decrease; do not turn.
6. On outside: Slip 3 stitches to left needle, Slip first two stitches together to right needle knitwise (they will turn and switch places), Slip 1 knitwise, pull first two together over third.
7. To close gaps, join wraps and stitches on either side of Bobble as described above.

Afterthought Bobble

If you have grown weary of a sweater that is just too plain, or you would like to dress up an older brother's hand-me-down but still perfectly good sweater for a younger sister, or perhaps you have just finished something and wish you'd thought of Bobbles in the first place, here is how to add them later. Furthermore, this makes it possible to have Bobbles in multiple colors and to work them with a smaller size needle, or you can make them very quickly with a crochet hook.

I am not sure this approach is any less trouble to do than the knitted-in sort, but the result is a perfectly respectable Bobble with no gaps on either side, and when it works, it works very well indeed.

1. Allow a 10- to 12-inch end of yarn and place a Slip Knot on a relatively small needle.
2. On that stitch, work a Better Bobble, firmly, as described above.
3. Break yarn, allowing a 10- to 12-inch end; pull end through last bobble stitch and tighten.
4. Hold Bobble on outside; on inside, use crochet hook to draw two yarn ends through fabric, one above and one below either a running thread or a stitch head.
5. Tie yarn ends together firmly in a knot and weave them into adjacent stitches; see Hiding Ends of Yarn.

Better yet, just tie the knots, cut the ends off, and leave them there to tickle the wearer, or stuff the ends inside the Bobble to fatten it up.

Edge Bobbles

We think of Bobbles as residing within a fabric, but they can take up position at the edges as well. Work them on the first row after casting on, adjacent to a selvedge stitch, on a picked-up stitch before working a border, or while you are casting off.

- Use one of the Compound Half-Hitch Cast-Ons and then work Bobbles spaced across first row. Use a Test Swatch to see if you prefer to have the Bobbles above the Knit or Purl side of the cast-on edge.
- Alternatively, use Knit or Cable Cast-On, spacing Bobbles along the edge as you cast on.
- On a Pullover Chained Cast-Off edge, work to position for Bobble. With one stitch on right needle, work Bobble on first stitch on left needle; with last Bobble stitch on right needle, pull second stitch over in usual way and then continue to cast off.
- To work Bobbles along a side edge, make them on the stitch adjacent to the selvedge.

Additive Techniques

The techniques discussed here are used to make loops of yarn, dainty bows, or knitted motifs that stand out from the surface of the fabric; although they are made as an integral part of the fabric, they look as if they might have been added later.

❖ Loop Stitch

Loops of yarn can be added to the surface of the fabric by working a stitch with additional wraps and then securing the loops to the stitch itself with a decrease.

These loops can be clustered in small tufty sections, scattered all over, lined up in neat horizontal or vertical stripes, or used for part of a border. They can be set on a smooth background of Stockinette, but are distinctive enough to hold their own when set amid more decorative stitch patterns.

Traditionally, the loops were used in a very utilitarian way to trap body heat on the inside of garments like mittens, hats, or vests. For an abundance of both warmth and charm, work the loops on both the inside and outside of a Garter Stitch fabric; keep in mind that the loops absorb quite a lot of extra yarn so space them out across the fabric a bit.

It is also possible to add loops to stitch patterns that do not specifically call for them, such as at the center of a motif or between two pattern repeats. For denser fluff, Knit with two or three strands of fine yarn held as one, and consider mixing yarns with different colors and/or textures.

Knotted Loop Stitch

The loops formed with traditional methods are not very secure in the fabric. Here is a new approach that keeps them in place quite dependably and offers the option of making one, two, or three loops at a time.

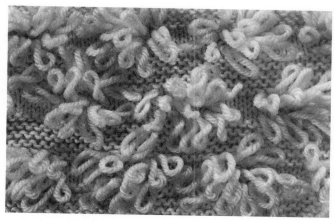

Knotted Loop Stitch.

1. Insert right needle into first stitch on left needle and Knit; do not discard.
2. Pass yarn to nearside between needle tips, around left thumb, and back through needle tips to farside; Knit same stitch on left needle farside, and then discard it and drop loop from thumb.
3. Pinch loop against fabric with thumb, insert tip of left needle into nearside of two new stitches on right needle, wrap yarn and Knit Two Together farside.
4. Pull up on yarn and down on loop to secure it.

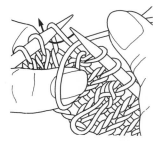

Knotted Loop Stitch: Step 2. Wrap yarn on thumb and then Knit same stitch farside.

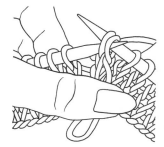

Knotted Loop Stitch: Step 3. Pinch loop and Knit Two Together farside.

Multiple Knotted Loop Stitch

1. Work as in Step 1, above, but do not discard; original stitch remains on left needle, and two new stitches are on right needle.
2. Wrap yarn again as in Step 1 to make second loop, and then Knit into nearside of same stitch and discard it.
3. Pinch two loops formed against fabric, wrap yarn on right needle as to Knit, and use left needle to pull all three stitches over wrap, one at a time or together.

Traditional Loop Stitch

This variation is found in many pattern books. However, the loops are formed on the farside of the fabric while you work, and they come undone all too easily; I recommend you use one of the techniques above, which make the loops more secure. On the other hand, if you are working in the round and want loops on the inside of something like a mitten for the warmth they add, this might be the best approach to use.

1. Insert right needle into first stitch on left needle as to Knit, wrap yarn under left forefinger or middle finger, back over top of finger, and around right needle tip; draw yarn through to form new stitch; maintain loop on finger and slip new stitch to left needle.
2. Insert right needle tip into farside of new stitch and original stitch on left needle and Knit Two Together; drop loop from finger and discard both stitches. Pull down on loop to tighten.
3. On next row, work stitch holding loop farside so it will twist.

Chain Loop

Instead of loops of yarn, this makes loops of stitches.

• Work as for one of the Chain Nubs, but continue the chain several more rows to make it longer; attach it with a decrease.

A loop made of a single stitch will be rather twisty, which can be a nice effect; a two-stitch version will lie more flat.

If you prefer, work the chain with a crochet hook, and then return the last stitch to the knitting needles to complete it.

Corded Loop

This loop is rounded instead of flat; work as for a Three- or Five-Stitch Nub.

1. Use a Multiple Increase on a stitch or a running thread.
2. Slip new stitches to left needle; draw yarn firmly past stitches on inside and Knit them again.
3. Repeat Step 2 until loop is as long as required.
4. Reduce number of stitches in cord to one in one of following ways:
   • If cord was worked on stitch: Use Multiple Decrease to reduce number of stitches in cord to one.
   • If cord was worked on running thread: Use a decrease to reduce cord stitches to one; work second decrease on remaining stitch and one adjacent stitch in fabric.

Alternatively, use a crochet hook and chain the loop with a decorative pattern.

❖ *Bow Knots*

Here is a charming variation on the loop theme that appeared in *Adventures in Knitting* by California knitter Barbara Aytes.† Yarnovers are used to make elongated loops that are pulled to the outside of the fabric and secured with a knot to form a little bow.

These loops could be especially nice on a garment for a little girl, but would also be beautiful done in something like a metallic yarn on an evening sweater for a very grown-up girl; no doubt there are many other possibilities.

Double Bow Knots.

Basic Bow Knot

1. Depending upon size loop required, make a double, triple, or quadruple Yarnover; Knit or Purl next stitch, and then make another multiple Yarnover of same size as first.
2. On return row, drop first Yarnover from needle to outside of fabric, work next stitch, drop second Yarnover from needle to outside.
3. Set work down on lap or table, pull both loops out firmly to even up stitches in fabric to either side and tie them together with a Square Knot.

Of course, you could drop all the loops across a row, and then set the work down and tie them into bows all at the same time.

Multiple Bow Knots

Several pairs of Bow Knots can be clustered together; here are some ways to change how they lie in the fabric:

1. Work Step 1 of Basic Bow Knot as many times across row as required for pattern.
2. On next row, drop loops on outside of fabric; do not tie.
3. Repeat Steps 1 and 2.
4. Set work down and knot pairs of loops corner to corner, one from Step 1, one from Step 3, joining upper left to lower right, upper right to lower left so they cross.

† Barbara Aytes, *Adventures in Knitting: More Than 100 Patterns, from Easy to Intricate* (Garden City, N.Y.: Doubleday & Co., 1968).

Use your imagination and place them where you will. For instance, you could knot the two left loops together, and then the two right loops together so the pairs are aligned vertically side-by-side. Or, consider setting a pair of loops on either side of two or three other stitches; knot the Bow firmly to cluster them together. Because the bows are tied securely, you can cut the loops if you prefer a fringier look.

Added Bows

Bows of this kind can also be added to a finished garment; while this does not make use of an increase or decrease technique, it does produce the same effect and so here they are. This approach offers the advantage that the bows can be made in a different yarn and/or color, and they can be added to an older garment to give it a fresh look; whether it is more or less trouble to do is for you to decide.

Before you begin, use a Test Swatch to try a few sample bows; undo the one you like best and measure the length of yarn required. Cut as many strands as you need ahead of time to make the work go more smoothly.

- Work on outside of fabric. Hold strand of yarn on inside and use crochet hook to pull one end through to right of a stitch, and then other end through to left of the stitch; tie into a bow knot as described above.
- Alternatively, use multiple strands of the same or different kinds of yarns; pull them through together or one at a time, line up the ends evenly and tie the knot, or knot each strand separately, if you prefer.

Surface Floats

In one way or another, these patterns all create their effects with strands of yarn drawn across the surface of the fabric. Some patterns of this kind have a subtle overall texture made up of little flecks of yarn, while in others the strands are bold and obvious. The strands can also be used to draw certain stitches tightly together to make pronounced surface textures, similar to what can be done with the Wrap technique.

❖ Pullovers

This technique involves pulling a stitch over one or more other stitches. Because this is a decrease, it requires a compensating increase to maintain the stitch count.

The pulled-over stitch encircles the others, forming a horizontal strand on the surface of the fabric; if the technique is worked on the outside of the fabric, the strand will slant up toward the left; if done on the inside it will slant up toward the right on the outside. The number of stitches encircled by the Pullover varies with the stitch pattern.

The increases that compensate for the Pullover can be lo-

cated adjacent to or within the pattern unit, or even on the row above or below. In the first set of examples here, a Yarnover is used for the Pullover; when made it is an increase, and when pulled over to complete the stitch, it serves as its own decrease. There are also patterns that use a Slip stitch for the pulled-over strand, and an increase is worked on one of the stitches that it will encircle.

Yarnover Pullovers

These examples use a Yarnover for the increase, and in two of them it leaves an Eyelet in the fabric. Other kinds of increases could be used, such as a Running Thread Increase, or the running thread itself could be pulled over, which would bind the stitches tightly together.

Yarnover with Stitch Pullover

- Yarnover, Knit 3; pull third stitch over first two stitches on right needle.

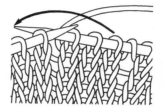
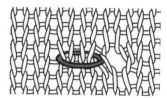

Yarnover with Stitch Pullover. Pull third stitch over first two stitches.

Yarnover followed by a Stitch Pullover.

Yarnover with Slip Stitch Pullover

- Yarnover, Slip 1 knitwise, Knit 2; pull Slip stitch over first two stitches on right needle.

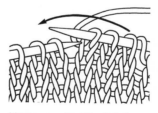
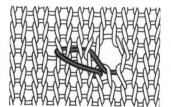

Yarnover with Slip Stitch Pullover. Pull Slip Stitch over first two stitches

Yarnover followed by a Slip Stitch Pullover.

Yarnover as Pullover

- Yarnover, Knit 2; pull Yarnover over first two stitches on right needle.

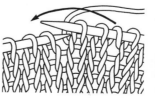
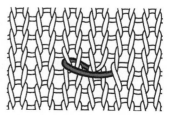

Yarnover as Pullover. Pull Yarnover over first two stitches.

Yarnover as Pullover.

If you used a Turned Yarnover, the result will be the same as a Basic Wrap Stitch.

Yarnover Within Pullover
- Knit 1, Yarnover, Knit 1; pull third stitch on right needle over other two stitches.

❖ Couching Stitch

Couching is an embroidery term for a yarn or cord that is laid across the surface of a fabric and fastened into place with decorative stitches; see Surface Decoration. In knitting, the term is often found in the name of patterns where stitches are drawn through the fabric and across the surface, but which do not include any inlaid material, although it is certainly possible to do so.

The Slip Stitch and the Pullover techniques can also be used to create somewhat the same effects; however, the Couching technique described here allows for greater variety because the strands can be drawn across the fabric horizontally, vertically, or diagonally. Also, it is easier to control the amount of yarn in the strands with this method so they either lie flat or draw the intervening stitches together to create surface texture.

Strands that float on the surface of the fabric are prone to snagging, so take the particular gauge you are working with into consideration; a strand longer than half an inch or so is somewhat impractical. Fortunately, these patterns are easy to adjust and once you understand how they work, you can change the number of stitches involved to meet your needs (in these examples the strand is pulled past three stitches).

Horizontal Couching Stitch

In the most basic version of the technique, the couching loop is pulled through and secured immediately before continuing across the row, as follows:

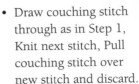

Horizontal Couching Stitch: Step 1. Insert needle between two stitches.

1. On outside: Insert right needle from nearside to farside between third and fourth stitch on left needle, wrap yarn as to Knit and pull couching stitch through fabric.
2. Slip 1 knitwise, insert left needle into nearside of slipped stitch and couching stitch and Knit Two Together farside; Knit next two stitches (those encircled by couching strand), and then continue row.

To allow enough yarn to the strand so it lies flat, stretch the stitches out along the left needle before knitting them. Also note that the couching strand encircles one less stitch than the number skipped in Step 1 because it is secured to the first of them.

Horizontal Couching pattern.

Here are two alternatives to try if you find the method above causes the couching stitch to enlarge:

- Draw couching stitch through as in Step 1, Knit next stitch, Pull couching stitch over new stitch and discard.
- Or, draw couching stitch through as in Step 1, Slip next stitch, insert left needle into nearside of slipped stitch and couching strand and Knit Two Together farside.

Diagonal Couching Stitch

This method makes it easier to control the amount of yarn in the strand and maintain even tension on the adjacent stitches. The couching strand is drawn through on one row, but not secured until the next; it will slope up slightly toward the right.

1. Draw couching stitch through as described in Step 1, above, and then continue across row, working the technique as often as required by pattern.
2. On next row, join each couching stitch and stitch to right of it on outside of fabric with a Right Decrease; couching stitch should be facing stitch of decrease.

If working flat, on inside row join couching stitch and next stitch with Purl Two Together; if working circular, on outside row join preceding stitch and couching stitch with Knit Two Together.

For a bolder look, Slip the couching stitch on the next row, and work it with a decrease on the following one; it will then stretch across three rows.

Knit Below Couching

Instead of carrying the couching stitch up past one or more rows, draw it through the fabric somewhere on a previous row, as follows:

1. Insert tip of right needle either into a stitch, or between any two stitches in a row below; wrap yarn around needle and draw through a couching stitch.
2. Slip next stitch, and then work Slip stitch and couching stitch together as for a Left Decrease.

Inlay Couching

If you want to create the appearance of true Couching, use the stitches to enclose a soft cord, narrow ribbon, or heavier strand of yarn. Work as follows:

- Hold inlay strand above left needle, move right needle below it to draw couching stitch through fabric in one of ways described above. Move inlay strand below needle and join couching strand to next stitch with decrease (or do so on next row, or slip it one more row and work it on following one).

Allow extra length to the inlay strand at both side edges; after Dressing the Fabric, adjust the width of the strand so it lies flat and does not pucker the fabric, and then attach it to the edge.

It is not necessary to place the inlaid material all the way across the row, or even along just one row.

For a partial row inlay, work as follows:

• Bring couching material through to outside of fabric at starting point, attach a length of it with couching stitches, and then bring it back through to the inside.

If you are using yarn for the inlay material, hide the ends in the usual way (see Hiding Ends of Yarn); if the inlay is ribbon, secure the ends with tiny stitches on the inside (see Sewing Wovens to Knits).

To attach the inlay material in a sinuous line or curve of some kind, plan the position on a Garment Chart (see Coordinating Stitch and Garment Patterns). Secure a section of the inlay material on one row, and then draw it up row-by-row, attaching it to as many stitches as needed in each row as described above.

Smocking

Horizontal Couching can be used on a ribbed fabric to pull the columns of Knit stitches together in patterns that resemble Smocking (for alternative knitted methods, see Wrap Stitches; and for the sewn method, see Needlework and Crochet).

The effect can be quite delicate if done on a Single Rib, or bold and highly textured when done on a Double Rib, as in this example:

1. On outside, skip past two Knit, two Purl and two Knit stitches (six in all) and insert right needle between last Knit stitch of group and next Purl stitch; wrap yarn as to Knit and draw through a couching stitch.
2. Transfer couching stitch to left needle, work Right Decrease joining it to next stitch, tensioning yarn firmly to draw intervening stitches together, and then work remaining stitches in pattern.
3. Four rows later, repeat as in Steps 1 and 2, but stagger pattern so Knit columns of previously smocked group are pulled away from each other, up to right and left.

In Step 2, the decrease draws the two Knit columns together across the intervening Purl column; the couching strand will be the backing stitch of the decrease and is drawn to the inside of the fabric.

Other variations involve changing the number of intervening rows, or the number of Knit and Purl stitches in the ribbing to adjust the spacing.

❖ Horizontal Chain Stitch

This technique is used to make a very decorative horizontal chain of stitches on the surface of the fabric. It is similar in appearance to the chain created by casting off within the fabric and then picking up the stitches again along the edge (see Picking Up Chained Cast-Off Edge), but this approach is easier and quicker to do.

The chain of stitches is very effective when used as a narrow decorative element between other stitch patterns, to set off a color change, or to define a distinct area of the garment, such as a yoke. There are two ways to do the same thing, so you can choose which way you prefer to work.

Basic Horizontal Chain Stitch

I first saw this technique in *Creative Knitting*, a book by the wonderfully imaginative and artistic knitter Mary Walker Phillips.†

1. Turn all stitches of row in one of following ways:
   • If working flat, on inside row use Purl Under for all stitches.
   • If working circular, on outside row use Knit Over for all stitches.
2. On next row, Knit into farside and then nearside of first stitch, and then continue as follows: [Slip 1 stitch from right to left needle, Knit second stitch farside, Knit first stitch farside, discard both stitches together], repeat between brackets across row.

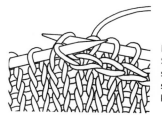

Basic Horizontal Chain Stitch: Step 2. Chain Stitch slipped to left needle; Knit second stitch farside, then Knit Chain Stitch farside.

Because the stitches have to be worked farside in Step 2, they need to be turned in Step 1 so they will not be twisted in the fabric.

The new stitches have a tendency to enlarge: carefully tighten each stitch while you work, or, if necessary, hold a smaller needle in your right hand to work Row 2.

† Mary Walker Phillips, *Creative Knitting: A New Art Form* (New York: Van Nostrand Reinhold Company, 1971).

Multiple Chains

Make a second chain by simply repeating the instructions above; there will be a plain row between the two. Or, if you want to use Chain Stitch on adjacent rows, work as follows:

Double row of Chain Stitch.

- For a flat fabric, work Step 1 and 2, above, and then turn and repeat Step 2 in Purl; the chain will appear on the outside of the fabric.
- For a circular fabric, use Knit Over to turn all the stitches in both Steps 1 and 2; for the second chain, repeat Step 2 on next round using plain Knit so new stitches will not be turned.

Contrast-Color Chains

For a more decorative chain, work with one or more contrast-color yarns in Step 2 of basic pattern, as follows:

- For Chain Stitch in a single contrast color: Knit second stitch farside with main color, and first stitch with contrast color.
- To make Chain Stitch with stitches in alternating colors: Knit second stitch with main color, first stitch with contrast color, and then Knit second stitch with contrast color, first stitch with main color. Alternate colors in this way across row.
- For three-color Chain Stitch: Always Knit second stitch with same color; alternate other two colors to first stitch of each pair.

Cast-Off Chain Stitch

The structure of this version is slightly different, but the general appearance is the same. Work on the outside of the fabric, as follows:

- Yarn nearside for Yarnover, Left Decrease; [Slip first stitch from right to left needle, yarn nearside for Yarnover, Left Decrease] repeat between brackets across row.

Use whichever version of a Left Decrease you prefer. Use firm tension when making the Yarnovers since they tend to enlarge; if necessary, work with a smaller-size needle in your right hand.

If necessary, the technique can also be done on the inside in Purl and the chain will appear on the outside. Work much as described above, but, after slipping the first stitch to the left needle, use a Purl-to-Purl Yarnover, and then Purl Two Together.

Decorative Fabric Structures

The stitch techniques discussed here are used alone to make an entire fabric (or large areas of one), each of them with a distinctive structure, texture, and appearance.

The first technique is another way to make Brioche fabrics that is unlike the Knit Below method described in The Stitches. Next is Tunisian Knitting, an old technique done in almost the same way as this version of Brioche, but to very different effect. Twice Knit is utilitarian, and primarily used for dense, sturdy fabrics. Finally, there is a group of patterns that create lively bias effects.

❖ Yarnover-Slip Brioche

As mentioned above, there are two distinctly different techniques that can be used to make Brioche fabrics.

This version is done using a combination of a Slip Stitch and a Yarnover; the latter will lie on top of the former and the two are joined on the next row with a decrease.

As you will see, the resulting stitch structure is identical to that created with the Knit Below technique, and the sample patterns here will produce the same fabrics as the instructions you will find in The Stitches. Whenever you are working a Brioche pattern, if for any reason you are having a problem doing it with one method, try the other to see if it is easier for you.

Brioche Rib

Cast on an uneven number of stitches plus two selvedge stitches, and work as follows:

1. Preparatory Inside Row: Purl 1, [yarn nearside for Yarnover, Slip 1, Knit 1], repeat between brackets across row. Turn to outside.
2. Knit 1, [Knit Two Together, yarn nearside for Yarnover, Slip 1] repeat between brackets across row, end Knit Two Together, Knit 1. Turn.
3. Purl 1, [yarn nearside for Yarnover, Slip 1, Knit Two Together] repeat between brackets across row, end Purl 1.
4. Alternate Rows 2 and 3 for length of fabric.
5. Final Row: Knit 1, [Knit Two Together, Knit 1], repeat between brackets across row.

Staggered Brioche Rib

As with the Knit Below version, the pattern can be staggered by working the pattern shown above for six or eight rows, and then working the same pattern for an equal number of rows, but in Purl.

To do this, use a Purl-to-Purl Yarnover, and work as follows:

- In Row 2, the pattern repeat is: Knit 1 [Purl Two Together, Slip 1, Yarnover], end Purl Two Together, Knit 1.
- In Row 3, the pattern repeat is Purl 1, [Slip 1, Yarnover, Purl Two Together], end Purl 1.

Syncopated Brioche. A staggered Brioche rib pattern.

> **The two Brioche techniques . . .**
>
> *There are some important differences between this technique and the Knit Below method.*
>
> *The latter uses a single technique, resembles plain Knit and Purl, and, because it has a simpler structure on the needles, any shaping required is easier to manage.*
>
> *The Yarnover-Slip method requires three techniques, a Yarnover, a Slip Stitch, and a Right Decrease, which seems somewhat more complicated; but once you get into the rhythm of working this way, you will find it easy enough to do, and in some situations it is preferable.*
>
> *This method often works better with a highly textured yarn; with the Knit Below method, it can be difficult to see where to insert the needle into the stitch. Also, there are some variations of these patterns that make use of the Yarnover in a slightly different way, and these can only be done with the method described here.*
>
> *Please see Tips for Brioche Patterns in The Stitches for suggestions on how to handle gauge, edges (casting on, casting off, and selvedges), and shaping for Brioche fabrics; those are suitable regardless of how you decide to work.*

❖ *Tunisian Knitting*

Stitch patterns of this kind are apparently based on very old, traditional Arabic knitting methods, which in British and American books are referred to as "Tunisian Stitch."

As you will see, the technique is done in a way that closely resembles the method used for Brioche patterns, above. However, there could not be a better example of how just one small change in knitting technique can produce a vastly different fabric.

A Tunisian fabric is rather tailored and geometric in appearance, and nicely resilient. There are visible holes between each stitch and, if done on somewhat larger needles, the fabric will be quite open; on much larger needles, it will turn into a netting.

I suspect these patterns are little known and oft neglected

because the common way of working them is somewhat problematic. The first instruction below is an alternative method that you may find easier; this is followed by the traditional method, so you will recognize it, and then an interesting variation on the theme.

Single Tunisian

This is a two-row pattern that begins on the inside for a flat fabric, but the instructions are the same for working circular.

1. On inside: yarn nearside, insert needle into first stitch as to Purl, wrap yarn as for Purl-to-Purl Yarnover, withdraw left needle, leaving stitch and Yarnover on right needle; repeat on every stitch across row; hold last Yarnover on needle and turn to outside. No new stitches are made on this row.

2. On outside: yarn farside [Slip 1 (the Yarnover), Knit 1, pull slipped Yarnover over stitch and discard]; repeat between brackets for each paired Yarnover and stitch across row; turn to inside.

Single Tunisian: Step 2. Slip the Yarnover.

3. Repeat Rows 1 and 2 to make fabric.

Notice that the Yarnovers made in Step 1 function merely to wind the yarn

Single Tunisian: Step 2. Knit the next stitch.

around the needle, one wrap for each stitch; if you were to take the needle out, the yarn would immediately fall free. Because no stitches are worked on the first row, it requires two pattern rows (two passes across the needle) to make one row in the fabric; it is especially important to keep this in mind when counting rows and calculating gauge.

In Step 2, when slipping the first Yarnover of the row, place tension on the yarn and insert the right needle on the nearside.

Once the stitches are made and discarded into the fabric, you will see that the Yarnover encircles the stitch in much the same way as the loop in the baseline of a Half-Hitch Cast-On. However, in this case the visible strand slopes up to the left, passing from below the running thread at the right side of each stitch to above the one at the left.

Consider using a contrast-color yarn,

Single Tunisian.

or one in a different texture for Row 1; if you are working flat, use the Slide technique to pick up the second yarn.

When done as described above, it is easy to make the mistake of Purling the stitch instead of slipping it; if you find yourself doing that, try working this way instead.

- Yarn nearside, Slip 1, Purl-to-Purl Yarnover, repeat across row.

Double Tunisian

With a slight modification, the Yarnover strand will encircle two stitches instead of one. If working flat, start on an inside row.

1. First row: Yarn nearside, Slip 1, [Slip 1, Purl-to-Purl Yarnover], repeat between brackets across row.
2. Second row: Yarn farside, Knit 1, [Slip the Yarnover, Knit 1, pass slipped stitch over], repeat between brackets across row.

Double Tunisian: Step 2. Slip first Yarnover.

Double Tunisian: Step 2. Knit the following stitch.

The first row here is the same as Row 1 of Single Tunisian, above, except there are two Slip stitches at the beginning of the row; make the first Yarnover with firm tension.

On the second row, push the Yarnover to the left of the first stitch with the needle tip and/or your left forefinger so you can Knit the first stitch. On all subsequent stitches, there will appear to be two Yarnovers on the left needle; Slip the first one, push the second one to the left, out of the way, and then reach the needle tip over it to Knit the stitch.

Traditional Single Tunisian

Here are the instructions for the basic technique as normally given, so you will know what has been changed and why; the resulting fabric is exactly the same, but once you try it, I think you will agree the version above is easier to do.

Here again, the pattern begins on the inside for a flat fabric; for circular, also work as written.

1. First row: [Yarn nearside, Slip 1 knitwise, Purl-to-Purl Yarnover], repeat between brackets across row; turn.
2. Second row: Use Knit Two Together farside to work every pair of stitches.
3. Repeat Rows 1 and 2 for pattern.

The stitches in the first row are slipped knitwise to turn them so they will not twist when Knit through the farside on the next row. On the return row, the Knit Two Together farside

will include the stitch and the Yarnover; it is all too easy to split the Yarnover strand when you do this, since it is on the farside, out of sight.

❖ Twice Knit

Here we have a family of stitch patterns that combine a basic decrease and an unconventional method of making the balancing increase.

If worked on the size needle that would be normal for the yarn, the technique produces extremely dense fabrics that are suitable for something like a belt, a bag, or a potholder. To make a fabric that is more supple, use needles two or three sizes larger than is normal for the yarn; make several Test Swatches to find the combination of yarn and needles that produces a fabric with the characteristics you want.

These instructions are all written for Stockinette, but the technique can also be done as for Garter Stitch, or even with Knit and Purl combined across a row. There is also an interesting variation done with two colors; see Double Strand Stitch.

Basic Twice Knit

1. On outside: [Knit Two Together, discard first stitch, retain second stitch on left needle]; repeat between brackets across row, ending Knit 1.
2. On inside: [Purl Two Together, discard first stitch, retain second stitch]; repeat between brackets across row, ending Purl 1.

Every decrease includes the stitch that was retained on the left needle after the previous pair was worked.

If you are working a flat fabric and prefer to start on an inside row, begin with Step 2, instead. For a circular fabric, Knit every row.

If you examine the structure of the fabric, you will see that it looks almost like embroidered cross-stitch, with each stitch overlapping the stitches to the right and left of it. Relaxed, however, only half of each stitch is visible, slanting up toward the right. On the Purl side, the slope of the stitches is more oblique, giving each row a corded look.

Basic Twice Knit.

Turned Twice Knit

When the technique is done as described above, the stitches tend to tighten up on the left needle. If you find it difficult to work into them, try this variation; it makes use of Turned Stitches, but the result is the same.

Turned Version Worked Flat

1. On inside: Work as in Step 2, above, but use Purl Two Together, wrapping yarn under needle to turn all new stitches on needle (see Purl Under in Turned Stitches).
2. On outside: Work as in Step 1, above, but Knit Two Together farside.

Turned Version Worked Circular

1. To begin, either work cast-on so all stitches are turned on needle or, on first round, turn each stitch before working decrease.
2. On subsequent rounds, work every pair of stitches with Knit Two Together farside, wrapping yarn over needle to turn new stitches.

Pullover Twice Knit

Here is another alternative to try if the stitches are tight on the needle and difficult to work; the stitches should be in standard position on the needle.

1. On outside: [Slip 1 knitwise, Knit 1 and retain discard stitch on needle; move left needle to nearside and pull Slip stitch over new stitch]; repeat between brackets across row.
2. On inside: Work in same way but in Purl; Slip stitch purl-wise and move left needle tip to farside to pull stitch over.

When working the Pullover in Step 2, you will find it is easier to pull the stitch over from the farside than the nearside, where it lies too close to the next stitch.

For a circular fabric, work only outside rows, as in Step 1.

Twisted Twice Knit

With this version, the stitches slope up toward the left instead of to the right.

- Work as for Basic Twice Knit with stitches in standard position on needle, and use Knit Two Together farside.

A row of Twisted Twice Knit alternating with a row of Purl Twice Knit will produce a horizontal herringbone pattern on one side, and on the other side, a corded effect that looks almost like columns of Knit stitches resting on their sides.

Herringbone Twice Knit. Alternating rows of Basic Twice Knit and Twisted Twice Knit.

Double Strand Twice Knit

Here is a new variation on Twice Knit that occurred to me when I happened to do a sample of the basic technique with a doubled strand of very fine yarn. The fabric has an unusual structure that is more supple than Basic Twice Knit. A variation of this technique can be done with two colors or with yarns of different textures; see Double Strand Stitch.

Cast on holding two strands of yarn as one and then work as follows:

1. [Insert needle tip between two strands of second stitch, and then into both strands of first stitch; Knit three strands together, discard first two strands, and retain third]; repeat between brackets across row. End Knit Two Together. Turn.
2. [Insert needle tip into both strands of first stitch, and then into first strand of second stitch; Purl three strands together; discard first two strands and retain third]; repeat between brackets across row. End Purl Two Together. Turn.

If you are working circular, use only Step 1 of the pattern. At the end of each round, the decrease will include two strands of the last stitch and one of the strands in the first stitch of the next round.

Tips for Twice Knit Fabrics

Here are some suggestions for working a fabric made with Twice Knit. Because these fabrics are so compressed in width, they require a special approach when casting on and off so the edges will not splay out. Also, it is necessary to adjust the normal methods of making increases and decreases to the special requirements of the technique.

Casting On for Twice Knit

This is very slow to do, but matches a Twice Knit fabric quite well.

- Use Knit Cast-On to place two stitches on the left needle; to continue, use Knit Two Together when adding each new stitch. Firmly tighten last stitch made before wrapping yarn for next stitch.
- Alternatively, use Cable Cast-On done with a smaller needle than will be used for the body of the fabric, or work a Half-Hitch Cast-On with a very firm tension on thumb yarn.

Casting Off for Twice Knit

Use Pullover Chained Cast-Off, working Twice Knit while doing so. Check results with a Test Swatch and, if necessary, adjust the size of the needle held in the right hand, using a larger one if the edge seems too tight, a smaller one if it seems too loose.

- Knit Two Together, discard one, pull right stitch over left and repeat.

Increases for Twice Knit
- Work a pair of stitches together as usual, and then slip first stitch purlwise to right needle instead of discarding it.
- Alternatively, Knit or Purl the pair together, and then work first stitch again; discard first stitch.

Decreases for Twice Knit
Work this at the very edge of the fabric; it will be obvious if done within the fabric.

- Work a pair of stitches together and discard.
- Alternatively, Knit three together, discard one; Knit three together, discard two; continue in pattern.

Twice Knit Applications
Because of its sturdy nature, Twice Knit is normally recommended for utilitarian purposes, but there are other interesting ways it can be used.

- A Twice Knit fabric lies flat and is quite well-behaved. Done with a needle large enough to produce moderate density in the fabric, it would serve very well for tailored vests, jackets, and hats. It is especially suitable for outerwear because the stitches overlap one another, making the fabric quite windproof, rather like Twined Knit. When done with fine yarn on relatively large needles, the result is a considerably softer fabric with a distinctive appearance.
- Old-fashioned knitted shoe liners, which were often fulled for warmth and durability (see Felting and Fulling), would be quite easy to do in Twice Knit instead, with no need to shrink the fabric; on the other hand, they might be even warmer and more cushiony if fulled.
- One of the interesting things about Twice Knit fabrics is that they will not ravel when cut; circular knitters who like to use Steeks, take note.

     This same quality also makes Twice Knit useful for the heels, toes, and soles of socks, because any spot that does wear through will not continue to ravel, and the density of the fabric makes it easy to use conventional darning to close the hole.
- The horizontal compression of Twice Knit works quite well as a way of drastically reducing fabric width to create gathering, such as if a few rows are placed between stripes made of Ruching.

❖ Bias Stitch Patterns
In the preceding sections we have looked at how paired increase and decrease techniques can be used to create surface texture and alter the structure and characteristics of a fabric. These same techniques are used in the applications discussed here, but in this case the results are smooth fabrics with columns of stitches that travel at an angle instead of vertically.

To create bias stitch patterns, the increase and decrease pairs are separated horizontally by several plain stitches; the new columns of stitches generated by the increases will travel up at an angle and several rows later will be absorbed by the decreases. The appearance of the fabric can be radically altered merely by changing the type of increase or decrease used, or their placement relative to one another.

Some published patterns specify which increase or decrease technique to use, while others do not. Whatever the case, please feel free to make substitutions—use a Test Swatch to try various alternatives and choose whichever techniques you think enhance the pattern and give the effect you want.

These Bias patterns make solid fabrics, but if a Yarnover is substituted for the increases used here, they would be transformed into Eyelet or Lace patterns.

Also see the Bias Mesh technique, which is done in an entirely different way and creates an openwork fabric.

About bias fabrics . . .
It is also possible to make a completely bias fabric by placing an increase at one side edge and a decrease at the other. This is not really a stitch pattern, since all the stitch columns and any decorative stitch pattern used will also slope, as will the side edges, which means the fabric will take on the shape of a trapezoid.

This is fun for a scarf or shawl, and for some specialized garment designs that take advantage of the shape created. Should you want to set the side edges vertical in order to make a conventional garment (the lower edge will then slope), develop a separate pattern for shaping the armholes and neckline using a Garment Chart; work the bias shaping and the garment shaping at the same time.

Chevron Patterns
Patterns with paired increases and decreases separated by several plain stitches will pull the area in between at an angle, resulting in alternating areas of bias, one sloping up to the left, the other sloping up to the right. These stitch patterns create handsome fabrics made up of columns of bias, sloping in opposite directions; they often have a rather formal, tailored look.

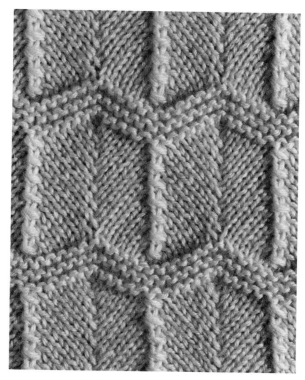

Welting Fantastic. A Chevron-type
pattern with Garter Stitch rows.

The bias effect set up by these patterns is so strong that it is also seen in the top and bottom edges, which tend to be pointed or scalloped. If several rows done in some other pattern or color are introduced between the Chevron pattern repeats, they will take on the bias contours as well, even though these rows contain no increases or decreases.

Stepped Patterns

Another variation on the theme is to place either the increases or decreases in a vertical column, while their opposite pairs

Dragon Skin pattern. A Stepped pattern with
increases at center and decreases at sides of motifs.

shift one stitch column to right or left, row by row; in other words, the number of stitches between the pairs constantly changes. If, for instance, paired increases are first stepped away from and then toward a center column of Double Decreases, the result is a diamond or petal shape.

Alternatively, the increases and decreases can be stepped in parallel fashion, each time moving one stitch to the right or left, always the same number of stitches apart; the result will be columns of bias stitches that travel in a zigzag fashion or in sinuous lines.

Wave Patterns

These kinds of patterns create soft, undulating wave-like effects in the fabric. Unlike the patterns described above, where each pattern unit consists of a single increase and a single decrease, these are done with paired groups; one group contains several increases and the one next to it will have an equal number of decreases.

The groups of increases and decreases can run parallel to one another the entire length of the fabric, in some cases set side by side, in others, separated by several plain stitches. Alternatively, they may remain parallel for several rows and then switch places to stagger the pattern (for an example, see Ostrich Plumes). Here again, plain rows can be introduced between pattern repeats, and these will take on the curved contours established by the primary pattern.

Tips for Bias Stitch Patterns

It can sometimes be a challenge to maintain the integrity of a bias stitch pattern in areas where a garment is shaped and this needs to be taken into consideration ahead of time. For instance, side edges may exhibit a certain amount of the contour established by the pattern; this can be very nice on a free edge, but can present a problem when seaming or adding borders.

Also, these stitch patterns can have a strong effect on top and bottom edges that remain visible, such as on a scarf or shawl. It is especially important to select an appropriate technique for these edges; some will prevent the edge from reaching its full decorative potential because they are not resilient enough to follow the contour of the pattern.

Here are suggestions for dealing with these aspects of working with bias patterns.

Garment Shaping

To shape the neckline, armhole, or sleeves of a garment with a bias stitch pattern, the easiest thing to do is to make use of the nature of the pattern itself. To increase, simply eliminate the decrease of a pair; to decrease, eliminate the increase of a pair, instead. Unfortunately, doing so eliminates the bias that lies between them, and the pattern will no longer look the same.

To avoid the problem entirely, select a garment design that requires little or no shaping (these patterns make beautiful skirts). Alternatively, consider working the fabric without shaping and cut out the garment pieces as for a woven fabric instead; see Steeks: Selvedges for Cut Openings.

Lower Edges

Because the lower edge may take on a pronounced scallop or chevron, it requires special consideration when casting on; see the discussion in Double-Needle Cast-On. Although that is not the only cast-on that could be used for this purpose, the explanation of why it is necessary to use a technique with those characteristics can be found there.

If you plan to use a ribbing at the lower edge of the garment, it will absorb most of the contour created by the stitch pattern; if the blousing above the ribbing is not smooth and even, try easing it in with a little steam; see Dressing the Fabric.

Side Edges

If the fabric will have exposed side edges, there is no need to use a particular Selvedge to accommodate contour, since most of them are soft enough to do so. Chain Selvedge works particularly well, as does either a Garter Stitch or Seed Stitch Selvedge.

If a contoured edge will be seamed, there are several ways to handle this successfully:

- In most patterns where the side edges exhibit some contour, they will go in on one side and out on the other. It is often possible to seam two edges in a conventional way with one side "nested" into the other; instead of a vertical seam, you will have one that follows the contours of the pattern.
- If the contour along the edge is pronounced and you prefer to eliminate it, use a straight, vertical seam within the fabric, turning the contoured area to the inside; it will make a pretty selvedge when steamed open and flat; see Seams for Wide Selvedges.
- If you will be faced with the challenge of joining a contoured edge to a straight one, consider overlapping them so the former remains visible.
- Also consider adding Edge Stitches to the pattern to fill in the contour at the sides; for suggestions, see Bias Patterns in the chapter Charted Stitch Patterns.

Seamed Upper Edges

In many cases the upper edge of a bias pattern will exhibit minimal contour and can be seamed in a conventional way, for instance at a shoulder; use a little steam to help it lie flat.

If there is more contour than can be absorbed in that way,

use one of the suggestions given above for a side seam. Keep in mind that a seam that follows the contour will only work if you establish the pattern on the two garment pieces so the two edges "nest" into one another; for more information, see Coordinating Stitch and Garment Patterns.

Free Upper Edges

If the upper and lower edges of the fabric will remain visible, such as on a shawl or a scarf, here are some suggestions for how to make them as compatible as possible:

- As with the cast-on edge, the cast-off edge needs to have adequate length so it can accommodate itself to the contour of the fabric. The easiest solution is to use a larger needle in the right hand when casting off; or see Picot Chained Cast-Off or Yarnover Chained Cast-Off for other alternatives.
- A fringe added to a border will often help to hide any differences in the two edges, and if it is only added to the peaks of the contour it may encourage the top edge to take on a shape more like that of the lower edge.
- In some cases, the best solution is to knit or crochet a border of some kind on both edges. Select one that is itself contoured in a compatible way to enhance the effect.

  Use a Provisional Cast-On so you can pick up the stitches at the lower edge to add the border.
- Many beautiful edging patterns that are worked narrow and long are ideal for this purpose. These can be sewn into place, or attached to free stitches while they are worked; see Picking Up to Join.

Eyelets, Mesh, and Lace

An Eyelet is a small hole in the fabric that is made with a paired Yarnover and decrease. Decorative openings of this kind can be included as one element within a larger, overall stitch pattern, but are often used alone, arrayed across a background of plain Knit, or clustered together to create small geometric motifs of some kind like diamonds or squares.

Eyelet Insertion is used to create narrow rows or columns of openwork on a solid background. This effect is similar to that seen in woven fabrics, where it is done either with embroidery techniques or by sewing two pieces of fabric to either side of a narrow strip of lace.

Mesh is an openwork fabric in which the Eyelets are set so close together horizontally and vertically that there is no background to speak of. While the number of mesh patterns is somewhat limited due to the nature of the technique, those that are available are quite distinctive and are commonly used for gloves, bags, and scarves. Some of these patterns cause the entire fabric to go on the bias, which can be used as part of the decorative effect.

Lace, one of the glories of the craft of knitting, is an openwork fabric that not only makes extensive use of Eyelets in all their forms, but combines them with all the other decorative stitch techniques as well. These beautiful fabrics can fairly be said to represent the ultimate expression of the knitter's art, the best of them done with great care using the thinnest and very finest of yarns.

The number of possible patterns for openwork fabrics of these kinds is vast and can seem overwhelming, but fortunately the basic techniques used are few and very easy to do. Even the most complex patterns are achieved with no more than slight variations of the basic techniques, and many of the simpler ones consist of small two- or four-row pattern repeats. Even knitters who do not think of themselves as having advanced skills can make these beautiful fabrics.

The discussion here is focused entirely on the basic techniques, with little or nothing said about the background fabric or how a particular technique can be combined with some other. However, once you understand the structure and behavior of each type of technique, how it is varied, and what its limitations and possibilities are, you will find any pattern in which it is used easy to understand and learn. This will not only allow you to select a pattern suitable for the project you have in mind, but will also help you gain the confidence to improve or modify a pattern, or even to create one of your own.

❖ Eyelets

As with other decorative techniques of this kind, Eyelets require paired increases and decreases in order to maintain the stitch count. The relationship between them, and which particular techniques are used, determine the appearance of the pattern.

The primary increase used for Eyelets is always a Yarnover because this makes the opening, although larger versions may include other kinds of increase techniques as well. Which decrease is used has a strong influence on the results—and whether the facing stitch belongs to the pattern unit, or to the background are the critical factors. In addition to the basic Single Eyelet, there are also Half-Double and Double Eyelets, which have larger openings.

The instructions here are written for working flat using Stockinette for the background; the pattern row is done on the outside in Knit, with plain Purl worked on the return row; for circular, simply work in Knit on every row. These patterns can also be done in Garter Stitch, which is common in many traditional patterns. While the resulting fabric is not as smooth and elegant as it would be in Stockinette, it is a good choice for reversible garments, such as shawls.

Single Eyelets

A Single Eyelet consists of a Yarnover either preceded or followed by a Right or Left Decrease.

In a Smooth Eyelet, the Yarnover is the primary element of the pattern, with the decrease done in a way that minimizes its effect and leaves the surrounding fabric undisturbed. In a Broken Eyelet, the decrease stitch has a visual presence equal to that of the Yarnover because the facing stitch creates a diagonal line adjacent to the opening.

To try these basic Eyelet units on a swatch, work on a background of Stockinette, with four or five plain stitches between each one, and several rows between each group, so they are set off clearly and you can see how different the results are with just a small change in the technique.

Left Smooth Eyelet

This Eyelet is nice and round with unbroken columns of stitches on either side because the background stitch to the left of the pattern unit is the facing stitch of the decrease.

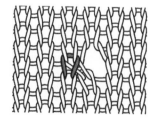

Left Smooth Eyelet.

- Yarnover, Knit Right Decrease.

Right Smooth Eyelet

This has the same general appearance as the one above, but the background stitch to the right of the pattern unit is the facing stitch of the decrease.

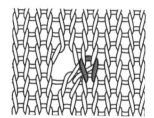

Right Smooth Eyelet.

- Knit Left Decrease, Yarnover.

Snowflake Pattern. Smooth Eyelets.

Left Broken Eyelet

In this case, the removed stitch is the facing stitch of the decrease, covering the background stitch to the left of the Eyelet. The appearance of the Eyelet is less round because of the angled stitch in the lower corner, which also has the effect of making the pattern unit seem larger than the smooth versions.

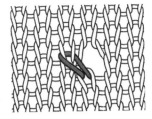

Left Broken Eyelet.

• Yarnover, Knit Left Decrease.

Right Broken Eyelet

The appearance of the Eyelet is the same as the one above, but the removed stitch covers the stitch to the right of the Eyelet.

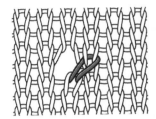

Right Broken Eyelet.

• Knit Right Decrease, Yarnover.

Eyelet Ribbing Patterns. Broken Eyelets.

Eyelet decrease options . . .

When a Yarnover follows a Left Decrease, the Slip Slip Knit version is easier to manage than the alternate Slip Knit Pullover. With the latter, the Yarnover strand covers the slipped stitch, making it more difficult to pick it up and pull it over; either decrease produces the same result.

The Left Smooth Eyelet and the Right Broken Eyelet are easier and quicker to do because they make use of a Right Decrease (Knit Two Together). Actually, I find the Purl Right Decrease (Purl Two Together) even faster, but I carry the yarn in my right hand, and those of you who carry it on the left may not find that to be the case. Nevertheless, it is an option when doing a simple pattern and working flat, since it is easy enough to work the eyelet on the inside in Purl, and then Knit the next row; for a complex pattern, it may not be worth the other changes that might be necessary to work that way.

Half-Double Eyelets

To increase the size of the Eyelets, two stitches are removed, one on either side of the Yarnover. The Yarnover replaces one of these stitches, and on the next row an increase is worked on the Yarnover to replace the other and restore the stitch count. When it is necessary to check the stitch count, therefore, do so only after completing the second row of the pattern repeat.

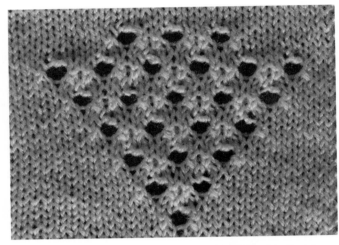

Arrowhead Eyelet pattern with Smooth Half-Double Eyelets.

Smooth Half-Double Eyelet

This Eyelet is round at the bottom; the removed stitches are hidden behind the stitches to either side.

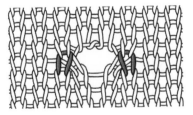

Smooth Half-Double Eyelet.

1. Outside Row: Knit Left Decrease, Yarnover, Knit Right Decrease.
2. Inside Row: Purl 1, Rib Increase on Yarnover, Purl 1.

Broken Half-Double Eyelet

The opening of this Eyelet is slightly angular at the bottom because the decreased stitches remain visible, covering the stitches to either side.

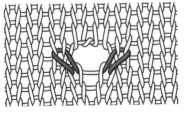

Broken Half-Double Eyelet.

1. Outside Row: Knit Right Decrease, Yarnover, Knit Left Decrease.
2. Inside Row: Purl 1, Rib Increase on Yarnover, Purl 1.

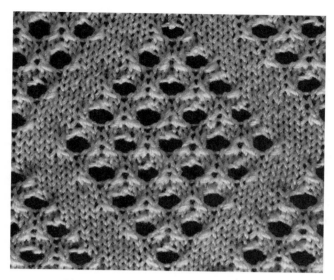

Diamond pattern. Broken Double Eyelets.

Double Eyelets

These are done in much the same way as the ones above, except a Double Yarnover is used to make the opening even larger.

Smooth Double Eyelet

This Eyelet is very open but somewhat less round at the top owing to the length of the Yarnover strand. The two removed stitches are hidden on either side at the bottom.

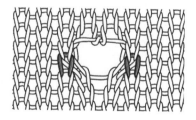

Smooth Double Eyelet.

1. Outside Row: Knit Left Decrease, Double Yarn-over, Knit Right Decrease.
2. Inside Row: Purl 1, drop first wrap of Double Yarnover, work Rib Increase on enlarged strand, Purl 1.

Broken Double Eyelet

Here the removed stitches slant out at the bottom, and the strands of the Yarnover slant in at the top, making the Eyelet angular at both the top and bottom.

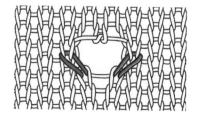

Broken Double Eyelet.

1. Outside Row: Knit Right Decrease, Double Yarnover, Knit Left Decrease.
2. Inside Row: Purl 1, drop extra wrap of Yarnover, work Rib Increase on strand, Purl 1.

Large Double Eyelets

There are patterns with larger Eyelets, but all are constructed on much the same principles as the ones discussed above. Here are some of the more common variations:

- In some patterns, only the Yarnover is done on the first row; on the next row, paired decreases are placed on either side of a Double Increase worked on the Yarnover.
- Where asymmetry is desirable, a Double Decrease can be used to one side of the Yarnover instead of placing single decreases on either side.
- The Multiple Yarnover Increase is particularly attractive when making a large Eyelet that calls for working three or more stitches onto a Yarnover strand.

❖ Horizontal and Vertical Eyelet Insertion

Here are the basic ways to set Single Eyelets into lines to create openwork stripes within a solid background. There are a great many variations here because the relative positions of the Yarnover and the decrease, as well as what kind of decrease it is, changes the appearance considerably.

Horizontal Eyelet Insertion

Rows of Eyelet Insertion are a charming way to set off a border or to define a yoke or a collar edge, and they often serve as a transition between two other stitch patterns.

Horizontal Eyelet Insertion.

This pattern can also be used to create the holes through which to thread a ribbon, such as on a bodice, for the edge of a baby bonnet, or perhaps for a drawstring. Also see the Picot Foldline, which uses Eyelet Insertion for the turning row of a hem edge.

- On outside, work a Single Eyelet on every pair of stitches across row; turn to inside and Purl one row.
- Alternatively, space the Eyelets several stitches apart across the row.
- The Eyelet pattern row can also be inserted between several rows of Garter Stitch, or, if the Eyelets are spaced out, just above and below each pattern unit.

Vertical Eyelet Insertion

Vertical or diagonal lines of Insertion are often placed between other kinds of patterns, such as small cables, or areas of mixed Knit and Purl stitches, and they often appear as one aspect of a Lace pattern with several other types of techniques.

With the smooth versions, the stitch columns to the right or left of the Eyelets remain unbroken because the decreased stitch is hidden behind them. With the corded versions, the facing stitch of the decrease slants across the column of stitches next to the Eyelet, giving it a nubby, cord-like appearance.

As with individual Eyelets, it is faster and easier to use a Right Decrease than a Left; therefore, either the Smooth Left Eyelet Column or the Corded Right Eyelet Column would be the best choice, if suitable for your pattern.

Smooth Left Eyelet Column

The strands dividing one Eyelet and the next slant upward to the left.

1. Outside Row: Yarnover, Knit Right Decrease.
2. Inside Row: Purl two stitches of pattern.

Smooth Right Eyelet Column

The strands of yarn between the Eyelets will slant upward to the right.

1. Outside Row: Knit Left Decrease, Yarnover.
2. Inside Row: Purl two stitches of pattern.

Corded Left Eyelet Column

The strands of yarn dividing the Eyelets slant upward to the left.

1. Outside Row: Yarnover, Knit Left Decrease.
2. Inside Row: Purl two stitches of pattern.

Corded Right Eyelet Column

With this version, the strands of yarn slant upward to the right.

1. Outside Row: Knit Right Decrease, Yarnover.
2. Inside Row: Purl two stitches of pattern.

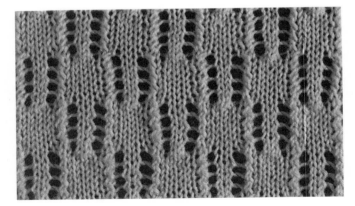

Checkered Acre. A Corded Eyelet pattern.

> **Note . . .**
>
> *On all outside rows after the first, when working the Left versions of the Eyelet Column, the decrease will include the stitch made on the previous Yarnover and the stitch to the left. When working the Right versions of the Eyelet Column, the decrease will include the stitch made on the Yarnover and the one to the right.*

Double Decrease Eyelet Column

The Eyelet Columns discussed above are frequently seen in pairs, a right and left flanking a plain stitch or two. A common variation on that theme is a column made up of pairs of Eyelets flanking a Center Double Decrease.

The resulting appearance will change slightly depending upon which of the three Double Decreases is used, but the basic approach is the same.

Double Decrease Eyelet Columns.

1. Outside Row: Yarnover, Double Decrease, Yarnover.
2. Inside Row: Purl three stitches of pattern.

❖ Diagonal Eyelet Insertion

Eyelets can be placed on the diagonal by stepping them one stitch to the right or left on each pattern row. There are two different ways of working, each resulting in a very different appearance.

In the first group, the Eyelets are divided by a decrease that produces a heavy bridge, either smooth or corded, between one Eyelet and the next.

In the second group the Eyelets are more open, divided by just two interlaced strands, and there is the option of forming a chain of stitches at the base of the diagonal.

Bridged Diagonal Insertions

The appearance of the bridge between one Eyelet and the next will be either smooth or corded depending upon the type of decrease used and its relationship to the Yarnover.

Bridged Diagonal Insertions.
Smooth version on right; Corded version on left.

The slope of the insertion column, whether up to the right or to the left, is controlled by the position of each Eyelet unit relative to the one below.

Smooth Left Bridge
1. On Outside: Knit Right Decrease, Yarnover.
   On subsequent rows, decrease will include stitch made on previous Yarnover and stitch to left.
2. All Inside Rows: Purl two stitches of pattern.

Smooth Right Bridge
1. On outside: Yarnover, Knit Left Decrease.
2. All Inside Rows: Purl two stitches of pattern.

Corded Left Bridge
1. On Outside: Knit Left Decrease, Yarnover.
2. All Inside Rows: Purl two stitches of pattern.

Corded Right Bridge
1. On Outside: Yarnover, Knit Right Decrease.
2. All Inside Rows: Purl two stitches of pattern.

Tin Lantern. A pattern with Bridged Insertions.

> **What's in a decrease . . .**
> *On all outside rows after the first, when working the Left Bridge versions, the decrease will include the stitch made on the previous Yarnover and the stitch to the left. When working the Right Bridge versions, the decrease will include the stitch made on the previous Yarnover and the stitch to the right.*

Open Diagonal Insertion

In these variations, the choice of decrease and its position before or after the Yarnover will determine whether there will be a chain of stitches below the line of Eyelets or not.

Here again the direction of the slope of the Insertion column is controlled by

Left: Chained Diagonal Insertion.
Right: Plain Diagonal Insertion.

the relationship between each Eyelet unit and the one below. The decrease always includes the stitch made on the previous Yarnover.

Chained Left Diagonal
1. On Outside: Yarnover, Knit Left Decrease.
2. All Inside Rows: Purl two stitches of pattern.

Chained Right Diagonal
1. On Outside: Knit Right Decrease, Yarnover.
2. All Inside Rows: Purl two stitches of pattern.

Plain Left Diagonal
1. On Outside: Yarnover, Knit Right Decrease.
2. All Inside Rows: Purl two stitches of pattern.

Plain Right Diagonal
1. On Outside: Knit Left Decrease, Yarnover.
2. All Inside Rows: Purl two stitches of pattern.

Zigzag and Diamond Insertion

While Diagonal Eyelet Insertion is often used to create simple lines of openwork on the fabric, the Chained version is favored to form zigzag and diamond shapes because the stitches at the base of the Eyelet emphasize the lines of the pattern.

The way this is done in many patterns often results in a break in the chain where it changes direction. Should you wish to connect the chain, add two rows to the pattern at the point where it switches direction; it is best to work out the change on a stitch chart.

Mrs. Montague's pattern.
Diamond Insertion with unconnected corners.

Chained Eyelets. Zigzag Insertion with connected corners.

Chained Eyelets: From Left to Right
1. Work Left Diagonal Chained Eyelets for first half of motif.
2. Work Left Diagonal Eyelet with a Smooth Bridge at turning point.
3. Use Right Diagonal Chained Eyelets for second half of motif.

Chained Eyelets: From Right to Left
1. Work Right Diagonal Chained Eyelets for first half of motif.
2. Work a Right Diagonal Eyelet with a Smooth Bridge at turning point.
3. Use Left Diagonal Chained Eyelets for second half of motif.

❖ Trellis Insertion
These patterns call for columns of Eyelet Insertion worked every row, with no plain rows in between. The instructions include examples of two-, three-, and four-stitch vertical columns of Trellis Mesh.

Narrow Trellis Insertion
As you work these versions, notice that on every row after the first, the decrease will include a Yarnover strand and the stitch that was made on the decrease in the row below.

Narrow Knotted Trellis
1. On outside: Knit Left Decrease, Yarnover.
2. On inside: Purl Right Decrease, Yarnover.

Narrow Zigzag Trellis
1. On outside: Yarnover, Knit Left Decrease.
2. On inside: Yarnover, Purl Right Decrease.

Narrow Trellis Insertions.
Left: Zigzag; Right: Knotted.

Medium Trellis Insertion
The next two variations are worked on a three-stitch unit, making the Eyelet column wider than the ones above.

Because the Yarnover strand is included in the decrease, the Eyelets take on a diamond shape.

Medium Knotted Trellis
1. On outside: Knit Left Decrease, Yarnover, Knit 1.
2. On inside: Purl Right Decrease, Yarnover, Purl 1.

Medium Trellis Insertions.
Left: Knotted; Right: Zigzag.

Medium Zigzag Trellis
1. On outside: Knit 1, Yarnover, Knit Left Decrease.
2. On inside: Purl 1, Yarnover, Purl Right Decrease.

Wide Trellis Insertion

And finally, a four-stitch unit that has two plain stitches; on all rows after the first, one stitch is worked on the previous decrease and one on the Yarnover strand; the new decrease includes the two plain stitches worked in the row below.

Wide Trellis Insertion.
Left: Knotted; Right: Zigzag.

Wide Knotted Trellis

1. On outside: Knit Left Decrease, Yarnover, Knit 2.
2. On inside: Purl Right Decrease, Yarnover, Purl 2.

Wide Zigzag Trellis

1. On outside: Knit 2 (first stitch and Yarnover), Yarnover, Knit Left Decrease.
2. On inside: Purl 2 (first stitch and Yarnover), Yarnover, Purl Right Decrease.

Frost Flowers. A pattern with Trellis Insertions.

❖ *Mesh*

Basic Single Eyelets, placed adjacent to one another both horizontally and vertically, will create a veil-like mesh, or netting. Patterns of this kind can be used for an entire openwork fabric, as is the case in the examples below; or small areas of mesh can be used to form a motif within a background done with a pattern that creates a solid fabric.

When Eyelets are set close together in this way, each one worked in exactly the same way, the fabric will exhibit a pronounced bias (for other ways to create bias, also see Bias Stitch Patterns, above, and Twist Stitch, in The Stitches). This is a permanent characteristic of the fabric, and is often used for decorative effect. Whether the bias travels to right or left is determined by the relative positions of the Yarnover and the decrease, and it can be eliminated entirely if the pattern alternates to balance the two effects.

Mesh fabrics benefit from being stretched and/or steamed open during finishing; see Dressing the Fabric. Also, they require special consideration when casting on and casting off to provide adequate width to the edge; see those chapters for suggestions.

To try these, work a sample on an even number of stitches, with a selvedge stitch at each side. The patterns either begin or end with a Yarnover, and it is all too easy to put one where it is not wanted, but fortunately any error will be made plain on the next row and can be corrected.

Bias Mesh

The fabric will lean toward the side that has the first Yarnover, away from the final decrease. In other words, if the sequence of Eyelets begins with a Yarnover, the fabric will bias to the right; if it ends with a Yarnover, it will bias to the left; it does not matter what type of decrease is used.

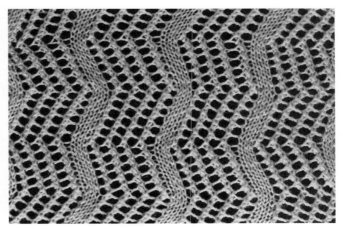

Rib Fantastic. Left and Right Bias Mesh.

Right Bias Mesh

- [Yarnover, Knit Right or Left Decrease]; repeat between brackets across row. Purl next row.

Left Bias Mesh

- [Knit Right or Left Decrease, Yarnover]; repeat between brackets across row. Purl next row.

Balanced Mesh

Here is an example of a Mesh pattern that balances the fabric so it does not exhibit bias.

Lace Check. A Balanced Mesh pattern.

1. [Yarnover, Knit Right Decrease]; repeat between brackets across row. Turn.
2. Purl all stitches. Turn.
3. [Knit Left Decrease, Yarnover]; repeat between brackets across row. Turn.
4. Purl all stitches. Turn.
5. Repeat Rows 1–4 for pattern.

Double Eyelet Mesh

This pattern also has no bias, and the effect is much more open. On all outside rows after the first, each decrease will include one of the stitches made with the Rib Increase on the Yarnover in the row below.

Double Eyelet Mesh.
Above: Left Decrease, Yarnover, Right Decrease.
Below: Right Decrease, Yarnover, Left Decrease.

1. Outside Row: [Knit Left Decrease, Double Yarnover, Knit Right Decrease]; repeat between brackets across row.
2. Inside Row: Purl across row; for every Yarnover, drop extra wrap and then work with Rib Increase.

Square Eyelet Mesh

This type of Mesh appears in old netting patterns where squares made up of Eyelets alternate with squares of Garter Stitch, each containing the same number of stitches. One of these Eyelets alone is not terribly attractive, but collectively they are more interesting because of their distinctive shape.

Square Eyelet Mesh.

There are two versions; one with a Single Yarnover, the other with a Double.

Single Yarnover Version

1. Knit 1, [Yarnover. Slip 2 stitches knitwise, one at a time; pass one slipped stitch over other and off needle. Slip a third stitch knitwise, pull second one over and off needle. Insert left needle into nearside of remaining slipped stitch and Knit farside], repeat between brackets across row, end Knit one.
2. Knit or Purl return row, working a Rib Increase on each Yarnover strand to restore the stitch count.

The technique in Step 1 is equivalent to Slip Chained Cast-Off, which makes the Eyelet flat on the top. Traditionally, the instructions for this mesh call for a Double Yarnover, but it tends to stretch out wider than the space occupied by the two decreased stitches and causes the fabric to splay out; if you want a larger Eyelet, work as follows.

Double Yarnover Version

In this version, the stitches are not worked before being cast off, which makes the fabric difficult to unravel; if that becomes necessary, undo each cast-off stitch individually.

- Work Step 1 above, but make a Double Yarnover, remove three stitches instead of two, and use a Multiple Yarnover Increase to restore the stitch count.

Trellis Mesh

Here are several ways to make an even more open version of mesh by working Single Eyelets not only side-by-side, but on every row instead of every other row. These types of patterns produce very handsome fabrics, they are extremely easy to do, and some look the same on both sides.

The two Trellis Mesh patterns discussed first have a radically different appearance, one nubby, the other smooth. Yet there is only a slight difference in how the patterns are worked, no more than a change in the relationship between the decrease and the Yarnover, and whether the Yarnover is the facing or backing stitch of the decrease on the next row.

I have provided Knit and Purl versions for each of them; the result is the same.

Nubby Trellis Mesh

Here is a delightfully nubby fabric that tends to lie nice and flat, and does not exhibit bias. Both the Yarnover openings and the nubs created by the decreases are staggered in vertical columns. You can work it in Knit or Purl, but I find the Purl version the easiest to do because I carry the yarn on the right; those of you who carry it on the left may prefer the Knit version. And either pattern can also be done with a Left Decrease instead.

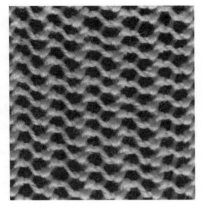

Nubby Trellis Mesh.

Knit Version

• [Knit Right Decrease, Yarnover]; repeat between brackets across row, and on every subsequent row.

Purl Version

• [Yarnover, Purl Right Decrease]; repeat between brackets across row, and on every subsequent row.

On all rows after the first, the Yarnover will be the right stitch of the decrease pair in the Knit version, and the left stitch of the decrease pair in the Purl version.

Smooth Trellis Mesh

These Trellis Mesh patterns make smoother fabrics that are more compressed than the Nubby version when first knit, and, if left in that condition, the stitch columns will appear to go on the diagonal. If the fabric is stretched open when it is dressed, the effect becomes more subtle but is still evident.

The first version of the pattern uses either a Knit or a Purl Right Decrease, which causes the stitch columns to appear to slope up to the right. The second version of the pattern slopes up to the left; it is best done with a Knit Left Decrease; the Purl Left Decrease is awkward to do. Whichever decrease you use, it will always include a Yarnover.

Also consider combining the right and left versions to create a zigzag effect by working several rows of one, and then several rows of the other.

Right Slope

• [Yarnover, Knit Right Decrease]; repeat between brackets across row, and on every subsequent row.
• Or, [Purl Right Decrease, Yarnover]; repeat between brackets across row, and on every subsequent row.

Left Slope

• Knit one, [Knit Left Decrease, Yarnover], repeat between brackets across row, and on every subsequent row.

Bias Trellis Mesh

To make a Trellis Mesh actually go on the bias, instead of just appear to do so, begin one row with a Yarnover, and end the next row with one.

1. [Yarnover, Knit Right Decrease], repeat between brackets across row.
2. [Purl Right Decrease, Yarnover], repeat between brackets across row.

To vary the pattern, you can use Knit on both rows, or use a Left Decrease instead.

❖ *Lace*

Lace is one of the glories of the knitter's art, yet you will find this section oddly brief. That is because all of the most important elements of Lace knitting have already been discussed above, including Increase and Decrease Techniques, Bias Stitch Patterns, and Eyelets and Mesh (above), and you will find more information and illustrations in Charted Stitch Patterns.

All that is left to do here, therefore, is to demonstrate that you now have the knowledge to make sense of even complex Lace patterns that use these techniques.

Lace Chevron

Purl Barred Scallop is an example of what a Chevron-type pattern looks like when done with a Yarnover Increase instead of with the closed increases that were used in the section on Bias, above. Also notice how the plain rows of Reverse Stockinette introduced between the pattern rows follow the contours set up by the bias.

Purl Barred Scallop Lace.

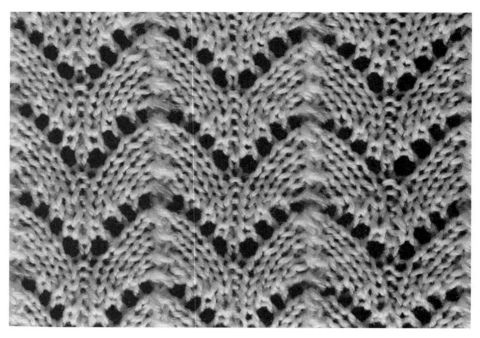

Horseshoe Lace.

Horseshoe Lace

This wonderful old lace is found in almost every pattern book because it is so pretty and so easy to do. The Yarnover Increases step toward Double Decreases set at the center of each motif.

The new stitch columns generated by the increases take on a soft curve toward the center where they are reabsorbed by the decreases.

Leaf-Patterned Lace

This is another common lace pattern that is quite simple to do. In this case, the Yarnover Increases are at the center and the decreases step out to each side, creating a diamond shape that is enhanced by using the facing stitches of the decreases to form a chain around the edges. Also, the motifs are staggered, with the middle of one adjacent to the beginning and end of the ones to either side.

Leaf-Patterned Lace.

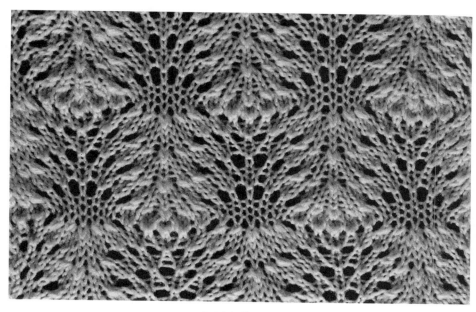

Ostrich Plumes.

Ostrich Plumes

This is a beautiful old cluster-type pattern that is done by setting groups of increases together within one motif, with the balancing decreases at the center of the adjacent motif. The paired increase and decrease motifs trade places on the next repeat, which greatly adds to the interest of the design; in other patterns of this kind, the two types of motif are more often lined up vertically.

Meander

Here is a beautiful example of a pattern where the number of stitches between the increase and its balancing decrease is held constant, but these pairs step to the right for several rows, and then to the left for several rows. Notice how the slope of the stitches that lie between each pair changes direction, always moving up out of the increases and then being absorbed by the decreases. The plain columns of stitches between each motif not only emphasize the undulating curve, but strengthen the vertical lines of the pattern.

Meander.

CHAPTER 13

Color Techniques

The introduction of more than one color to a knitted fabric livens things up considerably; as you will see, there are ways to do this that even beginning knitters will find easy, while others can challenge the expert.

The simplest patterns are horizontal stripes, which can be enhanced simply by varying the number of rows or by using yarns in different colors and textures. Vertical and diagonal stripes and more complex geometric motifs are made with the Stranded Color method, working with two colors at the same time.

Also, many patterns can be done by combining color and various stitch techniques to add lively surface texture. All of these reflect the underlying grid-like nature of the fabric; however, the Intarsia technique escapes this geometry and makes it possible to create free-form, painterly motifs.

Other ways to add color to a garment are discussed in the chapter on Surface Decoration, which includes needlework, appliqué, and trim, as well as beads and sequins. Those techniques can be used, either alone or in addition to one of the methods described here, to create color and textural effects that lie on the surface of the fabric.

Putting Colors Together

For anyone interested in learning how to design, or even for those who simply want to acquire greater confidence in choosing a pattern, some time spent learning more about how color can be used effectively is a good investment.

Many books have been written on color theory, including several specifically about designing for knits, and classes are available that teach how colors and shapes interact. However, you can do a great deal to train your eye in an informal way.

Wherever you are, pay attention to successful design—store windows, fashion magazines, books, television, and Internet sites are all rich resources. And by no means limit yourself to knits, nor just to clothing design—interior design is a good source of inspiration for color and pattern ideas, as are images of the natural world, such as flowers, insects, and birds.

When you see something you like, stop and think about why it appeals to you and analyze how it was done. Or challenge yourself by taking a design you do not particularly like and try to change it into something that is more appealing. Trace a pattern, or make several copies of it, and then use crayons or colored pencils to fill it in with different color combinations; cut pattern elements apart and reposition or resize them to see what will happen.

Another excellent exercise is to make several versions of charted color patterns for knitting—use one pattern with different color combinations, or use the same colors in several different patterns to see what effect a change of scale or difference in proportion between light and dark will have.

Pin the samples up and look at them from a distance. The stitches in a knit behave like the pixels of a digital photograph, the little squares of individual color that make up an image. If a color motif in a knitted fabric contains large stitches or is seen close up, the edge will appear to be stepped; if the stitches are small or seen from a distance, the edges will smooth out, just like when a digital photograph is enlarged or reduced.

Therefore, the gauge you use to make a fabric is a major factor in the appearance of the details in the design and it also determines how many motifs you can fit within the frame of the garment.

In addition to the scale factor, a biological phenomenon occurs called "optical mixing," which means that the smaller the bits of color, the more the eye blends them together into an entirely different one, just as if you had mixed paints on a palette. Similarly, your perception of a color seen separately will change when it is placed in close proximity to another. An interesting exercise is to cut various shapes out of different colored papers and put them next to or on top of one another to see how much they change. For instance, if you put two squares of the same color on top of two backgrounds in two other colors, the color of the squares on top will no longer look alike; the same phenomenon may be evident when you use different background colors in separate areas of a pattern for a pattern yarn in a single color.

These experiments with design and how the eye perceives color and pattern are fascinating and well worth trying. The important thing is to be playful and curious, and to remember that you learn something just as important from the examples you think of as failures as from those that succeed.

Blends and Stripes

To begin, here are several elementary but effective techniques that make it easy to add color to what might otherwise be a very plain design.

❖ Multiple Yarns

One of the simplest ways to introduce color to a knitted fabric is, in effect, to create your own yarn. If you hold two or more yarns together while you work, the individual colors and/or textures will blend together in the fabric, producing a tweedy effect and a new color that is the sum of its parts. At its simplest, you can combine two yarns for an entire fabric, but you can also change the colors held together to add variety to stripes or other types of color patterns (see Color Blending, below).

Multiple Yarns.
Two yarns held as one.

Notice that I said "textures," for you need not use the same types of yarns. In addition to blending colors, you can combine smooth with fluffy or nubby, thick with thin, or shiny with dull. Twist the yarns under consideration together, and then wrap them around your fingers to get an idea of the effect they will create in the fabric. Keep in mind that the thickness of the combined yarns needs to be suitable for the type of garment you plan to make—this is an opportunity to use those superfine yarns you might otherwise avoid.

Tips for Working with Multiple Yarns
Here are some suggestions for how to handle the yarns.

- *Keep a close eye on your work when using more than one yarn; it is all too easy to insert the needle between the strands instead of into the center of the stitch, or to miss a strand when you wrap the needle to make a stitch. The result will be stray loops on the surface of the fabric.*
- *Do not wind the yarns together into a single ball; you may find yourself with a terrible tangle. The stitches tend to take up more of a heavier strand than a thinner one, and less of a smooth yarn than a textured one. Instead, place each yarn in a separate container and only gather them together in your hand when you start to work.*
- *To keep the yarns from winding around each other when working flat, turn the work to the right at the end of one row and to the left at the end of the other.*

  When working in the round, stop from time to time and circle the needles and fabric in the opposite direction to untwist the yarns.

  Or, with either method, push the stitches back from the tip of the needle and let it hang from the yarn to unspin.

❖ Basic Horizontal Stripes

Another elementary way to add color is to do a few rows in one color, and then a few in another. Just attach a new supply of yarn along with the existing one, and switch back and forth between the two; for information on stranding the yarn up between rows, see Tips for Stranded Color.

When working circular, it is possible to make stripes of any number of rows; every round brings you back to where the other yarn is attached, and you have the option of dropping one and picking up the other.

Basic Stripes.

However, when working a flat fabric on single-point needles it takes two rows to bring you back to the side where the other yarn is attached. Therefore, when working this way it is impossible to make stripes with an odd number of rows. However, working on double-point needles makes it possible to use a technique called The Slide, which gets around that limitation (it is also used for patterns in Double-Fabrics).

The Slide

Use a pair of double-point needles or a circular one. For one-row stripes, work as follows:

1. On outside: With Yarn A, Knit across row. Drop Yarn A at left edge; do not turn.
2. Slide stitches back to tip of needle at right, pick up Yarn B, and Knit to end of row. Drop Yarn B; both yarns are at same edge of fabric; turn.
3. On inside: With Yarn A, Purl across row. Drop Yarn A; do not turn.
4. Slide stitches to right tip of needle, pick up Yarn B, and Purl to end of row; drop Yarn B; both yarns are at same edge of fabric; turn.
5. Repeat Steps 1–4 as needed.

Since you can slide the stitches to pick up whichever yarn you need next, it is easy to make stripes of any number of rows.

For instance, for three rows in one color, one row in another, work as follows:

- With Yarn A, work two rows, turning at the end of each row; work third row with Yarn A, drop it, and Slide. Pick up Yarn B and work one row, drop it, turn, and pick up Yarn A and repeat.

Color Blending

Color blending is a method of gradually shifting the color palette of either the background or foreground of a pattern. This approach can be applied to plain stripes done with several yarns, as described above, but is also interesting when used with the Stranded Color or Mosaic Patterns discussed below.

The concept is simple enough and there are several ways to apply it; here are some examples.

1. Select four yarns in closely related colors, and/or in different textures, and designate them Yarns A, B, C, D; these are background colors.
2. Select a fifth color that contrasts more strongly with the other four to use as the main yarn; call it M.
3. Work one stripe holding Yarns M and A.
4. For next stripe, retain Yarn M, drop Yarn A, and pick up Yarn B.
5. Continue in this way, working each stripe with Yarn M and the next yarn in the sequence of blending colors.

There are several other options for how to sequence the yarns; for example:

- Reverse the order, such as A, B, C, D, C, B, A.
- Hold A and B together for several rows, and then hold B and C together, next C and D, and finally D and A; repeat the sequence for the length of the fabric.

Fibonacci Stripes

An interesting design theory is based on what are called Fibonacci numbers, named for the medieval mathematician who first defined them. The Fibonacci series starts with 0 and continues with the sums of numbers paired according to a simple rule:

- $0 + 1 = 1$, $1 + 1 = 2$, $1 + 2 = 3$, $2 + 3 = 5$, $3 + 5 = 8$, and so on, to infinity.

    Notice that the two numbers on either side of the equal sign in one step are added together in the next step.

    Only the smaller Fibonacci numbers are of interest to knitters: 1, 2, 3, 5, 8, 13 . . .

The theory is that stripes made with rows of any Fibonacci number, in any sequence, will be aesthetically pleasing. In other words, you might use a stripe of 8 rows, and then one of 3, followed by one of 5, but never one of 4 or 9 rows. And of course, this need not be limited to plain stripes, since it would have the same effect when applied to more decorative ones, such as the Stranded Color patterns described below, although you may find few repeats with the number of rows that will fit the theory.

Stranded Color Patterns

Stranded Color patterns appear in many knitting traditions throughout the world, which means there is a wealth of designs to choose from and unlimited inspiration for new ones. The patterns consist of geometric motifs done in one color

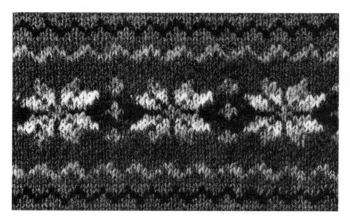

A Shetland Fair Isle pattern.

Traditional Fair Isle of the 1920s. Shetland Museum and Archives, photograph by J. Murray.

with the background in another; while many different colors may be used to create the overall pattern, it is rare for there to be more than two colors used in any one row.

Although a garment made with patterns of this kind looks complex, they are actually easier to do than you might think. The patterns are always charted (see Charted Color Patterns), and are usually done in plain Stockinette.

❖ Stranded Pattern Methods

To make patterns of this kind, two yarns are alternated to the stitches across the row, with one or more stitches done with one yarn, and then one or more stitches with the other. These are called "stranded" patterns because the yarn needed next

Diagram of Stranded Color pattern, looking down on stitches.

must be drawn past the stitches just made with the other yarn, leaving a horizontal strand on the inside of the fabric.

Simple variations of the standard knitting methods can be used to handle the yarns for these patterns, and there are two specialized techniques as well. The differences between them have primarily to do with the amount of manual skill required and the speed and ease of working, but they all produce the same result.

The easiest approach is to use a modification of your preferred knitting method; this speeds up the time it takes to get used to handling two yarns and is a real boon for those who are strongly right- or left-handed.

Another option is to use the technique of Slip Stranding; only one yarn is held at a time and it works equally well with any of the knitting methods.

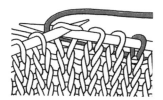

Stranding yarn past two stitches.

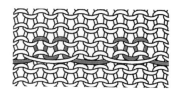

Stranded yarns on inside of fabric.

For anyone who wants to do these patterns frequently, however, it is well worth the effort to learn to carry one yarn in each hand, or both yarns at the same time in the left or right hand. This requires the most practice to achieve a consistent and satisfactory fabric, since few people are equally adept with both hands, but it is a fast and efficient way to work.

Regardless of which method you use, the most important thing is to provide just enough yarn to each strand so it is neither too loose nor too tight. If it is too loose, the stitches at either end will take up the extra yarn and enlarge; if it is too tight, it will bunch the fabric together. Here is the basic rule for how to measure out yarn to the strand:

- Before changing from one yarn to the other, spread the stitches last worked out along the right needle so there is a gap between each one that is roughly equal to the yarn width, and then work the next stitch.

Stranded Color pattern showing strands on inside.

The following instructions refer to Yarn A and Yarn B; these terms can be used to designate either the dark or light colors, respectively; or think of them as the background yarn and the motif yarn, if you prefer.

Stranding: Yarns Held to Left

If you carry the yarn on the left, you can work a Stranded Color pattern by holding one yarn on each of your first two fingers, or carry both yarns on your left forefinger with one close to the nail, the other between the first and second knuckles.

There are no special instructions required for working with two yarns instead of one in this way; simply use the needle tip to pick up whichever yarn is needed next from your left finger. Most people find it difficult to manage two yarns this way while working in Purl, so the method is primarily used for doing a circular fabric in Knit.

Whenever the pattern requires more of one yarn than the other, the two yarns will pass through your hand at a different rate, therefore, maintaining even tension can be a challenge. You may need to try several methods of holding the yarns to find which method works best for you—this is as much a matter of anatomy as it is of dexterity.

Stranding: Yarns Held to Right

There are three ways to hold both yarns to the right for a Stranded Color pattern, although the Right-Hand Method is by far the easiest to learn and to do.

The yarns can also be held on the first and second fingers of the right hand, but this makes Purl more of a challenge. However, there is an interesting alternative suggested by the method used for Twined Knit where each yarn is picked up by the forefinger as needed, and this makes Purl considerably easier. With either of these methods, a Knitting Belt, or some similar support for the needle, is a great help, but is not necessary.

Right-Hand Stranding

The Right-Hand Method of knitting is easily adapted for color patterns; it does not require learning a new skill but is more a matter of becoming accustomed to managing the two yarns and changing from one to the other.

Working this way is ideal if you have never done a color pattern before, do them only occasionally, or have tried one of the other methods and were unhappy with the result. You will find it just as easy to control the tension when working either Knit or Purl, which is why this method is a good choice if you want to do a Stranded Color pattern in a flat fabric.

When you pick up the yarns, have Yarn A pass between the first and second fingers and trail over the back of your hand, and have Yarn B pass between the third and fourth, or fourth and fifth fingers in the same way. Separating the yarns this way keeps them readily accessible and prevents tangling; having them trail over the back of your hand keeps them from getting caught between palm and needle.

You will be using just one yarn at a time to work the stitches, as follows:

1. Pick up Yarn A with thumb and forefinger, and work first group of stitches in that color.
2. Drop Yarn A, space last group of new stitches out along right needle, and pick up Yarn B; strand yarn past last group of stitches and work next group in that color.
3. Drop Yarn B, pick up Yarn A, and work next group of stitches as described in Step 2.
4. Continue in this way, alternating yarns to work as many stitches in each color as shown in pattern; always space stitches out on needle to measure yarn to strand, and strand yarn on inside of fabric.

There is no need to concern yourself with the tension of the inactive yarn; just let it trail through your fingers until you need it again and at that point adjust the tension to allow enough length to the strand.

Also, it is not necessary to wrap the yarns around each other every time you change from one color to the other, although you may see this recommended (however, see Twined Knit, where this is done after every stitch). Nothing is gained by this when making a Stranded Color pattern; it tangles the two yarns together and they will need to be unwound from time to time before the work can proceed.

Stranding with Two Right Fingers

Many knitters who work with the yarn on the right forefinger are adept at working color patterns with the second yarn carried in the same way on the middle finger. You may want to experiment and decide whether to tension the two yarns together, or to separate them, with one wrapped on your small finger and one on the ring finger, or some other combination that suits your hand and preferences.

- Work with yarn on forefinger in usual way; to work with yarn on middle finger, tilt hand slightly nearside to move forefinger out of the way in order to wrap yarn.
- To work in Purl, keep hand tilted toward nearside for both strands; if necessary, bend forefinger down to hold the yarn it carries out of the way when wrapping yarn with middle finger.

Stranding with Right Forefinger

Instead of holding both yarns poised above the needle with two fingers, with this method each yarn is picked up with the forefinger as needed; it works just as well for Purl as for Knit, so is ideal for working flat. This is similar to the method used for Twined Knit, and there are illustrations included with that material that you may find helpful for this purpose.

Hold yarns together in the palm of your hand or wrap them on your little finger in the usual way; insert your forefinger and middle finger between the two yarns to keep them separated, or keep one yarn on the nearside of your thumb; there is no need to place tension on either yarn until it is in use.

1. Draw hand down, away from needle tips, to put slight tension on two yarns, and move forefinger under Yarn A to pick it up.
2. Move hand back up into position and bring Yarn A past previous stitches in other color, measuring off adequate yarn to strand, work next stitches according to pattern, and then drop yarn from forefinger.
3. Draw hand down away from needle tips as before, and move forefinger under Yarn B to pick it up.

4. Move hand back up into position and bring Yarn B past previous stitches in other color and work next set of stitches according to pattern; drop Yarn B from forefinger.
5. Repeat Steps 1–4 to work pattern.

This seems complicated when described in words, but with a little practice the motions become very quick and smooth.

Yarn Ring

If you prefer to hold both yarns in the same hand, a Yarn Ring is a tool you can wear on your forefinger that is designed to keep the strands separated so they will not tangle together as much; see Tools.

There are two versions: one is a metal coil with a pair of loops on the top through which the yarns are threaded; the other is plastic with a series of pegs capped by a flat bar to keep the yarns in place.

Either tool will do the job, but I find they make it awkward to readjust the yarns as necessary to maintain tension; by all means try them for yourself and see if one or the other suits you.

Slip Stranding Method

Here is another way to do color patterns that can be used with any knitting method; it is as easy to do when working circular or flat, and in either Knit or Purl.

One yarn is used to work all the stitches of the motifs across the row, while slipping all the background stitches; then the other yarn is used for a second pass across the needle in the same direction, working all the background stitches and slipping the motif stitches. In other words, it takes two passes across the stitches on the needle to make one row of fabric. It might seem that having to manipulate all of the stitches twice in order to do a single row would be a very slow way of working. In fact, it goes along quite well, because the slipped stitches move from one needle to the next very rapidly.

When working circular, one round brings you back to where the other yarn hangs in wait and you can pick it up to work the next round. However, when working flat, at the end of the first pass across the stitches one yarn will be at the left side, the other at the right side. The solution is to work with a circular needle or a pair of double-point needles and use the Slide technique, described above; simply move the stitches from the left tip of the needle to the right tip to pick up the other yarn for the second pass across the stitches.

Slip Stranding a Flat Fabric

Slip all stitches purlwise with yarn stranded on inside of fabric. Work as follows:

1. On outside: With Yarn A, Knit all motif stitches, and Slip all background stitches purlwise with yarn stranded farside. At end of row, drop Yarn A; do not turn.

2. On outside: Slide all stitches to right needle tip, and pick up Yarn B; Knit all background stitches, and Slip all motif stitches with yarn stranded farside. At end of row, turn.
3. On inside: Work as described in Steps 1 and 2, but in Purl, and strand yarn on nearside.

The first two passes across the needle are used to make a single, outside row, and both yarns will then be together again at the edge. The next two passes are used to make a single, inside row, and the yarns will then be together at the other edge.

Slip Stranding a Circular Fabric

1. First round: Knit all motif stitches with Yarn A, and Slip all background stitches, with yarn stranded farside.
2. Second round: Knit all background stitches with Yarn B, and Slip motif stitches with yarn stranded farside.

At the end of two full rounds, all the stitches will have been worked once, completing a single row of the fabric.

Tips for Slip Stranding

A disadvantage of this method is that it can sometimes be difficult to keep track of where you are in a complex pattern. The problem is that on the first pass across the needle, the colors of the new stitches on the right needle will not accurately reflect the sequence of colors in the pattern because some of the stitches slipped will be the same color as those just worked.

Here are some suggestions that will help you keep your place in the pattern.

- *Be consistent, always working the motif stitches on the first pass, and the background stitches on the second, or vice versa.*
- *To check for accuracy after the first pass, look on the inside of the fabric; all the stitches with a strand below them were slipped, those with no strand were worked.*
- *After completing the second pass, check the new stitches on the needle to see if the completed pattern is correct before going on.*

Two-Hand Stranding

One of the fastest ways of doing Stranded Color patterns is to carry one yarn in each hand. Many knitters find this something of a challenge to learn, and it takes practice to develop even tension and produce a smooth, attractive fabric. However, if you think you will want to make Stranded Color patterns frequently, by all means have a go at this; learning it will be well worth the time you invest.

In those areas of the world where this is the traditional method, knitters work even complex patterns with ease, and you will undoubtedly encounter rather amazing claims regarding the speed they can achieve. Do not be intimidated by these stories. Keep in mind that these knitters have honed their skills with a lifetime of practice—most learned as children, knit frequently, and rarely do any other sort of knitting. Anyone who comes to the craft later in life, or only works this way occasionally, cannot expect to develop an equal facility. Besides, this is not a race; your comfort level while working is more important than speed, and you have only yourself to please.

First practice just the knitting method you have never used before; after you are comfortable with it, only then try to combine it with your customary method. Also, because Two-Hand Stranding is commonly done entirely in Knit while working in the round, it is a good idea to practice that way as well because Purl is somewhat more difficult; once you have some facility with Knit, then learn to Purl if you want to work flat.

- Hold Yarn A as for Right-Finger Knitting; hold Yarn B as for Left-Hand Knitting. Knit stitches with Yarn A according to pattern, space new stitches along right needle to measure yarn to strand, and then work next group of stitches with Yarn B, according to pattern. Alternate in this way across row.

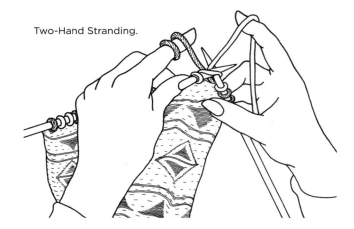

Two-Hand Stranding.

It is tempting to hold the yarn used for the majority of the stitches in a row in the hand with which you have the greatest facility. However, it is usually best to be consistent and always hold the background yarn in one hand and the pattern yarn in the other, regardless of which of them will be used for more stitches on any pattern row; for more information on why this is the case, see Theory of Color Dominance, below.

❖ Weaving-In Yarns

Most Stranded Color patterns are designed with a limited number of stitches between one color change and the next. This is done partly because it is more difficult to control the tension on longer strands, but also because the strands are prone to being snagged when the garment is put on or taken off.

The Weaving-In technique cures the problem of over-long strands by attaching them to the inside of the fabric while working a stitch with the other yarn. Most often the strand is caught at its midpoint, so instead of one long strand there are two shorter ones.

Keep in mind that the length of the strand is determined by the gauge of the fabric—a strand drawn past four stitches will be an inch long if the gauge is 4 stitches per inch, but only half an inch long if the gauge is 8 stitches per inch. (Mary Thomas discusses a fragment of Arabian color knitting some thousand years old, which she says is worked in silk at an astonishing 36 stitches to the inch; at that gauge, a strand drawn past even 9 stitches would be only ¼ inch long.†) A quick comparison of the scale of the pattern you plan to use with the gauge you expect to have will tell you whether weaving-in is something you want to consider.

When the strand is caught like this on the inside of the fabric, it may peek through on the outside. This is more likely to be the case if the fabric is

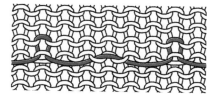

Strand woven in on inside of fabric.

knitted at a loose gauge; if the two yarns are in strongly contrasting colors; or if the garment fits tightly and the fabric is stretched taut in wear. The tweedy look this can create is not suitable for every garment design, but in some it is considered desirable; see Woven Intarsia. To get a realistic picture of how the finished fabric will look and behave, dress your gauge swatch; see Dressing a Swatch.

In addition to the practical purposes described here, a stranded pattern with systematically woven-in yarns can be beautiful when turned to the outside of a garment, as shown in the photograph on page 258. Also, the Weaving-In technique is used for Purl Inlay; however, in that application the woven-in yarn is not used for any of the stitches.

Weaving-in is done in slightly different ways depending on how you hold the yarns. While the first set of instructions below can be used with any method, those that follow are specific to each one.

Weaving-In: Lattice Method

This technique is worked in the same way as the Lattice Technique (see The Stitches); the yarns are stranded in the normal way across one row, and caught up against the inside of the fabric on the next.

---

† Mary Thomas, *Mary Thomas's Knitting Book* (New York: Dover Publications, 1972), p. 91.

It is easy to do and works with any method of holding the yarns for a color pattern, but it is a particularly welcome option if you hold both yarns on the right, because the alternatives are less than ideal.

Work a row of pattern; on next row, at the midpoint of a long strand, catch it up as follows:

- If working on outside, reach down on inside and lift strand onto left needle with right side of strand on nearside; Knit strand and next stitch together as for a Right Decrease.
- If working on inside, Slip next stitch, lift strand onto right needle with right side on nearside, insert left needle under strand and into stitch on farside and Purl strand and stitch together as for a Left Decrease.

While it is best to pick up the strand at its midpoint, if necessary, do this one stitch to right or left of center in order to work it together with a stitch in the same color yarn so it is less likely to be visible on the outside.

It is particularly important to allow enough yarn to the strand with this method of weaving-in, because it will be drawn up into the row above.

Weaving-In: Yarns in Two Hands

This is the most efficient method to use for weaving-in; however, how the two yarns are manipulated depends upon whether you are working in Knit or Purl, and whether the yarn to be stranded is held to the left or right. There are four sets of instructions to be learned, which may seem complicated at first, but once you are familiar with the technique it goes very quickly and becomes quite automatic.

Hold Yarn A in the left hand, Yarn B in the right hand. Work to the midpoint of a group of contrast-color stitches, and then catch the strand up on either side of the next stitch in one of the following ways.

Knit with Right Yarn/ Weave Left Yarn

1. Insert right needle into stitch as to Knit.
2. Shift left finger nearside so Yarn A leans against right needle tip.
3. Pass Yarn B to farside of Yarn A, wrap around needle as to Knit, and draw through new stitch.
4. Shift left finger farside, holding Yarn A away from needle tips; pass Yarn B between Yarn A and needle to Knit next stitch.

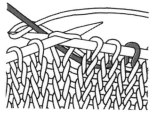

Knit with Right Yarn/Weave Left Yarn: Step 3.

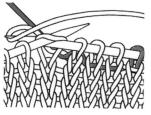

Knit with Right Yarn/Weave Left Yarn: Step 4.

Knit with Left Yarn/Weave Right Yarn

1. Shift left finger farside to hold Yarn A away from needles. Insert right needle into stitch and wrap Yarn B as to Knit, but do not draw through stitch.
2. Also wrap Yarn A around right needle as to Knit, to left of Yarn B.
3. Unwrap Yarn B from needle by passing it over Yarn A to left, and then under needle tip to farside; Yarn A remains wrapped on needle.
4. Draw Yarn A through to form new stitch.
5. Hold Yarn B in normal position and Knit next stitch with Yarn A.

Knit with Left Yarn/Weave Right Yarn: Steps 1 and 2.

Purl with Right Yarn/Weave Left Yarn

Hold both yarns on nearside.

1. Insert right needle into stitch as to Purl.
2. Move Yarn A against right needle tip.
3. Pass Yarn B to nearside of Yarn A, wrap around needle as to Purl, and draw through new stitch.
4. Move Yarn A to nearside, away from tip of right needle, pass Yarn B between Yarn A and needle, and Purl next stitch.

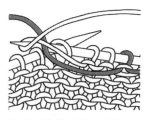
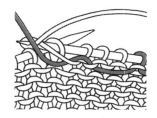

Purl with Right Yarn/Weave Left Yarn: Step 3.

Purl with Right Yarn/Weave Left Yarn: Step 4.

Purl with Left Yarn/Weave Right Yarn

Hold both yarns on nearside.

1. Insert right needle into stitch as to Purl.
2. Hold Yarn A to nearside, away from needle tips; wrap Yarn B under needle from nearside to farside. Lay Yarn A against right needle, to left of Yarn B.
3. Unwrap Yarn B from needle, passing it over Yarn A to left, and then under needle tip to nearside; Yarn A remains on needle.
4. Draw Yarn A through stitch as to Purl.

Purl with Left Yarn/Weave Right Yarn: Step 3.

Weaving-In: Yarns to Left

Whether you prefer to carry both yarns on the forefinger, or one on the forefinger and one on the middle finger, the important thing is to be consistent about how you weave-in to reduce how much the two yarns wind around each other.

Weaving-In: Yarns on Two Fingers

Hold Yarn A on forefinger and Yarn B on middle finger of left hand.

- To weave in Yarn B, reach needle over it and down on farside to pick up Yarn A; with yarn on needle, retrace path back into position and Knit next stitch.
- To weave in Yarn A, reach needle down on nearside and under it to pick up Yarn B; with yarn on needle, retrace path back into position and Knit next stitch.

Weaving-In: Yarns on One Finger

Hold Yarn A closest to fingertip and Yarn B between first and second knuckle.

- To weave in Yarn B, reach needle under it and up on farside to pick up Yarn A; with yarn on needle, retrace path back into position and Knit next stitch.
- To weave in Yarn A, reach needle over it and down on farside to pick up Yarn B; with yarn on needle, retrace path back into position and Knit next stitch.

Weaving-In: Yarns to Right

A strand can be woven in when holding both yarns to the right, but there is really no good way to do so. If the pattern you are using needs to have this done frequently, I recommend you use the Lattice Method of Weaving-In, described above, instead.

However, if you will only need to weave in the occasional strand, one of the methods described here will do. While the third one is the most complicated, once you get the hang of it, it is probably the best of the group.

In these instructions, clarity seems to be aided by referring to the "active yarn," which is being used to make stitches, and the "inactive yarn," which is being stranded.

Weaving-In: Right-Hand Method

- Drop active yarn to left, reach over and then under inactive yarn hanging below right needle and pick it up again.

Here is an alternative; no faster, but perhaps easier to do.

- Drop active yarn, pick up inactive yarn, pass it over active yarn and hold it against left needle; pick up active yarn again and work next stitch; drop inactive yarn and make next stitch.

Weaving-In: Right-Finger Method

This method of weaving in the yarns resembles that used to change the yarns for Twined Knit. For the latter, the yarns are wrapped around each other as they are alternated to the stitches; for this purpose, the wrapping method is much the same, but you continue with the same yarn as before.

Hold the yarns as for Twined Knit, with one on nearside of forefinger or thumb, and the other on farside of middle finger. The yarns are wrapped in one direction on the first side of a stitch, and in the other direction on the other side; the yarn not in use will be caught by the running thread. Work as follows:

1. To weave in to right of stitch: Drop active yarn from forefinger, reach over and then under inactive yarn and draw active yarn back over to nearside again; Knit or Purl next stitch.
2. To weave in to left of stitch: Drop active yarn, reach under and then over inactive yarn and draw active yarn back under to nearside; Knit or Purl next stitch.

It is important to alternate the direction in which the yarns are wrapped or they will wind around each other and you will need to stop and unwind them from time to time; if this happens, drop the needle and let it spin until they are separated again.

Weaving-In: Either Method

Here is an alternative that can be used with either method of holding the yarns to the right, on your finger, or in your hand. It is slow, but works quite well; the yarns will not tangle and the strand is caught on both sides of the stitch.

Weaving-In with Knit Stitch

1. Insert needle into stitch as to Knit. Draw inactive yarn under active yarn, and move it over right needle to nearside, past stitch with needle tips in it, and then over left needle to farside; hold yarn in place with left forefinger.
2. Wrap active yarn on right needle tip and Knit, drawing new stitch to nearside under inactive yarn; discard original stitch; inactive yarn will slide off left needle to farside.
3. Maintain inactive yarn on farside with left forefinger, and Knit next stitch to weave in that yarn on other side of previous stitch; drop inactive yarn.

Weaving-In with Purl Stitch

1. Insert needle into stitch as to Purl. Draw inactive yarn over active yarn and position across needles as described above.
2. Work Purl stitch and discard, leaving inactive yarn on left needle tip to right of next stitch.

3. Insert right needle tip under inactive yarn to Purl next stitch; drop inactive yarn from needle when discarding stitch and then return it to right of active yarn on nearside.

Stranding for Warmth

A garment done in fine wool with a Stranded Color pattern is both light and exceptionally warm—the sweater is, in a sense, lined with an extra layer of wool. (This is also true of the Twined Knit and Purl Inlay techniques.) But if you want a dense, sturdy fabric for a cold-weather vest or jacket, you might be interested in a technique that Mary Thomas calls "Corrugated Fabrics," or "Cartridge Pleating."†

A corrugated fabric has columns of stitches in contrast colors that are bunched tightly together. To do this, it is necessary to break one of the cardinal rules for Stranded Color work and pull each yarn firmly past the intervening stitches.

The color patterns that are most suitable for this are four- or five-stitch repeats done as vertical stripes, diagonals, or checkerboards. The technique can also be done with two yarns of the same color to take advantage of just the thermal benefits and pronounced surface texture.

- Draw yarn up very firmly to wrap first stitch after yarn change, and then return to normal tension so next stitches will not be too tight; use larger size needles, if necessary, to make softer fabric.
- For flat fabric, always hold both yarns together to work selvedge stitches in order to anchor last strand; a Stockinette Selvedge has more substance and works better for this purpose.

Be warned that a fabric of this kind requires a great deal of yarn. If you need to economize, perhaps do just the sleeves or the bodice this way. Another interesting application is to use a wide band of Corrugated Knit for a belt-like waist, creating a gathered peplum below, or, for a somewhat similar application, use it for the yoke of a jacket to gather the bodice.

❖ Tips for Stranded Color

Included here is information on gauge and estimating yarn requirements for Stranded Color patterns, suggestions for suitable cast-on techniques, how to shape a fabric with the minimum effect in a color pattern, and how to manage yarn supplies. Also, see the discussion on the Theory of Color Dominance, below, about various factors that can influence which color has a stronger presence in the pattern.

---

† Mary Thomas, *Mary Thomas's Knitting Book* (New York: Dover Publications, 1972), p. 99.

Making a Stranded Color Garment

Some practical aspects of making a Stranded Color garment are worth taking into consideration before you begin to work. The suggestions included here are particularly important if you are designing your own pattern, but you may also find them useful when working from a published pattern.

Stitch Gauge and Yarn Requirements

A garment made with a Stranded Color pattern requires a special approach to finding the gauge; see Gauge for Color Patterns.

Also, these patterns require considerably more yarn than the same garment style done in a single color, because the fabric has two layers, the stitches in one and the strands in the other. For information on how to estimate the amount of each color yarn to purchase for your project, see Garment Yardage, and Yardage for Color Patterns.

Casting On for Stranded Color Fabrics

One of the nicest ways to begin a fabric with a Stranded Color pattern is to use a technique suitable for casting on in two colors; see Alternating Cast-On for Single Rib, Alternating Cast-On for Double Rib, or one of the variations discussed in Contrast-Color Baselines. Also look at the Braided Cast-Ons, which provide the handsome edges common in many northern European knitting traditions.

Borders for Stranded Color Fabrics

A conventional ribbing can be done in horizontal stripes, but it requires special consideration when Purling a stitch that is in one color while working with a yarn that is a different color; for how to handle this, see Stripes in Ribbing, below.

A Single or Double Rib can also be done in vertical stripes—one color for the Purl stitches, the other for the Knit stitches; this is often seen in Fair Isle–type patterns.† The result is less elastic than a conventional ribbing; it is important to allow enough yarn to each strand. Some very pretty effects can be achieved with these kinds of patterns, particularly when the color for the Purl stitches is held constant while several colors are alternated every few rows for the Knit stitches.

Many traditional Stranded Color garments were made with a hem rather than a border, often with a name or initials worked into it, sometimes accompanied by a date.

---

† Many people refer to this as "Cartridge" ribbing, and in Shetland patterns it may be referred to as a "two-color basque," *basque* being a term used for a ribbed border. See Ann Feitelson, *The Art of Fair Isle Knitting: History, Technique, Color and Patterns* (Loveland, Colo.: Interweave Press, 1996), p. 53.

Shaping Stranded Color Garments

Garments made with color patterns are shaped in the usual ways; however, it is important to think about where to place the shaping elements, or which one to use to minimize disruption of the pattern. These suggestions are appropriate for any color pattern, not just those that are stranded.

Decreases in Color Patterns

- For a decrease that joins two stitches in different colors, select either a left or right decrease to control which one will be the facing stitch on the outside of the fabric.
- Alternatively, shift the position of the decrease to the right or left in order to work it on two stitches of the same color.

Increases in Color Patterns

When an increase is required where the pattern calls for stitches in different colors, there are three solutions.

- Use a Raised Increase and make one stitch in each color yarn.
- Knit a stitch with both yarns held as one; on next row, knit each stitch separately in order needed for pattern.

  Wrap the yarns so the color sequence is correct on the two new stitches, or rearrange the strands in the stitch before working them on the next row, if necessary.
- Use either a Crossed Stitch Yarnover Increase or a Running Thread Increase to add a stitch in color needed between two other stitches.

Following a Pattern

Most color stitch patterns are charted on a square grid, with each row of the chart equivalent to a row in the fabric; for details on how to read and write patterns of this kind, see Charted Color Patterns. As described there, it helps to place a guide on the chart that covers the rows above the one you are working from so they will not be distracting. The color sequence of the stitches on the left needle matches the charted pattern *below* the one you are currently following. To check your position, look at the relationship between the stitches in both of these rows on the chart.

For instance, if the pattern shows that the next three dark stitches should be centered above one dark stitch in the row below, a glance at the stitches on the left needle will tell you whether you are in the right place; there should be one light, one dark, one light.

Managing Stranded Yarns

Here are some suggestions for how to attach a new yarn supply, carry the color not in use up to a row above, and prevent or undo tangles.

Attaching Yarn Supply

- To introduce a new supply of yarn, whenever possible attach the yarn at the side edge of a flat fabric, or the beginning of a round of a circular fabric. Allow ends long enough to weave in on the inside during finishing; for more information, see Tying On Yarn and Hiding Ends of Yarn.
- A project with multiple color changes will leave lots of ends to work in later. You can do that, or try the approach used for Steeks on traditional Shetland Fair Isle sweaters—knot the two yarns together and cut the ends short; this leaves a little fringe on the inside that no one but you will see; see Steeks: Selvedges for Cut Openings.

Stranding Yarns Up Edges

- When working with different yarns, the one needed next will have to be carried up past rows made with the other color, either at the edge of a flat fabric or at the end of a round.

  If a yarn needs to be stranded past several rows, bind it to the fabric by wrapping one yarn around the other whenever they are together. Make sure to allow just enough yarn to this strand—if it is too short, it will draw the fabric up, and if it is too long, the adjacent stitches will enlarge.

  If the distance is greater than 2 or 3 inches, cut the yarn and reattach it when needed again.

- It can be difficult to make attractive visible edges on something like a blanket or shawl done with a color pattern, and each combination of technique and pattern will present unique challenges.

  In some cases you can use a Chain Selvedge and hold both yarns together to work the last stitch of every row; or use a Stockinette Selvedge and alternate colors to the edge stitches. This also anchors the yarn being stranded to the edge.

  Also, the Slide technique, discussed above, allows you to attach one yarn at each side, making it possible to either have each selvedge a different color, or to hold the yarns together to work the stitches in both selvedges.

- Also consider using a border at the side edges done in just one color; interlock that yarn with the other yarn at the intersection between the border and the main part of the fabric, as for Intarsia (see below).

Strand Length and Circular Knitting

There is a theory that if you turn a circular fabric inside out when working a color pattern—with the inside of the fabric on the outside of the circle—the strands will have to be slightly longer, ensuring that they will not bunch up the fabric.

The idea is that the circumference on the outside is slightly larger than that on the inside because of the thickness of the fabric, and as a result the strands will span a longer distance when they are made.

However, the length of each strand is fixed when the next stitch is made with that yarn. And since the arc formed by the surface of the fabric within the half-inch or so length of the strand is negligible, it is unlikely to have this effect.

Yarn Tangling

It can be difficult to keep the two yarns separate and untangled when you switch between them. Here are two methods you can use to unspin them:

- Push stitches back from needle tip, drop needle, and let it hang from yarn; pull two yarns apart and allow needles to spin until they unwind.

  The stitches will not slip off the needle because the hanging weight places tension on the yarn and tightens the last stitch or two.

- If a yarn is gaining or losing twist, see the suggestions for how to mitigate the problem, as well as how to correct for it, in Knitting Methods and Yarn Twist.

Theory of Color Dominance

The yarns stranded on the inside of the fabric lie parallel, one slightly above the other. Their relative position is determined by the knitting method used, and this may have a subtle effect on the appearance of a pattern. The theory of Color Dominance says the two colors of a Stranded Color pattern should always be held in the same way to control for this, with the yarn used for the pattern held so it strands below the one for the background.

At each color change, a stitch made with the strand that lies below will emerge very slightly lower in the row than one made with the yarn that rides above. As a result, the former may be somewhat larger and its color can appear more dominant in the pattern. This is most in evidence at a color change; therefore, the first and last stitches of a group may be enlarged but not those in between, and single stitches in spot patterns will be larger.

Many other factors determine the relative size of stitches and how a color pattern is perceived, such as the number of different colors used overall, their relative amounts, and the degree of contrast between them. Also, any difference in the size of the stitches is difficult to discern if they are small, easier if they are large, and soft yarns will blur any slight discrepancy in stitch size, whether this is caused by Color Dominance or simply by uneven tension.

Nevertheless, it is worth being systematic about how you handle the yarns for whatever benefit it provides; here are the rules for how to hold the yarns to determine which one strands above the other.

- Slip Stranding: Yarn used for first pass across needle will strand below yarn used for second pass.
- Two-Hand Stranding: Yarn held on left will strand below yarn held on right.
- Methods with yarns on or between two fingers: Yarn held closest to fabric will strand above yarn held farthest away.

   To maintain the same yarn as dominant, when working flat, switch position of yarns at end of each row.
- Yarns Held on Left Forefinger: Yarn held on tip of forefinger will strand above one held between two knuckles or on middle finger.

Intarsia Patterns

The Intarsia technique is used to make designs with larger areas of color than are possible in Stranded Color patterns—areas too wide to carry a yarn in one color past the stitches made in the other. Instead, each area of the pattern is done with its own small supply of yarn, and you switch from one to the other as you work across the row.

This means you can use a great many different colors on the same row and it opens up a wealth of design possibilities beyond the strict horizontal rows and vertical columns of a knitted fabric. Instead of patterns consisting of plain or patterned stripes, an Intarsia design can be made up of geometric or pictorial forms similar to those found in pieced quilts or woven tapestries.

The simplest Intarsia patterns consist entirely of identical geometric shapes, one set right next to the other. Some common examples would be a checkerboard pattern or a traditional argyle pattern of interlocking diamonds. These patterns can be done with just two colors, or as many different ones as you care to deal with.

In more complex Intarsia patterns, the shapes are more varied, similar to quilting patterns made up of various squares, rectangles, trapezoids, and diamonds, all fitted together as the components of larger motifs that repeat across the fabric. The most challenging versions resemble a "crazy quilt," with each area having a different shape, color, and texture, fitted together like a puzzle. For another approach that creates a similar effect, see Modular Garment Fabrics.

The Intarsia technique can also be used to make pictorial or

Masterpiece wool carpet from Alsace, 1781, 163 square cm.

abstract designs based on natural forms. The irregular shapes that define a pattern of this kind are distributed across a background usually done in a single color, or with large areas of color. Each area of the pattern will require a separate supply of yarn, both for the positive shapes of the design as well as for the negative shapes they create in the background.

A complex pattern might require a great many different yarns, all of them in play on a single row, all hanging in wait on the inside of the fabric until needed. A fabric festooned with these dangling yarns can look rather daunting if you have never done Intarsia before, but there are no special skills required. The patterns are normally done in plain Stockinette and only one yarn is used at a time. The only challenge lies in managing the yarns carefully, tying each one on neatly where it begins and ends, and changing from one to the other in a way that will leave no gaps in the fabric.

Because of the inherent nature of the technique, standard Intarsia is normally done only when making a flat fabric. While several methods can be used to work Intarsia in a circular fabric, only two are worth recommending; see Intarsia in the Round, below.

❖ *Basic Intarsia*

In order to work an Intarsia pattern, one yarn is used to work as many stitches as needed for the first area of color, and then another is tied on to work the stitches of the next area, with as many separate yarns as needed for each motif added across the row. The two yarns are interlocked (wound around each other) on the inside of the fabric at each color change to prevent gaps from appearing in the fabric. Each color is carried up row by row to continue its area of the pattern; a color can start and stop on any row, in any position, regardless of what is happening elsewhere in the pattern.

Interlocking Yarns

In a normal fabric, a running thread passes between two adjacent stitches, linking them together. However, when changing from one color to another in an Intarsia pattern, this link will be missing unless the two yarns are interlocked by wrapping them around each other before the first stitch is made with the next yarn. How to do this depends on the location of the yarn needed next and the nature of the pattern. A shape can have a different number of stitches on each row, and you may need to strand the yarn up and over at an angle to where it is needed next before interlocking it with the other yarn.

Keep in mind that the interlock can only be done between two Purl stitches on the inside of the fabric; it is for this reason that most Intarsia patterns are in Stockinette. Nevertheless, Purl stitches can be used within pattern motifs as long as they are not on either side of a color change, because this

would place the interlock on the outside of the fabric where it would be visible.

For the purpose of this example, Yarn A is used for the last stitch made, Yarn B for the next one.

Next Yarn Hanging to Left

- If Yarn B is hanging below left needle, pass Yarn A over it to left and hold temporarily out of the way; draw Yarn B under Yarn A to right and work next stitch.

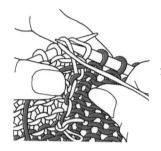

Interlocking with next yarn hanging to left.

Next Yarn Hanging to Right

- If Yarn B is hanging below right needle, draw Yarn A under Yarn B from left to right, and then back over it again from right to left; hold Yarn A temporarily against left needle and pick up Yarn B to work next stitch.

Interlocked yarns on inside of fabric.

Place tension on yarn held out of the way in order to form the interlock neatly between two stitches, and then drop it after first stitch is made with the other color.

Stranding Between Areas

Stretch the fabric out slightly when stranding to give it sufficient length. If you are tempted to strand past more than an inch, look for a way to interlock the strand with another yarn at its midpoint, or consider using the Lattice Method of Weaving-In (see above), binding the strand to the fabric with a stitch in a row above.

Wherever two pattern elements of the same color lie in relatively close proximity, use a single supply of yarn for both and strand between the last stitch of one and the first stitch of the other. Analyze the pattern before you begin to work and look for these opportunities. They reduce the number of yarns you need to tie on, and in some cases it is possible to travel quite a distance up the fabric in this manner, skipping from one area to another.

Managing Intarsia Yarns

Here are some tips for how to manage the yarns while you work.

- To calculate the amount of yarn needed for each area of the pattern, see Garment Yardage for Intarsia Patterns.
- To begin a new supply of yarn, allow a tail on the previous yarn long enough to weave in later; do the same with the new yarn. Press the two tails together against the inside of the fabric and begin to work with the new one. When you turn to the inside, stop and tie the ends together in a nice Bow Knot, which is easy to undo later when it is time to deal with all the ends during finishing.

Bobbins for Intarsia hanging on inside of fabric.
Classic argyle pattern of interlocking diamonds.

- Each yarn supply can be wrapped on a special bobbin designed for this purpose; see Tools. A bobbin has a slot to pass the yarn through so it will not unwind while you work; when the yarn gets too short, pass it back through the slot, unwind some more, and then refasten it. If you do not have bobbins on hand, use a Yarn Butterfly, or make an improvised bobbin from a bit of folded cardboard.
- The bobbins hanging from the fabric often tangle together while you work, which is a nuisance. One simple solution is to drop one bobbin over the needle to the nearside and leave the next on the farside, alternating them in this way so they are not side-by-side in close proximity.

    When all you need are relatively short lengths of yarn, it is often best to just let them all hang loose from the fabric instead of using bobbins. Even though the strands wrap around each other a bit, they tangle less and can easily be pulled free when needed. Use the bobbins only if the yarns are too long.
- What about all the little tails of yarn that will be left on

the inside? The traditional approach is to weave each end in to nearby stitches of the same color; see Hiding Ends of Yarn for more information. It is painstaking to do this neatly enough to leave no evidence on the outside, but is worthwhile if the inside will be visible from time to time. One alternative is to line the garment (see Linings); however, if only you will ever see the inside, a much quicker and simpler approach is to use a Square Knot to tie the yarns neatly together, and then cut the ends short; there will be no evidence of this on the outside.

Edges

Here are some suggestions for how to handle the edges of a fabric done with an Intarsia pattern when they will remain visible.

Selvedges for Intarsia

Any normal Selvedge pattern will work for an Intarsia fabric. However, if you are concerned that color changes at a side edge will not be neat, consider using one of the Double Selvedges or a solid color border of some kind so you can change from one Intarsia yarn to another within the fabric, instead.

Casting On for Intarsia

You can, of course, use any cast-on technique, but this clever approach allows you to cast on and begin the Intarsia pattern at the same time. You will be using a variation of the Contrast-Color Baseline technique described in Compound Cast-Ons.

1. Use Half-Hitch Cast-On, holding a single color on thumb for baseline.
2. Carry yarn for first color area on forefinger and cast on number of stitches required; drop yarn.
3. Pick up yarn needed for next color area, allow tail of yarn and pinch it against right needle; hold this yarn on left forefinger in usual way and cast on next group of stitches.
4. Repeat, adding all yarn supplies needed for first row of pattern.

Casting Off for Intarsia

Keep in mind that each cast-off stitch will lean to the left, on top of the adjacent stitch. To match the color of the stitch in the area below, work as follows:

Casting Off for Intarsia.

- On last row, work last stitch of each pattern area with color of the following area; when stitch is pulled over, it will match area below.

❖ *Intarsia and Stranded Combined*

There are three ways to combine the Intarsia and Stranded Color techniques in order to make color patterns that cannot be done with either technique alone.

With the first two, the Intarsia motifs will contain Stranded Color patterns; with the third, the Stranded Color pattern will have small areas of Intarsia.

Intarsia with Stranded Patterns

Two methods can be used to make areas of Intarsia that contain Stranded Color patterns.

Framed Patterns

An Intarsia pattern of this kind has a stranded pattern done in one color framed within a geometric Intarsia motif done in a second color, the whole set against a background in a third color—imagine a snowflake within a square or diamond.

• Tie on two colors for the motif and alternate them to the pattern and background stitches as for any Stranded Color pattern; use separate supplies of yarn at each side of the motif for the main background.

Striped Patterns

This type of pattern is characterized by a Stranded Color pattern that passes through a set of geometric Intarsia motifs. For instance, you could make a checkerboard pattern of squares in two alternating colors, and then add a Stranded Color pattern stripe done in a third color that runs through all of them, from one side of the fabric to the other.

1. Tie on separate supplies of yarn across the row for each area of Intarsia pattern; tie on another yarn at side edge to use for all stitches of Stranded Color pattern.
2. Work across row using Stranded Color yarn for pattern stitches, and pick up each Intarsia yarn in turn to work background stitches.

For a somewhat similar effect done with a different approach, see Mosaics and Other Color Techniques.

Stranded Patterns with Intarsia

Stranded Color patterns are almost always done with just two yarns on any row, because stranding more yarn than that on the inside would make for a much thicker garment.

However, you can introduce small amounts of other colors to areas of the design with the Intarsia technique. Just tie on short lengths of yarn wherever you want a few stitches in another color, and strand past these areas with the other two yarns.

When working circular, use motifs with a limited number of stitches and work as described in Small-Scale Intarsia, below.

❖ *Intarsia in the Round*

As mentioned above, Intarsia patterns are primarily used when making a flat fabric. The reason for this is quite simple; as you work across a row, each yarn will move from the first stitch on the right side of an area of color to the last stitch on the left side of it. When you turn at the end of a row, the yarns will again be in position at the right side of each area and can be used to work back across the stitches. However, after working one round of a circular fabric, all the yarns will still be on the left side of each area of color and inaccessible on the next round.

There is little difficulty in working a small motif, but larger ones are more problematic. There are several methods that can be used; however, all are more limited than conventional Intarsia, and two of them are quite problematic and are discussed here so you will recognize them should they be recommended to you.

Small-Scale Intarsia

If you want to introduce small Intarsia motifs into a circular garment, here is a quick and easy way to do so.

1. Start Intarsia motif at midpoint of yarn supply; after working stitches, one strand will be at each side of motif.
2. On next round, work first half of stitches with strand at that side of motif; pick up second strand from other side, draw across to midpoint, and work other half of stitches.
3. On subsequent rounds, draw strand from midpoint to work first half of stitches, and from opposite side to work second half of stitches.

Slip-Stranded Intarsia

Slip-Stranded Intarsia was traditionally used to showcase a single, often elaborate, multicolor motif in small garments such as on the back of mittens or the instep of socks; for a lovely example, see the Dalmatian sock done in this way in *Mary Thomas's Knitting Book* (she calls it "Festive Knitting").† There is, however, no technical reason to limit yourself to little things of that kind, because the approach can certainly be used for larger garments.

This technique is only suitable for the type of patterns discussed above in Intarsia with Stranded Patterns, where the main color of the fabric is also used for the background within the Intarsia motif. The Slip Stranding method is used to handle the yarns, and the Slide technique is used to move stitches to the location of the next yarn needed. To simplify the instructions, only two colors are used—Color A for the stitches of the motif and Color B for all other stitches.

Work with a set of double-point needles and cast on with

---

† Mary Thomas, *Mary Thomas's Knitting Book* (New York: Dover Publications, 1972), p. 112.

Color B. Place the number of stitches required for the widest row of the motif on one needle; distribute the remaining stitches evenly to the others. If you prefer, you can work with two circular needles instead of straight double-point needles—use a short circular needle for the motif stitches, and a longer one for all the other stitches, if necessary; for more information, see Working with Circular Needles.

Join the round and work to the row where the motif begins; at the needle bearing the motif stitches, attach Color A and continue as follows:

1. Knit all motif pattern stitches with Color A, and Slip all background stitches.

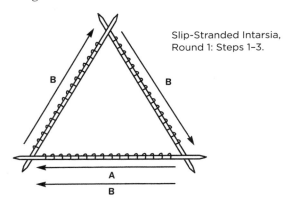

Slip-Stranded Intarsia, Round 1: Steps 1–3.

2. Slide stitches to right tip of needle to pick up Color B, Knit all background stitches, Slip all motif stitches.
3. Continue round with Color B, and return to needle bearing stitches of motif; Color A will be at left side.
4. Turn to inside, slide stitches to tip of needle to pick up Color A and Purl motif stitches, Slip all background stitches.

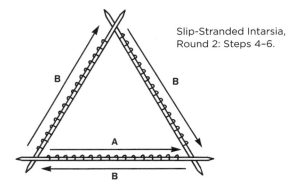

Slip-Stranded Intarsia, Round 2: Steps 4–6.

5. Turn to outside, slide stitches to tip of needle to pick up Color B and Knit all background stitches, Slip all motif stitches.
6. Continue round with Color B. At end of second round, Color A will be at right side of motif.

7. Repeat Steps 1–6. When motif is complete, break off Color A and continue working all stitches in round with Color B.

There are two alternatives.

• Combine Steps 1 and 2, holding yarns as for Two-Hand Stranding, alternating the colors to the pattern and background stitches of motif, and then work Steps 3–6 as described above.
• Instead of turning to the inside in Step 4, pick up Color A and work from left to right; see Bi-Directional Method.

Because this method relies on the Slide technique, it can also be used for a flat fabric if the stitches of the motif are on a separate double-point needle, whether circular or straight.

To make multiple motifs in this way, when working either flat or in the round, simply expand this concept, using as many needles as necessary.

Woven Intarsia

The Weaving-In technique, described in Stranded Color Patterns (above), can also be used as a means of working an Intarsia pattern in a circular fabric, but only when using two colors at a time. Instead of tying on a separate supply of yarn at the location of the motif, it is woven in across the entire width of the fabric until needed, at which point the background yarn is woven in to carry it across the pattern, in turn.

While often used for large-scale Intarsia patterns, the approach can be used for patterns of any size, and is by no means limited to working in the round. In fact, the most famous example of a garment done in this way is the designer Elsa Schiaparelli's famous Bowknot sweater of 1927, which was knit in flat pieces and sewn together.[†] Apparently Schiaparelli was as taken with the surface design possibilities inherent in this technique as she was by the unique fabric that it produces. The woven-in strands tend to peek through on the outside, giving it a tweedy look (less so in a firmly knit fabric than a loose one), and it has characteristics halfway between a woven and a knit because the strands reduce its resilience.

When weaving in the yarns, work consistently, either catching the strand with every stitch, every other stitch, or every third or fourth stitch, depending upon your gauge and the length of the strands, and how tweedy an effect you want on the outside. Also, unless you are catching the strand with every stitch,

---

† The technique, while used elsewhere, has become known as "Armenian knitting," because Armenian women in Paris knit this sweater and others like it for Schiaparelli; little is currently known about the history of this knitting method in their homeland. For more information, see Meg Swansen and Joyce Williams, *Armenian Knitting* (Pittsville, Wisc.: Schoolhouse Press, 2007).

Bowknot Sweater. Elsa Schiaparelli, early twentieth century, Paris.
Victoria and Albert Museum, London.

shift the point of weaving-in on each subsequent row so it is not always in the same column of stitches. Here are some suggested patterns.

- Stranding past two stitches: Start the weaving-in series on the second and fifth stitches of one row, and on the third and sixth stitches of the next row, the fourth and seventh of the next, etc., to make a twill pattern.
- Stranding past three stitches: Start the series with the second and sixth stitches on one row, and the fourth and eighth stitches on the next, and alternate in this way so the strands are always woven-in at the center of the strand below.

Circular Intarsia Worked in Rows

These two methods both employ the same approach—a circular fabric is worked as if it were flat, with alternating inside and outside rows. Each of them uses a device to join what would otherwise be the two side edges into a circle; the first has a pair of stitches that are linked at the join, the other uses two balls of yarn for the background that alternately strand across the join. In order to accomplish this, either the main color yarn for the background or a large Intarsia motif must occupy the area on either side of the join.

While it is technically possible to work an Intarsia pattern using these approaches, they are problematic; the stitches at the join tend to be distorted and there is some limitation on the kinds of patterns that can be done.

If there is a type of Intarsia pattern that you want to use for a circular garment and it cannot be done with either the Slip-Stranded or Woven Intarsia methods described above, I think you will achieve a far more satisfactory result if you simply knit a flat fabric and seam the edges. But try these; one or the other might work for you.

Seam Stitch Method

- Slip first stitch of round, continue in pattern; at end of round, work slipped stitch and then return it to left needle. Turn to inside and repeat, working in Purl.

In other words, the stitch slipped at the beginning of the round is worked at the end of it; therefore, the yarn crosses the join to link the two sides of the fabric.

Two-Yarn Method

Work with two balls of the main yarn, one for outside rows (Yarn A), one for inside rows (Yarn B). Tie the two yarns together, but cast on with only Yarn A; let Yarn B hang at beginning of cast-on edge.

• Work one round with Yarn A for background, adding separate supplies of yarn for motifs, according to pattern. Turn to inside of circle and work one round in Purl with Yarn B for background. Continue in this way, alternating background yarns for each round.

In other words, Yarn A is used on the outside for the odd-numbered rows; Yarn B is used on the inside for the even-numbered rounds. Each yarn will strand across the join only every other round.

Color and Stitch Techniques

Most color knitting is done in Stockinette, which provides a quiet background and allows color to be the primary focus of the design. However, the combination of stitch techniques and color makes it possible to add texture and depth to the surface of the fabric as well. Some of the most masterful examples of the interplay between color and stitch are found in the justly famous Bohus Stickning sweaters, designed and made between the 1930s and 1950s by the members of a knitting cooperative founded by Emma Jacobsson in Sweden.†

All of the basic techniques described in The Stitches, as well as those in Increase and Decrease Techniques, can be used in color patterns, although some are easier to deal with than others. Success depends on understanding the relationship between the color changes and the formation of the stitches, because they do not happen at the same time. The color of each stitch is determined when it is made on one row, but the structure and appearance of the stitch in the fabric is determined by which technique is used to work it on the next row.

This interaction is best explained by a discussion of color patterns that employ either Purl or Slip stitches, of which there are a great many. Once you understand how this works in these types of patterns, those that employ different kinds of techniques will make sense to you as well; for more illustrations, see Color Stitch Pattern Charts.

❖ *Color Patterns with Purl*

Simple color stripes done in Purl can add welcome texture to what might otherwise be a relatively plain pattern, and contrast colors can also be added to ribbings in a variety of ways.

---

† Wendy Keele, *Poems of Color: Knitting in the Bohus Tradition* (Loveland, Colo.: Interweave Press, 1995).

While Stranded Color patterns are conventionally done in Stockinette, they can also be done in Garter Stitch for a completely different look; and a wonderful technique called Shadow Knitting combines Stockinette and Garter Stitch in large-scale patterns that create interesting optical effects in the interplay of color.

Color in Purl Stripes

When a row of Purl stitches is worked on the outside of the fabric, there will be two parallel lines of little nubs directly below the right needle. The nubs on the top are the heads of the discarded stitches, while the nubs on the bottom are the running threads of the new stitches on the right needle; for more information on the structure of the stitch, see The Knit and Purl Stitches.

When stitches are Purled with a contrast color, the two sets of nubs discarded below the right needle will not only be in different colors, but each set will also contrast with the adjacent stitches above and below.

Here are some examples of the basic principles at work in color patterns of this kind. The instructions will specify whether a row of Knit or Purl should be placed on the outside of the fabric, but it does not matter whether this is done by working in Knit on the inside, or in Purl on the outside; it is the result that counts.

The following instructions all begin with the stitches on the left needle in Color A.

Flecked Purl Stripes

With this version, the colors change every row, and the result is a tweed.

1. With Color B, work one row of Purl on outside of fabric.
2. With Color A, work one row of Purl on outside of fabric. After Step 1, the new neutral stitches on the right needle will be in Color B, the Purl nubs below the needle will be in Color A, the running threads in Color B, and the discarded stitches in Color A.

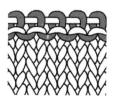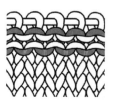

Far left: Flecked Purl: First row.

Near left: Flecked Purl: Second row.

After Step 2, the new neutral stitches on the right needle will be in Color A, the Purl nubs below the needle will be in Color B, the running threads in Color A, and the discarded stitches in Color B.

Purl Stripes with Flecked Edges

In this case, the stripe starts and ends with rows of Flecked Purl, as above, but it is a solid color in between.

1. With Color B, work first row of stripe in Purl on outside of fabric.
2. Continue with same color yarn for several rows in either Knit or Purl, or any combination of the two to make stripe.
3. With Color A, work first row of next stripe in Purl on outside, and then repeat Step 2.

Solid Purl Stripes

And here is how to make a Purl stripe with no flecks of contrast color at the bottom or top. Begin with Color A stitches on needle.

1. With Color B, work one row of Knit on outside of fabric.
2. Continue with Color B, working several rows of Purl on outside of fabric for stripe.
3. With Color A, work one row of Knit on outside.
4. For second stripe, continue with Color A, working Purl on outside of fabric for several rows.

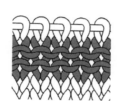

Solid Purl Stripe.

In other words, to make a solid color stripe with Purl stitches, work the first row of a new color in Knit; with all the stitches on the needle now in that color, you can work subsequent rows in the same color in either solid Purl, Garter Stitch, or any pattern of mixed Knit and Purl.

Purl in Intarsia

You can also work an Intarsia pattern with Purl on the outside as long as you use Knit for the first pattern stitch on any row. The simple rule is:

- If the stitch will be worked with a different color, Knit it; if it will be worked with the same color, you can Purl it.

> **Counting rows . . .**
> *When counting rows in a color stripe or Intarsia motif, also include the last row of new stitches on the needle; these will become part of the pattern when they are discarded into the fabric as you work the next row with a new color.*

Color in Ribbing Patterns

The general concepts introduced above in Color Patterns with Purl can also be applied to working stripes in ribbing.

Horizontal Stripes in Ribbing

To make solid color stripes in a ribbing, work as follows:

1. With Color A, work one row entirely in Knit on outside of fabric.
2. With Color A, work two or more rows in ribbing pattern.
3. With Color B, repeat Step 1.
4. With Color B, repeat Step 2.

If you eliminate Steps 1 and 3, the first row of every color change will have flecks of color in the Purl columns.

Horizontal Stripes in Single Rib.

The rows of Knit stitches will not seriously compromise the elasticity of the ribbing, particularly if it is worked at a firm gauge on relatively small needles for the size of the yarn.

Vertical Stripes in Ribbing

The Stranded Color method can be used to create vertical stripes in either Single or Double Rib. The strands reduce the resilience of the fabric somewhat, but the result is an attractive border that lies nice and flat. Sometimes called Cartridge Rib, it is often seen on traditional Fair Isle–type sweaters.

Here are the instructions for a Double Rib, which is most common:

1. On every outside row: [With Color A on farside, Knit 2; move Color B to nearside, Purl 2; return yarn farside]; repeat between brackets across row.
2. On inside rows: [Move Color B to farside, Knit 2, return yarn nearside; with Color A on nearside, Purl 2]; repeat between brackets across row.

In Step 1, Color A is used for the Knit stitches; therefore, it remains on the inside of the fabric for the entire row. Color B has to be moved to the outside of the fabric for the Purl stitches, and then back to the inside to strand past the Knit stitches.

Combination Stripes in Ribbing

Interesting and complex color effects can be achieved by combining the methods of making vertical and horizontal stripes in a Double Rib. Here are some suggestions:

- Cast on and use Color A for all Purl columns; in Knit columns, work Color B for several rows and then change to Color C for several rows, alternating two or more colors in this way the length of the ribbing.
- Work the ribbing pattern with Color A alone for several rows, and then work several rows with Color A used for

the Purl and Color B for the Knit columns. This will produce horizontal stripes separated by squares of color in the Knit columns.

Color in Garter Stitch

There are three interesting ways to do color patterns in Garter Stitch, and two are described here. One method is based on a simple adaptation of a Stranded Color pattern. The other is called Shadow Knitting, which consists of stripes done in a combination of Garter Stitch and Stockinette.

You can also work an Intarsia pattern in a fabric done in Garter Stitch, as long as you follow the rule described above for using Purl, and introduce any new color by working it in Knit on the outside of the fabric.

Stranded Color in Garter Stitch

Any Stranded Color pattern can be done in Garter Stitch, by working each row of a conventional pattern twice. The motifs will be enlarged, but the inherent compression in a Garter Stitch fabric somewhat offsets the increase in scale. These patterns are not reversible because of the strands on the inside.

For a flat fabric, work as follows:

Stranded Color pattern in Garter Stitch.

1. On outside of fabric: Work Stranded Color pattern row in Knit, in usual way. Turn.
2. On inside of fabric: work same pattern row in Knit again, but bring yarns to nearside to strand.

The outside row is easy enough, but stranding the inside rows can be a bit of a challenge because it is necessary to move the yarn last used to the nearside to strand, and move the yarn to be used next to the farside to Knit, and it is all too easy to forget to move them into position. Also, moving the yarns nearside and farside makes it somewhat more difficult to maintain an even tension, but with a little practice you will get into the rhythm of it.

For a circular fabric, first work the pattern row in Knit on the outside, and next work the same pattern row in Purl, moving the yarns to the farside to strand, as necessary.

Shadow Knitting

Here is a fascinating, yet very simple way to create a color pattern that changes its appearance depending upon the angle from which it is viewed. When seen from the front, some areas of color will be less obvious than when seen from the side, and as the fabric moves the pattern seems to constantly transform itself. The technique apparently originated in Japan, but was brought to the attention of the English-speaking knitting world in a charming book called *Shadow Knitting*, by Vivian Høxbro.†

Shadow Knitting pattern.
Shown with rows horizontal.

For all the visual interest, these are easy patterns to do because they consist of simple stripes: two rows in one color, two rows in the other. Cutting across these stripes, however, are large geometric patterns that move in and out of view. This magic is created by working parts of each stripe in Garter Stitch, and other parts of it in Stockinette.

The effect of this subtle change is quite striking. When seen from the side, the Purl rows in the areas of Garter Stitch are visually dominant, while the Knit rows in the Stockinette areas look more subdued, as if the color were dimmed. When viewed from the front, however, these relationships change, because the areas done in Knit become more visible and the effect of the Purls is reduced.

This interplay of color is enhanced by the amount of contrast there is between the colors used for the stripes—the less there is, the more subtle the pattern will be. It can be a challenge to select the right colors for a Shadow pattern because the inherent nature of these designs means the colors will interact strongly with one another and display many of the optical effects discussed in Putting Colors Together, above.

Also, these kinds of patterns are most successful when they contain relatively large and simple geometric shapes; you will need a larger Gauge Swatch to judge the overall effect. Color charts for Shadow patterns are not only easy to follow, but also, once you understand the technique, you will find it rela-

---

† Vivian Høxbro, *Shadow Knitting* (Loveland, Colo.: Interweave Press, 2004).

Shadow Knitting pattern. Shown with rows vertical.

tively easy to develop a pattern of your own. It is important to plot the color pattern on the garment chart just as you would do for an Intarsia Pattern; see Coordinating Stitch and Garment Patterns.

❖ Color Patterns with Slip Stitches

A Slip stitch, for all its simplicity, is also one of the most versatile and multifaceted of stitch techniques, and it can be used in a variety of ways to create interesting color patterns. Keep in mind that the color of a slipped stitch is determined when the stitch is first made in the row before it is slipped.

Miscellaneous Slip Stitch Color Patterns

• The simplest and most common way to create color patterns with Slip stitches is to strand the contrast-color yarns past them on the outside of the fabric. The strands create small horizontal flecks of color at the base of the Slip stitches, so the patterns consist primarily of tweeds and broken stripes of one kind or another.

  Because of the high proportion of Slip stitches, these fabrics tend to be dense unless worked on a relatively large needle size for the type of yarn. It is always a good idea to make a Test Swatch with the stitch pattern and yarns you will be using, and try several different needle sizes before choosing the one that produces a fabric that looks and feels right to you.

• Patterns done with the Lattice Technique are very effective when color is added. The contrast-color yarn is stranded past several consecutive Slip stitches on the outside of the fabric and is then caught up on a later row.

• Another simple approach involves slipping a stitch made in one color up past one or two rows containing stitches made in another color. Mosaics are the most common type of pattern that makes use of this technique (see below), but there are many others that produce different effects, such as the Crossed Stitch technique that pulls the slipped stitch up at an angle.

• Slip stitches are sometimes used to pull several rows together in order to make the intervening stitches puff out from the surface. These protruding areas can be further set off if the slipped stitches, and perhaps several adjacent rows above and below it, are done in a contrast color; see Embossed Motifs.

Mosaic Patterns

Barbara Walker defined and developed a special category of color Slip Stitch patterns that she called Mosaics, which were introduced in her *Second Treasury of Knitting Patterns*, and developed further in the *Third Treasury*, and in *Mosaic Knitting*.†

Mosaics are basically two-row color stripes done in either Stockinette or Garter Stitch, or a combination of the two, and the yarns are handled with the Slip Stranding method, working with one color at a time. Pattern is created by drawing contrast-color Slip stitches from one stripe up across the two rows of the next stripe. The patterns are always charted using a system unique to Mosaics; for more information, see Charted Color Patterns. The charts are as easy to follow as these patterns are to make.

In the following instructions, all stitches are slipped purlwise and the yarn is always stranded on the inside of the fabric:

1. Pattern Rows 1 and 2: Use Color A to work background stitches, and Slip all pattern stitches; all slipped stitches are Color B.
2. Pattern Rows 3 and 4: Use Color B to work background stitches and Slip all pattern stitches; all Slip stitches will be Color A.

The stitches worked may be Color A or Color B, but the slipped stitches will always be the color of the yarn not in use.

Because the patterns are formed by single Slip stitches (it is the rare pattern that calls for slipping two together), it is very easy to control the tension and make a smooth, even fabric.

Any Mosaic pattern you make in Stockinette will have the same gauge if done with the same yarn and needles; the same

---

† Barbara Walker, *A Second Treasury of Knitting Patterns* (New York: Charles Scribner's Sons, 1970); *A Third Treasury of Knitting Patterns* (New York: Charles Scribner's Sons, 1972); and *Mosaic Knitting* (New York: Charles Scribner's Sons, 1976).

Scarab—a Mosaic pattern. Light rows in
Stockinette, dark rows in Garter Stitch.

is true of patterns done in Garter Stitch. This makes it easy to combine several different Mosaic patterns in a garment—as long as all the patterns you use are done in Stockinette, for instance, there is no need to calculate a separate gauge for each one, nor adjust the number of stitches on the needle in order to switch from one to another.

While a Garter Stitch pattern gauge will not match that of a Stockinette pattern, the difference is seen mostly in the rows, so the two kinds of patterns can be combined fairly easily. Instead of calculating different gauges for them, develop a single gauge from a swatch that contains a representative sample of both types of patterns. This would also be the case if you want to use both Stockinette and Garter within a single pattern.

Mosaics and Other Color Techniques

Mosaic patterns are visually lively, but it is possible to enhance them further by combining the technique with other methods of working with color.

- While Mosaic patterns are commonly done with just two colors, it is certainly possible to mix things up and use different colors for each repeat, or select a main color for half the rows, and use more than one contrast color for the other rows. A simpler way to add variety is to use a solid color for half the stripes and a variegated color for the others.

Mosaics tend to have a very step-like appearance, and adding color in this way tends to soften this effect, changing them in sometimes remarkable ways.

- It is also possible to use Stranded Color techniques with Mosaic patterns, although this will change the nature of the fabric somewhat.

Select a main color to use for half the pattern rows, and choose two other colors that contrast with the main color to use for the rows between. Use one color between the first pair of Slip stitches, and the other color between the next pair, and alternate the two in this way across both rows of a stripe. Use the pattern chart to plan where to put the colors; interlock two yarns on the inside of the fabric where a Slip stitch occurs.

- You could also try combining a Mosaic pattern with Shadow Knitting. Work half the pattern rows in Garter Stitch with a single color, and work the other pattern rows in a combination of Garter Stitch and Stockinette, changing from one to the other according to a Shadow Knitting pattern.

- When the Intarsia technique is combined with Mosaics, it opens up some wonderful possibilities for color pattern. The Intarsia areas of the pattern cut across the horizontal Mosaic patterns, or float within them, creating a beautiful layered effect.

Here again, select a single yarn color for half the pattern rows, and tie on separate supplies of yarn to use for the other half, changing from one to the other as you work across these rows in the usual way. This is in many ways similar to the Intarsia and Stranded Combined, described above.

Brioche Color Patterns

The structure of a basic Brioche-type pattern is similar to that of a Single Rib—the two types of fabrics share the quality of having dominant columns of Knit stitches with Purl columns that recede, producing a reversible fabric that looks the same on both sides when done in a single color.

This structure is taken advantage of for color patterns, a great many of which create distinctive vertical stripes, which are otherwise difficult to achieve in a knitted fabric. There are also ways to make more subtle horizontal stripes of various kinds, or tweeds and spot patterns, and it is even possible to add areas of Intarsia. For an excellent selection of patterns of these kinds, see *Knitting Brioche*, by Nancy Marchant.†

---

† Nancy Marchant, *Knitting Brioche: The Essential Guide to the Brioche Stitch* (Cincinnati, Ohio: North Light Books, 2009).

Vertical Striped Brioche

The simplest type of color pattern for Brioche is vertical stripes, with all the Knit stitches on one side of the Fabric in Color A, and all the Knit stitches on the other side in Color B.

These instructions are for adding color to the Brioche Rib pattern found in Knit Below Brioche, but the same concept can just as easily be applied to the Yarnover-Slip Brioche version.

Work on a pair of double-point needles; cast on an uneven number of stitches with Color A, work Preparatory Row with Color B, and then continue as follows:

1. With Color A, Knit 1, [Knit Below, Knit 1]; repeat between brackets across row. Slide.
2. With Color B, Knit 1, [Purl 1, Purl Below]; repeat between brackets across row, end Purl 2; both colors are now at same side of fabric. Turn.
3. With Color A, Purl 1, [Purl Below, Purl 1]; repeat between brackets across row. Slide.
4. With Color B, Purl 1, [Knit 1, Knit 1 below]; repeat between brackets across row; both colors are again at same side of fabric. Turn.

Here are some things to keep in mind as you work a pattern of this kind:

- To make sure you are working with the correct color, look at the stitches on the left needle and pick up the yarn in the opposite color.
- If the Knit columns on the nearside of the fabric are in the same color as the yarn that you will use next, work the row in Knit; if they are in Purl, work the row in Purl.
- For variety, you can change the colors of the stripes, or continue the column in the same color but change from Knit to Purl; this can create interesting changes in your perception of the colors.
- It is also possible to introduce a great deal of movement into striped patterns of this kind through the use of increases and decreases, as well as with Crossed Stitch and Cable techniques.

Horizontal Striped Brioche

To make horizontal instead of vertical stripes, work as follows:

- To make single-row stripes, work two pattern rows of Brioche Rib with Color A, and then two pattern rows with Color B.
- To make two-row stripes, work four pattern rows of Brioche Rib with Color A, and then four pattern rows with Color B.

Brioche Rib with Horizontal Stripe. Rib reverses from Knit to Purl in lower half; the same colors are used throughout, but the dark yarn appears lighter in the lower portion.

Keep in mind that it takes two "passes" across the needle to give all the stitches in the fabric the form of a Brioche stitch (half are done on each pass); therefore, two pattern rows will make one-row stripes; four pattern rows will make two-row stripes.

For more variety, you can sequence through three or more colors.

Double Strand Stitch

Here is another way to blend two different color yarns into a tweedy fabric that has an unusual, supple structure. The technique suggested itself to me when I was making a sample of Basic Twice Knit with a doubled strand of very fine yarn because it was all I had on hand; this led to Double Strand Twice Knit, as well as this variation.

The technique tends to produce a very dense fabric; therefore, work with a considerably larger needle size than would be normal for the type of yarn used.

Hold the two contrast-color yarns as one (every stitch will have two strands, one in each color), cast on, and then work as follows:

- Knit one of two strands in first stitch; retain second strand on left needle. [Knit retained strand and one strand of next stitch together; discard]; repeat between brackets across row, end by Knitting remaining strand of penultimate stitch with both strands in last stitch.

Double Strand Stitch.

As you work, you may find it necessary to pull the second strand away with your left finger so you can work the first one.

This stitch technique looks best in plain Stockinette. For a flat fabric, there is no need to add a separate Selvedge stitch; the first and last stitches serve this purpose fine when worked in pattern.

When working circular, Slip one strand at the beginning of the first round; on all subsequent rounds, work one strand of the last stitch with one strand of the first stitch.

Working with two colors creates a tweed effect, and combining a smooth yarn and a textured one is also very effective; however, the structure of the fabric is interesting even when done with two yarns of the same color.

While you could control the pairing of yarns, so Yarn A is always the first strand, Yarn B the second strand in each stitch, it is a bit of a nuisance to try to line them up properly every time; taking them as they come creates a random effect that has its own charm and is much easier. If the yarns begin to wind around each other, drop the needles and let the yarns unwind every few rows.

For an interesting alternative, try working the technique in Balanced Twist Stitch; the facing stitches will slope in opposite directions row-by-row, creating a subtle herringbone effect.

❖ Other Stitch and Color Combinations

In addition to the methods used to integrate color into a stitch pattern, discussed above, there are also ways to combine color with a conventional stitch pattern, and these approaches are very easy to do.

Color Insertion

There are several ways to introduce color into a pattern that does not specifically call for it. For instance, it is easy to work a row or two of a stitch or color technique between pattern repeats, and some patterns can be done with one or more rows in a different color inserted somewhere within them. Here are some examples.

- Elongation techniques can be used to add a line of contrast color as well as a bit of openwork between repeats done in a different pattern.
- As with bias stitch patterns, some lace patterns have several rows of Garter Stitch set between or within the row

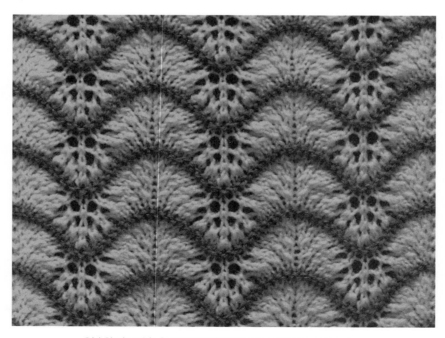

Old Shale with Garter Stitch stripe in contrast-color yarn.

repeats; it creates a nice effect when these are done in a contrast color.

- To liven up a plain fabric, introduce a few rows done in a contrast color with almost any sort of decorative stitch pattern; for ideas, see Increase and Decrease Stitch Patterns.

- In patterns that contain several stitch techniques, often one or more of them can be enhanced with a contrast color without otherwise changing the pattern. If these stitches are relatively close together, use the Stranded Color method; if they are farther apart, use Intarsia.

For instance, any pattern with Knots or Bobbles is very easy to do in this way. Similarly, all or some of the stitches

Latvian Mitten in Stranded Color Pattern with fringe, Braided Cast-On, and Herringbone Braid Insertion. Knitted by Melinda Mullins.

in a Cable can be done in a contrast color, and some Twist Stitch patterns lend themselves to this approach.

- To introduce a thin line of contrast color, either between pattern repeats or on a plain background, use Herringbone Braid; or consider Horizontal Chain Stitch.

Color and Pattern Repeats

Here are some suggestions for combining color with stitch pattern repeats, or portions of them.

- By far the simplest way to combine stitch pattern and color is to work all the rows of a pattern repeat in one color, and work the next repeat in another color to create textured stripes. Bias stitch patterns, which force the rows out of their horizontal path into undulations or chevrons, are particularly interesting when done this way.

- Another approach that can be used for stitch pattern repeats that are relatively wide is to work each one with a different color, tying on the yarns as for Intarsia.

- Ruching makes an interesting stripe when done in a contrast color; or use a contrast color for narrow stripes set between several ruched areas.

Color and Short Rows

The Short Row technique is an interesting way to introduce triangular blocks of color into a fabric.

For instance, you might use the concept for something narrow, like a scarf, and have one triangle of color sloping up from the left edge to the right, and the next in a contrast color sloping from the right edge to the left. Done this way, the angle of one triangle offsets the angle of the next, and the scarf will have straight sides.

Alternatively, you could use the application described in Short Row Curves to create a scarf with sinuous side edges: repeat a pattern several times in different colors, and then flip it so the triangles go in the other direction and repeat that several more times.

That approach to using Short Rows for color patterns need not be restricted to narrow widths; you could certainly add alternating triangles of color anywhere within a larger fabric; the angle of one will offset the angle of the other and the fabric will remain otherwise unaffected. And instead of triangular shapes, you can devise patterns for Short Rows to introduce curved areas, as well.

Stitch Techniques and Intarsia

Areas of color done with Intarsia can also contain stitch techniques.

- Purl adds a wonderful texture to Intarsia patterns—just remember to Knit the first row of a stitch column in a new color; see Color Patterns with Purl, above.

Sixteenth-century Italian silk tunic. Yellow and purple silk with metallic thread. Purl pattern outlined with intarsia on knit ground. The Metropolitan Museum of Art, Fletcher Fund, 194646.156.117.

- For even more texture, see Embossed Motifs, as well as Nubs, Knots, and Bobbles; any of these techniques are easy to include in an Intarsia pattern.
- A geometric Intarsia area can be made up of a single stitch pattern repeat; even a simple lace pattern repeat can be used in this way. If there is a minor difference in gauge between the Intarsia area and the background, a little steam will help; if it is more significant, increase or decrease a stitch or two when you start the area and restore the stitch count on the last row.

Color and Special Fabrics

In addition to the material discussed here, there are a variety of interesting ways to use color with the techniques described in the section on Special Fabrics, which includes Inlay, Felting and Fulling, Twined Knit, and the remarkable Double-Fabrics and Double-Faced Fabrics.

CHAPTER 14

Surface Decoration

The techniques in this chapter are borrowed from needlework and dressmaking, and have a long association with knitting. They make it possible to create effects that would be difficult or impossible to achieve otherwise. Furthermore, they lend themselves to afterthought and improvisation, making it easy to transform a plain garment into a festive one, to refresh the style of an older garment, or to cover damaged or stained areas.

Almost any embroidery or needlepoint technique can be used for a knitted fabric in much the same way it might be for a woven one. In addition, many beautiful trims are available at fabric stores and can be applied to the surface or edges of a knit; indeed, these materials are dazzling in their variety and include braids, flat tapes, ribbons, cords, laces, and even feathers. And of course, a great many patterns are available for narrow knitted or crochet trims that you can make separately and sew into place just as you would a woven one. Beaded or sequined trims are also available and can be used in the same way, or you can sew individual beads and sequins into place.

While you can make use of many of these techniques even long after a garment is made, several of them require designing the garment with the decorative finish in mind. Ribbing patterns, for example, provide an excellent background for Smocking, and some Eyelet patterns can be used to create openings for woven-in yarns or ribbons (for a similar effect done while knitting, see Couching or Inlay). The Needle Weaving technique requires controlled unraveling to free strands within the knitted fabric, which can then be gathered up and sewn into various patterns, or other materials can be woven into them. And, of course, beads and sequins can be knitted into the fabric as it is made.

Needlework and Crochet

The following techniques are all adaptations of traditional crafts that employ a needle to draw a thread, yarn, or ribbon through a fabric.

Crewel Embroidery, or Crewelwork, is a stitchery technique traditionally done with wool yarn. It is used to make free-form designs that are not restricted to the underlying geometry of the fabric, whether the warp and weft of a woven or the rows and columns of stitches in a knit. Designs are commonly derived from natural forms, such as flowers and foliage, and the result is a layered visual effect.

In contrast, decorative effects done with adaptions from Needlepoint or Counted Thread techniques follow the underlying grid-like nature of the fabric. These are normally done on stiffened woven fabrics with a precise number of threads per inch, but the designs can be readily adapted to the softer characteristics and different proportions of a knitted one.

Duplicate Stitch is similar to these, but is unique to knitting, since it replicates the shape of the stitches. The technique can be used to create geometric designs that resemble the motifs of Stranded Color Patterns, as well as the pictorial ones done with Intarsia.

And, of course, knitting's close relative, Crochet, can be used in a wide variety of ways to decorate the edges and surface of a fabric as well.

❖ General Tips

Special tools and materials are often required for projects of this kind, and the knitted fabric will need to be dressed (see Dressing the Fabric), and handled carefully when sewing or applying materials to the surface. Here are some suggestions that will help you achieve a smooth and even result.

Materials

Most knitters have a supply of leftover yarn on hand, often quite a lot of it, and these techniques provide an opportunity to use some of them. However, keep in mind that soft knitting yarns tend to abrade when drawn repeatedly through the fabric when used for sewing, and textured ones may be impossible to pull through the stitches. Furthermore, you may have specific colors in mind for a design and find, to your annoyance, that nothing in your supply is quite right.

For alternatives, look for silk or cotton embroidery thread or wool needlepoint yarns, which are intended for this purpose and are readily available in a great many colors. The better-quality materials of this kind are made with stable dyes that will not run (although it is always a good idea to test for this). Also, these yarns have multiple plies intended for easy removal, so the thickness of the yarn can be reduced to the size needed, or one or two plies can be added to a strand to thicken it.

Always work with relatively short lengths of about 20 inches, not only to prevent fraying, but also because this reduces tangling and requires less arm movement. Also, if you need to fix a mistake, or if a repair is ever needed, it is easier to replace a short length of stitching than a long one. For something that will be drawn in flat across the entire width or length of the fabric, cut multiple lengths sufficient to cover only a few rows or columns of stitches at a time, and/or start in the middle and pull the material through in opposite directions.

To add trim to the surface of a fabric, any good-quality sewing thread is suitable. I have seen warnings that nylon or polyester thread may "saw" through soft yarn as the garment moves in wear; if you share this concern, use cotton or silk thread. Also, if the sewn stitches will be part of the embellishment, silk thread has a beautiful sheen; if you prefer a heavier stitch, select silk buttonhole thread.

The compatibility of the materials you plan to use, both in wear and in terms of whether they can be cleaned in the same manner, is also important. For instance, if the label on a trim says "dry-clean only," this will dictate the care of the entire garment; if trims are washable, always preshrink them before application.

Tools

Most of the sewing techniques discussed below will require what is sometimes called a tapestry needle with a blunt tip and a large eye to accommodate thicker threads and yarns.

A normal sharp-tip needle is used for sewing on woven trims or to attach interfacing of any kind; because of the thickness of a knitted fabric, choose a relatively long needle.

To weave ribbons into a knit, there are special flat threaders with a slit instead of an eye; or you can use a bodkin, a type of tool that is clamped to the end of a ribbon or cord.

Needlework Patterns

Innumerable embroidery and needlepoint books are available that provide patterns you can adapt for decorating a knitted garment, or you can draw up an idea of your own. Patterns are usually printed on a square grid, or you can trace a design onto graph paper; in some cases, these designs will have to be modified to suit the rectangular shape of a knitted stitch, as is done for Intarsia patterns; see Coordinating Stitch and Garment Patterns. You will also find information there on how to plot the pattern on the overall garment shape, and how to work out the exact position for trims.

Fabric Behavior and Gauge

Many of these materials will add weight to a fabric, and this may affect the dimensions of the garment in wear. Make a swatch that is somewhat larger than normal, apply a proportional amount of trim to it, and then use the Weighted Gauge method to develop the pattern. If you plan to embellish a garment made from a published pattern, compare this trimmed gauge to the one specified and make any necessary adjustments to the instructions; for more information, see Matching Pattern Gauges.

Also keep in mind that an area decorated with a surface pattern may become less resilient than the surrounding fabric, and the two will no longer respond in the same way either in wear or when cleaned. For this reason, it is very important to give the fabric its final dimensions before using techniques of this kind; see Dressing the Fabric.

In some cases, it may be necessary to add support for a surface pattern or trim so the garment is not pulled out of shape in wear. This is particularly important if the added material is heavy or the design is concentrated in one area.

To support trim that will be sewn on only in certain areas, baste a commercial knit interfacing, soft gauze, or lightweight silk or rayon lining material cut on the bias to the inside of the fabric. Sew directly through all three fabrics: trim, knit, and facing. When you are done, turn to the inside and cut away any excess fabric around the edges to neaten things up. For a pattern that is distributed over the entire fabric, it may be best to interline the garment; see Linings.

Working Tips

When doing needlework or adding trim, work with the fabric laid flat and smooth on a table instead of in your lap. You may also want to take into consideration the dimensions in wear, which are often different from those of a garment lying flat (see Stitch Gauge, in particular, Drop: The Effect of Gravity, and Weighted Gauge Measurement). If necessary, pin the garment out on a firm, padded surface or use weights along the edges to maintain those dimensions as you work.

It is usually best to add surface decoration before assembling the pieces of a garment worked flat, but for a finished garment or one worked in the round, slide something like a small quilter's cutting board or firm piece of cardboard under the area you are working on to prevent sewing through both sides.

To attach a sewing thread for adding trim, skim the needle through a strand of yarn on the inside, or in a stitch that will be covered, and make a tiny knot. To attach yarn for needlework, either weave in the ends as you begin and end each motif (see Hiding Ends of Yarn), or put all this off until later and finish everything at the same time. For the latter, use a Simple Knot, or run the needle through an inch or two of adjacent stitches so the yarn is secure and will not pull through, but is still easy to pull out later and hide properly.

❖ Duplicate Stitch

Duplicate Stitch embroidery is done by drawing a contrast-color yarn through the fabric so it lies on top of, and exactly duplicates, some of the Knit stitches. This is usually done on a Stockinette fabric because it provides a flat, smooth ground that shows off the pattern nicely. However, it can also be ef-

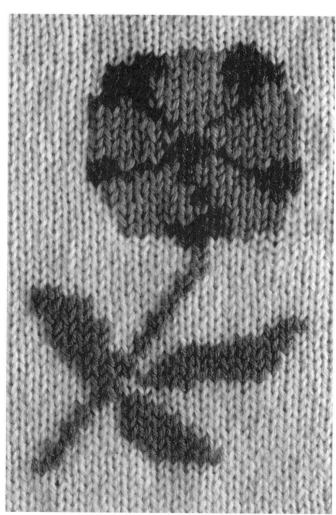

Duplicate Stitch.

fective when small amounts of duplicate stitch are tucked between areas done with various stitch techniques, for instance, in and around Cable patterns.

Duplicate Stitch works well for geometric patterns that resemble those done with the Stranded Color technique, as well as for the more fluid, naturalistic patterns often done with Intarsia. It lends itself to improvisation, especially for simple motifs, for spot patterns, or to add lines of color around or within pattern repeats.

The stitching is done on the outside of the fabric, working from right to left (or left to right if left-handed). After duplicating all the stitches in one row of a motif, the fabric is turned upside down to work back across the next row of the pattern.

A Stockinette fabric will look the same upside down, but a close examination will reveal that the running threads now appear to be the heads of stitches, and the heads of the stitches now seem to be running threads. For more information, see Working in the Opposite Direction.

However, the work proceeds exactly as it did with the fabric right side up, except there will be a half stitch instead of a whole one at the beginning and end of the group of stitches you are duplicating. Once you are familiar with this visual transformation it will be clear how to proceed.

Working a Duplicate Stitch Pattern

1. Bring yarn to outside through center of stitch in row below stitch to be duplicated.

2. Pass needle from right to left behind both sides of stitch in row above stitch being duplicated.

3. Insert needle into center of same stitch as in Step 1, and then out center of stitch to left.

4. Repeat Steps 2 and 3 across row for each stitch of motif.

5. After last duplicated stitch of row, bring needle out below running thread to left, and then insert from nearside to farside above running thread and out through center of same stitch.

6. Turn fabric around so bottom edge is up; it will appear that only half of stitch last sewn was covered. Insert needle into center of stitch in row that is now below next one to be

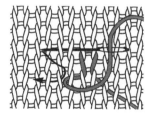

Duplicate Stitch: Steps 2–3.

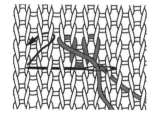

Duplicate Stitch: Repeating Steps 2–3.

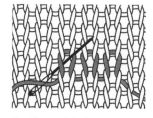

Duplicate Stitch: Step 5.

duplicated, and then out of center of stitch to left.

7. Insert needle behind both sides of stitch above one being duplicated, and then into center of stitch below it and out of the center of stitch to left. Continue to duplicate stitches in this way across row.

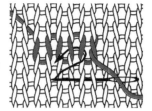

Duplicate Stitch: Step 6.

8. To cover half stitch at left end of row and anchor yarn for turn after Step 7, work as in Step 5, passing needle under running thread to left, then above it and out of the center of last duplicated stitch.

9. Turn fabric around with top edge up and duplicate stitches of next row in same way.

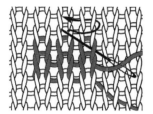

Duplicate Stitch: Step 9.

Step 5 anchors the yarn at the base of the last stitch sewn and positions it to work the stitch above after the fabric is turned around. If the next stitch to be duplicated is to one side, bring needle out of the center of whichever stitch is below it.

To create diagonal or vertical lines, proceed much as described above, duplicating one stitch and bringing the needle out in the center of the stitch below the next one you want to cover, anchoring yarn around running thread when necessary.

While all the instructions are written as if the fabric is positioned with the stitch columns vertical, in fact you might find it easier to work with it set at a slight angle, sewing up toward the left if right-handed, or up toward the right if left-handed.

❖ Embroidery

Any of the classic embroidery techniques can be done almost as easily on a knitted fabric as on a woven one. Crewel work is the best source for ideas and patterns because it is traditionally done with wool yarns rather than with fine threads.

Chain Stitch

Chain Stitch is the most compatible technique and the easiest to use for this purpose (it is the same as a basic crocheted Chain Stitch). It can be used to create horizontal or vertical lines, but there is no need to follow the underlying structure of the fabric. The stitch lends itself to making sinuous lines or outlines for motifs done in some other way, such as Intarsia.

The chain of stitches will be on the outside surface of the fabric, while the strand of yarn that is equivalent to a "running thread" passes between each sewn stitch and the next on the inside of the fabric.

Embroidered gloves. Dalarnas Museum, Falun, Sweden.

1. Thread tapestry needle, secure yarn on inside, and bring needle through fabric to outside.

2. Wrap yarn around left forefinger or make loop of yarn and hold against fabric.

3. Insert needle back through fabric where it emerged, and to outside again at base of next stitch, and then up through loop of yarn on forefinger.

4. Tighten stitch gently so it lies neatly on surface, neither too loose, nor nor too tight.

5. Repeat Steps 3–4 to create design; to finish, insert needle through fabric from nearside to farside at top of last Chain Stitch; secure yarn on inside.

❖ Needlepoint Stitches

Needlepoint and Counted Thread work are normally done on special fabrics with a balanced weave that forms a square grid, and they are stiffened to provide a firm base for even stitches that completely cover the surface. Nevertheless, these techniques can be adapted for use on a soft knit with stitches that are rectangular, not square, and there is no need to completely cover the underlying fabric.

In fact, decorative stitches of this kind look best when they

Cuffed socks with needlepoint-style embroidery.
Dalarnas Museum, Falun, Sweden.

have the same proportions as the knit stitches in the surrounding fabric; just use the latter as a base for whatever kinds of needlepoint stitches you want to use. However, this will change the proportions of the motifs, making them look tall and narrow unless the design is adjusted somewhat as is done for Intarsia patterns.

The simplest and easiest needlepoint technique is Cross-Stitch, and it serves as a good example of how stitches of this kind can be used.

Cross-Stitch

Set the fabric flat on a table and position it with the rows vertical or set at a slight angle.

Do not worry about attaching the yarn on the inside until you are done. Just slip the needle into the fabric nearby and bring it back out to the surface where you want to start the pattern. Press the tail of yarn against the fabric with your finger; once you have made a stitch or two, it will be secure. When finished with the stitching, draw the end of the yarn through to the inside and hide it in the usual way.

1. Bring yarn through fabric to outside below running thread at bottom left corner of first stitch of pattern.
2. Pass needle from right to left under both sides of stitch in same column, two rows up; yarn will cross over stitch in between from lower left to upper right.

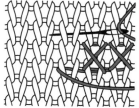

Cross-Stitch: Step 2.

3. Pass needle from right to left under same stitch as in Step 1, as well as under both sides of stitch to left; yarn will cross over stitch in between from upper left to lower right.
4. Repeat Steps 2 and 3 across row.

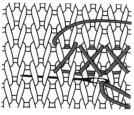

Cross-Stitch: Step 3.

You can, of course, make the cross-stitches larger or smaller, depending upon the look you want to achieve and the gauge of your fabric. On the inside of the fabric you will see two horizontal lines of stitching.

❖ Smocking

Smocking is a needlework technique used to produce precisely controlled, decorative tucks that gather the fabric below. It is often seen on skirt or bodice yokes, or at the top of a sleeve. Many books provide detailed instructions and patterns for smocking a woven fabric, and with some adjustments the basic principles and patterns can be applied to a knitted one.

One of the advantages a knitted fabric offers for a smocking pattern is that the columns and rows of stitches provide perfect guides—there is no need to mark and gather the fabric as you would a woven one. While a Stockinette fabric will do, a Single Rib is ideal for this purpose because the Knit columns can be drawn together and the Purl columns will recede.

There are two versions, and both are easy to do. The first leaves fewer strands on the outside of the fabric, which you may prefer for designs where a more subtle effect is needed; the other is more decorative. In either case, you will want to decide whether to use a yarn in a strongly contrasting color, or one that is the same or similar to the fabric.

Each smocking stitch includes two Knit stitches on either side of a Purl stitch; the two Knit stitches will be pulled tightly together, squeezing the Purl stitch out of the way toward the inside of the fabric.

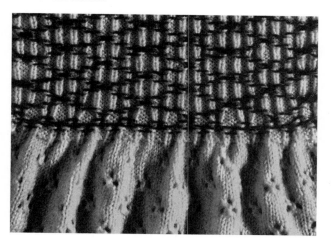

Smocking on Single Rib with Eyelet pattern.

Smocking: Version One

With this version, the strand that passes between the smocking stitches will be on the inside of the fabric; only the stitches that draw the columns of Knit stitches together are seen.

1. Attach yarn at right edge and then bring needle from inside to outside of fabric at left side of second Knit stitch.
2. Insert needle at right side of first Knit stitch of pair and then out to left of third Knit stitch; draw yarn through, pulling first two Knit stitches together.
3. Insert needle to right of second Knit stitch (in middle of pair last sewn), and then out to left of fourth stitch; draw second and third stitch together.
4. Repeat Step 3 across row to create pattern, always inserting needle to right of two Knit stitches and out to left of third one—two back, three forward.

In other words, insert needle two Knits to the right, and bring it out three Knits to the left.

Smocking: Version Two

With this version, you will see both the short strands that draw the pairs of Knit stitches together, as well as the slightly longer ones that pass between the pairs. Attach the yarn at the left edge of the fabric and bring the needle through to the nearside to the left of the first Knit stitch; work on the outside, as follows:

1. Insert needle into fabric to right of second Knit stitch and bring it out to left of first Knit stitch; draw yarn through and pull these two stitches together.
2. Insert needle to right of third Knit stitch and out at left side of second Knit stitch (right stitch of first pair); draw yarn through; pull these two stitches together.
3. Repeat Step 2 across row to create pattern.

In other words, insert needle three Knits to the right, and bring it out two Knits to the left.

If you sew with the needle below the yarn, the sewn stitch will lie parallel to, but slightly below the previous one; if you sew with the needle above the yarn, the sewn stitch will lie above the previous one.

Smocking Tips

For either version, if you prefer a bolder look, wrap the stitches twice before continuing to the next pair. Also, you can draw the yarn up tightly to bring the pairs of stitches close together, or more gently to leave more of the Purl background visible as contrast; this will also change how much gathering there is in the fabric below the smocked area.

To stagger the pattern, sew a pair of Knits in one row, then sew the next pair several rows up, and the following pair in the same row as the first. To hide the strand that passes between rows, after Step 2, pass needle to inside at right side of last pair and out again to left of next pair to be sewn.

Be careful to join two stitches of same row; if necessary, run a Yarn Marker through the stitches above or below the Smocking row before you begin.

Try the smocking pattern on a fairly large Gauge Swatch so you can see the full effect of the pattern and the gathers it creates. Measure the width of the smocked area to calculate the number of stitches needed for the width of the garment; this is particularly important when making a fitted garment, since the smocked area will no longer be resilient.

Note that similar effects can also be achieved with certain stitch techniques such as Wrap Stitches, Couching, and Pullover stitches.

❖ *Needle Weaving*

There is a lovely, traditional needlework technique used to create subtle openwork patterns, often called "drawn thread work" or "needle weaving," or, when used at the edges of tablecloths or napkins, "hemstitching."

In a woven fabric, several adjacent threads are pulled out of the fabric, leaving an open area with what looks like a "ladder" of threads that are then stitched together in various patterns. To create the same effect in a knitted fabric, instead of pulling threads as you would for a woven, use either a stitch technique to make a horizontal ladder or controlled unraveling for a vertical ladder.

Needle Weaving.

Once you have made the ladder in the fabric, you can use the patterns for needle weaving found in any standard embroidery book to complete the design. If you use a fine thread or a yarn in the same color as the knitted fabric for the needle weaving, the strands and open spaces of the knitted fabric will remain the dominant element of the pattern; use a yarn with a contrast color or texture to draw attention to the stitching instead.

A Horizontal Ladder is quite simple, but a Vertical Ladder requires more advance planning and some special techniques; however, once the ladder has been made in the fabric, the decorative stitching is the same.

Horizontal Ladder

- For a horizontal row, use one of the Elongation techniques.

Vertical Ladder

- Increase one stitch at base of ladder; continue working fabric. At top of ladder, drop stitch and unravel to base.

Make a one-stitch ladder if working with a thicker yarn, two stitches for a thinner one; try this on a Test Swatch first to decide on the effect you want.

Wide Vertical Ladder

For a wider ladder, work as for a Steek, and weave in multiple courses of a narrow ribbon or a thicker yarn. Keep in mind that the fabric will widen when the stitches are released, so you will want to test the effect with a fairly large Gauge Swatch. Also, take into consideration the effect this will have on the top and bottom edges. Here are some suggestions for how to integrate the woven area with the knitted fabric:

1. Insert Stitch Holder or Yarn Marker into stitches at bottom of ladder.
2. Position short needle at top and bottom of woven area; wrap weaving yarn or ribbon around needles to form equivalent of stitches.
3. At top, include the woven stitches with those of the knitted fabric on either side and continue above the area; or cast off the woven stitches with all the other stitches.
4. At bottom of area, stitches of fabric should be on hold, as for starting a Steek. Graft loops of woven material to stitches of fabric.

Alternatively, you can thread the weaving material through the stitches on hold as you go, sewing into one stitch on the holder each time you come to the bottom edge.

❖ Applied Materials

A wide variety of decorative effects can be achieved by sewing trims or other materials to the surface of a knitted fabric. As mentioned above in General Tips, it is important to take into consideration the characteristics of any material you would like to use before you begin.

For woven trims that will be sewn the length or width of the fabric, it is best if they are relatively soft and not too heavy. You are, of course, quite safe in selecting almost any sort of lace, or you can knit or crochet your own, even using 0000 needles and yarn barely thicker than a hair if you want an opportunity to display your skills on a small scale. Trims of that kind normally wind up on the edge of a pillow or hand towel; far better to have some beautiful lace on the front of your sweater

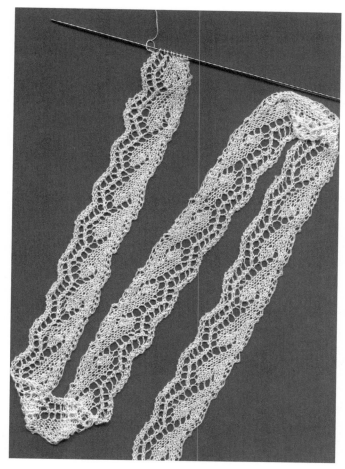

Cotton lace trim on size 0000 needles.

where it can be seen in all its glory—it will definitely earn you bragging rights.

Beautiful appliqué materials are also available from better sewing supply stores, or various fanciful shapes can be knitted or crocheted separately and sewn to the surface of your garment; a good source of inspiration is Nicky Epstein's book *Knitted Embellishments*.[†]

For the most part, there really are no particular instructions necessary here; minimal hand-sewing skills are all that are needed and a tiny hemstitch is the most common method used to apply trim.

Appliqué or Trim

You will find detailed information about how to sew woven appliqué and trim materials onto a knitted fabric in the mate-

---

[†] Nicky Epstein, *Nicky Epstein's Knitted Embellishments: 350 Appliqués, Borders, Cords, and More!* (Loveland, Colo.: Interweave Press, 1999).

rial on Sewing Wovens to Knits. Included are instructions for hand-sewing techniques and suggestions for the kind of interfacing materials to select when necessary to provide support for the trim on the inside of the garment.

Couching

In stitchery, couching is a technique that uses decorative stitches to attach a yarn, cord, or ribbon across the surface of a fabric. At its simplest, couching is used to create horizontal and vertical lines, but it is ideal for more fluid design elements, such as the stem of a flower, or to form the outline of a curvilinear shape.

The basic stitching is quite simple.

1. Draw one end of couching material through to inside of fabric and hold or pin into place on outside.
2. Thread needle with decorative embroidery thread or yarn; attach on inside and bring needle to outside immediately adjacent to lower edge of couching material.
3. Insert needle on other side of couching material, directly opposite where it emerged, and then pass it under fabric and out again about ¼ inch away from first stitch.
4. Repeat until couched material is sewn down.
5. Draw other end through to inside. Adjust width of couching material to width of knitted fabric as necessary, and then use needle and thread to sew two ends in place.

In Step 3, for basic Couching, the visible stitches cross the material at a right angle; you can, of course, use more elaborate embroidery stitches, such as cross-stitch or buttonhole stitch, if you prefer.

The couched material draws up a bit as you sew, so it is best not to pin it all in place ahead of time. Hold it down on the surface of the fabric with your left hand, or pin it just an inch or two beyond where you are working, and repin from time to time as you go. If you are not couching in a straight line, you might want to define the line to follow across the fabric by sewing in large basting stitches with a contrast-color yarn before you begin.

You can also create horizontal lines of couching within a knitted fabric by drawing a ribbon, cord, or decorative yarn behind a series of Slip stitches. Plan ahead, and make the Slip stitches the right size to accommodate the material you want to insert, using an Elongation technique if necessary. You can also make vertical or sloped lines, or even zigzags, by drawing a couching material under running threads stranded on the outside of Slip stitches, or under some of the decorative strands made with the Pullover technique or the Wrap technique, or do the same sort of thing as you work with the Inlay Couching technique.

Sewn-On Ornaments

A charming way to dress up a garment is to sew tiny decorative materials individually to the surface of the fabric. These items range from the amusing to the gorgeous—a trip to any bead or craft store should set your imagination racing. As long as there is some way to sew the item into place, it can be used. Also keep in mind that buttons can be used for purely decorative purposes as well, and they are available in a huge selection of colors and materials.

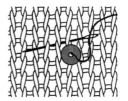

Sewing an individual sequin.

If the ornaments are not set close together, sew them on individually, rather than carrying the thread across the inside of the fabric from one to the next. While it is more time-consuming to knot the thread on and off for each one, the result is far more satisfactory because the resilience of the knit is preserved. This also means that if one ornament escapes, it will not take all its neighbors with it, making a repair much easier to manage.

If you are planning an embroidery pattern, consider stringing beads on the thread and setting them between or within the decorative stitches. You could, for instance, have a bead on each stitch used to sew trim or an appliqué into place, or beads could be incorporated into a smocking pattern.

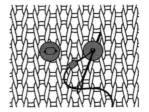

Sewing a sequin with a bead.

❖ Crochet

Crochet has traditionally been used to finish or adorn the edges of knitted garments, but the technique can be used in some lovely ways within a fabric as well. For instance, a beautiful crocheted lace edging can be set along the line of a yoke, down a sleeve, next to a button band, or around a neckline. The trim can be done separately and sewn into place, or anchored to the fabric as it is made.

A variety of crocheted patterns are available for making separate motifs such as flowers, leaves, bobbles, and so forth, that can be attached anywhere on the surface of a garment to add bold embellishment. You can use highly textured or even thin, delicate yarns for this purpose; because the trim is added later and the yarn is not repeatedly drawn through the fabric, it will not fray.

The most basic crochet technique, Chain Stitch, is particularly suitable for use as a surface pattern because it resembles a Knit stitch; it can be combined with other crocheted or needlework stitches, or used alone to create designs that travel across the surface of the fabric. The result will be similar to what can be done with the embroidery version, described above.

Chain Stitch on Purl

A column of Purl stitches set on a ground of Knit will recede and the Purl nubs provide perfectly spaced anchor points for a Crochet Chain. The chain of stitches will nest in the little "gutter" between the columns of Knit, flush with the surface of the fabric; it is a pretty effect.

1. Hold yarn on inside of fabric, insert hook below first Purl nub at base of stitch column, and draw through a loop.
2. Insert hook up under next Purl nub (or depending upon your gauge and the look you want, second or third nub), draw loop through fabric, and loop on hook to form Chain Stitch.
3. Repeat Step 2 for length of column; to secure last Chain Stitch, break yarn, draw end through stitch, and then draw it back to inside of fabric and secure.

You can also crochet a chain horizontally by working into the center of Knit stitches, or between two stitches.

One of the difficulties of doing this is that you will be working with the yarn on the inside where it is difficult to see and you have to fish for it with the hook (if the yarn is held on the outside, the running threads between each stitch will be visible, and they tilt the stitch to one side). Therefore, it is easiest to use the technique at the edges of the fabric where you can peer around to the other side; with a little practice, you do get the hang of finding the yarn, so it is not impossible to do this within the fabric as well.

Beads

A garment adorned with beads is certainly one of the more elegant expressions of the knitter's art, and even just a few of them scattered across the surface can transform the simplest design into one of high drama and glamour. For bold and dramatic effects, use shiny beads in a color that contrasts strongly with the yarn. Or, select beads that are the same color as the yarn, making use of their unique shapes and pronounced surface texture to create a more subtle effect.

Individual beads, or trims decorated with them, can be sewn onto the fabric, as discussed in Sewn-On Ornaments, above, and this technique works well when decorating relatively small areas or if you want to enhance a finished garment. However, this section focuses on how to incorporate the beads into the knitted fabric itself, which is a far more efficient way to work. The design potential is vast because it is easy to adapt a Brocade pattern, or almost any type of color pattern, for the purpose. For information on developing a chart you can work from, see Bead and Sequin Charts.

Because the beads are added to the fabric one at a time, no project of this kind will be a quickie knit; however, the skills required are modest and within the reach of every knitter. All that you need is a little patience.

It is a good idea to buy small amounts of the materials you think would be suitable for the project and try different kinds of patterns and techniques on a few Test Swatches before you decide how to work. This will reveal crucial information about the characteristics and appearance of the resulting fabric, and, if the results are not acceptable, there is little time and money lost and a great deal of information gained.

❖ Beading Materials

There are a surprising number of ways to incorporate beads into a knitted fabric, and they are great fun to work with. It is very easy to introduce beads into patterns that do not call for them—you can place beads on the Purl stitches of any Brocade pattern, for instance, or just tuck some in and around the elements of almost any decorative stitch pattern.

Beads can also be set on the contrast-color stitches of any Stranded Color or Intarsia pattern. They can be used to enhance certain details of the motifs within a pattern of this kind, or substituted for the contrast-color yarn. There are also some interesting ways to make use of beads in color patterns done with certain stitch techniques.

A bead can be situated in three places within the fabric: on the running thread, on the side of a stitch, or on the head of a stitch. Which location to use is partly a matter of preference; however, the type of decorative pattern or stitch technique used, the materials chosen, and the characteristics of the background fabric are factors to take into consideration.

For instance, one method might be preferable if the fabric needs to be relatively dense to support the weight of the beads; another approach might be selected because it helps maintain the beads on the outside of a relatively open fabric.

Yarns for Beading

Almost any yarn can be used for a beaded fabric, although some present more of a challenge than others. Before selecting a yarn, give some thought to the characteristics of the fiber: how the yarn was spun and how it is likely to behave over time are important factors. For more information, see the chapter

Fibers, and also Yarns; for now, here are some suggestions specifically for this purpose.

Suitable Yarns

- A yarn needs to be able to support the collective weight of the beads without stretching out of shape or breaking; individual beads may seem to weigh almost nothing, but a garment covered with them can be heavier than you might expect. Most yarns will stretch a bit when carrying the additional weight, less so if the beads are widely scattered across the fabric or used only in limited areas. This can be compensated for by using the technique of Weighted Gauge; however, if you are concerned by how much stretch the swatch reveals, it may be best to alter the pattern and use fewer materials, or select a different yarn. If you are truly enamored of the design just the way it is, consider lining the garment to provide it with support; see Linings.
- The yarn will be subjected to a certain amount of abrasion as the materials are threaded onto it, as you knit with them, and even as the garment moves in wear, and it must be able to tolerate this without fraying. Here again, this is of little concern if fewer beads are used, and certain methods can be used to reduce the potential for damage.

    To test for fraying, use the information in Estimating Quantities, below, to determine how many beads will be on a given length of yarn. String this number of beads on the yarn and slide them back and forth several times. Compare the appearance of the beaded strand to the yarn in the ball; if you see evidence of wear, reconsider your choice of yarn.
- If the yarn you would like to use for the project is too thick or textured to pass through the bead, or presents any of the problems discussed above, all is not lost. You can select a second yarn that is suitable, thread the materials onto it, and use it along with your main yarn to make the fabric; see Beading with a Carrier Yarn for the methods to use.

Suitable Fibers for Beading Yarn

- Silk filament yarn is exceptionally strong, lustrous and smooth, and is unlikely to fray. Yarns of this type are an excellent choice; however, they are expensive and not readily available. Some spun silk yarns may be suitable, but those made from noils (see silk yarns in the chapter Yarns), have a rough texture and tend to break easily.
- Wool crepe or *worsted-spun* yarns are a very good choice since they are strong and resilient. While there may not be a wide selection of these kinds of yarns available for

hand knitting, there are for machine knitting and they come in a wide variety of colors.

- Softer *woolen-spun* yarns can be used, and mohair looks wonderful with scattered beads peeking through the fuzz. However, fabrics made with these yarns are normally knit at a relatively loose gauge, and the more material added, the more likely it is that the garment will sag under the weight; also, these kinds of yarn abrade easily. As a result, it is best to work with relatively short lengths of yarn strung with only as many beads as needed, and tie on more as needed.
- Thin, smooth, firmly spun cotton and linen yarns are good choices for a beaded or sequined garment because they are strong and readily available. However, both cotton and linen weigh considerably more than silk or wool, and the addition of beads could make for a very heavy garment; also, cotton has a tendency to stretch.

    Success depends upon the right combination of design and materials. Select a pattern for a garment that is not too large, one made with an openwork stitch pattern of some kind, and/or one that has beads scattered farther apart. To compensate for stretch and assure the garment will fit, it is essential to develop the pattern from a Weighted Gauge.
- There are also polyester or nylon yarns, cords, and even narrow ribbons that can work well with beading. These materials are lightweight, strong, tend not to stretch, and even when very thin can easily bear the weight of beads. They are also ideal for use as a Carrier Yarn.
- If your yarn is made of a blend of fibers, the weaker or more fragile fiber should determine how suitable it is for your project.

Types of Beads

Beads are available in a stunning array of colors, shapes, and materials, including glass, wood, stone, metal, shell, bone, plastic, and various kinds of resins.

Glass seed beads are customarily used for knitting; they are ideal for the purpose and come in a wide variety of colors and several sizes that can accommodate yarn. However, any visit to a bead store will present other temptations, and if you are thinking of selecting something else, first take into consideration what makes a bead suitable for knitting.

- Some beads weigh considerably more than others; make a rough estimate of the total weight of the beads that will be used in the garment before making a purchase.
- The holes in some beads can be inconsistent; the opening may seem large enough on the outside but may narrow at the center, or have rough interior surfaces.

If you have your heart set on beads with this problem, and are only going to use a limited number of them, there are tools available at beading stores that can be used to refine and enlarge the holes.

- Select beads that can be subjected to the same sort of care required by the yarn. Some may be damaged by cleaning fluids, others by washing, and plastic beads are very heat-sensitive and should never be brought into contact with a hot iron.

- As always, if you have any misgivings about the suitability of the materials, buy a small amount and try them on a Test Swatch before making a final decision.

Tools for Beading

To string the beads on the yarn, you will need a needle that is thin enough to pass through the opening in the bead, but with an eye large enough to accommodate the yarn. Many beading needles are intended for use with fine thread or wire, but some are specifically designed to accommodate yarn. There are also additional tools you may find useful for a beading project.

Beading Needle

If the eye of the needle is large enough to thread the yarn and thin enough to pass through the bead, work as follows:

1. Thread yarn through eye of needle.
2. Insert needle through centers of several beads and slide them down onto yarn; repeat until all beads have been threaded.

Needle Threader

This tiny tool is used to draw thread through the eye of a needle for hand and machine sewing. At one end of the threader is a loop of very thin, flexible wire bent into a diamond-shape or oval. Work as follows:

1. Push wire loop through eye of needle.
   As the loop passes through the eye it will flatten, but once through it will open up again.
2. Thread yarn through loop and double end back 4 to 6 inches so it will not pull free, and then draw yarn through eye of needle.

Intermediary Thread

This works well if the yarn is simply too large to pass through the eye of the needle you have, even with the help of a threader.

1. Cut a 12- to 14-inch length of fine, strong thread and fold in half. Push center of doubled thread through eye of needle so loop emerges on other side.

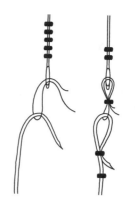

Intermediary thread for stringing beads.

2. Thread beading yarn into loop of thread and double yarn end back 4 to 6 inches.
3. Pass bead down across intermediary thread and then onto yarn.

Wire Bead Threaders

There are several simple, inexpensive devices sold at bead supply stores that are far better for stringing beads on yarn than a conventional needle.

- A split threader, or "big-eye" needle, consists of two thin wires attached at both ends, leaving a slit in the middle; they come in several sizes. Separate the sides at the center and pass the yarn through; you can insert either end of the wire into the beads for threading. This kind of threader can be reused, but it is quite delicate.
- Twisted wire threaders have a loop at one end. Thread the yarn into the loop, and then flatten it so it is thin enough to pass through the center of the bead. Insert the twisted end into the bead and then pull the bead down the wire onto the yarn. You will need a new threader each time you string more beads, but they are inexpensive and sold several to a package in various sizes.

You can also make a threader of this kind with any sort of thin flexible wire or strong thread.

- Cut 4 to 6 inches of wire, fold around pencil to make a loop, and twist ends together.

Dental floss, nylon fishing line, or buttonhole thread can be used in much the same way, but will need to be stiffened.

- Cut thread and fold in half around pencil, as above. Twist ends together and dab with liquid glue or nail polish starting about ¼ inch above cut ends; hold two ends taut until center is dry. Repeat with as many coats as necessary to stiffen thread; cut off unglued ends opposite loop.

Bead Spinner

A Bead Spinner is a small wooden bowl with a post in the center—sort of like an upside-down top. The beads are strung by means of a long, hooked threading needle.

This clever little device speeds up the process of threading small beads; it is available in bead stores or by mail, and may be worth the relatively modest investment if you plan to do beading projects regularly.

1. Thread yarn or intermediary strand into hooked needle. Pour beads into cup, and use post to spin bowl.
2. With beads flying around inside of cup, hold tip of hook against side near bottom. The beads will slip onto hook; slide them in groups down threader onto yarn.

It takes a bit of practice to find the right way to hold the hook inside the bowl, but once you get the hang of it, you will see the beads magically hop on the threader.

Miscellaneous Tools

Bead supply stores have many other tools and accessories you may find helpful if you often do beading projects.

- Bead Nabbers are little devices that scoop up beads and hold them for threading—much more efficient than bare fingers.
- Bead Stoppers consist of a metal spring coil with flaps or buttons on either side. Pinch the flaps together to bend the coil, insert the yarn or thread, and let them go. The stopper will grip the yarn and keep the beads from sliding off the end (and it can also be used to attach the yarn to the ball to keep it from unwinding).
- An inexpensive drill can be used to smooth or enlarge the hole in a bead.
- And, of course, storage supplies and sorting trays can keep things organized and are particularly useful if you want to thread beads of different colors.

Estimating Bead Quantities

Beads are sold loose in small bags or tubes, or strung on a cord tied in a loop. To estimate the number of beads needed for a project, and to determine how many to string on the yarn, use a modification of the method for calculating quantities of yarn needed; see Calculating Yarn Requirements, as well as Coordinating Stitch and Garment Patterns.

1. Use pattern chart to calculate how many beads will be in each square inch of fabric.
2. Use garment chart to find how many total square inches of fabric will be beaded.
3. Multiply the two results to estimate total number of beads needed.

Round the estimate up generously when buying the materials to compensate for the possibility of an error in calculation, losses, or a change of plans.

Materials per Pattern Repeat

If the beads will occupy only certain areas of the fabric, it may be easier to use a calculation of how many are needed for each pattern repeat instead.

- Calculate number of beads in one pattern repeat, determine how many repeats in the garment will have added material, and multiply to find number of beads needed.

Materials per Ball of Yarn

This information can also be used to determine how much material to string on each ball of yarn.

- Use number of beaded stitches per square inch and the yards per square inch from gauge to find how many beads to string per yard; use those figures to estimate total number of beads per ball of yarn.
- If you are using repeats for the calculation, find how many square inches of fabric each ball of yarn will make, and then determine how many beads will be in an area of fabric the same size and multiply.

Counting Beads

- Beads are sold in bags or tubes that contain a numbered quantity, so it is easy to determine how many to thread.

  When threading less than a full container, count the number needed into a small bowl before you begin.

Adjusting Amounts

- If you are concerned about abrading the yarn, if there are plain areas of knitting between decorated ones, or if there are sections done in different-color materials, thread only enough material to work a limited number of rows, and then break the yarn, thread on some more, and reattach it.
- If you find you did not string enough material, break the yarn at the end of a row, thread on more, tie the yarn back on, and continue with the work. If this occurs close to the end of the yarn, instead of breaking it, string the materials from the other end.
- To keep materials from sliding off the end of the yarn, double the yarn somewhere below the last bead and knot it or tie the end through the holes of a big button, or use a Bead Stopper (see Miscellaneous Tools, above).

❖ Multicolor Bead Threading

By far the most exquisite examples of beaded knitting have geometric or pictorial patterns done in multiple colors, and the most elaborate of these have a bead set on every single stitch.

Multicolored bead pattern on bonnet.
Lacis Museum of Lace and Textiles, Berkeley, California.

Traditionally done with tiny glass beads strung onto fine, strong silk, linen, or cotton yarn, this painstaking technique was used for small things like dainty purses, not only because the technique takes time and care, but also because a fully beaded item can be quite heavy.

Another traditional use of this technique is for multicolor bead patterns arranged in stripes at the edge of a collar or sleeve, or along the line of a yoke or center front opening. It is easy to adapt a Stranded Color or Intarsia pattern for a design of this kind. Instead of using a contrast-color yarn for the pattern, string contrast-color beads on the main yarn and set beads on the stitches of the motifs. Or, use two colors of yarn and string beads on the one used for the pattern, not on the one for the background.

Stringing Beads

When different colors of beads will be used across the rows, they need to be strung on the yarn in the order in which they will be used.

1. Arrange the beads in a divided tray or in several small bowls, one for each color.
2. Use a charted pattern and set a ruler under each row to help keep your place as you work. Start stringing with the last bead that will be used, reading the chart from the top down.
   - For a project worked in the round, read every line from left to right.
   - For a project worked flat, read from left to right on an outside row, and right to left on an inside row.
3. After stringing each row, lay the yarn flat under the charted pattern row and check the sequence of beads for errors before going any further. Once the pattern of beads is established on the yarn, the only way to correct it later will be to break the yarn and restring.

As a hedge against errors, string only enough beads for a limited number of rows, perhaps one or two vertical repeats of the pattern; when those have been used up, break the yarn, thread more beads, and continue. Mark the charted pattern clearly so you know where to start threading the next group of beads.

Also, when working with relatively short lengths of yarn, tie a stop of some kind on the end of the yarn so the beads will not slide off.

If you discover a bead of the wrong color after you have gone too far to want to rip, you can cut or break it off and replace it, but be careful not to damage the yarn as you do so.

Take up a strand of yarn about 12 inches long, thread on a bead of the correct color, and use the equivalent of Duplicate Stitch to replace the bead removed. Hide the ends of the strand on the inside; see Hiding Ends of Yarn.

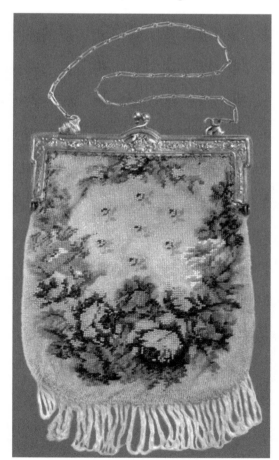

Beaded bag. Lacis Museum of Lace and Textiles, Berkeley, California.

❖ *Running Thread Beading*

This is by far the easiest way to add beads to a knitted fabric, and there are several variations. The basic technique is particularly suitable for Brocade patterns, or with any stitch pattern that makes use of a background of Purl stitches combined with other stitch techniques.

Variations of the technique also work well with Slip Stitch or Twined Knit patterns, in which the running thread is stranded past one or more stitches on the outside of the fabric. Finally, the technique also makes it possible to create loops of beads on an elongated running thread; also see Chain Loop Beading, below.

Basic Running Thread Beading

When a bead is set on a running thread between two stitches, it will lie horizontally in the fabric, with the holes facing right and left. In order to remain on the outside of the fabric it must have a pair of Purl stitches on either side.

Running Thread Beading. Bead set between two Purl stitches.

- Work Purl stitch on outside of fabric, bring bead up strand of yarn against right needle, and Purl next stitch.

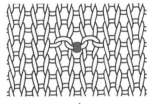

Running Thread Beading.

Work the second stitch with a relatively firm tension because the weight of the bead has a tendency to elongate the running thread.

An entire Reverse Stockinette fabric can be beaded in this way quite easily, but the approach is particularly effective in a pattern where Purl serves as the background for other stitch techniques. For instance, you could set beads on Purl rows that lie between pattern elements in a lace repeat or a cable pattern.

Running Thread Beading on Brocade pattern.

Slip Stitch Beading pattern.
Beads on yarn stranded past Slip stitches.

You can also use this approach for any Ribbing or Brocade pattern that contains pairs of Purl stitches; a Double Rib is the simplest example.

Slip Stitch Beading

Many stitch patterns make use of running threads stranded on the outside of the fabric past a Slip stitch, and these can easily be adapted for beading.

Because of the structure of the stitch, the beads cannot work their way through to the other side of the fabric, and there is no need to Purl adjacent stitches, as with the Basic Running Thread Beading method, above. Also, because the strand is slightly elongated, it can easily accommodate a larger bead, one that is oval instead of round, or several beads instead of just one.

The more Slip stitches there are in the pattern, the denser the fabric will be. To determine a gauge that strikes the right balance between a supportive fabric and one that is too stiff, make several Test Swatches using different needle sizes in order to find the best combination of pattern, yarn, and beads.

Work on the outside of the fabric, as follows:

- Yarn nearside, bring bead up against right needle, Slip next stitch, strand yarn past Slip stitch, yarn farside; continue with pattern.

There are other types of patterns in which the Slip stitches are the decorative element, not the running threads stranding past them. In these cases, the beads are set on the stitches instead; see Stitch Beading, as well as Hook Beading, below.

Twined Knit Beading

Twined Knit is a Scandinavian technique used to create dense, resilient fabrics. Two yarns are used at the same time and alternated to the stitches. To make a decorative pattern, one yarn is stranded on the outside of the fabric past a stitch formed with the other yarn; bolder patterns are made with Purl stitches flanking the strands or with strands on either side of a Purl stitch. The patterns are easy to enhance with beads set either on the strands or on the Purl nubs; for more information, see the chapter on Twined Knit.

Swag Beading

This charming method was traditionally used for small evening handbags. Multiple beads are set on the running thread between two stitches, forcing the fabric on either side apart. In some cases, the beads were set in columns, creating a wide stripe, but in most cases the number of beads was graduated, starting with more at the bottom and gradually decreasing in a carefully worked out progression toward the top.

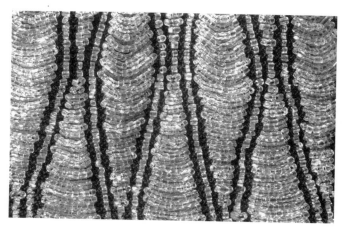

Swag Beading. Lacis Museum of Lace and Textiles, Berkeley, California.

Loop Beading

For an interesting decorative effect, you can make small loops of beads that hang down on the outside of the fabric.

- Bring three to five beads up to the needle between two stitches, allow sufficient yarn to the running thread to form a loop, and then make the next stitch.
- With an uneven number of beads, one will center at the bottom of the loop; this could be in a different color, or be slightly larger or a different shape than the others. The beads must be strung onto the yarn in the order in which they will be used; see Multicolor Bead Threading, above.
- A bead can be set on the running thread in the middle of a Chain Loop; see below.

❖ Stitch Beading

With this approach, the beads are set on a stitch instead of the running thread. On the next row, the stitch is worked with one of several different techniques that help maintain the bead on the surface of the fabric where it can be seen. The technique is slower to do and requires more steps than the methods discussed above, but a wider variety of patterns can be used to create a design.

The Twist Stitch technique has traditionally been used for beading of this kind. Another more decorative approach is to set the bead on a stitch that will be pulled over or across another one, such as with a Pullover or Crossed Stitch technique. Finally, it is also possible to set the bead on the head of a Purl stitch—this option is the most versatile.

While it is possible to use plain Knit for a beaded stitch, the result is not particularly satisfactory. The bead sits on one side of the stitch, distorting its shape, and, instead of sitting on the surface of the fabric, the bead lies within it and becomes less visible. It can be seen on both sides of the fabric, which might be appropriate for a reversible item, but any of the other beading methods can be used to set beads on both sides of a fabric to better effect.

One- or Two-Step Bead Setting

There are two ways to set the bead on a stitch so it will remain on the outside of the fabric. The first method is the conventional one, which takes a certain amount of practice before the work goes smoothly. The second method is considerably easier both to learn and to do, but requires an extra step; try them both and see which you prefer. In either case, it is best to work at a moderate gauge, with the size of the stitches proportional to those of the beads; if the stitches are too small, it is difficult to push the beads through them.

One-Step Bead Setting

1. Bring a group of beads up near or into your hand.
2. Work to position for next bead, bring single bead up yarn to needle, insert needle into stitch and wrap yarn as to Knit or Purl; bead should now be at base of stitch.
3. Draw bead and yarn through to form new beaded stitch and discard original stitch from left needle.
4. On next row, work beaded stitch according to pattern.

These are minimal instructions, since there are subtleties here that are helpful to know about. Here are some tips.

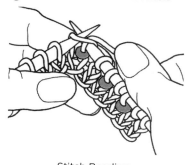

Stitch Beading.
Setting bead on a Knit stitch.

Managing the Beads

The trick here is to have the beads close enough to the needle so you can quickly separate one and move it into position, but not so close that they get in your way.

You may be able to position the group of beads in the palm of your hand; the yarn wrapped on your little finger for tension should prevent them from sliding down the yarn. If this does not work for you, find some way to bring the beads up closer to your hands, perhaps by setting something in your lap or working over a lap tray.

Knitting Methods

You can use any knitting method for this technique, but if you hold the yarn on the left, it will be somewhat easier to put the bead into the correct position for the next stitch because the yarn is drawn to the left past the space between the needles.

The beads are not as conveniently located when the yarn is held to the right, but of all the options, the Right-Hand Method makes it easiest to position the bead.

Depending upon the knitting method you use and type of stitch made, use your thumb or forefinger to encourage the bead to pass through the stitch. In some circumstances, the bead precedes the needle through the stitch, in some cases it follows it; see below for more details.

To Wrap Yarn for Knit

- Yarn held to left: With bead on farside at base of first stitch on left needle, insert right needle into stitch and wrap needle around yarn *above* bead; use either left or right forefinger to encourage bead to pass through stitch to nearside first, followed by needle bearing yarn.
- Yarn held to right: Position bead ¼ to ½ inch from first stitch on right needle and wrap yarn around needle; with bead now in position at base of stitch, push it through to nearside, followed by needle bearing yarn.

The initial distance of the bead from the needle depends upon the size of the stitches—it needs to be the length of one wrap around the needle. With practice you will learn to judge this distance fairly accurately, but from time to time it may be necessary to nudge the bead into place at the base of a stitch with your finger and then push it through.

To Wrap Yarn for Purl

- Yarn held to left: On nearside, position bead ¼ to ½ inch away from needle, pass needle around yarn just *below* bead; with bead at base of stitch, draw new stitch through to farside, pushing bead behind it with thumb.

    For a Twist Stitch pattern that requires a Turned Purl, bring bead up a little closer, insert right needle into stitch, and then move it over yarn *above* bead.

- Yarn held to right: On nearside, bring bead up into position as described above for Knit and wrap yarn; with bead now at base of stitch, push it through to farside first followed by needle bearing yarn.

    For a Twist Stitch pattern that requires Turned Purl, position bead at base of stitch and wrap yarn under needle.

Twist Stitch Beading patterns are described below.

Two-Step Bead Setting

Compared to one-step bead setting, you will find this method quick and easy to do. It does require two steps to set a bead, and the beads can be set no closer than every other stitch, but these are minor inconveniences.

1. To place bead, use Slip Stitch Beading method described above; bead is set on strand drawn past Slip stitch on either inside or outside of fabric, depending upon how stitch will be worked in Step 2.
2. On next row, work to Slipped stitch, and convert beaded strand into a beaded stitch in one of the following ways:
   - If stitch is to be in Knit on outside of fabric, strand bead on inside in Step 1. Lift beaded strand onto left needle, pull first stitch over bead, and discard.
   - If stitch is to be in Purl on outside, strand bead on outside in Step 1. Slip 1 knitwise, lift beaded strand onto right needle and pull slipped stitch over bead and discard; if necessary, return new stitch to left needle.
3. Work beaded stitch in one of ways described below.

This is the equivalent of repairing a stitch that has run down one row. Lift the strand onto the needle in standard position for a stitch, with the right side on the nearside of the needle. For a Twist Stitch pattern that requires a turned stitch, place left side of strand on nearside.

Twist Stitch Beading

It is traditional to use Twist Stitch for beading because the structure of the stitch prevents the bead from pushing through to the inside. However, Twist Stitches create bias in a fabric. There is no need to concern yourself with this if there will be only a small percentage of them in the fabric, but the more there are, or if they are clustered together in a small area, the more important it is to take this into consideration.

A Balanced Twist Stitch fabric has an equal number of stitches that cross to the left and right and, as a result, there is no bias. If you prefer to cross only the beaded stitches to the left because it is easier, an equal number of unbeaded stitches must be twisted to the right somewhere nearby in order to prevent bias.

On the other hand, there are Chevron patterns that take advantage of the tendency to bias, either by grouping several columns of Left Twist Stitch with several of Right Twist Stitch, or by working several rows that bias to the left, followed by several rows that bias to the right. While handsome on their own, these kinds of patterns are quite beautiful when beaded, because the structure of the fabric causes the lines of beads to slope as well.

Also, a bead set on a Twist Stitch will slant in the same direction as the stitch. If the pattern combines Right and Left Twist stitches, in close proximity, for instance, with one row twisted to the right, the next to the left, this will be quite visible; the beads will seem to be staggered instead of being lined up in vertical rows, as is the case with Running Thread Beading, above, or Stitch Head Beading, below.

Balanced Twist Stitch for Beading

The easiest way to work a Balanced Twist Stitch pattern is to twist stitches to the left on Knit rows and to the right on Purl rows. Regardless of whether the bead was set on the stitch using the One- or Two-Step method, here is how to work.

Left Twist Beaded Stitch

- If working on outside, position bead on nearside, insert right needle into stitch on farside, and Knit; wrap yarn over needle if new stitch is to be twisted on next row; under needle if it will not be.

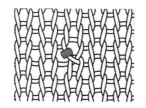

Left Twist Beaded Stitch.

- If working on inside, position bead on farside, insert needle into stitch above bead from left to right, and Purl.

Right Twist Beaded Stitch

- When working on inside, if stitch is not already in Turned position on needle, Slip knitwise and return to left needle; position bead on farside, insert needle into stitch below bead, and Purl.
- When working on outside, if necessary, first turn stitch as described above; then position bead on nearside, insert needle into stitch above bead, and Knit.

   When working with a yarn that is not resilient, inserting the needle into a beaded stitch in turned position can be a tight fit.

Decorative Stitch Beading

A number of decorative stitch techniques cause one side of a stitch to cross over one or more other stitches on the surface of the fabric, and it is easy to enhance these with a bead set on the facing stitch.

For instance, consider stitch patterns that contain Crossed Stitches, Pullover, Couching, or Threaded Stitch techniques.

Stitch Head Beading

With this method, the bead sits horizontally on the head of a Purl stitch on the outside of the fabric; it obscures the Purl nub behind it and claims all the attention. It is held in place by the two running threads to each side, so there is no need to Purl the stitches that flank the beaded stitch as with Running Thread Beading, above. Because the bead can be set on an isolated Purl stitch, this enlarges the number of patterns that can be used for this purpose.

Stranded Color patterns are a treasure trove of inspiration for beading in this way, since you can simply substitute a bead for each contrast-color stitch. Brocade patterns, with the motifs created in Purl, are another good source. However, for this type of beading, the charted pattern needs to be interpreted in a slightly different way, since it is necessary to set the bead on the stitch in the row below where it will be Purled. It is not difficult to use a charted pattern for this purpose, but you can also rewrite it, if you prefer; see Bead and Sequin Charts.

Basic Stitch Head Beading

Set beads on new stitches using one of the methods described above, and then work as follows:

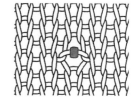

Stitch Head Beading. Bead set on head of Purl stitch.

1. Insert tip of needle into stitch beneath bead and either Purl on an outside row, or Knit on an inside row.
2. As stitch is discarded, bring yarn *under* bead to left and then to farside to work next stitch.

Stitch Head Beading: Step 1. Insert needle under bead to Purl.

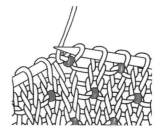

Stitch Head Beading: Step 2. Bring yarn under bead to secure it.

When working flat, it is easiest to set the bead on an inside row, and then Purl the beaded stitch on the outside of the fabric where you can see what you are doing better.

Beading on Yarnovers

You can create a charming effect in lace patterns by setting a bead on a Yarnover; when the Yarnover is worked on the next row, the result will be a bead hanging framed within an Eyelet.

1. On one row, yarn nearside, bring bead into position against right needle, and make Yarnover in normal way.
2. On next row, work beaded Yarnover as for Stitch Head Beading, above, so Purl nub is on outside of fabric and bead is set at top of Yarnover.

For a larger bead, or for a larger opening to frame the bead, use a Half-Double or Double Eyelet. In patterns that contain a Double Yarnover Increase, center the bead on the strand between the two stitches of the increase.

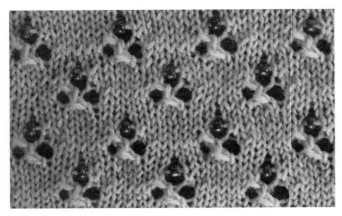

Beading on Yarnovers. Beads set on Yarnover in Eyelet pattern.

Beading on Lattice Strands

There are Lattice stitch techniques that make use of multiple Slip stitches, leaving one or more long strands on the outside of the fabric that are gathered up and worked with a stitch in a row above.

- Set two beads on the strand, and then in the row above, reach down with needle tip to pick up strand and work it with next stitch. A pair of oval beads would be nice for this technique, or you could set four tiny beads; two on either side of the stitch.

Chain Loop Beading

Here is another way to form a loop of beads on the outside of the fabric, in this case by working them into a chain of stitches; an uneven number of stitches in the chain works best.

- Work several Chain Stitches, set a bead on next stitch, and then work same number of stitches on other side of bead to form loop.
- Alternatively, work half the number of stitches in Chain,

set bead on running thread, and then work other half of stitches.
- Or, set a bead on the running thread between each Chain Stitch.

❖ Beading with a Carrier Yarn

As discussed above in Suitable Yarns, if the beads cannot be threaded on the yarn because it is too thick or too delicate, they can be strung on a separate Carrier Yarn, which is carried along with the main yarn to work the project.

There are several ways to make use of a Carrier Yarn for a project; here are some possibilities.

Multiple Yarns for All Stitches

This can be done with either the Running Thread or a Stitch Beading method.

- Hold Carrier Yarn and main yarn as one to work all stitches. For more information on combining yarns in this way, see Multiple Yarns.

For the main yarn, you might select one that is softly spun or textured, and use a very thin one such as silk filament or even a translucent "invisible" nylon thread for the Carrier Yarn.

You can also combine two or more strands of a thin yarn, such as one intended for lace or machine knitting. String the beads on only one of the yarns and include as many other strands as needed to create a yarn of whatever thickness seems appropriate for the garment. The yarns can be the same or different colors, or you can combine several different yarns; do make a Test Swatch to make sure the combined yarns are not too thick for the project.

Doubled Yarn for Bead Stitches

This only works with Stitch Beading.

- Hold main yarn and Carrier Yarn together to work only stitches with beads; use main yarn alone to work all other stitches, stranding Carrier Yarn on inside past these stitches as for a Stranded Color pattern.

This works best when the Carrier Yarn is considerably thinner than the main yarn so it does not appreciably enlarge the stitches when the two are held together. If the two yarns are the same color, there will be little evidence of the Carrier Yarn because the bead or sequin will obscure it; this is especially the case if the main yarn is textured.

Carrier Yarn for Bead Stitches

Here again, this is done with Stitch Beading and makes use of the technique for working Stranded Color patterns holding two yarns (see Two-Hand Stranding).

- Use Carrier Yarn alone to work all stitches with beads; use main yarn alone for all stitches without beads, and strand whichever yarn is not in use on inside past stitches done with other yarn.

Because the Carrier Yarn is used alone for each beaded stitch, it will be quite visible, although the main yarn and the beads will tend to dominate the visual effect. In appearance, it is similar to the effect produced by a slub yarn (see Novelty Yarns).

To do the equivalent of a Stranded Color pattern in this way, use the Carrier Yarn with the beads for the pattern stitches; this works best if the two yarns are about the same thickness.

Carrier Yarn for Regauged Stripes

- Use Carrier Yarn alone to bead several rows between areas of fabric done with main yarn.

The beaded rows done with the thin Carrier Yarn will be much more open than those done with the main yarn.

❖ *Beading on Edges*

Beads can be included while casting on or casting off, and can be incorporated into a selvedge. Here are some suggestions.

Casting On with Beads

- Half-Hitch Cast-On: String beads on tail of yarn held on thumb; bring one bead up against needle before making each stitch. Beads will be on half hitches at very edge of fabric.
- Alternating Cast-On: String beads on one or both yarns; bring bead up against needle between each stitch, or bring new stitch under baseline strand so it straddles a bead.
- Braided Cast-On: String beads on both yarns or just one.
- Woven Knit Cast-On: Set a bead on each stitch; because stitches are twisted as they are made, there is no need to work them in a special way on next row.

Beaded Selvedges

- Stockinette Selvedge or Garter Stitch Selvedge: Set bead on a selvedge stitch, and on next row either twist stitch toward fabric, or Purl it as for Stitch Head Beading.
- Chain Selvedge: Set bead on a selvedge stitch and slip this stitch on next row; on following row, push bead to either inside or outside strand of selvedge stitch before working it, as you prefer.
- Double Selvedges: Set bead on running thread between two stitches of selvedge, or use Stitch Head Beading and work second stitch set in Purl.

Casting Off with Beads

- Pullover Chained Cast-Off: Set bead on stitch, push bead to nearside, and then pull it over other stitch.
- Picot Chained Cast-Off: Set bead on stitch, Knit stitch again, and then work Pullover.
- Any Sewn Half-Hitch Cast-Off: String beads on sewing yarn; bring a bead up against fabric and sew next stitch.

❖ *Hook Beading*

This method makes it possible to use beads without stringing them on the yarn; instead, a crochet hook is used to draw the entire stitch through the opening in the bead. This approach requires beads with a large enough hole to accommodate a doubled strand of yarn. It is a slower way to work, because you must pick up the crochet hook each time, but it works fine when you just want to scatter a few beads across the fabric.

Hook Beading. Stitch is pulled through bead.

- Insert crochet hook into bead, and then through next stitch on left needle as to Knit; hook yarn and pull through stitch and bead, and then place new stitch carrying bead on right needle.

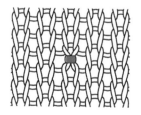

Hook Beading.

One interesting way to make use of this technique is to combine it with an elongated Slip stitch (see Wrap Elongation, which makes it possible to use larger beads).

- Carry the Slip stitch up as many rows as required by pattern. On row where stitch is to be worked, draw it through a bead and then secure it as described above.

Some charming patterns make use of Slip stitches drawn up past several rows and then "cabled" two or three stitches to right or left; these long strands set at an angle on the fabric would be ideal for oval-shaped beads.

Sequins and Paillettes

The word *sequin* derives from Arabic, and an early form of the word was the name of an old Venetian coin. The practice of adorning a garment with shiny disks comes from the custom of sewing small coins onto cloth, in equal measure a means to beautify it and to display the owner's wealth.

Today, a basic sequin is considerably smaller than a coin and made of plastic instead of precious metal; it may be smooth or faceted and has a tiny hole in the center. *Paillettes*, sometimes called spangles, are simply large flat sequins, with the hole set closer to the edge instead of in the center.

The sequin and paillette family has grown considerably and now includes a wild variety of geometric and figurative shapes. All of these tiny ornaments can be used to decorate a garment in much the same way as beads, but they create even more drama because they are larger. These are sometimes used to completely blanket the surface of a fabric, but, as with beads, they can also be set in stripes or used in designs adapted from Brocade, Stranded Color, or Intarsia patterns.

Please note that a garment decorated with sequins and paillettes will require special care when finishing and cleaning because moisture and heat can damage these materials; it is very important to ask about the care requirements before making a purchase.

❖ Sequins

To a great extent, working with sequins is similar to working with beads. The types of yarns that are suitable are the same as those discussed in Beading Materials, above (and this includes the possibility of using a Carrier Yarn); many of the tools mentioned there are useful as well.

However, sequins will only lie flat on the surface of the fabric if set on the stitches with either the One- or Two-Step Bead Setting technique, described above; a sequin set on a running thread will turn sideways, standing edge-out on the fabric.

General Tips for Sequins

Here is some general information about how to estimate the number of sequins to thread onto your yarn, how to thread them, and, if necessary, rethread them, and how to manage them while knitting.

Yarns for Sequins

While the same kinds of yarns used for beading can also be used for sequins, there is one distinction between the two that is worth taking into consideration when selecting your materials.

Because the strand of yarn holding the sequin passes across the surface to the hole in the center, it will be quite visible unless the sequins are set on every stitch so they overlap and hide it; doing so is not essential, however, and it severely limits the design possibilities.

If you prefer to scatter sequins across the fabric, tuck them in and around a stitch pattern, or use them to define motifs of various sizes and shapes, just as you might with beads, it will be necessary to accept the visible strand of yarn on the sequin as part of the decorative effect. If you prefer to minimize contrast, choose a sequin color that is as close as possible to that of the yarn, or use a Carrier Yarn that is the same color as the sequin, or perhaps colorless nylon.

Estimating Sequin Quantities

Sequins are sold loose in a plastic bag or strung on heavy thread, 1,000 per string. Strung sequins are by far the best choice for a project that requires a great many of them, since it is easy to transfer them in groups to the yarn. Loose sequins need to be dealt with individually, but if only a few will be needed, this is a more economical choice.

To decide how many to string each time, use the information in Estimating Bead Quantities, above. There is no point in trying to count individual sequins, since they are nested tightly together; instead, work as follows.

- Push sequins on strand together firmly, and measure length; divide measurement into total number of sequins on string to find sequins per inch.

    Thread however many inches worth of sequins you will need; allow a bit extra as a margin for error.

To Thread Sequins

The holes in sequins have sharp edges that will abrade a yarn far more than beads do. For this reason, it is best to string only as many as needed to work a limited area of fabric.

Also, before you begin threading, rewind your yarn to check for knots; if necessary, separate the yarn into smaller balls; it is a nuisance to discover a knot and have to rethread sequins, but if you need to do so, you will find instructions below.

The doubled thread bearing the sequins is tied in a circle. Untie it and, if necessary, place a Bead Stopper (see Miscellaneous Tools, above) on the loose ends, or tie these ends in a knot large enough to prevent the sequins sliding off.

Threading sequins.

To thread the sequins onto your yarn, work as follows:

- Pass the end of the yarn through the loop at the opposite end of the string, and then slide the sequins in small groups off the string onto the yarn.

Rethreading Sequins

If for any reason you need to rethread sequins, it will be necessary to transfer them back onto a string first.

- If possible, reuse the string on which they came, or use something similar, and restring so the convex side of the sequins faces the doubled end of string. Thread one end into needle and knot other end or use a Bead Stopper.

  Push small group of sequins together, and then pinch yarn around them tightly to open up a little space in the hole; slip needle in, trying not to catch yarn; slide sequins down needle onto thread.
- You can, of course, just pull any extra sequins off the yarn into a bowl or cup for storage; to rethread loose sequins on the yarn, use Intermediary Thread, above, as for beads, insert needle into concave side of each sequin and, after picking up a small group, slide them down thread and onto yarn.

Managing Sequins

The challenge in working with sequins is that they are very thin and nested tightly together on the strand, and it can be difficult to separate each one from its fellows in order to set it on a stitch; it helps to do this in stages.

1. Bring a group of sequins—about half an inch of them—up yarn closer to your hand.
2. Use thumb and forefinger to flatten group against yarn so they are slanted, and then push fingers apart in opposite directions to separate them slightly.
3. Next, bring three or four sequins closer to needle, and space them about an inch apart.

Spreading sequins along yarn.

The sequins will not move on the yarn easily, and once strung along the yarn they will more or less stay in place.

Do be careful to bring up only one sequin at a time; the difference between one and three sequins is fairly obvious, but the difference between one and two can be difficult to discern. With the sequins flattened against the yarn, look for the edge of the second one just back from the rim of the first.

Sequin Patterns

As mentioned above in the discussion on suitable yarns, sequins can be scattered across the fabric or tucked into and around other stitch patterns, just as you would with beads. Either twisting the stitch bearing a sequin or flanking it with

Purl stitches will keep the ornaments secure on the surface of the fabric.

For large sequined areas, you can work exactly as described for Balanced Twist Stitch for Beading, above. However, for an alternative that is simplicity itself, work as for Seed Stitch. The result will be very well-behaved sequins and a perfectly flat fabric that requires no blocking—a real boon since sequins cannot be steamed.

Sequined Seed Stitch

1. Place one sequin every other stitch on every other row, and stagger row by row—on the even-numbered stitches on one pattern row, and the odd-numbered stitches two rows up.

   Use either the One- or Two-Step method of setting sequin on stitch; for this pattern, the latter is more efficient.
2. On next row, work every stitch bearing a sequin so it is in Knit on outside of fabric; work all other stitches in Purl on outside.

In other words, the sequins are set on the Knit stitches and there are Purl stitches on either side. The head of the Purl stitch and the running threads to each side of it maintain the sequin on the outside of the fabric.

In this pattern, the sequins occupy every other row, but you can set them on the odd stitches of one row and the even stitches of the next if you want them closer together. If the sequined area does not occupy a full row, make sure to place a Purl stitch before the first and after the last sequin.

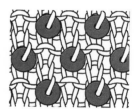

Sequined Seed Stitch.

As with beads set on a running thread between Purl stitches, consider placing sequins in the middle of the Purl column of a Double Rib, or in a column of paired Purls that flank a lace or cable pattern of some kind.

❖ Paillettes

As mentioned above, a paillette (sometimes called a spangle) is a flat plastic disc with a relatively large hole set close to the edge. The standard ones are the shape and size of a penny, but they are also available in a variety of geometric and figurative shapes and colors that challenge one another for brilliance and sparkle. I have even seen a garment with fluttery bits of silk organza sewn onto the surface that were called "paillettes," so the definition seems rather broad.

One characteristic that is true of all paillettes is that there is nothing subtle about them—they can do all the work of decorating a fabric by themselves. You can cover the entire surface of the fabric with them, set them in clusters to define geometric shapes such as squares or diamonds, place them in horizontal or vertical stripes on a plain ground, or scatter them between areas done in a decorative stitch or color pattern of some kind. Also, smooth, shiny paillettes look wonderful when tucked into textured yarns, particularly mohair.

Paillettes have several distinct advantages over beads or sequins. They are light in weight, which means there is less concern that the garment might sag, and they are larger, so you can use fewer and still gain a dramatic effect. Also, the hole in a paillette is large enough to accommodate all but the thickest yarns; however, they cannot be added to the fabric in the same way.

Setting Paillettes

Paillettes are too large to pass through a stitch, and they will not lie flat against the fabric if placed on the running thread. As a result, there is just one way to knit paillettes into the fabric and that is by drawing the entire stitch through the opening in a manner similar to Hook Beading, above. However, you can work as for either Knit or Purl and it is very easy to do.

Knit Version

- With yarn farside, pick up paillette and place hole against first stitch on nearside of left needle. Insert right needle tip through hole in paillette and into stitch as to Knit, wrap yarn, and draw new stitch through paillette; discard stitch.

The paillette will hang from the base of the new stitch.

Purl Version

- With yarn nearside, place paillette against first stitch on nearside of left needle, insert right needle tip into stitch as to Purl, and then through hole in paillette, wrap yarn as to Purl and draw new stitch through; discard stitch.

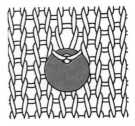
Paillette on Purl stitch.

The running threads will cross over the edge of the paillettes in a slight V shape, and hold it flat against the fabric.

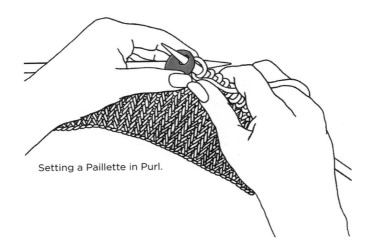
Setting a Paillette in Purl.

Part Four

SPECIAL FABRICS

CHAPTER 15

Double-Fabrics

Here is a set of ordinary knitting techniques applied in uncommon ways to create quite extraordinary results. The Double-Fabric technique makes it possible to knit two fabrics at the same time by interspersing the stitches for each of them on a single needle. This approach can be used to make double-thickness, fully reversible garments with mixed Knit and Purl or color patterns on both sides.

You will also find a variety of utilitarian applications of the technique described in Double-Fabric Insertion. These can be used to combine double-fabrics with single-thickness ones. This is an efficient way to make design details such as hems, casings, and pockets, working the two layers at the same time and eliminating the need to sew up during finishing. Perhaps the simplest and most useful of the Insertion techniques is the extraordinarily resilient Double-Fabric Ribbing, which combines a Basic Double-Fabric with rows of Single Rib.

In addition, the Singular Double-Fabric application —which, as the name suggests, has a somewhat contradictory nature—is used to make a conventional, single-thickness, circular fabric on two straight, single-point needles, working back and forth much as you would to make a flat fabric. This unorthodox approach is particularly useful for small items normally done with some frustration on a set of double-point needles (mitten thumbs, for instance), and this alone should win the technique a place in the hearts of many knitters. And for a charming variation of the Singular Double-Fabric application, you might want to try the Sock Trick, using the technique to work two socks simultaneously, in the round, on one set of double-point needles.

The remarkable decorative potential of the technique is seen primarily in the Double-Faced fabrics, which exhibit characteristics that are unlike anything else in knitting. The simplest of them have patterns that are the same on both sides, but done in a color or textural reversal; the more complex ones have entirely different patterns on each side. While the basic concepts of how to work these specialized patterns are introduced here, by necessity they are dealt with in greater detail in the chapter Charted Color Patterns because the written instructions are very long and difficult to follow; the charts are considerably easier to read.

From time to time while writing this material, I found it necessary to borrow terms used elsewhere in knitting and redefine them somewhat for this purpose, or even coin a new term when no other served as well. Before we go on to the instructions, therefore, I want to pause for some definitions; most of them are quite matter-of-fact, but the meaning of a few will become clearer as you work your way through the material.

Terminology

Double-Fabric The technique used to make these fabrics is commonly referred to as Double Knitting; unfortunately, that term is also used to refer to a particular thickness of knitting yarn. To clarify matters, I decided to use Double-Fabric instead because it conveys the idea of what is being done—making two fabrics, or the two sides of a circular fabric, at the same time.

Single-Fabric A short term used to refer to a conventional single-thickness fabric.

Double-Fabric Insertion An application used to make a section of double-fabric within a single-fabric.

Singular Double-Fabric An application used to make a circular, single-thickness fabric with a pair of straight needles. Also can be used to make two separate circular fabrics at the same time on a set of double-point needles or a circular one.

Double-Faced Fabric This term (or sometimes Double Cloth), is used in the textile industry for a reversible fabric, whether woven or knitted, made with specialized techniques. The yarns travel back and forth between what would otherwise be two separate fabrics, joining them into a single, interwoven structure with two outside faces. When decorative patterns are used, they may be the same on both sides, done as color or texture reversals, or entirely different.

Fabric A/Fabric B Terms used to distinguish two fabrics worked together on one needle, whether they remain entirely separate or are joined at one or more of the edges.

Set of Stitches A group of stitches on the needle that belong to one of the fabrics; there is one set of stitches for Fabric A, another set for Fabric B.

Nearside/Farside Fabric, or Nearside/Farside Stitch Relative terms used to refer to whichever fabric or set of stitches happens to be on the nearside or farside of the needles as you work.

Side A/Side B Used when the terms Fabric A and Fabric B do not apply, such as for the two halves of a fabric made with the Singular Double-Fabric technique, or for the two sides of a Double-Faced Fabric.

Fabric Face The surface of the fabric. The term "outside face" refers to a surface facing out and visible when on the needles; "inside face" refers to a surface that lies between the two fabrics.

When worn, a Basic Double-Fabric or a Double-Faced garment will have two outside faces and no inside face. A garment made with the Singular Double-Fabric technique is a conventional one, with an inside and an outside face, only one of which is intended to be visible in wear.

Pass The term "pass" is roughly equivalent to "row" when used to refer to the process of manipulating the stitches and discarding them into the fabric. However, with a Basic Double-Fabric pattern, a pass refers to working just one set of stitches and not the other. One pass adds a row of stitches to one fabric, the next pass adds a row to the other fabric, and two passes add one row of length to the overall, combined fabric. There are exceptions to this in some specialty applications and color patterns, and when working with two yarns at the same time.

For a Singular Double-Fabric, two passes are equivalent to one "round" when making a circular fabric in the conventional way.

With Double-Faced Fabric patterns, a pass generally refers to working all the stitches made with one yarn, regardless of which set they belong to; a second pass is used for the other color, and two passes equals a row.

The Slide A technique required for some color patterns, special techniques, or applications. Stitches are moved from one end of a double-point needle to the other so the next pass can be done without turning to the other side.

Interwoven Patterns Specialized color patterns used to create Double-Faced Fabrics.

Double-Fabric Patterns

The Basic Double-Fabric technique consists of a group of stitch patterns, any one of which can be used to make two fabrics at the same time. These patterns are done with two sets of stitches interspersed on a single needle; one set belongs to Fabric A, the other to Fabric B.

The first group of patterns contains the instructions for using one yarn for both fabrics; the second group has the instructions for working with two yarns at a time, one for each fabric, which is more challenging, but considerably quicker.

Following the instructions for the basic patterns, you will find a section that includes tips regarding suitable techniques to use for casting on, casting off, and shaping; how to calculate the gauge; and how to correct errors when necessary. This material also includes information about how to change from a single-fabric to a double-fabric (or vice versa); how to leave one or more of the edges open; and how to work two entirely separate fabrics. For an explanation of the terms used in the instructions, see Written Stitch Patterns.

I suggest you learn the basic techniques, and then skim through the others so you know what is possible; when you want to use one of the applications discussed in the section that follows this one, return here to the instructions for any of the specialized techniques needed for your project.

❖ The Basic Patterns

The instructions included here introduce the four basic methods used to make both fabrics in Stockinette. The patterns can be done in Knit or Purl, while working on either the inside or outside of the respective fabrics. (Several other variations are used with stitch and color patterns; see Decorative Techniques for Double-Fabrics.)

To master these methods, I suggest making a sampler swatch, no more than 4–6 inches wide. Just proceed from one set of instructions to the next until you have practiced them all. Work on relatively short, straight needles because they are comfortable when learning something new, and use a smooth, neutral-colored yarn so you can see the stitches and fabric structure clearly.

Estimate the number of stitches to use for the sample based on the gauge the yarn and needles would produce in a normal single-fabric done in Stockinette, and then double that number so you have enough stitches for two fabrics. Use Half-Hitch Cast-On to put an even number of stitches on the needle. The first stitch on the needle, and all odd-numbered stitches, will belong to the fabric on the nearside; the even-numbered stitches belong to the fabric on the farside.

On one pass across the needle, you will work one set of stitches and Slip those that belong to the other set. After turning the needle just as you do for flat knitting, do the next pass in the same way, but work the other set of stitches and Slip those worked previously. The instructions always begin with Fabric A on the nearside.

Pattern 1: Knit on Outside

With this approach, you will be working in Knit on the outside face of both fabrics; the Purl faces lie between the two, out of sight.

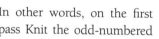

Pattern 1: Knit on Outside. Yarn farside, Knit Fabric A stitch.

1. First Pass: Work Fabric A stitches on nearside: [Yarn farside, Knit 1, yarn nearside, Slip 1 purlwise], repeat between brackets; turn.
2. Second Pass: Work Fabric B stitches on nearside: repeat same pattern.

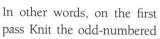

Pattern 1: Knit on Outside. Move yarn farside after slipping Fabric B stitch.

In other words, on the first pass Knit the odd-numbered stitches, and Slip the even-numbered stitches; on the second pass, do the same thing, but this time you will Knit the stitches that were slipped on the first pass, and Slip those that were Knit.

It is important to strand the yarn as indicated so it passes between the fabrics; if not done correctly, the strand will appear on the outside face of the other fabric. And because the strand is a running thread that passes between two stitches in the same fabric, if it takes a detour around a stitch of the other fabric, it will bind the two together.

Although both fabrics have Knit stitches facing out, you can see Purl nubs under every other stitch on the needle. These belong to whichever side of the fabric is currently on the farside of the needle. If you turn the fabric around, it will look the same. Also notice that, even though you are working flat, there are no selvedge stitches at the sides, simply a rounded fold of fabric.

While this particular pattern can be done with any knitting method, working with the yarn held to the left is easiest. With the yarn to the right, you must move it between the

needles after each stitch as you do for Single Rib. With it to the left, you can hold the yarn steady and simply move the right needle tip to the farside of the yarn to Slip a stitch, or to the nearside of it to Knit.

Pattern 2: Purl on Inside

This version produces exactly the same Stockinette fabric described above, but it is done by working in Purl on the inside faces of the fabric instead of in Knit on the outside.

Pattern 2: Purl on Inside. Yarn nearside, Purl Fabric B stitch.

You will be working on the set of stitches that belong to the fabric on the *farside* of the needle.

1. First Pass: Work Fabric B stitches on farside: [Yarn farside, Slip 1 purlwise, yarn nearside, Purl 1], repeat between brackets; turn.
2. Second Pass: Work Fabric A stitches on farside: repeat same pattern.

In other words, Slip the odd-numbered stitches with the yarn stranded farside, and Purl the even-numbered stitches.

Pattern 3: Knit on Inside

With this version, the Purl faces of the fabric will be facing out on both sides and the Knit faces will be hidden between the two. Here again, you will be working in Knit on the set of stitches that belong to the fabric on the *farside* of the needle.

1. First Pass: Work Fabric B stitches on farside: [Yarn farside for all stitches, Slip 1, Knit 1], repeat between brackets for one pass; turn.
2. Second Pass: Work Fabric A stitches on farside: repeat same pattern.

In other words, keep the yarn on the farside at all times; Slip the odd-numbered stitches and Knit the even-numbered stitches.

It is much easier to work this way because there is no need to shift the yarn from nearside to farside to strand past an intervening stitch.

Having the Purl faces of the fabric on the outside also makes it easier to fix an error such as a dropped stitch, because the released strands will be visible and accessible rather than hidden between the two fabrics on the inside.

If you want to have Knit on the outside of the finished garment, take the stitches off the needle and invert the fabric before casting off; use Alternating Cast-On, and also Separating Stitch Sets, both discussed below.

Knit Slip Variation

In her charming book *Notes on Double Knitting*,† Beverly Royce described a fast way of working a Double-Fabric with Purl on the outside. With this clever method, you can work one stitch and Slip the next in a single motion.

- Use pattern Knit on Inside, above, but with the following modification: Knit stitch of farside fabric, and, as you discard, immediately insert right needle purlwise into the next stitch of nearside fabric and Slip it. Repeat this motion on every pair of stitches and work in the same way on every pass.

Pattern 4: Purl on Outside

Once again Purl will be facing out on both sides, but in this case you will work in Purl on the set of stitches that belong to the fabric on the nearside of the needle. As with the version above, there is no need to move the yarn back and forth to strand past an intervening stitch, which makes this a quick way to work.

1. First Pass: Work Fabric A stitches on nearside: [Yarn nearside, Purl 1, Slip 1 purlwise], repeat between brackets for one pass; turn.
2. Second Pass: Work Fabric B stitches on nearside: repeat same pattern.

In other words, Purl the odd-numbered stitches and Slip the even-numbered stitches with the yarn stranded nearside.

If you want to work this way and then turn the Knit face to the outside, see the suggestion in Knit on Inside, above.

❖ *Basic Patterns with Two Yarns*

If you are comfortable working with two yarns when doing a Stranded Color pattern, you might want to try that here; things go along much more quickly when you do both sides of a double-fabric at the same time. However, keep in mind that this will require using one of the yarns to work in Purl.

For this reason, it is probably easiest to carry the yarn needed for the Knit stitches on the left, and the yarn needed for the Purl stitches on the right (which is how the instructions below are written), but it works just as well if you prefer to hold them the other way. You can also hold both yarns to the left or right, but because of the need to move them between the needles, it seems less efficient than holding one in each hand.

---

† Remarkably, Royce discovered the double-fabric techniques on her own when she was a young, beginning knitter. Later in her life, a typescript of what she had learned was circulated among knitting friends, who encouraged her to publish it as a small spiral-bound book. Schoolhouse Press deserves our gratitude for making this little-known work available to the larger knitting community in an expanded, illustrated edition. Beverly Royce, *Notes on Double Knitting* (Beverly Royce, April, 1981; expanded edition, Pittsville, Wisc.: Schoolhouse Press, 1994).

You can use this approach to make a conventional Basic Double-Fabric joined at the sides either by using two balls of the same yarn, or by taking one end from the inside and one from the outside of a center-pull ball. If you are making two entirely separate fabrics, use two yarns, either the same or in different colors or textures for a decorative pattern.

Knit on Outside of Fabric

1. To Knit stitch on nearside: Move both yarns to farside, Knit next stitch with left yarn.
2. To Purl stitch on farside: Move both yarns to nearside, hold left yarn away from needle to nearside, pass right yarn between it and needles to Purl next stitch.
3. Repeat these two steps across row; turn.

Purl on Outside of Fabric

This is the fastest way to work, because there is no need to bring the yarns back and forth between the needle tips.

- Hold right yarn on nearside, left yarn on farside. Purl all nearside stitches and Knit all farside stitches.

For either version, if you want to join the fabric at the side edges, always maintain the same yarn in the same hand so the yarns cross each other at the side edge—the yarn last used for Fabric A will be used next for Fabric B, and vice versa.

Some applications require leaving one or more side edges open, which is necessary if you want to make two separate fabrics. To do so, change the yarns from one hand to the other, always using the same yarn for the same side; see Open Side Edges for more details. Also see the information on working with two yarns in Double-Fabric Color Patterns.

To Complete a Sampler

You can use Joinery Cast-Off to finish the top edge of the sampler (see Casting Off Double-Fabrics), in which case the two fabrics will be linked on all four sides.

However, to get a good sense of how this technique works, just slide the stitches off the needles. The two sets of stitches will immediately separate at the top and your sampler will turn into a little pouch—a conventional, circular single-fabric joined

Double-Fabric off the needle.

at the bottom and the two sides. Consider this your introduction to the wonderful Singular Double-Fabric application, described below.

To secure the stitches at the top, thread a yarn through them as a holder, or pick up the stitches on a set of double-point needles and cast off in the usual way.

Making Double-Fabrics

Here is the information you will need to make a Basic Double-Fabric. Included are tips regarding gauge, correcting errors, casting on and off, how to shape the fabric, and how to handle seams.

Some of this material makes reference to techniques discussed in detail and illustrated elsewhere in this book. The comments here merely point out any differences or adjustments needed when using these techniques for double-fabrics.

Also included here are unique, specialized techniques needed for the Double-Fabric Insertion and Singular Double-Fabric applications that follow in the next section, such as how to leave one or more of the edges open, how to change from a single-fabric to a double-fabric or vice versa, and how to make a circular double-fabric.

❖ *Gauge for Double-Fabrics*

To determine gauge for a project of this kind, make the swatch with the yarn, needles, and double-fabric pattern you plan to use and dress it before measurement (see Dressing a Swatch).

The calculation is done in the same way as for a single-fabric—measure the width of the swatch and divide that number into the number of stitches cast on. As you will see, the stitch gauge will be twice as large as what it would be for a single-fabric because it represents the number of stitches in an inch, in *both* fabrics.

Row gauge is also done in the same way as for a single-fabric—measure length and divide into number of rows in one fabric. The result will be a normal-looking gauge, but this is fine for finding the number of rows to work in each fabric (although keep in mind that the number of rows is not the same as the number of passes required by the pattern).

If you made the sampler of Basic Double-Fabric techniques described above and used a needle of normal size for the yarn, you may have noticed that the stitches were slightly larger than expected.

This is because the stitches are interspersed on the needle. In order to work any two stitches in the same fabric, the yarn has to strand past a stitch of the other fabric that is temporarily between them, and this elongates the running thread. However, once the stitches have been worked and discarded, they will lie side by side within one of the fabrics and will then take up the extra length in the running threads and enlarge slightly. A few Test Swatches done prior to making your Gauge Swatch will help you select a needle size that produces a fabric with the characteristics you want.

When introducing sections of double-fabric within a single-fabric (see Double-Fabric Insertion), the two will have different gauges and this will be obvious unless some adjustment is made. You can work the double-fabric section with a firmer tension, but that is difficult to sustain; it is usually easiest to change to a needle one size smaller. In some cases, it may be best to treat the insertion like a change in stitch pattern and do a separate gauge for it.

❖ *Patterns and Stitch Sequence*

In the instructions above, the odd-numbered stitches belong to the fabric on the nearside, the even-numbered stitches to the fabric on the farside, but this arrangement is quite arbitrary.

If you prefer, you can alter the pattern sequences above and assign the even-numbered stitches to the fabric on the nearside—patterns that started with a Knit or Purl stitch would begin with a Slip stitch instead, and those that started with a Slip stitch would begin with a Knit or Purl. You can also work on an uneven number of stitches, in which case you would begin and end one side with Knit or Purl stitches, and the other side with Slip stitches.

What is important is not the number of stitches or their sequence, but being clear about which set belongs to which fabric and working accordingly. Once you understand how the technique is done, a glance at the fabric makes it obvious how to begin the next pass.

Also, whenever you are working a pattern where the last stitch is slipped (as with Pattern 1 and Pattern 4, above), you may find it easier to work the last stitch instead of slipping it before the turn. If you decide to do so, start the next pass by slipping that stitch and the next one, stranding the yarn as necessary nearside or farside, and then resume the basic pattern with the third stitch on the needle.

To help identify the two fabrics and keep track of whether you have worked an equal number of rows in both, mark Fabric A with a coilless pin or Yarn Marker, or take note of the location of the strand of yarn hanging from the cast-on edge. With a cast-on technique that requires a tail of yarn, it will be at the right corner when you begin the first pass; with a Knitted Cast-On technique, it will be at the left corner.

Some of the instructions below specify whether to work Fabric A or Fabric B, or Side A or Side B—and in some cases whether to work on the outside or inside of a fabric—but *not* whether to work in Knit or Purl because this depends upon which of the double-fabric patterns you choose. For the same reasons, the instructions may say to "position yarn" rather than specifying to move it nearside or farside; this should be understood to mean that the yarn must be moved as needed in order to either Knit or Purl the next stitch, or strand it past a slipped stitch, so it will lie between the two fabrics.

❖ *Casting On for Double-Fabrics*

Several standard cast-on techniques are suitable for double-fabrics, but they can look different when used for this purpose and often provide novel decorative possibilities. Try several edges and needle sizes on Test Swatches before deciding how you want to work.

When making a Basic Double-Fabric, all the stitches are cast on at the same time, joining the two fabrics at the bottom edge. However, for some of the Singular Double-Fabric applications discussed below, the bottom edge is left open, and this requires a special approach.

Ribbed Half-Hitch Cast-On

The Alternating Yarns Version of Ribbed Half-Hitch Cast-On works well for almost any double-fabric; it not only looks the same on both sides, but is very nice when done with two yarns for a color pattern. The edge is considerably more elastic than when used for a single-fabric because it contains twice as many half-hitches as there are stitches in the width of each fabric.

One-Yarn Version

Use a Twist Start and consider this the first stitch, and then cast on so that the sequence of edge stitches matches the sequence you will use for the double-fabric.

- For a nearside stitch first on needle, use Twist Start as first stitch and begin casting on with Purl, using yarn on forefinger for half-hitch, and then do a Knit with half-hitch from yarn on thumb.
- For a farside stitch first on needle, use Twist Start and begin casting on with Knit, and then Purl.

Two-Yarn Version

- If working with two yarns, join them with a Slip Knot, but do not count as first stitch. Start casting on with a Knit first, and then a Purl, or vice versa depending on pattern; drop knot at end of first pass.

A Ribbed Half-Hitch Cast-On edge usually remains quite tidy, but if you find it splays out a bit, make the half-hitches tighter than normal, or try one of the following tips:

- Increase tension on baseline yarn but not on yarn forming stitches.
- And/or, tuck each new stitch up close against preceding one on needle to shorten length of strand passing between one half-hitch and next.

Double-Needle Cast-On

For a wonderfully elastic, well-behaved edge that looks the same on both sides, try Double-Needle Cast-On. The edge is flat, with decorative Purl-like nubs running along each side, and it is quite distinctive when used for a double-fabric.

Stranded Cast-On

This cast-on is just as useful for a double-fabric as for a single-fabric and for all the same reasons, and it is done in the conventional way. When the time comes to pick up the edge, you can either keep the stitches interspersed on the needle and continue with a double-fabric, or separate them onto two needles, if necessary; see Separating and Interspersing Stitch Sets, and Casting On for Open Edge.

1. Use a Twist Start and begin cast-on with a "Knit" stitch, drawing yarn under other strand, followed by a "Yarnover"; end with a "Knit" stitch.
2. Turn and begin double-fabric pattern sequence: [Yarn nearside, Slip 1, yarn farside, Knit 1].

The above pattern sequence begins with a Slip stitch to avoid using a Yarnover as the last cast-on stitch; there are two other ways to avoid this:

- Use a Twist Start, begin with a "Yarnover," and cast on an uneven number of stitches, ending with a "Knit" stitch.
- Or, for an even number of stitches, end with a "Knit" stitch, turn and place a "Yarnover" on right needle, and then begin double-fabric pattern with next stitch.

Alternating Cast-On

Alternating Cast-On creates a rounded edge that does not look "cast-on" at all; in fact, the edge has so much in common with the structure of a double-fabric that they seem made for each other. Furthermore, when working with contrast-color yarns, all the stitches on the nearside of the edge will be in one color and all the stitches on the farside will be in the other.

Use a *very* small needle size for this cast-on.

- For a nearside stitch first on needle, use a Right Twist Start as first stitch of Fabric A; start Alternating Cast-On with a "Purl" stitch for Fabric B.
- For a farside stitch first on needle, use a Left Twist Start as first stitch of Fabric B; begin Alternating Cast-On with a "Knit" stitch for Fabric A.
- To start with a Slip Knot, begin cast-on sequence with either a "Knit" stitch for Fabric A, or a "Purl" stitch for Fabric B; drop Slip Knot at end of first pass.

This cast-on is the only one suitable for a double-fabric done with Purl on the outside, because when it is turned to the Knit side, the edge will look the same.

Other Cast-Ons

- Although not particularly elastic (and slow to do), a Cable Cast-On provides a handsome, tailored edge for a double-fabric. You could work it entirely in Knit, or alternate Knit and Purl.

- The Chained Cast-On family may also be useful in some situations.
- Picot Cast-On produces a serrated edge and can be done in two colors. The two sides look quite different and may provide just the right touch for some projects.

Casting On for Open Edge

It is also possible to cast on the stitches for a double-fabric and leave the lower edge open. Two approaches can be used: one leaves the lower edge open for a fabric worked in the round; the other is used to cast on for two fabrics that will remain entirely separate. These techniques require the temporary use of double-point needles, but you can continue on a single-point needle if you prefer.

Casting On for Circular Edge

The first version here is done with either Knit or Purl Half-Hitch Cast-On. The second makes use of Stranded Cast-On, and the stitches are later freed and picked up so they can be worked in some other way (see Working in the Opposite Direction).

Method One

1. Cast on number of stitches required for full circumference of fabric on double-point needle.
2. Starting with last stitch cast on, Slip half of stitches to second double-point needle.
3. Fold two needles side-by-side so stitch with yarn attached is on farside at right and folded edge is to left.

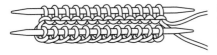

Casting On for Circular Edge: Step 3. Needles folded into position.

4. Slide two sets of stitches to right tips of needles, and then Slip stitches to third double-point needle one size smaller. Alternate one stitch from nearside needle, one from farside needle, as described in Interspersing Stitch Sets, below.
5. Slide interspersed stitches so yarn is at right tip and begin to work double-fabric pattern with needle of correct size for fabric.

The cast-on edge is closed at the folded corner, and the circle is joined when the first stitch is worked.

The smaller needle size suggested in Step 4 is necessary so the stitches will not be too tight when they are interspersed.

If you use Knit Half-Hitch Cast-On, the Knit side of the edge will be on the outside of both needles; if you plan to work the double-fabric pattern with Purl on the outside, use Purl Half-Hitch Cast-On instead.

Method Two

You can also use Stranded Cast-On for this purpose.

- Cast on all the stitches and begin the double-fabric pattern. To open the edge later, remove the strand to free the stitches and pick them up on a set of double-point needles as described in Separating Stitch Sets, below; either cast off the stitches immediately or continue working them in some other way.

Casting On for Separate Fabrics

To make two single-thickness fabrics, use a separate needle and supply of yarn to cast on each set of stitches, and then intersperse the two sets on one needle; see Interspersing Stitch Sets, below.

Or, cast on the stitches and intersperse them on a single needle at the same time using either Simple Cast-On or Half-Hitch Cast-On and two supplies of yarn, as follows:

Method One

It is easy to use Simple Cast-On for this purpose, but it can be a challenge to work the stitches the first time.

1. Make separate Slip Knots in each yarn and place Yarn A on needle first, and then Yarn B. Do not count Slip Knots as stitches; drop both at end of first pass.
2. Hold two yarns as for Knit Half-Hitch Cast-On. To place nearside stitch first on needle, hold Yarn A on thumb; to place farside stitch first, hold Yarn A on forefinger. Yarn is carried on thumb in usual way; yarn on forefinger should pass up nearside and over top of finger to needle (see Simple Half-Hitch from Forefinger).
3. Using Simple Half-Hitch Cast-On, start with Yarn A from either thumb or forefinger, and then alternate between two yarns to add as many stitches as needed.

Method Two

It is slightly more challenging to use Half-Hitch Cast-On when you want to make two separate fabrics, but the first row of stitches is considerably easier to do; use two supplies of yarn, and work as follows:

1. Measure off a tail for baseline and make a Slip Knot in each yarn; place Yarn A on needle first, and then Yarn B. Do not count Slip Knots as stitches; drop both at end of first pass.
2. On nearside of needle, pick up two Yarn A strands, hold in usual way for Knit Half-Hitch Cast-On with tail on thumb, and add one stitch; drop yarns.
3. On farside of needle, pick up two Yarn B strands and use Purl Half-Hitch Cast-On, Method Two, to add next stitch; drop yarns.

4. Alternate Steps 2 and 3 to cast on as many stitches as needed for Double-Fabric.

Always maintain the strands of one yarn supply on the nearside of the needle and the strands of the other on the farside in order to keep the two edges entirely separate.

If you prefer to work the double-fabric pattern with Purl on the outside, use Purl Half-Hitch Cast-On in Step 2 and Knit Half-Hitch Cast-On in Step 3.

❖ Shaping for Double-Fabrics

It is always easiest to shape a double-fabric at the side edges. This is usually done at the beginning of one pass in Fabric A, and at the beginning of the next pass in Fabric B.

A single increase will at least temporarily change the sequence of stitches on the needle. If a nearside stitch was first on the needle, after the shaping a farside stitch will be first, and if shaping is repeated on a subsequent row the sequence will change again. Adjust how you work the double-fabric pattern accordingly; a glance at the needle will tell you how to proceed. A double increase does not have the same effect.

When shaping is placed within a double-fabric, it is necessary to rearrange the interspersed stitches, either before a decrease, or while working an increase; this requires a few extra steps, but is otherwise quite simple to do.

Shaping with Short Rows can be done in a double-fabric much as for a single-fabric, although there are slight differences. The most common reason to use the technique is for the heels and toes of socks; see Singular Double-Fabrics, below.

Increases

The Raised Increase is the easiest and most unobtrusive technique to use for a double-fabric and it can be done either at the edge or within the fabric with equal success.

The following instructions are neutral, in that they do not specify whether to work Knit or Purl, because this depends upon which of the double-fabric patterns you are using. For the same reason, "position yarn" means to move it nearside or farside as necessary either to strand past a Slip stitch, or to work the next stitch.

Raised Increases at Side Edges

How to work the increase depends upon whether a stitch of the fabric on the nearside or farside is first on the needle.

To intersperse the new stitch between the originals, in some cases you may need to work the first step of the increase into the second stitch, and then Slip the first stitch before working the next half of the increase. In other cases, you may need to use the equivalent of a Slip Raised Increase, working the first

step below a stitch that will not be worked on that pass; Slip it with yarn nearside or farside, as necessary.

Nearside Stitch First

- Work both steps of Right Raised Increase into nearside stitch; new stitch belongs to fabric on farside.

Farside Stitch First

- Work first step of Right Raised Increase into second stitch below farside stitch (second row down). Position yarn as needed to either Slip stitch above or work it, depending upon double-fabric pattern used; new stitch belongs to fabric on nearside.
- Or, with yarn farside, move needle tip to left of first stitch and work first step of Raised Increase below second stitch on nearside. Position yarn as needed, Slip first stitch on needle; position yarn as needed and work second stitch on needle (above increase). New stitch belongs to fabric on nearside.

  In this case, it helps to lift the stitch below temporarily onto the needle to make the increase; it will be a bit tight because it has to be pulled past the intervening stitch.

- Or, at the end of previous pass, work a Left Raised Increase below last stitch; turn. Slip new stitch and then begin double-fabric pattern. New stitch belongs to fabric on nearside.

Double Raised Increase at Edge

To make the equivalent of a double increase, work a single increase at the end of one pass, turn, and then immediately work another at the beginning of the next pass; intersperse the new stitches as you do this.

Nearside Stitch First/Farside Stitch Last

1. At end of first pass, yarn nearside, Slip last farside stitch to right needle. Position yarn as needed and reach past the slipped stitch to work Left Raised Increase two rows below second stitch on right needle. Turn.
2. At beginning of second pass, new stitch is now first farside stitch. Reach past it and work first half of Right Raised Increase below second, nearside stitch. Yarn nearside, Slip first stitch, position yarn as needed and work stitch above increase.

Farside Stitch First/Nearside Stitch Last

1. At end of first pass, work Left Raised Increase on nearside stitch; turn.
2. At beginning of second pass, two farside stitches are now first on needle. Yarn nearside, Slip first stitch of

pair, position yarn, reach past second stitch and work first step of Right Raised Increase below next nearside stitch. Yarn nearside, Slip second stitch of farside pair, position yarn and work nearside stitch above increase.

Raised Increases Within Fabric

When a Raised Increase is done within the fabric, there will temporarily be a pair of stitches together on one side until the corresponding increase is done on the other side. When the second stitch is inserted between those two, it restores the normal sequence.

These instructions are for working in Stockinette and making the first increase in Fabric A, and the second in Fabric B. For a decorative stitch pattern, use any combination of Knit and Purl for the increase.

1. First Pass: Work a Right Raised Increase in Fabric A stitch (new stitch and original stitch will be side by side between two stitches of Fabric B); complete pass. Turn.
2. Second Pass: Work across Fabric B to pair of Fabric A stitches. Yarn nearside, Slip first stitch of Fabric A pair. Yarn farside, reach needle tip past second Fabric A stitch and lift stitch below onto left needle to work first half of Right Raised

Raised Increase Within Fabric: Step 2. On second pass, work first half of increase in second stitch.

Increase. Yarn nearside, Slip the second Fabric A stitch; yarn farside, work Fabric B stitch above increase.

If you are working the double-fabric pattern with Knit on the inside, the first increase would be made in Fabric B, the second in Fabric A.

And, of course, if you are making something that requires two increases in each fabric, such as for shaping the bodice of a circular garment, simply do the first pair close to one side edge and the second pair close to the other.

Rib Increase

A Rib Increase works nicely at the edge but is awkward to do within the fabric and offers no advantage over the Raised Increase, above; also, it binds the two fabrics together. Work the increase Knit/Purl or Purl/Knit depending upon which double-fabric pattern you are using. Regardless of whether you work the increase into a stitch of the fabric on the nearside or farside, the first stitch will belong to the other fabric; simply maintain the pattern on the next pass.

- If nearside stitch is first on needle, work Rib Increase; first stitch of increase belongs to fabric on farside.

- If farside stitch is first on needle, work Rib Increase on nearside stitch at end of pass; second stitch of increase belongs to fabric on farside.

Running Thread Increase

This increase leaves a little hole beneath it; it is quite obvious within the fabric, but less so at the edge, so you might want to try it there. Work in Knit or Purl, according to pattern.

- At beginning of pass, work Running Thread Increase into strand that passes across edge, between first two stitches on needle.

It is easiest to find the correct strand if a farside stitch is first on the needle; if that is the case, the new stitch will belong to the fabric on the nearside.

Yarnover Increases

This technique also works reasonably well at the edge, but it is slightly more noticeable than a Raised Increase. It is more complicated to do within the fabric because it takes four passes to complete and offers no advantage over the Raised Increase.

1. At side edge, make Yarnover on right needle and begin double-fabric pattern.
2. At end of next pass, work Yarnover farside so it will twist.

To make the Yarnover, either hold yarn on nearside and Knit next stitch, automatically forming Yarnover, or use a Purl to Purl Yarnover and Purl next stitch.

Decreases

A decrease at the side edge of a double-fabric is very easy to do and is unobtrusive and neat. In this case, you will be removing the last stitch on the needle; maintain your double-fabric pattern accordingly.

When a decrease is done within a double-fabric, it is necessary to rearrange the interspersed stitches in order to make the first one; this leaves a pair side by side in the other fabric, ready to be worked on the second pass.

In either case, work the decrease in Knit or Purl, depending upon which double-fabric pattern you are using.

Single Decrease at Edge

- If nearside stitch is first on needle, work a Left Decrease, joining it with a farside stitch; new stitch belongs to fabric on farside.
- If farside stitch is first on needle, use a Right Decrease; new stitch belongs to fabric on nearside.

- If nearside stitch is last on needle, work a Right Decrease; new stitch belongs to fabric on farside.
- If farside stitch is last on needle, use a Left Decrease; new stitch belongs to fabric on nearside.

Double Decrease at Edge

If you need to reduce the width more rapidly than one stitch at each side, use a Double Decrease. In this case, since two stitches are removed, one from each fabric, the double-fabric pattern will remain unchanged.

- At beginning of pass, work single decrease. Position yarn as needed and either work or Slip next stitch according to pattern, and then pull second stitch on right needle over first.
- At end of pass, work single decrease, turn. Slip decrease stitch, position yarn as needed and either work or Slip next stitch; pull second stitch on right needle over first.

Decrease Within the Fabric

As with the comparable increases, these instructions are for working one decrease in each fabric, first in Fabric A, and then in Fabric B. Use either a Left or Right Decrease done in Knit or Purl as necessary for your double-fabric pattern.

Begin the decrease with a nearside stitch first on left needle:

1. First Pass: With yarn held nearside, insert right needle tip from farside as to Purl into second stitch on left needle. Drop first stitch on nearside, Slip second stitch to right needle; yarn farside, pick up first stitch again on left needle. Stitches will trade places, leaving pair of Fabric B stitches on right needle, and pair of Fabric A stitches on left needle.

Decrease Within the Fabric: Step 1. Insert needle into second stitch on farside as to Purl; drop first stitch and then pick it up again.

2. Work decrease on pair of Fabric A stitches; pair of Fabric B stitches remains on right needle. Complete pass and turn.
3. Second Pass: Work across to Fabric B pair and make second decrease; stitches will again be interspersed on needle in normal way.

If you are working the double-fabric pattern on the inside face of the fabric, the first decrease will be in Fabric B and the second in Fabric A. To rearrange stitches on needle for decrease, start with a farside stitch first on the left needle and work as follows:

- On nearside, insert right needle into second stitch as to Purl and drop first stitch. Slip second stitch to right needle; pick up first stitch on left needle again. Work decrease on two Fabric B stitches now on left needle; work other pair of stitches on return pass.

Short Rows

A double-fabric can be shaped with Short Rows, but how to proceed depends upon the kind of pattern you are using and what kind of double-fabric you are making.

If you are making a Basic Double-Fabric, the Short Rows will bind the two fabrics together at the point where the wrap is done; this is acceptable for something like the shoulder line of a reversible garment because the two fabrics are treated as one.

For Singular Double-Fabrics, the two sides must be kept strictly separate, and the Short Row pattern is worked on only one side, or on one side and then the other.

Short Rows are not used for Double-Faced Fabrics because they are reversible fabrics and there is no "inside" face where the wraps can be hidden; see Double-Faced Fabrics.

Short Rows for Double-Fabrics

With this method, the two fabrics will be linked as the yarn travels between one side and the other at the Short Row turning point. Always start the wrap on the Purl side of the fabric.

1. First Pass: Work Fabric A stitches to turning point, wrap stitch, and turn.
2. Second Pass: If fabric is to be sloped at both right and left side, work to equivalent turning point in Fabric B, wrap stitch, and turn.
3. Repeat Steps 1 and 2 to complete Short Row pattern.

For Decreasing Short Rows: Reactivate all Fabric A stitches on one pass, working wrap and stitch together at each turning point in usual way, and then reactivate all Fabric B stitches on next pass.

For Increasing Short Rows: Work the previously wrapped stitch and then continue to the next turning point in Fabric A, wrap and turn; repeat in Fabric B.

Short Rows for Singular Double-Fabrics

This method of doing Short Rows is used with the Singular Double-Fabric technique for making socks and mittens.

The instructions are for working the entire Short Row pattern on only one set of stitches, working as for a flat fabric, first an outside row and then an inside row, always slipping the set of stitches that belong to the other side of the fabric to keep the two separate. In some applications, a Short Row pattern is done on just one side of the fabric, in others it is first completed on one side of the fabric and then repeated on the other side.

In a normal Short Row pattern, a stitch is slipped after the turn to create a smoother transition between rows. It is somewhat more complicated to do this here because that stitch is flanked by two stitches from the other side of the fabric and these have to be slipped as well.

In the instructions, these three stitches are slipped *before the turn*. Doing so helps keep you oriented in regard to which fabric you are working on. After the turn, the yarn will then be in the correct position to work the next stitch. Strand the yarn very firmly past all three so the wrap will not be elongated.

1. On outside, work to turning point in Side A and wrap next stitch as usual for Short Row.
2. Slip next three stitches from right needle to left—a Side B stitch, a Side A stitch, a Side B stitch—moving yarn as necessary to strand past these stitches between two sides of fabric; turn.
3. Draw yarn firmly past three stitches to work next Fabric A stitch and then continue across inside row of Side A. To slope at both sides, work second turning point in same position on other side. Turn.
4. Repeat Steps 1 and 2 to work Short Row pattern.

If you are working Decreasing Short Rows, wrap all stitches row by row, according to pattern. On next row, reactivate all wrapped stitches to one side of center, turn, and on following row reactivate all wrapped stitches on other side of center.

If you are working Increasing Short Rows, reactivate last stitch wrapped before wrapping next one.

❖ Correcting Errors in a Double-Fabric

Errors can be corrected in a double-fabric in much the same way as for a single-fabric, but there are some minor differences in how to approach the problems (for more information, see Correcting Mistakes in the chapter Working a Project).

Dropped Stitches

A dropped stitch can be worked back up to the needle in the usual way, but when doing a color pattern, it can be somewhat challenging to identify which strand belongs to the stitch that ran down.

- Pick up the dropped stitch with a crochet hook or cable needle and pull it away from the needles slightly to expose the strand lying between the two fabrics; in a Basic Double-Fabric, it will be attached to one stitch on the left needle, and to another below the right needle.

- In a Double-Faced Fabric, the strand will be attached to the two nearest stitches in the same color, regardless of which side of the fabric those stitches belong to. If the stitch has run down more than one row, it may be best to unravel the fabric in order to correct it unless the pattern is very simple.

Ripping Stitch-by-Stitch

For an error in the row you are working on, undo the stitches one-by-one, as you would in a single-fabric.

- For a Basic Double-Fabric, insert left needle from nearside to farside into stitch below first stitch on right needle, drop stitch above, and unravel; move yarn between needle tips if necessary and Slip next stitch directly from right needle to left needle.
- For a Double-Faced Fabric, adjacent stitches in same color can be undone as for a Single Rib fabric; Slip all stitches in other color.

    Depending upon the location of the yarn and the position of the stitches on the needle, sometimes you can undo two of them at once.
- If yarn is attached to second stitch on left needle, insert right needle into first stitch, and then into one below second stitch.
- If yarn is attached to first stitch, insert right needle tip into stitch below it, and then into next stitch on needle.

Ripping Rows

If an error is more than one or two rows down, fixing it will probably take less time if you pull the stitches off the needle and unravel.

Of course, the minute you do this, the stitches of a Basic Double-Fabric will separate and become a circular single-fabric. Pick up the stitches on a set of double-point needles one size smaller, fix the error, and then reintersperse them on a single needle again to continue; see Interspersing Stitch Sets, below.

Ripping Stitch Columns

Instead of unraveling rows, you can also drop a stitch from the needle and unravel it down to where an error is, much as you would for a single-fabric. This is the easiest way to correct a strand that wound up on the outside of the fabric, or to convert a stray Purl stitch to a Knit, for instance.

Doing so with several columns of stitches requires first separating them from the other set of stitches, correcting the error, and then interspersing them on the needle again when you are done. To do this with a color pattern requires a special approach because there are two sets of strands lying between the two fabrics and it may be difficult to determine which ones belong to the unraveled stitches.

Unraveling Multiple Stitch Columns

The instructions assume the error is on the nearside.

1. Drop first nearside stitch from left needle, Slip farside stitch to right needle, drop next nearside stitch from left needle; repeat if necessary. Unravel dropped stitches to error and correct.
2. Work stitches back up row-by-row using a pair of short double-point needles or a crochet hook and one needle; slide stitches to left tip of double-point needle used for correction. Slip one corrected stitch to main left needle, Slip one from main right needle to main left needle; repeat to intersperse stitches as before.

As you will see, once the stitches have been dropped from the needle, they will clearly belong to one fabric and will be side by side.

Unraveling Stitches in Color Patterns

If you need to unravel a stitch column in a color pattern, separate the released strands from all the others in the fabric as you unravel the stitches. Use a separate pair of short double-point needles for this purpose.

1. Place fabric flat on a table or in lap and turn it sideways, with needles bearing stitches to right.
2. Use needle held in left hand to unravel stitch column to row where error is; capture each released strand on needle held in right hand as you do so.
3. Fix error, and, with unraveled stitch on left needle, Slip first strand from right to left needle, pull next stitch over; repeat.

If more than one stitch is involved, rework the first stitch, Slip to right needle, and then rework next stitch on left needle using same strand, and so on. Transfer reworked stitches back to left needle and repeat process with next strand, or transfer needle with reworked stitches to left hand and slide stitches to right tip and repeat. At top, intersperse stitches again, as described above.

❖ *Single to Double and Back Again*

Double-Fabric Insertion applications also make use of specialized versions of the increase and decrease techniques to change from a single-fabric to a double-fabric, or vice versa. For this purpose, an increase is worked on or between every stitch, or a decrease is worked on every pair.

When changing to a double-fabric, in most cases the stitch columns of the original single-fabric continue without interruption above the row of increases and serve as Fabric A. The new, increased stitches serve as the basis for the new Fabric B, which in most cases will be on the inside of a garment.

Similarly, when changing from a double-fabric to a single

one, the decreases are worked so the Fabric B stitches stop on that row and the fabric continues on the Fabric A stitches.

Single- to Double-Fabric

Several increase techniques are suitable for use when changing from a single-fabric to a double-fabric. Try them on a Test Swatch before deciding how to work; you may find one or another easier to use and there are only subtle differences in the results.

If you plan to use a decorative pattern for the single-fabric, consider working one row plain prior to making the change to avoid distortion due to the increases. Also, select the needle size for the insertion based on a Test Swatch, or, if you are continuing in Stockinette, simply use a needle one size smaller to avoid an obvious change in gauge.

Slip Raised Increase

The Slip Raised Increase technique places the new stitches directly behind the original ones, ideally positioned for the second fabric. Work on an inside row of the single-fabric, as follows:

1. [Yarn farside, insert right needle up into Purl nub below first stitch and Knit, yarn nearside, Slip 1]; repeat between brackets across row. Turn.
2. With two sets of stitches now on needle, and a Fabric A stitch first, begin double-fabric pattern.

If you find it easier to do so, work into the left side of the stitches instead.

1. [Yarn nearside, Slip first stitch to right needle and then insert left needle up under Purl nub below it, yarn farside, Knit raised stitch]; repeat between brackets across row; turn.
2. A Fabric B stitch is first on needle; Slip it and begin working double-fabric pattern on original stitches of Fabric A.

Tension yarn firmly on first pass to encourage new Fabric B stitches to take their place behind the original stitches that now make up Fabric A. After working a few passes, tug down on the fabric to help the stitches line up smoothly.

Running Thread Increase

This is a very simple way to switch from a single-fabric to a double-fabric. Because a Running Thread Increase is worked between each stitch, the method produces one less than double the number of stitches in a flat fabric; for a circular fabric, the number will double.

This technique draws yarn out of the running threads and the stitches will tighten up considerably as you work. Use a smaller-size needle for the increase row; make a few Test Swatches to decide on needle size. If necessary, work the row prior to the increases on a needle one size larger to make the stitches temporarily bigger; they will shrink back to normal size after the increases are made and they are discarded into the fabric.

For a flat fabric, begin on inside row.

- Yarn nearside, [Purl 1, Purl Running Thread Increase], repeat between brackets across row; end Purl 1. Turn and begin double-fabric pattern.

Due to the uneven number of stitches, the first and last stitches on the needle belong to Fabric A.

For a circular fabric, work on outside and use the Knit version of this increase: the first stitch at the beginning of the round belongs to Fabric A, the last stitch to Fabric B.

Yarnover Increase

A Yarnover works well for this purpose, and often has less of an effect on the stitches in the last row of the single-fabric than some of the other techniques above. Begin on an outside row of the single-fabric, and work as follows:

- Knit all original stitches, working a Yarnover between each one. Turn and begin double-fabric pattern, slipping original stitches (which now belong to Fabric A) with yarn nearside; move yarn to farside to work Yarnovers and Knit them farside so they twist on discard.

If you prefer an even number of stitches, turn and at the beginning of the second pass work one Purl-to-Purl Yarnover on the right needle before starting the double-fabric pattern.

Bar or Rib Increases

These two closely related increase techniques can be worked on every stitch across the row to exactly double the number on the needle; both are easy to do.

- The Bar Increase is reasonably unobtrusive because the new stitches line up nicely behind the originals; use the Knit stitch of each increase for Fabric A and the "bar" for Fabric B.
- The closely related Rib Increase, with its Knit/Purl structure, pulls the stitches of the foundation row open slightly and leaves a visible effect in the fabric; you may consider this decorative in some situations and inappropriate in others.

Here again, if Knit is on the outside, use the Purl stitch of each pair for Fabric B and the Knit stitches for Fabric A, or vice versa if working with Purl on outside.

Double- to Single-Fabric

To change from a double-fabric to a single-fabric, simply reduce the number of stitches on the needle by half using one of the following decrease techniques. For this purpose, use the needle size needed for the main fabric because it will determine the size of the new stitches on the right needle.

Joinery Decrease

This simple method is appropriate for most purposes. The facing stitches of the decreases are those that continue in the single-fabric above the row in which they are done; the stitches of the inside portion of the double-fabric are the backing stitches of the decreases and stop on that row.

A farside stitch should always be the right stitch of each decrease pair; if a nearside stitch is first on left needle, Slip it to the right needle and then continue, as follows:

- Work a Knit or Purl Right Decrease on every pair of stitches across the row.

Pullover Decrease

With this method, the stitches of one fabric are pulled over the others and discarded. The fabric above the decrease row continues on the stitches of the inside fabric instead of on those of the outside, and the transition will be quite obvious.

Having the stitches change sides in this way can be used for decorative purposes when working with more than one color yarn. In that case, work the last row of the inside fabric in the color you plan to use for the fabric that continues above the decreases; those stitches are drawn to the outside and will remain visible.

Work the decrease on pairs of stitches, a farside stitch on the right, a nearside stitch on the left; if a nearside stitch is first on the needle, Slip it and then continue on the remaining stitches as follows:

Working on Outside

1. On nearside, insert right needle as to Purl into second stitch on left needle and pull it over first stitch and discard.
2. Knit remaining stitch of pair.
3. Repeat Steps 1–2 across the row.

Double- to Single-Fabric. Pullover Decrease, Working on Outside: Step 1.

Working on Inside

1. Slip decrease pair of stitches purlwise to right needle, either singly or together.
2. Move left needle to farside of right needle and insert into second stitch; pull it over first and off needle.
3. Move left needle to farside of right needle and insert into remaining stitch of pair; with both needle tips in stitch, Purl.
4. Repeat Steps 1–3 across the row.

Regardless of how you work, the pulled-over stitches encircle the base of the discarded stitches and lie one row lower in the fabric. This is used in some Double-Fabric Insertion applications to add slightly more length to one fabric for ease. The alternative is to work one less row on the set of stitches that will be pulled over.

❖ *Separating and Interspersing Stitch Sets*

In several of the Basic Double-Fabric applications described below, it may be necessary either to separate the interspersed stitches in order to continue with a single thickness, or to intersperse separate sets of stitches and continue as for a double-fabric.

Separating Stitch Sets

When interspersed stitches are separated, the fabric will open either into a conventional single-thickness circular fabric, or into two entirely separate fabrics, depending on how the edges were handled. For the former, transfer the stitches to a set of four double-point needles; for the latter, to two straight needles (if you prefer to work with a circular needle, begin doing so after separating the stitches).

Several methods can be used to separate the stitches; the first works well if you do not fear the stitches will run down, while the others are for when you have reason to be more cautious. It is helpful to use needles at least one size smaller for this purpose to ease the tension on the stitches; return to the correct size after the change has been made.

Method One

If the yarn is well behaved, or the fabric relatively narrow, the simplest and quickest way to separate the two sets of stitches is to pull them off the needle; the two fabrics will immediately come apart and you can pick up the freed stitches in the usual way for a single-thickness fabric; see Picking Up Freed Stitches.

Method Two

If you are working with a large number of stitches or a yarn that might unravel easily, a safer approach is to leave the stitches on the needle and separate them as they are transferred to a set of four double-point needles.

1. Hold needle with interspersed stitches in left hand, and a pair of double-point needles in right hand.
2. Slip a farside stitch from left needle to farside needle in right hand, and then a nearside stitch from left needle to nearside needle in right hand.
3. With half of stitches transferred, push stitches to centers of first pair of double-point needles, pick up second pair, and transfer remaining stitches in same way.

4. With stitches now on four needles, open fabric into a circle and either continue working as for a conventional single-thickness circular fabric, or cast off in usual way.

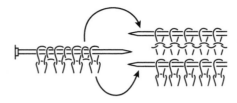

Separating Stitch Sets, Method Two: Step 2.

As you transfer the stitches in Step 2, work close to the tips of the needles, and hold the first stitches with your forefingers so they do not drop off as you work.

Method Three

For this method the stitches are transferred as described above, but to just two needles. This may be done prior to Grafting the stitches to close a top edge, or as a transitional step before beginning to work in the round. For the latter, use the Shetland Three-Needle Method, and, if you prefer, once the needles have opened into a triangle, introduce another needle or change to a circular one.

Refolding the Fabric

With the stitches separated and on two needles, as described in Method Three, above, you can reposition a Singular Double-Fabric so the stitches that were at the sides are moved within it; in other words, refold the fabric.

This can be useful if, for instance, you prefer to do any shaping at the sides where it is easier, and then move the shaped areas to the interior of the fabric.†

1. Hold two needles with separate sets of stitches in left hand; push stitches close to tips. Take up another needle in right hand, and use it to transfer several stitches one by one from left needle on farside to left one on nearside.
2. Turn pair of needles, slide stitches to other tips and repeat with equal number of stitches at other edge.
3. Continue in this way until stitches are repositioned as needed and there is an equal number on both needles.
4. Intersperse stitches again on a single needle below before continuing; see below.

Interspersing Stitch Sets

If you are making a conventional single-fabric in the round on a circular needle or a set of double-point needles, and

---

† Beverly Royce uses this method to shape the tops of thumbs or glove fingers; you may find some other applications for it. Beverly Royce, *Notes on Double Knitting* (Beverly Royce, April, 1981; expanded edition, Pittsville, Wisc.: Schoolhouse Press, 1994).

want to intersperse the stitches on a single needle in order to work as for a Singular Double-Fabric, use one of the following methods:

Method One

1. Distribute stitches evenly to four double-point needles.
2. Collapse circle of fabric so needles are side by side, a right pair and a left pair; stitch with yarn attached should be at left of second nearside needle. Hold single-point needle in right hand and start opposite where yarn is attached.

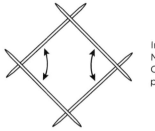

Interspersing Stitch Sets, Method One: Step 2. Collapse set of double-point needles.

Interspersing Stitch Sets, Method One: Step 2. Hold double-point needles parallel.

3. Slip one stitch from left nearside needle, next one from farside needle (or vice versa, depending on pattern); alternate in this way until all stitches from first pair of needles have been transferred and are interspersed on one needle.

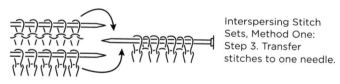

Interspersing Stitch Sets, Method One: Step 3. Transfer stitches to one needle.

4. Take up remaining pair of needles in left hand and transfer those stitches to same needle in right hand. Stitches from all four needles are now interspersed on single needle with yarn at tip.

Or, in Step 1, distribute stitches evenly to two circular needles and hold side by side as described; transfer all stitches to a single needle.

Method Two

If the yarn is well-behaved, it is often quicker and easier to slide pairs or small groups of stitches off the double-point needles and pick them up two at a time, as follows:

- Drop one stitch from each of left needles, or drop off a group of six or eight stitches. Pinch one pair together

below loops with left fingers, insert tip of right needle into farside stitch and then into nearside stitch so latter is left stitch of pair. Repeat with remaining stitch pairs until all are transferred and then do another group.

If you prefer to have a nearside stitch first, start by slipping one to right needle alone and then continue as described.

Method Three

If the stitches are off the needle for one reason or another, pick them up and intersperse them at the same time as described in Method Two, above.

- Flatten fabric so stitch with yarn attached is at left side. Make sure to start with the correct stitch; use your finger to trace the stitch column up from the corner of the cast-on edge to check. Begin picking up stitches at opposite side.

❖ Open Side Edges

With some Double-Fabric Insertion applications, it is necessary to leave one or both side edges open. The latter requires two yarns, but the former can be done when working with either one yarn at a time or two.

Variations on this application require working several rows in just one of the fabrics and not the other.

One Side Open

To leave one side edge open, simply work the Basic Double-Fabric pattern in a different sequence.

In the following instructions, Fabric A is on the nearside as you begin, Fabric B is on the farside; the right side will remain open and the left side will be closed. It is easy to alter this pattern to leave the other side open instead. Work in Knit or Purl, depending upon which Basic Double-Fabric pattern you are using.

1. Work Fabric A stitches in pattern for outside; Slip Fabric B stitches with yarn nearside; turn.
2. Work Fabric B stitches in pattern for outside; Slip Fabric A stitches with yarn nearside; turn.
3. Work Fabric B stitches in pattern for inside; Slip Fabric A stitches with yarn farside; turn.
4. Work Fabric A stitches in pattern for inside; Slip Fabric B stitches with yarn farside; turn.

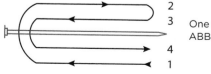

One Side Open, One Yarn. ABBA pattern sequence.

This is an ABBA sequence; to leave the left side edge open, instead, work an AABB sequence instead, or Steps 1, 4, 3, 2.

You can cast on to leave the bottom edge open, as described above, and also leave one side open. With the stitches still on the needle, this would be a flat fabric folded along one vertical side. To do this, work as follows:

- Use technique described in Casting On for Circular Edge, above, but do not close round. Fold left needle to farside or nearside, depending on double-fabric pattern; begin working with stitch with yarn attached. To control appearance of edge, use either Knit or Purl Half-Hitch Cast-On.

Both Sides Open

To leave both sides open it is necessary to use two yarns and always use Yarn A for Fabric A, and Yarn B for Fabric B, but you have the option of working with one yarn at a time, or both. All that is necessary is to alter the sequence of passes in the Basic Double-Fabric pattern.

Holding One Yarn at a Time

The first pattern variation is for an AABB sequence.

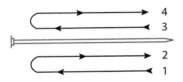

Both Sides Open: Holding One Yarn at a Time. AABB pattern sequence.

1. With Yarn A, work Fabric A stitches in pattern for outside; Slip Fabric B stitches with yarn nearside; turn.
2. Work Fabric A stitches in pattern for inside; Slip Fabric B stitches with yarn farside; drop Yarn A and turn.
3. With Yarn B, work Fabric B stitches in pattern for inside; Slip Fabric A stitches with yarn farside; turn.
4. Work Fabric B stitches in pattern for outside; Slip Fabric A stitches with yarn nearside; drop Yarn B and turn.

If you prefer, you can work ABBA:

- Attach one yarn at each side. With Yarn A, work on outside of Fabric A; turn. With Yarn B, work on outside of Fabric B, turn; work on inside of Fabric B, turn. With Yarn A, work on inside of Fabric A; turn.

Or you can work ABAB, instead:

- With Yarn A, work on outside of Fabric A; Slide. With Yarn B, work on inside of Fabric B; turn. With Yarn A, work on inside of Fabric A; Slide. With Yarn B, work on outside of Fabric B; turn.

Holding Two Yarns

When working with two yarns at the same time, you can leave one or both edges open; simply change how you hold the yarns at the end of each row.

- To leave both side edges open, always work Fabric A with Yarn A, and Fabric B with Yarn B, but change the yarns to the opposite hand at the end of every row so they cross at the side, binding the edge together.
- To leave only one edge open, maintain the yarns in the same hand at the end of one row to close the side, and change them at the end of the next to leave it open.

Working One Set of Stitches

In some applications, it is necessary or desirable to work just one of the two fabrics and not the other (or one side of a single-fabric); you will find this used in Casings and Welts, and also in several of the Singular Double-Fabric techniques. This can be done with one yarn or two.

1. On outside, Knit stitches of Fabric A, Slip stitches of Fabric B with yarn nearside. Turn.
2. On inside, Purl stitches of Fabric A, Slip stitches of Fabric B with yarn farside.

The stitches of Yarn B are never worked. Of course, you can work Fabric B instead of Fabric A, or Purl on the outside of the fabric rather than Knit, or, for that matter, work any stitch pattern you please.

In some situations, you would simply resume working on Fabric B again when appropriate; all the stitches might be cast off; or Joinery Decreases could be used to change to a single-thickness fabric.

❖ *Circular Double-Fabrics*

The Double-Fabric technique has many practical applications, but there are few reasons to make an entire garment with the method unless it is done with more than one color and is reversible. This means there are even fewer occasions to work a double-fabric garment in the round because you would normally want to see both sides. A sleeveless pullover that could be turned to one side or the other, hats, and perhaps wrist warmers, are rare examples of the kinds of circular garments that are suitable.

However, some of the utilitarian Double-Fabric Insertion applications are as suitable for use in a circular fabric as a flat one because it does not matter if the inside is seen. Also, some design details benefit from being done in the round with the Double-Faced Fabric technique, such as cuffs or necklines that can be turned up or down so both sides can be seen.

Working a Basic Double-Fabric in the round requires adjusting the pattern somewhat, and there are two options: the first is done with a single ball of yarn; the second requires two.

One-Yarn Circular Method

Cast on double the number of stitches needed for the circumference, as for a Basic Double-Fabric, and then redistribute the stitches to a set of double-point needles or a circular one. Join the round in the usual way, placing a Ring Marker on the needle between the first and last stitch. As you work, one fabric face will always be on the outside of the circle formed by the needle, and the other will face into the center.

With this method, the two fabrics are joined at the cast-on edge and also in a vertical line where the yarn travels between one fabric and the next at the end of each round. Because the doubled fabric cannot be turned inside out, the instructions assume you will be working Knit facing out on both sides.

1. Outer fabric: Knit outside stitches of Fabric A, Slip stitches of Fabric B with yarn nearside.
2. Inner fabric: Purl inside stitches of Fabric B, Slip stitches of Fabric A with yarn farside.

Many people like to knit in the round in order to avoid working in Purl, but you will notice that a circular double-fabric made in this way does indeed require that you Knit one round and Purl the next. However, the next approach offers an easy alternative.

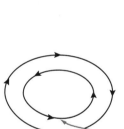

Circular Double-Fabric, One-Yarn Method. Knit outside fabric; Purl inside fabric.

Two-Yarn Circular Method

To make a circular double-fabric that is connected at the cast-on edge, but not vertically at the intersection of each round, cast on with two supplies of yarn, distribute the stitches, and work the round.

You can work with one yarn at a time or two. If you are comfortable holding one yarn in each hand, use one to Knit the outer fabric and the second to Purl the inner fabric; see Basic Patterns with Two Yarns, above.

If you prefer to work entirely in Knit, use one yarn at a time, as follows:

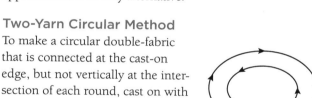

Circular Double-Fabric, Two-Yarn Method. Knit outside fabric clockwise; Purl inside fabric counter-clockwise.

1. On outside, with Yarn A, Knit stitches of Fabric A and Slip stitches of Fabric B with yarn nearside.
2. Pick up Yarn B, and at end of first outside round only, Slip first Fabric A stitch from left needle, and then wrap first Fabric B stitch as for Short Row turning point. Return both stitches to left needle and turn to inside of circle.
3. On inside, continue with Yarn B; Knit stitches of Fabric B and Slip stitches of Fabric A with yarn nearside; at end of first inside round only, work stitch and wrap together to join first round.

4. On all subsequent rounds, work Fabric A stitches with Yarn A on outside of circle, turn, and work Fabric B stitches with Yarn B on inside of circle.

If you look down on the circle of fabric and imagine the path of the two yarns, the one for the outer fabric will travel clockwise, and the one for the inner fabric will travel counter-clockwise. The two fabrics can be joined only at the cast-on and cast-off edges, or not at all.

❖ Casting Off Double-Fabrics

As with casting-on, familiar cast-off techniques work well for double-fabrics; however, some adjustments may be necessary to keep the edge neat because there are twice as many stitches for a given width as there would be in a single-fabric.

Joinery Cast-Off

This is an excellent cast-off for a double-fabric and it results in an edge with half the number of stitches, which is correct for a Basic Double-Fabric width; it also works well for some types of Double-Faced Fabrics.

Begin with a farside stitch first on left needle; if nearside stitch is first, Slip it to right needle and skip to Step 2.

1. Knit two together (left stitch of pair is Fabric A, right stitch is Fabric B).
2. With one stitch on right needle, Knit next two stitches together as in Step 1; with two stitches on right needle, pull second stitch over first and discard.
3. Repeat Step 2 to cast off all stitches.

When done in this way, the edge will have Knit below it on one side, and Purl below it on the other. To make them match, work as for Single Rib, casting off with alternate Knit and Purl Right Decreases.

Chained Cast-Off for Double-Fabrics

A standard Pullover Chained Cast-Off works well for both a Double-Fabric and a Double-Faced Fabric. Work the cast-off in pattern, using Knit for all nearside stitches and Purl for all farside stitches, so the fabric looks the same below the edge on both sides.

To prevent the edge from splaying out, work with a smaller size needle as described in the Basic Version; if this proves insufficient, try the Triple Version.

Basic Chained Cast-Off

1. Yarn farside, Knit 1, yarn nearside, Purl 1; with two stitches on right needle, pull second over first.
2. With one stitch on right needle, [yarn farside, Knit 1, pull second stitch over first; yarn nearside, Purl 1, pull second stitch over first]; repeat between brackets across row.

Triple Chained Cast-Off

This version reduces the number of stitches in the edge. You may even need to work with a needle a size *larger* to keep it from being too tight; try it on a Test Swatch to select needle size.

1. Work Step 1 as described above, but do three stitches in pattern and then pull second and third stitches over first.
2. With one stitch on right needle [work next two stitches in pattern; with three on right needle pull two over one]; repeat between brackets. At end of row, work last stitch alone, pull one over one, and secure last stitch.

Slip Chained Cast-Off

Another alternative is to use Slip Chained Cast-Off, which is quite firm and neat. Because the stitches are not worked prior to being cast off, the only way to adjust their size (and therefore the length of the edge) is to use a needle a size larger or smaller when working the row prior to casting off. Try this on a Test Swatch to select the needle size needed.

Work last row on double-point needle. Slide stitches to right needle tip. Begin with a farside stitch first on left needle; if nearside stitch is first, Slip it to right needle and skip to Step 2.

1. Pull second stitch on left needle over first and discard; Slip remaining stitch to right needle.
2. Repeat Step 1; with two stitches on right needle, pull second over first and discard.
3. Repeat Steps 1 and 2 to cast off all stitches; secure last stitch.

Grafted Cast-Off

The technique Grafted Edge for Single Rib is ideal for a double-fabric and produces an edge identical to that of Alternating Cast-On; this can be done with the stitches interspersed on the needle.

However, any sewn cast-off tends to abrade the yarn, and since double-fabrics have twice as many stitches for a given width, it is usually necessary to cast off using several lengths of yarn. Fortunately, it is easy to hide the ends between the two fabrics.

Casting Off for Open Edges

To leave the top edge of a Singular Double-Fabric open, separate the stitches as described in Separating Stitch Sets, above, and then cast off as for any single-fabric.

Alternatively, use one of the methods described here to cast off with the stitches still interspersed on the needle.

Open Edge, Two Yarns

1. Slip Side A stitch knitwise to right needle, drop Side B stitch from left needle on farside; on nearside, Slip next Side A stitch knitwise to right needle; on farside pick up dropped stitch on left needle.
2. With two turned Side A stitches on right needle and two Side B stitches on left needle, move Yarn A farside, insert left needle into nearside of two Side A stitches on right needle, and work Knit Left Decrease.
3. Yarn B nearside, work Purl Left Decrease on two Side B stitches.
4. Drop Side B stitch from right needle on farside, Slip one Side A stitch knitwise from left needle to right needle; pick up dropped stitch on left needle in standard position, and repeat Steps 2–4.

Always Slip a Side A stitch past a Side B stitch on the nearside, and Slip a Side B stitch past a Side A stitch on the farside. The Side A stitches are turned as they are slipped, to position them for the Knit Left Decrease. However, the Side B stitches have to be turned in the usual way prior to making the Purl Left Decrease.

Here are two suggestions for a quicker way to reposition the stitches:

• In Step 1, after slipping the first Side A stitch, reach the right needle tip past the Side B stitch on the farside and insert it into the next Side A stitch knitwise. Drop the Side B stitch off the left needle as you Slip the Side A stitch and then pick it up again. This may be difficult if your stitches are tight.
• In Step 4, reach past the Side B stitch on the nearside and insert the needle tip into the Side A stitch knitwise. Drop the Side B stitch as you Slip the Side A stitch and then pick it up again; this is easier to do.

Open Edge, One Yarn

With this version, the Side A stitches are cast off first and then the side B stitches; this can be used to finish the entire edge of a Singular Double-Fabric or for only a portion of the stitches within a fabric.

1. First step only: Yarn farside, drop first Side A stitch from left needle on nearside. Yarn nearside, Slip next Side B stitch to right needle. Yarn farside, pick up Side A stitch on left needle. Work Knit Left Decrease on two Side A stitches.
2. [Drop new Side A stitch from *right needle* on nearside. Yarn nearside, Slip next Side B stitch to right needle. Yarn farside, pick up dropped Side A stitch on left needle; work Knit Left Decrease on two Side A stitches.] Repeat between brackets to cast off all Side A stitches. Turn.
3. Working in Knit, use Pullover Chained Cast-Off on all Side B stitches; secure last stitch.

As you work Step 2, the Side B stitches will accumulate on the right needle; Side A stitches will be on that needle only long enough to make the next Left Decrease, which is the equivalent of Decrease Chained Cast-Off. The new stitch that results from each decrease is dropped so you can slip another Side B stitch to the right needle; when it is picked up again, there will be two Side A stitches together, ready for the next decrease.

❖ *Selvedges and Seams*

Worked in the usual way, a double-fabric does not have selvedge stitches because the edges are no more than the foldlines of a flattened circular fabric. This rounded edge can be seamed invisibly to maintain the reversibility of a garment; see Seams for Double-Fabrics, below.

However, selvedges are required for some Double-Fabric Insertion applications, or when sewing a double-fabric to a single one. Also, one type of Double-Faced pattern produces a fabric that resembles Single Rib and it requires selvedges when worked flat and seamed.

Selvedges for Double-Fabrics

A selvedge stitch on a double-fabric is worked in much the same way on a double-fabric as a single-fabric, but it needs to be worked immediately before or after another stitch or it will simply blend in with the rest of a double-fabric. How to do this depends on the sequence of stitches on the needle.

Stockinette Selvedge for Double-Fabrics

Add two stitches for selvedges to the number on the needle. On each side, there will be two stitches next to each other, with all the stitches between these pairs interspersed in the usual way. Use one of the following patterns, depending on whether the selvedge stitch is followed by a nearside or farside stitch; it is assumed that an even number of stitches are on the needle.

Method One

At right side, the selvedge stitch is followed by a Fabric A stitch.

1. First Pass: Knit 2 (the selvedge stitch and first Fabric A stitch); continue with double-fabric pattern; at end of pass, Slip 2 (a Fabric B stitch and the selvedge stitch). Turn.
2. Second Pass: Purl 1, Knit 1 (the selvedge stitch and first Fabric B stitch); continue with double-fabric pattern. At end of pass, Slip 2 (a Fabric A stitch and the selvedge stitch.) Turn.

Method Two

At right side, the selvedge stitch is followed by a Fabric B stitch.

1. First Pass: Knit 1, Slip 1 (the selvedge stitch and first Fabric B stitch); continue with double-fabric pattern; at end of pass Knit 2 (a Fabric A stitch and the selvedge stitch). Turn.
2. Second Pass: Purl 1, Slip 1 (the selvedge stitch and a Fabric A stitch); continue with double-fabric pattern. At end of pass, Purl 2 (a Fabric B stitch and the selvedge stitch). Turn.

Chain Selvedge for Double-Fabrics

1. First and Second Pass: Work selvedge stitches as described above.
2. Third and Fourth Pass: Slip selvedge stitches; work adjacent stitches according to double-fabric pattern.

Selvedges for Color Patterns

Color patterns often require more than one pass to add a row to one of the fabrics, but how to deal with the selvedge is much the same.

- Hold both yarns as one to work the selvedge stitch, choose one of them to use for the entire selvedge, or alternate the colors, using whichever one produces the effect you want on each pass.

Seams for Double-Fabrics

A double-fabric can be seamed invisibly in a way that fully preserves its reversibility, and there is no need for a selvedge. If you prefer to use a selvedge, it can be turned to the inside with a conventional Running Thread Seam, but the fabric will no longer be reversible.

As usual, it helps to leave enough yarn when casting on to use for sewing (see Seams); if you have not done so, hide the tail of yarn by drawing it between the two fabrics about 6 to 8 inches away from edge.

For a double-fabric with no selvedge, a Running Thread Seam will align the rows perfectly, and the join will be invisible.

The technique is done in the usual way, with one slight adjustment.

- Insert sewing needle under running threads at very edge of fabric (the one that connects the two fabrics), instead of ones lying between first and second stitch.
- In a fabric with larger stitches, it is best to seam using every running thread; for one with smaller stitches, it may be sufficient to insert sewing needle under two at a time.

Double-Fabric Applications

The most interesting and practical of the double-fabric applications are not used to make entire garments. Instead, they involve adding sections of double-fabric to a single-fabric.

These provide alternatives to the methods more commonly used to make design details with two layers of fabric, such as hems, casings, decorative welts and tucks, or even pockets and yokes.

With this approach, both layers are done at the same time, which makes these kinds of things quicker and easier to do and eliminates the need for sewing them into place. You will find helpful illustrations and information about the conventional methods used in the section on Constructing a Fabric; the text here covers only what is _different_ about doing them with the double-fabric techniques described above.

❖ _Double-Fabric Borders_

The borders described here can be used on any garment, not just double-fabric ones. By far the most common edge added to any knitted garment is a ribbing. The new Double-Fabric Ribbing discussed here is a variation of a conventional single ribbing and it has some unique characteristics.

You can also use the double-fabric technique for a hem on a top or bottom edge, or at a side edge such as for a center front opening. Casings are made in a similar way—they are no more than hems with the sides left open so that elastic or a drawstring can be inserted. Welts are tiny rolled hems that create a cord-like edge for a decorative finish. (Casings, welts, and their larger cousins, tucks, can be introduced within a fabric as well; see Double-Fabric Insertion, below.)

When working design elements of this kind on picked-up stitches, you also have the option of using a technique that encloses the edge within a section of double-fabric. This provides a nice finish for a neckline or armhole, and is of particular value for a cut edge.

Double-Fabric Rib

I developed this ribbing after publication of the first edition of _Principles of Knitting._[†] It combines rows of Single Rib (which provide elasticity) with rows of double-fabric (which provide stability). It is an expansive and resilient fabric, yet it retains its shape in wear even when made with inelastic yarns like cotton, rayon, and linen. It has a handsome appearance, with a subtle hint of horizontal stripes cutting across the vertical lines of the stitch columns.

Double-Fabric Rib can be substituted for a conventional ribbing at the lower edge of a garment body or sleeve, and its expandability makes it particularly good for round necklines or turtleneck collars. In contrast, its inherent stability also makes it a good choice for lapels and button bands, which have a sorry tendency to stretch out of shape when done in the usual way.

[†] June Hemmons Hiatt, "Perfect Ribbing for All Fibers," _Colorful Knitwear Design_ (Newtown, Conn.: The Taunton Press, 1994), pp. 84–86, and _Threads Magazine_ (August 1993), 48:44–46.

The double-fabric portions of the ribbing are, in effect, tiny casings into which you can insert elastic. This makes it an excellent choice for the waistline of a skirt, for instance, where the additional weight of the garment may require more support, or for the lower edge of a sweater bodice that will get hard wear. And because the elastic will not show on either side of the fabric, the ribbing is particularly effective for sleeve cuffs that will be turned up.

There will be a slight difference in the size of the stitches in the Single Rib rows compared to those in the double-fabric rows (see Gauge for Double-Fabrics, above). You can choose to accept that as an attractive feature of the ribbing, but for a more consistent appearance use two sets of needles—a smaller size for the double-fabric rows, and a size larger for the Single Rib rows. In addition, you will need a pair of even smaller needles just to cast on and work the first row (see Alternating Cast-On).

To Cast On Ribbing

Use smallest size needle and work as follows:

1. Use Alternating Cast-On to place required number of stitches on needle.
2. With same size needle, work one row of Single Rib; match ribbing pattern to stitches in cast-on edge: Knit stitches that look like Knits and Purl those that look like Purls.

To Make Ribbing

Begin alternating two needle sizes: a small one for the Double-Fabric portion, and one that is a size larger for Single Rib rows.

1. With smaller size needle, work double-fabric pattern: Knit all Knit stitches of ribbing and Slip all Purl stitches with yarn nearside.
2. If working flat, turn and repeat Step 1. If working circular, Slip all Knit stitches with yarn farside; yarn nearside, Purl all Purl stitches.
3. With larger size needles, work two rows of Single Rib.
4. Alternate Steps 1–3 until ribbing is length required. End with Step 3, using whatever needle size is required for fabric above ribbing.

Note that one repeat of the pattern, Steps 1–3, adds just _three_ rows to the length; the Single Rib portion adds two rows, but only half the stitches are worked on each pass of the double-fabric pattern, making just one more row.

To make a more rounded edge (although one that is less resilient), do not work the row of Single Rib after casting on; instead, begin working Steps 1–4 immediately.

If you are working the ribbing out from the fabric on picked-up stitches, consider using the enclosed edge described for any border, below. When ribbing is complete, cast off while working the Single Rib pattern to preserve elasticity, or use Grafted Cast-Off for Ribbing.

To Insert Elastic

- The tiny casings in this ribbing are one row deep and will accommodate the yarn elastic commonly sold in knitting stores; thread through casing with a tapestry needle.

  For a circular fabric or one that was seamed, insert elastic through a stitch, since there will be no side opening.

Double-Fabric Rib. Elastic inserted; ribbing is relaxed.

Double-Fabric Rib.
Ribbing is stretched open to show elastic is hidden.

- For wider, flat elastic, make the casing deeper by working two or three rounds of the double-fabric pattern between rows of Single Rib.

  This will no longer be a true ribbing, but rather a border of tiny double-fabric casings with a bit of Single Rib in between; see Multiple Casings, below. Still, it is attractive and effective. Work the pattern with open sides so you can insert the elastic later with a bodkin.

Double-Fabric Enclosed Edge

Here is an alternative way to pick up stitches and add a border to a neckline, armhole, or center front opening. The edge will be enclosed within a row or two of double-fabric, which hides it completely and provides a very nice finish. The technique is also ideal for a cut edge.† Two sample patterns are provided; the first is a conventional Single Rib, and the second is the double-fabric equivalent of a hemmed border of Single Rib.

---

† I first saw this technique in an article by Bee Borssuck, "Knitting Round on Straight Needles," *Threads Magazine* (August/September 1987); it was later included in their book *Hand Knitting Techniques from Threads* (Newtown, Conn.: The Taunton Press, 1991), pp. 24–27. Ms. Borssuck was an extraordinarily innovative designer and teacher who discovered the wonders of double-fabrics for hand knits on her own.

The instructions are for working flat, such as for a center front border. If you are adding a border to a neckline or armhole and working in the round, change the double-fabric pattern accordingly.

Enclosing an Edge

1. On outside of edge: Use technique Picking Up to Enclose an Edge, working into every selvedge stitch and making a Yarnover between each picked-up stitch; turn.
2. On inside: Work Fabric B: Knit Yarnovers farside; Slip picked-up stitches that belong to Fabric A with yarn nearside.
3. On outside, begin border pattern (see below).

In Step 2, the Yarnovers are Knit farside so they will twist on discard to tighten them up (see Twist Stitches). If you are working circular, on the first round, Slip the picked-up stitches of Fabric A with the yarn on the farside, and Purl the Yarnovers of Fabric B farside.

Enclosed Edge with Single Rib Border

- Begin Basic Double-Fabric pattern and work to depth required to enclose edge, usually 2–4 passes depending upon thickness of fabric. Change to Single Rib; Knit Fabric A stitches, Purl Fabric B stitches. To finish border, use Joinery Cast-Off or Grafted Cast-Off.

Enclosed Edge with Single Rib Border: Inside detail.

Enclosed Edge with Single Rib Border: Outside.

Enclosed Edge with Single Rib Hem

- Work Basic Double-Fabric pattern 4–6 passes, as needed to enclose edge; continue as double-fabric, but change to ribbing pattern, alternating Knit and Purl stitches in Fabric A, and Knit and Purl stitches in Fabric B. To finish border, use Chained Cast-Off, working in pattern, or

Grafted Cast-Off for Ribbing. Enclosed section of edge will be in Stockinette, border above in ribbing.

A Chain Selvedge works well on a fabric that will have a border of this kind because it reduces the bulk of the enclosed edge. However, the number of stitches picked up is determined by the number of selvedge stitches (along with any on hold or cast-off around the opening), and because the stitches are interspersed on the needle, it is more difficult to use increases or decreases to adjust the number to whatever is needed for the width of the border (see Adjusting Number of Stitches).

Instead of changing the number of stitches on the needle, consider using Regauging, and adjust the needle size instead. Also keep in mind that working a double-fabric tends to enlarge the stitches slightly. Therefore, plan to use whatever size needle will make the enclosed portion fit properly, and then switch to whatever size is appropriate for the border. Try all this on a relatively large swatch before deciding how to work.

Double-Fabric Hems

A hem normally consists of an extra length of fabric turned to the inside and sewn in place. With the Double-Fabric technique, you can make the outside and inside portions of the hem at the same time and there is no need to sew the latter into place. Not only does this save time and effort, but the result is a a very nice finish. Also see the methods suggested for making Double-Fabric Casings, below, which are simply hems with open sides.

In these instructions, it is assumed that the hem is done in Stockinette. For tips about coordinating the width of a hem with that of the fabric above when other stitch patterns are used, see Hems, Facings, Pleats, and Tucks.

Hem at Bottom Edge

The cast-on edge forms the foldline of the hem. Half-Hitch Cast-On or Cable Cast-On will create an edge similar to that of a standard Purl Foldline. One side of Picot Cast-On also produces an attractive edge, and if you use Alternating Cast-On there will be no foldline, just a rounded edge.

- Cast on twice number of stitches needed for width of hem (according to gauge), and begin using a Basic Double-Fabric pattern; work number of rows required for depth of hem. Use Joinery Decreases to reduce stitch count by half, and then continue garment in single-thickness on remaining stitches.
- If stitch pattern of main fabric is not Stockinette, adjust number of stitches on needle according to gauge on next row to maintain even fabric width.

- For a flat fabric that will not be seamed, work hem using one yarn for both inner and outer portion; side edges will be closed.
- For a circular fabric or for a flat fabric that will be seamed, work with two supplies of yarn as described for Both Sides Open, above, and also see Double-Fabric Casings, below.

Hem at Top Edge

The double-fabric pattern for a hem at a top edge is the same as that used for a bottom edge, but it begins and ends in a slightly different way.

- Double number of stitches on needle; see Single- to Double-Fabric, above. Begin Basic Double-Fabric pattern and work hem. Finish hem with Joinery Cast-Off.

The instructions assume the hem and the main fabric are both Stockinette; if not, in the row below where the hem begins, adjust the number of stitches on the needle to half that required for the width according to gauge.

Vertical Hem on Added Stitches

This double-fabric border forms the equivalent of a hem that runs the length of one side of the main fabric; it is worked at the same time as the main fabric on stitches added for this purpose. This makes a nice edge for the side of a blanket or for the center front opening of a jacket.

In these instructions the hem is set on the right side of the garment section (as seen from the outside), and once you understand the concept it is easy enough to apply to a border at the left side or at both sides.

Due to the difference in gauge between a single- and double-fabric, the border may not fit smoothly unless made with a needle of a different size than that used for the rest of the fabric. Do a small Test Swatch of just the border to select a

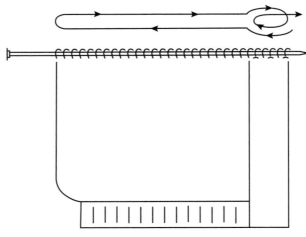

Vertical Hem on Added Stitches.

needle size that will produce a row gauge that closely matches that of the main fabric.

When using more than one needle, it helps to use a short circular one for the border because it will act as a stitch holder when not in use, but any double-point needle will do.

1. Cast on number of stitches required for width of single-fabric portion of garment, plus double number needed for width of border.
2. On outside, with smaller size needle, Knit Fabric A stitches of border, and Slip Fabric B stitches with yarn nearside. With main needle, continue across single-fabric width of garment section; turn and then work back across inside of main fabric to border.
3. With smaller size needle, Knit Fabric B stitches of border, and Slip Fabric A stitches with yarn nearside; turn. On outside, Knit Fabric A stitches of border; turn. On inside, Knit Fabric B stitches of border; turn.
4. Repeat Steps 2–3 for length of border.
5. If top of border will be picked up for collar, use Joinery Decreases to change to single-fabric, working toward main fabric; place border stitches on hold; if collar does not include border, use Joinery Cast-Off, worked in same direction.

Double-Fabric Casings

A casing at a top or bottom edge is a hem by another name, but the sides are left open so elastic can be inserted. The technique used here is also suitable for a hem in a flat garment that will be seamed, because the result will be smoother if the inner and outer portions of the side seam are sewn separately. You can work with one yarn or two.

Casing with Two Yarns

These instructions are for working the casing at a bottom edge; see below for how to add one to a top edge.

1. Make Slip Knot with two yarns and place on needle; do not count knot as stitch; discard at end of first pass. Cast on double number of stitches required for width of fabric.
2. Work double-fabric pattern as described in Both Sides Open, above, using one yarn for Fabric A, one yarn for Fabric B.
3. When casing is length required, break off one yarn and use Joinery Decreases to change to single-thickness fabric.
4. To finish, seam outer side edges, working from top down toward edge, and then turn to inside; insert elastic and then seam inner side edges from bottom up.

If you prefer, use a single yarn to cast on (perhaps in a contrast color for a decorative touch), and then attach second yarn to begin working double-fabric pattern. Also, consider using a thinner yarn for the inner portion of the hem to reduce bulk (for more information, see Gauge for Hems and Facings); try this on a Test Swatch first.

For a casing at a top edge, work as follows:

- Begin by doubling number of stitches on needle using second yarn; start with Step 2, above, and finish with Joinery Cast-Off in main or contrast-color yarn.

Casing with One Yarn

To make a casing or a hem with one yarn, use the technique described in Working One Set of Stitches, above.

1. Cast on double number of stitches required for width of fabric.
2. Begin double-fabric pattern, working *only* stitches of Fabric A; Slip stitches of Fabric B on every row, moving yarn nearside or farside as needed.
3. When casing is length required, work Joinery Decreases to change to single-thickness fabric.

The Fabric B stitches are never worked; the cast-on edge will be on the inside of the fabric, where the casing changes to a single-fabric.

To make an optional foldline on the middle row of the casing, work Purl on the outside of Fabric A.

To make a casing at a top edge, work as follows:

- Double number of stitches on needle, work casing as described above, and then finish with Joinery Cast-Off. Cast-off will be on inside of fabric.

Welted Edges

A welt is a tiny, rounded hem of about 3 to 5 rows, depending upon gauge (see Welts). It is a nice detail for an edge. It can be done when working flat or in the round, using either Knit or Purl or a combination of the two. (For a similar edge detail, see Knitted Cord.)

For a Welt at a top or bottom edge, work as described above for Casing with One Yarn. For an alternative at a bottom edge, begin with Alternating Cast-On and work a Basic Double-Fabric pattern for 3 to 5 rows and finish with Joinery Decreases.

Here are some suggestions for working a Welt on stitches picked up along a side edge. There are two options:

You can pick up the stitches in the conventional way; use a Chain Selvedge on the fabric to reduce bulk.

- On outside, pick up into every selvedge stitch along edge, turn, double stitches and work as described for Hem at Top Edge, above.

Alternatively, enclose the edge when you pick up the stitches for the welt; this is particularly nice for a cut edge.

Welt on Picked-Up
Stitches: Inside detail.

Welt on Picked-Up Stitches: Outside.

- Pick up stitches as described in Step 1 for Double-Fabric Enclosed Edge, above. Work number of rows needed to make Welt of size required and finish with Joinery Cast-Off as for a Hem at Top Edge.

A welt that encloses an edge generally requires one or two more rows than normal to accommodate the extra bulk.

A welt done on stitches picked up in the usual way is softer and lies next to the edge. One done on an enclosed edge wraps around the fabric, which makes it firm and tailored.

❖ Double-Fabric Insertion

The following applications are used to insert a portion of double-fabric within a single-fabric. Several interesting design elements—welts and tucks, or even yokes—can be added to a garment far more efficiently in this way than with the customary methods.

You can also add an interior casing at the waistline of a garment for elastic or a drawstring, or make multiple casings for decorative purposes. The technique is also an effective way to add pockets that require no sewing.

Insertion Welts and Tucks

As described above, a welt has a cord-like shape; a tuck is similar, but has more rows and a foldline so it lies flat. For more information, see Welts and Tucks.

Welts and tucks tend to widen somewhat because they are folded. You can mitigate their tendency to splay out by working with a smaller size needle; try this on a fairly wide swatch to select the needle size.

If the main fabric is not Stockinette, do a separate gauge and adjust the number of stitches in the main fabric to ex-

actly half as many stitches as needed before starting the welt or tuck; restore the original stitch count after the welt or tuck is complete.

Insertion Welts

- Double number of stitches on needle using one of techniques described in Single- to Double-Fabric, above. Begin double-fabric pattern, working only stitches of Fabric A; stitches of Fabric B are never worked; see Working One Set of Stitches, above.

  To complete welt, work Joinery Decreases across row and continue with single-fabric.

Insertion Tucks

A tuck is made in almost the same way as a welt, but is usually one-half to one inch in depth and has a foldline in the center row so it will lie flat.

- Work Tuck as for Welt, above, as many rows as needed for depth according to gauge; then work one row in Purl on outside to serve as foldline. Work same number of rows as before foldline, and finish with Joinery Decreases; continue with single-fabric.

Insertion Casings

A waistline casing for elastic or a drawstring can be inserted within the fabric using one of the approaches described for Both Sides Open, above. Work with two supplies of yarn, double the number of stitches on the needle, work the casing, and then use Joinery Decreases to return to a single-fabric.

If you want to use a drawstring instead of elastic, you will need openings on the outside of the casing at the center front, as well as at the sides. This is done by either changing the double-fabric pattern slightly or making a pair of buttonholes.

Drawstring Casing for Flat Fabric

In order to leave an opening at the center front of the garment, a flat fabric will need two casings, one on each side of a small group of stitches at the center front that remain single-thickness. In order to leave the side edges open, separate supplies of yarn are used for the inner and outer casings; you can break and reattach the main yarn as necessary, or use a second one in the same or a different color for the outer casing. Allow sufficient tails of yarn to hide during finishing; see Hiding Ends of Yarn.

Work with double-point needles or a circular one, and use the method described in Working One Set of Stitches, above; in this application you will be making the inner and outer portions of the casings separately, first one, and then the other.

1. Place markers on needle at either side of a group of stitches equal to about one inch at center of front garment section; number of stitches depends upon gauge.
2. On inside row, with main yarn, double every stitch except those in center portion. New stitches and center stitches belong to Fabric B; original stitches on either side of center belong to Fabric A and form right and left front outer casings. Turn.
3. Work even number of rows for inside portion of casing on Fabric B stitches only, Purl face of fabric is on inside of garment; Slip all Fabric A stitches and work center stitches as for single-fabric. End with inside row, break yarn.
4. Slide stitches to opposite needle tip and reattach yarn at other side. Beginning on inside, work left outer casing on Fabric A stitches only; Slip Fabric B stitches. At end of inside rows, turn at center front marker. Work same number of rows as inner casing and end with outside row at side edge; break yarn.
5. Slide stitches to right needle tip and attach yarn at other side edge. Work right outer casing on Fabric A stitches only; Slip Fabric B stitches. At end of outside rows, turn at center front marker. Work same number of rows as in Step 4 and end with inside row at side edge; turn.
6. On outside, work one row of Joinery Decreases on doubled stitches of casings to return to single-fabric.

The two side edges of the casing will be open at the center front; seam inside and outside of casing separately at sides of garment, as described for Casing with Two Yarns, above.

Drawstring Casing for Circular Fabric

1. Double all stitches except those in center front portion, as described above.
2. With main yarn, Knit only Fabric B stitches, and Slip Fabric A stitches with yarn farside; work as many rows as needed to complete inside casing.
3. Begin outer portion of casing on Fabric A stitches, working as for a flat double-fabric. [Knit across to right side of center front group of stitches, turn; Purl around to left side of center front group; turn]. Repeat between brackets for same number of rows as in Step 1.
4. On next round, work Joinery Decreases on all doubled stitches to return to single-fabric.

The last row in Step 3 is a partial inside row; it equalizes the number of rows on both sides; end where the round is joined at the side.

Buttonholes for Drawstring Casing

A pair of Eyelet Buttonholes set close together in the center front of the outer casing are nice for a thin drawstring. This application is done using a conventional double-fabric pattern, alternating rows of Fabric A and Fabric B.

1. On outside, work double-fabric pattern on Fabric A to within about half an inch of center front.
2. To work first buttonhole in casing, yarn nearside, Slip Fabric B stitch to right needle, make Purl-to-Purl Yarnover. Yarn nearside, rearrange next two stitches for decrease (see Decreases, above); with two Fabric A stitches together on left needle, move yarn farside and work Knit Right Decrease.
3. Work half-inch past center front of garment and then make second buttonhole in casing in same way. Complete pass.
4. On next pass, work Fabric B stitches; Slip Fabric A stitches, including Yarnovers.
5. On next pass, work Fabric A stitches, including Yarnovers to complete buttonholes.

You can make a larger Eyelet Buttonhole with a Double Yarnover, but this requires carrying the yarnover up an extra row and presents more of a challenge.

Multiple Casings

A series of Double-Fabric Casings, one immediately following the other, makes a charming overall fabric that looks like a down jacket. You can adjust the number of rows in the casings to create different looks—use large ones the entire length of a jacket, set several small ones at the lower edge of a bodice or sleeve for a decorative touch, or make a collar covered with tiny ones.

Here are some suggestions for how to make the transition between one casing and the next; all but one involve no more than a brief return to a single-fabric.

Decrease/Increase Method

1. Double number of stitches in single-fabric to make casing, work number of rows needed, and then reduce number of stitches by half, using Joinery Decreases.
2. Work one or two rows of single-fabric in any stitch pattern, and/or use a contrast color.
3. Double number of stitches for next casing. Repeat for as many casings as needed.

Multiple Casings: Decrease/Increase Method.

Single Rib Method

- Complete one casing. Change to a smaller size needle and work one or two rows of Single Rib (do not alter number of stitches on needle), working Knit on Fabric A stitches and Purl on Fabric B stitches. Return to larger needles and make next casing.

Threaded Stitch Method

A Threaded Stitch pattern also works well for the transition between one casing and the next. The stitches of the two fabrics will switch sides, binding the fabric together; there is no need to change the stitch count, and no rows are added between one casing and the next. If you are working with contrast-color yarns, one for each fabric, the colors will switch sides along with the stitches.

Complete one casing and then exchange pairs of stitches, working as for Joinery Decreases. Begin on outside; if a Fabric A stitch is first, Slip to right needle alone and then continue as follows:

1. Yarn nearside, insert right needle as to Purl into second stitch on left needle and pull over first stitch; retain stitch on right needle (do not discard), yarn farside, Knit remaining stitch of pair. Repeat on each pair of stitches; turn.
2. Make next casing: On first pass, Slip stitches worked on previous pass and work those that were pulled over and slipped; continue with double-fabric pattern.
3. Repeat Steps 1 and 2.

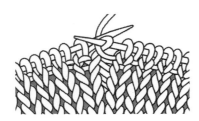

Threaded Stitch Method for making Multiple Casings: Step 1. Move yarn to nearside of stitch pulled over and Knit next stitch.

Quilted Casings

For a more pronounced effect, you can stuff casings with a filling of some kind.

- For a small casing of only a few rows, leave side edges open (see Open Side Edges, above), and then pull fill through with a bodkin; use material that will not shred, such as several strands of a softly spun bulky yarn.
- Or, insert roving or thick, soft yarn as you work. On one pass, carry yarn used for fabric in one hand and fill yarn in other hand, stranding it nearside and farside past every stitch so it lies between the two fabrics; see Purl Inlay for Warmth.

- To fill a deeper casing with quilt batting, separate the stitches onto two needles (see Separating Stitch Sets), insert material, and then hold the two needles side by side and use Joinery Decreases to close casing.

Quilted Casings.

Asymmetric Casings

For an interesting variation of the Multiple or Quilted Casings concept, close the casing with the Pullover Decrease technique described above, which causes Fabric A to rest one row lower than Fabric B. This provides a little extra ease on the outside so the fill can puff out more, while the inside face of the casing remains flat. Or, work one or two extra rows on outside fabric only, using the technique described in Working One Set of Stitches, above.

If you are making a casing for elastic, add an extra row or two in this way to the inside, instead; this will help it accommodate the extra thickness, leaving the outside undistorted.

Double-Fabric Pockets

These are the nicest pockets of all, I think. Making them with the double-fabric technique is quite easy, and because they are integral to the fabric there is no need to sew. For more information on pocket construction, see Pockets in the chapter on Openings.

To maintain a similar gauge in both the single-fabric portion and the visible pocket face, use a pair of needles one size smaller to work just the pocket stitches (a small circular needle works well for this because it acts as a stitch holder when not in use). Place the stitches of the main fabric on two other needles at each side of the pocket (if these are straight, use a third needle to work them).

Square Pocket

The pattern is written for a pocket and lining with Knit facing the outside of the garment.

Work the single-fabric to the row where the pocket begins, and continue as follows:

1. On inside, work to position for lower corner of pocket; place marker on needle. Work increases at base of pocket to double number of stitches for pocket lining, and then place marker at other corner. Work to end of single-fabric row. Turn.
2. On outside, work single-fabric to first marker; Knit Fabric A stitches, Slip Fabric B stitches with yarn nearside. At second marker, turn.
3. On inside, Purl Fabric B stitches, Slip Fabric A stitches with yarn nearside; at marker, turn.
4. On outside, Knit Fabric A stitches, Slip Fabric B stitches with yarn nearside; at marker, work single-fabric to end of row. Turn.
5. On inside, work single-fabric to first marker, Purl Fabric B stitches, Slip Fabric A stitches with yarn nearside; at second marker, work single-fabric to end of row. Turn.
6. Repeat Steps 2–5 until pocket is depth required.
7. Separate two sets of pocket stitches and cast off Fabric A; see Separating Stitch Sets, above; or, to cast off with stitches on needle, see Open Edge, One Yarn.

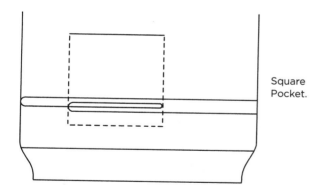

Square Pocket.

When starting the pocket in Step 1, the original stitches are for Fabric A, the outer portion of the pocket; the new, increased stitches are for Fabric B, which is the pocket lining.

To keep the open edge of the pocket from curling, work the last few rows of Fabric A in ribbing; see Double-Fabric Stitch Patterns.

Sloped Pocket

You can also make a sloped pocket opening with this technique. These instructions are for a right-hand pocket; reverse the instructions for a left-hand pocket. The outside portion of the pocket is worked somewhat as described in One Side Open, above, but in this case there are single-fabric portions to each side.

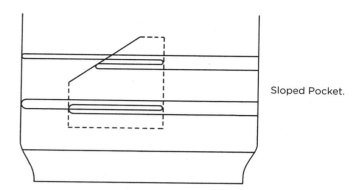

Sloped Pocket.

1. Work as described above for square pocket until interior pouch is depth required below where side opening begins.
2. On outside of single-fabric, work to first marker. Knit Fabric A pocket stitches, Slip Fabric B stitches with yarn nearside; with two stitches before second marker on left needle, adjust interspersed stitches and work Right Decrease. Turn.
3. Slip first stitch (the decrease stitch); Purl Fabric A stitches, Slip Fabric B stitches with yarn farside; at marker, turn.
4. Knit Fabric B stitches, Slip Fabric A stitches with yarn farside. At pocket opening, begin to work outside row of single-fabric pattern to edge; turn.
5. Work inside row of single-fabric pattern to pocket. Purl Fabric B stitches, Slip Fabric A stitches with yarn nearside. At second marker, begin working inside row of single-fabric pattern; turn at edge.
6. Repeat Steps 2–5 to make sloped edge until about one inch of pocket stitches remain interspersed on needle. Use Joinery Decreases to complete pocket and then work single-fabric across full width of garment section.

When the stitches are rearranged for the decrease in Step 2, a Fabric B stitch will become part of the main garment section to the left of the pocket; move the marker on the needle to reflect this, or simply take it off, since it will now be obvious where the pocket opening is located.

In Step 3, slipping the first stitch after the turn creates a Chain Selvedge on the pocket opening edge; you could work a decorative selvedge instead, which would help the edge lie flat.

To change the slope of the open edge, space the decreases out according to your stitch and row gauges (see Steps and Points for Gradual Slopes).

Yokes and Elbow Patches

For an interesting design detail and added warmth, consider a double-fabric yoke at the shoulder of a sweater or jacket. And you can add elbow patches to a sleeve using the same approach as described above for a patch pocket.

Shoulder Yoke

To begin yoke, work as for a Hem at Top Edge, above, using increases to change to a double-fabric. Shape the sides for armholes with decreases or increases as necessary (see Shaping for Double-Fabrics, above); to finish the top, use one of the following methods:

- To shape neckline opening of a yoke at center front of garment, use combination of Joinery Cast-Off and/or Joinery Decreases at top edge, as described in Vertical Hem on Added Stitches, Step 5, above.
- To slope shoulder, use Joinery Cast-Off in stepped fashion and then sew two shoulders together, or use Joinery Decreases in same way and then seam remaining stitches of two shoulders with Joinery Cast-Off.
- For more of a challenge but a nice result, use Short Rows for Double-Fabrics, described above, to slope each shoulder and then finish with Joinery Cast-Off.
- You can also insert batting into the yoke for extra warmth and a distinctive appearance. Work with Knit facing out on both sides, using double-fabric pattern for Working One Set of Stitches, above, shaping shoulders as needed. Separate stitches to insert batting as described for Quilted Casings, above, and then use Joinery Decreases and/or Joinery Cast-Off to finish.

Elbow Patches

Do you lean on your elbows? Then consider a double-fabric elbow patch to provide a little padding; think of it as a pocket that is closed at the top.

- Work as described for a square pocket, above, but instead of separating the stitches at the top to cast off the outside edge, work Joinery Decreases to complete the double-fabric portion and continue with the single-fabric.

  And, of course, you could actually pad the elbow patch with some thin batting, as for a Quilted Casing, above.

Singular Double-Fabrics

The Singular Double-Fabric technique is used to make a conventional single-fabric in the round. But instead of using a circular needle or a set of double-point needles, this technique is done on a set of straight needles, working back and forth just as for making a flat item.

You can make a circular garment of any kind or size in this way, but it is more often used for small items such as mittens, gloves, and socks. While many knitters thoroughly enjoy making these things in the conventional way (see Circular Knitting), some find managing the needles awkward and have trouble making a smooth transition at the intersections between them. Also, the fewer stitches there are on the needle, the more problems arise, and even experts can find this challenging—the needles seem to be all points and one of them will inevitably try to escape the job and hide under the sofa. The Singular Double-Fabric technique solves these issues.

The technique also makes it possible to work two circular items at the same time, but for this you must return to a set of double-point needles or one or two circular needles. For a project that employs this, try The Sock Trick, described below, and make two socks at the same time. Just the idea of doing this charms every knitter who hears about it, but the technique is aptly named because it is, indeed, somewhat tricky. I suspect few knitters will use it regularly, although it is a lot of fun to try at least once.

The first set of basic instructions here covers how to use the Singular Double-Fabric technique to make a simple cylinder open at one end and closed at the other. As unexciting as that might seem, it is useful for socks without heels, a child's mittens without thumbs, or even smaller things, such as the thumb of a mitten or the fingers of a glove.

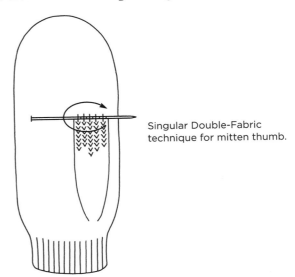

Singular Double-Fabric technique for mitten thumb.

The next set of techniques is for the options that make these garments fit better, like mittens with thumbs and socks with heels. Once you understand the basic concepts, you will be able to make even complex items using this approach—

Double-Fabric horse made by Beverly Royce.
Estate of Beverly Royce; photograph by Margaret Bruzelius.

the legendary stuffed horse made by Beverly Royce, which is illustrated here, stands proud as an example of the possibilities.†

In the instructions, the terms Side A and Side B refer to the two halves of the circular fabric and their respective sets of stitches; these might be the back and palm of a mitten, or the instep and sole of a sock. Two passes across the needle with the double-fabric method, one for Side A, the next for Side B, are equivalent to working one round in the conventional way on a set of double-point needles or a circular needle.

The applications described here make frequent use of the various special techniques for casting on and off, shaping, and separating or interspersing stitches—all of which are described in detail in Making Double-Fabrics, above. In some cases, no specific reference is given under the assumption that you are now familiar with how to work a specific technique, such as a decrease in a double-fabric. If you are at all uncertain about how to do any step, please look in that material. It is also assumed here that you are familiar with the Basic Double-Fabric patterns and no longer require instruction to move the yarn nearside or farside, as necessary, to Slip the interspersed stitches.

† Beverly Royce, *Notes on Double Knitting* (Pittsville, Wisc.: Schoolhouse Press, 1994).

❖ Singular Mittens and Socks

Mittens and socks are wonderfully easy to make with the Singular Double-Fabric technique. The instructions are written without specifying a stitch pattern or number of stitches; the concept then serves just as well for things like socks or mittens as it does for thumbs and glove fingers; it is up to you to decide matters of scale and detail.

When working in Stockinette, keep in mind that the most efficient option is to work with Purl on Outside, or Knit on Inside. However, with either of those patterns, the Purl side of the circular fabric will be on the outside as you work, so the item will need to be turned inside out when complete.

Tube Socks or Mittens

The technique has many applications, but tube socks are practical and easy as a first project and they are as nice for grown-ups as they are for children. Socks are often done with a variation of the Double-Fabric Double Rib pattern, below; by shifting the pattern one stitch to the left every one or two rows, the ribbing will spiral, which helps the socks shape to the foot without a heel. If your feet get cold in the middle of the night, you can pull on a tube sock any which way in the dark.

Working Edge to Tip

1. Use method described in Casting On for Circular Edge, above, to add number of stitches needed for full circumference.
2. Join round and begin a Basic Double-Fabric pattern, working stitches of Side A on one pass, and stitches of Side B on next pass; continue for as many rounds as needed for straight length of item.
3. Begin decreases at each side to shape tip (see Shaping Mitten Tips and Sock Toes, below), and finish using Grafted Cast-Off.

For something like a thumb or glove fingers, work the tube up from stitches either on hold or picked up around an opening; see Placeholder Thumb Opening, below.

Working Tip to Edge

1. Use Alternating Cast-On to add number of stitches needed for no more than half-inch in width.
2. Begin to work using a Basic Double-Fabric pattern, increasing at each side until number of stitches equals that needed for full circumference, and then work main portion to length needed.
3. To complete mitten or sock, either separate stitches and cast off in usual way, or see Open Edge, One Yarn, above.

If making a thumb, or fingers for a mitten or glove worked from the tip to the edge, place the stitches on hold instead of casting off.

Shaping Mitten Tips and Sock Toes

With the most common patterns used to shape the tip of a mitten or the toe of a sock, increases or decreases are set on either side of a pair of stitches at each side, every other round. This is done in the same way when using the Singular Double-Fabric method, except that the stitches must be rearranged first; see Shaping for Double-Fabrics, above.

Alternatively, eliminate the decorative column of stitches at both sides and simply work the shaping at the end of each pass; there is then no need to rearrange stitches. Or see the alternative discussed in Refolding the Fabric, above.

To create the type of slope used for most mittens or socks, either use double decreases or increases at each side on every other round, or single increases or decreases on every round. Or, devise a shaping pattern that creates a subtle curve instead of a slope; see Charting a Curve.

Thumbs

The double-fabric technique is a great asset for making anything small like a thumb for a mitten or glove; instead of fussing with a set of double-point needles, you can work on a pair of straight needles.

Here are the two most common approaches to making a thumb. Once you understand how it is done, you can apply it to making fingers for a glove.

Placeholder Thumb Opening

The simplest way to add a thumb to a mitten is to mark its position with a contrast-color yarn, as for the Placeholder Opening technique. These stitches are later removed, and the stitches above and below the opening are picked up to work the thumb.

The opening can be positioned at the side of the mitten or on the palm, according to the pattern, and this is done in the same way when working from tip down, or from edge up.

1. Use extra double-point needle and length of contrast-color yarn; in Side A work half number of stitches needed for circumference of thumb.
2. Slide stitches to right tip of needle. Pick up main needle again and work across placeholder stitches. Set aside extra needle and continue Singular Double-Fabric pattern to complete mitten.
3. To work thumb, use two needles to pick up and intersperse stitches from around opening. With left needle, pick up one stitch from below opening, one from above, and then Slip pair to right needle.

Withdraw placeholder yarn and repeat with next pair. Continue in this way to pick up all stitches; there will be one less stitch from above opening than from below.
4. Attach yarn and work thumb as described for mitten or sock, working edge to tip, as above.

When picking up stitches in Step 3, if there are gaps at the corner, pick up one or two extra stitches as necessary, and then decrease them again on the first round or two (also see information about Thumb with Gusset and Mini-Gussets, below).

Thumb with Gusset

A gusset is a diamond-shaped section of fabric added for ease and a better fit at the side of the mitten hand below the thumb. It can be worked up from the top of the border toward the base of the thumb, or from the thumb down. Tiny, mini-gussets are also sometimes added between thumb and hand of mitten to allow more freedom of movement.

Gusset from Wrist Up

Begin gusset increases above ribbing at wrist, two or three stitches in from one side; work as follows:

1. On first pass, work increase in Fabric A; on next pass, work matching increase in Fabric B. Continue shaping in same position every round or every other round, according to pattern, until number of stitches needed for full circumference of thumb has been added.
2. Slip interspersed gusset stitches to holder and then continue with remaining stitches to complete hand of mitten or glove.
3. To complete thumb, transfer interspersed gusset stitches to needle and work to tip as described above.

Gusset from Thumb Down

1. Work thumb from tip down and set aside.
2. Work hand of mitten from tip down to thumb position.
3. Intersperse thumb stitches on same needle with those of hand stitches and begin working them as one with Singular Double-Fabric technique, decreasing for gusset below thumb in same way that increases were used in above version.

Mini-Gussets

A mini-gusset consists of three or four stitches introduced between the thumb and the hand of the mitten; number of stitches depends upon gauge and size of mitten or glove.

Mini-Gusset Worked Up

1. Begin hand of mitten at wrist and work thumb gusset as described above; place thumb stitches on hold.
2. Increase 3 to 4 stitches in mitten hand; do not intersperse

stitches. Decrease same number of stitches on next two rounds.

3. Begin working thumb. For mini-gusset, pick up same number of stitches along base of mini-gusset in mitten hand; decrease stitches on next two rounds.

Mini-Gusset Worked Down

1. Work hand from tip down to position of thumb; on last two rounds, make increases at one side for mini-gusset.
2. Make thumb separately and add mini-gusset stitches at one side in same way; break yarn, leaving extra length.
3. Place needles with mini-gusset stitches of thumb and hand parallel; graft these stitches together with tail of yarn attached to thumb.
4. Transfer needle bearing remaining thumb stitches to right hand, and, with main yarn, begin working hand and thumb as one using Singular Double-Fabric technique, starting with Side A stitches of hand. Decrease on each side for main gusset below thumb as described above.

Singular Sock Heels

There are several ways to make sock heels, and all the conventional styles can be done with the Singular Double-Fabric technique.

A common type of heel makes use of a Placeholder Opening, and is done like a mitten tip; a heel with a similar shape can also be done with Short Rows. There is also the option of doing a heel flap and gusset. While this is somewhat more challenging than the other two styles, once you get the hang of it, it goes quite smoothly.

There are some differences in how these things are done with the stitches interspersed on the needle; however, if you are used to making socks, it should all seem quite familiar. Heels are usually done on half the stitches of the sock, which is quite convenient when using the Singular Double-Fabric technique because there is no need to count or redistribute stitches to other needles.

The patterns here are basic and intended to serve as examples; once you understand the concepts, they can be applied to sock patterns with different proportions and heel shapes.

Placeholder Heel

The heel opening is done in the same way regardless of whether you are working from edge to tip, or tip to edge.

1. Work to position of heel; with separate length of contrast-color yarn, work Side A stitches for Placeholder Opening. Slide stitches to right tip, take up main yarn, and work same stitches again.
2. Turn to Side B; on next pass, resume Singular Double-Fabric pattern and complete sock.

3. To finish heel, use two double-point needles to pick up and intersperse stitches from around opening, removing placeholder yarn, as described for Placeholder Thumb Opening, above.
4. Begin working heel stitches using Singular Double-Fabric technique, shaping at each side with decreases as for mitten or toe tip, above; to finish, graft stitches at center of heel.

Short Row Heel

To make a heel with the Short Row technique, work the sock either from the tip or from the edge to the position of the heel, and then finish the heel before continuing with the remainder of the sock.

The Short Rows are done only in the stitches of Side A of the sock; the stitches of Side B are never worked while the heel is being made (see Working One Set of Stitches, above). In most patterns, the heel is done on half the stitches and the center occupies one-third of these, but you can adapt the pattern to different proportions; the concept is the same.

Use Singular Double-Fabric pattern and work to position of heel.

1. Begin Decreasing Short Rows: Knit across outside of Side A stitches; wrap second-to-last stitch of heel; turn.
2. On next pass, Purl across inside of Side A stitches and wrap second-to-last stitch on other side of heel; turn.
3. Repeat Steps 1 and 2, working as for flat fabric on only Side A stitches; on each subsequent pass, wrap stitch before one previously wrapped.
4. When one-third of stitches remain active, reactivate those to each side: Knit across outside of Side A stitches and down side, working each wrap and stitch together, and then work last stitch; turn.
5. Purl across inside of Side A stitches, past center and down other side, working each wrap and stitch together; work last stitch and turn.
6. To make other half of heel cup, begin working Increasing Short Rows, again working only Side A stitches. Knit across outside of Side A stitches, wrap stitch to left of center third of stitches; turn.
7. Purl across inside of Side A stitches, wrap stitch to other side of center group of stitches; turn.
8. Repeat Steps 6 and 7, on each pass reactivating previously wrapped stitch, and then wrapping next one. On last two passes, reactivate second-to-last stitch on outside of Side A, work last stitch and turn; repeat on inside of Side A; turn.
9. On next pass, resume working Singular Double-Fabric pattern as before on both sets of stitches to make rest of sock.

Heel Flap and Gusset

These instructions for a heel flap and gusset do not specify which of the double-fabric patterns to use, so you can elect to work with Knit or Purl on the outside, and with any number of stitches in the usual proportions, or customized for fit.

All of the stitches for the sock are interspersed on a single-point needle with the center back of the sock at the right tip where the yarn is attached. Positioned in this way, the flap is folded vertically: half the flap stitches are Side A, half are Side B. The open side edges of the flap will be in the middle of the needle between the heel and the instep stitches; the latter remain inactive at the left end of the needle while the heel is made.

Work sock as for Singular Double-Fabric to position of heel. Then start at center of heel flap and work in AABB pattern sequence to leave two side edges open, as follows:

1. Work across on outside of Side A flap stitches to open edge, turn; work on inside of Side A stitches, slipping first stitch for Chain Selvedge; at center of flap, turn.

2. Work on inside of Side B flap stitches to open edge, turn; work on outside of Side B stitches, slipping first stitch for Chain Selvedge; at center of flap, turn.

3. Repeat Steps 1 and 2 for length of flap. For Stockinette Selvedge, do not Slip two stitches at open edges.

4. Continue with AABB pattern, but now begin to work decreases at each side of center group of heel stitches to cup heel according to pattern.
    - Start at center of heel flap; work across on outside of Side A to left of center group, rearrange stitches as necessary, and work decrease; turn. Work back across on inside of Side A, turn.

- Work across on inside of Side B and make matching decrease on other side of heel cup; turn, work across on outside of Side B to center of heel.
- Repeat this pattern as necessary to complete heel, and then pick up stitches on either side of flaps to join heel to instep of sock, as follows:

5. Start at center back and work across on outside of Side A heel stitches, pick up stitches along Side A of flap, and then work across remaining Side A stitches that have been on hold; turn.

6. Work across on outside of Side B stitches that have been on hold; pick up stitches along Side B of flap, interspersing each one with a stitch from Side A flap; continue across remaining Side B heel stitches to center back; turn.

7. Continue as for Singular Double-Fabric on all stitches of sock, working decreases for gussets on each side where heel flap meets instep. Rearrange stitches for decrease in Side A gusset, leaving pair of stitches in Side B for second decrease. Repeat on each round to complete gusset, and then continue with remaining portion of sock.

The Sock Trick

This clever technique was most famously described in Leo Tolstoy's *War and Peace*. In a charming scene set in the nursery, the servant Anna Makarovna is seated in a chair knitting a sock with the children gathered around her in a state of breathless anticipation. When the last stitch has been cast off, she pulls a second sock magically from within the first—she was actually knitting two at once. Tolstoy had more important things on his mind than the details of sock patterns, so it is not clear from his text just how Anna went about making two socks at the same time, but there are several versions here for you to choose from.†

The first set of instructions is for making a pair of bed socks with options provided for either a Short Row Heel or Placeholder Opening. Following that is the Ultimate Sock Trick for socks with heel flaps and gussets; while this requires patient attention to detail, it is not as difficult to do as you might think.

The technique is great fun to try at least once; however, it must be said that it offers little advantage over the usual way of making one sock. I suspect the only reason most knitters would do this more than once is to delight an audience of eager children, as Anna Makarovna did.

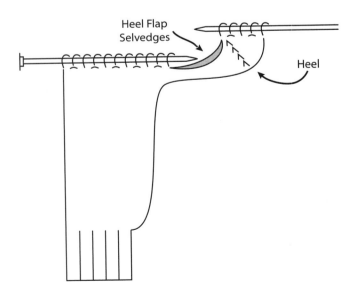

Singular Sock with Heel Flap: Pick up stitches along edges of Side A flap in Step 5, and then along Side B flap in Step 6.

---

† The Sock Trick was introduced to knitters in the United States first by Beverly Royce in her book *Notes on Double Knitting* (April 1981), and then by Margaret Bruzelius in "A Sock Within a Sock: The Enchanted 'War & Peace Method,'" *Vogue Knitting* (Spring/ Summer 1987), pp. 22–24.

Work with two supplies of yarn and a pair of short circular needles or a set of double-point needles, according to preference. You can hold two yarns at the same time; however, keep in mind that both yarns will need to be moved back and forth between each stitch in order to work with one and strand the other. Unless you are comfortable with that method, you may find it easier to work with one yarn at a time, doing one round for Sock A, and one for Sock B.

Top Down Pair of Socks

1. With two balls of yarn and one double-point needle, cast on as many stitches as needed for both socks, half with each yarn, as described in Casting On for Separate Fabrics, Method Two, above.
2. Redistribute the interspersed stitches to four double-point needles or two circular ones, and join the round. Begin to work using either a Single Rib or Double Rib pattern; see Double-Fabric Stitch Patterns, below.
3. Complete ribbing, change to Stockinette pattern, and work to row where heel begins.
4. Redistribute stitches so half are on one needle for heels, remainder divided between two others.
5. For Placeholder Openings, work Sock A heel stitches with contrast-color yarn as described above for Singular Sock Heels. Slide stitches to right needle tip and, with second contrast-color yarn, repeat for Sock B heel stitches.
6. Slide stitches to right needle tip and begin working with main yarns as before and complete socks.
   • Finish placeholder heel openings after socks are separated, as described for Singular Sock, above. Or, stop several rows above opening to do so: work heel in outer sock; for inner sock, pull it out between needles, work heel, and then tuck it back in before going on.
   • For Short Row Heels, work both heels before going on with remainder of sock, first in Sock A, and then in Sock B, as described above for a Singular Sock.
7. Complete foot of sock and then shape toes; to finish, remove needles and separate socks; pick up stitches of each toe on a pair of double-point needles, or intersperse them on one, and graft stitches.

For a heelless sock, work Steps 1 and 2 and then adjust the Double Rib pattern so it spirals, jogging the repeat one step to the left every other row; skip Steps 3–6, and finish as in Step 7.

Toe-Up Pair of Socks

In this case, each toe is first cast on and worked separately, and then one is put inside the other to continue with the stitches interspersed on a set of double-point needles.

To Make Toes

Cast on for each toe separately as described for Tube Socks or Mittens, Working Tip to Edge, above, and then use Singular Double-Fabric technique, shaping according to pattern. Work one toe with Knit facing out, and the other with Purl facing out.

Place one toe inside the other with either Knit or Purl facing out on both sides, (depending upon which double-fabric pattern you prefer), using one of the following methods:

• Separate and transfer stitches of one toe to pair of short circular needles or set of four double-point needles of same or smaller size than those used for socks; repeat with other toe. Put first toe inside second.

   Hold needles with two sets of Side A toe stitches parallel in left hand and intersperse stitches onto two double-point needles or a circular needle. Repeat with sets of Side B stitches.

• Alternatively, transfer Side A stitches of one toe to short circular needle or pair of double-point needles, and Side B stitches to straight double-point needle; repeat with other toe. Put one inside other and then continue as described above.

• Or, for a well-behaved yarn, simply take toe stitches off their respective needles, tuck one inside the other, line stitches up, and then pick up and intersperse them on needles, as described.

To Make Socks

With two sets of stitches for toes interspersed on needles, continue as follows:

1. Begin working socks in the round as for a Circular Double-Fabric, Two Yarn Circular Method: first Sock A on one round, and then Sock B on the next, or work holding two yarns and do both at once.
2. At position of heel, either insert stitches for Placeholder Opening, or work Short Row Heel pattern as described above, first in Sock A, and then in Sock B.
3. Work to where border begins; change to Single or Double Rib as described below in Double-Fabric Stitch Patterns. When ribbing is length required, use one of methods described in Casting Off for Open Edges, above.

The Ultimate Sock Trick

Here is the deluxe version of Singular socks with properly turned heels and gussets. This version is worked from the open edge down to the toe; if you prefer to work from the toe up, the heel flap and gussets are done in the same way, but they will be reversed in the sock. You might want to try the

Singular Sock described above before doing this; the methods are nearly the same.

1. Use two yarns and Casting On for Separate Fabrics, Method Two; place all stitches for both socks on straight double-point needle. After casting on, distribute stitches evenly to four double-point needles or two short circular needles; first stitch on each needle should be nearside stitch of outer Sock A.

2. Begin double-fabric pattern, using one yarn for outer Sock A, and other yarn for inner Sock B. Work to where heel begins. For stitches on double-point needles, redistribute, with half on one needle for heel flap, and remaining stitches evenly distributed to two needles.

3. Begin heel flaps, working back and forth as for a flat fabric using a Basic Double-Fabric pattern.

4. When flaps are length required, cup heels, making decreases on either side of center third of stitches, according to your pattern.

5. On outside of Sock A, work across to left side of center group of stitches, rearrange stitches as necessary, and make decrease; slide stitches back to right needle tip.

6. On inside of Sock B, work across to same position and make next decrease; turn. On outside of Sock B, work across to other side of center group of stitches and make decrease; slide stitches.

7. On inside of Sock A, work across to same position and make next decrease; turn.

8. Continue to make pairs of decreases at each side of heel, in each sock, until only center stitches remain.

9. On outside, work across Sock A heel stitches, and then pick up stitches on left side of heel flap. Continue around remaining Sock A stitches on other two needles, and then pick up stitches on other side of Sock A heel flap.

10. Repeat Step 9 for Sock B, but intersperse stitches picked up on each side of flap with those already picked up on each side of Sock A flap.

11. Begin working decreases for gussets at intersection between flaps and remaining stitches of socks; rearrange stitches to work first decreases in Sock A, and then work matching decreases on pairs of stitches left by this step in Sock B.

12. Continue in this way until stitches picked up along flaps have been decreased and original stitch count is restored. Complete feet of socks, shaping and grafting toe tips as described above.

Decorative Techniques for Double-Fabrics

Once you understand how to work the Basic Double-Fabric techniques, you will find it relatively easy to incorporate simple stitch or color patterns. Stitch patterns of mixed Knit and Purl are most suitable, but you can also make use of any others that are done on a single stitch, such as Slip Stitches and Twist Stitches.

Fortunately, a much wider range of color patterns can be used for these fabrics. Stripes and simple Stranded Color patterns are easy to manage and can be done as color reversals on opposite sides of the fabric.

For Double-Faced fabrics, however, it is not simply a matter of using a color pattern for decorative purposes; it is that the color pattern technique creates the *structure* of the fabric as well as its surface appearance. The yarns travel back and forth between the two sets of stitches on the needle, binding the two fabrics together to such an extent that the result resembles a single-fabric, but it has two outside faces.

By necessity, the color techniques used for these remarkable fabrics are introduced here only in their simplest form because the written patterns can be very lengthy and difficult to follow. Fortunately, even the most challenging of these patterns can be charted using the new system described in Charted Color Patterns. These special charts make the patterns considerably easier to do and also make it possible to adapt conventional Stranded Color and Mosaic patterns to Double-Faced Fabrics. This is important, because there are few published patterns of this kind available and even fewer of them have been charted.

❖ *Double-Fabric Stitch Patterns*

The patterns provided at the beginning of this chapter introduced how to Knit or Purl on either face of a double-fabric. Only a slight modification of those methods is required to work a pattern of mixed Knit and Purl on either or both fabric faces. (If you are unfamiliar with the method used to write the instructions, see Written Stitch Patterns.)

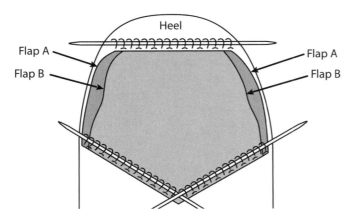

The Ultimate Sock Trick. Heel complete; ready to pick up flap edges in Steps 9 and 10.

Knit/Purl Stitch Patterns

To get a sense of the possibilities, cast on a multiple of four stitches, enough for a 2- to 4-inch swatch, and do a few rows of the following sample patterns: Single Rib, Double Rib, and Double Seed Stitch.

Instructions are provided for working with either one yarn at a time or two, and are suitable for working flat or in the round (such as for Singular Socks); it is assumed that a Fabric A stitch is first on the needle.

Double-Fabric Single Rib

Work with one yarn or two, as follows:

One-Yarn Method

- One yarn, every pass: [yarn farside, Knit 1, yarn nearside, Slip 1, Purl 1, Slip 1] repeat between brackets. Turn if working flat.

Two-Yarn Method

- Yarn A and Yarn B, every row: [Both yarns farside, with Yarn A Knit 1, Yarn A nearside; with Yarn B Knit 1, with Yarn A Purl 1, Yarn B nearside, Purl 1]; repeat between brackets. Turn if working flat.

Double-Fabric Double Rib

Cast on a multiple of eight stitches. The pattern has a pair of nested repeats, each one with two stitches, and each one done twice; these are alternated across the row (for more information about repeats, see Written Stitch Patterns).

One-Yarn Method

- One yarn, every pass: *2[Yarn farside, Knit 1, yarn nearside, Slip 1]; 2[Purl 1, Slip 1]*; repeat between asterisks. Turn if working flat.

Two-Yarn Method

- Yarn A and Yarn B, every row: *2[Both yarns farside, with Yarn A Knit 1; Yarn A nearside, with Yarn B, Knit 1]; 2[with Yarn A Purl 1, Yarn B nearside, Purl 1, Yarn B farside]*, repeat between asterisks; turn if working flat.

Double-Fabric Seed Stitch

There are two versions of Seed Stitch, one a variation of Single Rib, the other a variation of Double Rib; depending upon whether you are working with one yarn or two, use the appropriate pattern above as a model. These instructions are for working with one yarn; once you get the idea, you can modify the pattern to work with two, if you prefer.

- For Seed Stitch, cast on a multiple of four stitches. Work two passes as for Single Rib, above; on next two passes

work sequence: Yarn nearside, Purl 1, Slip 1, [Yarn farside, Knit 1, yarn nearside, Slip 1, Purl 1, Slip 1], repeat between brackets; end yarn farside, Knit 1. Alternate the two patterns for each round.

In other words, always Slip Fabric B stitches with yarn nearside; for Fabric A, position yarn as needed to either Knit a stitch with Purl below it, or Purl a stitch with Knit below it.

- For Double Seed Stitch, cast on a multiple of eight stitches; work pattern repeat for Double Rib, as given above, for two rows. On next two rows, start with the second of the nested repeats (the Purl stitches), followed by the repeat with the Knit stitches.

Double-Fabric Brocade Patterns

Once you understand how to do the patterns above, it should be clear how to work any Brocade-type pattern of mixed Knit and Purl stitches.

You can work a pattern on one side and do the other side in plain Stockinette, do both sides with the same pattern, or, for more of a challenge, use one pattern for Fabric A and a completely different one for Fabric B. For the latter, it is generally easier to work with one yarn and read one chart at a time, working the pattern for Fabric A, and then the one for Fabric B.

Also keep in mind that you can work patterns of this kind in a Singular Double-Fabric, which makes it possible to do a decorative pattern on the back of a mitten or the instep of a sock, and work plain Stockinette on the palm or sole, respectively.

❖ Double-Fabric Color Patterns

Customary methods of creating color patterns can be used for a double-fabric with little modification, and they are particularly well suited for use with any of the Insertion or Singular Double-Fabric applications discussed above.

To try the following techniques, use a pair of double-point needles and cast on enough stitches to make a sampler 4 or 5 inches wide.

To close the side edges, either add selvedge stitches and work them with both yarns held as one whenever they are together at the same side, or wrap the two yarns around each other to carry the color not in use up the edge, if necessary.

Horizontal Stripes

Stripes are easy and fun to do; you can work the same stripe on both faces, do a stripe on one face and not the other, or make stripes in different colors on each side.

These instructions are for simple one- and two-row stripes, working flat with Knit on the outside of the double-fabric.

The first group of patterns is for working with one yarn at a time; the instructions for working with two yarns at a time are below.

One-Row Stripe

Cast on and work several rows of a double-fabric pattern in the main color. Work a one-row stripe only in Fabric A, as follows:

1. Knit Fabric A stitches with stripe color, Slip Fabric B stitches; Slide.
2. Purl Fabric B with main color, Slip Fabric A stitches; turn.
3. Knit Fabric B stitches with main color; turn.
4. Knit Fabric A stitches with main color.

One-Row Color-Reversal Stripes

For one-row color-reversal stripes on both sides, change the sequence slightly.

1. Knit outside Fabric A with stripe color; Slide.
2. Purl inside Fabric B with main color; turn.
3. Knit outside Fabric B with stripe color; Slide.
4. Purl inside fabric A with main color; turn.

Two-Row Stripe

Fabric A has a two-row stripe; Fabric B is plain.

1. Knit outside Fabric A stitches with stripe color; turn.
2. Purl inside Fabric A stitches with stripe color; turn.
3. Purl inside Fabric B stitches with main color; turn.
4. Knit outside Fabric B stitches with main color; turn.
5. Continue with main color only, working double-fabric pattern on outside of Fabric A on one pass and outside of Fabric B on next pass to location of next stripe.

To make a stripe in Fabric B, in the same or a different color, attach another yarn for Steps 3 and 4; carry main yarn up side to use again with Step 5.

This pattern is an AABB sequence; it could also be done as ABBA, as follows:

- Knit outside Fabric A, Slide; Purl inside Fabric B, turn; Knit outside Fabric B, Slide; Purl inside Fabric A.

Working Stripes with Two Yarns

If you are comfortable holding two yarns at the same time, doing stripes is very easy.

- For one-row stripes in a color reversal, maintain yarns in same hands at end of row. On one row, use Yarn A for Fabric A, Yarn B for Fabric B; on next row, use Yarn B for Fabric A, and Yarn A for Fabric B.
- To make multi-row stripes, at end of row, wrap two yarns around each other to close side edge and then change yarns from one hand to the other, using same yarn for same fabric.

  To make next stripe: Maintain yarns in same hand at end of one row; transfer them on subsequent rows to continue color.

Stranded Color Patterns

Stranded Color patterns also work well for a Basic Double-Fabric. The pattern can be the same on both sides, or done with one side as a color-reversal, or you can even work different patterns on each side.

To give you an idea of how this works, here is a simple checkerboard pattern.

Double-Fabric Checkerboard

This is a color-reversal pattern—a dark square on one side will have a light square on the other side of it—although in such a simple arrangement it is difficult to see this because the two sides will look the same.

The pattern has the virtue of being easy to explain, and the important thing is to understand how it is done so you can apply it to a more complex Stranded Color pattern, if you prefer. Should you want to do so, it is only practical to work from a charted pattern—or from two of them, if you want a different pattern on each side. For another method of working somewhat similar reversible patterns, see Double-Faced Fabrics, below.

The instructions use the abbreviations C1 and C2 for "Color 1" (dark color) and "Color 2" (light color) yarns, respectively. Cast on a multiple of eight stitches; establish the pattern with a stitch of the nearside fabric first on needle. The pattern requires slipping groups of four stitches; after doing so, stretch them out on the right needle to allow enough yarn to the strand before working the next stitch, as when working a Stranded Color pattern.

Double-Fabric Checkerboard.

One-Yarn Method

1. First Pass: C1, Fabric A: [2(yarn farside, Knit 1, yarn nearside, Slip 1), Slip next 4 stitches, moving yarn nearside or farside as necessary]; repeat between outer brackets. Slide.
2. Second Pass: C2, Fabric A: [Slip next 4 stitches, moving yarn nearside or farside as necessary; 2(yarn farside, Knit 1, yarn nearside, Slip 1)]; repeat between outer brackets. Turn.
3. Repeat Steps 1 and 2, working same pattern in stitches of Fabric B.
4. Repeat Steps 1–3 again, to make two rows of pattern in each fabric.
5. Repeat Steps 1–4, but use C2 to work Step 1 and C1 to work Step 2 on each side; light-color squares are above dark-color squares, and vice versa.

To make a two-stitch vertical stripe instead of a checkerboard, repeat only Steps 1–3.

Two-Yarn Method

Alternate colors to make pattern first in Fabric A, and then in Fabric B.

1. First Four Passes: *2(yarns farside, Knit 1 with C1, yarns nearside, Slip 1); 2(yarns farside, Knit 1 with C2, yarns nearside, Slip 1)*; repeat between asterisks. Turn.
2. Next Four Passes: Change colors; work first repeat with C2 and second repeat with C1.

In Step 1 dark and light squares alternate for two full rounds (four passes), which makes two rows in the same pattern on both sides of the fabric; in Step 2 light and dark squares alternate for two full rounds.

Singular-Fabric Checkerboard

It is even easier to do a basic Stranded Color pattern when using the Singular Double-Fabric technique because you are simply making a conventional single-thickness fabric, while working in the round in an unconventional way.

Work with one yarn or two, first across the stitches of Side A, and then those of Side B; Slip the interspersed stitches in the usual way and move one or both yarns as needed. It is, of course, easiest to do this with Purl facing out, but most knitters prefer Knit facing out since it is easier to see the pattern develop.

Double-Faced Fabrics

These remarkable fabrics are made using the Basic Double-Fabric techniques in combination with Interwoven Color patterns, which are specialized adaptations of Stranded Color and Mosaic techniques.

Instead of strictly maintaining the separation between two sides in the usual way for a double-fabric, here that rule is broken. On any pass across the needle, a yarn is used for all stitches of the same color in both sets of interspersed stitches. Because the yarns travel back and forth between the two sides of the fabric, they are interwoven throughout their length and

Double-Faced Fabric: Color Reversal. Diamond pattern.

Double-Faced Fabric: Unlike Reversal. Cross and Stripe.

width and are no longer separable; this creates a hybrid fabric, half-way between a double-fabric and a single one.

Furthermore, the characteristics of the fabric are different depending upon the type of color technique used. Stranded Color patterns produce a slightly thicker fabric with Stockinette on both sides, while Mosaic patterns make a fabric that somewhat resembles a Single Rib.

These patterns may consist of the same motifs but reversed, with the yarn that makes the pattern on one side being used for the background on the other, or they can be entirely different. Also note that while patterns of this kind are conventionally called "color" patterns, they can be very effective when done with yarns of the same or similar color but with contrasting textures.

Interwoven Stranded Color patterns are ideal for a reversible garment such as a sleeveless jacket, while the resilient Interwoven Mosaic patterns are particularly appropriate for cuffs that turn up, or for collars and lapels. The two types are very effective when used together in one garment, but either will also work well when combined with conventional single-fabrics.

Some interesting patterns can also be done with a modification of the Twined Knit technique, where Purl stitches and running-thread strands are used on the outer faces of the fabric.

While the Double-Faced technique is rarely seen in contemporary knitting except in its simplest form, it is an old one, and there are beautiful, finely wrought nineteenth-century examples.† I suspect it fell into obscurity because the written instructions are very lengthy and difficult to follow, even when the pattern itself is relatively simple.

For this reason, the technique is introduced here in its simplest form; more information can be found in the chapter Charted Color Patterns. That material includes instructions for not only how to read and write the new specialized charts for these patterns, but also how to turn conventional color patterns into ones you can use for a double-faced fabric.

❖ Double-Faced Stranded Pattern

To give you an idea of how the technique is done, here are the instructions for making the same checkerboard pattern described above for a double-fabric, but rewritten here to produce a double-faced fabric, instead.

† For stunning examples of several double-faced items in the Museu Textil i d'Indumentaria, Barcelona, see Montse Stanley, *Reader's Digest Knitter's Handbook* (Pleasantville, N.Y.: Reader's Digest Association, 1993), p. 172.

Double-Faced Checkerboard

There are two versions of the Interwoven Stranded Color checkerboard pattern here; the first is done with one yarn at a time, the other is done holding two.

You may want to work a simple color-reversal pattern of this kind with both yarns at the same time because you can see the pattern develop immediately on the right needle, which is not the case when using one yarn at a time. However, with more complex patterns, it may be either impossible to do so or not worth the mental strain.

One-Yarn Method

1. First Pass: C1: [2(yarn farside, Knit 1, yarn nearside, Slip 1), 2(yarn farside, Slip 1, yarn nearside, Purl 1)]; repeat between brackets. Slide.
2. Second Pass: C2: [2(yarn farside, Slip 1, yarn nearside, Purl 1), 2(yarn farside, Knit 1, yarn nearside, Slip 1)]; repeat between brackets. Turn.
3. Repeat Steps 1 and 2.
   This completes two rows of pattern on each side of fabric.
4. Next Four Passes: Change colors; use C2 in Step 1 and C1 in Step 2.

Two-Yarn Method

To work a pattern of this kind with both yarns, you can hold one in each hand, or both to the left or right, but keep in mind that it will be necessary to Purl with both hands.

Also note that the instructions refer to moving the yarns nearside or farside, since both must be moved after every stitch; one is moved to place it in position to work the next stitch, and the other is moved to strand it between the two fabric faces.

1. First Pass: [2(yarns farside, with Yarn A Knit 1; yarns nearside, with Yarn B Purl 1); 2(yarns farside, with Yarn B Knit 1; yarns nearside, with Yarn A Purl 1)]; repeat between brackets. Turn.
2. Second Pass: [2(yarns farside, with Yarn B Knit 1; yarns nearside, with Yarn A Purl 1), 2(yarns farside, with Yarn A Knit 1; yarns nearside, with Yarn B Purl 1)]; repeat between brackets. Turn.
3. Repeat Steps 1–2 to complete second row of pattern in both fabric faces.
4. Next Four Passes: Alternate, doing Step 2 first and then Step 1.

Double-Faced Twined Knit

The unique decorative patterns used in the Twined Knit technique can also be adapted for a double-faced fabric. For a single-fabric, the technique is done with two supplies of yarn and the patterns are made with Purl stitches and running thread strands arranged on a background of Knit.

When these kinds of patterns are adapted for use with the Double-Fabric technique, all that is required is to strand the yarn wrong—on the outside of the other fabric face instead of between the two—which binds them together to create a Double-Faced fabric.

The patterns are noticeable when done in a single color; however, two colors can also be used to make vertical stripes and checkerboard patterns that create lively, optical effects.

Double-Faced Twined Knit pattern. Solid color reverse.

Shaping a Double-Faced Fabric

Shaping a Double-Faced Fabric is much the same as for a Basic Double-Fabric; it is easiest to do at the edges, and if increases or decreases are set within the fabric, what is done on one side must be done in the same position on the other side.

Because the yarns travel back and forth between the stitch sets, in some cases you can work an increase or decrease on both sides, and not wait to turn to the other side before doing the second one. However, the first priority is to maintain the integrity of the pattern, and so this may not always be possible.

Short Rows are not suitable for use with double-faced fabrics because there is no "inside" where the wraps can be hidden.

CHAPTER 16

Inlay

The Inlay technique is used to weave a secondary material into the stitches of a knitted fabric as it is made, either to create a decorative pattern or for utilitarian purposes. Because the inlay material is never used to make any of the stitches, the fabric usually has little resilience, resembling a woven more than a knit. For this reason, it is often recommended for a garment that would benefit from being stabilized, such as a straight skirt or perhaps a pillow cover, but it has advantages that recommend it for other items as well.

The ideal inlaid material is a narrow ribbon, but you can use any yarn in a contrast color or texture, including those that would be either too delicate or too textured to draw through with a needlework technique. While the Basic Inlay technique is primarily used to make simple stripes, some stitch patterns, as well as Stranded Color or Intarsia patterns, can be adapted for this purpose.

Purl Inlay is a variation that has both decorative and practical applications. It can be used to create an all-over color pattern with a unique surface texture, but is also used to weave in a soft wool or roving on the inside of a jacket or a mitten for extra warmth, or, in contrast, it can be used to add elastic to a waistband or cuff to guarantee its resilience.

Basic Inlay

The Basic Inlay technique is most often done on a plain Stockinette fabric because the added material is intended to be the primary focus and draw the eye. Typically, the strand is drawn on the outside of the fabric past every other stitch, or, at most, across pairs of stitches—a strand much longer than about ¼ inch is not advisable, both because it becomes increasingly difficult to control the tension as you work, and because it will be prone to snagging.

The description of how to do the technique is brief because it is so simple; the instructions here are followed by some suggestions for how to manage the yarns, as well as information about adapting various types of decorative patterns for this purpose.

❖ Basic Inlay Technique

If making a flat fabric, use selvedge stitches and attach the inlay material to the side edge, as you would a new supply of yarn. At the end of each row, work the selvedge stitch with the main yarn and the inlay material held together to anchor the strand at the side edge. Turn, and either Slip the first stitch for a Chain Selvedge, or work it with one or both yarns together for a Stockinette Selvedge.

Working a Basic Inlay Pattern
- For pattern, bring Inlay material to outside of fabric and work next stitch with main yarn; for background, bring Inlay material to inside of fabric and work next stitch.

Keep the stitches fully stretched out on the right needle when stranding past them so the inlay material is not so loose that it puckers, nor so tight that it constricts the intervening stitches.

Managing Width of Fabric
After working the first few rows, stop to check the width of the fabric; use the finished measurement from the schematic for this purpose, because the dimensions of a garment will change when it is dressed (see Dressing the Fabric).

- Lay tape measure on table and place fabric on top; hold on one side and stretch out other side to finished width. If Inlay material is too tight or too loose, use tip of needle to gently ease strand into place so it lies flat and smooth.

Recheck the width every inch or so. If the fabric looks too wide or the inlay material looks too loose, it is relatively easy to adjust.

- Pull strand out at selvedge to gather fabric slightly, and then ease stitches evenly around it across row; when it is correct width, cut loop at selvedge and knot material so it will not come undone. If fabric is too narrow, the only choice is to rip back and redo it.

Handling Inlay Material

There are two ways to handle the Inlay strand, both borrowed from methods used for the Stranded Color technique. The most efficient approach is to hold the main yarn in one hand and the inlay material in the other, as for Two-Hand Stranding; because the inlay material is never used to form a stitch, the technique is easier to do when used for this purpose.

However, if you find it difficult to handle two yarns simultaneously, or are having trouble regulating the tension on the inlay material with that method, you can use the Slip Stranding Method instead.

When working a Stockinette fabric, it matters very little how you hold the yarns, as long as you are consistent. However, there is a subtle but significant difference in the way the inlay material forms the pattern if it is held to the right or left, and this can be important when adapting a stitch or color pattern for this purpose.

Two-Hand Stranded Inlay

- If the inlay material is held to the right, it will strand above the running threads and the pattern will occur in the same row as the new stitches on the right needle, as with a Stranded Color pattern.
- If the inlay material is held to the left, it will strand below the running threads, and the pattern will occur in the row below the right needle, as is true of stitch techniques; see Color and Stitch Techniques.

Slip-Stranded Inlay

Work with a pair of double-point needles or a circular one, as follows:

1. First Pass: Work all stitches with main yarn; Slide stitches back to right needle tip.
2. Second Pass: Take up Inlay yarn and Slip every stitch, weaving yarn past stitches nearside or farside, according to pattern.

The pattern forms in the same row as the new stitches, which is suitable for use with Stranded Color patterns, as discussed below; however, it can be problematic when used with stitch techniques.

Inlay for Markers

There are occasions in knitting when it is helpful to mark a line along which you will later work, such as when it is necessary to pick up stitches within a fabric or to sew on something like a patch pocket. While the marker can be threaded in later with a tapestry needle, it can sometimes be difficult to work into exactly the right stitches and rows that way.

Instead, the marker yarn can be inserted with Basic Inlay. Select a contrast color in a smooth yarn or embroidery thread so it can be easily removed later without fraying the stitches or leaving lint behind.

❖ *Decorative Inlay Patterns*

It is easy to create stripe and twill patterns with inlay material and there is no need to do much, if any, advanced planning, which means you can improvise a bit. However, you can also adapt some Stranded Color and several kinds of stitch patterns for use with inlay material. Here are some ideas you might want to try.

Inlay Stripes and Twills

It is very easy to make simple horizontal, vertical, or diagonal stripes with the Inlay technique, or to do basic checkerboard-type patterns.

Inlay Stripes. Basic Inlay with variegated ribbon.

- Bring inlay material to outside of every other stitch, and stagger pattern row by row as for Seed Stitch, or use a Double Seed Stitch pattern, stranding past two stitches on two rows.
- To make inlay stripes, alternate inlay with plain rows done with main yarn alone.

  Or, use inlay technique for every row and change color of added material after several rows.
- For vertical stripes, bring inlay material to outside to strand past one or two stitch columns, always in same position for length of fabric.

  To make a wider vertical column, use an uneven number of stitches, with inlay material visible on odd-numbered stitches in one row of column, and even-numbered stitches in the next.
- For diagonal stripes and twill patterns of various kinds, work as for a vertical stripe, but shift pattern one stitch to left or right every row or two.

Stranded Color Patterns and Inlay

Some Stranded Color patterns can be adapted for the Inlay technique, but it is best to select those that create the pattern with no more than two stitches together. Simply use a normal color chart and substitute the inlay material for every contrast-color stitch, stranding it on the outside of the fabric while working all the stitches with the main yarn; see Charted Color Patterns.

If the pattern requires the inlay material to be stranded past more than two stitches on the inside, use the Weaving-In technique to prevent long strands from being snagged in wear. Alternatively, weave in on every stitch using Purl Inlay, below, which also helps maintain even tension as you work.

When using the technique for the entire fabric, you can hold the inlay material in either hand because it is of no consequence if the pattern appears in the row of discarded stitches or with those still on the needle.

However, if you are holding the inlay material on the left (see Two-Hand Stranded Inlay, above), it does matter when making stripes with plain areas in between. When it is time to change the color of the background yarn, do so when working the last row of the inlay pattern; the main yarn will form the new stitches on the needle and the inlay material will appear in the discard row below the right needle.

Stitch Patterns and Inlay

Brocade patterns of mixed Knit and Purl stitches can also be adapted for Inlay; work the fabric entirely in Stockinette and strand the inlay material on the outside of the fabric whenever the pattern calls for a Purl stitch. Here again, limit yourself to patterns that will require stranding past no more than two Purl stitches.

Alternatively, you can use the main yarn to work the pattern

Inlay Diamond Pattern. Inlay yarn substituted for Purl stitches in pattern.

in Knit and Purl, and strand the inlay material on the outside past every Knit stitch. When working this way, you will need to hold the inlay material on the left so it will appear with the Purl stitches in the discard row below the right needle.

A variety of other stitch techniques can be combined with inlay materials. The easiest approach is to work inlay on the plain rows between decorative pattern rows. However, you can also strand the inlay material through the background to highlight decorative patterns that include Slip Stitches, Crossed Stitches, or Bobbles, for instance. In some cases, you might want to rewrite a pattern to put an uneven number of stitches between pattern motifs so you can strand past odd-numbered background stitches on one row and even-numbered ones on the next for a Seed Stitch effect.

You might also consider using a hybrid technique, working some of the decorative stitches with the inlay material (such as a Bobble, perhaps), and stranding past background stitches as described for Basic Inlay, above. With all of these, you will want to hold the inlay material on the left, so it appears in the same row as the discarded stitches.

If you prefer to use the Slip Stranding method in combination with a stitch pattern of some kind, the material must be inlaid first, with the stitches worked according to pattern on the next pass. Depending upon the characteristics of the inlaid material and where it appears in the pattern, you may find it challenging to work this way if the material covers the stitches to such an extent that they become difficult to work; a Test Swatch should tell you quickly whether this is the case.

Finally, if you customarily hold the yarn to the right and prefer to work with one yarn at a time, you can also stop and pick up the inlay material before and after each stitch, bringing it to the nearside or farside as necessary for the pattern. This is a very slow way to work, but would be fine for small areas, and it provides better control of tension than other methods.

Purl Inlay

Purl Inlay is a variation of the Weaving-In technique done with Stranded Color patterns, where it is used when necessary to anchor one or the other of the yarns to the inside of the fabric if a strand would otherwise be too long.

The Purl Inlay technique described here is also done in Stockinette with two yarns, but one yarn is used for all the stitches, while the other yarn is simply woven in above and below the Purl nubs, and is attached by the running threads on either side. Because the inlay material follows a more sinuous path through the stitches than is the case with a Basic Inlay fabric, these fabrics are somewhat more resilient.

There are two decorative, all-over patterns done in Reverse Stockinette (Purl on the outside of the garment). With one, the strand passes above the Purl nubs in one stitch column and below it on the next and every row is the same, creating a vertical effect; with the other, the pattern is staggered for a handsome cell-like effect. To vary this somewhat, you can make Purl Inlay stripes alternated with stripes in plain Knit.

The technique can also be used to form motifs of one kind or another by working a defined area in Purl Inlay on a Stockinette ground. For the latter, either weave the material in on the Purl side of the background stitches to carry it across the row until needed, or work as for Intarsia, with a separate Inlay strand introduced for each motif. Also see the information on the Inlay Intarsia technique, below, where the contrast-color yarn is woven in across the row until needed for a motif.

Purl Inlay, staggered pattern.
Inlay material in dark color.

Purl Inlay, vertical pattern.

There are also two practical applications. The technique has traditionally been used to weave in a soft wool on the inside of a mitten or jacket for the thermal benefit it adds, and it can also serve as a means of incorporating elastic into a ribbing.

❖ Basic Purl Inlay

By far the easiest way to work Purl Inlay is to hold the inlay material in the left hand, the main yarn in the right; for illustrations, please see Weaving-In Yarns. The instructions here cover only the slight modifications needed when the technique is used for this purpose.

It is somewhat more challenging to do the technique while holding the inlay yarn on the right and the main yarn to the left, but it can be managed. And, while it is possible to hold both yarns to the left or right and weave in a strand from time to time in a Stranded Color pattern, it is not practical to work that way when weaving in on every stitch, as is done here.

If working a flat fabric, add selvedge stitches and use them to secure the inlay strand at each side, working these as described in Basic Inlay, above; they are not mentioned in the patterns below and, of course, are not needed for a circular fabric.

Inlay on Left, Main Yarn on Right

1. On outside, with both yarns on nearside, move inlay strand away from needle tips to nearside, pass stitch yarn between strand and needle, and Purl next stitch.
2. Insert right needle tip into next stitch as to Purl, move inlay strand against right needle, pass stitch yarn to nearside of strand to wrap on needle tip and Purl.
3. Repeat Steps 1 and 2 across row, and on all rows for circular fabric.
4. On inside, with both yarns on farside, move inlay strand to farside away from needle tips, pass stitch yarn between strand and needle, and Knit next stitch.
5. Insert right needle into next stitch as to Knit, move inlay strand against right needle; pass stitch yarn to farside of it to wrap on needle tip and Knit.
6. Repeat Steps 4 and 5 across row.

The pattern can be done in the same way on every stitch column, or staggered, simply by starting every other row with Step 2, instead of Step 1.

Inlay on Right, Main Yarn on Left

1. On outside, with both yarns on nearside, insert right needle into stitch as to Purl, move main yarn to nearside, away from needle tips, pass inlay yarn under right needle and up between tips; do not draw through stitch.

    Lay main yarn against needle to left and then unwrap inlay yarn from needle, drawing it firmly to right on nearside, leaving main yarn wrapped on needle; draw yarn through stitch as to Purl.
2. Hold inlay yarn to right and Purl next stitch with main yarn.
3. Repeat Steps 1 and 2 across row, and on all rows for circular fabric.
4. On inside, with both yarns on farside, hold main yarn away from needle, insert right needle into stitch and wrap inlay yarn as to Knit; do not draw through stitch.

Wrap main yarn around right needle as to Knit, and then unwrap inlay yarn, passing it back under needle to farside, leaving main yarn wrapped on needle; draw yarn through stitch as to Knit.

5. Hold inlay yarn to right and Knit next stitch with main yarn.

6. Repeat Steps 4 and 5 across row.

❖ Purl Inlay Applications

Here are a variety of ways to make use of the Purl Inlay technique for practical purposes.

Purl Inlay for Warmth

Inlay was traditionally used as an easy way to add considerable warmth to mittens;† for this purpose, however, the Purl face of the fabric is on the inside. The woven strands not only add another layer, but they cover the spaces between the stitches, making the fabric more windproof.

The ideal material for this purpose is roving, but any softly spun yarn will do. When planning a project, keep in mind that considerably less yarn is needed for a row of inlay than for stitches because it goes straight through; this is a good way to use up small amounts of leftover yarn.

You can also use the same yarn for both the fabric and the inlay, in which case a center-pull ball is convenient. Draw one strand from the outside of the ball, the other strand from the center as for Twined Knit (another technique that can be used to add warmth to a garment, but it maintains the resilience of a fabric).

Even though the inlay material is on the inside, it can show through slightly on the outside, particularly if it is thick, if the fabric is loosely knitted, or if the garment is stretched in wear. To minimize this effect, select an inlay material that is close in color to the main yarn, or, for a tweedy look, choose a soft and fuzzy yarn in a strongly contrasting color so it will peek through.

Purl Inlay for Reinforcement

The Purl Inlay technique can also be used to reinforce the palms of mittens, the heels and toes of socks, or even for something clever like the equivalent of elbow patches for a sweater or jacket that will get hard wear. For these purposes, consider a fine yarn to reduce bulk, and perhaps a true worsted yarn, or a sock yarn with added nylon for strength and resistance to abrasion.

---

† See the charming book of mitten patterns by Robin Hansen with Janetta Dexter, *Flying Geese and Partridge Feet: More Mittens from Up North and Down East* (Camden, Maine: Down East Books, 1986).

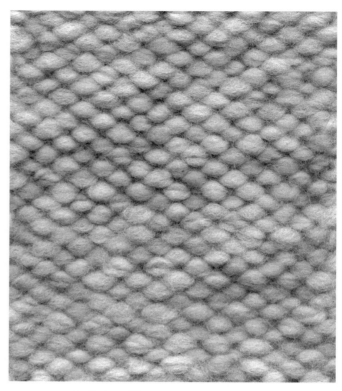

Purl Inlay with roving on inside of fabric.

Purl Inlay peeking through on outside of fabric.

Purl Inlay for Elastic

Ribbing at waist or wrists can often pull out of shape with wear, particularly when done in cotton or linen, since these fibers have little elasticity of their own. Adding elastic thread on the inside of the ribbing with Purl Inlay will definitely enhance the resilience and maintain it over time.

Use the fine yarn-like elastic sold on a spool, which comes in a variety of colors, or even soft ⅛-inch flat elastic if something more substantial is needed and the main yarn is bulky. While the elastic is unlikely to show on the outside, particularly if the color is close to that of the yarn, it will show on the inside, so this is not something you would want to do if the cuff is likely to be turned up in wear (for an alternative that hides the elastic completely, see Double-Fabric Rib).

This application works best with a Single Rib; the elastic is attached to the fabric on either side of each Purl stitch and strands past all the Knit stitches. It can also be used for a Double Rib; however, the elastic will strand past pairs of Knit stitches and may snag in wear.

As with all Inlay applications, stop at the end of a row to check the tension on the strand and make any necessary adjustments before going on. The elastic should strand smoothly through the stitches and draw the ribbing together in a natural way so it retains enough capacity to stretch as much as needed in wear.

If working a flat fabric, add selvedge stitches and begin the ribbing sequence with Knit/Purl, or Knit two/Purl two; use the selvedge stitches to secure the inlay strand at the side edges as described in Basic Inlay, above; they are not mentioned in the patterns.

Hold the elastic in your left hand and the main yarn in your right hand and begin on an outside row. (It is more difficult to manage the tension on the elastic when it is held in the right hand, because that method requires temporarily wrapping the inlay material on the needle, which stretches it; see Basic Purl Inlay, above.)

Inlay Elastic for Single Rib

1. On outside, with main yarn and elastic on farside, insert right needle into stitch as to Knit, move elastic against right needle, pass yarn to farside of it and wrap around needle; draw yarn through and discard stitch.

Inlay Elastic for Single Rib.

2. Move elastic away from needle to farside, bring main yarn between needle tips to nearside, and Purl.

3. Repeat Steps 1 and 2 across row. For circular fabric, work every row in same way. For flat fabric, turn.
4. On inside, hold elastic away from needle to nearside, move yarn between needles to farside, and Knit 1.
5. Move yarn between needles to nearside, hold elastic against tip of left needle, move right needle tip to farside of it and insert into next stitch as to Purl, pass yarn to nearside of elastic and around needle; draw yarn through and discard stitch.
6. Alternate Steps 4 and 5 across row; turn.

Inlay Elastic for Double Rib

1. On outside, with yarn and elastic on farside, hold elastic against right needle, pass yarn to farside of it, and Knit 2.

Inlay Elastic for Double Rib.

2. Move elastic away from needle to farside, bring yarn between needle tips to nearside, and Purl 2.
3. Repeat Steps 1 and 2 across row. For circular fabric, work every row in same way. For flat fabric, turn.
4. On inside, begin with yarn and elastic on nearside, move elastic away from needle to nearside, pass yarn between needles to farside, and Knit 2.
5. Move yarn between needles to nearside, hold elastic against tip of left needle, move right needle tip to farside of it and insert into next stitch as to Purl, pass yarn to nearside of elastic and around needle; draw yarn through and discard stitch. Repeat for second Purl stitch.
6. Alternate Steps 4 and 5 across row; turn.

Purl Inlay for Yarn Ends

The Purl Inlay technique can be used to hide the tails of yarn left where one supply stops and a new one is attached, although I think there is a more effective way to do this; see Hiding Ends of Yarn.

Inlay Intarsia

Purl Inlay is also used with a specialized type of Intarsia technique adapted for making circular garments. The contrast-color yarn is woven in on the inside of the garment until needed for a motif, and then it is used for the stitches while the main yarn is woven in on the inside, instead. If the fabric is relatively loosely knit, the woven-in yarn will peek through on the outside, creating a tweedy look. For more information, see Woven Intarsia.

CHAPTER 17

Twined Knit

A glove was uncovered in an archaeological excavation of an copper mine in Falun, Sweden. Now believed to date from around 1680, it seemed to have been knitted in an unusual way. This aroused the curiosity of Birgitta Dandanell, who learned it was made with a technique still in use in parts of rural Scandinavia. Called *Tvåändsstickning* in Sweden, and *Tvebanding* in Norway, it was largely unknown outside these regions until she wrote a book about it.†

As I was finishing the first edition of *Principles of Knitting*, I came across Ms. Dandanell's book *Tvåändsstikkat* and was able to visit her and then to learn something about the technique in Dalarna, Sweden, where it is still done. At the time, no information was available in English, my publishing deadline was at hand, and, while I included the material, it felt rushed and incomplete. Therefore, I am pleased to have the opportunity to expand somewhat here on this fascinating technique and, for those who want more details, to recommend Robin Orm Hansen's fine English translation of Ms. Dandanell's book, *Twined Knitting*.‡

The remarkable structure of this fabric is created in a very simple way: by working with two ends of one ball of yarn (or two balls) and alternating the yarns to the stitches, wrapping them around each other at every change. The strands cover the openings in the fabric and double its thickness.

The yarn used is typically finely spun wool that is worked on thin needles at a gauge of about 8–12 stitches to the inch (old examples often have stitch counts twice that, but many were slightly fulled). The result is a dense fabric with a complex structure that traps heat and keeps out the wind. These qualities were an obvious benefit in the cold

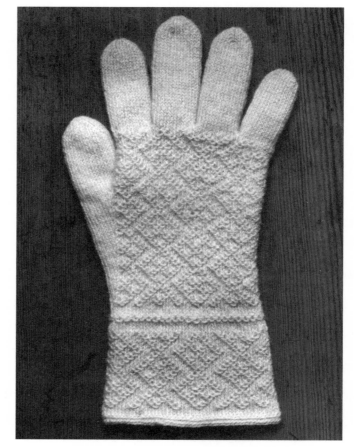

Twined Knit glove. Dalarnas Museum, Falun, Sweden.

---

† Birgitta Dandanell and Ulla Danielsson, *Tvåändsstickat* (Stockholm, Sweden: Dalarnas Museum and LTs Forlag, 1984). Translated by Robin Orm Hansen as *Twined Knitting* (Loveland, Colo.: Interweave Press, 1989).

‡ There was no English name for the technique when I first wrote about it; I called it "Stranded Brocade" because the term seemed to reflect something about the appearance of the decorative patterns. *Tvåändsstickat* in Swedish, *Tveband* in Norwegian, and *Tvebind* in Danish are translated as "Two-End" knitting or "Twisted" knitting. However, Hansen and Dandanell selected "Twined Knit" as the English translation, a choice I find euphonic and appropriate and am pleased to adopt here. (Although I confess a preference for Tvåändsstickat; unpronounceable as it seems to those who do not speak Swedish, I like the way it looks on the page.)

Scandinavian winters, but the handsome appearance of Twined Knit was also appreciated for its own sake, and garments of cotton or linen were often made for summer use.

The Knit face of the fabric looks like plain Stockinette, although the columns of stitches are somewhat narrower and have a slight twist, giving them a distinctive verticality. On the other side of the fabric, there is what looks like a firmly plied cord or braid below the Purl nubs, made up of the strands that pass behind each stitch. It has a handsome appearance and is sometimes used on the outside (or an edge is turned back to display it).

Furthermore, the Scandinavian knitters developed unique decorative patterns suggested by the inherent nature of the Twined Knit technique. These are simple Knit and Purl patterns that are enhanced by stranding a yarn past some of the stitches on the outside of the fabric. The decorative possibilities are expanded with the use of color patterns, and the finished garments were often lavishly embroidered.

Because the yarns are changed after every stitch, Twined Knit is not quick to do, and therefore was primarily used for small things like mittens and socks, for decorative borders on larger garments, and for knitted sleeves that were attached to plain bodices of woven fabric.

Basic Twined Knit

Twined Knit is no more than Knit and Purl stitches, but it takes practice to learn how to change the yarns and wrap them around each other between each stitch. Doing so is the equivalent of plying them together into a single, thicker yarn, and they need to be separated periodically in order to continue.

How firmly the yarns ply together and how challenging it is to separate them again depends on three factors: the type of yarn used, the direction in which the yarns are twined, and how the yarn is wrapped around the needle to form each stitch. The solution is to take these factors into consideration and change the method of doing Twined Knit slightly depending upon the kind of yarn you are using.

The first set of instructions below describes the technique as it is done with the traditional yarn, followed by a slight modification of the method that is best used for the type of yarns more commonly available. Also included are some variations of the technique that produce a fabric with most of the same characteristics but a slightly different appearance. Finally, there are some suggestions for how to untwine the yarns once they become so tangled you cannot go on.

But first, a brief explanation about what happens to the yarns when they are twined.

❖ *Yarns for Twined Knit*

Twined Knit is typically done with a two-ply Z-twist wool, of about 1800–2000 yards per pound, similar to lace or sock yarn. If you want the real thing, the yarn is available by mail order, but any good-quality wool of a similar thickness will do just fine, even if it is the more readily available S-twist. Also, a relatively smooth yarn, ideally one that is worsted-spun, will display the characteristics of the fabric and any decorative patterns to best advantage. (For more information about Z- and S-twist yarns, see Spinning and Plying Yarns.)

Traditionally, the yarn is wound into a center-pull ball, with one end drawn from the middle and the other from the outside, which is why the technique is also called "two-end knitting"; however, you can work with two separate balls if you prefer.

When doing Twined Knit with Z-twist yarns, the two yarns are wrapped around each other in a clockwise direction between each stitch. This removes the twist from a yarn of this type; it will get softer and thicker and the plies may begin to separate slightly. As a result, the two yarns will wrap around each other relatively loosely, and the twined area can be pushed toward the ball several times before it becomes so tangled that it is necessary to stop and separate the two.

However, if S-plied yarns are twined in this same direction, twist is added. Each yarn will get tighter and thinner and begin to kink up on itself; the two will tangle together easily, making it necessary to stop more often to separate them. Furthermore, many S-plied yarns are spun and plied more tightly than the yarns traditionally used for Twined Knit, which makes them even more prone to this. If possible, select a yarn that is more loosely plied; count how many plies there are in an inch; the lower the number, the better choice it will be.

The best solution is to twine S-plied yarns in the opposite direction and, if necessary, also change the direction in which the yarn is wrapped on the needle for the stitches; see S-Twist and Combined Method, below.

❖ *Twined Knit Methods*

It is apparently traditional to use either the Right-Finger Method or the Right-Hand Method for Twined Knitting.[†] As far as I know, knitting belts or sheaths (see Supported Needle

---

[†] Both the Right-Hand and Right-Finger Methods of knitting were traditional in Sweden well into the twentieth century, when the Left-Hand (Continental) Method of knitting was introduced in the schools. However, many knitters retained a preference for the older way of working and continued to use it at home; see *Twined Knitting*, pp. 8–9. Photos from Denmark show knitters using the Right-Hand Method for Twined Knit, holding the yarn with thumb and forefinger; see Tove Frederiksen, *Tvebinding* (Copenhagen: Clausen Bøger, 1982).

Methods) are not used in Scandinavia, but they are a great help with this technique; with the right needle held firm, the hand is free to manage the yarns and the work goes very smoothly. While the technique was not done with the Left-Hand (Continental) Method, you should be able to adapt the basic concepts to working that way, if you prefer.

The process of changing the yarns stitch by stitch will seem rather awkward at first, but it is a relatively simple movement; your hands will soon find their way and move along quite smoothly, if not quickly. Console yourself in knowing that even knitters who have used Twined Knit for a lifetime are not particularly speedy when doing it!

These fabrics are typically worked at a very firm tension, but do not worry about maintaining tension on the yarn not in use; once it is drawn out of the way, let it trail past your finger until needed. When you pick it up again, tighten the stitch it is attached to and then strand it past the intervening stitch. Once you are under way, the yarn used last will be attached to the first stitch on the right needle; the yarn to use next will be attached to the second stitch on the right needle.

Make a Slip Knot joining the two yarns and cast on an even number of stitches (do not count the knot); use Half-Hitch Cast-On or Braided Cast-On (which is more authentic). If working in the round, which is customary, distribute the stitches to four double-point needles; drop the Slip Knot from the needle and join the round to begin. Twined Knit can also be worked flat, and it is far more convenient to do so when first learning the technique, as well as when trying patterns or making a Gauge Swatch.

Twining Z-Twist Yarns

When working with Z-twist yarns, the two are wrapped around each other clockwise between each stitch, with the yarn used last passed over to the farside, and the yarn to use next drawn under to the nearside. The result will be twined strands that slope up to the right under the Purl nubs on the inside of the fabric.

There are three options here for how to do this.

Method One

1. Yarn last used is on nearside of forefinger, and other yarn is on farside of middle finger. Insert right needle into stitch and pinch fabric below crossed needle tips with left fingers.
2. Move right hand down, away from needle tips to put slight tension on yarns, and rotate back of hand toward farside so yarn used last is above other yarn.
3. Lift forefinger to release upper yarn and then move it down on nearside, insert it between two yarns, and pick up lower yarn on back of finger.
4. Withdraw middle finger and then reinsert it between two yarns and draw upper yarn to farside.

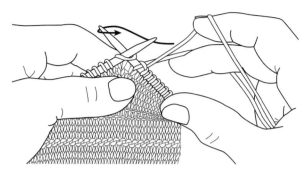

Twining Z-Twist Yarns, Method One: Steps 3–4.
Fingers in position for next stitch.

When the yarn is picked up this way, it will pass down the far-side of your forefinger to the needle tip, instead of down the nearside in the usual way. Because the yarn is farther from the tip of the needle, you will need to bend your forefinger slightly to wrap it for the next stitch. If you find this awkward, try one of the methods below.

Method Two

- Hold yarns and rotate hand as described above, but use thumb and forefinger to pick up yarn to use next.

Either hold yarn that way to make next stitch, as for Right-Hand Knitting, or do so as an intermediate step, next moving forefinger under strand so it passes down nearside of finger to needle tip.

Method Three

Here is the variation that I think is easiest to do if you prefer to carry the yarn on your forefinger in the usual way, with the yarn passing to the needle on the nearside. Instead of keeping the yarn not in use on the farside of the middle finger, keep it on the nearside of the thumb instead.

1. After last stitch, yarn last used is on farside of forefinger, other yarn on nearside of thumb; do not rotate hand.
2. Lift thumb to release yarn on nearside; reach thumb under that yarn and then over yarn last used to draw it back under to nearside.

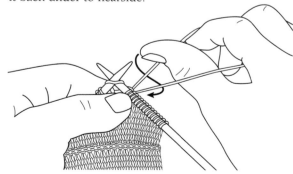

Twining Z-Twist Yarns, Method Three: Step 2.
Reach thumb over yarn last used and draw to nearside.

3. Reach forefinger down on nearside of yarn released from thumb and pick it up to use next.

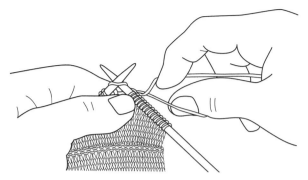

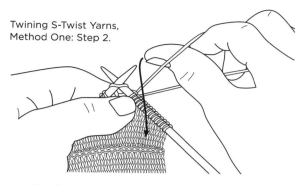

Twining S-Twist Yarns, Method One: Step 2.

Twining Z-Twist Yarns, Method Three: Step 3. Pick up other yarn on forefinger for next stitch.

Twining S-Twist Yarns

If you are working with the more readily available S-twist yarns, they will not ply as strongly together if you twine the two in the opposite direction, counter-clockwise; the one used last is passed over to the nearside, the one to use next is drawn under it to the farside.

The structure of the fabric will be the same, and there is a negligible difference in its appearance—the strands on the inside will slope up to the left instead of up to the right and the Knit stitches will lean slightly to the left instead of to the right.

Insert the needle into the stitch, pinch the fabric below cross, and then draw your hand down to put tension on the yarns; change yarns in one of the following ways:

Method One

When twining in this direction, it is a little easier if you hold the yarn not in use on the nearside of your thumb as described in Method Three, above. Work as follows:

1. Move hand down to put tension on yarns and then rotate back of hand toward *nearside* so yarn last used is above other one.

2. Drop forefinger down to release tension on yarn last used, and simultaneously move thumb up on farside of that strand and draw it to nearside. Press thumb against yarn on side of needle to hold in position.

3. Move forefinger down on farside and reinsert between two yarns to pick up yarn to use next.

Twining S-Twist Yarns, Method One: Step 3.

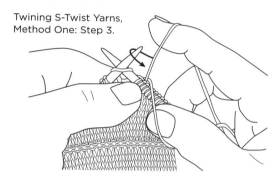

Purl side of Twined fabric. Bottom: Z-Twist Twining. Top: S-Twist Twining.

Method Two

If you prefer to hold the yarn not in use on the farside of your middle finger, change the yarns as follows:

1. Rotate hand as described above, but yarn last used will then be *below* other one.

2. Drop yarn last used from forefinger and raise finger under top yarn to pick it up.

3. Remove middle finger from between two yarns and reinsert it from farside to nearside, below yarn now on forefinger; pick up yarn last used and draw it to farside.

I find it helpful to push the lower yarn down slightly with my thumb to keep the yarns separated enough to reinsert my middle finger.

S-Twist and Combined Method

If you are working with an S-twist yarn that seems to tangle more than usual, it often helps to use the Combined Method of knitting, wrapping the yarn as for Standard Knit on one row, and as for Knit Over on the next (wrapping the yarn over the needle). Basically, one method compensates for any twist added or removed by the other. Of course, how much it helps depends on how many stitches there are on the needles, but when working something small like a sock or a mitten, you should be able to work longer stretches without having to stop and unwind the yarns.

Change the yarns between stitches as described above, but work them as follows:

To Work Circular

- On one round use Knit Over to turn stitches on right needle; on next round Knit turned stitches farside and wrap yarn under, in standard way.
- When working on a set of double-point needles or with the Two Circular Needles Method, on every round, use Knit Over on stitches of one needle, always knitting turned stitches farside, and use Standard Knit on stitches of next needle.

To Work Flat

- On inside rows, use Purl Under to turn stitches on right needle; on outside rows Knit turned stitches farside and wrap yarn in standard way.

❖ Unorthodox Approaches

There are two alternatives to working Twined Knit in the traditional way. While both will reduce or eliminate the problems with tangled yarns described above, they each produce a slightly different fabric in appearance and structure.

Alternating Yarn Changes

This method produces a fabric that is structurally the same as Twined Knit, but it looks somewhat different. On the Purl side of the fabric, the strands slant up to the right on one row and up to the left on the next. Traditionally, this is used for decorative purposes on the outside of the fabric, but not for an entire fabric (see Twined Purl Rows, and also Herringbone Braid, both below).

The Knit face is also changed, because the stitches lean slightly to the right on one row and to the left on the next, producing a zig-zag effect; it has a certain charm.

1. On one round, change yarns as described above for Twining Z-Twist Yarns.
2. On next round, change yarns as for Twining S-Twist Yarns.

While the two yarns will wind around each other over the course of one round, they will unwind on the next.

Stranded Two-End Knitting

Instead of twining the two yarns around each other after each stitch, you can simply draw each one directly past an intervening stitch, just as you would do for a Stranded Color pattern. This eliminates the problem of tangled yarns entirely and produces a warm and resilient fabric.

However, it does not qualify as a true Twined Knit. The Knit stitches will not have the distinctive striated appearance and

the Purl side will look quite different. Instead of rows with a cord-like appearance, the running threads will form a series of little swags. While this is unlikely to be seen on the inside of a garment, it is attractive.

Stranded Two-End Knitting.

In every other respect, the work proceeds in the same way; you can draw two strands from one ball of yarn or use two separate balls. Furthermore, all of the stitch and color patterns described below can also be used with this option, so it offers a reasonable alternative if you want to use the decorative patterns of Twined Knit with fewer of the real technique's challenges, and it also produces a softer fabric.

❖ Tips for Working Twined Knit

Here are a few suggestions on how to deal with the inevitable yarn tangling that accompanies this technique.

Separating Twined Yarns

When the yarns have been twined together to the point where the plied area is against your hand, push it down toward the ball of yarn.

- Insert left finger into space between two strands to maintain separation between them near the needle; then use fingers of right hand to push wound portion toward ball. Pick up yarns as before and continue.

You can do this several times before it becomes necessary to stop and unwind them completely in order to continue.

Spin the Ball

If you are drawing two ends from a single ball of yarn, which is the easiest way to work, you can simply hang the ball from the yarn and let it unspin, as follows:

1. Attach the yarn to the ball in one of the following ways so no more will pull free.
   - Wrap the yarns on your hand to form a big half-hitch, put it around the ball and tighten firmly.
   - Use a clip of some kind to attach the yarns to the side of the ball (see Bead Stopper for a convenient tool).
   - Or, insert a straight cable needle or small double-point needle into the side of the ball and wrap the yarns around it two or three times in a figure 8.
2. Lift the yarns up so the ball hangs free; it will spin on its own until the yarns are separated again.
3. Unfasten the yarn from the ball, draw out some more, and then refasten it so it is ready for the next time.

Spin the Needles

When working with two supplies of yarn, you can use the following approach to separate the strands; it is easy to do and also works with one ball.

- Push the stitches back from the tips of the needles slightly, and then drop them so they hang from the two strands of yarn; let them spin until they are unwound.

The needles may start spinning on their own, but if not, give them a little nudge and/or if necessary pull the two yarns apart to encourage them to completely unwind. The needles will not slip out when you do this; the hanging weight of the fabric will tighten the first few stitches and prevent it.

Untwining Two Yarn Supplies

Whether you spin the ball or the needles as described above, the two yarns will unply and both will also untwist. However, if you are working with separate balls of yarn, and you find they have gained too much twist and are kinking up, try unwinding and rebalancing them in a two-step process.

- Drop the needles as described above to unwind the two yarns. Fasten the yarn to each of the balls as described above; drop one and let it spin until balanced again and then repeat with the other.

Twined Knit Shaping

Increases and decreases can be worked in the usual way in a Twined Knit fabric, however, there is one increase that is somewhat unique.

- Insert needle into next stitch, bring yarn attached to second stitch over first and wrap around needle, then bring first yarn over second and also wrap on needle. Draw both yarns through stitch. On next row or round, work each stitch separately.

If you are working a color pattern, do not worry about twining the yarns in the normal order; place them on the needle so they will be in the correct sequence for the pattern.

Twined Knit Decorative Techniques

Twined Knit garments were traditionally decorated with various stitch and color patterns that are unique to these fabrics. Mittens and gloves were sometimes fulled slightly to increase warmth and durability, and then lavishly embroidered. Jackets seen in museum collections often had a woven bodice with knitted sleeves done in a combination of Twined Knit and Stranded Color or Intarsia patterns, or entire jackets were done in plain Stockinette with Twined Knit patterns used just for the borders.

The fabrics were densely knit on very fine needles, which made it possible to include elaborate patterns even within the small frame of a mitten, glove, or sock. The smooth worsted wool or cotton and linen yarns used, along with the characteristics of the fabric itself, gave the textured stitches great clarity.

❖ Stitch Patterns for Twined Knit

Decorative patterns for Twined Knit are made entirely with Knit and Purl, and the strands between the two stitches can also be placed on the outside of the fabric, somewhat like what is done with Slip Stitches. The resulting patterns have a distinctive appearance that is unique to this special fabric.

Several basic stitch and strand combinations serve as the fundamental units of the patterns, and once you understand how they are put together, you will find it easy to follow a pattern based on them (or even develop one of your own).[†]

These instructions are written for working circular because that is the way Twined Knit is normally done. If you prefer to work flat, it will be necessary to translate the instructions in the usual way; for instance, when working on the inside, if a Purl is required on the outside you will need to Knit, instead.

To help clarify how to manage the yarns when using Purl for decorative patterns, the instructions specify whether to bring a yarn to the outside or inside of the fabric (instead of nearside or farside, which are relative terms). Also, the terms "first yarn" and "second yarn" refer to the yarns attached to the first and second stitches on the right needle, respectively, as you begin a step.

Purl Stitches

Individual Purl stitches can be used in much the same way they are in any standard Brocade-style pattern; however, there are several variations that produce effects seen only in Twined Knit.

Single Purl Stitch

This is a conventional Purl stitch; the instructions simply specify how to change the yarns.

- Move second yarn to outside and Purl next stitch; return yarn to inside. Wrap two yarns in usual way and make next stitch with other yarn (now second on needle).

Twined Purl Rows

One row of Twined Purl will produce a subtle and attractive horizontal line of Purl nubs with a narrow cord below them formed by the sloping strands. However, Twined Purl is at its

---

† A good source of both traditional and contemporary patterns of this kind can be found in *Two-End Knitting* by Anne-Maj Ling, with English translation by Carol Huebscher Rhoades (Pittsville, Wisc.: Schoolhouse Press, 2004).

best when done on two adjacent rows, with the yarns twined in opposite directions on each one.

The result is a decorative braid effect that is commonly seen on mitten cuffs, the lower part of sleeves, or dividing two pattern areas, and it is often done in two or three colors; see Herringbone Braid, below.

Single Purl Row

For a circular fabric, work on the outside of the fabric; for a flat fabric, work either in Purl on the outside or Knit on the inside, as follows:

- For a braid that slants up to left, wrap yarns clockwise, as described for Z-Twist Twining, above.
- For a braid that slants up to right, wrap yarns counter-clockwise, as described for S-Twist Twining.

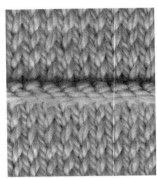

Twined Purl: Single Purl Row.

Double Purl Row

- Wrap yarns as for Z-Twist Twining on first row or round, and as for S-Twist Twining on second, or vice versa.

Deep Stitches

These two techniques are decorative Purl variations: the first one is a bolder version of the stitch, while the other is not a Purl stitch at all (it merely looks like one).

Twined Purl: Double Purl Row, also called Herringbone Braid.

Purl Deep Stitch

This technique is no more than Purl done with both yarns held together to create a double nub, and it can be used anywhere in a pattern where a bold effect is wanted.

1. On row below where Deep Stitch will be located, Knit one stitch with both yarns.
2. On next row:
   - For single Deep Stitch, Purl doubled stitch with one yarn. Discard stitch will have double Purl nub; new stitch on right needle will have single strand of yarn.
   - For multiple Deep Stitches arranged in vertical column, work doubled stitch with both yarns, and repeat

on subsequent rows. On final row, work Deep Stitch with single yarn.

Traditionally a column of two Deep Stitches was set at the center back of a stocking to create the illusion of a seam (apparently socks knit flat and sewn were once considered more stylish and desirable). If the stitches are twisted when worked, they will tighten up and the column will be more deeply recessed (see Twist Stitch).

Deep Stitches can also be arranged to create patterns similar to Single or Double Seed Stitch. For instance, to do the single version, use both yarns to work a stitch that has a single strand, and use one yarn to work a stitch made up of double strands.

Knit Deep Stitch

This technique can be used in patterns in somewhat the same way as a Purl Deep Stitch. Although called Deep Stitch, it is not done in the same way, with the two yarns held as one—instead, the yarn not in use is simply stranded past a Knit stitch on the outside of the fabric.

- Bring first yarn to outside and use second yarn to Knit next stitch; [switch position of yarns, and Knit next stitch], repeat between brackets as many times as needed for pattern.

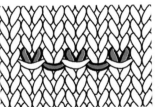 

Knit Deep Stitch. Stockinette fabric with alternate yarns stranding on outside.

Knit Deep Stitch. With first yarn on outside, Knit next stitch.

These stitches are sometimes set in pairs and lined up in vertical columns like Purl Deep Stitch; the result is more subtle because the strands lie flatter on the surface of the fabric than Purl nubs do. You could also use the technique across a row to create the illusion of Single or Double Ribbing without using actual Purl stitches.

Knit and Purl Combinations

Two fundamental Knit and Purl stitch combinations, both called Crook Stitch, are used for most Twined Knit decorative patterns. These pattern units can be scattered across a Knit background to create spot motifs or positioned to form diagonals and diamond shapes.

Alternatively, they can be lined up side-by-side to create

horizontal lines in a pattern, or they can be done across an entire row to make the pattern called Chain Path.

Crook Stitch

One Crook Stitch pattern unit is worked Purl-Knit-Purl with a strand passing on the outside of the middle Knit stitch; the other is done Knit-Purl-Knit with the strands flanking the Purl. When the latter is placed above the former, the motif is referred to as an "O," no doubt for its charmingly startled appearance.

Purl-Knit-Purl

1. Bring second yarn to outside and Purl next stitch; retain yarn on outside.

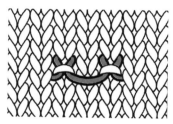

Crook Stitch: Purl-Knit-Purl.

Crook Stitch: Purl-Knit-Purl. Purling the third stitch of the pattern unit.

2. Use other yarn to Knit next stitch.
3. Purl next stitch with yarn on outside, and then return it to inside.

Knit-Purl-Knit

1. Bring first yarn to outside. Knit next stitch with second yarn on inside.
2. Purl next stitch with yarn on outside.
3. Knit next stitch with yarn on inside. Return other yarn from outside to inside.

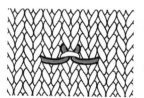

Crook Stitch: Knit-Purl-Knit.

Chain Path

Crook Stitch can be worked across an entire row to create a narrow stripe called Chain Path. If done on two adjacent rows, which is more common, the pattern units are usually staggered, with Purl-Knit-Purl worked on one row and Knit-Purl-Knit on the next, just as for Seed Stitch.

Chain Path.

Hold one yarn on the outside, the other yarn on the inside, and work as follows:

1. Purl 1, Knit 1 across row.
2. Knit 1, Purl 1 across row.

Here are several other options:

- For three-row stripe, repeat Step 1. For four rows, repeat Steps 1 and 2.
- For a simpler pattern, work with an uneven number of stitches and repeat Step 1 every row; if working flat, end each row Purl 1.
- Or, work columns of Knit and Purl like Single Rib; the result will not be as resilient.

Twined Knit Patterns: Horizontal lines in Chain Path, and patterns in Crook Stitch.

Some of you may recognize that Chain Path resembles working a basic Double-Fabric pattern with two yarns at the same time, and in fact, Twined Knit patterns work very well when adapted to double-fabrics; see Double-Faced Twined Knit.

❖ Color Patterns for Twined Knit

With some slight adjustments, all of the usual ways of adding color to a knitted fabric will work with Twined Knit, and the stitch techniques described above can be further enhanced by working them in contrast colors.

You can work with two balls of yarn, but for a more traditional approach, wind a center-pull ball with the first color, and then tie on the second color and wind it on the outside of the same ball; draw the first color yarn from the center, and the second color from the outside.

Color Pattern in Twined Knit.

Stripes and Checkerboards

The simplest way to add color to these fabrics is to work entirely in Knit and alternate the two colors stitch by stitch.

- To make contrast-color vertical stripes, always work each column of stitches in the same color.
- While not traditional, you could also use one solid color yarn and one variegated yarn; this produces the appearance of a solid stripe floating on a multicolored background.
- To make one-stitch checkerboard patterns, alternate the colors to the stitch columns row by row, or every two rows.
- For greater variety, combine stripes and squares to create patterns with very lively optical effects that are especially pronounced when done with strongly contrasting colors.
- Use the Knit Deep Stitch technique, above, stranding one color on the outside past a Knit stitch made in the other color; the result is a subtle layered effect with a geometric pattern created by the strands floating on top of the underlying stripe or checkerboard pattern.

Color and Stitch Techniques

It is also possible to make charming color patterns with Crook Stitch and Chain Path. When a contrast-color yarn is used for a Purl stitch, the discarded Purl nub, its flanking running threads, and the strands will create a flecked effect that can be charming; see Color Patterns with Purl.

One of the most common techniques that combine stitch and color are the variations on Herringbone Braids, which are made up of rows of Twined Purl. These braids are, by the way, just as lovely when used with conventional knitted fabrics.

Herringbone Braid

Herringbone Braid is not unique to Twined Knit—it is seen throughout northern Europe and the Baltic area—but the technique surely was born to this tradition. It is no more than Twined Purl worked on the outside of the fabric in two or three colors.

Herringbone Braid is commonly seen on mitten cuffs or the lower part of sleeves, but it makes a nice division between two pattern areas wherever it is set. It is also first cousin to Braided Cast-On, which is the standard way to start a Twined Knit garment.

Two-Color Braid

Working just one row of Purl on the outside of the fabric will produce the narrow cord described in Twined Purl Rows, above, but with strands in alternating colors. It is important to take certain aspects of working Purl with contrast-color yarns into consideration.

- When the fabric is worked in a single main color and the cord is done in two colors, the new stitches on the right needle and the strands below will alternate colors. However, the Purl nubs lying between them will all be in one color, that of the main fabric.

Two-Color Braid. Twined Purl in two colors.

- To have the Purl nubs also in two colors, work a preliminary row in Knit, alternating the two colors to the stitches.

On the next row, work each existing stitch with the same color so the strands and the Purl nubs match; or, work each stitch with the contrast-color yarn so the strands and the Purl nubs are in opposite colors.

Double Herringbone Braid

A Herringbone Braid is merely the Double Purl Row described above, done in two colors. Several variations are possible: you can work the strands so they slant in the same or opposite

Double Herringbone Braid shown with a Stranded Color pattern.

directions (the latter is more common), and you can line up the colors in both rows or stagger them, as described for the Two-Color Braid, above.

- If the second row is worked with the same sequence of colors (Color A above Color A, Color B above Color B), the colors in the herringbone will be lined up vertically.
- If the second row is done with Color A above Color B, Color B above Color A, the colors will be staggered.

Triple Herringbone Braid

For a three-color braid, use the same concepts discussed above to vary the direction of the slope and control the relationships between the colors in the respective rows.

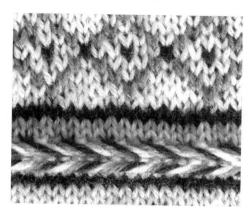

Triple Herringbone Braid.

- Always pick up the yarn farthest to the right to work the next stitch (the yarn attached to the third stitch on the right needle), and set it down to the left of the first strand.

    Draw the third yarn under the other two yarns to make the braid slope up to the right, and over them to make it slope up to the left.

Twined Knit and Stranded Color

More complex and interesting patterns can be done in Twined Knit by combining it with the Stranded Color technique. However, doing so means that from time to time it will be necessary to break the rule about strictly alternating the yarns.

- For a Stranded Color pattern containing small motifs of only a few stitches in the same color, wrap the two yarns only when the color changes.
- Or, work with three balls of yarn: one in a contrast color for the pattern stitches, and two others in the background color. Twine the background yarns in the usual way and strand the contrast-color yarn behind those stitches. When working the stitches of the motif, twine the contrast-color yarn first with one background yarn, then with the other.

    This is the best way to work larger motifs; it carries the background yarn past the motifs and maintains the

quality of the fabric. Three yarns will thicken the fabric somewhat, although with the thin yarns typically used for Twined Knit, this is generally not a problem.

- If areas of the pattern create long strands on the inside, consider attaching these to the fabric at the midpoint using the Lattice Method of Weaving-In.

Twined Knit and Intarsia

Traditional Twined Knit garments sometimes had widely separated Stranded Color patterns. Rather than carry the contrast-color yarn used for the motifs across the row, the Intarsia technique was used and each motif done with a separate supply of yarn; see Stranded Patterns with Intarsia, and Small-Scale Intarsia.

- Alternate the two main yarns across the row in the usual way. Tie on yarn for the Intarsia motif and continue the main yarns for the background stitches of the pattern, as described above for a Stranded Color pattern.

❖ *Twined Knit and Surface Decoration*

Because of the relatively firm nature of the fabric, Twined Knit is ideal for needlework. Garments were traditionally embroidered, both in freehand crewel-type patterns and in Cross-Stitch, and mitten cuffs and sleeve edges were often adorned with pile trim (see Loop Stitch). In addition, the technique welcomes the addition of beads.

Twined Knit and Beads

It is very easy to set beads on any Crook Stitch or Chain Path pattern using Running Thread Beading, described here, or Stitch Head Beading, or even to combine the two, with beads set on both the heads of the stitches and the strands.

The easiest thing to do is to string beads on both yarns so you can use either one when setting a bead; also keep in mind that you could string different color beads on each of the yarns.

Here are the instructions for Running Thread Beading; once you are familiar with using this easier technique with Twined Knit, you will be able to use Stitch Head Beading if you prefer.

1. Bring second yarn to outside and Purl one.
2. With other yarn on inside, Knit one.
3. Slide bead up yarn on outside, strand past previous Knit stitch, and Purl one; move yarn to inside.

❖ *Even Warmer Mittens*

Scandinavians know something about cold winters, and to enhance the exceptional thermal qualities of a Twined Knit fabric even more, items were often fulled slightly and mittens were sometimes lined with wool roving; see Purl Inlay for Warmth.

CHAPTER 18

Felting and Fulling

Felt is a fabric made from wool fibers that have been subjected to heat, moisture, and agitation; this causes them to shrink and permanently entangle into a dense mat. Felt is thought to be the oldest known textile, predating woven fabrics, and it would have been discovered quite naturally once sheep were domesticated; fleece-lined boots and sheepskin saddle blankets will felt without any effort beyond normal wear.

Considered one of the most remarkable and versatile textiles known, felt is wind, water, and flame resistant, cushions against shock and vibration, is an excellent heat and sound insulator, is extremely durable, and will not ravel when cut. These characteristics make it as useful today as ever, with applications ranging from industry to high fashion—felt is ideal for warm garments such as jackets or vests, hats, mittens, slippers and socks, as well as for practical items such as pillow covers and handbags.

Whereas felting is the technique of turning fiber directly into a fabric, fulling applies the same procedures to a fabric that has first been woven or knitted. A fulled fabric has some characteristics that are an improvement over a directly felted one; it tends to be more flexible and is less likely to tear under pressure, or to weaken and separate when repeatedly bent or folded.

Needle felting is a variant done without heat and moisture; instead, the fibers are entangled by repeatedly stabbing a barbed needle through them. While resembling felt in appearance, needle-felted textiles do not have all the characteristics of true felted or fulled fabric and are generally not as durable. However, the process is cheaper to do, and a mixture of fibers other than wool can be used to produce specific characteristics suitable for a variety of industrial applications.

In the craft world, wool needle felting has become popular as a way of making soft sculpture and toys, and can also be used as a means of decorating fulled items in a way that is similar to appliqué.

Felting

The process of making felt is quite different from that used for any other textile—it does not require tools such as needles or a loom, nor does it involve refined skills such as those needed for knitting and weaving. Instead, felting is done with a bit of manual labor at the kitchen sink or in the laundry room.

Felt is possible because of the unique properties that are inherent to wool fibers and what happens when they are subjected to certain conditions. However, success depends upon selecting the right materials—not all wools felt to the same extent, and some will not do so very well at all.

❖ Fibers for Felting

There is a full discussion of the structure and properties of wool fibers in the chapter Fibers, but for our purposes here, what is important is the behavior of these fibers under the conditions that cause felting.

Wool fibers are made of a protein called keratin; your hair and nails are made of the same material. The core of each fiber is filled with even thinner fibrils; these are relatively soft and elastic and are held together in bundles by the harder outside shaft of the fiber, the cuticle, which consists of overlapping triangular scales somewhat resembling those of a pine cone.

The cuticle will soften in warm water, which allows the fibrils to relax and curl, and the scales to open slightly at the tip. If fibers are subjected to agitation and pressure when in this condition, they will shrink in length, and the scales will interlock with one another, forming a dense, tangled mass. Once felting has taken place, the fibers can never be restored to their original condition.

Sheep's wool is the most common material used for felting; it is economical, readily available, and felts easily. Other wool fibers, such as camel, goat, or alpaca, will also felt, but they are more costly and produce fabrics with special characteristics.

For instance, camel's hair makes a rather fragile felt, while alpaca produces one that is dense and very hard. Various furs such as rabbit and beaver have traditionally been made into felt for hats, but these more expensive materials also require special manufacturing processes that add to their finished cost.† In some cases, blends of different types of wool are used to create felt with specific characteristics.

❖ *The Felting Process*

The first stage of felting involves carding and combing a clean wool fleece and then arranging the fibers in several thin perpendicular layers, called batts, which resemble fluffy blankets. The batt is placed on a cloth and rolled up and tied, or sandwiched between two cloths and basted together; these bundles hold the loose fibers together until the preliminary felting has occurred.

The second stage is called "hardening," or felting proper; the batt is saturated with hot, soapy water and then repeatedly rolled and/or beaten to promote felting. Some felters use alternating baths of hot and cold water; this is not essential, but often recommended as a way to "shock" the fiber and encourage it to felt as it alternates between relaxing and shrinking.

Soap acts as a "wetting agent" that changes the surface tension of the water, making it more slippery so it will penetrate the fibers more deeply; it also dissolves any residual grease or soil in the wool that might impede felting and frees the fibers to move more easily so they will entangle.

Modern detergent soaps are mild, but true soap is alkali, as is washing soda, a powder that can be added to the water. Alkalis are harsh and will soften the cuticle, the hard outer portion of the fiber. Making the water somewhat alkali can be helpful if the fiber resists felting or does not felt quickly enough, but should be done with caution; a mild acid like vinegar is then added to the final rinse to neutralize the alkali and prevent lasting damage to the wool (for more information, see Laundry Products).

In Mongolia and other communities of the steppes of Central Asia where felt probably originated, it is used for rugs and yurt dwellings as well as for garments. The felting is done outside and the batt is large, perhaps 6–8 feet x 12–18 feet. The fibers are carefully spread on a "mother felt," sprinkled with water, and rolled up around a thick wooden pole that is roped to the saddle of a camel or horse and then dragged across the ground. For smaller felts, several people kneel down and roll the tied batt back and forth repeatedly with their forearms.

In the third stage, the felting continues under more controlled conditions that refine the qualities of the fabric and perhaps its shape. In the last stage the surface of the felt is given a final finish.

---

† The expression "mad as a hatter" apparently refers to the symptoms of mercury poisoning suffered by traditional hat makers. This toxic chemical was used to treat beaver fur prior to felting; it loosened the hair from the pelt and made it mat together more readily.

Fulling

The transformation of an ordinary knitted fabric into one that has been felted or fulled rests entirely with the planning and finishing stages; the knitting itself is done in the usual way, and there are no special techniques required. Plain Stockinette is fine, as all but the boldest stitch patterns will lose definition and clarity when the fabric shrinks, but by all means consider the use of color. You will need to take several extra steps to develop a gauge and a pattern for a fulled garment because the dimensions will change radically.

❖ *Yarns for Fulling*

The degree to which any particular wool will felt depends upon the breed of the animal, its health, and even what it ate and whether it was sheared in the spring or fall, all of which will determine the qualities of the fiber. Also, the amount of twist put in the yarn during spinning and plying is a factor; because the fibers need to move during fulling, softly spun woolen yarns are the best choice.

Since the labels on knitting yarns rarely indicate what kind of sheep produced the wool, to say nothing of what it might have eaten for breakfast, you will need to do some research to find a good yarn for fulling. Yarn stores should be able to tell you which of their yarns felt well, and books on the subject often have recommendations, although the types of yarns available on the market change frequently and the information could be out of date.

Of course, a machine-washable yarn is not suitable because it has been treated to prevent shrinking and felting. On the other hand, some yarns that contain a mixture of fibers will felt if there is even as little as 20 to 25 percent wool in the blend.

If you have some yarn on hand and would like to try it, make a small Test Swatch and do all the things to it you are not supposed to do when washing a wool garment—put it in hot soapy water and scrub it well. If it starts to felt after five minutes or so, you have a good candidate for your project. If it felts, but slowly, or not as much as you would like, try a true soap or add some washing soda to the water and see if that helps.

❖ *Designing a Fulled Project*

As usual with any knitting project, a successful fulling project requires planning ahead. The Gauge Swatch requires special handling, and it is important to select a garment style that is suitable for a special fabric of this kind.

Here are some tips:

• In deciding on needle size, keep in mind that it is necessary for the fibers to move during fulling, so a loosely knit fabric will generally full more than a tightly knit one. You might want to make and full two or three gauge samples, each with a different size needle, to see which one gives the best result.

- Make the samples twice as large as normal to allow for shrinkage; see Gauge for Fulled Fabrics. Because a knitted fabric tends to shrink more in length than in width (this is due to the path of the yarn through the stitches and their arrangement in the fabric), a rectangle is better than a square.

- Write down the number of stitches and rows in the sample before it is fulled because they will be blurred and difficult to count later.

- Calculate the before and after gauges so you can judge how much the fabric changes. If possible, roughly recalculate the gauge several times during fulling by measuring the wet sample to determine how much and how quickly it changes.

- Keep a record of what you do as you full the sample—how much detergent you put in the water, how hot the water was, how long it took for felting to begin, and then how long it took to get to the point where it was finished to your satisfaction. This will guide you when you full the fabric.

- In planning a fulled item, it is a good idea to use simple shapes; remember, the resulting fabric will be considerably stiffer and denser than it was when first made.

- In general, flat pieces are easiest to manage for fulling, but give some thought to how you want to sew any seams that may be necessary; in general it is best to avoid seams because they can be bulky; see suggestions in Sewing Fulled Knits.

  For instance, you can make the front and back of a garment as one to avoid a side seam, leaving only the shoulder seam for later; or join the item at the shoulders and leave the sides open. However, you may then be faced with handling a fairly large piece of fabric and it is often easier to do separate pieces (be careful to subject them all to exactly the same treatment), and sew them together later.

- When fulling a circular garment, baste something like old sheeting or plastic wrap to the inside to prevent the two sides from felting to each other.

- Consistent shrinkage is sometimes difficult to achieve and an item may exhibit uneven edges. If you see evidence of this in the swatch, consider knitting a big rectangle of fabric, full it, and then cut out the garment pieces and sew them together. This makes it possible to cut away any irregular areas.

❖ *Traditional Hand Fulling*

This is the old-fashioned way to full, and it allows more precise control of the finished product. As you work, you can feel how well the fabric is fulling, concentrate your efforts in certain areas to make sure it fulls evenly, measure it whenever you want to check progress, and stop at just the right moment. It is fun, but fairly strenuous work—pick a day when you feel energetic.

Swatch for Fulling.

Same swatch after Fulling.

Select a hard, flat, waterproof surface that drains reasonably well. For small items, a flat-bottomed sink or sink drain will do; for larger ones, try the bathtub, a cellar floor with a drain, or even your driveway or patio on a nice day. (Fortunately, no camel is required.)

For a small item there is no need to roll it up in a bundle, but the instructions are otherwise the same.

Rolled Bundle

You will need something in which to roll the fabric. Old sheeting will do, but some kind of thin flexible plastic netting is ideal because it allows the water and soap to pass through freely (check at your local hardware or garden supply store for something suitable). Select a material that is larger in both dimensions than the item you plan to full.

1. Lay the fabric to be fulled down on the outer material and straighten it; check dimensions with a tape measure.
2. Pour on hot, soapy water to saturate the fabric thoroughly, and then roll it up in the cloth and tie it with any sort of string or flexible cord.

    If it makes the fabric easier to manage, try rolling it around something like a 2-inch wooden dowel or foam pipe insulation sleeve.
3. Write down your starting time. If you are using a strong soap or washing soda, wear rubber gloves. Pour on more hot water and then lean on the bundle with your full weight and roll it back and forth. Shift your hands to a new position on the roll frequently, and add more water as necessary to keep the whole thing fully saturated.
4. The fibers will shrink and crimp parallel to the direction of the roll, therefore, every five minutes or so, unroll the bundle, check how much fulling has taken place and again note the time. Place the fabric perpendicular to its original position, rewrap it, and continue rolling. If felting is taking place slowly, beat the bundle with a heavy rolling pin, or pick it up and repeatedly slap it down on the surface of the table.
5. Open the bundle and check for even shrinking. If you see inconsistencies, add more hot soapy water and scrub just those areas by hand. An old-fashioned washboard is ideal for this purpose, but any rough surface will do—try a dimpled dish drain, for instance.
6. When the fabric has fulled as much as you want, or it is willing or able to do, pour some more hot water on it, leave it to soak, and sit down to rest.
7. Once you have recovered sufficiently, thoroughly rinse the fabric with cold water, and use the spin-dry cycle of a washing machine to extract as much moisture as possible, or squeeze out as much as you can by hand and then roll it in dry towels.
8. At this point, the fabric should still have some residual stretch, so smooth it out, measure it, pull it into shape, pin it in place if necessary, and leave it to dry.

Flat Fulling

For some items, you might prefer to work with a flat bundle.

1. Lay the fabric down on one cloth, saturate it with warm soapy water, and then cover it with another cloth and "quilt" the whole together with large basting stitches, or pin or clamp the two cloths together around the item.
2. Add more hot soapy water and then use whatever means you have available to apply pressure and agitation. A heavy rolling pin is ideal because it can be used to both roll and beat the fabric, but you can use a large rubber mallet, a rug beater, or your feet—stomp on it, dance on it, have your kids jump up and down or roll around on it.

❖ *Machine Fulling*

The modern washer and dryer are great labor-saving devices for fulling. The only drawback is that it is more difficult to control the process, but with frequent checking it works reasonably well, particularly on simple garments where sizing is not critical.

Hot, soapy water and the agitation of the washing machine will only achieve a moderate amount of fulling by themselves; therefore, to increase the friction on the fabric, use a minimum of water and throw in some heavy clothing like old jeans (avoid anything that might bleed color, and do not use terry towels, since even old ones will give off lint); tennis balls or old flip-flops are often recommended for this purpose. Check the fabric at regular, timed intervals, and when it approaches the right conditions, use the rinse and spin cycles. To maximize shrinkage, you can throw everything in the dryer, but for more control over the finished product, check at frequent intervals and then use some of the finishing touches described in Traditional Hand Fulling, above, and let it air dry.

A front-loading washing machine is in many respects ideal for fulling because the rotary action repeatedly drops the contents on the floor of the drum; unfortunately, with many of these machines, it is impossible to open the door and check your progress. Nevertheless, even if you have one that cannot be paused, you might want to experiment on a large swatch. Use the shortest cycle possible, and perhaps reduce the water temperature somewhat to produce preliminary fulling and then finish the process by hand or in the dryer. On the other hand, if you are working with something that is reluctant to felt, a front-loading machine could be very effective, in which case, use the hottest water setting.

❖ *Shaping and Surfacing*

There are a variety of traditional ways to finish the surface of a fulled fabric and refine its shape. Experiment on your swatch before you work on the garment; here are some suggestions.

Steam Iron

A steam iron is an excellent tool for finishing a fulled fabric. It can be used to flatten the fabric and give it a very smooth surface, as well as to correct minor problems if the fabric has fulled unevenly.

To encourage further felting, or to correct uneven areas, work with the fabric before it has fully dried; to just touch up or finish the surface, allow it to fully dry before finishing.

The more steam there is, the better, but it also increases the likelihood of scalding burns, so keep your hands well out of the way; also, the wool will absorb a great deal of steam, so give the fabric time to cool a bit before moving it.

Set the iron temperature to "wool" and use a press cloth to prevent scorching; if your iron does not produce enough steam and the fulled item is dry, dampen the press cloth, or even use one that is thoroughly wet.

- To just flatten and smooth the surface, use a firm lift-and-press motion.
- To stretch the fabric out in some areas, slide the iron over the fabric and pull at the edges to help it take on the shape you want.
- If the felting is uneven in certain areas, push the fabric together to create a slight gathering, apply steam, and flatten with your fingers or a press cloth; repeat as necessary. When area has been eased together a bit, press iron straight down firmly and, without lifting it, slide it back and forth.

Surface Effects

- For a textured look, brush the surface with a teasel, a metal clothing brush, or a wire dog brush to bring up the surface fibers and give it a halo of soft fibers on the surface.
- Alternatively, for a very smooth look, hold a pair of scissors parallel to the surface and cut off all the fuzz, being very careful not to cut the fabric itself; or try an electric razor.

Shaping

Before the fabric has fulled as far as it will go, it can also be shaped.

- For something like a sleeve cap or shoulder area of a jacket, lay the fabric over a pressing ham, cover it with the press cloth, and steam heavily, pulling and stretching it to provide volume.

  Lay seam lines on a pressing roll, steam heavily, and either finger press or use the tip of the iron; do the same for any foldlines created during fulling that might otherwise set into the garment.
- For a hat, cut a piece of heavy foam the right size, or stuff the hat with a rolled-up towel or section of old sheeting. Pull it into shape and hold the iron about an inch away and blast it with as much steam as possible.

❖ *Decorating*

Fulled fabrics take well to many of the needlework techniques described in Surface Decoration, and can also be painted with fabric dyes. In addition, you can also use needle felting to add decorative motifs to the surface of a fulled item in much the same way as you would with appliqués. This can be done before or after the knitted garment is fulled.

There are excellent instructional books and videos available for needle felting, and the tools and materials are relatively inexpensive; it is fun to do, and an easy way to embellish a fulled project.

Fulled embroidered slippers, Dalarnas Museum, Falun, Sweden.

CHAPTER 19

Uncommon Shapes

Here you will find material on some oddities, like the Cord, which is the tiniest circular fabric; the Moebius fabrics, which have only one surface and one edge; and Medallion fabrics, which are flat fabrics made as you would a circular one on a set of double-point needles. Also included here are Modular fabrics, which are composed of small, individually knit pieces in a variety of geometric shapes that are joined together in one way or another, somewhat as you would a patchwork quilt. Medallions are often assembled in this way as well.

The techniques used for almost all of these are found elsewhere in the book; therefore, while you will find some instructions here, most of this material is a discussion of the possibilities along with references to where you will find more information.

Knitted Cord

A Cord is the smallest possible circular fabric, no more than a few stitches, but what it lacks in size, it makes up for in decorative value. Justifiably popular as a simple and effective way to finish an edge, it can also be sewn down on top of the fabric as trim (see Surface Decoration), or made as an integral part of the fabric (in which case it is known as a Welt).

The first set of instructions below consists of various methods used to make a separate cord that is later sewn into place; the second set of instructions is for making a cord and simultaneously attaching it to a side edge.

❖ *Separate Cords*

There are three ways to make an unattached cord. One method uses the Slide technique; another makes use of the Double-Fabric technique; and the third approach is done with a Knitting Spool, a very old device used to make cords, but which is now more often found in its role as a craft toy for children.

To make a cord in the conventional way, use a pair of short double-point needles and start with Simple or Knit Half-Hitch Cast-On, adding three to five stitches to the needle, depending upon gauge and the thickness of the cord you want.

Cord with Slide Technique

This is the most common way to make a cord; work as follows:

1. Knit stitches of cord.
2. Slide stitches to right needle tip; draw yarn across farside from left to right.
3. Knit first stitch; tighten new stitch on right needle firmly. Knit remaining stitches of cord.
4. Repeat Steps 2 and 3 to make cord of any length.

In other words, you will be working only on the outside of the fabric, from right to left, and drawing the yarn firmly across the inside between each row to draw the stitches into a circle.

The challenge is to tension the yarn firmly enough across the inside, but not make the stitches so tight that it is difficult to work into them on the next row. Nevertheless, there is likely to be a slight irregularity in the fabric at the join between rounds, so it is a good idea to sew the cord into place in a way that will hide it.

If you do not have double-point needles at hand, you can also do this with a straight needle; simply Slip the stitches from the right needle to the left at the end of every row instead of using the Slide technique. However, slipping all the stitches every row tends to make them a bit irregular, so the cord will not be quite as smooth as when it is done on double-point needles; it also takes twice as long to do.

Knitted Cord in Seed Stitch.

The instructions above are for working the cord in plain Knit, which is the way it is almost always done. However, you can also make a cord in Seed Stitch or Garter Stitch (Knit one row, Purl the next).

It is also possible to stuff the cord if you want to make sure it retains a nice rounded shape. You can use the soft cording material sold for upholstery, or just 4 to 6 strands of the yarn you are knitting with. Hold the stuffing material against the inside of the cord as you begin and then let it hang on the farside as you continue; always draw the yarn under the filling from left to right so it will be encased as you go.

Also, do dress the cord before applying it to the fabric; at the least, steam it a bit, stretch it out slightly, and let it relax.

Cord with Double-Fabric Technique

This is much easier to do and it will be truly seamless, with no evidence of the join between rounds. The pattern is the most basic Double-Fabric technique (see Pattern 1: Knit on Outside).

You could work on a pair of straight needles, but this is so tiny it is more easily done on a short pair of double-point needles. Cast on 5 stitches and work as follows.

1. 2[Knit 1, yarn nearside, Slip 1], end yarn farside, Knit 1; turn.
2. Yarn nearside, Slip 1, 2[Yarn farside, Knit 1, yarn nearside, Slip 1]; turn.
3. Repeat Steps 1 and 2 to make cord of any length.

Knitting Spool

A Knitting Spool is a very old device that has long been used to make cords. The spools are the smallest version of a frame knitting device (the inspiration for modern knitting machines), and circular sock knitting frames are still available. The littlest spools are primarily thought of as a child's craft toy, and are sometimes called a Knitting Nancy. They come in a variety of forms; some are plain polished wood, some are painted like little dolls, others are colored plastic. You can also find hand-cranked mechanical ones, and even battery-powered versions. They are available in craft stores or by mail order, and the manual ones are very inexpensive; if you find yourself making cords quite often, you might want to try one of these to see if it speeds things up a bit.

Knitting Spool. Photograph by Biopresto.

A spool is no more than a sturdy hollow tube, about 2 to 3 inches long, with 4 to 6 pegs or nails set on the top rim. The device always comes with instructions, but briefly, here is how it works:

1. Drop tail of yarn down center hole in tube. Start within circle of pegs and "cast on" stitches by looping a half-hitch around each one. Next, wrap yarn around outside of the circle of pegs and hold it taut.
2. Use pick supplied with spool to lift one stitch off a peg and over yarn; discard in the center. Work next stitch in turn, round and round, always wrapping yarn ahead of where next stitch is made.

After every round, give the tail of yarn a tug, and eventually the growing cord will emerge from the hole in the bottom.

❖ Attached Cords

A cord can also be attached to any edge of a fabric by means of decreases that join it to a stitch picked up along the edge, either ahead of time or as it is made; see Picking Up to Join. The first set of instructions produces a cord that is tightly and smoothly attached to the edge. This is followed by two options that you might want to try: one has decorative potential, and the other is not bound to the edge quite as tightly.

As small as it is, a cord does have a gauge, and when it is attached to the fabric as it is made, it is important to take this into consideration. The smoothest join is the result of picking up into one selvedge stitch per row, and this works well for a plain cord if the main fabric is also Stockinette, because there will be the same number of rows in both.

However, if you plan to attach a cord to a fabric made with any other stitch pattern (or to a horizontal edge), it may splay out or constrict the edge unless you make some adjustment. If you are attaching a cord to stitches picked up as you work, the best solution is to Regauge the cord. Select a different needle size for the cord to make the stitches somewhat larger or smaller as needed, to fit it to the fabric smoothly; try this first on the edge of your swatch. If you are attaching the cord to stitches picked up ahead of time, it is possible to adjust the number of stitches in the edge to match the number of rows in the cord.

The instructions here are written for attaching the cord to the right side of a fabric, which is the most convenient way to work. There are two other options: you can work on the inside, in which case convert the instructions below from Knit to Purl; or, perhaps easier, turn the fabric over and work from the top down so you can work on the outside.

Basic Attached Cord

1. Cast on 3 to 5 stitches for cord, plus one for join to main fabric.
2. Knit toward join, Slip last stitch knitwise. Insert left needle from outside to inside under selvedge stitch and Knit; pull slipped stitch over picked-up stitch and discard. Slide stitches to right tip of needle.
3. Repeat Step 2 to make Cord of any length, always stranding yarn firmly on inside before beginning next row.

Step 2 makes use of a Left Decrease that joins the last stitch of the cord to the stitch picked up in the selvedge. The cord wraps around the edge and completely covers it from view.

Cord with Visible Selvedge

You can make a very decorative attachment for a cord done in a contrast color by turning the selvedge to the outside as you pick it up. The column of selvedge stitches will lie between the contrast-color joining stitch and the cord, creating a vertical stripe. Make the selvedge as neat as possible in preparation for working this way.

1. At corner of main fabric, insert needle from outside to inside under full selvedge and pick up one stitch to use only for joining, and then cast on number of stitches needed for cord.
2. Work cord stitches; with yarn farside, Slip joining stitch knitwise, pick up new stitch under next selvedge stitch, and pull slipped stitch over.
3. Slide stitches to right tip of needle, stranding yarn with firm tension on farside, and repeat for length of edge.

Of course, there is no necessity to do this with a contrast color, in which case the joining stitch and the visible selvedge stitch will simply form a decorative, ridged column of two stitches lying between the cord and the main fabric. For another example of the technique, see the Garter Stitch Border done this way in Picking Up While Joining.

This cord has a tendency to turn to the inside of the fabric; steam it thoroughly and finger press it flat when finishing to discourage it from doing so.

Cord on Picked-Up Stitches

With this method, the stitches are all picked up along the edge ahead of time, turning the selvedge to the inside; the cord will lie alongside the edge of the fabric instead of wrapping around it.

- Start at opposite end of edge and pick up stitches; use Simple Half-Hitch Cast-On to add stitches for cord; make cord as described for Basic Attached Cord above; also see Picking Up to Join.

Corded Cast-Off

In this application, a rounded cord serves as the cast-off edge, but the same technique can be used to add a variety of borders, knitted narrow and long, as described in Horizontal Garter Stitch Border.

Corded Cast-Off.

Use a Double Increase to add three stitches to left needle at beginning of cast-off row, or, for a five-stitch cord, use Simple Half-Hitch Cast-On. On these stitches, work as follows:

1. Knit all but last stitch of cord; work Knit Left Decrease on next two stitches, joining stitch of cord to stitch of main fabric.

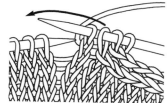

Corded Cast-Off. Pull last stitch of cord over next stitch of main fabric.

2. Slip three stitches back to left needle in normal position, with right side of stitches on nearside of needle, and then strand yarn past them on inside from left to right; draw yarn up firmly to pull first and last stitch together, forming cord.

3. Repeat Steps 2–3 to cast off. Work every row in same direction, toward main fabric.

4. To finish, with one stitch of edge remaining, Slip three stitches of cord to left needle, work a Double Left Decrease, Slip last stitch on left needle to right needle, and pull second stitch over first; secure remaining stitch. Or, work Double Left Decrease, Slip stitch from right needle to left needle, and work Knit Right Decrease on last two stitches.

It is important to pull the yarn taut as you begin Step 2, because this draws the first stitch tightly against the join, forming the cord.

Moebius

A moebius is a circular fabric with a twist; it does not have a right side or a wrong side, an inside or an outside. In fact, it has just one surface and just one edge. First described by two German mathematicians in the mid-nineteenth century, and named after one of them, August Ferdinand Möbius, the moebius is related to other strange geometric objects of interest primarily to mathematicians, but the basic version has several very practical applications in knitting, not least of which is that it makes a very nice scarf or shawl.

The classic way to understand a moebius is to take a long strip of paper; turn one end over so the paper has a half-twist across its width, and then glue or tape the two ends together. Next, draw a pencil line lengthwise down the center of the strip without lifting the tip (pull the paper under the pencil), and you will find the line appears on both "sides" of the paper. Similarly, if you run your finger along the edge, you will find there is only one edge, not two. There are other variations on the basic moebius, the simplest of which is a full twist.

Any knitter who has done this once will immediately think of applying it to a knitted scarf, and doing so might well have inspired the great designer Madeleine Vionnet to make her famous silk moebius scarves in the 1930s.[†]

The shape is inherently graceful and it is ideal for a scarf because it will not slide off in wear. You might want to plan the size so that when the scarf is pulled over your head it will sit at a flattering length without further adjustment. Or you can make it long enough so you have the option of folding it into two circles in order to snug it up closer around your neck for warmth. A shawl moebius is more or less waist length (shorter for a "shrug," longer for a jacket style), and the larger scale allows the twist in the fabric to lie flat at the center front in a very flattering way.

To decide on the measurement to use, take a long, narrow scarf, give it a half-twist, pin the two ends together into a moebius, and try it on. Reset the pins to shorten, if necessary, and once you have a look that appeals, unpin and measure the length.

Because both sides of the fabric will be visible, select a reversible stitch pattern; Seed Stitch and Double Seed Stitch are popular choices, but others are also suitable. For something more open, consider one of the Lace or Mesh patterns; see Increase and Decrease Stitch Patterns.

There is a very easy way to make a moebius, and a far more challenging way to do so. Take into consideration the direction and appearance of the stitch pattern you choose: with one method, stitch columns can run parallel either to the length or the width; with the other, the stitch columns can only run parallel to the length.

❖ Grafted Moebius

This is by far the easiest way to make a moebius, and there are two minor variations. With one, you will be casting on the width and knitting the length; with the other, you will cast on the length and knit the width. The only difference between the two is how to join the ends into the form of a moebius.

Lengthwise Grafted Moebius

1. Use Alternating Provisional Cast-On to put as many stitches on the needle as are needed for a normal scarf width, about 10 to 12 inches, and work to length required; do not cast off.

2. Pick up needle bearing cast-on edge and turn that end of fabric over to create a half-twist.

3. Bring needle bearing last row of stitches to meet cast-on stitches, folding scarf lengthwise. Allow sufficient yarn for one row of stitches, plus an end long enough to hide on inside, and Graft two sets of stitches together.

Alternating Provisional Cast-On inserts a circular needle along the lower edge that serves as a stitch holder. If you prefer not to have a needle hanging at the bottom while you work, use Stranded Cast-On instead; to prepare for grafting, use a double-point needle to pick up cast-on stitches and remove the baseline strand.

If the yarn you are using is not amenable to grafting because it is fragile or highly textured, you could also use Joinery

---

† Betty Kirke, *Madeleine Vionnet*, with foreword by Issey Miyake (San Francisco: Chronicle Books, 1998).

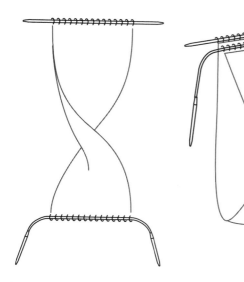

Lengthwise Grafted Moebius:
Turn one end of fabric over
to twist it on itself.

Lengthwise Grafted Moebius:
Bring needles together and
graft stitches.

Cast-Off, which will leave a line of cast-off stitches on one side and a seam on the other; this will be attractive, but obvious. Alternatively, consider joining the two sets of stitches with a decorative crochet stitch of some kind that looks the same, or, if not the same, is attractive on both sides.

Widthwise Grafted Moebius

If you would like to use a stitch pattern for the scarf that has a strong horizontal appearance, you might want to position it on the fabric so it runs lengthwise. Cast on enough stitches for the length of the scarf, knit the width in rows, and then cast off. Give the fabric one-half twist as described above, and join the two side edges; there are several options for how to do so:

- Use the Selvedge Nub Seam to create a simple, flat join; this works particularly well if you have a Garter Stitch Selvedge at both sides.
- Or, pick up stitches along each edge and then graft these stitches together; for a way to do this that looks nice on both sides of the fabric, see Picking Up to Enclose an Edge.
- Alternatively, use a Stockinette or Chain Selvedge; set aside the last selvedge stitches at each side before casting off. After casting off, unravel them and link the freed loops with a crochet hook, either in a plain chain, or with a decorative pattern of some kind (see Linked Seam).

❖ *Circular Knit Moebius*

This version is knitted with rows parallel to the length of the fabric, and stitch columns parallel to the width. It begins in the lengthwise center of the fabric and is worked out to the edge (it cannot be worked in the other direction, as with the Grafted Moebius, so there are fewer options in terms of decorative patterns).

You will need to use a relatively long circular needle; one 47 to 48 inches long is the best choice; a 36-inch cable may work if the needle tips are short. The method requires looping the cable on itself, and the circle formed must be large enough so that when you bring the two needle tips together to join the round you can grasp the loop of the cable as well. If the needle tips are too long and the cable too short, you will not be able to bring the tips together to work the stitches.

Also, as with any circular fabric, the width of the fabric must be longer than the length of the circular needle. However, in this case the cable is doubled on itself; therefore, if you are using a 48-inch needle, you will need to cast on enough stitches for an edge that is a minimum of 24 to 30 inches long; use your gauge and a measurement equal to the one you would use to make a Lengthwise Grafted Moebius, above, to determine the number of stitches needed.

There are three different methods that can be used to cast on and get started; once under way, the fabric is made in the same way.

Alternating Cast-On for Moebius

For this version, use two circular needles; a long one to use for making the moebius, and a shorter one (a 24-inch length is sufficient) to use along with the other just for casting on. Calculate a tail of yarn and work as follows:

1. Hold two needle tips parallel in right hand with longer cable needle above and shorter one below, make Slip Knot, and place it on lower needle. Use Alternating Provisional Cast-On to put twice number of stitches required for full length on two needles, half on each.
2. After casting on, draw lower needle tip (belonging to shorter cable) out to left so those stitches are on cable.
3. Stretch cast-on stitches out along two cables and make sure they lie parallel. Push stitches onto left tip of *lower* (shorter) circular needle and hold in left hand. Push stitches to right tip of upper cable and hold in right hand.
4. Bring right tip belonging to longer cable to meet left tip belonging to shorter cable to join round and create twist in moebius.
5. Begin working stitches in pattern. After working set of stitches on shorter circular needle, set it aside; all stitches will now be on longer circular needle, which is coiled in a double circle. Continue in the round to make fabric width required; always draw up yarn very firmly at the join.

Circular Knit Moebius,
showing cable in double circle.

4. Stretch cast-on stitches out along cable and bring needle tips together to join the round. Loops in cable should be parallel, bound together by cast-on stitches.
5. Slip Knot should be at left needle tip, which is connected to outer loop of cable; right needle tip is attached to inner loop. Bring right needle up across outer loop of cable to begin working; this creates twist for moebius.
6. Begin working into wrapped strands on needle, which will look like Yarnovers, half of which will be turned (see Turned Knit and Purl). Work into each stitch nearside or farside as needed so it will not twist on discard.
7. Continue to work around and around in pattern until fabric is width desired; always draw up yarn at join very firmly. Cast off.

This is a somewhat simpler way to cast on than the method described above, but Stranded Cast-On is less structured than Alternating Provisional Cast-On, and this makes it more difficult to create a neat, even center row for the fabric. Furthermore, working with two needles not only keeps the stitches even, but also makes it easier to determine if the two sets are lined up parallel and that the twist that creates the moebius is done correctly.

Moebius on Picked-Up Edge

An even simpler method is to use a single circular needle and Stranded Cast-On done in the conventional way on one needle; use a contrast-color yarn for the baseline strand and later pick up stitches along the other edge, as follows:

- After casting on, stretch the stitches the length of the cable and draw the tips together to join the round. Rotate the edge up, above the left needle tip, and begin picking up into the loops, removing the baseline strand as you go. Begin working the next round into the stitches on the left needle tip.

Working into the edge creates the twist in the moebius and the cable will form into a double loop after all the stitches have been picked up; there will then be twice as many stitches on the needle.

While working the first row this way is more time consuming, there will be no question about whether you are doing it correctly; the contrast-color yarn makes it very easy to determine if the edge is lined up parallel below the needles and is only twisted once to form the moebius. Also, the center row of the fabric is more likely to be smooth and even because the second set of stitches is simply wrapped around the contrast-color yarn baseline; those stitches will not be stretched out, which can happen with the method above, where they are wrapped around the cable.

Cast on as firmly and evenly as possible because this will form the center row of the fabric. It is also very important to draw the yarn up tightly when working the first stitch at the join to prevent unsightly gaps from forming there.

You will be working out from the center line of cast-on stitches in both directions (the tail of yarn will be in the middle). Notice there are Knit stitches under the needle on the first half of the round; after setting aside the shorter needle, there will be Purl stitches under the needle for the next half of the round. Establish your pattern accordingly; for Garter Stitch, for instance, Purl over Knits and Knit over Purls, or begin working in Seed Stitch or some other reversible pattern.

The cast-off edge will form the long edges of the scarf, and once that is done, the moebius is ready to wear.

Stranded Cast-On for Moebius

Instead of using two circular needles as described above, try this alternative using a single long one.

1. Form cable into circle with tips going in opposite directions. Hold looped cable and one needle in right hand with tip pointing left; let other needle tip hang from circle to your right.
2. Make Slip Knot and place on needle; there is no need to calculate a tail of yarn, but allow a tail long enough to hide when finishing.
3. Hold yarn on forefinger as for Left-Hand Method of knitting and use equivalent of Stranded Cast-On to put number of stitches for full length of edge on needle: treat cable as baseline strand, moving needle tip under cable from nearside to farside to pick up yarn for one stitch and make next stitch as for a Yarnover.

Larnach Castle pattern: Four modular units assembled into pattern block.
Estate of Mary Walker Phillips; photograph by Alain Ekmalian.

Modular Fabrics

Relatively small geometric shapes, called modules, can be knitted separately and sewn or crocheted together after they are all finished, or new ones can be attached to the others as they are made. The former approach resembles patchwork quilting, while the latter has some similarities to crochet.

Because Modular Knitting relies entirely upon techniques described elsewhere, you will find this section rather small. However, this should not be interpreted to mean it is without interest; on the contrary, there are heirloom pieces of patchwork knitting on display in museums, as well as contemporary designs of exquisite pattern and color.

❖ *Counterpanes and Coverlets*

Individual knitted modules with intricate patterns have traditionally been assembled in the manner of a patchwork quilt to make bed covers and crib blankets, or tablecloths and runners. There is a wealth of patterns for these things in old knitting books such as Weldon's, and more recently in Mary Walker Phillips's charming book *Knitting Counterpanes*.†

The simplest shapes are squares or diamonds that are started at a corner and made with increases and decreases; the

---

† PieceWork Magazine, *Weldon's Practical Needlework*, vols. 1–2 (Loveland, Colo.: Interweave Press, 1999–2004); original publications began in 1888. Mary Walker Phillips, *Knitting Counterpanes: Traditional Coverlet Patterns for Contemporary Knitters* (Newtown, Conn.: Taunton Press, 1989).

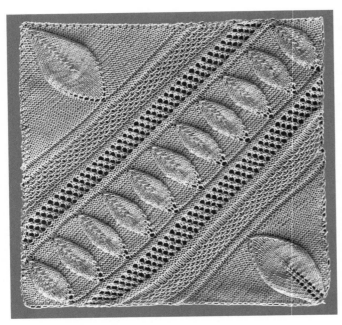

Module for Larnach Castle pattern, knitted by Mary Walker Phillips.
Estate of Mary Walker Phillips; photograph by Alain Ekmalian.

more challenging are done with the techniques described in Medallions, below.

The individual modules, or "patches," are conveniently small and portable, and there is a sense of satisfaction each time one is completed. However, once you have made as many pieces as needed, assembly is a different kind of project. Each square needs to be finished (washed and blocked to size), and the whole sewn or crocheted together.

This is easy enough to do with a relatively small item such as a crib blanket, but if you have been ambitious enough to make a counterpane for a bed, you will need a worktable that will support the weight and allow you to spread out a bit. And for something of that scale, you might want to take it to a good dry cleaners once it is all assembled and have them give it a final cleaning and steaming; blocking something this large yourself could be a real challenge.

Fine cotton or linen yarns were traditional for counterpanes, although keep in mind that these are very heavy (see Materials). If you prefer something lighter in weight, select a wool yarn or a blend of some kind; if you can afford it, consider silk.

If you substitute a different yarn and needle size for what is suggested in a pattern, each of the modules will be a slightly different size than originally specified, but fortunately, gauge is not critical for a project of this kind. If necessary, change the number of modules you make in order to adjust the overall dimensions, or add a decorative border around the edges. Alternatively, use a crochet pattern to join the modules together; this will add width and length throughout the fabric.

❖ *Medallions*

Medallions are flat fabrics in the shape of a disc, square, rectangle, or polygon. Small versions, called doilies, were popular a century ago, when they were used to decorate chair backs and arms (and, more practically, to protect the upholstery from soil), or they were set out on tabletops under a vase or fancy bowl. On a larger scale, the same techniques can be used to make a circle or half-circle shawl. Multiple copies of a medallion are often treated as a modular unit and assembled into counterpanes for a bed cover or lap robe, or for tablecloths or runners; I think it is safe to say that these are the most beautiful of all the modular shapes in knitting.

The distinctive characteristic of a medallion is that, in spite of it being a flat fabric, it is worked in the round on a set of double-point needles. To make a square or rectangle, the shaping pattern is set along four slopes that pass from the center to the corners; decorative patterns are normally set within each segment. To make polygons or circles, the number of slopes is increased, in effect dividing the fabric into the equivalent of pie slices; some patterns arrange the shaping in curves to create swirled segments, or they are distributed evenly around rows.

To plan a pattern of this kind, see Shaping Concepts, especially the information in Triangles and Circles, and also Charts for Internal Shaping. And for suggestions regarding how to plan a decorative pattern within the areas of the medallion, see Coordinating Stitch and Garment Patterns.

It is traditional to start a medallion on a very few stitches at the center; see Cast-Ons for a Center Start. However, in some cases you might want to start at the outer edge because there are more options with casting on than with casting off, or it could be that a particular stitch pattern is more attractive if worked in that direction. Also, the weight of the fabric makes it easier to manage the last few stitches at the center than if you start with them.

Medallion worked from edge toward center.
Notice lines of decreases between pattern repeats.

Medallion Modules and filler pieces for counterpane, in Margaret Murray's pattern,
knitted by Mary Walker Phillips. Estate of Mary Walker Phillips; photograph by Alain Ekmalian.

Medallion: Doily with swirled center. Increases distributed evenly throughout.
Lacis Museum of Lace and Textiles, Berkeley, California.

❖ *Modular Garment Fabrics*

It is more common today to use modular techniques for garments rather than household items. The scale of each unit is considerably smaller, and instead of being sewn together as for a counterpane, they are more often assembled with Joinery Decreases or by Picking Up Stitches.

Modular garments are frequently made of more varied components than counterpanes, and indeed some resemble a crazy quilt, with free-form shapes so varied they often defy description. More often, you will find patterns consisting of squares, rectangles, diamonds, or parallelograms; the simplest and most traditional pattern is probably what is known as *entrelac* (the French word for interlaced), which has contrast-color rectangles set on the bias to create the overall effect of a basketweave pattern.

These projects invite creativity and innovation, and their great charm rests not only in the variety of shapes and the changing direction of the knitted rows and stitch columns, but with the many color effects that can be achieved. Some modular items are precisely planned ahead of time using yarns in selected colors, while others are entirely improvised and made with whatever materials are at hand. Some of the patterns resemble what can be done with geometric Intarsia patterns, but the texture and appearance of the fabric is different.

Feel free to adapt any published pattern to your taste; there are always options regarding which shaping techniques to employ, or how to join one module to another. And, given that the modules are often very small in size, do consider using the Bi-Directional Method, which eliminates the need to turn at the end of each row.

If you are planning your project ahead of time, do a gauge swatch and make any adjustments in needle size before you begin working so you can be confident of the finished dimensions. If you prefer a more relaxed approach, it is a good idea to at least play with some Test Swatches beforehand to try the techniques you plan to use and see how well the materials and colors go together (see Stitch Gauge, and Putting Colors Together).

Here are descriptions of some of the basic methods used for modular knitting.

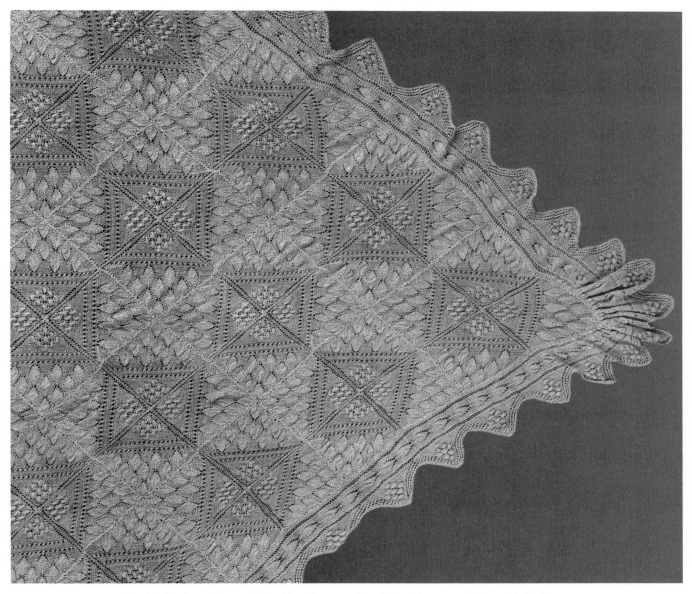

Hand-knitted counterpane. Brooklyn Museum; gift of Ida, Johanna, and Henry Mollenhauer.

Strips

You can make long vertical strips, each several inches wide, using a mixture of stitch patterns and/or color patterns in the manner of a sampler, or use stitch patterns with strong vertical elements, such as cables, or ones that have large, distinctive repeats. When assembled the result will resemble a geometric Intarsia pattern, but this approach is considerably easier to do because you can concentrate on working one pattern and color at a time. This method also makes it possible to work each strip with yarns that require different needle sizes for optimum gauge, something that would be awkward to do across a row of geometric Intarsia.

- Determine the gauge of each pattern used and vary the number of stitches in each strip in order to accommodate the scale of pattern repeats and to keep each strip the same width. If appropriate, also adjust the number of rows in each strip to make them all the same length. For any minor differences, you can rely on the resilience of knitting and a bit of steam to fit things together.

- Sew or link the selvedges together (see Selvedge Seams), or join them with a decorative crochet pattern of some kind.

Alternatively, you can use the technique Picking Up to Join, and attach the side of a new strip as it is made to the previous one.

• Strips can be aligned on the garment shape vertically, horizontally, or on the bias (see Coordinating Stitch and Garment Patterns).

Rectangular Modules, or *Entrelac*

The most traditional modular pattern is Entrelac, which consists of rectangles lying at right angles to one another, creating a basketweave effect. The edges of the fabric are usually made up of triangles that nest into the top, bottom, and sides, although these can be omitted to create an interesting serrated effect. The modules can be made in Stockinette, Garter Stitch, or any number of other stitch patterns, and/or in contrast colors.

The concept of "row" does not quite apply to a pattern of this kind. There are, of course, rows in the little modules, but the overall pattern is made up of tiers consisting of a series of modules set at an angle; those in one tier slant from right to left, those in the next tier slant from left to right.

The stitches that form the base of a rectangle are picked up along the side of a previous one. As each module is made, Joinery Decreases are used to attach it at one side to the free stitches left at the top of a module in the tier below.

The modules have twice as many rows as stitches, less one; decide on the number of stitches to use based on your gauge and the size module wanted. Use Simple Half-Hitch Cast-On or Knit Cast-On, because either requires only one strand of yarn, which works best for this technique. After casting on, the first step is to make a series of triangles that will serve as the base for the first tier; the instructions are for working in Stockinette; to work in Garter Stitch, simply Knit every row.

Base Triangles

1. On inside: Purl 2, turn; Slip 1, Knit 1, turn.
2. Purl 3, turn; Slip 1, Knit 2, turn.
3. Continue as in Step 3, but work one additional stitch every other row until there are enough stitches for one module on right needle; turn to inside and Purl across all stitches of triangle.
4. Repeat Steps 1–3 for each additional triangle, leaving stitches of previous triangle on right needle in wait.

When you are done, there will be a series of separate triangles on the needle, with just the tip of each one connected to the next.

The triangles are made with Short Rows, but it is optional whether to wrap the turning point. If you are working immediately above a cast-on edge, it is not necessary, but it is important to Slip the first stitch after the turn to avoid gaps in the edge. If you have worked several rows above the cast-on edge, or are starting a section of Entrelac above another portion of fabric, then do wrap the Short Rows.

Finnish Entrelac Stocking Top, 1890. Abo Akademi University, Turku, Finland. Photograph by Niklas Hulden.

Right-Side Triangles

Next, make a right "selvedge" triangle, one that will fill in along the vertical side edge of the fabric. The first side triangle you make will be joined to the stitches of the last lower edge triangle, forming a corner.

1. On outside, cast on number of stitches needed for one module.
2. Knit across all stitches but one; work Left Decrease, joining last stitch of side triangle with first stitch of base triangle; turn.

3. Purl 2; turn, Knit 1, Left Decrease; turn.

4. Purl 3, turn; Knit 2, Left Decrease; turn.

5. Continue in this way; at end of each inside row, work one additional stitch of those cast on; on outside row join last stitch of side triangle to stitch of base triangle with decrease.

The cast-on edge will form the side edge of the fabric, a new set of module stitches will be on the right needle, and the third side of the triangle will be joined to a base triangle.

Outside Tier

To make a tier of rectangles, you will be picking up into one side of a module in the tier below (or if this is the first tier, into the side of a base triangle), and joining the new module to the stitches on one side of the next module (or base triangle). Leave stitches of new side triangle unworked on right needle, and continue as follows:

1. On outside, pick up number of stitches for one module in side of module below, working into inner half of selvedge as to Knit (one stitch every other row; see Selvedges). Turn; Purl picked up stitches; turn.

2. Knit to last stitch of module, work Left Decrease, joining it to first stitch of next module. Turn; Purl to end of row; turn.

3. Continue as in Step 2; on each outside row, join last stitch of new module to stitch at top of adjacent module; work inside rows plain.

4. When no stitches remain in adjacent module, repeat Steps 1–3 for next module.

Using a Stockinette Selvedge on the free side of each module offers the most options for picking up and provides a smoother join when stitches are picked up along it. A Chain Selvedge can be too loose to make a neat join and it tends to distort the adjacent column of stitches, with the result that one side of each module will look visibly different.

Picking up into the inner side of the selvedge stitch tends to reduce the bulk of the join, but if it does not draw the modules neatly together, pick up under the full selvedge stitch, instead. On the other hand, if you are making something soft and relatively open, you might want to minimize the join as much as possible, and picking up into the outer strand of the selvedge stitch might work better. If the modules are done in Garter Stitch, see the suggestions for picking up into the side of a Diamond Module, below.

There will be an uneven number of rows in each module; therefore, you will need to adjust your pick-up pattern accordingly. You will be picking up into every other selvedge stitch, but may need to add an extra one at either the top or the bottom of the edge, depending upon what works best for your pattern.

After making the decrease that joins one module to another, to keep the stitches of the join as even as possible, after turning, tighten up the first stitch as you work it.

Left-Side Triangle

This triangle is started on stitches picked up along the side of the last base triangle, forming the corner of the fabric. One selvedge of the new triangle will be on the side of the fabric, one will be at the top.

1. Pick up stitches for one module along side of last module (or bottom triangle). Turn.

2. On inside, Purl; turn. On outside, Knit to last 2 stitches; Knit Right Decrease.

3. Repeat Step 2 until 2 stitches remain; turn.

Some patterns recommend working the decreases on the inside in Purl, and ending with one stitch, but this tends to make the triangle too long, and it curves out at the side. Working as described here scales it down a little and makes it tidier.

Inside Tier

The second tier starts on the inside of the fabric.

1. With two stitches on needle, pick up enough additional stitches for module, working as to Purl into top selvedge of side triangle; turn. Knit one row; turn.

2. Purl to last stitch and use Purl Right Decrease to join it to stitch of next module; turn. Knit one row; turn.

3. Repeat Step 2 until new module has been joined to all stitches of adjacent module.

4. Pick up stitches needed for next module into side of module in tier below; turn. Knit one row; turn. Repeat Steps 2 and 3.

5. Continue in this way, picking up stitches in side of one module and joining new module to top of another. At end of tier, make Right Side Triangle.

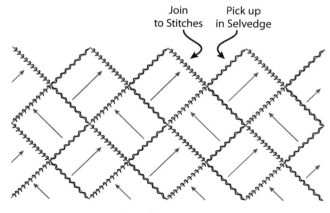

Join to Stitches   Pick up in Selvedge

Entrelac Diagram.

Top Triangles

To finish the top of an Entrelac fabric, make another tier of triangles. These instructions are for working the last tier on the inside of the fabric:

1. Work a Left Side Triangle and pick up stitches for next module; turn. Knit one row; turn.
2. Purl Right Decrease, work to last stitch and use Purl Right Decrease to join it to stitch of next module; turn. Knit one row; turn.
3. Repeat for each module across tier.

If you prefer to cast off on an outside row, complete the Right Side Triangle and then immediately cast off those stitches. Pick up stitches for the next module, and on each outside row, use a Knit Left Decrease on the first two stitches, and another Knit Left Decrease to join the last stitch with a stitch of the next module. Repeat across the row.

Entrelac Stitch Patterns

If Entrelac is done in Stockinette, the discrepancy between the stitch and row gauges alters the shape of the rectangles somewhat. The top edges of each module are stretched out in a slight curve where they connect with the side of another; the side edges of each module are compressed a bit and curve in along the line of picked-up stitches. This is characteristic of Entrelac and gives the fabric a distinctive, puffy surface texture that is quite charming, although it can be flattened somewhat with steam when finishing (see Dressing a Fabric).

Garter Stitch is more accommodating and the modules will lie flat. You can also use almost any decorative stitch pattern that has a repeat with twice as many rows as stitches; or, for one that is smaller, use a few plain rows of Garter Stitch at top and bottom, or at each side, to frame a repeat and provide a good edge for joining one module to another.

Diamond Modules

Another common modular technique is based on a diamond shape (a square set on end) done in Garter Stitch and shaped with double decreases. One of the more appealing things about these modules is the potential for color pattern. The yarn color can be changed on any outside Knit row to create textured stripes, and different color combinations can be used in each module, creating a very lively effect.

These are very easy to do, the effect is charming, and the variations in color and scale provide great potential for garment design.†

---

† Vivian Høxbro, *Domino Knitting*, English trans. (Loveland, Colo.: Interweave Press, 2002).

Diamond Modules: Made with Center Double Decreases slipped on next row.

Diamond modules always have an uneven number of stitches; one extra for the corner where the line of decreases will begin, and an equal number distributed to the two sides. The decreases cause the rows to angle up on each side, echoing the shape of the module.

The next module is started on the stitch remaining from the last one, and then half the stitches needed are picked up along its side; the other half of the stitches are then cast on. For best results, work as follows:

Casting On

Simple Cast-On is a good choice for these modules. It has the advantage of not requiring the use of a second yarn, and, after working the first row, the outside edge will be identical to one done with Purl Half-Hitch Cast-On, which blends in nicely with Garter Stitch. Knit Cast-On is more often recommended, but it makes a looser and bulkier edge, and picking up into it is less than ideal.

1. Determine your gauge and use Simple Cast-On to add number of stitches required for two sides of module; if possible, use smaller needle for this, and work cast-on firmly, tucking each stitch closely against next.
2. Turn to inside, and with main needle, Knit first stitch nearside (it will twist), and then Knit all remaining cast-on stitches farside (so they do *not* twist). There will be a row of Purl nubs on outside, above half-hitches of edge.

Most of the time you will be picking up into the selvedge of another module, but should you need to pick up into a Simple Cast-On edge, work into the outside strand of the half-hitch.

Making a Module

1. After casting on, work one inside row; turn.
2. Subtract three stitches from total number cast on; divide answer by two. Work that many stitches and then make a Center Double Decrease (see below); work same number of stitches after decrease. Work next row plain.
3. On each subsequent pattern row, there will be one less stitch before and after center decrease.
4. When three stitches remain, make a final double decrease; one stitch remains.
5. To make next module, begin with remaining stitch; pick up number of stitches needed for one side into selvedge of previous module and then cast on an equal number for other side.

For recommendations regarding which selvedge to use and how to pick up the stitches, see below.

Decrease Options

There are several decreases to choose from, but I find the Center Double Decrease particularly attractive for this purpose; it creates an attractive stripe down the center of the module; if you are planning something reversible, the inside is very subtle and unobtrusive.

- Slip 2 stitches knitwise, Knit 1, pull both slipped stitches over and off the needle.

For a more decorative effect, work as follows:

- Work Center Double Decrease on outside row; on inside, Slip center stitch with yarn nearside.

And if you want something quieter, try a Left Double Decrease:

- Slip 1, Knit two together, pass slipped stitch over.

Selvedges and Picking Up Stitches

When modules of this kind are done in Garter Stitch, there is no need to use a formal selvedge stitch; work the pattern from edge to edge. The edge will have a pair of strands at the end of every Knit row, and a tight little knot-like nub at the end of every Purl row. You can pick up into the strands, or into the nubs.

A new module begins with the single stitch remaining from the previous one; next, pick up the number of stitches needed for one side of the next module into the selvedge to the left of this stitch using one of the following approaches:

- Work with a pair of double-point needles in a smaller size than used for the fabric. Put the remaining module stitch on the right needle and pick up into the selvedge by in-

serting the left needle into the top strand of the nub and then Knit (each nub has two strands; one at the top that wraps to the farside, and one lower down that wraps to the nearside). This creates a nearly invisible join on both sides of the fabric (nice in any case, but important if you are planning something that will be reversible).

- Alternatively, pick up between the Purl nubs, working *into* the selvedge stitch instead of under it to reduce the bulk. This is easier to do, but is not quite as close a join; it creates a thin, cord-like join on the inside that is reasonably attractive.
- Many patterns recommend a Chain Selvedge, which is very easy to pick up into, but it forms a considerably looser join that is more obvious in the finished fabric.

After picking up the stitches, use Simple Cast-On, as described above, to add enough stitches for the other side of the module.

Changing Colors

Here are some suggestions for how to change colors when making modules of almost any shape.

- Always add a new color on an outside Knit row (for an explanation of why this is important, see Color in Purl Stripes).
- When starting a new color, use Weaving-In to hide the tail of yarn when working the first few stitches; this avoids the need to hide multiple tails of yarn later.
- Carry the yarns up one selvedge, always changing them in the same way to make the edge as neat as possible.
- The module described above will have an uneven number of rows (there is no return row following the last decrease). To start every module with the same color and end with the opposite color, work the last decrease with the color used for the two previous rows.

Other Geometric Modules

Almost any geometric shape can be used for a modular fabric—squares, rectangles, trapezoids, T- and L-shapes are common, and it is also possible to develop fan-shaped designs with curved edges; for a wealth of ideas, see the work of Horst Schulz.[†] You can nest smaller versions of the same shape within a larger one to create lively color and scale variations.

And instead of making diamond modules with decreases,

[†] Horst Schulz, *Patchwork Knitting* (East London, South Africa: Saprotex International, 1997).

Further back in time, Virginia Woods Bellamy patented her description of Modular Knitting; see *Number Knitting* (New York: Crown, 1952). Valid or not, the patent expired in 1965.

you could start with one stitch and use double increases instead, many of which are more decorative than decreases. After making the module, you will have enough stitches on the needle for two sides of the diamond; put one side on a holder (or cast off), start the next module on the center stitch, and attach it to the free stitches on the other side, row by row.

Garter Stitch is ideal for modules because it is inherently square, which means that the horizontal and vertical edges fit well together without distortion and the shaping is a systematic every other row. However, you can add additional surface interest to the fabric by combining areas of Stockinette with Garter Stitch.

For instance, alternate two rows of Stockinette with two rows of Garter, or add a square of Stockinette at the center or at a corner; in these cases, continue the Garter Stitch Selvedge to make it easy to join other modules at the sides. Also consider using the Garter Stitch version of Mosaic patterns; simply select a pattern repeat that fits within the module. If you want to insert a bit of decorative stitch pattern in the middle, use a narrow border of Garter Stitch all the way around to frame it.

Once you understand the concepts used to make and join modules, either picking up stitches, or casting on stitches as needed, it is easy to apply them to other shapes; simply use whatever combination of techniques is needed to start a new module and join it to its fellows.

Hybrid and Free-Form Modules

Some modular configurations and most free-form patterns are done in a combination of techniques and a variety of shapes, depending upon what seems to work best. Modules can be attached entirely to picked-up stitches, started on picked-up stitches and attached to free stitches, or stitches can be picked up as the next module is made, and crochet is used whenever it seems sensible to do so.

In crazy-quilt designs of this kind, use whatever stitch patterns and techniques strike your fancy; the differences in gauge will create surface contour, puffing out in some places and contracting in others, which will add another dimension to the overall effect.

It helps a great deal if you make a paper pattern of the garment sections to use as a guide. From time to time, stop and steam the fabric you have made, and lay it on top of the paper pattern to get a sense of how to proceed.

Color in Modular Patterns

Success with a modular design depends on a good mix of colors; while Entrelac patterns are traditionally done with just two, most of the others use a great many more than that. You may want to purchase a selection of yarns specifically for the project, but this is also a wonderful way to use up leftover bits of yarn. For inspiration in combining color for either Modular Knitting or Intarsia work, you cannot go wrong by looking at any one of the many books done by the master colorist, Kaffe Fassett, who started with knitting but has now branched off into needlework and quilting.

If you are working with what you have on hand, start by putting a variety of yarns in a shallow bowl or basket and mix them up good to see how compatible they are. Or, start with a main color, and then keep adding and subtracting yarns in other colors in amounts roughly proportional to how much of them you think will be used. If necessary, wind off smaller amounts from larger balls so you get a better sense of what they will look like in small areas, and then eliminate those that do not seem to fit with the others. You may find yourself with a good mix of colors but feel the need for one that repeats frequently throughout, in which case you may want to buy a ball or two to help pull the whole effect together.

As you make the fabric, periodically stand back to look at it from a distance. If something seems to be the wrong color, shape, or size, simply rip it out and put in something else. This is playful improvisation and the idea is to let the fabric develop in an organic way.

Part Five

STITCH AND COLOR PATTERNS

CHAPTER 20

Written Stitch Patterns

A stitch pattern is a set of instructions that specifies which techniques to use for every stitch in order to produce a fabric with a specific structure or decorative appearance. There are two distinctly different types of patterns: written and charted.

A written stitch pattern is in the form of a numbered list, and each item in the list contains the instructions for how to work one row of the pattern. Each instruction is written in the form of a short phrase made up of a series of steps that tell you how to work one or more of the stitches. The material here will help you learn to work from this type of stitch pattern.

As an alternative to the written method, patterns are also charted on a grid (like graph paper), using a set of symbols to represent the various stitch techniques instead of letter abbreviations. Each square in the chart represents a stitch and contains a symbol indicating how to work it. You will find detailed information on how to read and write stitch patterns in this form in the chapter Charted Stitch Patterns (and also see Charted Color Patterns, which are almost never seen in written form).

The equivalent information for written garment patterns can be found in the chapter Written Garment Patterns and, for the charted versions, in Charted Garment Patterns. Combined, the material in these four chapters will allow you to convert a complete set of pattern instructions into the form you like best, or even write one of your own.

Many knitters have a preference for one type of pattern or the other—some people find it challenging to keep their place in a written pattern, while others find it difficult to decipher the graphical information in a chart. However, both forms are used in published garment patterns and collections of stitch patterns, and it is important for you to understand how to work with either of them.

Stitch Pattern Terms

There is no single set of agreed-upon abbreviations or system of notation used for published written patterns. Many are done in one or another style that arose out of a regional knitting tradition, while some use methods developed by a particular publisher or designer. However, the information is presented in a somewhat similar way regardless of the particulars, and definitions are normally provided; once you are familiar with how patterns are written, you will find it easy to learn to read one that is initially unfamiliar to you.

In the material that follows, you will find examples of how abbreviations are put together in a format that conveys the instructions for any kind of pattern. But first, a Glossary of common terms found in published patterns, along with several that I prefer.

❖ Glossary of Abbreviations

As you will see in the discussions that follow, many of these abbreviations are combined with one another when it is necessary to convey more complex information, so the list has richer possibilities than its relatively short length suggests. You will undoubtedly encounter other abbreviations in published patterns and, as mentioned above, there is usually a key provided with definitions.

An abbreviation is usually capitalized only if it is at the beginning of a phrase, is a single letter, or, in some cases, because it stands for the name of a particular variation of a technique. While there are exceptions, the terms are not usually modified to specify tense or number because this can be understood from the context; for instance, there is generally no need to add endings such as "s," "ed," or "ing."

alt	alternate, alternating
approx	approximately
B	bobble

beg	begin/beginning
bel	below
bet or **betw**	between
bk	back
C	cable; or center
cc	contrast(ing) color
ccy	contrast-color yarn
ch	chain
c/off	cast off
c/on	cast on
circ	circular
cm	centimeter
cndl	circular needle
cont	continue
cr	cross
dbl	double
dec or **decr**	decrease
disc	discard
dpn	double-point needle
ea	each
ev	every
foll	following
fs	farside (relative term; refers to side of needle or fabric currently farthest from knitter; see nearside)
G = #/#	Stitch Gauge (number of stitches/rows)
gg	gauge
h	hand
in	inch
inc or **incr**	increase
incl	include/inclusive
ins	inside
K or **k**	knit
Kb	Knit Back (not used in this book; equivalent to Kfs)
Kfs	Knit farside (move right needle to farside of left needle to insert into next stitch)
KOv	Knit Over (wrap yarn over needle for Knit instead of under)
Ktog	Knit together
kw	knitwise (instruction to insert needle into stitch as to Knit)
L or **l**	left
LC	left cross, left cable, or light color, depending upon context
lh	left hand
lndl	left needle

M1	"make one," generic expression for an increase
mc	main color
mm	millimeter
mult	multiple
ndl	needle
ns	nearside (relative term; refers to side of needle or fabric currently closest to knitter; see farside)
num	number
o	over
outs	outside
P or **p**	Purl
patt	pattern
Pb	Purl Back (not used in this book; equivalent to Pfs)
Pfs	Purl farside (move right needle to farside of left needle to insert into next stitch)
pkup	pick up stitches
plso/prso	pass left or right stitch over
pnso	pass next stitch over
prev	previous
psso	pass slip stitch over
Ptog	Purl together
PUnd	Purl Under (wrap yarn under needle instead of over for Purl)
pw	purlwise (instruction to insert needle into stitch as to Purl)
R or **r**	right
RC	right cross or right cable
rem	remaining
rep	repeat
rep* . . . *	repeat instructions between symbols; same format used with parentheses or brackets instead of asterisks
ret	return
retR/retL	return stitch to right or left needle
rev	reverse
rh	right hand
rnd	round
rndl	right needle
rth	running thread
selv	selvedge
sep	separate
SKP	Slip Knit Pullover; one version of Left Decrease (Purl version rare); sometimes written SKpsso

sl and **slst**	Slip, and Slip stitch (always means to Slip purlwise)
slkw	Slip knitwise
sndl	straight needle
spn	single-point needle
SSK/SSP	Slip Slip Knit, Slip Slip Purl; variations of a Left Decrease
st/sts	stitch/stitches
str	strand
t	turn
tech	technique
tog	together
tpt	turning point
tw	twist
u	under
wk	work, as in work a stitch or work a row
wr	wrap
wyib	with yarn in back (not used in this book; see yarn farside)
wyif	with yarn in front (not used in this book; see yarn nearside)
wyon	wrap yarn on needle
x	times, as in mathematics
y	yarn
yfs	yarn farside (move yarn to farside between needle tips)
yns	yarn nearside (move yarn to nearside between needle tips)
yo	Yarnover
...	delimiters used to identify stitch pattern repeat; same format used with parentheses or brackets instead of asterisks
#	number
#/#	number of stitches and composition of a Cable; also see Gauge, above

❖ Terms in Written Instructions

The basic unit of a pattern instruction is an abbreviation of the name of a stitch technique, accompanied by a number that indicates how many times to work the technique or how many stitches to include in it. Here are some examples that cover most of the possibilities.

Abbreviations and Numbers

The simplest and most common terms in a pattern will have an abbreviation followed by a number that indicates how many times to work the same technique.

- K2 means "Knit the next two stitches."
- P3 means "Purl the next three stitches."

Combined Abbreviations

When more than one abbreviation is required to make it clear what to do, they are often combined, and the number of stitches to work is often set within the instruction.

- Sl2kw means "Slip 2 stitches knitwise."
- K2tog means "Knit 2 stitches together."

Techniques with Variations

When a technique can be done in more than one way, as is the case with some increases and decreases, a pattern might use a generic term and leave it for you to decide how to work. Others may be more specific.

- Inc, or M1, may indicate that an increase of any kind can be used, but a note accompanying the instructions may define this as standing for a particular type of increase.
- RDec or LDec are common; the latter leaves it optional which Left Decrease to use.
- SSK is quite specific as to how to make a Left Decrease, but the result would be the same in the fabric if you chose to use the SKP version (Slip 1, Knit 1, Pass Slip stitch over), instead.

There are many different kinds of cable patterns, and it is common for several to be combined in the same design. Because they are so varied, published patterns almost always provide definitions for whatever abbreviations are used. Here is the method I like to use for basic cables:

- The term LC 2/2 indicates a Left Cable "two over two"— in other words, two stitches drawn to the left on the outside of the fabric past two others. RC 2/2 is for a cable with two stitches drawn to the right past two others.

    If the pattern uses the same two cables throughout, this would be simplified as simply RC and LC.
- Using a similar abbreviation, a Right Cable "two over one," could be written RC 2/1, with two stitches drawn to the right on the outside past one other stitch.

    Or, this could be modified to KPRC 2/1 if the pattern was for two Knit stitches to be drawn to the right followed by a Purl stitch.

Pattern Repeats

A pattern repeat is one complete set of instructions consisting of a relatively small number of stitches and rows. Individually, the two aspects of the pattern are referred to as the "stitch repeat" and the "row repeat."

Each numbered line of the instructions provides the information needed to work one row of the fabric. The instructions consist of a set of steps written with the kinds of abbreviations described above. After working all the steps in a set of instructions once, you are to start at the beginning again with the first step, repeating the set as many times as necessary across the width of the fabric. When all the stitches of the row have been worked according to that set of instructions, then go on to work the next row of the instructions. Similarly, after working all the rows of the pattern once, begin again with the first row and repeat the entire pattern as many times as necessary for the length of the fabric.

Because each repeat is relatively small, a pattern can be used for projects of any size or gauge; more repeats are required for some, fewer for others. At the beginning of a written pattern, the number of stitches in the repeat is usually specified. This is referred to as the "multiple," and it is used to determine how many stitches to cast on so an even number of repeats will fit across the width of the fabric (for more information, see Pattern Multiples, below).

❖ Stitch Repeats

A set of instructions for a single row is written somewhat like a sentence, with the individual steps in the repeat separated by commas. The full repeat may also contain one or more "sub-repeats," each one of which is an even smaller series of steps that are to be worked more than once before going on to those that follow.

The primary repeat and any sub-repeats are set off by "delimiters," such as parentheses or asterisks, which make it clear where each set begins and ends.

While the number of steps in the instructions varies row by row, the number of stitches contained in each one of them is almost always the same.

Here is an explanation of the basic parts of a stitch repeat.

Steps in an Instruction

One row of instructions consists of a series of steps; each step consists of a letter abbreviation for a technique and a number indicating how many of the next stitches on the left needle should be worked with that technique. The individual steps are separated by commas.

This set of instructions is for one row of a pattern with a repeat that contains 12 stitches:

• P2, K3, YO, K2tog, K3, P2.

The instruction translates as, "Purl 2 stitches, Knit the next 3, make a Yarnover, and then a Right Decrease, Knit 3 more, and finally Purl 2."

When a complex technique requires several distinct steps, these are grouped without commas to indicate they should be treated as one step, as in this example of instructions for a repeat that contains 9 stitches:

• P2, K1, Sl2kw K1 p2sso, K1, P2.

The three abbreviations in the center group are not separated by commas; these describe the steps for a particular double decrease; if written out in words it would be "Slip 2 stitches knitwise, Knit 1, pull two slipped stitches over."

To simplify this, a pattern might substitute a single abbreviation like "DblDec" for "double decrease" or "CDDec" or "CDec2" for "center double decrease," and provide instructions for how to do the individual steps of the technique in the explanatory material.

The Primary Stitch Repeat

The repeat is commonly enclosed within asterisks, parentheses, or square brackets to set it apart from any steps that are done only at the beginning or end of a row (see Edge and Selvedge Stitches, below).

A repeat will then look something like this:

• K1 *K2, P3, K1, YO, SSK, K1, P3* K1.

The first K1 is worked only at the beginning of the row; the steps between the asterisks are for the repeat of 12 stitches, which are worked again and again across the row; the final K1 is worked on the last stitch of the row.

Some patterns assume you will understand to repeat the material within a pair of asterisks or parentheses, but more often than not there is a phrase of some kind that makes this explicit, and it will look like one of the following examples:

• *P5, K3* repeat from * to *.
• *P5, K3, rep from *.
• (P5, K3), rep between ( ).

My preference is to place the abbreviation "rep" (for repeat) *before* the set of terms within a bracket or parentheses, so you know what to do beforehand:

• Rep[P5, K3].

Sub-Repeats

When several steps of an instruction need to be done more than once, instead of writing them again and again, they are combined in a sub-repeat.

A small repeat of this kind is set apart by a different set of delimiters than those used for the main repeat. In other words, if asterisks are used for the main repeat, parentheses might be used for the sub-repeat.

A sub-repeat is always accompanied by a number that indicates how many times the steps within it should be worked before going on to the next step in the instruction, and will look something like this:

• *P2, (K2tog, YO) twice, P2, K1*.

The main repeat consists of everything between the asterisks; it starts with Purl 2 and ends with Knit 1. The two steps within the parentheses, Knit Two Together followed by a Yarnover, are steps in a sub-repeat, which is to be done twice before going on to the last two steps. Every time you work the main repeat, you would work the sub-repeat twice in its proper place.

If the same instruction was written with no sub-repeats, it would look like this:

- "P2, K2tog, YO, K2tog, YO, P2, K1."

There are different ways to indicate how many times a sub-repeat should be done; "twice," as used here is common, but you might see something like "three times," or, more briefly, "4x."

For these kinds of statements, I prefer to borrow from mathematics and write the number of times to do the sub-repeat before the parentheses, like this:

- [P2, 2(K2tog, YO), P2, K1].

In this example the full repeat is enclosed in square brackets instead of asterisks, and the sub-repeat is in parentheses. The number 2 before the sub-repeat indicates that those two steps are to be worked twice before going on to complete the remaining steps in the repeat.

More complicated patterns often contain several sub-repeats, as in this example:

- [P2, 2(K1fs, P2), K5, 3(P2, K1fs), K2].

This repeat starts with Purl 2, then there is a sub-repeat containing two steps that are to be done twice, followed by the Knit 5, followed by another sub-repeat of two steps done three times, before going on to the final Knit 2.

Pattern Multiples

Published stitch pattern collections intended for use when designing something customarily specify the number of stitches in the repeat. Often referred to as the "pattern multiple," this is a short phrase placed before the instructions. It tells you how many stitches are in the repeat, and how many extra stitches are needed for edge and/or selvedge stitches.

This information is used to calculate the number of stitches to cast on for a particular project, and it will look something like this:

- Cast on a multiple of 10 stitches, plus 4.

The "10 stitches" is the stitch pattern repeat, and the "plus 4" are edge and/or selvedge stitches (see below).

The multiple is used with some relatively simple math to determine how many full repeats will fit within the width of a fabric. It is important to know how to do this if you are designing something or want to alter a published pattern (the stitch pattern multiple does not appear in stitch patterns that accompany published garment patterns because these calculations have already been done for you by the designer).

Here is an example of how to use the multiple to calculate the number of stitches to cast on for a sample swatch if you wanted to just try a pattern. While this is a considerably simpler approach than what would be needed to plan a garment, the basic steps are the same (see Pattern Repeats and Garment Dimensions in the chapter Calculations for Pattern Design).

1. Assume the estimated gauge from the yarn label is 5.5 stitches/inch and you want to make a swatch about 6 inches wide.

   5.5 stitches per inch × 6 inches = 33 stitches

2. Next, determine how many repeats will fit evenly into this number of stitches. Although "multiple" is the term used for the number of stitches in the repeat, what actually needs to be done is a little division. Say the multiple is 10 stitches; work as follows.

   33 stitches ÷ 10 stitches in repeat =
   3 repeats, with 3 stitches left over

3. Because the extra 3 stitches amount to less than half a repeat, the simplest thing to do is just drop them.

   3 repeats × 10 stitches in repeat = 30 stitches

4. Now add the edge and selvedge stitches.

   30 + 4 = 34 stitches to cast on

Of course, if you wanted a larger sample, you might decide to add enough stitches for another full repeat; in this example, you would use 4 repeats and cast on 44 stitches instead.

It is important to fit an even number of repeats into the width of the fabric, even when doing something small and simple like a sample swatch. You may not be so concerned about the appearance of something like this, but it can be very confusing to deal with a partial repeat at one side—it is easy enough to end a row that way, but difficult to know which step of the instructions to start with for the next row.

❖ Row Repeats

Just as there are relatively few steps in a stitch repeat, there are a limited number of instructions in a row repeat. In many patterns half the rows are worked in plain Knit or Purl, and a single instruction usually serves for all of them; this considerably reduces the number of instructions needed.

And somewhat like the sub-repeats within an instruction, one or more rows may be repeated before the entire set is complete. In some cases a row is worked out of sequence; in other cases several rows are repeated at the end, before going on to do all of them again.

Instead of repeating an instruction, one row will simply refer to the instructions for another row. This simplifies a pattern considerably, making it easier to read.

Plain or Repeat Rows

Most stitch patterns are written for use when working a flat fabric, and it is common for the decorative stitch techniques to be worked on outside rows, with inside rows worked plain. Many decorative techniques look their best and are easier to do in Knit, and the plain rows in between provide them with a bit of background, or are used to complete techniques such as Yarnovers and Slip Stitches, which also appear in the next row.

In patterns of this type, it is only necessary to write specific instructions for half the rows. For instance, if the decorative pattern begins on Row 1, Row 2 might read simply:

- Purl all even-numbered rows.

Of course, if you plan to work a circular fabric, you would Knit those rows instead; for more information, see Inside and Outside Rows, below.

In some patterns of mixed Knit and Purl, one row may be just like the previous one, and the instructions might look like this:

- Row 2 and all even-numbered rows: Knit all Knit stitches; Purl all Purl stitches.

In other words, if you see a Purl stitch below the left needle, you are to Purl the stitch above; if you see a Knit stitch below the needle, you are to Knit the stitch above.

Row Sub-Repeats

Occasionally an instruction will specify that an instruction previously used for an outside row is to be worked on the inside instead. It will look like this:

- Row 4: Repeat Row 3.

In a case of this kind, the two rows will not necessarily look the same on the outside; what effect the instruction has will depend on the arrangement of stitches and it could mean there will be Knits above Purls and Purls above Knits, or Knits above Knits and Purls above Purls.

There are also patterns that use the same set of instructions on several rows, and the pattern will read something like:

- Rows 1, 3, and 5: *P3, K5, repeat from *.
  Rows 2, 4, and 6: *P5, K3, repeat from *.

In some patterns, several rows are repeated out of order. For instance, there might be unique instructions on each of Rows

1, 3, 7, and 9, with even-numbered rows worked in plain Knit or Purl, but then you might see:

- Row 5: Repeat Row 1.

In other words, after working Row 4, you are to skip back to the instructions in Row 1, and then go on to work Row 6 and continue with the remaining rows of the pattern. The odd-numbered row series is actually: 1, 3, 1, 7, 9.

There are also patterns where the rows in the second half are a repeat of those in the first half, but in reverse order. For instance, there might be instructions for Rows 1, 3, 5, and 7, and then you will see something like:

- Row 9: Repeat Row 5.
  Row 11: Repeat Row 3.

In this pattern, the row sequence is actually, 1, 3, 5, 7, 5, 3; then you start again with Row 1.

Inside and Outside Rows

Many patterns specify whether to begin on an inside or outside row of a flat fabric. As mentioned above, this is usually done so any special stitch techniques can be worked in Knit on an outside row. However, it is always important to consider whether starting the pattern as specified will be compatible with the appearance of the cast-on edge.

For example, say you plan to use a pattern that begins on an outside row, and you have used Knit Half-Hitch Cast-On. However, after turning to begin the first row, you would find yourself on the Purl side of the edge, and it would be better to start the pattern with an inside row instead. If you were to use Knit Cast-On, there would be no need to turn in order to begin, and starting with an outside row of the pattern would be fine, but if it started with an inside row, you would have a similar problem.

When a pattern starts in a way that is not appropriate for the cast-on you want to use, one solution is to begin with the last row of the stitch pattern instead of the first (it will, after all, lie below the first row of every subsequent repeat). Another way to solve the problem is to simply work one plain row before you begin. As discussed below, Preparatory Rows at the beginning and Final Rows at the end can help you start or end a pattern in a better way (they may also be used to prepare the stitches of one row for working the next).

Preparatory and Final Rows

A preparatory row is worked just once, immediately after casting on, or when making a transition from one stitch pattern to another within the fabric. This unique row may be present when the first row of a pattern repeat contains special techniques that cannot be done directly above a cast-on edge or a row containing any other special techniques. For instance, it is not ideal to begin a Knit Below pattern immediately above a cast-on edge or directly above a ribbing because it will cause distortion.

Also, the last row of a pattern may be done in a way that prepares stitches for techniques worked on the following row, which, of course, will be the first row of the next repeat. Whatever effect this has, it would not be available to the first row above a cast-on edge, and so a preparatory row is used as a substitute.

Similarly, a final row may be present when certain techniques that span more than one row need to be completed before casting off or changing to another stitch pattern. The first row of the next repeat would normally be in that position, but in its absence, an alternative is needed.

In some cases, a preparatory or final row is used simply to provide some visual separation between the cast-on or cast-off edge and the first and last rows of a decorative pattern, and they are equally useful when a pattern is inserted between other stitch patterns in the fabric. Even if these rows are not present in a pattern, you might consider adding them for these reasons.

Patterns for Flat or Circular Fabrics

Most collections of stitch patterns are intended for use when designing something of your own, and they are customarily written for working flat, with alternating inside and outside rows; it is assumed you will first try a pattern on a small sample and then make a flat gauge swatch. Stitch patterns are only written specifically for working in the round when they are part of a published garment pattern that is intended to be made in that way.

If you want to use a flat pattern but prefer to work in the round, or come across a circular pattern that you want to use for something made flat, you will need to translate the instructions so they will work for the application you have in mind.

To do this, all the Knit versions of any technique have to be changed to the Purl versions, the Purls to the Knits, and so forth, and the sequence of steps must be changed to match the direction in which the rows will be worked. Furthermore, flat patterns often require selvedge stitches, which are not used for circular knitting, and edge stitches, which are not always needed.

❖ Converting a Pattern

To translate a flat pattern for use when working in the round, you will only need to concern yourself with rewriting the inside rows. Of course, with any pattern that has plain rows on the inside, this is a simple matter; if the row was to be done as Purl, simply work in Knit, or vice versa.

However, when a pattern has unique instructions on all or most of the rows, it is not just a matter of changing Knit to Purl, or Purl to Knit. When making a circular fabric, the first stitch of a row is worked into the first stitch of the previous row, but when making a flat fabric, the first stitch of every inside row is worked into the last stitch of every outside row and the last stitch of a row is worked into the first stitch of the previous row. To read a pattern without rewriting it would require you to read one row from right to left, and the next from left to right; it is simpler to translate the instructions.

As you rewrite the instructions, you will also want to consider the role of any steps that are written outside the repeat in a flat pattern. These are either selvedge or edge stitches; the former are never used for a circular fabric, while the latter may be needed, depending on the pattern or how it is used.

Converting Instructions

To translate the instructions for an inside row so they can be used as an outside row, or vice versa, rewrite them as a "mirror image." To do this, read the steps *backwards*, from left to right, and then write them right to left, changing all Knits to Purls and Purls to Knits.

For instance, if the instructions for an inside row are written like this:

- P2, K3, P5, K3.

Then the same instructions for an outside row would be written:

- P3, K5, P3, K2.

In other words, the last K3 becomes the first P3, the first P2 becomes the last K2, and the two steps in the middle trade places and also change from Knit to Purl.

❖ Edge and Selvedge Stitches

Patterns written for working flat usually require selvedge stitches and may or may not need edge stitches as well. If these special stitches are included in a pattern, they will be written outside of the delimiters that define the repeat; in other words, before the first parenthesis or asterisk, or after the last one.

A flat fabric requires a selvedge stitch for any edge that will be seamed; the stitch at each edge will be absorbed into the seam, leaving the fabric the correct width and the decorative stitch pattern undisturbed. Selvedge stitches are also frequently used for a flat fabric that will not be seamed to provide a decorative visible edge when the main stitch pattern would not be attractive on its own, or perhaps to move any decorative stitch technique away from an edge so it will not be distorted. In those cases, they do add to the finished width of the fabric. Selvedge stitches are never used for a circular fabric.

It is important to know what purpose edge stitches serve before deciding whether to use them or not. They are commonly used to balance the appearance of a pattern at both sides of a flat fabric. In some cases, an edge stitch might be used in addition to a selvedge stitch in order to keep complex stitch techniques away from a seam.

Edge stitches are also added to the left side of a vertical pattern repeat that will not be worked the full width of the fabric (such as a cable pattern), so both sides will look the same. They also appear in patterns where the main motif changes its position, perhaps to create a spiral effect, or to stagger a motif horizontally. In these situations, the edge stitches consist of instructions for a partial repeat that appears at the beginning and end of only some rows.

Because edge and selvedge stitches serve such different purposes, it is important to determine whether they are needed or not, and this requires making sense of the pattern and thinking about how you will use it before you get started. A simple way to do this is with a Test Swatch, but charting the pattern will also make these things clear (see Charted Stitch Patterns).

Here are some examples of patterns that have selvedge or edge stitches.

Selvedge Stitches

A pattern with selvedge stitches will look something like this:

- K1, *P1, K1, P1, K4* rep from *, end K1.

It is safe to assume that one stitch at each side is a Selvedge Stitch, especially for a simple pattern that does not contain any special techniques, like this one. For a circular fabric, therefore, simply ignore the selvedges and work only the steps within the asterisks.

Selvedges with Edge Stitch

If the same pattern were to be used for an unseamed fabric, it would be best to add an edge stitch so the pattern will look the same at both sides.

In this case, the repeat is enclosed in brackets instead of asterisks to show what that option looks like:

- K1, rep[P1, K1, P1, K4], end P1, K1.

The Purl stitch worked at the end of the row is equivalent to the first stitch of the repeat at the beginning of the row.

For a flat fabric that will be seamed, include the selvedge stitches, but not the edge stitch; for one that is circular, ignore all three.

Edge Stitches as Partial Repeats

Here are several rows of a pattern that creates a spiral effect, which is done with edge stitches that shift the repeats stepwise within the fabric.

Row 1 and all odd-numbered rows, Purl.
Row 2: K1, rep[P5, K3].
Row 4: K2, rep[P5, K3], end P5, K2.
Row 6: K3, rep[P5, K3], end P5, K1.
Row 8: K4, rep[P5, K3], end P5.

The edge stitches at the beginning of each row shift the pattern one stitch to the left. This leaves too few stitches at the end of the row for a full repeat, so the edge stitches at the end of the instructions tell you how to work a partial repeat.

CHAPTER 21

Charted Stitch Patterns

A stitch chart is a graphic representation of a knitting pattern. Instead of the abbreviations and numbers used in the patterns described in Written Stitch Patterns, charted instructions are conveyed by means of symbols placed in the squares of graph paper; each square is equivalent to a stitch, and each symbol indicates which technique to use.

Published patterns are charted using a variety of different methods, most of them arising informally out of one or another regional knitting tradition. While similar in concept, they vary in the details, and all have limitations of one kind or another, whether in the types of patterns that can be charted, or how easy they are to read.

A good chart should provide you with a clear visual sense of which techniques are required and how they are used in the pattern, but ideally it will also give you a sense of what the fabric will look like. This will enable you to learn a new pattern more quickly, make it easier to keep your place in it as you work, and avoid errors because you can readily compare the fabric to the chart.

The stitch charting system discussed here is one that I developed in hopes of solving some of the problems and limitations often encountered with traditional methods. The result is not a radical departure and those of you who regularly work with charted patterns should find this system more or less familiar.

Immediately below, you will find a Glossary of the symbols preferred for this charting method, along with some traditional symbols that are included so you will recognize them and/or because they provide useful options for some patterns.

The Glossary is followed by a limited selection of sample charts accompanied by written instructions. This is not intended to be a comprehensive look at all the possibilities in charting; the goal is to introduce the underlying concepts used for all charts, and to explain how this method differs from others. The patterns were selected because they exemplify something about how charting is done; in some cases, several examples of the same pattern are presented using different methods so you can compare them.†

If you have never worked from charts before, this material should enable you to read one regardless of what method was used to make it, or even rewrite it using whatever method you prefer. The discussions that accompany each chart also suggest ways to modify a pattern, either to change its appearance somewhat or to make it more suitable for the application you have in mind. As you gain confidence in dealing with charts, you may be inspired to design your own patterns. Also included are instructions for how to translate written instructions into charted form, or vice versa.

Glossary of Symbols

As you will see, many of the more familiar symbols from other charting systems have been retained in this one, although some are used in different ways and there are several that are new. The first one listed for a particular technique is preferred, but the others are included both as options and so you will recognize them in published patterns.

My criteria for selecting a symbol were that it should resemble in some way the stitch it represents, be easy to read, and convey a good idea of what is actually taking place in the fabric.

Unique symbols are assigned only to the most basic techniques, but these are frequently modified in some way to indicate a variation of the technique so they can serve more than

---

† All of the stitch patterns included here were inspired and adapted from patterns found in Barbara Walker's books, *A Treasury of Knitting Patterns* (New York: Charles Scribner's Sons, 1968), and *A Second Treasury of Knitting Patterns* (New York: Charles Scribner's Sons, 1970).

one purpose. Techniques that are less common may have a symbol that combines two of the basic ones. When charting a pattern, you should feel free to use the symbols creatively, adapting them as needed to suit the pattern, or even make up some of your own.

For symbols used on garment charts, see Chart Symbols in the chapter Charted Garment Patterns.

❖ *Basic Stitch Techniques*

Here are the most basic symbols, used for the techniques discussed in The Stitches, along with some that can be used for Twined Knit patterns and Beading patterns.

Knit

In most charts, the most efficient symbol to use for the Knit stitch is none at all. In other words, it is assumed that every stitch will be Knit unless some other symbol occupies a square. This not only saves a considerable amount of writing when you are making a chart,

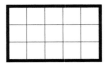

Knit indicated by squares with no symbol.

but it adds visual clarity, drawing your eye to the pattern stitches and making them easy to read. This works particularly well for any Rib or Brocade pattern, as well as for many lace patterns, although there are situations when this approach may not be sufficiently precise or unambiguous and a symbol is needed.

For some patterns it is important to use the symbol for Knit, shown on the left below, in order to indicate clearly what happens to each and every stitch. Also, when making a first, rough draft of a pattern chart, it helps to make a mark of some kind simply as a way of counting out stitches and keeping your place, and the symbol can then be omitted in the final draft if that would make the chart easier to read.

Whenever a pattern creates bias, the Knit symbol can be set at an angle to indicate the direction in which the stitches will be pulled; this can help you visualize what will happen in the fabric. The bias versions are shown on the right side of the chart.

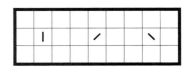

Knit symbols.

Purl

The small dot symbol, shown on the left, is often used to indicate a Purl stitch. The same symbol is also used in conjunction with many others when the Purl version of a particular technique should appear on the outside of the fabric.

The dash symbol shown at right is commonly used for Purl, and it looks quite like a Purl stitch; it is also quicker to write when drafting a pattern. It does, however, take up more space, and therefore does not work as well when combined with another symbol to indicate the Purl version of a technique. If you find it confusing to use two different symbols for the same thing, then use the dot; it works in every situation.

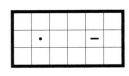

Purl.

Twist Stitch

A small hatch mark on a sloped line indicates that a Knit stitch should be worked so it will twist on itself to the right or left. As with the symbol for Purl, the mark can also be used in combination with other symbols to indicate that some other technique should be twisted as it is worked.

Just one method is used to make a Left Twist Stitch, but there are two ways to form a Right Twist Stitch (both produce the same result in the fabric). One version is used for a single stitch; it is turned first and then worked so it twists; the symbol shown here is used for that purpose.

The other approach is used for all-over patterns, where all or most of the stitches are turned on one row and then worked so they twist on the next. In patterns of this type, the technique is best explained with a note adjacent to the chart, and/or the symbol can be placed next to the row number, instead of within all the squares of the chart itself.

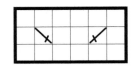

Twist Stitch.

Elongation

Two methods are used to elongate stitches; one for an entire row, one for individual stitches.

Multiple Wrap

These first symbols indicate that the yarn should be wrapped an extra time or two in order to elongate a particular stitch. The one on the left indicates a single extra wrap, although it could also be used for multiple wraps if the number required is made clear with a note adjacent to the chart that defines the technique.

Alternatively, the symbol on the right contains a number that indicates how many wraps are needed. Notice that the symbol touches the top line of the square to indicate that the wrap affects the *new* stitch, not the discard stitch; this leaves room below it for a Purl symbol when needed.

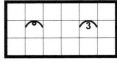

Multiple Wrap.

Needle Elongation

Needle Elongation requires the use of a larger needle on one of the pattern rows; because this affects every stitch in the row, it is easiest to simply indicate what is needed by circling the row number; an explanatory note can be used to specify the size needle to use.

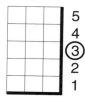

Needle
Elongation.

Slip Stitch

This symbol for Slip stitch is quite common; however, in this system it is used in a slightly different way.

In traditional charts, it is understood that if a square contains the bottom of the symbol, the stitch should be slipped; it should be slipped again if the symbol occupies a square in a row above. This stitch is then worked when a square above it contains a different symbol, usually for Knit or Purl.

However, in this system, the Slip stitch is worked when a square contains the top of the symbol; if a Purl dot is present, the Slip stitch is to be Purled on the outside of the fabric.

In some patterns, a Slip stitch may be involved in a decrease or in a Cable or Crossed Stitch technique. In these cases, the symbol can be placed at an angle, or it may share part of a square with another symbol.

Slip Stitch.

Twisted Slip Stitch

These symbols serve for a Twist Stitch technique used on a Slip stitch. For a Left Twist, the stitch is slipped purlwise when the lower portion of the symbol occupies a square, and it is Knit farside when the upper portion of the symbol occupies a square.

For a Right Twist, the stitch is slipped knitwise when the lower portion of the symbol occupies a square, and the turned stitch is Knit nearside when the upper portion of the symbol occupies a square.

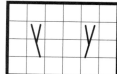

Twisted Slip Stitch.

Slip Stitch: Yarn Stranded Outside

The horizontal bar across the base of a Slip stitch symbol indicates that the yarn is to be stranded past the stitch on the outside of the fabric. In some patterns, there may be several Slip stitches side by side, with a single strand crossing all of them. If the stitches are slipped again on a subsequent row, there will be another strand.

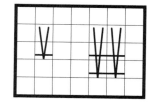

Slip Stitch.
Yarn stranded outside.

Lattice

The first symbol here shows the basic Lattice technique; a strand is passed on the outside of several Slip stitches and then picked up on a later row and worked together with a stitch.

The two symbols on the right represent the Multiple Lattice technique, where more than one strand is caught up on a later row. The one with the dotted lines indicates that the strands are on the inside of the fabric.

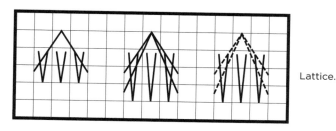

Lattice.

Knit Below and Brioche Stitch

This new symbol for the Brioche technique was designed to look as much as possible like the stitch in the fabric and serves equally well for either method of making this stitch: the Knit Below technique or the Yarnover-Slip technique. The little "tails" at each side of the Slip stitch symbol represent the strand that is equivalent to a Yarnover.

If you are using the Yarnover-Slip method of doing a Brioche pattern, when you come to a square containing the lower portion of the symbol, work the Yarnover and Slip stitch; when you come to a square containing the top of the symbol, work the decrease that joins the two. The symbol may be accompanied by a Purl dot when needed.

If you are using the Knit Below method, when you come to a square that contains the lower portion of the symbol, Knit or Purl as usual, whichever is convenient; when you come to the square that contains the top of the symbol in the row above and work the technique, these stitches will unravel.

Because these are generally allover patterns, it is rarely necessary to chart more than a single small repeat showing how to work the pattern.

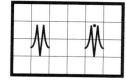

Knit Below/Brioche.

Multiple Knit Below

The two most common symbols used for the Knit Below technique are the little hoop shape or an arrow. Either one works well enough in a chart, but it does not resemble the fabric. When necessary, the symbol can be accompanied by a number if a pattern requires working into a stitch more than one row down, or you could elongate the symbol on the left so it includes the squares

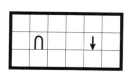

Multiple Knit Below.

for the stitches below that will be included when you work the technique.

Alternatively, you may prefer to use the new Knit Below symbol shown above, and simply elongate the Slip stitch portion of it to show how many stitches should be included when the technique is worked.

Ladder

The arrow passes through squares to show which stitches will later be unraveled; work them either as Knit or Purl, whichever is convenient. In some patterns the arrow may end at a row containing an increase, or, for a multiple ladder, at one that indicates a few stitches are to be cast on.

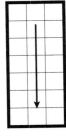

Ladder.

Cable Stitches

In her book *Charted Knitting Designs*, Barbara Walker worked out a very sensible and visually attractive system for charting cable patterns.† The lines indicating the facing stitches of the cable pass from the base of the squares where they originate to the top of the squares they will occupy when the step is completed. The two smaller lines slanting in the opposite direction indicate the origin and destination of the backing stitches.

The vertical lines that extend up and down from the cross indicate the path of the columns of Knit stitches that extend into and out of the Cable. These lines are optional but generally add visual clarity to a charted pattern. Despite the variety of Cable techniques, all of them can be charted using simple variations on this one symbol.

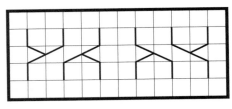

Cable Stitches.

Mixed Cables

If the backing stitches are to be Purled, the lines for them are replaced by the symbol for Purl. Although rare, there are also patterns that use Purl on the facing stitches, and the dot symbol placed in the appropriate square within the sloping lines would make this clear.

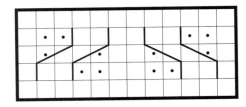

Mixed Cable of Knit and Purl.

† Barbara Walker, *Charted Knitting Designs* (New York: Charles Scribner's Sons, 1972).

Cable Stitch Option

Here is another commonly used symbol for the Cable technique. It clearly conveys what to do, but does not produce as vivid a picture of the pattern as the symbol above. Nevertheless, it is quicker to write, and you may find it useful when you are doing a rough draft of a pattern.

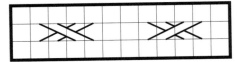

Cable Stitch, optional symbol.

Crossed Stitch

The Crossed Stitch is so closely related to a Cable that it makes sense to use a variation of the same symbol even though the working method may be different. In fact, there are so many methods of making a Crossed Stitch, the symbol would almost always need to be keyed to written instructions that specify the particular technique to be used.

The little hatch marks for the backing stitches are not present in the first Crossed Stitch symbol; they tend to clutter things up when only two stitches are involved. However, the vertical lines extending above and below

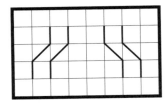

Crossed Stitch.

the Crossed Stitches are retained; these are especially useful in depicting the appearance of Crossed Stitch patterns that create columns of Knit stitches that "travel" across the fabric.

However, in patterns where the technique is worked repeatedly within the fabric to create textured effects, the backing stitches can be used to good effect, but the vertical lines above and below are not needed.

The traditional symbol for this technique is a little X symbol with an arrow tip on one, as shown.

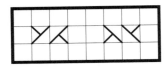

Crossed Stitch with backing stitches.

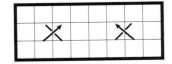

Crossed Stitch, traditional symbol.

Threaded Stitch

This symbol resembles the alternative shown above for a Cable Stitch, except a hooked line is used to indicate each facing stitch. Because only half of the facing stitch remains on the outside, this resembles the resulting fabric quite well.

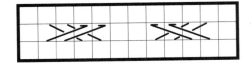

Threaded Stitch.

Wrap Stitch

These symbols show which stitches are included in a Wrap technique; the one on the left is a single Wrap, the one on the right is a Double Wrap.

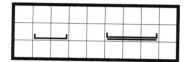

Wrap Stitch.

Loop Stitch

Easy to recognize and simple to use, this little symbol works nicely when a stitch pattern uses Loops only in certain areas; for an overall pattern, of course, you really do not need a chart at all.

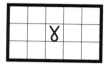

Loop Stitch.

Twined Knit

Four symbols are useful for the decorative techniques typical of Twined Knit patterns. The first pair are for Crook Stitch; the one on the left is Purl-Knit-Purl; the one on the right, Knit-Purl-Knit.

In the next pair shown, the one on the left represents the Deep Stitch, which is a Purl stitch made with two strands of yarn. It straddles the grid line because on one row, the new stitch is made with two yarns held as one, and on the next row, this doubled stitch is worked and discarded. The symbol on the right is used for Chain Path, where alternating yarns are stranded past every stitch on the outside of the fabric.

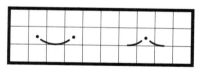

Twined Knit. Crook Stitch.

Twined Knit. Left: Deep Stitch; Right: Chain Path.

Beading

The symbol on the left is used for Running Thread Beading patterns. It is shown here on the line dividing two squares with Purl stitches on either side. However, a bead can also be set on a running thread that strands past a Slip stitch, in which case you could draw the little bead symbol at the bottom of that symbol. Similarly, if you wanted to set beads while working a Twined Knit pattern, the little bead circle could be combined with the symbols for that technique, which are shown above.

The symbol on the right is used for Stitch Head Beading. If the bead symbol is at the top of a square, it indicates a bead should be set on a new stitch; if the bead symbol is at the bottom of a square and there is a Purl dash above it, this means a beaded stitch should be Purled.

Here again, the bead symbol can be adapted to other uses; instead of a Purl stitch symbol in the square above, it could be a Twist Stitch, or the bead symbol could be set within or at the top of a Yarnover symbol.

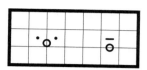

Beading. Left: Running Thread Beading; Right: Stitch Head Beading.

❖ Increase and Decrease Symbols

In many charting systems, a single symbol serves for any increase and another for any decrease; it is left to the knitter to determine the particular technique to be used, or a note may accompany the chart. However, the various techniques confer such unique characteristics to a fabric that I prefer to use more specific symbols for them.

Also, traditional charts write the symbols for both increases and decreases within a single square. In most cases, that is true of a decrease in this charting system, but not usually of an increase, which expands into an adjacent square and points up to the squares the new stitches will occupy in the row above.

Decorative increases and decreases are always paired in a pattern, and this approach generally works quite well, particularly for lace patterns where the pair consists of a Yarnover and a decrease. However, in some cases, the structure of the pattern is better displayed if the opposite is done, with the increase symbol in one square and the decrease symbol expanded into two or more squares; an example of this is shown in the chart for Berry Stitch, below.

Bar Increase

The barred, "Purl" portion of the symbol may lie to the left or right on the outside of the fabric.

Bar Increase.

Rib Increase

The dotted portion of the symbol indicates the position of the Purl stitch of the pair. The little circle suggests the way the yarn wraps around the head of the stitch when changing from Knit to Purl, or vice versa. See also the appearance of this increase when used on a Yarnover, below.

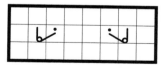

Rib Increase.

Raised Increase

The vertical line indicates the position of the original stitch; the sloping line shows the position of the new, increased stitch, whether on the right or left side. For a Double Raised Increase, sloping lines will be on both sides.

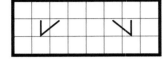

Raised Increase.

If you are using a Raised Increase in a Rib or Brocade pattern, you might want to work one or the other of the stitches as a Purl. The Purl versions shown indicate quite clearly whether it is the raised stitch that should be Purled, or the one on the needle above it.

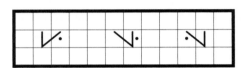

Raised Increase. Mixed Knit and Purl.

Slip Raised Increase.

The Slip Raised Increase combines this symbol with the one for the Slip stitch, which makes this variation of the technique quite clear.

Running Thread Increase

This increase is done between two stitches; therefore, the symbol is set between two squares. It can be written sloping to either the left or the right, depending upon the effect it causes in the fabric or to avoid conflict with an adjacent symbol, or perhaps simply because this would make the pattern easier to read.

For the Purl version, dot the symbol. The Twist version employs the little hatch marks used for the Twist Stitch symbol, above.

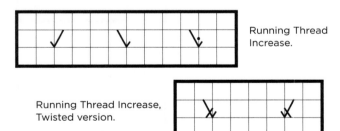

Running Thread Increase.

Running Thread Increase, Twisted version.

Yarnover

This is a new symbol for the Yarnover, and its use is explained in detail in the charting instructions below. When a square contains the bottom of the symbol, pass the yarn over the needle to form the Yarnover. When the square contains the top of the symbol, work the Yarnover strand as Knit on the outside, or, if it is dotted, work it as Purl on the outside.

While a Yarnover is made between two existing stitches, the symbol normally occupies a square on the chart that has become available because a decrease has removed a stitch nearby; the decrease symbol occupies a single square to leave room for the Yarnover.

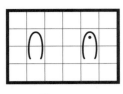

Yarnover.

Yarnover: Traditional

This is the traditional symbol for a Yarnover. It occupies a single square and indicates only that you should pass the yarn over the needle; the square above will contain a Knit or Purl symbol indicating that the Yarnover is treated as a normal stitch.

This symbol is convenient in patterns that are crowded with others that leave no room for the new version, above. It is effective at conveying what step to take, even if it does not match the fabric as closely.

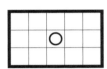

Yarnover, traditional symbol.

Multiple Yarnovers

The Yarnover symbol with the little loop at the top indicates the yarn should be wrapped more than once around the needle; if there are multiple wraps, a number can be used instead.

The next symbol shows a Double Yarnover Increase worked on a stitch (Knit, Yarnover, Knit).

The third symbol shows a Double Yarnover at the base of a Rib Increase (a Bar Increase could also be used). The symbol is expanded to include the squares that are affected by the change.

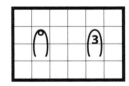

Multiple Yarnovers.

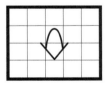

Double Yarnover Increase.

Double Yarnover with Rib Increase.

Multiple Increase

Here is a symbol for a Multiple Increase that is not specific to a particular technique, and so would require written instructions in a pattern. For instance, it would serve equally well for a Multiple Rib Increase or a Multiple Yarnover Increase.

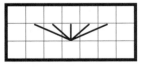

Multiple Increase.

Right and Left Decreases

These are quite self-explanatory; the sloping line indicates the slant

Right and Left Decreases.

of the decrease, whether to the right or to the left. If the decrease is to be Purled, a dot accompanies the symbol; if it is to be twisted, the Twist Stitch mark can be used.

When necessary, expand the symbol, writing the vertical line in one square, the sloped line in another.

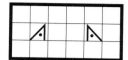 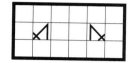

Purl Right and Left Decreases. **Twisted Right and Left Decreases.**

Double and Multiple Decreases

As with the single versions, two of the symbols for a Double Decrease slant in the direction the decrease will slant in the fabric: the Right and Left versions lean to either side, while the Center Double Decrease is upright. The symbol can be expanded into more than one square if necessary, with written instructions provided for the particular technique used.

The Multiple Decrease normally occupies a single square and is accompanied by a number that indicates how many stitches are worked together, but it could be written as an enlarged version of one of the Double Decreases, above, and include as many lines as there are stitches involved in the technique.

 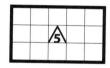

Double Decreases. **Multiple Decrease.**

Chain Nub

This technique is rarely seen and so hardly deserves to have a little symbol of its own, but it is difficult to use any combination of other symbols to convey the sense of what is required, so here it is.

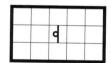

Chain Nub.

Bobbles

Because there are so many different ways to make a Bobble, the little diamond symbol, or just the letter "B" can be used to show its location. This would need to be accompanied by written instructions or a mini-chart providing the specifics about how to work the technique (see Teardrop Pendant, below). Use the same principle for a Nub or a Knot.

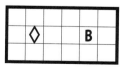

Bobble.

Embossing

For techniques of this kind, paired multiple increases and decreases are separated by several rows. In some patterns, a single symbol or inset box within the chart can be used along with brief written instructions. If the pattern is complex, it may be more practical to use a mini-chart placed next to the main chart to show the details; see the example in the chart for Mist Drops, below.

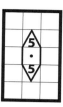

Embossing.

Pullover Stitch

The basic symbol for a Pullover is the hooked line that encircles the base of several new stitches (see Pullover technique). If the hooked end lies to the left, the Pullover is worked on the outside of the fabric; if it lies to the right, it is worked on the inside.

The symbol on the left starts within a square to indicate a Stitch Pullover. The one in the middle has a tiny Yarnover symbol set between two squares to show that a Yarnover is made in that position and then pulled over. The version on the right has a symbol indicating that a stitch is slipped knitwise before it is pulled over.

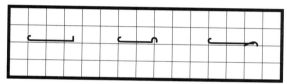

Pullover symbols.

Couching Stitch

This symbol for Couching resembles the appearance of the stitch in the fabric, and it can be drawn and positioned in different ways, as needed by the particular pattern. In this case, it shows that a loop should be drawn through two stitches in one row, and then attached two stitches to the right and up one row. However, there are different ways to accomplish this, and, as with many techniques where there are options, it would require written instructions accompanying the chart.

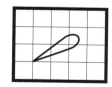

Couching Stitch.

Stitch Charts

The material below begins with basic information about how charts are organized and how symbols are used. This is followed by a section with several charted patterns that make use of basic stitch techniques. The first one, a simple Knit and Purl pattern, is accompanied by an explanation of how to read a chart.

The next section has charts that make use of decorative increase and decrease techniques. You will find examples of patterns that exhibit bias effects, several lace patterns, and some that make use of Embossing techniques. Finally, there is an example of a Twined Knit pattern and several charts for bead and sequin patterns.

The instructions that accompany the charts are written in the customary way for working a flat fabric; for an explanation of the abbreviations used and the form the instructions take, see Written Stitch Patterns. That material also contains an explanation of the basic components of any pattern: the repeat, the role of edge stitches, preparatory and final rows, and so on. Most of the stitch techniques used are discussed in the chapter The Stitches, as well as in Increase and Decrease Techniques, and Increase and Decrease Stitch Patterns; instructions are included here only for those that are more specialized.

Some of these patterns were chosen because they demonstrate ways in which this charting system differs from others. A few were selected because they are difficult to chart with traditional methods, but can be done with this one, or because they present unusual challenges and serve to illustrate some of the creative solutions you can use when faced with similar situations. The discussion accompanying the charts includes information about any optional edge stitches that appear in a pattern, and also provides suggestions for how to modify a chart if necessary for working either flat or in the round.

The best way to approach this material is with needles and yarn in hand. For each pattern you want to try, make a little Test Swatch, casting on just enough stitches for several repeats. (Use the estimated gauge on the yarn label to get an idea of how many stitches you will need for the width you want.) Selvedge stitches are not normally shown in a chart, but it is a good idea to add them to a swatch to keep any special stitch techniques away from the edge of the fabric; work them in any way you like at the beginning and end of each row.

If you want to make a sampler strip, working one pattern after another, use increases or decreases to adjust the number of stitches on the needle before starting a new one. This is important because a partial repeat at the end of a row will make it difficult to find your place in the next row of the chart.

❖ Introduction to Stitch Charts

A chart is written on a grid, and each horizontal line conveys the information about how to work one row of the pattern. The numbers written from right to left below the chart identify the stitches of a single repeat (in a written pattern, this information is referred to as the "multiple" and appears above the instructions). The numbers for a single row repeat are written on the right side from the bottom up. The charted numbering system corresponds to the way you knit, right to left, stitch by stitch, and bottom up, row by row.

One square in the chart is the same as one stitch on the needle or in the fabric. The information in each square tells you two things: First, the symbol it contains indicates which technique to use when working the next stitch on the left needle. Second, it tells you what the discarded stitch will look like in the fabric.

It is important to understand that a chart shows only what the pattern should look like on the *outside* of the fabric. This makes it very easy to read when making something in the round; simply read every row from right to left, just as shown.

However, it is more of a challenge when working flat because you need to read outside rows from right to left, *and inside rows from left to right.* Furthermore, as you read inside rows, the symbols need to be mentally translated into their opposite stitch forms—if a symbol indicates that a Purl stitch should appear on the outside of the fabric, and you are working an inside row, you would need to Knit that stitch instead; if the symbol indicates a Knit stitch should be on the outside, you would need to Purl that stitch on an inside row.

While it may seem confusing at first to have to mentally translate the instructions on the chart in this way, with a little familiarity what to do becomes automatic, and fortunately most patterns contain relatively few special techniques and they are generally worked only on outside rows, with the inside rows done plain. If you find a pattern challenging to read in this respect, feel free to make notes alongside the chart to remind yourself what to do, or even to rewrite the chart to show the inside rows as they are actually done; for an example, see Chart with Inside Rows in the material on Writing a Stitch Chart, below.

❖ Charts with Basic Stitch Techniques

The first group of charts is for patterns that make use of the most basic stitch techniques, such as Knit, Purl, and Slip stitches. Also included is an example of a Cable pattern and a Crossed Stitch pattern. After gaining familiarity with these, you should feel quite comfortable with reading charted patterns and be ready to go on to learn how to read charts that include increase and decrease techniques, discussed below, which are frequently more challenging.

Brocade Patterns

The two charts discussed first are made up of just Knit and Purl stitches. The simplicity of the first one, called Lozenge, will allow you to concentrate less on the pattern itself and more on how charting works. The second one, Diamond Brocade, is a little more challenging, and will give you additional practice working from a chart with just Knit and Purl before going on to patterns with other stitch techniques.

Lozenge

Here is a simple pattern with triangle motifs made of Knit and Purl stitches. There are two charts; the first is done using the methods I recommend, and it is accompanied by an explanation of how to read each row of the chart. The second chart is a more traditional version of the same pattern; it is included so you can compare this method with others to see what the advantages are, but also so you will become familiar with the types of charts you may encounter in published patterns.

Multiple of 5 stitches/8 rows.

Row 1: [P1, K4].   Row 5: [K4, P1].
Row 2: [P3, K2].   Row 6: [K2, P3].
Row 3: Repeat Row 2.   Row 7: Repeat Row 6.
Row 4: Repeat Row 1.   Row 8: Repeat Row 5.

First Chart

In this chart, blank squares indicate a Knit stitch, and the dot symbol is used for Purl. The chart includes several repeats of the pattern, with the primary one enclosed within darker lines. Extra repeats are not always included in published charts, but I think they give you a better sense of what the pattern will look like in the fabric, and how the repeats fit together horizontally and vertically.

However, when you read a chart, ignore the extra repeats and concentrate on just the primary one. Work each numbered step in the instructions once, and then repeat the same steps again and again to the end of the row or round, just as you would when reading the steps within the parentheses or the asterisks in written instructions.

To try this pattern, cast on a multiple of the number of stitches shown in the repeat; 20 or 25 stitches will do, just enough for a small swatch. Selvedge stitches are not shown on a chart, but you will want to add two for a flat fabric; work them according to preference at the beginning and end of each row. In this charting system, an arrow points to the first outside row; this pattern happens to be reversible, so it is a bit arbitrary in this case, but there is a subtle difference in the appearance of the two sides.

Read the chart as follows:

Row 1: Read the symbols from right to left. A Purl dot followed by four blank squares is the equivalent of the written instruction [P1, K4]; after working these 5 stitches, begin again with stitch 1 and repeat across the row.

Row 2: Read the symbols from left to right, starting with stitch 5. The written instructions say [P3, K2], but what you see on the chart are three empty squares for Knit and two with the Purl dot, which is just the opposite. The chart shows what the fabric looks like on the *outside*, but because you are working an inside row, you will need to Purl the stitches in columns 5, 4, and 3, and Knit the two stitches in columns 2 and 1.

Row 3: This is an outside row, and the chart shows three Purl dots and two blank squares, which matches the written instructions, [P3, K2].

Row 4: This is an inside row, and the chart shows that stitch 5 is a Knit—therefore, work it as Purl on the inside; stitches 4, 3, 2 and 1 are Purls—therefore, work them as Knit on the inside. This matches the written instructions, [P1, K4].

Rows 5–8: Continue in this way, reading right to left on outside rows, and left to right on inside rows.

In order to keep your place and follow the instructions as you work, it helps to place a ruler or piece of paper *above* the row you are reading ("sticky" notes work well for this because they stay in place). A guide of this kind draws your eye to the row

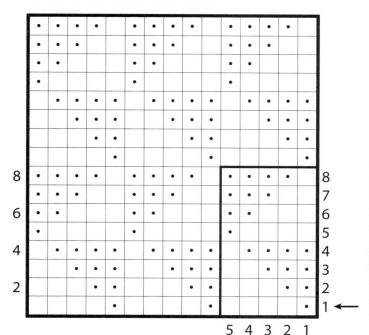

Lozenge. First chart.

Lozenge.

you are working on, and having it above the row leaves those below visible as well, which is important.

Imagine your right needle lying in the same position as the guide; to see if you did the last few steps correctly, or to find your place in the chart, compare the discarded stitches below your right needle with the symbols in the row below the guide.

Imagine the left needle lying *on* the row you are reading; the symbols in that row tell you what to do with the neutral stitches on that needle. The symbols in the squares one row down indicate what the discarded stitches below the left needle should look like. Therefore, when checking what to do next, look at both rows of the chart. The symbols in the row below the one you are reading will indicate something like: "there should be three Purl stitches below the left needle," while the current row will tell you something like "work a Knit, a Purl, and Knit above three Purl stitches."

Second Chart

Here is the same pattern charted in a more traditional way, with a symbol for Knit instead of empty squares, and a dash for Purl instead of a dot.

You will encounter many different types of charts in published patterns, and the important thing is to recognize that the underlying concepts are generally the same; what is different are the particulars—the symbols and how they are used. You should feel free to rewrite any chart into a form you are comfortable with, or even translate written instructions into a chart, as described below in Writing a Stitch Chart.

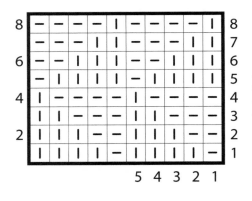

Lozenge. Second chart. A traditional chart using a symbol for Knit and a dash for Purl.

Diamond Brocade

Here is a lovely pattern that is a little more challenging than the one above. Here again, the second chart of the same pattern is done with traditional symbols so you can learn how to read one done that way as well.

This pattern has just 8 stitches, so for a sample swatch, cast on something like 24, 32, or 40 stitches, enough for three to five repeats, plus one edge stitch, and two selvedge stitches (always work the selvedge stitches separately; they are not

included in the instructions). Start reading the chart at the bottom right corner, Row 1, and compare it to the written instructions as you work.

Multiple: 8 stitches/8 rows; 1 optional edge stitch.

Row 1: Rep[K4, P1, K3], end K1.
Row 2: P1, rep[P2, K1, P1, K1, P3].
Row 3: Rep[K2, P1, K3, P1, K1], end K1.
Row 4: P1, rep[K1, P5, K1, P1].
Row 5: Rep[P1, K7], end P1.
Rows 6–8: Repeat Rows 4, 3, 2.
Final Row: Work after completing all row repeats, before casting off or changing to another pattern.

First Chart

This chart uses a dot for Purl and blank squares for Knit, and it is quite clear what the pattern will look like in the fabric.

The edge stitch at the left side of the chart is optional; it is only worked at the end of a row when needed to balance the pattern at both sides of an unseamed flat fabric. It is not used for a circular fabric, nor for a flat fabric that is to be seamed (the latter would need selvedge stitches at both sides).

You could also add a preparatory row to this pattern, perhaps to provide a little separation from the last row of a ribbing, or, if you are working flat and starting above a cast-on edge, it would then serve as the first inside row. As it happens, this pattern is reversible, and it does not matter how you start, but it is always a good idea to take this into consideration.

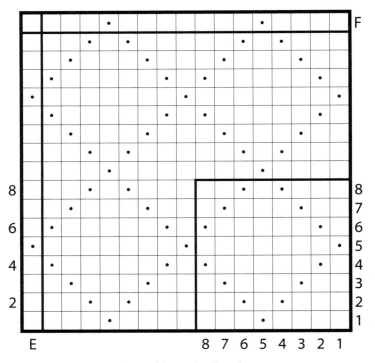

Diamond Brocade. First chart.

Diamond Brocade.

Second Chart

In many charting systems, the Knit symbol is a short vertical line (or sometimes a little V-shape that looks like the stitch), and the symbol for Purl is the short horizontal line. These are used in the next version of the same pattern to demonstrate how much more difficult it is to read a chart that uses a symbol for Knit.

However, using a dash for Purl instead of a dot is often a good option; it resembles the stitch and is somewhat quicker to write when drafting a chart, although it can be somewhat less versatile when used in combination with other symbols.

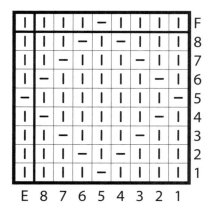

Diamond Brocade. Second chart with traditional symbols.

Slip Stitch Patterns

The two charts shown here are significant because they show an entirely new method of using the Slip stitch symbol. The first is a simple, allover pattern consisting of just Knit, Purl, and Slip stitches. The second is a pattern that has the yarn stranded on the outside of the fabric past a group of Slip stitches, and it is then caught up on a row above to create a little tent-like effect. Slip stitches also appear in several other patterns in the material below, where they are combined with other techniques.

Three-and-One Stitch

In this chart, the Purl stitches are represented by a dash instead of a dot; it is a nice option because it closely resembles the stitch.

The symbol used here for the Slip Stitch technique is also common to many charts. In the first chart of the pattern, however, it is employed in a new way; the second chart shows how the same symbol is used in the traditional way.

Also included is a drawing of the structure of the fabric so you can compare it with the two charts; this will help make it clear why this new approach to using the Slip Stitch symbol is an improvement.

> *Multiple: 4 stitches/4 rows; 1 optional edge stitch, a preparatory row, and a final row.*
> *Sl1yfs = Slip 1 stitch with yarn held on farside.*
> *Sl1yns = Slip 1 stitch with yarn held on nearside.*

Preparatory Inside Row: Knit.
Row 1: Rep[K3, Sl1yfs], end K1.
Row 2: K1, rep[Sl1yns, K3].
Row 3: Rep[K1, Sl1yfs, K2], end K1.
Row 4: K1, rep[K2, Sl1yns, K1].
Final Outside Row: Knit.

First Chart

This pattern has a preparatory row, which serves to separate the first row of Slip stitches from a cast-on edge or another stitch pattern. Depending upon how you plan to use the pattern, it may not be needed.

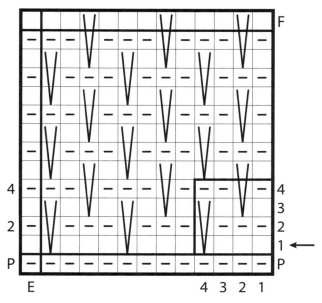

Three-and-One Stitch. First chart.

The pattern also has a column of edge stitches on the left; it is there to balance the pattern for an unseamed flat fabric, but is not needed for a seamed fabric or one worked in the round.

What is most important about this otherwise simple pattern, however, is the way the Slip stitch symbol is used. The symbol starts in Row 1, Column 4 and stops in Row 3 and it should be read to mean that the stitch is slipped in Rows 1 and 2, and worked on Row 3, where the top of the symbol occupies a square.

When used in this way, the symbol not only tells you exactly what to do at each step, but also, if you compare the chart to the drawing of the fabric, it matches the appearance and structure of the stitch in the fabric. In particular, note the single stitch that lies between the top of one Slip stitch and the bottom of the next one up.

Second Chart

Now look at the second chart of the same pattern, which uses the Slip stitch symbol in the conventional way. Here, the symbol spans only two rows, and it is read to mean that the stitch is slipped on each of those two rows. However, the square in the third row contains a symbol for Knit, meaning "Knit the next stitch." That the stitch happens to be a Slip stitch is not specified; it is treated as an ordinary stitch. In other words, the chart indicates the action to take, but not the nature of the next stitch on the left needle, nor the result in the fabric.

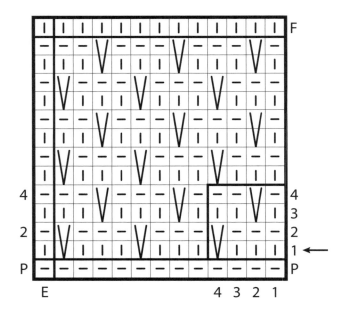

Three-and-One Stitch. Second chart
using Slip Stitch symbol in traditional way.

Three-and-One Stitch.

As a result, this chart makes it look as though there should be both a Knit and a Purl stitch between the top of one Slip stitch and the bottom of the next. However, the drawing of the fabric makes it clear there is only a single Purl stitch between the two; the top of the Slip stitch occupies the position where the chart makes it seem there is a Knit stitch. This discrepancy can cause confusion and make you think you have made an error.

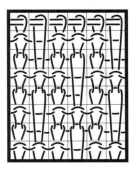

Three-and-One Stitch.
Diagram of fabric structure.

Little Lattice

Next is a lovely pattern that demonstrates the Lattice technique, where the yarn is stranded on the outside of the fabric past several Slip stitches, and then picked up on a later row.

The pattern is staggered horizontally, which means there are partial motifs at the beginning and end of the rows in the top half of the repeat. Writing the pattern in a way that accommodates the requirements of the stitch technique for these partial motifs is somewhat problematic.

The pattern works best for a flat, unseamed fabric with selvedge stitches that serve as anchors at each side for the picked-up strands in those partial motifs. Therefore, in this case the selvedge stitches are included in the written instructions and indicated on the chart with an S. You will find suggestions below for how to adapt the pattern for use in a seamed fabric or one worked in the round.

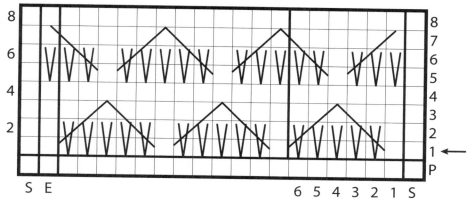

Little Lattice chart.

Multiple: 6 stitches/8 rows; 1 edge stitch, plus two selvedge stitches, and one preparatory row.

Sl5yns = Slip 5 stitches with yarn on nearside, or Sl3yns = Slip 3 stitches with yarn on nearside, etc.

L1 = Lattice technique: Insert right needle up under strand in row below, and then into next stitch on left needle and Knit, drawing yarn through stitch and under strand.

Preparatory Inside Row: Purl.

Row 1: K1, rep[K1, Sl5yns], end K2.

Row 2, and all inside rows: Purl.

Row 3: K1, rep[K3, L1, K2], end K2.

Row 5: K1, rep[Sl3yns, K1, Sl2yns], work last repeat Sl3yns, K1, Sl3yns, end K1.

Row 7: K1, rep[L1, K5], end L1, K1.

Row 8: Purl.

If this pattern were done without the selvedge stitches, the strands in the partial motif at each side of the fabric would be drawn up at an odd angle from the last stitch worked in the previous row, distorting the edge. The selvedge stitches are a good solution for a flat, unseamed flat fabric; the partial motif will look as it should and the pattern will be nicely balanced at both sides of the fabric.

However, if you use the pattern as shown for a seamed fabric or one worked in the round, these partial motifs will not align correctly when they are brought into position side by side. Instead of five stitches, there would be six stitches in the combined motif, and instead of one lattice strand caught up at the center, there would be two strands caught up by stitches on either side of the seam. Also, they would be further distorted in a circular fabric by the jog that occurs at the join between rounds.

One solution for a seamed fabric is to use a relatively wide selvedge on the left side, turning both the selvedge stitch and the edge stitch to the inside. While the strand in the partial

motifs would still not look entirely normal, there would be five stitches in the motif, making it the correct width, and the extra stitch present on the left side in the lower half of the repeat would be eliminated as well.

Two other solutions for either a seamed or circular fabric are probably more satisfactory because they avoid the need to have the half-motifs line up on either side of a seam or join. For the first, simply eliminate the partial motifs in the upper half of the pattern, replacing them with plain Knit background stitches. Or, work the pattern exactly as shown in the chart, and then add several columns of "fill" stitches at each side (such as Seed Stitch), so these meet at the seam or join between rounds. A vertical, intermediary pattern like this will separate the motifs of the Lattice pattern, and the partial ones would then make visual sense.

This is an excellent example of the advantage a chart provides in allowing you to analyze how a pattern works and to find solutions for different applications—none of this would be clear from written instructions.

Little Lattice.

Cable and Crossed Stitch Patterns

The Braided Cable stitch pattern shown next contains enough of that stitch technique's wonderful variety to convey all the basic principles involved. The Crossed Stitch Medallion that follows clearly shows how closely related the two techniques are, and how easy it is to slightly modify a symbol to suit a related method. The third chart of the Twilled Stripe pattern combines the Slip Stitch with the Crossed Stitch technique.

Braided Cable

Multiple: 11 stitches/8 rows; 2 optional edge stitches, and a final row.

LC2/1: Slip 2 stitches to cable needle, hold nearside, P1 from left needle, K2 from cable needle.

RC2/1: Slip 1 stitch to cable needle, hold farside, K2 from left needle, P1 from cable needle.

RC2/2: Slip 2 stitches to cable needle, hold farside, K2 from left needle, K2 from cable needle.

LC2/2: Slip 2 stitches to cable needle, hold nearside, K2 from left needle, K2 from cable needle.

Row 1 (Inside Row): K2, rep[K1, P4, K2, P2, K2].
Row 2: Rep[P2, LC2/1, RC2/1, LC2/1], end P2.
Row 3: K2, rep[P2, K2, P4, K3].
Row 4: Rep[P3, RC2/2, P2, K2], end P2.
Row 5: K2, rep[P2, K2, P4, K3].
Row 6: Rep[P2, RC2/1, LC2/1, RC2/1], end P2.
Row 7: K2, rep[K1, P4, K2, P2, K2].
Row 8: Rep[P2, K2, P2, LC2/2, P1], end P2.
Final Row: Repeat Row 1.

The first cable technique in the pattern is the Left Cross in Row 2, where stitches 3 and 4 are held nearside, stitch 5 is repositioned to Column 3 and Purled; then stitches 3 and 4 are Knit. Charts for these patterns generally use the dot for Purl and a blank square for Knit so the path of the stitches can be seen clearly.

The vertical lines drawn between one Cable and the next are optional and serve only to define the columns of Knit stitches. Ignore them as you work the pattern, because they convey only visual information, not an instruction of any kind. There is no need to include these lines in a chart, but, as you can see, it provides such a clear picture of the pattern that it is a nice touch.

In many cases a pattern like this is used as a vertical panel with other stitch patterns set to each side, therefore, only one stitch repeat is shown here. However, there are two row repeats, which makes it clear how the top of one repeat and the bottom of the next fit together. The two edge stitches at the left side are used to balance the pattern.

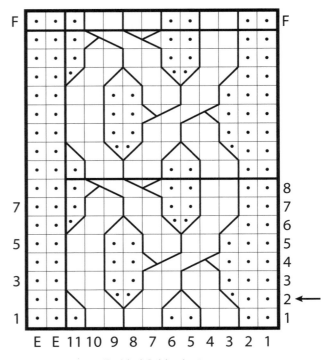

Braided Cable chart.

The chart also makes it clear that you could just as easily start on Row 3, 5, or 7, as on Row 1. You might want to choose one of those options in order to position the pattern on the garment or in relation to adjacent stitch patterns in a more attractive way (see Coordinating Stitch and Garment Patterns). This is the kind of thing a charted pattern makes evident that would not be clear in a written one.

Braided Cable.

Crossed Stitch Medallion

Here is an example of a Crossed Stitch pattern that causes columns of stitches to "travel" across the face of the fabric somewhat as a Cable does, but on a smaller scale.

Multiple: 7 stitches/12 rows; 2 optional edge stitches.
RC = Right Crossed Stitch.
LC = Left Crossed Stitch.

Row 1: Rep[K3, P1, K3].
Row 2: Rep[P3, K1, P3].
Row 3: Rep[K1, RC, P1, LC, K1].
Row 4: Rep[P2, K3, P2].
Row 5: Rep[RC, P3, LC].
Row 6: Rep[P1, K5, P1].
Row 7: Rep[K1, P5, K1].
Row 8: Repeat Row 6.
Row 9: Rep[LC, P3, RC].
Row 10: Repeat Row 4.
Row 11: Rep[K1, LC, P1, RC, K1].
Row 12: Repeat Row 2.

First Chart

Because a Crossed Stitch is made up of just two stitches, the little lines that indicate the backing stitches in a cable pattern are eliminated here. The symbol is quite clear without them when vertical lines are used to show how the columns of Knit travel between one Crossed Stitch and the next.

Second Chart

In other charting systems, the same pattern might be done with a symbol for Knit, the dash for Purl, and the alternate symbol for the Crossed Stitch, as in this small chart of the pattern. Here again, to my eye this chart is visually cluttered and more difficult to decipher, but charts of this kind are common and it is important to understand how to work from them, although you could certainly rewrite it.

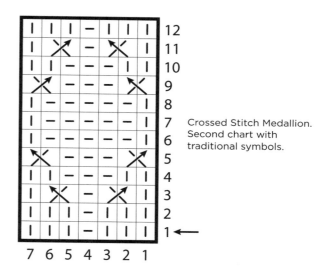

Crossed Stitch Medallion.
Second chart with traditional symbols.

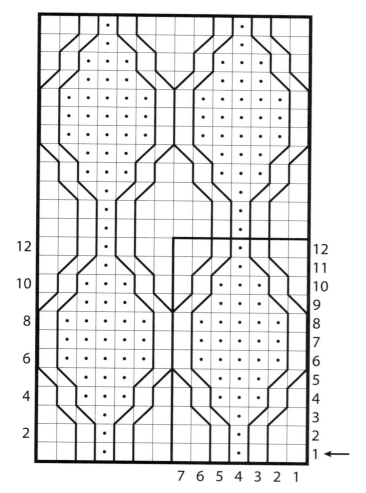

Crossed Stitch Medallion. First chart.

Crossed Stitch Medallion.

Twilled Stripe

Twilled Stripe uses an interesting technique that combines a Slip stitch and a Crossed Stitch. There is no particular symbol for this technique, nor need there be, because it is not that common. However, standard symbols used in an adaptive way serve very well to convey exactly what is required, particularly when keyed to some written instructions, as here.

> *Multiple: 7 stitches/8 rows; 2 optional edge stitches, and a preparatory row.*
>
> *LSlTw = Left Slip Twist: Knit the second stitch farside, Slip the first stitch knitwise, and then discard the second stitch.*

Preparatory Inside Row: K2, rep[P5, K2].
Row 1: Rep[P2, LSlTw, K3], end P2.
Row 2, and all inside rows: K2, rep[P5, K2].
Row 3: Rep[P2, K1, LSlTw, K2], end P2.
Row 5: Rep[P2, K2, LSlTw, K1], end P2.
Row 7: Rep[P2, K3, LSlTw], end P2.

The pattern could be used either as a single repeat with other stitch patterns on either side, or in multiple repeats for an all-over vertical stripe effect, as shown. When used across the entire width of the fabric like this, the edge stitches should be eliminated for a circular fabric or a flat fabric that is to be seamed.

Twilled Stripe.

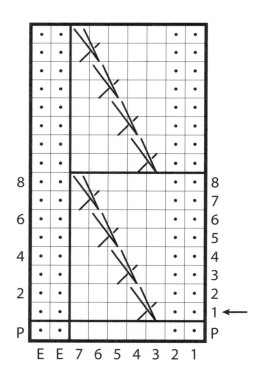

Twilled Stripe chart.

❖ *Writing a Stitch Chart*

Once you understand the basics of reading a chart, you will find that writing one is quite easy. You might want to learn to do this so you can improve the appearance of a chart done with some other method, revise a pattern in some way, or make a chart for a pattern that is only in written form.

Also included below is an example of a chart written with both outside and inside rows. You might want to put a chart in this form if you are working flat and find it difficult to mentally translate the instructions on the inside rows.

Stitch Charts from Written Patterns

If you would like to use a pattern that is in written form but prefer to work from a chart, you can make one of your own; it is really no more than "knitting" on paper, and it is a good way to learn a pattern before you actually pick up needles and yarn.

Graph paper of about four or five squares to an inch is ideal for charting; the squares are large enough to make it easy to write in the symbols and to read as you work.

You will need a ruler for drawing lines and it is best to use pencil for a draft version; once the chart is in finished form, either overwrite with a pen or make a new copy in ink. You might want to slip the finished chart into a plastic sleeve to keep it neat for the duration of your project, or make a copy that you can file away along with the gauge swatch and the yarn label for future reference.

Stitch patterns in published collections are normally written for working flat (see Written Stitch Patterns) because it is assumed you will be trying the pattern on a flat swatch; therefore, the instructions alternate inside and outside rows. To put the instructions into charted form, it will be necessary to write in symbols that show only what the result will be on the outside of the fabric. This is just like what you do when working inside rows from charted instructions, but in reverse.

Work as follows:

1. At lower right-hand side of paper, draw a horizontal line to define bottom of chart, and a vertical line to define right side.
2. Write number of rows to right of vertical line, from bottom up; draw a horizontal line across top to define row repeat.
3. If there are steps before repeat, count across an equal number of squares to left of first vertical line on chart and draw second vertical line.
4. Beginning in square to left of second vertical line, write numbers for stitch repeat under bottom line from right to left; draw vertical line to left of last number to define left side of repeat.
5. If there are steps after repeat, count across an equal number of squares in chart and draw another vertical line to define left side of chart.
6. Draw an arrow to right of number for first outside row; add inside row numbers up left side of chart.
7. Begin to follow instructions in written pattern, writing symbols into squares as for working real stitches on a needle. Write outside rows from right to left, and inside rows from left to right, translating Purls into Knit, or Knits into Purl on those rows as necessary.

If you want to include one or two more row repeats of a pattern, allow as many rows as needed above the primary repeat before drawing the horizontal line in Step 2. Similarly, for additional stitch repeats, before following instructions in Step 5, above, allow as many squares as needed to the left of the primary repeat and then draw the vertical lines.

Including extra repeats in a chart is not necessary, and many published charts do not do so. Personally, I find them particularly helpful as a means of learning how a pattern works, especially for patterns that have diagonal or staggered motifs, because they convey important information about the transition between repeats and how the shifting pattern elements fit together. However, if you find the extra repeats distracting when it comes time to work from the chart, you might want to make one that shows just the primary repeat.

As discussed in the chapter Written Stitch Patterns, any stitches that appear before and/or after the repeat could be either edge stitches or selvedge stitches, either of which are worked only at the beginning and/or end of a row. A chart will help you determine what purpose these stitches serve and decide whether to use them or not. Selvedge stitches are not included in the charts shown below; it is assumed you will add them for a fabric that will be seamed. If the pattern has unique preparatory or final rows, mark these with a "P" or an "F" and set them apart from the repeats with horizontal lines.

Many published patterns do not include the arrow pointing to the first outside row, nor the numbers on the left for the inside rows, but I think they are a nice touch; the latter help guide your eyes to the rows that need to be read from left to right and can be ignored when working circular. If they are not present in a published chart, feel free to add them.

After making a few charts, you will find that doing so is a very effective way to familiarize yourself with a pattern before you ever pick up the yarn and needles; it is, in a sense, practice knitting.

Chart with Inside Rows

Here is Diamond Brocade again, but in this version the chart has outside rows on the right and inside rows on the left, showing what the fabric looks like on both sides. This is not something you will encounter in a published pattern, but you can use the concept to rewrite any chart if you think it would be helpful.

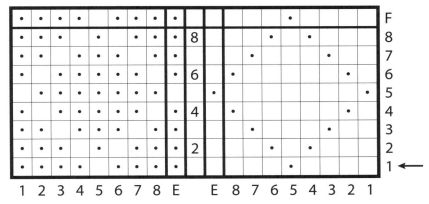

Diamond Brocade chart with outside rows on right, inside rows on left.

Done this way, both halves of the chart are read from right to left, and the squares in the left chart contain symbols that are correct for working on the inside of the fabric. There is no need to think about how to work a stitch on the inside so it looks like it should on the outside—in other words, a Knit is a Knit, and a Purl is a Purl, just as for outside rows.

Of course, there is no need to go to the trouble of making a double chart of this kind when every other row is plain, or for simple patterns that are quickly learned. However, for a more complex pattern, and especially for reversible patterns like this one, having inside rows would allow you to work more quickly and avoid errors.

❖ Charts with Decorative Increases and Decreases

Increase and decrease techniques frequently cause stitch columns to shift position away from the strict vertical that is normal in a knitted fabric. This has an effect on how a chart needs to be written, because the relationship of symbols in one row to those in the row above and below is no longer straightforward. However, both the appearance of the symbol and how it is used can help clarify the changes taking place and make it easier to read the chart.

The most common charting convention is to have increase and decrease symbols occupy a single square, regardless of how many stitches are added or removed or what the relationship of a symbol is to those in nearby squares. This method works reasonably well in terms of conveying what the individual steps in the pattern are; however, it rarely matches the structure or appearance of the fabric, and this can cause some confusion and make a chart difficult to follow.

In the charting system discussed here, a decrease symbol normally occupies just one square, even though two stitches are discarded in that position. The symbol points down toward the squares containing the stitches that are joined together and up to the square the new stitch will occupy, which helps clarify what is taking place.

The symbols for increases that are made on a stitch usually occupy more than one square; one belongs to the original stitch, and the other is available because a stitch elsewhere was removed by a paired decrease. However, in some patterns, the chart is improved by doing the opposite—restricting the increase to one square and expanding the decrease symbol instead.

The symbol for a Running Thread Increase is written between two squares, which reflects its position in the fabric, but it leans into the square the new stitch will occupy, either to the right or left, as needed to show what is happening in the fabric. In some cases, it may share a square with a decrease symbol, or a symbol for some other stitch technique.

A Yarnover is, in effect, an elongated running thread and is also made between two stitches, but it has a far greater effect in the fabric. The opening it creates spans two rows and the symbol occupies the same amount of space in the chart; half of it is in the square where the Yarnover is to be made, and half is in the square above where the strand is worked. This is similar to the way a Slip stitch symbol is used in this charting system; you make the Yarnover when you see the lower part of the symbol in a square, and you work the Yarnover when you see the upper part.

Most traditional charting systems use a circle within a single square for a Yarnover, and a Knit or Purl, or some other symbol is placed in the square above to indicate how the strand should be worked and discarded on the next row. This effectively shows what to do, but the chart gives the impression that the opening occupies just one row and has a stitch above it; however, that "stitch" is simply an instruction, and no actual stitch occupies that position in the fabric. While the new Yarnover symbol works best for most purposes, it is impossible to use in some lace and mesh patterns where Yarnovers are set close together in every row; in these cases, the older symbol is the better option.

Increase and Decrease pairs . . .

Increase and decrease techniques are always paired in decorative stitch patterns. The appearance of the two techniques, as well as their position in relation to each other, create different effects in the fabric (see Increase and Decrease Techniques). These pairs can be positioned in four different ways:

- *If an increase and a decrease are paired side by side, only their appearance is important; they will have no effect on the stitches to each side.*
- *When an increase and a decrease are paired but separated by other stitches, the stitches in between will slope away from the increase and toward the decrease; if the pairs are repeated in a series and spaced over several rows, the stitch columns between them will slope, creating a visible bias effect in the fabric.*
- *If the two are paired but separated by several rows, this not only causes bias, but also a temporary change in the stitch count on the needle; the fabric will draw in or protrude, creating dimensional effects.*
- *If several increases are grouped, and an equal number of decreases are grouped somewhere nearby, the stitch columns and rows will curve, creating wave effects.*

Several charts shown below demonstrate how these concepts can be put to use.

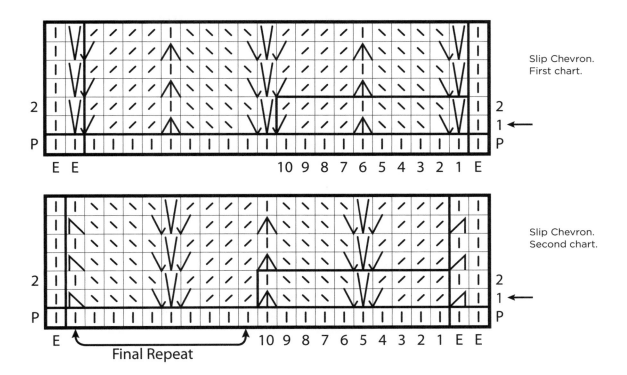

Slip Chevron.
First chart.

Slip Chevron.
Second chart.

Final Repeat

Bias Patterns

The two stitch patterns here have increases and decreases that are separated by intervening stitches, causing the stitch columns in between to slope. The first is a chevron-type pattern with increases and decreases set in straight vertical lines, giving it a very formal appearance. The next is an Eyelet pattern that has Yarnovers and decreases that change position, with the stitches in between chasing after them.

Slip Chevron

Here is a pattern I designed with a fancy Double Increase, no more than a pair of running threads on either side of a Slip stitch, that demonstrates how to adapt symbols to convey the instructions for a multistep technique. It also makes use of sloped Knit symbols to suggest the appearance of the bias that is set up between the separated increases and decreases.

For Both Charts

RDec = Right Decrease.

LDec = Left Decrease.

CDec2 = Center Double Decrease: Slip 2 together knitwise, Knit 1, pull 2 Slip stitches over.

RThInc = Running Thread Increase.

Sl1 = Slip 1 stitch purlwise.

First Chart

Multiple: 10 stitches/2 rows; 3 edge stitches, and a preparatory row.

Preparatory Row: Purl.

Row 1: K1, rep[Sl1, RThInc, K3, CDec2, K3, RThInc], end Sl1, K1.

Row 2, and all inside rows: Purl.

Notice there is one edge stitch on the right and two on the left. The outer ones serve to keep stitch techniques within the fabric and away from the edge. The second-to-last one is a Slip stitch, which is needed to balance the appearance of the pattern on both sides of an unseamed flat fabric. If you plan to work in the round, or make a flat fabric that is to be seamed, do not use the edge stitches; for the latter, add selvedge stitches instead.

Second Chart

Multiple: 10 stitches/2 rows; 3 edge stitches, and a preparatory row.

Preparatory Row: Purl.

Row 1: K1, RDec, rep[K3, RThInc, Sl1, RThInc, K3, CDec2], end final repeat K3, RThInc, Sl1, RThInc, K3, LDec, K1.

Row 2, and all inside rows: Purl.

This second chart of the same pattern shows another option. In this version, the repeat lines have been shifted so a seam or join would fall next to the decrease, instead of within the increase. This requires the use of a final repeat at the end of the row that is worked in a slightly different way than the others; when this sort of thing occurs in written instructions, the main repeat would be followed by words to the effect of "end final repeat . . ."

Slip Chevron. Center Double Decreases stand out from fabric.

It is often useful to consider shifting the repeat lines in this manner. You might do so to make a pattern easier to work in some way, as was the case here, but also as a way to start a pattern in a more advantageous way in relation to the garment pattern. In some cases it is better to start on a different row, or a different stitch, or both, and a chart makes it easy to see how to make an adjustment of this kind; for more information about why you might want to do this, see Coordinating Stitch and Garment Patterns.

Patterns like this one, with widely separated increase/decrease pairs, can pose challenges when garment pattern shaping is required, such as for an armhole or neckline. When one stitch of the pair is eliminated, the other must no longer be used or it will affect the stitch count; as a result, the stitches in that area will no longer be drawn on the bias, changing the appearance of the pattern at the edge of the fabric.

The sloped Knit symbols are optional, and you might find the chart easier to read if they are not used. However, they do help make the structure of the fabric clear, and this can be important when analyzing the pattern to determine how to use it.

By the way, Slip Chevron could be turned into a lace pattern simply by substituting a pair of Yarnovers for the Running Thread Increases and working the Slip stitch in between as plain Knit. Very small changes in arrangement or technique can result in strikingly different effects, and knowing this might inspire you to design your own patterns.

Track of the Turtle

This pattern has paired Yarnovers and decreases separated by four stitches; the decrease is to the left of the Yarnover in the first half of the repeat, and to the right of it in the second half. The stitches in between will always lean toward the decreases; therefore, the alteration in the arrangement of the pairs pulls the fabric into soft curves. Many lace patterns make use of this effect to create diamond or petal shapes in a pattern.

Multiple: 14 stitches/20 rows; 3 edge stitches, and a preparatory row.
LDec = Left Decrease.
RDec = Right Decrease.
YO = Yarnover.

Preparatory Inside Row: K3, P11, K3.
Row 1: P3, rep[K1, YO, K4, LDec, K4], end P3.
Row 2, and all inside rows: K3, [P11, K3].
Row 3: P3, rep[K2, YO, K4, LDec, K3], end P3.
Row 5: P3, rep[K3, YO, K4, LDec, K2], end P3.
Row 7: P3, rep[K4, YO, K4, LDec, K1], end P3.
Row 9: P3, rep[K5, YO, K4, LDec], end P3.
Row 11: P3, rep[K4, RDec, K4, YO, K1], end P3.
Row 13: P3, rep[K3, RDec, K4, YO, K2], end P3.
Row 15: P3, rep[K2, RDec, K4, YO, K3], end P3.
Row 17: P3, rep[K1, RDec, K4, YO, K4], end P3.
Row 19: P3, rep[RDec, K4, YO, K5], end P3.

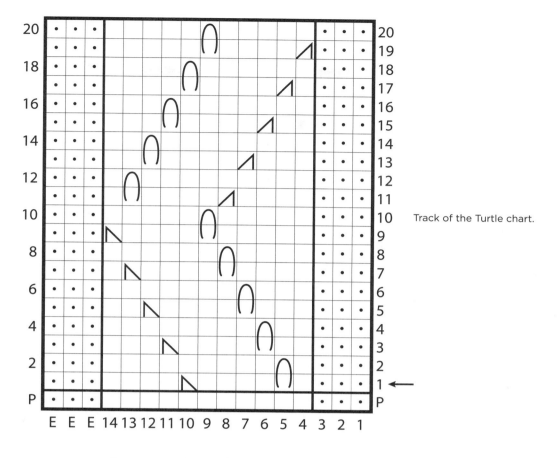

Track of the Turtle chart.

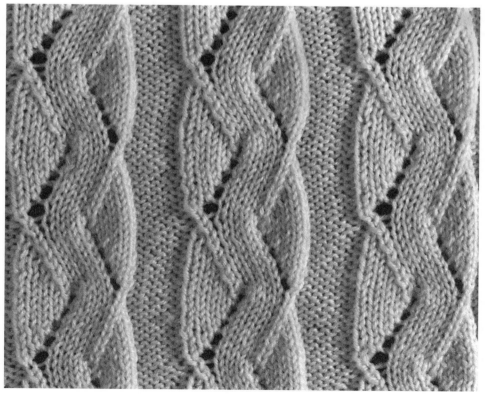

Track of the Turtle.

Lace Patterns

The first two lace patterns shown here, Elfin Lace and Pique Lace, make use of Double Decreases, and the latter has an unusual Double Increase. These are followed by Mist Drops, which has Yarnover and decrease pairs separated by several stitches, creating some of the same bias effects seen in Track of the Turtle, above, although the effect here is different because of the arrangement of the motifs.

These kinds of patterns can often present challenges because a literal translation of the written instructions may not produce a chart that resembles the fabric. The discussions accompanying each pattern explain how to make a first rough draft, analyze the pattern, and then rewrite the chart.

Elfin Lace

Two charts are shown for this lace pattern: the first uses the new Yarnover symbol as described above, and the second uses the traditional symbol. The pattern has both single and double decreases that are paired with Yarnover increases, with each balancing the other so no bias is created.

Also included is a drawing of the fabric with a grid superimposed on it, so you can compare it with the charts. I think you will agree that the chart with the new symbol correctly matches both what is occurring as you knit and what happens within the fabric.

Multiple: 8 stitches/16 rows; 3 edge stitches, a preparatory row, and a final row. Pattern requires selvedge stitches for a flat fabric.

RDec = Right Decrease.

LDec = Left Decrease.

CDec2 = Center Double Decrease.

Preparatory Inside Row: Purl.
Row 1: K1, rep[K4, YO, LDec, K2]; end K2.
Row 2, and all inside rows: Purl.
Row 3: K1, rep[K2, RDec, YO, K1, YO, LDec, K1], end K2.
Row 5: K1, rep[K1, RDec, YO, K3, YO, LDec], end K2.
Row 7: K1, rep[K3, YO, CDec2, YO, K2], end K2.
Row 9: K1, rep[YO, LDec, K6], end YO, LDec.
Row 11: K1, rep[K1, YO, LDec, K3, RDec, YO], end K2.
Row 13: K1, rep[K2, YO, LDec, K1, RDec, YO, K1], end K2.
Row 15: YO, rep[CDec2, YO, K5, YO], end CDec2, YO.
Final Outside Row: Knit.

First Chart

The preparatory and final rows of the pattern are optional, but they provide a little room above and below the Yarnovers in the first and last rows, and also keep these openings in the fabric away from something like a ribbing or a cast-off edge. If you were to set just one or two repeats of this pattern within the fabric like a stripe, there might be no reason to include them.

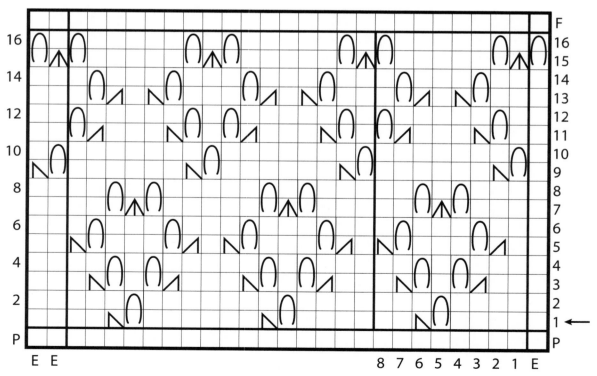

Elfin Lace. First chart with new Yarnover symbol.

The chart also has one edge stitch at the right and two at the left, which are used to accommodate the partial motifs at the beginning and end of the rows in the upper half of the repeat. This works well when the pattern is used for an unseamed flat fabric, in which case, you would also want to add selvedge stitches so the Yarnovers worked on the first and last stitches of Row 15 are positioned within the fabric and not at the edge.

However, these partial motifs are problematic should you want to use the pattern for a fabric that is to be seamed at the sides or worked in the round; the pattern would then need to be adjusted. For those applications, do not use the Yarnovers in Row 15; to maintain the stitch count, substitute single decreases for the doubles at the beginning and end of that row. Unfortunately, this positions the two decreases side by side at the seam or join, and the partial motifs that meet there will look different; the jog at the join in a circular fabric will further distort the motif (for more information, see Rows or Spirals in the chapter Circular and Flat Knitting).

A better solution might be to eliminate the need for these partial motifs to line up perfectly at the join or seam. One way to do this is simply not to use them; in the first repeat at the beginning of Rows 9–16, substitute plain Knit background stitches instead of stitches 1–4, and in the final repeat, work plain Knit on stitches 6–8. A second way to solve the problem is to retain the partial motifs on those rows, and to use a fill pattern of some kind on several stitches added at the beginning and end of the row (Seed Stitch is common), so they occupy either side of the join. In that case, you would want to retain the edge stitches and work the pattern exactly as shown in the chart.

Once again, this demonstrates how much helpful information a chart reveals that would not be apparent in written pattern instructions; it can make clear not only what the challenges would be if the pattern were to be used in a certain way, but also what the solutions might be.

Also notice just how simple a chart makes this pattern seem: in fact, this lovely lace is very easy to do. I have no doubt many people avoid lace knitting only because the written instructions look so daunting, but in most cases this is misleading. If charts do nothing more than persuade people that lace is within their abilities, they will have earned their keep.

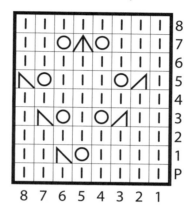

Elfin Lace. Second chart with traditional Yarnover symbol.

Second Chart

If you compare the traditional chart with the one using the new symbol for the Yarnover, and then compare both of them with the diagram and the photo of the fabric, it becomes clear why it is helpful to have a chart that resembles the fabric as much as possible. A chart of this kind is not only easier to learn, but after any interruption, you can quickly find your place in the pattern by comparing the chart to the fabric below your needles.

Elfin Lace.

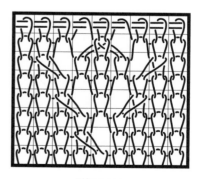

Elfin Lace.
Diagram of fabric structure.

Pique Lace

The first chart of this lace pattern is a direct transcription of the written instructions done with traditional symbols. A Test Swatch suggested ways to both improve the chart and modify the pattern, and the changes I made are shown in the second chart.

For Both Charts

YO = Yarnover, and YO2 = Double Yarnover (wrap yarn twice).
CDec2 = Center Double Decrease.
LDec = Left Decrease.
RDec = Right Decrease.
RibInc = Rib Increase; KP (Knit/Purl), or PK (Purl/Knit) on Double Yarnover.

First Chart

Multiple: 9 stitches/8 rows.

Row 1: Rep[K3, YO, CDec2, YO, K3].
Row 2: Purl.
Row 3: Rep[K2, LDec, YO, K1, YO, RDec, K2].
Row 4: Purl.
Row 5: Rep[K1, LDec, YO2, CDec2, YO2, RDec, K1].
Row 6: Rep[P2, KP on YO, P1, PK on YO, P2].
Row 7: Rep[2(LDec, YO), K1, 2(YO, RDec)].
Row 8: Purl.

Making a quick Test Swatch indicated that the chart was accurate, but it did not convey a good idea of how the specialized increase technique is done in Rows 6 and 7. It shows what looks like two Yarnovers, which is one way to convey the instruction for a Double Yarnover; there is a Knit stitch above one Yarnover symbol and a Purl above the next, but in effect, this is a Rib Increase worked into that Yarnover on the next row.

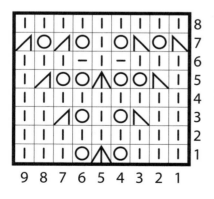

Pique Lace. First chart with traditional Yarnover symbol.

Second Chart

Multiple: 10 stitches/8 rows; 1 edge stitch, and preparatory and final rows.

Preparatory Inside Row: Purl.
Row 1: Rep[K4, YO, CDec2, YO, K3], end K1.
Row 2: Purl.
Row 3: Rep[K3, RDec, YO, K1, YO, LDec, K2], end K1.
Row 4: Purl.
Row 5: Rep[K2, RDec, YO2, CDec2, YO2, LDec, K1], end K1.
Row 6: P1, rep[P2, KPRibInc, P1, PKRibInc, P3].
Row 7: Rep[K1, 2(RDec, YO), K1, 2(YO, LDec)], end K1.
Row 8: Purl.
Final Outside Row: Knit.

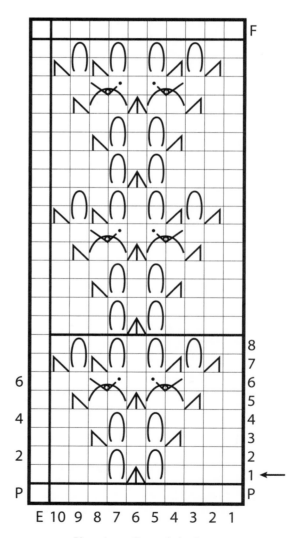

Pique Lace. Second chart with new Yarnover symbol and revised Decreases.

Pique Lace, worked according to the second chart.

The second chart of the same pattern has preparatory and final rows; these provide a little space between a ribbing or a cast-off edge and the Yarnovers in the first and last rows of the pattern.

This version also uses the new symbol for a Yarnover with a Rib Increase, which is fairly common in lace patterns; notice that one increase is worked as Knit/Purl, the other as Purl/Knit; the change is subtle in the fabric, but it makes the pattern easy to work. (Another option is to use Single Yarnovers instead of the Double versions on Row 6, which would make those openings smaller.)

The pattern looked somewhat undistinguished in the Test Swatch, and the solution was to reverse the right and left outside decreases so they would create a stronger line to define the motifs (see the explanation in Single Eyelets of the very different appearance of smooth and broken eyelets). And by the way, the Slip Slip Knit version of the Left Decrease is easiest to work after a Yarnover.

Notice that an additional stitch column has been added at the right side of the pattern (the repeat is now 10 stitches instead of 9). This provides a little separation for the two decreases in Row 7, which would otherwise be side-by-side when the pattern is used as a repeat.

An edge stitch has been added at the left to balance the pattern at both sides of a flat fabric; if the pattern is used as a single column between other kinds of stitch patterns, the edge stitch would serve to balance it in that setting as well.

Here again, one of the great advantages of charting is that it reveals the structure of the pattern so clearly that you can see ways to modify it, or even transform it into a somewhat different pattern. One of the things you may notice is the resemblance between Pique Lace and Elfin Lace. The basic motif is very similar, with only slight differences in the increase and decrease techniques used, and you will find many lace patterns based upon a small triangle motif of this kind. What is interesting is how the arrangement of motifs transforms the appearance of the pattern—here they are arranged in vertical columns, and in the other pattern they are staggered.

Mist Drops

Here is a charming pattern with Eyelets and a tiny Bobble set in the middle of a motif that has increases and decreases separated by several stitches, creating a soft, curved effect. The motifs are arranged in a half-drop—the widest part at the center of one motif is nested into the narrowest parts of the adjacent motifs.

Patterns of this kind can be challenging to chart because it is difficult to tell from the written instructions how the stitches actually line up. As a result, charting a pattern of this sort is often a two- or three-step process.

The first chart shown below is a direct transcription from the written instructions; while you could work from this chart, it looks rather confusing and clearly does not resemble the fabric. The second chart is a rough draft of a revision, done by analyzing the first to determine how the stitches relate to each other; the third chart is a finished one that clarifies everything.

I have used Knit symbols in these charts, partly to illustrate this as an option you might prefer, but also because the final chart exhibits bias, and the sloped Knit symbol helps to illustrate what the pattern will look like in the fabric.

Multiple: 14 stitches/16 rows; 1 edge stitch, and a preparatory row.

YO = Yarnover.

LDec2 = Double Left Decrease: Slip 1 knitwise, Knit 2 together, pass slipped stitch over.

B = Bobble: 5-stitch Double Yarnover Increase, turn; Purl 5 stitches, turn; LDec, Sl1, RDec, pull 2 stitches over.

Row 1: Rep[P1, K1, 2(YO, K1), P1, K3, LDec2, K3], end P1.

Row 2: K1, rep[P7, K1, P5, K1].

Row 3: Rep[P1, K2, YO, K1, YO, K2, P1, K2, LDec2, K2], end P1.

Row 4: K1, rep[P5, K1, P7, K1].

Row 5: Rep[P1, K3, YO, K1, YO, K3, P1, K1, LDec2, K1], end P1.

Row 6: K1, rep[P3, K1, P9, K1].

Row 7: Rep[P1, K4, B, K4, P1, K3], end P1.

Row 8: Repeat Row 6.

Row 9: Rep[P1, K3, LDec2, K3, P1, K1, 2(YO, K1)], end P1.

Row 10: Repeat Row 4.

Row 11: Rep[P1, K2, LDec2, K2, P1, K2, YO, K1, YO, K2], end P1.

Row 12: K1, rep[P7, K1, P5, K1].

Row 13: Rep[P1, K1, LDec2, K1, P1, K3, YO, K1, YO, K3], end P1.

Row 14: K1, rep[P9, K1, P3, K1].

Row 15: Rep[P1, K3, P1, K4, B, K4], end P1.

Row 16: Repeat Row 14.

First Chart

To rework the chart into something more understandable, the best thing to do is to analyze it from the top down, looking at the special techniques and lining them up with the stitches on which they are made. For instance, the double decreases at the top are clearly offset from the three stitches they have to be worked on; those stitches are outlined to make their association clear.

Second Chart

Next do a draft chart, and start by centering the decrease over the stitches below. As you continue to work down, it becomes clear that the Bobble is also centered under the decrease, as are the paired Yarnovers below it. Once the significant techniques are lined up, fill in the plain Knit stitches on either side. Next, fill in the mirror-image half of the motif at one side. As this is done, it becomes clear that the side edges are contoured.

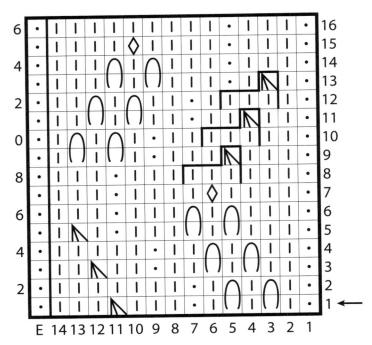

Mist Drops. First draft of chart.

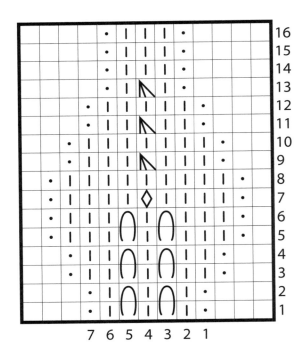

Mist Drops. Second draft of chart showing main motif.

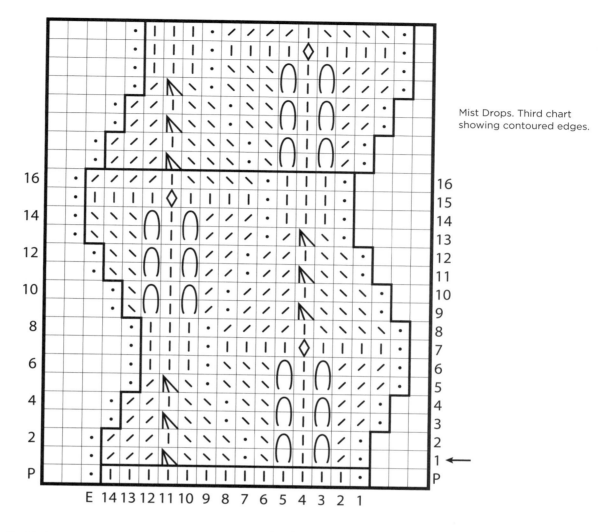

Mist Drops. Third chart showing contoured edges.

Third Chart

For the final chart I added a preparatory row to move the first Yarnovers away from a cast-on edge or ribbing and added an arrow indicating that Row 1 is an outside row.

This revised chart also reveals that the fabric will have asymmetric, scalloped side edges. These would be very attractive for something like a scarf or small blanket. Another option for an application of this kind would be to balance the pattern by adding a half-repeat, using edge stitches at the left side of the chart; simply fill in the symbols for the stitch columns that belong to the portion of the motif that occupies all the rows above those that start with stitches 2 through 7. The side edges of the fabric would then have a symmetric contour, but the stitch count would change radically, with considerably more stitches in some areas than in others.

Fabrics with contoured side edges present some challenges when they are to be seamed; for more information, see Tips for Bias Stitch Patterns. One way to make seaming easier is to add some plain edge stitches to fill in at the sides, as is done with the Berry Stitch pattern, below.

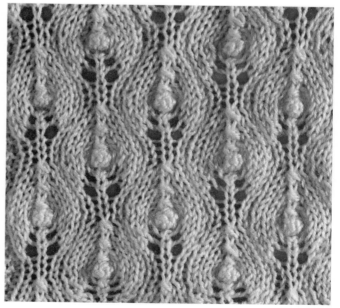

Mist Drops.

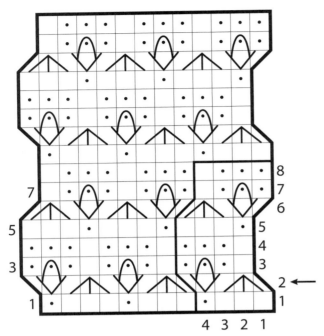

Berry Stitch chart showing scalloped edges.

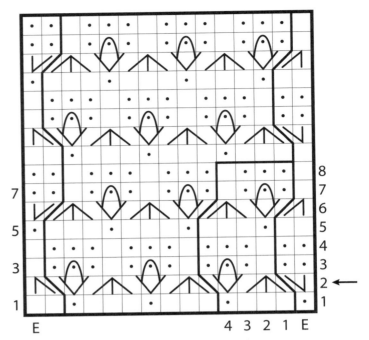

Berry Stitch chart with straight sides.

Embossed Patterns

Like Mist Drops, above, these patterns have increases and decreases separated by one or more rows.

The first one, Berry Stitch, provides an example of a chart where it is best to place the increase symbol in one square, and expand the decrease symbol.

The other two patterns have stitch counts that change radically row by row, and in these cases the most effective way to make the chart is by using blank squares to show that stitches are temporarily missing. There are options for how to do this, the choice between them being a matter of what seems to work best for you.

Berry Stitch

This highly textured pattern is done with a Double Yarnover Increase and a Center Double Decrease.

Multiple: 4 stitches/8 rows.
CDec2 = Center Double Decrease.
YOInc2 = In one stitch, K1, Yarnover, K1.

Row 1 (Inside Row): [K1, P3].   Row 5: [P3, K1].
Row 2: [CDec2, YOInc2].   Row 6: [YOInc2, CDec2].
Row 3: [K3, P1].   Row 7: [P1, K3].
Row 4: [K1, P3].   Row 8: [P3, K1].

While it might seem that the paired increases and decreases are set side by side, in fact this is an Embossed pattern: the "berry" that begins with an increase in Row 2 is actually completed with a paired decrease in Row 6.

Also, the motifs are staggered; in the lower half of the repeat the pattern row begins with an increase and ends with a decrease, while in the upper half, it is the opposite. This is what creates the scalloped side edges that appear in this chart, as well as in the fabric.

These edges would be charming on something like a scarf or small blanket; however, straight sides would make seaming easier. Therefore, in the second chart of the same pattern, I filled in the sides with half-motifs, and the symbols for the single decreases are expanded to indicate the relationship between the stitches above and below. A Raised Increase would work well for this, but you could also use a Yarnover and twist it on the return row to close it.

Berry Stitch. Swatch showing contour in edges.

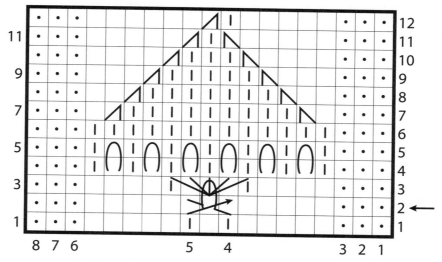

Rosebud. First chart with empty squares within pattern.

Rosebud

In this pretty pattern, the instructions call for casting on just eight stitches for each repeat; however, it is clear that portions of the pattern have considerably more stitches than that, due to multiple increases and decreases separated by several rows. As a result, the overall width of the chart is determined by rows 4 to 6, which have the largest number of stitches, and blank squares are used to indicate precisely how and where these changes occur.

Also notice that the knitted sample of the pattern shows several repeats treated as individual columns, each separated by vertical stripes of Seed Stitch framed by columns of Knit, which are not shown on the chart.

Multiple: 8 stitches/12 rows.
CSt/YO5 = Crossed Stitch with Multiple Yarnover: Slip 1 stitch to cable needle and hold on farside; K1; make Yarnover, wrapping yarn on needle 5 times; K1 from cable needle.
YOinc5 = 5-stitch Multiple Yarnover Increase: Drop extra wraps from previous Yarnover; on strand, P1, Yarnover, P1, Yarnover, P1.
KRDec and KLDec = Knit Right Decrease and Knit Left Decrease.
PRDec and PLDec = Purl Right Decrease and Purl Left Decrease.

Row 1 (Inside Row): [K3, P2, K3].
Row 2: [P3, CSt/YO5, P3].
Row 3: [K3, P1, YOinc5, P1, K3].
Row 4: [P3, K1, 6(YO, K1), P3].
Row 5: [K3, P13, K3].
Row 6: [P3, K13, P3].
Row 7: [K3, PRDec, P9, PLDec, K3].
Row 8: [P3, KLDec, K7, KRDec, P3].

Row 9: [K3, PRDec, P5, PLDec, K3].
Row 10: [P3, KLDec, K3, KRDec, P3].
Row 11: [K3, PRDec, P1, PLDec, K3].
Row 12: [P3, K1, KRDec, P3].

First Chart

As you can see, the Knit symbol is used in this chart. This is necessary because the number of stitches on the needle changes row by row, and empty squares, which would otherwise represent Knit, are needed to represent the absence of stitches instead. These empty squares are placed between the motif and the background, thus maintaining every stitch symbol above the one it will be worked into (the only blank square within the pattern is the one at the base of the motif). As you work from the chart, skip past the empty squares to read the next symbol to the left or right. If you prefer, you could leave the Knit squares empty, and shade the squares in the chart where stitches are missing.

The increase at the base of the motif is an unusual one and provides a good example of how charting symbols can be used creatively to define a technique for which no ready-made symbol exists. This hybrid symbol is a combination of a traditional Crossed Stitch symbol with the new Yarnover symbol at the center. In the next row, a five-stitch Multiple Yarnover Increase is worked on the first Yarnover. When accompanied by written instructions for the technique, the hybrid symbol indicates quite clearly what to do as you work the pattern.

Unfortunately, when you compare this chart to the fabric, you will notice that it does not convey the information that the Embossed motif is actually resting on a background of Purl stitches. The solution is shown in the second chart.

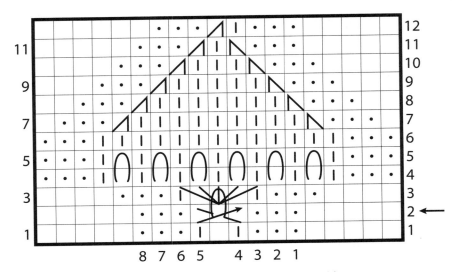

Rosebud. Second chart with empty squares at sides.

Second Chart

This next version of the same pattern provides a more accurate picture of what is happening, both in the fabric and as you work the pattern. The blank squares now lie between the pattern and the perimeter of the chart and the background Purl stitches follow the contours of the motif.

Nevertheless, while this version is far more accurate visually than the one above, it still makes it look as though the Purl background shifts, when in reality it stays pretty much in position while the motif puffs out owing to the extra stitches. Perfection escapes us, as it is wont to do; nevertheless, I think this chart is easier to work from and looks more like the fabric.

Teardrop Pendant

Here is a bold pattern of Seed Stitch outlined with Twist and Crossed Stitches and set on a background of Purl Stitch. There is also an embossed motif at the center, done with a series of increases on three rows, temporarily changing the stitch count; the matching decreases that restore it are located on the three rows above.

Both because of the length of the pattern, and because the techniques are simple and familiar ones, I have not included the written instructions with this chart, but you should find it relatively easy to read it without them.

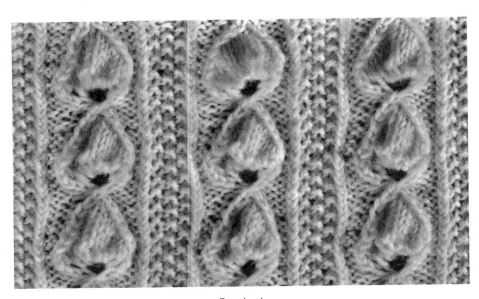

Rosebud.

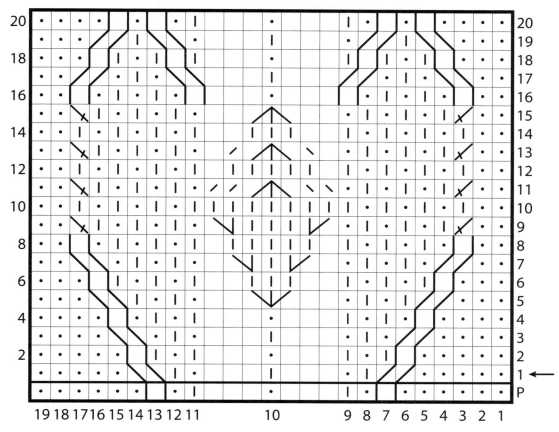

Teardrop Pendant. First chart with empty squares within pattern.

First Chart

In the first chart of the pattern, the details of how to work the embossed motif are included within the chart. As a result of the change in stitch count, blank squares indicating that there are no stitches in that position have to be set between the motif and the background. This version is effective in conveying what to do, but does not provide a good visual sense of the pattern.

Teardrop Pendant.

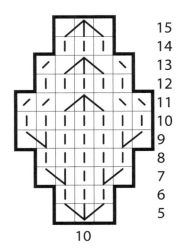

15
14
13
12
11
10
9
8
7
6
5

10

Teardrop Pendant. Chart for
Embossed pattern at center.

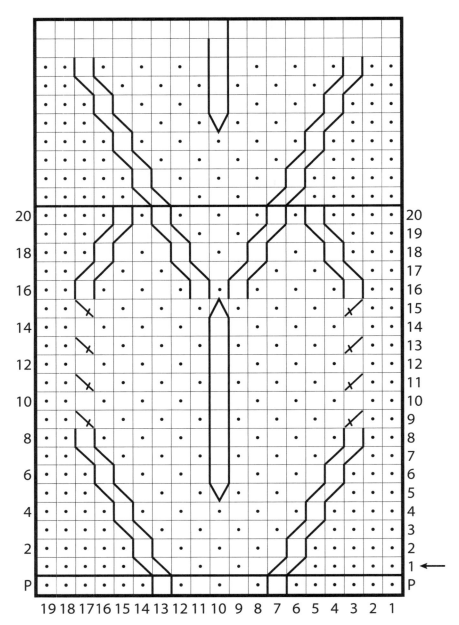

Teardrop Pendant. Second chart with no empty squares within pattern;
Embossed pattern in small chart at side.

Second Chart

A more successful alternative is to use a mini-chart, as shown in the second version. The mini-chart contains the instructions for just the embossed motif at the center of the pattern; it is set to one side and its position is marked within the main chart with the Embossing symbol.

The pattern for this center motif is easy to learn, and then you can concentrate on just the main chart, referring to the mini-chart only if you need a reminder. With no need for empty squares within the chart, the pattern for the background falls into place nicely and the whole becomes visually clear.

The general rule governing these situations is that if the motif is simple and the background complex, set the motif to one side. If they are both complex, or just the motif is, retain the motif within the pattern and use blank squares to deal with a change in stitch count.

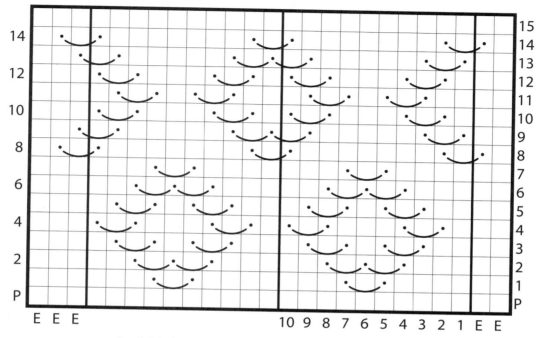

Crook Stitch Diamond. Twined Knit pattern with Crook Stitch.

❖ *Twined Knit Patterns*

The number of stitch techniques used in Twined Knit patterns is relatively limited, but they combine to make beautiful designs in the fabric. The most common one is Crook Stitch, which is a three-stitch unit of either Knit/Purl/Knit, or Purl/Knit/Purl. The yarns alternate to the stitches, and the one not being used to work a stitch is stranded past that stitch on the outside of the fabric.

These pattern units are arrayed in a variety of formations. The simplest arrangement is when they are staggered across the full width of two rows to create a stripe, but here is a chart showing a simple diamond shape made up of Crook Stitch to give you an idea of what a charted pattern of the technique looks like.

Twined Knit is commonly used for small items like mittens, but even so, you might want to position a pattern of this kind on a garment chart (see Coordinating Stitch and Garment Patterns).

Crook Stitch Diamond

This pattern really does not need written instructions; if you are familiar with the Twined Knit technique, it will be quite clear how to work from it.

- If a Purl symbol precedes and follows a strand symbol, work Purl/Knit/Purl version of Crook Stitch. Bring Yarn A to nearside and Purl a stitch; use Yarn B to Knit next stitch; strand Yarn A past new Knit stitch and Purl next stitch. Return Yarn A to farside, if appropriate for next step in pattern.

- If a strand symbol precedes and follows a Purl symbol, work Knit/Purl/Knit version of Crook Stitch. Bring Yarn A to nearside and Knit next stitch with Yarn B; Purl next stitch with Yarn A; Knit next stitch with Yarn B. Return Yarn A to farside, if appropriate for next step in pattern.

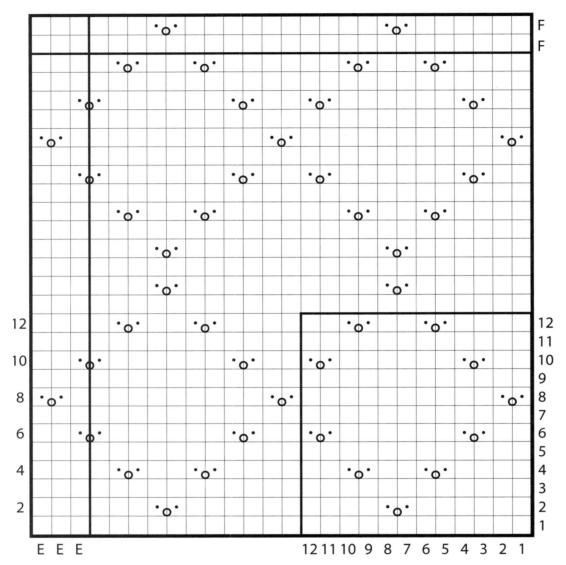

Running Thread Beading chart.

❖ *Bead and Sequin Charts*

Stranded Color and Brocade stitch patterns can be readily adapted for use as bead or sequin patterns with little or no modification; simply position the bead or sequin symbol wherever there is a contrast-color square in a color chart, or where there is a Purl in a stitch pattern.

Running Thread Beading Charts

The Running Thread beading technique requires Purl stitches on either side of each bead. Because the bead is positioned between two stitches, the best way to represent this on a chart is to place the bead symbol on the intersection of two lines, and write the Purl symbols into the squares on either side, as shown in this chart.

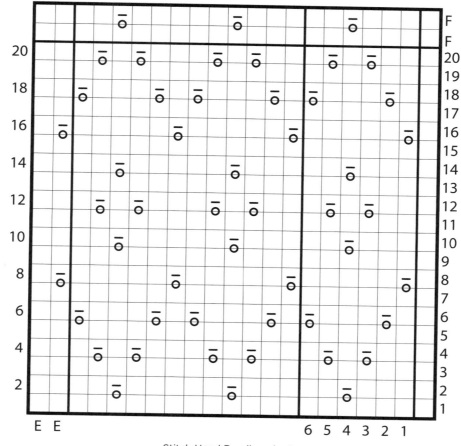

Stitch Head Beading chart.

Stitch Beading Charts

For Stitch Beading, the beads are set on the new stitches of one row, and only worked and discarded into the fabric on the next row as either a Purl or a Twist Stitch. To convey this information in a chart, the bead symbols are placed on the horizontal line dividing two squares, and the symbol for how to work the stitch is placed in the square above.

To work from a chart of this kind, when you see the bead symbol at the top of a square, set a bead as you work the next stitch. When you see the bead symbol at the bottom of a square, this means the next stitch should have a bead on it and you are to work it according to the pattern. The chart here is for Stitch Head Beading; therefore the Purl symbol is set above the bead symbol.

If you prefer to use Twist Stitch for the beaded stitches, you could use that symbol, but since all the stitches will be done the same way, another option is to just leave the square above empty. If necessary, a note accompanying the chart would make it clear to set a bead whenever there is a symbol at the top of a square, and to twist all beaded stitches on the next row. Keep in mind, however, that the simplest way to work this pattern in a flat fabric is to set the beads on an inside row, and Knit the beaded stitches farside on an outside row.

Stitch Head Beading pattern worked from chart.

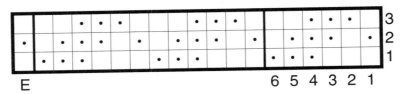

Brocade pattern used as basis for sequin pattern.

Sequin Charts

When sequins are used to blanket a fabric (or an area within one), they are typically set every other stitch and staggered row by row and no chart is needed.

However, when the sequins are used to define a motif, the pattern can be charted in a way that is similar to those for a beading pattern, but instead of the bead symbol being put on an intersection, it is positioned at the top of a square to indicate that a sequin should be set on a stitch. On the next row, the sequined stitch can be worked as a Twist Stitch, in which case no symbol really needs to be used.

Here is an example of a very small Brocade pattern converted from Knit and Purl, as shown in the first chart, to a sequin pattern with flanking Purl stitches. The configuration of Purl stitches that define the pattern is the same, but in the second chart they have been spaced out every other stitch to leave room for the Purl stitches, and every other row to give them a little background space. In this case, it is helpful to use the Purl symbols to make it clear how to work.

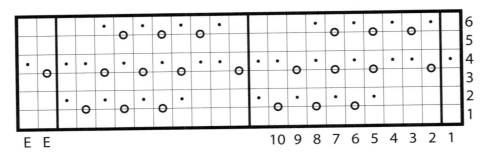

Pattern adapted for sequins with flanking Purl stitches.

CHAPTER 22

Charted Color Patterns

Each square in a color pattern chart represents a stitch, just like a stitch pattern chart. However, while one charting method works for all stitch patterns, each color technique requires a unique type of chart.

The charts used for Stranded Color or Intarsia patterns are similar in many respects and have been in use for a very long time; they should look familiar even if you have never worked from one. They are easy to understand because each square in the chart is simply colored in to show you which yarn to use for the next stitch.

Color stitch patterns are less often charted because their requirements are more varied. These charts have a dual task: to provide not just the information about which color to use, but which stitch technique to use as well. While charts for these kinds of patterns can be somewhat challenging to make, they are often far easier to work from than written instructions and they give you a good sense of what the fabric will look like.

In the case of Mosaic patterns, which are color patterns that employ Slip stitches, the charting system developed by Barbara Walker not only is easy to work from, but also makes it relatively easy to modify a pattern or develop a new one.† Color patterns that include other stitch techniques, including Purl as well as Slip stitches used in other ways, require different kinds of charts, and there are several examples of these shown below.

Finally, there is also a new method I developed to chart Interwoven patterns, which are used exclusively to make Double-Faced fabrics. This is significant, because the written instructions for these kinds of patterns are fiendishly long and difficult to follow; as a result, few of them are published. The charts made with the method described here not only are easier to work from, but also make it possible to develop your own patterns.

---

† Barbara Walker, *Charted Knitting Designs: A Third Treasury of Knitting Patterns* (New York: Charles Scribner's Sons, 1972).

Stranded and Intarsia Charts

Charts for Stranded Color and Intarsia patterns that accompany published patterns are normally printed in color, and in some books several different colorways may be provided as options. If a pattern is printed in black and white, the background squares are generally white, while the squares for the motif are black or gray; in some cases, geometric symbols or letters, or a fill pattern of some kind, might be used to indicate which color yarn to use instead, and a key will be provided.

If you do not want to use the colors suggested in a pattern, make a new copy on graph paper and fill in the squares with those you prefer; there is also computer software available that makes this very easy to do. It is an excellent idea to try a variety of color combinations in this way before purchasing yarn, or to get an idea of whether yarns you have on hand will work together.

You will undoubtedly find that even a small change, like simply switching the dark and light colors, can make a rather large difference in the appearance of a pattern. Also, if a chart is written for only two colors, you might want to see what it would look like if you introduced one or more different contrast colors on some of the rows.

Working from a Stranded Color or Intarsia chart is quite like working from a stitch pattern chart. You simply read the next few squares in a row of the chart to find which color yarn to use and work those stitches accordingly. However, an important distinction must be made between these charts and stitch pattern charts in regard to what is happening on the needles and in the fabric as you work.

On a stitch pattern chart, each row contains information about which techniques to use when working the neutral stitches on the left needle. To check your work to see if it is correct, you would look at the discarded stitches lying below the right needle. However, information about how to work the stitches is quite unimportant in a conventional Stranded Color or Intarsia pattern because they are all done in plain Stockinette; the

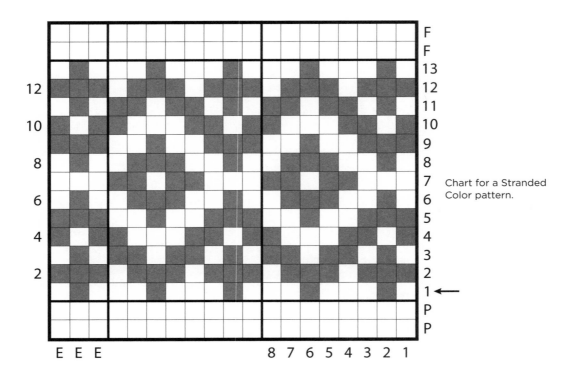

Chart for a Stranded Color pattern.

important information is what color yarn to hold as you work a particular stitch. Therefore, to see if you have worked the pattern correctly, compare the row you are reading on the chart to the colors of the stitches on the right needle. The stitches on the left needle, and those below the right needle, should have the same color sequence shown in the chart one row down.

To make sure you are reading the pattern correctly, check both of those rows. Doing so will tell you something like "work three red stitches onto one red, one blue, and one red stitch." If things do not match, either you are reading the wrong stitches in the chart, or you have made an error in the row below.

Most Stranded Color charts and some Intarsia patterns are built up out of repeats containing a specific number of stitches and rows, like a stitch pattern chart. This means they can be adapted for use with a pattern for any garment, accessory, or household item, regardless of the gauge. However, some Intarsia designs are not based on repeats; instead, the pattern must identify the color of each stitch in the entire fabric, or in major portions of it. As a result, these charts tend to be not only considerably larger and more challenging to make, but also unique to each project and its specific gauge.

❖ Stranded Color Charts

A Stranded Color chart is usually done on a 5-square-per-inch grid, like a stitch pattern chart, and is read in the same way—from the bottom up, from right to left on outside rows, and, if you are working flat, from left to right on inside rows.

If you are new to color knitting, the material below provides

instructions in how to read a charted pattern, including suggestions for approaches to managing more than one yarn.

Most Stranded Color patterns are basically horizontal stripes containing geometric motifs that are closely related to Brocade patterns of mixed Knit and Purl, and you will find a discussion below for how to convert one into the other.

Reading Stranded Color Charts

The chart shown here is a typical Stranded Color stripe pattern that includes two stitch repeats, with the primary one marked off by darker lines. A second dark line marks off the three edge stitches at the left side, which would be used to balance the appearance of the pattern in a flat fabric, but are not needed for one made in the round.

Selvedges are not shown in the chart, because the are optional; if used, work them according to preference. It is a good idea to include them on an unseamed flat fabric so the first and last stitches of the pattern do not turn to the inside, where they would be less visible. For a seamed fabric, add selvedges, but do not use the edge stitches; otherwise the repeats will not meet correctly on either side of the seam (see Edge and Selvedge Stitches). For working in the round, ignore the edge stitches; no selvedge stitches are needed.

This chart also has pairs of optional preparatory and final rows that can be used to give the pattern a little room above a cast-on edge or a ribbing, or below a cast-off edge, but they could also be used to provide a few rows of contrast color between this pattern and some other.

Stranded Color pattern (darker border not shown in chart).

Many Stranded Color patterns are designed for working in the round, but if you plan to work flat, even just to make a swatch, it is important to check the pattern for the occurrence of any solid color stripes with an uneven number of rows. These present a challenge when working a flat fabric (see Basic Horizontal Stripes), because you will end up at the edge opposite where the other yarn is attached. It is possible to break the yarn and Slide the stitches back to the right needle tip and reattach it, but the simplest thing to do is to add or subtract a row in the same color so all stripes have an even number of rows.

Several methods of handling more than one color of yarn while knitting a stranded pattern can be used, and color charts work equally well for any of them. A row on the chart matches a row of the fabric, and whether you alternate the colors as you work the stitches, or employ Slip Stranding and hold one yarn at a time, makes no real difference.

If you are making something in the round and alternating colors, you would read each row of the chart once from right to left, working some stitches in one color, some in the other. If you are making a flat fabric and alternating two colors, you would read one row from right to left working in Knit, and the next row from left to right working in Purl.

With the Slip Stranding method, you will need to make two passes across the stitches on the needle, once with each yarn, in order to make one row of fabric, and there are several options for how to work: two for working flat, and one for working in the round.

Slip Stranding a Flat Fabric

If you prefer to use Slip Stranding and are making a flat fabric, there are two different ways to read the pattern: one approach employs the Slide technique, and the other does not.

In these instructions, Yarn A is used for the pattern stitches, and Yarn B for the background stitches.

Method One

Attach both yarns at side edge and work an ABAB sequence, alternating first Yarn A, then Yarn B, as follows:

1. Outside Row, Yarn A: Read row of chart from right to left; Knit pattern stitches and Slip background stitches with yarn farside. Drop yarn and Slide stitches back to right needle tip.
2. Outside Row, Yarn B: Read same row of chart from right to left; Knit background stitches and Slip pattern stitches with yarn farside. Drop yarn; turn.
3. Inside Row, Yarn A: Read next row of chart from left to right; Purl pattern stitches and Slip background stitches with yarn nearside. Drop yarn and Slide stitches back to right needle tip.
4. Inside Row, Yarn B: Read same row of chart from left to right; Purl background stitches and Slip pattern stitches with yarn nearside. Drop yarn; turn.
5. Repeat Steps 1–4 for every two rows of pattern.

Method Two

With this method, the yarns are attached at opposite side edges and you work an ABBA sequence: first Yarn A, then two passes with Yarn B, and finally another pass with Yarn A, as follows:

1. Outside Row, Yarn A: Read row of chart from right to left; Knit pattern stitches and Slip background stitches with yarn farside. Drop yarn; turn to inside.
2. Inside Row, Yarn B: Read same row of chart again, but from left to right; Purl background stitches and Slip pattern stitches with yarn nearside. Turn.
3. Outside Row, Yarn B: Read next row of chart from right to left; Knit background stitches and Slip pattern stitches with yarn farside. Drop yarn; turn.
4. Inside Row, Yarn A: Read same row of chart from left to right; Purl pattern stitches and Slip background stitches with yarn nearside. Turn.

Slip Stranding a Circular Fabric

If you are working in the round, of course, there is no need to turn the fabric and all rows of the chart are read from right to left. Work as follows:

1. First pass, Yarn A: Read row of pattern from right to left; Knit all pattern stitches and Slip all background stitches with yarn farside. Drop yarn at end of round.
2. Second pass, Yarn B: Read same row of pattern again from right to left. Knit all background stitches and Slip all pattern stitches with yarn farside.
3. Continue in this way, working two passes across the stitches to complete one row of pattern.

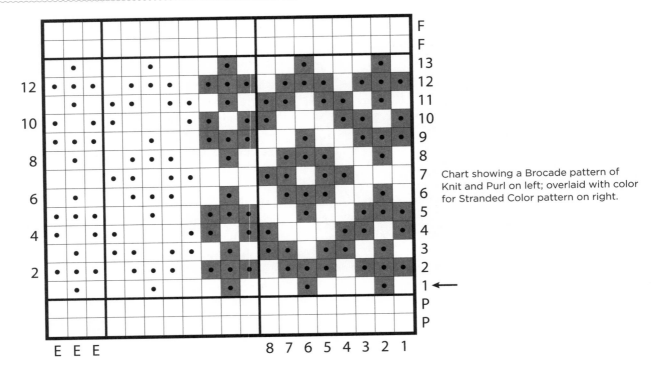

Chart showing a Brocade pattern of Knit and Purl on left; overlaid with color for Stranded Color pattern on right.

Making a Stranded Color Chart

Stranded Color stripe patterns are so plentiful that choosing among them is normally the biggest challenge you will face when starting a new project. Nevertheless, if you have gone through the books and magazines at hand and still have not found something that is just right, you might want to consider converting a Brocade pattern into a Stranded Color pattern.

Here is a chart of the same pattern shown previously, but its origins have been revealed. As shown on the left side of the chart, it started as a Brocade pattern of Knit and Purl; on the right, the squares have been filled in right over the Purl stitches to show what it would look like as a Stranded Color pattern instead.

In doing something of this kind, there is one limitation to consider. Stranded Color patterns normally have no more than about 5 stitches in the same color side by side because this limits the length of the strand in the contrast color that passes behind them. It is easier to control the tension on the yarn and make a smooth fabric if the strands are kept relatively short, and they are less likely to snag in wear; also, the work goes along more quickly.

However, this restriction does not apply to stitch patterns, many of which have more stitches than that grouped in either the motif or the background. Nevertheless, if you are interested in using a pattern of that kind, all is not lost.

First, keep in mind that the length of the strand depends upon your Stitch Gauge. Therefore, if your gauge is about 4 stitches to the inch it would be best to select a pattern with no more than 3 or 4 Knit or Purl stitches grouped together;

if you are working with a gauge of 8 or 9 stitches to the inch, you have more options when selecting a pattern.

If a pattern you like has more stitches grouped than you think are sensible given your gauge, there are two solutions to consider. First, you could introduce a stitch or two done in the contrast color at the center of a large group. For instance, if there would otherwise be a group of 9 stitches to strand past, on the chart, fill in the center stitch of the group with the contrast color, leaving 4 stitches at either side. The other alternative is to use the technique of Weaving-In, which attaches a strand at its midpoint to running threads on the inside of the fabric.

In many patterns, larger groups of stitches may occur on only one or two rows of the repeat. This means that if you choose the first solution and introduce some contrast-color stitches to the pattern, it is unlikely to radically alter its appearance; if you choose the second solution, you will not need to slow down to do the Weaving-In technique very often.

Given how compatible the two types of patterns are, you might also consider combining the Brocade version and the Stranded Color version of a pattern in the same fabric, either by using them in different areas, or alternating repeats of first one and then the other; see Purl in Color Stitch Charts.

Plotting Stranded Designs

Garment designs with Stranded Color patterns frequently make use of several different ones in a variety of color combinations. These can be plotted on a charted garment pattern, exactly as described for a stitch pattern; see Coordinating

Stitch and Garment Patterns. This makes it possible to determine the most advantageous placement of the decorative patterns in relation to the garment, such as centering a repeat at the lower neckline, or at the top of the sleeve, and also makes it easier to follow the color pattern while working a shaping pattern at the same time.

Here are some suggestions for how to plan a design of this kind and plot it on the garment chart:

- If the number of patterns you are going to work with is relatively limited, or only a few are repeated in a regular succession, a garment chart showing just the areas that are shaped is usually adequate; see Partial Charts.

- If you prefer to work with a greater number of patterns, it is probably a good idea to chart the entire garment, especially if the colors vary in each one. This may require either using larger graph paper, taping several sheets together, or charting different sections of the pattern on separate pages; see Chart Fragments.

- As you work out the details of the design, use pencil to draw preliminary horizontal and vertical lines that define the position of each pattern repeat on a draft of the garment chart.

- First establish a significant pattern at the neckline and top of the sleeve, because these are the visual focus points of the garment. Work down from there to position the remaining patterns.

    If necessary, adjust the length of the bodice or lower sleeve so there are enough rows for full repeats between the underarm and the lower edge or ribbing. If you need to make some adjustment in the number of rows, keep in mind that a half repeat set above a ribbing will usually look just fine; simply start on the center row of the chart, instead of on the first row.

- Take into consideration how each pattern repeat lines up on either side of a seam or at the join between rounds. You might want to add a few background stitches or fill stitches at the beginning and end of a row to avoid having partial repeats meet in an unattractive way on either side of a seam or join. In some cases you can add or remove a stitch or two, either within a motif or in the background between motifs, to change the number of stitches in the repeat so it will fit better.

- Because repeats differ in size, it is best to establish the number of stitches in the circumference of the garment based on the requirements of the repeat with the largest number of stitches; then check to see how the others fit within this frame.

    Whenever possible, select patterns with repeats that are multiples of one another, so the number of stitches in the smaller repeats all divide evenly into the number in the largest repeat.

Once you have the color patterns aligned on the garment chart correctly, make a final draft and draw in the horizontal and vertical lines to define their positions.

There is no need to fill in every stitch with the relevant colors; however, you might want to color in one repeat of each pattern around the perimeter of the garment chart to get a better sense of how they all relate to one another and to the shape of the garment. Having the decorative pattern plotted on the shaping pattern in this way provides information about how to start each row of a pattern as the stitch count on the needle changes, which helps you keep your place and speeds up the work.

❖ *Intarsia Charts*

The Intarsia technique is used to create two different types of color patterns, geometric and pictorial. Geometric Intarsia patterns are relatively easy to plan because they function like stitch or color pattern repeats, although the color used for each repeat may be highly variable.

Pictorial Intarsia patterns present more of a challenge in planning because there is often little or no repetition and they need to be superimposed on a portion of, or even all of a garment chart; in the latter case, the charts can be quite large. Depending upon your gauge and the size of the garment, it may be necessary to divide the pattern into sections, with the lower bodice on one piece of graph paper and the upper bodice on another.

Plotting a Geometric Intarsia Pattern

Geometric Intarsia patterns are based on repeats, like stitch patterns or Stranded Color patterns. A familiar example would be an argyle pattern or a checkerboard.

While you can chart a pattern of this kind on the squares of graph paper, just as you would a stitch pattern or Stranded Color pattern, keep in mind that the result will look shorter and wider in the fabric. To determine the overall size of the pattern in the fabric, divide the number of stitches and rows in the repeat by your stitch gauge and row gauge, respectively.†

---

† The difference between the proportions of the squares in a chart and those of a knitted stitch has the same effect on every type of decorative pattern, whether it is based on stitch or color techniques. If you compare the appearance of a Stranded Color pattern chart to the result in the fabric, you will see that the former looks taller than the latter. However, with the exception of some Intarsia patterns, there is usually little reason to take this into consideration because the result in the fabric does not look so different that it is objectionable.

If the proportions do not seem right to you, add a few rows to the pattern so it will look the way you want it to.

To plot a pattern of this kind on a garment chart, draw an overlay grid that represents the number of stitches and rows in the repeat (see the information in Coordinating Stitch and Garment Patterns). Draw in any other lines you think would be helpful, and then use colored pencils to fill in the pattern elements. If the pattern within each grid is at all complex, you might want to color in only the repeats that meet the outer lines of the garment chart. This helps define how to start each row of the pattern and keep your place as you work.

Plotting a Pictorial Intarsia Motif

Unlike Stranded Color patterns or geometric Intarsia patterns, which are based upon repeats, a pictorial Intarsia pattern is plotted on a garment chart according to a particular gauge. As a result, the pattern will be suitable for that project and no other; in order to use the same Intarsia design for a garment pattern with a different gauge, you would need to make an entirely new chart.

In this respect, a pictorial Intarsia pattern is equivalent to a schematic for a garment design; both are drawn according to dimensions that must be converted into a certain number of stitches and rows for a charted pattern.

Because graph paper is made up of squares and knitted stitches are rectangles, the proportions of a garment chart are longer and narrower than a schematic drawing; similarly, an Intarsia design will look elongated in a chart, but it will then have the correct proportions in the fabric. If you were to draw the Intarsia design directly on graph paper it would be distorted in the fabric (see General Information in the chapter Charted Garment Patterns).

There is software available to help design a pattern of this kind, but if you do not have access to those tools, here is the information you will need to make a chart in the traditional way, with a pencil, a ruler, and some graph paper.

The pictorial Intarsia design shown here is not an overall pattern, like those described above. It is a single motif that could be scattered across a sweater bodice or used to decorate a handbag or pillow cover. For applications of that kind, copies of the motif could be flipped horizontally and/or vertically to produce a more lively effect. Here, it has the advantage of being small in scale and will serve adequately to demonstrate how to plot something of this kind on a garment chart.

The original drawing of this simple floral design is 5 square inches; therefore, when drawn on graph paper it would require 25 squares horizontally and vertically.

If you were to knit a pattern drawn with those proportions onto a square grid, but your actual stitch gauge was 5.7 stitches and 7.9 rows per inch, the result in the fabric would

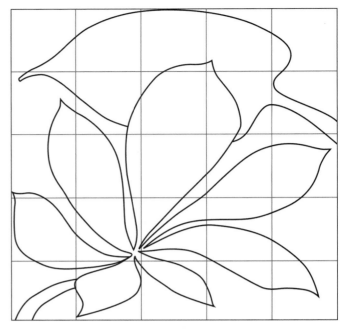

Pictorial Intarsia motif. Draft of design with grid overlay.

have a different shape. Instead of being 5 square inches, it would be:

25 stitches/5.7 Stitch Gauge = 4.4 inches wide

25 squares/6.3 Row Gauge = 3.2 inches high

In other words, considerably smaller, no longer square, and not what you had in mind. Instead, elongate the drawing of the motif so it matches the gauge of the garment chart.

Transferring the Pattern

Draw the garment chart according to gauge on 10-squares-per-inch graph paper. Draw a schematic of the motif on 5-squares-per-inch paper with the proportions you want it to have in the garment.

1. Draw lines around motif to frame design; if graph paper does not have a 1-inch overlay, draw horizontal and vertical lines across it to superimpose a grid on the drawing.
2. Measure height and width of design and use gauge to determine how many stitches and rows will be required to make something that size; allocate that number of squares to the motif on the garment chart.
3. On the garment chart, decide on the placement of the Intarsia motif. Draw a frame for the design on the graph paper enclosing the correct number of squares according to the gauge.
4. For the interior lines within the frame, round your gauge numbers up or down to whole or half-inch numbers and draw a grid that reflects this approximate gauge.

5. Copy the lines of the motif from each square in the original drawing, to the rectangles drawn on the grid, elongating the original lines of the design slightly to fit the proportions of the grid based upon your gauge.

As an example of how to round the numbers up or down for Step 4, the gauge above would be changed from *G* = 5.7/7.9, to *G* = 6/8 instead, which is close enough for the purposes of transferring the pattern.

If you round the numbers up or down and the result is a gauge that includes .5, first draw vertical lines that include squares equal to your gauge times 2, and then divide these areas in half, drawing lines in the middle of the graph paper squares.

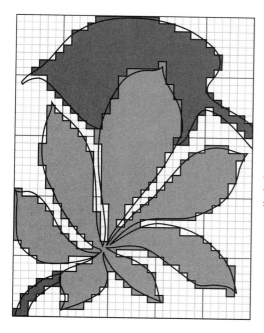

Pictorial Intarsia motif. Transferred to chart with stitches stepped off.

Stepping Off the Pattern

After transferring the drawing to your new grid, step off the lines on the graph paper more or less as you would for stepping off the lines of a shaping pattern (see Charting Slopes and Curves).

- Step off the squares that lie within or on the lines that define each element of the motif. Once the pattern has been stepped off to your satisfaction, fill it in with colored pencils, if you have them; if not, mark each area with letters representing whichever yarn color you plan to use.

Plotting an Overall Intarsia Pattern

If you are dealing with a pattern that will be plotted across the entire fabric, the approach is very much the same, but on a larger scale; see the example of an Intarsia pattern in the chapter Charted Garment Patterns.

First, make a garment chart for the pattern on 10-squares-per-inch graph paper. Then make a schematic of your garment design on 5-squares-per-inch graph paper, ideally with a 1-inch overlay grid (or use a ruler to draw an overlay grid on the paper). It is difficult to show the details of an Intarsia design on a schematic drawn at the usual scale of one square per inch (see Drawing Schematics); therefore, enlarge it to at least half-scale by using 2 squares per inch instead. If you think it necessary, tape several pages together and draw it at full-scale. Then work as follows:

1. Draw the Intarsia design on the schematic with realistic proportions.
2. Round the numbers in your gauge up or down, as described above for the motif, and draw an overlay grid on the garment chart that approximates the number of stitches and rows there will be in every inch of the fabric.
3. Transfer the pattern from the squares of the schematic to the rectangles of the garment chart, elongating the proportions in each one.
4. Step off the pattern along the lines of the design and fill in the colors.

Computer-Assisted Intarsia Design

A complex Intarsia design is obviously a fairly challenging project. There is specialized software available that makes it considerably easier to make a chart (although some programs do not allow the input of precise gauge numbers that include tenths). If you do not have access to software of this kind, but do have a computer, there are other resources you can use that can help speed up the process of making the chart.

Gauge-Based Grid

Internet-based software is available that you can use to create a grid that exactly matches your gauge, with rectangles instead of squares. You can draw your pattern on this paper with the proportions you want it to have in the fabric, and it will turn out the way it should.

1. Using the software, input your gauge to customize the graph paper.
2. Print out the paper and draw the schematic diagram of the garment on it according to its actual dimensions.
3. Overlay the Intarsia design on the schematic, drawing it with correct proportions.

Image Editing Tools

Another alternative is to use any simple photo editing software that allows you to change the proportions of an image.

For this approach, you will need conventional graph paper in both 5- and 10-squares-per-inch sizes, and access to a scanner and a printer.

Because of the scale of the pattern, you will probably find it necessary to divide the schematic and the chart into separate sections for upper and lower bodice, and upper and lower sleeve. However, in the following example of how to do this, the instructions have been simplified, and include only the overall dimensions and number of stitches and rows required; it should be clear how to proceed if you are dealing with a divided pattern.

1. Make a half-scale schematic drawing of garment. For garment 20 inches wide and 24 inches long, schematic will be 10 inches wide and 12 inches long. Draw Intarsia design on schematic with correct proportions.
2. For garment chart, find overall stitches and rows required, as in this example:

   Multiply Stitch Gauge by width: 5.7 × 20 = 114 stitches.

   Multiply Row Gauge by length: 7.9 × 24 = 190 rows.

   On 10-squares-per-inch graph paper, overall chart would be 11.4 inches wide, and 19 inches tall (make separate calculations for divided sections).
3. Scan schematic to make digital image and use photo editing tool to change dimensions from an overall 10 × 12 inches to 11.4 × 19 inches to match dimensions of garment chart. (Make sure to uncheck default setting for "retain proportions," so it is possible to adjust length and width separately.)
4. Separate pattern into two sections (lower and upper bodice) to fit paper, insert 10-squares-per-inch graph paper into computer, and print out design.
5. Draw lines around design to define dimensions and contours of garment chart and step off lines. Next, step off squares that define elements of Intarsia pattern and color in.

Color Stitch Pattern Charts

Patterns that employ both color and stitch techniques are somewhat more challenging to chart than plain color ones, but the benefits of a chart are considerable compared to working from most written instructions.

The charting system created by Barbara Walker for the Mosaic patterns that she defined and developed has become readily available, and you will find instructions below for how to work from one of these.

Also included here is an example of a Stranded Color chart with Purl stitches (which are easy to add in the same way to Intarsia patterns), and another example that uses Slip stitches to make a tweed pattern. Finally, there is an unusual pattern that is done with Short Rows.

Combined, these patterns should give you a good idea of how color stitch charts work, and since few of them are available, you will then be able to make your own based on written instructions.

❖ *Mosaic Pattern Charts*

Charts for Mosaic patterns are as easy to work from as a Stranded Color pattern, but differ in several important ways.

Mosaics are made up of two-row solid color stripes; both rows are worked in exactly the same way and with the same yarn; therefore, a single row on the chart is sufficient for two rows of the pattern. These patterns contain true Slip stitches that remain in the fabric, which are always the color of the stitches in the stripe below; when pulled up into position, they interrupt the continuity of the stripe above, forming the pattern.

In some respects, working a Mosaic pattern is similar to using the Slip Stranding method for a Stranded Color pattern, but because there is rarely more than one stitch slipped in any position (two is the maximum), the work goes very quickly.

The charts will have the squares for the dark color filled in, and those for the light color left blank. Of course, when you make your own chart, you can color the squares in as you please to get a better sense of what the pattern will look like and to try different color combinations; there is a brief discussion of several options for varying these patterns below.

Reading a Mosaic Chart

As you can see on the chart below, each row is numbered twice, with the odd numbers on the right, the even on the left. This is helpful when working a flat fabric; the numbers on the left can be ignored when working in the round.

Slip all stitches with the yarn stranded on the *inside* of the fabric. The instructions are written for working flat; therefore, Slip stitches with yarn farside when working outside rows, and Slip them with yarn nearside when working inside rows.

The abbreviation DC is used for the dark-color, LC for the light-color yarn.

Reading the chart is very simple; begin with an outside row:

1. With DC, read row of chart from right to left and work one stitch for every black square and Slip one stitch for every white one; turn.
2. Continue with DC for next row; work same stitches as on previous pass, and Slip all stitches previously slipped; turn.

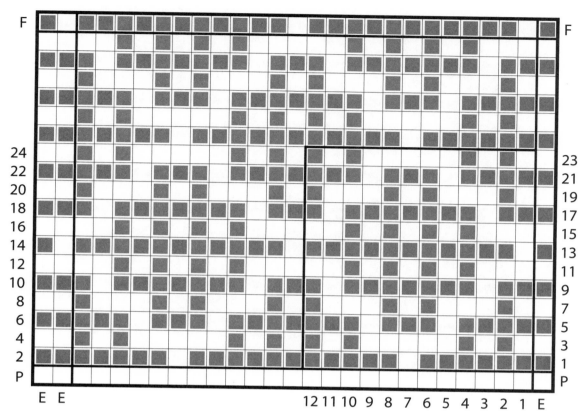

Mosaic pattern chart.

3. With LC, read next row of chart from right to left. Work one stitch for every white square and Slip one stitch for every black square; turn.
4. Continue with LC for next row; work same stitches as on previous pass, and Slip all stitches previously slipped; turn.
5. Repeat Steps 1–4, working each row of instructions twice with same yarn.

You will find there is no real need to read the chart when working the second row of each stripe. Simply let yourself be guided by the stitches on the needle, and work all those in the same color as the yarn you are working with and Slip all those in the contrast color.

The colors always alternate: work the first pattern row twice with the yarn represented by the black squares, then work the next pattern row twice with the yarn represented by the white squares. Of course, you could decide to use the light color yarn for the black squares and the darker one for the light squares (as a matter of fact, these patterns invite color reversal effects).

The two preparatory rows are required to form the foun-

dation for the contrast-color stitches in the first row of the pattern. It is easiest to accomplish this by using a Half-Hitch Cast-On and then working one additional row before starting Row 1 of the pattern.

Notice that a stripe always begins and ends with a stitch, never a Slip stitch. It is customary to include selvedge stitches on a Mosaic chart for this purpose, and they also conveniently serve to indicate which color to use for that pair of rows. Of course, if you are knitting in the round, you have no need of them, but the information they contain about which color yarn to use for each pair of rows remains valid.

It is sometimes said that there is no need to worry about partial repeats with a Mosaic pattern because the second row of each stripe is always identical to the first. This means that, unlike other stitch or color patterns, there will be no confusion about how to start the second row when you are working flat, even if you have ended with a partial repeat. Nevertheless, I prefer to balance the appearance of the pattern at both sides of a fabric, and usually adjust the number of stitches in the width of the fabric to accommodate full repeats.

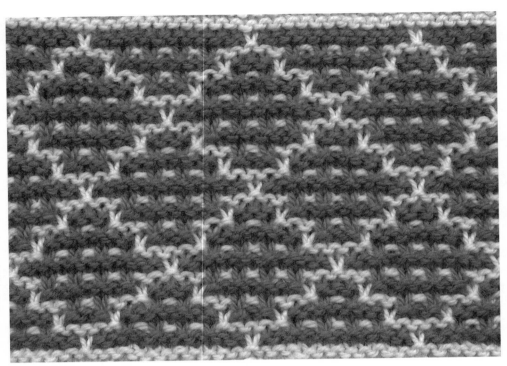

Mosaic pattern shown in chart. Pattern done entirely in Garter Stitch.

Mosaic pattern shown in chart.
Pattern done in a color reversal; white stitches in Garter Stitch and dark stitches in Stockinette.

Mosaic Variations

Mosaic charts are customarily done in two colors, but it is quite easy to add more to test the effect of other combinations; the most common option is a color reversal.

Another possibility is to use a third color for one or more of the stripes in a row repeat, or to maintain one yarn as the background color and alternate two contrast colors for the row repeats. Other interesting effects can be achieved by using a solid color yarn for half the rows, and a variegated yarn for the others; you can also combine Mosaic patterns with the Intarsia technique.

Mosaic patterns are typically done entirely in either Stockinette or Garter Stitch. However, there is no information provided in the chart about how to work the stitches, although quite a few variations are possible.

You can, for instance, combine the two within a row repeat, working Garter Stitch on pattern rows, and Stockinette on background rows, or vice versa. Another approach is to do one stitch repeat in Stockinette, the next in Garter Stitch, or alternate working the row repeats that way, or do both. Or you could use Garter Stitch for everything but the slipped stitches.

If you want to vary the pattern in any of these ways, it is a good idea to chart several repeats both horizontally and vertically to show any color effects you want to use. In a pattern of mixed Stockinette and Garter Stitch, you might want to circle certain row numbers or stitch column numbers to indicate how to work them.

When using Garter Stitch only in some areas, write the Purl symbols in where necessary and then fill the squares with relatively transparent colors so they will be visible. And, of course, remember that the first row of every stripe must be in Knit on the outside of the fabric, so the Purl symbols only refer to the second row (for an explanation of what happens if you work a row of Purl in a contrast-color yarn, see Color Patterns with Purl in the chapter Color Techniques). If you do use Garter Stitch, keep in mind that these fabrics are not reversible; the Slip stitches create the pattern on only one side of the fabric.

❖ *Purl in Color Stitch Charts*

Purl stitches add texture to Stranded Color or Intarsia patterns, and it is relatively easy to adapt almost any pattern of that kind to include them. However, you will achieve the most attractive result if you work Purl only on a stitch of the same color as the yarn being used for the new stitch. (For a superb example, see the illustration of the Italian silk tunic on page 280, which has Intarsia motifs done in Garter Stitch.)

This is not an ironclad rule, and some interesting effects can be created by breaking it. If you Purl a stitch while working with the contrast-color yarn, the head of the discarded stitch will be one color and the running threads on either side of it will be the other color and the result will be a tweedy effect in the fabric; see Color Patterns with Purl in the chapter Color Techniques.

A chart for a color pattern that includes Purl stitches must provide both the information that is normally on a stitch pattern chart (how to work each stitch), and the information that is normally on a color pattern chart (which color yarn to use).

Stranded Color Pattern with Purl

Here is the same Stranded Color chart shown earlier, but Purl symbols have been added; notice that they are not centered within the square in the normal way for a stitch pattern chart, but instead lie on the line separating two stitches of the same color. As you follow the pattern, use whatever color yarn is shown in the square for the next stitch; work all the stitches in Knit unless there is a Purl symbol at the *bottom* of the square; work those stitches in Purl.

Positioning the Purl symbol in this way makes the chart not only relatively easy to read, but also accurately represents what happens within the fabric. The head of a Purl stitch lies at the base of the new stitch and the running threads lie close to the sides of the discard stitch; combined, they occupy the space between two rows, just as the symbol sits on the line between two squares.

Make a small swatch to try the pattern; here are written instructions for the first half of the pattern that you can compare to the chart; once you have gone that far, you should have the idea and can decide which you prefer.

Multiple of 8 stitches, plus 3 edge stitches and 2 selvedge stitches.
LK = Knit with Light Color, LP = Purl with Light Color.
DK = Knit with Dark Color, DP = Purl with Dark Color.

Selvedge stitches are not included in chart or instructions, but add them for a flat swatch. Work at end of row with both yarns held as one to anchor stranded yarn; Slip knitwise at beginning of outside row; Slip purlwise at beginning of inside row.

Preparatory Rows: Cast on with light color and work one inside row; tie on second color; turn and work as follows:
Row 1: Rep[LK1, DK1, LK3, DK1, LK2], end LK1, DK1, LK1.
Row 2: DP1 K1 P1, rep[LP1, DP1 K1 P1, LP1, DP1 K1 P1].
Row 3: Rep[LK1, DP1, LK1, DK1 P1, LK1, DP1 K1], end LK1, DP1, LK1.
Row 4: DP1, LP1, DP1, rep[DK1, LP3, DK1 P1, LP1, DP1].
Row 5: Rep[DP1 K1 P1, LK2, DK1, LK2], end DP1 K1 P1.

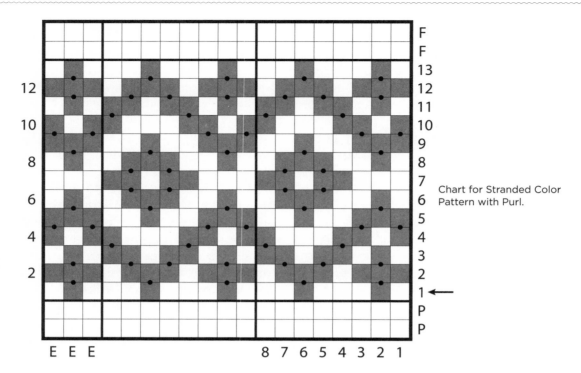

Chart for Stranded Color
Pattern with Purl.

Row 6: LP1, DK1, LP1, rep[LP1, DP1 K1 P1, LP2,
    DK1, LP1].
Row 7: Rep[LK3, DK1 P1, LK1, DP1 K1], end LK3.
Rows 8–13: Continue per charted instructions.
Final two Rows: Stockinette.

It is important to return the yarn used for Purl to the inside
of the fabric before working a stitch in the other color. It will
be obvious if you make a mistake because the next time you
try to use the yarn it will be in the wrong position. If this happens, Slip the completed stitches to the left needle, bring the
yarn between the needle tips, and then Slip the stitches back
to the right needle again and continue.

Stranded Color Pattern with Purl.

It takes some practice to learn to control the tension for a
pattern like this; if the first stitch at a color change is Purl, it is
tempting to draw the strand up too tightly as you move it into
position to make the stitch; make sure to stretch the stitches out
on the right needle to provide sufficient length to the strand.

After working the first Purl stitch with a stranded yarn, apply a
little extra tension to tighten the stitch on the needle, drawing
any extra yarn out of it so it will not enlarge (this will tighten
only the stitch and not the strand).

It is usually best to add Purl to only one of the colors used
in the pattern; this not only provides some background contrast, but also makes the pattern easier to work.

❖ Slip Stitch Color Patterns

Mosaics are by no means the only color patterns that employ
Slip stitches, but other types of patterns that use the technique
require a different approach to charting them. The method used
to chart the patterns below involves separating the two pieces
of information needed—which color to use to make the next
new stitch, and how to work the stitch that will be discarded.

The symbols for the technique are written into each row in
the normal way for a stitch pattern; these determine the form
of the discarded stitches in the fabric below the right needle.
Which yarn to use is indicated by the color of the row number. However, because the yarn held as you work determines
the color of the new stitches on the right needle, that color
appears not on the same row of the chart, but *in the row above*.

This sounds complicated, but it is actually not that difficult to
make charts of this kind and they are surprisingly easy to work
from. Because the method is suitable only for charting color patterns that are done with one yarn color for any row, simply pick
up the correct yarn according to the color of the row number,
and read the symbols in each row of the chart square by square,
just as when working from a stitch pattern chart.

Actually, just looking at the color of the row number is

enough information for you to work from one of these patterns, which means there is really no need to fill in the colors on the rows as well. However, doing so provides a much better idea of what the pattern will look like, and is also useful when you need to check your work for accuracy and/or find your place in the pattern.

Three-Color Tweed

Here is a very simple Slip Stitch pattern done in three colors. The yarn is stranded past the Slip stitches on the outside of every other row, leaving a small horizontal fleck of contrast color at the base of those stitches. There is a good selection of patterns of this kind available, and all produce attractive, tweedy fabrics that are suitable for any number of applications.

When worked with a needle size normal for the thickness of the yarn, these fabrics are quite firm because of the number of Slip stitches they contain. Done that way, they are wonderful for jackets and vests; for a softer fabric, simply increase the needle size.

The best way to really get a sense of how this works is to try it on a swatch. Here is an explanation of the first six rows of the pattern; by the time you have done those, you should be able to follow the rest of the pattern from the chart without the help of written instructions.

Preparatory Rows: Cast on and work one inside row with dark color. This determines color of stitches in Preparatory Row and stitches on needle.

Row 1, on outside: Knit with light color. New stitches on right needle are light color, and Slip stitches are dark color, as shown in Row 2. Running threads stranded on outside of Slip stitches are light color. Discarded stitches below right needle are dark color.

Row 2: Purl on inside with light color. All new stitches on right needle are light color, as shown in Row 3. Stitches discarded from left needle will be mixture of Slip stitches in dark color and plain stitches in light color.

Row 3: Knit with medium color. New stitches on right needle are medium color, and Slip stitches are light color, as shown in Row 4. Yarn is stranded farside past Slip stitches; no running threads appear on outside of fabric. Discarded stitches will all be light color used in Row 2.

Row 4: Purl with medium color. All new stitches on right needle are medium color, as shown in Row 5. Stitches discarded from left needle will be mixture of Slip stitches in light color and normal stitches in medium color.

Row 5: Knit with dark color. All new stitches on right needle are dark color, and Slip stitches are medium color, as shown in Row 6. Running threads stranded on outside of Slip stitches are dark color. Stitches discarded from left needle will be medium color used in Row 4.

Row 6: Purl with dark color. All new stitches on right needle will be dark color, as shown in Row 7. Stitches discarded from left needle will be mixture of Slip stitches in medium color, and plain stitches in dark color.

Rows 7–12: Continue with charted instructions.

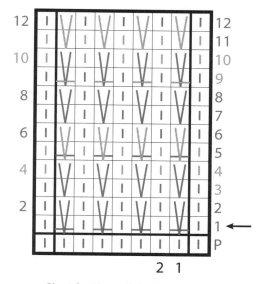

Chart for Three-Color Tweed,
a Slip Stitch pattern.

Three-Color Tweed.

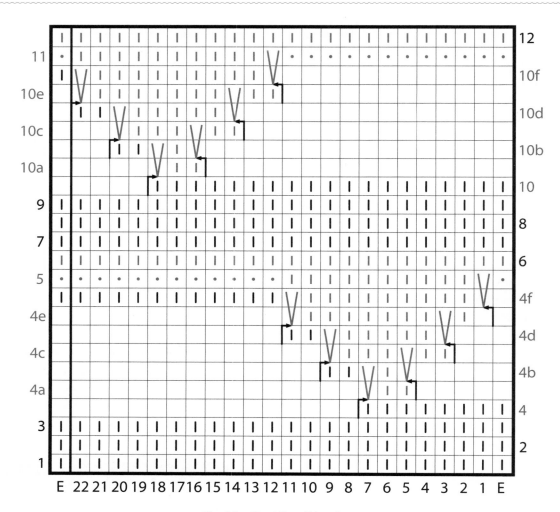

Chart for Short Row Triangles.

❖ Color Short Row Patterns

There are not very many color patterns that exploit the Short Row concept as a stitch technique, but it can be used to create interesting combinations of color and texture in a fabric (in fact, these patterns could also be done in a solid color for just the texture).

A chart for a pattern that uses this technique not only has to indicate what color and which stitch technique to use, but it must also indicate that some stitches are missing because extra rows are worked in certain areas, and not in others. This can be done by leaving blank spaces within the chart, in a way that is similar to the Rosebud and Teardrop Pendant patterns in the chapter Charted Stitch Patterns, which have a temporary change in the stitch count on certain rows.

Short Row Triangles

This pattern makes use of the Short Row symbols shown in Charted Garment Patterns. There is no need to wrap a stitch at the turn as is done when using Short Rows to shape a fabric.

Multiple of 22 stitches/12 rows, plus two edge stitches. Selvedge stitches are not shown, but it is helpful to add them for a swatch; work according to preference.

DC = Dark Color.

LC = Light Color.

Row 1 (inside): With dark color, Purl.

Row 2 DC: Knit.

Row 3 DC: Purl.

Row 4 LC: K1, rep[K7, turn; Sl1, P2, turn; Sl1, K4, turn; Sl1, P6, turn; Sl1, K8, turn; Sl1, P10, turn; Sl1, K21], end K1.

Row 5 LC: K1, rep[K11, P11], end K1.

Row 6 DC: Knit.

Row 7 DC: Purl.

Row 8 DC: Knit.

Row 9 DC: Purl.

Row 10 LC: K1, rep [K18, turn; Sl1, P2, turn; Sl1, K4, turn; Sl1, P6, turn; Sl1, K8, turn; Sl1, P10, turn; Sl1, K10], end K1.

Bobbles set against contrast-color Triangles in Purl.

Row 11 LC: K1, rep[P11, K11], end K1.
Row 12 DC: Knit.

The rows with Short Rows are marked 4a, 4b, and so on, to indicate that you are to work only the stitches of the motif. The symbols used at the turning points should be quite clear, and after each turn the first stitch is slipped.

Having the empty squares within the chart makes it quite large, and this Short Row motif is easy to do and quick to learn. Another option would be to use a mini-chart, showing just the Short Row pattern, with a line drawn within the larger chart showing where to position it (for an example, see Teardrop Pendant in Charted Stitch Patterns); however, there is no need to do that here because the background is a simple stripe.

❖ *Charting Other Stitch Techniques*

Many other stitch techniques can be included in color patterns, and the method used to chart them depends on how they are done. Patterns that require working with one yarn at a time, like those above, are relatively easy to chart, while Stranded Color patterns present somewhat more of a challenge.

A Bobble, for instance, is made entirely with the yarn in hand and will be the same color as the new stitches on the right needle; an example is shown here set on a background of Purl stitches.

Wrap Stitches, Couching Stitches, and Slip Stitches or Yarnovers that are used as a Pullover technique will all be the color of the yarn in hand.

Threaded Stitches, Twist Stitches, Crossed and Cable Stitches are discarded into the fabric and will all be the color

Short Row Triangles.

used on the previous row. These are more likely to appear in a Stranded Color pattern and the best approach to charting is to insert the stitch symbols into the chart first, and then add the information about the color.

Double-Faced Fabric Patterns

Interwoven color patterns were introduced in the material on Decorative Techniques for Double-Fabrics. This highly specialized technique is used not simply to add a color pattern to a fabric in the conventional sense; the color technique itself produces a different and completely unique fabric structure: the Interwoven Pattern technique is *how* Double-Faced Fabrics are made.

To get an idea of what is at work here, imagine that you are making a circular fabric, and you work one pattern on half the stitches and a different pattern on the other half of the stitches (or a color reversal of the first pattern). Next, you wave a magic wand that flattens the circular fabric to such an extent that the two halves are inseparably merged—the result would be a single-thickness, flat fabric with two outside faces. That is what you will be doing with this color technique.

In order to make a Double-Fabric, two sets of stitches are interspersed on the needle, one set for each side of the fabric; the basic method of working the stitches keeps the two sets carefully separated and the fabric is joined only at the edges (see The Basic Patterns in the chapter Double-Fabrics). However, for a Double-Faced fabric, both patterns are worked *at the same time;* the contrast-color yarns travel back and forth between the two sets of stitches, which links the two sides of the fabric into a single-thickness fabric with two outside faces.

There are three different kinds of Interwoven patterns.

An Intarsia-type Interwoven pattern is made using the Basic Double-Fabric technique for the background, but with two colors, one for each side. The pattern consists of small Intarsia-type figurative or geometric motifs widely spaced across the two fabric faces. The two colors change sides, with the background color on one side used for the stitches of the motif on the other. This binds the two fabrics together into a Double-Faced Fabric. If the motifs are large enough, it is even possible to create a trapunto effect by separating the two sets of motif stitches and filling the interior with wool fiber or soft yarn, as shown in the photographs opposite.† The stitches are then interspersed on the needle again to close the now prominent motif and continue with the background.

A Stranded Color Interwoven pattern is typically a simple color reversal. The same pattern is done on both sides, but the background color on one side is used for the pattern on the other side. These are well-behaved fabrics that lie flat and smooth; they are thicker than a single-thickness fabric, but not as thick as a Double-Fabric. While it is technically possible to use a different pattern on each side, the result is not always satisfactory because the strands passing between the two faces of the fabric tend to peek through to the outside unless the fabric is quite firm.

The Interwoven Mosaic patterns are far more interesting because the technique not only makes it possible to use two entirely different patterns on each side of the fabric, but they are considerably easier to work than the others. There is also a wealth of patterns to choose from that combine well with one another. These fabrics are somewhat thinner than those made with a Stranded Interwoven pattern; they lie flat and have considerable elasticity, and in fact, resemble a Single Rib in many respects. Because they are reversible, they make an excellent choice for hat brims, for collars and cuffs, or perhaps for a nice vest.

Jane F. Neighbors' book, *Reversible Two-Color Knitting*, contains a variety of patterns of this kind, but unfortunately, the written instructions look formidable even to the experienced and this has limited their use.‡ What you will find here is a method of charting Interwoven patterns that not only makes them somewhat easier to do (it must be said they can be rather challenging), but also allows you to develop your own patterns (and since few patterns are available other than in Neighbors's book, which is out of print as of this writing, this is important).

While charting patterns of this kind takes a certain patience, it is not at all difficult to do once you get the idea. As you will see, the result is a simple, relatively easy-to-read graphic guide for making these remarkable fabrics.§

Actually, three charts are required—separate ones for the patterns that will appear on each face of the fabric, and one that combines those two into a chart that you can work from.

❖ Stranded Interwoven Charts

Stranded Interwoven patterns can be charted in two different ways.

With one method, the information from each row of the pattern is placed in a *register*; the lower rows in each register contain the pattern for Side A, and the upper rows in each register contain the pattern for Side B. The numbers for the two patterns are staggered on two rows below the chart to reflect the sequence of stitches on the needle; the odd-numbered stitches belong to Side A and the even-numbered stitches to Side B.

With the second method, the information from both patterns is merged on a single row, just as the stitches are interspersed on the needle; the odd-numbered squares are for one pattern, the even-numbered squares for the other pattern.

There are also two ways to work a pattern of this kind. You can hold one yarn at a time, making two passes across the stitches for each row and using the Slide technique to return to the other yarn. Or, you can hold both yarns at the same time, working all the stitches in the row on one pass. Either chart is suitable, regardless of how you hold the yarn; try them both and choose the one you find easiest to follow as you work.

---

† Trapunto is a form of quilting where motifs are outlined with stitching and then stuffed to make the surface protrude.

‡ Jane F. Neighbors, *Reversible Two-Color Knitting* (New York: Charles Scribner's Sons, 1974; out of print).

§ The method used to chart these patterns was introduced in the first edition of this book, but the graphics were minimal and less than ideal, and the explanations made something sufficiently challenging seem even more so. I am hoping the necessarily brief discussion here will help clarify the concepts.

Interwoven Intarsia pattern with trapunto. Center motif has been filled;
background worked in Stranded Interwoven pattern of Fleur-de-Lis.

Interwoven Intarsia pattern with trapunto. Second side in color reversal.

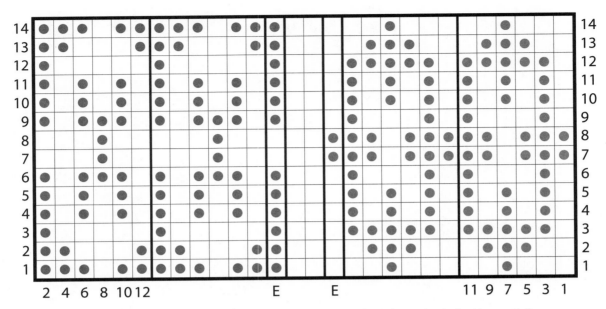

Enchained, a Stranded Color pattern. Original chart on right; color reversal of pattern on left.

Enchained

This pattern is from Neighbors's book; it is a color reversal of a Stranded Color pattern that she calls Enchained.†

The first step is to make a chart of the original Stranded Color pattern and another of the color reversal, and number them as shown. On the right side of the chart, Side A has only odd numbers written from right to left, and, on the left, Side B has only even numbers written from left to right.

The reason for this numbering system is that once in the fabric, the two patterns will then be back to back, and the stitch represented by the number 2 square in the left pattern will be behind the stitch represented by the number 1 square in the right pattern.

Chart with Registers

The first Stranded Interwoven chart is done with registers, each one containing a pair of rows. The lower row in each register contains the information from the Side A chart, and the upper row has the information from the Side B chart.

In this pattern, the upper half is a mirror image of the lower half. This is quite convenient, because only the first seven rows have to be charted; simply read the same rows in reverse to make the second half of the pattern.

† Neighbors, *Reversible Two-Color Knitting*, p. 120.

1. Draw a horizontal line at bottom and a vertical line at right side to define bottom and one side of chart.
2. For row registers, draw horizontal lines every two rows equal to maximum number of rows in one pattern, plus one empty row between each register to make chart easier to read.
3. Write stitch repeat numbers below bottom line in two rows, with odd numbers in lower row, and even numbers staggered one column to left in upper row, as shown.
4. Add odd and even row numbers next to each register on right side, and even numbers next to every other register on left side.
5. Transfer information from first row of Side A pattern to lower row in Register 1. Work from right to left and draw dark and light colors only into squares with odd numbers; leave all squares with even numbers blank.
6. Next, transfer information from first row of Side B pattern to upper row in Register 1. Read Side B chart from left to right, but fill dark and light colors into every other square from right to left, matching stitch numbers in both charts.
7. Repeat for other rows of pattern, transferring information from every row of Side A to lower row of each register, and information from every row of Side B into upper row of each register. Read Side A chart rows from right to left and Side B rows from left to right; fill in all squares in working chart from right to left.

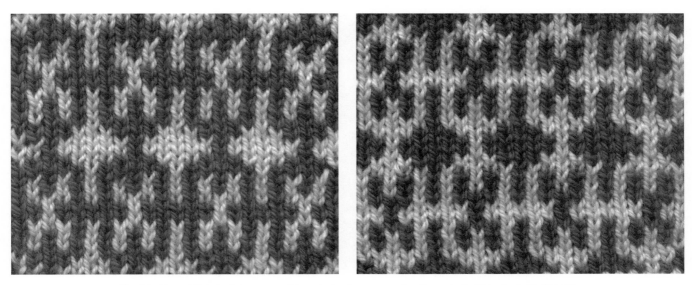

Double-Faced Fabric: Interwoven Stranded color-reversal pattern. Left: Side A; right: Side B.

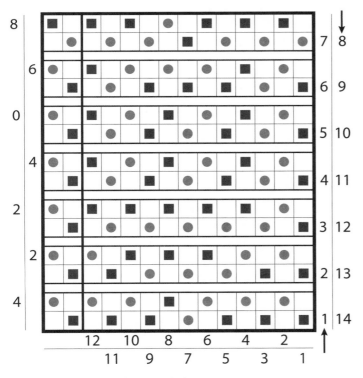

Enchained, a Stranded Interwoven pattern:
chart with registers.

As an example of how to do Step 6, start by filling in the color from square 2 in the Side B chart, to square 2 in the upper row of Register 1, then fill in the color of square 4, and continue in this way until all the even-numbered squares have been filled in; every other square will be left blank.

When you are done, the lower row of every register will have blank squares for all the even-numbered stitch columns; the upper row of every register will have blank squares for all the odd-numbered stitch columns. This is equivalent to separating the stitches of a Double-Fabric onto two needles and holding them parallel (see Separating and Interspersing Stitch Sets). As with a conventional Stranded Color pattern, you can work this pattern holding one yarn at a time or both; there are pros and cons to each method.

To work from the chart, I strongly recommend that you place a guide of some kind above the row you are reading to help you keep your place. You might find it helpful to cut out a window in a piece of paper or cardboard that is exactly the size of a single register; clip it in place on your pattern so you only see the row you need to read next.

One-Yarn Method

If you prefer to hold one yarn at a time, you will work all the stitches on both sides of the fabric that should be in that color on the first pass; then Slide the stitches to pick up the other yarn and, on the second pass, work all the stitches that should be the other color; after two passes, one row is complete on both sides of the fabric.

The difficulty with this is that when you do the first pass across the stitches, some of the stitches slipped will be the same color as the one you are working with, which makes it very difficult to check to see whether you have worked the pattern correctly. It is only on the second pass across the stitches that the pattern will emerge in the proper sequence on the right needle.

Tie the two contrast-color yarns together with a Slip Knot and cast on a multiple of two pattern repeats (half for each side of the fabric), plus two selvedge stitches; use Knit Half-Hitch Cast-On or Alternating Cast-On. Work one row in either color, drop the Slip Knot from the needle and untie.

The selvedge stitches are useful for anchoring the yarns at each side; Slip them at the beginning of each row and work them at the end of each row, in Knit on an outside row, in Purl on an inside row.

DC=Dark Color
LC=Light Color

Register 1 and odd-numbered registers: Read pattern from right to left.

1. With DC: Knit all DC pattern stitches in lower row of register, and Purl all DC pattern stitches in upper row. Slip all LC stitches in lower row with yarn farside, and Slip all LC stitches in upper row with yarn nearside. Slide.
2. With LC: Knit all LC stitches in lower row of register, and Purl all LC stitches in upper row. Slip all DC stitches in lower row with yarn farside, and Slip all DC stitches in upper row with yarn nearside. Turn.

Register 2 and even-numbered registers: Read pattern from left to right.

3. With DC: Knit all DC stitches in upper row of register, and Purl all DC stitches in lower row. Slip all LC stitches in lower row with yarn nearside, and Slip all LC stitches in upper row with yarn farside. Slide.
4. With LC: Knit all LC stitches in upper row of register and Purl all LC stitches in lower row. Slip all DC stitches in lower row with yarn nearside, and Slip all DC stitches in upper row with yarn farside. Turn.

After completing Rows 1–7, read them again from the top down for Rows 8–14 to complete the pattern. As before, read odd-numbered registers from right to left, and even-numbered registers from left to right.

Yikes! Indeed, but with a little practice it will become easier.

Here are some tips that should help you gain facility with working from the chart.

- When both colors are together at the same side of the fabric, begin a new row. When one color is at each side, read the same row again, in the same direction.
- It helps you keep your place and remember what to do next if you always work the colors in the same sequence. It does not matter if you use the dark color first, or the light color first; what matters is that you do it the same way every time.
- When you begin a new row, pay closest attention only to the squares in the color you will work with next. For instance, if you are working with the light color, and there are something like three LC squares one after the other in the lower register and only DC squares above them, think "K3." If you see two LC squares together in the upper register, think "P2." Simply Slip all the DC squares with yarn nearside or farside, as necessary.
- If you have any difficulty reading the even-numbered rows on the chart from left to right, simply turn the chart upside down. Read from right to left and Knit the stitches in what will then be the lower row of the register and Purl those in the upper row.

Enchained Written Instructions

To give you an idea of what written instructions for the pattern look like, here are the first two rows so you can compare them to the chart; if you were not already convinced that a chart makes it considerably easier to work one of these patterns, this should be persuasive.

The selvedge stitches are not included in the pattern; work them as described above.

Row 1, DC: Rep (3[Sl1yfs, P1], K1, Sl1yns, 2[Sl1yfs, P1]), end Sl1yfs, P1. Slide.

Row 1, LC: Rep (3[K1, Sl1yns], Sl1yfs, P1, 2[K1, Sl1yns]), end K1, Sl1yns. Turn.

Row 2, DC: K1, Sl1yns, rep(K1, Sl1yns, 3[Sl1yfs, P1], 2[K1, Sl1yns]. Slide.

Row 2, LC: Sl1yfs, P1, rep(Sl1yfs, P1, 3[K1, Sl1yns], 2[Sl1yfs, P1]. Turn.

Two-Yarn Method

If you prefer to hold both yarns at the same time, you can work just once across the stitches for each row, which makes things go more quickly, and you can see the pattern appear immediately in the color of the stitches on the right needle. However, it can be difficult to control the tension and produce an even fabric.

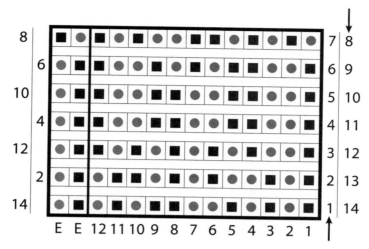

Enchained, a Stranded Interwoven pattern:
chart showing pattern interspersed on single rows.

You can hold both yarns in one hand, but the yarns tend to tangle together more than if they are separated by holding one in each hand; see Two-Hand Stranding. However, the latter technique not only requires familiarity with both the Right-Hand and Left-Hand Methods of knitting, but also requires equal skill at working Knit and Purl with both hands, since a mixture of the two stitches will be worked on every row.

Both yarns have to be passed between the needle tips after each stitch is worked; one may be used for the next stitch and the other stranded, or both may be stranded. Position both farside in order to Knit a stitch in the lower register with one of the yarns; position both nearside in order to Purl a stitch in the upper register with one of them.

1. Read Register 1 from right to left: With DC, Knit all pattern stitches in lower row of register and Purl all pattern stitches in upper row. With LC, Knit all background stitches in lower row of register and Purl all background stitches in upper row of register. Turn.
2. Read Register 2 from left to right: With DC, Knit all pattern stitches in upper row of register and Purl all pattern stitches in lower row. With LC, Knit all background stitches in upper row of register and Purl all background stitches in lower row. Turn.
3. Continue in this way to work all registers of pattern. With either yarn color, Knit Side A stitches and Purl Side B stitches when reading pattern from right to left, and Purl Side A stitches and Knit Side B stitches when reading pattern from left to right.

Chart with Interspersed Patterns

Here is the same pattern done by interspersing the two patterns in a single row just as the stitches are on the needle.

1. Draw horizontal line for bottom of chart and vertical line for right side. Number rows up right side, and write in all numbers for stitch repeat from right to left at bottom.
2. Transfer information from first row of Side A pattern to odd-numbered stitches in first row.
3. Transfer information from first row of Side B pattern to even-numbered stitches in first row.
4. Repeat for every row of pattern.
5. Draw left vertical line for repeat and horizontal line at top.

One-Yarn Method

To read a chart with the stitches interspersed on one row while working with one yarn at a time, read from right to left on odd-numbered rows, and left to right on even-numbered rows, and work as follows:

Row 1, DC: Knit all DC stitches in odd-numbered columns, and Purl all DC stitches in even-numbered columns; Slip all LC stitches with yarn nearside or farside, as necessary. Slide.

Row 1, LC: Knit all LC stitches in odd-numbered columns, and Purl all LC stitches in even-numbered columns; Slip all DC stitches with yarn nearside or farside, as necessary. Turn.

Row 2, DC: Knit all DC stitches in even-numbered columns, Purl all DC stitches in odd-numbered columns;

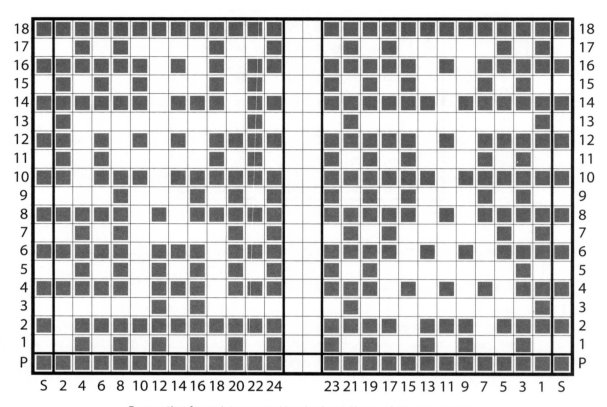

Preparation for an Interwoven Mosaic chart. Charts of Dancers pattern.
Male dancer on left; female dancer on right.

Slip all LC stitches with yarn nearside or farside, as necessary. Slide.

Row 2, LC: Knit all LC stitches in even-numbered columns, Purl all LC stitches in odd-numbered columns; Slip all DC stitches with yarn nearside or farside, as necessary. Turn.

Two-Yarn Method

To read a chart of this kind holding both yarns at the same time, work as follows:

Row 1: Knit all stitches in odd-numbered columns, using DC or LC as shown in square; Purl all stitches in even-numbered columns in same way; move yarn not in use to nearside or farside as necessary. Turn.

Row 2: Knit all stitches in even-numbered columns, using DC or LC as shown in square; Purl all stitches in odd-numbered columns in same way; move yarn not in use to nearside or farside as necessary. Turn.

❖ Interwoven Mosaic Charts

Interwoven Mosaic patterns make it possible to create a Double-Faced fabric with two entirely different patterns on each side. These patterns are charted using the register method described above, with the instructions for one pattern in the lower row of the register, and the instructions for the other pattern in the upper row of the register.

The only restriction in terms of which Mosaic patterns to select is that it is best to choose those that have the same number of stitches and rows in the pattern repeat, or to have one that is a multiple of the other. In other words, if you find a pattern you like with a repeat of 12 stitches and 18 rows, select another that is the same size, or 6 stitches and 9 rows, or 4 stitches and 6 rows. The result will be a single repeat on one side for every two or three repeats on the other side.

These patterns can only be done holding one yarn at a time, and each pattern row is done twice. There is no need to read the chart when working the second row because it is an exact

Double-Faced Fabric with Interwoven Mosaic pattern of Dancers.
Male dancers are on one side of the fabric and female dancers are on the other side.

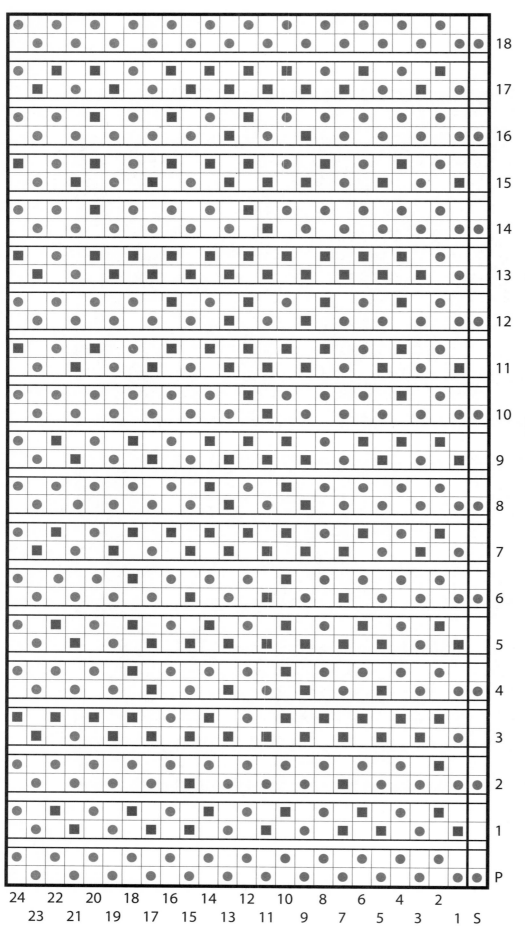

Interwoven Mosaic chart of Dancers pattern.

repeat of the first; simply Knit or Purl all the stitches in the same color, and Slip the others, stranding the yarn appropriately nearside or farside.

Dancers

Here is a wonderful pattern from one of Barbara Walker's books, of male and female dancers.† With the Interwoven Mosaic technique, you can work the two patterns on opposite sides of the same Double-Faced fabric: the male dancer on one side, the female dancer on the other.

First, make the two charts showing the separate patterns in the usual way for a Mosaic chart, but number them in preparation for an Interwoven chart. The chart for Side 1, showing the female dancer, has odd numbers written from right to left below the chart. The chart for Side 2, showing the male dancer, has even numbers written from left to right. The color symbol showing which yarn to use for each row is at the right side next to the numbers.

Making an Interwoven Mosaic Chart

To make the combined chart, work as follows:

1. Draw the bottom horizontal line and the vertical line at the side. Draw parallel lines every two rows for the registers; skip a row to make it easier to read the chart. Write the row numbers alongside the registers. Add the symbols for which color to use for each row at the right side.
2. Add the stitch numbers below the chart, odd numbers two rows down, and even numbers offset one square to the left in the row above. Fill in the dark color squares for Side 1 in the lower row of the register, matching the stitch numbers in the original chart to those in the Interwoven chart; as a result, the symbols will be in every other square. Draw the vertical line at the left side.
3. Fill in the dark color squares for Side 2 in the upper row of the register, but read the original chart from left to right and write the symbols in from right to left to match the stitch numbers in the two charts.
4. Fill in the light color squares in both rows of the register; every other square will be blank. Check your work before going on.
5. Repeat to fill in the pattern on the remaining registers.

It helps a great deal to place a ruler above the row you are reading on the original chart. If you are dealing with charts that have quite a few rows, as in the one shown here, you may find it helpful to place a ruler vertically to help you find the correct stitch column in the upper rows.

Working from an Interwoven Mosaic Chart

Tie two contrast-color yarns together with a Slip Knot and cast on a multiple of the number of stitches in the combined repeat, plus two selvedge stitches; drop Slip Knot at end of first row. Slip the selvedge stitches at the beginning of every row; Knit them at the end of the Side 1 row, and Purl them at the end of the Side 2 row.

Preparatory Rows: Use DC (dark color) to work two rows of Single Rib.

Register 1A (read from right to left): Knit all LC stitches in lower row of register, Purl all LC stitches in upper row of register, and Slip all DC stitches with yarn nearside of a Purl stitch, and farside of a Knit stitch. Turn.

Register 1B (read from left to right): Repeat Row 1. Knit all LC Knit stitches and Purl all LC Purl stitches; Slip all DC stitches with yarn nearside or farside, as necessary. Turn.

Register 2A: Knit all DC stitches in lower row of register, Purl all DC stitches in upper row of register, and Slip all LC stitches with yarn nearside of a Purl stitch and farside of a Knit stitch. Turn.

Register 2B: Repeat Row 2. Knit all DC Knit stitches and Purl all DC Purl stitches; Slip all LC stitches with yarn nearside or farside, as necessary. Turn.

Work every register in the same way, using same yarn for both rows.

As you will see, it is really unnecessary to read the chart when working the second row of each pair. Simply work the stitches as they present themselves: Knit the Knits and Purl the Purls in the same color, and Slip all the others.

Strand the yarn rather firmly past the Slip stitches; do not stretch the stitches out on the right needle as you would with a Stranded Color pattern. Keep in mind that these stitches are interspersed on the needle, but they will be back to back in the fabric; you want the stitches on the same side to draw together to hide the strands that pass between the two fabric faces. When you dress the fabric, pull it down sharply to encourage the stitches to align properly and help the fabric draw together (see Dressing a Fabric).

---

† Walker, *Charted Knitting Designs*, p. 207.

Here are some tips for following the pattern:

- When you see a series of symbols in the same color, such as stitches 3–6 in Register 2, think "rib 4" and work K1, P1, K1, P1.
- When you see a series of alternating pairs of colors, such as stitches 1–4 in Register 1, think "2 pairs" and, for that example, K1 P1 for the first pair, and Slip the next pair.
- Sometimes there will be a single Slip stitch. In Register 2, for example, there is a 4-stitch series and then a 7-stitch series separated by a single Slip stitch. Think "rib 4, Slip 1, rib 7."

Recognizing sections of the pattern like this will help you memorize the instructions more quickly and by the time you work the second or third repeat you should be zipping right along. If you find it helpful, chart a second stitch repeat to the left of the first so you can see the end of one repeat alongside the beginning of the next; you will then find you can pick out larger segments of the pattern. For instance, if there is a "rib 4" at the end and a "rib 6" at the beginning, it will be clear that you can work a "rib 10."

Part Six

PATTERN DESIGN

CHAPTER 23

Stitch Gauge

auge is a pair of numbers that tells you how many stitches and rows there are in every inch of a knitted fabric. This information is found by making a Gauge Swatch, a small sample of the fabric, and then measuring it and doing a few simple math calculations.

When designing a garment, the gauge is used to determine how many stitches and rows are needed to make it a certain length and width, as well as to develop the patterns for shaping contoured areas, such as the neckline, armholes, and sleeves.

When working from a published pattern, the gauge of the fabric you make has to be the same as the one specified in the instructions in order for the garment to be the correct size. Because each person's knitting is unique, the first step is to make one or more swatches to find what size needle you need to use to match the pattern gauge. Unfortunately, many people either do not do this, or find they cannot match it exactly, or think they have done so only to discover that the finished garment turns out the wrong size anyway.

This chapter introduces a more accurate and efficient system for making and measuring a swatch to find the gauge than the methods commonly used. It also provides a variety of options for how to do this depending upon what you are making, and whether you are designing something or working from a published pattern. Some projects require greater precision for a good fit, while with others you can take a more relaxed approach. Also, several modifications of the method are useful for certain kinds of specialized patterns and techniques.

Information obtained from a swatch can also be used to calculate how much yarn you will need if you are designing something, or want to substitute a different yarn for the one called for in a pattern.

About Gauge

It is probably fair to say that gauge was not all that important until relatively recently. A far more limited range of materials was available in the past, and whether the yarns were homespun or millspun, knitters would have been intimately familiar with their characteristics. Having worked with the same yarns throughout their lives, they would have known exactly what to expect from them, and they typically made a very narrow range of simple garment styles using favorite well-worn needles.

Times have changed. When today's knitters begin a project, both the yarn and the style of the garment are likely to be new. A Gauge Swatch allows you to familiarize yourself with the materials and techniques you will be working with so you know what to expect. Not making one means you take a considerable risk of ripping and reworking, accompanied by an underlying anxiety about whether the final result will be worth the effort, or worse, that you finish the garment and discover that it does not fit.

For those of you who enjoy a relaxed approach to your knitting but would prefer fewer setbacks and better outcomes, I would like to persuade you to look upon a swatch as an aid to creativity. Even if a precise gauge is not all that important for the item you are making, the swatch provides a way to master the techniques you plan to use, to test the interplay of yarn with color or stitch pattern, and to develop the confidence to improvise to your heart's content.

And if you are one of the many knitters who do make Gauge Swatches, but have problems trying to match the gauge for a pattern, or are frustrated by things that still do not fit quite right, I want to reassure you that the problem does not rest with you—it is that the methods recommended for finding gauge are flawed and unreliable. The method described here will provide you with a gauge you can trust.

If I had to select a single chapter in this large book that I think would make the most difference to every knitter, it would be this one. There is nothing more important to the fit of any garment you knit than an accurate stitch gauge. I am going to repeat that, with emphasis: *There is nothing more important to the fit of any garment you knit than an accurate stitch gauge.*

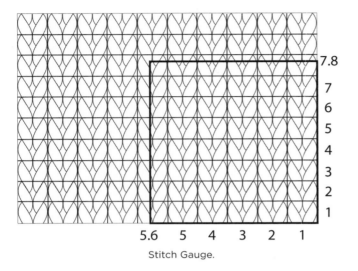

7.8
7
6
5
4
3
2
1

5.6   5   4   3   2   1

Stitch Gauge.

❖ Traditional Methods for Gauge

Two methods of finding gauge are commonly recommended in published patterns and books on knitting techniques.

The first method calls for making a swatch of about 4 inches square. Next you are instructed to use a ruler and set straight pins in the swatch to mark off a 2-square-inch area, and then count the stitches and rows within it. Unfortunately, it is difficult to set pins precisely or count stitches accurately because of the soft and flexible nature of a knitted fabric. This is particularly true with a complex stitch pattern, especially if you are working with a textured yarn or one in a dark color.

In addition, there is no way to be very precise about any partial stitch that falls within the marked area. While fractions of a stitch might seem inconsequential, not including them in the calculations to find gauge can create surprisingly large differences in the finished size of a garment. This is because any small error made will be multiplied by the full length and width of the garment (see the explanation for this in Five Steps to Accurate Gauge, below).

Another commonly used method requires you to make a swatch with a specified number of stitches and the recommended needle size, and then measure it from edge to edge. To achieve the gauge specified in a pattern, the resulting swatch must have certain dimensions, usually 4 inches square. Unfortunately, it is rare for the swatch to turn out exactly the size required, and the only option then is to make a new swatch with a different needle size; if that also fails, most knitters are at a loss as to what to do.

Furthermore, few instructions include the advice to wash the swatch before finding the gauge, but this is of critical importance, as the discussion in Dressing a Swatch, below, makes clear. Many even suggest making the gauge in Stockinette, regardless of what sort of a stitch pattern is used for the garment itself. Unfortunately, a swatch made in a different pattern and not dressed prior to being measured will guarantee an inaccurate gauge.

While discouraging to think about, this list of problems with conventional methods of doing gauge has the virtue of pointing toward the solutions. In the following material, you will find a thorough discussion of all the components that determine gauge, as well as suggestions for how to deal with each of them in a way that produces a major improvement in accuracy.

Is it "Tension," or is it "Gauge"?

A Gauge Swatch is sometimes referred to as a tension swatch. However, while the tension placed on the yarn as you knit is one of the factors that produces the gauge, this is not what is measured, and is not relevant to what you need to know.

The term gauge is used in reference to the quantity of something within a particular measurement; in this case, it is the number of stitches in a given area of a knitted fabric.

The Gauge System

The first and most important thing to understand is that a gauge is unique to a particular fabric, and there are five variables that determine what it is; these are discussed first.

Next, there is a brief explanation of the five steps you can take when making and measuring a swatch that will provide you with an accurate gauge. These will be discussed in greater detail throughout the chapter.

The method presented here for making a swatch and finding gauge is different in almost every respect from the traditional approach. It is easy to do, you can trust the results, and I think once you understand how it all works, you may even find, as I do, that making a swatch is a pleasurable way to begin any project.

❖ The Five Variables

The unique characteristics of a knitted fabric are determined by five variables: your hands, the needles you use, the knitting method you prefer, the yarn you work with, and the stitch or color pattern you choose.

If any one of these things changes, the gauge of the fabric will change. Therefore, the swatch must be made in exactly the same way as the fabric of the garment itself.

The Hands

As you knit, the yarn passes through your hands in a way that is as individual as you are. How you hold and wrap the yarn, and the amount of tension you place on it will affect the size of the stitches—and, therefore, the gauge. This means that you cannot work on someone else's knitting, nor have anyone work on yours, without a change in gauge.

Similarly, the gauge of a fabric made when you are first learning a stitch or color pattern may be different from what it will be once you feel comfortable with it. For this reason, it is a good idea to practice the pattern on a Test Swatch, a small sample swatch (see below), before making the Gauge Swatch itself.

The Needles

When you wrap the yarn to form a stitch, the needle measures out a precise amount to each stitch—the larger the diameter of the needle, the larger the size of the stitches. Therefore, any change in needle size will produce a change in gauge.

What is less obvious, but also true, is that even the material of which the needle is made can influence how the yarn wraps and how the stitches move along the needle as you knit, and this can change the gauge. A smooth metal needle offers considerably less resistance to the yarn than one made of wood or bamboo, and this will not only change the tension in your hands as you work, but the stitches may be very slightly smaller because the yarn wraps more closely around the needle with less effort on your part.

Even changing from straight to circular needles can have an effect, because this slightly alters the position of your hands and the movements you make. Finally, the sizes of the needles produced by one manufacturer may be subtly different from those produced by another.

In short, it is essential to knit the Gauge Swatch with the same kind of needles you plan to use for the garment.

The Knitting Method

The method of knitting will also affect the gauge, and most people cannot switch from one method to another without causing a visible change in the fabric.

You may see evidence of this in a garment if the lower bodice was done in the round, while the portion above the armholes was done flat; there will often be a visible line across the fabric where the change occurred. Something of this kind can also happen if you simply change the way you hold the yarn as you work.

It does not matter whether you hold the yarn in your right or left hand, work the rows from right to left or left to right, or work flat or circular. The important thing is to be as consistent as possible.

The Yarn

Of course, the thickness of the yarn will affect the size of the stitches, and therefore the gauge: thick yarns produce fewer stitches and rows per inch than thin ones. However, even yarns that appear to be the same size may take up into the fabric in very different ways depending upon their other characteristics, and this will affect the gauge as well.

Smooth, silky yarns will pass through your hands more easily than soft, fuzzy ones. One yarn may be spun and plied more or less firmly than another that otherwise looks similar, and, if the fiber content is different, one may have more resilience than the other.

A slight but significant change in gauge can even occur when you work with two yarns that are the same but were dyed a different color, because some dye colors add more volume to a yarn.

Therefore, if you plan to substitute a different yarn for the one specified in a pattern, a new Gauge Swatch is required, even when the two yarns appear to be similar, or even if the labels suggest they will produce the same gauge.

The Pattern

Every stitch or color pattern imparts unique characteristics to the fabric. Even when made with the same number of stitches, the same needles and yarn, some patterns produce fabrics that are dense and compressed, while others are open.

In addition to the unique qualities imparted by the pattern itself, the techniques they contain may alter your tension. For instance, you may knit more loosely when making something of just Knit and Purl, but more firmly when doing something that contains techniques that require greater manipulation of the yarn and stitches, causing you to put more tension on the yarn.

Similarly, a Stockinette swatch made in a single color will not tell you what the gauge will be for a color pattern done in Stockinette because the way you hold and manage two yarns will change how you knit. If you plan to add beads or sequins, or do any surface decoration like embroidery or smocking, these will also change the characteristics of the fabric and, therefore, the gauge.

For these reasons, the swatch must be made with the same pattern used for the garment; if there is more than one pattern, you will need to make a separate swatch for each, or combine them into one swatch that is representative.

❖ Five Steps to Accurate Gauge

In addition to the five variables that determine the gauge of a fabric, there are five aspects of making and measuring a swatch for gauge that determine its accuracy.

The swatch needs to be large enough to minimize the

effect of error in measurement, and requires unrestrained edges so it will lie perfectly flat. It will need to be "dressed," that is, washed and steamed or blocked before it is measured.

Also, it is important to use a gauge that represents what the fabric of the garment will be like when you wear it long after it has been finished. Finally, this method makes use of gauge numbers that include tenths of an inch to improve accuracy.

Here is a brief explanation of why these things are important; they will all be discussed in greater detail below.

Swatch Size

A swatch can be sized in proportion to the garment, but needs to be relatively large for accurate measurements because any error made will be multiplied by the full circumference and length of the garment. A larger swatch means that if an error is made, it will represent a smaller percentage of the total measurement.

For instance if you make a ⅛-inch error when measuring a 2-inch-wide swatch, this represents a 6 percent difference; however, if you make that same error when measuring a 6-inch swatch, it would only be a 2 percent difference. In other words, a larger swatch will improve the accuracy of the results and provide insurance against any mistakes.

Unrestrained Edges

Taking the measurements is really quite simple because the swatch is measured from edge to edge and there is no need to set pins or count stitches. This makes it easy to read the ruler and include those important little eighths of an inch.

However, it also means that you need to work edges in a way that will not restrict the swatch, nor interfere with accurate measurement. You will find information below regarding which selvedges are best for a swatch, and how to cast on and cast off.

Dressed and Raw Gauge

Just as the swatch must be made in exactly the same way as the garment, before you measure it to find the gauge it must be dressed—washed and steamed, and/or blocked, in exactly the same way as you plan to clean the garment.

As you will see in the discussion below, this will permanently change the characteristics of the fabric, which changes the gauge. In other words, the gauge of the fabric just off your needles is not the same as the gauge of the fabric you will wear and, of course, it is the latter that should be used for the project.

However, it is also a good idea to calculate what I call the "Raw Gauge," the gauge of the fabric as it emerges from your needles, before it has been dressed. This is the gauge to use if you want to measure the length or width of a fabric as you are making it; see Measuring a Work in Progress.

Drop: The Effect of Gravity

The fabric will be transformed once and forever when it is washed the first time. However, it will also change every time you wear it because the hanging weight of the garment will alter the proportions of every stitch; they will get longer and narrower, and this will immediately change the gauge. The weight of the garment may also cause the yarn to stretch, which can further affect the gauge.

Small garments or those made with very lightweight and resilient yarns are not susceptible to this effect, but most of the things you knit will exhibit some amount of drop.

Because of this, there are two ways to measure: The Flat Gauge method is suitable for things that weigh very little or will lie flat in use; it is also used to calculate the Raw Gauge. The Weighted Gauge method is used for everything else; it will provide you with the gauge of the garment you will wear over time, not the one the garment has lying on a table or tucked away in a drawer.

Calculating Gauge

When it comes time to calculate the gauge, all you need to do is divide the number of stitches by the width of the swatch, and the rows by the length. In many cases, the answer will include a decimal number, and, just as it was important to include eighths of an inch when measuring, it is very important that any tenths are included in the gauge.

If the tenths are omitted, or rounded up or down when doing the calculations to find the number of stitches and rows for the pattern, it will make a surprisingly large difference in the size of the finished garment; see Those little tenths . . . , below.

Test and Gauge Swatches

There are two kinds of swatches discussed here and both are important. Of course, those of you who are dubious about making any sort of swatch may now be wondering how I am going to persuade you to make more than one. Bear with me: I think you will find that they are well worth doing, and indeed they are likely to save you time and effort in the long run.

Test Swatches are little preliminary samples that are quick and easy to do. They provide you with critically important information about the materials and techniques you plan to use and help you plan how to make the larger Gauge Swatch, including which needle size to use.

The Gauge Swatch is the one you will dress and measure in order to find out how many stitches and rows there are in every inch of the fabric. If you are working from a published pattern, you will need to make a swatch in order to determine if your gauge matches the one specified in the instructions. When designing a pattern, Gauge is used to determine how many stitches and rows there need to be to make the fabric the width and length needed, and to develop patterns for the shaping.

❖ *Making Test Swatches*

This is an invitation to sit down and play with your new yarn for a little while. Test Swatches need only be about 2 inches square, they are fun to do, and will provide you with very important information. How to make them and how to use them depends on whether you are working from a published pattern or designing something yourself.

Published pattern instructions will specify the required gauge and provide a recommended needle size. While it is necessary to match the gauge, it is important to understand that the needle size shown is exactly what it says—*recommended*. It is the size used by the designer to develop the pattern; however, you may need a different size needle in order to make a fabric with the same gauge.

It is frustrating to make an entire swatch only to find that the gauge does not match and that you then need to make another one with a different needle. You can save yourself a lot of time if you first make one or two little Test Swatches to decide which needle size to use for the larger Gauge Swatch.

When designing something, Test Swatches serve as the equivalent of an artist's sketchpad—they let you try out your ideas and decide on the particular combination of yarn, needles, and stitch or color pattern that you want to use. In the process of experimenting in this way, you may be surprised by what you discover, and perhaps try things you would otherwise not have considered. You might even decide that you do not like the yarn at all! Think of this as valuable information gained with little investment of time or money.

Test Swatches. Same stitch pattern, three needle sizes.

Actually, even if you are planning to make something from a published pattern, a Test Swatch may persuade you it is not such a good idea after all. If you discover the yarn and pattern are not appealing, you will have lost only one ball of yarn and very little time, and you can make something else. Better to find out after 2 square inches, than after making several inches of the garment itself!

Test Swatches for a Pattern

If you will be working from a published pattern, it normally takes no more than three of these little samples to discover which size needle will produce a gauge closest to that required by the pattern. The worst thing that can happen is that you will feel a bit like Goldilocks—one needle will be too small, the next too big, and the third just right.

Make the first little swatch using the needle size suggested in the pattern instructions. Or, if your knitting is typically looser or tighter than what you encounter in most pattern instructions, rely on experience and start with a size larger or smaller.

Use the gauge given in the pattern to calculate the number of stitches needed for a swatch about 2 inches wide, and then adjust that number to enough for an even number of repeats of the stitch pattern. (For more details on how to calculate the number of stitches to use, see Making a Gauge Swatch, below; for an explanation of stitch pattern repeats, see Written Stitch Patterns.)

Work as follows:

1. Use Stranded Cast-On, work about 2 inches in length (or a minimum of a full row repeat of the pattern), and then use Stranded Cast-Off to finish.
2. Wash and block or steam sample as for a Gauge Swatch; see below.
3. Measure width of swatch from edge to edge and divide into number of stitches cast on to find estimate of stitch gauge (there is no need to use row gauge for this purpose).
4. If estimated gauge has fewer stitches per inch than specified in pattern, use a smaller needle size and make another Test Swatch; if it has more stitches per inch than specified, use a larger needle size.

Do not skip Step 2; for why this is so important, see Dressing a Swatch, below.

Test Swatches for Designing

In the early stages of designing, you may want to try several different yarns and a variety of stitch or color patterns. It is a great time-saver to make a sampler instead of individual test swatches, switching from one pattern or needle size to another until you discover what you think works best.

1. Determine number of stitches needed for first pattern as described for the Test Swatch, above, and use Stranded Cast-On.
2. Work several row repeats, or an inch or two of each pattern—less if one does not seem promising, more if it does.
3. Adjust number of stitches on needle as necessary when switching from one pattern to another; always work with full pattern repeats.

When changing from one stitch pattern to another, you may also need to change the needle size, using a smaller one for a lace pattern, a larger one if the next pattern tends to be dense. Use a few increases or decreases at each side to change the number of stitches to whatever is needed for even repeats of the pattern (see Pattern Repeats and Garment Dimensions).

If you are working with a yarn that will tolerate it, stop from time to time and give the fabric a good blast or two of steam, gently smooth the swatch open, and pat it flat so you can see what it really looks like.

Once you find a combination of yarn and pattern you like, use just that portion of the sampler to estimate the gauge and calculate the number of stitches to use for the main Gauge Swatch. Or, if you want to be certain you like it, make one last separate Test Swatch, wash it first, and then measure it (for why it is a good idea to do this, see Other Uses for a Test Swatch, and Dressing a Swatch, below).

Test Swatches for Improvising

It takes a certain amount of time and effort to do a real Gauge Swatch, and in some situations it makes sense to just proceed on the basis of what you have learned from a few Test Swatches instead.

However, before deciding whether to do this or not, give some thought to the consequences of being well under way with your project and finding you have a problem with gauge. You do not want to spend more time making corrections than it would have taken to make the swatch.

If you are making something small, or are working with a bulky yarn done on big needles and find you need to rip it out, the loss of time and effort might be negligible. However, if you are using a fine yarn and needles and a complex pattern, any setback becomes a more serious matter, especially if you have a lot of stitches on the needle or are working in the round. Also, some yarns are rather fragile, and ripping out can noticeably change their characteristics. You may not be able to reuse the yarn, or you may have to make use of it in ways that will hide the damage (see Recycling Yarn).

Nevertheless, if you want to proceed on the basis of a gauge taken from a Test Swatch, here are some suggestions that will help minimize the risks:

- Make the Test Swatch slightly larger, about 3 inches square, wash and/or steam it, and estimate the gauge as described above.
- If you are making something that will be large and heavy, please see Weighted Gauge, below, for how to take into consideration the behavior of the fabric in wear.
- If possible, start the project with a small section, such as a sleeve, to minimize how much work would be lost if it is necessary to rip back and begin again.
- Check for accuracy after you have worked a few inches of the fabric; see Measuring a Work in Progress, below.

Other Uses for a Test Swatch

Test Swatches are also extremely useful for trying out some of the techniques you plan to use for a design, and they give you an opportunity to learn something about the characteristics of the yarn.

- A swatch is a good way to try different methods of casting on or casting off, and to learn the stitch techniques used in the pattern.

  You might also want to make a separate swatch to practice buttonhole techniques or an embroidery pattern, or use it to practice picking up stitches along the edge.
- It is a good idea to wash the Test Swatch to see if the color bleeds, particularly if you will be doing a multicolor pattern. In some cases dyes can be stabilized (see Unstable Dyes), but if you do not want to make the effort, it may be best to select a different yarn.
- If you have any doubts about how suitable the yarn might be for a garment intended for hard use, you might want to test for abrasion. When the swatch is dry, rub the fabric against itself, or rub a coarse rag over the surface of the swatch. If the fabric seems to mat, develops "pills," or the stitch pattern blurs and loses distinction, the yarn may not be appropriate for what you have in mind.

  If you notice color on the rag when you rub the swatch (often referred to as "crocking"), it may be that the dye is not stable, was not set properly, or that excess dye was not rinsed out.

❖ Making a Gauge Swatch

Once you have done a few Test Swatches and settled on a needle size, it is time to make the larger swatch that you will use to calculate the gauge.

While it is important to make the swatch exactly as you will make the fabric of the garment—same yarn, same needles, same stitch or color pattern—there are some options in regard to how big the swatch should be and how to handle the edges.

Also, the swatch for a circular fabric is slightly different from one intended for a flat fabric, as are those for certain kinds of patterns or fabrics, such as when you are combining multiple stitch patterns, or want to add beads or sequins.

Sizing a Swatch

As discussed above in Five Steps to Accurate Gauge, a larger swatch helps to minimize the effect of any error in measurement, but the size can be in proportion to the size of the item you plan to make.

- Plan to make the swatch roughly square, with a width no smaller than about 15 percent of the widest measurement of your garment.

   For a sweater with a 40- to 50-inch circumference, make a 6- to 8-square-inch swatch.

   For a child's sweater with a 20-inch circumference, one of 3 to 4 inches will do.
- No swatch should be smaller than 3 to 4 inches no matter what you are making, nor do I think one much larger than 8 inches is ever necessary.
- The smaller the swatch, the more important it is to measure very carefully; see Flat Gauge, below.

Swatch Patterns

Once you have decided on the overall size of the Gauge Swatch, use the information from your Test Swatch and work as follows to find the number of stitches to cast on and rows to work.

1. Multiply estimated stitch and row gauges by dimensions of planned swatch.

   Estimated stitch gauge × width of swatch = approximate number of stitches to cast on

   Estimated row gauge × length of swatch = approximate number of rows to work

2. Next, adjust number of stitches and rows so swatch contains full pattern repeats.

   Approximate number of stitches ÷ stitches in one pattern repeat = number of repeats in swatch

3. Any remainder means there are extra stitches, but not enough for a full repeat; either subtract extras, or add enough for another repeat.

   For example, if the swatch is 6 inches wide and has a gauge of 5 stitches per inch, it should have 30 stitches. However, if the pattern has a stitch repeat of 4, then:

   30 stitches ÷ 4 = 7.5 repeats

   Adjust the number of stitches up or down as needed for full repeats:

   4-stitch repeat × 7 = 28 stitches, or

   4-stitch repeat × 8 = 32 stitches

4. Add any edge stitches and selvedge stitches if needed.
5. Adjust number of rows in same way to accommodate full pattern repeats.

For more information on repeats and stitch multiples, and an explanation of edge stitches and selvedge stitches, see Written Stitch Patterns.

Swatch Edges

The measurement of the swatch is taken from edge to edge, and should include *only* the stitch pattern. For this reason, all four sides need to be handled in a special way.

- Stranded Cast-On and Stranded Cast-Off are ideal for swatches because they do not form edges in the usual sense, nor will they restrict them in any way.

   Unrestrained edges are particularly important because the dimensions of the swatch will change when it is dressed, and these edges can be stretched out to match whatever characteristics it takes on, and the swatch will lie flat for measurement.
- The first and last stitches of any fabric will normally become the equivalent of selvedge stitches, whether this was intended or not (this is not the case for some stitch patterns that lie very flat, such as Garter Stitch or Seed Stitch). For most patterns, therefore, it is best to use a Stockinette or Chain Selvedge, either of which tends to turn to the inside of the fabric, making it relatively easy to exclude them when measuring.

   When you dress the swatch, use your fingers to press the selvedges firmly against the inside of the fabric while it is still damp from washing, or while still warm with steam.
- Knitted fabrics commonly curl at the edges, although dressing the swatch usually helps make it lie flat enough for measurement. If a Test Swatch indicates that the curl is strong enough to be a problem, consider using a small Garter Stitch border for all four edges.

   Use a single or double Garter Stitch Selvedge at the sides, and three rows of Garter Stitch at the top and bottom, starting and ending with a Purl row on the outside. The swatch is then measured within this border.

   If it would then be difficult to distinguish the border from the main stitch pattern, insert contrast-color Yarn Markers on each side between a stitch column of the border and one in the main stitch pattern, and just above and below the rows of the top and bottom borders; measure between the markers.

Swatches for Circular Fabrics

Because your gauge may differ when working flat or circular, it would seem logical to make a swatch in the round if that is how you will make the garment. However, this will not only

Swatch for a Circular Fabric. Knots tied at each side.

consume twice the amount of time and yarn as a flat swatch of the same size, but it is more difficult to measure accurately because of the fold at each side.

The best solution is to work flat, but only on outside rows; use a circular or double-point needle and make the swatch as follows:

1. Develop pattern for swatch as described above.
2. Work an outside row in pattern, and then break yarn, leaving a 4- to 5-inch tail.
3. Slide stitches back to right needle tip, allow a similar length of tail, and reattach yarn at edge; work next outside row.
4. Knot pairs of yarns together at edges so columns of stitches at each side will not enlarge.

❖ Dressing a Swatch

Tension placed on the yarn while you knit stretches the fibers. They will relax in the warmth and moisture of the cleaning process and recover their natural condition, which in turn alters the proportions of the stitches. This significantly changes the appearance, the feel, and the dimensions of the fabric, and these changes are permanent.

What this means is that the fabric that emerges from your needles does not have the same gauge as a fabric that has been dressed. It also means that a garment made on the basis of a gauge taken from a swatch that was not dressed might fit well—but only until it is cleaned for the first time. Once that is done, the size of almost all garments will change; some moderately, some radically. This also has important implications for those knitters who like to make a garment in the round from the top down so they can try it on to check the fit.

Similarly, many patterns contain instructions to knit a certain number of inches to the armhole, or between armhole and shoulder. Unfortunately, a measurement of this kind will be misleading unless you make use of the Raw Gauge (the gauge of the fabric as it emerges from your needles); see Measuring a Work in Progress. Knowing the Raw Gauge also provides the means to check whether your true gauge is correct before you go too far. For more information, see Working with Raw Gauge.

If you think you will want to know the Raw Gauge, find it *before you dress the swatch,* using the same method described for Flat Gauge, and write the gauge down so you have it when needed.

Washing a Swatch

While it is safe to wash most yarns, and washing is cheaper than dry cleaning (see Cleaning and Dressing a Knit), do read the care instructions on the yarn label beforehand; you may also find the information in the chapter on Fibers and the one on Yarns of interest.

If you have any doubts about how to proceed, make and wash a little Test Swatch before making the larger Gauge Swatch.

Here are simplified instructions for washing a swatch (for recommendations for the kinds of detergents to use, see Laundry Products).

1. Add small amount of mild detergent to bowl of cool water and submerge swatch. Swish it around to make sure it is completely saturated, but do not scrub; allow to soak for 5 to 10 minutes.
2. Rinse swatch under cool tap water to remove suds, or fill bowl repeatedly with successive rinses until water runs clear.
3. Squeeze swatch without twisting to remove excess water, lay flat on clean towel, and roll up inside. Press down firmly on roll to help towel absorb moisture from swatch; unroll, move swatch to dry area of towel, and repeat.
4. Lay swatch down on countertop or other nonabsorbent surface, stretch it gently but firmly in both dimensions to open it up, straighten sides, and square corners. Make it look pretty, pat it gently, and leave it untouched to dry.

If you have used Selvedges, turn the swatch face down and press them firmly against the inside of the fabric so they will not be included in the edge-to-edge measurement.

Blocking or Weighting a Swatch

- If you are working with a fiber that should not be subjected to steam, or are making something like a lace shawl or scarf that benefits from being blocked, then handle the swatch in the same way you will the garment before measuring for gauge; see the information on Blocking in the chapter Cleaning and Dressing a Knit.
- For a heavy garment, or one made with a yarn that has little resilience (like cotton or linen, for instance), take hold of the top and bottom edges and stretch the swatch firmly before setting it down to dry.

   Or, instead of leaving it to dry lying flat, clip it to a skirt hanger, smooth it out, stretch it lengthwise, and hang it up to dry. For more information, see Weighted Gauge, below.

Steaming a Swatch

Most knitted fabrics benefit from a bit of steam finishing after they are washed, much as woven ones do. This encourages the fibers to relax and the yarn to settle into the pattern structure, leaving the fabric soft, smooth, and even. It not only helps to display the stitch or color pattern to ideal effect, but also allows the fabric to take on the finished proportions that it will have when the garment is worn.

While steam is safe for all natural fibers, it will damage many of the manufactured ones; as with washing, please check the yarn label and read the relevant information in the chapters on Fibers and Yarns; if you have any concerns about how to proceed, experiment with your Test Swatch ahead of time.

1. Set iron to temperature that is appropriate for fiber and hot enough to produce steam, or use garment steamer appliance.
2. Place terry towel or washcloth on ironing board, place swatch with outside face down on towel. Hold iron about an inch above fabric, and saturate it with steam. Do not allow soleplate of iron to touch fabric (although see Pressing a Swatch, below); if necessary, protect swatch with press cloth.
3. When swatch is just cool enough to handle, but still slightly warm and damp, grasp side edges, stretch fabric gently, and then let go, allowing it to spring back; repeat with top and bottom edges to help swatch find its natural shape and dimensions. If swatch has Selvedges, use fingertips to press them flat against inside of fabric so they will not be included in measurement.
4. Allow steam to dissipate, turn swatch face up, and repeat Step 3.
5. Finally, steam one last time, smooth swatch out, true corners, and straighten edges; if edges are contoured, shape them so everything is even and the same on all sides. Allow swatch to cool and dry before moving.

If you are working with a vegetable fiber such as cotton or linen, stretch the swatch lengthwise gently but firmly, and hold it until it is cool (see Weighted Gauge, below).

If the edges of the swatch curl, the sides will normally curl to the inside, the top and bottom to the outside. To correct for this as much as possible, in Step 2 flatten out the sides with a press cloth, and then apply steam; leave the press cloth in place to hold the edges as the swatch cools. Turn the swatch over and repeat to steam out the curl on the top and bottom as well.

Pressing a Swatch

It is not customary to press hand-knit fabrics today, although it was more common in the past and there is no reason not to do so. In fact, true pressing produces some very interesting and beautiful effects. Furthermore, pressing a knit tends to stabilize the gauge, so the dimensions are less likely to change with time and wear; for more information, see the discussion on Pressing in the chapter Cleaning and Dressing a Knit.

If you want to experiment with what will happen, first try pressing one of your Test Swatches; if you like the result, only then press your main swatch.

The appearance of a pressed swatch may be dramatically different from one that has simply been dressed in the usual way; if you decide to do this to your Gauge Swatch, of course, you must be prepared to press the garment as well.

Dry Cleaning a Swatch

Most knitting yarns can be washed, even when the label says to dry clean only. Nevertheless, there are good reasons for dry cleaning an item instead of washing it. You may find it more convenient, or have concerns about color fading or bleeding, or the finished item may be too large to handle at home.

If this is the case, you might seriously consider taking your little swatch to the cleaners before you measure for gauge. Perhaps this seems excessive, but it may be the only way to discover whether the gauge will change, and it is particularly worthwhile if you are unfamiliar with any of the fibers in the yarn (show the cleaner the label with the fiber content).

Even if you plan to dry clean the garment, you may want to preserve the option of washing it, should you need to. If a Test Swatch indicates the yarn is washable, but cleaning will be a convenience, you might want to wash the Gauge Swatch and plan to wash and dress the garment once, immediately after it is made, and then dry clean it in the future.

Also, if you plan to add sequins, beads, or decorative trim to the finished fabric, and have any misgivings about washing the garment after they are applied, you might want to consult with the cleaner about care requirements. You will be investing extra time and expense to add these things, and you do not want to find yourself with a garment that is impossible to clean.

Characteristics of a Dressed Swatch

After dressing the Gauge Swatch as described above, you will notice a considerable transformation in the appearance and characteristics of the fabric. Most fabrics will feel quite different, the stitch or color pattern will open up, and the texture of the yarn might change.

Some of these things may not have been evident in a little Test Swatch, and can only be fully appreciated in the larger Gauge Swatch.

Texture and Pattern Definition

One of the most obvious changes you will notice in a Dressed Swatch is the appearance of any stitch or color pattern.

Fabrics done with stitch techniques tend to flatten considerably, and the distinction between different pattern elements will be more apparent. Columns of Knit and Purl stitches will be straighter and the background will be smoother; techniques with texture will stand out more, and the structure and details in the pattern will be more apparent.

If you used a Lace pattern, the change is particularly dramatic, as all the Yarnovers will open up and the directional flow of the stitch columns will be clear.

The change in a fabric made with color patterns is often subtle, but you will notice that it is more smooth and regular,

Swatch before Dressing.

Swatch after Dressing.

and the pattern motifs will be more clearly defined against the background.

Hand

This is a term used to describe how a fabric feels, and it refers to such things as relative softness, whether it is thick and plush or flat and smooth, and whether it drapes or is somewhat stiff. A yarn may feel relatively coarse as you work with it, but may soften when washed. Many stitch patterns are highly textured when first made, giving a rather thick, firm hand to a fabric, but when washed they may flatten out, feel thinner, and have more drape.

Bloom

Many yarns become fuzzier after the first wash. This is referred to as "bloom," and it may blur the details of a stitch or color pattern.

Bloom is more common with "natural" wools that were minimally processed, especially if they still contain lanolin. Cleaning the fabric removes any residues of oils, excess dye, dirt, and foreign matter left in the yarn, and this will affect its appearance and behavior.

Coned yarns intended for machine knits are also likely to bloom because they are sometimes coated to keep them smooth, reduce lint, and prevent snagging.

While it is important to discover this characteristic before you begin to work, if a yarn exhibits bloom, it does not mean that something is wrong with it—simply that you are seeing its true nature for the first time.

If you are surprised . . .

Given the transformation a fabric can undergo when dressed, you may be surprised by what you discover. The fabric might be attractive but in unexpected ways; you may decide it is not suitable for the project you had in mind, but might be useful for something else. Perhaps you like the yarn but not when used with that particular stitch pattern.

If you find the yarn is not suitable for what you had in mind, you will have lost a minimum amount of time and the cost of a single ball of yarn (and consider yourself fortunate not to have wasted time and money making a garment you would not have liked); return the rest of what you purchased to the store and make another selection.

Check the store's return policy when you make a purchase, keep all unused yarn in its original packaging, and save your receipt. Do not expect them to take back any balls of yarn with missing or torn labels, or those that you have tried and rewound.

Measuring and Calculating Gauge

Three different methods can be used to measure a swatch to find the gauge; once you have taken the measurements, the calculations used to find the gauge are the same regardless of what you are making.

The Flat Method is good for small projects or those that are light in weight, items that will lie flat in use, or for when exact size is not an issue. This method is also used for Test Swatches, and for finding Raw Gauge, which is the gauge of the fabric before it has been dressed. While the latter is not a gauge you can use to plan a garment, nor should it ever be used to determine if your gauge matches that of a published pattern, it can be useful if you need to check your progress as you work.

The Weighted Method is best used for any but the lightest garments because it takes into consideration the phenomenon of "drop," discussed above, which is the effect of gravity on the proportions of a garment in wear.

The Average Gauge Method is used for things like ribbings, where the resilience of the fabric is important, as well as for some garments designed to cling to the body, such as socks or perhaps a camisole.

Before going on to the instructions, here is some general information you will find useful no matter how you measure.

❖ Measuring a Swatch

It helps to place the swatch on a contrast-color surface for measurement so you can see the edges clearly. A metal or plastic ruler is more accurate for measurement than a cloth tape measure, which can stretch, and will not help to flatten the swatch at the edges; if the fabric tends to curl at the sides, you can ease them under a ruler to straighten them out.

Do not include selvedges in the width measurement or the count of stitches. If you added a border of Garter Stitch, measure between Purl nubs on all sides; if you used contrast-color Yarn Markers, measure between those. Similarly, if you used Stranded Cast-On and Stranded Cast-Off, measure between the strands that pass through stitches.

If side edges scallop, they usually go in on one side and out in the same place on the other side; as long as you measure from one side to the next, it does not matter; take several measurements in different locations and average the results. Top and bottom edges may also be irregular; ignore the contour and measure from the first to the last row; repeat in more than one location to check for accuracy and average the results.

Always measure carefully to the eighth of an inch, or 2 mm. Because the gauge is multiplied by the full width or circumference of the garment, any error will be multiplied as well; for more information, see Calculating Basic Gauge, below.

Flat Gauge

The Flat Gauge is the easiest and most fundamental method of measuring the swatch. It is the method to use when making small things like children's wear, socks, mittens, and scarves, or for particularly lightweight garments made with fibers that have considerable resilience and tend to hold their shape (see Yarns). It is also ideal for projects that will generally lie flat themselves, such as small tablecloths, pillow covers, and so on. Also use this approach for measuring Test Swatches, or for measuring a swatch prior to dressing it in order to find Raw Gauge.

1. Lay dressed swatch down on hard surface and use ruler or metal tape and measure to an accuracy of ⅛ inch (or 2 mm).
2. Set ruler across middle of swatch, lined up evenly with a row of stitches, and measure swatch from edge to edge.
3. Set ruler vertically in middle of swatch, line it up with a column of stitches, and measure full length.

Weighted Gauge

If you have encountered the problem of a garment that seemed to grow with wear, blame gravity. As discussed in Five Steps to Accurate Gauge, above, this phenomenon is called "drop," and its first effects will begin to happen as soon as you put a garment on—its own hanging weight will cause each stitch to become longer and narrower, and the overall dimensions of the garment will change.

In effect, the gauge of a garment is different in wear than when it is folded in your dresser drawer. The amount of drop a garment undergoes will vary, depending upon the stitch pattern, the density of the fabric, and the size and weight of the garment.

Additional changes will occur more slowly. With time, the fibers themselves gradually stretch owing to the weight of the garment, and how much they do depends on their characteristics and how the yarn was spun, as well as the environment in which the garment is worn and how much wear it gets.

Some fibers have more resilience than others and will recover their original condition when cleaned, but with time and wear many will lose their ability to do so. This is particularly the case for larger garments that are densely knit or made of an inelastic or heavy fiber like cotton or linen.

Also keep in mind that any fiber will relax in the presence of warmth and moisture, and human beings often produce these very conditions. (If you walk back to work after lunch on a hot day, you could find that your lovely cotton sweater has grown a size.)

To make a garment that will fit correctly throughout its wearable life, it is necessary to take drop into consideration when calculating the gauge. This is done by weighting the swatch for measurement to simulate the condition of the garment in wear (for another way to help stabilize the gauge, see Pressing a Swatch, above).

1. Insert thin knitting needles through stitches along top and bottom edges of swatch. If garment was worked side to side, insert needles into every second or third selvedge stitch along each edge, instead.
2. Smooth stitches out along needles so swatch hangs naturally, and is neither compressed nor stretched out at edges.
3. To weight swatch, pass 20- to 24-inch-long string or doubled strand of yarn through center of a full ball of same yarn used for project. Make a Slip Knot at each end of strand, and place knots on bottom needle, one on either side of swatch.
4. Pick up top needle and allow ball of yarn to hang freely from bottom of swatch and use hard ruler to measure swatch as described above for Flat Gauge.

To free both of your hands for measuring, clip the top needle to a skirt hanger, or find some other way to hang the swatch.

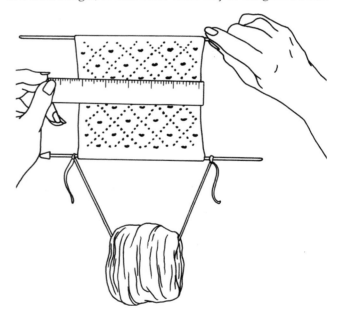

Weighted Gauge. Swatch weighted with ball of yarn.

Gauge for Heavy Fabrics

Some garments or types of yarn should be weighted more heavily than others. For certain kinds of designs you might want to develop a pattern based on separate gauges for different areas of the garment.

- If a fabric is particularly dense or if the garment will be large, use two balls of yarn as a weight instead of one.

  If the fabric is relatively open and light, and the yarn

is made of a lightweight fiber such as silk or mohair, use whatever remains of the ball you used for the swatch.

- When working with heavy, inelastic fibers like cotton or linen, wash and hang the swatch wet; tug down on the lower edge and leave to dry. And/or stretch the swatch lengthwise when steaming or pressing. Then use Weighted Gauge to measure.

- If you are designing a large, heavy item like a coat, develop the garment pattern from more than one gauge taken from the same swatch.

  Weight the swatch more heavily to determine the gauge for the area between the underarm and the shoulder where drop will have the greatest effect. Weight the swatch less to find a second gauge for the area between the hem and the armhole.

- Similarly, you might want to use a Weighted Gauge for the pattern of a bodice and a long sleeve, but a Flat Gauge for a short sleeve or a collar.

❖ Calculating Basic Gauge

To calculate the gauge, use the measurements of the swatch and the number of stitches and rows it contains. It is a good idea to write the latter information down when you make the swatch, but if necessary, you will need to count them; if possible, count pattern repeats and multiply by number of stitches and rows in the repeat (for information about repeats, see Written Stitch Patterns).

I highly recommend using a calculator to find the gauge, since it makes doing the necessary math fast, accurate, and painless. However, calculators are not designed for fractions; therefore, you must first convert any eighths in the measurement to decimals.

For instance, if your swatch measures something like 6⅛ inches, change this number into its decimal form of 6.125 inches; see Tips for Doing the Math, in the chapter Calculations for Pattern Design.

Use number of stitches and rows for this calculation; do not include selvedge stitches, if present.

Stitches in Swatch ÷ Measured Width = Stitch Gauge

Rows in Swatch ÷ Measured Length = Row Gauge

I recommend a very simple notation system for writing gauge, with stitches always written first and rows second; see Gauge Notation, below. For instance, a gauge with 6.3 stitches per inch and 7.6 rows per inch would be written as G = 6.3/7.6. (Published patterns often use other methods; see Gauge and Needle Size in the chapter Written Garment Patterns.)

It is important to retain the numbers to the right of the decimal point in the measurements when calculating the gauge.

You can safely round the answer up or down, but *do not drop the tenths.* In other words, if the answer is something like 5.73, use 5.7 for the gauge; if it is 5.785, use 5.8 for the gauge.

Those little tenths . . .

If you have any doubt about the importance of those tiny tenths of an inch, let me give you an example.

- *Assume a gauge of 5.7 stitches per inch, and a garment that will be 50 inches in circumference. Calculate the number of stitches needed:*

  50 inches × Dressed Gauge of 5.7 = 285 stitches

- *If you were to persuade yourself that three-tenths of a stitch does not seem important, and that it would be much easier to work with a gauge of 6 stitches to the inch, you would cast on:*

  50 inches × rounded-up Stitch Gauge of 6 = 300 stitches

- *To see how much difference 15 extra stitches will make, use the actual gauge to find out how wide the garment would be if you cast on that many more stitches:*

  300 stitches ÷ Dressed Gauge of 5.7 = 52.6 inches

- *Perhaps you thought 5.5 would do well enough:*

  50 inches × rounded-down Stitch Gauge of 5.5 = 275 stitches

- *Again, check to see what difference this makes:*

  15 extra stitches ÷ Dressed Gauge of 5.7 = 2.6 inches

  275 stitches ÷ Dressed Gauge of 5.7 = 48.25 inches

In the first example, the result would be a garment more than 2½ inches too large; in the second, it would be almost 2 inches too small.

❖ Working with Raw Gauge

Raw gauge is the gauge of the fabric as it emerges from your needles, before it has been dressed. Because there are occasions when it is useful to check the dimensions of a work in progress, it is helpful to know what this gauge is.

Measure the swatch as you would one that has been dressed, using the Flat Gauge method described above; calculate the gauge in the usual way and write it down in your notes so you have it at hand should you need it.

Then go on to find the Dressed Gauge; after doing so, you may find it interesting to compare the two.

1. Multiply the garment width by the Raw Gauge to find number of stitches.
2. Divide that number by the Dressed Gauge to find true width of fabric.

Step 1 tells you how many stitches to cast on according to the Raw Gauge; Step 2 will tell you how big the garment would be after you washed it the first time. If you had any doubts about the value of dressing a swatch prior to measuring and calculating the gauge, the answer might persuade you otherwise.

Nevertheless, there are times when it is helpful to know what the Raw Gauge is; here are some suggestions for how to use it effectively.

Checking Gauge Accuracy

Whether you have decided to take a precise or a more casual approach to planning a project, it is an excellent idea to use the Raw Gauge to check for accuracy after you are under way.

Stop when you are a few inches above the lower edge, or above the ribbing, and measure the width; to find out how wide it should be, work as follows:

Number of Stitches Cast On ÷ Raw Stitch Gauge = Fabric Width

If the dimensions are what you expected, you can continue with peace of mind, knowing your gauge was correct and the garment will turn out to be the size wanted. For a garment styled with a more precise fit, you might want to check again a few inches below where you will begin the armhole shaping, or before starting a sleeve cap.

If the measurements are not what they should be, you will have to decide if the difference is acceptable or if you need to rip out and start over again; before doing so, take a more accurate measurement by dressing the work on the needles.

Dressing a Work in Progress

If you check the width of a fabric using the Raw Gauge, as described above, and the result gives you any reason to think the gauge you are working from was not accurate, you may have to start over again.

However, before you take the radical step of ripping everything out, first remeasure your Gauge Swatch and recalculate the gauge. If it is correct, this either indicates that you calculated the Raw Gauge wrong, or that something about how you are working has changed.

The safest thing to do is to dress the fabric you have made, right on the needles, and then measure the width.

1. If necessary, transfer stitches to one or more metal or plastic circular needles that are long enough so fabric can be stretched to full width.

2. Wash and/or steam fabric as described above for Dressing a Swatch and lay flat to dry, or block fabric instead.
3. Measure length and width.

You could save considerable time by just using steam instead of washing the fabric and waiting for it to dry; this would not be quite as accurate, but it will give you a good idea about whether there is a problem.

Even if your gauge is accurate, it is a very good idea to dress a work in progress when making something like a skirt, where correct length is critical. When you are a few inches from the finished length, wash the skirt on the needles as described above, and hang it to dry to maximize lengthwise stretch (see Weighted Gauge, above). Measure again when it is dry, and if necessary adjust the number of rows worked before doing the shaping pattern between hip and waist, or, if you worked from the top down, before casting off.

If a final measurement indicates that you need to rip something out, keep in mind that the yarn you have already used and dressed in this way will have been altered. See the information in Recycling Yarn for how to handle the yarn you ripped out; it may be best to use it for ribbings or other details of the garment. At the very least, steam it to get the kinks out and allow it to relax before working with it again, or even wind the yarn into a skein and wash it.

Measuring a Work in Progress

Measuring a work in progress to check for length is not an accurate enough method to rely upon in terms of making something the correct size; for this you will want to work a certain number of rows, but it does provide a quick way to check your progress.

For instance, you might want to measure the length to see if you are getting close to the row where you are supposed to begin the armhole shaping. This is particularly useful if the fabric makes counting rows difficult and you would rather not have to do that more than once.

Length Measurement × Raw Row Gauge = Number of Rows

Of course, this is just an estimate, and once you get closer to the armhole, you will want to do a careful count to find exactly how many more rows you need to work.

By the way, another, even quicker way to check your progress is to count by stitch pattern row repeats:

Number of Row Repeats × Number of Rows in Repeat = Rows Worked

❖ Calculating Average Gauge

Average Gauge is a special approach that takes the elasticity of the fabric into consideration. While it is primarily intended for ribbings, in certain circumstances it is appropriate for other stitch patterns as well, particularly when you are making a garment that will have a close fit.

Some ribbing patterns are primarily decorative and will lie flat in the fabric, in which case the gauge should be calculated in the normal way, as described above. However, a ribbing pattern placed at the waist, wrist, or neckline of a garment has work to do—it is expected to be elastic, drawing the fabric against the body. Unfortunately, ribbings often stretch out of shape with wear, or do not fit well in the first place. There are several reasons why this happens, all of them having to do with gauge in one way or another.

Pattern instructions commonly call for the ribbing to be worked on the same number of stitches as the body of the garment, but on needles two sizes smaller. This is a form of Regauging, which, when combined with the inherent qualities of the ribbing itself, will cause it to narrow relative to the main fabric, gathering it slightly. However, this approach means that the number of stitches in the ribbing is determined not by its own requirements, but by the gauge of whatever stitch or color pattern is used for the body of the garment, and these can vary widely.

Consider two sweater designs, both the same size and made with the same yarn and needles; the body of one is done in a cable pattern, while the other has an eyelet pattern. Cable patterns draw in and typically require considerably more stitches for a given width of fabric than an eyelet pattern, which opens out. If you were to work the ribbing with the same number of stitches as the body, the one done with the cable pattern would have more stitches and a much larger circumference than the one done with the eyelet pattern.

This difference still does not take into consideration whether the person who will wear the garment has wide or narrow hips in relation to the bust or chest measurement, nor whether the ribbing is to sit at the waist, the high hip, or the low hip.

I do not know how this formula came into use, or why it has had such a long career, but I would like to see it abandoned and invite you to ignore an instruction of this kind in any pattern you work from.

Basically, you can hardly use a needle too small when making a ribbing, regardless of the thickness of the yarn. The more stitches there are per inch, and the smaller they are, the more stretch and resilience the ribbing will have, and the more likely it is to retain its elasticity.

Average Gauge for Ribbing

Use a Test Swatch to determine the size needle to use, make a separate Gauge Swatch of the ribbing, as described below,

and then use the Average Gauge Method described here to measure the swatch and calculate the gauge. Use that gauge and a measurement of the body to find how many stitches to cast on for the ribbing. When the ribbing is done, change to the needle size and number of stitches needed for the pattern in the fabric above.

Ribbing Swatch

- Make a ribbing swatch no smaller than 3 inches wide, and 2 or 3 inches long.

   Start with Stranded Cast-On or Alternating Cast-On, and finish with Stranded Cast-Off so edges will be unrestrained.
- Dress swatch in normal way. Do not stretch it widthwise when washing or steaming, but it often helps to give it a tug lengthwise before allowing it to dry.

Calculating Gauge for Ribbing

For a ribbing to hug the body, it should be neither stretched to its maximum, nor completely relaxed in wear; in other words, it needs to be stretched out slightly so it will cling. However, it would be difficult to take a measurement of the fabric under those conditions in any consistent or dependable way.

The solution is to use a little simple mathematics, instead. The method is easy, it takes very little time to do, and the wonderful thing about it is that it really works.

1. Find Relaxed Gauge of ribbing using method described above for Flat Gauge.

Number of Stitches ÷ Relaxed Width = Relaxed Stitch Gauge

Number of Rows ÷ Relaxed Length = Relaxed Row Gauge

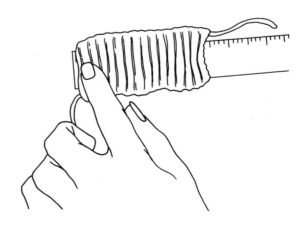

Average Gauge for Ribbing. Measuring Relaxed Gauge.

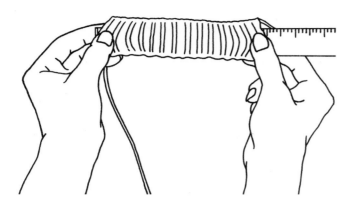

Average Gauge for Ribbing. Measuring Stretched Stitch Gauge.

2. Next, find Stretched Stitch Gauge, as follows:

Hold left edge of swatch against left edge of ruler. Take hold of opposite edge and stretch swatch along ruler as far as it will go (this is why unrestrained edges are important).

Number of Stitches ÷ Stretched Width = Stretched Stitch Gauge

3. Then find Stretched Row Gauge, as follows:

Take side edges in both hands again and stretch swatch as far as it will go, but lay it down across ruler to measure length.

Number of Rows ÷ Stretched Length = Stretched Row Gauge

4. Finally, take the two gauges and average them:

Relaxed Stitch Gauge + Stretched Stitch Gauge ÷ 2 = Average Stitch Gauge

Relaxed Row Gauge + Stretched Row Gauge ÷ 2 = Average Row Gauge

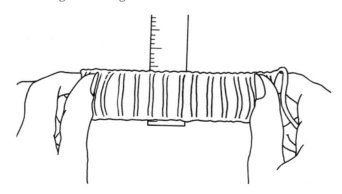

Average Gauge for Ribbing. Measuring Stretched Row Gauge.

Using Average Gauge

You can use Average Gauge just as you would a normal gauge to calculate the width and length of a ribbing at the lower edge of a bodice or sleeve; it reduces the width of the fabric by roughly 20 percent.

- For width, multiply Average Stitch Gauge by a body measurement taken from where ribbing will be, whether that is low or high hip, waist, or wrist, as needed.
- Multiply Average Row Gauge by whatever length is required for ribbing.
- Cast on and work ribbing, and then use increases or decreases to adjust number of stitches on needle as needed to change to main pattern of fabric above (see Horizontal Shaping in the chapter Calculations for Pattern Design, or the same topic in Charted Garment Patterns).

Also use Average Gauge in much the same way to determine the number of stitches to pick up around the opening of a neckline (see Picking Up Stitches). Because the ribbing will be stretched out a bit at the join between the two fabrics, it will help support the shape of the neckline. The edge of the ribbing will exhibit the Relaxed Gauge, which means the entire ribbing will have sufficient residual stretch so it can be pulled over the head.

If the ribbing will be deeper than an inch or two, you might want to use Regauging in addition to Average Gauge, by progressively changing the needle size over the length of the ribbing. This is a particularly good approach to use for a turtleneck, a sleeve cuff, or cap; see Turned-Back Ribbing.

A border for something like a sleeveless armhole or a V-neckline will also require decreases to shape the deep curve or point at the bottom of the opening; see V-Neckline Design.

Average Gauge for Negative Ease

The Average Gauge concept can be applied to any stitch pattern that will be used in a design intended to cling closely to the body, such as a camisole, a form-fitting vest, or socks.

However, in designs where only a moderate amount of cling is needed, instead of using Average Gauge, it may be sufficient to use a normal stitch gauge and reduce the number of stitches by 5 or 10 percent instead; for more information, see Ease Allowances.

❖ *Gauge for Special Patterns*

In some cases, you will need to modify the basic method of making a swatch and calculating gauge for certain types of fabrics or patterns. For instance, when a garment design includes several different stitch patterns, you would normally make a swatch for each one because they will all have different gauges. However, it often makes more sense to combine smaller patterns into one swatch and treat them as a single larger pattern, and this requires a different method of calculating and using the gauge when planning a design.

Also included here are some tips for how to handle the swatch for a fabric that will have beads, will be fulled (see Felting and Fulling), or one made for a Double-Fabric.

Coordinating Multiple Stitch Patterns

When a design includes several different stitch patterns arranged in vertical or horizontal panels, each major pattern requires its own swatch; narrower ones that will be used together in the fabric can be combined in a single swatch and then treated as a single stitch repeat (for information about repeats, see Written Stitch Patterns).

Once you find the relevant dimensions and gauges of the various patterns, it is relatively easy to work out even a complex design of this kind by means of a chart; see Coordinating Stitch and Garment Patterns.

Swatches for Vertical Patterns

• For a single, wide vertical pattern, make a swatch consisting of one stitch repeat and at least one full row repeat; dress the swatch in the usual way.

Calculate only the row gauge; there is no need to find the stitch gauge. If the stitch pattern is used just once in the fabric, only the width it contributes and the number of stitches it contains is important.

• If several similar, relatively narrow vertical patterns will be arranged side by side, combine them into one swatch and treat them as if they were a single pattern. As with the large panel, all you need is the information on the number of stitches and overall width and the row gauge.

• If the combined decorative patterns are not wide enough to occupy the full garment width, it is common to use a textured fill pattern of some kind. Small portions of this pattern are set between the primary, decorative ones, or at each side of the garment to make up the difference.

Swatch for Vertical Patterns.
Combined patterns for a central panel.

If the fill pattern will occupy anything more than about half an inch on either side, do a small Test Swatch to find a gauge for it and determine exactly how many stitches to use.

• If the row gauges of different panels that will be used side by side are not the same, they may not lie smoothly together in the fabric. To check for this, make each swatch with the same number of rows. If they are different lengths, try to equalize them when they are dressed by lengthening some, widening others.

A knitted fabric is quite flexible and you may be able to fit them together reasonably well this way, but if it does not work, it may be best to select a different pattern; the only alternative is to use Short Rows.

Swatches for Horizontal Patterns

Similar dynamics are at work when dealing with multiple stitch patterns that are set horizontally, in the equivalent of stripes.

In this case, however, it is the stitch gauge of each pattern that is important.

• Make a separate swatch for each stitch pattern used. To change from one pattern to next, adjust number of stitches on needle by spacing shaping units evenly across a single row; see Horizontal Shaping in the chapter Calculations for Pattern Design, or the same topic in Charted Garment Patterns.

• If several patterns are similar and likely to have the same gauge, combine them in one swatch and treat it as a single large row repeat; dress swatch and calculate number of stitches needed for width.

The length each pattern will contribute to the garment is measurable, and the number of rows is simply equal to one repeat.

• Measure lengths of all swatches, and add together to determine length of combined patterns in garment.

As with vertical panels, a filler pattern may be needed at the top and bottom, or between each primary decorative pattern, to achieve the necessary length for the garment.

Gauge for Borders

A border of any kind is a separate stitch pattern, and will have its own gauge.

• When making a narrow vertical border, a dressed Test Swatch is usually sufficient to find out how many stitches to cast on for the width.

• A border on stitches picked up along a side edge of a fabric is as wide as the main fabric is long, and it is important to make a swatch large enough to do an accurate gauge. Pick up stitches evenly along the edge, and then use the border gauge to develop. For more information about why this is important, see Adjusting Number of Stitches in the chapter Picking Up Stitches; for information on developing the pattern, see Horizontal Shaping in the chapter Calculations for Pattern Design.

Gauge for Color Patterns

Color patterns have their own gauge just as stitch patterns do. If you use several different Stranded Color patterns in one fabric, as long as you are consistent in the way you strand the yarn, they are all likely to have the same gauge.

However, if one pattern has considerably more background than pattern stitches, its gauge might be somewhat different than that of a pattern where the number of background and pattern stitches is closer to equal.

If you have any concern about this, do separate Test Swatches for the patterns, dress them, and compare the estimated gauges. If this confirms a discrepancy, make a separate full-size swatch for the pattern that is different from the others, find the gauge, and develop a pattern for it as described in Swatches for Horizontal Patterns, above.

Mosaic pattern gauges are all the same, as long as you work them in a consistent way. However, if you change from one done entirely in Stockinette to one done in Garter Stitch, the gauge will change. Use a Test Swatch to see if the difference is enough to merit adjusting the number of stitches between one and the other. If the difference is minor, include a representative sample of patterns when making the Gauge Swatch.

Of course, you cannot change from a solid-color fabric to a color-patterned one, or from Stranded Color to Intarsia, without a change in gauge. On the other hand, if an area in a different pattern is only a few rows (like a solid color stripe between Stranded Color stripes), a knitted fabric is flexible enough to accommodate the difference, and a little steam is a great encouragement when you want two patterns to settle in together. Use your judgment and perhaps make a few Test Swatches before deciding how fussy you want to be.

Gauge for Decorated Fabrics

If you plan to use beads or sequins in a pattern, include them in the swatch. These materials may not seem to weigh very much, but collectively they do (this is particularly true of beads), and it is important to take drop into consideration.

You might want to wash the swatch and hang it wet, and/or hang a bag of beads from the bottom of the swatch along with a skein of yarn when measuring for Weighted Gauge; this is the best approach to use if steam will damage the decorative materials.

For a fabric that will later be embroidered, or if you plan to add trim, it is especially important that it be given the finished dimensions before these kinds of things are added to the surface. In most cases, therefore, it is best to use the Weighted Gauge method (and do pre-shrink a woven trim or dress a knitted trim before it is applied).

Furthermore, you might also want to use your swatch as a way to test how you will add these elements to the fabric. Once you have done so, recheck the gauge to see if length and width are stable and the gauge remains the same.

Gauge for Double-Fabrics

Make a swatch for a Double-Fabric just as you would for a single-layer fabric, and find the gauge using the Flat or Weighted Gauge method, above. However, there are a few things to keep in mind.

- Use the stitch gauge in the normal way to find the number of stitches needed for the width of one fabric, and then multiply by 2 to add the stitches needed for the second fabric.
- The row gauge also represents the number of rows in one fabric, or, to think of it another way, the number of rows in the combined fabric. Keep in mind that working the pattern usually requires two passes across the stitches to make each one of those rows; for more information, see Double-Fabrics.

Gauge for Fulled Fabrics

Fulling a fabric changes its dimensions radically, and therefore it requires a special approach to finding the gauge; for more information see Fulling.

It is a very good idea to make several swatches in order to test how well the yarn will full and what the timing needs to be in order to achieve the degree of shrinkage you want.

- Make a square swatch with a width equal to about 20 percent of the largest garment measurement, but no less than about 8 inches wide.
- Write down the number of stitches and rows used before fulling the swatch because it can be very difficult to count stitches afterward.
- Calculate the Raw Gauge so you can compare it with the fulled gauge to see how much it has changed.
- Full the swatch exactly as you will the garment and then calculate the gauge in the normal way.
- You may notice that a fabric shrinks more in one dimension than another, but your gauge will reflect this, so there is no need for concern.

❖ *Matching Pattern Gauges*

The instructions for a published garment pattern require that you match the gauge specified in order to produce a garment of the size shown in the schematic; however, it is difficult to do this very precisely.

Furthermore, you may not be able to rely on the accuracy of the gauge in many published patterns. There is no way to know if the designer dressed the swatch or how they calculated the gauge. It is also quite likely that the measurements shown in the schematic were taken from the garment lying flat and do not reflect how much of an effect drop could have when it is worn.

Under the circumstances, the best thing to do is to make a swatch and calculate the gauge according to the instructions provided here. Then use your gauge and the measurements from the pattern's schematic, or the dimensions provided in the written instructions, to alter the pattern slightly so it will fit correctly. You will find several suggestions below for how to do this.

Also, some patterns recommend that you work a certain number of inches to a given point in the pattern, instead of specifying a certain number of rows. Before you begin, use your gauge to calculate how many rows to work; this will be more accurate than relying on the Raw Gauge and a measurement of the fabric.

Gauge Notation

In published patterns, you will frequently see gauge written as something like "5 stitches and 7 rows per inch," or perhaps "13 stitches/15 rows = 2 inches," or "23 stitches and 30 rows in 4 inches." The latter two methods are used as a way to avoid fractions or decimal numbers.

You can convert any of these to the gauge notation recommended here by dividing the number of stitches or rows by the number of inches.

The two examples above would look like this:

13 stitches ÷ 2 = 6.5

15 rows ÷ 2 = 7.5

G = 6.5/7.5 (meaning a Gauge of 6.5 stitches per inch and 7.5 rows per inch)

Or like this,

23 stitches ÷ 4 = 5.7

30 rows ÷ 4 = 7.5

G = 5.7/7.5

Gauge and Pattern Size

If you have made a swatch and the gauge does not match the one in the pattern, and you have no other options regarding the size needle to use, first see what would happen if you used the instructions for one of the other garment sizes. This approach works reasonably well for garment designs that are intended to have a loose, easy fit.

1. Check width of fabric using your gauge and instructions for each size, as follows:

Number of Stitches for Size A ÷ Your Stitch Gauge = Width of Fabric

Number of Stitches for Size B ÷ Your Stitch Gauge = Width of Fabric

2. Compare results to measurements indicated in schematic.
3. Work from whichever set of instructions produces a fabric that is closest to dimensions needed for garment to fit.

If your gauge produces a width that is acceptable with any one of the pattern instructions, the length will probably be all right as well.

In some cases, you may find your stitch gauge matches, but your row gauge does not, in which case you can usually make some simple alterations to adjust the garment length; see below. The reason for this discrepancy may be uneven row tension, either on your part or on the part of the pattern designer; for more information, see Tension in the chapter The Stitches, and also Change in Tension on Knit and Purl Rows in the chapter Knitting Methods.

Pattern Alterations

If none of the instructions for other sizes in the pattern will work for the gauge you have, the alternative is to rewrite the pattern somewhat.

One way to do this is to use your gauge and the measurements provided in the schematic to change the number of stitches and rows needed in areas of the garment where the pattern is relatively simple.

This is also the approach to use when taking drop into consideration; use the Weighted Gauge method and the dimensions in the schematic to rewrite the pattern somewhat.

- To alter the length, change the number of rows between the lower edge and the armhole of a bodice.
- To alter the width, change the number of stitches at the center of the front and back so there will be no change in the shaped areas of the neckline or shoulders.

If you feel it is necessary to rewrite a pattern in a way that does involve a slope or curve (such as for the shoulder, or the armhole and sleeve), the best thing to do is to chart a new garment pattern, using your gauge and the measurements provided; see Charted Garment Patterns. If you are dealing with written instructions, also see Charts from Written Garment Patterns.

Stitch Gauge Ratios

The Gauge Ratios are two numbers that represent the difference between your stitch and row gauges and the ones called for in the pattern. These numbers are used to recalculate the instructions for slopes and curves, and they simplify the amount of math that needs to be done.

This approach is particularly useful if you like a garment

style but prefer to use a different yarn and/or stitch pattern and all of the instructions need to be rewritten.

To Find the Gauge Ratios

New Stitch Gauge ÷ Original Stitch Gauge = Stitch Gauge Ratio

New Row Gauge ÷ Original Row Gauge = Row Gauge Ratio

To Adjust Length and Width

Stitch Gauge Ratio × Original Number of Stitches =
New Number of Stitches

Row Gauge Ratio × Original Number of Rows =
New Number of Rows

To Adjust a Slope Pattern

Here is an example of how to use a Gauge Ratio to rewrite the pattern for a slope.

Say the pattern gauge is G = 4.5/6 and your gauge is G = 5.2/7.3. The pattern instruction reads: "Decrease 1 stitch each side every 10 rows 7 times." This means 7 stitches will be decreased over 70 rows, so there are 10 rows between each decrease.

1. Divide your gauge by the pattern gauge to find the ratios:

   5.2 stitches per inch ÷ 4.5 stitches per inch = a stitch ratio of 1.15

   7.3 rows per inch ÷ 6 rows per inch = a row ratio of 1.22

2. Use Stitch Ratio to change number of stitches to be decreased.

   7 stitches × 1.15 = 8.05 stitches; round down to 8 stitches to decrease in new pattern

3. Use Row Ratio to change number of rows between each decrease:

   10 rows × 1.15 = 11.5 rows; option to round down to 11 or up to 12 rows in between decreases in new pattern

It is easier to work with an even number of rows between decreases, therefore, round up and rewrite the pattern as: "Decrease 1 stitch each side every 12 rows 8 times."

To Adjust a Curve Pattern

• A curve in a knitted fabric is a series of tiny slopes, one after the other; see Curved Shaping, in the chapter Calculations for Pattern Design. To rewrite the pattern using the Ratios, simply recalculate each one of the separate steps in the instruction in the same way as described above.

Calculating Yarn Requirements

A Gauge Swatch can be used to make fairly precise estimates of the amount of yarn required for a project.

It is always a good idea to buy just one ball of yarn, make some swatches, and find the gauge before deciding whether to invest your time and money in a project. Then develop the pattern and calculate how much more yarn you will need to purchase using the information here.

If you have a design idea for some yarn you have on hand, it is important to know if there is enough; if not, you can then modify the design so there will be. If you are working from a pattern and want to alter it in some way, or perhaps substitute another yarn, you can calculate the amounts needed.

There are two sets of formulas here. One gives you a rough estimate of how much yarn is required. The other is more detailed for those times when you really need to know exactly how much yarn is needed. This can spare you the decidedly unpleasant experience of nearing the end of a project only to realize you do not have enough to finish it.

Also included here is information about how to calculate the amount of time a project is likely to take. For those of you who are knitting something to sell, or if you are planning to make a gift for a birthday or holiday, this can help you decide whether to proceed with what you have in mind, or perhaps take on something more or less ambitious.

❖ *Stitch Yardage*

It is very useful to know exactly how many stitches one yard of the yarn you will be working with will make. At the very least, this information will take the guesswork out of deciding whether you will make it across one more row before you run out.

Of greater importance, however, is that this figure also provides the basis for the other calculations that will tell you how much yarn you need for any project. For that purpose, you will also need to know how many yards it takes to make a square inch of the fabric.

Stitches per Yard

The number of stitches per yard is just as unique to a given combination of needles, yarn, and stitch pattern as is gauge. Every time you wrap the yarn around the needle, a certain amount of yarn is measured out to each stitch. Some techniques require more or less yarn than others—a pair of Crossed Stitches, for instance, will require more yarn than if the same two stitches were worked individually.

It is quite easy to obtain the figure for stitches per yard while making the swatch (a Test Swatch is not wide enough to use for this purpose), and once you have it, you can calculate the yardage required for a garment of any size, or determine whether you can substitute one yarn for another.

1. Work about an inch of Gauge Swatch. At beginning of next row, measure one yard of yarn from where it is attached to last stitch; tie a Slip Knot in yarn to mark length.

2. Continue in pattern to knot; keep track of how many rows were worked, and count how many stitches are in final partial row.

3. Calculate how many stitches were made with one yard:

(Number of Rows × Number of Stitches per Row) + Number of Stitches Worked in Partial Row = Number of Stitches per Yard

Be careful not to pull the knot out when it works its way up close to your hand.

If one yard is not enough to include a representative sample of the pattern and all stitch techniques used, tie the knot at two yards, or even five yards, and work in the same manner. Use the formula above, which will give you the total number of stitches worked, and then adjust as follows:

Total Number of Stitches ÷ Number of Yards = Stitches per Yard

Yards per Square Inch

Next, find how many yards of yarn it will take to make 1 square inch of the fabric. Complete the swatch, dress it, and calculate the gauge. Then work as follows:

1. First use gauge numbers to find stitches per square inch.

Stitches per Inch × Rows per Inch = Stitches per Square Inch

2. Then find yards per square inch.

Stitches per Square Inch ÷ Stitches per Yard = Yards per Square Inch

Round the number up or down to tenths, but do not drop the tenths.

Yards per Square Inch for Color Patterns

Finding the yardage required for a color pattern is more challenging. For instance, in a Stranded Color pattern, both the stitches and the strands take up yarn, and as the pattern changes the amount of each color absorbed continually changes as well. This is further complicated if you combine several different patterns in one garment, as is common.

If you are using more than one color pattern, make the swatch long enough to include an example of each one so it is as representative as possible of the finished fabric. Alternatively, make a sampler of patterns that have a similar percentage of background and pattern stitches.

As you work, keep track of how much of each yarn is used to make the entire swatch. This example assumes you are using two yarns, Color A and Color B.

1. Cast on for swatch, measure off two to five yards of Color A, and tie knot to mark position; repeat with Color B.
2. Begin to work patterns. When knot is at last stitch made, untie it, measure off same amount again, and tie another knot.

3. Dress and measure swatch and calculate gauge, and then calculate yardage per square inch for each color as follows:

Swatch Length × Swatch Width = Square Inches of Swatch

Yards Used for Color A ÷ Square Inches of Swatch = Yards of Color A per Square Inch

4. Repeat for Color B, then add two results to find total yardage per square inch needed.

5. To find percentage of each color, work as follows:

Yards of Color A per Square Inch ÷ Total Yards per Square Inch = Percentage of Color A per Square Inch

Patterns often require different amounts of each color; therefore, keep a separate record of how many knots you tie in each one. For the last rows of the swatch, tie knots at one yard, and then count how many stitches you worked with each color on the last row. If part of a yard remains, measure it and subtract from the total yarn used for that color.

❖ Square Inches of Fabric

Once you have calculated the yards per square inch, the next step in finding out how many yards of yarn you will need is to determine the total number of square inches in the garment.

To do this, use the measurements from the schematic drawing, or the dimensions of the garment provided in a written pattern, and one of the two methods described here. The approximate method is good for most purposes; use the precise method when it is essential to know exactly what to expect.

Approximate Square-Inch Method

In the following equations, note that *width of front + width of back* may be substituted for the Maximum Circumference of the bodice.

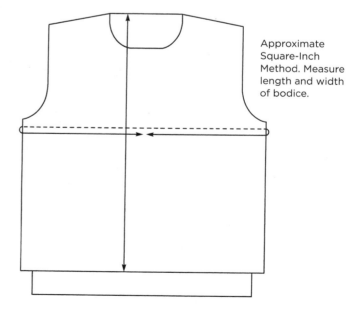

Approximate Square-Inch Method. Measure length and width of bodice.

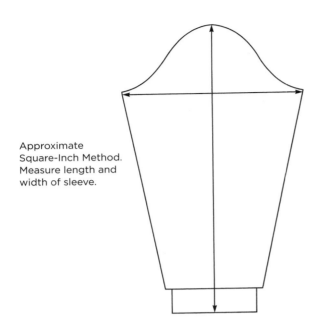

Approximate Square-Inch Method. Measure length and width of sleeve.

Bodice Length × Maximum Circumference =
Square Inches of Body

Sleeve Length × Maximum Sleeve Circumference =
Square Inches of Sleeve

Body + 2 Sleeves = Total Square Inches of Fabric

If the bodice is shaped, use the width measurement at the widest part, usually at the underarm. If the front and back bodice widths are different, add them together to find the circumference.

To find the bodice length, use the measurement from the lower edge to the center back neck or the top of shoulder line, whichever is longer. The sleeve length is a measurement from the top of the cap at the shoulder to the lower edge and the widest sleeve circumference is usually equivalent to the width of the sleeve at the underarm.

If there are any other sections of the garment that will require a substantial amount of yarn, such as a large collar, calculate the square inches for those sections separately and add them in. Always calculate ribbings separately.

Precise Square-Inch Method

The calculations used in the Approximate Square-Inch Method, above, provide a generous estimate because nothing is deducted for areas removed by shaping. For most purposes, it is best not to subtract those areas because this builds in an allowance of extra yarn in case you miscalculate or alter the pattern after you begin to work.

There are times, however, when the amount of yarn is already fixed, and it is crucial to know whether you have the correct amount. In these cases, you will need to make a more precise estimate. Work as follows.

To Calculate Bodice Area

For the bodice, first find the square-inch figure as described in the Approximate Square-Inch Method, above. Then square off the areas that will be removed to shape the neckline and armholes, eliminating any slopes or curves, and then calculate as follows:

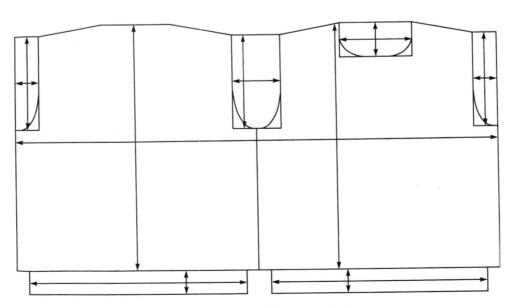

Precise Square-Inch Method. Measuring the bodice.

1. First find area to subtract for armholes.

    *Armhole Length × Armhole Width × 2 =
    Area to Subtract for Armhole*

2. Next find area to subtract for neckline.
   For a round neckline:

    Neckline Width × Neckline Depth = Area to Subtract for Neck

    For a V-neckline:

    *(Back Neckline Width × Neckline Length) ÷ 2 =
    Area to Subtract for Neck*

3. Subtract these areas from square-inch figure for bodice to get more precise yardage:

    *Area of Sleeves + Area of Body − Armhole Area − Neck Area =
    Square Inches of Fabric*

To Calculate Sleeve Area

Treat the sleeve caps and the sleeve body (from wrist to underarm) separately.

Imagine turning one cap and one sleeve upside down and placing them adjacent to their counterparts from the second sleeve, as shown in the illustration. The result is a trapezoid, and the area is width times length, just as for a rectangle or square.

Find the areas as follows:

*Sleeve Width at Wrist + Sleeve Width at Armhole =
Combined Sleeve Width*

Combined Sleeve Width × Sleeve Length = Area of Sleeves

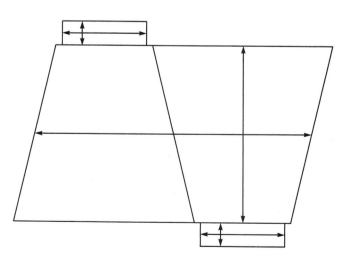

Precise Square-Inch Method. Measuring the lower sleeve.

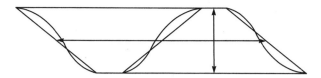

Precise Square-Inch Method. Measuring the sleeve cap.

*Width of Cap at Center Top + Width of Cap at Armhole =
Combined Cap Width*

*Combined Cap Width × Sleeve Cap Length =
Area of Sleeve Caps*

If the garment contains large areas done with different patterns that will have appreciably different yarn requirements (for instance, if the bodice is Stockinette and the sleeves a lace pattern), calculate the square inches and yardage for each area separately and then add those figures together to find the total for the entire garment.

It is particularly important to calculate amounts needed for ribbings separately, because they require considerably more yarn than other kinds of patterns.

❖ Garment Yardage

After you work out how many square inches of fabric there will be in the garment, and have calculated the figure for yards per square inch, then find out how many yards of yarn are required. First check the yarn label for the number of yards or meters in each ball or skein; if this information is not available, see Measuring a Skein, below, to determine what it is.

Yardage for Solid Color Garment

1. First find total yarn yardage required for garment.

    *Square Inches of Fabric × Yards per Square Inch =
    Yardage for Garment*

2. Then use yardage for garment and yardage of ball of yarn to find how many are needed.

    *Yards for Garment ÷ Yards per Ball or Skein =
    Number of Balls or Skeins Required*

Remember, it is always better to have too much yarn than too little, and you will need some for your swatch; if you can, always buy an extra ball to be on the safe side.

If the yarn label does not provide total yards or meters, or if this information is not available from the yarn store or from the manufacturer's web site, there is a way to obtain it without too much trouble; see Measuring a Skein, below.

An example . . .

I once bought two large skeins of beautiful merino wool at an outlet store that carried overruns from knitwear designers; there was no label. I used an umbrella swift to measure the yardage (see Measuring a Skein, below) and designed a pattern for a sweater. I first used the Approximate Method, above, to calculate the yardage and thought there was more than enough yarn.

The yarn was thin so I doubled it and used size 2 mm needles; the gauge was close to 8 stitches to the inch and it was a large sweater. It would not be a trivial setback if my calculations were wrong.

The front was done and the back half finished when I started to worry. I used the Precise Method to check and it indicated there would barely be enough yarn. I decided to keep going, and when the last stitch was cast off and the seams were sewn, I had 14 inches of yarn left. That was very anxious knitting, indeed, but the sweater was a success and has given me many happy years of wear.

Yardage for Color Patterns

When working any color pattern, you not only need to find out how much yarn is required for the entire garment, but how much you need of each color.

You can do this without too much trouble by using the stitches-per-yard figures from the swatch, as described above, and then estimating how much of the total area each color occupies in the garment.

Stripes are quite easy, of course, because all that is needed is to find how much yardage is required for the garment and then divide in half, or thirds, and so on, to find how much is needed for each color.

Stranded Color and Mosaic patterns are also relatively easy, but Intarsia patterns present some challenges.

Garment Yardage for Stranded Color Patterns

The method of finding the stitches-per-yard figure for each color in a Stranded Color pattern, above, was a bit of a challenge, but once you have it, it is easy to work out how much of each color will be needed for the garment:

*Garment Yardage ÷ Yards per Square Inch of Color A =
    Total Color A*

Repeat for each color needed. Work in the same way for a Mosaic pattern.

Garment Yardage for Intarsia Patterns

Most Intarsia patterns are done in plain Stockinette, in which case you can make a single swatch in one color to find the gauge, the stitches-per-yard figure, and that for yards per square inch. Then calculate the total yarn requirements for the garment.

The next step is to calculate how much of the total is needed for each color you will use. The approach to use for geometric patterns is quite straightforward, but pictorial patterns present more of a challenge. However, Intarsia patterns are usually overlaid on a garment chart, which helps make this somewhat easier to do; see Coordinating Stitch and Garment Patterns.

The instructions are for finding the amount of yarn needed for each color used in a geometric Intarsia pattern; you will find tips below for how to calculate the amount needed for a pictorial pattern.

First, find the number of stitches there are in one motif, and then find the yardage, as follows:

*Stitches in Width of Motif × Rows in Length of Motif =
    Total Number of Stitches in Motif*

Stitches in Motif ÷ Stitches per Yard = Yardage for Motif

*Yardage for Motif × Number of Motifs in Each Color =
    Total Yards of Color Needed*

Be generous with your estimates, and add something for all the little tails of yarn left behind each time you start and finish a motif.

Here are some suggestions for how to calculate the amount of yarn you will need for a non-geometric pattern.

- For each major motif, square off pattern on chart and use formulas above for Geometric Intarsia Yardage.
- For minor motifs, find the number of stitches in several of them and then average the number. Use that number to find the yardage needed for one, and then multiply by how many motifs of a similar size there are in each color.
- Find total yardage needed for garment, subtract amounts for main and secondary motifs from amount required for entire garment; remainder is amount needed for background color.

❖ Measuring a Skein

If the label does not indicate the yardage (or if there is no label), and you cannot obtain the information from the store or the manufacturer, there are several simple methods to determine what it is.

The best approach depends upon having a Yarn Swift or a Niddy-Noddy. A swift is an umbrella-like device used to hold a skein of yarn and it expands to fit any diameter. Normally it is used to hold a skein while you wind the yarn into a ball, but it can be used to turn a ball back into a skein as well. A niddy-noddy is a hand-operated tool (with a charming name) that is also used to make a skein from a ball, but the length of the skein is fixed.

If you have one or the other, it makes it quite simple to determine the yards in a skein.

1. To set size of skein on a swift, place a measuring tape around center of ribs where skein will be, then open swift up until circumference measures one yard.

    If you prefer to make a 2-yard skein, measure off a length of yarn to use as a guide for the circumference.
2. Attach yarn to one arm of swift and spin to wind yarn out of ball.
3. Calculate yardage.

Number of Strands in Skein × Circumference = Yardage

If the yarn is already in skein form, place it on the swift, count the number of strands, and then measure the circumference and calculate yardage. If these tools are not available, wrap the yarn around a chair back or a friend's outstretched arms instead, and then measure the circumference of the skein and count the strands.

About Wraps per Inch

You may come across suggestions to use a concept borrowed from weaving called Wraps per Inch (WPI) as a way of comparing two yarns.

The yarn is wrapped evenly around a ruler so the strands lie side by side and fill one inch and then the strands are counted. The same thing is done with another yarn. The idea is that if the number of wraps is the same for both yarns, one can be substituted for the other.

Of course, the reliability of the technique depends upon your wrapping in a perfectly consistent way each time, with an even tension and all the strands nestled in just the same way next to one another.

Perhaps you detect that I am somewhat dubious. I have tested this method (and invite you to do the same) by carefully wrapping the same yarn ten different times to see how much variation there was, and it was considerable. Of course, if you are comparing your WPI to someone else's, it is even more likely that there will be differences in the way the wrapping is done.

❖ Gauge and Yarn Substitution

From time to time, you may prefer to use a yarn other than the one called for in a published pattern. Perhaps you like the pattern but not the recommended yarn, the yarn recommended is no longer available, or you have a yarn on hand that you want to use instead.

There are several things to take into consideration before you decide how, or even whether to proceed.

- Use a yarn that is as similar as possible to the one recommended by the pattern, ideally one made of the same fiber, with the same or very similar yardage per ounce or gram; for more suggestions about selecting an alternative, see Yarn Substitution in the chapter on Yarns.
- If you have both yarns on hand, make Test Swatches of each one and find the stitches-per-yard figure as you do so. Then wash and dress the swatches and find the gauges. If the two gauges and the stitches-per-yard figures are very similar, you can safely substitute one yarn for the other.
- If you only have the yarn you would like to use on hand, the best you can do is to calculate the Dressed Gauge and compare it to the gauge required by the pattern.

❖ Timing Your Work

If you are faced with making something that has to be done by a certain date, it is very helpful to have a way to determine how long it will take to do. Faced with the reality, you may go ahead with it, choose a different project, or perhaps decide it would be quite impossible to finish in time.

Be warned that you might feel faint the first time you see these numbers because they are generally larger than you expected, or perhaps wanted to know about. (But remember, some of the nicest things we do in life are those we might never have had the courage to try if someone had told us exactly what would be required; marriage and children come to mind).

1. Make first inch or so of swatch. At beginning of row, set timer for 5 minutes and work in pattern until alarm rings. Keep track of number of rows and count number of stitches in final partial row.

    Alternatively, set timer while calculating stitches-per-yard figure, and get both figures at the same time.

*Number of Rows × Number of Stitches per Row
+ Number of Stitches in Partial Row =
Number of Stitches Knit in 5 Minutes*

*Stitches in 5 Minutes ÷ 5 = Stitches per Minute × 60 =
Stitches per Hour*

Or, conversely:

Stitches in 5 Minutes × 12 = Stitches per Hour

2. Then find time required.

*Stitches per Square Inch × Square Inches of Fabric =
Total Stitches in Garment*

Stitches in Garment ÷ Stitches per Hour = Hours of Work

Remember, this figure is an approximation. The 5 minutes of timed knitting will include a certain amount of time for turning the work, pulling yarn out of the ball, and shifting stitches up and down the needles, so it is a relatively accurate estimate of how long it takes to knit that particular stitch pattern.

If you want to include a little more of these practicalities in your estimate, time how long it takes you to knit the entire swatch instead.

Swatch Width × Length = Square Inches of Swatch

*Total Time to Knit Swatch ÷ Square Inches =
  Time per Square Inch*

*Time per Square Inch × Square Inches of Garment =
  Time for Project*

Of course, this still does not include planning, ripping, counting stitches or rows, or the details of finishing, to say nothing of telephone calls, the distractions of children and pets, or getting slowed down by a really good episode of your favorite television show. As we all know, these things are inevitably part of the time taken to knit an actual project.

CHAPTER 24

Measurements and Schematics

If you have a concept for something that you would like to design, the first step in developing a pattern for it is to decide on the basic contours and determine the measurements of every section of the garment. These are recorded in the form of a schematic, a small line drawing that shows the proportions of the garment and all the relevant dimensions. The schematic is then used in conjunction with your Stitch Gauge and the information in Calculations for Pattern Design and Charted Garment Patterns to write the pattern instructions.

However, it can be a challenge to design a garment that has good proportions and fits well. One solution to the difficulties this can pose is to base your design on an existing garment that you know is flattering and comfortable, or on a knitting or sewing pattern that is similar to what you want to make. These have been professionally designed and, therefore, the most critical elements of a successful design—the proportions of the shoulder and neckline, and those of the sleeve and armhole, have all been worked out for you. This leaves you free to concentrate on selecting the yarn and the stitch or color pattern and working out the details of the pattern.

The first set of instructions below describes how to draw a schematic based on the measurements of a typical pullover-type sweater. This is followed by information on how to adapt a sewing pattern for use as the basis of a knitted design, taking the measurements from the individual pieces more or less as you would from a garment; the schematic is then drawn in the same way.

While you could simply make a list as you do this, the best approach is to record these measurements directly in the form of a schematic. While a schematic is not essential for a simple project, making one is easy and serves to check the accuracy of your measurements and whether the different pattern pieces fit together the way they should.

If you prefer to develop an entirely original design, you will also find step-by-step instructions for how to take body measurements (you might also need to do this in order to check the fit or alter a published knitting pattern or a sewing pattern). The final dimensions of a garment are based on these measurements plus "ease," which is an amount added to the length and width for comfort and stylistic reasons; guidelines for how much to add are included.

Following this is a discussion of the design of the upper bodice areas of a garment—the shoulder, armhole, and sleeve—which are without question the most challenging aspects of a pattern. Due to space constraints, this material covers only the basics of a subject that could fill a separate book. However, this information can be enhanced by also working with sewing patterns. You will gain skills doing this and acquire a familiarity with the proportions and subtleties of fit in these areas of a garment that will provide you with a much wider scope of design possibilities.

As you can see, this material provides several options for how to approach a design, and you might find it useful to skim through all of it first, just to see what is here. Read the introductory material for how to take measurements and draw a schematic, as well as those on the various aspects of garment design, and then return to the particular instructions that are most relevant for the project you have in mind.

Keep in mind that all of the concepts discussed here can be applied to the design of anything, not just a sweater. You would use exactly the same approach to taking measurements and drawing a schematic if you wanted to make a hat, a handbag, slippers, a stuffed toy, or a pillowcase.

General Tips

Before going on to the detailed instructions, here is some general information about how to take measurements regardless of whether you are starting with an existing garment or using a sewing pattern (details specific to measuring the body are discussed with that material below). Also included here are some general guidelines for how to draw a schematic on graph paper, which makes it very easy to make all the lines nice and straight and record the dimensions accurately.

❖ Basics of Taking Measurements

To measure a garment, you can simply lay it out flat and smooth on a table. However, it is important to understand that the dimensions of many knitted garments are different in wear than when lying flat on a table or folded in a drawer—they become longer and narrower because of the weight and flexibility of a knitted fabric (see Drop: The Effect of Gravity). If you are dealing with a garment that you think is heavy enough to exhibit drop, it is important to take this into consideration.

Put the garment on a padded hanger and use a tape measure to take preliminary measurements of the full length and width of the bodice and sleeves. Then lay it down flat and, using a tape measure, stretch it out to give it the hanging dimensions; if necessary, pin or weight the garment edges to hold them in place.

In order to take the detailed measurements needed, an angle rule (L-shaped) is helpful, but you can improvise with two rulers, or combine a tape measure and a ruler. For a knitted fabric, measure along the rows and columns of stitches; for a woven fabric, measure parallel to the threads.

There is no need to measure any slopes or curves on a garment or sewing pattern in order to draw a schematic.† Knitting pattern instructions for shaping any area will specify how many stitches to add or remove over a certain number of rows; the edge will slope or curve automatically as a result of working the pattern correctly. To develop a set of pattern instructions, the area to be shaped is defined as a triangle, and to find the number of stitches and rows to work, all you need are the stitch gauge and the length and width measurements of the triangle (see Shaping Concepts in the chapter Calculations for Pattern Design).

Measurements can be taken of the full width of a garment or sewing pattern piece, but as you will see, many schematics only show one vertical half of the bodice and sleeve. For a drawing of that kind, either divide a full width measure-

ment in half, or measure from the center line of the garment or pattern piece when making the drawing. Of course, when developing the pattern you will use the full width (or the circumference) to find the number of stitches needed, therefore it is a good idea to write these measurements down on the schematic, as well.

When measuring a knitted bodice and sleeve, do not include any ribbings or details such as borders or collars, whether worked on picked-up stitches or sewn into place; measure these areas separately. If a ribbing gathers the fabric, stretch it out so the garment lies flat and/or measure a few inches above it. For a garment made of woven fabric, measure from seam to seam (do not include selvedges) and measure cuffs, collars, plackets, etc., separately.

Always measure to an accuracy of $1/8$ inch; for why this is important, see Five Steps to Accurate Gauge. Then convert all fractional measurements to decimal numbers to make the pattern calculations easier to do; see Tips for Doing the Math in Calculations for Pattern Design. Of course, there is no need to bother with this conversion if you measure in centimeters.

❖ Basics of Drawing a Schematic

Before going on to an example of how to measure a garment and draw a schematic, here are some general tips:

- A schematic is a simple line drawing done on 4-squares-per-inch graph paper; the grid makes it easy to count off measurements and draw straight lines. Treat one square as equal to an inch (graph paper with a 5-squares-per-inch grid does not line up with the quarter-inch marks on a ruler).

  An 8.5 × 11-inch sheet of graph paper will have 34 horizontal and 44 vertical squares, which is more than enough to accommodate even a relatively large pattern. To make a larger schematic, treat each square as ½ inch, or even ¼ inch.

  If you do not have graph paper on hand, simply measure off the lines, treating each quarter-inch mark on the ruler as equivalent to an inch, and square up the corners as best you can.

- For basic designs, draw just one vertical half of the bodice and sleeve. If the front and back bodice have the same dimensions, one drawing will serve for both; superimpose a line for the front neckline below the one defining the back neckline.

  A full width schematic may be needed for any design that is asymmetrical, or when necessary to show areas of decorative pattern or placement of pockets and button bands; see Design Details, below.

- Start the schematic by drawing two lines on the graph pa-

---

† The exceptions to this rule are when a measurement of the armhole is needed to design the sleeve cap, or when adding a border to a slope, such as for a V-neckline; see Armhole and Sleeve Cap Design, and V-Neckline Design, both below.

per in the shape of a "T." The vertical line represents the center of the garment, and the horizontal line represents the back neck at the highest point of the shoulders, or the top of the sleeve, or the waist of a skirt.

- All measurements are taken in relationship to the "T" drawn on the schematic. Length measurements are counted down the vertical line square by square and marked with a "point"; if there is a related width measurement, it is counted across from that position and marked with a second point. Place any marks for half- or quarter-inch measurements within a square. Once all measurements have been marked, draw lines to connect the points. Write length and width measurements adjacent to the relevant lines.

- Add notes regarding techniques and methods of construction if needed. Write down information on yarn, needle size, and gauge, and identify the decorative pattern you plan to use by title and page number if it is from a book, or attach a copy. And finally, if the first schematic you draw is a little the worse for wear by the time you finish, make a clean copy.

Drawing Schematics

The material below provides detailed, step-by-step instructions for how to take measurements and draw a schematic, first from a garment such as a sweater, next from a sewing pattern, and finally from the body.

Taking the measurements of the first two is quite similar, although there are certain steps taken to prepare a sewing pattern beforehand that are not needed for a knitting pattern. Taking the measurements of the body, of course, requires an entirely different approach.

However, the process of drawing the schematic is the same for all of them. Once you understand how to take measurements and make a schematic drawing, you can apply the same general concepts to measuring anything you want to make—you could, for instance, copy the dimensions of a handbag, a stuffed toy, or even measure your dog for a sweater.

❖ *Schematics from Garments*

The following instructions cover how to measure a simple, pullover-style sweater and draw the schematic as you do so. Once you understand how this is done, you can apply the basic principles to any type of garment, knitted or woven, even if the shaping is more complex. And as you will see, the same approach is used to measure sewing patterns, and is similar to how you would measure an individual, and then record the information, both of which are discussed below.

Measuring and Drawing a Bodice

1. **Back Neck Width:** Measure garment between two highest points of shoulders, straight across back neck (ignore any back neck shaping, if present). Divide by 2.

   On schematic, mark Center Back Neck Point at top of "T," and then count squares across equal to half width of neck and mark Shoulder/Neckline Point.

2. **Shoulder Width and Slope:** Position angle-rule down from Shoulder/Neckline Point and across to Shoulder/Armhole Point and measure length and width.

   On schematic, count squares down from Shoulder/Neckline Point and across to mark Shoulder/Armhole Point.

3. **Front Neckline Depth:** Measure from Center Back Neck Point to lowest point of Front Neckline (do not include any collar or ribbing).

   On schematic, count squares down vertical line and mark Neckline Depth Point.

4. **Upper Chest Width:** If armhole is shaped, position angle-rule down from Center Back Neck Point and across to narrowest part of armhole and measure length and width. Or, measure between armholes at narrowest point and divide by 2.

   On schematic, count squares down and across to mark Upper Chest Width Point.

5. **Underarm Width:** Position angle-rule down from Center Back Neck Point and across to widest point of garment at underarm and measure length and width. Or, measure full width of garment at underarm and divide by 2.

   On schematic, count squares down and across to mark Underarm Width Point.

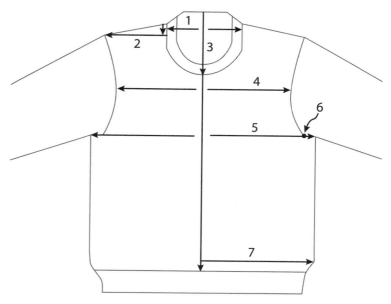

Measurements of Garment Bodice.

6. Inner Underarm Width: On schematic, count back one square (more or less depending on garment style) from Underarm Width Point and mark Inner Underarm Point. If garment is large and armhole is deeply curved, measure horizontal portion at underarm and mark width on schematic.

7. Full Bodice Length and Lower Edge Width: Measure down from Center Back Neck Point and then across to side of garment; do not include ribbing, if present.

   On schematic, count squares down and mark Full Bodice Length Point, and then count squares across and mark Lower Edge Width Point.

Completing the Bodice Schematic

Draw in all horizontal and vertical lines to connect the points, as follows:

1. Draw a slope from Shoulder/Neckline Point to Shoulder/Armhole Point.
2. Draw horizontal line between Underarm Width Point and Inner Underarm Point.
3. Draw a slope or a curve down from Shoulder/Armhole Point to within a few squares of Inner Underarm Point, and then draw a deep curve between those two points to complete armhole.

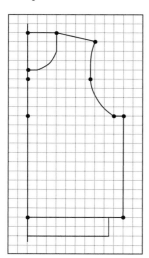

Draft Schematic of a Bodice, showing measurement points.

4. Draw horizontal line from Full Bodice Length Point to Lower Edge Width Point.
5. Draw vertical or sloped line down from Underarm Width Point to Lower Edge Width Point.
6. To draw in the neckline, work in one of the following ways:
   • For a curved neckline, draw 1- to 2-inch vertical line down from Shoulder/Neckline Point, and 2- to 3-inch horizontal line across from Neckline Depth Point and curve corner to join two lines.

   • For V-neckline, draw vertical line down 1 to 2 inches from Shoulder/Neckline Point, and then draw slope from there to Neckline Depth Point.

For more information in regard to Step 3, see Armhole and Sleeve Cap Design, below. Also see the information regarding the Raglan Shoulder style, which should make it clear how to measure a garment with that sleeve style.

Measuring and Drawing a Sleeve

The next step is to make a schematic drawing of one vertical half of the sleeve, just as you did for the bodice.

A sleeve is divided into two main areas: the lower sleeve, between wrist and underarm, and the sleeve cap, between underarm and shoulder. In most garments, the sleeve cap has a roughly triangular shape, with sloped or curved sides.

To begin, draw the "T" lines on the graph paper and work as follows:

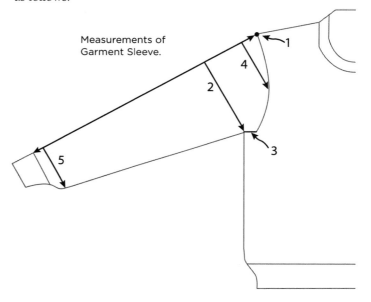

Measurements of Garment Sleeve.

1. Sleeve Cap Top Width: Measure flat area at top of cap and divide in half.

   On schematic, count across from top of vertical line and mark Cap Top Width Point.
2. Sleeve Cap Length and Underarm Width: Set angle-rule down along fold of sleeve and across to underarm; measure both length and width.

   On schematic, count squares down vertical line from top and then across to mark Underarm Width Point.
3. Inner Underarm Point: Count one square back from Underarm Width Point and mark (or use measurement equal to one used for bodice).
4. Sleeve Cap Midpoint: For shaped cap, measure from Sleeve Cap top to Inner Underarm Point and divide by 2; set

angle-rule across from this point and up along fold of sleeve at center of cap and measure length and width.

On schematic, count squares down vertical line for length and across to mark Cap Midpoint.

5. Full Sleeve Length and Lower Edge Width: Measure down along fold from where sleeve meets shoulder to lower edge above ribbing, if present, and across to measure width of sleeve.

On schematic, count measurement down along vertical line of schematic and mark full Sleeve Length Point, and then across to mark Lower Edge Width Point.

Completing the Sleeve Schematic

1. Draw sloped line from Sleeve Cap Top Width to Inner Underarm Point.
2. Draw horizontal line between Underarm Width Point and Inner Underarm Point.
3. Draw sloped line from Underarm Width Point to Lower Edge Width Point.
4. Draw horizontal line from Sleeve Length Point to Lower Edge Width Point.

If sleeve cap is shaped, draw S-curve out between Sleeve Cap Top Width to Sleeve Cap Midpoint, and somewhat deeper curve between that point and Inner Underarm Point.

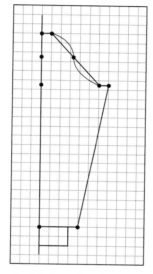

Draft Schematic of a Sleeve. Dots are measurement points.

❖ Schematics from Written Patterns

If you plan to work from a published knitting pattern that does not provide a schematic, you might want to consider drawing one from the written instructions before you begin to work. This will allow you to check the size and shape of the pattern, discover errors, and determine if you need to make any alterations.

To draw a schematic from the pattern, "knit" it onto the graph paper. If necessary, use the gauge provided by the pattern to convert the number of stitches and rows specified in the pattern into horizontal and vertical measurements in inches (see Calculations for Pattern Design).

Next, draw the "T" lines on graph paper, and count out these measurements, one square per inch, mark the relevant points, and connect the dots, just as described above.

❖ Schematics from Sewing Patterns

The instructions provided above for how to measure a garment and draw the schematic serve equally well for taking the measurements from a sewing pattern. While these instructions focus entirely on working with a sewing pattern for a garment like a sweater, the basic concepts apply equally to patterns for accessories such as hats, gloves, and handbags, as well as for toys, or household items like pillow covers.

A sewn garment is constructed in a markedly different way from a knitted one, and it is important to analyze the pattern carefully before you start in order to decide how it needs to be adapted for this purpose.

For instance, sewing patterns include a wide allowance for selvedges along all seams, while for a knit all that is needed is one extra stitch, and some seams can be eliminated entirely. Similarly, hems and facings are either not needed or can be simplified in a knitted fabric.

Sewn garments often have a greater variety of separate pieces than would typically be used for a knitted one. These may be necessary to refine the fit, introduce stylistic details, or as a means of finishing the raw edges of a woven fabric—think of princess seams, darts, peplums, and plackets. In a hand-knit fabric, these aspects of a design are more often done as an integral part of the construction.

If you are not familiar with sewing, it is best to start with a simple style. Sewing pattern instructions always include schematic drawings of the pattern pieces so you can see the shape of each one. This will give you a good idea of whether the pattern is suitable for a knit before you purchase it.

However, once you gain confidence working with sewing patterns, you will find you can adapt almost any pattern regardless of how complex the design might be. A few tips on basic alterations are included here, but for anything more extensive, you may want to refer to an instruction book on sewing pattern alterations. Also keep in mind that you do not need to copy the pattern exactly, or even use all of it; you may want to borrow only some elements of a design, such as the sleeve and armhole proportions or an interesting neckline and collar style.†

---

† If you want to sell a knitting pattern that you developed on the basis of a generic sewing pattern (such as a basic pullover or cardigan), this would not be considered a violation of copyright; first, because designs of that kind are commonplace and, second, because you will have substantially altered the end product. However, if the sewing pattern was done by a known garment designer, you could be in violation of copyright if you sold a pattern that retained enough elements of the original for it to be recognizable as being the work of that designer. To avoid this, alter the proportions, color, pattern, and design details (such as a collar), to the point where the original pattern that served as a source of inspiration has been transformed into your own, unique design.

When sewing, it is customary to make a sample garment out of inexpensive material such as muslin so it can be tried on for fit. This may seem like too much trouble, but for a complex project, you may find it worth the time and effort, especially if you are altering the pattern. Alternatively, fuse the paper pattern to a piece of lightweight interfacing so it will be flexible and sturdy enough to pin or baste together, and then try it on.

The Pattern Pieces

Sewing pattern sizes are generally quite different from those of retail clothing; consult the index of the pattern book for the details on the body measurements and sizes before you purchase a pattern. Also, some pattern companies provide general guidance about "ease" allowances (the amount added to the body measurement for movement or style considerations), and this can give you a general idea of how the pattern will fit.

To begin, cut the sewing pieces apart roughly, outside the lines, just to separate them from the larger paper on which they are printed. Then, press the pieces with a warm, dry iron so they lie smooth and flat. You might want to trace a copy of the pattern to preserve the original in case you make a mistake or want to use it later for sewing; art supply stores sell rolls of inexpensive tracing paper in various widths.

Examine each piece carefully and study the sewing instructions to see how the garment is assembled. The itemized steps will reference a unique number printed on each pattern piece. You can safely ignore most details about how to sew and finish the seams—what is important is to look at how the pieces fit together. As you do so, begin to think about what aspects of the design may be necessary for a sewn garment, but not needed for a knitted one.

Pattern Lines

There are a variety of lines on a pattern, and it is important to familiarize yourself with what all of them mean.

- Many patterns include more than one size on a single sheet of paper. Mark the lines for your size in colored pen beforehand, or simply cut the pieces out along the size lines you want to use and ignore the others.
- Multi-size patterns make it possible to adjust the fit by redrawing pattern lines to blend two sizes together, and it is usually fairly self-evident how to do this. For instance, you might want to use one size line for the upper armhole, but redraw the lower portion of the line to connect it with a different size line for the bodice width at the underarm.
- Notice the "grain line" arrow on each pattern piece. On a woven fabric, the pattern would be positioned with this arrow aligned on a lengthwise thread; in a knitted fabric

this is equivalent to a column of stitches. All measurements of the pattern pieces should be taken parallel or perpendicular to the grain line.

- Some pattern pieces, usually the back bodice, are half width and the center line will be marked with arrows indicating it should be positioned on a lengthwise fold of the fabric. This reduces the amount of pinning and cutting that needs to be done. With a pattern piece of this kind, use the width measurement as is when drawing a half-width bodice schematic; double it for use in developing pattern instructions or for a full-width schematic.
- Seam lines will usually have one or more triangular notches on them; these serve as guides for lining up two pattern pieces at their edges.
- Woven fabrics require a selvedge (also called a seam allowance), which is normally ⅝ inch. For a hand knit, one column of stitches is adequate (see Selvedges), therefore, those on the sewing pattern can be eliminated. However, there are differences among various patterns in regard to how the selvedge is handled.

  Some patterns show two parallel lines at the edges; the outer one is the guide for cutting out the fabric, the inner one indicates where the piece will be sewn. The area in between is the width of the selvedge. For a knit pattern, either trace or cut piece out along the sewing lines, instead.

  Other patterns show only the cutting line (this is true of all multi-size patterns), and it will be necessary to draw the sewing line within the pattern, parallel to the cutting line. Using a transparent ruler, draw a line ⅝ inch in from the cutting line; swivel the ruler as necessary to trace curves. Cut or trace along the line you have drawn to eliminate the selvedge.

- Lines or dots will mark the position of pocket openings or patch pockets. Also, buttonholes are marked with short lines; button positions with an X.

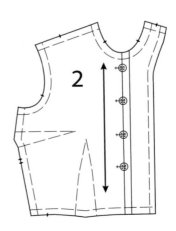

Typical Sewing Pattern. Inner dashed lines are sewing lines. Facing to right of buttons can be eliminated. Darts are optional.

- Darts are in the shape of a triangle; pleats have parallel lines with an arrow that shows the direction in which the fabric should be folded; gathering will be indicated by the same lines but will be marked "Gather." See Darts and Pleats, below, for more information on how to deal with these elements.

Seams

A knitted garment typically requires fewer seams than a woven one, or indeed can be made without any seams at all. Before you eliminate a seam, however, check to see how the pattern pieces relate to one another.

- Place the center front line on top of the center back line and put the shoulder seams together, lining up the notches. If the side seams also line up in a straightforward way, it is safe to eliminate the latter.
- If the side seam is shaped, you may want to straighten it and gather the extra width at the lower edge of the fabric with a ribbing, instead. When tracing the pattern, simply redraw the side line and extend the bottom line to meet it; do front and back the same.

  If you prefer to retain the shaping, it will be necessary to develop a pattern for increases placed at the side edges. If working circular, eliminate the seam and work the same pattern of increases within the fabric instead; see Steps and Points and/or Charting Slopes and Curves.
- Some patterns will have a shoulder seam offset from the natural shoulder line to the bodice front. If you prefer to have it centered at the top, line up the front and back patterns at the center and sides, and then fold the back shoulder extension into place over the front so the seam lines meet and pin it into place. Cut the back pattern piece along the fold to transfer the back extension to the front pattern piece.

Pattern Design Details

After examining how the pattern fits together, look at various design details with an eye to how they can be done in a knitted fabric (or whether they should be eliminated).

Hems, Facings, and Borders

The raw edges of a garment made from a woven fabric must be finished in some way. Folded hems and facings are common, or a facing may be a separate piece that is sewn on at a side edge. An edge might be encased in a binding, or a placket might both enclose the edge and extend beyond it. Before tracing the sewing pattern, decide how you want to handle these details; many are not needed for a knit, or can be done without

sewing. For more information about these design elements, see Hems, Facings, Pleats, and Tucks.

- If there is a hem on the sewing pattern, a foldline may be shown, or only the measurement of its depth may be indicated.
- To substitute a ribbing or some other decorative stitch pattern that lies flat, fold the pattern hemline into position. The folded edge is equivalent to the cast-on edge; make the ribbing equal to the measurement of the hem depth.
- Vertical facings, such as for a center front opening, may be shown as an extension of a pattern piece with the foldline marked. Either fold the facing into place on the inside of the pattern piece, or cut it off before tracing the pattern. In some cases, the facing will be a separate piece that is sewn into place; this can be ignored, in which case, eliminate the selvedge.
- Plackets and button bands can be knitted as one with the main fabric. Here again, they may be shown as an extension of the main pattern piece, in which case they can be folded into place and retained when you trace the lines.

  If the piece is separate, lay the placket seam line on top of the bodice seam line and pin or tape into place; trace the pieces as if they were one.

  Or, if you prefer to sew the placket to the edge or work it on picked-up stitches (see Picking Up Stitches), trace and measure placket piece separately.
- Many sewing patterns have a shaped back neckline, which is rarely done in a knitted pattern. This does improve the fit, but requires a pattern for the shaping. If it does not appear to be essential to the design, you can eliminate it by drawing a horizontal line between the Shoulder/Neckline Points, instead.

Yokes

If you are planning to use a shirt or jacket pattern, it may have a shoulder yoke at the back, and less often, at the front. You can either eliminate this, or incorporate it as a design detail without a seam.

- To remove the yoke, overlay the seam line of the yoke pattern piece (not the cutting line) on that of the lower front or back bodice piece; pin or tape into place and trace the two as if they were one.
- To retain the appearance of the yoke, consider using a different stitch or color pattern in that area to set it off. Pin yoke into place as described above and measure length from Center Back Neck Point; draw line on schematic to show where pattern will change.

Darts and Pleats

Darts are not often used in hand knits, but they are common in sewing patterns, especially for fitted styles. However, they can enhance the appearance of a knitted garment and may be essential to a good fit for someone with a large bust, and it is relatively easy to develop the knitting instructions for them; see Charts for Internal Shaping.

On the other hand, removing darts from a sewing pattern may require fairly extensive alterations; for the most part, how to do so is beyond the scope of this material. However, a basic explanation of how darts function can be found in the discussion of designing a knitting pattern for Darts, below, and this may help you make an alteration of this kind for a relatively simple design.

Pleats are also less common in hand knits, but can be effective if you are working with relatively thin yarns; for more information, see Hems, Facings, Pleats, and Tucks. The most likely place you will encounter pleats in a sewing pattern is at the bottom of a sleeve above a cuff. You can choose to retain them, but it is much simpler to replace the cuff with a ribbing that gathers the extra width of the sleeve instead of folding it out.

Sleeve Caps and Armholes

One of the great advantages of working with sewing patterns is that they provide an armhole and sleeve cap that you can be sure will fit well together.

However, these areas often have more complex shaping in a sewing pattern than is the case with a typical knitting pattern. The armhole may be deeply curved, and the sleeve cap often has an S-curve instead of a slope. While it might be tempting to straighten these lines to simplify working the pattern, they do improve the fit and appearance of the garment, and you will find a remarkably easy method for developing pattern instructions for something like this in Charting Slopes and Curves.

If the pattern has a raglan sleeve and armhole, notice that the sleeve cap covers not just the upper arm, but actually replaces the shoulder area of the bodice, and the top edge of the cap serves as a portion of the neckline. The top of the cap may also have a dart that serves to slope the shoulder and sleeve.

In addition, the armholes of the front and back bodice, as well as the sloped lines at the right and left sides of the sleeve cap, are of different lengths because of where they meet the neckline, and they will require separate pattern instructions. For more information on raglan design, see Bodice and Sleeve Design.

Pattern Alterations

If you have a sewing pattern that requires some alterations, try to make the adjustments in areas that have little shaping. You can either fold extra width or length out of the paper pattern, or cut it apart and spread it open to add the necessary amounts.

If you make an adjustment in one pattern piece, make an equivalent change in the one to which it will be joined. After making an alteration, set the two pieces side by side or pin them together to make sure they match.

Keep in mind that when dealing with one vertical half of a pattern, you will need to add or remove only one half of a measurement for an alteration of width. In other words, if you decide to add ½ inch to the width of the garment, alter the pattern piece by ¼ inch.

If possible, use an 18-inch-long clear plastic ruler with ⅛-inch marks (sold at sewing stores), and work as follows:

Bodice Alterations

Distribute width changes between the neck and shoulder areas. This need not be an even distribution; you might want to change the neckline less than the shoulder, or vice versa, depending upon body measurements. Length alterations are quite simple and can usually be done at the lower edge.

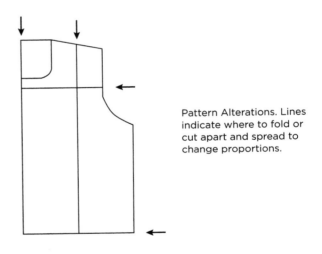

Pattern Alterations. Lines indicate where to fold or cut apart and spread to change proportions.

Neck Alterations

- To make neck narrower: Draw new center line parallel to original within pattern; either cut off latter or trace pattern along new line.
- To make neck area wider: Trace pattern, drawing new center line outside of original one.

Narrower Shoulder

1. Draw vertical line full length of pattern, centered on shoulder.
2. Set ruler on line with edge measuring width to be removed and draw second line parallel to first.
3. Fold pattern, bringing two lines together, and tape or glue into place.
4. Set ruler on Shoulder/Neckline Point and Shoulder/Armhole Point and redraw shoulder slope line.

Wider Shoulder

1. Draw vertical line centered on shoulder, as described above. Draw a horizontal line anywhere across pattern piece at right angle to grain line to act as guide.
2. Cut pattern piece apart along vertical line.
3. Place one pattern piece on tracing paper and tape or glue into place.
4. Set ruler on cut line and measure off amount to add; draw second line parallel to first.
5. Set other half of pattern piece against vertical line, use ruler to align two pieces on horizontal guide line, and tape or glue into place.
6. Redraw shoulder slope line as described above.

Length Alterations

- To add length to bodice, trace pattern and then add amount needed to lower edge; to reduce length, fold pattern up at bottom before tracing.
- If sides are shaped, set ruler at Underarm Width Point and Lower Edge Width Point and redraw sloped line.

Sleeve and Armhole Alterations

Sleeve length between underarm and lower edge can easily be changed just as for the bodice, as described above. However, changing the depth of an armhole or width of a sleeve is considerably more challenging because any change in one will require an equivalent change in the other.

While these instructions are intended for altering a sewing pattern prior to taking measurements and drawing the schematic, the same procedure can be followed to alter a schematic made from garment measurements, or one you designed on the basis of body measurements.

The instructions here assume the alteration begins with a change in the depth of the armhole (which is simpler to do), followed by a comparable change in the width of the sleeve; the concept is the same if you start by changing the width of the sleeve, instead.

To Lengthen Armhole

1. Draw horizontal line across armhole, as described above.
2. Cut pattern apart and paste or tape upper bodice piece to sheet of tracing paper. Draw an extension of vertical grain line on tracing paper to act as guide.
3. Place ruler along cut edge, measuring off amount to add, and draw second line on tracing paper, parallel to cut edge.
4. Place lower bodice piece along horizontal line, matching grain line, and paste into place.

To Shorten Armhole

1. Set ruler at narrowest part of armhole (Upper Chest Width) and draw horizontal line, or start midway between lowest point of neckline and top of deep curve at base of armhole.
2. Draw second line parallel to first defining amount to remove.
3. Bring lines together to fold out area and pin or tape into place.

To Make Sleeve Narrower

1. Set ruler down vertically, 3 to 4 inches from center of sleeve; if necessary, move closer to center if ruler does not fall within lower edge of sleeve. Draw line full length of sleeve.
2. Place ruler along sloped sleeve cap line and measure from top of vertical line drawn in Step 1 to mark amount folded out in armhole. From this point, draw second vertical line parallel to first.
3. Bring two lines together to fold out width.
4. Redraw slope between Inner Underarm Point and top of sleeve cap.

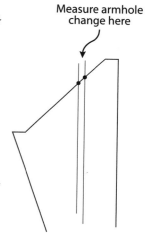

Measure armhole change here

Sleeve Alteration. Mark measurement of armhole alteration on this line.

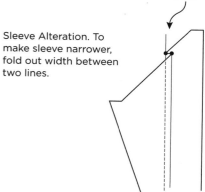

Fold

Sleeve Alteration. To make sleeve narrower, fold out width between two lines.

To Make Sleeve Wider

1. Draw vertical line as described in Step 1, above. Draw horizontal line at right angle to grain line to serve as guide.
2. Cut along vertical line, and paste one piece into place on tracing paper.
3. Extend ruler along sloped sleeve cap line past cut line, and mark measurement added to armhole on tracing paper.
4. Line up second pattern piece with mark on sleeve cap line and with horizontal guide line; paste into place.
5. Redraw slope between Inner Underarm Point and top of sleeve cap.

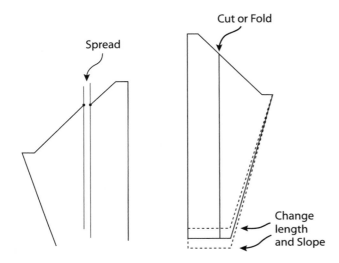

Sleeve Alteration. After altering sleeve length and/or width, redraw slope at side.

Sleeve Alteration. To make sleeve wider, cut pattern on line and spread apart.

Where to measure . . .

It is important to measure the amount to add or remove along the sloped seam line of the cap because it will be sewn to the armhole and the two must match.

If you want to change the width of the sleeve, but not the length of the armhole, it is necessary to redesign the sleeve proportions, as described in Bodice and Sleeve Design, below.

❖ *Schematic from Body Measurements*

An original design begins with measurements of the body, and you will find step-by-step instructions here for how to do this. If you are planning to publish your design, another option is to use standard garment industry measurements (which are readily available), or those found in the appendix of any sewing pattern catalog. However, if you are making something for an individual, whether it is an original design or an alteration of an existing pattern, it is always best to take measurements so you can customize the fit.

The person to be measured should wear their usual undergarments and form-fitting clothing such as a leotard or T-shirt. Also have them wear a narrow belt, or tie a tape or cord around the natural waistline. You will need a cloth tape measure and a straight ruler. You may also find it helpful to have some masking tape or tailor's chalk to mark the clothing at key points as guides for the measurements.

As you take the measurements, you can write them down as a numbered list, or you might want to draw a rough draft of a body schematic, either while taking the measurements or afterward. Not only does this serve as a permanent graphic record of the information, but it can be a useful aid when developing a design. For instance, you can place a sheet of tracing paper on top of the body schematic and draw preliminary sketches as a way to test your ideas about the garment proportions and style.

However, body measurements only provide a starting point for a design. Before drawing the final schematic, you will need to add a minimum of extra width or length for comfort and movement; more may be added for stylistic reasons. This is called "ease," and you will find some general guidelines below regarding how much to add for different garment styles.

Torso and Hip Measurements

1. Back Neck Width: Drape tape measure around neck as if it were a scarf, with two ends hanging straight down in front. Face person and use ruler to measure width between two outer edges of tape.

   If the person has a broad neck or rounded upper back, position a whole number on the tape at one side of the neck and note the measurement at the same point on the opposite side; subtract smaller number from larger.
2. Front Neck Depth: With tape in position as above, hold ruler parallel to floor, just above two prominent bones at hollow of neck (the clavicles), and count down from number on tape at shoulder.

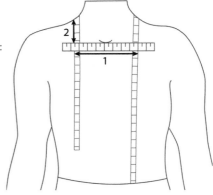

Neck Measurements: Step 1. Back Neck Width; Step 2. Front Neck Depth.

3. Shoulder Slope Depth: With tape in place around neck, position any whole number mark at shoulder. Hold ruler parallel to floor with upper edge level with top of shoulder where it meets the arm (if you find it helpful, place your hand flat on top of shoulder at arm and position top edge of ruler against palm). Count down from number on tape to top of ruler.

4. Waist Length: Pull one end of tape measure down to waistline and note measurement at shoulder; for women, this measurement should go over full bust.

5. Chest Point: With tape in position as in Step 4, count down from shoulder to most prominent point of chest.

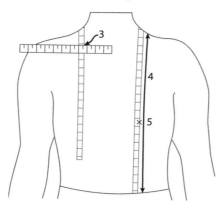

Torso Measurements: Step 3. Shoulder Slope Depth; Step 4. Waist Length; Step 5. Chest Point.

6. Armhole Depth: Set edge of ruler as high as possible in underarm, parallel to floor. Measure from top of shoulder at arm to top of ruler.

7. Upper Front/Back Chest Width: Set second ruler in other underarm as in Step 6 and measure across front chest from top of one ruler to the other; take same measurement across back.

   If you do not have two rulers, substitute stiff cardboard or stretch the tape across the chest and use your fingers to find the highest point where the underarm meets the chest.

8. Full Chest/Bust: Place tape under arms at widest part of chest/bust, position it parallel to floor and measure circumference.

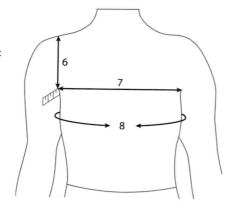

Torso Measurements: Step 6. Armhole Depth. Step 7. Upper Front/Back Chest Width. Step 8. Full Chest/Bust.

9. Center Back Length: Have person bend head down and locate prominent bone at base of back neck; measure from there to waist.

   Alternatively, if person is wearing T-shirt, measure down from bottom of neckline trim. Or, if you have two tape measures, leave one around neck as described above, and measure from top of tape to waist.

10. Shoulder-to-Shoulder: Measure straight across widest point of shoulders at base of neck. If upper back is rounded, take separate measurements of front and back.

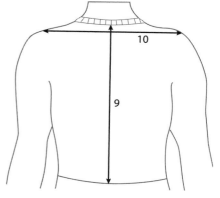

Back Measurements: Step 9. Center Back Length. Step 10. Shoulder-to-Shoulder.

11. Waist: Measure circumference of body at natural waistline.

12. High Hip Length and Width: Locate pelvic bones on each side of abdomen and mark with piece of masking tape or chalk; measure straight down to mark or tape from waistline. Place measuring tape parallel to floor at chalk line or masking tape, and measure body circumference. If suitable, take separate front and back measurements between side seams of garment being worn.

13. Full Hip Length and Width: Locate most prominent point of back or side hip and mark with piece of masking

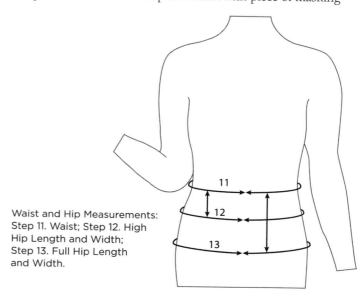

Waist and Hip Measurements: Step 11. Waist; Step 12. High Hip Length and Width; Step 13. Full Hip Length and Width.

tape or chalk as in Step 12. Measure straight down from waistline to mark or top of tape. Position measuring tape parallel to floor at chalk mark or masking tape and measure circumference. If suitable, take separate front and back measurements between side seams of garment.

Arm Measurements

1. Neck-to-Wrist: The most useful length measurement for the arm is taken from the center back neck to the wrist. To determine full sleeve length for any garment style, subtract garment shoulder width from this measurement.

   There are several alternatives for how to take this measurement on the body, depending upon whether you want to include a certain amount of Ease (see below):

   • With arm straight out to side, parallel to floor, measure from Center Back Neck, across shoulder and along arm to indentation between wrist bone and hand. This measurement will require addition of ease to sleeve length, see below.

   • Or, have person hold arm straight down at side with back of hand extended up, palm down and parallel to floor. Measure from center back neck, across top of shoulder, down arm to top of hand. Sleeve length may require additional ease depending upon garment style.

   • Alternatively, have person place hand on hip with elbow out to one side, and measure from Center Back Neck across shoulder and down over elbow to wrist bone. This adds adequate ease to sleeve length.

2. Upper Arm Circumference: Measure around widest part of upper arm, usually about 1 to 3 inches below highest point of underarm.

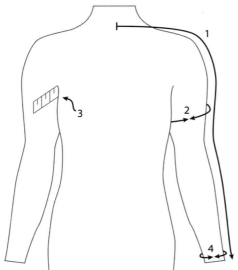

3. Underarm Width: With arm down at side, center ruler high in underarm as in Torso Measurements, Step 6. Note ruler numbers visible at front and back of arm; subtract smaller number from larger to find full underarm width, and divide by 4.

4. Wrist Circumference: Measure circumference over wrist bone; do not draw tape tight; divide by 2.

The measurement in Step 3 is a reasonable amount to use for the customary shaping at the base of the armhole on the front and back of the bodice, and at each side of a sleeve cap; the armhole is typically curved sharply in to meet this line. Most published patterns remove ½ to 1 inch in this area, but taking a measurement is more accurate for someone with large arms.

Ease Allowances

Ease is the difference between the body measurements and the garment measurements; it is determined before the schematic is drawn.

Movement Ease is the minimum amount of added length or width needed to allow for comfortable wear. Design Ease is quite arbitrary, and is based primarily on stylistic considerations.

Width Ease

• Movement Ease: For a slim fit that is close to the body, the rule of thumb is that you should be able to "pinch an inch" at each side of the bodice. Because this means you would be pinching the front and back of the fabric together, it is the equivalent of 2 inches of extra fabric at each side.

   This means you would add 4 inches to the Full Chest circumference, and 2 inches to the upper arm circumference. On a schematic showing one vertical half of the pattern, it would be an additional 1 inch in width.

• Design Ease: For average fit, add enough to pinch 2 inches—4 to 6 inches added to Full Chest measurement, and 2 to 4 inches for the upper arm circumference. For a loose fit, add 6 to 8 inches or more to the chest measurement, and 4 to 6 inches or more to the upper arm.

Negative Ease

• Items like mittens, socks, hats, or camisoles are often designed with Negative Ease, meaning that five or ten percent is subtracted from the body measurement. The garment will be slightly stretched in wear, and due to the natural elasticity of a knitted fabric, it will cling to the body; for more information, see Average Gauge for Negative Ease in Stitch Gauge.

Arm Measurements: Step 1. Neck-to-Wrist; Step 2. Upper Arm Circumference; Step 3. Underarm Width; Step 4. Wrist Circumference.

Length Ease or Blousing

A knitted garment with a ribbing that draws in to hug the body at hip, waist, or wrist will be more comfortable in wear if a small amount is added to the length of the bodice or sleeve as movement ease. This creates some blousing above the ribbing and allows the arm to be raised without disturbing the position of the garment at the hip or wrist; more can be added for stylistic reasons.

To determine the amount of ease to allow, first decide length of bodice between center back neck and where you want lower edge to sit at hip; then decide length of sleeve from shoulder to wrist. Next decide on depth of ribbing.

- For no blousing, include ribbing in overall bodice or sleeve length, drawing line within schematic to define depth above lower edge.
- For slight blousing, add half of ribbing depth measurement to bodice or sleeve length, drawing lines on schematic equidistant above and below the line for the lower edge.
- For average blousing, add full depth measurement of ribbing below lower edge line of bodice or sleeve schematic.

Existing Ease

If you are developing a design based on a sewing or published knitting pattern, and you want to check the fit or need to make an alteration of some kind, a comparison of pattern and body measurements is not helpful because there is no direct way to determine how much ease has been added.

The best approach is to ignore the overall pattern dimensions and focus on any difference between the actual body measurements (yours, or whoever you are knitting for) and those provided in the appendix of the pattern book.

In other words, if your bust measurement is 1 inch larger than that specified in the pattern book for the size, add 1 inch to the circumference of the garment. Divide the change equally, front and back, right and left sides, as described in Pattern Alterations, above. Whatever ease was added to the pattern will remain unaffected, as will the overall proportions of the design.

Bodice and Sleeve Design

Undoubtedly, the most challenging aspect of garment design is the upper bodice. Not only is this area the most visible part of a garment, but both function and appearance are equally important. The shoulders support the garment, and the armholes, sleeves, and neckline all converge on that horizontal line; all of these elements need to fit together smoothly in order for the garment to be attractive and comfortable.

Furthermore, these elements are all interrelated and have to be designed together—if the width of the neckline changes, so does the width of the shoulder; if the slope of the shoulder changes, the armhole will change; if the armhole changes, the width and shape of the sleeve will have to change as well.

In the material below, the basic shoulder styles are defined first, and this discussion includes an explanation of how each one affects the behavior of the garment in wear. This is followed by instructions for how to design the two most challenging styles, a set-in sleeve with a shaped armhole, and a raglan sleeve.

The material on sleeves and armholes is followed by information about how to customize the fit of a garment by adjusting the contours of the neckline, shoulder, and armhole, and by making use of darts. And finally, there is some information about adding borders to a V-neckline, which can be challenging to design.

❖ Shoulder Styles

There are four basic variations of the shoulder line, and each of them requires a different type of armhole and sleeve design. (In pattern drafting and tailoring, an armhole is often called an "armscye," an old and quaintly descriptive word derived from "arm's eye.")

The garment shoulder can match the natural shoulder width, it can be wider so it drops down the arm, it can be shorter so the top of the sleeve cups the outer shoulder, or it can be eliminated entirely as in a raglan design (where it is replaced by an extended sleeve cap).

As mentioned above, the overall sleeve length for any garment can be found by subtracting the garment shoulder width from a measurement taken from the center back neck to the wrist.

Straight Shoulder

The most basic sweater design is a tube knit straight up from waist to shoulder. The sleeve is another tube that may taper from shoulder to wrist. In the most radically simple versions, there is no shoulder slope, and the armhole is a vertical slit; a slight refinement is an armhole that is notched about an inch into the bodice.

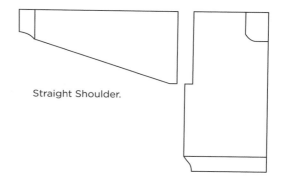

Straight Shoulder.

Because the shoulder is straight, with no slope, and neither the top of the sleeve nor the armhole is shaped, the former is attached at a right angle to the bodice. If the sleeve is narrow and the armhole relatively short, the garment will bunch up at the underarm when the arm is down at the side; one solution is to insert a gusset at the underarm to open up that area and add ease.

The style can be made considerably more comfortable by lengthening the armhole and making the sleeve wider so there is no fabric close under the arm. In a design of that kind, the upper bodice and sleeve will drape into soft folds when the arm is down at the side.

To draw a schematic for this style, the bodice is basically a rectangle; if you prefer, mark the Inner Underarm Point and draw a line straight up from there to define the shoulder width. The depth of the armhole is equal to half the width of the sleeve.

Drop Shoulder

As with the Straight Shoulder described above, in this design type the garment shoulder is wider than the shoulders of the body, extending down the arm an inch or more. The underarm point is dropped to provide some ease, and the armhole is slightly shaped with a slope or curve. The sleeve is relatively wide and has a shallow cap with sloped or slightly curved sides.

A deep armhole and wide sleeve assure there will be no fabric near the underarm. And because some areas of the fabric are removed by shaping the sleeve cap and armhole, the sleeve is attached at a slight angle to the bodice.

With the arm down, the fabric of the sleeve and bodice on either side of the armhole will have a pronounced vertical drape, and the bottom edge of the bodice will hang lower at the sides than at the center front. (If supported by a ribbing, this effect will be present, but not as obvious.)

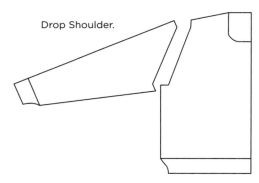

Drop Shoulder.

When the arm is raised, however, the lower side edge of the garment will also rise, and the wrist may be exposed. This happens because of the deep armhole, which means that the measurement from lower edge to underarm, and from underarm to wrist, is shorter on the garment than the equivalent measurement on the body.

A garment of this kind is comfortable to wear either on its own or over another garment, but it is bulky if worn underneath another garment unless it too has a generous armhole and sleeve.

Natural Shoulder

A garment designed with a sleeve that reaches the top of the arm will have a shoulder width that matches, or is narrower than, the body width.

The armhole is curved and shallow, fitting close at the underarm, and is intended for what is often called a "set-in" sleeve, which is relatively narrow and has a tall, triangular cap with curved, S-shaped sides. This shape allows the cap to be inserted into the space carved out of the bodice by the armhole shaping, and the sleeve will be set at a relatively steep angle.

While the S-shaped curve of armhole and cap are not essential to a forgiving knitted fabric, they enhance the fit of a garment with a relatively close fit, and developing the pattern instructions is easier to do than you might think (see Charting Slopes and Curves).

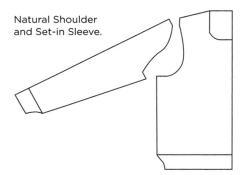

Natural Shoulder and Set-in Sleeve.

The upper portion of the curve adds a slight amount of width so the sleeve and bodice are not stretched across the upper arm and outermost portion of the shoulder. The lower portion of the curve removes a considerable amount of fabric near the underarm, making the sleeve comfortable even though it fits close to the body.

Also, because the garment underarm point is normally quite high, the measurements from lower bodice edge to underarm and from underarm to wrist more closely approach those of the equivalent body measurements. This provides the arm with a comfortable range of motion, and there will be little or no movement of the garment at the lower edge or at the wrist, as is seen in Drop Shoulder styles.

This sleeve and shoulder style is comfortable when worn beneath another garment such as a coat or jacket, but can only be worn over something else that is relatively thin and close fitting.

Raglan Shoulder

A raglan sleeve is joined to the bodice with a sloped or curved line between underarm and neckline. The sleeve cap is extended to cover the shoulder, eliminating a shoulder seam entirely. (In sewn garments, a raglan sleeve cap has a dart at the top to slope the shoulder and lower sleeve, but this is usually not done in a knit because the fabric will contour itself to the body somewhat.)

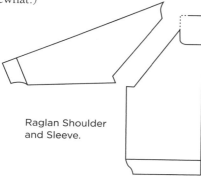

Raglan Shoulder
and Sleeve.

This style allows considerable variability in the design, as the armhole may be high at the underarm or dropped down, and the sleeve may be narrow or wide. In wear, the garment may show many of the same characteristics as either the dropped or natural shoulder garment design, depending upon the proportions and the location of the underarm point.

Because there is no seam or join of any kind at the armhole, a garment with a raglan sleeve allows very comfortable movement and adapts easily to different body proportions.

❖ *Armhole and Sleeve Cap Design*

Once you have decided on the type of shoulder line, the next step is to decide on the depth of the armhole, and the length and width of the sleeve. Because of the way all the parts relate, there are several variables, and changing a measurement of one will alter the dimensions of another.

The essential body measurement for sleeve length is from center back neck to wrist. Within this overall measurement, if the garment shoulder width is made narrower, the sleeve will have to be longer; if the shoulder is wider, the sleeve will be shorter.

It is usually fairly easy to decide on the relative measurements of shoulder width and sleeve length, but the dynamic relationship between armhole length, sleeve width, and shape of sleeve cap is more complex.

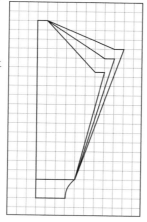

Relationship between
sleeve width and length
of cap.

For a Straight Shoulder Design with little or no armhole shaping, the armhole length is simply equal to half the width of the sleeve.

For a Drop Shoulder or Natural Shoulder Design, there are more options. Because the sloped sides of the cap are sewn to the armhole, sleeve width can be reduced somewhat. If the sleeve is narrower, the cap will be taller; if the sleeve is wider, the cap will be shorter.

Armhole depth and sleeve width are stylistic decisions and relatively easy to determine based on body measurements and ease. However, the proportions of the sleeve cap are more challenging to determine.

In the material below, you will find a simple, efficient, and accurate method to find the length needed for any sleeve cap. Once you have the measurements of sleeve width and sleeve cap length, you can develop a set of pattern instructions, either by using the formulas provided in the chapter Calculations for Pattern Design, or by using the even simpler graphic method described in Charted Garment Patterns.

The first set of instructions is for the design of a set-in sleeve cap for a garment with a natural shoulder and a shaped armhole; the second set is for a raglan sleeve.

Set-In Sleeve Design

First design the bodice and draw a schematic showing the proportions of the shoulder and armhole. Then use these measurements to make a half- or full-scale schematic drawing of just the armhole, from the Shoulder/Armhole Point to the Underarm Width Point so you can take an accurate measurement of its length.

To make the larger scale drawing, for every square on the bodice schematic, count off two squares for half-scale, or four squares for a full-scale diagram of the armhole. Work as follows:

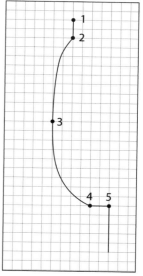

Shaped Armhole Drawing
for Set-in Sleeve Design.
Measure from #2 to #4
along curved line.

Shaped Armhole Drawing

1. Shoulder/Armhole Point: Mark point in center about an inch below top of paper.

2. Sleeve Cap Top: Count down from Shoulder/Armhole Point and mark amount that will be cast off at top of sleeve cap; usually about 1 inch (indicates where top of sleeve will be sewn into place at top of armhole).

3. Upper Chest Width Point: Count down from Shoulder/ Armhole Point and across to left to mark Upper Chest Width Point.

4. Armhole Length: From Shoulder/Armhole Point, count down and across to right to mark Inner Underarm Point.

5. Underarm Point: Count across from Inner Underarm Point and mark Underarm Width Point.

6. Draw Armhole Contour: Draw sloped or curved lines connecting Sleeve Cap Top Point, Upper Chest Width Point, and Inner Underarm Point.

7. Measure Armhole Contour: Place tape on edge, contoured to line of armhole; measure from Sleeve Cap Top Point, 2, to Inner Underarm Point, 4. This measurement equals length of slope on each side of sleeve cap.

Sleeve Cap Drawing

A sleeve cap has the shape of a triangle, and in order to write the pattern instructions for shaping it correctly you will need to know all three of its dimensions.

The sloped side of the sleeve cap will be sewn to the armhole, which can be measured as described above. The width of the sleeve is a design decision, based on upper arm circumference and ease. You can use this measurement and Stitch Gauge to find the number of stitches to decrease (if working the cap from the bottom up) or increase (if working from the top down).

However, what remains unknown is the length of the cap and how many rows to work. Fortunately, if you know any two of the measurements of a triangle (in this case, the length of the sloped side of the cap and the width of the sleeve), you can find the third.

There are two ways to do this; one method requires the use of a calculator with a square root function and some dim memories of high school geometry (see Triangles and Circles in the chapter Calculations for Pattern Design). The other is a purely mechanical approach that you can use if you do not have a calculator that can do a little algebra, nor any memory of geometry (or perhaps a distinct aversion to both).

Diagram Method for Sleeve Cap Length

If you do not have a calculator, or would rather not even try to use math formulas, here is a delightfully easy alternative. It does require another simple drawing, but this takes very little time to do and it will fit on the other side of the paper you used for the full-scale drawing of the armhole.

I guarantee that this simple, diagrammatic method will give the correct length cap for any sort of sleeve and armhole design you can think of, for all those you have yet to think of, and for any size or shape garment you might have occasion to make.

Draw the following diagram at the same scale as the Shaped Armhole Drawing, above.

1. Shoulder/Armhole Point: Draw line full length of paper, about an inch from left side.

2. Width at Top of Sleeve Cap: From first vertical line, count across half of width to be cast off at top of sleeve cap (usually about 1 inch), and mark Top Sleeve Cap Width. At this point, draw a second vertical line, to right of and parallel to first vertical line.

3. Baseline of Sleeve Cap at Underarm: Draw horizontal line about an inch from bottom of paper, at right angle to first line and full width of paper.

4. Sleeve Width: Start at intersection of horizontal line and left vertical line and count one-half sleeve width across to right and mark Underarm Width Point.

5. Underarm Width: From this point, count back along baseline width for portion cast off at underarm (usually about 1 inch) and mark Inner Underarm Point.

6. Draw Armhole Length Slope: Place the 0 mark of a ruler at Inner Underarm Point. Hold that end of ruler securely in position, and pivot upper end down along right vertical parallel line until you reach measurement on ruler of armhole length taken from full-scale drawing, above; draw sloped line to represent side of sleeve cap.

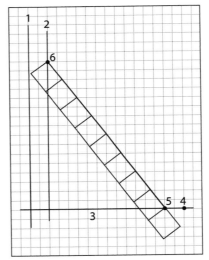

Diagram Method for Sleeve Cap Length: Step 6. Slope ruler down between Inner Underarm Point #5 and line #2 to find slope of sleeve cap.

7. Top Cap Width: Draw a horizontal line from top of slope to left vertical line to define flat portion cast off at top of sleeve cap.

8. Length of Cap: Count squares or measure from Center Top Point to baseline to find length of cap.

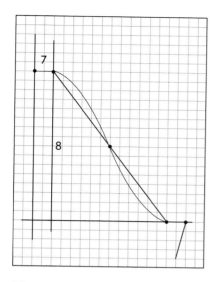

Diagram Method for Sleeve Cap Length. Draw in slope and curve for sleeve cap; line #7 is top of cap at shoulder; line #8 is length of cap.

Diagram Method for Cap Width and Length

If you are uncertain about how wide you want the sleeve to be, it is also possible to use this system to find both width and cap length at the same time. Graph paper with a 1-inch grid overlay makes it easy to count by inches.

1. Draw two vertical lines on left side of graph paper, as described in Steps 1–2, above; do not draw horizontal line at bottom of schematic.
2. Near top of page, draw horizontal line between two verticals. At intersection with left line, mark Center Top Cap Point; at intersection with right line mark Top Cap Width Point.
3. Place 0 mark of ruler at Top Cap Width Point and slope it down until cap length measurement from armhole intersects with desired sleeve width, less 1 inch; mark Inner Underarm Point.
4. Draw horizontal line through Inner Underarm Point—to left across two vertical lines to define base of sleeve cap, and to right about 1 inch; mark Underarm Width Point.

Raglan Sleeve Design

A raglan sleeve design is quite unlike that of a conventional armhole and sleeve. Because of where the front and back armhole meet the neckline, there will be four entirely different slopes on a pattern of this kind.

The triangle that defines the front and back armhole will have the same width, but a different length, which means each slope requires a separate pattern. The same is true of the triangle that defines the sleeve cap, and in addition, these measurements are entirely different from those of the front and back armholes.

In the raglan schematic shown here, the bodice back is positioned above the front and the sleeve is opposite where it will be attached to the armhole. Another option would have been to line them up side by side at the underarm, which is a bet-

ter orientation if you plan to work in the round. Having them aligned in ether way makes it easy to measure correctly and draw both schematics with the same dimensions.

Raglan Bodice Schematic

In most respects, the bodice schematic for a raglan sleeve design can be drawn in the conventional way—except, of course, that there is no shoulder. To allow for this, work as follows:

1. Count all length measurements from Center Back Neck Point along vertical line for front and back schematics.
2. Depth of Underarm Point is determined by style of garment: Add Shoulder Slope Depth and Armhole Depth, and then add length ease.
3. Count all width measurements across and mark Shoulder/Neckline Point, Lower Edge Width Point and Underarm Width and Inner Underarm Points.
4. Draw in lines to define schematic; upper area of bodice at shoulder will be missing.
5. Mark points where front and back sleeves meet neckline, usually about 1 inch in from Shoulder/Neckline Point on back neckline, and about 2 inches down from Shoulder/Neckline Point on front.

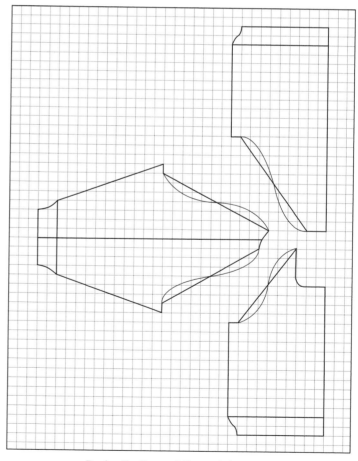

Raglan Bodice and Sleeve Schematic.

Raglan Sleeve Cap Design

A variation of the approach described above for finding the length of a set-in sleeve cap can also be used to design a raglan sleeve. However, because the front and back armholes have different measurements, the right and left sides of the cap are also different, and the top of the cap includes the contour of the front and back neckline. First draw schematics of the front and back armholes so you can measure them, and then design the sleeve cap.

Raglan Armhole Schematics

To measure the length of the front and back armhole slopes accurately, it is best to enlarge the schematic to half-scale with one square in grid equal to ½ inch, or even full scale with one square in grid equal to ¼ inch. You only need to draw the upper quadrant of the front and back bodice, between shoulder and underarm and between the center of the bodice and the underarm.

Once you have made the drawing, take the following measurements:

- Measure front armhole slope from Inner Underarm Point to side of neckline.
- Measure back armhole slope from Inner Underarm Point to back neckline.

Raglan Cap Design

To draw the schematic of the raglan cap based on these measurements, work as follows:

1. Draw vertical line at center of paper; mark Shoulder/Neckline Point.
2. From Shoulder/Neckline Point, count squares across to right equal to number between Shoulder/Neckline Point, and Front Armhole/Neckline Point on front bodice schematic (usually 2 inches). From this point, draw second vertical line, parallel to first and full length of page.
3. From Shoulder/Neckline Point, count up and across to left (usually 1 inch), and mark Back Armhole/Neckline Point. Draw gently curved line from Front Armhole Neckline Point to Back Armhole/Neckline Point to define top of sleeve cap.
4. At bottom of paper, count squares across from first vertical line drawn in Step 1, to mark measurement equal to sleeve width at Inner Underarm Point from bodice schematic; draw a faint vertical line a few inches long to act as a guide.
5. Place 0 mark of ruler at Front Armhole/Neckline Point and swivel it down until length measurement of front bodice armhole meets vertical line drawn in Step 4; mark Inner Underarm Point and draw slope for right side of cap.
6. Draw horizontal line to right and left of Inner Underarm Point marked in Step 5 to define length of sleeve cap.

Count across to right and mark Underarm Width Point (usually 1 inch).

7. Count equal measurement across to left and mark Inner Underarm Point and Underarm Width Point for back of sleeve.
8. Draw slope from left Inner Underarm Point to Back Shoulder/Neckline Point.
9. Draw horizontal line between two Underarm Width Points; count up from this line to Shoulder/Neckline Point to find cap length.

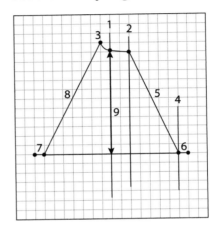

Design of Raglan Sleeve Cap.

The sloped or curved line drawn in Step 3 should equal the measurement of the area of the neckline that the top of the sleeve cap will occupy, usually 2 to 4 inches, depending on garment style and size. The back neck portion will wrap around the neck when the sleeve cap is attached to the back armhole.

As with the design of a set-in sleeve, a raglan design will fit better if the armhole and sleeve slopes are changed to a gentle S-curve. The outward curve provides ease over the widest part of the shoulder and upper arm, and the inward curve removes excess fabric at the underarm. This is more important if the garment underarm point is high and the sleeve is narrow.

To decide on sleeve width as you find cap length, work more or less as described above in Diagram Method for Cap Width and Length. Work as described above for Steps 1–3 but do not draw in vertical line in Step 4; simply decide on width as you swivel ruler down.

❖ Customized Fit

The above instructions for taking measurements of the body can be used to draw a schematic for any basic design. However, the most flattering garment is one that is customized to fit the individual. Some people have one arm longer than the other, one shoulder sloped more than the other, a particularly broad upper back, or a rounded back neck.

Here are a few tips for adjusting the fit for these sorts of things.

Broad Back

If you are designing a garment for someone who has a broad back, you can make the upper chest width wider there than in the front. To do this, use a single schematic for front and back, and simply draw in two different armhole lines, both converging at shoulder and underarm, but one wider than the other.

This not only provides width across the back, but rotates the entire armhole and upper sleeve slightly toward the front, making the garment more comfortable in wear.

Unless the difference in the two contours is extreme, this normally does not require any change in the shape of the sleeve cap. However, you might want to consider shifting the center point of the sleeve where it meets the shoulder about ¼ inch toward the back of the armhole to make the back slope of the sleeve slightly longer.

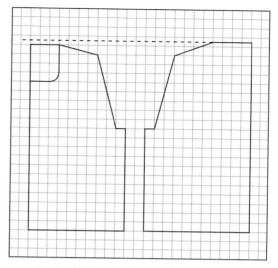

Bodice Design for Rounded Upper Back.
Back neckline is higher than front;
dotted line shows difference.

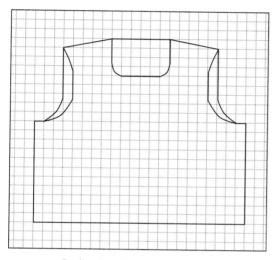

Bodice Design for Broad Back.
Back upper chest width is wider than front.

Rounded Upper Back

As discussed below, you can add darts to accommodate a rounded upper back, but these are somewhat challenging to design and work, and will be visible in the garment. For a simpler alteration, raise the back neck instead. This provides additional length at the center of the garment back so the lower edge is not drawn up.

Draw separate front and back bodice schematics.

1. On back bodice schematic, draw horizontal line for back neck ½ to 1 inch higher than on front.
2. Draw new slope from Shoulder/Neckline Point to Shoulder/Armhole Point.

Because the back shoulder slope is slightly steeper, it will also be ever so slightly longer, but the difference is minor and a knitted fabric is forgiving. Furthermore, as long as the front and back

shoulders have the same width, they will have the same number of stitches, so they can be seamed with Joinery Cast-Off.

You can combine this alteration with that shown above for a Broad Back, redrawing the center vertical line of the back schematic as needed. As long as the shoulder width, armhole length, and side seam length match, the front and back garment pieces will fit together.

Different Shoulder Slopes

If one shoulder is lower than the other, take separate measurements of the body to find the respective shoulder depth measurements.

Draw a full width schematic showing different shoulder slopes; this will lower the armhole on one side of the body relative to the other. Work as follows:

1. Draw first half of schematic showing higher Shoulder/ Armhole Point.
2. Draw second half of schematic starting with lower Shoulder/Armhole Point.
3. Count down from lowered Shoulder/Armhole Point and across to mark Underarm Width and Inner Underarm Points.

The slope of the two shoulders will be different, but the widths of the shoulders will be the same, which means they will have the same number of stitches and you can use Joinery Cast-Off for the seams.

Also, the proportions of the armhole should be the same on both sides of the schematic, one is simply set slightly lower to reflect the different shoulder slope.

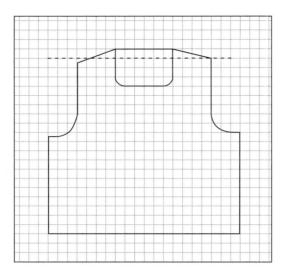

Bodice Design for Different Shoulder Slopes.
Dotted line shows difference.

Because the armhole is unchanged, there is no need to alter the shape of the sleeve cap. However, this alteration may change the length of the sleeve on the lowered side.

- Take separate measurements of right and left arms from center back neck to wrist and compare. If necessary, shorten sleeve that will be sewn to lowered armhole between wrist and underarm.

❖ *Darts*

Another way to refine the fit of a garment is through the use of darts, which serve to add volume to the interior. Darts are particularly useful for fitted styles and also serve to shape dimensional items such as hats, sock toes, and heels, or to sculpt items like stuffed toys.

A dart has a triangular shape, with the point facing into the fabric and the wide base at an edge or seam; the material within the triangle is removed. When a dart is made in a woven fabric, it is folded into place and sewn along the sloped side between point and base; in a knitted fabric, the area is removed with shaping techniques.

In a knitted fabric, vertical darts, as well as those that slope up at an angle, are done with a pattern of increases or decreases set in a line at the center of the dart. Horizontal darts are done with Short Rows. Once you have the measurements of the dart, you can develop a set of pattern instructions by using the formulas provided in the chapter Calculations for Pattern Design, or with the graphic method described in Charted Garment Patterns.

However a dart is made, the result is that a measurement taken within the fabric will be wider or longer than a parallel measurement taken at the edge. This volume added within the fabric causes it to bend or cup out, and it will no longer lie flat.

For the bustline, darts may be placed pointing up from the waistline, in from the side or armhole, or down from the shoulder—or even in all three positions. A "princess seam," which originates at the shoulder and ends at the waist, is, in effect, a double dart with the points meeting at the bust.

Small darts can also be used to add volume for a high rounded back. These are usually placed pointing down from the neckline and/or shoulder, but horizontal darts can also be hidden in the transition between the lower bodice and a yoke.

Another subtle and interesting use of a dart is at the elbow. This adds length to the back of the sleeve, which causes the lower half of the sleeve to bend forward in a manner that follows the natural line of the arm, and reduces strain on the fabric when the elbow is bent.

There are also several very common darts in garments that we rarely think of as such; one is the slope of the shoulder, another is a slope at the side seam between the lower edge and underarm of a bodice or sleeve, and another is the top curve of a sleeve cap, which also has the effect of a dart.

A gusset is a type of double dart in the form of two triangles set head-to-head entirely within a fabric. These are sometimes used to provide ease at the underarm, with half the gusset set within the bodice, and the other half above it, within the sleeve. Tiny gussets are also found in mittens or gloves, with one half set at the base of the thumb and the other within the hand.

Front Bodice Darts

If you think it is important to add darts to a bodice front, here is an extremely simplified method you can try.

First, take a circumference measurement *under* the bust. Draw a schematic showing a vertical half of the bodice and use that measurement, plus ease, to determine width of bodice.

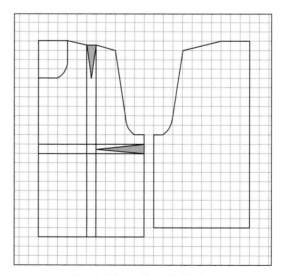

Front Schematic with Darts.
Front is longer and wider than back;
shaded areas are removed with shaping techniques.

Next, add darts to the pattern by using an approach similar to that described for making alterations in a sewing pattern; see Bodice Alterations, above. Work as follows:

1. Determine amount of width to add to interior by subtracting under-bust circumference from full-bust measurement; divide by 2. This is amount to add on front to schematic for one vertical dart.

2. Draw vertical line centered on shoulder and cut schematic apart on line. Spread two pieces apart by amount equal to measurement found in Step 1, and paste down on graph paper, matching grid lines.

3. Draw vertical shoulder dart centered on spread areas, as shown; darts in this location are normally 3 to 4 inches long.

4. Find amount of interior length to add to interior by subtracting Center Back Length from Front Shoulder/Neck to Waist Length (see Torso and Hip Measurements, Step 4). Add this length to lower edge of front schematic.

5. Draw horizontal line on pattern representing location of bust dart; usually 2 to 3 inches below underarm point.

6. Draw horizontal bust dart centered on this line, as shown. Depending upon size of item and amount of fullness added, a dart in this location is normally 4 to 6 inches long.

The front and back schematics will now have different dimensions. The front will be wider at the shoulder and longer at the side seam. However, when the dart pattern is worked in the fabric, the extra width and length will be removed from the front bodice edges so they equal those of the back bodice, and will be retained within the fabric where the volume is needed.

Technically, a dart would also be needed at the lower edge if the bodice ends at a fitted waistline; however, for most sweaters, the extra width can simply be gathered into a ribbing. Or if the garment is intended to hang straight, the extra width may be needed to cover the abdomen, but if not, the side seam can be sloped in to remove it.

To check the accuracy of your work and get a sense of what the effect will be in the garment, make a larger schematic (one square per half inch), cut it out and fold the darts into place. Take particular note of the shape of the garment at the edges; all seam lines should line up and have the same dimensions as before the change.

Back Bodice Darts

To add volume for a rounded upper back, make separate front and back schematics.

1. Draw front schematic according to design; mark length to waist on center line (Torso and Hip Measurements, Step 4).

2. Determine width to add to back by subtracting front upper chest width from back upper chest width and divide

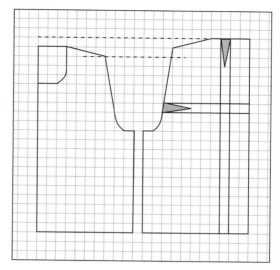

Back Bodice Darts. Back is wider and taller than front; dotted lines show difference. Shaded areas are removed with shaping techniques.

answer by 2; this is amount of change in one vertical half of pattern. Draw lower half of back schematic using this width; mark waist point at same length as in Step 1, above.

3. From back waist point, count up Center Back Length measurement (Torso and Hip Measurements, Step 9) and mark Center Back Neck Point.

4. Decide whether to add extra width to neck or shoulder, or both; in sample schematic shown, it is added at neck. Draw horizontal line to define neck width; draw parallel vertical lines within neck area to define width and location of dart.

5. From Shoulder/Neckline Point, draw in shoulder slope as for front schematic, and draw armhole from shoulder to underarm. Note that armhole depth is longer on back schematic.

6. Draw parallel horizontal lines just above curve of armhole; distance between lines is equal to difference in armhole depth and shows size and location of dart.

7. Draw neck and armhole darts centered between parallel lines. Neckline darts are usually no more than about 2 inches long, and both shoulder and armhole darts are normally 2 to 3 inches long (less if width added is small).

You might consider hiding the armhole dart by including it in the transition between the lower bodice and the equivalent of a yoke done in a different stitch or color pattern.

❖ V-Neckline Design

A border for a V-neckline can be designed in one of two ways. It can lie flat around the neck, or rise up around the back and sides of the neck. The two versions require a slightly different approach to drawing the schematic.

It is quite straightforward to determine the finished depth of the opening at the center front of a V-Neckline (with the border inserted), because this is a design decision. However, it takes a few more steps to determine the depth of the opening in the main fabric *before* the border is inserted. When making the bodice, you will need to separate the fabric at that point, and use a decrease pattern to shape the slope of the neck opening.

Interior Border for V-Neckline

This border is inserted *within* the bodice, replacing what would otherwise be part of the main fabric; it will lie flat around the neck.

1. Draw schematic of vertical half of front bodice.
2. Based on garment style, determine finished depth of V-neckline, counting down and across from Shoulder/Neckline Point; mark Center Front Neckline Point.
3. To define edge of border, start at Shoulder/Neckline Point and draw vertical line down, equal in length to depth of shoulder slope; from that point, draw sloped line to Center Front Neckline Point.
4. From Center Back Neckline Point, count down depth of border and draw line parallel to back neckline.
5. For inner front neckline edge of main fabric, place ruler at point where horizontal line drawn in Step 4 meets shoulder, and draw line down and then at a slope, parallel to lines drawn in Step 3.

You will need three patterns to make this neckline; one for the slope of the front neckline on the bodice, one for picking up the stitches around the opening for the border, and one for the miter pattern at the center front. See the information on both V-Necklines and Miters in Calculations for Pattern Design, and also see Charting a Gradual Slope.

To develop the pattern for the number of stitches to pick up for the border, you will need a measurement of the sloped edge of the main fabric. You can find this using the calculation in Formulas for Triangles in Calculations for Pattern Design, or simply make a full-scale drawing of the neckline opening and measure the front and back necklines.

The miter at the center front of the border is usually done with double decreases worked on every row of the border. However, a diagram of the miter makes it obvious that there are probably more stitches that should be removed than there are rows available. Fortunately, the natural slope of the shoulder will draw the border up slightly and take up some of the slack. And to make sure the border lies flat, try one of the following approaches:

- If the border will be a ribbing, which is common, determine the number of stitches needed by using the length of the inner edge and Average Gauge for Ribbing. As explained there, this will mean that the length at the outer edge of the border will be less than that at the inner edge because the latter is stretched out slightly; this also helps support the entire neckline so it keeps its shape.

To check how well this will work, find the number of stitches as described, and divide by the Relaxed Gauge to find the length of the outer edge. If it will be too tight, try the following, instead:

- If Average Gauge will make the border too tight, calculate the number of stitches based on the Relaxed Gauge, and then reduce the total by 5 to 10 percent.
- And/or, consider Regauging the border by reducing the needle size once or twice as you work it.

Exterior Border for V-Neckline

This version of a border for a V-neckline rises up around the sides and back of the neck; it fits more like a ribbing for a round neckline, which makes it slightly more complicated to draw.

1. Draw single schematic to represent both front and back bodice.
2. Count across from Shoulder/Neckline Point and mark depth of border on horizontal line representing back neckline.
3. Based on garment design, determine finished Center Front Neckline depth, count down from Center Back Neck and mark.
4. Draw faint horizontal line above and parallel to back neckline at a distance equal to depth of border (width is yet to be determined).

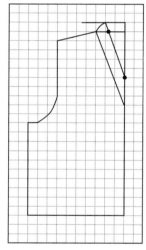

Exterior Border for V-Neckline.

5. For finished edge of front border, draw slope from mark made on back neckline in Step 2, down to mark made for Center Front Neckline depth in Step 3; and then extend slope up to meet horizontal line drawn in Step 4. Redraw horizontal line at defined width for finished edge of border at back neck.
6. For inner edge of neckline opening in main fabric, draw line parallel to slope drawn in Step 5 from Shoulder/Neckline Point to center front line.
7. Draw small angled line from Shoulder/Neckline Point up to point where slope drawn in Step 5 meets horizontal line drawn in Step 4.

CHAPTER 25

Calculations for Pattern Design

The chapter on Stitch Gauge provides essential information about how to make a sample of the fabric you plan to use for the design and find its gauge. The chapter on Measurements and Schematics discusses how to design a knitted garment by taking measurements and then making a small line drawing that shows its shape and dimensions.

Here you will learn to put the gauge and dimensions together and use some simple mathematical formulas to develop a set of pattern instructions to work from (see Written Garment Patterns for more information). Included are several examples of how the formulas can be applied to various aspects of garment design.

This material begins with definitions of the type of shaping most often done, followed by an introduction to the basic calculations used to find the number of stitches and rows needed for width and length; these are also used in one way or another to develop more specialized and complex shaping patterns. Also included is information about how to adjust the dimensions to accommodate the particular stitch or color pattern you want to use.

Following this is information about how to define an area to be shaped and to select the appropriate formulas needed to develop patterns for more complex areas like sleeves, armholes, shoulders, and necklines.

The basics of how to do this are the same whether you want to develop a written garment pattern or a charted one, which is a graphic version using symbols on a grid (see Charted Garment Patterns). While the written system relies entirely on the formulas discussed here, the charted system uses only the two most basic ones for length and width, which makes it considerably easier to use.

Even if you come to prefer the charted method for most purposes, it is important to understand what kinds of shaping can be done and how the formulas are applied in order to develop a pattern, and these things are explained here. Also, there may be times when you do not have the necessary graph paper at hand to make a chart, want only to check the accuracy of some pattern instructions, or need to make a few minor alterations.

The best approach is to skim through this material to gain an overview of the contents. The most important thing to understand is *what* the formulas do so you know which one to use in order to find what you need to know. Then go back and learn just those things that are useful to you as the need arises.

Shaping Concepts

The first task in developing a pattern for shaping any knitted item is to define the nature of the change—whether this will involve a slope or a curve at an edge, or will be internal to the fabric—and then to define the dimensions of the area affected.

With one exception, any area where a change takes place in the dimensions and shape of the fabric can be defined as a triangle. The base of the triangle is the width of the fabric, made up of stitches; the height of the triangle is the length of the fabric, made up of rows.

The shaping pattern creates the sloped side of the triangle. If a certain number of increases or decreases are spaced out over a certain number of rows, the number of stitches on the needle will gradually change and the slope will appear as the fabric gets wider or narrower. This means it is not necessary to know the angle of any slope, and rarely necessary to know its length (for the exceptions, see Triangles and Circles, below).

What is important is to understand which calculation and which numbers you need to use in order to get the answers needed in different circumstances. First, here are some definitions, and then an introduction to the formulas.

❖ *Types of Shaping*

There are four basic kinds of changes that can take place: a gradual slope, an acute slope, or a curve, all of which can be defined as a triangle; in addition to these, there can be a horizontal adjustment in width. The characteristics of the change, and where it takes place in the fabric, will determine both the pattern and the techniques that are used to work it.

Gradual Slopes

A gradual change in the dimensions of a fabric can be represented by a triangle that is taller than it is wide. A shaping pattern of this kind is done with increase and decrease techniques used no more frequently than one per row (most often, one per row at each side of the fabric). The sloped side edges of a sleeve are perhaps the most familiar example of this.

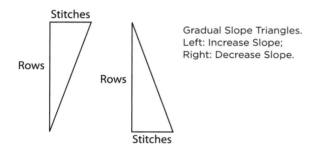

Gradual Slope Triangles.
Left: Increase Slope;
Right: Decrease Slope.

If the shaping techniques are worked a few stitches away from the edge, all of the stitch columns in between will also slope. This is sometimes done to create a decorative detail when shaping an armhole; see Shaping a Fabric.

If the shaping pattern is set within a three-dimensional fabric instead of a flat one, the result is quite different because the change is contained and the fabric will gain or lose volume at the interior. This can also have an effect at an upper or lower edge, but in most situations this is not obvious. For instance, vertical lines of shaping set within a hat will have an effect on the lower edge, but a ribbing will obscure this.

Acute Slopes

An acute slope is one where the triangle that defines the area is wider at the base than it is tall. This indicates that a large number of stitches need to be added or removed quickly, and using just one increase or decrease per row is insufficient. Instead, the shaping is done by Casting On or Casting Off, or with Short Rows, and each of these approaches will have a markedly different effect on the fabric.

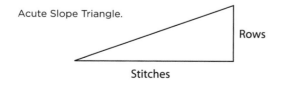

Acute Slope Triangle.

A familiar example of an acute change at an edge is the slope of a shoulder line, where casting off is used to remove groups of stitches at the beginning of several rows. The reverse of this is seen when stitches are cast on at a side edge for something like a dolman sleeve; see Side or Mid-Fabric Cast-Ons.

An acute slope can also be set within the fabric using the Short Row technique, where it will form the equivalent of a dart and create volume. Here again, the change will affect the side edge, but this will be hidden within the seam.

If repeated, the same kind of Short Row pattern can also be used to make contoured collars and scarves, and then the change is seen at the edge of the fabric, as well as within it; see diagram in Short Row Curves.

Curved Shaping

A curve in a knitted fabric actually consists of a combination of several short gradual and/or acute slopes set at different angles, one after the other. The soft, flexible nature of the knitted fabric blends this series of individual slopes into what looks like one smooth curve.

The most common areas of a garment design where curves appear are shaped armholes and sleeve caps, and you will find examples of how to develop a pattern for these below. Curves are also seen in designs for hats, sock toes, and mitten tips.

The overall area with a curved edge is first defined in the usual way as a triangle, as if you were going to develop a pattern for a straight slope. However, this overall area is then divided up into multiple smaller triangles, each of them with a different slope and each of them requiring its own pattern.

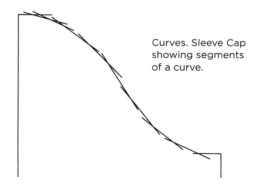

Curves. Sleeve Cap showing segments of a curve.

Working out the pattern for a basic curve using the calculations described below requires quite a few steps, and it must be said that it is far easier to do this with the charted system described in the next chapter. Nevertheless, there may be times when you will want or need to develop a pattern in this way, and knowing how to do so will enhance your understanding of what is at work here.

Horizontal Shaping

A change of this kind is distributed evenly across the width of the fabric, instead of over the length.† The most common example of this is gathering, which is done by spacing multiple increases or decreases evenly across a row. (A similar effect can be achieved with the Regauging technique, which does not concern us here because no calculations are involved, but it will be familiar to you from the ribbings commonly placed at the lower edge of a bodice or sleeve.)

Paradoxically, the same type of shaping pattern can also be used to prevent gathering. A familiar application of this is when stitches are picked up along an edge to add a border of some kind (see Picking Up Stitches). Because the row gauge of the original fabric is unlikely to match the stitch gauge of the one that is added to it, increases or decreases are spaced evenly across a row before starting the new pattern so the two will be the same width.

A similar approach is used when several different stitch patterns are set in horizontal stripes or in large areas of a garment. Each of the patterns will have a unique gauge, and in order to maintain the fabric at the same width throughout, it is necessary to adjust the number of stitches on the needle when changing from one to the other.

Horizontal shaping can also be used to create a gradual change in volume if the pattern is repeated on several subsequent rows. This approach is sometimes used as a way to shape the crown of a hat, for instance. It is also seen in some sweater designs where it is employed to narrow the upper bodice and sleeve; in effect, the change in contour that would ordinarily be done at the armholes and sleeve cap is distributed evenly around the circumference of the garment, instead.

❖ *The Basic Formulas*

This material requires an understanding of no more than simple arithmetic and a little elementary geometry. The instructions are written in such a way that even if you are not comfortable with math, you can simply substitute the numbers needed for your project for those in the examples. Having a calculator at hand will make things as quick and painless as possible, although you could do any of this with paper and pencil.

Of course, formulas will not provide good answers unless you provide them with good numbers, so first a word about accuracy, dealing with fractions and decimals, and working with a calculator.

---

† Because no slope is involved, the concept of the triangle, discussed above, is not particularly useful when developing a written horizontal shaping pattern, but it is when using the charted method; see Charted Garment Patterns.

Tips for Doing the Math

Before going on to the details about the formulas and how to use them, here is some preliminary information regarding the kinds of numbers you will be working with and the type of calculator to use; if math is not your strong point, you should find this helpful.

Inches and Decimals

As discussed in Five Steps to Accurate Gauge, it is important to include any eighths of an inch when taking a measurement, whether that is of a garment or a gauge swatch. However, before the numbers can be entered into a calculator, they have to be converted to decimals (numbers based on tenths, instead of eighths).

Here is a list of fractions of an inch converted to their decimal equivalents:

$\frac{1}{8}$ = .125
$\frac{1}{4}$ = .25
$\frac{3}{8}$ = .375
$\frac{1}{2}$ = .5
$\frac{5}{8}$ = .625
$\frac{3}{4}$ = .75
$\frac{7}{8}$ = .875

If you do not have this list at hand, you can use your calculator to make the conversion by simply dividing the number to the left of the slash (the numerator) by the one to the right (the denominator). For instance, divide 1 by 8, or 3 by 8, etc.

The numbers to the right of a decimal point represent a percentage (a fraction) of something. The first number to the right of the decimal point is a tenth, the second is a hundredth, the third is a thousandth (you can safely ignore any numbers that appear to the right of the third one).

When using the formulas for stitch gauge, or when doing any calculation that includes a measurement, *use these decimal numbers exactly as shown*; your results will be far more accurate. For instance, if you measure something and find it is 20 and $\frac{3}{8}$ inches, you will substitute .375 for the $\frac{3}{8}$ and enter the number 20.375 into your calculator.

The answer, however, can be simplified, as discussed below.

Rounding Up or Down

It is customary to drop some of the numbers to the right of the decimal to make certain calculations easier; this is called "rounding," and how this is done determines how accurate the answer will be.

To find the Stitch Gauge, for instance, you would divide the number of stitches in a fabric by its width, and you might get an answer that includes several numbers to the right of the decimal point. However, a gauge is sufficiently accurate if you work with no more than the tenths, but those are *very* important (see Those little tenths . . . in the chapter Stitch Gauge). The result should look something like this: G=5.7/6.3, with stitches per inch written first and rows per inch second.

However, instead of just dropping any of the other numbers to the right of the tenth, round each one up or down first. Look at the number farthest to the right of the decimal; if it is below 5, drop it; if it is at or above 5, drop it and add 1 to the number to the left of it. Repeat with the number that is now farthest to the right.

For instance, if you have used the formula for gauge and get an answer like 6.273, simplify it as follows: The 3 at the right is less than 5, so simply drop it. The next number is 7, and since it is greater than 5, drop it and round the 2 up to 3. The number you will work with is then 6.3.

While you need to retain the decimals in the gauge and in any measurement in order to accurately determine the number of stitches or rows in any area of the pattern, if the *answer* contains a decimal, it has to be rounded up or down to a whole number because, of course, you cannot knit part of a stitch or part of a row.

So, to summarize, the rules are:

- Retain as many as three of the numbers to the right of the decimal point for a measurement.
- Round up to tenths for the Stitch or Row Gauge.
- Round up to whole numbers for stitches and rows.

Calculators

For most of the formulas described here, you can use a very basic calculator that does just simple math. However, the formulas for triangles and circles require a "scientific" calculator that has three important buttons, or "functions," that are used in basic geometry (which deals with the shapes and sizes of things). As you will see, all you need to do is enter the right numbers in the right sequence, as shown in the formulas below, and push the right buttons on the calculator, and it will provide you with the correct answer.

The first button needed is for the exponent, which looks like this: x^2. It is used to "square" a number; in other words, to multiply a number by itself. The second one is the square root button, which looks like this: $\sqrt{}$. The square root simply undoes an exponent, turning it back into the number that was multiplied by itself. And the third magic button is for "pi," which looks like this: π. It is used for any formula that involves a circle.

Many inexpensive calculators have these functions, but if you do not have one that does, most computers come with a calculator application (usually several types are included for specialized purposes; select the scientific calculator in the menu). You can download one, or use one on the web.

Defining the Area of Change

The development of any pattern begins with the basic formulas, below, which are used to determine the number of stitches and rows contained within the triangular area where the shaping will take place (see Types of Shaping, above). Here are the steps you will need to take before using any of the formulas.

1. Use stitch gauge and measurement from schematic to find number of stitches that will be on needle before change takes place.
2. Use same approach to find number of stitches that will be on needle after change takes place.
3. Subtract smaller number from larger to find how many stitches need to be added or removed.
4. Use row gauge and measurement from schematic to find number of rows over which change will take place.

The next steps in developing the particulars of a pattern depend upon what kind of shaping needs to be done.

Formulas for Width and Length

Regardless of how complicated the shape of any garment might be, developing any aspect of the pattern begins with finding how many stitches and rows are needed to make the fabric a particular width and length.

This is done using the first two formulas here; they are the only ones you will need to make a pattern for something in the shape of a square or rectangle. Variations of these basic formulas are also used to coordinate the number of stitches needed for length and width with the number needed for any decorative stitch or color pattern.

Width and Length

The two most basic formulas are used to find out how many stitches and rows are needed to make a fabric a particular width and length. They also appear as part of the multi-step formulas that are used to develop a pattern for shaping.

Width Formula

Stitch Gauge (Number of Stitches per Inch) × Width of Fabric = Number of Stitches in Width

Length Formula

Row Gauge (Number of Rows per Inch) × Length of Fabric = Number of Rows in Length

Variations on the Formula

You can switch the elements of the formulas around and divide to find other information. Width or length can be found by dividing the number of stitches or rows by the gauge. And, of course, gauge is found by dividing the number of stitches by width, or rows by length.

Pattern Repeats and Garment Dimensions

Any garment made with a stitch or color pattern will look far better if there are full, rather than partial repeats on either side of a seam or at the join between rounds. It is also more attractive to have a full repeat meet a neckline at the center front, or perhaps at the top of a sleeve because these areas are so visible in wear. And if you are making a flat, unseamed item such as a scarf, you will want full repeats on all four edges.

The difficulty is that pattern repeats come in a variety of sizes, and the number of stitches and rows needed to accommodate full repeats in the fabric is often not the same as the number of stitches and rows required for the length and width of the fabric based on the gauge.

If there is a discrepancy, which is common, it will be necessary to do a few more calculations to find out how many stitches and rows to add to or subtract from the length and width of the garment in order to accommodate full pattern repeats.

You will find more information about how to do this in Coordinating Stitch and Garment Patterns, along with illustrations that make clear what is needed, but here is how to do this using just the formulas:

Width Adjustment for Repeats

To find how many stitch repeats will fit into the number of stitches needed for width according to gauge, work as follows:

Number of Stitches for Width (or Circumference) ÷ Number of Stitches in Repeat = Number of Repeats

If you are using a calculator and the answer contains a decimal number, it represents a partial repeat—there are extra stitches, but not enough of them for a full repeat. (If you are using paper and pencil and long division, the answer may contain a remainder, which is the exact number of stitches that are left over.)

You must then decide whether it would be best not to include the extra stitches, making the fabric slightly narrower, or better to add more to accommodate a full repeat, making it wider. Which is preferable depends upon the size and style of the garment, how much ease is already built into the design, and how much bigger or smaller it would be if you did one or the other.

Here is how to find out what the difference would be so you can decide what to do:

1. Drop decimal number or remainder from answer and find number of stitches in width using whole repeats.

Number of Repeats × Stitches per Repeat = Stitches in Width

2. Find width of fabric with adjusted number of stitches.

Stitches in Width ÷ Stitch Gauge = Width of Fabric

If dropping the extra stitches would make the fabric too narrow, add enough stitches for another repeat in Step 1 and do the same calculations again to see how wide the fabric would then be.

Large repeats can be particularly problematic, because adding or removing enough stitches to have an even number of them can appreciably change the size of the garment. How to solve this depends upon the circumstances, but here are some suggestions:

- While unorthodox, you might consider using an uneven number of repeats in the circumference. This solution works reasonably well for a circular fabric, but not for one that is flat and will be seamed.

    In a circular fabric, the result would be two repeats on either side of the join between rounds on one side, but only a single repeat in the equivalent position on the other side of the garment (where a seam would be if you were working flat). This is unlikely to be noticeable, except at the underarm, where the pattern on each side would meet the sleeve in a different way.

    In a flat fabric, the seam would pass between two repeats on one side and through the center of a repeat on the other side; while a well-done seam could make this difficult to discern, it is not ideal.

- It is more common to solve a problem of this kind by making use of what are called "filler patterns" at the sides of the garment—little one- or two-stitch textured patterns such as Seed Stitch or Double Seed Stitch. These allow you to use the number of stitches required by the gauge and an even number of repeats, with the filler pattern occupying the extra stitches.

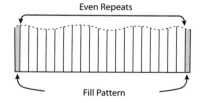

Repeats and Garment Dimensions. Add fill pattern at each side.

- Another possibility is to consider altering the primary stitch pattern slightly by adding or removing a stitch somewhere within the repeat. The best way to work out something like this is with a charted pattern; see Charted Stitch Patterns.

    Keep in mind that changing the number of stitches in a small repeat will make a large difference; if just one stitch is added or removed it will be multiplied by the number of repeats needed for the width. Changing the number of stitches in a larger repeat will have less of an effect; with fewer repeats across the width, the multiplier is smaller.

Length Adjustment for Repeats

Work in much the same way as described above to decide how many row repeats to use in the length of the item. For a bodice, as in the example here, you will want to find the number of rows from the bottom to the center front neckline; use a similar approach if you want to locate the pattern at the beginning of a yoke or at the top of a sleeve.

Use your schematic drawing to find the measurements needed, and work as follows:

1. Find length to neckline (or other design detail).

   Overall Length – Depth of Neckline =
   Length from Lower Edge to Neckline

2. Find number of rows to neckline.

   Length to Neckline × Row Gauge = Rows to Neckline

3. Find number of repeats that fit in length to neckline.

   Rows to Neckline ÷ Rows in Repeat = Number of Repeats

Here again, if the answer includes a decimal number, use the formulas described above for adjusting the width (substituting rows for stitches) to find what the difference in length would be if you used one repeat more or less.

You will find it easier to make length adjustments to accommodate row repeats than to adjust widths for stitch repeats. Here are some suggestions:

- If a half repeat of the pattern is attractive, consider using that at the neckline.
- Alternatively, a partial repeat at the bottom of a garment will be considerably less noticeable, especially if there is a ribbing.
- Consider the use of a filler pattern or just a few plain rows of Stockinette at the bottom.
- Also consider changing the size of the repeat by adding or removing one or more plain rows within it, or between repeats.

❖ Steps and Points

As described in Shaping Concepts, above, the formulas for width and length are the basis for all the other kinds of patterns that may be needed to shape a knitted fabric, such as those for slopes, curves, and horizontal changes in width.

The patterns for these kinds of things are done by means of what I call Steps and Points, which is both a way of describing how a particular type of change takes place in the fabric and a set of formulas that are the tools you can use to develop a pattern for any shape, no matter how complex.

It is really more accurate to describe a slope in a knitted fabric not as a smooth straight line, but as a series of steps,

and this also describes the nature of the pattern that is needed to create it.

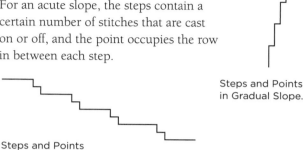

Steps and Points
in Gradual Slope.

Steps and Points
in Acute Slope.

- For a gradual slope, the steps are the rows worked with no change in width, and the points designate the rows where an increase or decrease is placed.
- For an acute slope, the steps contain a certain number of stitches that are cast on or off, and the point occupies the row in between each step.
- With a horizontal change, the steps consist of stitches worked plain, and the points designate stitches that are to be increased or decreased.

The formulas here are used to find how many stitches or rows are in each step, which in turn determines the location of the points. However, variations in the arrangement of steps and points may be necessary due to the particulars of the slope or its location, and the formulas need to be applied in a slightly different way to reflect this.

For instance, a gradual slope could begin or end with either a step or a point; an acute slope will always begin with a step, but need not end with one. Furthermore, the distribution of stitches or rows to the steps does not always work out evenly; when a formula produces a remainder, it means there are extras that need to be allocated to some of the steps.

These differences are quite easy to deal with in terms of the formulas, but it is important to recognize what is needed for a particular aspect of your design. The examples provided below show how to develop a pattern for specific garment areas, which will help make these things clear.

Steps and Points for Gradual Slopes

For a gradual slope, there is never more than one increase or decrease per row; the more plain rows there are between each shaping technique, the more gradual the slope will be.

The steps consist of the plain rows worked with no change in width, and the points are where the shaping is placed.

Basic Formula for Gradual Slope

For a basic pattern, work as follows:

Rows in Area of Change ÷ Stitches to Increase or
Decrease (Points) = Rows per Step

Variations for a Gradual Slope

In some patterns it is necessary to start with a step and end with a point, or vice versa, or even start and end with a step, or vice versa. Here are various ways to alter the basic formula to meet the particular circumstances.

More Points than Steps

Many gradual slope patterns begin and end with a point, but the customary way to write the pattern instructions for a slope specify working an increase or decrease on the *last* of a specified number of rows.

Therefore, it is necessary to work the row with the first point as a separate step; the remaining series starts with a step and ends with a point.

Steps and Points for Gradual Slope. More Points than Steps.

Work as follows:

Number of Points – 1 = Number of Steps

Number of Rows – 1 = Number of Rows Distributed to Steps

Number of Rows in Steps ÷ Number of Steps =
    Number of Rows per Step

The resulting instruction might read:

Decrease 1 stitch at beginning of next row, then decrease 1 stitch at beginning of every 4th row 8 times.

Equal Steps and Points

In some cases, a pattern will begin with a step and end with a point, or vice versa.

For instance, when shaping the lower half of a sleeve worked up from the wrist, the slope could begin immediately with an increase point on the first row, and end with a step at the underarm. In this case, ending the slope with a step is important because it positions the last increase a few rows below the underarm, away from where stitches will be cast off to start the armhole.

Steps and Points for Gradual Slope. Equal Steps and Points.

If the sleeve is worked from the top down, the sequence will start with a step and end with a point.

Either way, there are an equal number of steps and points in the series, which makes it easy to work out the distribution of rows, as follows:

Number of Rows ÷ Stitches to Increase or Decrease (Points) =
    Number of Rows per Step

The instructions for working from the wrist up are somewhat more challenging to write because you need to have a separate step for the increase on the first row, as well as one at the end.

An instruction might look something like this:

Increase 1 stitch at beginning of next row, then every 5th row 11 times; work 4 rows to underarm.

While it is not customary, the instruction could also be written as follows:

(Increase 1 stitch at beginning of next row, then work 4 rows plain), repeat 12 times.

If the sleeve is worked from the top down and the pattern is reversed, the instruction is much simpler to write:

Decrease 1 stitch at beginning of every 5th row 12 times.

More Steps than Points

Gradual slope patterns can also begin and end with a step; you might use this arrangement for a sleeve if you prefer to place the first increase well above the gathering caused by the ribbing, and also position the last one below the underarm.

Here is how to proceed:

Steps and Points for Gradual Slope. More Steps than Points.

Number of Stitches to Increase or Decrease (Points) + 1 = Number of Steps

Number of Rows ÷ Number of Steps =
    Number of Rows per Step

After finding how many rows are in each step, set one step aside to place at the end of the series and write the pattern:

Increase 1 stitch at beginning of every 7th row 10 times, work 7 rows plain.

Distributing Extra Rows

If there is a remainder in a calculation for a gradual slope, drop any numbers to the right of the decimal and rework the pattern as follows:

1. Find number of rows that can be distributed evenly to the steps.

Number of Rows per Step × Number of Steps =
    Number of Rows Distributed Evenly

2. Find number of extra rows.

Total Rows – Number of Rows Distributed Evenly =
    Extra Rows

3. Distribute one extra row to each step until all are absorbed.

The pattern might look something like:

Decrease 1 stitch at beginning of every 6th row 3 times,
then decrease 1 stitch at beginning of every 5th row 4 times.

In other words, there were three extra rows in the example and they were distributed to the first three steps.

A distribution of this kind produces steps of different sizes and, therefore, two different slopes. If this would be noticeable in the garment, it might be better to intersperse the steps of different sizes across the length of the slope, instead of placing all the steps of one size at the beginning and the others at the end.

For instance, in the above example, you could work one step with 5 rows, then one with 6 rows, and continue to alternate them in this way to even out the slope.

This is a more difficult instruction to develop and to write using the method described here, but it would appear automatically in a charted garment pattern, and would also be easier to follow as you work.

Steps and Points for Acute Slopes

A step in an acute slope consists of a group of stitches that are cast on or off, or set aside with Short Rows, and there is a turning point at the end of each row in between.

Basic Formula for Acute Slope

To develop the pattern for a slope of this kind, work as follows:

Number of Stitches to Add or Remove ÷ Rows in Area of Change =
Stitches per Step

When casting off, two rows are needed for each step: the step is done at the beginning of one row, and then another row is needed to work back to the same edge where the work is turned to work the next step. To make a smooth transition between steps, one stitch is normally decreased at the turning point at the end of the second row before turning to work the next step. Because this decrease is on a different row, the points are separated from the steps in the instructions.

When casting on at a side edge, or when using Short Rows within the fabric, the steps are worked at the end of a row instead of at the beginning, and the first stitch after the turn is slipped to smooth out the transition between rows. Because the Slip stitch causes no change in the number of stitches on the needle, there is no need to separate it out in the formula.

Depending on the situation, the series may begin with a step and end with a point, meaning there would be an equal number of them, or the pattern can begin and end with a step, and there will be one fewer point, as in this example.

Variations for an Acute Slope

Here are the formulas for developing a pattern for an acute slope using a cast-on or cast-off technique, or Short Rows.

Cast-Off for Acute Slope

1. Find the number of steps (one every other row):

Rows ÷ 2 = Number of Steps

2. Find the number of turning points:

Number of Steps − 1 = Number of Points

3. Separate out the number of stitches needed for the decreases at each point to find the number that will be distributed to the steps:

Number of Stitches − Number of Points =
Stitches Distributed to Steps

4. Find how many stitches are in each step:

Stitches Distributed to Steps ÷ Number of Steps =
Stitches per Step

The pattern might read something like:

(Cast off 4 stitches at beginning of row, turn; decrease
1 stitch at end of row); rep between parentheses 4 times;
cast off last step of 4 stitches.

Or it might say:

*Cast off 4 stitches at beginning of next row, turn; decrease
1 stitch at end of next row*; repeat between * and * 4 times;
cast off remaining 4 stitches.

Or more briefly:

Cast Off: 4-1-4-1-4-1-4-1-4.

If you need a pattern that ends with a point, it will have an even number of steps and points; use the same formula above, but omit Step 2.

Cast-On or Short Rows for Acute Slope

If you are casting on an acute slope, or developing a slope pattern for Short Rows, use the same approach as for casting off, but skip Steps 2 and 3 because there are no decreases needed at the turning points. A stitch is typically slipped after the turn, but this does not change the number of stitches in each step.

The pattern might look something like this:

5(Cast on 4 stitches at end of row, turn, Slip 1,
continue to end of row, turn). 20 stitches cast on.

In this type of pattern notation, the number 5 before the

parentheses means to work the instructions within five times; it is the same as having "5 times" after the instructions.

Distributing Extra Stitches

If the number of stitches does not divide evenly into the number of steps, it means extra stitches need to be distributed. If you have done this with arithmetic, the remainder equals the number of extra stitches; if you have used a calculator, drop the numbers to the right of the decimal point and work as follows:

1. Find number of stitches that can be distributed evenly to steps.

   Stitches per Step × Number of Steps =
   Stitches Distributed Evenly

2. Subtract number of evenly distributed stitches from total number needed for slope.

   Total Stitches – Evenly Distributed Stitches = Extra Stitches

3. Distribute one extra stitch to as many steps as necessary.

In other words, if there were 26 stitches to be distributed to 4 steps, there would be 6 stitches in each step with two stitches left over.

To distribute them, put one extra stitch in each of two steps; the pattern would then read something like:

Cast on 7 stitches at end of every other row 2 times,
6 stitches at end of next row; always Slip first stitch
after turning between steps.

Or, briefly:

Cast On: 7-7-6.

Steps and Points for Horizontal Shaping

When shaping is distributed across a single row, the points are where the shaping techniques are placed, and the steps consist of the plain stitches in between. In a change of this kind, adjacent stitch columns close over a space where a stitch was removed with a decrease, or they spread apart to accommodate a new stitch added with an increase.

The arrangement of steps and points for horizontal shaping depends entirely on whether you are working flat or in the round. In addition, the pattern needs to be modified depending upon what kind of shaping technique you will be using.

For instance, a decrease involves two stitches, while an increase could be worked between two stitches or into one, and the formula needs to be adjusted accordingly.

As with slopes, if there are extra stitches, either distribute them equally to as many steps as necessary at the beginning and end of the row, or evenly across the entire row.

Formula for Horizontal Shaping in a Flat Fabric

If you are making a flat fabric, the pattern will start and end with a step so the first and last shaping techniques are away from the seams. This means there will be one fewer point than there are steps.

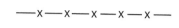

Steps and Points for Horizontal Shaping in a Flat Fabric.

Increase Pattern

If working increases into stitches, separate them from all the others:

Total Stitches – Number of Increases (Points) =
Stitches Distributed to Steps

Points + 1 = Number of Steps

Stitches Distributed to Steps ÷ Number of Steps =
Stitches per Step

If working increases between stitches, do not subtract points from total stitches.

After distributing the stitches to the steps, separate one step from the others and place it at the end of the pattern sequence.

In the briefest type of pattern notation, a pattern of this kind might read as follows:

10(k4, incr1), end k4.

Decrease Pattern

Work as above, but subtract two stitches for each point.

After reserving one step for the end of the sequence, the pattern might look something like:

Work decrease on every 5th and 6th stitch across row;
end Knit 4.

In other words, you would work 4 stitches plain and then work the decrease on the next two stitches.

Or, the instruction might be written more briefly:

K4, K2tog, repeat betw * and * across row, end K4.

Formula for Horizontal Shaping in a Circular Fabric

If you are making a circular fabric, the pattern will start with a step and end with a point, which means there will be an equal number of both. The last point falls at the end of the round, followed by the first step at the beginning of the next round.

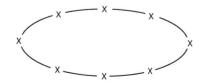

Steps and Points for Horizontal Shaping in a Circular Fabric.

Increase Pattern

- For an increase between two stitches, divide total stitches by number of points to find number of stitches per step.
- For an increase into a stitch, subtract one stitch for each point, and divide remaining stitches to steps.

Decrease Pattern

- Subtract two stitches for each point; divide remaining stitches by number of points to find number of stitches per step.

Triangles and Circles

While fairly uncommon, some designs require the measurement of a slope. One of these is for the design of a sleeve cap, where a measurement of the sloped armhole is needed. Another is the pattern for a border on a V-neckline (see V-Neckline Design), and there is also one approach to making a triangular shawl design where this is also needed.

Unfortunately, a typical schematic drawing is not large enough to use for an accurate measurement of a slope. One solution is to make a full- or half-scale drawing of the area, instead (see Bodice and Sleeve Design in Measurements and Schematics) but the quickest approach is to use the mathematical formulas discussed below.

Another type of design that requires a special formula for developing the pattern is a Medallion, which is a flat fabric in the shape of a circle. Few people today make the exquisite lace doilies that were so popular in late-nineteenth-century décor. However, should you ever want to make one, or a full or half-circle shawl (a Medallion on a grand scale), this formula will make it very easy to do.

Formulas for Triangles

For those of you who remember what you learned in geometry class, here is the Pythagorean Theorem; it defines the mathematical relationship between the parts of a right triangle:

$$A^2 + B^2 = C^2$$

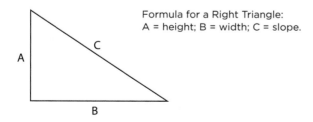

Formula for a Right Triangle:
A = height; B = width; C = slope.

In the drawing of a triangle shown here, *A* is the height (rows), *B* is the base (stitches), and *C* is the hypotenuse (slope). If you know two of the three numbers, and have a calculator

with geometric functions, you can find the missing number (called the unknown). Most often you will know the first two, the height and the width, and that will allow you to find the length of the slope.

Finding a Slope

To find the measurement of the slope of a triangle, work as follows:

1. Enter the number for *A* and push x^2.
2. Push the plus sign.
3. Enter the number for *B* and push x^2 again.
4. Push the equal sign.
5. When the answer appears, push $\sqrt{}$.

You will want a calculator with the square root sign, but if it does not have the exponent sign, you can manage; instead of Steps 1 to 4, above, enter $A \times A + B \times B$, press the equal sign, and then press the square root sign.

For an example of how this can be applied when developing a pattern, see V-Necklines, below.

Finding Length or Width

In those rare cases where you already know the length of the slope and one of the other measurements, you can find the one that is missing:

$$A^2 = C^2 - B^2$$

In this example, the height is not known; work as follows:

1. Enter the number for *C* (length of slope) and push x^2.
2. Push the minus sign.
3. Enter the number for *B* (width) and push x^2.
4. Push the equal sign.
5. When the answer appears, push $\sqrt{}$.

Of course, if you know the width instead of the length, just switch *A* and *B* and work the same way.

You will find an example of how useful this can be for designing a certain type of triangular shawl, below.

Formulas for Circles

Only two measurements are needed to plan a pattern for a circular item such as a Medallion or a half-circle shawl; see Shaping Within a Fabric.

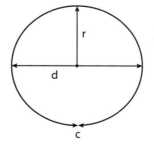

Formula for a Circle: d = diameter; r = radius; C = circumference.

The drawing of a circle above shows the *diameter = d*, which is a measurement through the center of the circle from edge to edge. The *radius = r*, which is half the diameter. The *circumference = C*, which is a measurement all the way around the edge.

If you know just one of these measurements, you can find the other by using pi (π), which is a special number used just for this purpose. Actually it is an infinite number, but for knitting it is fine to use the short form, which is 3.14. Fortunately, you do not even have to remember that number as long as you have the pi button on your calculator; it will remember for you.

The basic formula uses *C* for the circumference and *d* for the diameter and looks like this:

$$C = d \times \pi$$

Finding Circumference

Here is how to find the measurement of the circumference of something when you already know the diameter:

Enter the number for d, push π, and then push the equal sign.

Or, if your calculator does not have a button for π:

Enter the number for d, push the multiplication sign, enter 3.14, and then push the equal sign.

If you know the radius (a measurement from the edge to the center of the circle), use the following formula to find half the circumference:

$$\tfrac{1}{2}C = r \times \pi$$

In other words, multiply the radius times 3.14.

If you know the radius and want to find the full circumference, simply multiply the answer times 2, or use the following formula:

$$C = 2r \times \pi$$

Finding Diameter

While there are likely to be fewer occasions when you know the circumference and want to find the diameter, here is how to do so:

$$C \div \pi = d$$

And, of course, to find the radius, simply divide the diameter by 2.

Ratio of Circumference and Radius

Here is another piece of information you might find useful:

- If the radius doubles in length, the measurement of the circumference doubles as well.

In brief, this means that if you know the circumference of a circle with a radius of 2 inches, it will be twice as large when the radius is 4 inches.

Formula for Shaping a Circle

And finally, to find how many evenly distributed increases or decreases to use every round to make a flat, circular fabric such as a Medallion (see below), a circular shawl, or a ring-patterned yoke for a sweater, work as follows:

Stitch Gauge ÷ Row Gauge = Gauge Ratio

Gauge Ratio × 2π =
Number of Increases or Decreases per Round

If you want to space the increases out more, or fit them into a decorative pattern, here is the general concept of how to do so:

Number of Increases or Decreases per Round × 2 =
Number Every Other Round

Number of Increases or Decreases per Round × 4 =
Number Every Fourth Round

Garment Shaping Examples

The above material describes the basic concepts and provides the formulas you can use to develop a pattern for any kind of slope or curve. Here are some examples that show how to apply this information to some of the more common areas of a garment design.

The first group is made up of shaping done at the edges of a fabric; the second group consists of shaping done within the fabric.

❖ *Edge Shaping Patterns*

Here are practical examples of various design details that require a slope at a side edge. Two are examples of gradual slopes, one for the lower portion of a sleeve, the other for a V-neckline; and two are examples of acute slopes, one for a cast-off shoulder line, and one for a cast-on dolman sleeve.

Lower Sleeve Shaping

A sleeve is normally shaped between wrist and underarm. All you need to do is develop the pattern for one slope because the other slope will be worked in the same way. Therefore, use width measurements taken from a schematic showing one vertical half of the sleeve, as shown.

The instructions assume the sleeve is worked from wrist to underarm. There is a step at the beginning and at the end, so there will be one more step than there are points.

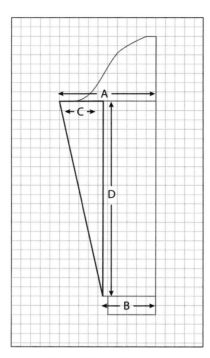

Lower Sleeve Shaping.
Triangle defines area of shaping.

Determine the pattern for the sloped side, as follows:

1. *A* is half width of sleeve at underarm, *B* is half width at wrist; subtract smaller measurement from larger, to find total width to add to slope side, *C*.

    A - B = C

2. Multiply width to add by stitch gauge to find number of stitches to add at side (points).

    C × Stitch Gauge = Number of Increases for Full Width (Points)

3. To find number of rows from wrist to underarm, use measurement of *D* and row gauge.

    D × Row Gauge = Rows in Area of Change

4. Use formula More Steps Than Points, above, to distribute rows to steps.
5. If Step 4 produces a remainder, use formula for Distributing Extra Rows.
6. Set one step aside to place after last increase.

Once you have developed the pattern for the slope on one side of the sleeve, make it clear in the instructions that it should be worked on the other side of the sleeve in the same way.

Increase 1 stitch at beginning and end of every 5th row 3x, every 6th row 11x; work 5 rows to armhole.

V-Necklines

The shaping for a V-neckline opening provides a good example of a gradual slope. The fabric is divided at the center front, half the stitches are placed on a holder, and then each side of the neckline is worked separately. One side of the neck would start on the outside of the left front; the other side would begin on the inside of the right front; the pattern is otherwise the same.

The shaping pattern begins with a decrease on the first row; therefore, the slope starts with a point and ends with a step, which would normally mean an equal number of steps and points. However, it is easiest to write an instruction with an increase or decrease placed on the last of a series of rows (as in "decrease every 5th row"). Therefore, the first decrease point is set aside in a pattern like this, and the remaining rows are distributed to the steps; this creates a pattern that starts and ends with a step.

Use the measurements from a schematic and work as follows:

1. A is full neckline length measurement and B is equal to half of back neckline width. Use gauge to find number of stitches and rows involved in pattern.
2. Separate one point and one row to start pattern at center front, and then use formula for More Steps than Points to find slope pattern; distribute any extra rows to steps in usual way. Set one step aside to work after last increase.

The instructions for the slope would then read something like this:

Decrease 1 stitch at beginning of first row, then decrease 1 stitch every 4th row 10 times, every 3rd row 4 times; work 3 rows to shoulder.

Here again, if you prefer a more even slope, you could intersperse the steps with three rows among those that have four, instead of separating them.

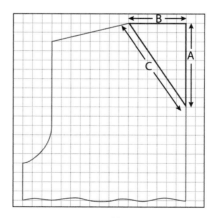

V-Neckline.
Triangle defines area of change.

Shoulder Slope

The shaping of a shoulder line requires an acute slope, one where the triangle that defines the change is considerably wider than it is tall.

There are three ways to work: the stitches can be cast off in steps; the slope can be done with Short Rows first, and then all the stitches cast off at once; or after working the Short Rows, the front and back shoulders can be seamed with Joinery Cast-Off.

A pattern of this kind starts and ends with a step.

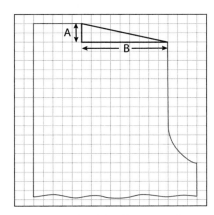

Shoulder Slope.
Triangle defines area of change.

1. Find rows in length.

   A × Row Gauge = Rows in Pattern

2. Find stitches in width.

   B × Stitch Gauge = Stitches in Pattern

3. Use Formula for Acute Slope to develop pattern.

The pattern written out in abbreviations might look something like this:

3(cast off 6 stitches at beginning of row, turn, decrease 1 stitch at end of following row); turn and cast off remaining 6 stitches.

As noted above, the number 3 means to work all instructions inside the parentheses three times. However, the quickest way to write a stepped cast off pattern is like this:

Cast off: 6-1-6-1-6-1-6.

Dolman Sleeve

The approach to working out a pattern for casting on in steps at a side edge is similar to that for a shoulder slope, however, there is no need to separate out stitches for the points.

For instance, a dolman sleeve, which is worked as one with the bodice, could be done either by casting on in steps, or all the stitches could be cast on at once and then the slope made with Increasing Short Rows (see Side or Mid-Fabric Cast-Ons).

In either case, the casting on is done at the end of a row instead of at the beginning, as for casting off. After turning at the end of a row, the recommended procedure is to slip the first stitch of each interim row to smooth out the jog between steps.

Curves

The two most common areas in a garment that have curved edges are the armhole and the sleeve cap. The design of this area is discussed in detail in the chapter Measurements and Schematics, where the necessary measurements are taken from a full-scale or half-scale drawing.

Developing a pattern of this kind is much easier to do using the charting system described in the next chapter (see Charting a Curve), but if you do not have graph paper on hand this example of a sleeve cap will give you an idea of how to proceed; an armhole is done in the same way.

First define the overall sleeve cap as a triangle, and then divide it into several smaller ones. Each of these smaller areas is also represented as a triangle; each short slope represents one segment of the curve, and each requires its own pattern. When worked, the individual slopes, each at a different angle, will blend into a curve.

Here is an example of a shaped sleeve cap; you can work out the pattern for an armhole in the same way.

1. Draw a 1-inch overlay grid on top of a full-scale drawing (or a half-inch overlay grid on top of a half-scale drawing).
2. Draw in short horizontal and vertical lines to define triangles of various sizes for each part of the curve where the line approaches a slope. The triangles will be different sizes.
3. For each triangle, measure the width and multiply times stitch gauge; measure the length and multiply times row gauge to find stitches and rows involved.
4. Use formulas for gradual or acute slopes, above, as needed to find pattern for each segment of the curve.

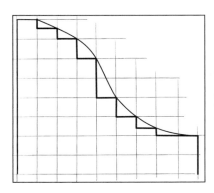

Sleeve Cap Shaping. Draw one-inch overlay grid on schematic to define segments of curve.

❖ *Horizontal Shaping Patterns for Borders*

The number of stitches to pick up along a vertical edge of a fabric, such as when adding a border to a center front opening, is determined by the number of rows in the fabric (see Picking Up Stitches).

The number of stitches needed for the border is determined by a measurement of the length of that edge (taken from the schematic, or from the dressed fabric itself), multiplied by the gauge of the border pattern that will be worked on the picked-up stitches.

Unfortunately, the number of rows in the main fabric and the number of stitches needed for the width of the border are almost never the same. This means that after picking up the stitches, it will be necessary to use either increases or decreases evenly spaced across one row to adjust the number of stitches on the needle before starting the border.

Pattern for Vertical Border

A pattern of this kind will normally start and end with a step; work as follows:

1. Determine number of stitches to pick up (usually equal to number of rows in side edge).
2. Multiply edge measurement by border stitch gauge to find number of stitches needed for border.
3. After finding number of stitches in Steps 1 and 2, subtract smaller number from larger to find how many stitches to increase or decrease.
4. Use Steps and Points for Horizontal Shaping formula to distribute stitches to steps.
5. Distribute any remainder stitches evenly to steps.

Write the pattern, remembering to set aside one step at end; it will look something like this:

   2(K5, K2tog), 9(K6, K2tog), end K5, K2tog, K5.

Notice there are two steps with 5 stitches each at the beginning and end of the pattern, but all the steps in the middle have 6 stitches.

Pattern for Sloped Border

If you are planning to add a border to a V-neckline, you need to take a few extra steps to find the measurement of the sloped edge. Then you can use the Stitch Gauge of the border pattern to find how many stitches are needed.

One solution is to make a full-scale drawing of the neckline; the other is to use the formula for a right triangle, above.

If you look at the drawing of the V-neckline above that shows the triangle defining the area of change, *A* is the full length of the opening from the back neck, and *B* is the width of the back neck.

You can then use your calculator to find *C*, the length of the slope, as follows:

$$A^2 \times B^2 = C^2$$

Then find the number of stitches for the border.

   C × Border Stitch Gauge =
   Number of Stitches for Border at each Side

   B × 2 = Width of Back Neck

   Width of Back Neck × Border Stitch Gauge =
   Number of Stitches for Border at Back Neck

❖ *Shaping Within a Fabric*

The same calculations used to create slopes or curves in flat fabrics are also used to create volume at the interior of a fabric. All that is needed is to set the slope or curve within the fabric instead of at the edge and repeat it in a balanced way in several locations.

Darts

Darts are another way to create shaping within a garment, and you will find illustrations and an explanation of how they work in the chapter Measurements and Schematics.

A vertical dart is simply two gradual slopes set side by side within the fabric. To develop the pattern, all you need to know are the dimensions of the length and width of the triangle that describes one half of the dart. Use these measurements with your gauge to find the number of stitches and rows involved and work out the pattern as for any other slope. The pattern is worked using either pairs of single increases or decreases, or double ones set at the center of the dart.

A horizontal dart is a pair of acute slopes; the lower one will look like a shoulder slope; the upper one is simply an upside-down version of the same pattern. Work the first half of the dart with Decreasing Short Rows, reactivate all the stitches, and then work the second half of the dart with Increasing Short Rows.

A gusset is a type of double dart with a triangular or diamond shape that is set entirely within the fabric, away from any edge. A large one is sometimes set at the underarm of a sweater to provide ease, and tiny ones are often inserted between the thumb and palm of a mitten or glove. The lower part of the gusset is made with an increase pattern, the upper part with a decrease pattern. Socks also have a type of gusset, one on each side below the ankle that serve to reduce the number of stitches between the heel and the instep.

Interior shaping of this kind interrupts any decorative stitch or color pattern. This generally looks quite normal because we are so familiar with the seams in garments made of woven fabric. However, if there are any options as to the placement of the dart, you might want to locate it where it will least disturb the pattern; see the discussion on how to coordinate the two in Internal Shaping and Decorative Patterns in the chapter Charted Garment Patterns.

Miters

Miters are quite similar to darts in the way they are made, but instead of creating volume within a fabric, they are used to create angles in a flat fabric. The pattern is developed on the basis of the length and width of the triangle as for any slope.

Miters appear in several places that will be familiar to you: at the center of a V-neckline opening (or similarly at the underarm of a border for an armhole in a sleeveless garment), or at the corner of a border on a shawl or blanket. The latter is easy to do because the corner is square.

If the border is joined at one side to stitches picked up along the edges of the main fabric, the stitch columns will run perpendicular to those of the main fabric at the top and bottom edges and parallel at the side edges; a miter of this kind is done with Short Rows. If the border is worked out from stitches picked up around the main fabric, the stitch columns at the top and bottom will run in the same direction as the main fabric and those at the side will be perpendicular; this kind of miter is done with increases set at the corner (or if worked from the edge toward the center, with decreases). However they are worked, miters enable the border to turn the corners neatly.

To develop the pattern for a square miter, work as follows:

1. To find number of stitches in miter pattern, multiply width of border by stitch gauge.
2. To find number of rows in miter pattern, multiply width of border by row gauge.
3. For miter requiring Short Rows, see Formulas for Acute Slope, above.

   For miter done with increases or decreases, see Formulas for Gradual Slope.

Even though the miter is square, there will be more rows than stitches because of the rectangular shape of a stitch.

Also see the discussion of the design of borders for V-Necklines in Measurements and Schematics.

Square Miter at corner of border.

Segments

For simple, symmetric shapes like a hat, a mitten tip, or a sock toe, the garment design is divided into equal segments, which are then treated like a decorative stitch or color pattern repeat.

All that is needed is to develop a pattern for the decreases used to curve the side of one segment just as described above for a sleeve cap; the pattern is then done in the same way on both sides of each segment, either with pairs of decreases, or with double decreases.

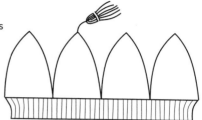

Circular Hat Diagram. Curved lines of segments are where shaping takes place.

In this little drawing of a round watch cap, there are four segments. The base of each segment is one-quarter of the circumference of the hat; the height is equal to the number of rows in the length of the hat. All of the stitches will eventually be removed with double decreases, which will draw the sides of the four segments together so they meet at the top of the cap.

Medallions

A Medallion is also worked in the round; however, the shaping is distributed in a way that allows the fabric to lie flat instead of creating volume as for a hat or a mitten tip (see Uncommon Shapes). There are two types of Medallions; one is a circle, the other is a polygon (a shape with three or more sides like a triangle, a square, or something with five, six, or more edges).

To plan a pattern for a circular Medallion, you could start by deciding on the measurement from the edge to the center, or by deciding on the measurement around the outer edge (the circumference). To find out how many stitches to increase or decrease on every round, or every few rounds, use the Formula for Shaping a Circle, above.

To make a polygon, the internal shaping is arranged like the spokes of a wheel, dividing the Medallion into several equal-sized triangular segments—each segment will have a flat outer edge. The simplest polygon is a square with four segments; it is made with double decreases (or double increases) evenly distributed along the spokes that pass from the center to the corners.

All you need is to develop the pattern for one of the triangles:

Stitch Gauge × Length of One Side =
  Number of Increases Between Center and Edge

Row Gauge × ½ Length of One Side =
  Rows to Center

Use the formulas under Steps and Points to work out the pattern for distributing the increases evenly to the rows; the same pattern is used for all four segments.

It is also easy to make a Medallion pattern with eight segments; simply start by multiplying your Stitch Gauge times half the length of one side.† Of course, if you add enough "spokes," a polygon will begin to resemble a circle. In fact, you could use the Formula for Shaping a Circle and instead of distributing the increases evenly across a round, you could arrange them in a spoke-like pattern instead.

---

† Anyone familiar with geometry will immediately recognize that the segments in the diagram of the Medallion are not right triangles. Rather than burdening the general reader with the formulas for cosines, I am simplifying here and relying on the flexibility of a knitted fabric to create the effect; in fact, arranging the increases in a spoke pattern would angle the edges, as shown. For those of you who are comfortable with these calculations and are seeking perfection, you will know to divide 360 by the number of segments to find the angle, A; determine the lengths of two sides (the spokes), and then apply the formula: $a^2 = b^2 + c^2 - 2bc × cosA$ to find the third side (the edge).

Critters

And finally, should you want to make more fanciful things, such as stuffed toys of one kind or another, all that is necessary is to break them down into components and develop each area of the pattern using one of the approaches described above for any slope or curve.

Because nearly every aspect of the design will be unique, such as the head, body, legs, etc., there may be quite a few separate patterns. The challenge is in drawing the schematic of the design and finding the dimensions needed.‡

Here again, at the risk of repeating myself too often, I strongly recommend that you go on to learn the charted method of developing a pattern, because it makes this much quicker and easier to do, and the patterns are very easy to follow.

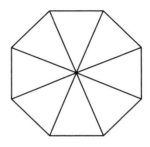

Medallion. Each "spoke" is a radius. Use formula for a circle and divide circumference by number of segments to plan pattern.

---

‡ For a beautiful example of subtle shaping, do see the toy horse on page 333, which not only is perfectly made, but was done with the Double-Fabric technique.

CHAPTER 26

Charted Garment Patterns

A chart is a graphic representation of a pattern that is diagrammed on a grid in somewhat the same manner as a schematic (see Measurements and Schematics). However, while the schematic is a small drawing that shows just the overall shape and basic dimensions of an item, the larger pattern chart shows details regarding the number of stitches and rows in critical areas where the shaping takes place.

A garment chart based on the dimensions shown in a schematic serves two purposes. First, it is an extremely efficient tool that you can use to develop a set of pattern instructions for an original design. Then, the completed chart provides clear, easy-to-read instructions from which you can work.

Once you are familiar with how to make a chart, you will also find it easy to translate a written pattern into charted form. Doing so is an excellent way to familiarize yourself with the pattern and check its accuracy before you begin to work on the project.

Basic Garment Charts

The instructions for how to draw a chart, below, are based on a typical pattern for a simple bodice (like a pullover sweater), which is the most common type of knitted garment. The same basic approach would be used for something like a vest or jacket.

Also included is information about how to chart patterns for garments like hats or mittens, and these same concepts can be applied when making patterns for items like handbags or stuffed toys. Once you are familiar with how charting is done, you will be able to develop a charted pattern for anything you can knit, regardless of how complex the shape might be.

❖ *General Information*

Before we turn to the instructions, here is some preliminary information about how charting is done, the kind of graph paper to use, how to reconcile the difference between the squares of graph paper and the rectangular shape of a knitted stitch, and how to save space on the paper by drawing just those areas of the pattern that are relevant.

To draw the chart, you will need graph paper, a ruler, a pencil, and an eraser for corrections. You will be using the measurements from the schematic drawing of your design, the stitch gauge, and some basic math (see Tips for Doing the Math in the chapter Calculations for Pattern Design) to find the number of stitches and rows needed in every area of the pattern where a change takes place. If you are making a chart based on a published pattern that does not include a schematic, you can use the information provided in the written instructions.

Once you have a chart that fits together and makes sense, you may want to make a final, clean copy in ink. Write the dimensions and the number of stitches or rows alongside the lines, and make notes in the margins around the chart regarding anything you think might prove useful later. Scribble away; this is your pattern.

Grid

Unlike a schematic drawing, where one square represents an inch, one square in a garment chart represents a stitch. In this, it more closely resembles a stitch or color pattern chart (see Charted Stitch Patterns, and Charted Color Patterns), although a garment chart is much larger.

Because a garment chart may include a considerable number of stitches and rows, it is customarily done on 8½ × 11 paper with a grid of 10 squares to the inch, which means it can include as many as 85 stitches and 110 rows (or 110 stitches and 85 rows if turned sideways).

However, for most purposes, only critical areas of the garment need to be charted (see Partial Charts, below), and most patterns will fit on paper of this size. If the pattern requires a larger number of stitches and rows, you may need to use 11 × 14-inch graph paper, or you can tape several sheets together.

If possible, select the type of graph paper that has a 1-inch overlay of darker horizontal and vertical lines on top of the base grid. This allows you to count by tens at a glance, which not only makes it easier to develop the pattern, but also makes it easier to follow as you knit.

Proportions

The squares of the grid will accurately convey information about the relative position of every stitch in the pattern, but they do not correctly represent the shape of knitted stitches, which are rectangles. Because of this discrepancy, the proportions of the charted garment will appear tall and narrow.

While this distortion may look odd at first, it is of no consequence, because unlike a schematic, it is not the shape of the garment that is important here; what is needed is the information about what to do with each and every stitch.

These proportions also mean that you cannot simply draw the garment shape onto the grid according to the measurements alone. While the chart would look right, the fabric would turn out to be the wrong size.

You may come across what is called "knitter's graph paper," which has a grid of 5 by 7 squares per inch. The idea is that this is a typical gauge for a Stockinette fabric and, therefore, a chart can be made by drawing the pattern according to its measurements. However, it is quite rare for a gauge to be exactly that size, and unfortunately even a minor difference between your actual gauge and that of the paper will be multiplied by the dimensions of the garment (see Those little tenths). As a result, there is really almost no situation in which you could use paper of that kind to make an accurate pattern.

However, computer programs are available that will print graph paper in a grid size that exactly matches whatever gauge you specify, including one with numbers that include tenths of an inch, which is important because no gauge is accurate

without them. Paper of this kind is particularly helpful for Intarsia patterns and can speed up the development of any pattern, although, as you will see, it is not necessary and ordinary graph paper will do fine.

Partial Charts

The significant information conveyed by a chart is not what stays the same, but only what changes and where. Therefore, only areas that have slopes and curves are charted, and it is rarely necessary to show an entire garment section.

For instance, there is no need to chart the portion of the garment between the lower edge and the underarm if it is worked on a constant number of stitches. A simple notation on the chart indicating how many stitches to cast on at the lower edge, and how many rows to work to the underarm is sufficient.

Furthermore, if the front is just like the back, one chart will do for both, and if the right and left sides of the garment are the same, only one vertical half need be shown.

Therefore, a pattern might consist of one chart showing a vertical half of the sleeve, and another chart for just the upper quadrant of a bodice, between the center front and the armhole, and from the underarm to the shoulder and back neckline. The front neckline shaping is superimposed below that of the back neckline; work from one or the other as necessary. (In fact, you can abandon all resemblance to the shape of a garment, and place fragments of the chart anywhere they will fit on the page; see Chart Fragments, below.)

While a partial chart shows the pattern for shaping just one edge, it is understood to mean that it should be repeated at the opposite edge. In other words, if there is an increase or decrease at the beginning of a row, another one is worked in the same position at the other side (depending upon circumstances or preference, this might be at the end of the row, or at the beginning of the next row). Similarly, if the chart shows stitches cast off at the beginning of a row, the same cast-off pattern is repeated at the beginning of the next row on the other side.

When working from a chart that includes a vertical half of a garment section, keep in mind that at any point in the pattern the number of stitches on the needle will be twice what is shown if you are making a flat fabric, and four times the amount if making one in the round. My preference is to include a note that indicates what the total stitch count should be at critical points in the pattern, but a 10-square overlay grid makes it easy to count, in any case.

The only exceptions to the use of partial charts are when a decorative pattern or some asymmetry in the garment design must be carefully plotted over the entire width and length of the pattern, or when it is necessary to show the relationship of a complex stitch or color pattern to the shape of the garment. You will find several examples of these kinds of charts in Coordinating Stitch and Garment Patterns, below.

❖ Drawing a Chart

The instructions here are for making a chart of a simple bodice pattern suitable for something like a pullover sweater. You will be using the same general approach to drawing a garment chart as you did for drawing a schematic (see Drawing Schematics), but instead of each square being equivalent to an inch, here they are equivalent to stitches and rows instead.

Simply count squares across and draw a horizontal line to define the number of stitches in any area of the pattern and count squares up or down and draw a vertical line to indicate the number of rows in any area. Then connect those lines with sloped or curved lines to define the shaped areas of the pattern. As you will see, the latter will cut across the squares of the grid, indicating exactly how many stitches are on the needle before and after any change takes place, and revealing the exact location of every shaping technique.

In effect, the pattern for any slope or curve will magically appear on the chart—there is no need to use any of the other formulas described in Calculations for Pattern Design. The speed and accuracy with which this can be done is quite remarkable and opens up a world of design possibilities.

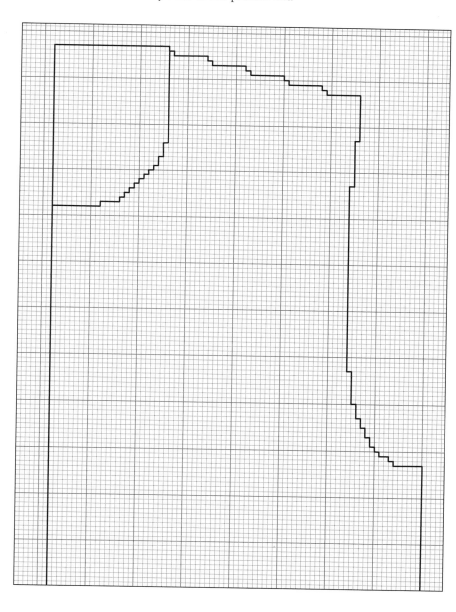

Partial Garment Chart. Typical chart showing only shaping of armhole and shoulder.

Basic Chart from a Schematic

Work from the measurements shown on the schematic drawing of the pattern. To begin the chart, draw a vertical line at one side of the graph paper to represent the center of the garment section and mark the Center Back Neck at the top of this line; then continue as follows.

1. To find number of stitches or rows in any area of pattern, use gauge and measurements from schematic in one of these formulas:

   Vertical Measurement × Row Gauge = Number of Rows in Pattern

   Horizontal Measurement × Stitch Gauge = Number of Stitches in Pattern

2. Calculate number of rows in every aspect of design involving length, such as for shoulder slope, center front neck, underarm, and so on. Count first by tens using overlay grid, and then square by square to mark off exact numbers of rows needed.
3. Next, do calculations for every aspect of design involving width, such as shoulder width and underarm width; for each of these, count across from one of the marks on center line and make second mark.
4. Draw all horizontal and vertical lines to connect marks. Before drawing in any slopes and curves, see information below.

When doing the width calculations in Step 3, any edge that will be seamed or have stitches picked up along it will need a selvedge, so add one stitch to the answer.

There is no need to set the selvedge stitch apart in any way, but you might want to draw a short vertical line to delineate the selvedge stitch column at the bottom right corner of the chart; write an "S" underneath to make it clear the selvedge is present and part of the stitch count.

A sleeve chart is done in the same way, counting down along the center vertical line to establish the underarm point and sleeve length, and then counting widths across from those points.

Charting Slopes and Curves

A knitted garment is shaped by adding or removing stitches, either along the edges or within the fabric. The relative positions of the shaping techniques, how many there are, and how close together or far apart they are, determine the characteristics of the change. If set near an edge, the shaping will cause it to slope or curve, which is what is needed for a neckline, shoulder, armhole, or sleeve. If done within the fabric, the shaping will create the volume needed to make something like a hat, a sock, or a mitten.

The different approaches that can be used to shape a fabric are described in Types of Shaping, and Defining the Area of Change in the chapter on Calculations for Pattern Design. Also explained there is the concept of "steps and points," which is both a useful way to understand what is actually happening in the fabric where a change occurs, and an essential aspect of developing a set of pattern instructions.

Briefly, shaping can be done in four basic ways:

- A *gradual slope*, such as for the lower half of a sleeve, is done with increases or decreases. In this type of slope, a step is a set of rows worked at a constant width, and a point is where a shaping technique is located, causing a change in the width of the fabric.
- An *acute slope*, such as for a shoulder, is done with casting off, casting on, or Short Rows. A step consists of a group of stitches, and the point is where the work is turned at the beginning or end of the row between each step.
- A *curve*, such as for an armhole or sleeve cap, is a variation of one or the other of these kinds of slopes. Instead of a constant number of stitches or rows in each step, the number varies.
- *Horizontal shaping* takes place across a single row and may be done either to create gathering, to adjust the number of stitches needed when changing from one stitch or color pattern to another, or to shape interior contours. In this case, the steps are sets of stitches worked plain, the points are where a shaping technique is positioned.

As you can see on the partial garment chart shown on the previous page, a slope or curve drawn on a garment chart cuts across the grid, and wherever it touches the corner of a square it makes it clear that the fabric width has changed—there is one less square included in the chart.

The information conveyed by a chart is much easier to read if you make it explicit, by stepping the line around the square at each point where these changes occur.

Charting a Gradual Slope

Depending upon what precedes and follows the shaped area, a gradual slope might start or end with a step or a point (see Steps and Points). In some cases, you might want to start the slope immediately, while in others, it could be better to have a few plain rows at the beginning and/or end. You will find practical examples of both approaches below.

Point-to-Point Slope

1. At top of area on chart that will be shaped, draw a line down and then under one square to define last point of pattern.
2. Draw slope from that point down to bottom of area, closing gap in chart.

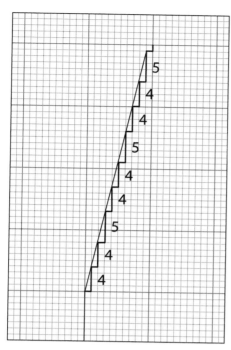

Point-to-Point Slope.
A slope that starts and ends with a point.

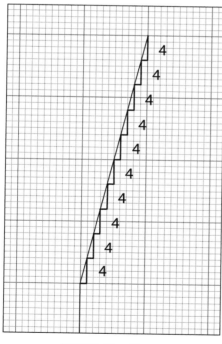

Point-to-Step Slope.
A slope that starts with a point at the
bottom and ends with a step at the top.

Point-to-Step Slope

- Draw line from top to bottom of area that will be shaped, closing gap in chart.

Stepping Off a Slope

It helps to use a ruler for this; work as follows:

1. Draw horizontal line under first point; out for an increase, in for a decrease.
2. Position ruler vertically with edge at first point and note where it intersects with slope above.
3. Draw vertical line from first point to intersection, and then draw a horizontal line under the adjacent square to mark next point.
4. Reposition ruler on that point and repeat.

Always step off pattern entirely on the inside of the slope for decreases, or on the outside of the slope for increases; do not allow the stepped line to cross the sloped line from one side to the other.

After stepping off the points on a chart, you may notice that some of the steps have a different number of rows. This occurs when the number of rows does not divide evenly into the number of steps; the extra rows are automatically distributed throughout the sloped line as it is drawn on a chart. (When using formulas to develop a pattern, several calculations are required to work out a distribution of this kind; see Distributing Extra Rows in the material on Steps and Points for Gradual Slopes.)

In the adjacent illustrations, the first shows a point-to-point slope. It has the same number of rows and the same number of stitches are either increased or decreased, but three of the stitches in the last step have been distributed to other steps, changing the pattern. It helps to write the number of rows in each step alongside the line so there is no need to count squares while working the pattern, especially if the pattern is irregular like the one shown. The second shows a point-to-step slope with four rows in each step.

Charting an Acute Slope

Acute Slopes are done with casting off, casting on, or Short Rows. In these situations, the steps contain the stitches that are added or removed (or are temporarily set aside with Short Rows), and a second row is required to work back to where the next step will be worked. Notice in the sample charts below that, unlike a gradual slope, the stepped line of an acute slope straddles the slope, which cuts through the middle of the two-row jog between steps.

Step-to-Step Cast-Off Slope

A cast-off pattern starts at the beginning of a row, and a single stitch is decreased at the turning point at the end of the next row to smooth out the transition between steps. This is indicated on the chart by a little one-square jog between steps. This first example begins and ends with a step.

1. Define area with number of stitches and *uneven* number of rows and draw in slope.
2. Starting at top look down along slope to where line crosses intersection of two squares. Draw horizontal line across and down to this point, then jog one square across and one down for decrease.
3. Repeat Step 2 to define all steps and points.

If the steps vary in size, you may find it helpful to write the number of stitches in each one above the slope, as shown.

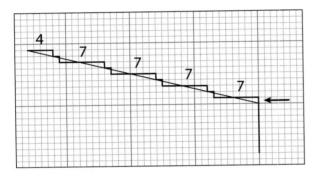

Step-to-Step Cast-Off Slope.
Jogs between steps are decrease points.

Step-to-Point Cast-Off Slope

A pattern that begins with a step and ends with a point will require an even number of rows. If it starts and ends with a step, however, it will require an uneven number of rows; if necessary, add or subtract a row depending upon your sense of what is appropriate. In some cases you may want to decide this on the basis of where the slope will start or end in relation to the surrounding fabric, or to maximize or minimize the angle of the slope.

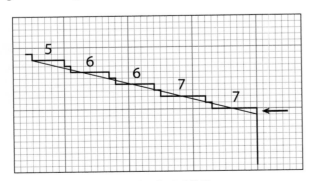

Step-to-Point Cast-Off Slope.

- Work as described above, but define area with *even* number of rows, and draw in last point at top of slope before drawing line, as shown. Step off slope in same way.

Cast-On, or Short Row Slope

Casting On and Short Rows are done at the end of a row, and after turning, the first stitch is slipped (the last stitch of the previous step). Because there is no decrease needed at the turning point, the stepped line goes straight down two rows, and a pattern of this kind always starts and ends with a step.

- Work as described for Step-to-Step Slope, but at each point where line intersects two squares, draw vertical line straight down, without a jog.

When working Short Rows, remember to include the slipped stitch in your count as you work the return row. Also keep in mind that, for Increasing Short Rows, the first stitch of every step after the first will be wrapped; include it in your count of how many stitches to work in each step.

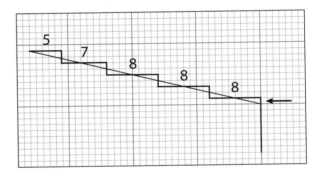

Cast-On, or Short Row Slope.
No jogs between steps needed.

Charting a Curve

When you examine the area defined by a curved line, you will notice that it describes a complex sequence, with shaping set close together in some areas, and farther apart in others. The chart for a curved acute slope will indicate varying numbers of stitches in the steps; one for a gradual slope will have different numbers of rows in the steps. And some curves, such as for an armhole or sleeve cap, will contain both acute slopes and gradual ones.

When drawing a chart of this kind, first work in light pencil so you can make any necessary corrections as you decide how you want to step off the line. Here are some tips for how to do so.

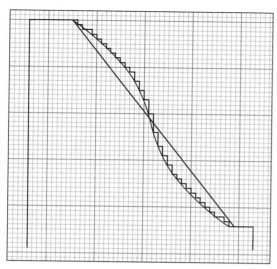

Charting a Curve. Example of curved sleeve shaping.

- As with the slopes above, lightly mark the points wherever the slope touches the intersection of two grid lines.
- When two points on the slope are separated by one or more squares horizontally, step it off as described above for an acute slope.
- When two points on the slope are separated by more than one square vertically, step it off as described above for a gradual slope.
- In some areas, such as in the middle of an armhole, the pattern may continue at a constant width for several inches; draw a vertical line.
- If the pattern seems unnecessarily complicated in certain areas, consider making minor adjustments to the shape of the curve to smooth things out a bit.

    Keep in mind that the curve is elongated on the chart; therefore, if you change its contour, check widths in several locations to make sure the fabric will have the correct proportions.

- To make the pattern easier to read as you work from it, add brief written instructions alongside the line.

    For instance, you might write something like, "1 every 6R" near one area, and "1 every 4R" near another, and so on.

Charting Horizontal Shaping

For horizontal shaping, a series of increases or decreases are spaced across a single row. While this kind of shaping does not involve a slope, an abstract slope drawn on a chart can be used to develop a pattern for this kind of change in the width of the fabric.

The slope is drawn in a slightly different way, depending upon whether you are working flat or circular. The former requires a step at the beginning and end of the pattern; the latter starts with a step and ends with a point, or vice versa.

Horizontal Shaping for Flat Fabric

1. Draw horizontal line, one square per stitch, equal to number of stitches on needle before shaping is done.
2. At one end of horizontal line, draw vertical line, one square per stitch, equal to number of stitches to increase or decrease, plus one.
3. Draw slope connecting line drawn in Step 2 with opposite end of horizontal line, making a triangle.
4. Mark points along slope wherever it touches intersection of two grid lines.
5. Count and mark number of squares between each point.

The vertical line includes one extra stitch because a pattern of this kind requires a step at the beginning and end of the row. As you will see in the instructions for horizontal shaping in a circular fabric, if that extra square is not included, the slope will produce a pattern that starts with a step and ends with a point.

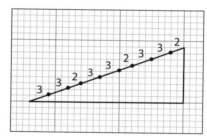

Horizontal Shaping for Flat Fabric. Pattern begins and ends with a step.

Horizontal Shaping for Circular Fabric

1. Draw horizontal and vertical lines as described above; use half number of stitches in the circumference, and half number of stitches to be increased or decreased.
2. Draw slope from top of vertical line to opposite end of horizontal line.
3. Mark points and count off steps as described above.

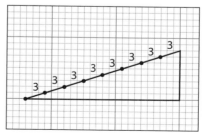

Horizontal Shaping for Circular Fabric. Pattern begins with a step and ends with a point.

Horizontal Shaping Patterns

After defining the pattern, you may want to write a note that specifies how to work the shaping techniques; there are differences depending upon whether they are increases or decreases.

For Increases

- Work increase on last stitch in each step, except final one.
- Or, work increase at point, between last stitch of one step and first stitch of next step.

For Decreases

- Work decrease including last stitch of one step and first on next step.
- Or, work decrease on last two stitches of each step, except final one.

Charts from Written Garment Patterns

Translating written knitting instructions to charted form is really no more than "knitting" on paper. If the pattern does not provide a schematic, it is best to start by drawing one based on the measurements given before doing the garment chart (see Schematics from Written Patterns); however, this is not essential and you can develop the chart based entirely on the written instructions.

If you find you cannot match the gauge provided in the pattern, use the measurements provided and the gauge you do have to chart the pattern; see Matching Pattern Gauges.

Use a pencil to do a rough draft, and once you are sure the pattern is accurate, make a copy in ink, if you prefer. For a conventional sweater pattern, start by making a note on the chart indicating the number of stitches to cast on, and the rows to work to the underarm. If the pattern provides only measurements of length, use your gauge to find the number of rows needed.

Then chart half the upper bodice, more or less as described above, except work from the bottom up, following the instructions step-by-step. Because you will be making a partial chart, remember to divide the number of stitches by 2 for a flat pattern or by 4 if it is a circular pattern.

1. Draw vertical line on left side of page to represent center of bodice; draw horizontal line to represent bottom of chart at underarm. Count across the horizontal line to mark underarm point.
2. Follow pattern instructions for shaping armhole. Count across squares to left to indicate number cast off at underarm, and then step off slope. Draw up and around a square for a decrease, counting squares up and draw vertical line for rows with no change.
3. When neckline shaping begins, step off shaping at center line of chart; continue stepping off armhole shaping at other edge.
4. Pattern for shoulder shaping, whether done with casting off or Short Rows, requires stepping off an Acute Slope.

For instance, when stepping off an armhole slope, if the pattern reads, "Decrease one stitch every other row five times," step off the line, over one square, up two, over one, up two, and so on, five times, just as you would when knitting actual stitches and rows.

The neck opening will normally end with a vertical line that meets the last step of the shoulder. To complete the chart, simply draw a horizontal line to define the back neckline.

If the shoulder and front neckline pattern do not connect on the same row, or if a count of the number of stitches in the back neckline is not correct, check the instructions again to find the error.

Chart Variations and Applications

It is easy to see how the basic methods of drawing a schematic and charting a pattern could be applied to any related garment style; you could omit the sleeves for a vest, open the center front for a cardigan sweater, lengthen the garment into a tunic, or enlarge it into a jacket or coat. Those kinds of projects may be the sorts of things you would have occasion to do frequently, but charting can also be used to make patterns for *anything* you might have occasion to knit. If you can describe the shape of something in a schematic drawing, you can make a chart for it.

The material that follows will provide you with some additional tools for charting so you can apply it in a wider variety of circumstances. To begin, there are a few simple but useful tips about fitting a large chart onto the paper, beyond what is discussed in Partial Charts, above. Also included are a few symbols that you might find useful, similar to those used for stitch charting. You will also find information about how to change the size of a pattern, or alter the proportions of a garment, if necessary.

Of greater significance, however, is the information below about making charts for items that require internal shaping, such as hats and mittens. As you will see, the methods used to do this make it possible to chart a pattern for any shape you can imagine.

❖ Chart Details

The idea of using partial charts as a way to fit a larger pattern on a page was discussed above, but you can take that a step further and break the chart into even smaller pieces, if necessary, to fit it on the graph paper.

Also, there are a few symbols shown here, similar to those used for stitch pattern charts, that you might find useful for adding details of the pattern to a garment chart.

Chart Fragments

When necessary to save space, feel free to abandon all efforts to make the chart resemble the shape of a garment, particularly when the chart is one that only you will use. Instead, place disconnected segments of the chart anywhere they will fit on the page.

- Place the chart for the armhole curve in one position on the paper, and that for the neckline shaping and shoulder slope wherever it will fit in another area of the paper. Draw an arrow from the end of the armhole curve to the start of the shoulder slope. Draw another arrow from the row on the armhole curve where the front neckline shaping begins to the chart for the latter. Or, just label each segment clearly so you know where to look next.
- Similarly, the chart showing the slope of the sleeve between wrist and underarm does not need to be connected to the chart for the sleeve cap. Place them in any convenient position, or put the slope on one side, and the cap on the reverse of the page.

Chart Symbols

Here are some symbols that I have found useful for indicating details on garment charts. If you feel the need for a symbol not included here, make up some of your own; also see the Glossary of Symbols in the chapter Charted Stitch Patterns.

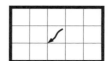

Attach Yarn symbol.

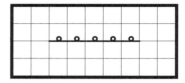

Cast-On Stitches symbol.

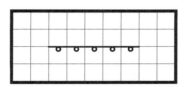

Cast-Off Stitches symbol.

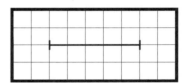

Opening symbol.

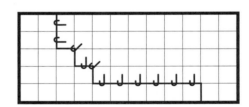

Pick Up Stitches symbol.

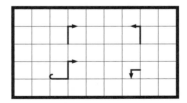

Short Row symbols.

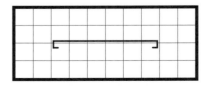

Stitches On Hold symbol.

❖ *Charts and Pattern Size*

In addition to being an excellent way to work out a pattern, a chart can be used as a tool for making adjustments in the size of the pattern, and it can also be drawn so it illustrates more than one size option.

Multi-Size Charts

It is common for published patterns to include a range of sizes, with the charts for the smaller sizes set inside those of the larger.

- To make a chart with multiple sizes, draw the one for the small size first, and then draw the lines for the other sizes outside of it.

  A chart showing more than three sizes can be visually confusing; if you plan to design for more than that, make more than one multi-size chart.

- To follow a pattern of this kind, work within whichever set of lines is appropriate for the size you have chosen, and ignore the lines for the smaller or larger sizes.

  Should you find that the lines for the other sizes are visually distracting as you work, mark those you need to follow with a highlighter pen.

- Multi-size charts make size alterations easy to do; see below.

Alterations

You can use a chart to make two kinds of alterations to an existing pattern—a change in the dimensions, and/or a change in the gauge.

  Either use new measurements and the pattern gauge to find the number of stitches and rows to adjust, or use the existing pattern measurements and a different gauge to do so.

  If the pattern is written, make a chart of it according to the instructions first, and then alter the chart as needed.

- To alter a charted multi-size pattern, change dimensions by blending the line for one size with that of another.
- To alter depth of neckline, use gauge to determine number of rows to add or remove, and mark new position on chart. Redraw line and step off stitches for new pattern. A change of this kind is also likely to require a change in the pattern for any collar or border.
- To alter length of a sleeve between wrist and underarm, redraw slope as shown for a V-neckline.
- Any change in the length of an armhole or width of a sleeve is more challenging and requires redrawing the schematic before making a new chart; see Bodice and Sleeve Design.
- To change a cardigan into a pullover, eliminate lines that define border or button band and draw center front line to match back of bodice.

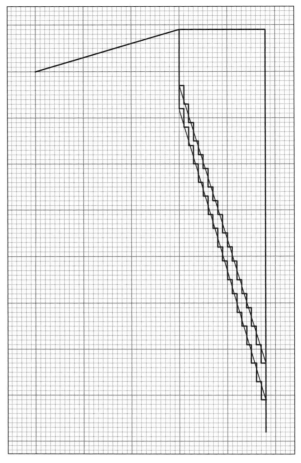

Alterations: Example of V-neckline.
Redraw line in new position and step off slope.

  To make a pullover into a cardigan, draw border or button band that straddles center front line.

❖ *Charts for Internal Shaping*

The charts discussed above illustrate the instructions for flat garment pieces shaped at the outer edges, but there are many situations where shaping is done within the fabric instead.

  Of course, all the shaping is done within the fabric for circular garments such as hats, socks, and mittens, but flat fabrics may also have internal shaping, such as for darts in a bodice, or to make shaped collars or peplums. There are several ways to represent shaping of this kind in a chart.

  The shaping for a small circular garment such as a cap or a mitten (as well as for Medallions) requires gradual slopes that run the length, or part of the length of the fabric. A partial chart is all that is needed for something like this; it shows just one segment of the garment and it will look somewhat like a slice of pie, as if the fabric had been cut apart along the slopes.

  In the case of a sock or mitten, the chart will show one-half of the stitches in the circumference; for a hat it would be one-quarter or less. The chart is then treated just like a stitch or color pattern repeat, and is read from right to left as many times as necessary based on the number of stitches in the circumference and the size of the segment.

For shorter Gradual and Acute Slopes set within a fabric, such as for darts, a normal garment chart is drawn according to its widest overall dimensions and the shaped area is set within it (see Darts in the chapter Measurements and Schematics). The dart will have the shape of a triangle with the sides stepped off in the usual way.

General Information for Internal Shaping

Here are some tips for how to read and write charts for patterns that require shaping set within the fabric instead of at the edges.

- The squares between two slopes, or between a slope and a straight vertical or horizontal line within a fabric, should be thought of as empty—these are the stitches that are removed by the shaping and you just skip over them as you read from the chart. If you prefer, shade the area to make it clear that there are no stitches in that area.
- If there is a vertical line on one side of the area and a slope on the other side, shaping is done with single increases or decreases.
- If there is a slope or curve on both sides of the area, shaping is done with double increases or decreases, or perhaps paired single versions of the techniques.
- Some patterns have vertical columns of stitches set between two curves or slopes, in which case that area remains at a constant width, and single increases or decreases are used on either side.
- An Acute Slope done with Short Rows may have a slope on one side of the triangle and a straight line on the other; or there may be two Short Row Slopes, and, after completing one pattern, another one is done in reverse.

Below you will find several charts that demonstrate internal shaping of this kind. The charts shown here are not real patterns, which of course would depend on a particular gauge and measurements, but they serve to illustrate how this is done.

Charting a Hat Crown

The adjacent chart shows one segment of a hypothetical cap worked in the round. It is very narrow, which means it would represent perhaps one of six or eight segments, depending upon the size of the hat and its gauge.

Each segment is treated just as you would a color pattern repeat; after working across from right to left once, simply read the pattern again for the next group of stitches.

The crown of this cap is shaped with a curve, and there is

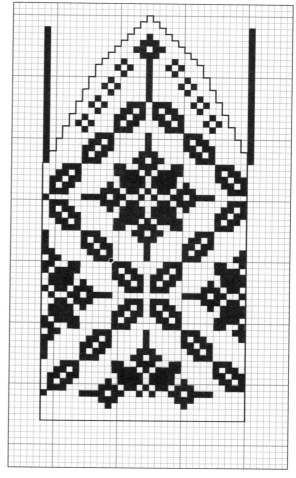

Charting a Hat Crown. Chart shows one segment that is treated like a pattern repeat.

a single column of stitches at each side. The squares between these two stitch columns and the stepped curves are empty; these represent the stitches removed by the shaping.

To read the pattern, you would work a single dark-colored stitch at the beginning of the repeat, and then a single decrease; work the color pattern within the segment, and then on the left side work another single decrease followed by another single dark-colored stitch. When the pattern is repeated, the two dark stitches will be side by side, creating a vertical stripe flanked by the decreases.

To develop a chart of this kind, work as follows:

1. Determine circumference of hat and divide by 4 (or 6, etc.); multiply by gauge to find number of stitches. Adjust number to requirements of decorative pattern, as necessary. Draw horizontal line on chart with squares equal to number of stitches in one segment.

2. Decide on length of hat; multiply by gauge to find number of rows; adjust number to requirements of decorative pattern, as necessary. Count up from center of horizontal line to mark top.

3. Decide on length of segment side before shaping begins, multiply by row gauge, count up from horizontal line and mark at each side.

4. Draw curve starting at mark placed in Step 3 and ending at center top mark; step off curve to develop pattern. Repeat for curve on other side of segment.

Charting Mitten Patterns

There are far simpler mittens than the example shown here, but this chart has the virtue of illustrating the possibilities. It shows the contours of the mitten and all necessary shaping, but also provides a good example of how to plot a decorative pattern on a garment chart (for more information, see Coordinating Stitch and Garment Patterns, below).

While the chart may appear complicated at first glance, it should be clear after studying it a bit how it is done. Once again, it is merely a matter of translating width and length

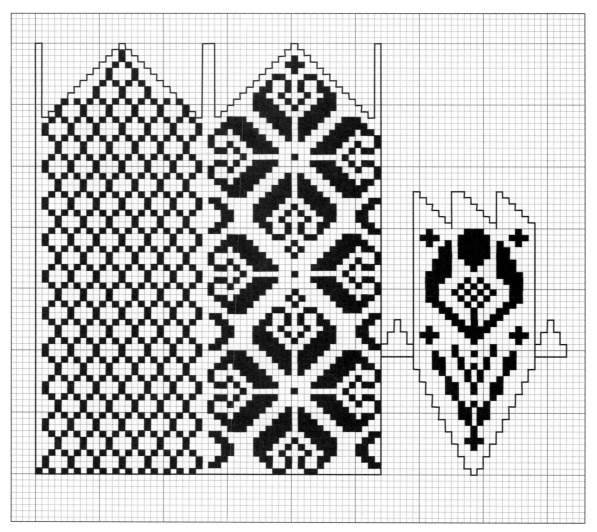

Charting Mitten Patterns. Palm at left, back in middle, thumb at right, with small gusset on either side.

measurements into stitches and rows and, after plotting these on the grid, drawing in the slopes or curves and stepping off the pattern.

As you can see, the shaping at the tip of the thumb and the tip of the mitten resembles that of the shaping for the crown of a hat, above. Also, not only does the thumb have a gusset (half is worked in the palm, the other half in the thumb), but this is a "handed" mitten, with different surface patterns on the palm and the back, and as such requires "mirrored" construction.

It is certainly possible to work the second mitten from the same chart by simply imagining the thumb on the other side of the mitten. If you find that challenging, you could make a second chart, but there are two simpler options: Photocopy the chart, cut the three parts of the pattern apart, and paste them down on another sheet of paper with the thumb to the left and the palm to the right of the back, and then recopy the pattern. Or, if you know how to do so, scan the pattern and use graphics software to simply flip the chart horizontally and print out another copy.

Charted Dart Patterns

A vertical dart consists of a pair of gradual slopes that meet within the fabric; on the chart, the squares between the two slopes should be considered empty, and you skip over them when reading the chart. The slopes are stepped off as for any gradual slope, and the pattern can be worked either with paired single increases or decreases, or double ones.

A horizontal dart can be done either with a single Short Row pattern, or with a pair of them. The latter will look somewhat like a pair of shoulder slopes, one above the other; the first half of the dart is done with Decreasing Short Rows, and, after reactivating all the stitches, the second half is done with Increasing Short Rows. Here again, there will be an empty triangular space within the chart that indicates where stitches are missing. For more information about the design of darts, see Darts in the chapter Measurements and Schematics.

Also keep in mind that any dart will interrupt the lines of a stitch or color pattern. It is a good idea to plot the decorative pattern on the garment pattern chart to see the relationship between the two; for an example of this, see the horizontal dart pattern discussed in Coordinating Stitch and Garment Patterns, below.

Short Rows can also be used to curve an entire fabric, such as for a collar or peplum; the technique creates side edges with different length measurements, as shown in the chart above. The pattern is simply repeated every few rows, depending upon the amount of curve required (also see the diagram and an explanation of this in Short Row Curves).

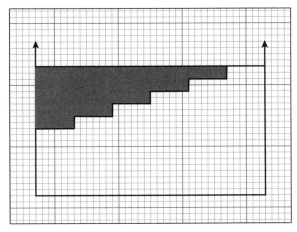

Short Row pattern for acute slope. Shaded area will be eliminated by short rows, making one side of fabric longer than the other, causing it to curve.

❖ *Coordinating Stitch and Garment Patterns*

It is important to plot the relationship between any decorative stitch or color pattern and the contours of the garment pattern. At the very least, you will want to have enough stitches in the width of the fabric to accommodate whole repeats, but it is also a good idea to position a full repeat at the center front neckline or at the top of a sleeve, where it will be highly visible (for more information on adjusting the width and length of a garment for this purpose, see Pattern Repeats and Garment Dimensions in the chapter Calculations for Pattern Design). Based on this, you can then determine how to start the pattern at the lower right corner of the garment.

It would be tedious and time-consuming to fill in the squares of an entire chart with color or stitch technique symbols for the decorative pattern. Fortunately, that is really not necessary. Instead, plot the decorative pattern onto the chart by drawing lines that define the number of stitches and rows in the stitch or color pattern repeat.

If you like, also fill in a bit of the pattern around the edges of the chart, where it meets slopes or curves; this makes it easy to check your work for accuracy because you will quickly see any discrepancy between the chart and the appearance of the fabric.

Having the repeats drawn on the chart in this way serves as an effective visual guide that will help you keep your place while working complex areas of the pattern. For example, instead of counting off the rows between the armhole shaping and the neck shaping, you can look at the chart and quickly see that the neck starts on, say, the second row of the fourth repeat after the underarm, which is so much easier.

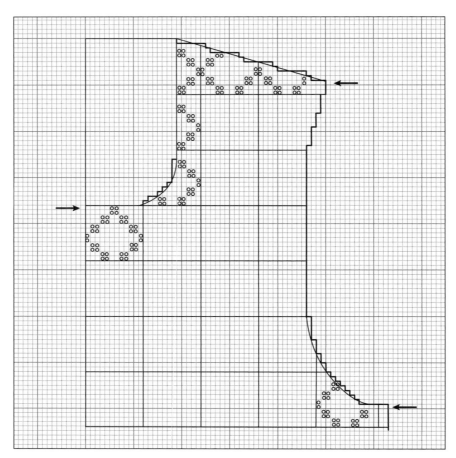

Coordinating Stitch and Garment Patterns.
Lines drawn for pattern repeat, with some of pattern filled in.

Once you have plotted the pattern on the upper bodice or sleeve cap, then determine how to start the pattern on the first row so it will come out right at the top. To do this, you will need to know the number of rows from the lower edge (or from the top of the ribbing) to the underarm and then find how many repeats this number of rows will accommodate. Once you know where the first row of the garment pattern would fall within the decorative pattern, you can coordinate the two, if necessary, either by adding or subtracting a few rows from the garment, or by starting the decorative pattern on a different row.

Plotting Pattern Repeats

Draw the lines that represent the stitch or color pattern repeat in faint pencil first so you can make changes, if necessary, and analyze the result to see how the decorative pattern interacts with any slope or curve.

1. Draw horizontal line from center to outer edge of chart where top of pattern repeat selected as focal point will be positioned.
2. Draw series of lines parallel to first, each one enclosing same number of squares on chart as there are rows in repeat.
3. Draw vertical line from top to bottom of chart where side of pattern repeat selected as focal point will be positioned.
4. Draw series of lines parallel to each side of line drawn in Step 3, each enclosing same number of squares on chart as there are stitches in repeat.

Here are some options to consider when deciding how to position the decorative pattern.

- Consider whether to center the repeat at the focal point, or have one repeat on either side of it.

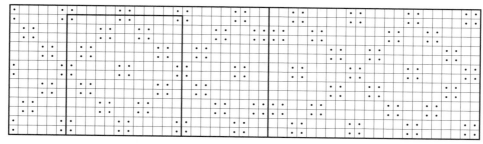

Plotting Pattern Repeats.
Stitch pattern chart shows partial repeat at side seam.

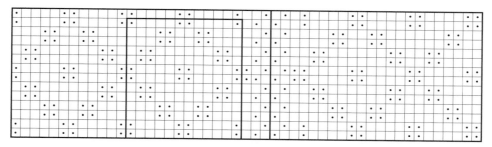

Plotting Pattern Repeats.
Stitch pattern chart shows partial repeat replaced by fill pattern.

- A slope or curve will cut across the decorative pattern repeats in various places. Examine these areas closely and look for any situation where a shaping technique conflicts with a stitch technique, or where shaping cuts across a color pattern and leaves an odd fragment of a motif, and consider whether any change should be made.

  For instance, you might be able to adjust the contour of curve, alter the width in a critical area slightly, or shift the shaping up or down a row or two to avoid conflicts. Alternatively, reposition the decorative pattern in some way; merely shifting it up or down a row can often eliminate a potential problem.

Plotting Pattern with a Stitch Chart

Once you have located a repeat at the center front neckline and plotted it across the garment chart, then consider how it lines up at the lower corner, where you will start to work.

This area is not shown on your garment chart, but you can calculate how many repeats will fit in the rows between the first row and the underarm. Then use a stitch pattern chart as an aid in making any necessary adjustments. For instance, you might want to start the pattern with the middle row if that would help it line up in a better way at the neckline.

Also notice that the first stitch pattern chart shown here shows the stitch repeat meeting the seam in an unattractive way. In the second chart, a fill pattern has been added at the sides to avoid that problem.

Internal Shaping and Decorative Patterns

Darts cut across any stitch or color pattern, distorting them in one way or another. If you superimpose a chart of a Short Row pattern on top of a chart for the stitch or color pattern, you can analyze what would happen if you moved the Short Row pattern up or down a few rows, and decide where to position it so it cuts across the decorative pattern in the least problematic way.

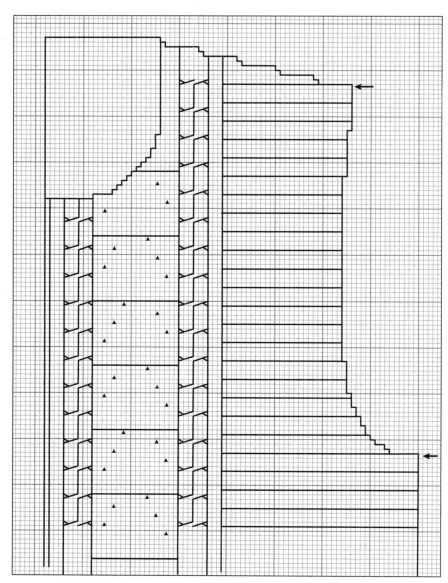

Coordinating Multiple Patterns.

Coordinating Multiple Patterns

When large areas of a garment section have different stitch patterns, say at the yoke, or perhaps in a panel down the center front, draw lines on the chart so you know when to switch from one pattern to the other.

If necessary, chart the full width of the bodice or sleeve so the relationship of each element to the garment, as well as their relationship to one another, is clear.

Intarsia Patterns

Those glorious Intarsia patterns are really quite easy to work from a chart, and the one shown here is very economical in that the back, front, and sleeve are all superimposed on one another and on the color pattern. For patterns that do not repeat, as this one does, separate charts of each section of the garment would have to be made.

Making a chart for an Intarsia pattern does have its challenges because of the difference between the squares on the graph paper and the rectangular shape of a knitted stitch; see the discussion of Proportions under General Information, above.

This is not a problem if you are planning to work an Intarsia pattern that is basically geometric, which can be handled much as you would any color pattern and plotted on the chart according to the number of stitches and rows.

Intarsia Pattern. Front and back bodice the same;
front neckline shown; sleeve superimposed on bodice.

However, any pictorial, free-form pattern is more of a challenge because the pattern is transformed from its normal appearance to one that is elongated on the chart, which represents the number of stitches and rows needed according to gauge, not the dimensions of the motif.

There are three ways to deal with this.

- Use computer software to generate a grid that exactly matches your gauge; see Grid under General Information, above. This makes it possible to draw the pattern on the graph paper using its actual proportions and is the easiest solution.
- Alternatively, draw the pattern using its actual proportions on normal graph paper, scan the result, and then use computer software to alter the proportions to match your gauge. This requires doing some math to find exactly how to adjust the size, but otherwise works reasonably well.
- Finally, you can draw a 1-inch overlay grid on the original drawing, and then draw rectangles on the chart that include the number of stitches and rows that will be in each inch of the fabric.

Transfer the shape of the lines within each of the squares on the original drawing to the respective rectangles on the chart. This is somewhat painstaking and slightly imperfect, but it is the way it was always done before computers offered other solutions; for an example of this, see the Intarsia chart in Charted Color Patterns.

Part Seven

MATERIALS

CHAPTER 27

Fibers

The fibers used in knitting yarns can be grouped into five main classifications: proteins, vegetables, a hybrid category known as the regenerated fibers, synthetics, and metallics.

The protein fibers are provided by animals, most often sheep, but also by various members of the goat and camel families, the silkworm, and some fur-bearing animals such as rabbit and possum. Vegetable fibers are derived from plants, and the most common ones used for textiles are cotton and flax (linen); ramie and hemp also appear, but they are less often found in knitting yarns.

Regenerated fibers occupy a somewhat ambiguous area; the most common are the rayons, which are made from cellulose, the primary material of all plants. However, the raw material is chopped up and chemically dissolved, and then reformed into fibers in a manufacturing process similar to that used to make synthetic fibers. The most common rayons are made from wood pulp, but newer ones are now being made from bamboo and several other materials.

The animal, vegetable, and regenerated fibers are usually referred to as "natural" because they derive from renewable resources—the animals and plants that replenish themselves year after year. This is intended to distinguish them from the synthetic fibers that are made primarily from petrochemicals and natural gas. To be perfectly accurate, these raw materials are also "natural" in origin; the real difference is that they are derived from nonrenewable resources.

Because of concerns about the environmental impact of making any textile, producers and manufacturers are searching for new raw materials and are also developing new methods of processing them that have fewer negative consequences. There is increased recognition that even the methods used to produce textile materials derived from renewable resources is not always environmentally benign; how animals and plants are raised and how the materials they provide are turned into usable fiber are currently being subjected to new scrutiny and improvements are being made. Similarly, the kinds of fibers currently made from petrochemicals may very well be derived from bio-sources in the near future, which would be both cleaner to produce and renewable.

Nevertheless, if these things matter to you, as I hope they do, natural fibers can still be thought of as superior to synthetics in terms of the environmental consequences of making them. However, you will find in the following discussion that I tend to favor them not entirely because of ecological concerns, but due to their inherent characteristics and suitability for knitting yarn. While synthetic fibers are usually designed to mimic the feel and behavior of a natural fiber, most have yet to match what Mother Nature has already done for us so beautifully.

On the other hand, synthetic fibers are considerably cheaper to produce than the more labor-intensive natural fibers, and for many knitters this can be an important factor. Also, they are often marketed as easy to care for and "allergy-free," although I am not entirely persuaded by many of those claims. It seems to me that the best reason to use yarns made from synthetic fibers is to take advantage of whatever unique and positive characteristics they offer that are *not* available in a natural fiber.

I am also a great believer in using materials of the best possible quality for any knitting project, even if they cost slightly more. Most things we make require a significant investment of time and care, and good materials are not only a pleasure to work with, but also guarantee that the garment will provide lasting satisfaction.

Personally, I am willing to pay a premium to work with good yarns, not least because I consider this a form of tithing. It is important to support those who produce things we care about by favoring them with our business. If budgetary considerations are an important factor for you, look for sales (for instance, buy wool in the summer and cotton in the winter, or purchase discontinued stock), or at the very least, reserve a percentage of what you have to spend for something truly special. This is no different than buying everyday household items like paper towels from a chain store at a discount, but buying your fresh vegetables at a farmer's market or specialty retailer at a premium.

Similarly, while Internet purchases can be efficient and economical, if you want to have a local yarn store, it is important to spend at least some of your money there. The personal service and sense of community you will gain are priceless—you will soon forget about the few extra dollars something might cost you at the yarn store, but long remember happy hours around their table and be grateful for the help you received and the knowledge you gained.

Protein Fibers

Any fiber produced by an animal, whether hair, down, fleece, or fur, is a protein fiber, meaning its chemical composition is primarily made up of "keratin," the same protein found in human hair and fingernails. However, there are many animals not represented on the list of those that contribute fibers for knitting yarns because their hair is not conducive to spinning or is too short or coarse to be useful.

Technically, the Wool Products Labeling Act of the United States Federal Trade Commission defines wool as "the fiber from sheep or lambs, as well as fiber from Angora or Cashmere goats, camels, alpacas, llamas and vicuñas."

But when most people think of wool, they think of sheep's wool, and that is how I will use the term here; to distinguish the others, I will refer to them as specialty wools. Furthermore, because of the preeminent position of wool in knitting, I will discuss it at some length but will be more brief with the others, as they share many characteristics with it and need only be discussed in the ways in which they differ.

❖ Wool

The wool fiber comes from domesticated sheep, whose covering of thick hair is called a "fleece." There are many different breeds of sheep, some of them now obscure but true descendents of ancient stock; most are the result of selective breeding programs that have gone on since Roman times.

The Merino and the Rambouillet (often called the French Merino) produce extremely high quality fleeces. The Merino sheep originated in Spain, but Elizabeth I of England acquired some with the defeat of the Spanish Armada. She used them to establish the famed English wool industry, which in turn helped finance the expansion of the British Empire. Queen

Merino ram, Australia. Photograph by C. Goodwin, 1998.

http://commons.wikimedia.org/wiki/File:Poll_Merino.jpg

Elizabeth's sheep have vast numbers of descendents in Australia and New Zealand, and they now produce most of the world's wool.

Ancient breeds of sheep that originated in particular regions of the world are still raised on small farms and their fleece is primarily sold to hand spinners. A very few breeds, such as the Shetland Sheep, are strongly associated with certain popular knitting traditions and this has kept them in relatively large-scale commercial production, but that is rare.

The Fleece

Some breeds of sheep produce a short, tightly crimped (wavy or curly), fine wool used primarily for woolen yarns; others have longer, shaggier fleeces that produce the long-staple fibers preferred for worsted yarns (for the difference between the two, see Yarns). Finally, there are breeds with coarse coats that are useful for such things as rug yarn.

Fleece color ranges from white through all shades of gray and brown to black. White wool is preferred, as it can be dyed any color, but natural fleece colors are also appreciated, particularly by hand spinners. In order to protect the fleece from damage, sheep that produce the finest grades of wool are sometimes kept in roofed pens or in enclosed pastures where underbrush is kept out, and they may even wear coats.

Very old breeds of sheep would shed in the spring and the wool was gathered, but modern sheep are sheared.† The

---

† Some wool was plucked from where it had caught on fences and shrubs, an activity referred to as "woolgathering"; this was apparently a somewhat idle pastime, because the word has long been used to mean "daydreaming."

fleece is removed in one piece and weighs an average of 10 pounds (one Merino ram produced a record 50 pounds). The best wool comes from the shoulders, sides, and backs, as this receives the least wear and tear while on the sheep. Fleece sheared from animals under seven or eight months of age is called "lamb's wool" and is softer and finer.

The fleeces are graded for color, fineness, staple (length), and crimp (the amount of natural elastic curl or waviness in the fiber) and then sorted by quality. As a general rule, the longer the staple, the coarser and more lustrous it is. "Kemp" is hard, straight, shiny hair found mixed in with some fleeces. It does not dye or spin well and must be removed; breeding programs strive to eliminate it.

The wool fiber ranges from 1 to 18 inches in length and anywhere from 8 to 70 microns in diameter (a micron = .00004 inch); the finest Merino is around 15 microns. The Bradford wool "count" is a number representing a relationship between fineness and micron diameter, and the higher the number the finer the wool. The Merino count falls between 60 and 90, while the count for most wool used in knitting yarns lies somewhere between 40 and 60.

At one time, the very finest Shetland lace yarn was collected by "rooing," running the hands through the fleece on the necks and backs of the sheep where the softest and less damaged wool could be found. These fibers are so delicate that they are not carded, just straightened gently by hand or with a comb and then spun 5 to 10 fibers at a time into a two-ply yarn as thin as a human hair. Sarah Don, in her book *The Art of Shetland Lace*, tells us that a Mrs. Peterson of Unst, one of the last of the renowned lace knitters, said it took her a year to spin one and a half to two ounces of yarn and another year to knit the yarn into a 6-foot-square gossamer "ring" shawl—so-called because it can pass through a woman's wedding ring![†]

Sharon Miller, in her wonderful book on Shetland Lace, *Heirloom Knitting*, says very little of this hand-spun worsted yarn is still made.[‡] To give you an idea of how fine it is, two ounces of worsted wool fingering (sock) yarn is about 230 yards; two ounces of a two-ply lace weight yarn contains about 560 yards, which means that the two single-plies of which it is made would be 1,120 yards long; but two ounces of single-ply hand-spun Shetland lace wool is an astonishing 5,600 yards!

Before it can be spun into yarn, the wool is usually "scoured," which means it is cleaned in a detergent bath. In addition to removing soil, this also removes the natural oil called lanolin,

which, while on the sheep, softens the fibers and acts as a water repellent. The lanolin is collected and sold as a by-product for use in cosmetics and in various industrial applications. If the wool still contains other foreign material after scouring, it may be cleaned further with carbonization or freezing, either of which breaks down any remaining foreign material, which can then be combed or shaken out.

The poorest-quality wool is made from recycled materials, in which case the label should say it is "reprocessed wool." The technical term for yarn of this kind is "shoddy," and so-called "ragg" yarn is often made of one strand of shoddy and one of an inexpensive woolen yarn. New wool will be labeled "virgin wool"; however, this is not an indication of quality, only that it went directly from fleece to yarn.

Wool Fiber

The wool fiber has a complex structure. The surface is covered by a thin membrane called the "epicuticle," which is responsible for two of wool's remarkable characteristics. This membrane is water repellent, which means a wool garment will resist the absorption of water. A light rain tends to bead up, water-based spills will sit on the surface and can be blotted off, and a sweater will actually float for a while (especially if the wool still contains lanolin).

But the epicuticle will allow water *vapor* to pass through, which is absorbed into the center of the fiber. This means that wool "breathes," not only responding to the humidity in the air, but absorbing and evaporating moisture from the body. Wool can hold up to 30 percent of its weight in moisture before the surface feels damp because the outer epicuticle remains dry. This characteristic also prevents the buildup of static electricity, which not only means you will never get a shock when wearing wool, but also that it will not attract lint and soil.

Fine wool fiber. Photomicrograph by Leo Barish, Albany International Research.

† Sarah Don, *The Art of Shetland Lace* (London: Bell & Hyman, Ltd., 1986).

‡ Sharon Miller, *Heirloom Knitting: A Shetland Lace Knitter's Pattern and Workbook* (Lerwick, Shetland: The Shetland Times, 2002).

Beneath the thin coating of the epicuticle is the cuticle, the outer structure of the fiber, which is covered with triangular scales attached only at their base. There may be anywhere from 600 to 3,000 of them per inch, and the higher the number, the higher the quality of the wool and the warmer the fiber will be, because heat is trapped in the scales. The scales also cause the fibers to cling together, which is what makes wool easy to spin into yarn. Dye readily penetrates the cuticle and is absorbed into the fiber; if correctly done this means the color is more durable because there is no dye on the surface.

Within the cuticle lies the hollow cortex, which contains long, spindle-shaped cells called "fibrils." However, the fibrils occupy only about 20 to 40 percent of the space; the rest is air. Therefore, in addition to the heat that can be stored in the scales, and between the fibers in the yarn, heat is also stored in the cortex; the result is that wool garments are exceptionally warm for their weight.

The fibrils give wool its natural curl; they are extremely elastic and resilient, and can stretch and bend without breaking and then return to normal. In the presence of moist heat, the fibrils temporarily rearrange their molecular structure, which means that wool takes a "set," just like your hair, stretching out or contracting, holding a crease or releasing wrinkles, depending upon the circumstances.

Another significant characteristic of wool is that it is naturally flame retardant. It shrinks from flame, burns very slowly, and self-extinguishes, which makes it very safe for you and for your little lambs.

The outer scales and the elastic fibrils also play a dual role in the ability of the wool fiber to "felt," or shrink and mat together when subjected to warmth, moisture, and agitation. While felt is a remarkable textile, it is not desirable to have a garment felt by accident (see Felting and Fulling), therefore, it is important to wash any wool garment appropriately. Fortunately, this is very easy to do; simply wash in cool water without agitation (actually, wool can be washed in warm water safely as long as it is not agitated; for more information, see Washing a Knit). Wool is somewhat weaker wet than dry and should be handled gently when washed. Dry heat is damaging, which is why wool is always steam pressed and why the iron temperature must be set carefully.

In spite of how easy wool is to care for, people are accustomed to laundering clothing without much concern for the details; in response to complaints about shrinkage due to improper laundering, the wool industry developed "machine washable" wool that is not supposed to felt. The original method used to do this involved a chlorination process that blunted or burned off the scales, making it impossible for felting to take place, but this also made the wool harsh and weak. Newer processes coat the fibers with a plastic resin that glues the scales down.

Many knitters appreciate the easy-care aspects of wool that has been treated in this way. Also, because the resin coating makes the fibers slick, these yarns are given a slightly tighter twist in spinning; both things make them smoother and, as a result, many people find washable wool soft and comfortable to wear.

However, easy care comes at a cost. Critics say the yarn is slippery and manufacturers concede that it stretches out of shape because it has lost its natural resiliency. Dyes do not penetrate the plastic coating very well, which means that colors are more likely to fade. The coating also prevents heat from being trapped in the scales or from penetrating the fiber, therefore it is likely that these wools are not as warm as untreated wool; heat can only be trapped between the fibers in the yarn, not within the fibers themselves. And finally, the resin will gradually wear off unless the wool is washed in cold water; people who were persuaded they could safely wash wool garments in the machine are often surprised to find they do eventually shrink.

If plastic-coated "washable" wool has given up some of its more desirable qualities and still has to be laundered in cold water just like natural wool, I have to say it is difficult to understand exactly what has been gained.

Wool Allergies

Allergies are on the rise in the general population, most of which are acquired, while others, such as the varied and poorly understood skin condition called "eczema," seem to be inherited.

Many people claim an allergy to wool, but according to the medical literature that is extremely rare, perhaps nonexistent. After all, wool is made from the same protein as human hair and fingernails, and people have worn wool for millennia without complaint. (It has always aroused my suspicion that an "allergy to wool" first appeared around the same time that synthetic fibers were introduced; it was unheard of before then.)

Nevertheless, there are things about some wools that could cause people to think they are allergic to it, even if they are not. There is no question that any coarse, hairy yarn worn next to the skin will be irritating, but this simply causes a "contact dermatitis," a fancy way of saying itchy, red skin. A true allergy sets off an internal response (runny nose and eyes, swelling, extensive rash), while contact dermatitis is confined only to the area of the skin that was irritated.

People who suffer from eczema are particularly sensitive to allergens and skin irritants, although they are just as likely to react to any prickly fiber as to wool. In fact, some people complain about acrylic yarns in this regard, because the fine fibers have sharp, cut ends that can irritate. Furthermore,

Coarse wool fiber. Photomicrograph by Leo Barish, Albany International Research.

some acrylics do not wick moisture away, and warm damp skin makes eczema worse. Wool, on the other hand, absorbs moisture from the skin without feeling damp, so it keeps you dry.

While pure wool is not known to cause allergies, there are things associated with it that can. Some "natural" wool is not thoroughly cleaned before it is spun, which means it is likely to contain what I have seen referred to as "barnyard."† In addition to dander, sheep sweat, and other waste products, a freshly sheared fleece contains microscopic amounts of grasses, pollen, seeds, and any number of insect bits and pieces. If these things are not thoroughly washed and carded out before the wool is spun into yarn, they can definitely cause allergic reactions among the susceptible.

And while relatively rare, some people are allergic to lanolin (the sheep's equivalent of the natural oil in your hair). Lanolin is present in some wool yarn, either in trace amounts, or because it was deliberately left in the wool or added back in later. This is sometimes done to make the yarn more waterproof and give it the authentic feel (and the faint sheepy aroma) of the wool used for a fisherman's sweater.

Worsted-spun wools tend to be very clean because of the extra processing they undergo, as is washable woolen-spun yarn (for the difference between the two, see Yarns). Alpaca, which is also a "wool," is extremely smooth, and many people with sensitive skin find it quite comfortable. Silk is another very smooth protein fiber that does not seem to cause problems, but it is costly and is primarily found blended with wool in knitting yarns.

People with eczema find cotton and linen very comfortable because these fibers are not only smooth, but they also wick

warmth and moisture away from the skin; for a warmer garment you might want to try a linen and silk blend, or a silk and wool blend.

And finally, it is possible for people with allergies to react to certain dyes, or even to chemical or detergent residues left in a yarn during processing. Some of this might be mitigated by washing the wool prior to working with it. While that is an extra chore, it may make the difference between being able to use a yarn or not; consider buying one ball of yarn to see whether this provides a solution.

There are also a limited number of "organic" yarns on the market that are made from fibers produced without harmful chemicals and left undyed (although if they undergo less processing, they may not be as clean as other yarns). Also keep in mind that the dyes used for synthetic yarns are added to the raw material before the fiber is made, and therefore are not on the surface where they would come in contact with your skin.

Some evidence indicates that allergy problems have increased in the general population because we live in too "clean" an environment. Exposure to a certain amount of natural soil in early childhood encourages a healthy immune system and helps prevent the development of allergic reactions. This leads me to think that perhaps people who have worn wool from earliest childhood do not react to it. And this suggests that making wool garments and blankets might be a very good thing to do for babies and young children as a way to guarantee that they will be able to wear it throughout their lives. Of course, the tender young should have the benefits of the softest possible wool next to their skin, so lamb's wool would seem to be just the thing.

❖ Specialty Wools

Several other fibers called "wool" do not come from sheep. Some are common in knitting yarns, others are so costly or rare that little is available, or they have characteristics that make them somewhat less desirable.

Mohair

The all-white Angora goat probably originated in the Himalayas, but it came to fame as a producer of wool in Ankara, Turkey, whence its name (Ankara is also the original home of the Angora rabbit; see below). South Africa and the United States are now the largest producers of mohair.

The goats are sheared twice a year, and just as young sheep give us lamb's wool, young goats give us kid mohair, the finest and softest grade; mohair from older animals is more coarse, and is typically used for upholstery. The Angora goat is unusual in that it has a single coat of fine wool. Most wool-producing animals have double coats; the outer one is not useful for yarn and must be combed out.

---

† Alden Amos, *The Alden Amos Big Book of Handspinning* (Loveland, Colo.: Interweave Press, 2001), p. 36.

Angora goat. Photograph by Trisha M. Shears (Ltshears), 2007.

http://commons.wikimedia.org/wiki/File:Angora_003.jpg

Cashmere fiber. Photomicrograph by Leo Barish, Albany International Research.

The mohair fiber is between 4 and 12 inches long, with a diameter of 20 to 60 microns. The cortex of mohair contains air pockets, making the fiber very light in weight, with excellent insulating properties. Mohair is extremely hard wearing; before cheaper synthetics came on the market, it was favored for upholstery that would get heavy use, such as for railroad car and theater seating.

The fiber has considerably fewer scales than wool, which makes it smooth and lustrous; it does not felt easily and takes dye beautifully. However, because it is so smooth, the yarn must be spun tightly to prevent it from falling apart. Only the finest and softest mohair is used for knitting yarns, which means it is generally costly. To make it more economical to work with, mills brush the surface of the yarn, giving it the familiar halo effect (smooth, unbrushed kid mohair yarn is a rare luxury), which produces a yarn that is best knitted on relatively large needles so the fluff is not compressed; a little goes a long way. These fabrics trap and hold warm air, making the garments both weightless and very warm (although mohair is prickly, and may not be a good choice for someone with sensitive skin).

Mohair sheds soil easily and therefore is easy to care for, but it is slightly more sensitive to chemicals than wool; wash in a mild, pH-neutral detergent.

Cashmere

The Cashmere goat originated in the Himalayas, taking its name from the province of Kashmir in northern India, although the finest cashmere today comes from Mongolia and China. The goat has two coats: the "beard," the coarse, hairy outer coat, and an undercoat of fine wool down. Both are combed from the goat when the animal sheds and then separated (traditionally the animals were not sheared, but that is less true today). One goat produces only a few ounces of down each year, which is the reason it is so expensive.

The down fibers are 1 to 3½ inches long and average 14 microns in diameter (somewhat finer than Merino wool); it ranges from light tan to brown in color, and is usually bleached before it is dyed.

Cashmere has fewer scales than sheep's wool, giving it a silky feel and resistance to felting; however, this also makes it more difficult to spin into yarn that wears well. Inexpensive cashmere yarn is made from the shortest fibers; it is prone to shedding and does not wear well. Several other goat breeds, and some other animals, produce down with similar characteristics that may be substituted for true cashmere without the consumer's being aware of the difference; read labels carefully.

The fiber does not resist moisture the way sheep's wool does, and in general is more fragile. It is also more susceptible to alkalis; wash carefully. Due to its delicate nature, cashmere is only suitable for gently worn garments, and because of its expense, it is most often found blended with wool or silk.

Australian cashmere goats. Photograph by Paul Esson, 2008.

http://commons.wikimedia.org/wiki/File:Australian_Cashmere_Goats.jpg

Bactrian camel, Cincinnati Zoo.
Photograph by Trisha M. Shears (Ltshears), 2010.

Vicuña, near Arequipa, Peru.
Photograph by Alexandre Buisse (Natfodd), 2007.

Camel

The wool-producing Bactrian camel, the one with two humps, is native to the high desert steppes of central Asia and must endure extremes of heat and cold. The wool was traditionally collected when the animal shed great clumps of hair in the spring. On the caravans, the last camel in line bore the baskets in which the hair of the entire herd was collected.

The outer coat of coarse hair is up to 15 inches long, the undercoat of wool down is 1 to 5 inches in length, and the two must be separated by combing. Camel down averages 20 microns in diameter, only slightly less fine than Merino wool.

The beautifully distinctive "camel color" is an integral part of the fiber and cannot be bleached; it is usually sold undyed or dyed darker. The fiber is very lightweight and has excellent insulating properties, but like the other downy fibers, it is fragile. Because the resemblance is so close, sheep's wool is sometimes used as an unlabeled substitution for more expensive camel wool.

Vicuña and Guanaco

The graceful, lovely, long-necked vicuña is the smallest member of the South American branch of the camel family, and lives at altitudes of 16,000 feet in Peru. The animal was nearly hunted to extinction by the 1960s, but is now protected by the Peruvian government, and herds have recovered in numbers.

These shy animals remain wild, but the indigenous people corral them in large herds for shearing every third year. Each animal produces only about one pound of wool each time, so very little of it is ever available, and when it is, it is extremely expensive. Vicuña down is the finest and most delicate of any of the wool fibers, being just 2 inches in length and averaging 13 microns.

The guanaco is a larger relative of the vicuña with a wider range in South America. It was also hunted close to extinction but is now protected in most countries. The guanaco is more difficult to herd into confined areas for shearing, which means very few are domesticated, and the fiber is not produced in commercial quantities. This beautiful fleece is slightly less fine than vicuña, but when available, it is extremely expensive. If you come across yarn containing either guanaco or vicuña and want to try it, make something small that will not receive hard wear.

Llama and Alpaca

At about 5 feet, the llama is the tallest of the South American camel group and it is quite tame, having long served as the chief beast of burden in the high Andean plateau. It has a

Guanaco, Torres del Paine National Park, Chile.
Photograph by Mary Frances Howard, 2005.

http://commons.wikimedia.org/wiki/File:Unshorn_alpaca_grazing.jpg

Unshorn alpaca grazing.
Johann Dréo, from Château-Thierry, France, 2007.

thick, coarse outer coat and a soft undercoat that is indistinguishable from alpaca (see above). However, because of the outer coat, the llama is less attractive as a commercial producer of fiber than the alpaca.

The South American alpaca was indispensable to the Incas. It has a shorter neck and heavier body than the llama and produces an extraordinary fleece with no kemp and little waste. There are several breeds; the most common used for commercial fiber are the huacaya and the suri. They are sheared twice a year (the unsheared hair can grow to 30 inches) and come in a rich array of fifteen basic colors and many shades in between.

Compared to wool, alpaca fiber has relatively flat, smooth scales, which makes it sleek and lustrous, with less crimp and elasticity; this means it does not felt easily, and tends not to pill. It is also considerably denser (heavier) than wool, and garments knitted with alpaca yarn have a characteristic silky drape; it is important to take drop into consideration when designing anything (see Stitch Gauge). The alpaca fiber has a

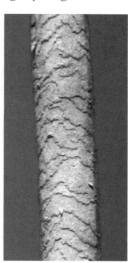

Alpaca fiber.
Photomicrograph by
Leo Barish, Albany
International Research.

medulla, a hollow core at the center of the cortex that traps air, making it even warmer than wool, and it has similar moisture and vapor properties, making it very comfortable to wear. The staple length averages 4 to 8 inches, and at 22 to 29 microns in diameter it is only slightly less fine than mohair, which it resembles in some respects; alpaca is also worsted-spun, which holds smooth fibers like these in the yarn better.

Musk Ox and Bison

Qiviut (pronounced *kiv-ee-uht*) is an extraordinary fiber that comes from the musk ox, an animal native to the Arctic that migrated into North America during the Pleistocene period between 100,000 and 200,000 years ago. It is a unique animal whose closest relatives are sheep and goats (not cattle, as the name might suggest), and it is about half the size of an American bison, which it somewhat resembles.

Programs began in the 1950s to domesticate this wild creature, and by the 1970s, a hand-knitting cottage industry using qiviut wool was established in the remote, scattered native American villages of Alaska. The Musk Ox Producers Cooperative sends the fiber out for spinning into very fine yarn, distributes the yarn to the membership, and then sells the knitted lace garments they produce. The fiber is still scarce and very little yarn is sold to the commercial market; what is available is very expensive.

The animals have a shaggy outer coat and an undercoat that is shed in the spring, which can be pulled out from under the outer coat in large sheets, producing six to seven pounds of fine down; they are not sheared.

The fiber closely resembles cashmere, but the color ranges from soft pale gray-brown to taupe and light brown; the natural colors are very beautiful, but the fiber also dyes well. Qiviut

http://commons.wikimedia.org/wiki/File:Musk_ox_.jpg

Musk ox, Stratford, Quebec. Photograph by Circeus, 2005.

Bison, Luneburg Heath Park, Germany. Photograph by Quartl, 2009.

http://commons.wikimedia.org/wiki/File:Bison_bonasus_qtl2.jpg

is an extremely durable fiber that does not shrink, and is both stronger and warmer than wool.

The great American Bison is making a return to the American plains, and fiber from these magnificent animals is newly available in knitting yarn. Its characteristics resemble those of fine sheep's wool, but it tends to be warmer, does not felt, and has no lanolin, an advantage for those who are sensitive to it. Because this fiber is still relatively rare, it is expensive, but hopefully the herds will increase and more will become available.

❖ *Silk*

This glorious fiber was used in China long before it was first mentioned in written records over four thousand years ago. Sericulture, the production of silk from domesticated moths, spread to Japan and India around A.D. 300 and from there to the rest of the world. The finest silk produced today still comes from its earliest homelands.

http://commons.wikimedia.org/wiki/File:Silk_worms.jpg

Silk worms feeding on mulberry leaves, Vietnam. Photograph by Dennis Jarvis, 2009.

Silk is given to us by two species of moth, one domesticated, one wild. The life cycle is brief. The moth lays four to six hundred eggs and then dies; the larvae hatch and feed on carefully selected chopped mulberry leaves for about a month as they grow into caterpillars.

When it is time for the metamorphosis from caterpillar to moth, the insect begins to spin its cocoon, moving its head in a figure eight while secreting two continuous protein filaments called "fibrin" that are encased in sericin, a gummy substance. After two or three days of work, the result is a silk cocoon a little larger than a peanut shell.

The largest cocoons are set aside to hatch into moths and continue the cycle; the others are heated to kill the chrysalis (the stage of the insect's life spent within the cocoon), and then the cocoons are washed in warm soapy water to soften the sericin and release the filaments. If the sericin is not removed from the filaments, the fiber has a slightly rough hand and a unique odor, and is called raw silk. The fiber color depends on the diet, and while white is preferred for dyeing, there is natural yellow and green silk. Wild silk, known as "tussah," is brown in color and is both coarser and stronger than domestic silk.

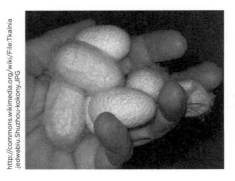

http://commons.wikimedia.org/wiki/File:Tkalnia jedwabiu.Shuzhou-kokony.JPG

Silk cocoons, China. Photograph by Kwz, 2007.

Continuous silk filaments, averaging 1,000 yards long, are unreeled from each cocoon and twisted with others directly into yarn.† Damaged cocoons, and those from which the moth has emerged, contain broken filaments that are cut into staple lengths and handled much like any other fiber; the shortest fibers are carded and woolen-spun; the longer fibers are combed and worsted spun.

Broken cocoons may also be stretched out over a hoop frame into a cap shape called "mawata," or stretched over a square frame and called "silk hankies"; there may be 20 to 30 cocoons or more in each. Silk in this form was traditionally used for padding in quilts and clothing, but can also be spun. It is possible to lift a layer from the mawata or hankie, stretch it

---

† It takes 5,500 silkworms to produce about 1 pound of silk; silk thread contains 45–50 filaments.

Silk filament.
Photomicrograph by
Leo Barish, Albany
International Research.

out into something that roughly resembles a roving, and then knit from it directly. However, it can be a challenge to handle because the filaments are so fine and strong they catch on your hands and can even cut; working with silk top or a true roving is easier to manage because the fibers are aligned.

The silk filament is very smooth, translucent, and lustrous, about 10 microns in diameter (finer than any wool) and exceptionally strong. (My understanding is that there is only one protein fiber that is stronger, and that is spider web.) Silk shares many characteristics with wool. It has nearly the same ability to absorb moisture and retain heat, but it is slightly lighter in weight and pills less. The fiber is elastic, although it recovers more slowly than wool, and will neither shrink nor stretch appreciably, making knitted silk garments quite stable.

Silk resists mildew and moths, but is susceptible to perspiration, which causes it to discolor and deteriorate. The fiber is weaker wet than dry, and is damaged by dry heat and alkalis; it burns reluctantly and will self-extinguish. Silk can be dry cleaned or washed like wool with a pH-neutral detergent; use steam and a moderate iron temperature. Silk and wool make a beautiful blend in yarn; the former provides a smooth sheen, the latter greater elasticity.

❖ *Fur*

Fur is very difficult to spin into yarn, and even when blended with another fiber such as wool, it tends to shed. Angora rabbit fur is the only one common in knitting yarns; while mink and possum have appeared in yarns, only the latter is available in any quantity.

Angora

The fiber we call "angora" is produced by a domesticated rabbit, of which there are three main varieties: English, French, and German (like the angora goat that gives us mohair, the angora rabbit originated in Ankara, Turkey). The latter two countries are the main commercial producers of angora yarn, although the fur comes from many different countries. Hand spinners often raise their own rabbits and produce limited quantities of high-quality angora yarn. The rabbit may be either combed or clipped to obtain the fur, which contains both down and stiffer guard hairs that must be removed prior to spinning.

The angora fiber is very fine, 13–15 microns in diameter and 1–4 inches in length, and it is smooth and inelastic with a silky hand. It is warmer than wool, has the same absorbency, and is very prone to felting.

Because the fur fiber is so smooth, angora yarns have a reputation for shedding, although hand-spun angora yarns are not as guilty of this because only the long staple is used and the yarn is spun more tightly so the fiber is firmly held in the yarn. Nevertheless, angora is a fuzzy yarn with lots of little ends sticking out like brushed mohair; it is not for sensitive skin. Angora is often blended with silk or wool to create yarns that are smoother and more resilient than angora alone.

Angora sweaters are usually worked up on relatively large needles to allow room for the yarn to fully expand. Because the fiber has no elasticity, plan the dimensions of any garment carefully and allow for sufficient wearing ease. The fiber is extremely warm for its weight, and because it felts easily, close-fitting garments tend to mat at the underarm; therefore, it is best used for garments worn over another item of clothing, such as a vest or jacket, or for accessories like hats and scarves.

Angora can be cleaned as for any other protein fiber, and the cold air-fluff cycle on an automatic dryer is sometimes suggested as a way to loft an angora garment after it has been packed away. I have also heard claims that putting an angora garment in the freezer helps to keep it fluffy and prevent matting.

Possum

The possum was introduced to New Zealand and, in the absence of predators, soon became a pest. In an attempt to deal with this, efforts were made to popularize the fur, and as a result, some has found its way into knitting yarn; because of where it comes from, it is only found blended with merino wool.

The yarn has a luxurious softness that is often compared to cashmere; the hair shaft is hollow and traps heat, making possum fibers considerably warmer than wool. However, as with other fur, it is difficult to spin into durable yarn, and it tends to shed. Also, it cannot be dyed, and some of the natural tan color will appear in any yarn blend; this tends to become increasingly visible as the fur emerges from the yarn with wear.

Vegetable Fibers

While protein fibers retain heat and keep us warm, vegetable fibers conduct heat away from the body and keep us cool. Conveniently for us, Mother Nature has provided both summer and winter garb, so we can have sweaters all year round.

However, while wool is perfection itself for knitting, the vegetable fibers present some challenges. Because of its inherently flexible structure, any knitted garment is liable to sag from its own weight, giving up something in width as it gains in length, and causing yarns to stretch (see Drop: The Effect of Gravity). Wool, being relatively lightweight and elastic, works against this tendency, helping to support the shape of a garment. The vegetable fibers are relatively heavy, which exacerbates the problem, and, because they lack elasticity, garments made from these fibers tend to stretch out of shape unless these things are taken into consideration when planning a design (see Weighted Gauge).

It is, for instance, a good idea to reduce the weight of a garment, and thin or softly spun yarns are a better choice than dense, thick ones; smaller-scale garments are better than large ones. Heavily embossed stitch patterns will add to a garment's weight, so it is often better to select something smoother or more open. It is quite hopeless to expect ribbed waists and wrists to retain any elasticity; while ribbing can be used as a flat border pattern, it will not draw in unless elastic is added on the inside. While this may seem like quite a few restrictions, a garment designed with these things in mind will be quite successful and satisfying to wear.

❖ *Cotton*

The earliest known place of cultivation of the cotton plant is India, and the oldest fragment of cotton textile dates to about 3,000 B.C. Some of these ancient textiles were spun of fibers from a species of cotton so fine the fabrics were transparent and their qualities have never been duplicated.

Indian cotton was one of the rare commodities Columbus was seeking on his voyage, and it is interesting to know that he found the people of South America wearing it. It is speculated that cotton migrated with the earliest Americans from Asia, which would make cotton cultivation a very old practice indeed. The plant grows best in hot climates, and the southern United States, South America, Egypt, China, and the Soviet Union are the major cotton-producing areas. More cotton is used in the world than any other fiber.

Cotton is so ubiquitous, it is difficult to imagine life without it. However, the methods used to grow and process cotton are increasingly criticized because of the damage done to the environment. Cotton cannot be grown on a large scale without extensive use of fertilizers and pesticides, and cleaning

http://commons.wikimedia.org/wiki/File:Cotó_dins_la_càpsula.JPG

Cotton plant. Photograph by Victor M. Vicente Selvas, 2010.

and preparing the fiber for spinning produces harmful waste products. Efforts are being made to respond to these concerns; however, one of the proposed solutions raises another set of questions, and that is the use of genetically modified cotton that is insect- and disease-resistant. Due to these issues, there is growing demand for organic cotton, and some of this is available in knitting yarns.

The cotton plant produces first a flower, then a pod (called the "boll") containing a mass of cotton fibers surrounding the seeds. When the pod opens, the cotton is picked and passed through a cotton gin that removes the seeds and short fibers, called "linters" (these are now recycled for use in the production of some types of rayon).

The cotton fiber has a hollow core called the "lumen," surrounded by concentric layers of cellulose that somewhat resemble the rings of a tree, but with a spiral or twisted pattern that gives it some elasticity. The living fiber is like a hollow

Cotton fiber. Photomicrograph by Leo Barish, Albany International Research.

tube, but once picked it wilts, flattening and curling up. This natural curl gives the fiber its soft loft and comfortable feel.

The cotton fiber varies in length and color depending upon the type of plant and the growing conditions; the whiter the color and the longer the fiber, the higher the quality (there is a relatively rare, naturally brown cotton that some craftspeople prize for its unique color, and some colored cottons have been grown).

The fiber absorbs moisture readily and conducts heat away from the body, making it comfortable in a hot climate, but not in a cold one. Not only does it not insulate well, but once wet it is slow to dry and tends to cling—if you are wet and cold in cotton, you can quickly become dangerously wet and cold; change clothes as quickly as possible. On the other hand, if you want to cool off on a really hot day, wear wet cotton; as the water slowly evaporates, you will feel refreshed.

Cotton is a heavy fiber, has little elasticity, and it stretches in wear, primarily from its own weight. As mentioned above, it is important to take this into consideration when planning a garment (see Weighted Gauge). However, cotton also exhibits what is called relaxation shrinkage, which means that washing in warm water and using a hot dryer will restore it to its original condition again, although its ability to recover will lessen with time.†

Cotton is weaker than silk or linen, stronger than rayon or wool, and stronger wet than dry. "Mercerized" cotton has been treated with an alkali that causes the fiber to swell and straighten, making it stronger, more lustrous, and better able to absorb dye. Cotton sheds soil and stains readily when washed with either soap or detergent, and it can be bleached if necessary (chlorine bleach should be properly diluted and the fabric neutralized afterwards; see Cleaning and Dressing a Knit). Cotton is susceptible to mildew if stored damp and makes an excellent meal for silverfish, particularly if soiled; always put it away clean and perfectly dry.

❖ Linen

Linen comes to us from the flax plant, which grows in cool, temperate climates with good rainfall. It has a beautiful flower and so is sometimes grown as an ornamental plant; in addition to textiles, it also produces linseed oil and edible seeds.

Fragments of linen textiles survive from Egypt and Europe that are some six to seven thousand years old, and evidence of its cultivation indicates it was in use long before that; dyed linen

Flax flower. Photograph by H. Zell, 2009.

fibers have been found in Georgia dating to 30,000 years ago. Aside from wool, which it predates as a textile fiber, linen was the most important fabric in western Europe until the arrival of imported cotton. Linen is more labor-intensive than cotton, even when production is mechanized, making it more costly.

Flax produces what is called a "bast" fiber: long, stiff cellulose strands taken from the outer stalk of the plant. The plant is pulled out of the ground, the seeds and leaves are removed, and then the stalk is "retted," either exposed to the action of moisture and bacteria that rot and break down the outer layer, or to chemicals that accomplish the same thing.

Next, the stalk is "heckled," crushed and beaten in order to remove the woody portions of the stem and free the fibers, which range from 5 to 20 inches or more in length. Flax fibers are smooth and lustrous and naturally cream or tan in color; they are often left undyed, but take color very well. Linen

Flax fiber (linen). Photomicrograph by Leo Barish, Albany International Research.

---

† Cotton yarns are placed under tension when loomed or knit into fabric and will stretch; if the fabric is not washed afterward to promote relaxation shrinkage (a step sometimes skipped to economize), garments made from it will shrink when the consumer washes them for the first time.

yarns made of long-staple flax are smooth, lustrous, and will not pill. Those spun from shorter lengths will be softer, fuzzier, and less strong, and these are spun like cotton.

Linen is the strongest of all the fibers discussed here, natural or synthetic, and it gets smoother, softer, and more lustrous with age and proper care; actually, new linen is not as nice as old linen. (Many woven linen garments today are not in fashion long enough for them to age well, so the full benefits never become apparent. You can get a sense of what is possible with these fabrics only if you have an old treasured linen nightgown, or your grandmother's linen sheets or tablecloths.)

Linen is even more comfortable than cotton in a hot climate. It not only absorbs moisture, but dries more quickly, wicking excess moisture along the fiber shaft where it can evaporate and conduct heat away from the body. Those with skin sensitivities find it very comfortable, both because of this, and because it is so smooth.

Like cotton, linen is a heavy fiber and is even less elastic; however, it is stable and will neither shrink nor stretch appreciably. While woven linen wrinkles badly, this is not a consideration with knitted fabrics. A knitted linen garment will give a lifetime of pleasure if the inherent characteristics of the fiber are taken into consideration when planning a design.

Linen can be safely dry cleaned but is easily washed, and since it is even stronger wet than dry, you need not fuss over it. It is damaged by acids but not by alkalis, meaning strong detergents and soaps are quite safe. Linen tolerates hot dryers and iron temperatures, but will burn if exposed to flame. Avoid repeatedly creasing the fabric, which will cause wear lines and break the fibers. Chlorine bleach is tolerated, if it is used infrequently and the fabric is neutralized afterward. If stored damp, linen is susceptible to mildew, but not to insects or rot.

❖ Ramie

Ramie is another bast fiber, taken from a tall, leafy plant of the nettle family that grows in semitropical areas. It is similar in many respects to linen and has been used for textiles almost as long.

It is a strong, lustrous white fiber that is processed and spun like linen; it is absorbent and takes dye well, and is particularly appreciated in tropical climates for its resistance to mildew. However, it is coarser and more brittle than linen, and because it is labor-intensive, even more expensive. If found in knitting yarns at all, it is most likely to be in a blend with another fiber.

❖ Hemp

Hemp is the fiber derived from a plant of the cannabis family (a variety that does not produce psychoactive materials in usable quantities). It is one of the oldest textile plants, is extremely easy to grow, and requires no fertilizers or pesticides, which makes it of great interest to those concerned about textile production and the environment.

Hemp was traditionally used for paper—the Gutenberg Bible is printed on hemp paper, Thomas Jefferson wrote a draft of the Declaration of Independence on it, both he and George Washington grew hemp on their farms, and that good printer, Ben Franklin, had a hemp papermaking business.

Because it is a bast fiber, hemp is processed like linen and has similar characteristics, although the fiber is even longer. However, it is more difficult to free from the plant, and it is coarser; therefore linen is preferred for most garment textiles.

Hemp insulates better than cotton, is warmer in cold weather, cooler in hot weather, and, like ramie, is resistant to mildew. It absorbs and holds dye well, which means it is less prone to fading. There are some knitting yarns available in either pure hemp, or hemp blended with wool, cotton, or rayon.

Regenerated Fibers

Natural fibers like linen and cotton are processed directly from plants, which are all made up primarily of cellulose. In the mid-twentieth century, chemical processes were developed to dissolve the cellulose in plants, removing everything else, and this raw material is then reformed into what are called "regenerated" textile fibers.

While the particulars differ, this means the cellulosic raw materials are processed in much the same way as synthetic materials derived from petroleum or natural gas. The first fiber made in this way was rayon, which was derived from wood pulp. Because the fiber is produced by means of manufacturing and chemical processes, rayon occupies an ambiguous place in most people's thinking; it is neither entirely "natural" nor really a "synthetic." The distinction between the two is really one of whether or not a fiber is made from a renewable resource, which puts rayon firmly in the "natural" category.

While early rayon showed promise, it had poor strength and did not hold up well in wear. However, recent developments in processing methods, as well as the use of a wider variety of raw materials, have brought about significant improvements, and modern rayons have many positive characteristics.

One of the most important of the new materials used for making a type of rayon is bamboo, which is proving to be very popular in knitting yarns. Other raw material sources for regenerated fibers are introduced with some regularity, including a few based on proteins, although most are too new yet to assess with any confidence.

❖ *Rayons*

Rayon was the first manufactured fiber derived from a natural material—cellulose derived from wood pulp or cotton linters.

The raw material is first chopped up and then subjected to various chemical baths that separate out the cellulose, which is formed into large blotter-like sheets that are dried and aged. In the next step, the sheets are crumbled and the material is redissolved into a thick solution resembling honey. In the final stage, this solution is extruded through a "spinneret," a device resembling a showerhead (but inspired by the silkworm), into an environment that instantly hardens it into long filament strands.

Almost every stage of the manufacturing process can be changed to produce slightly different characteristics in the fiber, or the fiber can be treated in various ways after it is extruded to give it distinctive qualities. The filaments can be cut into long or short staple, depending upon what kind of yarn is wanted: some have a smooth and silky feel with beautiful drape and luster, some are so soft that they resemble cotton, and some are even sueded to resemble leather. This means there can be many different types of rayon.

The most common are rayon viscose, rayon acetate, and triacetate. These were originally marketed as "imitation silk," although with experience it became clear that rayon was relatively weak, especially when wet, it shrank when exposed to heat (dry cleaning is usually recommended), and it was susceptible to mildew. With time, the early rayons took their place primarily as a less expensive substitute for cotton, not silk.

Newer "high wet-strength modulus" (HWM, or modal rayon), is a significant improvement over rayon viscose. Lyocell (under the brand name Tencel) is another improved rayon-type fiber with unique characteristics. Furthermore, the manufacturing processes used for these new types of rayon serve as an example of what can be done to mitigate environmental damage in textile production because all chemicals used in the processing are recycled.

These modern rayons are considerably stronger and have improved elasticity, and they can tolerate higher heat, which makes them easier to care for. While the elasticity of these fibers has been improved compared to the earlier rayon viscose, it is still less elastic than wool; however, they are considerably stronger and are now considered to be more durable than cotton. They also take dye beautifully and resist fading, and some are treated to prevent shrinkage, or to produce water or wrinkle resistance. Newer rayons intended for specialized purposes may incorporate Outlast® technology, a patented "climate control" additive that acts to regulate body tempera-ture; it is incorporated into the fiber during manufacturing (and is also used in some acrylics).†

In knitting yarns, rayon is most often found blended with cotton or linen, which helps to reduce the price of these natural fibers, and because the feel and behavior of rayon can be tailored to the type of yarn wanted, these blends can be quite successful. Rayon is also found in many blended synthetic novelty yarns to provide some of the characteristics of cotton at less cost.

However, you will want to read labels carefully, because many yarns still contain rayon viscose rather than one of the newer versions of rayon. Also read care requirements on the label because while improved, even the newer rayons require special handling. The fiber is damaged by both alkalis and acids, so it is important to use a mild pH-balanced detergent (a normal laundry detergent can be much too harsh); if bleaching is necessary, use an oxygen rather than a chlorine bleach. Rayons are susceptible to mildew, bacteria, and insects; store them clean and dry.

❖ *Bamboo*

The new bamboo yarns on the market have generated great interest. They are advertised as an ecologically sound alternative to cotton because the plant grows rapidly with no need for fertilizers and pesticides. The Federal Trade Commission has, however, acted to stop some of the more deceptive and extravagant claims being made about bamboo fibers.

Some marketing gave the impression that bamboo fiber was taken directly from the plant in the same way that linen or ramie is, but this is not true. Basically, it is a rayon, made from dissolved cellulose derived from bamboo, and therefore, it shares the same general characteristics of other rayons.

While bamboo may be the raw material used, the origin of the cellulose is only one factor among many that determine what a fiber is like; manufacturing processes control many others, such as how elastic it is, whether it is smooth like silk or crimped like wool, or how well it absorbs moisture or takes on dye, for instance. Nevertheless, because bamboo grows extremely quickly, it could prove to be more environmentally benign than rayon derived from wood, which grows very slowly.

---

† Outlast® was developed for NASA for use in clothing worn in outer space or at high altitudes, and for extreme terrestrial environments, but it is now finding its way into commercial products. It is most effective when the fibers that contain the material are worn directly against the skin or in very close proximity to the body; it is now appearing in some knitting yarns intended for socks, mittens, and hats.

❖ Paper

Washi, the handmade paper of Japan, is made from the inner bark of the paper mulberry tree. It is remarkably durable and flexible and was traditionally made into clothing (in particular for Shinto religious garb), but was also used for wrapping paper, book binding, origami, household accessories, and even toys. It has recently become available as yarn; the paper is simply cut into very narrow ribbon-like strips of continuous length. When knitted, the resulting fabric has a charming crispness and irregularity; it can be laundered as for rayon.

❖ Azlons

The same type of manufacturing processes used to make rayon have also been applied to regenerated fibers made from protein instead of cellulose. Some of this material is derived from animal sources, like casein (from milk), chitin (from beetles), and feathers. Others are made from plant proteins such as alginate (seaweed), or derived from crops like soy, corn, and peanuts.

For centuries, casein was used as the basis of an extraordinarily durable paint, which has reappeared on the market recently as a result of consumer interest in environmentally safe products. The first attempts at using casein for a regenerated fiber occurred in the 1940s, when it was primarily found blended with wool, with which it shared some characteristics. However, it was weak, had a sour-milk odor when warm, and was not successful.

Soy protein was first used as a regenerated fiber in 1938, but it also failed to compete successfully with either natural fibers or the newly introduced synthetics. However, efforts were renewed in 2000 in China, one of the world's largest growers of soy, and changes in the manufacturing process have led to improvements in the fiber. It is now found blended with natural and synthetic fibers in knitting yarns.

Major investments are being made in developing fibers based on a combination of corn protein and cellulose from other plants, which are referred to as PLA fibers, as well as newly introduced fibers derived from kelp (seaweed). Manufacturing processes are far more sophisticated today, and the chemistry of basic materials is better understood. Some of these things are proving to be successful textile fibers and more will be introduced.

However, it is sobering to read the exaggerated claims made for earlier fibers and realize how many of them failed (rayon never became a viable substitute for silk, for instance). When you buy yarn containing a fiber your grandmother would not recognize, or there are terms on the label you do not understand and perhaps cannot pronounce, exercise a certain amount of healthy skepticism and caution. Buy one ball and put it through its paces (see Test Swatches); see what happens if you do *not* follow the care instructions—wash it, steam it, stretch it, rub it hard, leave it out in the sun. And the true test of any yarn is to make something and wear it for a while; it will only be with time and experience that we know whether these new fibers will live up to the claims made for them, but it is fun to try new things.

Synthetic Fibers

Synthetic fibers begin as a thick chemical soup; like rayon, the solution is forced through the holes of a spinneret and the fluid emerges into a controlled environment that causes the liquid to congeal into long, continuous strands called filaments. This process is very like what the silkworm has been doing all along and similar to that used for the regenerated cellulose fibers discussed above.

Of the many synthetic fibers on the market, only five appear in knitting yarn: nylon, polyester, acrylic, olefin, and the elastomerics, like spandex. Each of these has different characteristics, but they all have some things in common.

Synthetic fibers are hydrophobic, or water-resistant. This means water remains on the surface of the fiber rather than being absorbed into it, as is the case with natural fibers. This quality has several positive and negative aspects.

On the one hand, the fibers dry quickly after wetting, and they resist water-based stains. This is the basis of the "wash and wear" claim. On the other hand, they have an affinity for oil- and grease-based stains, which can penetrate the fiber. Because water cannot enter the fiber, this kind of soil can only be removed by dry-cleaning solvents. Another criticism of synthetics is that they tend to absorb odors, most of which are bound to the oils in perspiration, which is why they cannot be washed out.

This hydrophobic quality is also responsible for making garments of synthetic fibers feel clammy; while some newer synthetics have been developed with the ability to wick moisture (and heat) away from the body where it can evaporate, many do not have this quality. This lack of absorbency also causes synthetics to build up static electricity, a problem more serious when selecting carpeting than knitting yarn, perhaps, but a factor to keep in mind. In addition to the possibility of shock, static electricity attracts and holds lint and soil in a fabric.

And finally, the fibers themselves do not trap heat; the warmth provided by a synthetic garment is the result of heat trapped in the air pockets that lie between one fiber and another within the yarn, and within the structure of the fabric itself.

Unfortunately, many synthetic yarns pill badly because the tangled fiber ends are so strong that once caught up together, they do not separate. Also, the filaments are cut into staple lengths that mimic natural fibers in one way or another, and the cut ends tend to be sharp, giving some of these yarns a prickly feel on the skin, which some people find irritating.

And finally, most synthetic fibers are very sensitive to heat and should never be washed in hot water or dried at high temperature. The fibers are also thermoplastic, which can be good or bad, depending upon circumstances. Woven synthetic fibers can be given permanent folds or pleats, when appropriate heat and pressure is applied. In a knitted fabric, even hot steam can make them permanently wilt; on the other hand, it is also possible to create an interesting silk-like drape by steaming or pressing them with a warm iron.

When exposed to flame, these fabrics will melt into a puddle of plastic that sticks to skin. This can cause serious burns; be extremely careful when wearing synthetic garments near any open flame and consider carefully whether you want your children to wear them at all!

On the positive side, synthetic fibers are generally lightweight, very strong and resilient, and fabrics made of them are therefore durable and retain their shape well. Most are colorfast because they are solution dyed (the color is introduced before the fiber is extruded), and none of them are of any interest to mildew or moths. When first made, the filaments are very smooth, almost slippery, but manufacturers have developed a variety of techniques for changing the shape of the filaments in cross-section, and adding crimp or texturizing the surface to give them characteristics that mimic those of natural fibers or that create some other desirable quality.

In fact, by far the best reason to use synthetic yarns is their wild variety and whatever characteristics they have been given that cannot be found in natural fibers. Some are simply good fun, others are glamorous, but most bring something new and novel to knitting and this is a welcome addition to the choices we have.

❖ Nylon

Nylon was invented right before World War II but was not available on a wide scale until the war ended. It has, of course, lent its name to one of the most justifiably popular products on the market, women's nylon stockings, which caused a sensation when they were introduced.

Nylon belongs to the polyamide family, a word you may see on some yarn labels instead of nylon. Nylon fibers are lightweight, very strong, abrasion resistant, and elastic. They do not stretch out of shape and will shrink only with high water temperatures, although a too-hot iron can cause the fiber to soften or melt.

The fiber is very easy to wash, and any detergent is safe, but some dry-cleaning solvents are harmful. Light-colored nylon can pick up dyes from other fabrics, giving it a yellow or a gray cast; it is best washed alone or only with other white fabrics. Only oxygen-based bleach should be used for stains.

In knitting yarns, nylon is most often combined with natural fibers, which gain the advantage of its strength and elasticity. Since very little of it is required to accomplish this goal, and because its other characteristics are not particularly desirable in knitted fabrics, you will rarely see a yarn containing more than 10 to 20 percent nylon, at which level it is very unobtrusive but effective.

It is at its most useful combined with wool in sock yarns, and is so strong the wool will wear away long before the nylon does (instead of a hole in the sock, you will have a nylon lattice window). Small quantities of nylon yarn are also available for carrying with a yarn for just the heels and toes, and it also appears in fine elastic threads and yarns used in knitting; see Elastomerics, below.

❖ Polyester

Polyester of one sort or another has become the most common synthetic fiber since its introduction in the early 1950s. Like nylon, it is made in many different variations with a wide range of applications.

These fibers are relatively strong and elastic, although less so than nylon, and have excellent resilience. Because of its economy, polyester is frequently blended with natural fibers, often in amounts no greater than 40 percent to allow the characteristics of the natural fiber to dominate. Garments made with yarns blended with polyester tend to hold their shape without sagging through repeated wearings; polyester is particularly successful when blended with cotton because it contributes strength and resilience to the yarn and reduces the

Polyester fiber. Photomicrograph by Leo Barish, Albany International Research.

weight of garments. Modifications of the shape and surface of polyester are also bringing it closer to the feel of silk and wool, although it has few of their other characteristics.

Polyester can be dry cleaned, machine washed in any normal detergent, and machine dried at low heat. These fabrics will shrink at high heat; reduce iron heat to the lowest setting that will produce steam. When cleaning a blend, take the properties of both fibers into consideration. For instance, in a cotton-polyester blend, clean it as for a polyester.

❖ Acrylics

Acrylic is basically a vinyl plastic that is made into fibers that are intended to mimic the feel and appearance of wool. Since their introduction in the 1950s, acrylics of one kind or another have become the most common synthetics used in knitting yarns.

Pure acrylic yarns are marketed as an economical and "non-allergenic" alternative to wool (for wool "allergy," see above), or they are blended with wool or other natural fibers to reduce their cost. Blends are often quite successful, because they offer some of the characteristics of all the fibers used. The fibers can also be manufactured in a variety of textures that are impossible to achieve with natural fibers, and these characteristics are often effectively exploited in the novelty yarns.

Acrylic yarn is relatively elastic, very soft to the touch, lightweight, and lofty. Even though no heat is absorbed into the fiber, air spaces within the yarns and in the fabric structure will trap body heat. Modern acrylics have been developed with improved wicking ability, which means they are far better at regulating heat than earlier versions, especially if they incorporate Outlast® technology into the fiber (see the note in Rayons, above), making them more comfortable to wear.

Acrylics are subject to the usual problems with grease stains and odors described above, although some progress is being made with newer acrylics to mitigate this. They are moderately strong fibers, although less so when wet, and can be dry cleaned or laundered; they tolerate oxygen bleaches and are colorfast.

However, acrylics are *extremely* heat sensitive and must never be washed in hot water or put in a hot dryer because they will literally start to melt; at the very least they will go limp and stretch out of shape. The best approach is to hand wash in cool water and air dry; the centrifuge action of the washing machine will remove most of the water, which means they will dry very quickly.

Acrylics, unless specifically marked "flame retardant," will ignite and burn readily, creating a molten plastic that can attach to the skin and cause serious burns. (A closely related fiber, modacrylic, most often used in pile and fake-fur type fabrics and children's garments, is apparently fire retardant and self-extinguishing.)

❖ Olefins

There are two main types of olefin fibers, polypropylene and polyethylene, both made from natural gas. The latter is primarily used for packaging materials and does not interest us.

Polypropylene, however, is an exceptionally strong, very lightweight, inexpensive, and abrasion-resistant fiber. It is commonly used for industrial textiles, indoor-outdoor carpeting, and upholstery. More recently, however, it has appeared in machine-knit undergarments and light sweaters designed for active sports, for which its wicking ability is appreciated; it is rarely used in hand knitting yarns.

Polypropylene pills with a vengeance, builds up static electricity, attracts and holds lint and hairs tenaciously, has a great affinity for grease and oil stains and for perspiration and other odors, and it melts at relatively low temperatures. In short, it is altogether unpleasant to deal with and to wear. If you want long underwear, wool is best, silk is nice, and cotton is fine; all are easy to care for and will stay beautiful, fresh, and clean for a long, long time.

❖ Elastomerics

The one synthetic fiber that is clearly superior to a natural one is made from polyurethane. Technically known as "elastomeric" fibers, spandex, elastane, and Lycra will stretch just as far as rubber, but are stronger and less prone to deterioration. These are most often used for stretch woven and machine-knit fabrics that are made into undergarments, swimming suits, and other active wear.

Some attempts have been made to introduce spandex into knitting yarns, usually as a core wrapped with a natural fiber yarn. This has not been particularly successful for hand knitting because it is extremely difficult to work with consistent tension. However, most good knitting stores carry a small supply of fine nylon spandex yarns in a basic range of colors that can be worked into ribbings at waist and wrists to preserve elasticity. These can be machine washed and dried, but should not be bleached; whites will turn yellow in hot water.

Metallics

Gold and silver were once woven into priceless fabrics intended for the favored few. However, they were quite impractical; not only were they heavy, but the thin metals tarnished and broke.

Glitter is no longer reserved for the elite and is now democratically and economically available to all. And we have the advantage that modern metallic yarns are lightweight, reasonably durable, and permanently shiny. They come in three forms.

Silver-plated thin gauge wire and color-tinted copper wire are available on spools in different thicknesses and in 10- to

25-foot lengths. These wires are flexible enough for knitting and are suitable for making jewelry and small accessories. Some coated wire is available that is softer to the touch; this looks less obviously like wire, but has the characteristic combination of being both stiff and flexible.

Extremely fine steel yarn blended with silk or wool has recently become available as a knitting yarn. Because it is so thin, it is almost always knitted along with another yarn. This yarn behaves far more like a normal one; however, it has shape-retention: if the fabric is crumpled, it will retain the contours, giving it a unique appearance.

More often, however, small amounts of metal are combined with a conventional synthetic knitting fiber. For instance, sheets of colored aluminum can be coated with an adhesive, sandwiched between layers of polyester, and heat set. Or metal dust is deposited on a polyester film and sealed with resin. The resulting material is cut into filaments and texturized before being spun into yarn.

Yarns of this kind are not particularly strong or soft and so are usually plied with wool or acrylic. All of these are heat-sensitive, but otherwise should be treated like any other synthetic fiber; read the care instructions on the label for the specific needs of each yarn.

CHAPTER 28

Yarns

It used to be that knitters had a very limited number of yarns to work with. In many cases, they had raised the sheep or grown the linen or cotton and then spun the yarn themselves. The characteristics of the yarn would be well known, and they would knit it up into a customary garment style with their favorite pair of needles (often their only pair of needles).

There is comfort in the familiar, but this is not the situation most of us now find ourselves in. When knitters today start a project, they may be dealing not just with a new yarn, but new needles, a pattern for a garment style they may have never made before, and which might require unfamiliar techniques. Adventurous, yes; but perhaps asking quite a lot.

A basic understanding of how yarn is made can help you decide whether the one used in a published pattern is something you want to work with, or it may help you select a yarn that is suitable for something you want to design.

The chapter on Fibers provides information on the characteristics of the basic materials used for making yarns. Here you will find a general discussion of the different ways that fibers can be spun into yarn and what kinds of yarns are suitable for different types of garments. Also included is information on how yarns are normally wound into forms you can knit with (and how to wind it yourself), and how to interpret the information on labels. You will also find some general advice about how to substitute another yarn for the one called for in a published pattern.

Making Yarn

The steps taken to turn any fiber into yarn are quite similar, although there are subtle but important differences depending on the characteristics of the fiber and the type of yarn that will be produced. The first step is carding, which is the process of blending the fibers together; for certain types of fibers, this is followed by combing, which aligns them. Spinning is the process of drawing the fibers out of the combed or carded mass and twisting them together into a strand of yarn called a "single" or a "ply." Finally, two or more strands are normally "plied" together, twisted into a yarn of the required thickness.

❖ Carding and Combing

Natural fibers come in various "staple" lengths, which are natural to the plant or animal that produced it; cotton, for instance, is very short, linen is long, and wool is in between. "Filament" fibers are extremely long, and are produced only by the silkworm and synthetic manufacturing processes. To a great extent, the natural length of the fiber determines how it will be spun; however, filaments are usually cut into staple lengths that resemble those of one of the natural fibers so they can be spun in the same way.

After a natural fiber has gone through the preliminary stages of being cleaned and prepared for spinning, the first step is to smooth the fibers out so there are fewer tangles. This is done using a process called "carding."

Hand spinners use "carding paddles," which consist of a pair of rectangular wooden pads with sturdy handles on one side, and a leather or rubber surface on the other that is studded with fine bent wires; the paddles look like giant dog brushes.

A small bunch of fibers is laid on the wires of one paddle, the wires of the other paddle are set down on top and the two are drawn in opposite directions several times. This blends the fibers, and draws out the shortest lengths and any foreign material. The carded fibers are rolled off the paddle and are then ready for spinning. The process is basically the same in a

http://commons.wikimedia.org/wiki/File:Wiik_Kardande_flicka.jpg

Girl Carding Wool, 1883, by Maria Wiik (Finnish). Oil on canvas.

mill, but with large, wire-covered rotating drums substituted for the paddles.

Hand spinners roll short staple off the paddle in the direction in which it is carded, forming a little cigar shape called a "rolag." The fiber can be spun directly from a rolag, but more often several are combined and drawn out with a slight twist into a thick, soft rope of fibers called a "roving." A "pencil roving" is drawn out further and given slightly more spin; this can be used as-is for knitting (Icelandic yarn is of this type).

For long staple fibers, carding is followed by combing, which aligns the fibers so they all lie in the same direction; this also removes lengths shorter than a few inches. Long fibers are referred to as "top" and the shorter ones are called "noil." Noils retrieved from combing are usually blended back into carded yarns.

Long staple fibers are rolled off the paddle from side to side, parallel to the carding, and then combed. The combed fibers may be drawn directly out of the end of the rolag and spun into yarn, or folded over the forefinger and drawn out from the center, but more often they are first combined and drawn out into what is called a "sliver" (pronounced *sly-ver*), which is similar to a roving, but the fibers lie parallel and no twist is introduced.

Linen has the longest staple of any natural fiber, and the strongest. It is "hackled" (repeatedly drawn through a group of what look like long, sharp nails) to align the longest fibers, called "line," and remove the shorter ones, called "tow." The long fibers are more typically used for weaving; the shorter ones are spun into yarns for knitting.

Silk is reeled directly out of a cocoon in a single long, continuous filament that is so fine it is difficult to see, and three or four of them are twisted into thread as they are unreeled. If the cocoon has been damaged or broken, the filament is no longer continuous, and these shorter lengths of silk are used for "spun" silk, which is the type used in knitting yarns.

Like silk, manufactured fibers are produced in the form of long, continuous filaments. Because of the way they are made, no carding or combing is necessary before spinning. However, mills typically cut the filaments into whatever staple lengths are thought suitable for the type of yarn wanted and then it is spun in much the same way as a natural fiber.

❖ *Spinning*

Two primary methods are used to spin any fiber into yarn, one for short staple fibers, and the other for long staple fibers. There are variations on how each of these can be done, depending upon the fiber, the staple length, and the type of yarn desired.† The equipment used by mills mimics hand-spinning techniques, but on a giant scale.

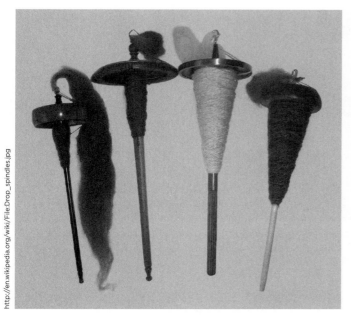

http://en.wikipedia.org/wiki/File:Drop_spindles.jpg

Top-whorl drop spindles. Photograph by Pschemp, 2010.

The basic process of spinning involves drawing a few fibers at a time out of the combed or carded mass and twisting them together by means of a drop spindle or a spinning wheel. A spindle is a relatively short stick with a weighted "whorl" or disc on one end; it is suspended from the yarn and is given a quick twist with the fingers to set it in motion. A spinning wheel is mounted on a frame with the equivalent of a spindle and the motion of the wheel is transferred to the spindle.

As the fibers are twisted together, they are held together in the yarn by friction and compression. Yarns with some natural surface texture, like wool, hold together quite readily; those that are smoother, like linen or alpaca, require more twist to bind them together. You can get a sense of how this works simply by pulling a few strands out of an ordinary cotton ball and twisting them in your fingers as you do so. As you will see, the first ones drawn into a yarn by the twist will pull those that follow after them. If only a few fibers are drawn out of the

mass at a time, the yarn will be thinner; if more twist is applied, it will be both thinner and firmer.

The "long-draw," or woolen-spun method, is used for any short staple, carded fiber, not just for wool. The twist is applied as one hand draws the mass of unaligned fibers (or the end of the roving) away from the turning spindle. The result is soft, plush yarn with visible ends that give it a somewhat fuzzy surface. This is the most common type of knitting yarn because it is suitable for a wide variety of garments. While it tends to be relatively weak (a strand can be broken easily), this matters less once it is within the structure of the knitted fabric.

The "short-draw," or worsted-spun method, is used for long staple, combed fibers. The aligned fibers are first drawn out between the two hands for several inches; the hand closest to the spindle then releases, allowing the twist to move up into the fiber; these steps are then repeated. Worsted-spun yarns are smoother, stronger, and more elastic than woolen-spun yarns. They also resist abrasion, which means they are less likely to fuzz, pill, or show other signs of wear over time, and they knit up beautifully. Semi-worsted is, as the name suggests, halfway between a woolen and a worsted; it is long-staple wool that is not combed, but it is spun like worsted.

Long, smooth linen fibers are also worsted-spun, but require slightly different handling. A large bundle of combed fibers is tied to a distaff, a pole held under one arm or attached to the spinning wheel.‡ The fiber ends are drawn into the yarn

Spinning fibers into yarn. The draft zone demonstrated by Ted Myatt. Photograph by Michael Wade, 2011.

---

† For an excellent and highly readable introduction to spinning, please see Alden Amos, *The Alden Amos Big Book of Handspinning* (Loveland, Colo.: Interweave Press, 2001).

‡ The word "distaff" comes from the German words for flax and staff, or pole. The word is also used when referring to women, as in the phrase, "the distaff side of the family," because it was they who did the spinning. Men often did the weaving, although this was clearly not thought to be their most essential occupation, because when referring to the male side of the family, the opposite of distaff is "spear side."

http://en.wikipedia.org/wiki/File:Reine_Berthe_et_les_fileueses_1888.jpg

Reine Berthe et les fileuses (*Queen Bertha and the Spinners*), 1888, by Samuel Albrecht Anker (Swiss).
A romantic depiction of Queen Bertha of Kent (541–580), with young girls spinning flax.
Musée Cantonal des Beaux-Arts, Lausanne.

a few at a time; the smoothest linen yarn is "wet-spun," meaning it is kept slightly damp during spinning. However, most linen knitting yarns are made from relatively short staple fibers, and these are carded and woolen-spun, like cotton.

When yarn is twisted to the left as it is spun, it is referred to as "Z-twist"; when twisted to the right, "S-twist." Linen tends to naturally twist to the right, so is traditionally spun S-twist, but most other fibers are spun Z-twist. The resulting strand is called a "single" or a "ply." But a single is not yet a proper yarn that you can knit with; for that you really need yarn with more than one ply.

❖ Plied Yarn

In order to form true yarn, two or more singles are twisted together to form what is called a "plied" yarn; this adds strength

as well as dimension. If the singles were given a Z-twist when spun, they will be plied together with an S-twist, and almost all knitting yarns today are in this form. Linen and some wools are spun S-twist and plied Z-twist, but the latter is now uncommon.

The singles are slightly over-twisted when spun. The fibers can tolerate a certain amount of twist without protest, but if they are twisted too far, resistance will occur (and at some point, they will break). If the yarn is allowed to hang free, the fibers will relax and the yarn will unspin slightly to release the excess twist; in this condition, the yarn is considered balanced.

If two singles containing extra twist are brought together and twisted in the opposite direction from which they were spun, they will actively wrap around each other; done correctly, the resulting two-ply yarn will be perfectly balanced, with the amount of twist in the singles equalized by the amount of twist given to the yarn when plied. It is the tension between the twist imparted to the singles and the amount imparted when they are plied that holds the combined yarns together so they will not simply unwind and come apart.

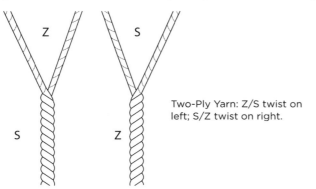

Two-Ply Yarn: Z/S twist on left; S/Z twist on right.

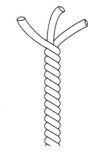

Three-Ply S-Twist Yarn.

Over-Twisted Yarn

If you were to knit with an over-twisted single (one prepared for being plied, but still alone in the world), whatever you make with it is likely to go on the bias—the extra tension in the fibers will be released into the fabric.

If not made correctly, plied yarn can also have too much twist in it, and the same thing will happen; it is rare to find this to be true of yarns made by large mills, since their manufacturing processes tend to be very precise, but it may occur with hand-spun yarns.

To test a yarn to see if it is well balanced, allow about a yard of yarn to hang down in a U-shape and then gradually bring the two strands together. If they hang straight down in a relaxed way, the yarn is balanced. If they just take a few leisurely turns around one another, there is little reason for concern. But if they actively twist together and resist coming apart again, the yarn has excess twist and needs to be rebalanced.

The solution is quite simple; either drop your knitting and let the needles unspin the twist from the yarn, or clip or tie the strand of yarn to the side of the ball and let it hang from the yarn and unspin.

It is a good idea to do this frequently as you work because the process of wrapping the yarn around the needle to form each stitch either adds twist or removes it from a yarn, depending upon the knitting method used; see Knitting Methods and Yarn Twist. For some projects, you might want to consider working with the Combined Method of knitting because the yarn is wrapped in one direction for Knit and the other for Purl, which can help keep the yarn balanced.

Twist can also be added when yarn is drawn from the top of a cone or from a center-pull ball. An easy way to prevent this is to place the yarn supply on a spool of some kind so it can be unreeled (drawn off from the side instead of being drawn from the top), or simply leave the ball on your ball winder (or even leave the skein on your umbrella swift).

And finally, a small amount of twist is added simply by turning the fabric around and around as you work; if you are working flat, you might want to develop the habit of turning it away from you at the end of one row, and toward you at the end of the next. In any case, the twist added by drawing off a new supply of yarn from the ball or turning the needles as you work can be corrected in the same way—by either letting the fabric or the ball hang to unspin, as described above.

The amount of twist in a single or plied yarn can be temporarily "set" by putting a skein on a swift under moderate tension (see Tools), applying steam, and letting it dry thoroughly. However, the next time the yarn is washed or even just steamed, this "set" will be released. In other words, it may make it easier to work with, but any extra twist in the yarn could still show up in your finished fabric.

❖ Dyes

It is well beyond the scope of this book to go into all the different dye types and methods that are used, nor is such a highly technical discussion really necessary. However, some general information is useful.

Natural fibers may be "stock" or "top" dyed, meaning they are dyed before spinning; the dye thoroughly penetrates the fibers, which means the color is much less likely to fade or run. Often labeled "dyed in the wool," the approach is more expensive because it requires extra steps and careful blending of the fibers. It is commonly used to make tweed and heather yarns, and the resulting colors have great subtlety and depth.

However, it is far more common and economical for the mills to dye yarn rather than fiber, as this allows them greater flexibility in responding to changing fashions in color. Because of the structure of the yarn, the dye does not penetrate as deeply as when fibers are dyed prior to spinning.

Some yarns are made up of singles that were dyed different colors and then plied together. Artisan dyers also paint yarns, dabbing or pooling color onto a skein of yarn or using tie-dye techniques. Not only is each skein of yarn unique, but when it is knitted, the effect the areas of color will produce depends upon the width of the fabric, the gauge, and the stitch pattern, which means that no two items are alike (no two socks are even alike).

For the knitter, it matters less how the yarn was dyed than whether it is colorfast. Some dyes may fade in sunlight, in water, in dry-cleaning solutions, or with exposure to perspiration. Reputable manufacturers indicate on the label if the yarn is colorfast under all or some of those conditions. If the label is marked "dry clean only," it may be because the dye used is not fast in water, or it may mean the manufacturer is concerned that someone will not know how to wash the item correctly. In the absence of information on the label, there are certain tests you can conduct at home; see Unstable Dyes in Cleaning and Dressing a Knit.

One of the advantages of synthetic fibers is that they are solution dyed, which means the color is added to the liquid chemical mixture prior to extruding the filaments. This is done because once the fiber is formed, it will resist the penetration of the dyes, and the great advantage of this being done is that the color is locked inside the fibers, and will not fade or bleed.

Yarn Types

Straight, smooth yarns made up of plies that are all of the same uniform type are referred to as "simple," or "classic," yarns. Many people mistakenly believe that the number of plies in the yarn is a designation of its thickness, but this is not necessarily true. A four-ply yarn made of very fine singles will be considerably thinner than a two-ply yarn made of thicker, softly spun singles.

❖ Classic Yarns

Classic woolen and worsted knitting yarns are smooth, with a consistent thickness throughout. They are typically made up in two- and three-ply versions from the same size singles, which is convenient for the mill, as well as for the knitter; the two-ply would be suitable for lighter garments, the three-ply suitable for heavier ones.

However, this only applies when the two yarns are made by the same mill with the same singles; another mill might start with singles that have a slightly different thickness, which means that its two-ply or three-ply yarn will not be comparable.

Most knitters do not concern themselves much about whether a yarn is two-ply or three-ply. However, if you have a choice of ply between two yarns that are otherwise about the same thickness, you might want to give some thought to how you plan to use the yarn. A three-ply yarn is rounder and will make plump-looking stitches; a two-ply yarn is flatter and will produce a smoother fabric surface; this is subtle, but you are likely to notice the difference in a stitch or color pattern with a lot of detail.

❖ Novelty Yarns

What are called "novelty," or "complex," yarns come in many different forms. It is impossible to cover all the possibilities that exist because they are highly individual and new variations take their turn on the market every year; there are, however, some common types.

Cord or cable yarns are made by plying together several already-plied yarns. In other words, a mill might start with two very fine S-twist singles combined in a Z-twist yarn, and then ply two or more of these two-ply yarns with an S-twist. Because cords typically contain extremely fine singles, the fibers are closely held in the yarn, which makes it smooth, strong, and lustrous with a distinctive pebbled look. Many cord yarns are cotton, but wool versions are available that are more loosely plied and very plush.

One way of adding texture to a simple yarn is to rough up the fiber ends. Mohair, for instance, is a long smooth worsted-spun fiber plied into a very fine yarn, and the surface is then brushed to raise the ends, giving it a characteristic fuzzy halo. You can create a similar effect with a woolen yarn after you have knit it into a fabric by using some equivalent of a "teasel," which is a dried seed pod with a thorny surface that was traditionally used to raise the nap on woven textiles.

A far more subtle texture is seen in crepe yarns, which are made from over-twisted singles; these yarns have a great deal of elasticity. Normally only available in relatively thin yarns,

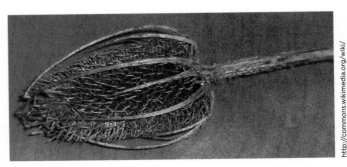

Teasel, the dried pod of a thistle, used to raise ends of yarn or nap of fabric. Photograph by Loggie, 2007.

they were favored by hand knitters in the 1940s and 1950s for beautiful blouses, dresses, and suits that held their shape well.

Another yarn that was popular in that era was bouclé, which is made of one single that is more tightly twisted than the other. The high-twist strand will curl around the more relaxed one, doubling back on itself to form tiny loops along the yarn. Contemporary bouclé yarns are thicker and the loops are quite pronounced; some mohairs are made this way. The loops can make them a little challenging to knit with because they can catch on the needle tip.

"Gimp" is made up of one thin and one thick ply and for "spot," or "nub" yarns, one ply is intermittently bunched up tightly in sections around the other as the two are plied. "Slub" yarns are made up of one normal single and one that was spun unevenly so it alternates thick and thin; the loosely spun sections form soft, thickened bumps on the yarn.

Instead of being plied, two soft singles may simply be held together by a third, "binder" yarn. In some cases, the core yarn is simply a thin roving wrapped with a very fine, almost thread-like binder yarn that holds it together; in others the core yarn is wrapped with two binder yarns in a double-helix pattern.

Chenille (which means caterpillar in French) was originally made by cutting strips from a specially woven fabric by hand. However, in the 1990s new methods of producing chenille yarns were developed, and have since been improved upon. Filament fibers that make up the pile are laid across two firmly spun core yarns, which are then plied tightly together to hold the pile in place. Because the core yarns are given a high twist, this can cause bias in the fabric; see Knitting Methods and Yarn Twist. Nylon-core yarns may be heat set to prevent the pile from shedding. The highest-quality chenille is made from cotton, and this is the easiest type to work with and to care for, but there are also rayon and synthetic chenilles. The yarn needs to be knit at a firm, close gauge to prevent what is called "worming"; acrylic chenille is particularly prone to stretching and will work its way out of the structure of a relatively loose fabric, forming unsightly loops on the surface. Follow care instructions on the label; most chenille can be washed, but should be dried flat.

Novelty yarns.

Chainette yarn is basically a knitted cord (see Uncommon Shapes); its appearance as a knitting yarn is relatively recent, but the technique has long been used to make things like tassels and lanyards.

Ribbon yarns may be woven narrow, but synthetic ribbons are more often strips cut from woven fabrics that have heat-melted edges. As mentioned in the chapter Fibers, paper ribbon yarns are also cut strips; the best of these are made from *washi*, the traditional handmade Japanese paper that is remarkably durable and can be laundered.

❖ *Yarn Labels*

It is worth your while to read labels carefully before you buy any yarn. Laws about truth in marketing have grown increasingly stringent, and therefore, more information is available to you now than was the case before. Nevertheless, there are both sins of commission and omission in labeling.

Fortunately, when a yarn contains high-quality materials the manufacturer generally wants you to know about it. A label may mention that a yarn is worsted wool or combed or mercerized cotton because these are more expensive to produce and the information is provided to justify the cost. Similarly, labels will always draw attention to the presence of the

finer and more precious fibers, such as Merino wool, lamb's wool, kid mohair, alpaca, or cashmere. However, do read the fine print; I once saw a label marked "cashmere/wool" on the front, and on the back found that the yarn was actually 80 percent wool and 20 percent cashmere.

A label may also point out that the fiber comes from a country with a reputation for producing excellent material. However, even places justly famed for mohair, silk, or wool, for example, also produce poorer grades of these fibers, which may find their way into the knitting yarns you purchase. Some labels, for example, trumpet that the yarn contains "pure virgin wool"; however, this only means the wool is new, not that it is soft or of a high quality, and it may not even mean that 100 percent of the yarn fiber is of that type.

Unfortunately, price is not a very accurate measure of the quality of a yarn. A high price may instead indicate a high-fashion novelty or designer yarn, a large advertising budget, a fancy store in a high-rent neighborhood, or an import, but the quality of the yarn itself may be average or poor. Keep in mind that the label may tell us who has designed and marketed the yarn, but not necessarily what mill manufactured it, and one mill may sell to several different labels.

Your only assurance of quality, therefore, is the reputation of the yarn manufacturer, the store you patronize, and your own experience with both. Ask questions and use your hands to confirm the label's claim; buy one ball, take it home and make a swatch and then test it (see Test Swatches).

On the back of the label, you will often find suggested needle sizes and sometimes the average number of stitches per inch in Stockinette. Unfortunately, this information is problematic, for several reasons. First, American yarn manufacturers suggest needle sizes that produce a much looser fabric than is customary in Europe, so you need to take into consideration where the yarn is from and guess what sort of fabric they had in mind. Also keep in mind that you may not be able to produce that exact gauge with the needle size suggested, or you may not be working in Stockinette (see Matching Pattern Gauges).

The labels will also have information indicating the name or number of the color and frequently a dye-lot number. The dye-lot number is very important. It designates all the yarn dyed at the same time and, therefore, guarantees that the color of each ball of yarn bearing that number will match all other balls similarly labeled. It is very important that the yarn you use for any solid-color project all has the same dye lot. The difference between one dye lot and another will generally not be apparent to the eye when looking at the balls of yarn in the store, but will be obvious once the two yarns are worked up side by side in the fabric.

For this reason, check the label on every ball you want to purchase to make sure the dye lot numbers match. Be especially careful if labels are missing or look like they came off at some point and were replaced. Ask the shopkeeper for a fresh supply from a box in storage if you have any doubts. Of course, if you are dealing with a multi-colored pattern, dye lot will not be nearly as important, as long as balls from different dye lots are well separated by other colors.

Finally, a good label will indicate the care requirements. Part of the information will be written out, and some will be conveyed by internationally recognized symbols. Wool labels will also indicate if the yarn has been mothproofed or if it is "Superwash," which means it has been treated to prevent shrinkage during laundering; these yarns can be machine washed (although the protection can be lost over time; see the discussion in Wool Fiber).

Yarn Names and Sizes

Manufacturers and pattern magazines frequently use a variety of traditional terms when referring to a size or type of knitting yarn. Unfortunately, few of these terms reveal anything useful to the uninitiated, and some of them are quaint or obsolete; rarely are they very descriptive of the real characteristics of the yarn.

The terms used specify that a yarn is a certain "weight" because yarn has traditionally been sold by weight; therefore, instead of describing yarns in terms of their thickness, we speak of them as either "heavy" or "light" instead of thick or thin. These terms tend to confuse the issue, and fortunately, more manufacturers, shops, and pattern magazines now refer to the various yarn sizes simply as "super fine," "fine," "medium," "bulky," and "extra bulky," which are far more appropriate and helpful.

Lace-weight, or super fine, yarn is for shawls, scarves, baby garments, and sometimes for socks.

Fingering is a relatively thin yarn, somewhat thicker than lace-weight; it is commonly used for gloves, mittens, and stockings, but previously it was often used for lightweight sweaters and vests as well.

What Americans call "sport weight" yarn is somewhat thicker than fingering and is roughly equivalent to what the British refer to as "jumper weight," a jumper being what Americans call a pullover sweater.

"Shetland" has come to be a generic term for yarns that resemble in some way the traditional yarn of Shetland, and more often it indicates a heather blend rather than a yarn size. Traditional Shetland yarn is a relatively thin yarn made of wool from a distinct breed of native sheep (at a minimum, a traditional Fair Isle garment was normally done at a gauge of 8 to 12 stitches per inch), the fibers were dyed in the wool with organic dyes, and the colors were blended. Today Shetland wool is made into yarns in a variety of thicknesses to satisfy the interests of the international market, and some labeled Shetland may not even be from the Shetland Isles (although the wool may be from the native Shetland sheep). This wool is quite variable in quality; some of these yarns are fine and soft, while others are less so.

What the British call "double-knitting" yarn is a medium-thick, woolen spun yarn, and it is equivalent to what Americans now refer to as "worsted weight." Both of these terms lead to some confusion. Americans confuse "double-knitting" with Double-Fabrics, which are entirely different, and, as discussed above, worsted is a method of spinning yarn in a variety of thicknesses.

You may also come across the term "fisherman" or "Aran" used to refer to a medium-thick yarn that is used for the traditional Aran sweater style.

Both "bulky" and "chunky" are used when referring to thick yarns intended for jumbo size needles, and "Icelandic" yarn is basically pencil roving (see above).

Weight and Yardage

Yarn is sold primarily by weight; most European yarns are sold in 50-gram balls (1.75 ounces), while American yarns are usually 2 ounces (56.7 grams); skeined yarn is usually 100 grams or 4 ounces.

Unfortunately, what a knitter really needs to buy is yardage (meters). It is not how much the yarn weighs that matters, but how much of it is taken up by each stitch and how many stitches and balls of yarn it takes to make the garment.

Furthermore, there is no really accurate way to calculate the amount of yarn to buy based on weight, while the method based on yardage is more accurate; see the discussion of how to calculate Garment Yardage in the chapter Stitch Gauge. The discrepancy between how the yarn is sold and what the knitter requires has led to a great deal of guessing and frustration when it comes to purchasing yarn.

You may come across various charts or formulas that suggest so many ounces for a man's sweater, so many for a woman's, etc. Given the number of yarns on the market today and the wide variety of garment styles (and sizes of people), these approaches are quite obsolete and were only suitable when knitters worked repeatedly with the same yarn. Furthermore, every stitch pattern absorbs a different amount of yarn.

I have also seen it suggested that you weigh an existing sweater similar to the one you want to make to determine how much yarn to purchase. Aside from the problems discussed above, this might work reasonably well for synthetic fibers, but natural fibers respond to humidity in the environment, and as they take in or give off moisture, the weight may vary. This is particularly true of wool, which can absorb a great deal of moisture yet remain dry to the touch (see Fibers). Weigh a wool sweater on a dry day and you will think you need twenty ounces of yarn to make a garment just like it; weigh it on a damp day and it will tell you to buy twenty-six ounces.

Also keep in mind that two yarns of the same fiber and weight may have different yardages due to the way they were spun. Conversely, different fibers may have the same yardage but considerably different weights due to their inherent density. For instance, if you compare cotton fibers and wool fibers of the same length, the latter will weigh less; linen will weigh more than cotton; silk less than wool.

Fortunately, most yarn labels now indicate both the weight and the length of yarn in each ball, sometimes in both grams/meters and ounces/yards, which is much appreciated. However, it would be far better for knitters if the manufacturers would package and sell yarn by standard lengths and let the weights come out willy-nilly instead of the other way around.

It would be far more convenient to purchase 100 yards, 200 yards, or 300 yards of yarn than to be faced with some balls that have 168 yards or 223 yards, packaged that way because the weight happens to be the same. This would not only make yarn requirement calculations easier for designers, it would make it much easier for the average knitter to substitute one yarn for another in a pattern (see below), and would vastly simplify price comparisons for all concerned.

Windings

Yarn is wound into many different shapes, and you may find it useful to know their names and how to put yarn into whatever form you find convenient.

A "skein" or "hank" refers to yarn wound into a large circle. In order to keep the strands from tangling, the skein is tied in two places, twisted on itself, and then folded in half; one folded end is pulled through the other to secure the bundle. Yarn sold in this form is often more economical than yarns wound into balls because it eliminates one step in the manufacturing process.

If you purchase yarn in a skein, you will need to wind it into a ball before you can work with it. The only alternative is to sling it diagonally between shoulder and waist like a general's ribbon and unloop the yarn from around your neck as you knit; hang it on a hook when not in use.

More often, however, yarn is wound from a skein mounted on some kind of support—such as an umbrella swift, a chair back, or a friend's outstretched arms—that holds it open in a circle and keeps it intact so it will not tangle.

The yarn may be wound into a nice round ball, but more commonly it is turned into what is called a "center-pull ball," which is done on a core of some kind. Yarn wound like this allows you to pull the end either from the outside or the inside, or both if you want to double the thickness (also see Twined Knit).

Machine knitters generally purchase "coned yarn," which is relatively thin yarn wound on sturdy cardboard cones and sold in ½-pound or 1-pound amounts.

Slippery yarns that do not hold together in a ball are sold on a straight cardboard core.

❖ Hand Winding

A ball of yarn is just what it suggests—nice, round, and softball-sized, and suggestive of home because manufacturers do not wind yarn into this form; the shape presents packaging problems and the balls will not stay put in the store. If you have wound yarn into a ball, do keep it in a basket or bag as you work because it will not stay put for you either; cats find this very entertaining.

Winding a ball of yarn is a simple, peaceful procedure, to be valued as an opportunity for daydreaming or conversation, depending upon whether you are alone or have help.

- Place the skein on some kind of support, as described above. Hold the tail of yarn in the palm of your hand and make a large Yarn Butterfly; hold on to the tail, but remove the butterfly from your fingers and fold it in half. Start winding the yarn over the butterfly, your thumb, and two or three fingers.

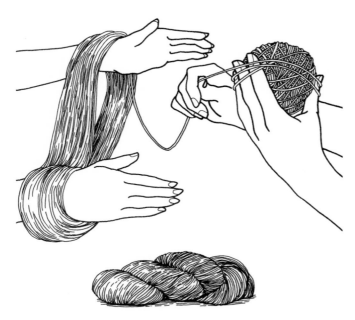

Hand-winding a ball of yarn. Twisted skein at bottom.

Every few wraps withdraw your yarn-covered fingers, turn the growing ball to another position and let your fingers get caught up again. Wrap the yarn gently, just tight enough to stay in the ball, and each time around, wrap in a different place to distribute the yarn evenly; the result should be squeezably soft. If the yarn is wrapped too tightly, it will stretch out and lose its resilience in storage; if necessary, rewind it so it is softer.

If you manage to keep hold of the tail of yarn while doing this, you will have a "center-pull" ball, which means you can draw the yarn off from the inside, and/or the outside.

❖ Dowel Winding

Another traditional way of making a center-pull ball is to wind it on a wooden dowel, a wooden spoon handle, or, better yet, a proper tool called a "nostepinde," or "nostepinne," (pronounced *noh-ste-pin*), which in one dialect or another is the Scandinavian term for a special yarn-winding tool.

A nostepinne is a tapered dowel about 10 to 12 inches long, with a shaped handle and, in some models, a narrow neck where the yarn can be tied on. For any of you who sail, they look just like a "belaying pin," which sailors use for tying on ropes. And since sailors whittle and carve away when there is no other work to be done, it should come as no surprise to find that nostepinnes are often beautifully carved (and in this, resemble knitting sheaths).

With a little practice, you will find that you can quickly and easily wind a beautiful center-pull ball of yarn using no more than this simple tool. Mount the skein in one of the ways described above, and work as follows:

1. Make a Slip Knot and drop it over tip of nostepinne and tighten around neck, or grasp end of yarn with handle in left hand. Hold with tip pointing up to right and hold yarn from skein in right hand (or swap everything if left-handed).
2. Tightly wrap yarn about 20 to 30 times around center of dowel, from base toward tip, each strand lying next to the last (or push together firmly), to form a 1½- to 2-inch-wide wrapping to serve as starting base.
3. Bring next wrap down across farside of dowel to lower left and hold in position with left thumb.
4. Begin to wind, rotating nostepinne in left hand (either toward or away from you), while wrapping yarn from lower left to upper right, around the back and down to lower left again. Lay each strand down no more than about ⅛ to ¼ inch away from last one.

If you wrap the yarn around the dowel just above and below the last strand, the result will be an egg-shaped ball. If you wrap it on the outside of the last strands at top and bottom, you can wind a "cake" shaped ball, just like a mechanical ball winder. To do this, guide the wraps with your forefinger positioned at the top left shoulder of the ball, and your middle finger at the bottom right; curl your other fingers around the handle and use your thumb to turn the dowel as you bring the yarn up from the left.

The ball will soften down a bit when taken off the dowel, which is good insurance against winding too tightly. It takes some practice to wind neatly and evenly and get the tension

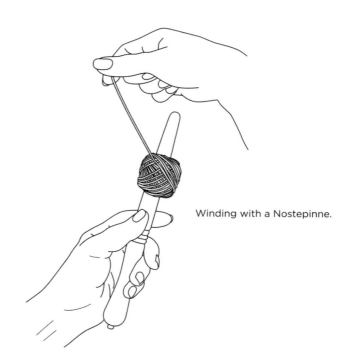

Winding with a Nostepinne.

just right, but it is a pleasant pastime and no expensive tools are required (although there are beautiful carved nostepinnes available, if you want to indulge yourself).

❖ Ball Winders

The faster, more convenient yarn-winders sold in stores (see Tools) wind a center-pull ball just like one done on a nostepinne. The result will be precisely wound and have a perfect "cake" shape, with flat sides, top and bottom. These balls are very well behaved and stay put wherever you place them.

Here again, you will need some support for the skein, but because ball winders work very quickly it is far better to use an umbrella swift than to ask a friend to keep up. The swift can be adjusted to any skein circumference, holds the yarn at just the right tension, and spins as you wind the yarn.

However, the temptation is to wind very quickly, which places the yarn under tension and will make the ball too tight. Go at a slower pace and use your non-winding hand to guide the yarn. You will also want to have your guide hand ready to stop the swift from spinning if you stop winding, or you will find it has spilled extra yarn on the floor.

After you have wound the yarn, take the ball off the core of the winder and give it the squeeze test; if it feels even a little too firm it is a good idea to rewind it. Place the ball of yarn on the floor under your guide hand, take the end from the center of the ball, feed it to the winder, and rewind.

If you have a tight ball of yarn that was left for any length of time, return it to skein form using a skein winder, or a niddy-noddy, wash it (see Recycling Yarn), and then rewind it before use. Left too long, the yarn may never recover its original resilience; how much it does recover depends upon the type of fiber, how tight the ball was, and how long it was left in that condition. The yarn is not necessarily ruined, but you will want to take this into consideration before deciding how to use it; as usual, make a good-sized Gauge Swatch, dress it, and see what happens.

When working color patterns with the Twined Knit technique, it is convenient to wind one color on the outside of another, although the risk is that the ball will get too big unless you wind half a skein of each.

❖ Mill Windings

Manufacturers wind yarns into several other center-pull ball shapes. When soft, delicate yarns are wound into a center-pull ball, they frequently collapse somewhat into a fat doughnut shape (or think bagels), and the label is passed through the center of the ball to hold it together.

Fine yarns with a lot of yardage are often wound into a cylinder, about 2 inches in diameter and 6 to 8 inches long; the label is passed around the middle.

Ribbons sold for knitting, and other smooth, slippery yarns are wound on a cardboard core with a label covering all but the very ends to keep the strands in place. However, the yarn can only be drawn from the outside, and unfortunately, once the label is removed these kinds of yarns do not stay wound. The solution is to slip the yarn into a "sleeve" (see Tools), or cut off the foot of a nylon stocking, and use that.

Weavers and machine knitters purchase fine yarn in long lengths wound on a cone about 8 to 10 inches tall. While these yarns are rarely used alone for hand knitting, the cone makes it easy to combine several strands into a thickness that is suitable. And while the cones are not particularly portable (a quality knitters prefer), yarn in this form offers several advantages; it stands at attention next to your favorite chair and will not wander away, it stays neat to the last yard, the yarn can be pulled off very easily, and best of all, there are no knots (machine knitters will not tolerate that sort of thing).

General Yarn Information

Here is some general information about yarn you may find useful, including tips about selecting the right yarn for a project or what to take into consideration when substituting another yarn for the one recommended in a published pattern. Also included are tips for how to remove one or more plies from a yarn if you need to thin it for one reason or another.

❖ Selecting a Yarn

There are several factors to take into consideration when selecting a yarn for a particular garment. You might want a thinner yarn made from a soft fiber for a garment that will be worn indoors and close to the skin. For warmth, you might prefer something softer that will trap heat effectively, or perhaps a thin yarn for a Stranded Color pattern (because the fabric is, in effect, lined with the strands, it will be quite warm). For an outdoors, sporty garment, something thicker and coarser may be perfectly acceptable or even more appropriate, but also consider thin to medium-thickness worsted yarns, because they are far more durable.

Soft, woolen-type yarns are the most common yarns used for knitting, and have many appealing characteristics. They have a wide range of acceptable needle sizes that can be used, as they will loft into the stitches in a relatively loosely knit fabric or compress down into a more firmly knit one. They do well for both color and stitch patterns, although with time they tend to fuzz up a bit and obscure the details; for this reason, it is often best to select bolder patterns. The softer twist leaves more space between fibers, meaning items made from these yarns tend to be somewhat warmer and cozier than those made from a worsted-type yarn.

Balls of yarn in different shapes.

However, they are not as strong as worsted-spun yarns and are far more prone to abrasion and felting and are, therefore, less suitable for hard wear. Also, because more fiber ends are on the surface of a woolen-spun yarn, they will pill more, and sensitive individuals may find them a bit more irritating against the skin, especially if the yarn was not made with a naturally soft fiber (the cut ends of synthetic fibers can be particularly sharp and prickly).

The short, downy fibers like cashmere make relatively fragile yarns that tend to shed; the highest-quality yarns are made with the longest of these fibers and tend to be very expensive. As a result, they are primarily used for small items like scarves, and for lace shawls; because lace opens up, it requires less yardage. Luxury fibers are frequently blended with another fiber for reasons of both economy and strength.

Worsted-spun yarns are expensive to produce, and the fibers used are normally of high quality; fewer yarns of this kind are available for knitters. True worsted yarns have greater strength and resistance to abrasion and soil, and they are more elastic than woolen yarns. Since there are fewer ends, and the ends are tucked well into the yarn, a garment made from a worsted is more likely to be comfortable against the skin.

Also, because there are fewer ends on the surface, worsted-type yarns display stitch techniques clearly and produce crisp details in color patterns, and can be worked into fabrics with a relatively tight gauge to produce rich pattern detail. Because the fibers are aligned, these yarns also have a slight sheen that can impart a subtle elegance to a fabric.

Crepe and bouclé yarns make fabrics with a subtly textured, pebbly surface and a quiet dull appearance. Because of the tight spin, they do not pill and tend to be very resilient. They have traditionally been favored for knitted dresses, suits, and blouse-like sweaters that have a very nice drape and good shape retention. Wool crepe yarns are comfortable even in warm weather. For knitters who are not accustomed to working with smaller needle sizes, two or more strands can be combined, or one strand can be carried with a thicker yarn, which can be used to add color and texture; see the discussion in Multiple Yarns.

Few of the novelty yarns do justice to stitch techniques, which are obscured by pronounced texture. However, these yarns are often well displayed when Purl stitches are used on the outside, as the nubs and running threads heighten the textural effect.

Moderately textured yarns are excellent for beginning knitters. It is easier to control tension, they conceal uneven stitches and minor errors, can be worked up on larger needles, and working in plain Knit or Purl makes a project go quickly and produces gratifying results.

Mohair and angora are also worked on large needles to allow the yarn to fluff out as much as possible in the fabric; this means only the boldest stitch or color patterns are effective.

Hand-knit yellow dress with Intarsia flowers;
probably crepe yarn or worsted. Knitter unknown;
American Textile History Museum, Lowell, Massachusetts.

Icelandic-type yarns, which are really a loosely spun single or a fine roving, are weak and may come apart under tension, although this is less of a factor once it is knitted into the fabric. The Right-Hand Method of knitting is the safest one to use because it allows you to handle these yarns very gently. These fabrics can be very warm and cozy, but they may pill and abrade; therefore garments made from roving should not be expected to provide hard wear. This is not the case if you decide to knit with unspun silk; the long filaments are exceedingly strong and will not break, so any knitting method is suitable, as is almost any sort of stitch or color pattern.

There are various woven ribbons sold for knitting, usually in silk, rayon, or polyester. When ribbon knitting was popular in the 1940s, pattern instructions called for putting the spool on a rod of some kind to allow the ribbon to unreel, so no twist would be added. Relatively large needles were used and the ribbon was wrapped carefully for every stitch so it would lie as flat and smooth as possible in the fabric. The most common stitch pattern used was Balanced Twist Stitch.

The fabric was carefully steam-pressed flat in finishing, giving the stitches an overlapping, scaly appearance; in synthetic fabrics, the stitches could be permanently heat set. A fine ribbon-knit garment is a painstaking creation with a unique and beautiful surface texture and drape—they are absolutely luscious to wear. Most people today knit with ribbon as they would with any other yarn, allowing it to crumple into the stitch, and the effect is quite different, albeit still attractive.

❖ *Yarn Substitution*

When faced with the necessity of substituting a yarn for the one recommended in a published pattern, there are two important things to keep in mind. Of course, you will want to find a yarn that allows you to match the stitch gauge, but also look for one that has the same characteristics as the original so the fabric will have the qualities the designer intended. This means the best selection would be another yarn of the same fiber and type—in other words, do not substitute a worsted for a woolen, or a cotton for an acrylic, or a textured yarn for a smooth one.

However, even two wools or two cottons that appear similar could have been spun and plied in different ways and they may have characteristics that are not obvious to the eye. To check for this, compare the weight and yardage numbers on the label. If, for instance, one 50-gram ball has 160 yards, and the other weighs the same but has only 120 yards, the latter will be slightly thicker than the former. As a rough guideline, if there is more than a 20 percent difference in the yardage of two balls of the same weight, it is probably not the best choice for the project.

A pattern will always say how many balls of a yarn to buy, and may indicate how many yards or meters there are in each ball. If the length of the yarn you would like to substitute is slightly different, multiply the yardage of the recommended yarn by the number of balls required to find the total length. Next, divide the result by the yardage shown on the label of the ball of the yarn you prefer. If one yarn is sold in grams and meters, you will have to first convert ounces and yards to grams and meters, or vice versa, before doing the calculation.

You may come across suggestions to use a rough calculation based on WPI, or "Wraps per Inch"; but see the discussion on that subject for reasons why I do not recommend it.

I do not want to discourage you from substituting another yarn for the one called for in a published pattern, even one that is quite different, because this is a wonderful way to learn how to design. If you think a yarn is suitable for the garment design, you can use the dimensions shown in the schematic and make use of the stitch or color pattern as a basis for a slightly different version.

However, because the yarn will produce a different stitch gauge, you will need to rewrite the pattern instructions. The safest thing to do is to buy just one ball of the yarn, take it home and make a gauge swatch to discover how it will behave. If you decide to go ahead with it, please see the information in Pattern Alterations in the chapter Stitch Gauge.

❖ Yarn Direction, or Nap

There is some discussion about whether yarn has a "nap," or "direction." The idea is that the yarn will remain smoother with fewer ends raised if you start working from one end of the yarn instead of the other.

However, people who manufacture yarn do not recognize this distinction, and there is no physical reason for the yarn to display this characteristic with the spinning techniques they use. After all, every fiber has two ends, and it is just as likely for one end to be sticking out of the yarn as for the other end to do so, especially if it is woolen-spun with fibers going every which way.

Hand spinners, however, will sometimes claim that worsted and semi-worsted yarns made with long staple fibers do have a "direction" because they sometimes fold the combed fibers over their finger and draw the fibers out from the center of the fiber mass. In other words, the folded ends of the fibers are pulled into the yarn first, the tips and cut ends last, which means there are half as many ends in one direction as in the other. Therefore, if you run it through your fingers in the direction opposite to which it was spun, more ends will be teased out of the yarn.

However, this is a relatively minor distinction, and after all, the yarn will pass through the knitter's hands but once. Furthermore, there is no way for anyone to know which end is which unless you have the opportunity to ask the spinner. And given that most knitters work with woolen-spun yarn containing short staple fibers that are not aligned in the yarn, it really does not matter.

❖ Unplying Yarn

If you are working with a plied yarn and want to thin a small amount of it for use when sewing a seam, or perhaps to reduce the bulk of a hem or facing (see Hems, Facings, Pleats, and Tucks), it is easy enough to do.

Unplying a Small Length

For sewing up, you only need to thin about 24 inches or less of the yarn. If it is a 3-ply yarn, remove one ply; if it is a 4-ply yarn, you have the option of removing one or two plies. Work as follows:

1. Draw off amount of yarn needed from ball, and then fasten it so no more will unwind. Either clip yarn to ball with something like a Bead Stop, or insert a short double-point needle into side of ball and wrap yarn around it two or three times in a figure 8.
2. Take up end of yarn and separate ply; hold one portion in each hand. Suspend ball from length of yarn and pull ply apart; ball will spin rapidly as ply separates.
3. When ball stops spinning, set it down and cut off yarn.

The yarn is likely to kink up a bit with residual twist; let the ends hang free and encourage it to unwind a bit and balance itself.

Unplying a Larger Supply

If you need to unply a larger supply of yarn to knit with, work as described above, but after Step 2, continue as follows:

- Set down ball and one portion of separated ply. Take other portion and let end hang free so it unspins some of its twist and then wind it into a small Yarn Butterfly and secure with a half-hitch. Repeat with other portion of ply.

    Unwind more yarn from ball, and separate that length in the same way. Working with one at a time, let each Yarn Butterfly hang down to unspin extra twist, undo the half-hitch holding it, and wind up the next portion of separated ply. Continue in this way to separate as much yarn as needed.

This requires some patience, but it works well enough. You may want to make a fairly good estimate of how much yarn you will require beforehand to make sure you do no more than necessary; see Calculating Yarn Requirements.

CHAPTER 29

Tools

Every craft needs its tools and needs them to be efficient and effective. It also helps if they fit well in your hand, are finely made of good materials, and are handsome to look upon.

Knitting makes few demands, really no more than a small selection of needles and a supply of yarn. The needles, well cared for, can last a lifetime, yet are relatively inexpensive.There are also specialized needles that are helpful to have on hand; these are used to temporarily hold stitches, for picking up, making repairs, or sewing.

In addition to needles, there are a variety of other tools that are convenient in one way or another, but relatively few of them are essential. These include counting devices, markers, storage materials for yarns, needles, and other small tools, various items that are helpful when dressing a finished fabric, as well as tools that will help you wind yarn efficiently.

Needles

Knitting needles come in a variety of shapes, sizes, and materials, and represent a relatively minor investment. While traditional knitters had just one or two favorite sets, most knitters today have fairly large collections, long and short, straight, double-point, and circular—in other words, just the right needle for any sort of project.

While not technically a needle, crochet hooks are also useful in knitting; it is not really necessary to have an entire set in a full range of sizes, but it is a good idea to have several in sizes that match those of the knitting needles you use most often.

You will also want to have a "tapestry" needle, which is used for sewing seams and hiding yarn ends, and perhaps one of the specialty needles used for picking up stitches and making repairs. It is also convenient to have several stitch holders available for when you need to put stitches on hold temporarily. And if you plan to do a cable pattern, you will need the specialized tool used to manipulate the stitches.

Knitting Needles

When you think about it, a knitting needle is a marvel of elegant simplicity, an old and simple tool that is still perfectly suited to its task. Oh, there have been a few improvements over the years; needles today are stronger, rustproof, lighter in weight, more precisely sized, and so on, but it would be difficult to imagine any improvement in the concept.

What is wanted from knitting needles? Ideally, they should be light in weight, strong enough to resist bending out of shape or breaking, and polished so they offer little resistance to the stitches. It helps if the tips are tapered just so, and can be inserted into the stitches easily yet not split the yarn.

Types of Needles

Needles come in three basic forms: single-point, double-point, and circular. Most knitters have collections that include a range of sizes in all three types. While single-point needles can only be used for flat knitting (although see Singular Double-Fabrics for the exception), the others can be used for both flat or circular knitting.

Double-Point Needles

The oldest form of knitting needle is the straight double-point (pointed at both ends), originally used for all knitting, but now reserved primarily for small items knit in the round. They are sold in sets of four or five, in a full range of sizes, and can be from 6 to 18 inches in length.

Double-point needles can be used to knit a garment of any size, flat or circular; when necessary to accommodate more stitches, longer needles can be used, or another needle added. The knitters of Shetland are known to use just three needles, two for the stitches and one to work with, but that seems to be a unique approach; they also preferred 14- to 18-inch needles when using a knitting belt or sheath (see below, and Shetland Three-Needle Method). But most knitters today use shorter lengths, which are suitable for the ever-popular socks and mittens.

Single-Point Needles

Single-point needles have a point at one end and a cap at the other to prevent the stitches from slipping off, and can only be used for knitting flat. Sold in pairs, they come in a full range of sizes, and in 6- to 14-inch lengths. These needles appeared in the mid-nineteenth century along with knitting patterns for fashionable garments, which, with their more complex styling and shape, are easier to make in flat sections.

Single-point needles serve this purpose very well but for one minor flaw. While the formation of each stitch requires relatively slight movements at the point, the result is a rather large motion at the opposite end, and the longer the needle, the larger the motion. The capped end of a 14-inch needle can rise and fall as much as 2 to 4 inches or more with each stitch (depending upon the knitting method used), which means the knitter is repeatedly lifting and lowering the weight of the fabric hanging from the needle. This repetitive motion puts stress on hands, wrists, and elbows and can cause injury; even working with a needle just 2 inches shorter can make a positive difference.

Circular Needles

The circular needle, called "twin pins" in Britain, consists of two needle tips joined by a length of fine nylon cable; they can be used for either flat or circular knitting. These are sold in a full range of sizes and in lengths ranging from 12 to 60 inches, measured tip to tip. Since their appearance shortly after World War I, they have gradually replaced double-point needles for all but the smallest items, and they are supplanting the long single-points for flat knitting as well.

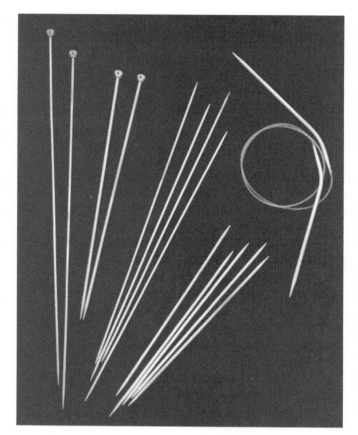

Assortment of knitting needles. Single-points at left, double-points in center, circular needle at top right.

These needles are really quite wonderful because the work is drawn into a circle and the fabric is supported in your lap, relieving you of its weight and cutting down on fatigue. Furthermore, the thin cable encourages the stitches to move off the shaft, which speeds things along, and when you are not knitting, the fabric can be pushed back from the tips onto the cable, which then acts as a stitch holder.

A further benefit is that it is impossible to lose one of the pair, as often happens with straight needles. Even better, you can fit into even the narrowest chair (or airplane seat) and still manage to knit without risk of poking your neighbor.

When working flat, the length of the needle is irrelevant as long as the stitches will fit on it; you can knit the smallest item on even a 36-inch circular needle should that be all you have at hand. For knitting in the round, however, the circumference of the fabric must be at least two inches larger than the length of the needle. The 24-inch length is generally best for most things; not too long, not too short, it will comfortably hold even a large garment, particularly since stitches crowd together more closely on a cable than on the shaft of a straight needle.

The little 12- and 16-inch lengths are somewhat problematic, because their tips are so small it is difficult to gain a purchase for your hands. However, many people prefer them to working on a set of double-points, which must otherwise be used for smaller circumferences, and they are also popular for working in the round with two circular needles (see Circular Knitting).

Circular needles are made in all of the materials described below, except solid steel (although I have some old ones in steel). Some have straight tips, while others have a slight bend in the needle shaft that fits the palm of the hand. The critical factor is the join between the shaft and the cable, which needs to be smooth so the stitches will not snag as they make the transition between cable and tip, and strong so the tip does not separate from the cable. Modern manufacturers have solved these problems, and metal circular needles are now excellent tools to work with. Plastic circular needles are a continuous length of extruded nylon; this makes them very smooth because there is no joint between cable and tip.

There are also sets of circular needles on the market with interchangeable needle tips that can be screwed onto cables of various lengths. These sets allow you to create whatever combination of needle size and cable length you require, although the tips are only available in sizes larger than 3.5 mm. Extra tips and cables are available separately, so the sets can be customized and expanded. The initial investment is a rather serious one; however, the sets come in a compact storage case, which not only keeps them ordered but is nice for travel.

Jumper, or Flex Needles

Jumper needles are a hybrid; they look somewhat like a circular needle except that they are a pair; a needle tip is attached to one end of each cable and there is a stop at the other end. The design is intended as a substitute for long straight needles, which can be inconvenient and tiring to work with.

This was an innovative solution to the constant motion of a long, straight needle; because the cable is soft, it will curve down and rest in the lap instead of sticking out to the side, and the weight of the growing fabric will be supported.

However, they seem to be well named, because the cable tends to jump around at every turn and many people find this distracting. Furthermore, they offer little advantage to working with a conventional circular needle, which can be used for working either flat or in the round.

Cro-Needles

While little known today, one of the oldest types of knitting needle may very well be a straight needle with a crochet hook at one end and a point at the other. These are still used by some knitters who work with what I call the Thumb Method of knitting, and they provide certain advantages with the Left-Hand Method as well. While it is possible to use them to work flat, they are best for circular knitting.

Somewhat more common is a cable version that is wonderful for picking up stitches; see Circular Cro-Needle, below.

Needle Materials

The original knitting needles were made of whatever materials could be fashioned by hand—commonly bone, ivory, tortoiseshell, or wood. The earliest metal needles were made of steel wire; later lightweight aluminum needles were introduced, and eventually various plastics as well.

Beautifully crafted needles of smooth hard woods and bamboo are a pleasure to look at and to work with, and many people prefer them for their quiet performance and the way they feel in the hand. Unfortunately, they are breakable, especially in the thinner, small sizes, and the wood ones are often costly. Another factor to consider is that no matter how highly polished they are, needles made from these materials are not as smooth as metal needles. As a result, they create a certain amount of friction or drag on the stitches.

This can be advantageous if you generally work at a very loose tension or are using a slippery yarn, because the resistance makes it less likely that a stitch will drop off or that a needle will slip out of the stitches entirely. However, if you knit at even moderate tension, the needles will drag on most yarns, which can slow your progress and cause fatigue.

If you doubt me, do a test: knit with a standard wool yarn for five or ten minutes using a wood or bamboo needle, and then switch to a metal one and note the ease with which the stitches move along the shaft. A smooth needle can make a big difference in terms of time and effort saved over the course of even an hour's knitting.

Many people like needles made of synthetic materials for their quiet, warm feel and for their economy, and they are available in a variety of integral colors. However, most are considerably more flexible than needles made from other materials and have relatively rounded tips. This can make them less than ideal for some stitch techniques or for anyone who works at a relatively firm tension, because it is more difficult to insert the tip into each stitch. The needles are generally not stiff enough to be effective in small sizes, but their light weight makes them ideal for large, jumbo size needles.

Cellulose acetate plastic is harder than other types (this is the same plastic used for eyeglass frames), which means the needles tend to be stiffer, the tips can be given a more pronounced point, and the material can be polished to a smoother finish than other types of plastics. They have a rather nice heft and warm feel to them, and some people like that they are made from renewable materials (cotton linters or wood pulp, the same raw material used to make rayon).

The most common metal used for needles today is aluminum; it is inexpensive, relatively lightweight, and reasonably strong. Needles of this kind used to be available in a variety of colors, but more often now they have a neutral matte gray coating that reduces glare from what would otherwise be a shiny surface. These coatings may wear off the tips with time, but this does not affect the performance of the needles.

Hollow steel, brass, and nickel-plated brass needles are also available (some people are allergic to nickel; read the label carefully if this is a concern). These materials are light in weight, take a fine point, and are highly polished, which speeds up the knitting and reduces fatigue. However, the slick surface can make it difficult to manage some smooth yarns and it reflects light, which can be hard on the eyes when working under a lamp. Nevertheless, for most yarns, and with indirect light, these are superb tools.

Double-point needles are also available in solid steel. They are exceptionally smooth, strong, and flexible, and have excellent points, but the material is heavy and needs to be wiped dry to prevent rust from developing when the needles are stored. Those recommended for lace work are available in 6-inch lengths and come in the very smallest sizes available for knitting, ranging from .5 mm (American size 00000000) to 2.0 mm (American size 0).

It is important to keep in mind that needles made of different materials can change the tension with which you knit. Make sure to knit your gauge sample on the same type of needle you will use for the garment (see The Five Variables, in Stitch Gauge).

Comparative Needle Sizes

There are three different systems commonly used for needle sizes: the metric system in Europe, the traditional British system, and the American system. Each uses a series of numbers (and often diameters) that have no relation to the others. Fortunately, the metric size is becoming more standard, and many needle packages are now marked with both the metric size and the American or British size. Straight needles will have the size printed on the head; some circular needles now have the size printed on the shaft.

Needles made by different manufacturers, even when marked with the same size, can have subtly different dimensions. This is less true with the wider adoption of metric sizing; nevertheless, it pays to use a needle gauge (see below) to check the size before using a brand that is new to you, especially when dealing with handcrafted needles.

It does not matter what size a needle is, as long as it will produce the gauge you want, and also that you use the same needle for the entire project. Subtle size discrepancies between needles actually give you a way of adjusting gauge. For instance, if you were trying to match a pattern gauge and found that neither a 3.25 mm needle nor a 3.5 mm was quite right, you might be able to find one made by a different manufacturer that is closer to 3.3 or 3.4 mm; see the chart in the Appendix.

❖ *Specialized Needles*

There are several other needle-type tools used in knitting that serve purposes other than making the stitches. These are special purpose items that help get a particular job done.

Cable Needle, or Cable Holder

Cable stitch patterns require transposing sets of stitches by taking some off the needle temporarily, working another set, and then replacing the first. The device used for this purpose is called a cable needle, or cable holder. These little tools come in three sizes, for fine, medium, and heavy-weight yarns, and there are four different designs on the market.

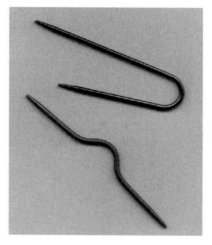

Cable Holders.

One version is a tiny straight needle about three inches in length. The second is the same except that it has a dip in the center where the transferred stitches nest while the other set of cable stitches is worked from the main needle. Either of these must be held along with the left needle or it may slip out of the stitches while the other stitches of the cable are worked. The third type is bent something like a fish hook, with one tip shorter than the other, and it can safely be allowed to hang from the fabric as the other set of stitches is being worked. With any version, the stitches can be slipped on and off the same end of the holder, or slipped onto one end and worked off the other end.

Those who enjoy working cable designs know quite well how easy it is to lose these little tools; I have heard rumors that they can be found in the same place as lost socks. I have no advice about the socks, but you can attach a cable tool to your

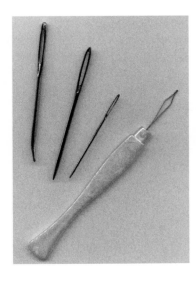

Cro-Needle Pick-Up Tool with
Hook Needle Repair Tool in center.

work. The hooked version can be tucked into the fabric and will stay put, obediently waiting for the next cable. Or, instead of a true cable needle, use a blunt-tipped tapestry needle with a large eye. Thread it with a length of smooth yarn or cord and knot it around a selvedge stitch where it will be ready at hand when you need it.

Another option is a cable tool that consists of a very short needle mounted on a ring that is worn on one finger like a thimble. This is particularly convenient when working multiple cables in close succession, although the stitches must be slipped back to the main needle to be worked. And it must be said that it looks like a lethal weapon on your finger.

Cro-Needle Pick-Up Tool

This type of cro-needle is made like a conventional circular needle, but it has a knitting needle tip at one end, and a crochet hook at the other. It is an ideal tool for picking up stitches around a neckline, down the center front of a cardigan, or along one side of a shawl; the stitches can then be worked from the end with the knitting needle tip.

- Hold yarn in left hand, insert hook under selvedge stitch, catch yarn and draw it through; stitches accumulate on cable.
- If working in the round, hold needle tip end of tool in left hand and standard circular needle in right hand, and begin working picked-up stitches.
- If working flat, break yarn and slide stitches to end with needle tip; reattach yarn and begin working picked-up

stitches. Or, pick up stitches using tail of yarn so main supply is attached at needle tip; see Picking Up with Cro-Needle.

Hook Needle Repair Tool

This is a clever device, well worth having in your tool kit. It looks like a tiny 3-inch cro-needle, with a crochet hook at one end and a knitting needle tip at the other.

It is ideal for reworking a dropped stitch because you can use whichever end serves the purpose best; you can slide it through the fabric, to position it correctly for dealing with a Knit or Purl stitch. It can also be used as a cable needle: use the hook to slip the stitches off the left needle and knit the stitches off the needle end of the tool.

Crochet Hooks

Crochet hooks are very useful for knitters and you will want to have several in the sizes that are closest to the knitting needle sizes you use most often. They are available in plastic, aluminum, and steel; the former two are lighter in weight, the latter are smoother and favored for relatively thin yarns. Some crochet hooks have a steel tip with a thicker plastic handle to provide a better grip.

Hooks are very useful for finishing exposed edges with various decorative borders. Additionally, crochet hooks are used in some techniques for casting on, casting off, and sewing up, and they are convenient for reworking stitches that have run down; see those sections for more information.

❖ *Sewing Needles*

For many finishing tasks, you will need what is called a "tapestry" needle, which has a blunt tip and an eye large enough for yarn. Some of the needles are straight and look like large versions of a regular sewing needle. Another version has a

Tapestry needles; version with bent tip at left. Yarn threading tool at right.

slightly flattened, bent tip that is useful for lifting a stitch off a needle, or for hiding ends of yarn on the inside of the fabric. The bent tip makes the job of seaming or grafting stitches go very quickly because you can go in one stitch and out the other in one smooth motion.

There is no need to be very precise about the size of a sewing needle, but they are often conveniently sold in sets with small, medium, and large sizes.

It is impossible to thread an end of soft yarn through the eye of a needle; instead, allow several inches, fold the yarn end over the eye of the needle, and pinch it very tightly. Slide the pinched yarn off the needle, and then push the folded end through the eye.

There are also large versions of conventional needle threader devices on the market. A threader tool has a loop of flexible wire attached to a handle, or to a small, flat tab of metal. Insert the wire into the eye of the needle, pass the yarn through the loop, and draw it back through the eye of the needle.

Other Tools

Here you will find a discussion of a variety of tools that are also useful in knitting. Not all are essential, but most are useful and they represent a minor investment.

First, there are various accessories that are used in association with needles, such as tip protectors (to prevent stitches from falling off when you are not knitting), gauges to check needle size, and storage containers of various kinds. Also included here is information about knitting belts and sheaths, which are used to hold the right needle when working with one version of the Right-Finger Method of knitting.

Next, you will find a brief discussion of a variety of counters and other devices that help you keep your place as you work a pattern.

Finally, there are also quite a few tools that are helpful for managing yarns, either in preparation for knitting, or while you are working, as well as those that are used for dressing and finishing a fabric after you are done with the knitting itself.

❖ *Needle Accessories*

In addition to the needles themselves, there are several tools associated with the use of needles that are very helpful to have on hand.

Stitch Holders

As you work a project, it is sometimes necessary to place a group of stitches on hold. The simplest and most economical way to deal with this is to use a tapestry needle and insert

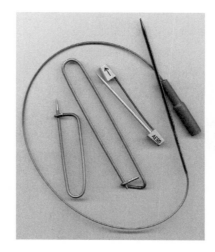

Stitch Holders, with cable version on outside.

a length of contrast-color yarn, string, or embroidery thread through the stitches. However, it is far more convenient to use one of the various types of stitch holders sold for this purpose because they are rigid and function like a miniature knitting needle, making it easy to transfer the stitches back and forth between needle and holder.

The smallest holders are variations of a coilless pin, which is a safety pin without the coil at the bottom that could snag the yarn. Another type of holder is a tiny single-point needle with a spring-held cap that snaps over the tip; there is also a double-point needle version with two caps, which makes it possible to take the stitches off from either end.

Finally, there is a version available for holding a large number of stitches that resembles a jumper needle. It has a small needle tip, a long cable, and a stop at the other end. You draw the cable into a circle and lock the tip into a hole in the end stop. However, in my experience, the lock is not always as secure as it should be. I find it easiest to use a conventional circular needle or a few double-point needles with tip protectors; simply use any needle that is the same size or smaller than the one you are working with.

Needle Size Gauge

A needle size gauge is a flat piece of rectangular or circular metal. One type has holes punched in it that are the diameter of standard needle sizes; another has notches around the edge. Either drop the needle into the slot to see if it will fit, or pass it into the hole; if the slot or hole is too small the shaft of the needle will not fit; if the hole is too large there will be space around the needle; the size is indicated when the needle fits the hole exactly.

Some of these are plain utilitarian objects, others have a touch of whimsy (there is a charming one that looks like a sheep, for instance), while newer ones can be quite decorative.

A Chamber's Bell Knitting Gauge, patented in 1847, England; based on the British Standard Wire Gauge. Victoria and Albert Museum, London.

It is very useful to have a gauge at hand if you regularly work with double-points or circular needles that are not marked; unless you keep them in their original package, you cannot be sure what size a needle is until you measure it. Furthermore, it is not a bad idea to check your needle size whenever you start a new project; you might have inadvertently stored one in the wrong package.

Tip Protectors

When working with straight needles or double-point needles, it is very helpful to use tip protectors, which are small rubber or plastic caps that fit on the needle tips and prevent the stitches from falling off when you set your work aside. This is particularly important when the width of the fabric is large in relation to the length of the needle. Some versions are designed to fit on two needle tips, and so do double duty: they not only keep the stitches in place but keep your needles together, as well.

However, if you do not have tip protectors on hand, simply wrap some of the yarn around the tip. For short needles, you can wrap it several times, first around one end, then around the other in a figure-8 motion.

Needle Storage

A wide variety of storage containers are available for your needle collection. Most are made of cloth or see-through plastic; some lie flat; others roll up. There are configurations for either straight needles in various lengths, or circular ones. There are also plastic tubes with screw-on lids that work very well, and these come in various lengths.

If you like straight needles, an attractive vase is a nice way to store them near where you usually sit to knit. They tend to get mixed up with one another, but one solution is to use the little plastic coils that wrap around a pair of straight needles, or a set of double-point needles; the coils come in different colors that help you identify which needle you want to reach for.

Knitting Belt or Sheath

As described in Knitting Methods, there are several devices that can be used to support one needle as you work, although they are rarely seen today.

The knitting belt is a leather pouch pierced with small holes and stuffed with horsehair; a short section of belt with a buckle is attached to one end, a longer section of belt is attached to the other. The pouch is positioned at the right waist or hip and you insert one tip of a double-point needle into one of the holes; the horsehair in the pouch will hold the needle firmly at whatever angle is convenient for you. With the needle fixed in place, there is no need for the right hand to support the weight of the needle or growing fabric, and this frees the right forefinger to act solely as a shuttle, cutting down on fatigue and speeding the work.

Knitting Belt; leather stuffed with horsehair.

A wooden knitting sheath, or stick, acts on the same principle. The most basic ones look somewhat like a narrow dowel with a hole drilled into the end. The shaft is inserted into a waistband or a belt tied around the waist. The sticks were often charmingly carved and quite attractive, and with some versions the end opposite where the needle is inserted is shaped to fit the waist and hip.

However, the hole in these sheaths accepts only one size needle. Since they were traditionally used by knitters who always worked with the same needles and yarn, and made the same style garments time after time, this was no disadvantage to them, but it limits the concept today. The knitting belt is far more versatile, although, for contemporary knitters, a limitation is that it accepts only double-point needles in relatively small sizes; a 3 mm is about the largest it will accommodate unless you enlarge a hole.

Knitters familiar with the concept but lacking a knitting belt or a lovingly carved knitting stick have used various other devices to accomplish the same task. One of the more charming of these substitutions is a bunch of feathers bound together like a miniature duster and tied to the waist, quills to the rear and vanes to the fore, which serves to hold the needle nearly as well.

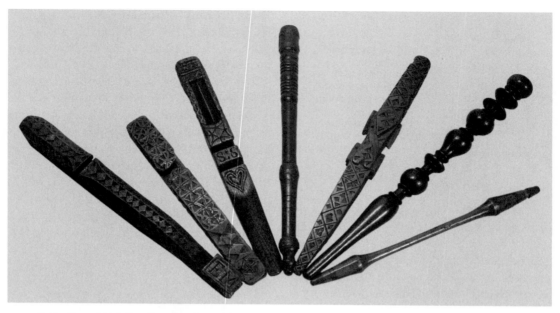

Collection of Knitting Sheaths. Copyright Brecknock Museum & Art Gallery, Brecon, Powys, Wales.

If you have no geese in the yard to provide feathers, you can even just tie a scrap of cloth into a good strong knot, tuck the ends into your waistband, and insert the needle into the knot.

❖ *Miscellaneous Tools*

Here is a small assortment of tools that in one way or another help keep track of where you are in a pattern, along with a brief mention of a very common tool used to measure gauge.

Counters

I strongly recommend that a count be kept of the rows you work; it is far more accurate than measuring the fabric; see Measuring a Work in Progress. To keep track of where you are, all you need is pencil and paper; use either hatch marks in groups of five, or make a check or dot next to completed rows on the garment pattern. Of course, when you are working with a decorative stitch or color pattern, you can simply take a quick count of repeats, instead of counting individual stitches or rows.

However, several devices are available for keeping count of rows; the most common one is barrel shaped, with a hole through the center so it can be slipped onto a straight knitting needle. It has little windows that display numbers printed on two dials, and it will count up to 99. Unfortunately, they make the head of the needle even heavier and, of course, cannot be placed on a circular needle or double-point needles. But if you have one and like using it, run a strand of yarn through the counter and hang it from the fabric or around your neck, or pin it to your clothing instead.

Another alternative is a chain of 10–20 rings that hangs from the needle; to keep count, slip your needle into the next link in the chain at the end of every row, or round. And, of course, there are now digital counters, either stand-alone devices or applications for your phone.

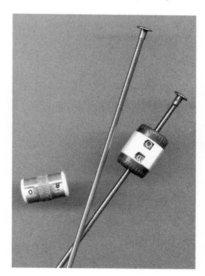

Counters: Vintage barrel counters with steel single-point needles.

Stitch Gauge Rulers

A gauge ruler has a little cutout window in the center of a metal plate; it is intended to measure stitches and rows per inch. If you have not done so already, please read the section on Stitch Gauge for why I do not recommend that method of determining gauge; all you need to do the job accurately is an ordinary ruler or a measuring tape.

Ring Markers

These are little colored metal or plastic rings that can be slipped onto the knitting needle between two stitches to mark the end of a round, to mark the location of a shaping pattern, or to indicate where a pattern changes. They are sold in small and large sizes or in packages of mixed sizes so they will fit on any needle you might use.

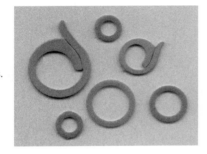

Ring Markers.

Basic rings are inexpensive, lightweight, and handy; if you have none available, cut a plastic drinking straw into thin rounds, or make a Slip Knot in a short length of contrast-color yarn and use that. Or, for a bit of indulgence, some are available that look like bracelet charms—jewelry for your needle.

Split Ring Markers can be used either on the needle or to mark a stitch within the fabric; there are locking markers that look like fat little safety pins that can be used in the same way.

Magnetic Board

This is a metal book stand that holds a knitting pattern at a readable angle. It has a magnetic guide that you place above or below the row of the pattern that you are following.

❖ *Yarn Handling Tools*

The following tools are all associated with managing the yarn in one way or another. Here again, some of these are tools you will definitely want to have available, while others are options.

Niddy-Noddy

The traditional tool for hand-winding a skein is a niddy-noddy (such a charming name), which consists of three sticks: a middle one, which is usually a shaped dowel with a hand grip in the center, and two bars perpendicular to it at top and bottom that are set at right angles to one another.

The bars tip up slightly at the end to hold the yarn as it is wound; one might tip down at the end to facilitate removing the skein.

- Think of the two halves of the top bar as 1 and 2, the two halves of the bottom bar as 3 and 4. Tie the yarn to one arm and then wind it by hand, down from 1 to wrap around 3, up and around 2, and then down and around 4; repeat.

  To wind efficiently, simultaneously bring the yarn to the niddy-noddy, and twist the niddy-noddy back and forth to bring the correct arm to meet the yarn.

A niddy-noddy also functions as a measuring device. They come in different sizes that wind skeins of specific lengths; most are 1½ or 2 yards, but some are smaller. Because the length of a single wrap is known, you can simply count wraps as you wind to determine how much yarn you have.

Yarn Swifts

Most knitting yarns today come already balled, but some of the more traditional yarns, such as those from smaller mills,

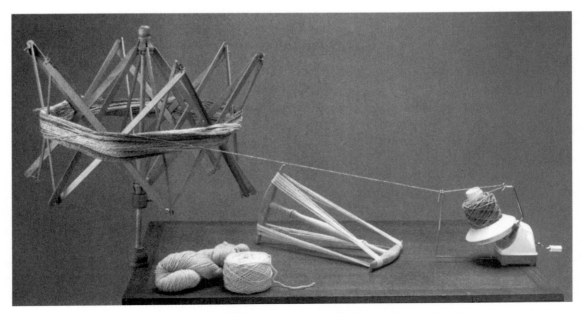

Yarn Swift mounted at left; skein and wound ball on table at left front;
Niddy-Noddy in center; Ball Winder at right.

hand spinners, or artisan dyers, are usually available in skein form, and the yarn will need to be wound into a ball before you can work with it. You can, of course, use the tried-and-true alternative of a chair back or a friend's outstretched arms, the latter being the most companionable method, but it is easiest to use an umbrella swift to make a skein.

A swift clamps on to a table edge and has six or eight arms mounted to a center pole that can be lifted into position to hold a skein of almost any size. The pole spins on its axis, allowing you to unwind the yarn.

There are also skein-winders available. Some are umbrella swifts with a handle on top that faciliates winding; simpler ones have arms that resemble the arrangement of a windmill, and others are wall- or table-mounted and have adjustable pegs set on a frame.

- To use an umbrella swift as a winder, lift the arms into place and wrap a tape measure around the middle of the extended arms; readjust the height until you reach the measurement you want for the skein.

   Set your ball of yarn in a box nearby to keep it from bouncing around or rolling away. Attach the yarn to one arm of the skein and then push the swift to set it spinning; hold the yarn in your other hand to act as a guide and to tension the yarn. If you want to know the yardage, count the number of wraps on the swift before you remove the skein.

Should you ever need to recycle yarn, you will want to skein and wash it before knitting with it again; see Recycling Yarn in the chapter Working a Project.

Nostepinne, or Nostepinde

This is a very simple, traditional tool for winding a center-pull ball of yarn by hand (see illustration in Yarns). The word is Scandinavian and its spelling and pronunciation vary with the particular language or dialect, but the tool is common to knitting. It was probably modeled on the belaying pins used by sailors along the side of the ship to fasten their lines. It is no more than a short dowel with a handle at one end, a slight indentation or "neck," and a slightly tapering tip; the whole is about 10 to 12 inches long. If you do not have a proper "nostie," you can use a plain length of dowel, or an even more traditional version, a wooden spoon handle. For how to use this tool, see Windings in the chapter on Yarns.

Ball Winders

A ball winder is a hand-operated mechanism that winds a ball from a skein in a fraction of the time it would take to do by hand; see Windings in the chapter on Yarns. Winders are not only useful for dealing with skeined yarns, but also for rewinding balls of yarn that have grown messy, or when you need to recycle yarn from something you had to rip out.

The yarn is wound into a center-pull ball with a "cake" shape, a disc with a flat top and bottom and straight sides. This is a very convenient form because you can draw the yarn off the outside or from the center of the ball, or both, as the case may be, and the yarn stays put and will not roll around, as a hand-wound ball tends to do.

The ball needs to be wound with sufficient tension that it will hold together when you are done, but not so firmly that the yarn is stretched; the finished ball should feel soft and plush. To use the winder, guide the strand with one hand and wind with the other. Be careful not to put too much tension on the yarn with the guiding hand, and wind at a moderate speed; the faster you wind, the more likely it is that the ball will be too firm.

Because the yarn is wound around a fixed plastic cone, it will collapse on itself slightly when removed and this will relax the yarn. Nevertheless, if you find yourself with a ball that feels too firm, it is best to rewind it at a gentler tension.

Some ball winders have an extra arm that makes it possible to combine two yarns. The yarns are not plied (no counter-twist is put on the separate yarns before they are brought together); they are simply wound together into a single ball. However, it is not advisable to combine two dissimilar yarns in one ball because they tend to take up into the fabric in unequal amounts, with more of one drawn out of the ball than the other. The result can be a serious tangle and the challenge of either separating the two or abandoning the yarn entirely.

If you want to work with two strands of the same yarn, simply pull one end from the outside, the other from the inside of a center-pull ball and hold them together in your hand as you knit.

Ball Holders and Reels

Balls of yarn tend to escape across the floor and under the chair. You can put the yarn in any sort of box (a shoe box will do) and punch a hole in the top to feed the strand through. I keep mine in a lined basket deep enough to keep the ball from leaping over the side.

If you want portability, there are clear plastic containers available with a hole in the top to feed the yarn through, guaranteeing that the ball will stay put. Older ones looked like little plastic beehives; newer ones look like a thermos.

When working with several colors in a pattern, it can be a challenge to keep the different yarns all nicely separate and untangled. At one time there were wooden stands like a table-top Lazy Susan tray that could be spun around; it had upright pegs that held the different balls of yarn. A more contemporary version is a clear plastic container with several compartments.

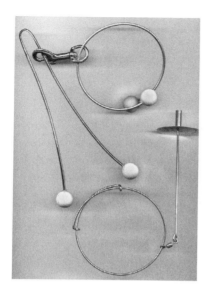

Yarn Ball Holders. The loop is worn on the wrist; the stick on the right, or the V-shape at upper left, holds a ball of yarn.

snap down around it to hold it in place; a little notch in the cup serves as an outlet for the yarn. You can just unwrap the yarn from within the slit between the two cups.

If you need bobbins and have none on hand, you can quickly make some from small folded pieces of cardboard about 2 inches long; cut a notch in one end and wedge the yarn in to keep it from unwinding.

Intarsia Bobbins. The slit is in the notch at the top.

A certain amount of twist is added to a yarn when it is pulled off the top of a ball or cone; the only way to avoid this is to unreel the yarn; see Knitting Methods and Yarn Twist. Small reels are not readily available for knitters, but they can be found wherever weaving supplies are sold.

You can also make something from inexpensive materials that will work. Find a sturdy box and cut two indentations on the top edge, one opposite the other. Cut a narrow dowel to fit, or use a straight needle that has lost its mate; put it through the center of the ball of yarn, and drop it into the indentations.

There are also traditional yarn holders that could be worn; one form is like a bracelet with a stick hanging from it to hold the yarn, another is a hook that is tucked in the waistband.

Yarn Sleeves

Also known as "yarn bras," these are pierced nylon tubes of the kind used to hold delicate fruit at the market, and they fit around a ball of any size or shape. They are particularly handy for holding slippery yarns together (for example, ribbon yarns are notorious for coming unwound). The sleeves are very inexpensive, but for an even more economical alternative, use a section of old nylon stocking cut to any convenient length.

Bobbins

Flat, plastic bobbins are designed for holding the small supplies of yarn used when working an Intarsia pattern. They are roughly in the shape of a square with a center bar. One end of the plastic frame has a slit in it that can be held open; you pass the yarn through the slit and wind it around the center bar. Release the slit and it closes the frame to keep the yarn in place; open it up and unwind more yarn, as needed.

Another type of bobbin looks like a yo-yo. The yarn is wound around the center core and the outer cup-like parts

Unfortunately, the more bobbins you have hanging from the fabric, the more they tangle up with one another. As discussed in the material on working Intarsia patterns, one solution is hang every other bobbin on the nearside, the others on the farside, or to simply do without. Leave the yarn hanging down from the fabric and just pull the next strand you need free from the others, dropping it again when you are done and need to pick up the next one; they tangle less than you think they might, and often less than the bobbins do.

Yarn Ring

This device is a ring that is worn on the tip of the forefinger; it keeps the yarns separated when working color patterns.

One version is a coiled metal ring with two eyes through which the yarns are fed. The other is plastic with pegs that create divisions to keep the yarns separated; a cap snaps down on top to contain the yarns after they are inserted.

The device works quite smoothly for Knit but is somewhat awkward for Purl because the yarns twist around one another, making it more difficult to wrap the correct yarn on the needle tip.

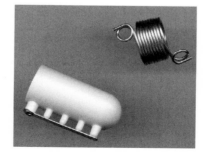

Yarn Rings for Stranded Color work.

If you have had trouble working with more than one yarn in one of the more conventional ways (see Stranded Color Patterns), a guide of this kind might prove helpful. The difficulty comes whenever you need to rewrap the yarns for tension. Because the yarn has been fed through the ring, you have to reach around with the other hand and pull the yarns down and rewrap them in order to position your finger the correct distance from the needle.

Bead Stopper

This clever tool is designed to keep beads from sliding off the yarn. It is a metal spring, no more than an inch long, with a round finger tab at each end. Press the tabs together to bend the spring and open the coil on one side, and then release the coils around a strand or two of yarn to pinch them into place.

It can also be used to clip the yarn to the ball so you can let it unspin if it has started to kink up on itself; see Knitting Methods and Yarn Twist. This is particularly handy when doing Twined Knit, which uses two yarns that are wrapped around one another after every stitch, meaning they need to be unspun frequently.

❖ Finishing Tools

Sewing needles and crochet hooks have already been discussed (see above); here are some other tools you might need for finishing a project.

Blocking Boards

A blocking board is a padded, cloth-covered or foam board that you can use for pinning out an item to dry. The fabric is usually printed with a one-inch grid, which makes it easy to give the item its finished dimensions.

Blocking Pins and Wires

Blocking pins and wires are made of rustproof steel and are used to hold the fabric in position. The pins come in either a T-shape or U-shape that will not slip through the fabric.

The flexible steel wires are inserted along the edges or folds of a fabric, and then the wires are pinned into place, instead of pinning the fabric itself; see Blocking for more information.

Seam Clips and Pins

Seam clips are miniature versions of the kind of spring clips sold for use in the kitchen to close up bags of chips and crackers. They are used to hold two fabric edges together for seaming.

If you are planning to seam with the two edges side by side, instead, you can use blocking pins, although they are less secure. It is far better to use larger size locking marker rings mentioned above, or simply tie the two edges together every few inches with a short strand of contrast-color yarn; see Seams for more information.

Part Eight

WORKING A PROJECT

CHAPTER 30

Working a Project

The material in this chapter provides useful information about how to decide on a new project and carry it out from beginning to end. You will find tips for selecting a pattern or yarn, along with suggestions for various tools you might want to have on hand, and information about caring for a work in progress.

Also included are techniques you can use to keep track of where you are in a pattern by counting stitches and rows and/or using markers to guide your work, and there are instructions for various ways to tie on new supplies of yarn, along with a selection of useful knots, for when needed.

Because we all make mistakes, you will find detailed instructions for how to fix them, whether it is simply a matter of picking up a stray stitch or repairing more serious problems. And if you have had to rip out a lot of yarn, you will also find suggestions for how to recycle it.

Knowing how to handle these mundane tasks will make your work go more smoothly and contribute in innumerable subtle ways to a finished project that you will be proud of.

Choosing a Project

For many of us, the look and feel of a certain yarn, a charming pattern spotted in a magazine, or just the urge to have knitting in hand is what gets a project going. However, it is a good idea to hold all these impulses in check long enough to give some serious consideration to what it is we are about to embark upon, for most garments involve a considerable investment of time and money, especially the former.

Making your choice requires careful attention to several factors: the details of the design and how suitable it is for the person who will wear it, the characteristics of the yarn, and how compatible both the yarn and any stitch or color pattern are with the style of the garment.

❖ Selecting a Garment Pattern

Whether you are designing something yourself, or planning to use a published pattern, the first step is to decide on a style that is appropriate for the person, for the season, and for the use it will be put to.

If the garment is for yourself, give some thought to what you need in your wardrobe. Perhaps you have a beautiful skirt or handsome pair of slacks that you do not wear very often for lack of a pullover that works with it. Maybe there is a blouse you would wear more often if you had a cardigan that matched. Or a jacket you might get more wear out of if you had just the right scarf or vest. If this is where you start, you will solve many problems at once, for these things may decide not just the style of the garment, but the kind of yarn and the color.

Another approach is to use the design of a favorite garment that has always worked well in your wardrobe as a model for something new. Or, if you try on something you like in a store, use it as a concept for what you want to make. Take a picture of it, or take notes on the details of fit and style, and then see if you can find a similar pattern, or design one of your own.

If you are knitting for someone else, of course, the safest

thing is to ask them what they would like, but when you are planning a surprise, a bit of detective work is in order. Be alert to what that person wears, the colors they like, and what flatters them. Is their style casual or formal? Perhaps they are involved in a sport or other activity that suggests a theme. Some people enjoy dramatic, contrasting color combinations, others a quieter, monochromatic palette.

If you are looking for a published pattern, keep in mind that the pictures are always of attractive, carefully posed models. However, few of us look like models, nor will we always stand around in attractive poses. Fortunately, if a schematic drawing is included, it will reveal details of the garment that you might otherwise miss when looking at the photo.

First, check the measurements and compare them to your own; this will tell you how much ease there is and whether the garment is meant to fit loose or hug the body more closely (see Measurements and Schematics). Then analyze key design elements for whether or not they will be flattering.

Pay particular attention to the shape and size of the neckline and the style of the armhole and sleeve, as these are critical areas in terms of both fit and appearance. Cap sleeves and sleeveless garments enhance only the prettiest arms. Open or round necklines and small collars enhance the appearance of a short neck, while cowls, turtlenecks, ruffles, and large collars flatter a longer one. Yokes make shoulders seem broader, especially if done in a contrast color.

Pay close attention to where the garment falls against waist or hips. A blouson style adds softness to a figure with straight lines, while anything that hits at the widest part of the hips can make them look even wider. (But keep in mind that it is relatively easy to adjust the length of almost any garment between the lower edge and the underarm.) Short jackets are flattering to the petite figure and to anyone who is slender because they make the legs look longer. Vests are versatile because they look just as nice under a jacket as over a shirt, and they are good for almost any figure type.

❖ Selecting a Yarn

If you are deciding whether to make a particular pattern, give careful thought to the yarn that is used and what kind of care it will require. Most yarns can be washed, but if dry cleaning is recommended, this will be an additional, ongoing expense that you may want to take into consideration.

If the yarn represents a serious investment, you might want to buy just one ball to try it out; most stores will hold enough yarn in the same dye lot for a few days while you decide. Do some Test Swatches to get a feel for how the yarn behaves and what it feels like when you work with it; this is also an opportunity to learn the stitch or color pattern to see what you think of it.

Wash the swatch to get a good idea of what the finished fabric will really be like (and check the wash water for colorfastness). Finally, hold the swatch up against your cheek in front of a well-lit mirror to see whether the color is flattering to your complexion; hold the swatch up against clothes in your wardrobe to see how compatible it will be with other items.

Doing this gives you time to think, away from all the seductions of the yarn shop. After all of this sober reflection, you may decide your original idea was a mistake. Please do not think of your time and money as wasted; focus instead on how much time and effort you have saved. Go back and try again—you are likely to make a much better selection the second time.

Of course, there are many wonderful projects that start, not with a pattern, but with the yarn. If you find a yarn you really like but have no idea what to make with it, someone at the store can usually direct you to a selection of published patterns that use that yarn or one that is similar. Many shops have swatches made up so you can get a better sense of what the yarn feels and looks like when knitted up. And if you want to try designing something yourself, see the material in the section on Pattern Design.

Consider the size of the yarn in relation to the type of garment you want to make. Something made in a bulky yarn will be quick to do and have a bold charm, but may be too heavy for indoor wear. Stitch patterns done in thick yarns will take on a grand scale and give the fabric a pronounced

Stitch pattern in relatively thick yarn. Swatch is 5 inches wide.

Stitch pattern in medium yarn. Swatch is 3 inches wide.

Stitch pattern in relatively thin yarn.
Swatch is 2¼ inches wide.

surface texture; color patterns that require stranding will in-crease the thickness of the fabric and make a warm garment even warmer.

Medium-weight yarns are excellent for most purposes and can be worn comfortably indoors when the heat is turned down, outdoors on a cool day, or under a jacket or coat on a cold one. They work very well for cardigans or light jackets that serve as layering pieces in your wardrobe. Nearly any stitch pattern can be used to good effect, although those based on Eyelets will leave rather large holes. Intarsia patterns and color stripe patterns are also very effective, but again, keep in mind that Stranded Color patterns add extra thickness and warmth.

Thinner yarns are by far the most versatile, as they are suit-able for almost any type of garment. Yarns of similar size can be used to make elegant lace shawls, cozy socks and mittens, warm sweaters done in Stranded Color patterns, or hard-wearing ganseys, traditionally done at 9 or 10 stitches to the inch (dense and warm, they protected British fisherman out at sea in Britain's worst weather). And if you prefer something that knits up more quickly, thin yarns can be doubled or even tripled, which gives you the opportunity to blend colors to create tweed effects.

While it is always more fun to go to the yarn store and

revel in the lovely colors and textures, you may already have a supply of yarn at home, and it would be economical, sensi-ble, practical, and altogether righteous of you to do something about it at last. Almost every knitter has a stash of previously purchased yarn; some of us have quite a lot of it.

Usually what happens is that you impulsively buy a pat-tern and some yarn, and get started, full of enthusiasm. Then a big project comes up at work, or your son's graduation is suddenly closer than you thought, and your knitting sits ne-glected for several months, and then is put away. With time you may begin to wonder what it is you liked about it. Give the remaining unused yarn to a retirement home or a charity resale store; far better for it to find a good home and apprecia-tive hands than to fill a dark corner in your closet.

If you still like the yarn, but not the pattern, the situation can be salvaged. Rip out whatever you started (be brave, it happens to us all), and then skein, wash, and rewind the yarn; see Recycling Yarn, below. Also determine the yardage so you know exactly how much you have (see Measuring a Skein). If possible, reserve the ripped-out yarn for ribbing, collars, pocket linings, etc., or blend it with a yarn of a different color and texture, because it may have a subtly different look from yarn that has never been knit up.

❖ Selecting a Decorative Pattern

When you are designing your own garment, you will want to select not only a suitable yarn, but a stitch pattern that is appropriate to the style, as well. The drape, weight, and texture of the fabric are aspects of garment design that are just as important as color or shape. Also, some stitch patterns have a sporty look, some are fancy, and others are very tailored.

A pattern may consist of a technique that draws the stitches together, making a dense fabric that would be just right for outerwear such as a jacket or hat; others are inherently softer or more open and are better for summer or even fancy evening wear. Subtle, textured stitch patterns are best done in a smooth yarn because the details tend to be obscured by a yarn that is too soft or fuzzy, and variegated or highly textured yarns can overwhelm all but the boldest patterns.

The appearance of a stitch pattern can also change depending upon whether it is worked firmly on a smaller size needle, or with a larger needle to make it more open. There are no rules that dictate what gauge to use, so take time to play with the yarn before you decide what to do with it. Pick a stitch pattern you like and make up three small swatches using a different needle size for each one (see Making Test Swatches in the chapter Stitch Gauge for more information). Wash the one you like best so you can see what it will really look like when finished. Then make your gauge swatch with the needle size that gave the best result.

Also give some thought to whether the decorative pattern will enhance, not just the garment, but also the figure. A stitch pattern with vertical lines is slimming and adds an appearance of height, while horizontal lines do the opposite. A bold stitch or color pattern on an oversize garment can work well for those of medium build, but may upstage a small person or exaggerate the proportions of a large one. Bulky, nubby, or fuzzy yarns will add volume, while smooth ones are slimming.

Working Tips

This section contains general suggestions about the more mundane aspects of working a project. While admittedly not the most interesting aspect of knitting, these details contribute to making the project more satisfying to do and help produce a better result.

Included is material on how to keep track of where you are in a pattern, how to tie on additional yarn, and how to correct mistakes.

❖ Getting Started

Before you get started, make sure that you have any tools that will be required—the correct size and length needles, stitch holders and markers, measuring tape, and a bag or basket that will keep the project clean as you work on it. Use a needle size gauge to check the size of each circular needle, because some are not marked and it is easy to accidentally put one away in the wrong package.

If you are working from a published pattern, read the instructions through so you know what to expect. Familiarize yourself with any special techniques used in the garment pattern by practicing on a swatch beforehand. In some cases, you might want to make a substitution, selecting a different method of casting on, a better buttonhole, or a neater shoulder line than that suggested.

If it is a written pattern, consider converting it to charted form; charted patterns are not only easy to read while you work, but allow you to anticipate details, which helps the work go more smoothly; see Charted Garment Patterns.

❖ Swatches and Gauge

Making a swatch to measure and calculate the gauge is, by far, the most important preliminary step in starting any new project. If you have not already done so, please read the discussion in Stitch Gauge about why this step is so essential to a successful project.

And as discussed there, even before you make the gauge swatch, I would like to encourage you to sit down and play for a while with your yarn and needles. Test Swatches are a wonderful way to practice the stitch or color pattern, learn the techniques that will be needed, and get a feeling for the characteristics of the yarn.

Save your Gauge Swatch, at least for the duration of the project; if you have any reason to question the accuracy of your gauge calculations after you are underway, you will want to have it to figure out what is wrong.

❖ Record Keeping

Take notes as you go; should your work be interrupted for any length of time, these reminders can get you started again more quickly. Notes are especially important if you are designing something yourself or altering a published pattern. Even if you decide not to proceed with a project you may have learned something worthwhile. An understanding of why a particular combination of yarn and pattern did not work might suggest another use for the yarn, or provide information about what kind of yarn would work better.

Whatever level of detail you prefer, find a record-keeping system that suits you, be it a computer program, index cards, a notebook, or all three. Here are a few suggestions:

- Keep one yarn label so you have the information on fiber content, dye lot, yardage, and care recommendations. Staple it to the receipt in case you need to return anything, or to have for future reference should you ever want to use that brand again.

- I like to staple the Gauge Swatch to a large index card containing all of the above information, along with the title and page number of a published stitch or color pattern, or that of a garment pattern. Having this not only provides a nice memento of the project, but the information may be useful when planning other projects in the future. Do the same with any Test Swatches you found interesting.

- In addition to making note of the Gauge itself, also record the number of stitches and rows in the swatch, its dimensions, and the size needle used. Include any of the information you may have regarding stitches per yard for the decorative pattern, and yarn requirements for the garment pattern; see Calculating Yarn Requirements.

- You might want to make a copy of the pattern so you have one to work from; save the original in case you need a fresh copy. Also, consider enlarging the pattern to make it easier to read as you work.

- Mark off rows as you go, and take notes when you work a challenging area such as the armholes and sleeve cap; these may prove useful when you make the other garment section with the same shaping. Also make a note if you substitute a different technique for the one indicated, or make any alterations in the dimensions of the pattern.

- Keep all materials related to a single project together; large plastic storage bags are helpful for this sort of thing.

❖ Caring for Work in Progress

It is nice to have some sort of a container to keep all your assembled materials together while you work on a project.

A zippered bag is useful for all the little things you carry along—measuring tape, markers, pen or pencil, stitch counter, tapestry needle, crochet hook, cable stitch holders, and tip protectors.

If you have a favorite chair at home where you always knit, a large lined basket is ideal. If you are not always at home, knitting bags of various kinds are available at craft stores and yarn shops, but even a sturdy plastic shopping bag will do.

Keep your knitting clean. One of the more sensible suggestions I have seen is to put what you are working on in a pillowcase (and a zippered pillow cover is ideal). Spread out on your lap, this makes a clean surface for you to rest the fabric on as you knit, and it will protect your clothing from lint.

Do wash your hands before you pick up your knitting, especially if the yarn is a light color or delicate, or keep packages of wipes in your knitting bag.

When you must put your knitting down, try not to stop mid-row, as this tends to stretch out the fabric at the gap between the needles. When this is unavoidable, here are some tips to prevent stretching:

- If you are working on circular needles, slide the stitches onto the cable to loosen the tension on them, and tuck the tips into the fabric in opposite directions.

- If you are working on straight needles, fold the fabric so the needles are side by side, hold them as one and wrap some of the yarn around the needle tips to keep them in position and prevent the stitches from falling off.

❖ Counting Stitches and Rows

Yarn shops sell counters of various sorts that work well for keeping track of the number of rows worked (see Tools). However, if you are working with a stitch or color pattern, it is far easier to count the repeats, with their fixed number of stitches and rows. To keep track of where you are in a shaping pattern, tick off each row on a chart, or make a note in the margin of a written pattern.

Should you need to count stitches and rows to find out where you are, the simplest thing to do is to count by stitch or color pattern repeats whenever possible. Multiply the number of repeats by the number of stitches or rows for that portion of the count.

To count individual stitches and rows, work as follows:

- Put fabric down on firm surface in good light and use tip of needle as pointer; stick it into center of each stitch as you count.

   If possible, count across a plain row, or up a column of plain stitches, or work on Purl side and count nubs.

- For complex stitch patterns, see illustrations in The Stitches that show the structures of various techniques; these will help you identify the stitches in the fabric.

- If your count is interrupted, insert needle or cable needle into stitch to mark your place and make note of row or stitch number.

❖ Markers

There are several types of markers that can be used to help you keep track of where you are in a pattern; some are available at stores, but it is easy to make your own.

One type is carried on the needle to mark off a position within the stitches, the other is set within the fabric as an aid in counting stitches or rows; see Tools.

Ring Markers

Yarn shops sell metal or plastic Ring Markers of two kinds. One type rides on the needle between two stitches to identify the beginning of a round in circular knitting, the position where a certain technique needs to be worked, or the boundaries between two different stitch patterns.

Just slip one on the needle wherever you think it would be

helpful, and use as many of them as you please. Every time you encounter a marker, simply slip it from one needle to the other, and carry it up row by row as you work.

If you do not have any on hand, you can make an equivalent with a bit of contrast-color yarn. Cut a 4- to 6-inch length of yarn, put a Slip Knot in the center, and slip it on the needle in the required position; these are also softer under your hands as you work.

A split Ring Marker is another type that can be placed on the needle, or on a stitch; you might do the latter to mark a position to count from, for instance. There are also coilless pins available that can be used in the same way; see Tools.

Yarn Markers

Markers can also be set within the fabric either on a single stitch, across a row, or vertically, alongside a column of stitches.

This might be done to keep count of rows, or when necessary to mark the position of something like a pocket or where decorative trim will be added.

A marker of this kind can also be inserted later by threading a length of yarn into a tapestry needle and weaving it through the fabric, but it is much easier to do this while you are working, as follows:

Running Thread Marker

1. Cut strand of contrast-color yarn about 12 inches long and fold in half. Insert right needle under running thread, place loop of marker yarn on needle and draw under running thread (as for a Running Thread Increase).
2. Insert left needle into nearside of marker "stitch," wrap *both* ends of marker yarn around right needle, and Knit.
3. Pull two ends of marker yarn through discarded stitch and gently tighten it into a knot around running thread.

A smooth yarn makes these markers easier to remove later and leaves no lint behind.

Running Thread Markers.

If this is an afterthought, you can crochet the marker yarn onto the running thread, as follows:

- Hold folded end of marker yarn on outside with looped end facing crochet hook. Reach up under running thread and hook loop, then hook two ends and pull through loop; tighten into place.

Row Marker

If you need to mark a row for something like pocket placement, or just as a line to measure or count from, lay it in as you work.

Use smooth contrast-color yarn slightly longer than fabric width, and work as follows:

- To begin, allow tail on marker yarn and pinch end against fabric on nearside; hold other end in hand not carrying main yarn. Work across row and, every few stitches, move marker yarn between needles to other side of fabric.

Alternatively, use technique described in Purl Inlay to weave marker yarn in on inside of fabric.

Row Marker woven in with Purl Inlay.

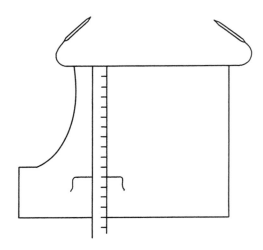

Measuring from a Row Marker.

Stitch Column Marker

If you need to mark a vertical line in the fabric, work as described above for a Row Marker, but move the marker yarn nearside and then farside every few rows, always between the same two stitch columns.

Cast-On Edge Markers

As you cast on, it can be a real nuisance to have to keep recounting stitches every time your attention lapses for a moment, especially when there are a lot of them.

You could place Ring Markers on the needle every ten or twenty stitches, but they are large enough to distort the cast-on edge; it is best to use a contrast-color length of yarn, instead.

Stitch Column Marker.

There is an added advantage to doing this if you are planning to work in the round. When it comes time to join the round it will be quite obvious if the cast-on edge is twisted over the needle, because the contrast-color marker yarn will betray it.

Marking a Finger Cast-On Edge

You can use the same technique to mark any of the cast-on techniques that employ a tail of yarn, as for the familiar Knit Half-Hitch Cast-On.

1. Take length of contrast-color yarn slightly longer than fabric will be wide, make Slip Knot at one end, and place on needle.
2. Make Slip Knot in main yarn and place on needle.
3. Hold two strands of main yarn for casting on to left in usual way; hold marker yarn on right forefinger (as for Right-Finger Method of knitting), or let hang from needle.
4. Begin casting on; after every ten or twenty stitches, pass marker yarn from farside to nearside or vice versa, under needle tip and over two strands of yarn used for casting on.

When you are done, you need only count up by tens or twenties to make sure you have the correct number of stitches.

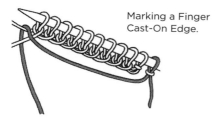

Marking a Finger Cast-On Edge.

Once you are sure of your stitch count, begin to work first row and release the marker yarn each time you come to it between two stitches.

Marking a Knit Cast-On Edge

- Hold main yarn according to preference and hold marking yarn in other hand, as for working with two yarns for a Stranded Color pattern.

As above, count off stitches as you cast on in groups of ten or twenty. Pass marking yarn between needle tips, nearside or farside, after making new stitch but before transferring it to left needle.

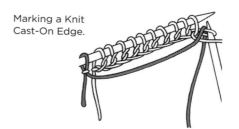

Marking a Knit Cast-On Edge.

❖ Tying On Yarn

When all the yarn in one ball has been used up, you will need to tie on another in order to continue. The important thing is to do this in a way that leaves little or no evidence of where it happened.

Of course, any join between two yarns will leave two ends. These need to be secured and hidden on the inside in a way that prevents the stitches from coming undone or enlarging, and keeps the ends from poking through and becoming visible on the outside.

By far the easiest thing to do is to tie on new yarn at an edge that will be seamed; a selvedge acts as a convenient little closet where the yarn ends can be hidden.

However, there are many situations where it is preferable or necessary to tie the yarn on within the fabric. Circular garments, of course, have no edges, although you can treat the join between rounds as if it were a selvedge. If you have used a Steek, tie on the new supply of yarn in the center of it; the ends will be cut away when it is opened (see Steeks).

Even when working flat, you may want to tie on within the fabric if you might run short of yarn and want to conserve every inch; it would be wasteful to stop well short of the end to tie on at a selvedge. And, of course, Intarsia and Entrelac patterns have yarn tied on all over the place, leaving innumerable ends to deal with, or you may be tying yarn on for some decorative needlework.

There are two ways to tie on yarn within the fabric. One approach involves joining the two yarns together in a way that weaves the ends in as you work the next few stitches. The other starts the new yarn, but leaves the ends to be secured and hidden on the inside later, during finishing (see Hiding Ends of Yarn).

Unfortunately, no matter how you join the yarns or weave the ends into the fabric, the last little bit may refuse to stay put because the fabric is stretchy. I have yet to find any solution to this short of acceptance—hide most of the end using whatever method you choose, and cut the rest off. If you catch an end trying to poke through the fabric to the outside, free up about an inch on the inside, and leave it there; a slightly longer length is less likely to slip through than a shorter one, and only you will see it.

While it is usually best to avoid using a knot to secure an end, in some cases this is necessary, especially when dealing with a slippery yarn or one with low resilience, such as linen. Using a knot will allow you to cut an end off short. You will find some suggestions below for several knots that can be tucked in unobtrusively on the inside; your fingers may find it, but it will not be visible on the outside, if done right.

Finished Tie-Ons

Here are several ways to start a new yarn in a way that leaves no ends to hide later. Which of these approaches to use depends to a great extent on the characteristics of the yarn, and what kind of stitch or color pattern you are using.

Double Yarn Tie-On

One of the most common methods of starting a new supply of yarn is to knit with the old and new yarn held as one. Of course, this approach is not suitable for multi-color patterns or when changing from one color to another.

1. With about 20 inches of original yarn left, pick up new yarn several inches from end and hold both yarns together with the two ends going in opposite directions.
2. Begin to work, leaving new end hanging on inside of fabric at starting point; after working about 1 inch (number of stitches will depend upon gauge), drop end of previous yarn on inside and continue with new yarn alone.
3. At your convenience, cut off two ends about an inch or two from fabric surface, or as an option, knot ends to Purl stitch on inside and then cut short.

Because the ends are woven in to the stitches, they have the same contour, and therefore the same elasticity, as the rest of the fabric.

However, because you are temporarily knitting with a yarn that is twice as thick as normal, those few stitches will be enlarged and this may be visible in the fabric. If you are using a nubby or fuzzy yarn, or a highly textured stitch pattern, the difference in size may not be very noticeable. However, if you

are using a smooth yarn and a stitch pattern with relatively little surface texture, this irregularity in the fabric could be quite obvious.

To prevent the short ends of yarn left behind from pulling free of a stitch, turn to the inside and use a crochet hook to work the last inch of yarn back the way it came, tucking it into a few Purl nubs nearby. This works well enough for wool, but may not be sufficient to keep a smoother yarn from popping through to the outside; if you are concerned about this possibility, it is better to use a Simple Knot to tie the end securely on the inside; see below.

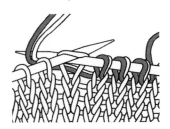

Double Yarn Tie-On.

Purl Inlay Tie-On

This method of weaving in the yarn ends as you begin to work is borrowed from a color technique called Purl Inlay. It must be done while working in Knit on the outside, or in Purl on the inside of the fabric.

1. Leave about 12-inch ends on both yarns. Transfer original yarn to other hand and pick up new yarn; hold yarns as for working Stranded Color Pattern with two yarns; see Two-Hand Stranding.
2. Pinch both ends against fabric to begin, and use new yarn to work one or two stitches.
3. Begin using Purl Inlay to weave end of original yarn in on inside of fabric for 4 to 6 inches.
4. If working flat, on next row work across to join, pick up end of new yarn and repeat Step 3, weaving in other end in opposite direction.

   If working circular, on next round, weave in end of new yarn in same direction as original yarn.

This is very simple to do, and works quite well, although the end will not have the same elasticity it has when woven in with the shape of a stitch. With smooth yarns, you may want to secure each end with a tiny knot on a Purl nub.

To achieve the same thing after the fabric is finished, thread the yarn end through a tapestry needle and weave it in along the running threads.

Twined Knit Tie-On

Here is an alternative to the above approaches that does not thicken the stitches and is very easy to do. In this case, the technique is borrowed from Twined Knit.

1. With 12 or more inches of original yarn remaining, pick up new yarn and allow end of equal length.
2. Press tail of new yarn against inside of fabric and using Twined Knit technique, alternate one stitch with new yarn, one stitch with original yarn until only a few inches of original yarn remain. Drop it and continue with new yarn.
3. On next row, at point in fabric where join occurred, pick up tail of new yarn and alternate yarns to stitches again, as in Step 2.

This is quite clever, and eliminates the problems caused by doubling the yarn.

If you are working flat, you will be working in the two ends in opposite directions; if working circular, they will be parallel, one row above the other.

Felted Splice

This method is somewhat similar to the Double Yarn Tie-On, in that both yarns are held together to work several stitches. However, with this approach, the yarn is thinned first to prevent the stitches from being enlarged.

It can be challenging to do this well, and it only works with wool because the technique relies upon the yarn's ability to felt.

1. Start at end and separate plies of both yarns for about 10 or 12 inches (see Plied Yarn for more information).
2. Cut some of ply in each yarn to staggered lengths. For two-ply, cut one ply off at half length of other; for three-ply, remove a third from one, two-thirds from the other.
3. Place thinned yarns side by side with ends going in opposite directions. Overlap each long single with a shorter one, and wrap them around one another to re-ply them much as possible.
4. Moisten your hands and rub the spliced ends rapidly between your palms to encourage them to felt. When they are clinging together and seem unlikely to separate again, cut off any ends left behind.
5. Work next stitches without placing too much tension on yarn.

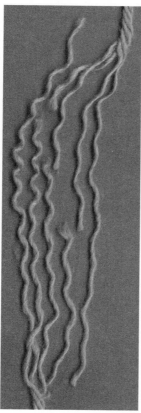

Felted Splice. Plies separated and cut, ready to be felted.

As an alternative, you can also interlock the two yarns, and felt the end of each yarn back on itself.

Russian Splice

With this approach, the two yarns are looped around one another and each end is threaded back into its own yarn with a tapestry needle. Thread the first end on needle and work as follows:

1. Insert needle back into same yarn as tail, parallel with the ply, and draw it through about 2 to 3 inches; there will be a loop at tip, where yarn was doubled back on itself.
2. Grasp loop at one end, and pull needle through to expose eye; then pull tail of yarn through and remove needle, leaving end of yarn exposed.
3. Thread other end of yarn into tapestry needle, pass needle through loop formed in first yarn, and repeat Steps 1 and 2.
4. Hold looped end of one yarn in right hand and grasp exposed end in left hand; pull to tighten loop until it almost disappears. Then stretch and smooth doubled portion of yarn in other direction until exposed end is absorbed into yarn; cut off any extra, if necessary. Repeat with other yarn.

Russian Splice.

In Step 1, push the yarn against the needle tip to soften and loosen the plies.

The joined yarns will be twice as thick, which presents the same problems as the Double Yarn Tie-On, above. Also, this will only work with conventionally plied yarns of at least moderate thickness; it would be difficult to do with thin yarns and is unlikely to work at all with many textured or novelty yarns.

It has to be said this is quite a bit of work for little advantage over other methods. However, it does suggest an interesting way to tame the last little ends on the inside; see Duplicate Stitch and Sewn Splice in the chapter Finishing Techniques.

Unfinished Tie-Ons

Here are several ways to attach the yarn, leaving the ends to be hidden later during finishing.

Duplicate Stitch Tie-On

This method of starting within the fabric produces a join that in some ways resembles the Double Yarn Tie-On, above, but it does not thicken the stitches and so is less obvious.

1. Stop working with original yarn when 12-inch end remains; allow same length end for new yarn.
2. Pinch two ends against fabric to hold them in place and begin using new yarn; release ends after a stitch or two.
3. When convenient, tie two ends together with Bow Knot, below.
4. During finishing, untie knot, interlock two yarns as for Intarsia, and weave each end in opposite directions on inside of fabric with Purl Duplicate Stitch; see Hiding Ends of Yarn.

It is obviously more trouble to weave yarns in later during finishing than to just knit with the two of them; however, there is much to recommend this approach.

First, because you never knit with more than one yarn, the stitches will not be enlarged as they are with the Double Yarn Tie-On, above. Although the fabric will feel thicker if you run it through your fingers, it will not look as if it is.

Second, each woven-in end will have the same contour and elasticity as the stitches, a characteristic this technique shares with the Double Yarn Tie-On and the Felted Splice, but which is not the case with the Purl Inlay Tie-On, above.

And because it is done during finishing rather than while knitting, you can choose to weave it in along whichever stitches will hide it best. In some patterns, the row above or below may provide a better hiding place than the one the join actually occurred on. This is particularly helpful with open stitch patterns like lace (especially for something reversible like a shawl or scarf), as well as for Intarsia or other color patterns, because you can weave the ends in with stitches of the same color.

Tie-On at Selvedge or Join

All the methods described above for tying on within the fabric are fine when necessary; however, whenever possible, the ideal place to do so is at the selvedge.

It is simplicity itself to attach the yarn at the edge, and easy to run the ends through some of the selvedge stitches later to tuck them away; there is no possibility that they will ever show through on the outside.

1. Use Stitches per Yard calculation to determine length of yarn needed for one row. When there is less than that amount left at beginning of row, break yarn, leaving 12-inch end.

2. Allow same length end on new yarn, press two ends against fabric and begin to work with new yarn; or tie together with Taut-Line Hitch, below.
3. Before starting next row, tie two ends together with Bow Knot.
4. After seaming edge, untie knot, interlock ends, and weave one end up along selvedge, the other down.

This method adds a negligible amount of bulk to a selvedge, and better to have it there than in the middle of the fabric. Here are some additional tips:

- If the garment will be seamed on one edge and not on other, or if stitches will be picked up along other edge, tie on yarn only at edge that will be seamed.
- If a border will be added to side edge, tie two yarns together between main fabric and selvedge stitch. Hide ends within selvedge of picked-up stitches or seam after border is attached.
- For flat fabric with all edges visible, tie on yarn within fabric, or between selvedge and first stitch of main fabric.

  For latter option, hide ends in selvedge stitches with equivalent of Duplicate Stitch, working one end down edge, the other up. Run last inch or so of each end into adjacent fabric.

Knots

Knots are often considered to be unacceptable in knitting, but I have come to think of them as necessary in some cases. Some yarns are simply too smooth or slippery to tame in any other way. And if there must be a knot, here are several to choose from.

Simple Knot

A Simple Knot is useful in any number of situations, especially where you want something quick and easy.

It can be used as a temporary attachment, such as when tying on yarn at an edge or within the fabric. It will help to keep the stitches on either side of the join from stretching out too much, and it is easy to undo when it is time to weave the ends in permanently.

1. Thread yarn end into a tapestry needle and pass it around another yarn, or under a nearby Purl nub or running thread.
2. Loop yarn on itself so it looks like a cursive lowercase "e" (a half-hitch). If end lies on top of the strand, pass needle up through loop; if end lies below the strand, pass needle down through the loop. Tighten it on itself.

Always knot the yarn to the corner of a Purl nub or running thread to make it as unobtrusive as possible.

If you are dealing with yarn ends that are prone to coming

loose, a Simple Knot can be helpful. For instance, you might want to knot an end about an inch away from where you plan to cut it off, before you have finished weaving it all in.

Simple Knot. Tied on to outside strand of selvedge stitch.

Purl Knot

This little knot is very easy to do and resembles a tiny Purl stitch. It is done with the yarn threaded into a tapestry needle and is nice to use for permanently securing an end of yarn on the inside of the fabric, either at the edge or within it.

1. Pass needle up through Purl nub or running thread, and then back down through same strand, forming a loop.
2. Insert needle up through loop, but do not draw through. Pinch loop against needle and pull on yarn to tighten, and then pull needle through.

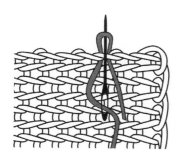

Purl Knot on selvedge.

Tuck the knot in at the corner of the nub, close to an adjoining stitch, instead of in the middle of it.

Tightening the loop around the needle before pulling it all the way through prevents tangles.

Here are some tips for using this knot in different circumstances:

- If you are tying on the yarn at a selvedge, leave a tail of yarn to weave in later. Pull down on the tail to tighten the loop.
- If you are tying on within the fabric, weave the tail in first, tie the knot, and then continue.
- If you are knotting the yarn after weaving the tail in, weave in another inch of yarn before cutting it off.
- If you are working with a smooth yarn that might not be secure, tie a second knot on the same nub, or on an adjacent one.

Taut-Line Hitch

This is a good way to tie one yarn to another; you can make the knot anywhere along a second yarn, slide it up into position against the fabric where it will stay put, and leave it there, or slide it down and off when it is no longer needed.

Strand A is passive and on left; Strand B is on right.

1. First wrap: Pass Strand B over to left and under Strand A and then bring end to nearside above where two strands cross.
2. Second wrap: Repeat Step 1 above first wrap and then tighten first two wraps around Strand A so they are side by side.
3. Third wrap: Make next wrap in same way below first wrap, bringing end out to nearside in space between this wrap and two above.
4. Pull on Strand B to tighten last wrap up against first two. To position knot, pull down on end of Strand A with left hand and hold taut; with right hand, slide knot up into position.
5. To undo, pinch knot between thumb and forefinger and pull Strand A up until it comes free; knot will fall open; there is no need to undo it.

Taut-Line Hitch.

You may recognize these wraps as simple half-hitches, just like the ones that form the edge of any Half-Hitch Cast-On.

Square Knot

There are occasions when you will want to tie two yarns together permanently, and one of the neatest ways to do so is with a classic Square Knot.

This knot lies flat against the fabric, and the ends naturally go in opposite directions, which is convenient for weaving them in. You can use it to tie on at a selvedge or within the fabric.

- Hold one yarn end in each hand. Wrap right end over left to farside, and then under it to nearside; pull two ends to tighten against fabric.

Wrap left end over right to farside, and then under it to nearside and up through circle formed; tighten against first half of knot. If necessary, retighten first half of knot before tightening second half.

Square Knot.

- This knot can also be used to simply join two yarns together when not attached to a fabric. Tie both halves of the knot, grasp all *four* strands and pull in opposite directions to tighten. The problem is, there is no way to predict where the knot in the yarn will appear within the fabric, but it can be undone and repositioned, if necessary.

Bow-Tie

This is probably the simplest and most effective way to tie two yarns together temporarily when tying on a new supply in the middle of a row, or for Intarsia (and it looks charming, as well).

1. Press tails of both old and new yarn against fabric and begin to work with new one.
2. On next row, stop when you encounter two yarn ends, set work down with inside of fabric facing up, and tie a bow knot, exactly as for a shoelace.
3. When convenient, untie just bow part of knot, and then weave ends in on inside of fabric.

Weaver's Knot

You may come across advice to use this classic knot; however, it is more suitable for weaving than it is for knitting.

The Weaver's Knot is ideal for tying two yarns together so they will not come apart when stretched at tension on a loom. There is no comparable situation in knitting, and the knot is relatively prominent compared to others; your fingers will definitely find it.

Glue

Yes, I said glue. Flexible fabric glues, available at sewing stores, are used to keep raw edges from raveling. If you are working with something like a ribbon or other slippery yarn that simply will not stay put, you really can resort to glue, with no apologies.

The knot will be a bit stiff and your fingers might notice, but it will not be visible on the outside of the fabric. Even better, you can then cut any yarn ends off short, close to the knot. This eliminates the risk that an end will become visible, and the inside of the fabric will look much neater.

- Make one of the knots described above. Place a drop of fabric glue on a piece of wax paper. Dip a toothpick in

the glue; roll it on the paper so you have no more than absolutely necessary, and then dab a tiny amount on the knot; repeat as necessary and let dry.

If the fabric will be against your skin, try to dab the glue into the side of a stitch, or between two strands, hiding it within the fabric so you are less likely to ever feel it.

❖ Correcting Mistakes

First, console yourself—it happens to everybody. Fixing something usually does not take as much time as you fear it will. When faced with an error you need to correct, the important thing is to understand the structure of the stitch or stitches involved; Knit and Purl are relatively easy, but some stitch techniques can pose more of a challenge; if necessary, look at the illustration of the structure of the stitch technique you need to fix in The Stitches.

The methods suggested here for repairing things are intended to minimize the possibility that any other stitches will run while you are fixing the first problem, and also ensure that you wind up with the correct number of stitches on the needle when you are done.

Unraveling Stitches

When an error has occurred in the row you are currently working on, unravel the stitches one by one, as follows:

To Unravel a Knit Stitch

1. Insert tip of left needle from nearside to farside into stitch below right needle.
2. Drop stitch above off right needle and pull on yarn to unravel stitch; retain stitch below on left needle.

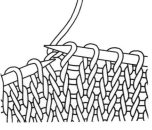

Unravel a Knit Stitch.

To Unravel a Purl Stitch

- Insert left needle up under Purl nub below right needle, then drop and unravel stitch on right needle, as described above; retain stitch below on left needle.

Continue in this way, stitch by stitch, until you have worked back to the error that needs to be corrected.

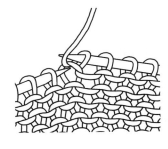

Unravel a Purl Stitch.

To Unravel Other Stitch Techniques

A Slip stitch, of course, can simply be slipped back to the left needle without change. If a stitch was slipped knitwise and is turned on the needle, insert the left needle into the stitch on the nearside from right to left and slip it back, turning it again so it is then in standard position with the right side of the stitch on the nearside of the needle.

If more than one stitch was included in a technique, such as a decrease or a Crossed Stitch technique, it helps to study its structure in the fabric so you understand how to insert the needle in order to pick up both stitches in the row below at the same time. Pull up on the yarn so you can see how it passes through the stitch or stitches below. If necessary, rearrange the unraveled stitches once they are on the needle.

When undoing a Cable Stitch pattern, work the pattern in reverse, slipping the first group of stitches to a cable needle, holding it nearside or farside as needed, and then slipping the next group of stitches to the left needle, followed by those on the cable needle.

Unknitting

When you are ripping out fragile yarns like mohair and angora, or those that are highly textured, be gentle to avoid fraying. The process of ripping back stitch-by-stitch can sometimes be damaging, particularly if a technique involved more than one stitch. If the method above becomes problematic, try the following approach instead:

1. Insert left needle into stitch below right needle as described above.
2. Remove right needle from stitch above, and then insert it into stitch now on left needle, either as to Knit or Purl.
3. Unwrap yarn around needle, reversing motion used to make stitch, and then draw yarn out of stitch while removing right needle.

Having both needles inserted into the stitch opens it up, allowing the yarn to be pulled through with less stress and abrasion because it slides around the needle and catches less against the yarn of the stitch.

Ripping Back Rows

You may be tempted to think that the mistake you discovered several rows down will not really show very much, that it is too much trouble to fix, and that you just want to keep knitting. But you will know the problem is there, and it may really spoil the pleasure you would otherwise have in wearing what you have made.

Also, it is not a good idea to put the problem away, thinking you will fix it later; the danger is that later may never come. Speaking from experience, I have found it is best to get the pain over with quickly—the minute you find the mistake, rip things out and get back to your knitting immediately. After you have fixed the mistake, you will quickly forget that it even happened.

In most cases, if the mistake is more than two rows down, the quickest thing is to take the stitches off the needle. Rip down close to where the mistake was made, and then pick them up on the needle again. Then rip stitch-by-stitch across the row to the problem.

Here is how to do this safely.

Mark Error

1. Place a Running Thread Yarn Marker or coilless pin in fabric where error is located. Pull stitches off needle.
2. Hold fabric down with one hand and with other, pull up on yarn to unravel stitches. After freeing 2 or 3 yards of yarn, wind yarn back on ball so it will not tangle.
3. Rip down to one row above marker, and stop.
4. Pick up stitches as described below.

If yarn is fragile, rip slowly and gently and ease the yarn out of the stitches with your fingers when it gets caught.

Picking Up Freed Stitches

If you have to rip out several rows, stop one row above the error and then pick up the stitches, as follows.

Use a needle two or three sizes smaller than one used for fabric; it will be easier to insert into the stitches and will put less tension on them, which helps prevent adjacent stitches from unraveling before you can pick them up. Work as follows:

1. Hold needle in one hand and fabric in other, according to preference; start at side where yarn is attached to first stitch and work more or less as described for unraveling stitches still on the needle, above.
2. Insert needle into stitch below first free loop and pick it up with right side of stitch on nearside of needle; pull yarn to unravel stitch above. Continue in this way across row.

    If fabric is on right, insert left needle into stitch under free loop from nearside to farside.

    If fabric is on left, insert right needle into stitch under free loop from farside to nearside.
3. With all stitches on smaller needle, use main needle again and rip back partial row stitch-by-stitch to error.

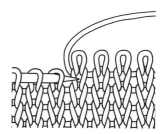

Picking Up Freed Stitches. Rip down one more row as you pick up.

In Step 2, if a stitch runs down before you can get it on the needle, pick up both stitch and strand. If this is not automatically corrected as you work Step 3, fix it when working the first row after correcting the original problem; see Repairing a Dropped Stitch, below. And, of course, if stitches have been off the needle, put any turned stitches in standard position, and make a careful stitch count before going on.

Rip Stop

Here is another approach that makes it impossible to miss a stitch or have one run down. It is a good technique to use for a slippery yarn, such as ribbon or a smooth silk, and is ideal for stitch patterns with complex techniques.

Use the smallest size circular needle you have (or one at least two or three sizes smaller than the one used for the fabric). Identify the first plain Knit row below the row where the error occurred. Work on the outside of the fabric, as follows:

1. Insert tip of needle from farside to nearside into each stitch in row; right side of stitch should be on nearside of needle (see Picking Up Within a Fabric). Also pick up selvedge stitches at sides, if present.
2. With all stitches on needle, remove main needle above and rip down to row where needle was inserted.
3. Do a careful stitch count, then slide stitches so one with yarn attached is at needle tip and begin to work again.

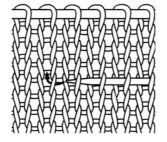

Rip Stop. Pick up stitches in a row below, before ripping out ones above.

If you do not have a small enough needle on hand, thread a smooth, contrast-color yarn or string into a tapestry needle and thread through stitches as described in Step 1.

Before beginning to work again, slip each stitch from one needle to the other, checking to make sure they are in the correct position on needle and none have run down.

Dropped Stitches

There are any number of reasons a stitch might drop off the needle, or the needle might slip out of a group of stitches. It is easy to get stitches back on the needle; every knitter will eventually become practiced at doing so.

If a stitch drops off unnoticed, however, it will run down into the fabric and need to be worked back up into position again. This kind of mistake can be relatively easy to fix if it is caught quickly, but if you have gone several rows beyond where it happened, it presents more of a problem.

What usually alerts you that something is wrong is that the stitch or color pattern does not line up properly, a stitch count comes out incorrect, or you simply stopped to admire your progress and noticed that something was amiss. At that point, you have very little choice but to rip back to the row where the stitch was dropped, and then work it back up again to the needle (for alternatives, see Orphaned Stitch, below).

Stitches Off Needle

If the needle has slipped out of a group of stitches accidentally, generally they won't go anywhere if you handle the fabric carefully. In fact, when the stitches first come off, they may still be lined up sideways, just as they were on the needle, waiting for you to slip them right back on again.

However, if they have been off the needle for a while, or if the fabric has been moved, they will gradually turn shoulder to shoulder. To pick them up again, work as follows:

• Pinch fabric below free stitches to prevent them from running down any farther. Insert needle through center of first stitch from farside to nearside so right side of stitch is on nearside of needle. Repeat until all stitches are back on needle.
• If a stitch is uncooperative and you find it difficult to insert the needle correctly, or one runs down before you can capture it, just pick them up as best you can and worry about putting them right later.
• Before going on, slip stitches back and forth between the two needles, checking each one until you are sure they are all in the correct position; if a stitch has run down, work it back up to the needle as described below.
• Count all stitches on needle before starting work again.

Once you've handled this situation a few times, it won't seem quite the frightening event it does the first time.

Repairing a Dropped Stitch

If a stitch has run down just one row, it will look just like a slipped stitch does, with a running thread stranding past it.

This is easy enough to correct, but you must be careful to position the stitch in relation to the strand correctly before reworking it. How to do so depends upon whether it is to be a Knit or a Purl stitch on the outside of the fabric.

Repairing a Dropped Knit Stitch

1. Position dropped stitch on nearside, and running thread on farside.
2. With left needle, pick up stitch in standard position first, and then pick up running thread in same way.

3. With strand on tip of needle and stitch to its left, insert right needle tip into stitch and pull it over running thread; discard on farside.

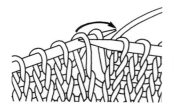

Repairing a Dropped Knit Stitch. Lift stitch over running thread.

Repairing a Dropped Purl Stitch

1. Position dropped stitch on farside, and running thread on nearside.
2. Pick up stitch on right needle in standard position, and then pick up running thread in same way.
3. With strand on tip of needle and stitch to its right, reach left needle tip on farside and insert into stitch; pull it over running thread and discard on nearside.

Repairing a Dropped Purl Stitch. Pull stitch over strand to recreate stitch.

Correcting Long Runs

If a stitch has run down more than one row, it will leave an open ladder of strands as evidence of its travels, and all you have to do is follow the ladder down to where the wayward stitch can be found. Keep it from going any farther by picking it up on a cable stitch holder or a short double-point needle.

Work across the row to where the dropped stitch should be, and push stitches well back from both needle tips, or place tip protectors on the needles.

You can use the knitting needles you have been working with to repair the run if it is not too far down, but it is easier to manage if you use a crochet hook to work the stitch back up, as follows:

Correcting a Run in Stockinette

1. For a column of Knit stitches, work on outside of fabric. Each stitch should be on nearside of its running thread; if necessary, use hook to pull stitch through to nearside.
2. Insert hook into stitch from nearside to farside with hook facing up; catch lowest running thread and draw it through stitch.

Correcting a Run in Stockinette. Use crochet hook to work stitch back up to needle.

3. Repeat as necessary for each running thread and then place last stitch on needle.

For a column of Purl stitches, work on inside of fabric, in the same way.

For a long run, or when working with a textured or fuzzy yarn, you might want to stop and make sure the running threads are lined up in the correct sequence before working the stitch back up. First secure dropped stitch, and lay fabric down on a table; work as follows:

- Use a long straight needle and weave it over and under all running threads. Check each strand to make sure sequence is correct and they are lined up row by row. Pick up hook and begin working stitch back up, taking one strand at a time from above or below needle.

Be careful not to place any unnecessary tension on the stitch or the strands as you work to avoid drawing yarn out of adjacent stitches. Once the run is repaired, you may have to ease yarn into or out of those stitches to get things looking as if nothing had happened.

Correcting a Run in Mixed Knit and Purl

If you are repairing a run in a column with both Knit and Purl stitches, first make sure you understand what the sequence of stitches should be according to your stitch pattern. Examine the fabric on either side of the run so you know exactly which stitch column and row of the pattern has the problem.

Work as described above, but change from one side of the fabric to the other as needed for Knit and Purl. This requires temporarily removing the hook from the stitch and inserting it again from the other side. To keep it from running down again, hold a small double-point needle in your other hand and transfer the stitch to it while you change the position of the hook; or use the repair tool that has a needle tip at one end, and a hook at the other (see Hook Needle Repair Tool).

Correcting a Run to an Increase

A stitch column originating on an increase technique can run no farther than that point.

- If the increase was a Yarnover, the running thread at the base of the ladder will be the Yarnover strand, which will be longer than the other running threads. Pull the second running thread under the bottom one to form the first stitch. Then work this stitch up through the remaining running threads in the usual way.
- If the increase was on a running thread, the strand freed from a stitch will be longer than the running thread below it, where the stitch originated; pull the upper, long running thread under the short one at the base of the run.

- If it was a Raised Increase, pull the first running thread through the stitch *below* the one that running thread is attached to on right or left, as necessary.
- For a Rib Increase, the strand at the bottom of the run will be connected to two stitches on either side in the usual way, and it will be slightly longer than a normal running thread. The original

Correcting a Run to an Increase. Stitch column based on a Raised Increase.

increase was pulled through a stitch to the right or left, in the row below the one the strand is connected to. Decide which stitch the increase was made on, and look to see if the stitch above is a Knit or a Purl; pull the strand through the stitch below in the opposite direction—if there is a Knit stitch above, pull it through as to Purl, or vice versa.

Correcting a Run to a Decrease

If a stitch runs to a row that contains a decrease technique, it too will unravel and the run will then involve two stitch columns below that point. You will recognize that this has happened if the ladder abruptly widens.

1. Work both stitches up to row where decrease should be, as described in Reworking Partial Sections, below.
2. Pick up both stitches on hook, facing stitch first, as follows:

Correcting a Run to a Decrease. Stitch column based on a Right Decrease.

   For left decrease, have left stitch at needle tip and right sides of stitches on *farside* of hook; draw running thread through both stitches.

   For right decrease, have right stitch at needle tip with right sides of stitches on *nearside* of hook; draw running thread through both stitches.

Orphaned Stitch

As mentioned above, if you continue to work several rows after a stitch dropped off the needle, the ladder will start somewhere within the fabric instead of directly below the needle, and the fabric will narrow above it. When this happens, there will not be sufficient yarn in the running threads above the dropped stitch to form new stitches in those rows.

The best way to correct the situation is to rip all the rows down to the point where the stitch dropped off the needle, work the stitch up from the bottom of the ladder to the needle, and then reknit.

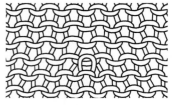

Orphaned Stitch. A stitch dropped off, unnoticed.

If that is not something you care to do, here are two other makeshift solutions, and which one to use depends on the project at hand.

Stealing Yarn

If you think the fabric is forgiving enough, you can try working a tiny bit out of each of the four or five stitches to either side of where the stitch is missing in order to elongate the running threads enough to make new stitches out of them. This will have to be done on every row, all the way up to the needle; it can be time-consuming and tends to distort the fabric on either side of the repair, but if the fabric is textured, it may not be obvious.

- Work carefully with needle tip, pulling up on side of a stitch to draw some of its yarn out, then pull loop formed into next stitch, and then out of that one into next. Work stitch up one row with yarn drawn into space between stitch columns. Repeat for next row up until stitch is at needle again.

Tying In an Orphaned Stitch

If you think the fabric will not really miss the stitch that dropped down, secure it in place by weaving in a strand of yarn in a way that effectively creates a decrease in that position.

1. Work dropped stitch up to top of ladder of freed running threads to row where fabric narrows. Temporarily secure it on inside with cable stitch holder or small double-point needle.
2. Thread tapestry needle with separate strand of main yarn. On inside, start five or six stitches to one side of dropped stitch, and weave yarn in as for Duplicate Stitch (see Hiding Ends of Yarn).
3. At dropped stitch, pass needle through stitch from nearside to farside, and then into stitch to left in same way to begin forming equivalent of a decrease.
4. Work duplicate stitch into stitch in row above, and then pass needle from farside to nearside through both stitches below, completing decrease.
5. Finally, weave yarn into stitches to left of dropped stitch with Duplicate Stitch, as in Step 2.

This gives as subtle a fix as possible, and if you take care to weave the strand in evenly it will not be noticeable, particularly if the stitch pattern or yarn provides other distractions for the eye.

If the yarn is slippery or inelastic, you might want to secure the Duplicate Stitch yarn with a tiny knot on a stitch head somewhere near the repair where it will be the most unobtrusive.

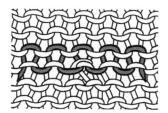

Tying In an Orphaned Stitch. Use length of yarn and Purl Duplicate Stitch to tie orphaned stitch to fabric with equivalent of a decrease.

Reworking Partial Sections

There may be times when you need to rip down an entire group of stitches to correct an error and knit them back up again. This is not a task I can recommend to an inexperienced knitter; even those who are confident of their skills will pause to carefully weigh their options beforehand. Doing a repair of this kind may require more time than it would take you to re-knit the part you would have to rip out, and reknitting might be far more pleasurable than fussing with this sort of repair.

Nevertheless, if the alternative is to rip out several inches of challenging knitting, it may be worth the effort (it is most tempting to those who work in the round because ripping means taking out the entire circumference, not just a flat half).

Success depends upon a real understanding of the stitch pattern, and great care must be taken not to distort the stitches—not only those reworked, but those on either side. Should you think that Stockinette would make this easier to do, you are correct in that the stitches are easy to deal with, but it is the most unforgiving of fabrics—any irregularity in the repaired area is likely to be quite obvious.

Nevertheless, if you have the incentive and the patience, here is how to proceed. First, mark off the pertinent section on a copy of your stitch or color pattern chart so you are quite sure of exactly what you must do every step of the way.

1. Drop whatever group of stitches are involved off needle and rip down to point where error is. Push remaining stitches back from needle tips or use tip protectors so none will slip off while you work.
2. Use pair of short double-point needles of same size as those used for project; pick up stitches at base of run.
3. Hold needle with stitches in left hand.
   - To make Knit stitch, place first running thread on left needle tip and use right needle tip to lift stitch over strand and discard on farside. Slip new stitch to right needle.
   - To make Purl stitch, slip next stitch knitwise to right needle, lift running thread strand onto needle tip,

reach around on farside and pull stitch over strand and discard on nearside. Alternatively, turn to inside and work as for Knit.
4. Slide stitches back to right needle tip at end of each row and repeat with next.
5. At top, slip stitches to main needle and continue.

The running threads will be under some tension as you work the stitches back up. As a result, some of the reworked stitches may be irregular, there is likely to be a gap on either side of the area, and the stitches on either side of it may have tightened up.

Use your needle tip to gradually work yarn out of any enlarged stitches and into those that are too tight. This takes some patience and going over things a few times, but usually you can get it to look as if they are all perfectly normal stitches and nothing unfortunate had ever happened to them.

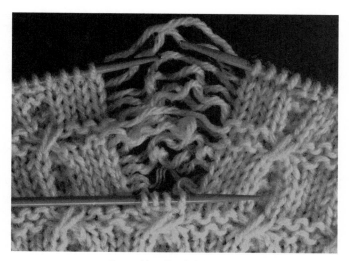

Reworking Partial Section.

Major Repairs

If you discover an error after the fabric has been cast off, or find a hole in the fabric that needs repair, here is what to do.

Grafted Repair

This is suitable for fixing an error on one row.

1. Snip a stitch at center of problem area and open fabric as many stitches to each side as necessary (see Separating a Fabric).
2. Pick up freed stitches above and below opening on relatively thin double-point needles.
3. Thread tapestry needle with length of matching yarn and graft stitches into opening (see Grafting Within a Fabric).
4. Hide ends left by weaving in yarn, as well as ends of unraveled yarn, using Duplicate Stitch, as described in Hiding Ends of Yarn.

Repairing a Hole

If you are dealing with a hole in a garment that involves more than one row, try the following approach:

1. Open up damaged area as described for the Grafted Repair, above. Unravel as many stitches as needed to leave ends long enough to secure on inside.
2. Pick up stitches below opening and running threads above it on double-point needles as for a Placeholder Opening.
3. Take length of yarn sufficient to replace missing stitches, plus about 20 inches for weaving in ends when done.
4. Thread repair yarn in tapestry needle, start at bottom of opening, and weave one end in through 4 to 6 stitches at one side of first row with Duplicate Stitch. At opening, tie original and repair yarn together with Square Knot.
5. Use repair yarn and separate double-point needle to re-knit row of stitches at base of hole.
6. Rethread tapestry needle with yarn, and duplicate one stitch on inside at side of opening. Pull yarn out of needle again and reknit stitches of next row.
7. Repeat Steps 5–6 until hole is filled.
8. Graft last row of reworked stitches to bottom of stitches in fabric above.
9. Remove yarn from tapestry needle and tie repair yarn and original yarn together in Square Knot. Rethread needle and weave end of repair yarn through stitches at other side with Duplicate Stitch.
10. On inside, make sure all knots in original yarn are secure and set close to fabric; cut off ends, leaving about 1 inch, and leave where they are.

If this is for something like a sock, knots are not ideal. If possible, leave ends of original yarn a little longer when you open the area up, interlock them with the repair yarn, and weave them in using a tapestry needle or crochet hook to finish.

Recycling Yarn

If you have had to make a major repair that involved ripping out a considerable amount of yarn, give some thought to the condition it is in before deciding whether to reuse it.

Some yarn is more fragile than others and may be damaged by the process of unraveling, especially if it has been ripped out more than once. If the yarn looks thin and frayed and you use it again, the fabric may look different in that area.

At the very least, the unraveled yarn will have stitch kinks in it, and it is a good idea to smooth them out before reknitting with it; yarn in this condition can take up into the fabric in a different way than smooth yarn and this can change the gauge.

Here are several tips for how to recycle yarn:

- If yarn can be steamed, hold a steam iron over the ironing board and draw the strand of yarn under it to straighten out the kinks. I have sometimes done this as I rip—set the fabric down on the ironing board and rip as you draw the yarn under the steam.

  If you are working with a center-pull ball (see Yarns), first rewind the ball to the point where you will begin to rip it out. With the ball on your winder, start to rip, drawing the yarn beneath the steam; stop every 5 yards or so, and wind more on to the ball. When you are done, give the whole ball of yarn several good blasts of steam.

- Alternatively, wind the yarn out of a ball into a skein using a niddy-noddy or an umbrella swift (see Tools). Use a steamer appliance to apply copious steam to the skein; adjust swift to tighten and expand skein slightly to stretch yarn smooth and remove kinks (do not stretch too tight).

  Or, secure the skein so it will not tangle; take one full circle of the yarn and use it to make two half-hitches around the mid-point of the skein; repeat at the opposite end and then knot the yarn end to itself. Lay the skein down on the ironing board and steam it; gently stretch it to remove the kinks. Repeat until the yarn seems smooth enough (if necessary, retie or slide the half-hitches to new locations and steam the areas where the yarn was tied first). Allow to dry thoroughly and then rewind yarn into a ball.

- If steaming the skein does not work well enough, wash the tied skein, just as you would a sweater (see Washing a Knit); minimize movement in the water so it will not tangle. Rinse and squeeze out as much water as possible, roll up in a towel, and squeeze out more. Then, place the skein on a plastic hanger and hang up to dry. If the yarn has any residual kinks, steam it, and then rewind into a ball.

- If a comparison between used and unused yarn shows signs of wear, break off the used part and wind into a separate ball. Reserve this yarn, but use it only if you have to. If possible, use this yarn for areas of the garment other than the main fabric. Any difference between it and the unused yarn is less likely to show up in a ribbing, for instance; alternatively, use it for sewing up.

  If it is absolutely necessary to reuse it for the main fabric, consider alternating it with unused yarn, row by row, to help blend it in.

CHAPTER 31

Written Garment Patterns

A knitting pattern consists of two sets of instructions. One set provides detailed information about how to make an item the correct size and shape, whether it is a garment, an accessory, or something for the home, and this is what is discussed here.† The other set tells you how to work each stitch to produce a particular decorative pattern; for information about that aspect of a pattern, see Written Stitch Patterns, Charted Stitch Patterns, or Charted Color Patterns.

Most garment patterns are accompanied by a photograph of the item in an appropriate setting so you can see what it will look like. Generally, a pattern will also include a schematic, a simple line drawing showing the shape and dimensions of each section, such as the sleeve and bodice; see Measurements and Schematics.

While less common, some patterns also provide a garment chart, a graphic representation of the pattern for shaping areas like the sleeve cap or armhole; this type of pattern is described in Charted Garment Patterns.

If you are unfamiliar with any of the techniques used in the pattern, try them on a Test Swatch or two before you begin. You might also want to refer to the relevant discussions in this book and decide for yourself how to work various details; there are usually options that are worth considering and one or another might improve the results or suit you better without substantially altering the pattern itself.

---

† For the sake of brevity, I primarily use the term "garment" throughout these instructions because that is what most knitters make most of the time. In some cases the instructions can be understood to apply equally to household items like pillows or accessories like handbags, but when necessary these kinds of things are dealt with explicitly.

Written Garment Patterns

Originally, patterns were developed by knitters for their own use, and they generally consisted of no more than brief notes of some kind, perhaps accompanied by a simple sketch. When a pattern was shared with a neighbor or friend, anything not written down was conveyed orally. Nothing more was needed because the styles and techniques used within each regional knitting tradition would have been familiar to every knitter since childhood.

When knitting patterns began to be published it became necessary to expand on the details and include what was previously unwritten. To save space, publishers used a spare writing style with a compressed sentence structure that eliminated all non-essential words and substituted abbreviations for the names of techniques. The terms used were undoubtedly those already familiar to the pattern writers and publishers from their own knitting tradition, which they then formalized in some way.

Patterns published in different parts of the world still exhibit the legacy of these regional differences, and as a result there is still no single, agreed-upon system for how to write knitting patterns. Fortunately, they all convey the same kind of information, and once you are familiar with reading one sort of pattern, any of the others will be relatively easy to interpret. Also, most publishers include a glossary that explains the techniques and abbreviations used. Those listed in the chapter Written Stitch Patterns are common in many patterns; also included there are several that I have found useful. Here you will find a detailed discussion of how these terms are combined to convey the pattern instructions in a clear and concise way.

Written instructions are divided into sections. The first deals with the preliminaries, such as the required gauge, the garment dimensions, and the necessary tools and materials. This information is normally followed by the instructions for any stitch or color pattern.

Next is the main section of the pattern, which contains specific instructions for how to work every aspect of the garment. And last, details will be provided for how to finish the item.

The material below explains each of these things in turn, with the exception of the information on stitch and color patterns, which have their own chapters.

❖ Pattern Sizes

Published patterns generally include instructions for a range of sizes in a design; for a simple garment this might be only small, medium, large, and extra-large—written S, M, L, XL. For garments that require a more precise fit, there will be a numerical set of chest or bust measurements (for a skirt these would be hip measurements), that is written something like:

To fit 36 (38, 40, 42) inches.

Ready-to-wear sizes are rarely used since they tend to change over time, and those in many countries differ; if a size of that kind is used, a key to body measurements will usually be provided in the back of the pattern book.

This type of notation, consisting of a series of numbers with all but the first enclosed in parentheses, is a form that will be used again and again throughout the pattern. All other numeric instructions, such as for how many stitches to cast on or rows to work, and so on, will have the relevant number for the smallest size first, and those pertinent to the other sizes in the same relative position within the sequence.

After deciding on your size, use only the number that appears in the same position within the notation for every instruction in the pattern, and ignore the others. For instance, in the example given above, if you plan to make the size 40, the only number you need to look at when following any instruction will be the second-to-last one in the sequence.

Before you start to work, it is a good idea to mark all the numbers that are correct for your size throughout the pattern; circle each one, or use a highlighter pen so they are easy to identify.

❖ Garment Dimensions

The pattern size is based on a body measurement; however, the garment itself will usually have a larger measurement because extra width will have been added to allow for ease or because the style requires a looser fit.

The pattern will provide the finished dimensions of the garment either in written form or as a schematic—a drawing of the main pattern pieces. These pattern dimensions will be given in the same way as the sizes. For instance, you might see:

Width at underarm 44 (46, 48, 50) inches.

As with the sizes, the only number that is important to you is the one in the same position as your size.

The difference between the body measurement and the garment measurement tells you something about how the garment will fit. For instance, if the pattern is for a 38 chest, and the garment measures 44 inches in circumference at the underarm, there is 6 inches of ease.

You might also want to compare any other measurements provided in the pattern to the body measurements of the person who will wear the garment. Pay particular attention to the width of the shoulders and length of the sleeve, as they are critical to a good fit. Unfortunately, sleeve length alone is not particularly useful; to check on what the measurements really mean, work as follows:

• Divide shoulder width in half and add to sleeve length. Measure person from center back neck to wrist and compare.

Keep in mind that if a sleeve has a ribbing at the wrist, it would ordinarily have some ease for movement as well, and should be about an inch or two longer than the actual body measurement; see Ease Allowances. For more information on altering pattern instructions, see Pattern Alterations in the chapter Stitch Gauge.

❖ Yarn and Other Materials

In the first part of the pattern, you will also find information regarding the yarn to use—the brand, and perhaps a name or number for a particular color (called the "dye lot"). How much yarn to buy will also vary with the size of the garment, and will be indicated with the same notation, such as,

9 (10, 11, 12) 50-gram balls of XYZ wool, color #652.

You can certainly select a different color than the one suggested; however, if you prefer to use a different yarn entirely, choose something that has the same characteristics; see Yarn Substitution. The yarn listed in the pattern has qualities the designer thought suitable for the style of the garment; in addition, it is important that your choice is similar enough that it will produce the gauge required in the pattern.

The pattern may also provide a list of other tools and materials needed, such as stitch holders, a sewing needle for finishing, or perhaps things like the size and number of buttons, or type and length of zipper when appropriate.

Gauge and Needle Size

The first step in any pattern is the instructions for how to make and measure a Gauge Swatch, a 4- to 6-inch square sample of your knitting made with the same stitch or color pattern used for the garment. The pattern gauge may be shown in the form of a small graphic of a knitted fabric that has the stitch gauge at the bottom, the row gauge at the side, and the needle size in the middle.

If the information is written only in words, it might look like this:

With size 5 needle, 26 stitches and 34 rows = 4 inches.

Another way to say the same thing is:

On size 4 needle, 18 stitches / 25 rows in 10 cm.

Or, the gauge may be given alone, such as:

5 stitches and 7 rows per inch.

The instructions will almost always warn you that your gauge must match the one in the instructions or the garment will not fit. Believe it. Should you be tempted to skip this step and just get on with your knitting, please read the discussion in Stitch Gauge about why that is not a particularly good idea.

Actually, even if you are going to make a swatch, read that chapter anyway, because it is full of useful information about why swatches are so important and provides detailed instructions for how to measure and calculate an accurate gauge. The method recommended there is quite different from that found in most published patterns, but as long as you match the gauge in the instructions, it does not matter how you obtain it. You will also find suggestions there for what to do if you find you cannot match the gauge, or what to do if the stitch gauge matches, but the row gauge does not, which are rather common problems.

Most patterns will require at least two needle sizes, usually one for the main fabric and a smaller one for the ribbing. Whether the pattern specifically says so or not, it is very important to understand that these are "recommended" needle sizes.

The primary needle is the one the designer used to calculate gauge and make the garment. However, your hands and knitting tension are unique, and you may need to use a different size needle in order to match the gauge specified. For instance, if the pattern says to use a size 5 needle, you may need to use a size 4 or a size 6; see Matching Pattern Gauges. It is a good idea to do several small, preliminary Test Swatches as a way to select the needle size to work with before you make the larger Gauge Swatch.

The needle size recommended for a ribbing is customarily two sizes smaller than the one used for the main fabric. However, I strongly suggest that you use a considerably smaller needle size for ribbing—the smaller the needle size the more elastic the ribbing will be—and that you make a separate Gauge Swatch and calculate the number of stitches used for the ribbing based on a body measurement; see the information in Average Gauge for Ribbing.

❖ The Pattern

Following all these preliminaries, you will finally get to the actual pattern. If the garment is constructed in flat pieces there will be separate instructions for the front, back, sleeves, and so on, or, if it is worked in the round, for the body and the sleeves. There may be additional instructions for anything added to the main sections, such as a neckline or collar.

Cast-On and Ribbing

The first instruction will be for casting on a number of stitches, and it will read something like the following:

With size 4 ndl, cast on 70 (74, 78, 82) stitches.

In many patterns, this will be followed by the instructions for a ribbing:

Work K1 P1 rib 20 (22, 24, 26) rows.

Bodice

After the ribbing, the next instruction will generally require you to change to the larger needle and begin the stitch or color pattern used for the body of the garment; for more information about reading this part of the pattern, see Written Stitch Patterns, and/or the material in Charted Stitch Patterns and Charted Color Patterns.

This instruction might look like:

With size 6 needle, begin stitch pattern.

For most sweaters, the length between the ribbing and armholes is a straight stretch of knitting. The pattern may specify either a certain number of rows or inches, such as,

Work in pattern 14 (15, 16, 17) inches to armhole.

Or

Change to #6 needle; work in pattern to row 70 (75, 80, 85).

Because the dimensions of the fabric will change when it is dressed (washed and steamed, or dry cleaned), a measurement taken while you work will not be the same as that of the finished garment; see Measuring a Work in Progress.

For this reason, it is far better to work a certain number of rows, instead of a measured length. If the pattern does not specify the number of rows (as in the first example), multiply the length to the underarm times the row gauge to find it.

Shaping

There are two kinds of basic shaping instructions: those that are spaced across a single row, and those that are spaced along the length of the fabric. You will find more information about this aspect of working a pattern in the chapter Shaping a Fabric, and the various techniques used are described in Increase and Decrease Techniques.

Horizontal Shaping

Shaping that is spaced across a single row most often occurs when the pattern calls for you to switch from one stitch pattern to another, because each one is likely to have a different gauge and require a different number of stitches for the width (for more information, see Shaping a Fabric). In this case, the instructions might read something like:

Increase every 7th stitch across row, work last 6 sts in pattern; 78 sts on needle.

This means you are to work six stitches plain, then work an increase on the seventh stitch, work another six stitches and another increase, etc., and then work the final six stitches at the end of the row.

The pattern will usually tell you how many stitches should be on the needle after working any shaping; it is always a good idea to count them before going on to make sure you increased or decreased accurately.

Vertical Shaping

Shaping is also done at the side edge of the fabric, spaced along the rows to create the slope of a sleeve, for instance. If the pattern requires increases, it might read something like the following:

Increase 1 stitch each side every 7 (8, 9, 10, 11) rows × 6.

In other words, the pattern calls for working one increase at each side, and then working a certain number of rows at a constant width before another increase is needed.

You can work the increases at each side of the same row, or at the beginning of the next two rows.

In the above example, if you put the shaping at each side of the same row, you would work six more rows before making another increase. If you put the shaping at the beginning of the next two rows, you would work five more rows after the last increase.

Contour Shaping

You will encounter another kind of shaping instruction for armholes and sleeve caps. A pattern of this kind will usually tell you to cast off several stitches at the beginning of each of the next two rows, which indents the side edge sharply for the underarm. A very simple armhole might have no further

shaping, but most are also sloped or curved above this, and the pattern will read something like this:

Decrease 1 stitch each side every other row twice, every 4th row twice, every 6th row once.

This means you are to work a decrease on the first and last stitch of, say, row 56 and row 58 (every other row twice), then again on rows 62 and 66 (every fourth row twice), and finally on row 72 (six rows later).

The pattern to shape a sleeve cap or a neckline will read much the same.

Acute Slopes

Shoulder lines have a steep slope and are done by casting off the stitches or using Short Rows. An instruction to cast off shoulder stitches might read:

Cast off 4 stitches at beginning of each row 3 (4, 5, 6) times.

Because you can only cast off at the beginning of a row, the stitches at the other side will be removed on the next row.

This instruction is actually simplified, because it is usual to decrease one stitch at the end of every intervening row to ease the transition between cast-off steps. For more information on Acute Slopes, see the chapters Calculations for Pattern Design, and Charted Garment Patterns.

Also note that the shoulder could be sloped with Short Rows and then seamed with Joinery Cast-Off, which gives a much smoother result. You can substitute that approach whenever a pattern says to cast off in steps.

Borders

There may also be instructions for picking up stitches to add a ribbing or collar to the neck opening, for how to work the button band on a cardigan, or perhaps for how to work the sleeves from the armhole down. For all of these techniques, see the chapter Picking Up Stitches.

Finishing

And finally, there will be a section on finishing details that may include instructions for how to wash and shape the finished garment; for more information, see Dressing the Fabric. And for details on sewing the Seams and tucking away ends of yarn, see the chapter on Finishing Techniques.

CHAPTER 32

Cleaning and Dressing a Knit

A knitted fabric cannot be thought of as finished until it has been "dressed," washed or dry cleaned and then blocked and/or steamed.

As careful as you may have been while knitting a fabric, it has been much handled in the process and will need to be freshened up for wear. Of far greater importance, however, is the fact that the fabric will undergo a profound change during its first cleaning, and its characteristics and dimensions will never be the same as they were when the stitches first came off your needles (see the discussion in Stitch Gauge).

Several different methods can be used to clean and dress a knitted fabric, and the choice of which approach to use depends primarily on what fiber the yarn was made of, what kind of a stitch pattern was used, and how large the knitted item is.

Cleaning a Hand Knit

Obviously, the long-term cost of care is much less if you can wash the garment, and this is safe for most yarns, even when the label "suggests" dry cleaning. A warning not to wash a yarn may be on the label because the yarn manufacturer is concerned that the consumer will not use the proper water temperature or detergent. You can find out for yourself what will happen to the yarn by washing a good-sized Test Swatch.

There are, however, many good reasons to dry-clean a garment, not least of them being the convenience. Furthermore, it requires some effort to educate yourself about which cleaning products to use for safely cleaning a hand knit. Nevertheless, there is much to recommend it, including economy.

The following discussion includes some of the pros and cons, as well as extensive material on home cleaning materials, both for general laundry and for stain removal.

❖ Dry Cleaning

While most knitting yarns can be washed, there are times when it is appropriate or desirable to dry-clean a garment. If you have any reason to be concerned about the stability of the dyes (for more information, see the chapter on Yarns), particularly in a multicolored garment, dry cleaning is probably the best option.

You may also want to dry-clean a garment that is badly soiled or stained, and of course there may be times when you do not have the facilities or the time to hand wash it. Finally, if the garment is large and heavy, like a coat or blanket, it could be too cumbersome to wash at home.

When it comes time to send a precious hand knit to a dry cleaners, ask around for recommendations about where to take it. A good choice is a cleaner that handles wedding gowns or high-end designer clothing on a regular basis, since they will be more familiar with handling fine fabrics and will take better care of it. If there are any unusual fibers in the yarn, show the cleaners the yarn label; just as they rely on the care labels inside clothing, they will appreciate knowing what the fiber content and manufacturer's recommendations are so they know how to deal with it.

❖ *Laundry Products*

Before going on to talk about how to wash a knitted fabric, first it is important to discuss laundry products. An overwhelming number of choices are on the market; some are sold to the general consumer for day-to-day laundry chores, others are intended specifically for fine textiles such as hand knits, hand wovens, quilts, and embroidered pieces.

With few exceptions, you will not find specific product recommendations here because formulations can change, or a product may not remain on the market. Instead, there is general information about what to look for in any product you are thinking of using.

A good source of current information and recommendations are companies that sell materials to textile artists for dyeing, spinning, weaving, or felting. Another is the textile department of a museum, or a dealer in handmade or antique textiles that provides care advice for their products. And, of course, the Internet provides a wealth of information, although so much of it can be difficult to sift through.†

In addition, it is important to understand what the yarn will tolerate before selecting a product to use for cleaning it. You will find information about the characteristics of fibers commonly used in knitting yarns in the chapter on Fibers, and included there are specific care requirements for each one, as well as a general discussion of dyes.

This chapter focuses on how to clean a knitted item. However, before we turn to those instructions, first a few definitions:

- Soil is due to general wear and requires laundering the entire garment.
- Stains, or spots, consist of foreign material concentrated in one area. These materials usually need to be removed prior to general laundering because they may spread or permanently set if not dealt with beforehand.
- Bleach does not clean; it is used to remove discoloration caused by soil and stains; in other words, it acts on the color, not the stain itself, so any residue can no longer be seen.

    Mildew, tomato, coffee, and tea are a few familiar things that can leave permanent color in the fabric even after spot removal and laundering.

What follows here is a discussion of some of the ingredients in common cleaning products, including two things that may matter more in terms of the long-term health of your precious hand knits than which detergent you use—pH and water.

While some of the following might seem like a bit too much chemistry when all you want to do is wash a sweater, I think you will find it interesting and informative. It will help you understand more about what to look for on labels and decide which products to use on a regular basis, or what to do if your usual ones are not available.

pH

The most important thing to take into consideration when cleaning any fabric is the pH of the wash water, which is a measurement of how acidic or alkaline it is.‡ The fibers commonly used in many knitting yarns have different tolerances for acids and alkalis, which are the primary ingredients in cleaning products, but all of them can be damaged by strong ones.

At 7, pure, distilled water is neutral on the pH scale, which ranges from 0 to 14; a low number indicates an acid, and a high one indicates an alkali.

Here is a list of the pH of common household items.

Lemon juice: 2	Water: 7
Vinegar: 2–3	Baking soda: 8.5
Wine: 3.5	Borax: 9
Tomato juice: 4	Washing soda: 11
Coffee: 5	Ammonia: 11–12
Milk 6.5	Household bleach: 14

The difference between two numbers on the scale is not a simple progression; it means something is ten times stronger or weaker. In other words, ammonia is ten times more alkali than washing soda.

You can buy inexpensive pH test strips (narrow strips of coated paper) in many pharmacies or on the Internet. When a test strip is dipped in liquid, the tip will change color; simply match it to the color chart on the container to find the pH.

You will come across frequent mention of "neutralizers" in the material below; this term refers to any material that can be used to bring the pH of a solution back toward the center of the scale; an acid can be used to neutralize an alkali, and an alkali will neutralize an acid.

While many household cleaners are harsh, keep in mind that they are meant to be diluted in water, which makes them weaker. An understanding of pH will enable you to use these

---

† The U.S. Department of Health and Human Services, National Institutes of Health, maintains a Household Products Database on their website that you can search either by ingredient or product for complete information.

‡ The definition of the term "pH" is not entirely clear, but it is generally accepted that the "p" is related to power or potency, and the "H" to hydrogen.

ingredients without the risk of damaging your garments. While anything safe for the fabric is probably safe for your skin, you still might want to wear rubber gloves.

Water

Most of us are familiar with the idea that water can be "hard" or "soft." Hard water has more minerals in it (those of primary importance being calcium and magnesium). Aside from taste, this has little significance in terms of human health (in that respect, hard water is preferable to soft).

What is of most interest here is that hard water tends to make detergents less effective; the minerals bind with the detergent, leaving little or none of it available for cleaning. Instead of suds, the water will turn cloudy and there may be a gray scum on the surface that is difficult to rinse off; it sticks to the basin or bathtub, leaving a dirty ring behind, and some remains in the fabric, making it dull and dingy and giving it a greasy feel.

Hard water requires considerably more detergent to do the job (two to four times as much, or more), and is also damaging to plumbing. Since these costs can add up, many people have their water systems treated with either chemicals or filtration. If you do not know how hard your water is, there are test kits available, or your city may provide information on water quality.

An easy way to see if you have a problem is to put a half cup of warm water in a glass container with a screw cap; add 3 drops of liquid detergent, put the lid on, and shake. If there are no suds and the water clouds, try 3 more drops; if that does not do it, double it again; any amount beyond about 6 drops indicates the water is probably hard. If the water is not hard, bright white suds will float on top of clear, sparkly water.

If you do have a problem, but water treatment is not affordable or possible for you (or you are not at home), there are some things you can do to mitigate the problem.

For general laundry and cleaning, select detergents that specify on the label that they contain water softeners. For laundering by hand, select a mild liquid detergent with no added ingredients, and then soften the water yourself.

One of the most common and safest ways to do this is with citric acid, which is available in powdered form, but you can also just squirt a little lemon juice in the wash water before adding the detergent.

Another common way to soften water is with washing soda (sodium carbonate, an alkali; see below). It is sold in most supermarket laundry sections; the box will provide information about how much to use for various purposes.

Both citric acid and washing soda will bond with the minerals in hard water, preventing them from reacting with the soap; the softened water will be sudsy, will clean more effectively, and be easier to rinse, leaving things sparkling clean instead of dull or streaky.

However, both will make the wash water more alkali, so it is a good idea to use pH strips to find out how much to use. To launder most protein fibers, keep the pH below 8–9; for vegetable fibers and manufactured fibers, below 10–11. Once you have a system worked out, just do it the same way each time, perhaps adding a little more or less depending on how soiled the item is.

Detergents and Soaps

Soaps and detergents have different ingredients and work in different ways.

Old-fashioned soap would seem to be just the thing to use for something old fashioned like a hand knit. However, in general, a true soap has a pH of about 12, which is very alkali and at the outer limit of even what vegetable fibers can tolerate.

Most liquid dishwashing detergents are mild, with a pH of 6–8, which is ideal for hand knits made with any yarn. However, laundry detergents are normally in the range of pH 10–12; this is safe for vegetable fibers and manufactured fibers, but not for protein fibers.

The most important ingredients in detergents are surfactants. These compounds contain molecules with one end that attaches itself to oil and grease, and another end that attaches itself to water; then the whole little package floats up to the surface carrying the soil with it. The agitation of a washing machine is intended to help the water and detergent thoroughly penetrate, so these molecules can dislodge the soil and lift it off the clothing.

Many laundry detergents also contain washing soda and "whiteners" or "brighteners," which are normally a form of oxygen bleach, and some also contain enzymes. All of these ingredients are discussed below in Stain Removal; all but the first should be treated with skepticism and caution.

The simplest, most economical, and safest thing to do is to wash a hand knit in a liquid dishwashing detergent; if possible, select one with no more than two or three ingredients. If something is badly soiled, wash it a second time, and/or see the list below of common household cleaners that can be used to boost its cleaning power.

Museum conservation departments often use an inexpensive product called Orvus® for cleaning textiles. It is pH neutral, has a single surfactant, sodium laurel sulfate (the most common ingredient in most detergents), and no other additives. It is sold as a paste that dissolves in water, but otherwise is used like any other detergent.

You will undoubtedly come across detergents sold specifically for washing delicate fabrics of wool, silk, or linen. Most are far more expensive than ordinary liquid dishwashing detergents, some are remarkably alkali, and I see no advantage in using them.

When more alkali substances are used, it is important to minimize the amount of time the fabric is in the wash water (generally, no more than 15 to 20 minutes), rinse it thoroughly, and neutralize the final rinse; see below. If you are concerned about exposing your skin to washing products, wear rubber gloves.

If you are traveling and have no mild detergent available, you can safely use your shampoo. After all, your hair is a fine protein fiber, and most good shampoos are pH balanced (inexpensive shampoos can be harsh, and baby shampoo, of all things, is strongly alkaline; because it is the opposite of an acid, it will not sting the eyes).

There are any number of "natural" or "green" products sold; however, there is little agreement about what the terms really mean or which products deserve to use them; any manufacturer can put them on a label. Also keep in mind that many completely natural products can still be dangerous to you or a fabric when used in concentrated form or in the wrong way.

Nevertheless, manufacturers who are trying to make environmentally safe products deserve our support and appreciation and the Internet provides a wealth of information about the ingredients used in almost anything you might want to buy. If you are concerned about these things, I strongly encourage you to read labels and make your selections carefully.

Neutralizers and Softeners

Acids and alkalis are opposites, and one will neutralize the other.

- Washing a fabric with relatively alkali cleaning products to improve soil removal can leave a residue in the fabric that will cause it to deteriorate over time.

   Rinse well, and neutralize the fabric by adding a mild acid to the final rinse water. A little lemon juice or white vinegar will do, and the odor will evaporate by the time the garment dries.
- Fabric softeners deposit a waxy substance on the fibers that cuts down on static electricity and softens fabrics; it causes woven fabrics to be smoother and require less ironing.

   Used in moderation in the final rinse water, they can do wonders for a yarn that is not naturally soft, making it much more comfortable against the skin. It is also my impression that they impart a slight gleam to the fibers; perhaps it is the wax reflecting light.

   However, these products can build up in the fibers over time, making them look dull and feel almost greasy.

Furthermore, they reduce moisture absorption, making cotton and linen less comfortable to wear on a hot day (and your towels less good at their job). If you suspect this is happening, stop using the softener and it will gradually wash out.

- Lanolin is a natural oil in the wool fleece that adds a bit of luster to the yarn, enhances its natural tendency to repel water, and keeps it from getting dry or brittle with age. Washing in warm water and detergent will remove the lanolin, although there are rinses on the market that will add it back in if you prefer.

   Traditional fishermen's sweaters in Europe were often made with yarn spun "in the grease," which means that the lanolin was left in the yarn; a faintly sheepy aroma will betray its presence. I rather like it, but it is far more appropriate for a garment worn at sea or when walking the dog than it is for the office or the dining room (and it will be more fragrant after walking the dog, when you and the sweater are warm and damp).

❖ *Stain Removal*

Stains become more difficult to remove with time. In most cases, the safest course is to take the garment to a dry cleaner as soon as possible.

If you act quickly and use the right product, you may be able to remove a stain entirely, although there is some risk of making it worse. Nevertheless, there are times when it is best to take matters into your own hands.

It is important to understand which stain removal products are safe for the yarn. (If the yarn is a blend, check the label—which is a good argument for saving one.) Also read the label on the cleaning product and pay particular attention to warnings about how it should *not* be used.

Here are some general suggestions.

- In some cases, the stain will sit on the surface of the fabric, and most of it can be blotted up into an absorbent paper towel or cotton rag before it penetrates the garment.

   Do not press the towel or rag against the fabric; touch it lightly to the top of the stain and allow it to wick off. Then treat any residue, which will be considerably smaller than it might have been.
- Try the cleaning product on a Test Swatch (and this is a good argument for saving your swatches), some leftover yarn, or a seam on the inside of the garment to make sure it will not affect the color.
- To treat a small stain that has penetrated the fabric, place the fabric face down on an absorbent surface such as an old towel or a rag, and pour water or a cleaning solution through from the other side of the fabric.

Move to a clean area of the absorbent material and repeat; use a cotton swab, a rag, or a paper towel to press the soiled area down against the underlying material, encouraging it to draw the stain out of the fabric.

Use cold water first; hot water can set many stains. Only use hot water if it is a grease stain with no other ingredient, or any other ingredient has been removed, leaving only grease behind.

- If stain removal involves a paste or spray-on solvent that dries to a powder, set hair dryer on cold and blow off from opposite side, or use vacuum on low power to lift it off; cover nozzle with hand or nylon stocking so it does not suck up fabric.

  Stain removal for knitted garments should never involve rubbing, because this will damage the yarn, mat the fabric, and press the stain into the fibers.

- Synthetic fibers absorb grease and oil into their structure, but resist water, which sits on the surface. These stains require solvents that are safe for the particular fiber. In most cases, it is best to have the item dry cleaned. If the yarn is a blend, notify the cleaner of the fiber content.

Stain Removal Ingredients

Here is a list of common household cleaning products that can be used for stain removal or in the wash water to launder a hand knit. They are all reasonably safe when used according to the instructions on the label; however, some should not be used for certain fibers.

Alcohol

- Common drugstore alcohol can be effective for fruit and vegetable stains (including wine), grass stains, and some inks. It can damage acetate and acrylic fibers, and may affect dyes.

Ammonia

- Very effective for grease-based stains, but strongly alkali; use product without scent or color. Can be used for stain removal or added to wash water to strengthen detergent.

  Dilute according to instructions on label; do not breathe fumes, and *never mix with chlorine bleach (it forms a lethal gas)*. If possible, check pH of water before adding garment to water.

Baking Soda

- Baking soda (sodium bicarbonate) will neutralize *both* acids and alkalis; it is safe and harmless.
- For dried stains, use a wet paste of baking soda and vinegar (also see Borax, below); recommended for many stains, including blood and ink.

- Sprinkle on liquid and grease stains that have not yet dried. It may become gummy as it absorbs material; do not press into fabric.

  Allow paste to partially or fully dry; shake or brush off, or use hair dryer set on cold or vacuum on low with covered nozzle (see above).

Bleach

- Chlorine bleach is a strong alkali with a pH of 14. It does not remove stains; instead it removes discoloration left by stains and may bleach fabric color as well. It is not safe for concentrated use; always dilute in water; residue remaining in fabric can damage fibers; therefore, rinse thoroughly.

  Never use chlorine bleach on protein fibers; it is reasonably safe for cotton, rayon, and linen if used infrequently. Test solution on seam, a Test Swatch, or leftover yarn before using.

  To use, dab dilute bleach on stain with cotton swab, or corner of a rag. As soon as stain disappears, rinse and then launder item and neutralize last rinse (see above).

- Hydrogen peroxide in a 3 percent solution is a mild bleach (do not use stronger solution sold for bleaching hair), and is generally safe for all fibers when used according to directions; minimize time of exposure and use a neutralizing rinse. It is often suggested as one ingredient in homemade cleaning solutions and for stain removal; also see oxygen bleach, below.

- Oxygen bleaches and laundry pre-wash stain treatments usually contain detergent surfactants as well as sodium percarbonate. In hot water, the latter breaks down into its components, washing soda and hydrogen peroxide.

  These products are normally sprayed on to loosen stain before laundering, or added to wash water to boost detergent cleaning power and are considered quite safe and effective for vegetable fibers like cotton and linen.

  However, oxygen bleaches are alkali, with a pH of 10–12, which is high enough to damage protein fibers if the solution is concentrated and exposure is longer than 10 to 15 minutes. Also, any residue left in a fabric of any kind can cause damage over time; rinse thoroughly, and/or add a neutralizer to the final rinse.

- A solution of water and baking soda mixed with either vinegar, lemon juice, or hydrogen peroxide is often recommended as a bleach solution that can be made at home.

Borax

- Sodium borate (there are several chemical formulations; all will have "borate" as part of the name, as in "perborate") is a natural mineral that can be safely mixed with most other cleaning products.

When dissolved in water at recommended amounts, it stabilizes pH in the range of 8–9.5. It also softens water, makes detergent more effective, and some formulations release hydrogen peroxide, which will act as a mild bleach.

- A paste of borax and water is a good all-purpose stain remover; add either baking soda or washing soda to increase strength. Works well on tomato-based stains, oil or grease stains, grass stains, and mildew.
- For laundering, use ¼ cup borax and 1–2 tablespoons liquid detergent in warm water; soak for 20 minutes and then rinse well.

Nail Polish Remover

- Acetone fingernail polish remover will damage protein fibers and dissolve acrylics.
- Non-acetone polish remover (usually ethyl acetate, also found in wine) is much safer and is often effective for ink stains.

Oxalic Acid

- An organic compound derived from plants; commonly used as a wood bleach and in some polishing compounds (for example, Bar Keepers Friend®).

A paste of oxalic acid and water may remove rust and tannin stains, such as those left by brown tea, coffee, some dry leaves, red wine, and coffee, which are notoriously difficult to remove by any other means.

Vinegar

- White vinegar is a common, safe household cleaner, often mixed in equal amounts with water. May also be safely mixed with many other cleaning products such as ammonia, and baking soda.

It is a mild acid that can be used to neutralize rinse water used for items washed with alkali detergents, or when washing soda has been added to wash water with liquid detergent.

Washing Soda, or Soda Ash

- Washing soda (sal soda or soda ash) is sodium carbonate, a moderately strong alkali made from salt and limestone; it is available as a boxed powder in supermarkets. Use in laundry to soften water; it also helps dissolve oil, grease, and alcohol-based stains so they can be lifted off by the detergent.

Water

In some cases, water (or plain carbonated water) will dissolve a fresh stain, and this is often the best thing to try first. Pour it through from the side of the fabric opposite from where the stain was deposited.

- The general rule is cold water for non-grease stains, hot water for greasy ones.

However, hot water can set non-grease stains; therefore, if stain contains any other ingredient, use cold water first and do not use hot water until other material has been completely removed.

Wool can tolerate hot water if it is simply poured through this way (also see washing instructions, below).

- Cold salt water is excellent for blood stains; dissolve salt in hot water and cool with an ice cube or two before using.

Stain Removal Compounds

Here is some general information about commercial products sold for stain removal, along with a recipe for one you can make yourself.

Commercial Powder Spot Removers

- Spray-on spot removers that dry to a powder come in various formulations; read label for suitability and warnings. These work best on smooth, woven surfaces and can be difficult to remove from yarn.

Apply and let dry; shake as much of the powder off as possible; if necessary, use a hair dryer set on cold to blow the powder off from the inside of the fabric. Or, use a hand-held vacuum to suck it off from the outside; put it on the lowest possible speed and place your hand in front of the nozzle or cover with nylon stocking so it does not draw the fabric into the hose.

Detergents for Stain Removal

- For a protein fiber, dab liquid detergent into the stain; for a vegetable fiber, make a paste of powdered detergent and water.

Let sit for a few minutes and rinse by pouring water through from inside out (hot for grease stains, cold for all other stains).

Enzyme Cleaners

- These cleaners usually contain an enzyme of some kind that breaks down organic material such as milk, blood, or urine; they also contain a detergent surfactant to lift the stain out after it is released from the fabric. Enzymes of one kind or another are fairly common ingredients in laundry detergents, especially those sold for washing diapers; this type of cleaner is also sold in spray bottles for treating pet stains.

To see if an enzyme is present in a cleaning product, check the ingredient list for any word that ends in *-ase* (common ones are protease, amylase, and lipase).

Never use an enzymatic cleaner on protein fibers such as silk or wool, because they will weaken or even dissolve the yarn.

Laundry Pre-Wash Treatments

- Sold in spray bottles for spot treatment prior to laundering; usually some form of liquid detergent plus an oxygen bleach; see above.

Orange Oil Cleaners

- Cleaning solvent made from orange rinds; some formulations are pH neutral. Potent degreaser; will also remove some glues. Dilute in alcohol (will not dilute in water). There are concerns about toxicity, but these products are reasonably safe at normal concentrations; nevertheless, wear gloves.

Homemade Pre-Wash Stain Treatment

- ¼ cup ammonia, ¼ cup white vinegar, ⅛ cup baking soda, 1 tablespoon liquid detergent, 2 cups water. Shake in spray bottle and apply.

❖ *Washing a Knit*

I understand the competing demands of work, family, friends, domestic chores and time to knit. Nevertheless, I think many people have an exaggerated idea of how much effort is required to hand wash a sweater; it is really quite simple to do and takes very little time.

The first strategy, however, is to do so infrequently because it can cause wear or fading. So be careful when you eat, watch where you put your elbows, wear a good deodorant, shake the garment out gently and hang it in the air to freshen it from time to time!

If a garment was a "quickie knit," is expected to have a short but serviceable life, and the fiber is amenable to that sort of treatment, by all means, use the washer and dryer. It can work just fine for some things, but do see Machine Washing and Machine Drying, both below, for how to avoid potential damage.

When an item does need to be cleaned, the following information should be helpful.

Water Temperature

The ideal temperature of the washing water depends primarily on the type of fiber, the type of soil, and the stability of the dye.

General soil can be washed out with water of any temperature, although detergents are usually more effective in hot water. However, because you may not know the nature of the soil, and some stains can be set by hot water, the best approach is to do a first wash with cold water, a second wash with warm or hot water (depending on the fiber), and then rinse in cold water.

Wool fabrics will felt in hot water *only if agitated*; however, if left to soak quietly and undisturbed there is little danger of that. Nevertheless, to be on the safe side, use cold or warm water, not hot.

Cotton, linen, and rayon can all be safely washed in hot water. Surprisingly enough, cotton fibers do not actually shrink. The fiber stretches in wear and lacks the elasticity to recover, but when placed in a hot dryer it exhibits what is called "relaxation" shrinkage, and returns to its original condition. This is also true of rayon, but linen is more stable. Cotton and linen are stronger wet than dry, while rayon is weaker and should be handled very gently when washed.

Most manufactured fibers used in knitting yarns are heat sensitive and should be washed only in cold water.

Some dyes, particularly blacks and reds, will fade more quickly, especially in hot water, and it may be best to dry clean them to preserve their color; if washing is necessary, do so infrequently and use only cold water.

Hand Washing

Doing this is somewhat like baking bread; you deal with it lovingly every now and then for just a few minutes, and then ignore it for a while.

1. Use a basin large enough to comfortably hold garment; add cold water and about a teaspoonful of mild detergent to start.
2. Push fabric into water until it is fully immersed; slosh it around a little bit to encourage thorough penetration of soapy water; leave to soak for ten or fifteen minutes.

    Do not scrub the fabric against itself; this will fray the yarn, may cause pilling or felting, and could drive the soil into the yarn rather than eliminating it.

    Most soils will be released from the fabric without any other activity on your part. Some soil is water soluble, and the remainder will be lifted off by the action of the detergent.
3. The detergent will have a finite capacity to dissolve soil. If suds disappear, follow first wash with a second one using warm water.
4. After washing, do not remove garment from water; let water out of basin. Gently push garment against side or bottom of basin to force soap and water out.

    To avoid stretching the fibers and straining the seams, do not wring the water out of the garment, or even lift it out of the basin; water is very heavy, and a knitted garment can hold a great deal of it.
5. Fill basin with cool rinse water and drain again as described in Step 4. Repeat as necessary until water runs clear.
6. Leave garment to drain in sink for an hour or so; if possible, lay it on a tilted dish drain and let gravity remove some of the water.

If you are concerned about dye stability, and/or garment is made with more than one color yarn, remove from basin immediately.

To speed drying time, remove as much excess water as possible.

- Roll garment up in a large heavy towel and push down on it in several places with your full weight; turn over and press again; repeat with a second towel if necessary.
- Alternatively, use the spin cycle of a washing machine. This is quite safe—the garment will be flattened by centrifugal force against the side of the tub, but will not be stretched or abraded in any way. If it is a heavy garment, balance the load by putting a towel on the opposite side of the tub.

Machine Washing

Cotton, linen, and most rayons will stand up quite well to machine washing. Even wool can be washed if the label is clearly marked *superwash* or *machine washable*.

Agitating a knitted garment can be hard on the yarn (rayon is weaker wet than dry), particularly if there are other garments in the same wash water. Yarns are more likely to fade and develop "pills" (those nasty little knots of fiber on the surface) than if they are washed by hand.

However, the machine is reasonably safe if you exercise care; the most conservative approach is to stand over the machine and control the process.

1. Turn garment inside out and wash by itself; use cold water, a mild detergent, gentle cycle, and shortest time.
2. Start wash cycle, allow a few minutes of agitation to help moisture and detergent penetrate fibers, and then turn machine off; let garment sit in soapy water to soak for 10 to 20 minutes.
3. To finish, switch to rinse cycle, agitate for a few minutes, and then let soak for a few minutes; repeat until water runs clear.
4. After final rinse, let spin cycle run.

Starch, or Sizing

Starch is thought of as a bit old fashioned these days, but it still has its place if you are interested in knitting things like cotton or linen lace tablecloths or curtains. Traditional starch is no more than cornstarch dissolved in cold water and serves two functions.

First, starch is used to stiffen the fabric in order to maintain the smooth, open appearance of a decorative pattern; it will help it retain the shape given to it by blocking (see below).

Second, starch acts as a "sacrificial layer," a term used for things like floor polish and shoe polish, as well as for fabric starch. These renewable outer layers are intended to absorb wear and soil, protecting the material underneath.

Starch is added to the final rinse water and stiffens when it dries; when used in this way the knitted item is blocked (pinned out to dry), as described below. There are also spray-on versions that can be used on something pinned out for blocking, or during ironing.

Sizing is a broader term referring to products used to create various specialized surface finishes on woven fabrics. These are typically plastic resins of one kind or another that are intended to be permanent and are normally applied at the mill. However, some types of sizing are available in aerosol form for home use; these work just like starch and can be removed with washing or dry cleaning.

The advantage of starch is its economy and simplicity, and it is traditional for the kind of knitted items for which you might use it. However, it is a vegetable product, and therefore attractive to insects. For this reason, it is not advisable to put something into storage unless the starch has been thoroughly washed out. This is not the case with the spray-on sizings; if you have used that kind of product, the item can be put into storage without concern.

Unstable Dyes

To check for dye stability make a Test Swatch exactly as you will the garment; there are two tests you might want to make.

First, some dyes will "crock," which means excess dye is sitting on the surface of the fiber and can wear off. To test for this, take a clean, white rag and rub the back of the dry swatch fairly vigorously to see if color comes off on the rag.

Next, to determine if the dye is stable when washed, place the swatch in a clear glass bowl filled with cool water and a small amount of the detergent you plan to use for laundering. Allow it to set for half an hour, remove the sample, allow the water to settle, and check it for color.

Some excess dye may very well come out in the first few washings without serious loss of color in the yarn. Therefore, rinse the sample and let it dry, and then check it against a ball of yarn to see if there is a noticeable change.

There are products available from textile craft suppliers that are used to wash off excess surface dye, or which act as dye fixatives to stabilize those that bleed; these are specific to certain types of dyes. You will have to skein and treat all the yarn, but if you really like it in every other respect, or cannot return what is left, this may be worth the effort. (Even after treatment, do not use the yarn for a project with more than one color).

If the garment will frequently be worn outside in strong light, also test for light fastness. Place a Test Swatch on a windowsill or table that receives direct sunlight, and cover one-half the swatch with something like a piece of cardboard or aluminum foil. Signs of fading can show up within a few hours, but to be on the safe side, leave the swatch exposed for a day or two. There may be no reason to give up on the yarn if there is slight evidence of fading, but you will want to store the garment away from the light and never leave it in the back window of your car!

Dressing a Fabric

Dressing is the process of finishing a fabric after it has been washed. Several methods can be used to do this, alone or in combination, but they are all intended to accomplish the same thing—to smooth the surface of the fabric, display the pattern to advantage, and give the item even edges and finished proportions.

The important thing is to understand how dressing works and which methods are suitable for different yarns, types of fabrics, and garment styles.

When the fabric first comes off the needles, it is not in truly finished condition. The yarn will have stretched because of the tension placed on it while you work with it, and the stitch or color pattern is normally somewhat collapsed upon itself and bunched up, giving the fabric an uneven appearance.

Washing relaxes the fibers and allows them to recover from being stretched, and this in turn allows the stitches to settle into the fabric more comfortably. Neither the yarn nor the fabric will ever return to exactly the same condition they were in before being washed the first time; these changes are permanent (see Dressing a Swatch in the chapter Stitch Gauge for more information).

Dressing techniques are then used to open up the fabric so the stitches are of a consistent size and evenly spaced, and the fabric takes on its finished dimensions. To some extent, these changes are transient, because the stitches and the yarn will continue to respond to their environment.

The stitches will change their shape in response to gravity and the hanging weight of the garment in wear. This tends to stretch the yarn, and how well it recovers depends on its characteristics and the resilience of the fibers it contains; with time and age many yarns lose the capacity to recover, and gradually the garment will stabilize in a stretched condition.

What you want, of course, is a garment that fits well even after you have worn it for a while, and dressing the fabric after it is made plays an important role in achieving that goal. More significant in this respect is an accurate Stitch Gauge, and if that is done correctly, dressing the fabric is the last step in a process that begins before you start to knit.

Several approaches to dressing a garment are discussed below. In some cases, laying the garment out flat to air-dry is all that is needed; a wet knit is very malleable, and it can be smoothed out quite readily.

Blocking is a method of stretching and pinning out a damp fabric and leaving it to dry. Steaming softens and relaxes the fabric after it has dried. Steam is sometimes used as a substitute for blocking, or in conjunction with it, but it is not suitable for all yarns because some fibers can be damaged by the heat. Machine drying is very hard on fabrics and should be used only for certain kinds of yarns, and only when necessary.

While long thought of as taboo, there are times when it is appropriate to press (iron) a knitted fabric. There are also garments that benefit from being hung up to dry in order to maximize lengthwise stretch and stabilize the dimensions. This is particularly important if you have made separate flat garment pieces, which should be dressed before they are sewn together so seams will not pucker.

In short, there is no one single approach to use. Everything depends upon what kind of a knitted item you are dealing with, and it is important to take into consideration all of its components—the fiber, the yarn, the stitch and/or color pattern, as well as the size and the style of whatever it is you have made.

Below you will find information that can help you decide what to do.

❖ *Air-Drying*

Most knitted fabrics benefit from being air dried, as opposed to machine dried. The latter is hard on these fabrics and in some cases can cause either shrinkage or stretching. Nevertheless, there are circumstances when you may want to resort to careful machine drying, and/or you may have a garment that can tolerate it reasonably well; before deciding whether to use the dryer, please see the discussion below.

Air drying can be done in three ways: by simply laying the garment out on a flat, moisture-proof surface, by hanging it to dry, or by blocking. The first two are quite simple; the third requires some effort and special equipment.

Drying Flat

This approach works well for most garments, and is particularly suitable for those made with acrylic yarns. Some items may need to be blocked the first time they are dressed, but may not need to have that done afterward, in which case you can use this simpler approach, perhaps followed by a bit of steam if the yarn will tolerate it.

After washing the item as described above, lay it out to dry as follows:

1. Spread out a large dry towel on a flat surface and lay garment on top; if necessary, protect surface with sheet of plastic.
2. Stretch item out fully extended, so surface is smooth and edges are straight; push ribbing together as tightly as possible.

3. After an hour or two, change wet towel for dry one. Turn item over to expose other side to air and stretch out as before. Repeat as necessary.

4. When item is still slightly damp, remove towel. Use tape measure and stretch and smooth it out to finished length and width dimensions. Make all edges straight, line up stitch columns and rows at right angles, and leave undisturbed until thoroughly dry.

A towel placed under the garment will wick moisture out of the item, but there is no need to leave two thick, wet fabrics sitting there, one on top of the other. Changing wet towels for dry ones speeds the process up considerably.

If you have squeezed the water out of the garment into a towel after washing, or used the spin cycle on the washing machine as described above, there is actually no need for a towel at all. Simply lay the garment down directly on the countertop and turn it over from time to time.

The fabric will only take on the finished proportions in the relatively brief period when it passes from damp to dry, so you need have no concern about handling it before then. Also, if you plan to steam the garment later, it does not matter much what dimensions it has while drying, since the steam will alter them.

If you do not have a good location where you can spread out a wet garment, there are inexpensive drying racks available for knits. These have a mesh fabric secured in a frame that can be suspended over a bathtub or set on the floor or a table. The mesh allows the air to pass through the item, which speeds drying time. If possible, place it near an open window or turn on a nearby fan to circulate the air.

Hanging to Dry

If you are dealing with a particularly heavy garment, or if you used a yarn made of a fiber that has a tendency to stretch, use Weighted Gauge for the pattern.

You can block or steam the garment to the length it will have in wear, or hang it up to dry and let gravity do the job. Water is heavy and it will stretch the fabric; there will then be no surprises when you wear it.

This is a useful approach to use for something like a skirt or coat, where length is critical. Complete all but the last few inches of a skirt, or work from the lower edge to the underarm of a coat, and then wash and hang the fabric to dry; tug down on it to maximize length (for more information, see Measuring a Work in Progress). When dry, check the length and then work the last few rows needed, or rip some out if it is too long.

You may also want to hang separate garment pieces to dry in order to maximize inherent stretch prior to sewing up. Seams have little or no ability to stretch, and if you sew them prior to dressing the fabric, the seam may pucker as the fabric around it stretches in wear.

The simplest way to maximize lengthwise stretch is to use a skirt hanger, or even old-fashioned clothespins, if you have them.

- Clip skirt hanger to bottom, straight edge of garment. If possible, run dressing wire through lower edge so it is perfectly straight, and then clip hanger to wire.
- If item is unfinished, leave it on needle and clip hanger to needle or to cable of circular needle.

Blocking

Blocking can be thought of as a substitute for steaming a knitted fabric. At one time, the only alternative was a heavy iron and a damp press cloth, which are not ideal. Instead, knits were more often pinned into shape and left to dry, or they were put on a stretcher of some kind (see below).

Because a knitted item will permanently change the first time it is washed and dressed (whether steamed or blocked), this step requires a certain amount of care and attention.

However, yarns can stretch in wear, some more than others, and more so if the garment is heavy. Therefore the proportions given to the garment when dressed are not entirely permanent. When washed again, the yarn will relax and recover somewhat, and the garment will need to be dressed again. In other words, the dimensions of the garment change with time and circumstances, although most will stabilize at some point.

Because of this, it is important to have realistic expectations about what blocking can achieve and what it does. Basically, the size and shape of a garment is determined in the knitting, and the one that fits best is made according to a Stitch Gauge that takes into consideration the hanging weight of the garment (see Weighted Gauge).

Blocking is best thought of as an alternative to steaming and pressing. It is the approach to use when a yarn will not tolerate steam heat, or when an item is too large to manage on an ironing board. It is particularly helpful for dressing lace and highly textured stitch patterns that need to be opened up to display their true characteristics. Many items need only be blocked the first time they are dressed; afterward they can usually just be left flat to dry, and then touched up with a bit of steam if the yarn likes that sort of thing.

There are three ways to block a fabric. You can pin it into place, use long steel "dressing wires" inserted along the edges, or place it on a stretcher frame. If it dries a bit while you are doing this, use a spray bottle to remoisten it.

Stretchers

A stretcher is the old, traditional method of blocking.

One type, used for shawls and scarves, consists of a square wooden frame with pegs or holes set evenly all around. The

Shetland lace shawl on a stretcher. National Museum of Scotland.

fabric is attached by sewing it to the frame with strong yarn or cord. Each side is attached temporarily, and then all the ties are adjusted until the shawl is stretched straight and true.

Another type of stretcher is used for sweaters. It consists of a T-shaped frame on a stand. The body is pulled over the center frame and adjustable bars are inserted inside the sleeves.

There are also flat board frames in a range of sizes for socks and gloves that can be hung up for drying.

Blocking Pins

One of the most common ways to block a garment of any kind is to use stainless steel T-pins (they do not rust). This requires a surface into which you can insert the pins.

If the item is small, the ironing board will do. Something larger can be pinned out on a thick terry towel set on a table or countertop; if necessary, weight the towel around the edges to hold it in place. Or put the towels down on a large sheet of plastic spread out on a mattress or the floor. There are also padded "blocking boards" available that have a convenient 1-inch grid printed on the fabric cover.

Lay the item down on the surface and straighten it out in a natural way. Use the measurements from the schematic drawing or the written instructions of the pattern. You will need a tape measure, but it is also helpful to have a long metal or plastic ruler to straighten edges and align stitch columns and rows.

Blocking a Garment

These instructions are for blocking a typical pullover sweater.

1. Set pins at bottom edge first; place close together to avoid scalloping. If there is a ribbing, set pins above it, and do not stretch it out widthwise.
2. Measure from shoulder at neckline to lower edge and set one pin.
3. Measure width of back neckline and set second pin at other shoulder. Then place several pins across width of back neck.
4. Measure across from where shoulder meets sleeve to establish shoulder width. Set one pin there, and then several more along sloped line of shoulder. Repeat on other side.
5. Measure straight down from shoulder/sleeve pin to establish armhole depth. Pull garment out at underarm and temporarily set first pin.
6. Measure across from that pin to establish underarm width; set second pin. Check to make sure garment is straight and true in relation to shoulders and adjust these pins as necessary.

Fair Isle sweater on a stretcher. Photograph by J.D. Rattan.
Shetland Museum and Archives.

7. Set pins close together down along sides between underarms and lower edge; stop several inches above ribbing, if present.

8. Move sleeve out at natural angle to underarm and armhole. Measure from shoulder to wrist to establish length and set pin at vertical fold, several inches above ribbing if present.

9. Measure sleeve width at underarm; set one pin at underarm and another opposite on fold.

10. Set pins close together along sleeve foldline between shoulder and pin set at wrist. Make sure all stitch columns and rows are at right angles and edges are straight and true; adjust pins as necessary and leave to dry.

Blocking Lace

If you are blocking a lace shawl or scarf, it will need to be stretched open considerably more than other types of knitted fabrics, and stretched more firmly.

Lace often has scalloped or pointed edges, and pins are set at each one to emphasize their contours.

Here are some suggestions:

• For a triangular shawl, establish width of straight edge first; pin points into place and then set pins across the width. Next measure and pin the length of the center point.

Set a straight edge of some kind between top and bottom pins to act as a visual guide (even a folded sheet or towel laid next to the shawl will establish a straight line), and pull each point of the contoured side edge out to the guideline and set pins.

- If there is a contoured border on all four sides, establish widths and lengths and pin the corners into place first, and then work as described above.
- For a lace garment, pin out as for any other. To emphasize pattern at lower edges, if possible, line up points on front and back of bodice and sleeve and set one pin through both.

Dressing Wires

Dressing wires or blocking wires are a convenient alternative to working with pins alone, and are an excellent investment. These are stainless steel wires in a variety of thicknesses and several lengths (like a set of very long, straight double-point needles), which are inserted along the edges of the fabric, and then pinned into place (see Blocking Pins and Wires).

The wires are quite versatile and considerably reduce the number of pins needed (use just a few spaced evenly along the wire), and the edges will be perfectly straight.

- For a lace shawl or scarf with scalloped edge, insert wire into one stitch at tip of each scallop in same position where blocking pin would be set.

    With wires set around all edges, pin one into place and then square off others, stretching wires out to give fabric finished dimensions.

- For a garment, run one wire through join between back neck and border. Weave second wire into stitches of lower edge, or into row of stitches above ribbing. Then insert wires inside fold of sleeve and side of bodice. For a seamed garment, turn it inside out and insert dressing wires into selvedges.

    Pin wire at top into place first, then one at bottom. Measure and position those at sides of bodice and pin it into place, and finally sleeves.

❖ Steaming and Pressing

In many cases steam can be used as a substitute for blocking. The warmth and moisture will relax the yarn and stitches and the item can be shaped to its finished dimensions and allowed to cool.

Steam can also be used to finish what blocking cannot do. For instance, you might block a garment and then use steam to shape and contour a collar or a lace cuff or peplum, to soften the foldlines of the sleeves, or to provide a finish to a seam or shape the shoulders or sleeve cap. Steam can also be used to reverse blocking that was less than successful, or to stretch something even farther when necessary.

Before we talk about how to use steam, it is important to understand that all steam generated by an iron is the same temperature. The heat setting on the iron controls only how hot the soleplate and water chamber get. This in turn determines how rapidly the water inside will boil, and therefore how much steam is produced.

The only way to control the amount of hot steam the fabric is exposed to is by reducing how much there is; lower the iron temperature, and/or adjust the distance between the iron and the fabric.

A press cloth acts as a barrier that will protect a fabric from direct contact with the hot iron soleplate. A dry press cloth can also keep the fabric from receiving too much steam. A wet press cloth, however, is used with a dry iron to generate steam and the wetter it is, and the hotter the iron, the more steam will be produced.

Because steam is produced by irons, I want to take pains to point out that a knitted garment is usually not *ironed* in the sense of pressing the heavy iron down the way you do with a woven fabric. I say usually because, while it has long been thought of as taboo to press a knitted fabric, it can be advantageous in some cases (see below).

For most purposes, however, never let the iron rest on the garment; hold it about half an inch away so only the steam penetrates the fabric. (A steamer appliance is an excellent tool for this purpose because there is no hot soleplate, and therefore no mistake can be made.)

The steamed fabric will retain heat and moisture for a minute or two and will be too hot to touch. Furthermore, whatever "set" the steaming imparts to the fabric will be lost if you move it too soon. Therefore, wait for the fabric to cool and dry before moving it.

Steam is wonderful for most yarns containing protein and vegetable fibers. It softens and fluffs up the yarn and takes away any of the hardness you may feel after a garment has been washed and dried.

However, some fibers are sensitive to heat and can be easily damaged by steam. This is true of almost all the manufactured fibers common in knitting yarns, such as acrylic, nylon, and polyester.

These fibers are "thermoplastic," which means that if they are heated to a certain temperature they will soften (and if the heat is too high, they will melt), and when held in a fixed position until cool, they will be permanently "set." This means a garment made of these fibers can be given certain characteristics and dimensions in a far more permanent way with steam than with simple blocking, but it must be done with great care.

The best thing to do is practice on several Test Swatches to see what effect a moderate amount of steam heat will have on the fabric. There is usually a polyester setting on an iron;

however, it is intended for pressing and generates very little steam. Instead, increase the iron temperature to the setting for silk, and keep it at a careful distance from the fabric when steaming, and/or protect the fabric with a dry press cloth.

Basic Steaming

Whatever you are working on, use a surface large enough to lay the garment out flat. An ironing board will do for small items, but large items may hang off the board and stretch out in unintended ways. If possible, set heavy towels on a counter, the carpet, or on a table protected by plastic.

To enhance the texture of stitch pattern elements, set the outside face of the fabric down on the towel. Turn a circular or seamed garment inside out and insert toweling between the front and back, and inside the sleeves.

Work as follows:

1. Hold iron a minimum of 1 inch above surface of fabric and dose it with steam, more or less depending upon type of yarn. Avoid seams and folds as much as possible; if necessary reduce exposure to steam in these areas by covering with a dry press cloth.
2. While fabric is warm and damp with steam, smooth fabric, straighten edges, and make everything square and true; check dimensions with tape measure.
3. Apply more steam as necessary; leave piece undisturbed and allow to thoroughly dry before moving.
4. For garment, turn right side out. Insert rolled towel or other pressing aid such as a seam roll into sleeve,† cover with press cloth, and steam down center to eliminate any foldline; press with fingertips or heel of hand.
5. Repeat with bodice sides whether seam is present or not. For shoulders, use pressing ham or rolled wash cloth.

Here are some tips for handling special cases:

- For something like a hat, stuff with rolled or wadded fabric.
- For a collar, lay in sections over seam roll, or roll hand towel up lengthwise and fit under collar and then steam. For lapels, insert folded towel between lapel and main fabric.
- For gathered peplum, or gathered lace trim on sleeve or lower edge, work with small sections. Spread a few inches along edge out flat, and point iron toward gathers to steam.

---

† There are various padded forms available for sewing and tailoring that are useful for this purpose; seam rolls are long and narrow, mitts fit over your hand like a hot pad and are useful for small items or specific areas, and "hams" are shaped, well, just like a ham, and are useful for shoulder and neckline areas.

- To finish buttonholes, sew them closed with a bit of contrast-color yarn. Lay face down on towel, lay press cloth on top, and steam thoroughly; press gently with heel of hand. Allow fabric to dry thoroughly and then remove sewing yarns.

Steam can also be used in conjunction with blocking. After the fabric is dry, give it a good blast of steam and allow it to cool before you remove the pins. This will relax and soften the yarn, and help stabilize the shape you have given it.

Pressing

It is rare today for anyone to press a knitted fabric; however, there are good reasons to do so and it is worth knowing the considerations.

Pressing sets the fabric in a far more permanent way than if it had been simply blocked and/or steamed. Therefore, you will want to give the garment its finished dimensions with more conventional means first. Lace is particularly amenable to pressing; the pattern will be displayed to great effect and is more likely to remain open.

Always try this on a Test Swatch first, adjusting the pressure used when ironing to achieve the desired effect. If you decide to go ahead, of course, you will need to press your final Gauge Swatch as well; if you calculate the gauge on the basis of a pressed swatch, you will have to press the garment, because simple blocking and/or steaming will not produce the same finished dimensions.

Also keep in mind that pressing is really only successful with yarns that are smooth; those that are fuzzy and plush will gain little from this approach, or will even have their best qualities destroyed.

Linen is very strong and these fabrics take on a wonderful silky hand and a beautiful sheen when pressed. This is also true of fabrics made with cotton and rayon yarns, and even smooth worsted-spun wool yarns respond beautifully to being pressed.

Manufactured fibers such as polyester and acrylic are thermoplastic and can be permanently set by the application of heat; carefully controlled pressing can radically alter the feel and appearance of the fabric. It is particularly important to try this on Test Swatches first; set the iron temperature carefully and use a press cloth to avoid direct contact with the soleplate. Actually, it is fun to experiment with these things—some will be disasters (the fiber will melt), while others can prove very interesting.

Classic ribbon knits were traditionally done with Twist Stitch patterns, using a special method of handling the ribbon that kept it flat and relatively uncrushed on the needle. In finishing, the fabric was firmly pressed to flatten the stitches, giving them a uniquely scale-like appearance.

Ribbon is customarily worked in a more casual way today, with the yarn allowed to crumple into the stitches; however, these fabrics can still benefit from pressing. The stitches will be crimped into micro-pleats, and the fabric takes on a wonderful drape. Please take fiber content into consideration when setting iron temperature and use a press cloth.

And one final tip: if you have picked up stitches along a cut edge, pressing can flatten the join very effectively. Set the edge on a seam roll, lay a press cloth on top, steam, and then press firmly. The seam roll will protect the fabric on either side, and only the join will be pressed.

❖ Machine Drying

If you want to make a garment and have the convenience of machine washing and drying, read the yarn label carefully. After calculating gauge, wash and dry your Gauge Swatch to test what will happen to the fabric; remeasure it afterward to see if there has been any change.

Even if the yarn label says a yarn can be machine dried, the tumbling action is hard on clothing; the abrasion can fuzz the surface and cause color fading and pilling. The latter is a particular problem with manufactured fibers like acrylics.

At the very least turn the garment inside out to protect the exterior and put it in the dryer alone so it will not be pounded by other clothing. Better yet, to reduce the amount of time it is tumbled, lay the item flat to air-dry and when it is still slightly damp, put it in the dryer for a short time.

Yarns containing protein fibers like silk and wool should not be dried because the heat and abrasion of the dryer is damaging and their characteristics can change. Wool will felt unless it is labeled "superwash." This means it has been coated to prevent shrinkage, but this protection can wear off with repeated laundering (see the discussion under Wool Fiber in the chapter Fibers).

Many labels recommend machine washing acrylic yarns, and this is quite safe as long as you are very careful to use *low temperatures*, but they should not be put in the dryer; these fibers are "thermoplastic," which means they will deform or even melt at higher temperatures, and tend to stretch even with moderate heat.

Also, the label on yarns that contain a blend of acrylic and superwash wool may also recommend machine washing and drying, but keep in mind the caution about acrylic and heat, and that the superwash protection in wool tends to lessen with time.

Cotton and linen yarns often benefit from a bit of time in the dryer and can tolerate heat; they will soften and recover from having been stretched out in wear.

This is also true of rayon, but be careful, because this fiber is weak when wet and can be damaged by being dried for too long, especially if other garments are in the dryer at the same time. It is a good idea to lay the garment flat until almost dry, and then give it just a few minutes alone in the dryer.

❖ Storage

Knitted garments tend to be highly seasonal and usually spend some portion of every year tucked away. Please put them away clean; any soil left on the garment will attract insects, damage dye, and weaken fibers.

It is an excellent idea to fold the garment differently every time you put it away to prevent the formation of wear lines and fiber breakage along the folds. If you are concerned about this, pad the garment with tissue.

The ideal way to store your knits is in zippered cotton or linen storage bags. Plastic storage containers are not advisable; if the fabric is only slightly damp, you invite mildew and rot; if it is very dry the fibers cannot regain any moisture from the environment and may break and deteriorate. Do not place the item in contact with wood, which contains acids that can harm fibers; if you have an unlined blanket chest or dresser drawers, wrap the knit in cloth or paper to protect it.

As a general rule, it is best not to hang knitted garments because that places a strain on shoulder seams and the fibers will stretch. Coats and suits that have been stretched in finishing, especially those with linings, can be left on padded hangers just as a garment of woven fabric would be, although this is not ideal. Fulled fabrics or those knitted in firm, inelastic stitch patterns will not be affected.

CHAPTER 33

Finishing Techniques

When you are done knitting the last stitch, there is still more to do before the garment is truly finished. At the very least, there are seams to sew if you have worked flat, and for almost anything you make, ends of yarn will need to be hidden away. There may also be zippers or buttons to deal with, or times when you want to sew on trim or even add a lining.

For some items, you will want to use Grafting, sewing in a line of knitted stitches instead of having a seam. And while Steeks are dealt with during the making of a circular garment, they require sewing techniques to finish them, which are also discussed here (as well as in Selvedges and Steeks).

None of these things are hard to do, or even very time-consuming, but after all those contented hours of knitting most of us are suddenly in a hurry to try on our new treasure and get started on the next project. And, it must be said that many knitters do not enjoy this phase, although I would like to persuade you to reconsider. I confess to rather enjoying the fussy details of sewing a perfect seam and making the inside of a garment look beautiful, and I find hand sewing quite pleasurable; it is simply another needle craft that has its own satisfactions.

You will find quite a few options here, and one technique or another should help you deal with almost any challenge that presents itself. Slow down, take the time to do the job well, and you will be amply rewarded with a garment that has a finish worthy of your efforts.

General Tips

Here are some suggestions for how to prepare a fabric before you do any finishing, along with recommendations for what kind of needles and yarn or thread to use for sewing.

❖ Preparing the Fabric

For almost all of the sewing or finishing tasks you will deal with, it is important to dress the fabric beforehand (see Dressing a Fabric, and also Dressing a Swatch in the chapter Stitch Gauge), because the garment dimensions will be permanently changed; if this is not done, the fabric may pucker on either side of a seam as it stretches in wear.

This is also important if you are sewing on any kind of decorative trim; both trim and any interfacing used will need to be pre-shrunk, as well. An exception to this is Grafting, which is simply another way to make knitted stitches, and it is best to wait and dress the garment after this is done.

Before you start to do any sewing, it helps to tuck any yarn ends hanging from the edge temporarily out of your way. Tie them into a Yarn Butterfly, or use a crochet hook to pull the ends through the fabric a few inches away from the seam; after you are done, pull them out again and weave them in properly.

❖ Yarns for Sewing

The yarn used for the fabric may not always be the best choice for sewing up unless it is smooth, well-behaved, and relatively strong. Because it will be repeatedly drawn through the fabric, a knitting yarn will begin to fray, and the longer the seam, the more serious the problem will be. Furthermore, highly textured yarns can be difficult or impossible to pull through the stitches, fragile ones may break, and bulky yarns make bulky seams.

Embroidery thread or needlepoint yarns of cotton, silk, or wool are excellent alternatives. There is a large selection of colors to choose from, so it is likely you can find a good match for your garment; all of them are intended for sewing and less prone to fraying. Also, these yarns are loosely plied so it easy to remove one or more plies to make them thinner (while this can also be done with many knitting yarns, it is usually more difficult; see Unplying Yarn).

Regardless of what kind of yarn you use, the general rule is to work with a length no more than about 20 to 24 inches long, not including the end drawn through the needle; for longer seams, use several separate lengths, tying them on as needed.

❖ *Sewing Needles*

To sew knitted fabrics together, you will want to use what is called a tapestry needle, which has an eye large enough for yarn and a blunt tip that will pass between stitches and not through them. These are readily available from knitting stores and they come in several lengths and thicknesses suitable for either thin yarns and tiny stitches or thicker yarns and fatter stitches. One version has a bent tip that is very convenient when used for any task that requires inserting it into individual stitches, and it also helps with sewing seams.

For sewing wovens to knits, you will need a sharp needle, and because of the thickness of the knitted fabric, it is best to select one that is relatively long.

❖ *Try It First*

If you will be using a technique that is new to you, or you are unsure how it will work with the fabric, try it first on a swatch.

- To practice a seam, make two relatively narrow Test Swatches, 3 or 4 inches long, with the selvedge you plan to use.

  Alternatively, make the swatches with a Stockinette Selvedge on one side and a Chain Selvedge on the other. Try one seam; if you do not like it, take it out and try a different approach on the sides with the other selvedge.
- To try a grafting technique, make two wider swatches. If they will be joined at the tops, do not cast off; if the top of one will be joined to the bottom of the other, use a Provisional Cast-On for the latter.
- If you plan to attach a patch pocket, make a 2-inch-square mini-version; after you have used the swatch to calculate gauge, sew the little pocket on to practice the technique.
- Similarly, practice how to bind an edge, sew on trim, or cut and sew a Steek. Make a separate swatch, or use any swatch you have left over from another project for this purpose.

❖ *Attaching Yarn*

You will find several ways to attach a new supply of yarn to a fabric while you are making it in Tying On Yarn; here the focus is on how to attach a yarn for sewing a seam.

Yarn Butterfly for Seaming

One of the most efficient ways to attach the yarn to the fabric for sewing a seam is to leave a long enough tail of yarn when you cast on; it will be there waiting for you when it is time to sew up. Wrap the end into a Yarn Butterfly to keep it tidy and out of your way.

You can do something similar at the top, as well: before casting off at the underarm of a bodice or sleeve, allow a length for sewing, break the yarn and tie it into a Yarn Butterfly. Allow another long tail, reattach your main yarn supply, wrap that end into a Yarn Butterfly as well, and continue knitting. You will then have two tails of yarn to use for seaming: one for the side seam, one for the sleeve. If you have also left one at the bottom you will have two at the top, one for each side of the sleeve seam.

If you want to remove a ply to thin the yarn, sew about 2 inches of the seam before doing so. In effect, this weaves in the tail of the ply, so there will be no need to deal with it later.

Tying On Yarn for Sewing

The simplest way to attach a separate strand of yarn for a seam is to just pinch the tail against the fabric until you have the seam underway; weave the tail into the selvedge of the finished seam later.

This works reasonably well for wool, but may not do for smooth or slippery yarns, which can start to pull out of the seam. For these it is better to use the Purl Knot; allow a tail to weave in later and tie the yarn to the outside strand of the first selvedge stitch just above the edge. Or use the Button-Stop, below.

Button-Stop

Here is a clever way to attach a sewing yarn temporarily; it also works nicely for attaching yarn for sewing something within the fabric, like a pocket.

1. Thread yarn for sewing in tapestry needle. Draw yarn through two holes of a large button, and knot end to itself close to button.
2. Skim yarn through fabric an inch or two away from where you will start; button will stop at fabric, out of the way, and prevent yarn end from pulling through.
3. After completing seam, cut knot, remove button, and pull end of yarn out of fabric so it is at seam. Thread tail of yarn into needle and weave in on inside (see Hiding Ends of Yarn).

Selvedge Seams

The most common seams are those that join the sides of a bodice and the lower half of the sleeves. These are the easiest seams to do because the edges match and the number of rows in the two fabrics is the same, so everything lines up nicely.

Whether these seams will be successful is partly determined before you even start to work on the project, because choosing the right selvedge is as important as how it is sewn. Decide what kind of seams you want to use, and then select a selvedge that will be compatible (see Selvedges).

Before going on to discuss the types of seams used for selvedges, here are some general tips that will help you make a smooth, even seam on these kinds of edges.

❖ *Tips for Selvedge Seams*

There are several things you can do when making the main fabric that will produce a selvedge that is easy to sew. Also, it is important to dress the fabric before seaming to make sure it is the right length. Finally, for a smooth finish, give some attention to how well the cast-on or cast-off edge lines up at a seam.

Making Selvedges for Seams

Always work the selvedge consistently. The most common side seam is worked into the running threads next to a Stockinette Selvedge, and you will get a much better result and find it easier to sew if you always Knit the selvedge stitch on the outside of the fabric and Purl it on the inside of the fabric. This is especially important if a decorative stitch pattern is used within the fabric itself because it guarantees that the running threads will be available on the inside of the fabric where they are needed for sewing.

For the same reason, work all shaping within the fabric, and not on the selvedge stitch itself (see discussion in Selvedges). If an increase or decrease includes a selvedge stitch, more than one stitch must be turned to the inside when seaming, as shown in the illustration. This will distort the seam on the outside and add bulk to the selvedge on the inside.

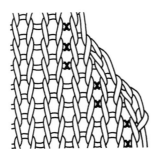

Decreases worked into selvedge will make seam bulkier; Xs show where seam is sewn.

When tying on a new supply of yarn as you work, attach it to a selvedge stitch and not within the fabric unless you plan to turn the selvedge to the outside, which may be done for decorative purposes. In that case, tie the yarn on between the first and second stitches of the main fabric, instead, so the running threads adjacent to the selvedge can be used for the seam.

Seam Length

To make sure the seam is the correct length, dress the fabric before sewing, and then measure it and compare the dimensions to those on the schematic or in the pattern instructions. To make sure the seam does not draw up and gather as you sew, here are a few tips:

- Measure the edge, divide into eighths, and set coilless pins or Yarn Markers as guides. As you sew, when you come to a pin, stop and measure to make sure you are not drawing the seam up too tightly.
- Pull the sewing yarn up just enough to bring the sides of the seam together without gaps, and no more. Stretch the seam slightly after drawing it together and let it spring back naturally. These steps help preserve some elasticity and prevent the seam from being too tight.

Edges and Seam Corners

One tiny detail that is worth your attention when sewing any seam is to make sure the two corners are perfectly lined up so the visible cast-on or cast-off edge looks continuous.

This can be done with the equivalent of Duplicate Stitch (which is normally used as a decorative embroidery stitch), by sewing a stitch across the gap that looks just like all the others in the edge. Finishing the edge corner in this way not only makes it look much nicer, but it helps you start the seam with the rows perfectly lined up.

Corners at Cast-On Edge

Duplicating a stitch for a cast-on edge depends on which technique you used (it is not necessary to do this for Alternating Cast-On, as there is no discernible edge). To determine how to sew a stitch across the corner that matches the path of the yarn in the edge, look at the illustrations for the technique you used in Casting On and compare them to your fabric.

If you have used a Half-Hitch Cast-On, after sewing seam, finish corner as follows:

- Thread yarn end left over from casting on into tapestry needle, insert needle into other fabric from outside to inside between half-hitch in cast-on edge and first running thread; draw yarn through to inside; turn to inside and hide end in selvedge.

If there is no tail of yarn at one of the corners, you can use the sewing yarn to do much the same thing, either when beginning or ending the seam.

Corners at Cast-Off Edge

You will also find instructions and an illustration for a technique that can be used for duplicating a stitch to join the corners of a cast-off edge at the top of a seam in Finishing Circular Fabric Edge.

While it is used there to complete the edge of a circular fabric, the same concept can be applied to draw the corners of a seamed fabric together.

❖ Stockinette Selvedge Seams

The following seams work best for a Stockinette Selvedge; there are three options. The first is the easiest to do and draws the two fabrics together firmly and smoothly. The next pulls them together a little more gently, which in some cases looks a bit more natural. It is also a good option for some stitch patterns, as is the third technique, which is a mixture of the first two.

Running Thread Seam

This is the most common way of joining two knitted fabrics. The seam is sewn into the running threads that lie between the selvedge and the first column of stitches. It is also called the Mattress Stitch Seam, or the Invisible Seam (which it is). Done well, this seam is difficult to find when looking at the outside of the fabric.

There will be one running thread passing into and out of the selvedge for every row. This makes it easy to line up the two columns of stitches perfectly, shoulder to shoulder on either side of the seam. It is a good durable seam, yet retains some resilience if not sewn too tightly.

Work on the *outside* of the fabrics with the edges set side by side; you will have more control and get a smoother result if the two pieces are lying flat on a table instead of in your lap.

Thread a tapestry needle and attach the yarn to Fabric A on the left; if appropriate, duplicate a stitch of the cast-on or cast-off edge across the gap to draw the corner together, as described above.

For each sewn stitch, pass the needle under the running thread next to the selvedge, first in one fabric, and then in the other, row-by-row.

1. To begin, pass sewing needle from inside to outside below first running thread in Fabric A, immediately above cast-on edge.

2. In Fabric B, pass sewing needle into space below first running thread and out space above it. Do not draw seams together; leave strand about an inch long between edges of two fabrics.

3. In Fabric A, pass needle into space below first running thread (where yarn emerges from last stitch sewn), and out space above it. Draw yarn through, leaving strand about an inch long between two edges.

4. Repeat Steps 2 and 3, each time drawing yarn under a single running thread and leaving yarn laced between two edges until about an inch of seam has been loosely sewn.

5. Draw laced yarn up through all stitches, just enough to pull two sides of fabric together smoothly without gathering seam. Continue inch by inch for length of seam.

For most fabrics, you will want to sew under every running thread, inserting your needle into the space where the yarn emerged from the last stitch sewn on that side of the fabric; the result will be two strands of yarn in each space between the running threads. However, for a fabric made with a thin yarn and tiny stitches, it may be sufficient to work under two at a time.

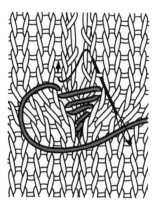

Running Thread Seam.
Sew under running threads next to selvedge stitches.

After working the first inch of the seam, check to make sure the rows are lined up perfectly; if not, pull out the yarn and start over again to realign them.

If the seam starts to gather, use the tip of your sewing needle to loosen the yarn between the edges of the fabric and then retighten it more gently; if necessary, pull the seam lengthwise as you draw the yarn up.

Selvedge Seam

This method of sewing up also produces a nice seam with a Stockinette Selvedge. It is nearly invisible on the outside of the fabric, and is slightly less bulky on the inside than the Running Thread Seam described above.

The two columns of stitches adjacent to the seam will be somewhat farther apart than with one done with a Running Thread Seam, but subtly so. In a soft fabric, this seam may look a bit more natural, because the latter can pull the stitch columns almost too closely together.

You can do this seam with the fabrics lying flat on a table, or place them with the outside faces together and hold the edges up as you sew.

Selvedge Seam Sewn Face-to-Face

Place the outside faces of the fabric together, Fabric A on the nearside and Fabric B on the farside; hold edge up and work from right to left.

Notice that the outermost strands of the selvedge stitches tilt down toward the inside faces of the fabric; the inner strands of the selvedge (those closest to the fabric) lie closer to the very top of the edge.

1. In Fabric A, pass needle under inner half of selvedge stitch (closest to fabric) from seam toward fabric.
2. In Fabric B, insert needle under inner half of first selvedge stitch from fabric toward seam, and then under inner half of next selvedge stitch to left from seam toward fabric. Draw yarn through.
3. In Fabric A, insert needle under inner half of first selvedge stitch from fabric toward seam, and then under inner half of next selvedge stitch to left from seam toward fabric. Draw yarn through and tighten seam gently.
4. Alternate from side to side in this way for length of seam.

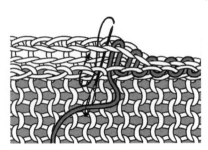

Selvedge Seam Sewn Face-to-Face.

You will be passing the yarn into and out of the center of each selvedge stitch, and the result will be that the sewn stitch passes around the *head* of each selvedge stitch, turning it to the inside.

Always insert the needle into the same selvedge stitch that the yarn emerged from previously—in other words, work through each stitch twice.

This method will work on a Chain Selvedge if it is not too loose, but you might want to make a pair of swatches and try it first because it has a tendency to leave gaps in the seam.

Selvedge Seam Sewn Lying Flat

If you prefer, work with the edges side by side, placing the *inside* faces up with Fabric A at the left and Fabric B at the right, and work as follows:

1. In Fabric A, bring needle to outside in space below first running thread, and then out through center of first selvedge stitch from edge toward fabric.
2. In Fabric B, pass needle into center of first selvedge stitch from fabric toward edge, and then through center of selvedge stitch above it from edge toward fabric.
3. Repeat Step 2 in Fabric A; insert needle into stitch with sewing yarn in it from previous step, and bring it out in next stitch above.

4. Continue alternating from side to side in this way, always sewing into each stitch twice, and out stitch above.

Combination Seam

You can also sew up using the Running Thread Seam in one fabric and the Selvedge Seam in the other fabric. This is a good solution if the stitch patterns in the two fabrics are not the same.

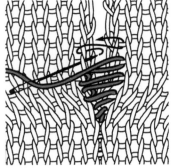

Combination Seam. Running Thread Seam on one side; Selvedge Seam on the other.

Linked Seam

This technique is discussed by Montse Stanley as a way to join two Stockinette Selvedges; the result resembles the Crochet Seam, below.† One selvedge is unraveled and pulled through the other; therefore, the last stitch at the top needs to be set aside so it can be released later.

After working the last row of the fabric, allow about a 12-inch tail and break the yarn; draw the end through the top selvedge stitch and drop it from the needle. Reattach the main supply of yarn to the fabric, increase one stitch to serve as a new selvedge stitch for the fabric above, and continue working.

To link the seam, release the top stitch and unravel the entire column of selvedge stitches; you may want to pick them up on a needle to keep them in order and readily available.

1. Place fabrics with outside faces together and edge with released selvedge stitches on farside.
2. Insert crochet hook under both sides of selvedge stitch of fabric on nearside, catch first free selvedge stitch and draw it through; maintain stitch on hook.
3. Insert hook on nearside under next selvedge stitch to left, catch next free selvedge stitch and draw it through.

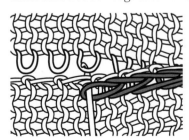

Linked Seam. Draw one selvedge through the other.

† Montse Stanley, *Knitting Your Own Designs for a Perfect Fit* (Newton Abbot, England: David & Charles Publishing, 1982).

4. With two stitches on hook, draw left stitch through one to right.

5. Repeat Steps 2–4 for length of seam. At top, pull tail of yarn through last stitch and weave that end into seam.

When the selvedge is unraveled, every pair of stitches released will turn into a single, larger stitch, like that of a Chain Selvedge. Each of them must not only pass through the other fabric, which will absorb some of their length, but there is only one for every two rows of the fabric and, when relinked, the new selvedge may be somewhat tight or less resilient.

Two Stockinette Selvedge stitches have more yarn than one Chain Selvedge stitch. Therefore, if a Test Swatch indicates the seam is too tight, try it with a Chain Selvedge on the left side of one fabric, and a Stockinette Selvedge on the right side of the other fabric. Release the Chain Selvedge and pull it through every other stitch of the Stockinette Selvedge.

Having a Chain Selvedge on both sides tends to make a Linked Seam that is too loose, but you could also try that and see if it works for your project; it may be successful in a relatively open fabric, for instance.

For a decorative touch, release both edges, work on the outside with a crochet hook, and link them with a decorative join.

The technique can also be used to link a selvedge to other kinds of edges. You could, for instance, attach the side edge of a narrow collar to a neckline in this way. However, the number of stitches in the two edges would not match. You would have to space the links out, skipping some of the stitches in the remaining selvedge, which might look irregular; it might be better to simply sew the collar into place, or join it to picked-up stitches (see Picking Up to Join).

❖ Garter Stitch Selvedge Seams

A Running Thread Seam is quite successful on a Garter Stitch Selvedge (regardless of whether the rest of the fabric is also in Garter Stitch). The selvedge will be nubby on the inside, but not too bulky in a medium to fine yarn. The following Selvedge Nub Seam is also quite successful.

Selvedge Nub Seam

This seam works very well for a Stockinette or a Garter Stitch Selvedge, as well as for a fabric worked entirely in Garter Stitch or Seed Stitch. It is a good choice for sewing together modular pieces, or for sewing a border on to a reversible fabric, because the two edges are butted against one another, and not turned to the inside.

Do not add selvedge stitches to the number of stitches cast on for the width, and use the same yarn for sewing up as was used for the fabric because some of it will show on the outside.

When butting two edges together in this way, it might seem tempting to sew into the sides of the selvedge stitches, but do-

ing so will stretch them out, leaving unsightly gaps; the nubs along the edge are tighter, and will not stretch out.

Set fabrics side by side with outside faces up; Fabric A is to the left and Fabric B to the right.

- Use a relatively thin tapestry needle, and insert straight up through Fabric A nub, then up through its mate in Fabric B; make next stitch in Fabric A nub, and then again in a Fabric B nub. Repeat, working back and forth, row by row.

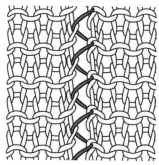

Selvedge Nub Seam. Shown in Garter Stitch.

The yarn will appear to take a zigzag course between the two fabrics, but the rows will line up once drawn together because the nub on one side is a row higher than the nub on the other (each one lies on the intersection of two rows).

❖ Chain Selvedge Seams

Several methods can be used to sew a Chain Selvedge; none produce a seam as neat as one done on a Stockinette Selvedge, but it is possible to achieve a very satisfactory result. Try one or another of these options on a Test Swatch: if neither of the first two work well, use the Selvedge Seam instead.

Two-Row Chain Selvedge Seam

A Chain Selvedge has only one stitch for every two rows of the fabric, which means the stitches are large and open, and it is easy to see where to sew. The seam will not be as thick as one with a Stockinette Selvedge, it looks very nice on the inside, and lies quite flat.

- Sew as for Running Thread Seam, but insert needle under pairs of running threads that lie close together between selvedge and first column of stitches.

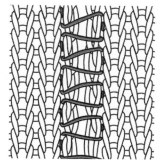

Two-Row Chain Selvedge Seam.

This seam may not close up as smoothly and neatly as a Stockinette Selvedge Seam, especially if the fabric was knit loosely or in an open stitch pattern, and it may gape if the garment fits tightly. If that is the case, try the option below.

One-Row Chain Selvedge Seam

While a Chain Selvedge has only one stitch for every two rows, there will be two running threads, one per row, and you can often improve the appearance of this seam if you sew under each one, as for a Stockinette Selvedge.

However, the two strands lie closely together in pairs, and it is not always easy to separate one from the other in order to insert the sewing needle. See the illustration of a Chain Selvedge in the chapter Selvedges and Steeks and also examine your Gauge Swatch to learn how to identify the two strands.

As you work, pull the selvedge away from the fabric so you can see the pair of running threads. To make the first stitch, it helps to insert the needle under both strands first, and then tease the lower one away from the upper one with the tip of the needle; for the next stitch, the second strand will be left behind and is easy to pick up.

Selvedge Seam for Chain Selvedge

You can also use the Selvedge Seam for a Chain Selvedge; the result can be satisfactory if you want to minimize the bulk of the selvedges on the inside.

Work as described for the Stockinette Selvedge Seam, above, with the fabrics either side by side, or with the outside faces together and the edges up.

On each side, always pass the needle from the fabric toward the seam, and then from seam toward fabric so the yarn passes around the head of the selvedge stitch.

General Sewing Techniques

The following material covers techniques for sewing seams that do not line up quite as cooperatively as Selvedge Seams with perfectly matched rows. The most common situation you will encounter of this kind is setting in a sleeve, where both the sleeve cap and the armhole have been shaped and the two fabrics have a different number of rows. But there may also be times when you need to sew top or bottom edges together, or an edge of that kind to a side edge; you may need to sew a collar to a neckline or perhaps a patch pocket onto the middle of the fabric.

You will find techniques and general information for handling these kinds of things and many others in the following material, which begins with a discussion of basic hand-sewing

techniques. These can be used for any number of different applications, including those times when you want to sew woven fabrics to knits, such as for applying trim or linings.

❖ Hand-Sewing Techniques

The following hand-sewing techniques are commonly used for sewing two knitted fabrics together in any situation where a Selvedge Seam is not possible. Many of them are also used for sewing woven fabrics to a knit.

Depending upon the application, you will want to select the right type of needle and sewing material. For sewing two knitted fabrics together with yarn, use a tapestry needle and the yarn suggestions described above in General Tips.

If you are sewing a woven to a knit, you will need a sharp needle; select one that is relatively long, because knitted fabrics are thicker than wovens. Any type of sewing thread is suitable, but there is some evidence that silk or cotton thread is less abrasive to yarn than polyester thread. Silk thread is the best choice for sewing on beautiful trims; it is both strong and resilient, and it has a beautiful sheen should any of the stitches be visible.

Backstitch and Prickstitch

Backstitch is a basic hand-sewing technique that is typically used for seams that need to be strong and stable. It is a good choice for seaming relatively heavy garments like jackets or coats, for sewing on collars and lapels, and for sewing together two fabrics that do not have the same number of rows. It is also the best method to use when stabilizing a shoulder or neckline with seam tape.

Each stitch doubles back on itself, which can add bulk to the seam, but usually this is not a serious problem. However, you might want to consider sewing up using a thinner yarn than that used for the fabric; see Yarns for Sewing, above.

Prickstitch is a variation done in the same way, but with much smaller stitches on one side than the other; it is not often used for seams, but is a good choice for something like attaching trim or sewing a zipper into place.

Sewing a Knit with Backstitch

Place the two fabrics with outside faces together and set coilless pins at 1-inch intervals to hold the seam together evenly, or baste fabrics together, as described below. After basting, check length of seam against measurement from schematic before you begin to sew.

Attach the yarn, hold the edges of the fabrics up, and work from right to left, as follows:

1. To begin, insert needle under selvedges of both fabrics from nearside to farside; draw yarn through.

2. Insert needle under selvedges from farside to nearside about ¼ to ½ inch to left; draw yarn through.
3. Insert needle from nearside to farside about ⅛ to ¼ inch to right; draw yarn through.
4. Repeat Steps 2–3 to sew seam.

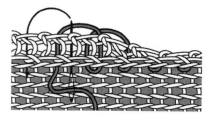

Backstitch Seam.

Basically, you are sewing two steps to the left, and back one step to the right. The closer the stitches on the nearside are to each other, the stronger the seam will be.

The stitches on the other side of the fabric will be twice as long and will overlap, each one starting in the middle of the previous one. Size the sewn stitches in proportion to the knitted fabric, making longer stitches in a more open fabric or one made with a thicker yarn.

If you prefer, you can also work from left to right. Insert the needle two steps to the right, and bring it out one step to the left. The overlapped stitches will be on the nearside.

You can pass the needle into the spaces between stitches, or between running threads; however, if the fabric is loosely knit, you might get a better result if you use a tapestry needle with enough of a point to sew through the yarn of the knitted stitches in order to make smaller sewn stitches.

If the knitted fabric is thick, it may not be possible to pass the needle from farside to nearside and back again with one movement (a tapestry needle with a bent tip is useful for this). If necessary, pass the needle through one way and draw up the yarn, and then pass it back through in the other direction as a separate step.

For most purposes, tighten each stitch gently to retain some resilience in the seam; only tighten it more firmly if you need a stable seam that will maintain a precise length.

Sewing Wovens with Backstitch

The method of working Backstitch is the same regardless of what kind of material you are sewing. However, if you are sewing two woven fabrics, or a woven to a knit, you will be using a sharp needle and normal sewing thread, and there is no need to concern yourself with selvedges or working between stitches.

When sewing two wovens, work as described above, one step to the right, two steps to the left. To help sew in a nice straight line, you might want to baste things together first, or draw a chalk line as a guide.

When sewing a woven to a knit, you can pierce all the way through both fabrics, but if the knit is thick, fuzzy, or loosely knit, it may be sufficient to skim the needle through the yarn instead.

To minimize the appearance of visible stitching and still sew a fairly strong seam, use Prickstitch instead. Make a very tiny stitch on the nearside and a long stitch on the farside; for more information, see Trims, Appliqués, and Zippers, below.

Running Stitch Seams

This stitch gets its name because the needle "runs" through the fabric, making several small stitches one after the other before the thread is pulled through, each one the same size and distance apart. This seam is not as strong as a Backstitch Seam, but it is quicker and less bulky.

Running Stitch for Knits

• Insert needle through fabric from nearside to farside just under selvedge, then bring it back through from farside to nearside about ¼ inch away; repeat, making as many stitches as will fit on the needle before drawing it through.

Use a stitch length appropriate to the garment and the kind of seam you need; smaller stitches will pull the fabric together more tightly than large ones.

It helps to bend the fabric back against the needle tip as you work, first in one direction, then in the other so the needle passes straight through the fabric instead of at an angle.

Because a knitted fabric is relatively thick, even with a long needle it is difficult to do more than two or three stitches at a time. You will have more control and produce a neater seam if you do one stitch at a time. Of course this is slower, but the result will be almost the same as the Running Thread Seam described for a Stockinette Selvedge, above.

• For every stitch, insert needle perpendicular to surface of fabric, right under selvedge, draw through and tighten thread. Make one stitch from nearside to farside; place next about ⅛ inch away from farside to nearside.

If the stitches are small, try not to split the yarn; if you meet resistance to the blunt-tipped needle, reinsert it. However, if the fabric was made with a thicker yarn and has larger stitches, it may be best to use a sharper needle and sew through the yarn of the knitted stitches in order to pull the seam together effectively.

If you want to strengthen a Running Thread Seam, you can sew it first in one direction, and then again in the other direction, sewing the second set of stitches in the gaps of the first.

Running Stitch for Wovens

This stitch can be used for sewing two wovens when the seam will not be under stress, or to finish the raw edge of a woven so it will not ravel. It can also be used to attach appliqués with finished edges if you want visible stitching. It is the quickest, easiest stitch to do.

- Place two fabrics together with edges aligned. Move needle down through fabric and then back up ⅛ to ¼ inch away; repeat, taking three or four stitches before drawing needle and thread through.

Running Stitch.

- To finish raw edge of a woven, turn edge under ¼ inch and press. Use Running Stitch ⅛ inch from folded edge, taking tiny stitches.
- For an appliqué, it may be difficult to make even stitches by inserting the needle into and out of the fabric. Instead, insert the needle straight down through the fabric, perpendicular to the surface, draw the thread through, and then bring it straight out again to finish the stitch. Also see Prickstitch, above, a variation of Backstitch that is useful for this purpose.

   For the most even stitching, use a ruler and chalk to mark the position of every stitch on the appliqué before sewing.

Basting Stitch

Basting is no more than a long Running Stitch; it is used to sew two things together temporarily, such as if you wanted to assemble a garment in order to try it on.

   More often, however, it is used to position two fabrics correctly before sewing them permanently, such as for a patch pocket, for attaching a sleeve to an armhole, or when sewing on an appliqué or other trim.

- Use Running Stitch, above, but make each stitch about ½ inch long.

It is not necessary to make the stitches equal length on both sides of the fabric; in a thick fabric, it is often easier to make a long stitch on the farside of the fabric, and a shorter one on the nearside.

Whipstitch Seam

This is a very elementary method of sewing a seam in a knitted fabric. Instead of the sewn stitches running parallel to the edge, as is the case with the methods discussed above, they cross over the selvedge on both sides of the fabric. If sewn loosely the two fabric edges will be butted together; if sewn firmly, the sewing will encase the seam and create a rather prominent ridge; in either case, the sewing yarn will be visible.

   Whipstitch is most successful when no effort is made to hide it. It is sometimes used to join lace borders to the center section of a shawl; a flat seam is desirable for something reversible, and the open nature of the seam blends in reasonably well with an open stitch pattern. Using Whipstitch in either of the ways described here is also a good option when sewing seams in a fulled fabric, or other particularly thick or dense knitted fabric, in which case it may be also be done with a contrast-color yarn as a decorative detail.

Whipstitch for Encased Selvedges

Place the two outside faces of the fabrics together, hold edges up, and sew through both at once; the entire edge is enclosed in the seam.

- Insert needle from right to left between selvedge and adjacent column of stitches and bring it out in same place in other fabric. Draw yarn over edge and repeat.

   Sew between every running thread, or between every other one to make stitches as even as possible, and draw yarn up rather firmly to make a ridge, or less firmly to make wider stitches and a flatter join.

For a decorative seam, position the fabrics with the inside faces together to turn the seam to the outside and sew with a contrast-color yarn.

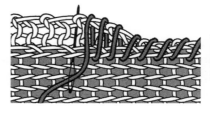

Whipstitch Seam. Decorative seam on outside of fabric.

Whipstitch for Flat Seam

- Place Fabric A to left, Fabric B to right, outside faces up with the selvedges side by side. Thread yarn in tapestry needle and attach on inside of Fabric B and bring through to outside of Fabric A. To sew Whipstitch, insert needle from nearside to farside between running threads next to selvedge in Fabric B and then from farside to nearside between running threads next to selvedge in Fabric A; repeat to sew seam.

Insert needle into each space between running threads just once. You have the option of sewing so the yarn passes horizontally between two selvedges on the inside and at an angle on the outside, or vice versa; draw yarn up gently, just enough to draw edges together.

Overcasting

This stitch is commonly used to bind the raw edge of a woven fabric to keep it from raveling. This is more quickly done by machine, but you might have occasion to use it if you do not have a sewing machine at hand.

- Bring needle through to outside a scant ⅛ inch from edge of woven, and then repeat about ¼ inch away. Draw thread up just enough to encase edge; if drawn too tightly, it will pucker.

Overcasting.

Hemstitch

This technique is used to attach linings and facings to the inside of the fabric, to tack down the edges of a zipper tape, or to sew appliqués or trim to the outside.

Sewing a Lining

If there is a raw edge on the woven fabric, first turn it under and press.

Use a single strand of thread, knot it, and work from right to left, as follows.

1. Pass needle up through edge of woven, catching no more than a few threads next to fold.
2. Pass needle up under Purl stitch or running thread closest to edge of woven fabric.
3. Repeat Steps 1–2, making each new stitch in woven about ¼ inch away from previous one.

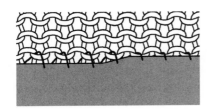

Sewing a Lining.
Sewing Woven to Knit with Hemstitch.

Only a tiny stitch will be visible, lying perpendicular to the edge of the woven fabric; the thread that passes from one stitch to the next will be hidden under the folded edge of the woven fabric. This not only produces a nearly invisible hem, but there will be no long threads to snag in wear. Another option is to skim the needle through the yarn of the knitted fabric, being careful that it does not show on the outside.

Sewing Trim

If you are using Hemstitch to sew appliqués or woven trim to the outside of the fabric, instead of passing the thread around a knitted stitch, or skimming the needle through the yarn, pass it all the way through the fabric to anchor it more securely.

If the material is heavy, or if you are concerned that the thread might abrade the yarn, baste interfacing on the inside of the fabric (see below). Sew through trim, knit, and interfacing; in effect, this sandwiches the knitted fabric between the woven interfacing and the trim, which will protect the fabric and keep it from being pulled out of shape. Adjust the method as follows:

- Instead of taking the tiny stitch in Step 2, above, insert the needle down through the knit to make the stitch perpendicular to the folded edge, and then bring it out again ¼ inch away along the edge of the woven, in position for the next stitch.

Catchstitch

This is an excellent method of sewing any woven fabric to a knit where it is important to maintain as much resilience as possible. Catchstitch is often used to attach linings to a hem, or to tack the edge of a facing down on the inside of a fabric.

The stitches will be visible on the inside; to prevent them from showing through on the outside, skim the sewing needle through the yarn, or sew under a Purl nub or running thread.

Attach thread to inside of woven and bring needle through to outside; you can work with the folded edge of the woven above where you will sew, or below. Work from left to right as follows.

1. Insert needle from right to left parallel to edge of woven to make a ⅛-inch stitch.
2. Pass needle up under closest Purl nub or running thread, about ⅛ to ¼ inch to right.
3. Repeat Steps 1–2, each time making next stitch ⅛ to ¼ inch to right of previous stitch.

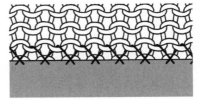

Sewing Woven to Knit with Catchstitch.

Each time you make a new stitch, the thread will cross over the strand passing from the previous stitch, forming a tiny X; this allows the two edges to move in relation to one another; it preserves the resilience of the knit, and the sewn stitches are less likely to break.

❖ *Other Seaming Techniques*

The Selvedge Seam techniques discussed above depend upon matching selvedges and a row-by-row alignment between the two fabrics. This will not work for fabrics made with different stitch patterns, which are more than likely to have an unequal number of rows. The same is true if you need to join a side edge to a top or bottom edge, or a sloped edge to a straight edge.

In these situations, use one of the following suggestions:

- Use Backstitch to sew seam, drawing yarn up gently to preserve some resilience and avoid puckering.
- Or, place fabrics on table with outside faces up and edges side by side; join the two with coilless pins set at even intervals, and use the Combination Seam.

  Use the Running Thread Seam technique on the side where you may have to work occasionally under two selvedge stitches at a time in order to line things up, and the Selvedge Seam technique on the side where you can work evenly into every pair.

Crochet Seam

If you are handy with a crochet hook, there is a wealth of patterns that can be used to make a decorative, visible seam on the outside of the fabric. This is an excellent way to join borders for a lace fabric, or when joining modular patches for a coverlet (see Modular Fabrics), or as the equivalent of a basting stitch.

Here is how to use it to make a conventional seam on the inside of the fabric.

Place outside faces of two fabrics together, hold edges up, and work from right to left.

1. Insert crochet hook beneath pair of selvedge stitches, one in each edge, hook yarn and draw loop through fabric.
2. Insert hook under pair of selvedge stitches to left. Draw loop through fabric and loop already on hook. Repeat for length of seam.

Crochet Seam.

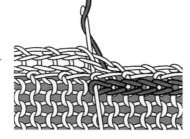

Crochet Options

Here are several other convenient things you can do with crochet during finishing.

- If you want to try a garment on, use a simple crochet chain to baste a seam together, and then just zip it off again. Place the two edges together and chain between the selvedge and the first column of stitches.
- Baste a sleeve into an armhole with a crochet chain before sewing it; in this case, do so about ¼ to ½ inch away from the edge where you will sew. There is no need to worry about making even stitches.
- Use crochet to chain in a contrast-color Yarn Marker to act as a guide for patch pocket placement; then crochet-baste the pocket into place for sewing.

  Or, make the pocket with either a Chain or Garter Stitch Selvedge, and use a Single Crochet Chain on the outside to fasten the pocket into place between the selvedge and the main fabric.

Machine-Sewn Seams

Machine knits are often seamed on a sewing machine or serger (an overlock sewing machine for edges). This is less commonly done for hand knits, but works very well in certain situations, particularly when sewing wovens to knits; see below. Sewing machines are also useful for binding an edge with a bias woven fabric, which is particularly successful when used for the cut edge of a Steek, but it can also be used to sew a sleeve into an armhole.

However, machine sewing is less successful when it is important to line up two fabrics row by row, because the pressure foot tends to push the top fabric out of alignment with the one underneath. Even when that is not a factor, it is important to baste the pieces firmly together. Some machines have special pressure feet for knits that help to keep the two fabrics aligned and, of course, thinner knits are easier to manage than thicker ones.

❖ *Specialty Seams*

While the instructions above focused on how to seam, here are some suggestions for how to deal with sewing together edges that require a special approach for one reason or another.

Turning Selvedges Outside

If you sew a Running Thread Seam while working on the *inside* of the fabric, the two columns of selvedge stitches will lie side by side on the outside of the fabric, forming a ridged line that is quite handsome. Either a Stockinette or Chain Selvedge will work, but the latter is particularly attractive.

Turning Selvedges Outside.

Of course, for this seam to be successful, the selvedges must be smooth and even. Do not tie on any yarns at the selvedge, and work all shaping within the fabric, not on the selvedge.

For a Stranded Color pattern, hold both colors as one for every selvedge stitch, or carefully alternate the colors stitch by stitch.

Seam for Turned-Back Cuffs

To seam sleeve cuffs that will be turned up, work as follows:

1. On inside of fabric, work Running Thread Seam from cast-on edge to second or third row above center of cuff.
2. Turn to outside of fabric, bring yarn through next running thread, and complete rest of seam.

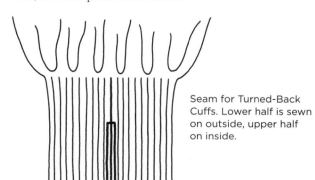

Seam for Turned-Back Cuffs. Lower half is sewn on outside, upper half on inside.

The selvedge will be on the outside of the fabric in the lower half of the cuff and on the inside in the upper half; when folded into position, no selvedge will be visible.

Use the same approach to seam a hat that has a ribbing that will be folded up around the ears.

Seams for Wide Selvedges

Some traditional sweater designs are made with relatively wide Steeks, somewhat more like the selvedges used for a woven fabric. Stitches are picked up around the opening between the Steek and the main fabric, and this wide selvedge with its cut edge is turned to the inside and hemmed into place (see Sewing and Cutting Steeks, below).

A wide selvedge is also worth consideration for things besides Steeks because it lies very flat on the inside of the fabric. In some circumstances, it may be more unobtrusive and softer for a seam than the ridge formed by a typical narrow selvedge. Also, you can use a simple open stitch pattern of some kind for the selvedge, which will not only make it thinner than the surrounding fabric, but will look attractive on the inside.

Also, if the decorative stitch pattern you plan to use for the fabric leaves an irregular edge that could be difficult to seam, a wide selvedge might be a better solution than using a conventional one; also see Tips for Bias Stitch Patterns in the chapter Increase and Decrease Stitch Patterns.

Here is a good approach to use for sewing a seam of this kind.

1. When dressing fabric, fold all stitch columns to be included in selvedge to inside and steam slightly to flatten.
2. To sew, lay fabric face up with folded edges side by side and use Running Thread Seam, working between two stitch columns of fabric.
3. To finish, turn to inside of fabric and gently flatten seam and selvedge with steam and a press cloth.

By the way, a wide selvedge also offers a clever way to let out a growing child's sleeveless vest. Make the vest a larger size, and then sew up using a wide selvedge at sides and shoulders. Tack the selvedge to the edges with tiny stitches so it will not show on the outside. When the child grows too large for the garment, open up the seams and resew them using a one-stitch selvedge, in the usual way.

You could even use this idea for a garment with a sleeve, if you were willing to disassemble the entire garment and sew it back together in a bigger size for a bigger kid.

There is a risk that the outside face of the garment will fade more than the selvedge due to sun exposure or laundering; you might want to wash it inside out and unfold the edges for drying to expose them to more light.

Seaming Top or Bottom Edges

It is easy enough to join two cast-off or cast-on edges with Backstitch, working just under the edge. However, the result will be a bulky seam, and it is better to avoid sewing these edges entirely. Any of these options can be used for seaming a garment worked side to side.

- For top edges, do not cast off and seam them together; use Joinery Cast-Off instead. And consider placing the inside faces of the fabric together as you do so, to turn the cast-off edge to the outside for a decorative effect.
- For a bottom edge, start with a Provisional Cast-On; to seam, free the stitches of the cast-on edge, pick them up on a needle, and then use either Joinery Cast-Off or Grafting.
- Also see Grafting to a Cast-Off Edge, below.

Sewing in Sleeves

A sleeve cap and armhole not only have different contours, but a different number of rows. This means the two edges cannot be lined up and sewn row by row as for a conventional side seam, and it is necessary to use Backstitch or a firm Running Stitch for the seam.

Sew up with your knitting yarn if it is strong and smooth; otherwise, see the yarn suggestions above in Yarns for Sewing.

1. Join shoulders and sew sleeve seam and side seam in bodice.
2. Turn bodice inside out, put sleeve inside bodice so outside faces of two fabrics are together, and line up edges.

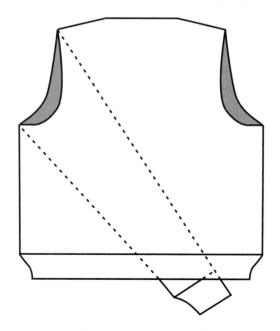

Sewing in Sleeves. Bodice is turned inside out; outside faces of bodice and sleeve are together.

3. Baste two fabrics together about ½ inch away from edge, or use coilless pins to join edges at 1-inch intervals.
4. Sew seam with Backstitch or Running Stitch. Pass needle through in one direction perpendicular to edge immediately under selvedge and draw yarn through. For next stitch pass needle back in other direction in same way.

In a thin fabric, you can put the needle through in one direction and immediately back through in the other, which is much faster. However, the needle travels at an angle, and when sewing a thicker, softer knit, this makes it more difficult to keep the two fabrics lined up and to insert the needle carefully under the selvedge.

Do not pull stitches too tight; stop from time to time to check the measurement of the armhole and stretch it out or snug it up a bit, if necessary.

Dolman Sleeve Seams

If you are dealing with a garment that has stitches cast on somewhere along the side, such as for a dolman sleeve, the sides of the bodice will have selvedges, but the sleeves will have cast-on and cast-off edges, and you will need to join both types of edges in a continuous seam.

For something like this, work as follows:

1. When making garment, add stitches for sleeve with Stranded Cast-On at Side Edge, and use Stranded Cast-Off at top.
2. To seam, turn to inside, free stitches at top and bottom edges of sleeve and pick up on circular needles; hold needles side by side and seam edges with Joinery Cast-Off working from wrist toward sides of bodice.
3. Break yarn, allowing enough to complete seam, and use Running Thread Seam for side edges between sleeve and lower edge; be careful to sew first cast-on stitch and first selvedge stitch together to close any gap that may exist.

Sewing Fulled Knits

Fulled fabrics are thick and tend to be somewhat stiff, and conventional seam techniques will not work well. However, there are good alternatives. The fabric is firm, so use a long, relatively sharp needle.

- For a decorative seam, emphasize the bold nature of the fabric by using Whipstitch and a contrast-color yarn, sewing the seam on the outside of the fabric, as described above.
- Overlap the two edges, and use a decorative embroidery stitch or crochet to sew them together. To make sure the stitching is perfectly even, use chalk to make ¼ to ½ inch marks along the edge to serve as a guide. To keep the fabrics aligned as you sew, use double-sided adhe-

sive tape (available at sewing supply stores) between the two edges.

- Apply a decorative ribbon or woven braid over the two edges to cover the seam. Whipstitch the two fulled fabric edges together first, place the braid on top, and then use sewing thread, a sharp needle, and Hemstitch to sew the braid into place (see Sewing Wovens to Knits, below). To be on the safe side, you might want to cover the inside of the seam, as well. If the fulled fabric is not too thick, you might be able to use a sewing machine to sew the trim into place.

❖ Sewing Within a Fabric

Attaching a pocket or sewing a hem into place are about the only times you would have any reason to sew one piece of knitted fabric to the interior of another. The method given here is the traditional one; however, a better result can usually be achieved by grafting edge stitches to the inside of the fabric, as described in Grafting a Hem, below. Another approach is to use the Joinery Decrease Hem discussed in Hems, Facings, Pleats, and Tucks.

A far more common reason to sew within the fabric is when finishing a Steek, which is a type of internal selvedge. In addition to the methods described here, also see the instructions for Bound Edges, below.

Sewing a Hem

In most books, Hemstitch is recommended for sewing up a hem, more or less as you would to sew a hem of woven fabric.

- Take one stitch into the baseline of the edge and the next into a running thread or Purl nub of the fabric.

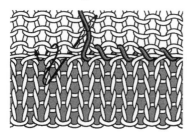

Sewing a Hem.

The line of sewn stitches will be less elastic than the fabric and can also cause a slight indentation along the sewing line that is visible on the outside of the garment.

An alternative that preserves more resilience in the fabric is to use Catchstitch, described above.

Sewing a Pocket Lining

If you have made a single-thickness pocket lining that needs to be sewn to the inside of the main fabric, there is no need to turn the pocket selvedge to the inside; sew it down flat to reduce bulk.

- Sew into outer strands of selvedge stitches of pocket and into Purl nubs on inside of fabric. Sew back and forth between the two as for Hemstitch; draw yarn up gently to avoid distorting the outer fabric.

❖ Sewing and Cutting Steeks

A Steek is a type of selvedge worked within a fabric where it will later be cut open; it is used for armholes, necklines, or center front openings in circular garments.

Before the fabric is cut, the stitch columns on either side of the cutting line need to be machine or hand sewn to secure them so they will not unravel. These two columns of stitches then serve as the selvedges and will be turned to the inside when the sleeve is attached to the armhole, or a border is added to the center front or neckline.

The fabric is normally cut open as one step in the process of making the garment, but the instructions are here in Finishing because what is required are sewing techniques that also have other applications.

Actually, what is thought of as a Steek (traditionally, a few stitches worked in a contrasting pattern of some kind) is not really necessary. You can cut a knitted fabric anywhere as long as you allow one column of stitches on either side of the cutting line to serve as selvedges; work whatever shaping is needed within the fabric, adjacent to these stitch columns. Traditionally, stitches are also set aside at the base of the opening, but even this is unnecessary; you can just sew across the bottom of the opening to secure it, as well.

If you would rather not bother with having to work a shaping pattern, you can make a rectangle or tube of knitted fabric and cut out as much of the fabric as needed to form armholes or neckline, just as you would when using a sewing pattern and a length of woven fabric. If that is the approach you take, dress the fabric beforehand (see Dressing a Fabric).

Securing the edges and cutting a fabric open is really quite easy, but it does produce a certain amount of anxiety the first time anyone tries it; practice on a Test Swatch before you sew and cut your garment.

The hand-sewn methods are described here, but it is quick and convenient to use a sewing machine if you have one; see Machine-Sewn Steek, or Bound Edges, below.

Hand-Sewn Steek

The first two techniques make use of classic hand-sewing stitches that are used here in a special way; the first is Backstitch, discussed above for use as a seam, and the second is Catchstitch, which is primarily used for woven fabrics, but here functions like a machine-sewn zigzag stitch.

If necessary, mark the cutting line on the fabric with a strand of contrast-color yarn before you begin to sew.

Use a sharp needle and ordinary sewing thread for this, or buttonhole thread if you need something thicker and stronger.

Steek Sewn with Backstitch

Hold fabric sideways and sew from left to right along the first column of stitches next to the marked cutting line. Insert needle *into* yarn of stitches, not between them, and wherever one strand of yarn meets another sew through both yarns to lock them together.

Attach yarn at left edge and work as follows:

1. To begin, insert needle about ⅛ inch to right and bring it back out at starting point; make second stitch in same location to secure top edge of Steek.
2. Sew with Backstitch; insert needle about ¼ inch to right and bring it back out ⅛ inch to left. Repeat for length of selvedge.
3. If necessary, sew across bottom of what will be cut opening, and then turn fabric around and sew up other side of selvedge in same way.

To make the edge more secure, sew a second line of stitching just like the first in the other half of the same column of stitches.

Steek Sewn with Catchstitch

This is an unconventional use of Catchstitch, a hand-sewing stitch normally used to attach a lining to a hem or facing. In this application, it serves almost like the zigzag stitch of a sewing machine. Normally Catchstitch is sewn loosely, and the stitches are spaced farther apart, but for this application make each stitch next to the previous one and sew rather firmly to lock the strands of the stitches together. Also, as described for sewing with Backstitch, above, wherever two strands of yarn meet, sew through both.

Hold fabric sideways and sew from left to right into the now-horizontal column of stitches, directly below where the fabric will be cut.

1. Start at left edge of fabric and secure edge first. Sew two ⅛-inch stitches, one on top of the other, in lower side of first knit stitch and then repeat in upper side of stitch.
2. Sew parallel to cutting line. Make a ⅛-inch-wide stitch in lower half of knitted stitch, immediately to right of previously sewn stitch, and then sew next stitch to right of previously sewn stitch in upper half of knitted stitch. Repeat for length of Steek.
3. Turn top edge of fabric up and sew across bottom of Steek.
4. Turn fabric sideways in other direction and work as in Step 2 along stitch column on other side of where fabric will be cut.
5. To secure edge, sew two pairs of stitches at top of Steek, as described in Step 1.

Crocheted Steek

Crochet is another technique suggested for securing a Steek prior to cutting, and it is easy to do. However, it is only effective for wool, which tends to felt a bit around the cut edge, making it less likely to ravel.

Furthermore, the crocheted edges will be bulky if done with the same yarn used for the fabric. If you can find a reasonable color match, use a thinner yarn, or even better, use something like embroidery thread or needlepoint tapestry yarn, and thin it by removing one or more ply.

If necessary, baste a strand of contrast-color yarn along the cutting line to act as a guide. Turn the fabric sideways so the stitch columns are horizontal, and work on outside of fabric.

Typically, each crocheted stitch is used to join two sides of one column of Knit stitches, or the left side of the stitches in one column and the right sides of those in an adjacent column (it does not matter if you cut a fabric open between two columns, or down the center of one; see Working in the Opposite Direction).

Because you will be holding the fabric sideways, the instructions refer to the upper strand and the lower strand of the knitted stitches. Work from right to left, as follows:

1. Insert hook under lower and upper strand of one stitch (or adjacent stitches), catch yarn and draw loop through.
2. Insert hook under lower and upper strands of stitch to left, hook yarn and draw through loop.
3. With two loops on hook, draw left loop through right loop; one loop remains on hook. Repeat for length of Steek.
4. Chain across bottom of where fabric will be cut, and then up other side.

To make the Steek more secure, use a thin yarn or thread and a small size hook; insert hook *into* the yarn of the stitches instead of around them, and work at least twice into each one.

Machine-Sewn Steek

You can also machine sew the stitch columns on either side of a cutting line, which is much faster than hand sewing (see the illustration in Steeks: Selvedges for Cut Openings). However, this may stretch the fabric unless it is stabilized in some way beforehand. Here are some suggestions for how to proceed:

- Place tear-away stabilizer under the edge before sewing (available at most sewing stores), or use tissue paper so yarn will not be drawn into the bobbin.
- Stretch fabric slightly *widthwise* while sewing to keep the fabric from stretching lengthwise; this also helps you see better where to sew.
- Use zigzag stitch set to medium length, and as wide as possible. Sew directly down the center of a stitch

column, or between two columns, catching all or most of the sides of the stitches to right and left.

- If the machine offers other options besides a basic zigzag stitch, use one of the stitches that take multiple steps; select one that the sewing machine manual suggests for toweling or heavy knits.

- If the machine will only do straight stitch, use two lines of sewing on the column of stitches, first down the strands in one half, then down the strands in the other half. Repeat on the other side of the cutting line.

- Some machines have a "walking" foot that helps pull bulky or stretchy fabrics past the needle and minimizes stretching.

- Alternatively, see Bound Edges, below.

Sewing Wovens to Knits

Woven fabrics are frequently used in supporting roles for knitted garments. For instance, it is traditional to back center-front openings with grosgrain ribbon to provide support for the buttons and buttonholes and to stabilize the length; zippers are often more effective for sporty jackets than buttons and also stabilize an edge.

Also, seam tape can be used to stabilize a shoulder or neckline that threatens to stretch out of shape, and interfacing is often needed as a backing for trim of one kind or another. Woven pocket linings are less bulky than knitted ones and are easy both to sew in and to replace, if necessary. And while rarely done today, some garments benefit from the addition of a full or partial lining.

In addition, there are some very interesting garment designs that combine knitted and woven fabrics. Traditional Scandinavian garments often had woven bodices and knitted sleeves, for instance, and there is no reason not to do the opposite and add woven sleeves to a knitted bodice. You might want to sew knitted trims onto woven fabrics—lace edgings for a pillowcase or hand towel are common examples, but the concept could easily be extended to sewing a bit of lace trim onto a sweater.

The sewing methods and thread used for these purposes are the same as those you would use for sewing any woven fabric. The only difference is that one of the fabrics you will be sewing into is made of soft and flexible yarns, which requires minor adjustments in the methods used.

❖ *Preparing Materials*

It is especially important to dress the knitted fabric to stable, finished dimensions before attaching any woven fabric because the latter is not resilient. And it is just as important to pre-shrink the woven materials beforehand, as well.

Always check the care requirements on the label first, but most lining fabrics can be machine washed and dried. Before doing so, run a line of zigzag stitch on cut edges to prevent fraying, or cut raveled edges off later. Use the delicate cycle and, if possible, take the fabric out of the dryer while still damp and press with a dry iron. If the material is not washable, steam press it thoroughly.

For small pieces of interfacing, decorative trim, ribbons, and zippers, rinse in hot water, roll flat in a towel and squeeze out as much moisture as possible, and then press with a dry iron or air dry.

❖ *Faced or Bound Edges*

Woven facings and edge bindings can be very useful in knitted fabrics. As mentioned above, it is customary to face the inside of the center front opening of a cardigan sweater with grosgrain ribbon to support the weight of buttons and stabilize the buttonholes.

Traditional Scandinavian sweaters often had a knitted or woven facing sewn to the cut edges of a Steek, both to secure it and cover it on the inside of the garment. Center front openings and necklines were sometimes faced on the outside with a decorative ribbon. Either approach adds little or no bulk to the edge and is not difficult to do.

Woven bias bindings can also provide a way to prevent a neckline from stretching out of shape, or a wider bias facing could be cut to fit the shape of the neckline, sewn to the edge, and turned to the inside.

A bound edge is also a nice way to finish the visible edges of a knitted fabric on either side of a decorative zipper, as described below, or to cover the edge of a pocket opening.

Pre-folded bias seam binding is available at sewing stores in a wide variety of colors and several different widths. Because of how soft and thick a knitted fabric can be, wider bindings are easiest to work with and can be trimmed to fit after they are applied.

You can also make your own binding by cutting 2-inch bias strips from lightweight silk, cotton, or linen fabric. A bias binding will not fray, and can be contoured with a steam iron if you are dealing with a curved edge (see Shaping for a Cut Opening).

Bound Edges

The example here is for a bound selvedge; there are only minor differences when using this approach for a Steek; see below.

Select a pre-folded bias binding and steam out all but the narrowest fold, or cut bias binding from any suitable fabric.

1. On outside of knitted fabric, lay edge of binding along selvedge, and baste into place. Check to make sure length is correct; if necessary, pull up basting thread, or stretch edge and remeasure and then fasten thread to stabilize length.

2. Machine sew using straight stitch along fold in binding (about ¼ inch from edge).

3. Remove basting thread and fold binding over stitching. Steam press bound edge only, using press cloth to protect knitted fabric.

4. Turn binding to inside of fabric, wrapping it around cut edge; steam press again and baste into place.

5. On outside, use straight stitch to sew "in the ditch," where the folded edge of the binding meets the knitted fabric.

6. Turn to inside and, if necessary, trim binding close to stitching.

Bound Edges. Binding basted and sewn into place.

Bound Edges. Binding folded into place and sewn.

To make the edge as neat on the inside as it is on the outside, instead of using a sewing machine in Step 5, fold the edge of the binding under on the inside and hand sew into place with Hemstitch. If you do not have a sewing machine, you can bind the entire edge by hand, using Backstitch in Step 2.

To bind the edge of a Steek, work as described above, with the following changes.

• Baste the edge of one bias binding along the left side of the cutting line, and another on the right side. Sew both bindings into place as described in Step 2, above, making sure to sew across any cast-on or cast-off edge. Cut Steek open and complete Steps 3–6.

Taping Shoulders

If a shoulder seam stretches out, the sleeve of the garment will hang lower on the arm. To stabilize the seam at its correct length, sew a piece of seam tape to the shoulder selvedge on the inside.

1. Determine correct measurement for shoulder width and cut piece of seam tape ½ inch longer; fold two cut edges under about ¼ inch and press.

2. Baste seam tape to shoulder seam, gathering it up evenly to fit.

3. Use Whipstitch to sew tape to underlying selvedge.

4. Turn garment to outside and apply steam to shrink knit to fit length of tape.

For a somewhat neater look, use tiny running stitches to fasten tape to either side of the selvedge.

Buttonhole Facings

A grosgrain or satin ribbon sewn behind buttonholes and buttons is a classic finishing detail that helps to stabilize the opening edges (see Woven Facings in the chapter Hems, Facings, Pleats, and Tucks).

For the button side of the border, sew both sides of the grosgrain to the fabric with Hemstitch; sew on the buttons, passing the needle through both the knit fabric and the facing.

For buttonholes, the facing will need to be cut open and attached to the edges of the buttonholes on the inside. There are several ways to do this:

Slashed Opening

Use this method for horizontal buttonholes.

1. Use Hemstitch to sew ribbon to inside of buttonhole band along outer edge.

2. On outside, insert straight pins through knitted fabric and ribbon at inner and outer points of each buttonhole to

mark location. Turn to inside and make chalk marks on ribbon between pins.

3. Cut ribbon along chalked line from inner edge to outer point of buttonhole.

4. Turn two slashed edges of ribbon under to form V-shaped opening and steam lightly.

5. Sew slashed edges to knitted fabric with tiny Hemstitches, skimming needle into yarn so it is not visible on outside; reinforce ribbon at corner of slashed opening with several tiny stitches across point.

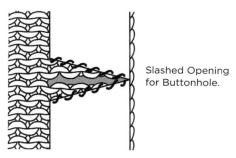

Slashed Opening for Buttonhole.

The advantage to this is that the ribbon will reinforce the point of the buttonhole where it is under strain, and will also keep it from stretching out, yet the slash maintains the resiliency of the opening so the button can pass through.

However, if it seems best to stabilize the buttonhole to keep it from stretching out, sew down the inner edges of the ribbon on each side of the opening.

Machine-Sewn Opening

This approach works well for both horizontal and vertical buttonholes.

1. Baste ribbon into place on inside of button band, and insert pins to mark location and size of knitted buttonholes on facing.

2. Use chalk to mark location of buttonholes; remove basting stitches and take ribbon off knit.

3. Work machine-sewn buttonholes at markings.

4. Sew long edges of facing to inside of fabric with Hemstitch.

5. Use Hemstitch to sew facing edges of buttonholes just inside openings of knitted buttonholes; work so the facing cannot be seen on the outside.

In Step 2, if chalk does not remain on ribbon, mark buttonhole locations with thread before machine stitching.

Hand-Sewn Buttonhole

1. Work Steps 1 and 2, above.

2. To make buttonholes in ribbon, use tiny Running Stitches to sew a narrow oval about ¼ inch away around each buttonhole marking on facing.

3. Slash buttonhole open within oval of stitches, and then use tip of scissors to cut tiny notches from slashed edge toward running thread stitches.

 Hand-Sewn Buttonhole. Stitch around opening and slash; turn under and press.

4. Turn cut edge of each buttonhole under to form hemmed opening; press into place.

5. Attach facing to inside of button band and sew folded edge of facing buttonhole just inside knitted buttonhole opening.

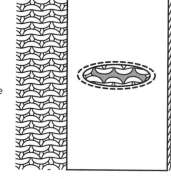

Hand-Sewn Buttonhole. Sew edge of facing just inside knitted buttonhole opening.

Sewing On Buttons

A button can be sewn onto a knit in the same way it would be sewn onto any woven fabric. You can use the knitting yarn, but a better choice is silk buttonhole thread, or color-matched needlepoint or embroidery thread.

Because of the soft nature of a knitted fabric, it is a good idea to support the decorative button in some way on the inside. Here are some suggestions:

- Position small button on inside of fabric, and decorative button on outside; sew through both at same time. To finish, knot thread between support button and fabric.

- Instead of a small button, cut small square of felt, or bias piece of canvas or denim, about ¼-inch square; hold it on inside of fabric under decorative button and sew through both at once.

- On heavy knits, consider using button with a shank, or make a thread shank as you sew. When the button is inserted into the buttonhole, a shank provides room underneath it for the thickness of the knitted fabric.

❖ Trims, Appliqués, and Zippers

Here are some suggestions for sewing trim or decorative appliqués to the surface of the fabric, along with tips for sewing in zippers.

Sewing on Trim

When attaching trim to the outside of the fabric, you have the option of using decorative stitching or sewing invisibly, depending upon the effect you want to achieve.

Part Eight: Working a Project

- For decorative stitching, consult any embroidery book for inspiration and work with silk or cotton embroidery thread, or wool needlepoint yarn.
- To invisibly attach something light in weight, use Hemstitch to attach the trim at the very edge. If the trim is heavier, consider using Prickstitch (a variation of Backstitch), which will be more secure.

Interfacing for Appliqués

An appliqué, or any kind of heavy trim, benefits from the support that interfacing provides. The classic choice for something like this is silk organza, but a lightweight, firmly woven linen or cotton also works well; even thin felt could be a good choice.

Cut the interfacing about an inch larger than the trim on all sides. If possible, cut on the bias, otherwise finish edges so they will not ravel.

1. Pin and baste interfacing into place on inside.
2. Pin appliqué or trim to outside.
3. Sew through all layers—appliqué, knitted fabric, and interfacing—using Hemstitch or Prickstitch.

Due to the thickness of the layers, it is probably easiest to sew in two steps; insert the needle straight down through all fabrics and draw full length of thread through; then insert needle up through all fabrics to outside in same way for next half of stitch.

❖ Sewing In a Zipper

Zippers are a nice way to finish a jacket or cardigan front, but it can be a challenge to keep the yarn from snagging in the zipper teeth, especially if it is fuzzy.

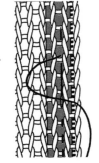

Sewing In a Zipper. Sew with Backstitch next to selvedge.

- Consider a decorative zipper that is intended to remain visible and has large, smooth teeth. Set the edges of the knitted fabric alongside the teeth, instead of covering them, so the yarn is less likely to get caught. Working on outside, sew into place with Backstitch, working around running threads in fabric, or even around heads of selvedge stitches.
- Alternatively, bind the selvedge of the center front opening with leather or firmly woven fabric of some kind; see Faced or Bound Edges, above.
- To conceal a separating zipper in a center front opening, make a facing similar to one for buttonholes, and line with grosgrain ribbon. Sew one side of the zipper to the selvedge on the inside of the border, and sew the other selvedge to the outside of the zipper alongside the teeth.

❖ Linings

Lining a hand-knit garment is done less often today than it used to be, perhaps because fewer knitters are making the tailored suits, coats, and jackets for which a lining is such a nice addition.

However, if you are tempted to make a Chanel-inspired jacket, a lining is a beautiful finishing touch; or you might want to consider lining just the sleeves of a jacket to make it easier to take on and off. Also, a knitted skirt will hold its shape better with a lining.

Commercial lining fabrics are usually made of rayon, but for a special garment consider lightweight silk. To preserve the resilience of the knitted fabric as much as possible, consider cutting the lining on the bias, or try to find a suitable stretch woven.

Making a Lining

If you have used a sewing pattern as a basis for a garment design (see Schematics from Sewing Patterns), it may have separate pieces for a lining, or you can make a lining pattern from the main pieces. Otherwise, use the measurements from the schematic of your knitted garment pattern to make a full-scale pattern for the lining.

The lining will be attached between the main fabric and any borders; plan the size and shape accordingly. For instance, the lining will be sewn to the inner edge of a center front border, below any neck border, and above any border at lower edge and wrist.

To basic length and width, add ⅝-inch selvedge allowances as necessary for all seams and edges. Also add an allowance of 2 to 4 inches at the center back for a pleat, and about a 1-inch allowance to length for movement ease.

1. Clean and dress knitted fabric (see Cleaning and Dressing a Knit), and then sew together.
2. Preshrink lining fabric and iron while still damp, or steam press when dry.
3. Cut out and sew lining together and finish seams as necessary.
4. Fold vertical pleat at center back and sew 4 to 5 inches down from top and up from bottom; press fold into place, and press all seams flat.
5. Mark and turn under all edges to be sewn to knitted fabric, press, and baste into place.

Attaching a Lining

To attach lining, work as follows:

1. Turn knitted garment inside out and slip lining into place with inside of both fabrics together; pin at neckline and center front opening.

2. Use Hemstitch to sew lining at all edges.

3. Use Catchstitch under folded edge to attach lining above lower borders of bodice and sleeve.

If you want to add a lining just to the sleeve, assemble garment and then add sleeve lining as follows:

1. Sew seam of sleeve lining and finish raw edges; press flat.

2. Turn up hem at lower edge, baste and press.

3. Sew line of stay-stitching ½ inch from raw edge of lining sleeve cap to prevent stretching; cut notches in selvedge from edge to line of stitching, about one inch apart around upper portion of sleeve cap (this allows edge to turn under smoothly). Turn sleeve cap selvedge under ⅝ inch and press.

4. Turn garment inside out and put lining on knitted sleeve. Sew folded edges of lining sleeve cap to selvedges of armhole in knitted fabric. Use Catchstitch to tack hemmed lower edge of lining to sleeve above ribbing; skim the sewing needle and thread through the yarn so none of the stitches will show on the outside.

Grafting

Grafting is a sewing technique that creates a horizontal, stitch-to-stitch join between two pieces of knitted fabric that exactly duplicates the structure and appearance of Knit or Purl stitches. Done well, you should not be able to identify the grafted join when it is finished, even with close inspection.

Most often grafting is used as a substitute for a seam when it is important to preserve the resilience of the fabric. However, it may also be used to rejoin two pieces of fabric that have been separated, to join the top of one fabric to the side of another, to hide a seam when its appearance is undesirable, or as a way of reducing the bulk of a seam at a top edge.

Each of these applications requires slight modifications of the technique to adapt it to the purpose.

❖ *General Technique*

Due to the challenge of duplicating any complex stitch technique, Grafting is normally used to join (or rejoin) two sets of stitches that are both in Stockinette, or at most a relatively simple combination of Knit and Purl stitches.

Fortunately, many stitch patterns have plain rows between the decorative ones, where grafting can sometimes be managed, or you might want to introduce a row or two of plain Knit to make the grafting possible.

In order to recreate the stitches by sewing, you will want to have a good understanding of the structure of Knit and Purl and the path the yarn takes through the stitches; see the illustrations in The Stitches.

Yarns for Grafting

Grafting is a sewing technique, and therefore the entire length of yarn used is repeatedly pulled through each stitch, which causes it to fray. For this reason, the technique may be difficult or even impossible to do with many slubbed, nubby, or fuzzy yarns, or with any yarn that is particularly delicate.

Even yarns that are rather smooth and strong will start to thin out after a while; therefore, it is best to work with several shorter lengths. While this necessitates hiding extra ends of yarn on the inside of the garment later, that is better than stitches that look thin and uneven.

Lining Up Fabrics for Grafting

When joining two fabrics, it is important to understand how the stitches line up when you join the top of one to the top of another, such as for a shoulder or a sock toe, or a top to a bottom, or when rejoining a fabric that has been separated (see Separating a Fabric).

When dealing with a top-to-bottom join, there will be stitches on one needle, and running threads on the other, and there will be one less of the latter. When grafted, the running threads will nest between the stitches, and the result will be that the stitch columns of both fabrics line up perfectly and will look just as if they had been worked continuously.

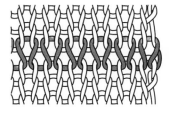

Lining Up Fabrics for Grafting. Top to bottom join lines up.

However, when you graft the tops of two fabrics together, they will be head to head, with an equal number of stitches on the two needles. This is problematic because, when joined, one set of stitches functions as running threads that fit between the other set of stitches. As a result, one fabric will be offset a half-stitch in relation to the other.

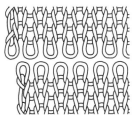

Lining up Fabrics for Grafting. Tops of two fabrics will not line up perfectly.

This offset will not be visible within a Stockinette fabric because it looks the same right side up as it does upside down. However, with other stitch patterns, particularly those that have strongly vertical lines, the offset will be in evidence all the way across the fabric.

The only solution is to trick the eye into not seeing it by introducing several rows of Stockinette at the top of both fabrics, which also makes it easier to work the grafting pattern. If that is not acceptable, it may be necessary to find another method of joining the two fabrics.

The offset will also affect the side edges of the fabric; it will jog in on one side and out on the other. While this can be hidden in a side seam, it will be visible at the edges of a blanket or shawl, and will be more noticeable if the stitches are large.

Holding the Work

The safest approach to grafting two edges is to have each set of stitches on a separate needle. It is possible to graft with the stitches off the needle, and this makes it easier to see where you are going and what the path of the yarn should be, however, there is a risk of having stitches unravel.

Nevertheless, this is often done for sock or mitten tips because there are so few stitches and wool does not unravel as easily as some other yarns.

There are also options for how to position the stitches. You can place the fabrics down on a table top, with the outside faces up and one needle set above the other. Or, you can hold the needles parallel with the inside faces together.

It is easier to see what you are doing with the fabrics lying flat, but holding the needles parallel goes a bit faster, and that is the approach used in the instructions below.

In either case, have the tips of the needles facing to the right; if necessary, work another row on one fabric, or slip the stitches to a double-point needle and slide the stitches to the right tip.

❖ Basic Grafting Patterns

The Stockinette grafting pattern is the most common one used. In the first set of instructions, the steps are written out in some detail for those who are learning to do this; the second set is a briefer version that you can refer to once you are familiar with the process.

The grafting pattern variations that follow are more formulaic. In each of them, there will be a preliminary step that is used to begin the pattern sequence.

Basic Grafting on Needle

This is by far the most common method of grafting. Pay attention to what is happening as you work and you will soon make sense of it; it is not at all difficult to do.

To begin, thread the yarn coming off the first stitch on one of the needles into a tapestry needle. Hold the needles parallel in your left hand, with the tips facing to the right.

Preliminary Steps

1. Pass sewing needle through first stitch on near needle from right to left as to Purl; draw yarn through stitch.

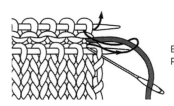

Basic Grafting: Preliminary Steps.

2. Pass sewing needle through first stitch on far needle from left to right as to Knit; draw yarn through. Retain both stitches on knitting needles.

The Grafting Sequence

Repeat the following steps across the width of the fabric.

Near Needle

1. Insert sewing needle into first stitch on needle from left to right as to Knit, drop stitch from needle; draw yarn through.

Basic Grafting Sequence: Near Needle.

2. Insert sewing needle into next stitch from right to left as to Purl and draw yarn through; retain stitch on knitting needle.

Far Needle

1. Insert sewing needle into first stitch on needle from right to left as to Purl; drop stitch from needle, and draw yarn through.

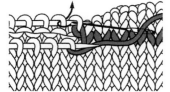

Basic Grafting Sequence: Far Needle.

2. Insert sewing needle into next stitch from left to right as to Knit and draw yarn through; retain stitch on knitting needle.

Abbreviated Pattern

In the following instructions, "near" or "far" refer to the position of the respective needles; "hold" or "drop" refer to retaining the stitch on the needle or dropping it off, respectively. The instruction to Knit or Purl simply means to insert the sewing needle into the next stitch in the same way you would when inserting the knitting needle.

Insert sewing needle into the stitches and work as follows:

1. Preliminary: Stitch on near needle as to Purl, hold; stitch on far needle as to Knit, hold.
2. Near needle: Knit, drop; Purl, hold.
3. Far needle: Purl, drop; Knit, hold.

As you work, always bring the yarn under the needle tip as you switch between the two fabrics; do not pass it over the needle.

Moving the sewing needle between the two fabrics creates one side of a stitch. Moving the sewing needle horizontally between two stitches of the same fabric creates a running thread. If you get the running threads in the right place, the sides of the grafted stitches lying between the two fabrics will position themselves correctly.

Never drop a stitch from the knitting needle until it has two strands of yarn in it. The first stitch on the needle should always have one strand of yarn in it before you begin the sequence for each pair on that needle. If there is no yarn in the stitch, it means you have either missed a step or dropped a stitch from the needle. Retrace the path of the yarn to find the error; if necessary draw the yarn out of the grafted stitches and pick them up on the needle again.

After dropping a stitch from the needle, draw the yarn up carefully and make each stitch the same size as the one next to it. Stop and examine the edge after sewing two or three stitches; if they are uneven, use the tip of your sewing needle to draw yarn into or out of them, as needed.

At the end of the row, weave the end of the yarn into the selvedge, just as you would for an end left by tying on a new supply of yarn.

Basic Grafting off Needle

As discussed above, it is much easier to make sense of the grafting patterns if you are working with the stitches off the needle. If you are a confident knitter and the yarn you are working with is not slippery and shows little tendency to unravel, you may prefer to work this way.

Before you begin, lightly steam the freed stitches; this sets them so they are less likely to run down. Alternatively, run a length of thin contrast-color cord through each set of stitches. Since the cord is softer than a needle, it will allow the stitches to lie flat in much the same way as when they are free; remove it when you are done.

Grafting off-needle is most often done for sock or mitten tips, and these short lengths represent a minimal challenge. Also, the fabric is usually Stockinette and the stitches should

look familiar, but if you have any doubts about the path of the yarn, see the drawing of the Knit stitch in The Stitches; there are also drawings of other stitch techniques there, if you are dealing with some other kind of pattern.

❖ *Grafting Other Stitch Patterns*

Here are some suggestions for how to use Grafting when faced with two fabrics that were done in a pattern other than Stockinette.

Garter Stitch Grafting

To graft the top of one Garter Stitch fabric to the bottom of another, make sure there is a row of Purl below the stitches on both needles. Graft Knit stitches in between as for the Basic Grafting pattern.

Single Rib Grafting

This will line up properly only when grafting the top of one section of fabric to the bottom of another.

The grafting sequence has four steps, two for the Knit stitches on each needle and two for the Purl stitches. The first stitch of the Single Rib sequence is a Knit.

1. Preliminary Step: Near stitch as to Purl; Far stitch as to Knit.
2. Near needle: Knit, drop, draw yarn through; Knit, hold.
3. Far needle: Purl, drop, draw yarn through; Purl, hold.
4. Near needle: Purl, drop, draw yarn through; Purl, hold.
5. Far needle: Knit, drop, draw yarn through; Knit, hold.
6. Repeat Steps 2–5 across row.

Double Rib Grafting

As with Single Rib, this can only be done successfully when grafting the top of one section to the bottom of another.

After the preliminary step, the sequence has eight steps, one for each needle, and one for each of four possible combinations of stitches: two Knit, two Purl, a Knit then a Purl, or a Purl then a Knit; it begins with a pair of Knit stitches.

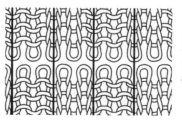

Double Rib Grafting, top to top showing offset. Only a top-to-bottom join will line up.

1. Preliminary Step: Near stitch as to Purl; Far stitch as to Knit.
2. Near needle; two Knit stitches: Knit, drop, draw yarn through; Purl, hold.
3. Far needle; two Knit stitches: Purl, drop, draw yarn through; Knit, hold.

4. Near needle; one Knit, one Purl: Knit, drop, draw yarn through; Knit, hold.

5. Far needle; one Knit, one Purl: Purl, drop, draw yarn through; Purl, hold.

6. Near needle; two Purl: Purl, drop, draw yarn through; Knit, hold.

7. Far needle; two Purl: Knit, drop, draw yarn through; Purl, hold.

8. Near needle; one Purl, one Knit: Purl, drop, draw yarn through; Purl, hold.

9. Far needle; one Purl, one Knit: Knit, drop, draw yarn through; Knit hold.

10. Repeat Steps 2–9 across row.

Grafting Mixed Knit and Purl

Should you have occasion to graft a fabric where the pattern is something other than Stockinette, Garter Stitch, or a basic ribbing, here are the instructions, broken down so you know how to recreate a Knit stitch or a Purl stitch wherever it happens to be.

In these instructions, "first pass" means the first time the yarn is drawn through a stitch, and "second pass" is the second time the yarn is drawn through that same stitch.

Because the stitches on the far needle cannot be seen as you work, you may want to chart the stitch patterns of both fabrics as a guide so you know whether to work as for Knit or Purl.

Knit Stitch on Near Needle
1. First pass as to Purl.
2. Second pass as to Knit.

Knit Stitch on Far Needle
1. First pass as to Knit.
2. Second pass as to Purl.

Purl Stitch on Near Needle
1. First pass as to Knit.
2. Second pass as to Purl.

Purl Stitch on Far Needle
1. First pass as to Purl.
2. Second pass as to Knit.

❖ *Grafting to an Edge*

From time to time, you might want to graft one edge to another instead of using a conventional seam. This is often a good choice when faced with joining two dissimilar edges; done well, the result will look seamless.

Grafting to a Cast-Off Edge

Grafting offers no support to the line of a garment, particularly when used at the shoulder; more than likely, the shoulder will stretch out, making the sleeve longer. The approach described here gives the shoulder line the appearance of a grafted join, with the support provided by a cast-off edge.

This is also a good technique to use when joining two top edges that have stitch patterns or color patterns that would not line up correctly for true grafting.

Cast off the stitches of one shoulder; leave the stitches of the other on the needle. Place the outside of each fabric face up, with the cast-off edge above the needle bearing the stitches; have the tip of the needle pointing to the right. Work as follows:

1. Thread yarn into tapestry needle and pass needle from farside to nearside through center of first stitch above cast-off edge.

2. Insert sewing needle into first stitch on knitting needle from right to left, as to Purl; retain stitch on needle.

3. Pass yarn from nearside to farside through center of same stitch above, then from farside to nearside through stitch to left.

4. Insert sewing needle into first stitch on knitting needle from left to right as to Knit; drop stitch from needle.

5. Repeat Steps 2–4 until all stitches have been joined.

Grafting to a Cast-Off Edge.

On the outside, the fabrics will have the seamless appearance of grafting; on the inside, the single line of cast-off stitches will support the shoulder line. You can work in the same way to join free stitches to a cast-on edge.

The grafting technique can also be used to join two cast-off edges or a cast-off and a cast-on edge, grafting above one and below the other, but while the appearance is quite good, the seam itself is wide and stiff and has little to recommend it.

Grafting to a Selvedge

There are times when you may find it necessary to graft stitches to a selvedge. For instance, you could work a hemmed center front border on picked-up stitches, and instead of casting off the last row and sewing it into place, graft the stitches to the selvedge, instead.

Perhaps you want to design a garment with one section worked vertically and another horizontally, in which case any seam would join a top and a side edge. Grafting the last row of one fabric to the selvedge of the other would create a far more attractive seam than sewing the two together in the conventional way.

In these situations, the number of stitches in one fabric is unlikely to match the number of rows in the other. In order to coordinate the two, use increases or decreases to adjust the number of stitches on the needle before grafting; develop a pattern for this as you would for stitches picked up along an edge; see Horizontal Shaping in the chapter Calculations for Pattern Design, and/or Horizontal Shaping for Flat Fabric in the chapter Charted Garment Patterns.

There are then two different ways to work, depending upon whether you will be grafting to the outside or the inside of the fabric.

Working on Outside

This approach turns the selvedge to the inside of the garment and produces a result nearly identical to picking up the stitches and working in the other direction.

To graft the top edge of a fabric to a selvedge, place the needle bearing the stitches below the selvedge with the outside of both fabrics facing up.

1. Graft stitches off needle in normal way, working entirely in Knit or in a combination of Knit and Purl (see patterns above).
2. Along selvedge, pass needle under running threads that lie between selvedge and first column of stitches within fabric, as for a Running Thread Seam.

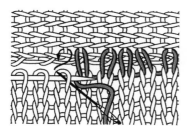

Grafting to a Selvedge. Working on Outside.

If you adjusted the number of stitches on the needle, consistently work either under every running thread, or under two at a time.

If you did not adjust the number of stitches on the needle, work under one running thread for some stitches, and under two for others to space the grafted stitches along the edge.

Working on Inside

Use this version to hem a border to a selvedge where stitches were picked up. Fold the border into position on the inside of the fabric, then graft as follows:

1. Pass sewing needle into first stitch from right to left as to Purl; retain stitch on needle.
2. Pass needle up under side of selvedge stitch directly above, and then back down under side of selvedge stitch to left.

3. Pass needle into first stitch as to Knit and drop it from needle.

Make sure to line up the columns of stitches in the border accurately when you begin so it will not be skewed. If necessary, thread a contrast-color yarn down one or more columns of stitches to act as a guide (see Yarn Markers).

If you find a row of grafted stitches adds too much bulk to the join, graft the stitches off the needle, but work into the selvedge with an Overcast stitch, instead.

Grafting to a Mixed Edge

A very nice finish for a circular neckline opening is a ribbed border turned down and hemmed into place. Securing the border with grafting helps to preserve the elasticity of the neckline. You will, however, be sewing the border to stitches at the center back and front of the neckline, and to selvedges at the sides.

For best results, use a very fine needle to make the ribbing and calculate the stitch gauge and pickup pattern carefully (see Average Gauge for Ribbing, and also Picking Up Stitches).

Pick up and work the ribbing on the *inside* of the fabric; if you do this on the outside, it will be very difficult to pull the set of needles through the neck opening in order to graft the hem.

Pick up around edge as to Purl as follows:

1. Purl all stitches of neck edge that are on holders, and pick up stitches into selvedge from farside to nearside as to Purl.
2. Begin border pattern on next round.
3. To graft collar stitches to neckline, work entirely in Knit or Purl, according to preference.
4. Graft into stitch columns in all areas where neckline stitches were originally on holders. Graft into selvedge in areas where stitches were picked up (see Grafting to a Selvedge, above).

❖ *Grafting Within a Fabric*

Grafting is often the best technique to use for sewing a hem into place, or attaching a patch pocket to the outside of a fabric, because it will preserve the elasticity of the fabric.

Grafting a Hem

Sewing down a hem on the inside is commonly done with Hemstitch. However, a grafting technique produces a more satisfying result, both in terms of appearance and behavior. If you are planning to fold a hem up from the bottom edge, use a Provisional Cast-On, free the stitches and pick them up on a needle for grafting. If you are folding a hem down, such as for a waist, leave the stitches on the needle or use a stitch holder.

In both of these situations, you will be grafting on the inside of the fabric, which, more often than not, will be in Purl.

Determine which row within the fabric you want to graft into and mark the row *below* with a Yarn Marker (or plan ahead and insert this as you work that row). In order to line the columns of stitches up accurately so the hem will not be skewed, thread in several Stitch Column Marker yarns across the width, inserting them along a column of stitches from the edge to the horizontal marker yarn.

Break the knitting yarn, allowing a length for sewing, and thread it into a tapestry needle. Turn up hem so needle bearing stitches is aligned with Row Marker:

1. Pass sewing needle through first stitch on knitting needle from right to left as to Purl; retain stitch on needle.
2. Pass sewing needle up under running thread within fabric, then down under running thread to left to create a Purl nub.

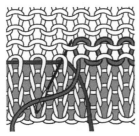

3. Pass sewing needle through first stitch on needle from left to right, as to Knit; drop stitch from needle.
4. Repeat Steps 1–3 until all of stitches have been worked off knitting needle.

Grafting a Hem.

If fabric was seamed, sew equivalent of a stitch to join hem at selvedge on each side.

Grafting a Patch Pocket

The nicest way to sew on a patch pocket is to use a version of Running Thread Seam for the sides, and Grafting for the bottom edge.

Begin the pocket with Knit Half-Hitch Cast-On for the lower edge and use Stockinette Selvedge for the sides. When dressing the pocket, use a press cloth and steam to flatten the column of selvedge stitches against the inside of the pocket.

Insert Yarn Markers in the main fabric as guides for the pocket placement. Put the pocket on the placement lines and baste into place.

To sew the pocket, start at the top right corner and work as follows:

1. Sew side edge in place with Running Thread Seam, sewing under running threads adjacent to selvedge of pocket, and under running threads between two columns of stitches in main fabric, just under edge of pocket.
2. To sew bottom edge, bring yarn out in center of first stitch of main fabric below corner of pocket.
3. Pass needle behind both sides of first stitch in pocket, directly above cast-on edge.
4. Insert needle into stitch that yarn emerges from in main fabric below pocket, and then out center of stitch to left.

5. Pass needle behind both sides of stitch in pocket to left of last one duplicated.
6. Repeat Steps 4–5 across bottom of pocket.
7. At corner, turn and work as in Step 1 to sew other side of pocket with Running Thread Seam.

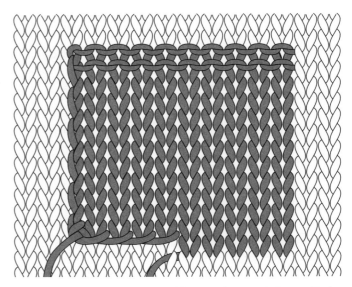

Grafting a Patch Pocket. Right side sewn; bottom being grafted.

As you will see, the Running Thread Seam will turn the pocket selvedge to the inside and line the rows of the pocket up with the rows in the fabric.

At the bottom, the Duplicate Stitch will completely cover the strands in the cast-on edge and it will look as if the stitch columns in the main fabric simply continue uninterrupted into the pocket.

Both the selvedges and the cast-on edge will be turned inside the pocket, but the pocket itself will look almost seamlessly joined to the fabric. It's a very nice effect.

Here is an alternative that leaves the bottom edge much softer:

- To make patch pocket, use Stranded Cast-On, increase one stitch each side for selvedges, and complete pocket. Sew sides with Running Thread Seam, free stitches of bottom edge, and graft them into place. However, the bottom edge will lack the stabilizing effect of a cast-on edge.
- You can use the same technique to attach a pocket lining to the inside of a fabric.

Miscellaneous Finishing

Here are all those little housekeeping details that need to be done before the garment is presentable and ready to wear.

❖ *Hiding Ends of Yarn*

Whenever you start or finish knitting, tie on a new supply of yarn, or change colors, you will leave an end of yarn that will need to be hidden on the inside of the fabric during finishing.

Actually, it doesn't have to be hidden; only you will see them, but it does make the inside of the garment look so much nicer if you tuck them away. On the other hand, some of those gorgeous Shetland Fair Isle sweaters have a multitude of tiny knots on the inside where the color changes occurred or the fabric was cut open, and the yarn ends are just cut off about half an inch long and left like a little fringe (see Knotted Steek). Because the yarn is so fine, you hardly notice they are there. So much for those who say never tie a knot and always hide the ends.

However, in most garments, the yarn ends are intermittent and randomly placed, and leaving them just hanging there makes the inside look a bit messy. If you are the only one who will ever see them, you have to decide for yourself whether you think it important to tuck them away. If the garment is something like a cardigan and the inside may show, or if it is a gift for someone, the incentive to make the interior neat becomes more compelling. Personally, I find a nicely finished interior very satisfying—quite like having a nice lining in a jacket.

If the garment was made in flat pieces and sewn together, the selvedge is a very convenient place to hide yarn ends. However, if you knit it in the round, tied on yarn for Intarsia or for embroidery, or sewed on a pocket, the ends will be within the fabric rather than at an edge, and they must be hidden in a way that leaves no evidence on the outside.

Even more of a challenge is an item made with exposed edges, such as a scarf, a shawl, or a blanket, where both the inside and outside of the fabric will be visible.

Here are some suggestions for how to work, depending upon the circumstances.

Hiding Yarn Ends in Selvedge

To hide ends of yarn along an edge wherever a new supply has been tied on or left at the corner of a cast-on or cast-off edge, weave them into the selvedge after the seam has been sewn.

1. Untie any temporary knot used and thread yarn coming off the lower row into tapestry needle. Tighten up selvedge stitch that yarn emerges from and wrap two yarn ends around one another once to interlock them.
2. Weave in first end down along selvedge 4 to 5 inches; insert needle from right to left into outer half of every selvedge stitch.
3. Remove yarn from needle, stretch seam out as far as it will go, and cut end off close.

Hiding Yarn Ends in Selvedge.

4. Thread other yarn end into needle and work it up along selvedge in same way.

Working the ends in opposite directions helps to keep the selvedge from getting bulky. If you are working from a cast-on or cast-off edge, of course, there will only be one end to hide.

Hiding Yarn Ends Within a Fabric

Several methods can be used to tie on yarn within the fabric (see Tying On Yarn). The yarn can be woven in as the next stitches are worked, or the ends can be hidden later.

The most common method of hiding ends of yarn left on the inside of the fabric is to weave it into either the running threads or the Purl nubs for several inches. However, when the fabric is stretched out, the tip can work its way free and may poke through to the outside.

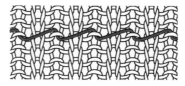

Hiding Yarn Ends Within a Fabric. Shown on Single Rib.

One solution is to consider a Knot (see the chapter Working a Project), which in some cases may be the only reasonable solution, or try one of the Duplicate Stitch methods discussed here.

Hiding Yarn Ends with Duplicate Stitch

The best approach to hiding ends of yarn on the inside of the fabric is to use the equivalent of Duplicate Stitch, which is a decorative embroidery technique that duplicates the form of a Knit or Purl stitch. In this case, however, the technique is used for purely practical purposes on the inside of the fabric.

The sewn stitches will have the same contour and resilience as the rest of the fabric, which means an end will be less likely to pull free when the fabric is stretched.

Purl Duplicate Stitch

1. Thread one end of yarn into tapestry needle. Interlock two yarns by wrapping them around one another once.
2. Pass needle up through running thread in row above, and down through next running thread in same row to make Purl nub.
3. Pass needle down through head of stitch in row below, then up through head of adjacent stitch to make running thread.
4. Repeat, always working twice into each nub for as many stitches as necessary; cut end of yarn.
5. Repeat with other end of yarn in opposite direction.

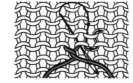

Hiding Yarn Ends with Purl Duplicate Stitch.

Knit Duplicate Stitch

1. If yarns are on outside of fabric, draw them through to inside; do not interlock. Thread tapestry needle, and weave yarn attached to stitch on right from right to left across gap, and other end from left to right.
2. Bring needle out through center of stitch to right or left in row below break.
3. Pass needle behind two sides of stitch in row above.
4. Insert needle into center of same stitch below, and then out center of adjacent stitch in same row. Repeat as necessary.

Duplicate Stitch for Other Patterns

- For Garter Stitch, follow path of yarn, working Knit below and Purl above, or vice versa.
- For a complex stitch pattern, hide yarn ends on a plain row, instead; otherwise, follow path of yarn in adjacent stitches as best you can; if necessary, skip some.
- For color patterns, hide ends only on stitches of same color; this may require working end in vertically or on a slope, instead of horizontally.
- For slippery yarns, or those with little resilience, interlock yarns at break, weave yarn almost all the way in; then use a Simple Knot to attach yarn to itself, finish weaving in and cut off end. If yarn pulls free, knot will stop it.

Duplicate Stitch with Separate Plies

- To reduce the bulk of an end woven in to the fabric, separate the plies, thread one into a tapestry needle, and use the Duplicate Stitch approach to weave it in; repeat to weave each ply in on different rows.

Duplicate Stitch and Sewn Splice

- Another way to tuck the ends in securely is to separate the plies, and use a tapestry needle with a relatively sharp point to skim the needle *through* the yarn of the Purl nubs and running threads (do not sew into the vertical sides of the stitches) as you work the Duplicate Stitch. This is a good way to prevent ends from coming free because they will be encased in the yarn of the stitches.

❖ Inserting Elastic

While knitted fabrics are generally very resilient, there are occasions when it is necessary to insert elastic. Knitted ribbings are often not strong enough to support the weight of a skirt, for instance, or may lose resilience with wear. There are several types of elastic that are suitable, and different ways to attach them to the fabric.

You can create casings for elastic as you make the fabric (see Double-Fabric Casings), weave in thread elastic on the inside of a fabric, make sewn or crochet casings, or make a casing from a length of woven fabric.

Elastic Thread

The method used to weave in elastic thread while you knit is described in Purl Inlay. However, if this is an afterthought, you can also weave it in later with a tapestry needle. Select elastic that will blend in with the color of the fabric as much as possible so it will not show on the outside.

To avoid having to adjust the width of the elastic after it is inserted, divide the fabric into quarters and insert Yarn Markers or coilless pins as guides. The general rule for the length of elastic to use is a body measurement less ten percent. Measure what remains of the elastic at each marker to see if you are drawing it through evenly.

1. Knot elastic to a seam, or pass it around a stitch head and knot it to itself, leaving sufficient length at end to hide later.
2. Pass needle up under stitch head in each Purl column, then strand past Knit stitches. Pull elastic through after every few stitches and adjust length.
3. At edge, knot elastic to itself, weave a short end back through fabric and cut it off.
4. Repeat every row or every other row for depth of ribbing.

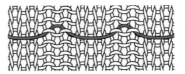

Elastic Thread. Shown on Double Ribbing.

Another possibility is to thread the elastic in using Duplicate Stitch, as described above; this is more trouble to do, but can be very effective.

Sewn Yarn Casing

A sewn yarn casing on the inside of a ribbing works well for soft, flat elastic no more than ¼ inch wide; make as many casings as needed for depth of ribbing. Use a fairly strong needlepoint or embroidery thread, matched in color to the knit.

This approach is used for a garment worked in the round, or already seamed; after insertion, the ends of the elastic are overlapped and sewn together. It is suitable for delicate garments that will not be subjected to hard wear because the yarns of the casing may snag on the inside.

Length of elastic is normally body measurement less ten percent, plus 2 inches to overlap ends. Measure width of elastic against fabric to find how many rows to include in each casing; stitch into rows above and below this area; if necessary, insert Yarn Marker as guide.

Thread tapestry needle with yarn and work from left to right, as follows:

1. Pass needle from right to left behind two sides of a Knit stitch in row at top of casing.

2. Repeat in stitch column to right, in row at bottom of casing.
3. Continue in this way, making one stitch at bottom, one at top.
4. Insert elastic in casing. Pull ends out to overlap, safety pin together and try garment on for fit. Adjust length, if necessary.
5. Sew overlap securely by machine or hand.

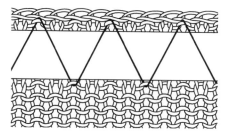

Sewn Yarn Casing.

The elastic can move freely within the casing; to prevent it from twisting, divide waist into quarters and mark; at each mark, use sewing thread to tack the lower edge of the elastic to a Purl nub.

Crocheted Casing

This version is like the one above, but it is considerably stronger.

1. Insert hook under Knit stitch at top of casing, draw through a loop; crochet a chain equal to width of elastic.
2. Insert hook two stitch columns to right at bottom of casing, and draw through a loop; crochet chain equal to width of elastic.
3. Repeat, always skipping one column of Knit stitches between each chain.

Woven Casings

A woven casing for elastic is very nice, particularly because the elastic will not be in contact with your skin and there will be no threads to snag; it is also much easier to do this than the options above. However, because the fabric will be gathered up by the elastic, the casing will be slightly thicker than a sewn or crocheted casing; therefore, select a very lightweight fabric or soft ribbon.

- Cut length of facing fabric equal to knitted fabric width. If you are using a woven fabric, turn under the edges ¼ inch and press.

  Use Hemstitch to sew the top edge of the fabric just below the cast-on or cast-off edge of the ribbing. Sew the other edge to the stitches in the first row of the ribbing, next to the main fabric (see Sewing Wovens to Knits).

❖ *Edgings*

To a great extent, knitted fabrics can be pre-finished by selecting a stitch pattern for the edges that will lie flat. Ribbings and non-curling stitch patterns such as Seed Stitch are obvious choices, and there are also a variety of decorative selvedges that can be used on side edges (see Selvedges).

However, there are many beautiful stitch patterns knit narrow and long that can be worked up separately and sewn on, or attached during the knitting (see Picking Up to Join). And there are also beautiful crocheted edgings that are often much easier to do and can be added later.

There is one minimal and unobtrusive edging you are unlikely to find elsewhere, and since it is so useful, I will include it here. It is particularly good for finishing a selvedge that didn't turn out neatly enough to be visible. It is also a good choice for an edge sewn along a zipper, for instance, or for finishing something like a bonnet.

Single Crochet Turned Edge

1. Fold column of selvedge stitches toward inside of the fabric.
2. Insert crochet hook between two running threads adjacent to selvedge and then through center of selvedge stitch underneath. Hook yarn and draw through a loop.
3. Insert crochet hook between two running threads one or two rows up, hook yarn and draw loop through fabric and loop already on needle.
4. Repeat Step 3 length of selvedge, adjusting size of stitches so they are even and do not constrict fabric.

Single Crochet Turned Edge.

Fringe

Fringe can make a nice finishing touch for shawls, scarves, blankets, and pillow covers. Elementary fringes are very easy to make and to attach. There are also a wide variety of decorative knotting patterns for more elaborate fringes that are available in knit or crochet stitch pattern books, or in any elementary book on macramé.

To add a fringe, plan ahead and use a method of casting on or casting off that leaves openings. On a side edge, use Chain Selvedge, or crochet a border that will accommodate the fringe.

Fringe and pompom gauges are available at most knitting shops and include instructions for their use; simply wrap the yarn around the gauge as many times as needed and cut off.

Knotted Fringe

Attaching fringe to a cast-on or cast-off edge is very easy to do and can be added later, even much later, if you want to give something a new look.

Use a gauge to cut yarn to length needed and work as follows:

1. To attach fringe, fold in half, insert large crochet hook through edge of knitted fabric and pull folded end through, forming a loop.
2. Hook all ends of fringe and draw through loop, and then pull ends down to tighten knot against edge.

Knotted Fringe.

Unraveled Fringe

This fringe must be planned for ahead of time, because it is worked along with the fabric at one side edge.

To decide how many stitches to use for the fringe, cast on ten stitches and work one row. Take the stitches off the needle, pinch the yarn where it comes off the last stitch and unravel exactly one row. Measure the length of the unraveled strand; you may need more or fewer stitches, depending upon the length of the fringe you want.

1. Cast on extra stitches at one side for fringe.

Unraveled Fringe. Knitted edge partially unraveled.

2. Work these stitches in Stockinette entire length of fabric.
3. Before casting off, drop fringe stitches from needle and unravel from top to bottom.
4. Cut looped ends and tie each pair of strands together to keep first stitch columns within fabric from enlarging.

You can also add a fringe of this kind to a top or bottom edge. With the stitches on a needle, cast on extra stitches for width of fringe base and knit it long and narrow, joining it to the stitches of the main fabric at one side (see Picking Up to Join). On last row, cast off several of the stitches close to the join, then drop and release the others to make the fringe and finish as described in Step 4, above.

REFERENCES

APPENDIX

Here are some numbers you may find useful.

Conversion Charts

Standard Lengths and Weights
1 inch = 2.54 centimeters
1 yard = 0.91 meter
2 centimeters = 0.79 inches
5 centimeters = 1.97 inches
1 meter = 1.09 yards
2 ounces = 56.7 grams
50 grams = 1.75 ounces

Conversion Formulas

Multiply by	To Convert	To	
2.54	inches	centimeters	0.3937
30.48	feet	centimeters	0.0328
0.9144	yards	meters	0.000621
6.452	sq. inches	sq. centimeters	0.155
28.35	ounces	grams	0.0352
0.4536	pounds	kilograms	2.2045
	To Find	Multiply	By

Needle Sizes
(All Bernat/Aero and Clover except noted)

Metric	American	British
1.25	0000	16
1.50	000	15
1.75	00	14
2	0	
2.25	1	13
2.3	1[1]	
2.75	2	12
2.8	2[1]	
3		11
3.125	3[4]	
3.25	3	10
3.3	3[1]	
3.5	4	
3.75	5	9
3.8	5[1]	
4	6[2]	8
4.25	6	
4.5	7	7
5	8	6
5.25	9[4]	
5.5	9	5
5.75	10[4]	
6	10	4
6.5	10.5	3
7	10.5[3]	2
7.5		1
8	11	0
9	13	00
10	15	000

[1]Leisure Arts   [2]Inox   [3]Phildar   [4]Boye

GLOSSARY

Active Stitches   Stitches on needles available to be worked. *See also* Inactive Stitches.

Acute Slope   A slope formed at edge of fabric using casting-on or casting-off techniques, or formed within fabric using Short Row technique. *See also* Gradual Slope.

Average Gauge   A specialized form of Stitch Gauge used primarily for sections of fabric intended to be highly elastic, such as ribbing, or for garments intended to fit tightly.

Back   In this text used only when referring to section of a garment worn on back of body; opposite of Front. In other books and in many published patterns, refers to side of fabric on needles that is currently facing away from knitter, to position of yarn relative to needle, or to side of stitch on farside of needle. *See also* Front; Inside; Outside; Nearside; and Farside.

Backing Stitch   Stitch or stitches of a Cable, Crossed Stitch, or decrease that are pulled past one or more stitches on inside of fabric and not visible on outside. *See also* Facing Stitch; Outside.

Balanced Yarn   A relaxed yarn; one where the amount of twist given to each separate strand of the yarn is balanced by the amount of twist used to ply strands together. Unbalanced or over-twisted yarn will kink up on itself and cause bias in the knitted fabric. *See also* Ply; Twist.

Ball Winder   A mechanical device for winding a ball of yarn.

Baseline   Outermost strands of cast-on edge; used to bind first row of stitches to needle.

Beading   A method of adding beads to a fabric as it is knitted, or methods used to sew beads on to finished fabric; similar methods are used for adding Sequins or Paillettes.

Bias   Columns of stitches that travel at an angle within fabric instead of vertically; done with stitch techniques for decorative purposes, or may be unintended characteristic of entire fabric due to over-twisted yarn. *See also* Twist.

Bi-Directional Method   Working one row as for Standard Method with new stitches accumulating on right needle; next row as for Reversed Method, with new stitches accumulating on left needle.

Binding Off   *See* Casting Off.

Binding On   *See* Casting On.

Blended Yarn   Yarn made up of two or more fibers blended together. *See also* Classic Yarn; Novelty Yarn.

Blocking   Method of dressing a fabric by stretching and pinning it into place for air-drying or during steam finishing; used to display stitch pattern and establish finished proportions. *See also* Dressing.

Bobbin   Holder for a small supply of yarn; used for Intarsia color patterns. *See also* Yarn Butterfly.

Bobble   A group of stitches worked tightly together to form a round ball-shaped decorative element on surface of fabric; terms for small versions are Nub, Knot, or Popcorn.

Braid   A horizontal line of strands on surface or at edge of fabric formed by a stitch or cast-on technique that creates a decorative, braid-like effect.

Brioche   A family of stitches used to make fabric with a cellular structure and excellent thermal properties; also called Honeycomb. *See also* Knit Below.

Brocade   Decorative patterns formed with a combination of Knit and Purl stitches, exclusive of Rib patterns.

Butterfly   *See* Yarn Butterfly.

Cable Holder or Cable Needle   A small hooked or bent needle used for holding and moving stitches when doing a Cable Stitch technique.

Cable Stitch   A decorative technique that creates sinuous lines of stitch columns that stand out from the surface of the fabric; achieved by changing positions of two or more groups of stitches. *See also* Cable Holder; Crossed Stitch.

Casing   Doubled section of fabric through which elastic or drawstring can be inserted; can be made by hemming top or bottom edge, or within fabric by means of Double-Fabric technique, or in any position by sewing woven fabric or tape to inside of knitted fabric.

Casting Off or Binding Off   Technique used to secure stitches to prevent unraveling; forms top edge of finished fabric. May also be used to create a decorative, horizontal Chain effect, or openings within a fabric. *See also* Sewn Cast-Off.

Casting On or Binding On   Techniques used to secure first stitches on needle; forms lower edge of fabric. *See also* Provisional Cast-On.

Center-Pull Ball   A ball of yarn that has both ends accessible; one from the outside, one from the center.

Chain   Any set of stitches that resembles a knitted stitch column or single line of crochet stitches; also an instruction to make a single chain of crochet stitches. *See* Stitch Column.

Chart   A set of instructions for either a stitch or garment pattern done by means of symbols and/or lines on graph paper.

Chevron   A stitch technique creating alternating columns of bias stitches. *See* Bias.

Circular Knitting   Method used to make a seamless, three-dimensional fabric with a spiral row structure; also called Knitting in the Round.

Circular Needle   A type of double-point needle consisting of two short needle tips connected by a long, thin plastic cable; used for both Flat and Circular Knitting. Called "twin pins" in Great Britain.

Classic Yarn   Relatively smooth yarn of consistent size, and made up of 2–4 identical plies. *See also* Blended Yarn; Novelty Yarn.

Cluster   A group of stitches pulled tightly together creating an embossed effect on surface of fabric.

Color Reversal Patterns   Color patterns with background and motif colors reversed in subsequent repeats; in Double-Faced fabrics, reverse is on opposite side of fabric.

Color Stitch Patterns   Patterns that combine color pattern and stitch techniques.

Combined Method   Variation of Left-Hand Method; one row is worked so new stitches are in Standard Position (right side of stitch on nearside of needle), and one row is worked so new stitches are in Turned position (left side of stitch on nearside of needle).

Continental Method   *See* Left-Hand Method.

Cord   Smallest circular fabric consisting of 3–5 stitches; or a firm, smooth, string-like yarn.

Couching   A stitch technique used to pull a loop of yarn across face of fabric for decorative effect. In embroidery, decorative stitches used to attach cord or yarn across surface of fabric.

Crossed Stitch   A pair of stitches that are crossed, with one pulled to right or left past other on face of fabric; closely related to Cable Stitches. In some published patterns (and in first edition of this book), called Twist Stitch.

Decrease   A stitch technique used to work two or more stitches together, leaving one on needle. May be used to reduce number of stitches on needle to make fabric narrower; also paired with increases in decorative stitch patterns, leaving fabric width unaffected.

Discard or Discard Stitch   An instruction to drop a stitch from needle into fabric after a new stitch has been formed on it; the stitch is thus discarded into the fabric. *See also* New Stitch.

Double Decrease or Increase   Technique used to remove or add two stitches in one position, instead of one; primarily used in decorative stitch patterns.

Double-Fabric   A double-thick fabric with two outside faces; also, a method of knitting two fabrics simultaneously on a single needle.

Double-Fabric Insertion   Method of inserting a section of Double-Fabric within a conventional single-thickness fabric. Can be used for hems, borders, casings, and pockets.

Double-Faced Fabric   A single-thickness fabric with two outside faces.

Double Knit   Term used for Double-Fabric technique in other books and many published patterns. *See* Double-Fabric.

Double Knitting Yarn   British term for a particular thickness of yarn; often abbreviated in patterns as "DK."

Double-Point Needles   Straight needles with pointed tip at both ends; packaged with four to five needles in a set. Most often used for Circular Knitting; more often now, only for items with a small circumference. *See also* Circular Needle.

Double Rib   Common elastic border pattern consisting of alternating pairs of Knit and Purl stitch columns. *See also* Single Rib.

Double Stranding   A method of working two-color Stranded patterns with one yarn held in each hand.

Dressed Gauge   A stitch and row gauge taken from a knitted sample that has been cleaned and smoothed out as for a finished fabric. Used for calculating number of stitches and rows required for fabric shape and size. *See also* Dressing; Flat Gauge; Gauge; Raw Gauge; Stitch Gauge; and Weighted Gauge.

Dressing   Method of cleaning and finishing a fabric so it has the correct proportions and a smooth surface that displays stitch and color patterns to full advantage.

Drop   Change in proportions of a garment caused by hanging weight of fabric in wear.

Dropped Stitch   A stitch that is either allowed to drop off needle, or one that has dropped off accidentally.

Duplicate Stitch   A surface embroidery technique that exactly duplicates Knit stitches in fabric; also used as method of hiding ends on inside of fabric during finishing.

Ease   Width or length added or subtracted to body measurements for purposes of comfort or style when developing a garment pattern; used to determine finished proportions of design. *See also* Negative Ease.

Edge Stitch   A number of stitches added to one or both sides of a stitch pattern; not part of Stitch Repeat. Used to balance pattern elements at edges of fabric, or to fit a stitch pattern repeat to fabric width.

Elongation   Techniques used to make some stitches of a row, or one or more rows, larger than others.

E-loop   *See* Half-Hitch.

Embossing   Stitch patterns that create a strongly defined, raised texture on fabric surface.

End   *See* Yarn End.

Entrelac   *See* Modular Fabric.

Eyelet   A small round opening in fabric. In Eyelet patterns, openings are spaced across a background of solid fabric; in Lace patterns, half or more of fabric consists of Eyelets. *See also* Yarnover.

Face   Flat surface of fabric. *See also* Inside; Outside.

Facing Stitch   Stitch or stitches of a Cable, a Crossed Stitch, or a decrease that are pulled past other stitches and remain visible on outside of fabric. *See also* Backing Stitch.

Farside   A relative term referring to whichever side of fabric on needles is facing away from knitter at any time; to that half of stitch on needle that is farthest from knitter; to whichever needle tip is positioned farthest from knitter; or to position of yarn in relation to needle. *See also* Nearside.

Felting   Process used to permanently mat wool fibers together to form a fabric. *See also* Fulling.

Final Row   Row worked after completion of decorative pattern repeat, either below a cast-off edge or before beginning a new pattern; not part of pattern repeat. *See also* Repeat; Row Repeat.

Finishing   Techniques used to assemble individual sections into completed garment, weave-in yarn ends, and sew on trims.

Flat Gauge   Stitch Gauge taken from sample of knitted fabric that is lying flat when measured. *See also* Weighted Gauge.

Flat Knitting   A method of working back and forth on rows of stitches to create a flat piece of knitted fabric. *See also* Circular Knitting; Row.

Foldline   A stitch technique used on a row or column of stitches that encourages fabric to fold along that line.

Fourchette   A small diamond-shaped Gusset used between thumb and fingers of mittens or gloves to provide ease for movement.

Front   In this text, used only when referring to section of a garment worn on front of body. In other books and many pattern instructions, refers to side of fabric on needles that is currently facing knitter, to side of stitch on nearside of needle, or to position of yarn relative to needle. *See also* Back; Inside; Outside; Nearside; and Farside.

Fulling   Process of felting a woven or knitted wool fabric. *See also* Felting.

Gansey   *See* Guernsey.

Garter Stitch   Elementary stitch pattern of alternating Knit and Purl rows; creates a compact, highly elastic fabric with horizontally corrugated appearance.

Gauge   Number of stitches and rows per inch or centimeter in a given fabric; used to determine number of stitches and rows required for finished dimensions of fabric. *See also* Dressed Gauge; Flat Gauge; Gauge Swatch; Raw Gauge; Stitch Gauge; and Weighted Gauge.

Gauge Swatch   A small sample of a knitted fabric used to find gauge. May also be called Tension Sample.

Gradual Slope   A slope formed with increases and decreases, either within a fabric or at edges. *See also* Acute Slope; Short Rows.

Grafted Hemstitch   A method of sewing a hem that reproduces the form and resilience of Knit stitches; related to Grafting and to Duplicate Stitch.

Grafting   Sewing technique that re-creates structure and appearance of a row of knitted stitches; invisibly joins free stitches of two fabrics, or free stitches to a finished fabric edge; alternative to a seam. Also called Kitchener Stitch.

Guernsey   Traditional style of pullover sweater from Channel Islands. Also called Gansey or Jersey.

Gusset   A triangular area inserted into fabric to provide ease, most commonly at underarm of sweater or at base of thumb in mitten or glove.

Half-Drop   Staggered and/or partially overlapped decorative motifs in stitch or color pattern; beginning of one motif is at midpoint of adjacent motifs.

Half-Hitch   A strand of yarn looped back on itself around needle or another stitch; also called an e-loop, from its resemblance to cursive letter. Basic structure of large family of cast-on techniques.

Honeycomb   Related stitch patterns that create fabrics with a cellular structure and appearance, and excellent thermal properties. *See also* Brioche, as well as Knit Below.

Horizontal Shaping   Method of altering dimensions of fabric by distributing shaping techniques horizontally across a single row instead of vertically across several rows.

Inactive Stitches   Stitches on hold and not currently being worked; used in Short Rows or when fabric is temporarily divided. *See also* Active Stitches.

Increase   A stitch technique used to add stitches to needle to make fabric wider; or for decorative purposes, paired with decreases in decorative stitch patterns, leaving fabric width unaffected.

Inlay   A method of weaving in a second yarn, ribbon, or roving that is not itself knitted; has decorative and practical applications.

Insertion   A vertical, sloped, or horizontal stripe of decorative openwork made with Eyelet techniques. Or, a section of fabric worked in a different pattern, or a different direction, and inserted between two other sections of fabric. *See also* Double-Fabric Insertion.

Inside   In this text, face of fabric not intended to be seen in wear or use; opposite of Outside. Commonly referred to as "wrong side" in other books and many published stitch and garment patterns. *See also* Outside; Front; Back; Nearside; and Farside.

Intarsia   Technique used to create geometric or pictorial patterns using more than one color yarn on every row; similar to woven tapestry in appearance.

Interlock   A technique for joining two yarns to prevent holes in fabric where two sections of Intarsia pattern meet.

Interwoven   A color pattern technique used to create Double-Faced Fabrics.

Jersey   *See* Guernsey.

Jog   A visible irregularity at join between rounds due to spiral structure of circular fabric.

Joinery   Technique used to join two sections of fabric using either decreases or casting off instead of sewing.

Kitchener Stitch   *See* Grafting.

Knit   One face of basic stitch (Purl is opposite face); or, technique used to place Knit aspect of stitch on nearside of fabric. Also used to refer to a fabric made using the technique of knitting, and to the process of making a knitted fabric.

Knit Back   *See* Knit Farside.

Knit Below   Method of working into a stitch below one on needle; used for Brioche or Honeycomb stitch patterns, or in other patterns to create highly textured effects on surface of fabric.

Knit Farside   Instruction to Knit a stitch in Standard Position on needle so it will Twist in fabric, or to work a Turned Stitch so it will not twist. *See* Farside; Standard Position; Turned Stitch; and Twist Stitch.

Knit Over   Instruction to wrap yarn over needle instead of under for a Knit stitch; new stitch will be turned on needle. *See* Turned Stitch.

Knitting Belt   A belt connected to an oval pad stuffed with horsehair and pierced with holes; worn at waist or hip and used to support one end of a double-point needle. *See also* Knitting Sheath or Stick; Supported Needle Method.

Knitting in the Round *See* Circular Knitting.

Knitting Needles Tools used to manipulate stitches and form knitted fabric. Made in a variety of materials, sizes, and lengths; pointed at one end or both. *See also* Circular Needle; Double-Point Needles; and Single-Point Needles.

Knitting Sheath or Stick A short shaped and/or carved stick with a hole in one end; worn tucked in belt or waistband and used to support one end of a double-point needle. *See also* Knitting Belt; Supported Needle Method.

Knitwise Instruction to insert needle into stitch as if to Knit; used when result will not be a basic Knit stitch in fabric.

Knot Small version of a Bobble.

Lace A highly decorative, openwork fabric consisting of Eyelets and other stitch techniques set close together.

Ladder A vertical column of running threads left within a fabric by an accidentally dropped stitch, or done as a decorative stitch technique. *See also* Run.

Lattice A stitch technique used to pull a strand of yarn placed on outside of the fabric up into row above to create a tent-like effect.

Left-Hand Method A method of knitting in which yarn is carried on left forefinger; often called Continental Method.

Make One *See* Increase.

Markers Various objects in the shape of small circles, or contrast-color thread or cord, that are set within a fabric for purposes of measurement or counting, or which are placed on needle to facilitate correct positioning of pattern elements or shaping.

Medallion A flat knitted fabric worked in the round and having a circular or polygonal outer edge.

Mesh An extremely open, netlike fabric related to Lace.

Mini-Chart A small stitch or garment chart adjacent to main one; provides instructions for a particular technique or motif used in small area of larger decorative pattern.

Miter A slope set within a border to form a corner using decreases, increases, or Short Row technique; causes stitch columns and rows of one section to travel at right angle to adjacent section.

Modular Fabric A knitted fabric made up of separate pieces sewn together, or one made by joining pieces worked in different directions, often in different colors or materials, as they are made. Most common version is known as Entrelac.

Moebius A geometric object with a single face and single edge; scarves and shawls can be knitted in this shape using specialized techniques.

Mosaic Pattern A type of color stitch pattern consisting of two-row stripes and Slip stitches.

Motif A distinctive shape created by stitch or color techniques, set against a plain background and repeated to form a decorative pattern.

Multiple Number of stitches in pattern repeat; used to determine number of stitches to cast on for width of fabric. *See also* Repeat; and Stitch Repeat.

Multiple Decrease or Increase Technique used to add or remove more than two stitches in same position.

Narrow A now-obsolete term for reducing width of a fabric.

Natural Fibers A fiber obtained from a plant or animal. *See also* Regenerated Fibers; Synthetic Fibers.

Nearside A relative term referring to whichever side of fabric is facing toward knitter at any time; to that half of stitch on needle that is closest to knitter; to whichever needle tip is positioned closest to knitter; or to position of yarn in relation to needle. Opposite of Farside. *See also* Front.

Needle Size A number designating circumference of knitting needle (see chart in Appendix).

Negative Ease Amount subtracted from body measurements for purposes of style and fit when determining width of a garment pattern; used if design is intended to cling to body. *See also* Ease.

Neutral Stitch A stitch on needle; one not yet given a particular stitch form in fabric.

New Stitch A loop of yarn pulled through an existing stitch to form a new, neutral stitch on needle.

Niddy-Noddy A tool used to wind a skein of yarn.

Nostepinde, or Nostepinne A tool used to hand-wind a ball of yarn; affectionately referred to as a "nostie." Popular name is Scandinavian; tool appears in other cultures by other names.

Novelty Yarn A variety of textured yarns with unconventional structure; often made up of several plies with different fibers and characteristics; or any yarn that is not plied in the conventional way. *See also* Classic Yarns.

Nub *See* Bobble.

Outside   In this text, that face of fabric intended to be seen in wear or use; opposite of Inside. Commonly referred to as "right side" in other books and many published stitch and garment patterns, but the latter term is used in this text only as opposite of "left side." *See also* Inside; Back; Front; Farside; and Nearside.

Over   An alternate term for Yarnover; not used in this text.

Paillette   Flat round disk, usually plastic, which is an enlarged version of a Sequin, but with hole close to edge instead of in center. Can be knitted into fabric or sewn on later. *See also* Beading.

Panel   A narrow vertical or horizontal section of a fabric worked in a distinctive pattern.

Parlor Method   Method of knitting by holding right needle positioned above thumb, and grasped between thumb and forefinger.

Pattern   Refers to a set of written or charted instructions for a decorative stitch technique, or to a complete set of instructions for making a garment, accessory, or household item, which can also include a stitch or color pattern.

Pick Up/Picking Up   The process of drawing new stitches through existing ones along edge or within a completed fabric in order to attach another section of fabric; used instead of a seam.

Picot   Generally refers to a tiny rounded point at an edge created with a cast-on technique or stitch technique.

Placeholder Stitches   Temporary stitches inserted into fabric using separate strand of contrast-color yarn; later removed to create opening in fabric. Used for buttonholes, thumb openings, pockets, and sock heels.

Ply   A single strand of yarn; a number of separate plies are twisted together (plied) to make a single heavier strand of yarn.

Popcorn   *See* Bobble.

Preparatory Row   Used prior to working first row of a stitch or color pattern as transition above a cast-on edge, or between one pattern and another; not part of pattern repeat. *See* Stitch Repeat.

Provisional Cast-On   Method of putting first stitches on needle so that running threads can later be accessed in order to work new section of fabric down from edge, or to finish edge in some way, or to join it to another edge.

Pullover   A stitch technique used to pull one stitch over another and off needle for discard. Most often used for casting off, but also seen in decorative stitch techniques.

Purl   One face of basic stitch. Also, a technique designed to place Purl aspect of stitch on nearside of fabric. *See also* Knit; Purl Nub; Reverse Stockinette; and Stockinette.

Purl Back   *See* Purl Farside.

Purl Farside   Method of working into farside of a stitch in Standard Position on needle so it will Twist, or working a Turned Stitch so it will not Twist. *See also* Knit Farside.

Purl Nub   Head of discarded stitch; short horizontal strand visible on Purl side of fabric; used on outside of fabric as primary decorative element in Brocade patterns.

Purl Under   Instruction to wrap yarn under needle instead of over for a Purl stitch; new stitch will be turned on needle. *See also* Turned Stitch.

Purlwise   Instruction to insert needle into stitch as if to Purl; used when result will not be a Purl stitch in fabric.

Raw Gauge   A gauge taken from an undressed sample of fabric that has not been washed, steamed, or blocked.

Regauging   A method of altering width of fabric by changing needle size or yarn thickness instead of changing number of stitches on needle.

Regenerated Fibers   Fibers formed from chemicals extracted from raw material of vegetable or animal origin. Rayon is the most common regenerated fiber.

Repeat   A single complete stitch pattern unit that is worked multiple times across width and length of fabric. *See also* Multiple; Row Repeat; Stitch Repeat.

Reversed Method   Knitting method done with stitches of previous row on right needle; as existing stitches are worked, new stitches accumulate on left needle; opposite of Standard Method. *See also* Bi-Directional Method.

Reverse Stockinette   Purl side of a Stockinette fabric.

Ribbing   A variety of stitch patterns used to make vertical columns of alternating Knit and Purl; produces a resilient fabric structure commonly used for borders at wrists, waistlines, and within a fabric for gathering. *See also* Welt.

Right-Finger Method   A method of knitting in which yarn is carried and manipulated by right forefinger.

Right-Hand Method   A method of knitting in which yarn is carried and manipulated by right thumb and forefinger.

Right Side   In this text used only in common sense of a relative direction; opposite of left. In other books and many published pattern instructions, refers to face of fabric that will be on outside of garment in wear; opposite of Wrong Side. *See also* Outside.

Rip   Process of unravelling stitches or rows to correct an error or reduce length of fabric.

Round   In Circular knitting, a single set of stitches set side by side on needle or in fabric, and aligned perpendicular to vertical stitch columns. Number of rounds determines length of fabric. Equivalent to a row in Flat Knitting, but distinguished by spiral structure in fabric. *See also* Jog.

Row   In Flat Knitting, a single set of stitches set side by side between two edges of fabric, and perpendicular to vertical stitch columns. Number of rows determines length of fabric. Equivalent to a round in Circular Knitting, but distinguished by strict horizontal arrangement.

Row Repeat   In stitch pattern, a single set of instructions for how to work each of several rows to create fabric structure or decorative pattern; set is repeated multiple times to create a horizontal stripe, or for entire length of fabric.

Ruching   Method of creating horizontal bands of gathering within fabric, either by means of a change of needle size, or change of yarn.

Run   A series of running threads left in fabric where a stitch has unraveled. *See also* Ladder.

Running Thread   Portion of yarn that passes horizontally between one stitch and next; also, a short horizontal strand in fabric that has same structure and appearance as a Purl Nub, but is upside down. May form base for a certain type of Increase.

Schematic   A small line drawing of garment pattern showing proportions and component parts of design, and their measurements.

Seam Stitch   A column of stitches used to create illusion of a seam. *See* Stitch Column.

Selvedge   A stitch at a side edge that is either decorative or will eventually become part of a seam.

Sequin   A small, disc-shaped ornament with hole in center; either sewn to finished fabric, or added to stitches while knitting. *See also* Beading; Paillette.

Sewing Needles   In knitting, specialized large-eye needles used to assemble sections of fabric and hide yarn ends during Finishing; also used for embroidery techniques done on knitted fabrics. *See also* Tapestry Needle.

Sewn Cast-Off   Method of securing last row of stitches and creating finished edge by sewing stitches with yarn and tapestry needle instead of by using a knitting technique.

Shaping Techniques   Increase and Decrease techniques, Short Rows, or Regauging; used to contour or change width of fabric.

Shetland Three-Needle Method   Method of working a circular fabric using three double-point needles instead of four or five; stitches are distributed to two needles and worked with third.

Short Rows   A technique for working partial rows to create volume within a fabric or contour at a side edge; patterns make use of changing number of Active and Inactive Stitches over several rows.

Single-Point Needles   Straight needles with a point at one end and a cap at the other; used for Flat Knitting and for Singular Double-Fabrics.

Single Rib   Common elastic border pattern consisting of alternating Knit and Purl stitch columns. *See also* Double Rib.

Singular Double-Fabric   A method of making a circular fabric using a pair of single-point needles and the Double-Fabric technique.

Skein   A long length of yarn wound into a large circle and tied so it will not tangle; often called a "hank" of yarn.

Slide   Technique used when working flat fabric on double-point needles; stitches are moved from one needle point to other instead of turning fabric at end of row. Makes it possible to work next row in same direction as last; most often used for managing yarns in color patterns.

Slip Knot   A simple, sliding knot used to attach yarn to needle in order to begin casting on.

Slip Stitch   A stitch passed from one needle to another without being worked. May be done as one step in complex stitch technique, or as decorative technique; yarn is stranded past stitch on inside, or on outside where it will be visible.

Slip Stranding   A method used for making color patterns by working with one yarn at a time; all pattern stitches are worked with one yarn, and all background stitches are worked with the other; stitches not worked with yarn in hand are slipped.

Slope   A sloping line either within or at edge of a fabric; used to create internal volume or contoured edge.

Smocking   An embroidery technique used to create decorative gathering.

Splice   A method of joining two ends of yarn by plying them together so diameter and appearance resembles that of a single strand.

Split Stitch   Caused by drawing new stitch through yarn of original stitch, instead of through center of stitch; an error.

Split Yarn   Yarn with one or two plies removed to make it thinner. Also, evidence in fabric of a Split Stitch.

Standard Method   Most common method of knitting; existing stitches of previous row are on left needle; as row is worked, new stitches accumulate on right needle.

Standard Position   Conventional position of stitches on needle: right side of stitch is on nearside of needle. *See also* Turned Stitch.

Steek   An internal selvedge; designated area that is later cut open to make armholes and center front openings; primarily used in Circular Knitting.

Stepped Cast-Off   Method of casting off step-wise over several rows to create a sloped edge.

Steps and Points   A method of calculating distribution of shaping techniques either at edge or within a fabric, or to develop a pattern for picking up stitches.

Stitch   A single loop of yarn within fabric or on needle; number of stitches on needle or in a row (or round) determines width of fabric; number of stitches aligned vertically determines length. *See also* Discard Stitch; Neutral Stitch; New Stitch; and Turned Stitch.

Stitch Column   A single vertical column of stitches, each one pulled through stitch below; number of stitch columns determines fabric width. *See also* Row.

Stitch Form   The particular appearance or structure of a stitch in the fabric; form imparted by using one or another specialized stitch technique to work a neutral stitch on the needle before it is discarded into the fabric.

Stitch Gauge   Number of stitches and rows per inch or centimeter produced by any unique combination of hands, yarn, needle, and stitch pattern; used to determine number of stitches and rows required for a given width and length of fabric.

Stitch Gauge Ratio   A formula for translating instructions derived from one gauge to instructions based on another gauge.

Stitch Head   The top portion of the stitch; visible in the fabric at the base of the new stitch; also called the Purl Nub, and resembling appearance of Running Thread in fabric.

Stitch Holder   Small tool resembling a knitting needle, or a length of yarn or cord that is used to securely hold temporarily Inactive Stitches.

Stitch Repeat   A set of instructions for a group of stitches that is repeated across full or partial width of fabric to create a particular fabric structure or decorative effect.

Stitch Technique   A specialized method of manipulating a neutral stitch before it is discarded so it will have a particular form and structure in the fabric. *See* Stitch Form.

Stockinette   Most basic stitch pattern in knitting, with Knit used exclusively on outside face of fabric and Purl on inside. Also called Stocking Stitch. Purl face is referred to as Reverse Stockinette.

Stocking Stitch   *See* Stockinette.

Strand   A single length of yarn, but, more specifically, a relatively small length of yarn that passes horizontally across one or more stitches. Strand is on outside of fabric in decorative stitch patterns, on inside as consequence of yarns alternating to stitches in color patterns, or past each stitch in Twined Knit.

Stranded Color Patterns   A type of color knitting in which two yarns alternate; each one is stranded on inside of fabric past stitches made with other yarn; used to create geometric patterns, primarily in Stockinette.

Stranding   The technique of carrying a second yarn across the inside of the fabric in Stranded Color work, or past a Slip Stitch on the outside of the fabric in some decorative stitch patterns. *See* Strand; Stranded Color Patterns; and Slip Stitch.

Supported Needle Method   A knitting method that employs a device for supporting the right needle. *See also* Knitting Belt; Knitting Sheath or Stick.

Surface Decoration   Decorative patterns or materials added to surface of completed fabric; may be done with needlework techniques, or by sewing on trim, appliqués, or ornaments such as beads, sequins, or paillettes.

Swatch   A small sample of knitted fabric. *See also* Gauge Swatch, Test Swatch.

Swift   A device that holds a skein of yarn and spins on its axis so the strand can be unwound into a ball; some versions are used for winding yarn into a skein.

Synthetic Fibers   Fibers derived from chemical and manufacturing processes. *See* Natural Fibers; Regenerated Fibers.

Tail of Yarn   A measured length of yarn used as the baseline in certain methods of casting on.

Tapestry Needle   A blunt-tipped, wide-eyed needle used for sewing with yarns for Finishing techniques, or for Duplicate Stitch and other embroidery patterns. *See also* Sewing Needles.

Tension May be used to describe whether a knitted fabric was worked firmly or loosely, to refer to tension placed on yarn while forming stitches, or in reference to Gauge.

Tension Sample *See* Gauge Swatch.

Test Swatch Small swatch used to select needle size, practice decorative stitch or color pattern, and determine yarn characteristics; made prior to Gauge Swatch.

Thermal Properties The characteristics of a fiber or fabric that are conducive to capturing and preserving heat.

Threaded Stitch A decorative technique in which one or more stitch is pulled through the center of one or more other stitches.

Thumb Method Very old method of knitting with yarn attached to bodice or passed around back of neck; yarn is manipulated by left thumb when forming stitches.

Tuck Decorative effect created by folding fabric on itself within interior; may be horizontal or vertical; may be done with stitch technique, or later by sewing into place.

Tuck Stitch In machine knitting, a stitch with same structure as one created by Knit Below technique in hand knitting.

Tunisian A form of knitting originating in Middle East; now more commonly, a set of stitch techniques that produce a particular fabric structure.

Turn Act of turning needle bearing stitches at end of row in order to work back in other direction; used in Flat Knitting, in Short Rows, or when casting off.

Turned Stitch A stitch positioned with left side of stitch on nearside of needle instead of in Standard Position; used as one step in some complex decorative stitch techniques. In Turned Left-Hand Method, all stitches on needle are turned; in Combined Method, new stitches are turned only when working Purl rows.

Turning Point A point within a fabric where needle is turned so work can continue in the other direction instead of completing a full row or round; used in Short Rows and for Casting Off.

Twice Knit A technique where each stitch is worked together with stitches on either side; produces an extremely dense fabric structure that does not ravel.

Twined Knit A unique knitted structure made by alternating two yarns to stitches; traditional technique found in Scandinavia.

Twist A characteristic of spun or plied yarn; fibers are twisted to right or left as yarn is spun; separate strands of yarn are plied together with twist opposite to that used for spinning. Over-twisted yarn can cause fabric to bias. *See also* Balanced Yarn; Ply.

Twist Start Simple method of attaching yarn to needle to begin casting on.

Twist Stitch A decorative stitch turned at its base so it is twisted on itself; in some published patterns (and in first edition of this book), called Crossed Stitch.

Two Circular Needles Method Method of working a circular fabric with two circular needles, one for each half of stitches.

Tying On Various methods used to attach a new supply of yarn to a fabric as it is being worked.

Unravel Literally, to disentangle. To pull yarn out of fabric and thus reduce number of completed stitches or rows, or to undo one or more columns of stitches. May occur accidentally, but also done to correct an error, or as step in a decorative stitch technique. *See also* Ladder; Run.

Weaving In Primarily a technique for catching a strand of yarn against inside of fabric when working Stranded Color patterns. Also used as a means of inserting elastic or separate strand of yarn for thermal benefit; to weave-in yarn ends; or to carry contrast-color yarn across inside of fabric for Woven Intarsia. *See also* Inlay.

Weighted Gauge A Stitch Gauge taken from a swatch that is weighted to mimic effect of drop exhibited by a garment in wear. *See* Drop.

Welt In this text used to refer to any horizontal or vertical corded effect within fabric. Also, British term for ribbing at waistline and wrist.

Wicking Ability of a fiber to transmit moisture away from body so it can evaporate.

Woolen-Spun A spinning technique used to make relatively soft yarn from short, carded fibers; not restricted to wool.

Work Even To continue in an established pattern, or on same number of stitches without change.

Worsted-Spun A spinning technique used to make relatively firm, smooth yarn from long, combed fibers; not restricted to wool.

Woven Intarsia A method used for large-scale Intarsia

patterns; secondary colors are carried across background and attached to inside of fabric using Weaving-In technique.

Wrap   Yarn wrapped around several stitches to create decorative effect; method of wrapping yarn around needle to form a new stitch; also method used to wrap a stitch in order to prevent a gap at Turning Points when working Short Rows.

Wrong Side   Used in other books and many knitting instructions to refer to face of fabric not intended to be seen in wear. Not used in this text. *See also* Inside.

Yarn   Long continuous strands consisting of fibers that are spun (twisted together) and then plied to create yarns of different characteristics and thickness. Created from a wide variety of fibers of both natural and manufactured origin. *See also* Classic Yarn; Novelty Yarn.

Yarn Butterfly   A small supply of yarn wrapped into a tiny skein and tied to prevent it from coming undone. *See also* Bobbin.

Yarn End   A relatively short length of yarn left hanging from fabric as a result of casting on or off, or from tying on new supply of yarn at edge or within fabric; often referred to as a "tail." Hidden on inside during finishing process.

Yarn Nearside/Farside   An instruction to pass yarn between needles to side of fabric currently facing knitter, or side that is facing away, respectively. In other books and many pattern instructions, commonly written as "yarn front/back" or "yarn forward/back."

Yarnover   Yarn passed over needle to form new stitch; decorative increase technique fundamental to knitted lace; creates an opening in fabric. Can be used as a basic increase if opening is closed by twisting Yarnover when worked.

BIBLIOGRAPHY

In addition to supplementing the footnotes in the text, the following bibliography lists the contents of my knitting library. Whenever I made specific reference to a book in the text, it is cited there in a footnote, but all of these books have influenced me in one way or another, challenging my assumptions, suggesting avenues to be explored, providing answers to questions, or revealing subtle details about a technique or an application. They have been both a rich resource and a constant reminder of the endless creativity of knitters; the debt I owe to the authors for all I learned from them is immense, and their contribution to this craft we love is present on every page of *The Principles of Knitting*.

Abbey, Barbara. *Barbara Abbey's Knitting Lace*. Pittsville, Wisc.: Schoolhouse Press, 1993.

———. *The Complete Book of Knitting*. New York: A Studio Book, The Viking Press, 1971.

———. *Susan Bates Presents: 101 Ways to Improve Your Knitting*. New York: Studio Publications, 1949.

Allen, John. *Fabulous Fairisle: A Complete Guide to Traditional Patterns and Classic Styles*. New York: St. Martin's Press, 1991.

Alweil, Judi. *Ribbon Knits: 45 New Designs to Knit and Crochet*. Newtown, Conn.: Taunton Press, 1998.

Amos, Alden. *The Alden Amos Big Book of Handspinning: Being a Compendium of Information, Advice, and Opinions on the Noble Art and Craft*. Loveland, Colo: Interweave Press, 2001.

Aytes, Barbara. *Adventures in Knitting: More Than 100 Patterns, from Easy to Intricate*. Garden City, N.Y.: Doubleday & Co., 1968.

———. *Knitting Made Easy*. Book Club ed. New York: Doubleday & Co., 1970.

Baber, M'Lou. *Double Knitting: Reversible Two Color Designs*. Pittsville, Wisc.: Schoolhouse Press, 2008.

Barr, Lynne. *Reversible Knitting: 50 Brand-New Groundbreaking Stitch Patterns*. New York: STC Craft/A Melanie Falick Book, 2009.

Bartlett, Roxana. *Slip-Stitch Knitting: Color Pattern the Easy Way*. Loveland, Colo.: Interweave Press, 1998.

Beeton, Isabella Mary. *Beeton's Book of Needlework*. Preface by Samuel Butler. London: Chancellor Press, 1986. Originally published in Great Britain by Ward, Lock and Tyler, 1870. The Project Gutenberg eBook edition, 2005.

Belcastro, Sarah-Marie, and Carolyn Yackel. *Making Mathematics with Needlework*. Wellesley, Mass.: A K Peters/CRC Press, 2007.

Bellamy, Virginia Woods. *Number Knitting*. New York: Crown, 1952.

Bennett, Helen. *Scottish Knitting*. Aylesbury, England: Shire Publications, Ltd., 1986.

Bohn, Annichen Sibbern. *Norwegian Knitting Designs*. Oslo, Norway: Grondahl & Son, 1965.

Bordhi, Cat. *Socks Soar on Two Circular Needles: A Manual of Elegant Knitting Techniques and Patterns*. Friday Harbor, Wash: Passing Paws Press, Inc., 2001.

———. *A Treasury of Magical Knitting*. Friday Harbor, Wash.: Passing Paws Press, Inc., 2004.

Borssuck, Bee. *Hand Knitting Techniques from Threads*. Newtown, Conn.: Taunton Press, 1991.

———. "Knitting Round on Straight Needles." *Threads Magazine* (August/September 1987).

Bredewold, Ank, and Anneke Pleiter. *The Knitting Design Book*. Asheville, N.C.: Lark Books, 1988.

Briar, J. C. *Charts Made Simple: Understanding Knitting Charts Visually*. Corvallis, Ore.: Glass Iris Publications, 2011.

Brittain, Judy. *The Bantam Step-by-Step Book of Needle Craft*. Bantam ed. New York: Bantam Doubleday Dell, 1980.

Brown-Reinsel, Beth. *Knitting Ganseys*. Loveland, Colo.: Interweave Press, 1993.

Bruzelius, Margaret. "A Sock Within a Sock: The Enchanted 'War & Peace Method.'" *Vogue Knitting* (Spring/Summer 1987), pp. 22–24.

Budd, Ann. *A Knitter's Handy Book of Patterns: Basic Designs in Multiple Sizes and Gauges.* Loveland, Colo.: Interweave Press, 2002.

Bulls, Alette. *Strikkebok.* Oslo, Norway: H. Aschehoug & Co. (W. Nygaard), 1933.

Bush, Nancy. *Folk Knitting in Estonia: A Garland of Symbolism, Tradition and Technique.* Loveland, Colo.: Interweave Press, 1999.

———. *Folk Socks: The History and Techniques of Handknitted Footwear.* Loveland, Colo.: Interweave Press, 1994.

———. *Knitted Lace of Estonia: Techniques, Patterns, and Traditions.* Loveland, Colo.: Interweave Press, 2008.

———. *Knitting on the Road: Sock Patterns for the Traveling Knitter.* Loveland, Colo.: Interweave Press, 2001.

———. *Knitting Vintage Socks: New Twists on Classic Patterns.* Loveland, Colo.: Interweave Press, 2005.

Buss, Katharina. *Big Book of Knitting.* New York: Sterling Publishing, 2001.

Carr, Sandy, Josie May, and Eleanor Van Zandt. *The Knit Kit.* London: Collins, 1985.

Carroll, Alice. *Complete Guide to Modern Knitting and Crocheting.* New York: Wm. H. Wise & Co., 1949.

Carroll, Amy. *The Pattern Library: Traditional Knitting.* New York: Ballantine Books, 1983.

Carroll, Amy, and Dorothea Hall. *The Pattern Library: Knitting.* New York: Ballantine Books, 1981.

Chatterton, Pauline. *Scandinavian Knitting Designs.* New York: Charles Scribner's Sons, 1977.

Christoffersson, Britt-Marie. *Swedish Sweaters: New Designs from Historical Examples.* Newtown, Conn.: Taunton Press, 1990.

Compton, Rae. *The Complete Book of Traditional Guernsey and Jersey Knitting.* New York: Arco Publishing, 1985.

———. *The Complete Book of Traditional Knitting.* New York: Charles Scribner's Sons, 1983.

Cooper, Marie Jane. *The New Guide to Knitting and Crochet.* London: J. S. Cooper, 1847. The Project Gutenberg eBook edition, 2011.

Crockett, Rena. *Flawless Knit Repair.* The Woodlands, Tex.: Rena Crockett, 1998.

Dandanell, Birgitta, and Ulla Danielsson. *Tvåändsstickat.* Stockholm: Dalarnas Museum and LTs Förlag, 1984.

———. *Twined Knitting: A Swedish Folkcraft Technique.* Translated by Robin Orm Hansen. Loveland, Colo.: Interweave Press, 1989.

Debes, Hans M. *Føroysk Bindingarmynstur.* Tórshavn, Faroe Islands: Føroyskt Heimavirki [Faroese Home Industries Council], 1986.

Dexter, Janetta. *Traditional Nova Scotian Double-Knitting Patterns.* Halifax, Canada: Nova Scotia Museum, 1985.

Don, Sarah. *The Art of Shetland Lace.* London: Bell & Hyman, Ltd., 1986.

———. *A Practical Handbook of Traditional Designs: Fair Isle Knitting.* New York: St. Martin's Press, 1983.

Dreiblatt, Martha "Marti." *A Handy Knitting Library.* Vol. 4. Garden City, N.Y.: Blue Ribbon Books, 1949.

Druchunas, Donna. *Arctic Lace: Knitting Projects and Stories Inspired by Alaska's Native Knitters.* Fort Collins, Colo.: Nomad Press, 2006.

Duckworth, Susan. *Susan Duckworth's Knitting.* New York: Ballantine Books, 1988.

Duncan, Ida Riley. *The Complete Book of Progressive Knitting: The Fundamentals of Knitting.* New York: Liveright Publishing, 1971.

Durant, Judith. *Knit One Bead Too: Essential Techniques for Knitting with Beads.* North Adams, Mass.: Storey Publishing, 2009.

Eichenseer, Erika, Erika Grill, Betta Krön, and Günter Standl. *Omas Strickgeheimnisse.* Rosenheim, Germany: Rosenheimer Verlagshaus, 2000.

Elalouf, Sian. *The Knitting Architect.* Amityville, N.Y.: Knitting Fever, Inc., 1982.

Emery, Irene. *The Primary Structures of Fabrics: An Illustrated Classification.* Washington, D.C.: Watson-Guptill Publications/Whitney Library of Design, The Textile Museum, 1995.

Epstein, Nicky. *The Knit Hat Book: 25 Hats from Basic Shapes.* Newtown, Conn.: Taunton Press, 1997.

———. *Knitting Beyond the Edge: The Essential Collection of Decorative Finishes.* New York: Sixth & Spring Books, 2006.

———. *Knitting on the Edge: The Essential Collection of 350 Decorative Borders.* New York: Sixth & Spring Books, 2004.

———. *Knitting over the Edge: The Second Essential Collection of 350 Decorative Borders.* New York: Sixth & Spring Books, 2005.

———. *Nicky Epstein's Knitted Embellishments: 350 Appliqués, Borders, Cords, and More!* Loveland, Colo.: Interweave Press, 1999.

Erlbacher, Maria. *Twisted-Stitch Knitting: Traditional Patterns and Garments from the Styrian Enns Valley.* Translated by Char Dickte. Pittsville, Wisc.: Schoolhouse Press, 2009. Originally published Austria, 1982.

———. *Überlieferte Strickmuster aus dem steirischen Ennstal.* Part 1. Trautenfels, Austria: Verein Schloß Trautenfels, 1999.

———. *Überlieferte Strickmuster aus dem steirischen Ennstal.* Part 2. Trautenfels, Austria: Verein Schloß Trautenfels, 1985.

———. *Überlieferte Strickmuster aus dem steirischen Ennstal.* Part 3. Trautenfels, Austria: Verein Schloß Trautenfels, 1999.

Evans, Ethel. *This Is Knitting.* New York: Macmillan Publishing Co., 1948.

Falick, Melanie D. *Knitting in America: Patterns, Profiles, and Stories of America's Leading Artisans.* New York: Artisan, 1996.

Fanderl, Lisl. *Bäuerliches Stricken 1: Alte Muster aus dem alpenländischen Raum.* Rosenheim, Germany: Rosenheimer Verlagshaus, 1978.

———. *Bäuerliches Stricken 2: Strümpfe, Jacken und Westen nach alten Mustern aus Museen und Privatbesitz.* Rosenheim, Germany: Rosenheimer Verlagshaus, 1979.

———. *Bäuerliches Stricken 3: 165 Muster aus Bauern- und Bürgerhäusern.* Rosenheim, Germany: Rosenheimer Verlagshaus, 1980.

Farson, Laura. *New Twists on Twined Knitting: A Fresh Look at a Traditional Technique.* Woodinville, Wash.: Martingale & Co., 2009.

Fassett, Kaffe. *Glorious Knits: Designs for Knitting Sweaters, Dresses, Vests and Shawls.* New York: Clarkson N. Potter, Inc., 1985.

———. *Kaffe Fassett's Pattern Library.* Newtown, Conn.: Taunton Press, 2003.

———. *Kaffe's Classics: 25 Favorite Knitting Patterns for Sweaters, Jackets, Vests, and More.* Boston: Little, Brown and Company, 1993.

Fee, Jacqueline. *The Sweater Workshop.* Loveland, Colo.: Interweave Press, 1983.

Feitelson, Ann. *The Art of Fair Isle Knitting: History, Technique, Color and Patterns.* Loveland, Colo.: Interweave Press, 1996.

Føroyskt Heimavirki [Faroese Home Industries Council]. *Føroysk bindingarmynstur.* Tórshavn, Faroe Islands: Faroese Home Industries Council, 1983.

Fournier, Nola, and Jane Fournier. *In Sheep's Clothing: A Handspinner's Guide to Wool.* Loveland, Colo.: Interweave Press, 1995.

Frederiksen, Tove. *Tvebinding.* Copenhagen: Clausen Bøger, 1982.

Fredholm, Inger. *Sticka till barnen.* Stockholm: Wahlström och Widstrand, 1983.

Freeman, June. *Knitting: A Common Art.* Aberystwyth, Wales: Aberystwyth Arts Centre Publications, 1986.

Frost, Jean. *Jean Frost Jackets: Fabric, Fit and Finish for Today's Knits.* Sioux Falls, S.D.: XRX Books, 2003.

Furuta, Yo. *"How To" 1: 101 Ways to Seam, Join, & Pick Up Stitches.* Yo's Needlecraft, Vol. 3, No. 1. Tokyo: Nihon Vogue, 1987.

Gainford, Veronica. *Designs for Knitting Kilt Hose and Knickerbocker Stockings.* Edinburgh: Scottish Development Agency, 1985.

Galeskas, Beverly. *Felted Knits.* Loveland, Colo.: Interweave Press, 2003.

———. *The Magic Loop: Working Around on One Needle; Sarah Hauschka's Magical Unvention.* East Wenatchee, Wash.: Fiber Trends, 2002.

Gibson-Roberts, Priscilla A. *Ethnic Socks & Stockings: A Compendium of Eastern Design and Technique.* Sioux Falls, S.D.: XRX Books, 1995.

———. *Knitting in the Old Way.* Loveland, Colo.: Interweave Press, 1985.

Gibson-Roberts, Priscilla A., and Deborah Robson. *Knitting in the Old Way: Designs and Techniques from Ethnic Sweaters.* Fort Collins, Colo.: Nomad Press, 2004.

Gilchrist, Lee. *Twice-Knit Knitting.* New York: Grosset & Dunlap, 1970.

Goldstein Gallery, Dept. of Design. *The Magic Knitting Needles of Mary Walker Phillips.* St. Paul: University of Minnesota, Goldstein Gallery, 1987.

Gottfridsson, Inger, and Ingrid Gottfridsson. *The Swedish Mitten Book: Traditional Patterns from Gotland.* Asheville, N.C.: Lark Books, 1984.

Gravjord, Ingebjørg. *Votten I Norsk Tradisjon.* Oslo: Landbruksforlaget, 1986.

Grayson, Martin, ed. *Encyclopedia of Textiles, Fibers and Nonwoven Fabrics.* New York: John Wiley & Sons, 1984.

Guðjónsson, Elsa E. *Notes on Knitting in Iceland.* Reykjavik, Iceland: Elsa Guðjónsson, 1985.

Handbook of Wool Knitting and Crochet. Augusta, Maine: Needlecraft Publishing Company, 1918. The Project Gutenberg eBook edition, 2008.

Hansen, Robin. *Fox, Geese and Fences: A Collection of Traditional Maine Mittens.* Camden, Maine: Down East Books, 1983.

Hansen, Robin, and Janetta Dexter. *Flying Geese and Partridge Feet: More Mittens from Up North and Down East.* Camden, Maine: Down East Books, 1986.

The Harmony Guides. Vol. 1, *Knitting Techniques: All You Need to Know About Hand Knitting.* London: Collins & Brown, Ltd., 1998. Originally published by Lyric Books, 1986.

The Harmony Guides. Vol. 2, *450 Knitting Stitches.* London: Collins & Brown, Ltd., 1998. Originally published by Lyric Books, 1986.

The Harmony Guides. Vol. 3, *440 More Knitting Stitches.* London: Collins & Brown, Ltd., 1998. Originally published by Lyric Books, 1987.

The Harmony Guides. Vol. 4, *250 Creative Knitting Stitches.* London: Collins & Brown, Ltd., 1998. Originally published by Lyric Books, 1990.

Harrell, Betsy. *Anatolian Knitting Designs.* Istanbul: Redhouse Press, 1981.

Hartley, Marie, and Joan Ingilby. *The Old Hand-Knitters of the Dales.* 5th ed. Leeds, England: Smith Settle Publishing, 2001.

Harvey, Michael. *Patons: A Story of Handknitting*. Berkshire, England: Springwood Books, 1985.

Harvey, Michael, and Rae Compton. *Fisherman Knitting*. Shire Album #31. Aylesbury, England: Shire Publications, Inc., 1978.

Haxell, Kate, and Luise Roberts. *Decorative Knitting*. North Pomfret, Vt.: Trafalgar Square Books, 2005.

Heathman, Margaret. *Knitting Languages: Knitting Terms Translated into English*. Pittsville, Wisc.: Schoolhouse Press, 1996.

Hewitt, Fruze, and Billie Daley. *Classic Knitted Cotton Edgings*. Sydney, Australia: Kangaroo Press, 1987.

Hiatt, June Hemmons. "Perfect Ribbing for All Fibers." In *Colorful Knitwear Design*, pp. 84–86. Newtown, Conn.: Taunton Press, 1994. Originally published in *Threads Magazine* 48 (August 1993): 44–46.

———. *The Principles of Knitting*. 1st ed. New York: Simon & Schuster, 1989.

Hinchcliffe, Frances. *Knit One, Purl One: Historic and Contemporary Knitting from the Victoria and Albert's Collection*. London: Faber & Faber, 1985.

Hochberg, Bette. *Fibre Facts*. Santa Cruz, Calif.: B. Hochberg, 1981.

———. *Handspinner's Handbook*. Santa Cruz, Calif.: B. Hochberg, 1980.

Hollingworth, Shelagh. *The Complete Book of Traditional Aran Knitting*. New York: St. Martin's Press, 1983.

———. *Traditional Victorian White Work to Knit and Crochet for the Home*. New York: St. Martin's Press, 1987.

Høxbro, Vivian. *Domino Knitting*. English translation. Loveland, Colo.: Interweave Press, 2002.

———. *Shadow Knitting*. Loveland, Colo.: Interweave Press, 2004.

Hyde, Nina. "Fabric of History: Wool." *National Geographic* 173, no. 5 (May 1988).

Itten, Johannes. *The Elements of Color: A Treatise on the Color System of Johannes Itten Based on His Book, The Art of Color*. Edited by Faber Birren. Translated by Ernst van Hagen. New York: Van Nostrand Reinhold Co., 1970.

Jensen, Åse Lund. *Strik Noget Andet*. Copenhagen: Borgen, 1976.

Jensen, Candi. *Knitting Loves Crochet*. North Adams, Mass.: Storey Publishing, 2006.

Jerome, Susan, ed. *The Art of Knitting 1892: Facsimile Reproduction of the Original Edition from The Butterick Publishing Co. (Limited), London and New York*. Easton, Conn.: Piper Publishing, 2003.

Johnson, Melissa. *Knitting Essentials: Knitter's Historical Pattern Series*. Vol. 1. Oak Hill, Va.: Pastime Publications, 2000.

Johnson, Wendy, and Susanna Hansson. *Bohus Stickning: Radiant Knits: An Enchanting Obsession*. Minneapolis, Minn.: One

of Susannas and Saga Hill Designs, 2009. Exhibition catalogue for "Radiant Knits: The Bohus Tradition," the American Swedish Institute, 2009.

Kagan, Sasha. *The Sasha Kagan Sweater Book*. New York: Ballantine Books, 1985.

Keele, Wendy. *Poems of Color: Knitting in the Bohus Tradition*. Loveland, Colo.: Interweave Press, 1995.

Khmeleva, Galina. *Gossamer Webs Design Collection: Three Orenberg Shawls to Knit*. Loveland, Colo.: Interweave Press, 2000.

Khmeleva, Galina, and Carol R. Noble. *Gossamer Webs: The History and Techniques of Orenburg Lace Shawls*. Loveland, Colo.: Interweave Press, 1998.

Kinzel, Marianne. *First Book of Modern Lace Knitting*. New York: Dover Publications, 1972. Originally published Calgary: Artistic Needleworks Publications, 1961.

———. *Second Book of Modern Lace Knitting*. New York: Dover Publications, 1972. Originally published London: Mills & Boon, Ltd., 1961.

Kirke, Betty. *Madeleine Vionnet*. Foreword by Issey Miyake. San Francisco: Chronicle Books, 1998.

Kjellberg, Anne. *Strikking I Norge*. Norwegian ed. Oslo: Norges Husflidslag, Landbruksforlaget, 1987.

Klift-Tellegen, Henriette van der. *Knitting from the Netherlands: Traditional Dutch Fishermen's Sweaters*. Asheville, N.C.: Lark Books, 1985.

Kopp, Ernestine, Vittorina Rolfo, and Beatrice Zelin. *Designing Apparel Through the Flat Pattern*. 5th ed. New York: Fairchild Publications, 1981

———. *How to Draft Basic Patterns*. 2nd ed. New York: Fairchild Publications, 1980.

The Ladies Work-Book, Containing Instructions in Knitting, Crochet, Point-Lace, &c. London: John Cassell, n.d. The Project Gutenberg eBook edition, 2005.

Ladies Work-Table Book, Containing Clear and Practical Instructions in Plain and Fancy Needlework. New York: J. Winchester, 1844. The Project Gutenberg eBook edition, 2009.

Lambert, Miss. *My Knitting Book*. London: John Murray, 1843. The Project Gutenberg eBook edition, 2010.

Lavold, Elsebeth. *Viking Patterns for Knitting: Inspiration and Projects for Today's Knitter*. Translated by Robin Orm Hansen. North Pomfret, Vt.: Trafalgar Square Books, 2000.

Lee, Ruth. *Contemporary Knitting for Textile Artists*. London: Batsford, 2008.

Leszner, Eva Maria. *Knitted Lace Designs of Herbert Niebling: Translation of Gestrickte Spitzendecken*. Berkeley, Calif.: Lacis Publications, 2009.

Lewandowski, Marcia. *Folk Mittens: Techniques and Patterns for Handknitted Mittens*. Loveland, Colo.: Interweave Press, 1997.

Lind, Vibeke. *Knitting in the Nordic Tradition*. Asheville, N.C.: Lark Books, 1984.

Ling, Anne-Maj. *Two-End Knitting*. Translated by Carol Huebscher Rhoades. Pittsville, Wisc.: Schoolhouse Press, 2004.

Lorant, Tessa. *The Batsford Book of Hand and Machine Knitted Laces*. Newton Abbot, England: David & Charles Publishing, 1982.

———. *Knitted Lace Collars*. Somerset, England: The Thorn Press, 1983.

———. *Knitted Lace Doilies*. Somerset, England: The Thorn Press, 1986.

———. *Knitted Lace Edgings*. Somerset, England: The Thorn Press, 1981.

———. *Knitted Quilts and Flounces*. Somerset, England: The Thorn Press, Somerset, 1982.

———. *Knitted Shawls and Wraps*. Somerset, England: The Thorn Press, 1984.

Macdonald, Anne L. *No Idle Hands: A Social History of American Knitting*. New York: Ballantine Books, 1988.

Marchant, Nancy. *Knitting Brioche: The Essential Guide to the Brioche Stitch*. Cincinnati, Ohio: North Light Books, 2010.

Marshall Editions, Ltd. *The Knit Kit*. New York: Villard Books, 1985.

Mathieson, Elizabeth Laird. *The Complete Book of Knitting*. Cleveland, Ohio: World Publishing Co., 1947.

Matthews, Anne. *Vogue Dictionary of Knitting Stitches*. New York: Quill, 1984.

McCormack, Mary A. *Spool Knitting*. New York: A. S. Barnes & Company, 1909. The Project Gutenberg eBook edition, 2007.

McGregor, Sheila. *The Complete Book of Traditional Fair Isle Knitting*. New York: Charles Scribner's Sons, 1982.

———. *The Complete Book of Traditional Scandinavian Knitting*. New York: St. Martin's Press, 1984. Originally published London: B. T. Batsford, Ltd., 1984.

———. *Traditional Knitting*. London: B. T. Batsford, Ltd., 1983.

Mee, Cornelia. *Exercises in Knitting*. London: David Dogue, 1846. The Project Gutenberg eBook edition, 2007.

Melville, Sally, and Elaine Rowley. *Sally Melville Styles*. Sioux Falls, S.D.: XRX Books, 1998.

Meyers, Belle. *Knitting Know-How: An Illustrated Encyclopedia*. New York: Barnes & Noble Books, 1982. Originally published New York: Harper & Row, 1981.

Miller, Sharon. *Heirloom Knitting: A Shetland Lace Knitter's Pattern and Workbook*. Lerwick, Shetland Islands, Scotland: The Shetland Times, Ltd., 2002.

Mon Tricot & Plus, Step-by-Step Knitting. Paris: Ste. Ediclaire et Cie, 1980.

Mon Tricot Knitter's Basic Book. 2 vols. Mon Tricot Monthly Nos. D17 and D18. Paris: Compagnie des Editions de l'Alma, n.d.

Mon Tricot Knitting Dictionary: 900 Stitches and Patterns. Translated by Margaret Hamilton-Hunt. New York: Crown Publishing, 1971.

Morse, Linda. *Luxury Knitting*. New York: Sixth & Spring Books, 2005.

Moss, Jean. *Sculptured Knits*. Sioux Falls, S.D.: XRX Books, 1999.

Murray, Margaret, and Jane Koster. *Complete Home Knitting Illustrated*. London: Odhams Press Ltd., ca. 1940.

Nehring, Nancy. *The Lacy Knitting of Mary Schiffmann*. Loveland, Colo.: Interweave Press, 1998.

Neighbors, Jane F. *Reversible Two-Color Knitting*. New York: Charles Scribner's Sons, 1974.

New, Debbie. *Unexpected Knitting*. Pittsville, Wisc.: Schoolhouse Press, 2003.

Newton, Deborah. *Designing Knitwear*. Newtown, Conn.: Taunton Press, 1998.

Nicholson, Heather. *The Loving Stitch: A History of Knitting and Spinning in New Zealand*. Auckland: Auckland University Press, 1998.

Norbury, James. *The Family Knitting Book*. London: Paul Hamlyn, 1969.

———. *Knit with Norbury*. London: Odhams Press, 1952.

———. *Traditional Knitting Patterns*. New York: Dover Publications, 1973. Originally published London: B. T. Batsford, 1962.

Norbury, James, and Margaret Agutter. *Odhams Encyclopaedia of Knitting*. London: Odhams Press, ca. 1950.

Oberle, Cheryl. *Folk Shawls: 25 Knitting Patterns and Tales from Around the World*. Loveland, Colo.: Interweave Press, 2000.

———. *Folk Vests: 25 Knitting Patterns and Tales from Around the World*. Loveland, Colo.: Interweave Press, 2002.

Pagoldh, Susanne. *Stickat från Norden*. Stockholm: Anfang Forlag, 1987.

Palmer, Marilyn. *Framework Knitting*. Shire Album 119. Aylesbury, England: Shire Publications, Ltd., 1984.

Paterson, Annie S., ed. *The Big Book of Needlecraft*. London: Odhams Press, 1935.

Pearson, Michael. *Michael Pearson's Traditional Knitting: Aran, Fair Isle and Fisher Ganseys*. New York: Van Nostrand Reinhold Co., 1984.

Phildar. *Hand Knitting Stitches*. Paris: Phildar, 1985.

Phillips, Mary Walker. *Creative Knitting: A New Art Form*. New York: Van Nostrand Reinhold Co., 1971.

———. *Knitting*. New York: Franklin Watts, 1977.

———. *Knitting Counterpanes: Traditional Coverlet Patterns for Contemporary Knitters*. Newtown, Conn.: Taunton Press, 1989.

———. *Step-by-Step Knitting: A Complete Introduction to the Craft of Knitting*. New York: Golden Press, 1967.

Piecework Magazine. *Weldon's Practical Needlework*. Vols. 1–10. Edited by Jeane Hutchins. Facsimile editions. Loveland, Colo.: Interweave Press, 1999–2004. Original publications began in 1888.

Piiri, Reet. *Estonian Gloves*. Translated by Tiina Mällo. Tartu, Estonia: Estonian National Museum, 2002.

Porter, Kristi. *Knitting for Dogs*. New York: Touchstone, 2005.

Praakli, Aino. *Kirikindad: Patterned Mittens: Reconstructions of Mittens Based on the Collection in the Estonian National Museum*. Tartu, Estonia: Eesti Rahva Museum [Estonian National Museum], 2003.

Pretl, Julia S. *Bead Knitted Bags: 10 Projects for Beaders and Knitters*. Minneapolis, Minn.: Creative Publishing International, 2006.

Price, Lesley Anne. *Kid's Knits: Irresistible Hand Knits for Infants and Children to Age Five*. New York: Ballantine Books, 1984.

Radcliffe, Margaret. *The Essential Guide to Color Knitting Techniques*. North Adams, Mass.: Storey Publishing, 2008.

Rådström, Anne Marie. *Wålstedts—mastare I ull*. Stockholm: LTs Forlag, 1986.

Reade, Dorothy. *25 Original Knitting Designs*. Eugene, Ore.: Dorothy Reade, 1968.

Riego de la Branchardière, Éléonore. *Knitting, Crochet, and Netting with Twelve Illustrations*. London: S. Knights, 1846. The Project Gutenberg eBook edition, 2011.

Righetti, Maggie. *Knitting in Plain English*. New York: St. Martin's Press, 1986.

Roberts, Patricia. *Patricia Roberts Collection*. London: W. H. Allen, 1981.

Robinson, Debby. *The Encyclopedia of Knitting Techniques*. Emmaus, Pa.: Rodale Press, 1987.

Robson, Deborah, ed. *Handspun Treasures from Rare Wools: Collected Works from the Save the Sheep Project*. Loveland, Colo.: Interweave Press, 2002.

Robson, Deborah, and Carol Ekarius. *The Fleece and Fiber Sourcebook: More Than 200 Fibers from Animal to Spun Yarn*. North Adams, Mass.: Storey Publishing, 2011.

Royce, Beverly. *Notes on Double Knitting*. Expanded ed. Pittsville, Wisc.: Schoolhouse Press, 1994. Originally published Langdon, Kans.: Beverly Royce, 1981.

Rutt, Richard. *A History of Hand Knitting*. Loveland, Colo.: Interweave Press, 2003. Originally published London: B. T. Batsford, Ltd., 1987.

Ryder, H. P. *Cycling and Shooting Knickerbocker Stockings*. London: Macmillan and Co., 1896. The Project Gutenberg eBook edition, 2011.

Schreier, Iris. *Reversible Knits: Both Sides Right*. Asheville, N.C.: Lark Books, 2009.

Schulz, Horst. *New Patchwork Knitting: Fashion for Children*. East London, South Africa: Saprotex International, 2000.

———. *Patchwork Knitting: Pullovers, Jackets, Waistcoats*. East London, South Africa: Saprotex International, 1997.

Schurch, Charlene. *Mostly Mittens: Traditional Knitting Patterns from Russia's Komi People*. Asheville, N.C.: Lark Books, 1998.

———. *Sensational Knitted Socks*. Woodinville, Wash.: Martingale & Co., 2005.

Scoville, Barbara. *The Heirloom Knitter Presents Heavenly Cotton Facecloths*. Vol. 1. South Jordan, Utah: Barbara Scoville, 1997.

———. *The Heirloom Knitter Presents Heavenly Cotton Face Cloths*. Vol. 2. South Jordan, Utah: Barbara Scoville, 1997.

———. *The Heirloom Knitter Presents Heavenly Cotton Hand Towels*. South Jordan, Utah: Barbara Scoville, 1998.

———. *The Heirloom Knitter Presents Heavenly Cotton Soap Socks . . . and More*. South Jordan, Utah: Barbara Scoville, 1997.

Smith, Mary, and Chris Bunyan. *A Shetland Knitter's Notebook*. Lerwick, Shetland Islands, Scotland: Shetland Times, Ltd., 1991.

Smith, Mary, and Maggie Twatt. *A Shetland Pattern Book*. Lerwick, Shetland Islands, Scotland: The Shetland Times, Ltd., 1986.

Stanfield, Leslie, and Melody Griffiths. *The Encylopedia of Knitting: A Step-by-Step Visual Guide*. Philadelphia: Running Press, 2000.

Stanley, Montse. *Creating and Knitting Your Own Designs for a Perfect Fit*. New York: Harper & Row, 1982.

———. *Handknitter's Handbook*. Newton Abbot, England: David & Charles Publishing, 1986.

———. *Knitting Plus: Simple, Stunning Techniques for Embroidering Knitting*. London: B. T. Batsford, Ltd., 1989.

———. *Knitting Your Own Designs for a Perfect Fit*. Newton Abbot, England: David & Charles Publishing, 1982.

———. *Reader's Digest Knitter's Handbook*. Pleasantville, N.Y.: Reader's Digest Association, 1993.

Starmore, Alice. *Alice Starmore's Book of Fair Isle Knitting*. Newtown, Conn.: Taunton Press, 1988.

———. *The Celtic Collection: Twenty-Five Knitwear Designs for Men and Women*. North Pomfret, Vt.: Trafalgar Square Books, 1993.

———. *Charts for Color Knitting*. Mineola, N.Y.: Dover Publications, 2011.

———. *Scandinavian Knitwear: 30 Original Designs from Traditional Patterns*. New York: Van Nostrand Reinhold Co., 1982.

———. *Sweaters for Men: 22 Designs from the Scottish Isles*. New York: Ballantine Books, 1989.

Stewart, Evelyn Stiles. *The Right Way to Knit, Book 1: A Manual for Basic Knitting.* Columbus, Ohio: Knit Services, 1967.

————. *The Right Way to Knit, Book 2: Basic Knits; How to Block and Finish.* Columbus, Ohio: Knit Services, 1967.

Stove, Margaret. *Creating Original Hand-knitted Lace.* Berkeley, Calif.: Lacis Publications, 1995.

————. *Wrapped in Lace: Knitted Heirloom Designs from Around the World.* Loveland, Colo.: Interweave Press, 2010.

Strawn, Susan M. *Knitting America: A Glorious Heritage from Warm Socks to High Art.* Minneapolis, Minn.: Voyageur Press, 2007.

Stuever, Sherry, and Keeley Stuever-Northup. *Intarsia: Workshop for Hand and Machine Knitting.* 3rd ed. Guthrie, Okla.: Sealed with a Kiss, Inc., 1998.

Sundbø, Annemor. *Everyday Knitting: Treasures from a Ragpile.* 2nd English language ed. Kristiansand, Norway: Torridal Tweed, 2001.

————. *Setesdal Sweaters: The History of the Norwegian Lice Pattern.* Kristiansand, Norway: Torridal Tweed, 2001.

Susan Bates, Inc. *Learn to Knit: Knitting for Beginners.* Chester, Conn.: Susan Bates, Inc., 1978.

Swansen, Meg. *Handknitting with Meg Swansen.* Pittsville, Wisc.: Schoolhouse Press, 1995.

————. *Meg Swansen's Knitting: 30 Designs for Hand Knitting.* Loveland, Colo.: Interweave Press, 1999.

Swansen, Meg, and Joyce Williams. *Armenian Knitting.* Pittsville, Wisc.: Schoolhouse Press, 2007.

Szabo, Janet. *The "I Hate to Finish Sweaters" Guide to Finishing Sweaters.* 2nd ed. Kalispell, Mont.: Janet Szabo, 2000.

Taylor, Gertrude. *America's Knitting Book.* New York: Charles Scribner's Sons, 1968.

Tellier-Loumagne, Francoise, and Sandy Black. *The Art of Knitting.* Melbourne, Australia: Thames & Hudson, 2005.

Thomas, Mary. *Mary Thomas's Book of Knitting Patterns.* New York: Macmillan Publishing Co., 1945. Originally published London: Hodder and Stoughton Ltd., 1943.

————. *Mary Thomas's Knitting Book.* New York: Dover Publications, 1972. Originally published London: Hodder and Stoughton, 1938.

Thompson, Gladys. *Patterns for Guernseys, Jerseys & Arans: Fishermen's Sweaters from the British Isles.* 3rd ed. New York: Dover Publications, 1979.

Threads Magazine. *Colorful Knitwear Design.* Newtown, Conn.: Taunton Press, 1994.

————. *Great Knits: Texture and Color Techniques.* Newtown, Conn.: Taunton Press, 1995.

————. *Knitting Around the World.* Newtown, Conn.: Taunton Press, 1993.

Tillotson, Marjory. *The Complete Knitting Book.* New York: Pitman & Sons, Ltd., 1940. Originally published in 1934.

Tortora, Phyllis G. *Understanding Textiles.* New York: Macmillan Publishing Co., 1982.

Trotzig, Eva. *Stickning: Tradition och Kultur.* Swedish ed. Stockholm: LTs Forlag, 1980.

Upitis, Lizbeth. *Latvian Mittens: Traditional Designs and Techniques.* St. Paul, Minn.: Dos Tejedoras, 1981.

Van Stralen, Trudy. *Indigo, Madder and Marigold: A Portfolio of Colors from Natural Dyes.* Loveland, Colo.: Interweave Press, 1993.

Vogel, Lynn. *Twisted Sisters Sock Workbook.* Loveland, Colo.: Interweave Press, 2002.

Vogue Knitting Magazine Editors. *Vogue Knitting: The Ultimate Knitting Book.* New York: Sixth & Spring Books, 2002.

Walker, Barbara G. *Charted Knitting Designs: A Third Treasury of Knitting Patterns.* New York: Schoolhouse Press, 1996. Originally published New York: Charles Scribner's Sons, 1972.

————. *A Fourth Treasury of Knitting Patterns,* Pittsville, Wisc.: Schoolhouse Press, 2001.

————. *Knitting from the Top.* New York: Charles Scribner's Sons, 1972.

————. *Learn to Knit Afghan Book.* New York: Charles Scribner's Sons, 1974.

————. *Mosaic Knitting.* Pittsville, Wisc.: Schoolhouse Press, 1997. Originally published New York: Charles Scribner's Sons, 1976.

————. *Sampler Knitting.* New York: Charles Scribner's Sons, 1973.

————. *A Second Treasury of Knitting Patterns.* New York: Charles Scribner's Sons, 1970.

————. *A Third Treasury of Knitting Patterns.* New York: Charles Scribner's Sons, 1972.

————. *A Treasury of Knitting Patterns.* New York: Charles Scribner's Sons, 1968.

Waller, Jane. *Classic Knitting Patterns from the British Isles: Men's Hand-Knits from the '20s to the '50s.* London: Thames and Hudson, 1984.

Waterman, Martha. *Traditional Knitted Lace Shawls.* Loveland, Colo.: Interweave Press, 1998.

Watts, Miss. *The Ladies Knitting and Netting Book.* 2nd series. 2nd ed. London: John Miland, 1840. The Project Gutenberg eBook edition, 2010.

Westman, Berit. *Tvåändsstickning: Grunderna.* Västerås, Sweden: Sätergläntan, 2004.

Williams, Joyce. *Latvian Dreams: Knitting from Weaving Charts.* Pittsville, Wisc.: Schoolhouse Press, 2000.

Wilson, Janet. *Classic and Modern Fabrics: The Complete Illustrated Sourcebook.* New York: Thames & Hudson, 2010.

Wiman-Ringquist, Gia. *100 Landskaps-Vantar.* Västerås, Sweden: ICA-Förlaget, 1982.

Wintzell, Inge. *Sticka Mönster: Historiskt om Stickning i Sverige*. Swedish ed. Stockholm: Nordiska Museet, 1980.

Wiseman, Nancie M. *The Knitter's Book of Finishing Techniques*. Woodinville, Wash.: Martingale & Co., 2002.

———. *Knitting with Wire*. Loveland, Colo.: Interweave Press, 2003.

———. *Lace from the Attic: A Victorian Notebook of Knitted Lace Patterns*. Loveland, Colo.: Interweave Press, 1998.

Wong, Andrea. *Portuguese Style of Knitting: History, Traditions, and Techniques*. Powell, Ohio: Andrea Wong Knits, 2010.

Wright, Mary. *Cornish Guernseys & Knit-Frocks*. Penzance, Cornwall, England: Alison Hodge, 1979.

Zilboorg, Anna. *Fancy Feet: Traditional Knitting Patterns of Turkey*. Asheville, N.C.: Lark Books, 1994.

———. *45 Fine and Fanciful Hats to Knit*. Asheville, N.C.: Lark Books 1997.

———. *Knitting for Anarchists*. Petaluma, Calif.: Unicorn Books, 2002.

———. *Magnificent Mittens: The Beauty of Warm Hands*. Sioux Falls, S.D.: XRX Books, 1998.

Zimmermann, Elizabeth. *Elizabeth Zimmermann's Knitter's Almanac: Projects for Each Month of the Year*. New York: Dover Publications, 1981. Originally published New York: Charles Scribner's Sons, 1974.

———. *Elizabeth Zimmermann's Knitting Workshop*. Pittsville, Wisc.: Schoolhouse Press, 1981.

———. *Knitting Around, or, Knitting Without a License*. Pittsville, Wisc.: Schoolhouse Press, 1989.

———. *Knitting Without Tears*. New York: Charles Scribner's Sons, 1971.

———. *Knitting Workshop*. Pittsville, Wisc.: Schoolhouse Press, 1981.

INDEX

Bold page numbers indicate illustrations.

A

abbreviations of knitting terms,
  383–385
  combining, 385
  in written garment patterns, 603
  See also charting symbols
abrasion
  in sewn cast-offs, 88, 92
  testing for, 290, 460
acetate, 552
acrylic fibers, 555
active stitches, 655
  in Short Rows, 97
Acute Slopes, 504, 510–511, 655
  calculating steps and points for,
    508, 510–511, 515
  casting off for, 85, 510
  casting on for, 510–511
  charted patterns for, 522,
    523–524, 531
  with Short Rows, 510–511
  in written garment patterns, 606
  See also Curves; Gradual Slopes;
    slopes
Adjusting Number of Stitches,
  115–116
  with Increases and Decreases, 115
  for slopes and curves, 115–116
  and spacing a pickup, 116
*Adventures in Knitting: More Than 100
  Patterns, from Easy to Intricate*
  (Aytes), 232
Afterthought Bobble, 230

Afterthought Pocket, 144
Air-Drying, 615–619
alcohol, 611
*The Alden Amos Big Book of Handspin-
  ning* (Amos), 543n, 559n
alkalis, 608–610, 611, 612
allergies, 542–543
alpaca wool, 545–546
Alterations, 473, 488–490, 528
  and adapting sewing patterns,
    488–490
  to customize fit, 498–500
  with garment charts, 387, 528
  in garment length, 473
  in garment width, 473
  and gauge, 472–474
  keeping records of, 588–589
  measurements for, 490–493
  relation of stitch and garment
    pattern, 531–536
  releasing edge for, 127–130
  in shape or size of neckline, 528
  in sleeve length, 528
  See also Charted Garment Patterns;
    pattern making
Alternating Cast-On, 56–58
  with beads, 299
  for Double-Fabrics, 310
  for Double Rib, 57–58
  with Grafted Cast-Off for Ribbing,
    90
  for Multicolor Ribbings, 58
  removing, 128
  for Single Rib, 57
Alternating Provisional Cast-On,
  59–60

for Center Start, 60–61
  Knit, 59–60
  for Moebius fabrics, 368–370
  Purl, 60
Alternating Yarns Version, of Ribbed
  Half-Hitch Cast-On, 45
Alternative Brioche Method, 189
aluminum needles, 574
ammonia, 611
Amos, Alden, 543n, 559n
angora, 548, 568
  ripping out, 597
Anker, Samuel Albrecht, 560
Applied Materials, 287–288
appliqués, 287–288, 640
Aran yarn, 564
"Armenian knitting," 270n
Armenian Knitting (Swansen and
  Williams), 270n
Armhole and Sleeve Cap Design,
  495–498
armholes
  adapting from sewing patterns,
    488
  adding ease in, 492
  altering length of, 489
  body measurements for, 491, 492
  in calculation of yardage
    requirements, 476–477
  charting, 524–525, 526
  in circular knitting, 30–31, 75–79
  curves for, 95–96, 504, 515
  with cut opening, 30, 75–79,
    635–636
  darts for, 500, 501
  facings for, 153–155

The Principles of Knitting: Methods and Techniques of Hand Knitting
was produced under the auspices of Touchstone

Senior Editor Michelle Howry

Produced by Wilsted & Taylor Publishing Services

Project management Christine Taylor

Copyediting Nancy Evans

Design and composition Jody Hanson

Proofreading Jennifer Brown

Indexing Jennifer Uhlich

Production assistance
Andy Joron, Melody Lacina, Mary Lamprech, Laurel Muller,
Evan Winslow Smith, Yvonne Tsang, and LeRoy Wilsted

Printer's devils
Lillian Marie Wilsted and Elsa Hanson-Schiffgens

The book was composed in Berkeley Old Style with Mrs. Eaves and Gotham display.
The paper is 55 lb. Glatfelter Offset. It was printed and bound by Courier Westford, Inc.